The HarperCollins World Reader

Antiquity to the Early Modern World

MARY ANN CAWS

Chief Editor
City University of New York

CHRISTOPHER PRENDERGAST

Editor
City University of New York

HarperCollins*CollegePublishers*

The section on Africa was initially developed by Richard Bjornson: It is dedicated to his memory.

Acquisitions Editor: Lisa Moore
Developmental Editor: Dawn Groundwater
Project Coordination, Text and Cover Design: York Production Services
Cover Illustration: Eisen: Chiryu/Horse Country in Full-moon.
c. 1845. Ronin Gallery, New York.
Photo Researcher: Sandy Schneider
Production Manager: Willie Lane
Compositor: York Production Services
Printer and Binder: R. R. Donnelley & Sons Company
Cover Printer: The Lehigh Press, Inc.

For permission to use copyrighted material, grateful acknowledgment is made to the copyright holders on pp. 1399–1406, which are hereby made part of this copyright page.

The HarperCollins World Reader: Antiquity to the Early Modern World
Copyright © 1994 by Mary Ann Caws

Library of Congress Cataloging-in-Publication Data

The HarperCollins world reader : antiquity to the early modern world / [edited by] Mary
    Ann Caws. Christopher Prendergast.
        p.   cm.
    Includes bibliographical references and indexes.
    ISBN 0-06-501382-4
    1. Literature—Collections.   I. Caws, Mary Ann.   II. Prendergast, Christopher.
    PN6014.H3125   1994
    808.8—dc20   93-39305
                                                                              CIP

93 94 95 96 9 8 7 6 5 4 3 2 1

Brief Contents

Detailed Contents

SECTION III
East Asia: Early and Middle Periods 600

SECTION IV
Medieval Europe   788

SECTION V
Early and Classical Middle East 930

SECTION VII
Early Modern Europe   1078

Preface

The HarperCollins World Reader assembles in one place—within the limits imposed by length—the selections that all the various editors together have chosen to form the best grid through which to perceive interlocking and yet separate currents of world literatures. The editorial team comprises over forty regional editors, consultants, and essayists, each with specialized knowledge in particular areas, as well as hundreds of reviewers with extensive experience as instructors of world literature.

In bringing together this diversity of texts and presentations, we have tried to offer a sensible and sensitive balance of new and familiar material, considering not only what is most teachable, but also what is most readable at the present moment. Alongside the main currents of traditional literatures, we wanted to represent voices previously neglected, some quieter, some louder. *The Harper-Collins World Reader* seeks to promote interactive reading within a comparative perspective. While each regional section fits into the overall structure governed by a *world* perspective, we have made every attempt to retain the specific and often contrasting styles of the readings and commentaries. Since a "world reader" is not a just a selection of readings, but also the person reading the world through them, our diverse ways of seeing and constructing viewpoints proved essential to this complicated project.

The Organization:
A New Way of Thinking

The HarperCollins World Reader provides a great range of material from very old to very new, in a manageable number of pages. Our team of specialized editors has taken great care to stress the specific character of the particular regions for which they were responsible. The literary content and arrangement of the individual sections are determined by their own cultural context rather than by Western or Eurocentric preconceptions. The expertise of our editors provides *The HarperCollins World Reader* with a rich diversity in both selections and genres giving a variety that would not usually be available from a small number of specialists.

We begin with The Ancient Mediterranean World, which is built around three distinct phases in this period of civilization (heroes, cities, and empires)—phases that brought the ancient Near East and Greek cultures into contact with one another in a cross-fertilization we see elsewhere throughout Asia, the Middle East, and Africa. This multicultural perspective that opens the book prepares the way for the crossweave of material throughout. South Asia, East Asia, the Middle East, and Africa are approached in the light of their own literary chronology, so that the time periods with which we are most familiar, such as "the middle ages" or the "Renaissance" (Early Modern Europe in this reader), become largely irrelevant for them. This approach enables instructors to teach what is most critical within a particular tradition, according to its own conceptions, following the intellectual and geographic currents or interrelations. The comparative perspective is encouraged through a Comparative Table of Contents by Theme found on page 1382 at the end of the book.

What Is So Exciting About
The HarperCollins World Reader?

Reading takes vitality, energy, imagining. "You have," said the French philosopher Gaston Bachelard, "to imagine too much in order to have enough." We have all had to imagine a great deal in order to present this much, knowing that we could not possibly represent everything we would have liked to. We are particularly proud of the special features we have been able to include in this text:

- A global perspective in selections taken from all regions of the world and an organization representative of new conceptions and ways of thinking about these literatures
- Marginal as well as mainstream voices in literature, particularly the inclusion of women's voices
- A wide range of genres: poems, short stories, tales, legends, essays, letters, journals, and plays
- Exceptional translations: many of the works are translated for the first time within these pages. In some cases, such as the Bible and Dante, different translations are used for different parts of the work, so that the original is seen from more than one point of view. The Bible, for example, is rendered in four different versions, each with its own particular style and relevance; the King James version, which has had such an influence on English-language literature, the New International Version, the Jerusalem Bible translation, and the Revised Standard Version
- Extensive pedagogical support in the teaching of this material, including introductions that guide students through the historical, cultural, geographic, linguistic, and literary background of each region, with special attention to gender relations. Most selections are also preceded by a headnote that provides a brief biographical background on the author as well as specific information on the importance of each selection in the literary history of its region and period
- Artwork from around the world in a four-color insert, as well as interior black-and-white images preceding each section and within text selections, are included to visually enhance and complement the literature selections
- An Afterword on translation by Jorge Luis Borges
- A comparative chronology of world cultures
- An alternate Comparative Table of Contents organized by theme
- An essay on how to read and write about world literature

Acknowledgments

All the many people who have given their time and effort to *The HarperCollins World Reader* join me in hoping that its readers will find their own world widened in these pages.

Throughout the intensive and lengthy work required here, all of us were encouraged by the hundreds of world literature instructors who responded to questionnaires and telephone surveys and/or reviewed the manuscript in various drafts—sharing with us their experience in teaching this subject and their hopes for its future. They have all guided our progress and helped us shape this text to meet the needs of the changing emphasis in such a vast field undergoing constant metamorphosis.

Sydney Aboul-Hosn, Pennsylvania State University

Michael Aishelman, University of Virginia

Stanley Alexander, Stephen F. Austin State University

Liahna Babener, Montana State University

Richard Badessa, University of Louisville

Lea Baechler, Columbia University

Robert Baggs, University of Massachusetts at Amherst

Christopher Baker, Lamar University

Sylvan Barnet, Tufts University

Tita Baumlin, Southwest Missouri State University

David Benson, University of Connecticut

Paula Berggren, Baruch College, City University of New York

Ronald Bogue, University of Georgia

Max Braffet, Southwest Texas State University

Ward Briggs, University of South Carolina

Michael Bright, Eastern Kentucky University

Steven Buccleugh, Auburn University

Arthur Buck, West Virginia University

Roland Bush, California State University—Long Beach

Davey Carozza, University of Wisconsin—Milwaukee

Gerome Coffee, Montana State University

Arthur Coffin, Montana State University

Linda Coleman, University of Maryland

John Coumes, Southeastern Louisiana State University

Robert O. Crespi, University of California—Santa Cruz

Thomas Dasher, Valdosta State College

Frank Day, Clemson University

Steward DeSchell, Boston University

Caroline Eckhardt, Pennsylvania State University

Beverly Freer, Western Oregon State College

Catherine Gannon, California State University—San Bernardino

Patricia Gardner, Utah State University

Pat Garret, Louisiana Tech University

Sharon Gravett, Valdosta State College

Donald Gray, Indiana University

Sue Greene, Towson State University

MaryJean Gross, Southwest Texas State University

Donald Haberman, Arizona State University

John Hagge, Iowa State University

Sarah Hansom, University of Rhode Island

Janice Harris, University of Wyoming

Donald Hassler, Kent State University

Walter Hesford, University of Idaho

E. W. Hirschberg, University of South Florida

Ruth Hoberman, Eastern Illinois University

Rebecca Hogan, University of Wisconsin—Whitewater

Phil Holcomb, Angelo State University

Gail Houston, Brigham Young University

Ann Howard, University of Nevada at Las Vegas

Chris Hudgins, University of Nevada at Las Vegas

Ilinka Johnstine, Indiana University

Steve Kaplan, University of Southern Colorado

George Kennedy, University North Carolina—Chapel Hill

Scott Kiserman, University of Maryland

Andy Knoedler, University of Colorado at Boulder

Sidney Knoles, North Carolina State University

Gene Koppel, University of Arizona

Eleni Kourduriotis, Columbia University

Tom Kovach, University of Alabama

Douglas Krienke, Sam Houston State University

Tom LaPointe, Rutgers University

Rick Leahy, Boise State University

John Leavey, University of Florida

Catherine Lederer, Southwest Missouri State University

Jae Lee, Portland State University

Joan Levine, Boston University

John Locke, University of Arkansas

Marilyn Malina, University of Rhode Island

Marilyn Manners, University of California at Los Angeles

Nicholas Margaritis, Western Washington University

Harriet Margolis, Oakland University

Joellen Masters, Boston University

Donovan McDonough, St. Michael's College

John McNamara, University of Houston

Ronald McReynolds, Central Missouri State University

John Mercer, Northeastern State University

Mona Oliver, Northeast Louisiana University

Lee Paterson, Duke University

Donald Pattow, University of Wisconsin—Stevens Point

Robert Philipson, New York University

Pamela Pittman, Central Oklahoma State University

Jeff Portnoy, University of Nevada at Las Vegas

William Potts, Oregon State University

Richard Priebe, Virginia Commonwealth University

Renee Ramsey, Indiana State University

Pete Richardson, University of North Texas

Frances Rippy, Ball State University

Jean Roberts, The American University

Gregory Sadlek, University of Nebraska at Omaha

Alfred Shivers, Stephen F. Austin State University

Conrad Shynaker, University of Central Arkansas

Rachel Skalitzky, University of Wisconsin—Milwaukee

Bob Skulachy, Columbia University

Bill Streipberger, University of Washington

Johnye Strickland, University of Arkansas

Paula Sunderman, Mississippi State University

John Tanner, Brigham Young University

Pat Taylor, Western Kentucky University

Cammy Thomas, Millsaps College

Paul Trout, Montana State University

Laura Tulley, State University of New York at Binghamton

William Ulmer, University of Alabama

Martin Wallen, Oklahoma State University

Steve Ward, North Dakota State University

Thomas Wheeler, University of Tennessee at Knoxville

Charles Whitney, University of Nevada at Las Vegas

Gary Williams, University of Idaho

Bruce Wilson, St. Mary's College

John Wilson, University of Maine, Orono

Elaine Wise, University of Louisville

Richard Wolf, Mississippi State University

Joe Zavadil, University of New Mexico

Many thanks to those whose counsel was essential at various stages in this project:

Ammiel Alcalay, Queens College, CUNY

Haskell Block, SUNY, Binghamton

Richard Brod, Modern Language Association

Patrick Cullen, College of Staten Island and Graduate School, CUNY

Manthia Diawara, New York University

Robert Enright, Border Crossings, Manitoba

Daniel Gerould, Graduate School, CUNY

David Gordon, Hunter College and the Graduate School, CUNY

Judy Goulding, Modern Language Association

Barbara Harlow, University of Texas

Carolyn Heilbrun, Graduate School, CUNY

Michael Holquist, Yale University

Gerhard Joseph, Lehman College and the Graduate School, CUNY

Amy Mandelker, Graduate School, CUNY

Nancy K. Miller, Lehman College and Graduate School, CUNY

Stephen Nichols, Johns Hopkins University

Burton Pike, Graduate School, CUNY

Edward Said, Columbia University

Grace Schulman, Baruch College, CUNY

Brian Swann, Cooper Union

Special thanks go to our authors of the Instructor's Manual:

Madeline Aria, Columbia University

Olga M. Davidson, Brandeis University

Tita Baumlin, Southwest Missouri State University

Louise Forsyth

Eric Haralson, Hofstra University

Randall Huff, University of San Francisco

Martha S. Grise, Eastern Kentucky University

Sharon Gravett, Valdosta State University

David Buerher, Valdosta State University

My warmest gratitude to each of the regional editors, art editors, and essayists for their prompt and generous support through all the stages of this project, in which each of them played an integral part. I could not have imagined such enthusiastic cooperation before beginning, and now in ending, I can only wish them easier projects from now on. May their glory be as great as their patience has been.

Without the determination and perseverance of my editors at HarperCollins, this massive project would never have seen the light of day: I want to thank Laurie Likoff, Betty Slack, and in particular Lisa Moore for her confidence in the project and in me; Marian Wassner, whose imaginative zeal took it through the early development stage; and Dawn Groundwater for carrying it through. Thanks also to Clifford Browder, Jeff Brown, Tom Maeglin, and to Terry-lynn Grayson at York Production Services for her patience in overseeing the whole production.

I also want to thank the poet/translators Robert Fagles and C. W. Williams for their friendship and assistance; the Slatkin family for their welcome and their care; my students Angela Bargenda and Kiyoko Ishikawa, for helping out; Liangyan Ge for helping with the Chinese sections; and the Henri Peyre Institute for the Humanities for its support. Particular thanks to William Kurzyna for preparing the comparative cultures addition, and to Matthew Rorison Caws for his steadfastness in editing, in counseling on geography, and in preparing the comparative table of contents by theme (with a team consisting of Anna Gebbie, Amy Stein, and Laura Rabhan). It would be impossible for me to express sufficient gratitude, from all of us, to Mark Getlein, whose infinitely intelligent research and imaginative solutions are responsible for the Historical Background appended to the introductions to each section (a massive job in which he was aided by David Cantor, Tan Lin, and Gordon Tapper).

Finally, my special gratitude to Gloria Loomis for her encouragement and understanding; to Boyce Bennett, for his unfailing good humor; and to all my friends who moved from bewilderment at the scope of this undertaking to a guarded fascination with its outcome.

Mary Ann Caws
Chief Editor

PUBLISHER'S NOTE: *The HarperCollins World Reader* is available in three formats. For one-semester courses, it is available as a single volume edition (ISBN: 065007506). For two-semester courses, *The HarperCollins World Reader* is available in split versions: *The HarperCollins World Reader, Antiquity to the Early Modern World* (which begins with Section 1, The Ancient Mediterranean World, and ends with Section VIII, The Early Americas) (ISBN: 065013824), as well as *The HarperCollins World Reader, The Modern World* (which begins with Section IX, Modern South Asia, and ends with Section XVIII, Writing Across Boundaries) (ISBN: 065013832).

In addition, HarperCollins has made available an extensive teaching resource package to support *The HarperCollins World Reader*. For more information on any of the following resources, please contact your HarperCollins representative or write to: English Literature Marketing Manager, HarperCollins College Publishers, 10 East 53rd Street, New York, NY 10022.

- *The Odyssey*, translated by Richmond Lattimore, can be packaged with *The HarperCollins World Reader*, Antiquity to the Early Modern World, at a 60% discount off the list price for *The Odyssey*.
- *100 Years of Solitude*, by Gabriel Garcia Marquez, can be packaged with *The HarperCollins World Reader*, The Modern World, at a 60% discount off the list price for *100 Years of Solitude*.
- *Issues in World Literature*, by Mary Ann Caws with Pat Laurence, City College, City University of New York, and Sarah Bird Wright, College of William and Mary. This book of essays was written specifically to accompany this text and can be packaged with *The HarperCollins World Reader* gratis for students. The essays include: "The World Reader and the Idea of World Literature" by Christopher Prendergast, City University of New York; "Reading a World" by Mary Ann Caws, City University of New York; "Whose Canon Is It Anyway?" by Barbara Christian, University of California at Berkeley; "Literature and Politics" by Susan Rubin Suleiman, Harvard University; "The Politics of Genre" by Stephen Heath, Jesus College, Cambridge University; "Speaking of Writing and Writing Speech: The Orality and Literacy of Literature" by Christopher Miller, Yale University; "Gender Reading" by Susan Gubar, Indiana University, Carolyn Heilbrun, City University of New York, bell hooks, Oberlin College, Mrya Jehlen, University of Pennsylvania, and Catharine R. Stimpson, Rutgers University; "Place, Exile, and Affiliation: Migrant and Global Literatures" by Shirley Geok-lin Lim, University of California at Santa Barbara; "Culturally Variable Ways of Seeing: Art and Literature" by Mary Beard, Newnham College, Cambridge University; "Periods and Ideologies" by Earl Miner, Princeton University; "Making Room for the Avant-Garde" by Marjorie Perloff, Stanford University.
- Comprehensive *Instructor's Manual*, by a team of experienced world literature instructors, provides in-depth coverage of each region and each selection from an historical, literary, and pedagogical perspective. The *Instructor's Manual* includes sample syllabi, a glossary of literary terms, and for each section of the text, an overview of the historical and literary issues of the region and period with a special focus on the role of women; a pronunciation guide; and classroom strategies, such as suggestions for making connections between texts across cultures and periods, ideas for using media in the classroom, discussion questions, topics for writing, and an extensive bibliography.
- *Writers on Writers* videotape, depicting Anton Chekhov's story "Enemies" (included in Section XIV: Modern Europe) through an original screenplay by Jamaica Kincaid and followed by an interview with Kincaid in which she reads from her work (including "Girl," in Section XV: The Caribbean) and discusses adapting works across cultures. This videotape is produced through an exclusive partnership among HarperCollins College Publishers, WGBH (Boston), and the British Broadcasting Corporation. It is only available through HarperCollins and is free to adopters of *The HarperCollins World Reader*. A library of other high-quality audio- and videotapes is also available to qualified adopters of *The HarperCollins World Reader*.

The HarperCollins World Reader

Back panel of a throne of Tutankhamen.
Egyptian, Eighteenth Dynasty
(fourteenth century B.C.E.).

SECTION I
The Ancient Mediterranean World

This section brings together a number of ancient texts from Mesopotamia and the regions surrounding the Mediterranean Sea. The selections encompass a span of time ranging from the third millennium B.C.E. to the second century of the common era, and they are drawn from the civilizations of Sumer, Akkad, Babylonia, Egypt, Israel, Greece, and Rome.

In considering this broad arc of time and these diverse civilizations under a single heading, we are already making a significant and, we believe, long overdue departure from the conventional viewpoint, which has tended to oppose two great unities: "The Ancient Near East," comprising Mesopotamia, Egypt, and Israel, and "The Classical World" of Greece and Rome. In the ancient Near East (to reduce this notion of opposition to its essence), religion and mysticism were thought to dominate; in the classical world, humanism and rational inquiry were considered to have sprung into being in a moment of unprecedented cultural genius. This view adequately served the eighteenth- and nineteenth-century European scholars who formulated it, for it allowed them to concentrate on what they saw as the two most direct sources of their own culture: the religion of the Hebrews (including Jesus) and the humanism of Greece. But it could be maintained only through an oversimplification of both Greece and Israel and the wholesale exclusion of other bodies of material that archaeology and scholarship have steadily brought to light.

Antiquity can no longer be adequately described as a bipolar opposition of two unified cultures, the one based in Athens, the other in Jerusalem; rather, it should be reconceived as an extended, multipolar system of historically related and often interdependent civilizations, a region at once disunified and yet still coherent in interesting ways. Both geographically and culturally, the ancient Mediterranean world encompassed North Africa, Palestine and the Fertile Crescent stretching to Babylon between the Tigris and Euphrates rivers, Asia Minor, Greece, and Italy, to speak only of the areas of greatest literary production. Archaeological evidence amassed during the past two centuries has shown that these different regions were in constant contact, as is vividly evident in the Greek adaptations of the norms of Egyptian sculpture or the transmission of what eventually became the Roman alphabet from the Semites to the Greeks via the Phoenicians.

The ancient Mediterranean included literary cultures of great antiquity as well as those of later origin. The oldest writing systems in the world, Egyptian hieroglyphics and Sumerian cuneiform, were created early in the third millennium B.C.E., and many of the literary forms of later antiquity — lyric and epic poetry, historical texts, hymns and religious texts, and stories for pure enjoyment — were first explored by the Sumerians, their successors in Babylonia and Assyria, and the Egyptians. The literary production of most of these older cultures continued through the first millennium B.C.E., overlapping first with the Hebrews and a variety of other groups (Phoenicians, Minoans, Mycenaeans, Chaldeans, and Hittites, to name but a few), and then with the Greeks and Romans.

The literatures of the ancient Mediterranean share "family resemblances" in their exploration of questions about the construction of the cosmos and of human society within it, about the nature of mortality and the relationship of the gods to the mortal realm, and about human social relations, both individual and collective. The writers of antiquity were keenly aware of the degree to which their societies were responding to the other societies around them. Indeed, a recurrent theme in ancient literature is the definition of a culture in relation to its surroundings and in relation to its own past, a process that often involved either incorporating or purging elements transmitted from abroad. The wanderings of Odysseus in the *Odyssey,* for example, reinforce what it is to be Greek by looking at what is not Greek. The first writers of the Hebrew Bible adapted older polytheistic creation myths to serve their own belief in a single god; later writers revised some of their efforts, in all probability ridding them of residual traces of polytheism that were no longer acceptable. When empires were created through conquest, more complex moral and philosophical issues of cultural contact evolved. Seen in this light, for example, the Egyptian *Hymn to the Aten* shows a developed awareness of the diversity of the cultures under Egyptian rule.

The readings we have selected here emphasize the interrelations and overarching coherence of the ancient Mediterranean world. We have aimed not for a survey that represents each culture equally but instead for illuminating juxtapositions, progressions, and contrasts. To encourage a new approach, we have chosen not to isolate the selections by culture, nor to interweave them in a single, extended chronological sequence. Rather, we have grouped the readings under three headings: The World of Heroes, The World of the City, and The World of Empire. The headings are not thematic (though they can be used as a springboard for thematic discussion), but reflect three broad stages in a pattern of development largely shared by these civilizations. We propose them as a framework for considering the literature of the ancient Mediterranean in the light of changing perspectives through which its various peoples sought to understand their existence. Headnotes to the selections draw attention where appropriate to the diverse roles of literature in these societies and invite readers to make connections across cultures, across categories, and over time.

The surviving literature of the ancient world generally reflects the concerns and perspectives expressive of the male-dominated societies that produced it. There is little direct testimony that helps us to understand the experience and the viewpoint of women in these societies. In an effort to use what indirect evidence we have, we have made a point of including texts in which women figure prominently as heroines or goddesses. The *Hymn to Demeter*, though in all probability composed by a man, is particularly noteworthy in its representation of the institution of marriage from a female point of view, focusing on the separation of mother and daughter. The lyrics of the Greek poet Sappho included here are among the few surviving texts from a woman's hand. Fragmentary as they are, they offer us an invaluable opportunity to recover a female poetic voice—one that responds powerfully to those of her male counterparts.

We expect that readers will discover here material that is both surprising and moving; and we hope that these readings will provide a new sense of the vitality of the cultures of the ancient Mediterranean.

Historical Background

Mesopotamia

Mesopotamia, the "land between the rivers," encompassed an area roughly equivalent to present-day Iraq. The city-states that made up the civilizations of Mesopotamia clustered along the Tigris and Euphrates rivers, whose waters fed the irrigation systems that supported the vast husbandry needed to sustain urban life. But while an abundance of fertile land made Mesopotamia desirable, a lack of natural boundaries made it difficult to unite and vulnerable to invasion, and its political history is a stormy one.

Civilization first arose in Sumer, the southernmost portion of Mesopotamia, around 3500 B.C.E.; a dozen Sumerian city-states emerged as powers some seven hundred years later. With their invention of writing by 3300 B.C.E., the Sumerians became the first people to leave behind not just artifacts, but words. Sumerian script is known as cuneiform, meaning wedge-shaped (from the Latin *cuneus*, "wedge"). Its characteristic triangular marks were made by pressing a reed stylus into a damp clay tablet, which was subsequently left to bake to rock-like hardness in the sun. Cuneiform spread by trade, conquest, and diplomacy throughout Mesopotamia. Adapted by each people to the needs of their own language, it served as the regional writing system for over three millennia. The complexities of cuneiform took many years to master, and literacy was the special skill of an elite class of scribes trained to staff the vast religious/political bureaucracies typical of Mesopotamian societies.

Shortly after 2400 B.C.E. the Sumerians were conquered by a Semitic people from Akkad, the neighboring region to the north. The two cultures had long been in contact, and the Akkadians had already adopted many elements of Sumerian civilization, including writing. The Akkadians established the first known empire, which stretched from the Mediterranean to the Persian Gulf. The empire did not last long, however, and fell to invaders around 2250 B.C.E. Toward the end of the following century, the Sumerians regained control over Sumer and Akkad, but when their capital city, Ur, was sacked by invaders 108 years later, this empire, too, disintegrated into independent city-states.

A second Semitic people, the Amorites, who had established their capital in Akkad in Babylon, were the next to unify the region, extending their rule throughout Mesopotamia to create the Babylonian Empire in the mid-1700s B.C.E. As had the Akkadians before them, the Babylonians built their civilization on the foundations laid by the Sumerians. The language of business and government was Akkadian, but scribes were required to master Sumerian as well, and Sumerian culture was studied intensively. A city of unrivaled splendor, Babylon became the cultural center of Mesopotamia, a reputation it kept for some thousand years, long after its political power had faded.

The Sumerian and Babylonian literature in this section dates from this first cycle of Mesopotamian history. The subsequent history of the region should also be briefly told, for its names are linked to the fates of the other peoples of the ancient Mediterranean. Raided by the Hittites, an Indo-European speaking people who had settled in Asia Minor (present-day Turkey), and other invaders, the Babylonian Empire crumbled around 1600 B.C.E. Numerous small kingdoms rose and fell over the ensuing 500 years, but the next sizeable empire was built by the Assyrians from the north of Mesopotamia, who brutally subjugated not only all of Mesopotamia but also Syria, Palestine, and even Egypt. Assyrian rule was notoriously harsh, yet as custodians of the now many-layered civilization of Mesopotamia the Assyrians were scrupulous, and in their great library at Ninevah were preserved the writings of Babylon and Sumer. The Assyrian Empire fell in 612 B.C.E., and Babylon enjoyed a final cultural flowering with the Neo-Babylonian Empire, ruled by yet another Semitic people, the Chaldeans. Their empire lasted until 539 B.C.E. when the entire region was conquered from the east by the Persians.

Egypt

As in Mesopotamia, civilization in Egypt grew up along a river, the 750-mile length of the Nile. But while the Tigris and Euphrates were prone to disastrous and unpredictable floods (the floods of Mesopotamian myth are rooted in experience), the Nile was gentle and reliable. Each year, on schedule, it swelled, overflowed its banks, and then receded, depositing a nutrient-rich layer of silt over the farmland. Protected to the south by a series of cataracts and to the east and west by vast deserts, Egypt developed with relatively little interference from outsiders for much of its long history.

Civilization emerged in Egypt at roughly the same time it appeared in Sumer. The two regions were probably in contact, and the Egyptians may have even learned the idea of writing from the Sumerians. Unlike cuneiform, which began inauspiciously as a method for noting transactions and inventories, Egyptian hieroglyphs were from the start intended to record spoken language. As in Mesopotamia, the complexities of the writing system gave rise to a professionally trained scribal class. Throughout Egyptian history, literacy was the privilege of scribes and priests and a source of considerable power. Whether there is any direct connection between cuneiform and hieroglyphics is a matter of ongoing debate; what is certain is that Egypt had developed its own form of writing by about 3100 B.C.E., for that is when we find recorded the name of its first king, Narmer, who unified the regions of Lower (northern) Egypt and Upper (southern) Egypt into a single country. The subsequent history of Egypt unfolds against the successions of thirty ruling dynasties and is marked by three eras of great stability and achievement known as Old Kingdom, Middle Kingdom, and New Kingdom.

The Old Kingdom comprises the Third to Sixth Dynasties (c. 2700 – 2200 B.C.E.). This period saw the construction of the greatest of the pyramids — colossal tombs filled with treasure to accompany the king (or *pharaoh,* from the Egyptian word for *great house* or *palace*) on his journey to the afterlife. Having ruled on earth as a god incarnate, he would now rejoin the gods in immortality.

High taxes, a string of crop failures, and the crippling expense of lavish burials brought an end to the Sixth Dynasty; nobles rebelled, reclaiming their provinces, and civil war ensued. Order returned with the Middle Kingdom, presided over by the kings of the Eleventh and Twelfth Dynasties (c. 2050–1800 B.C.E.). Instead of grandiose tombs, these rulers focused on public works (today's "infrastructure") such as irrigation projects. They also extended the kingdom to the south with the conquest of gold-rich Nubia. Civil wars of succession followed the Twelfth Dynasty, and Egypt suffered a major invasion for the first time when a largely Semitic people known as the Hyksos entered from Palestine and conquered the Delta region.

Toward the middle of the sixteenth century the Egyptians finally mobilized to expel the invaders. They pursued the Hyksos all the way into Palestine, thereby ushering in the New Kingdom (c. 1570–1090 B.C.E.), Egypt's age of empire. The kings of the Eighteenth Dynasty reclaimed Nubia and extended Egyptian rule from Palestine north through Phoenicia (roughly present-day Lebanon) and east through Syria to the Euphrates. Their capital city, Thebes, surpassed even Babylon in magnificence, and tribute poured in from the conquered as well as from neighboring powers. During the mid-fourteenth century, most of Egypt's Middle Eastern possessions fell away from the empire. The kings of the Nineteenth Dynasty entered into extended warfare with the Hittites (who had expanded into the region) to recapture the territories, but they were eventually forced to settle for a peace treaty in 1269 B.C.E.

Egypt's long decline had begun. Priests and merchants gained power; kings lost it. Libyans invaded from the west in 940 B.C.E. and established a dynasty. Two centuries later, the Kushites of Nubia conquered Egypt from the south and founded the Twenty-fifth Dynasty. The Assyrians were next, invading from the east and subsuming Egypt into their empire in 671 B.C.E. They were quickly routed (with help from Greek mercenaries), but in 525 B.C.E. the country fell again, this time to the Persians. Two hundred years later, Alexander the Great conquered the country for Greece, and under the Greek dynasty that he installed, Egypt passed into the Hellenistic Age.

Hebrews

Our major source for the history of the Hebrews is their great work, the Bible. Historians must approach it warily, however, being careful to sift historical fact from religious and poetic truths. A seminomadic people, the Hebrews probably did, as the Bible narrates, come out of Sumer and migrate to the southeastern

Mediterranean sometime after 1900 B.C.E. Later, some of them moved on to Egypt, most likely during the period of Hyksos occupation. With the advent of the New Kingdom, the Hebrews would have been forced into service as laborers on the vast construction projects typical of Egyptian rulers. Eventually, many Hebrews left Egypt and sought to rejoin the rest of their people in Palestine. The Bible sets the story of their departure during the reign of Ramses II, which would place it shortly after 1300 B.C.E.

In a loose confederation of twelve tribes—an era known as the days of judges (temporary leaders in times of military danger)—the Hebrews successfully carved out a territory for themselves in Palestine by 1200 B.C.E. In an attempt to fend off invasions from a people who were eventually to be known as the Philistines, the Hebrews later regrouped as a monarchy and reached their greatest glory as a temporal power under Kings David and Solomon in the tenth century. After 922 B.C.E., the realm split into two kingdoms: northern Israel, with its capital at Samaria; and southern Judah, with its capital at Jerusalem. Israel fell to the Assyrian Empire in 722 B.C.E.; its people were deported (the famous "ten lost tribes" of Israel) and replaced with other settlers. Judah withstood the Assyrian assault but fell in 586 B.C.E. to the conquering forces of the Neo-Babylonian Empire, which exiled a great portion of the population to Babylon. Seventy years later, the Persian conquerors of the Neo-Babylonian Empire allowed the Jews to return to their homeland, and many did.

Although it retained a large measure of autonomy, the new state of Judah was under foreign domination for most of the rest of its existence, belonging first to the Hellenistic empire of Egypt, then to the Roman Empire. In response to uprisings in the early part of the common era, the Romans destroyed Jerusalem in 70 C.E. and again in 132 C.E., putting an end to the Hebrews' unity and independence as a people until the founding of the state of Israel in the twentieth century.

Greece

The Greek peninsula was the site of two Greek-speaking civilizations in the ancient world. The first was built by the Mycenaeans (so-called after their most important city, Mycenae), who took over the peninsula around 2000 B.C.E. Their chief teachers in the arts of civilization were the Minoans, whose vigorous culture on the island of Crete was already fully established. (The pupils repaid their teachers none too handsomely, conquering Crete in 1450 B.C.E.) The Mycenaeans were seafaring traders, but also pirates and raiders, and they probably did, as later Greek epics relate, destroy the city of Troy on the coast of Asia Minor, although we do not know under what circumstances.

Starting around 1200 B.C.E., a new wave of barbarian tribes, the Dorian Greeks, descended into the peninsula, overwhelming the Mycenaeans, who fled to the Aegean Islands and eventually settled the Aegean coast of Asia Minor. For the next several hundred years, our historical record is a blank. These "dark years" of Greek history are especially intriguing to scholars. It appears now that toward the end of their dominance the Mycenaeans knew writing, which they had either adapted from the Minoans or directed the Minoans to adapt for them. While we have no indications that their script, known as Linear B, was ever used for anything but palace inventories, its sudden and total eclipse is a mystery which at the very least underscores the fragility of literacy in the ancient world. When the Greeks begin to write again, in the eighth century B.C.E., their script bears no traces of Linear B, but instead employs a new concept, the alphabet. The first alphabet, known as Old Canaanite, was developed around 1500 B.C.E. in the eastern Mediterranean. From it all alphabets—such visually diverse systems as Hebrew, Arabic, and Latin—ultimately derive. Its immediate descendant was Linear Phoenician, the alphabet adapted by the Greeks, whose decisive contribution was the addition of letters to represent vowel sounds. Interestingly, the intellectual forefront of the new Hellenic culture (from *Hellas,* the ancient Greek name for *Greece*) was not the peninsula but the Asia Minor coast—a region called Ionia—where the first philosophers and poets arose among the descendants of the displaced Mycenaeans.

Greece developed as a confederation of fiercely independent, intensely competitive city-states. Their political development was diverse, and they variously experienced (and named) four major forms of government: monarchy, oligarchy, tyranny, and democracy. In a mountainous country with little arable land, overpopulation was a constant concern. Between 750 and 550 B.C.E. Greece established numerous colonies along the Black Sea coast and at key points around the Mediterranean, thus siphoning off potentially disruptive excesses of Greek citizens while at the same time creating new opportunities for trade. By the end of this period, Athens and Sparta had emerged as the two most important and powerful city-states.

The main foreign threat to Greece was Persia, which began to amass a huge empire in the mid-sixth century. (Remember that the Persians conquered the Neo-Babylonian Empire in 539 B.C.E. and Egypt in 525 B.C.E.) Extending their rule across Asia Minor, the Persians subjugated the cities of Ionia in 549 B.C.E. (The subsequent flight of many Ionian Greeks did much to spread Hellenic culture throughout the Greek world.) In 499 B.C.E. the Ionians rebelled and appealed to Athens for help; Greece entered into war with Persia, dramatically triumphing in 479 B.C.E. after coming perilously close to defeat.

Athens, whose fleet had been largely responsible for the last-minute victory, emerged from the conflict with a new sense of energy and self-confidence. It became the leading city-state of Greece and entered into an astonishing period of artistic and intellectual vigor known as the Golden Age. To combat the continuing Persian threat, Athens formed and led the Delian League, a naval alliance that succeeded in reclaiming Ionia in 468 B.C.E. At this point, the alliance could have disbanded, but Athens now repressed any attempts at secession. The Athenians claimed to be leading a union of democratic states, an example to the rest of Hellas. To some of its members, but especially to Sparta and its allies, the league had become the Athenian empire, and they accused Athens of tyranny. Mounting tensions led to the Peloponnesian War in 431 B.C.E. The war, which pitted Sparta against Athens, eventually involved—and exhausted—all of Greece. Athens surrendered in 404 B.C.E. and was stripped of its empire.

The politically unstable and economically depressed Greece of the fourth century left ample opportunity for a strong, decisive leader. Such a person emerged in Macedonia, a region just north of Greece, in Philip II, who conquered Greece and forced its city-states into a league to wage a campaign against Persia. After Philip's assassination in 336 B.C.E., his twenty-year-old son, Alexander, took command. With an army drawn from Macedonia and the Greek league, Alexander reclaimed Asia Minor, Syria, Palestine, and Egypt from the Persians. He defeated the Persian king decisively in Mesopotamia in 331 B.C.E., then marched on to conquer the rest of the Persian Empire, reaching as far as India. Alexander died suddenly at the age of thirty-two, and his vast empire was carved into three: the Ptolemaic Empire (Egypt and Palestine; Ptolemy was the name of the new dynasty Alexander had installed in Egypt); the Seleucid Empire (Alexander's Asian conquests, including most of the eastern provinces of the former Persian empire); and Macedonia and Greece.

In this configuration, the ancient Mediterranean passed into the Hellenistic (meaning Greek-like—that is, based in Greek culture) Age. The Seleucid Empire soon splintered into various kingdoms, and Greece regained independence from Macedonia. The light of Hellenism was to burn brightest and longest in Alexandria, Egypt, the capital of the Ptolemies, and it is with the fall of this city in 30 B.C.E. to a new power, Rome, that historians date the end of the Hellenistic Age.

Rome

Rome was probably no more than a collection of villages—the meeting place for a group of tribes called the Latins—when the Etruscans conquered it after 625 B.C.E. The Etruscans had established the first civilization in Italy, probably during the ninth century B.C.E. Under the Etruscan kings, Rome grew into an important city-state; its people worshipped the Etruscans' gods and observed their customs, and they mastered the Etruscan arts of building and writing. (The Etruscans had adopted the alphabet, along with other elements of their civilization, from the Greeks, who had colonized the southern portion of Italy. Etruscan writing has never been deciphered. Along with an undeciphered Minoan script known as Linear A, it remains one of the most tantalizing "locked doors" of the ancient Mediterranean world.)

In 509 B.C.E. the Romans overthrew their Etruscan king. Determined never again to suffer the absolute power of a monarch, they founded their independent state as a republic (from the Latin *res publicum,* which roughly translates as "something that concerns everyone"), governed by two chief executives (*consuls*), each elected to a one-year term, and an advisory body of nobles (*patricians*) called the senate. As the republic evolved, ordinary citizens (*plebeians*) gradually won the right to elect one of the consuls as well as their own body of representatives.

During the early phase of the republic, to 133 B.C.E., Rome expanded through warfare and alliances to become the dominant power of the Hellenistic Age. After first subduing all of Italy, Rome fought and destroyed the great naval power of Carthage (a wealthy city in Africa near present-day Tunis, originally founded as a Phoenician colony), in the process gaining control over Sicily, Sardinia, Corsica, Spain, and the portion of Africa around Carthage itself. To the east, Rome subdued a newly militant Macedonia, established power over Greece, forced the Seleucid Empire out of Asia Minor, and extended its protection to Egypt and Judea.

During the late phase of the republic, Rome suffered three civil wars as rival generals led their armies against each other for control of the state. The empire continued to grow, for each general consolidated his power base by conquest.

The last of these wars ended in 30 B.C.E., with the victory of Caesar Octavian over the combined forces of Mark Antony and Cleopatra, the queen of Egypt.

With the triumph of Octavian, the republic effectively came to an end, for he ruled as Augustus, Rome's first emperor. To ensure stability and legitimize his rule, Augustus preserved republican institutions such as the senate. For the rest of its history, Rome would be ruled in this way—a thinly disguised dictatorship we call the empire. During the first two centuries of the common era, Roman dominion reached its greatest extent, and the empire stretched from Britain to the Euphrates and around the entire perimeter of the Mediterranean.

Culturally, Rome came of age in the Hellenistic world, and its artistic thought was shaped by Greece. Roman literature flowered first in the late republic and reached its classical peak in the Augustan Age. The majority of the Roman selections here are drawn from this most creative period.

Further Readings

Alter, Robert, and Frank Kermode, eds. *The Literary Guide to the Bible*. Cambridge: Harvard University Press, 1987.

Boardman, John, Jasper Griffin, and Oswyn Murray, eds. *The Oxford History of the Classical World*. Oxford: Oxford University Press, 1986.

Burkert, Walter. *The Orientalizing Revolution: Near Eastern Influence on Greek Culture in the Early Archaic Age*. Cambridge: Harvard University Press, 1992.

Hallo, William, and W. K. Simpson. *The Ancient Near East: A History*. New Haven: Yale University Press, 1974.

Ogilvie, R. M. *Roman Literature and Society*. Harmondsworth, England: Penguin Books, 1988.

Saggs, H. W. F. *The Greatness That Was Babylon*. New York: New American Library, 1962.

Vernant, J. P. *The Origins of Greek Thought*. Ithaca, N.Y.: Cornell University Press, 1982.

ANONYMOUS (c. 1500 –1200 B.C.E.)

Ancient Babylon

Enuma Elish, the Babylonian creation epic, recounts the origins of the gods and of the world, culminating in the birth of Marduk, patron god of Babylon. The forces of chaos, embodied in the goddess Tiamat and her children, threaten to take over the universe until Marduk leads the defense. After Tiamat's defeat, Marduk declares Babylon the ritual center of the world. He establishes cosmic order with the movements of the planets and the division of time, and he creates humanity to serve the gods.

The text is preserved on clay tablets written during the first millennium B.C.E., but the epic was probably composed earlier, perhaps sometime between 1500 and 1200 B.C.E. Presumably many of the elements of the story are much older still. The epic was used ritually, recited or performed during the annual festival for the new year in Babylon. The audience at this celebration included all of the royal governors, courtiers, and officers, and it was at this time that the king's mandate to rule as Marduk's earthly representative was renewed.

The epic's creation myths show many parallels to later accounts in the Bible and in Hesiod's *Theogony*. Its vivid dialogue and action invite comparisons with the epics of Homer, the *Epic of Gilgamesh,* and the *Erra Epic.*

from *Enuma Elish*

The Babylonian Creation Epic

Tablet 1

When skies above were not yet named,[1]
Nor earth below pronounced by name,
Apsu, the first one, their begetter
And maker Tiamat, who bore them all,[2]
Had mixed their waters together,   5
But had not formed pastures, nor discovered reed-beds;
When yet no gods were manifest,
Nor names pronounced, nor destinies decreed,
Then gods were born within them.
Lahmu (and) Lahamu emerged, their names pronounced.[3]   10
As soon as they matured, were fully formed,

Translated by Stephanie Dalley.

---

1. The Babylonians called the epic by its opening words, *Enuma Elish,* "When skies above."
2. Apsu, father of the primeval gods, is the personification of the body of freshwater beneath the earth. Tiamat, "Ocean," is the primordial mother of the gods.
3. Primeval heroes, controllers of water and fishing.

Anshar (and) Kishar[4] were born, surpassing them.
They passed the days at length, they added to the years.
Anu[5] their first-born son rivalled his forefathers:
Anshar made his son Anu like himself,   15
And Anu begot Nudimmud[6] in his likeness.
He, Nudimmud, was superior to his forefathers:
Profound of understanding, he was wise, was very strong at arms.
Mightier by far than Anshar his father's begetter,
He had no rival among the gods his peers.   20
The gods of that generation would meet together
And disturb Tiamat, and their clamour reverberated.
They stirred up Tiamat's belly,
They were annoying her by playing inside Anduruna.[7]
Apsu could not quell their noise   25
And Tiamat became mute before them;
However grievous their behaviour to her,
However bad their ways, she would indulge them.
Finally Apsu, begetter of the great gods,
Called out and addressed his vizier Mummu,   30
    "O Mummu, vizier who pleases me!
    Come, let us go to Tiamat!"
They went and sat in front of Tiamat,
And discussed affairs concerning the gods their sons.
Apsu made his voice heard   35
And spoke to Tiamat in a loud voice,
    "Their ways have become very grievous to me,
    By day I cannot rest, by night I cannot sleep.
    I shall abolish their ways and disperse them!
    Let peace prevail, so that we can sleep."   40
When Tiamat heard this,
She was furious and shouted at her lover;
She shouted dreadfully and was beside herself with rage,
But then suppressed the evil in her belly.
    "How could we allow what we ourselves created to perish?   45
    Even though their ways are so grievous, we should bear it patiently."
Mummu replied and counselled Apsu;
The vizier did not agree with the council of his earth mother.
    "O father, put an end to their troublesome ways,
    So that she may be allowed to rest by day and sleep at night."   50
Apsu was pleased with him, his face lit up
At the evil he was planning for the gods his sons.

---

4. "Whole Sky" and "Whole Earth."
5. "Sky," patron god of Uruk, head of the older generation of gods.
6. A name for Ea or Enki, god of wisdom and

incantations, who sent the Seven Sages to teach the arts and skills of civilization to humanity.
7. Name of the gods' dwelling.

Mummu hugged him,
Sat on his lap and kissed him rapturously.
But everything they plotted between them   55
Was relayed to the gods their sons.
The gods listened and wandered about restlessly;
They fell silent, they sat mute.
Superior in understanding, wise and capable,
Ea[8] who knows everything found out their plot,   60
Made for himself a design of everything, and laid it out correctly,
Made it cleverly, his pure spell was superb.
He recited it and it stilled the waters.
He poured sleep upon him so that he was sleeping soundly,
Put Apsu to sleep, drenched with sleep.   65
Vizier Mummu the counsellor (was in) a sleepless daze.
Ea unfastened his belt, took off his crown,
Took away his mantle of radiance and put it on himself.
He held Apsu down and slew him;
Tied up Mummu and laid him across him.   70
He set up his dwelling on top of Apsu,
And grasped Mummu, held him by a nose-rope.
When he had overcome and slain his enemies,
Ea set up his triumphal cry over his foes,
Then he rested very quietly inside his private quarters   75
And named them Apsu and assigned chapels,
His own residence there.

[In the ensuing 350 lines, omitted here, Qingu and other gods urge Tiamat to avenge the death of her husband. She assembles an army, which Ea and his allies hesitate to oppose, until Ea's son Marduk agrees to lead the defending forces.]

Tablet IV

They founded a princely shrine for him,
And he took up residence as ruler before his fathers, (who proclaimed)
    "You are honoured among the great gods.
    Your destiny is unequalled, your word (has the power of) Anu!
    O Marduk, you are honoured among the great gods.   5
    Your destiny is unequalled, your word (has the power of) Anu!
    From this day onwards your command shall not be altered.
    Yours is the power to exalt and abase.
    May your utterance be law, your word never be falsified.
    None of the gods shall transgress your limits.   10
    May endowment, required for the gods' shrines
    Wherever they have temples, be established for your place.

---

8. God of Wisdom.

O Marduk, you are our champion!
We hereby give you sovereignty over all of the whole universe.
Sit in the assembly and your word shall be pre-eminent!   15
May your weapons never miss, may they smash your enemies!
O lord, spare the life of him who trusts in you,
But drain the life of the god who has espoused evil!"
They set up in their midst one constellation,
And then they addressed Marduk their son,   20
    "May your decree, O lord, impress the gods!
    Command to destroy and to recreate, and let it be so!
    Speak and let the constellation vanish!
    Speak to it again and let the constellation reappear."
He spoke, and at his word the constellation vanished.   25
He spoke to it again and the constellation was recreated.
When the gods his fathers saw how effective his utterance was,
They rejoiced, they proclaimed: "Marduk is King!"
They invested him with sceptre, throne, and staff-of-office.
They gave him an unfaceable weapon to crush the foe.   30
    "Go, and cut off the life of Tiamat!
    Let the winds bear her blood to us as good news!"
The gods his fathers thus decreed the destiny of the lord
And set him on the path of peace and obedience.
He fashioned a bow, designated it as his weapon,   35
Feathered the arrow, set it in the string.
He lifted up a mace and carried it in his right hand,
Slung the bow and quiver at his side,
Put lightning in front of him,
His body was filled with an ever-blazing flame.   40
He made a net to encircle Tiamat within it,
Marshalled the four winds so that no part of her could escape.
South Wind, North Wind, East Wind, West Wind,
The gift of his father Anu, he kept them close to the net at his side.
He created the evil wind, the tempest, the whirlwind,   45
The Four Winds, the Seven Winds, the tornado, the unfaceable facing wind.
He released the winds which he had created, seven of them.
They advanced behind him to make turmoil inside Tiamat.
The lord raised the flood-weapon, his great weapon,
And mounted the frightful, unfaceable storm-chariot.   50
He had yoked to it a team of four and had harnessed to its side
"Slayer," "Pitiless," "Racer," and "Flyer;"
Their lips were drawn back, their teeth carried poison.
They know not exhaustion, they can only devastate.
He stationed on his right Fiercesome Fight and Conflict.   55
On the left Battle to knock down every contender.
Clothed in a cloak of awesome armour,
His head was crowned with a terrible radiance.

The Lord set out and took the road,
And set his face towards Tiamat who raged out of control. 60
In his lips he gripped a spell,
In his hand he grasped a herb to counter poison.
Then they thronged about him, the gods thronged about him;
The gods his fathers thronged about him, the gods thronged about him.
The Lord drew near and looked into the middle of Tiamat: 65
He was trying to find out the strategy of Qingu her lover.
As he looked, Qingu's mind became confused,
His will crumbled and his actions were muddled.
As for the gods his helpers, who marched at his side,
When they saw the warrior, the leader, their looks were strained. 70
Tiamat cast her spell. She did not even turn her neck.
In her lips she was holding falsehood, lies, wheedling,
   "[How powerful is] your attacking force, O lord of the gods!
   The whole assembly of them has gathered to your place!"
The Lord lifted up the flood-weapon, his great weapon 75
And sent a message to Tiamat who feigned goodwill, saying:
   "Why are you so friendly on the surface
   When your depths conspire to muster a battle force?
   Just because the sons were noisy (and) disrespectful to their fathers,
   Should you, who gave them birth, reject compassion? 80
   You named Qingu as your lover,
   You appointed him to rites of Anu-power, wrongfully his.
   You sought out evil for Anshar, king of the gods,
   So you have compounded your wickedness against the gods my fathers!
   Let your host prepare! Let them gird themselves with your weapons! 85
   Stand forth, and you and I shall do single combat!"
When Tiamat heard this,
She went wild, she lost her temper.
Tiamat screamed aloud in a passion,
Her lower parts shook together from the depths. 90
She recited the incantation and kept casting her spell.
Meanwhile the gods of battle were sharpening their weapons.
Face to face they came, Tiamat and Marduk, sage of the gods.
They engaged in combat, they closed for battle.
The Lord spread his net and made it encircle her, 95
To her face he dispatched the evil wind, which had been behind:
Tiamat opened her mouth to swallow it,
And he forced in the evil wind so that she could not close her lips.
Fierce winds distended her belly;
Her insides were constipated and she stretched her mouth wide. 100
He shot an arrow which pierced her belly,
Split her down the middle and slit her heart,
Vanquished her and extinguished her life.

He threw down her corpse and stood on top of her.
When he had slain Tiamat, the leader,   105
He broke up her regiments; her assembly was scattered.
Then the gods her helpers, who had marched at her side,
Began to tremble, panicked, and turned tail.
Although he allowed them to come out and spared their lives.
They were surrounded, they could not flee.   110
Then he tied them up and smashed their weapons.
They were thrown into the net and sat there ensnared.
They cowered back, filled with woe.
They had to bear his punishment, confined to prison.
And as for the dozens of creatures, covered in fearsome rays,   115
The gang of demons who all marched on her right,
He fixed them with nose-ropes and tied their arms.
He trampled their battle-filth beneath him.
As for Qingu, who had once been the greatest among them,
He defeated him and counted him among the dead gods,   120
Wrested from him the Tablet of Destinies,[9] wrongfully his,
Sealed it with (his own) seal and pressed it to his breast.
When he had defeated and killed his enemies
And had proclaimed the submissive foe his slave,
And had set up the triumphal cry of Anshar over all the enemy,   125
And had achieved the desire of Nudimmud, Marduk the warrior
Strengthened his hold over the captive gods,
And to Tiamat, whom he had ensnared, he turned back.
The Lord trampled the lower part of Tiamat,
With his unsparing mace smashed her skull,   130
Severed the arteries of her blood,
And made the North Wind carry it off as good news.
His fathers saw it and were jubilant: they rejoiced,
Arranged to greet him with presents, greetings gifts.
The Lord rested, and inspected her corpse.   135
He divided the monstrous shape and created marvels (from it).
He sliced her in half like a fish for drying:
Half of her he put up to roof the sky,
Drew a bolt across and made a guard hold it.
Her waters he arranged so that they could not escape.   140
He crossed the heavens and sought out a shrine;
He levelled Apsu, dwelling of Nudimmud.
The Lord measured the dimensions of Apsu
And the large temple which he built in its image, was Esharra:

---

9. A book recording everyone's fate.

In the great shrine Esharra, which he had created as the sky,   145
He founded cult centres for Anu, Ellil, and Ea.[10]

Tablet V

He fashioned stands for the great gods.
As for the stars, he set up constellations corresponding to them.
He designated the year and marked out its divisions,
Apportioned three stars each to the twelve months.
When he had made plans of the days of the year,   5
He founded the stand of Neberu[11] to mark out their courses,
So that none of them could go wrong or stray.
He fixed the stand of Ellil and Ea together with it,
Opened up gates in both ribs,
Made strong bolts to left and right.   10
With her liver he located the Zenith;
He made the crescent moon appear, entrusted night (to it)
And designated it the jewel of night to mark out the days.
  "Go forth every month without fail in a corona,
  At the beginning of the month, to glow over the land.   15
  You shine with horns to mark out six days;
  On the seventh day the crown is half.
  The fifteenth day shall always be the mid-point, the half of each month.[12]
  When Shamash looks at you from the horizon,
  Gradually shed your visibility and begin to wane.   20
  Always bring the day of disappearance close to the path of Shamash,[13]
  And on the thirtieth day, the year is always equalized, for Shamash is
    responsible for the year."
Marduk grouped the spittle of Tiamat and made clouds scud.
Raising winds, making rain,
Making fog billow, by collecting her poison,   25
He assigned for himself and let his own hand control it.
He placed her head, opened up springs: water gushed out.
He opened the Euphrates and the Tigris from her eyes.
He piled up clear-cut mountains from her udder,
Bored waterholes to drain off the catchwater.   30
He laid her tail across, tied it fast as the cosmic bond
And placed the Apsu beneath his feet.

---

10. The tablet ends with the following postscript: "146 lines. Fourth tablet 'When
skies above.' Not complete. Written according to a tablet whose lines were can-
celed. Nabubelshu son of Naid-Marduk,
son of a smith, wrote it for the life of
himself and the life of his house, and
deposited it in Ezida."

11. "Crossing Place," the name of the planet
Jupiter.
12. The word for the fifteenth day of the
month, *shabattu*, is related to the Hebrew
term "sabbath."
13. The sun god.

He set her thigh to make fast the sky,
With half of her he made a roof; he fixed the earth.
When he had designed earth's cult, created its rites,   35
He threw down the reins and made Ea take them.
The Tablet of Destinies, which Qingu had appropriated, he fetched
And took it and presented it for a first reading to Anu.
[The gods of] battle whom he had ensnared were disentangled;
He led (them) as captives into the presence of his fathers.   40
And as for the eleven creatures that Tiamat had created,
Smashed their weapons, tied them at his feet,
Made images of them and had them set up at the door of Apsu.
     "Let this be a sign that will never in future be forgotten!"
The gods looked, and their hearts were full of joy at him.   45
Lahmu and Lahamu and all his fathers
Embraced him, and Anshar the king proclaimed that there should be a reception
     for him.
Anu, Enlil, and Ea each presented him with gifts.
Damkina his mother exclaimed with joy at him;
She made him beam [inside (?)] his fine (?) house.   50
Marduk appointed Usmu, who had brought his greetings present as good news,
To be vizier of the Apsu, to take care of shrines.
The Igigi[14] assembled, and all of them did obeisance to him.
The Anunnaki,[15] each and every one, kissed his feet.
The whole assembly collected together to prostrate themselves.   55
They stood, they bowed, "Yes, King indeed!"
His fathers took their fill of his manliness,
[They took off his clothes] which were enveloped in the dust of combat.
With cypress they sprinkled his body.
He put on a princely garment,   60
A royal aura, a splendid crown.
He took up a mace and grasped it in his right hand.
He set a dragon at his feet,
Slung the staff of peace and obedience at his side.
Lahmu and Lahamu made their voices heard and spoke to the Igigi,   65
     "Previously Marduk was our beloved son
     But now he is your king. Take heed of his command."
Next they spoke and proclaimed in unison,
     "LUGAL-DIMMER-ANKIA is his name.[16] Trust in him!"
When they gave kingship to Marduk,   70
They spoke an oration for him, for blessing and obedience.
     "Henceforth you shall be the provider of shrines for us.
     Whatever you command, we shall perform ourselves."

---

14. A group of younger gods.
15. A group of fifty gods, sons of Anu and
     judges of the underworld.

16. Sumerian for "King of the gods of heaven
     and earth."

Marduk made his voice heard and spoke,
Addressed his words to the gods his fathers,   75
 "Over the Apsu, the sea-green dwelling,
 In front of Esharra, which I created for you,
 Where I strengthened the ground beneath it for a shrine,
 I shall make a house to be a luxurious dwelling for myself
 And shall found his cult centre within it,   80
 And I shall establish my private quarters, and confirm my kingship.
 Whenever you come up from the Apsu for an assembly,
 Your night's resting place shall be in it, receiving you all.
 Whenever you come down from the sky for an assembly,
 Your night's resting place shall be in it, receiving you all.   85
 I hereby name it Babylon, home of the great gods.
 We shall make it the center of religion."
The gods his fathers listened to this command of his, and said,
 "Babylon, whose name you have just pronounced,
 Found there our night's resting place forever!"[17]   90

Tablet VI

When Marduk heard the speech of the gods,
He made up his mind to perform miracles.
He spoke his utterance to Ea,
And communicated to him the plan that he was considering.
 "Let me put blood together, and make bones too.   5
 Let me set up primeval man: Man shall be his name.
 Let me create a primeval man.
 The work of the gods shall be imposed (on him), and so they shall be at leisure.
 Let me change the ways of the gods miraculously,
 So they are gathered as one yet divided in two."   10
Ea answered him and spoke a word to him,
Told him his plan for the leisure of the gods.
 "Let one who is hostile to them be surrendered (up),
 Let him be destroyed, and let people be created (from him).
 Let the great gods assemble,   15
 Let the culprit be given up, and let them convict him."
Marduk assembled the great gods,
Gave (them) instructions pleasantly, gave orders.
The gods paid attention to what he said.
The king addressed his words to the Anunnaki,   20
 "Your election of me shall be firm and foremost.
 I shall declare the laws, the edicts within my power.

---

17. Twenty fragmentary lines follow, ending
 with a postscript identifying the tablet's
 ownership—rather pointedly—as "Palace

of Assurbanipal, king of the world, king of
Assyria."

Whosoever started the war,
And incited Tiamat, and gathered an army,
Let the one who started the war be given up to me,   25
And he shall bear the penalty for his crime, that you may dwell in peace."
The Igigi, the great gods, answered him,
Their lord Lugal-dimmer-ankia, counsellor of gods,
    "It was Qingu who started the war,
    He who incited Tiamat and gathered an army!"   30
They bound him and held him in front of Ea,
Imposed the penalty on him and cut off his blood.
He created mankind from his blood,
Imposed the toil of the gods (on man) and released the gods from it.
When Ea the wise had created mankind,   35
Had imposed the toil of the gods on them—
That deed is impossible to describe,
For Nudimmud performed it with the miracles of Marduk—
Then Marduk the king divided the gods,
The Anunnaki, all of them, above and below.   40
He assigned his decrees to Anu to guard,
Established three hundred as a guard in the sky;
Did the same again when he designed the conventions of earth,
And made the six hundred dwell in both heaven and earth.
When he had directed all the decrees,   45
Had divided lots for the Anunnaki, of heaven and of earth,
The Anunnaki made their voices heard
And addressed Marduk their lord,
    "Now, O Lord, that you have set us free,
    What are our favours from you?   50
    We would like to make a shrine with its own name.
    We would like our night's resting place to be in your private quarters, and to
       rest there.
    Let us found a shrine, a sanctuary there.
    Whenever we arrive, let us rest within it."
When Marduk heard this,   55
His face lit up greatly, like daylight.
    "Create Babylon, whose construction you requested!
    Let its mud bricks be moulded, and build high the shrine!"
The Anunnaki began shovelling.
For a whole year they made bricks for it.   60
When the second year arrived,
They had raised the top of Esagila in front of the Apsu;
They had built a high ziggurrat[18] for the Apsu.
They founded a dwelling for Anu, Ellil, and Ea likewise.

---

18. A terraced pyramid crowned with a temple.

In ascendancy he settled himself in front of them,   65
And his 'horns' look down at the base of Esharra.
When they had done the work on Esagila,
And the Anunnaki, all of them, had fashioned their individual shrines,
The three hundred Igigi of heaven and the Anunnaki of the Apsu all assembled.
The Lord invited the gods his fathers to attend a banquet   70
In the great sanctuary which he had created as his dwelling.
  "Indeed, Bab-ili is your home too![19]
  Sing for joy there, dwell in happiness!"
The great gods sat down there,
And set out the beer mugs; they attended the banquet.   75
When they had made merry within,
They themselves made an offering in splendid Esagila.
All the decrees and designs were fixed.
All the gods divided the stations of heaven and earth.
The fifty great gods were present, and   80
The gods fixed the seven destinies for the cult.
The Lord received the bow, and set his weapon down in front of them.
The gods his fathers looked at the net which he had made,
Looked at the bow, how miraculous her construction,
And his fathers praised the deeds that he had done.   85
Anu raised (the bow) and spoke in the assembly of gods,
He kissed the bow. "May she go far!"[20]
He gave to the bow her names, saying,
  "May Long and Far be the first, and Victorious the second;
  Her third name shall be Bowstar, for she shall shine in the sky."   90
He fixed her position among the gods her companions.
When Anu had decreed the destiny of the bow,
He set down her royal throne. "You are highest of the gods!"
And Anu made her sit in the assembly of gods.
The great gods assembled   95
And made Marduk's destiny highest; they themselves did obeisance.
They swore an oath for themselves,
And swore on water and oil, touched their throats.
Thus they granted that he should exercise the kingship of the gods
And confirmed for him mastery of the gods of heaven and earth.   100

Anshar gave him another name: ASARLUHI.[21]
  "At the mention of his name we shall bow down!
  The gods are to pay heed to what he says:

---

19. "Babylon" is written phonetically in this
    line as "Bab-ili," to emphasize its meaning
    of "Gate of God."

20. The bow is apparently treated as a mani-
    festation of Ishtar.

21. Originally a separate god, with powers of
    magic and healing, here assimilated with
    Marduk.

His command is to have priority above and below.
The son who avenged us shall be the highest! 105
His rule shall have priority; let him have no rival!
Let him act as shepherd over the dark-headed people, his creation.
Let his way be proclaimed in future days, never forgotten.
He shall establish great offerings for his fathers.
He shall take care of them, he shall look after their shrines. 110
He shall let them smell the offering, and make their chant joyful.
Let him breathe on earth as freely as he always does in heaven.
Let him designate the dark-headed people to revere him,
That mankind may be mindful of him, and name him as their god.
Let their interceding goddess pay attention when he opens his mouth. 115
Let offerings be brought [to] their god and their goddess.
Let them never be forgotten! Let them cleave to their god.
Let them keep their country pre-eminent, and always build shrines.
Though the dark-headed people share out the gods,
As for us, no matter by which name we call him, he shall be our god. 120
Come, let us call him by his fifty names!
His ways shall be proclaimed, and his deeds likewise!"[22]

With fifty epithets the great gods
Called his fifty names, making his way supreme.
May they always be cherished, and may the older explain to the younger. 125
Let the wise and learned consult together,
Let the father repeat them and teach them to the son.
Let the ear of shepherd and herdsman be open,
Let him not be negligent to Marduk, the Ellil of the gods.
May his country be made fertile, and himself be safe and sound. 130
His word is firm, his command cannot alter;
No god can change his utterance.
When he is angry, he does not turn his neck aside;
In his rage and fury no god dare confront him.
His thoughts are deep, his emotions profound; 135
Criminals and wrongdoers pass before him.

The scribe wrote down the secret instruction which older men had recited in his
    presence,
And set it down for future men to read.
May the peoples of Marduk whom the Igigi gods created
Weave the tale and call upon his name 140
In remembrance of the song of Marduk
Who defeated Tiamat and took the kingship.

---

22. An extended listing follows, but is omitted here. Some names are of formerly independent gods, now identified with Marduk; others describe various aspects of his power.

ANONYMOUS (c. 2300 B.C.E.)
Egypt

Pyramid texts are among the oldest writings in the world. They were found carved on the interior walls of the pyramids of rulers from the Fifth and Sixth dynasties of Egypt (c. 2500–2180 B.C.E.). The texts consist of incantations and spells to ensure the king's resurrection and his success in earning immortality as a god in the afterlife. In order to achieve immortality, the soul had to purify itself and defeat a variety of hostile underworld forces. Priests recited the texts during the several stages of the burial itself and again during subsequent offerings of food and drink at the tomb. The texts of Unas are the best preserved of the examples that have come down to us. The last king of the Fifth Dynasty, Unas died around 2300 B.C.E.

Although the emphasis on cannibalism in the first selection soon disappeared from the tradition of pyramid texts, the practice is reflected in the many regional myths of generational succession among the gods. Hesiod's *Theogony*, for example, tells of how the god Zeus triumphed over his father, Cronos, who devoured his own children in order to forestall the succession to his throne. The brief second selection shows Unas in a far humbler relationship to the gods he hopes to rejoin.

from *The Pyramid Texts of Unas*

[Sky rains, stars darken]

Sky rains, stars darken,
The vaults quiver, earth's bones tremble,
The planets stand still
At seeing Unas rise as power,
A god who lives on his fathers,   5
Who feeds on his mothers!

Unas is master of cunning,
Whose mother knows not his name;
Unas's glory is in heaven,
His power is in the horizon;   10
Like Atum, his father, his begetter,
Though his son, he is stronger than he!

The forces of Unas are behind him,
His helpers are under his feet,
His gods on his head, his serpents on his brow,   15
Unas's lead-serpent is on his brow,

Translated by Miriam Lichtheim.

Soul-searcher whose flame consumes,
Unas's neck is in its place.

Unas is the bull of heaven
Who rages in his heart,   20
Who lives on the being of every god,
Who eats their entrails
When they come, their bodies full of magic
From the Isle of Flame.[1]

Unas is one equipped who has gathered his spirits,   25
Unas has risen as Great One, as master of servants,
He will sit with his back to Geb,[2]
Unas will judge with Him-whose-name-is-hidden
On the day of slaying the eldest.
Unas is lord of offerings who knots the cord,   30
Who himself prepares his meal.

Unas is he who eats men, feeds on gods,
Master of messengers who sends instructions:
It is Horn-grasper in Kehau who lassoes them for Unas,
It is Serpent Raised-head who guards, who holds them for him, 35
It is He-upon-the-willows who binds them for him.
It is Khons, slayer of lords, who cuts their throats for Unas,
Who tears their entrails out for him,
He the envoy who is sent to punish.
It is Shesmu[3] who carves them up for Unas,   40
Cooks meals of them for him in his dinner-pots.

Unas eats their magic, swallows their spirits:
Their big ones are for his morning meal,
Their middle ones for his evening meal,
Their little ones for his night meal,   45
And the oldest males and females for his fuel.
The Great Ones in the northern sky light him fire
For the kettles' contents with the old ones' thighs,
For the sky-dwellers serve Unas,
And the pots are scraped for him with their women's legs.   50

He has encompassed the two skies,
He has circled the two shores;
Unas is the great power that overpowers the powers,
Unas is the divine hawk, the great hawk of hawks,
Whom he finds on his way he devours whole.   55

---

1. A heavenly region.
2. The god of earth, known as the father of the gods.
3. The god of oil and wine.

Unas's place is before all the nobles in the horizon,
Unas is god, oldest of the old,
Thousands serve him, hundreds offer to him,
Great-Power rank was given him by Orion, father of gods.

Unas has risen again in heaven,   60
He is crowned as lord of the horizon.
He has smashed bones and marrow,
He has seized the hearts of gods,
He has eaten the Red, swallowed the Green.[4]
Unas feeds on the lungs of the wise,   65
Likes to live on hearts and their magic;
Unas abhors licking the coils of the Red
But delights to have their magic in his belly.

The dignities of Unas will not be taken from him,
For he has swallowed the knowledge of every god;   70
Unas's lifetime is forever, his limit is eternity
In his dignity of "If-he-likes-he-does if-he-hates-he-does-not,"
As he dwells in the horizon for all eternity.
Lo, their power is in Unas's belly,
Their spirits are before Unas as broth of the gods,   75
Cooked for Unas from their bones.
Lo, their power is with Unas,
Their shadows are taken from their owners,
For Unas is of those who risen is risen, lasting lasts.
Nor can evildoers harm Unas's chosen seat   80
Among the living in this land for all eternity!

[Unas is gods' steward, behind the mansion of Re]

Unas is gods' steward, behind the mansion of Re,
Born of Wish-of-the-gods, who is in the bow of Re's bark;[5]
Unas squats before him,
Unas opens his boxes,
Unas unseals his decrees,   5
Unas seals his dispatches,
Unas sends his messengers who tire not,
Unas does what Unas is told.

---

4. The "Red" is the crown of Lower Egypt (the northern half of the country, "lower" because farther down the Nile); the "Green" is Wadjet, the cobra goddess of Lower Egypt.

5. Probably a reference to the goddess Maat ("Truth"), daughter of Re.

HESIOD (EIGHTH CENTURY B.C.E.)
Greece

The *Theogony* names Hesiod as its author, but our only information about him comes from the purportedly autobiographical references within the poems ascribed to him, especially *Works and Days,* in which the narrator relates that his father fled poverty in Asia Minor and came to mainland Greece. Although the alphabet was introduced into Greece in the early eighth century B.C.E., we cannot say whether Hesiod was literate. The *Theogony,* however, clearly belongs in the tradition of oral composition and performance. Like the *Iliad* and the *Odyssey,* it is composed in dactylic hexameter (the meter characteristic of epic verse), uses a special amalgam of dialects adapted to the meter, and includes "formulas"— repeated phrases that facilitated oral composition.

The *Theogony*'s account of how the cosmos came into being and of the genealogy and social order of the gods is representative of a widespread type of literary composition describing the creation of the universe; the opening of Genesis (and its subsequent genealogies) may be said to be another example. The *Theogony* draws on traditional mythological material, and its account shows remarkable parallels with a second millennium B.C.E. Hittite text from Asia Minor as well as with the Babylonian *Enuma Elish* in this section. Hesiod traces hundreds of deities descended from three lineages: the Night, the Sea, and Heaven and Earth. Those descended from Heaven and Earth are given prominence because Heaven and Earth are also the progenitors of the current and (we are to understand) permanent divine regime under the leadership of Zeus, whose rule (after struggles detailed in the *Theogony*) is now beyond challenge.

from *Theogony*

[Now let us begin with the Olympian Muses]

Now let us begin with the Olympian Muses who sing for their father Zeus and delight his great soul, telling with harmonious voices of things past and present and to come. Sweet song pours from their mouths and never wearies; the house of their father Zeus the Thunderer laughs as the lily-like voice of the goddesses floats through it; the peaks of snowy Olympus and the homes of the gods echo with the sound. They lift their immortal voices to celebrate first the venerable primeval generation of the gods, born from Mother Earth and huge Father Sky, and then the gods who are descended from them and from whom all blessings flow. Secondly, they honor Zeus, the father of gods and men, both at the beginning and at the end of their song, since he is the greatest of the gods and the first in power. Next the Olympian Muses, the daughters of Zeus the lord of the aegis, delight the soul of Zeus on Mount Olympus by singing of mankind and of

Translated by Norman O. Brown.

the mighty Giants. These Muses were born in Pieria to Mnemosyne [Memory], the queen of the hills of Eleuther, after her union with Father Zeus the son of Cronus; their nature is forgetfulness of evil and rest from cares. On nine successive nights did Zeus the lord of wisdom unite with her, going to her sacred bed unknown to the rest of the gods; and when the year was up, as the seasons revolved and the months waned and many days had passed, she gave birth to nine daughters all of one mind, all with spirits dedicated to song, all carefree in their hearts. A little way from the topmost peak of snowy Olympus were they born, and that is where their smooth dancing floor and their beautiful home is; near them the Graces and Passion keep festive house. As soon as they were born, this immortal choir went in procession to Olympus, glorying in the beauty of their voice. The dark earth echoed all around as they sang, and under their feet a lovely sound leaped up as they went to their father—their father the king of heaven, the sole possessor of the thunder and the blasting lightning-bolt, who by his power conquered his father Cronus, who in his wisdom assigned to each of the gods their properties and settled their privileges.

Such was the song of the Muses whose home is Olympus—nine daughters of great Zeus: Clio and Euterpe and Thalia and Melpomene; Terpsichore and Erato and Polyhymnia and Urania; also Calliope; Calliope is the most exalted of them all, since it is she who attends on the majesty of kings. Whenever the daughters of great Zeus observe the birth of one of those appointed by Zeus to be kings and decide to honor him, they pour sweet dew upon his tongue, and the words flow like honey from his lips. All the people look up to him as he in judgment gives straight verdicts; with his sure eloquence he knows how to bring even large disputes to a quick end. Kings must have strength of mind for this—that they may secure redress for people who are wronged in the market place, their gentle words winning eager consent. Such a king, as he enters the assembly, receives worship like a god and gentle reverence: he is conspicuous in the assembled multitude. Such is the sacred gift of the Muses to mankind. It is the gift of the Muses and of the archer-god Apollo that makes men on earth singers and musicians; it is the gift of Zeus that makes men kings. Fortunate is the man whom the Muses love: sweet words flow from his lips. If someone has sorrow and is sick at heart and stunned with fresh trouble on his mind, and if a servant of the Muses sings of the glorious deeds of men in former times or of the blessed gods whose home is Olympus, he quickly forgets his bad thoughts and no longer remembers his troubles: the gifts of these goddesses instantly divert the mind.

Daughters of Zeus, I greet you; add passion to my song, and tell of the sacred race of gods who are forever, descended from Earth and starry Sky, from dark Night, and from salty Sea. Tell how in the beginning the gods and the earth came into being, as well as the rivers, the limitless sea with its raging surges, the shining stars, and the broad sky above—also how they divided the estate and distributed privileges among themselves, and how they first established themselves in the folds of Mount Olympus. Relate these things to me, Muses whose home is Olympus, from the beginning; tell me which of them first came into being.

[First of all, the Void came into being]

First of all, the Void came into being, next broad-bosomed Earth, the solid and eternal home of all, and Eros [Desire], the most beautiful of the immortal gods, who in every man and every god softens the sinews and overpowers the prudent purpose of the mind. Out of Void came Darkness and black Night, and out of Night came Light and Day, her children conceived after union in love with Darkness. Earth first produced starry Sky, equal in size with herself, to cover her on all sides. Next she produced the tall mountains, the pleasant haunts of the gods, and also gave birth to the barren waters, sea with its raging surges—all this without the passion of love. Thereafter she lay with Sky and gave birth to Ocean with its deep current, Coeus and Crius and Hyperion and Iapetus. Thea and Rhea and Themis [Law] and Mnemosyne [Memory]: also golden-crowned Phoebe and lovely Tethys.[1] After these came cunning Cronus, the youngest and boldest of her children; and he grew to hate the father who had begotten him.

Earth also gave birth to the violent Cyclopes—Thunderer, Lightner, and bold Flash—who made and gave to Zeus the thunder and the lightning-bolt. They were like the gods in all respects except that a single eye stood in the middle of their foreheads, and their strength and power and skill were in their hands.

There were also born to Earth and Sky three more children, big, strong, and horrible, Cottus and Briareus and Gyes. This unruly brood had a hundred monstrous hands sprouting from their shoulders, and fifty heads on top of their shoulders growing from their sturdy bodies. They had monstrous strength to match their huge size.

[Of all the children born of Earth and Sky]

Of all the children born of Earth and Sky these were the boldest, and their father hated them from the beginning. As each of them was about to be born, Sky would not let them reach the light of day; instead he hid them all away in the bowels of Mother Earth. Sky took pleasure in doing this evil thing. In spite of her enormous size, Earth felt the strain within her and groaned. Finally she thought of an evil and cunning stratagem. She instantly produced a new metal, gray steel, and made a huge sickle. Then she laid the matter before her children; the anguish in her heart made her speak boldly: "My children, you have a savage father; if you will listen to me, we may be able to take vengeance for his evil outrage: he was the one who started using violence."

This was what she said; but all the children were gripped by fear, and not one

---

1. These are some of the more benign members of the generally violent older generation of gods called Titans. Of Crius little is known; Hyperion and Thea are the parents of Helios, the sun; Iapetus is the father of Prometheus; Rhea is the mother of Zeus; Themis, the guardian of social order among the gods, bore Zeus a number of children, including the Seasons and the Fates; Mnemosyne is the mother of the Muses; Coeus and Phoebe are the parents of Leto, who bore Apollo and Artemis to Zeus; and Tethys is a goddess of the sea and the wife of Ocean.

of them spoke a word. Then great Cronus, the cunning trickster, took courage and answered his good mother with these words: "Mother, I am willing to undertake and carry through your plan. I have no respect for our infamous father, since he was the one who started using violence."

This was what he said, and enormous Earth was very pleased. She hid him in ambush and put in his hands the sickle with jagged teeth, and instructed him fully in her plot. Huge Sky came drawing night behind him and desiring to make love; he lay on top of Earth stretched all over her. Then from his ambush his son reached out with his left hand and with his right took the huge sickle with its long jagged teeth and quickly sheared the organs from his own father and threw them away, backward over his shoulder. But that was not the end of them. The drops of blood that spurted from them were all taken in by Mother Earth, and in the course of the revolving years she gave birth to the powerful Erinyes [Spirits of Vengeance] and the huge Giants with shining armor and long spears. As for the organs themselves, for a long time they drifted round the sea just as they were when Cronus cut them off with the steel edge and threw them from the land into the waves of the ocean; then white foam issued from the divine flesh, and in the foam a girl began to grow. First she came near to holy Cythera, then reached Cyprus, the land surrounded by sea. There she stepped out, a goddess, tender and beautiful, and round her slender feet the green grass shot up. She is called Aphrodite by gods and men, because she grew in the *froth*,[2] and also Cytherea, because she came near to Cythera, and the Cyprian, because she was born in watery Cyprus. Eros [Desire] and beautiful Passion were her attendants both at her birth and at her first going to join the family of the gods. The rights and privileges assigned to her from the beginning and recognized by men and gods are these: to preside over the whispers and smiles and tricks which girls employ, and the sweet delight and tenderness of love.

[More genealogies follow, culminating in the account of the birth of the children of Cronus and Rhea.]

[Rhea submitted to the embraces of Cronus]

Rhea submitted to the embraces of Cronus and bore him children with a glorious destiny: Hestia, Demeter, and Hera, who walks on golden sandals; Hades, the powerful god whose home is underground and whose heart is pitiless; Poseidon, the god whose great blows make the earth quake; and Zeus the lord of wisdom, the father of gods and men, whose thunder makes the broad earth tremble. As each of these children came out of their mother's holy womb onto her knees, great Cronus swallowed them. His purpose was to prevent the kingship of the gods from passing to another one of the august descendants of Sky; he had been told by Earth and starry Sky that he was destined to be overcome by his own son. For that reason he kept a sleepless watch and waited for his own children to be born and then

---

2. The word *aphros* in Greek means foam; the poet associates it here with the name of the goddess (although the words are not actually etymologically related).

swallowed them. Rhea had no rest from grief; so, when she was about to give birth to Zeus, the father of gods and men, she begged her own dear parents, Earth and starry Sky, to help her contrive a plan whereby she might bear her child without Cronus' knowing it, and make amends to the vengeful spirits of her father Sky. Earth and Sky listened to their daughter and granted her request; they told her what was destined to happen to King Cronus and to his bold son. When she was about to give birth to great Zeus, her youngest child, they sent her to the rich Cretan town of Lyctus. Huge Mother Earth undertook to nurse and raise the infant in the broad land of Crete. Dark night was rushing on as Earth arrived there carrying him, and Lyctus was the first place where she stopped. She took him and hid him in an inaccessible cave, deep in the bowels of holy earth, in the dense woods of Mount Aegeum. Then she wrapped a huge stone in baby blankets and handed it to the royal son of Sky, who then was king of the gods. He took the stone and swallowed it into his belly—the fool! He did not know that a stone had replaced his son, who survived, unconquered and untroubled, and who was going to overcome him by force and drive him from his office and reign over the gods in his place.

The young prince grew quickly in strength and stature. After years had passed Cronus the great trickster fell victim to the cunning suggestions of Mother Earth and threw up his own children again. The first thing he vomited was the stone, the last thing he had swallowed; Zeus set it up on the highways of the earth in holy Pytho under the slopes of Parnassus, to be a sign and a wonder to mankind thereafter.

Zeus also set free his father's brothers from the cruel chains in which their father Sky had in foolish frenzy bound them. They gratefully remembered his kindness and gave him the thunder and the lightning-bolt and flash, which huge Earth had kept hidden till then. In these weapons Zeus trusts; they make him master over gods and men.

[The *Theogony* goes on to recount the gift of fire to men by the Titan Prometheus, the creation of the first woman, and the Olympian gods' victorious struggle, under Zeus's leadership, against the Titans, whom they relegate permanently to the netherworld. The poem ends with an account of the children born to the Olympian gods.]

THE BIBLE

(EARLY FIRST MILLENNIUM B.C.E.)
Babylon

Genesis, meaning "beginning," is the first of the five books of Moses with which the Bible begins. These books are known collectively in Hebrew as the Torah, or "law." Chapters 1 through 11 form the opening section, a primeval history that serves as a prelude to the history of the Hebrew people and their relations with

God. The stories in these chapters are modeled after older Near Eastern accounts of creation, flood, and the subsequent ordering of the world such as those found in the *Enuma Elish* and the *Epic of Gilgamesh*.

Genesis is the product of several stages of composition, reflecting successive reworkings of these polytheistic stories to suit an increasingly monotheistic religion. The initial account, known as the Yahwistic version (from *Yahweh,* the name given to God by the Hebrews), probably dates to around the time of Solomon (the early tenth century B.C.E.). This version was revised by a later writer known as the Elohist (from *Elohim,* the name that he gave to God). Still later, a writer or group of writers known as the Priestly source made further revisions.

The process has left interesting differences between the two creation stories given here. Genesis 1 is a Priestly account of creation. It may have replaced an earlier, less strictly monotheistic account. (Several psalms preserve elements of stories in which Yahweh must defeat other primordial forces in order to establish the world.) The Yahwistic story of Eden that follows portrays a more mysterious and tentative relationship between God and his creation.

from **The Bible**

GENESIS 1–11

[*The Creation Story*]

1

In the beginning God created the heavens and the earth. Now the earth was formless and empty, darkness was over the surface of the deep,[1] and the Spirit of God was hovering over the waters.

And God said, "Let there be light," and there was light. God saw that the light was good, and he separated the light from the darkness. God called the light "day" and the darkness he called "night." And there was evening, and there was morning—the first day.

And God said, "Let there be an expanse between the waters to separate water from water."[2] So God made the expanse and separated the water under the expanse from the water above it. And it was so. God called the expanse "sky." And there was evening, and there was morning—the second day.

And God said, "Let the water under the sky be gathered to one place, and let dry ground appear." And it was so. God called the dry ground "land," and the gathered waters he called "seas." And God saw that it was good.

Then God said, "Let the land produce vegetation: seed-bearing plants and trees on the land that bear fruit with seed in it, according to their various kinds."

New International Version

1. "The deep," *tehom* in Hebrew, is related to Akkadian "Tiamat."
2. Whereas *Enuma Elish* shows the primeval gods being born from the mingling of Apsu and Tiamat, the Bible pointedly shows God beginning by *separating* the two—natural, not divine—bodies of water.

And it was so. The land produced vegetation: plants bearing seed according to their kinds and trees bearing fruit with seed in it according to their kinds. And God saw that it was good. And there was evening, and there was morning—the third day.

And God said, "Let there be lights in the expanse of the sky to separate the day from the night, and let them serve as signs to mark seasons and days and years, and let them be lights in the expanse of the sky to give light on the earth." And it was so. "God made two great lights—the greater light to govern the day and the lesser light to govern the night. He also made the stars. God set them in the expanse of the sky to give light on the earth, to govern the day and the night, and to separate light from darkness. And God saw that it was good. And there was evening, and there was morning—the fourth day.

And God said, "Let the water teem with living creatures, and let birds fly above the earth across the expanse of the sky." So God created the great creatures of the sea and every living and moving thing with which the water teems, according to their kinds, and every winged bird according to its kind. And God saw that it was good. God blessed them and said, "Be fruitful and increase in number and fill the water in the seas, and let the birds increase on the earth." And there was evening, and there was morning—the fifth day.

And God said, "Let the land produce living creatures according to their kinds: livestock, creatures that move along the ground, and wild animals, each according to its kind." And it was so. God made the wild animals according to their kinds, the livestock according to their kinds, and all the creatures that move along the ground according to their kinds. And God saw that it was good.

Then God said, "Let us make man in our image, in our likeness, and let them rule over the fish of the sea and the birds of the air, over the livestock, over all the earth, and over all the creatures that move along the ground."

> So God created man in his own image,
> in the image of God he created him;
> male and female he created them.

God blessed them and said to them, "Be fruitful and increase in number; fill the earth and subdue it. Rule over the fish of the sea and the birds of the air and over every living creature that moves on the ground."

Then God said, "I give you every seed-bearing plant on the face of the whole earth and every tree that has fruit with seed in it. They will be yours for food. And to all the beasts of the earth and all the birds of the air and all the creatures that move on the ground—everything that has the breath of life in it—I give every green plant for food." And it was so.

God saw all that he had made, and it was very good. And there was evening and there was morning—the sixth day.

2

Thus the heavens and the earth were completed in all their vast array.

By the seventh day God had finished the work he had been doing; so on the seventh day he rested from all his work. And God blessed the seventh day and made it holy, because on it he rested from all the work of creating that he had done. This is the account of the heavens and the earth when they were created.[3]

When the LORD God made the earth and the heavens, no shrub of the field had yet appeared on the earth and no plant of the field had yet sprung up; the LORD God had not sent rain on the earth and there was no man to work the ground, but streams came up from the earth and watered the whole surface of the ground. And the LORD God formed man from the dust of the ground[4] and breathed into his nostrils the breath of life, and man became a living being.

Now the LORD God had planted a garden in the east, in Eden; and there he put the man he had formed. And the LORD God made all kinds of trees grow out of the ground—trees that were pleasing to the eye and good for food. In the middle of the garden were the tree of life and the tree of the knowledge of good and evil.

A river watering the garden flowed from Eden, and from there it divided; it had four headstreams. The name of the first is the Pishon; it winds through the entire land of Havilah, where there is gold. (The gold of that land is good; aromatic resin and onyx are also there.) The name of the second river is the Gihon; it winds through the entire land of Cush. The name of the third river is the Tigris; it runs along the east side of Asshur. And the fourth river is the Euphrates.[5]

The LORD God took the man and put him in the Garden of Eden to work it and take care of it. And the LORD God commanded the man, "You are free to eat from any tree in the garden; but you must not eat from the tree of the knowledge of good and evil, for when you eat of it you will surely die."

The LORD God said, "It is not good for the man to be alone. I will make a helper suitable for him."

Now the LORD God had formed out of the ground all the beasts of the field and all the birds of the air. He brought them to the man to see what he would name them; and whatever the man called each living creature, that was its name. So the man gave names to all the livestock, the birds of the air and all the beasts of the field.

But for man no suitable helper was found. So the LORD God caused the man to fall into a deep sleep; and while he was sleeping, he took one of the man's ribs and closed up the place with flesh. Then the LORD God made a woman from the rib he had taken out of the man, and he brought her to the man.

The man said,

"This is now bone of my bones
and flesh of my flesh;
she shall be called woman,
for she was taken out of man."[6]

---

3. This is the conclusion to the Priestly account of creation. Next comes a different ("Yahwistic") account of the creation of humanity.

4. "Man" in Hebrew, adam, is here derived from "ground," adamah.

5. Eden is thus located in southern Mesopotamia.

6. "Woman," ishshah, is seen as formed from "man," ish.

For this reason a man will leave his father and mother and be united to his wife, and they will become one flesh.

The man and his wife were both naked, and they felt no shame.

3

Now the serpent was more crafty than any of the wild animals the LORD God had made. He said to the woman. "Did God really say, 'You must not eat from any tree in the garden'?"

The woman said to the serpent, "We may eat fruit from the trees in the garden, but God did say, 'You must not eat fruit from the tree that is in the middle of the garden, and you must not touch it, or you will die.'"

"You will not surely die," the serpent said to the woman. "For God knows that when you eat of it your eyes will be opened, and you will be like God, knowing good and evil."

When the woman saw that the fruit of the tree was good for food and pleasing to the eye, and also desirable for gaining wisdom, she took some and ate it. She also gave some to her husband, who was with her, and he ate it. Then the eyes of both of them were opened, and they realized they were naked; so they sewed fig leaves together and made coverings for themselves.

Then the man and his wife heard the sound of the LORD God as he was walking in the garden in the cool of the day, and they hid from the LORD God among the trees of the garden. But the LORD God called to the man, "Where are you?"

He answered, "I heard you in the garden, and I was afraid because I was naked; so I hid."

And he said, "Who told you that you were naked? Have you eaten from the tree that I commanded you not to eat from?"

The man said, "The woman you put here with me—she gave me some fruit from the tree, and I ate it."

Then the LORD God said to the woman, "What is this you have done?"

The woman said, "The serpent deceived me, and I ate."

So the LORD God said to the serpent, "Because you have done this,

"Cursed are you above all the livestock
and all the wild animals!
You will crawl on your belly
and you will eat dust
all the days of your life.
And I will put enmity
between you and the woman,
and between your offspring and hers;
he will crush your head, and you will strike his heel."

To the woman he said,

"I will greatly increase your pains in childbearing;
with pain you will give birth to children.

Your desire will be for your husband,
and he will rule over you."

To Adam he said, "Because you listened to your wife and ate from the tree about which I commanded you, 'You must not eat of it.'

"Cursed is the ground because of you;
through painful toil you will eat of it
all the days of your life.
It will produce thorns and thistles for you,
and you will eat the plants of the field.
By the sweat of your brow you will eat your food
until you return to the ground,
    since from it you were taken;
    for dust you are
    and to dust you will return."

Adam named his wife Eve, because she would become the mother of all the living.[7]

The LORD God made garments of skin for Adam and his wife and clothed them. And the LORD God said, "The man has now become like one of us, knowing good and evil. He must not be allowed to reach out his hand and take also from the tree of life and eat, and live forever." So the LORD God banished him from the Garden of Eden to work the ground from which he had been taken. After he drove the man out, he placed on the east side of the Garden of Eden cherubim and a flaming sword flashing back and forth to guard the way to the tree of life.

4

Adam lay with his wife Eve, and she conceived and gave birth to Cain. She said, "With the help of the LORD I have brought forth a man."[8] Later she gave birth to his brother Abel.

Now Abel kept flocks, and Cain worked the soil. In the course of time Cain brought some of the fruits of the soil as an offering to the LORD. But Abel brought fat portions from some of the firstborn of his flock. The LORD looked with favor on Abel and his offering, but on Cain and his offering he did not look with favor. So Cain was very angry, and his face was downcast.

Then the LORD said to Cain, "Why are you angry? Why is your face downcast? If you do what is right, will you not be accepted? But if you do not do what is right, sin is crouching at your door; it desires to have you, but you must master it."

Now Cain said to his brother Abel, "Let's go out to the field." And while they were in the field, Cain attacked his brother Abel and killed him.

Then the LORD said to Cain, "Where is your brother Abel?"

"I don't know," he replied. "Am I my brother's keeper?"

---

7. "Eve" means "living."

8. "Cain" sounds like the Hebrew for "brought forth."

The LORD said, "What have you done? Listen! Your brother's blood cries out to me from the ground. Now you are under a curse and driven from the ground, which opened its mouth to receive your brother's blood from your hand. When you work the ground, it will no longer yield its crops for you. You will be a restless wanderer on the earth."

Cain said to the LORD, "My punishment is more than I can bear. Today you are driving me from the land, and I will be hidden from your presence; I will be a restless wanderer on the earth, and whoever finds me will kill me."

But the LORD said to him, "Very well: if anyone kills Cain, he will suffer vengeance seven times over." Then the LORD put a mark on Cain so that no one who found him would kill him. So Cain went out from the LORD's presence and lived in the land of Nod[9] east of Eden.

Cain lay with his wife, and she became pregnant and gave birth to Enoch. Cain was then building a city, and he named it after his son Enoch. To Enoch was born Irad, and Irad was the father of Mehujael, and Mehujael was the father of Methushael, and Methushael was the father of Lamech.

Lamech married two women, one named Adah and the other Zillah. Adah gave birth to Jabal; he was the father of those who live in tents and raise livestock. His brother's name was Jubal; he was the father of all who play the harp and flute. Zillah also had a son, Tubal-Cain, who forged all kinds of tools out of bronze and iron. Tubal-Cain's sister was Naamah.

Lamech said to his wives,

"Adah and Zillah, listen to me;
wives of Lamech, hear my words.
I have killed a man for wounding me,
a young man for injuring me.
If Cain is avenged seven times,
then Lamech seventy-seven times."

Adam lay with his wife again, and she gave birth to a son and named him Seth,[10] saying, "God has granted me another child in place of Abel, since Cain killed him." Seth also had a son, and he named him Enosh. At that time men began to call on the name of the LORD.

5

This is the written account of Adam's line.

When God created man, he made him in the likeness of God. He created them male and female; at the time they were created, he blessed them and called them "man."

When Adam had lived 130 years, he had a son in his own likeness, in his own image; and he named him Seth. After Seth was born, Adam lived 800 years and had other sons and daughters. Altogether, Adam lived 930 years, and then he died.

When Seth had lived 105 years, he became the father of Enosh. And after he

---

9. "Nod" means "wandering."   10. "Seth" probably means "granted."

became the father of Enosh, Seth lived 807 years and had other sons and daughters. Altogether, Seth lived 912 years, and then he died.

When Enosh had lived 90 years, he became the father of Kenan. And after he became the father of Kenan, Enosh lived 815 years and had other sons and daughters. Altogether, Enosh lived 905 years, and then he died.

When Kenan had lived 70 years, he became the father of Mahalalel. And after he became the father of Mahalalel, Kenan lived 840 years and had other sons and daughters. Altogether, Kenan lived 910 years, and then he died.

When Mahalalel had lived 65 years, he became the father of Jared. And after he became the father of Jared, Mahalalel lived 830 years and had other sons and daughters. Altogether, Mahalalel lived 895 years, and then he died.

When Jared had lived 162 years, he became the father of Enoch. And after he became the father of Enoch, Jared lived 800 years and had other sons and daughters. Altogether, Jared lived 962 years, and then he died.

When Enoch had lived 65 years, he became the father of Methuselah. And after he became the father of Methuselah, Enoch walked with God 300 years and had other sons and daughters. Altogether, Enoch lived 365 years. Enoch walked with God; then he was no more, because God took him away.

When Methuselah had lived 187 years, he became the father of Lamech. And after he became the father of Lamech, Methuselah lived 782 years and had other sons and daughters. Altogether, Methuselah lived 969 years, and then he died.

When Lamech had lived 182 years, he had a son. He named him Noah and said, "He will comfort us[11] in the labor and painful toil of our hands caused by the ground the LORD has cursed." After Noah was born, Lamech lived 595 years and had other sons and daughters. Altogether, Lamech lived 777 years, and then he died.

After Noah was 500 years old, he became the father of Shem, Ham and Japheth.

6

When men began to increase in number on the earth and daughters were born to them, the sons of God saw that the daughters of men were beautiful, and they married any of them they chose. Then the LORD said, "My Spirit will not remain in man forever, for he is mortal; his days will be a hundred and twenty years."

The Nephilim were on the earth in those days—and also afterward—when the sons of God went to the daughters of men and had children by them. They were the heroes of old, men of renown.

The LORD saw how great man's wickedness on the earth had become, and that every inclination of the thoughts of his heart was only evil all the time. The LORD was grieved that he had made man on the earth, and his heart was filled with pain. So the LORD said, "I will wipe mankind, whom I have created, from the face of the

---

11. "Noah" sounds like the Hebrew for "to comfort."

earth—men and animals, and creatures that move along the ground, and birds of the air—for I am grieved that I have made them." But Noah found favor in the eyes of the LORD.

This is the account of Noah. Noah was a righteous man, blameless among the people of his time, and he walked with God. Noah had three sons: Shem, Ham and Japheth.

Now the earth was corrupt in God's sight and was full of violence. God saw how corrupt the earth had become, for all the people on earth had corrupted their ways. So God said to Noah, "I am going to put an end to all people, for the earth is filled with violence because of them. I am surely going to destroy both them and the earth. So make yourself an ark of cypress' wood; make rooms in it and coat it with pitch inside and out. This is how you are to build it: The ark is to be 300 cubits long, 50 cubits wide and 30 cubits high.[12] Make a roof for it and finish the ark to within one cubit of the top. Put a door in the side of the ark and make lower, middle and upper decks. I am going to bring floodwaters on the earth to destroy all life under the heavens, every creature that has the breath of life in it. Everything on earth will perish. But I will establish my covenant with you, and you will enter the ark—you and your sons and your wife and your sons' wives with you. You are to bring into the ark two of all living creatures, male and female, to keep them alive with you. Two of every kind of bird, of every kind of animal and of every kind of creature that moves along the ground will come to you to be kept alive. You are to take every kind of food that is to be eaten and store it away as food for you and for them."

Noah did everything just as God commanded him.

7

The LORD then said to Noah, "Go into the ark, you and your whole family, because I have found you righteous in this generation. Take with you seven pairs of every kind of clean animal, a male and its mate, and two of every kind of unclean animal, a male and its mate, and also seven pairs of every kind of bird, male and female, to keep their various kinds alive throughout the earth. Seven days from now I will send rain on the earth for forty days and forty nights, and I will wipe from the face of the earth every living creature I have made."

And Noah did all that the LORD commanded him.

Noah was six hundred years old when the floodwaters came on the earth. And Noah and his sons and his wife and his sons' wives entered the ark to escape the waters of the flood. Pairs of clean and unclean animals, of birds and of all creatures that move along the ground, male and female, came to Noah and entered the ark, as God had commanded Noah. And after the seven days the floodwaters came on the earth.

In the six hundredth year of Noah's life, on the seventeenth day of the second month—on that day all the springs of the great deep burst forth, and the

---

12. A cubit was about eighteen inches.

floodgates of the heavens were opened. And rain fell on the earth forty days and forty nights.

On that very day Noah and his sons, Shem, Ham and Japheth, together with his wife and the wives of his three sons, entered the ark. They had with them every wild animal according to its kind, all livestock according to their kinds, every creature that moves along the ground according to its kind and every bird according to its kind, everything with wings. Pairs of all creatures that have the breath of life in them came to Noah and entered the ark. The animals going in were male and female of every living thing, as God had commanded Noah. Then the LORD shut him in.

For forty days the flood kept coming on the earth, and as the waters increased they lifted the ark high above the earth. The waters rose and increased greatly on the earth, and the ark floated on the surface of the water. They rose greatly on the earth, and all the high mountains under the entire heavens were covered. The waters rose and covered the mountains to a depth of more than twenty feet.[13] Every living thing that moved on the earth perished—birds, livestock, wild animals, all the creatures that swarm over the earth, and all mankind. Everything on dry land that had the breath of life in its nostrils died. Every living thing on the face of the earth was wiped out; men and animals and the creatures that move along the ground and the birds of the air were wiped from the earth. Only Noah was left, and those with him in the ark.

The waters flooded the earth for a hundred and fifty days.

8

But God remembered Noah and all the wild animals and the livestock that were with him in the ark, and he sent a wind over the earth and the waters receded. Now the springs of the deep and the floodgates of the heavens had been closed, and the rain had stopped falling from the sky. The water receded steadily from the earth. At the end of the hundred and fifty days the water had gone down, and on the seventeenth day of the seventh month the ark came to rest on the mountains of Ararat. The waters continued to recede until the tenth month, and on the first day of the tenth month the tops of the mountains became visible.

After forty days Noah opened the window he had made in the ark and sent out a raven, and it kept flying back and forth until the water had dried up from the earth. Then he sent out a dove to see if the water had receded from the surface of the ground. But the dove could find no place to set its feet because there was water over all the surface of the earth; so it returned to Noah in the ark. He reached out his hand and took the dove and brought it back to himself in the ark. He waited seven more days and again sent out the dove from the ark. When the dove returned to him in the evening, there in its beak was a freshly plucked olive leaf! Then Noah knew that the water had receded from the earth. He waited seven more days and sent the dove out again, but this time it did not return to him.

By the first day of the first month of Noah's six hundred and first year, the

---

13. In Hebrew, "fifteen cubits."

water had dried up from the earth. Noah then removed the covering from the ark and saw that the surface of the ground was dry. By the twenty-seventh day of the second month the earth was completely dry.

Then God said to Noah, "Come out of the ark, you and your wife and your sons and their wives. Bring out every kind of living creature that is with you—the birds, the animals, and all the creatures that move along the ground—so they can multiply on the earth and be fruitful and increase in number upon it."

So Noah came out, together with his sons and his wife and his sons' wives. All the animals and all the creatures that move along the ground and all the birds—everything that moves on the earth—came out of the ark, one kind after another.

Then Noah built an altar to the LORD and, taking some of all the clean animals and clean birds, he sacrificed burnt offerings on it. The LORD smelled the pleasing aroma and said in his heart: "Never again will I curse the ground because of man, even though every inclination of his heart is evil from childhood. And never again will I destroy all living creatures, as I have done.

> "As long as the earth endures,
> seedtime and harvest,
> cold and heat,
> summer and winter,
> day and night
> will never cease."

9

Then God blessed Noah and his sons, saying to them, "Be fruitful and increase in number and fill the earth. The fear and dread of you will fall upon all the beasts of the earth and all the birds of the air, upon every creature that moves along the ground, and upon all the fish of the sea; they are given into your hands. Everything that lives and moves will be food for you. Just as I gave you the green plants, I now give you everything.

"But you must not eat meat that has its lifeblood still in it. And for your lifeblood I will surely demand an accounting. I will demand an accounting from every animal. And from each man, too, I will demand an accounting for the life of his fellow man.

> "Whoever sheds the blood of man,
> by man shall his blood be shed;
> for in the image of God has God made man.

As for you, be fruitful and increase in number; multiply on the earth and increase upon it."

Then God said to Noah and to his sons with him: "I now establish my covenant with you and with your descendants after you and with every living creature that was with you—the birds, the livestock and all the wild animals, all those that came out of the ark with you—every living creature on earth. I establish my covenant with you: Never again will all life be cut off by the waters of a flood; never again will there be a flood to destroy the earth."

And God said, "This is the sign of the covenant I am making between me and you and every living creature with you, a covenant for all generations to come: I have set my rainbow in the clouds, and it will be the sign of the covenant between me and the earth.[14] Whenever I bring clouds over the earth and the rainbow appears in the clouds, I will remember my covenant between me and you and all living creatures of every kind. Never again will the waters become a flood to destroy all life. Whenever the rainbow appears in the clouds, I will see it and remember the everlasting covenant between God and all living creatures of every kind on the earth."

So God said to Noah, "This is the sign of the covenant I have established between me and all life on the earth."

The sons of Noah who came out of the ark were Shem, Ham and Japheth. (Ham was the father of Canaan.) These were the three sons of Noah, and from them came the people who were scattered over the earth.

Noah, a man of the soil, proceeded to plant a vineyard. When he drank some of its wine, he became drunk and lay uncovered inside his tent. Ham, the father of Canaan, saw his father's nakedness and told his two brothers outside. But Shem and Japheth took a garment and laid it across their shoulders; then they walked in backward and covered their father's nakedness. Their faces were turned the other way so that they would not see their father's nakedness.

When Noah awoke from his wine and found out what his youngest son had done to him, he said,

"Cursed be Canaan!
The lowest of slaves will he be to his brothers."
He also said,
"Blessed be the LORD, the God of Shem!
May Canaan be the slave of Shem.
May God extend the territory of Japheth;
may Japheth live in the tents of Shem,
and may Canaan be his slave."

After the flood Noah lived 350 years. Altogether, Noah lived 950 years, and then he died.

10

This is the account of Shem, Ham and Japheth, Noah's sons, who themselves had sons after the flood.

The sons of Japheth: Gomer, Magog, Madai, Javan, Tubal, Meshech and Tiras.

The sons of Gomer: Ashkenaz, Riphath and Togarmah.

The sons of Javan: Elishah, Tarshish, the Kittim and the Rodanim. (From

---

14. Compare God's literal rainbow to Marduk's bow personified as Ishtar in *Enuma Elish*.

these the maritime peoples spread out into their territories by their clans within their nations, each with its own language.)

The sons of Ham: Cush, Mizraim, Put and Canaan.

The sons of Cush: Seba, Havilah, Sabtah, Raamah and Sabtecah.

The sons of Raamah: Sheba and Dedan.

Cush was the father of Nimrod, who grew to be a mighty warrior on the earth. He was a mighty hunter before the LORD; that is why it is said, "Like Nimrod, a mighty hunter before the LORD." The first centers of his kingdom were Babylon, Erech, Akkad and Calneh, in Shinar. From that land he went to Assyria, where he built Nineveh, Rehoboth Ir, Calah and Resen, which is between Nineveh and Calah; that is the great city.

Mizraim was the father of the Ludites, Anamites, Lehabites, Naphtuhites, Pathrusites, Casluhites (from whom the Philistines came) and Caphtorites.

Canaan was the father of Sidon his firstborn, and of the Hittites, Jebusites, Amorites, Girgashites, Hivites, Arkites, Sinites, Arvadites, Zemarites and Hama-thites.

Later the Canaanite clans scattered and the borders of Canaan reached from Sidon toward Gerar as far as Gaza, and then toward Sodom, Gomorrah, Admah and Zeboiim, as far as Lasha.

These are the descendants of Ham by their clans and languages, in their territories and nations.

Sons were also born to Shem, whose older brother was Japheth; Shem was the ancestor of all the sons of Eber.

The sons of Shem: Elam, Asshur, Arphaxad, Lud and Aram.

The sons of Aram: Uz, Hul, Gether and Meshech.

Arphaxad was the father of Shelah, and Shelah the father of Eber.

Two sons were born to Eber: One was named Peleg, because in his time the earth was divided; his brother was named Joktan.

Joktan was the father of Almodad, Sheleph, Hazarmaveth, Jerah, Hadoram, Uzal, Diklah, Obal, Abimael, Sheba, Ophir, Havilah and Jobab. All these were sons of Joktan. The region where they lived stretched from Mesha toward Sephar, in the eastern hill country.

These are the sons of Shem by their clans and languages, in their territories and nations. These are the clans of Noah's sons, according to their lines of descent, within their nations. From these the nations spread out over the earth after the flood.

11

Now the whole world had one language and a common speech. As men moved eastward, they found a plain in Shinar[15] and settled there.

They said to each other, "Come, let's make bricks and bake them thoroughly." They used brick instead of stone, and tar instead of mortar. Then they said, "Come, let us build ourselves a city, with a tower that reaches to the heavens,

---

15. Babylonia.

so that we may make a name for ourselves and not be scattered over the face of the whole earth."

But the LORD came down to see the city and the tower that the men were building. The LORD said, "If as one people speaking the same language they have begun to do this, then nothing they plan to do will be impossible for them. Come, let us go down and confuse their language so they will not understand each other."

So the LORD scattered them from there over all the earth, and they stopped building the city. That is why it was called Babel[16]—because there the LORD confused the language of the whole world. From there the LORD scattered them over the face of the whole earth.

THE BIBLE (SIXTH CENTURY B.C.E.)
Babylon

The Book of Job—one of the greatest wisdom texts of antiquity and a searching challenge to the very limits of human wisdom—explores the theological as well as the psychological implications of God's willingness to permit suffering on earth. The book thus explores on a personal level the same problems that were being raised in earlier works: the sacking of Babylon in the *Erra Epic*, Antigone's outcry against Creon's rule in Sophocles' play. As great as the problems of misrule might be when the responsible figure is a mortal king or the god of pestilence, the problem is even more severe in the context of monotheism, where God alone is ultimately to blame.

In developing his searching inquiry, the author of the poetic body of the Book of Job used an old second-millennium folktale, perhaps written down around 900 B.C.E. and appearing here as the prose frame at the beginning and end of the book. Probably writing during the period of exile in Babylon during the sixth century B.C.E., the poet structured his poem in the form of an initial outcry by Job, followed by a series of speeches by Job's friends Eliphaz, Bildad, and Zophar. Each friend makes three speeches attempting to mollify Job or to justify God's actions. In the course of their speeches, they begin increasingly to accept many of Job's premises, while his replies become increasingly ironic, often parodying commonplaces from wisdom literature and the Psalms. Following the friends' speeches and Job's final reply, God suddenly speaks from the whirlwind and silences Job, in the enigmatic inner conclusion that occurs before the return to the prose frame story.

Job's unrelenting quest for justice and his open accusations of God clearly disturbed the book's ancient editors, and the text as it appears in the Bible shows different attempts to soften Job's later speeches and to strengthen the friends' replies. The version presented here removes the major alterations: two long

---

16. I.e., Babylon; the writer intentionally ignores the name's actual meaning, "Gate of God," ironically suggesting instead that *babel* derives from *balal,* "to confuse."

speeches that must originally have been made by the friends but were later given to Job, and a repetitive set of speeches later added in and attributed to a new character named Elihu.

from The Bible

The Book of Job

1

There was a man in the land of Uz,[1] whose name was Job; and that man was perfect and upright, and one that feared God, and eschewed evil.

And there were born unto him seven sons and three daughters.

His substance also was seven thousand sheep, and three thousand camels, and five hundred yoke of oxen, and five hundred she asses, and a very great household; so that this man was the greatest of all the men of the east.

And his sons went and feasted in their houses, every one his day; and sent and called for their three sisters to eat and to drink with them.

And it was so, when the days of their feasting were gone about, that Job sent and sanctified them, and rose up early in the morning, and offered burnt offerings according to the number of them all: for Job said, It may be that my sons have sinned, and cursed God in their hearts. Thus did Job continually.

Now there was a day when the sons of God came to present themselves before the LORD, and Satan[2] came also among them.

And the LORD said unto Satan, Whence comest thou? Then Satan answered the LORD, and said, From going to and fro in the earth, and from walking up and down in it.

And the LORD said unto Satan, Hast thou considered my servant Job, that there is none like him in the earth, a perfect and an upright man, one that feareth God, and escheweth evil?

Then Satan answered the LORD, and said, Doth Job fear God for nought?

Hast not thou made an hedge about him, and about his house, and about all that he hath on every side? thou hast blessed the work of his hands, and his substance is increased in the land.

But put forth thine hand now, and touch all that he hath, and he will curse thee to thy face.

And the LORD said unto Satan, Behold, all that he hath is in thy power; only upon himself put not forth thine hand. So Satan went forth from the presence of the LORD.

And there was a day when his sons and his daughters were eating and drinking wine in their eldest brother's house:

King James Version.

---

1. Probably Edom in southern Palestine; interestingly, Job is not a Hebrew, though he calls upon the God of Israel.

2. Literally, "the Accuser."

And there came a messenger unto Job, and said, The oxen were plowing, and the asses feeding beside them:

And the Sabeans[3] fell upon them, and took them away; yea, they have slain the servants with the edge of the sword; and I only am escaped alone to tell thee.

While he was yet speaking, there came also another, and said, The fire of God is fallen from heaven, and hath burned up the sheep, and the servants, and consumed them; and I only am escaped alone to tell thee.

While he was yet speaking, there came also another, and said, The Chaldeans[4] made out three bands, and fell upon the camels, and have carried them away, yea, and slain the servants with the edge of the sword; and I only am escaped alone to tell thee.

While he was yet speaking, there came also another, and said, Thy sons and thy daughters were eating and drinking wine in their eldest brother's house:

And, behold, there came a great wind from the wilderness, and smote the four corners of the house, and it fell upon the young men, and they are dead; and I only am escaped alone to tell thee.

Then Job arose, and rent his mantle, and shaved his head, and fell down upon the ground, and worshipped;

And said, Naked came I out of my mother's womb, and naked shall I return thither: the LORD gave, and the LORD hath taken away; blessed be the name of the LORD.

In all this Job sinned not, nor charged God foolishly.

2

Again there was a day when the sons of God came to present themselves before the LORD, and Satan came also among them to present himself before the LORD.

And the LORD said unto Satan, From whence comest thou? And Satan answered the LORD, and said, From going to and fro in the earth, and from walking up and down in it.

And the LORD said unto Satan, Hast thou considered my servant Job, that there is none like him in the earth, a perfect and an upright man, one that feareth God, and escheweth evil? and still he holdeth fast his integrity, although thou movedst me against him, to destroy him without cause.

And Satan answered the LORD, and said, Skin for skin, yea, all that a man hath will he give for his life.

But put forth thine hand now, and touch his bone and his flesh, and he will curse thee to thy face.

And the LORD said unto Satan, Behold, he is in thine hand; but save his life.

So went Satan forth from the presence of the LORD, and smote Job with sore boils from the sole of his foot unto his crown.

And he took him a potshered to scrape himself withal; and he sat down among the ashes.

---

3. Nomads from Arabia.   4. A people from southern Mesopotamia.

Then said his wife unto him, Dost thou still retain thine integrity? curse God, and die.

But he said unto her, Thou speakest as one of the foolish women speaketh. What? shall we receive good at the hand of God, and shall we not receive evil? In all this did not Job sin with his lips.

Now when Job's three friends heard of all this evil that was come upon him, they came every one from his own place; Eliphaz and Temanite, and Bildad the Shuhite, and Zophar the Naamathite[5] for they had made an appointment together to come to mourn with him and to comfort him.

And when they lifted up their eyes afar off, and knew him not, they lifted up their voice, and wept; and they rent every one his mantle, and sprinkled dust upon their heads toward heaven.

So they sat down with him upon the ground seven days and seven nights, and none spake a word unto him: for they saw that his grief was very great.

3

After this opened Job his mouth, and cursed his day.

And Job spake, and said,

Let the day perish wherein I was born, and the night in which it was said, There is a man child conceived.

Let that day be darkness; let not God regard it from above, neither let the light shine upon it.

Let darkness and the shadow of death stain it; let a cloud dwell upon it; let the blackness of the day terrify it.

As for that night, let darkness seize upon it; let it not be joined unto the days of the year, let it not come into the number of the months.

Lo, let that night be solitary, let no joyful voice come therein.

Let them curse it that curse the day, who are ready to raise up their mourning.

Let the stars of the twilight thereof be dark; let it look for light, but have none; neither let it see the dawning of the day:

Because it shut not up the doors of my mother's womb, nor hid sorrow from mine eyes.

Why died I not from the womb? why did I not give up the ghost when I came out of the belly?

Why did the knees prevent me? or why the breasts that I should suck?

For now should I have lain still and been quiet, I should have slept: then had I been at rest,

With kings and counsellers of the earth, which built desolate places for themselves;

Or with princes that had gold, who filled their houses with silver:

Or as an hidden untimely birth I had not been; as infants which never saw light.

There the wicked cease from troubling; and there the weary be at rest.

---

5. Job's friends are from northwestern Arabia.

There the prisoners rest together; they hear not the voice of the oppressor.

The small and great are there; and the servant is free from his master.

Wherefore is light given to him that is in misery, and life unto the bitter in soul;

Which long for death, but it cometh not; and dig for it more than for hid treasures;

Which rejoice exceedingly, and are glad, when they can find the grave?

Why is light given to a man whose way is hid, and whom God hath hedged in?

For my sighing cometh before I eat, and my roarings are poured out like the waters.

For the thing which I greatly feared is come upon me, and that which I was afraid of is come unto me.

I was not in safety, neither had I rest, neither was I quiet; yet trouble came.

4

Then Eliphaz the Temanite answered and said,

If we assay to commune with thee, wilt thou be grieved? but who can withhold himself from speaking?

Behold, thou hast instructed many, and thou hast strengthened the weak hands.

Thy words have upholden him that was falling, and thou hast strengthened the feeble knees.

But now it is come upon thee, and thou faintest; it toucheth thee, and thou art troubled.

Is not this thy fear, thy confidence, thy hope, and the uprightness of thy ways?

Remember, I pray thee, who ever perished, being innocent? or where were the righteous cut off?

Even as I have seen, they that plow iniquity, and sow wickedness, reap the same.

By the blast of God they perish, and by the breath of his nostrils are they consumed.

The roaring of the lion, and the voice of the fierce lion, and the teeth of the young lions, are broken.

The old lion perisheth for lack of prey, and the stout lion's whelps are scattered abroad.

Now a thing was secretly brought to me, and mine ear received a little thereof.

In thoughts from the visions of the night, when deep sleep falleth on men,

Fear came upon me, and trembling, which made all my bones to shake.

Then a spirit passed before my face; the hair of my flesh stood up:

It stood still, but I could not discern the form thereof: an image was before mine eyes, there was a silence, and I heard a voice, saying,

Shall mortal man be more just than God? shall a man be more pure than his maker?

Behold, he put no trust in his servants; and his angels he charged with folly:

How much less in them that dwell in houses of clay, whose foundation is in the dust, which are crushed before the moth?

They are destroyed from morning to evening: they perish for ever without any regarding it.

Doth not their excellency which is in them go away? they die, even without wisdom.

5

Call now, if there be any that will answer thee; and to which of the saints wilt thou turn?

For wrath killeth the foolish man, and envy slayeth the silly one.

I have seen the foolish taking root: but suddenly I cursed his habitation.

His children are far from safety, and they are crushed in the gate, neither is there any to deliver them.

Whose harvest the hungry eateth up, and taketh it even out of the thorns, and the robber swalloweth up their substance.

Although affliction cometh not forth of the dust, neither doth trouble spring out of the ground;

Yet man is born unto trouble, as the sparks fly upward.

I would seek unto God, and unto God would I commit my cause:

Which doeth great things and unsearchable; marvellous things without number:

Who giveth rain upon the earth, and sendeth waters upon the fields:

To set up on high those that be low; that those which mourn may be exalted to safety.

He disappointeth the devices of the crafty, so that their hands cannot perform their enterprise.

He taketh the wise in their own craftiness: and the counsel of the froward is carried headlong.

They meet with darkness in the daytime, and grope in the noonday as in the night.

But he saveth the poor from the sword, from their mouth, and from the hand of the mighty.

So the poor hath hope, and iniquity stoppeth her mouth.

Behold, happy is the man whom God correcteth: therefore despise not thou the chastening of the Almighty:

For he maketh sore, and bindeth up: he woundeth, and his hands make whole.

He shall deliver thee in six troubles: yea, in seven there shall no evil touch thee.

In famine he shall redeem thee from death: and in war from the power of the sword.

Thou shalt be hid from the scourge of the tongue: neither shalt thou be afraid of destruction when it cometh.

At destruction and famine thou shalt laugh: neither shalt thou be afraid of the beasts of the earth.

For thou shalt be in league with the stones of the field: and the beasts of the field shall be at peace with thee.

And thou shalt know that thy tabernacle shall be in peace; and thou shalt visit they habitation, and shalt not sin.

Thou shalt know also that thy seed shall be great, and thine offspring as the grass of the earth.

Thou shalt come to thy grave in a full age, like as a shock of corn cometh in in his season.

Lo this, we have searched it, so it is; hear it, and know thou it for thy good.

6

But Job answered and said,

Oh that my grief were throughly weighed, and my calamity laid in the balances together!

For now it would be heavier than the sand of the sea: therefore my words are swallowed up.

For the arrows of the Almighty are within me, the poison whereof drinketh up my spirit: the terrors of God do set themselves in array against me.

Doth the wild ass bray when he hath grass? or loweth the ox over his fodder?

Can that which is unsavoury be eaten without salt? or is there any taste in the white of an egg?

The things that my soul refused to touch are as my sorrowful meat.

Oh that I might have my request; and that God would grant me the thing that I long for!

Even that it would please God to destroy me; that he would let loose his hand, and cut me off!

Then should I yet have comfort; yea, I would harden myself in sorrow: let him not spare; for I have not concealed the words of the Holy One.

What is my strength, that I should hope? and what is mine end, that I should prolong my life?

Is my strength the strength of stones? or is my flesh of brass?

Is not my help in me? and is wisdom driven quite from me?

To him that is afflicted pity should be shewed from his friend; but he forsaketh the fear of the Almighty.

My brethren have dealt deceitfully as a brook, and as the stream of brooks they pass away;

Which are blackish by reason of the ice, and wherein the snow is hid:

What time they wax warm, they vanish: when it is hot, they are consumed out of their place.

The paths of their way are turned aside; they go to nothing, and perish.

The troops of Tema looked, the companies of Sheba waited for them.

They were confounded because they had hoped; they came thither, and were ashamed.

For now ye are nothing; ye see my casting down, and are afraid.

Did I say, Bring unto me? or, Give a reward for me of your substance?

Or, Deliver me from the enemy's hand? or, Redeem me from the hand of the mighty?

Teach me, and I will hold my tongue: and cause me to understand wherein I have erred.

How forcible are right words! but what doth your arguing reprove?

Do ye imagine to reprove words, and the speeches of one that is desperate, which are as wind?

Yea, ye overwhelm the fatherless, and ye dig a pit for your friend.

Now therefore be content, look upon me; for it is evident unto you if I lie.

Return, I pray you, let it not be iniquity; yea, return again, my righteousness is in it.

Is there iniquity in my tongue? cannot my taste discern perverse things?

7

Is there not an appointed time to man upon earth? are not his days also like the days of an hireling?

As a servant earnestly desireth the shadow, and as an hireling looketh for the reward of his work:

So am I made to possess months of vanity, and wearisome nights are appointed to me.

When I lie down, I say, When shall I arise, and the night be gone? and I am full of tossings to and fro unto the dawning of the day.

My flesh is clothed with worms and clods of dust; my skin is broken, and become loathsome.

My days are swifter than a weaver's shuttle, and are spent without hope.

O remember that my life is wind: mine eye shall no more see good.

The eye of him that hath seen me shall see me no more: thine eyes are upon me, and I am not.

As the cloud is consumed and vanisheth away: so he that goeth down to the grave shall come up no more.

He shall return no more to his house, neither shall his place know him any more.

Therefore I will not refrain my mouth; I will speak in the anguish of my spirit; I will complain in the bitterness of my soul.

Am I a sea, or a whale, that thou settest a watch over me?[6]

When I say, My bed shall comfort me, my couch shall ease my complaint;

Then thou scarest me with dreams, and terrifiest me through visions:

So that my soul chooseth strangling, and death rather than my life.

I loathe it; I would not live alway: let me alone; for my days are vanity.

---

6. Job ironically compares himself to the conquered Tiamat in *Enuma Elish*.

What is man, that thou shouldest magnify him? and that thou shouldest set thine heart upon him?

And that thou shouldest visit him every morning, and try him every moment?

How long wilt thou not depart from me, nor let me alone till I swallow down my spittle?

I have sinned; what shall I do unto thee, O thou preserver of men? why hast thou set me as a mark against thee, so that I am a burden to myself?

And why dost thou not pardon my transgression, and take away mine iniquity? for now shall I sleep in the dust; and thou shalt seek me in the morning, but I shall not be.

8

Then answered Bildad the Shuhite, and said,

How long wilt thou speak these things? and how long shall the words of thy mouth be like a strong wind?

Doth God pervert judgment? or doth the Almighty pervert justice?

If thy children have sinned against him, and he have cast them away for their transgression;

If thou wouldest seek unto God betimes, and make thy supplication to the Almighty;

If thou wert pure and upright; surely now he would awake for thee, and make the habitation of thy righteousness prosperous.

Though thy beginning was small, yet thy latter end should greatly increase.

For inquire, I pray thee, of the former age, and prepare thyself to the search of their fathers:

(For we are but of yesterday, and know nothing, because our days upon earth are a shadow:)

Shall not they teach thee, and tell thee, and utter words out of their heart?

Can the rush grow up without mire? can the flag grow without water?[7]

Whilst it is yet in his greenness, and not cut down, it withereth before any other herb.

So are the paths of all that forget God; and the hypocrite's hope shall perish:

Whose hope shall be cut off, and whose trust shall be a spider's web.

He shall lean upon his house, but it shall not stand: he shall hold it fast, but it shall not endure.

He is green before the sun, and his branch shooteth forth in his garden.

His roots are wrapped about the heap, and seeth the place of stones.

If he destroy him from his place, then it shall deny him, saying, I have not seen thee.

Behold, this is the joy of his way, and out of the earth shall others grow.

Behold, God will not cast away a perfect man, neither will he help the evil doers:

---

7. Materials for making paper and pens.

Till he fill thy mouth with laughing, and thy lips with rejoicing.

They that hate thee shall be clothed with shame; and the dwelling place of the wicked shall come to nought.

9

Then Job answered and said,

I know it is so of a truth: but how should man be just with God?

If he will contend with him, he cannot answer him one of a thousand.

He is wise in heart, and mighty in strength: who hath hardened himself against him, and hath prospered?

Which removeth the mountains, and they know not: which overturneth them in his anger.

Which shaketh the earth out of her place, and the pillars thereof tremble.

Which commandeth the sun, and it riseth not; and sealeth up the stars.

Which alone spreadeth out the heavens, and treadeth upon the waves of the sea.

Which maketh Arcturus, Orion, and Pleiades, and the chambers of the south.

Which doeth great things past finding out; yea, and wonders without number.

Lo, he goeth by me, and I see him not: he passeth on also, but I perceive him not.

Behold, he taketh away, who can hinder him? who will say unto him, What doest thou?

If God will not withdraw his anger, the proud helpers do stoop under him.

How much less shall I answer him, and choose out my words to reason with him?

Whom, though I were righteous, yet would I not answer, but I would make supplication to my judge.

If I had called, and he had answered me; yet would I not believe that he had hearkened unto my voice.

For he breaketh me with a tempest, and multiplieth my wounds without cause.

He will not suffer me to take my breath, but filleth me with bitterness.

If I speak of strength, lo, he is strong: and if of judgment, who shall set me a time to plead?

If I justify myself, mine own mouth shall condemn me: if I say, I am perfect, it shall also prove me perverse.

Though I were perfect, yet would I not know my soul: I would despise my life.

This is one thing, therefore I said it, He destroyeth the perfect and the wicked.

If the scourge slay suddenly, he will laugh at the trial of the innocent.

The earth is given into the hand of the wicked: he covereth the faces of the judges thereof; if not, where, and who is he?

Now my days are swifter than a post: they flee away, they see no good.

They are passed away as the swift ships: as the eagle that hasteth to the prey.

If I say, I will forget my complaint, I will leave off my heaviness, and comfort myself:

I am afraid of all my sorrows, I know that thou wilt not hold me innocent.

If I be wicked, why then labour I in vain?

If I wash myself with snow water, and make my hands never so clean;

Yet shalt thou plunge me in the ditch, and mine own clothes shall abhor me.

For he is not a man, as I am, that I should answer him, and we should come together in judgment.

Neither is there any daysman betwixt us, that might lay his hand upon us both.

Let him take his rod away from me, and let not his fear terrify me:

Then would I speak, and not fear him; but it is not so with me.

10

My soul is weary of my life; I will leave my complaint upon myself; I will speak in the bitterness of my soul.

I will say unto God, Do not condemn me; shew me wherefore thou contendest with me.

Is it good unto thee that thou shouldest oppress, that thou shouldest despise the work of thine hands, and shine upon the counsel of the wicked?

Hast thou eyes of flesh? or seest thou as man seeth?

Are thy days as the days of man? are thy years as man's days,

That thou inquirest after mine iniquity, and searchest after my sin?

Thou knowest that I am not wicked; and there is none that can deliver out of thine hand.

Thine hands have made me and fashioned me together round about; yet thou dost destroy me.

Remember, I beseech thee, that thou hast made me as the clay; and wilt thou bring me into dust again?

Hast thou not poured me out as milk, and curdled me like cheese?

Thou hast clothed me with skin and flesh, and hast fenced me with bones and sinews.

Thou hast granted me life and favour, and thy visitation hath preserved my spirit.

And these things hast thou hid in thine heart: I know that this is with thee.

If I sin, then thou markest me, and thou wilt not acquit me from mine iniquity.

If I be wicked, woe unto me; and if I be righteous, yet will I not lift up my head. I am full of confusion; therefore see thou mine affliction;

For it increaseth. Thou huntest me as a fierce lion: and again thou shewest thyself marvellous upon me.

Thou renewest thy witnesses against me, and increasest thine indignation upon me; changes and war are against me.

Wherefore then hast thou brought me forth out of the womb? Oh that I had given up the ghost, and no eye had seen me!

I should have been as though I had not been; I should have been carried from the womb to the grave.

Are not my days few? cease then, and let me alone, that I may take comfort a little,

Before I go whence I shall not return, even to the land of darkness and the shadow of death;

A land of darkness, as darkness itself; and of the shadow of death, without any order, and where the light is as darkness.

11

Then answered Zophar the Naamathite, and said,

Should not the multitude of words be answered? and should a man full of talk be justified?

Should thy lies make men hold their peace? and when thou mockest, shall no man make thee ashamed?

For thou hast said, My doctrine is pure, and I am clean in thine eyes.

But oh that God would speak, and open his lips against thee;

And that he would shew thee the secrets of wisdom, that they are double to that which is! Know therefore that God exacteth of thee less than thine iniquity deserveth.

Canst thou by searching find out God? canst thou find out the Almighty unto perfection?

It is as high as heaven; what canst thou do? deeper than hell; what canst thou know?

The measure thereof is longer than the earth, and broader than the sea.

If he cut off, and shut up, or gather together, then who can hinder him?

For he knoweth vain men: he seeth wickedness also; will he not then consider it?

For vain man would be wise, though man be born like a wild ass's colt.

If thou prepare thine heart, and stretch out thine hands toward him;

If iniquity be in thine hand, put it far away, and let not wickedness dwell in thy tabernacles.

For then shalt thou lift up thy face without spot; yea, thou shalt be steadfast, and shalt not fear:

Because thou shalt forget thy misery, and remember it as waters that pass away:

And thine age shall be clearer than the noonday; thou shalt shine forth, thou shalt be as the morning.

And thou shalt be secure, because there is hope; yea, thou shalt dig about thee, and thou shalt take thy rest in safety.

Also thou shalt lie down, and none shall make thee afraid; yea, many shall make suit unto thee.

But the eyes of the wicked shall fail, and they shall not escape, and their hope shall be as the giving up of the ghost.

12

And Job answered and said,

No doubt but ye are the people, and wisdom shall die with you.

But I have understanding as well as you; I am not inferior to you: yea, who knoweth not such things as these?

I am as one mocked of his neighbour, who calleth upon God, and he answereth him: the just upright man is laughed to scorn.

He that is ready to slip with his feet is as a lamp despised in the thought of him that is at ease.

The tabernacles of robbers prosper, and they that provoke God are secure; into whose hand God bringeth abundantly.

But ask now the beasts, and they shall teach thee; and the fowls of the air, and they shall tell thee:

Or speak to the earth, and it shall teach thee: and the fishes of the sea shall declare unto thee.

Who knoweth not in all these that the hand of the LORD hath wrought this?

In whose hand is the soul of every living thing, and the breath of all mankind.

Doth not the ear try words? and the mouth taste his meat?

With the ancient is wisdom; and in length of days understanding.

With him is wisdom and strength, he hath counsel and understanding.

Behold, he breaketh down, and it cannot be built again: he shutteth up a man, and there can be no opening.

Behold, he withholdeth the waters, and they dry up: also he sendeth them out, and they overturn the earth.

With him is strength and wisdom: the deceived and the deceiver are his.

He leadeth counsellers away spoiled, and maketh the judges fools.

He looseth the bond of kings, and girdeth their loins with a girdle.

He leadeth princes away spoiled, and overthroweth the mighty.

He removeth away the speech of the trusty, and taketh away the understanding of the aged.

He poureth contempt upon princes, and weakeneth the strength of the mighty.

He discovereth deep things out of darkness, and bringeth out to light the shadow of death.

He increaseth the nations, and destroyeth them: he enlargeth the nations, and straiteneth them again.

He taketh away the heart of the chief of the people of the earth, and causeth them to wander in a wilderness where there is no way.

They grope in the dark without light, and he maketh them to stagger like a drunken man.

13

Lo, mine eye hath seen all this, mine ear hath heard and understood it.

What ye know, the same do I know also: I am not inferior unto you.

Surely I would speak to the Almighty, and I desire to reason with God.

But ye are forgers of lies, ye are all physicians of no value.

O that ye would altogether hold your peace! and it should be your wisdom.

Hear now my reasoning, and hearken to the pleadings of my lips.

Will ye speak wickedly for God? and talk deceitfully for him?

Will ye accept his person? will ye contend for God?

Is it good that he should search you out? or as one man mocketh another, do ye so mock him?

He will surely reprove you, if ye do secretly accept persons.

Shall not his excellency make you afraid? and his dread fall upon you?

Your remembrances are like unto ashes, your bodies to bodies of clay.

Hold your peace, let me alone, that I may speak, and let come on me what will.

Wherefore do I take my flesh in my teeth, and put my life in mine hand?

Though he slay me, yet will I trust in him: but I will maintain mine own ways before him.

He also shall be my salvation: for an hypocrite shall not come before him.

Hear diligently my speech, and my declaration with your ears.

Behold now, I have ordered my cause; I know that I shall be justified.

Who is he that will plead with me? for now, if I hold my tongue, I shall give up the ghost.

Only do not two things unto me: then will I not hide myself from thee.

Withdraw thine hand far from me: and let not thy dread make me afraid.

Then call thou, and I will answer: or let me speak, and answer thou me.

How many are mine iniquities and sins? make me to know my transgression and my sin.

Wherefore hidest thou thy face, and holdest me for thine enemy?

Wilt thou break a leaf driven to and fro? and wilt thou pursue the dry stubble?

For thou writest bitter things against me, and makest me to possess the iniquities of my youth.

Thou puttest my feet also in the stocks, and lookest narrowly unto all my paths; thou settest a print upon the heels of my feet.

And he, as a rotten thing, consumeth, as a garment that is moth eaten.

14

Man that is born of a woman is of few days, and full of trouble.

He cometh forth like a flower, and is cut down: he fleeth also as a shadow, and continueth not.

And dost thou open thine eyes upon such an one, and bringest me into judgment with thee?

Who can bring a clean thing out of an unclean? not one.

Seeing his days are determined, the number of his months are with thee, thou hast appointed his bounds that he cannot pass;

Turn from him, that he may rest, till he shall accomplish, as an hireling, his day.

For there is hope of a tree, if it be cut down, that it will sprout again, and that the tender branch thereof will not cease.

Though the root thereof wax old in the earth, and the stock thereof die in the ground;

Yet through the scent of water it will bud, and bring forth boughs like a plant.

But man dieth, and wasteth away: yea, man giveth up the ghost, and where is he?

As the waters fail from the sea, and the flood decayeth and drieth up:

So man lieth down, and riseth not: till the heavens be no more, they shall not awake, nor be raised out of their sleep.

O that thou wouldest hide me in the grave, that thou wouldest keep me secret, until thy wrath be past, that thou wouldest appoint me a set time, and remember me!

If a man die, shall he live again? all the days of my appointed time will I wait, till my change come.

Thou shalt call, and I will answer thee: thou wilt have a desire to the work of thine hands.

For now thou numberest my steps: dost thou not watch over my sin?

My transgression is sealed up in a bag, and thou sewest up mine iniquity.

And surely the mountain falling cometh to nought, and the rock is removed out of his place.

The waters wear the stones: thou washest away the things which grow out of the dust of the earth; and thou destroyest the hope of man.

Thou prevailest for ever against him, and he passeth: thou changest his countenance, and sendest him away.

His sons come to honour, and he knoweth it not; and they are brought low, but he perceiveth it not of them.

But his flesh upon him shall have pain, and his soul within him shall mourn.

15

Then answered Eliphaz the Temanite, and said,

Should a wise man utter vain knowledge, and fill his belly with the east wind?

Should he reason with unprofitable talk? or with speeches wherewith he can do no good?

Yea, thou castest off fear, and restrainest prayer before God.

For thy mouth uttereth thine iniquity, and thou choosest the tongue of the crafty.

Thine own mouth condemneth thee, and not I: yea, thine own lips testify against thee.

Art thou the first man that was born? or wast thou made before the hills?

Hast thou heard the secret of God? and dost thou restrain wisdom to thyself?

What knowest thou, that we know not? what understandest thou, which is not in us?

With us are both the grayheaded and very aged men, much elder than thy father.

Are the consolations of God small with thee? is there any secret thing with thee?

Why doth thine heart carry thee away? and what do thy eyes wink at,

That thou turnest thy spirit against God, and lettest such words go out of thy mouth?

What is man, that he should be clean? and he which is born of a woman, that he should be righteous?

Behold, he putteth no trust in his saints; yea, the heavens are not clean in his sight.

How much more abominable and filthy is man, which drinketh iniquity like water?

I will shew thee, hear me; and that which I have seen I will declare;

Which wise men have told from their fathers, and have not hid it:

Unto whom alone the earth was given, and no stranger passed among them.

The wicked man travaileth with pain all his days, and the number of years is hidden to the oppressor.

A dreadful sound is in his ears: in prosperity the destroyer shall come upon him.

He believeth not that he shall return out of darkness, and he is waited for of the sword.

He wandereth abroad for bread, saying, Where is it? he knoweth that the day of darkness is ready at his hand.

Trouble and anguish shall make him afraid; they shall prevail against him, as a king ready to the battle.

For he stretcheth out his hand against God, and strengtheneth himself against the Almighty.

He runneth upon him, even on his neck, upon the thick bosses of his bucklers:

Because he covereth his face with his fatness, and maketh collops of fat on his flanks.

And he dwelleth in desolate cities, and in houses which no man inhabiteth, which are ready to become heaps.

He shall not be rich, neither shall his substance continue, neither shall he prolong the perfection thereof upon the earth.

He shall not depart out of darkness; the flame shall dry up his branches, and by the breath of his mouth shall he go away.

Let not him that is deceived trust in vanity: for vanity shall be his recompence.

It shall be accomplished before his time, and his branch shall not be green.

He shall shake off his unripe grape as the vine, and shall cast off his flower as the olive.

For the congregation of hypocrites shall be desolate, and fire shall consume the tabernacles of bribery.

They conceive mischief, and bring forth vanity, and their belly prepareth deceit.

16

Then Job answered and said,

I have heard many such things: miserable comforters are ye all.

Shall vain words have an end? or what emboldeneth thee that thou answerest?

I also could speak as ye do: if your soul were in my soul's stead, I could heap up words against you, and shake mine head at you.

But I would strengthen you with my mouth, and the moving of my lips should asswage your grief.

Though I speak, my grief is not asswaged: and though I forbear, what am I eased?

But now he hath made me weary: thou hast made desolate all my company.

And thou hast filled me with wrinkles, which is a witness against me: and my leanness rising up in me beareth witness to my face.

He teareth me in his wrath, who hateth me: he gnasheth upon me with his teeth; mine enemy sharpeneth his eyes upon me.

They have gaped upon me with their mouth; they have smitten me upon the check reproachfully; they have gathered themselves together against me.

God hath delivered me to the ungodly, and turned me over into the hands of the wicked.

I was at ease, but he hath broken me asunder: he hath also taken me by my neck, and shaken me to pieces, and set me up for his mark.

His archers compass me round about, he cleaveth my reins asunder, and doth not spare; he poureth out my gall upon the ground.

He breaketh me with breach upon breach, he runneth upon me like a giant.

I have sewed sackcloth upon my skin, and defiled my horn in the dust.

My face is foul with weeping, and on my eyelids is the shadow of death;

Not for any injustice in mine hands: also my prayer is pure.

O earth, cover not thou my blood, and let my cry have no place.

Also now, behold, my witness is in heaven, and my record is on high.

My friends scorn me: but mine eye poureth out tears unto God.

O that one might plead for a man with God, as a man pleadeth for his neighbour!

When a few years are come, then I shall go the way whence I shall not return.

17

My breath is corrupt, my days are extinct, the graves are ready for me.

Are there not mockers with me? and doth not mine eye continue in their provocation?

Lay down now, put me in a surety with thee; who is he that will strike hands with me?

For thou hast hid their heart from understanding: therefore shalt thou not exalt them.

He that speaketh flattery to his friends, even the eyes of his children shall fail.

He hath made me also a byword of the people; and aforetime I was as a tabret.

Mine eye also is dim by reason of sorrow, and all my members are as a shadow.

Upright men shall be astonied at this, and the innocent shall stir up himself against the hypocrite.

The righteous also shall hold on his way, and he that hath clean hands shall be stronger and stronger.

But as for you all, do ye return, and come now: for I cannot find one wise man among you.

My days are past, my purposes are broken off, even the thoughts of my heart.

They change the night into day: the light is short because of darkness.

If I wait, the grave is mine house: I have made my bed in the darkness.

I have said to corruption, Thou art my father: to the worm, Thou art my mother, and my sister.

And where is now my hope? as for my hope, who shall see it?

They shall go down to the bars of the pit, when our rest together is in the dust.

18

Then answered Bildad the Shuhite, and said,

How long will it be ere ye make an end of words? mark, and afterwards we will speak.

Wherefore are we counted as beasts, and reputed vile in your sight?

He teareth himself in his anger: shall the earth be forsaken for thee? and shall the rock be removed out of his place?

Yea, the light of the wicked shall be put out, and the spark of his fire shall not shine.

The light shall be dark in his tabernacle, and his candle shall be put out with him.

The steps of his strength shall be straitened, and his own counsel shall cast him down.

For he is cast into a net by his own feet, and he walketh upon a snare.

The gin shall take him by the heel, and the robber shall prevail against him.

The snare is laid for him in the ground, and a trap for him in the way.

Terrors shall make him afraid on every side, and shall drive him to his feet.

His strength shall be hungerbitten, and destruction shall be ready at his side.

It shall devour the strength of his skin: even the firstborn of death shall devour his strength.

His confidence shall be rooted out of his tabernacle, and it shall bring him to the king of terrors.

It shall dwell in his tabernacle, because it is none of his: brimstone shall be scattered upon his habitation.

His roots shall be dried up beneath, and above shall his branch be cut off.

His remembrance shall perish from the earth, and he shall have no name in the street.

He shall be driven from light into darkness, and chased out of the world.

He shall neither have son nor nephew among his people, nor any remaining in his dwellings.

They that come after him shall be astonied at his day, as they that went before were affrighted.

Surely such are the dwellings of the wicked, and this is the place of him that knoweth not God.

19

Then Job answered and said,

How long will ye vex my soul, and break me in pieces with words?

These ten times have ye reproached me: ye are not ashamed that ye make yourselves strange to me.

And be it indeed that I have erred, mine error remaineth with myself.

If indeed ye will magnify yourselves against me, and plead against me my reproach:

Know now that God hath overthrown me, and hath compassed me with his net.

Behold, I cry out of wrong, but I am not heard: I cry aloud, but there is no judgment.

He hath fenced up my way that I cannot pass, and he hath set darkness in my paths.

He hath stripped me of my glory, and taken the crown from my head.

He hath destroyed me on every side, and I am gone: and mine hope hath he removed like a tree.

He hath also kindled his wrath against me, and he counteth me unto him as one of his enemies.

His troops come together, and raise up their way against me, and encamp round about my tabernacle.

He hath put my brethren far from me, and mine acquaintance are verily estranged from me.

My kinsfolk have failed, and my familiar friends have forgotten me.

They that dwell in mine house, and my maids, count me for a stranger: I am an alien in their sight.

I called my servant, and he gave me no answer; I intreated him with my mouth.

My breath is strange to my wife, though I intreated for the children's sake of mine own body.

Yea, young children despised me; I arose, and they spake against me.

All my inward friends abhorred me: and they whom I loved are turned against me.

My bone cleaveth to my skin and to my flesh, and I am escaped with the skin of my teeth.

Have pity upon me, have pity upon me, O ye my friends; for the hand of God hath touched me.

Why do ye persecute me as God, and are not satisfied with my flesh?

O that my words were now written! oh that they were printed in a book!

That they were graven with an iron pen and lead in the rock for ever!

For I know that my redeemer liveth, and that he shall stand at the latter day upon the earth:

And though after my skin worms destroy this body, yet in my flesh shall I see God:

Whom I shall see for myself, and mine eyes shall behold, and not another; though my reins be consumed within me.

But ye should say, Why persecute we him, seeing the root of the matter is found in me?

Be ye afraid of the sword: for wrath bringeth the punishments of the sword, that ye may know there is a judgment.

20

Then answered Zophar the Naamathite, and said,

Therefore do my thoughts cause me to answer, and for this I make haste.

I have heard the check of my reproach, and the spirit of my understanding causeth me to answer.

Knowest thou not this of old, since man was placed upon earth,

That the triumphing of the wicked is short, and the joy of the hypocrite but for a moment?

Though his excellency mount up to the heavens, and his head reach unto the clouds;

Yet he shall perish for ever like his own dung: they which have seen him shall say, Where is he?

He shall fly away as a dream, and shall not be found: yea, he shall be chased away as a vision of the night.

The eye also which saw him shall see him no more; neither shall his place any more behold him.

His children shall seek to please the poor, and his hands shall restore their goods.

His bones are full of the sin of his youth, which shall lie down with him in the dust.

Though wickedness be sweet in his mouth, though he hide it under his tongue;

Though he spare it, and forsake it not; but keep it still within his mouth:

Yet his meat in his bowels is turned, it is the gall of asps within him.

He hath swallowed down riches, and he shall vomit them up again: God shall cast them out of his belly.

He shall suck the poison of asps: the viper's tongue shall slay him.

He shall not see the rivers, the floods, the brooks of honey and butter.

That which he laboured for shall he restore, and shall not swallow it down: according to his substance shall the restitution be, and he shall not rejoice therein.

Because he hath oppressed and hath forsaken the poor; because he hath violently taken away an house which he builded not;

Surely he shall not feel quietness in his belly, he shall not save of that which he desired.

There shall none of his meat be left; therefore shall no man look for his goods.

In the fulness of his sufficiency he shall be in straits: every hand of the wicked shall come upon him.

When he is about to fill his belly, God shall cast the fury of his wrath upon him, and shall rain it upon him while he is eating.

He shall flee from the iron weapon, and the bow of steel shall strike him through.

It is drawn, and cometh out of the body; yea, the glittering sword cometh out of his gall: terrors are upon him.

All darkness shall be hid in his secret places: a fire not blown shall consume him; it shall go ill with him that is left in his tabernacle.

The heaven shall reveal his iniquity; and the earth shall rise up against him.

The increase of his house shall depart, and his goods shall flow away in the day of his wrath.

This is the portion of a wicked man from God, and the heritage appointed unto him by God.

21

But Job answered and said,

Hear diligently my speech, and let this be your consolations.

Suffer me that I may speak; and after that I have spoken, mock on.

As for me, is my complaint to man? and if it were so, why should not my spirit be troubled?

Mark me, and be astonished, and lay your hand upon your mouth.

Even when I remember I am afraid, and trembling taketh hold on my flesh.

Wherefore do the wicked live, become old, yea, are mighty in power?

Their seed is established in their sight with them, and their offspring before their eyes.

Their houses are safe from fear, neither is the rod of God upon them.

Their bull gendereth, and faileth not; their cow calveth, and casteth not her calf.

They send forth their little ones like a flock, and their children dance.

They take the timbrel and harp, and rejoice at the sound of the organ.

They spend their days in wealth, and in a moment go down to the grave.

Therefore they say unto God, Depart from us; for we desire not the knowledge of thy ways.

What is the Almighty, that we should serve him? and what profit should we have, if we pray unto him?

Lo, their good is not in their hand: the counsel of the wicked is far from me.

How oft is the candle of the wicked put out! and how oft cometh their destruction upon them! God distributeth sorrows in his anger.

They are as stubble before the wind, and as chaff that the storm carrieth away.

God layeth up his iniquity for his children: he rewardeth him, and he shall know it.

His eyes shall see his destruction, and he shall drink of the wrath of the Almighty.

For what pleasure hath he in his house after him, when the number of his months is cut off in the midst?

Shall any teach God knowledge? seeing he judgeth those that are high.

One dieth in his full strength, being wholly at ease and quiet.

His breasts are full of milk, and his bones are moistened with marrow.

And another dieth in the bitterness of his soul, and never eateth with pleasure.

They shall lie down alike in the dust, and the worms shall cover them.

Behold, I know your thoughts, and the devices which ye wrongfully imagine against me.

For ye say, Where is the house of the prince? and where are the dwelling places of the wicked?

Have ye not asked them that go by the way? and do ye not know their tokens,

That the wicked is reserved to the day of destruction? they shall be brought forth to the day of wrath.

Who shall declare his way to his face? and who shall repay him what he hath done?

Yet shall he be brought to the grave, and shall remain in the tomb.

The clods of the valley shall be sweet unto him, and every man shall draw after him, as there are innumerable before him.

How then comfort ye me in vain, seeing in your answers there remaineth falsehood?

22

Then Eliphaz the Temanite answered and said,

Can a man be profitable unto God, as he that is wise may be profitable unto himself?

Is it any pleasure to the Almighty, that thou art righteous? or is it gain to him, that thou makest thy ways perfect?

Will he reprove thee for fear of thee? will he enter with thee into judgment?

Is not thy wickedness great? and thine iniquities infinite?

For thou hast taken a pledge from thy brother for nought, and stripped the naked of their clothing.

Thou hast not given water to the weary to drink, and thou hast withholden bread from the hungry.

But as for the mighty man, he had the earth; and the honourable man dwelt in it.

Thou hast sent widows away empty, and the arms of the fatherless have been broken.

Therefore snares are round about thee, and sudden fear troubleth thee;

Or darkness, that thou canst not see; and abundance of waters cover thee.

Is not God in the height of heaven? and behold the height of the stars, how high they are!

And thou sayest, How doth God know? can he judge through the dark cloud?

Thick clouds are a covering to him, that he seeth not; and he walketh in the circuit of heaven.

Hast thou marked the old way which wicked men have trodden?

Which were cut down out of time, whose foundation was overflown with a flood:

Which said unto God, Depart from us: and what can the Almighty do for them?

Yet he filled their houses with good things: but the counsel of the wicked is far from me.

The righteous see it, and are glad: and the innocent laugh them to scorn.

Whereas our substance is not cut down, but the remnant of them the fire consumeth.

Acquaint now thyself with him, and be at peace: thereby good shall come unto thee.

Receive, I pray thee, the law from his mouth, and lay up his words in thine heart.

If thou return to the Almighty, thou shalt be built up, thou shalt put away iniquity far from thy tabernacles.

Then shalt thou lay up gold as dust, and the gold of Ophir as the stones of the brooks.

Yea, the Almighty shall be thy defence, and thou shalt have plenty of silver.

For then shalt thou have thy delight in the Almighty, and shalt lift up thy face unto God.

Thou shalt make thy prayer unto him, and he shall hear thee, and thou shalt pay thy vows.

Thou shalt also decree a thing, and it shall be established unto thee: and the light shall shine upon thy ways.

When men are cast down, then thou shalt say, There is lifting up; and he shall save the humble person.

He shall deliver the island of the innocent: and it is delivered by the pureness of thine hands.

23

Then Job answered and said,

Even to day is my complaint bitter: my stroke is heavier than my groaning.

Oh that I knew where I might find him! that I might come even to his seat!

I would order my cause before him, and fill my mouth with arguments.

I would know the words which he would answer me, and understand what he would say unto me.

Will he plead against me with his great power? No; but he would put strength in me.

There the righteous might dispute with him; so should I be delivered for ever from my judge.

Behold, I go forward, but he is not there; and backward, but I cannot perceive him:

On the left hand, where he doth work, but I cannot behold him: he hideth himself on the right hand, that I cannot see him:

But he knoweth the way that I take: when he hath tried me, I shall come forth as gold.

My foot hath held his steps, his way have I kept, and not declined.

Neither have I gone back from the commandment of his lips; I have esteemed the words of his mouth more than my necessary food.

But he is in one mind, and who can turn him? and what his soul desireth, even that he doeth.

For he performeth the thing that is appointed for me: and many such things are with him.

Therefore am I troubled at his presence: when I consider, I am afraid of him.

For God maketh my heart soft, and the Almighty troubleth me:

Because I was not cut off before the darkness, neither hath he covered the darkness from my face.

24

Why, seeing times are not hidden from the Almighty, do they that know him not see his days?

Some remove the landmarks; they violently take away flocks, and feed thereof.

They drive away the ass of the fatherless, they take the widow's ox for a pledge.

They turn the needy out of the way: the poor of the earth hide themselves together.

Behold, as wild asses in the desert, go they forth to their work; rising betimes for a prey: the wilderness yieldeth food for them and for their children.

They reap every one his corn in the field: and they gather the vintage of the wicked.

They cause the naked to lodge without clothing, that they have no covering in the cold.

They are wet with the showers of the mountains, and embrace the rock for want of a shelter.

They pluck the fatherless from the breast, and take a pledge of the poor.

They cause him to go naked without clothing, and they take away the sheaf from the hungry;

Which make oil within their walls, and tread their winepresses, and suffer thirst.

Men groan from out of the city, and the soul of the wounded crieth out: yet God layeth not folly to them.

They are of those that rebel against the light; they know not the ways thereof, nor abide in the paths thereof.

The murderer rising with the light killeth the poor and needy, and in the night is as a thief.

The eye also of the adulterer waiteth for the twilight, saying, No eye shall see me: and disguiseth his face.

In the dark they dig through houses, which they had marked for themselves in the daytime: they know not the light.

For the morning is to them even as the shadow of death: if one know them, they are in the terrors of the shadow of death.

"He is swift as the waters; their portion is cursed in the earth: he beholdeth not the way of the vineyards.

Drought and heat consume the snow waters: so doth the grave those which have sinned.

The womb shall forget him; the worm shall feed sweetly on him; he shall be no more remembered; and wickedness shall be broken as a tree."

He evil entreateth the barren that beareth not: and doeth not good to the widow.

He draweth also the mighty with his power: he riseth up, and no man is sure of life.

Though it be given him to be in safety, whereon he resteth; yet his eyes are upon their ways.

They are exalted for a little while, but are gone and brought low; they are taken out of the way as all other, and cut off as the tops of the ears of corn.

And if it be not so now, who will make me a liar, and make my speech nothing worth?

25

Then answered Bildad the Shuhite, and said,

Dominion and fear are with him, he maketh peace in his high places.

Is there any number of his armies? and upon whom doth not his light arise?

How then can man be justified with God? or how can he be clean that is born of a woman?

Behold even to the moon, and it shineth not; yea, the stars are not pure in his sight.

How much less man, that is a worm? and the son of man, which is a worm?[8]

26

But Job answered and said,

How hast thou helped him that is without power? how savest thou the arm that hath no strength?

How hast thou counselled him that hath no wisdom? and how hast thou plentifully declared the thing as it is?

To whom hast thou uttered words? and whose spirit came from thee?

Dead things are formed from under the waters, and the inhabitants thereof.

---

8. At this point, an ancient editor has inserted several lines from Job's reply (verses 1–4 of Chapter 26), thereby attributing the balance of Bildad's speech to Job.

Hell is naked before him, and destruction hath no covering.

He stretcheth out the north over the empty place, and hangeth the earth upon nothing.

He bindeth up the waters in his thick clouds; and the cloud is not rent under them.

He holdeth back the face of his throne, and spreadeth his cloud upon it.

He hath compassed the waters with bounds, until the day and night come to an end.

The pillars of heaven tremble and are astonished at his reproof.

He divideth the sea with his power, and by his understanding he smiteth through the proud.

By his spirit he hath garnished the heavens; his hand hath formed the crooked serpent.

Lo, these are parts of his ways: but how little a portion is heard of him? but the thunder of his power who can understand?

27

Moreover Job continued his parable, and said,

As God liveth, who hath taken away my judgment; and the Almighty, who hath vexed my soul;

All the while my breath is in me, and the spirit of God is in my nostrils;

My lips shall not speak wickedness, nor my tongue utter deceit.

God forbid that I should justify you: till I die I will not remove mine integrity from me.

My righteousness I hold fast, and will not let it go: my heart shall not reproach me so long as I live.

Let mine enemy be as the wicked, and he that riseth up against me as the unrighteous.

For what is the hope of the hypocrite, though he hath gained, when God taketh away his soul?

Will God hear his cry when trouble cometh upon him?

Will he delight himself in the Almighty? will he always call upon God?

I will teach you by the hand of God: that which is with the Almighty will I not conceal.

Behold, all ye yourselves have seen it; why then are ye thus altogether vain?

Zophar replied: This is the portion of a wicked man with God, and the heritage of oppressors, which they shall receive of the Almighty.

If his children be multiplied, it is for the sword: and his offspring shall not be satisfied with bread.

Those that remain of him shall be buried in death: and his widows shall not weep.

Though he heap up silver as the dust, and prepare raiment as the clay;

He may prepare it, but the just shall put it on, and the innocent shall divide the silver.

He buildeth his house as a moth, and as a booth that the keeper maketh.

The rich man shall lie down, but he shall not be gathered: he openeth his eyes, and he is not.

Terrors take hold on him as waters, a tempest stealeth him away in the night.

The east wind carrieth him away, and he departeth: and as a storm hurleth him out of his place.

For God shall cast upon him, and not spare: he would fain flee out of his hand.

Men shall clap their hands at him, and shall hiss him out of his place.

28

Surely there is a vein for the silver, and a place for gold where they fine it.

Iron is taken out of the earth, and brass is molten out of the stone.

He setteth an end to darkness, and searcheth out all perfection: the stones of darkness, and the shadow of death.

The flood breaketh out from the inhabitant; even the waters forgotten of the foot: they are dried up, they are gone away from men.

As for the earth, out of it cometh bread: and under it is turned up as it were fire.

The stones of it are the place of sapphires: and it hath dust of gold.

There is a path which no fowl knoweth, and which the vulture's eye hath not seen:

The lion's whelps have not trodden it, nor the fierce lion passed by it.

He putteth forth his hand upon the rock; he overturneth the mountains by the roots.

He cutteth out rivers among the rocks; and his eye seeth every precious thing.

He bindeth the floods from overflowing; and the thing that is hid bringeth he forth to light.

But where shall wisdom be found? and where is the place of understanding?

Man knoweth not the price thereof; neither is it found in the land of the living.

The depth saith, It is not in me: and the sea saith, It is not with me.

It cannot be gotten for gold, neither shall silver be weighed for the price thereof.

It cannot be valued with the gold of Ophir, with the precious onyx, or the sapphire.

The gold and the crystal cannot equal it: and the exchange of it shall not be for jewels of fine gold.

No mention shall be made of coral, or of pearls: for the price of wisdom is above rubies.

The topaz of Ethiopia shall not equal it, neither shall it be valued with pure gold.

Whence then cometh wisdom? and where is the place of understanding?

Seeing it is hid from the eyes of all living, and kept close from the fowls of the air.

Destruction and death say, We have heard the fame thereof with our ears.

God understandeth the way thereof, and he knoweth the place thereof.

For he looketh to the ends of the earth, and seeth under the whole heaven;

To make the weight for the winds; and he weigheth the waters by measure.

When he made a decree for the rain, and a way for the lightning of the thunder:

Then did he see it, and declare it; he prepared it, yea, and searched it out.

And unto man he said, Behold, the fear of the Lord, that is wisdom; and to depart from evil is understanding.

29

Moreover Job continued his parable, and said,

Oh that I were as in months past, as in the days when God preserved me;

When his candle shined upon my head, and when by his light I walked through darkness;

As I was in the days of my youth, when the secret of God was upon my tabernacle;

When the Almighty was yet with me, when my children were about me;

When I washed my steps with butter, and the rock poured me out rivers of oil;

When I went out to the gate through the city, when I prepared my seat in the street!

The young men saw me, and hid themselves: and the aged arose, and stood up.

The princes refrained talking, and laid their hand on their mouth.

The nobles held their peace, and their tongue cleaved to the roof of their mouth.

When the ear heard me, then it blessed me; and when the eye saw me, it gave witness to me:

Because I delivered the poor that cried, and the fatherless, and him that had none to help him.

The blessing of him that was ready to perish came upon me: and I caused the widow's heart to sing for joy.

I put on righteousness, and it clothed me: my judgment was as a robe and a diadem.

I was eyes to the blind, and feet was I to the lame.

I was a father to the poor: and the cause which I knew not I searched out.

And I brake the jaws of the wicked, and plucked the spoil out of his teeth.

Then I said, I shall die in my nest, and I shall multiply my days as the sand.

My root was spread out by the waters, and the dew lay all night upon my branch.

My glory was fresh in me, and my bow was renewed in my hand.

Unto me men gave ear, and waited, and kept silence at my counsel.

After my words they spake not again; and my speech dropped upon them.

And they waited for me as for the rain; and they opened their mouth wide as for the latter rain.

If I laughed on them, they believed it not; and the light of my countenance they cast not down.

I chose out their way, and sat chief, and dwelt as a king in the army, as one that comforteth the mourners.

30

But now they that are younger than I have me in derision, whose fathers I would have disdained to have set with the dogs of my flock.

Yea, whereto might the strength of their hands profit me, in whom old age was perished?

For want and famine they were solitary; fleeing into the wilderness in former time desolate and waste.

Who cut up mallows by the bushes, and juniper roots for their meat.

They were driven forth from among men, (they cried after them as after a thief;)

To dwell in the clifts of the valleys, in caves of the earth, and in the rocks.

Among the bushes they brayed; under the nettles they were gathered together.

They were children of fools, yea, children of base men: they were viler than the earth.

And now am I their song, yea, I am their byword.

They abhor me, they flee far from me, and spare not to spit in my face.

Because he hath loosed my cord, and afflicted me, they have also let loose the bridle before me.

Upon my right hand rise the youth; they push away my feet, and they raise up against me the ways of their destruction.

They mar my path, they set forward my calamity, they have no helper.

They came upon me as a wide breaking in of waters: in the desolation they rolled themselves upon me.

Terrors are turned upon me: they pursue my soul as the wind: and my welfare passeth away as a cloud.

And now my soul is poured out upon me; the days of affliction have taken hold upon me.

My bones are pierced in me in the night season: and my sinews take no rest.

By the great force of my disease is my garment changed: it bindeth me about as the collar of my coat.

He hath cast me into the mire, and I am become like dust and ashes.

I cry unto thee, and thou dost not hear me: I stand up, and thou regardest me not.

Thou art become cruel to me: with thy strong hand thou opposest thyself against me.

Thou liftest me up to the wind; thou causest me to ride upon it, and dissolvest my substance.

For I know that thou wilt bring me to death, and to the house appointed for all living.

Howbeit he will not stretch out his hand to the grave, though they cry in his destruction.

Did not I weep for him that was in trouble? was not my soul grieved for the poor?

When I looked for good, then evil came unto me: and when I waited for light, there came darkness.

My bowels boiled, and rested not: the days of affliction prevented me.

I went mourning without the sun: I stood up, and I cried in the congregation.

I am a brother to dragons, and a companion to owls.

My skin is black upon me, and my bones are burned with heat.

My harp also is turned to mourning, and my organ into the voice of them that weep.

31

I made a covenant with mine eyes; why then should I think upon a maid?

For what portion of God is there from above? and what inheritance of the Almighty from on high?

Is not destruction to the wicked? and a strange punishment to the workers of iniquity?

Doth not he see my ways, and count all my steps?

If I have walked with vanity, or if my foot hath hasted to deceit;

Let me be weighed in an even balance, that God may know mine integrity.

If my step hath turned out of the way, and mine heart walked after mine eyes, and if any blot hath cleaved to mine hands;

Then let me sow, and let another eat; yea, let my offspring be rooted out.

If mine heart have been deceived by a woman, or if I have laid wait at my neighbour's door;

Then let my wife grind unto another, and let others bow down upon her.

For this is an heinous crime; yea, it is an iniquity to be punished by the judges.

For it is a fire that consumeth to destruction, and would root out all mine increase.

If I did despise the cause of my manservant or of my maidservant, when they contended with me;

What then shall I do when God riseth up? and when he visiteth, what shall I answer him?

Did not he that made me in the womb make him? and did not one fashion us in the womb?

If I have withheld the poor from their desire, or have caused the eyes of the widow to fail;

Or have eaten my morsel myself alone, and the fatherless hath not eaten thereof;

(For from my youth he was brought up with me, as with a father, and I have guided her from my mother's womb;)

If I have seen any perish for want of clothing, or any poor without covering;

If his loins have not blessed me, and if he were not warmed with the fleece of my sheep;

If I have lifted up my hand against the fatherless, when I saw my help in the gate:

Then let mine arm fall from my shoulder blade, and mine arm be broken from the bone.

For destruction from God was a terror to me, and by reason of his highness I could not endure.

If I have made gold my hope, or have said to the fine gold, Thou art my confidence;

If I rejoiced because my wealth was great, and because mine hand had gotten much;

If I beheld the sun when it shined, or the moon walking in brightness;

And my heart hath been secretly enticed, or my mouth hath kissed my hand:

This also were an iniquity to be punished by the judge: for I should have denied the God that is above.

If I rejoiced at the destruction of him that hated me, or lifted up myself when evil found him:

Neither have I suffered my mouth to sin by wishing a curse to his soul.

If the men of my tabernacle said not, Oh that we had of his flesh! we cannot be satisfied.

The stranger did not lodge in the street: but I opened my doors to the traveller.

If I covered my transgressions as Adam, by hiding mine iniquity in my bosom:

Did I fear a great multitude, or did the contempt of families terrify me, that I kept silence, and went not out of the door?

Oh that one would hear me! behold, my desire is, that the Almighty would answer me, and that mine adversary had written a book.

Surely I would take it upon my shoulder, and bind it as a crown to me.

I would declare unto him the number of my steps; as a prince would I go near unto him.

If my land cry against me, or that the furrows likewise thereof complain;

If I have eaten the fruits thereof without money, or have caused the owners thereof to lose their life:

Let thistles grow instead of wheat, and cockle instead of barley. The words of Job are ended.

[Chapters 32–37 in the received text, omitted here, are a latter addition in which a new character, Elihu, is abruptly introduced. Elihu's long speech reiterates the three friends' argument. The text then resumes.]

38

Then the LORD answered Job out of the whirlwind, and said,

Who is this that darkeneth counsel by words without knowledge?

Gird up now thy loins like a man; for I will demand of thee, and answer thou me.

Where wast thou when I laid the foundations of the earth? declare, if thou hast understanding.

Who hath laid the measures thereof, if thou knowest? or who hath stretched the line upon it?

Whereupon are the foundations thereof fastened? or who laid the corner stone thereof;

When the morning stars sang together, and all the sons of God shouted for joy?

Or who shut up the sea with doors, when it brake forth, as if it had issued out of the womb?

When I made the cloud the garment thereof, and thick darkness a swaddling-band for it,

And brake up for it my decreed place, and set bars and doors,

And said, Hitherto shalt thou come, but no further: and here shall thy proud waves be stayed?

Hast thou commanded the morning since thy days; and caused the dayspring to know his place;

That it might take hold of the ends of the earth, that the wicked might be shaken out of it?

It is turned as clay to the seal; and they stand as a garment.

And from the wicked their light is withholden, and the high arm shall be broken.

Hast thou entered into the springs of the sea? or hast thou walked in the search of the depth?

Have the gates of death been opened unto thee? or hast thou seen the doors of the shadow of death?

Hast thou perceived the breadth of the earth? declare if thou knowest it all.

Where is the way where light dwelleth? and as for darkness, where is the place thereof,

That thou shouldest take it to the bound thereof, and that thou shouldest know the paths to the house thereof?

Knowest thou it, because thou wast then born? or because the number of thy days is great?

Hast thou entered into the treasures of the snow? or hast thou seen the treasures of the hail,

Which I have reserved against the time of trouble, against the day of battle and war?

By what way is the light parted, which scattereth the east wind upon the earth?

Who hath divided a watercourse for the overflowing of waters, or a way for the lightning of thunder;

To cause it to rain on the earth, where no man is; on the wilderness, wherein there is no man;

To satisfy the desolate and waste ground; and to cause the bud of the tender herb to spring forth?

Hath the rain a father? or who hath begotten the drops of dew?

Out of whose womb came the ice? and the hoary frost of heaven, who hath gendered it?

The waters are hid as with a stone, and the face of the deep is frozen.

Canst thou bind the sweet influences of Pleiades, or loose the bands of Orion?

Canst thou bring forth Mazzaroth in his season? or canst thou guide Arcturus with his sons?

Knowest thou the ordinances of heaven? canst thou set the dominion thereof in the earth?

Canst thou lift up thy voice to the clouds, that abundance of waters may cover thee?

Canst thou send lightnings, that they may go, and say unto thee, Here we are?

Who hath put wisdom in the inward parts? or who hath given understanding to the heart?

Who can number the clouds in wisdom? or who can stay the bottles of heaven,

When the dust groweth into hardness, and the clods cleave fast together?

Wilt thou hunt the prey for the lion? or fill the appetite of the young lions,

When they couch in their dens, and abide in the covert to lie in wait?

Who provideth for the raven his food? when his young ones cry unto God, they wander for lack of meat.

39

Knowest thou the time when the wild goats of the rock bring forth? or canst thou mark when the hinds do calve?

Canst thou number the months that they fulfil? or knowest thou the time when they bring forth?

They bow themselves, they bring forth their young ones, they cast out their sorrows.

Their young ones are in good liking, they grow up with corn; they go forth, and return not unto them.

Who hath sent out the wild ass free? or who hath loosed the bands of the wild ass?

Whose house I have made the wilderness, and the barren land his dwellings.

He scorneth the multitude of the city, neither regardeth he the crying of the driver.

The range of the mountains is his pasture, and he searcheth after every green thing.

Will the unicorn be willing to serve thee, or abide by thy crib?

Canst thou bind the unicorn with his band in the furrow? or will he harrow the valleys after thee?

Wilt thou trust him, because his strength is great? or wilt thou leave thy labour to him?

Wilt thou believe him, that he will bring home thy seed, and gather it into thy barn?

Gavest thou the goodly wings unto the peacocks? or wings and feathers unto the ostrich?

Which leaveth her eggs in the earth, and warmeth them in dust,

And forgetteth that the foot may crush them, or that the wild beast may break them.

She is hardened against her young ones, as though they were not hers: her labour is in vain without fear;

Because God hath deprived her of wisdom, neither hath he imparted to her understanding.

What time she lifteth up herself on high, she scorneth the horse and his rider.

Hast thou given the horse strength? hast thou clothed his neck with thunder?

Canst thou make him afraid as a grasshopper? the glory of his nostrils is terrible.

He paweth in the valley, and rejoiceth in his strength: he goeth on to meet the armed men.

He mocketh at fear, and is not affrighted; neither turneth he back from the sword.

The quiver rattleth against him, the glittering spear and the shield.

He swalloweth the ground with fierceness and rage: neither believeth he that it is the sound of the trumpet.

He saith among the trumpets, Ha, ha; and he smelleth the battle afar off, the thunder of the captains, and the shouting.

Doth the hawk fly by thy wisdom, and stretch her wings toward the south?

Doth the eagle mount up at thy command, and make her nest on high?

She dwelleth and abideth on the rock, upon the crag of the rock, and the strong place.

From thence she seeketh the prey, and her eyes behold afar off.

Her young ones also suck up blood: and where the slain are, there is she.

40

Moreover the LORD answered Job, and said,

Shall he that contendeth with the Almighty instruct him? he that reproveth God, let him answer it.

Then Job answered the LORD, and said,

Behold, I am vile; what shall I answer thee? I will lay mine hand upon my mouth.

Once have I spoken; but I will not answer: yea, twice; but I will proceed no further.

Then answered the LORD unto Job out of the whirlwind, and said,

Gird up thy loins now like a man: I will demand of thee, and declare thou unto me.

Wilt thou also disannul my judgment? wilt thou condemn me, that thou mayest be righteous?

Hast thou an arm like God? or canst thou thunder with a voice like him?

Deck thyself now with majesty and excellency; and array thyself with glory and beauty.

Cast abroad the rage of thy wrath: and behold every one that is proud, and abase him.

Look on every one that is proud, and bring him low; and tread down the wicked in their place.

Hide them in the dust together; and bind their faces in secret.

Then will I also confess unto thee that thine own right hand can save thee.

Behold now behemoth, which I made with thee; he eateth grass as an ox.

Lo now, his strength is in his loins, and his force is in the navel of his belly.

He moveth his tail like a cedar: the sinews of his stones are wrapped together.

His bones are as strong pieces of brass; his bones are like bars of iron.

He is the chief of the ways of God: he that made him can make his sword to approach unto him.

Surely the mountains bring him forth food, where all the beasts of the field play.

He lieth under the shady trees, in the covert of the reed, and fens.

The shady trees cover him with their shadow; the willows of the brook compass him about.

Behold, he drinketh up a river, and hasteth not: he trusteth that he can draw up Jordan into his mouth.

He taketh it with his eyes: his nose pierceth through snares.

41

Canst thou draw out leviathan with an hook? or his tongue with a cord which thou lettest down?

Canst thou put an hook into his nose? or bore his jaw through with a thorn?

Will he make many supplications unto thee? will he speak soft words unto thee?

Will he make a covenant with thee? wilt thou take him for a servant for ever?

Wilt thou play with him as with a bird? or wilt thou bind him for thy maidens?

Shall the companions make a banquet of him? shall they part him among the merchants?

Canst thou fill his skin with barbed irons? or his head with fish spears?

Lay thine hand upon him, remember the battle, do no more.

Behold, the hope of him is in vain: shall not one be cast down even at the sight of him?

None is so fierce that dare stir him up: who then is able to stand before me?

Who hath prevented me, that I should repay him? whatsoever is under the whole heaven is mine.

I will not conceal his parts, nor his power, nor his comely proportion.

Who can discover the face of his garment? or who can come to him with his double bridle?

Who can open the doors of his face? his teeth are terrible round about.

His scales are his pride, shut up together as with a close seal.

One is so near to another, that no air can come between them.

They are joined one to another, they stick together, that they cannot be sundered.

By his neesings a light doth shine, and his eyes are like the eyelids of the morning.

Out of his mouth go burning lamps, and sparks of fire leap out.

Out of his nostrils goeth smoke, as out of a seething pot or caldron.

His breath kindleth coals, and a flame goeth out of his mouth.

In his neck remaineth strength, and sorrow is turned into joy before him.

The flakes of his flesh are joined together: they are firm in themselves; they cannot be moved.

His heart is as firm as a stone; yea, as hard as a piece of the nether millstone.

When he raiseth up himself, the mighty are afraid: by reason of breakings they purify themselves.

The sword of him that layeth at him cannot hold: the spear, the dart, nor the habergeon.

He esteemeth iron as straw, and brass as rotten wood.

The arrow cannot make him flee: slingstones are turned with him into stubble.

Darts are counted as stubble: he laugheth at the shaking of a spear.

Sharp stones are under him: he spreadeth sharp pointed things upon the mire.

He maketh the deep to boil like a pot: he maketh the sea like a pot of ointment.

He maketh a path to shine after him; one would think the deep to be hoary.

Upon earth there is not his like, who is made without fear.

He beholdeth all high things: he is a king over all the children of pride.

42

Then Job answered the LORD, and said,

I know that thou canst do every thing, and that no thought can be withholden from thee.

Who is he that hideth counsel without knowledge? therefore have I uttered that I understood not; things too wonderful for me, which I knew not.

Hear, I beseech thee, and I will speak: I will demand of thee, and declare thou unto me.

I have heard of thee by the hearing of the ear: but now mine eye seeth thee.

Wherefore I abhor myself, and repent in dust and ashes.

And it was so, that after the LORD had spoken these words unto Job, the LORD said to Eliphaz the Temanite, My wrath is kindled against thee, and against thy two friends: for ye have not spoken of me the thing that is right, as my servant Job hath.

Therefore take unto you now seven bullocks and seven rams, and go to my servant Job, and offer up for yourselves a burnt offering; and my servant Job shall pray for you: for him will I accept: lest I deal with you after your folly, in that ye have not spoken of me the thing which is right, like my servant Job.

So Eliphaz the Temanite and Bildad the Shuhite and Zophar the Naamathite went, and did according as the LORD commanded them: the LORD also accepted Job.

And the LORD turned the captivity of Job, when he prayed for his friends: also the LORD gave Job twice as much as he had before.

Then came there unto him all his brethren, and all his sisters, and all they that had been of his acquaintance before, and did eat bread with him in his house: and they bemoaned him, and comforted him over all the evil that the LORD had brought upon him: every man also gave him a piece of money, and every one an earring of gold.

So the LORD blessed the latter end of Job more than his beginning: for he had fourteen thousand sheep, and six thousand camels, and a thousand yoke of oxen, and a thousand she asses.

He had also seven sons and three daughters.

And he called the name of the first, Jemima; and the name of the second, Kezia; and the name of the third, Keren-happuch.[9]

And in all the land were no women found so fair as the daughters of Job: and their father gave them inheritance among their brethren.

After this lived Job an hundred and forty years, and saw his sons, and his sons' sons, even four generations.

So Job died, being old and full of days.

ANONYMOUS (SECOND MILLENNIUM B.C.E.)
Assyria/Babylonia

This haunting Akkadian poem describes the struggle for control of the underworld between Ishtar, the goddess of love, and her sister Ereshkigal, the queen of the underworld. Ereshkigal defeats Ishtar but spares her life on the condition that she surrender her husband, Dumuzi, as hostage.

The Descent of Ishtar dates from sometime during the second millennium B.C.E. The poem was performed in the Assyrian capital of Nineveh in connection with an annual ritual that featured the bathing and anointing of a statue of Dumuzi. It is based on an earlier Sumerian poem, *The Descent of Inanna,* in which Dumuzi is described as dying and rising again, thus causing seasonal fertility. (A

---

9. In this return to the folktale frame, Job's
new daughters have names meaning Dove,
Cinnamon, and Horn of eye-shadow.

similar mythical explanation of seasonal renewal can be found in the story of Persephone's abduction in the *Hymn to Demeter*.) *The Descent of Ishtar's* chilling description of the underworld House of Dust later found its way into the *Epic of Gilgamesh*, where it serves to motivate Gilgamesh's horror of death and leads to his subsequent search for immortality.

The Descent of Ishtar to the Underworld

To Kurnugi, land of no return,[1]
Ishtar daughter of Sin[2] was determined to go;
The daughter of Sin was determined to go
To the dark house, dwelling of Erkalla's god,[3]
To the house which those who enter cannot leave, 5
On the road where travelling is one-way only,
To the house where those who enter are deprived of light,
Where dust is their food, clay their bread.
They see no light, they dwell in darkness,
They are clothed like birds, with feathers. 10
Over the door and the bolt, dust has settled.
Ishtar, when she arrived at the gate of Kurnugi,
Addressed her words to the keeper of the gate,
    "Here gatekeeper, open your gate for me,
    Open your gate for me to come in! 15
    If you do not open the gate for me to come in,
    I shall smash the door and shatter the bolt,
    I shall smash the doorpost and overturn the doors,
    I shall raise up the dead and they shall eat the living:
    The dead shall outnumber the living!" 20
The gatekeeper made his voice heard and spoke,
He said to great Ishtar,
    "Stop, lady, do not break it down!
    Let me go and report your words to queen Ereshkigal."
The gatekeeper went in and spoke to Ereshkigal, 25
    "Here she is, your sister Ishtar,
    Who holds the great *keppū*-toy,[4]
    Stirs up the Apsu in Ea's presence."
When Ereshkigal heard this,
Her face grew livid as cut tamarisk, 30
Her lips grew dark as the rim of a pitch-coated vessel.

Translated by Stephanie Dalley.

1. *Kurnugi* is Sumerian for "Land of No Return."
2. The moon god (also spelled Su'en).
3. *Erkalla*, "The Great City," is another name for the underworld. It is ruled by Ereshkigal

and her husband Nergal, who is often assimilated with Erra; he is called Herakles in Greek.
4. Perhaps a top, made to spin with a whip.

"What brings her to me? What has incited her against me?
Surely not because I drink water with the Anunnaki,
I eat clay for bread, I drink muddy water for beer?
Should I weep for young men forced to abandon their sweethearts?   35
Should I weep for girls wrenched from their lovers' laps?
Should I weep for the infant child, expelled before its time?
Go, gatekeeper, open your gate to her.
Treat her according to the ancient rites."
The gatekeeper went. He opened the gate to her.   40
  "Enter, my lady: may Kutha give you joy,[5]
  May the palace of Kurnugi be glad to see you."
He let her in through the first door, but stripped away the great crown on her
    head.
  "Gatekeeper, why have you taken away the great crown on my head?"
  "Go in, my lady. Such are the rites of the Mistress of Earth."   45
He let her in through the second door, but stripped away the rings in her ears.
  "Gatekeeper, why have you taken away the rings in my ears?"
  "Go in, my lady. Such are the rites of the Mistress of Earth."
He let her in through the third door, but stripped away the beads around her neck.
  "Gatekeeper, why have you taken away the beads around my neck?"   50
  "Go in, my lady. Such are the rites of the Mistress of Earth."
He let her in through the fourth door, but stripped away the fasteners at her
    breast.
  "Gatekeeper, why have you taken away the fasteners at my breast?"
  "Go in, my lady. Such are the rites of the Mistress of Earth."
He let her in through the fifth door, but stripped away the girdle of birth-stones
    around her waist.   55
  "Gatekeeper, why have you taken away the girdle of birthstones around my
    waist?"
  "Go in, my lady. Such are the rites of the Mistress of Earth."
He let her in through the sixth door, but stripped away the bangles on her wrists
    and ankles.
  "Gatekeeper, why have you taken away the bangles from my wrists and ankles?"
  "Go in, my lady. Such are the rites of the Mistress of Earth."   60
He let her in through the seventh door, but stripped away the proud garment of
    her body.
  "Gatekeeper, why have you taken away the proud garment of my body?"
  "Go in, my lady. Such are the rites of the Mistress of Earth."
As soon as Ishtar went down to Kurnugi,
Ereshkigal looked at her and trembled before her.   65
Ishtar did not deliberate, but leant over her.
Ereshkigal made her voice heard and spoke,
Addressed her words to Namtar her vizier,

---

5. Kutha was a city sacred to Nergal; here the
name is used for the underworld itself.

'Go, Namtar, send out against her sixty diseases:
Disease of the eyes to her eyes,   70
Disease of the arms to her arms,
Disease of the feet to her feet,
Disease of the heart to her heart,
Disease of the head to her head,
To every part of her.'   75
After Ishtar the mistress of the land had gone down to Kurnugi,
No bull mounted a cow, no donkey impregnated a jenny,
No young man impregnated a girl in the street,
The young man slept in his private room,
The girl slept in the company of her friends.   80
Then Papsukkal, vizier of the great gods, hung his head, his face became gloomy;
He wore mourning clothes, his hair was unkempt.
Dejected, he went and wept before Sin his father,
His tears flowed freely before king Ea.
    "Ishtar has gone down to the Earth and has not come up again.   85
    As soon as Ishtar went down to Kurnugi
    No bull mounted a cow, no donkey impregnated a jenny,
    No young man impregnated a girl in the street,
    The young man slept in his private room,
    The girl slept in the company of her friends."   90
Ea, in the wisdom of his heart, created a person.
He created Good-looks the playboy.[6]
    "Come, Good-looks, set your face towards the gate of Kurnugi.
    The seven gates of Kurnugi shall be opened before you.
    Ereshkigal shall look at you and be glad to see you.   95
    When she is relaxed, her mood will lighten.
    Get her to swear the oath by the great gods.
    Raise your head, pay attention to the waterskin,
    Saying, 'Hey, my lady, let them give me the waterskin, that I may drink water
        from it.'"
                                    (*And so it happened. But*)   100
When Ereshkigal heard this,
She struck her thigh and bit her finger.
    "You have made a request of me that should not have been made!
    Come, Good-looks, I shall curse you with a great curse.
    I shall decree for you a fate that shall never be forgotten.   105
    Bread begged from the city's bakers shall be your food,
    The city drains shall be your only drinking place,
    The shade of a city wall your only standing place,
    Threshold steps your only sitting place,
    The drunkard and the thirsty shall slap your cheek."   110

---

6. Literally, "His appearance is bright."

Ereshkigal made her voice heard and spoke;
She addressed her words to Namtar her vizier,
   "Go, Namtar, knock at Egalgina,
   Decorate the threshold with coral,
   Bring the Anunnaki out and seat (them) on golden thrones,   115
   Sprinkle Ishtar with the waters of life and conduct her into my presence."
Namtar went, knocked at Egalgina,
Decorated the threshold steps with coral,
Brought out the Anunnaki, seated (them) on golden thrones,
Sprinkled Ishtar with the waters of life and brought her to her (sister).   120
He let her out through the first door, and gave back to her the proud garment of
   her body.
He let her out through the second door, and gave back to her the bangles for her
   wrists and ankles.
He let her out through the third door, and gave back to her the girdle of birth
   stones around her waist.
He let her out through the fourth door, and gave back to her the fasteners at her
   breast.
He let her out through the fifth door, and gave back to her the beads around her
   neck.   125
He let her out through the sixth door, and gave back to her the rings for her ears.
He let her out through the seventh door, and gave back to her the great crown for
   her head.
   "Swear that she has paid you her ransom, and give her back (in exchange) for
   him,
   For Dumuzi, the lover of her youth.
   Wash (him) with pure water, anoint him with sweet oil,   130
   Clothe him in a red robe, let the lapis lazuli pipe play.
   Let temple prostitutes raise a loud lament."
Then Belili[7] tore off her jewellery,
Her lap was filled with eyestones.
Belili heard the lament for her brother, she struck the jewellery from her body,   135
The eyestones with which the front of the wild cow was filled.
   "You shall not rob me (forever) of my only brother!
   On the day when Dumuzi comes back up, (and) the lapis lazuli pipe and the
   carnelian ring come up with him,
   (When) male and female mourners come up with him,
   The dead shall come up and smell the smoke offering."   140

---

7. Sister of Dumuzi; in the longer Sumerian   seasonal return from the underworld in the
   version, she pleads for Dumuzi's periodic   Greek myth.
   release. Compare this with Persephone's

ANONYMOUS (SEVENTH CENTURY B.C.E.)
Greece

The *Homeric Hymn to Aphrodite* and the *Homeric Hymn to Demeter* (from both of which we give substantial selections here) belong to a body of poems in epic meter that in antiquity were generally attributed to Homer. Linguistic and stylistic evidence has since disproved the attribution, although the poems clearly draw on traditional mythology and story patterns. As a genre, the hymn was highly popular in the archaic and classical periods of Greece (the seventh to the fifth centuries B.C.E.). The hymns ascribed to Homer are thought to have been composed for performance at public religious festivals as preludes to epic songs.

The *Homeric Hymn to Aphrodite* opens by acknowledging the irresistible power of Aphrodite, the goddess of erotic love. All beings mortal and divine (with only three exceptions) are helpless before her, and even Zeus, the supreme deity, has often been at her mercy. In the subsequent narrative, Zeus turns the tables on the goddess, causing her to fall in love with a young man—Anchises, a cousin of the Trojan king, Priam. Disguising herself as a girl from the countryside, Aphrodite seduces Anchises. His poignant expression of fear when he discovers her identity reflects the peril inherent in mortal-immortal liaisons—a recurrent motif in early Greek mythology and literature. From this union of Aphrodite with Anchises, however, the Trojan hero Aeneas will be born. Aphrodite predicts for him an endless line of descendants, which, centuries later, becomes an important thematic element in Vergil's *Aeneid*.

Homeric Hymn to Aphrodite

Muse, tell me the things done by golden Aphrodite,
the one from Cyprus,[1] who arouses sweet desire for gods
and who subdues the races of mortal humans,
and birds as well, who fly in the sky, as well as all beasts
—all those that grow on both dry land and the sea.   5
They all know the things done by the one with the beautiful garlands, the one
     from Kythera.[2]
But there are three whose minds she cannot win over or deceive.
The first is the daughter of aegis-bearing Zeus, bright-eyed Athena.
For she takes no pleasure in the things done by golden Aphrodite.
What does please her is wars and what is done by Ares,   10
battles and fighting, as well as the preparation of splendid pieces of craftsmanship.

Translated by Gregory Nagy.

---

1. Aphrodite is always associated with the island of Cyprus, thought to have been either the place of her birth or the island onto which she first stepped after her birth in the sea, as described in Hesiod's *Theogony*.
2. According to Hesiod, after Aphrodite's birth in the sea, she drifted near the island of Kythera before reaching Cyprus.

For she was the first to teach mortal humans to be craftsmen
in making war-chariots and other things on wheels, decorated with bronze.
And she it is who teaches maidens, tender of skin, inside the palaces,
the skill of making splendid pieces of craftsmanship, putting it firmly into each
  one's mind.   15
The second is the renowned Artemis,[3] she of the golden shafts: never
has she been subdued in lovemaking by Aphrodite, lover of smiles.
For she takes pleasure in the bow and arrows, and the killing of wild beasts in the
  mountains, (hunter)
as well as lyres, groups of singing dancers, and high-pitched shouts of celebration.
Also shaded groves and the city of just men. (Art of music)   20
The third one not to take pleasure in the things done by Aphrodite is that young
  Maiden full of honorableness,
Hestia,[4] who was the first-born child of Kronos, the one with the crooked mind,
as well as the last and youngest, through the Will of Zeus, holder of the aegis.[5]
She was the Lady who was wooed by Poseidon and Apollo.
But she was quite unwilling, and she firmly refused. (virgin/hearth)   25
She had sworn a great oath, and what she said became what really happened.
She swore, as she touched the head of her father Zeus, the aegis-bearer,
that she would be a virgin for all days to come, that illustrious goddess.
And to her Father Zeus gave a beautiful honor, as a compensating substitute for
  marriage.
She is seated in the middle of the house, getting the richest portion.   30
And in all the temples of the gods she has a share in the honor
Among all the mortals, she is the senior goddess.
These are the three that she could not persuade in their minds.
As for all the rest, there is nothing that has escaped Aphrodite:
none of the blessed gods nor any of mortal humans.   35
She even led astray the perception of Zeus, the one who delights in the thunder,
the one who is the very greatest and the one who has the very greatest honor as his
  share.
But even his well-formed mind is deceived by her, whenever she wants,
as she mates him with mortal women with the greatest of ease,
unbeknownst to Hera, his sister and wife,   40
who is the best among all the immortal goddesses in her great beauty.
She was the most glorious female to be born to Kronos, the one with the crooked
  mind,
and to her mother, Rhea. And Zeus, the one whose resources are inexhaustible,
made her his honorable wife, one who knows the ways of affection.
But even upon her Zeus put sweet desire in her heart   45
—desire to make love to a mortal man, so that

---

3. The chaste goddess of the hunt is Apollo's
sister.
4. Hestia, whose name means "hearth" or
"fireplace," was the first child swallowed by

her father Cronus and the last disgorged,
according to Hesiod.
5. The aegis is Zeus' shield.

not even she may go without mortal lovemaking
and get a chance to gloat at all the other gods,
with her sweet laughter, Aphrodite, lover of smiles,
boasting that she can make the gods sleep with mortal women,   50
who then bear mortal sons to immortal fathers,
and how she can make the goddesses sleep with mortal men.
And so he put sweet desire in her heart—desire for Anchises.
At that time, he was herding cattle at the steep peaks of Mount Ida, famous for its
     many springs.
To look at him and the way he was shaped was like looking at the immortals.   55
When Aphrodite, lover of smiles, saw him,
she fell in love with him. A terrible desire seized her in her mind.
She went to Cyprus, entering her temple fragrant with incense,
to Paphos.[6] That is where her sacred precinct is, and her altar, fragrant with
     incense.
She went in and closed the shining doors.   60
Then the Graces bathed her and anointed her with oil
—the kind that gives immortality, glistening on the complexion of the gods, who
     last for all time.
Immortal it was, giver of pleasures, and it had the fragrance of incense.
Then she wrapped all her beautiful clothes around her skin.
She was decked out in gold, Aphrodite, lover of smiles.   65
She rushed toward Troy, leaving behind fragrant Cyprus.
Making her way with the greatest of ease, high up among the clouds.
She arrived at Mount Ida, famous for its many springs, nurturing mother of beasts.
She went straight for the herdsmen's homestead, up over the mountain. Following
     her came
gray wolves and lions with fierce looks, fawning on her;   70
bears too, and nimble leopards, who cannot have their fill of devouring deer,
came along. Seeing them, she was delighted in her heart, in her thoughts,
and she put desire where their hearts were. So they all
went off in pairs and slept together in shaded nooks.
She in the meantime came to the well-built shelters   75
and found him left all alone at the herdsmen's homestead,
that hero Anchises, who had the beauty of the gods.
All the others went after the herds, along the grassy pastures,
while he was left all alone at the herdsmen's homestead,
pacing back and forth, playing tunes on his lyre that pierce the inside.   80
She stood before him, the daughter of Zeus, Aphrodite,
looking like an unwed maiden in size of length and appearance.
She did not want him to notice her with his eyes and be frightened of her.
When Anchises saw her he was filled with wonder as he took note
of her appearance and size of length and splendid clothes.   85
For she wore a robe that was more resplendent than the brightness of fire.

---

6. A city in Cyprus.

She had twisted brooches, and shiny earrings in the shape of flowers.
Around her tender throat were the most beautiful necklaces.
It was a thing of beauty, golden, decorated with every sort of design. Like the moon
it glowed all around her tender breasts, a marvel to behold.   90
Seized with love, Anchises said to her:
"Hail, my Lady, you who come here to this home, whichever of the blessed ones
      you are,
Artemis or Leto or golden Aphrodite
or Themis of noble birth or bright-eyed Athena.
Or perhaps you are one of the graces, you who have come here. They are the ones   95
who keep company with all the gods and are called immortal.
Or you are one of those Nymphs who range over beautiful groves,
or one of those Nymphs who inhabit this beautiful mountain,
and the fountainheads of rivers and grassy meadows.
For you, on some high peak, in a spot with a view going all round,   100
I will set up an altar, and I will perform for you beautiful sacrifices
every year as the season comes round. And I wish that you in turn may have a
      kindly-disposed heart towards me.
Grant that I become a man who is distinguished among the Trojans.
Make the genealogy that comes after me become a flourishing one. And make me
live a very long life and see the light of the sun,   105
blessed in the midst of the people. And let me arrive at the threshold of old age."
Then Aphrodite, daughter of Zeus, answered him:
"Anchises, most glorious of earth-born men!
I am no goddess. Why do you liken me to the female immortals?
No, I am a mortal. The mother that bore me was a woman.   110
My father is Otreus, famed for his name. Maybe you have heard of him.
He rules over all of Phrygia, with its strong-walled fortresses.
But I know your language as well as my own.
The nursemaid who brought me up in the palace was a Trojan. Ever since I was
      a small child,
she brought me up, having taken me from my dear mother.   115
That is why I know your language as well as my own.
But then, the one with the golden wand, the Argos-killer Hermes, abducted me,
taking me from a festival of song and dance in honor of Artemis, the one with the
      golden arrows.
There were many of us nymphs there, maidens worth many cattle as bride-price.
We were having a good time, and a crowd so large that you couldn't count them
      was standing around us in a circle.   120
Then it was that the one with the golden wand, the Argos-killer, abducted me.
He carried me over many fields of mortal humans
and over vast stretches of land unclaimed and unsettled, where wild beasts,
eaters of raw flesh, roam about, in and out of their shaded lairs.
I thought that my feet would never again touch the earth, grower of grain.   125
And he said that I, in your bed, the bed of Anchises, would be called your
lawfully-wedded wife, and that I would give you splendid children.

But once he pointed this out and made note of it, straightaway
he went back, that powerful Argos-killer, to that separate group, the immortals.
I in the meantime reached you here, and there is an overpowering compulsion
    that I have in me.   130
In the name of Zeus, in the name of your parents, I appeal to you as I touch your
    knees.
Your parents must be noble, for base ones could never have conceived such a one
    as you.
Take me, virgin that I am, inexperienced in making love,
and show me to your father and to your caring mother
and to your brothers, those born from the same parents.   135
I will not be an unseemly in-law for them, but a seemly one indeed.
And send a messenger quickly to the Phrygians, trainers of swift horses,
to tell my father and my mother, however much she grieves.
They will send you plenty of gold, and woven clothing as well.
Take these abundant and splendid things as dowry.   140
After you have done so, prepare a lovely wedding-feast
that gives honor to both humans and immortals."
After she said these things, she put sweet desire in his heart
and Anchises was seized with love. He said these words, calling out to her:
"If you are mortal, and if a woman was the mother who gave birth to you,   145
and if Otreus is your father, famed for his name, as you say he is,
and if you have come here because of the Immortal Conductor,[7]
Hermes, and if you are to be called my wife for all days to come,
then it is impossible for any god or any mortal human
to hold me back, right here, from joining with you in making love,   150
right now, on the spot—not even if the one who shoots from afar, Apollo himself,
takes aim from his silver bow and shoots his arrows that bring misery.
Then, O lady who looks like the gods, I would willingly,
once I have been in your bed, go down into the palace of Hades below."
So saying, he took her by the hand. And Aphrodite, lover of smiles,   155
went along, with her face turned away and her eyes downcast,
towards the bed, all nicely made, which had already been arranged for the lord,
all nicely made with soft covers. And on top lay skins of
bears and lions, who roar with their deep voices,
which he himself had killed on the lofty mountainsides.   160
And when they went up into the sturdy bed,
he first took off the jewelry shining on the surface of her body
—the twisted brooches and the shiny earrings in the shape of flowers.
Then he undid her girdle and her resplendent garments.
He stripped them off and put them on a silver-studded stool,   165
Anchises did. And then, by the will of the gods and by fate,

---

7. Hermes, the divine messenger, conducts
   travelers to their destinations and guides
   the souls of the dead to the underworld.

he lay next to the immortal female, mortal male that he was. He did not know
  what he was really doing.
But when the time comes for herdsmen to drive back to the fold
their cattle and sturdy sheep, back from the flowery pastures,
then it was that Aphrodite poured sweet sleep over Anchises,   170
sweet and pleasurable. She in the meantime put back on her beautiful clothes,
  which covered again the surface of her body.
Now that her skin was again beautifully covered over, the resplendent goddess
stood by the bed, and the well-built roof-beam
—her head reached that high up. And beauty shone forth from her cheeks
—an immortal beauty, the kind that marks the one with the beautiful garlands,
  the goddess from Kythera.   175
Then she woke him from his sleep and called out to him, saying:
"Rise up, son of Dardanos! Why do you sleep such a sleep without awakening?
See if I look like
what you noticed when you first saw me with your eyes."
So she spoke, and he, fresh out of his sleep, straightaway heeded her word.   180
As soon as he saw the neck and the beautiful eyes of Aphrodite,
he was filled with fright and he turned his eyes away, in another direction.
Then he hid his beautiful face with a cloak,
and, praying to her, addressed her with winged words:
"The first time I ever laid eyes on you, goddess,   185
I knew you were a god. But you did not speak to me accurately.
Now I appeal to you by touching your knees, in the name of Zeus the holder of the
  aegis,
don't let me become disabled, don't let me live on like that among humans!
Please, take pity! I know that no man is full of life, able,
if he sleeps with immortal goddesses."   190
He was answered by the daughter of Zeus, Aphrodite:
"Anchises, most glorious of mortal humans!
Take heart, and do not be too afraid in your thoughts.
You should have no fear of that I would do any kind of bad thing to you,
or that any of the other blessed ones would. For you are dear indeed to the gods.   195
And you will have a dear son, who will be king among the Trojans.
And following him will be generations after generations for all time to come.
His name will be Aineias, since it was an unspeakable[8] grief that took hold of
  me—grief that I had fallen into the bed of a mortal man."

[Aphrodite's speech continues, pointing out examples of other gods who fell in love with
mortals but acknowledging her extreme embarrassment at sharing their vulnerability. The
hymn ends with the goddess informing Anchises that his son will be raised by mountain
nymphs, and warning him to conceal the identity of his son's mother and his encounter with
her.]

---

8. Aphrodite connects the name of Aineias
with the Greek adjective *ainos,* meaning
"unspeakable, terrible"; the two words are
not actually related etymologically, although they sound alike.

ANONYMOUS (SEVENTH CENTURY B.C.E.)
Greece

The *Homeric Hymn to Demeter* exhibits the hallmarks of oral composition in its meter, diction, and style (including the use of repeated phrases, or formulas). It can be dated, though only approximately, to the mid- or late seventh century B.C.E. As with the *Hymn to Aphrodite,* the ancient attribution of this hymn to the poet of the *Iliad* and *Odyssey* is certainly incorrect, but we have no positive evidence to determine its true authorship.

The *Hymn's* subject is the grief of Demeter, goddess of the fruits of the earth, over the rape of her daughter Persephone by Hades, god of the underworld. Significant above all are the consequences of Demeter's wrath, both at Hades— who has taken the girl to live with him in the underworld—and at Zeus, Persephone's father, who sanctioned the rape. Demeter withdraws from the company of gods and withholds her fertility functions, so that the earth is made barren; famine results, threatening human beings with extinction and depriving the gods of their due offerings. The motif of a god's withdrawal, with resulting universal infertility, occurs in ancient Egyptian, Babylonian, Ugaritic, and Hittite mythology, which add to their parallels with the *Hymn to Demeter* the distinctive feature that the gods themselves are threatened with starvation.

Despite pleas from the gods on Olympus, Demeter does not relent until she has seen her daughter and has secured her return from the underworld for at least part of every year—those seasons when the earth is fruitful. In its central section, the *Hymn* suggests that because Demeter—disguised as an old woman, in her chosen exile from Olympus—was hospitably received by the people of Eleusis (a town near Athens), she revealed to them in return the secrets of agriculture and the mysteries that promise happiness after death. Throughout antiquity, Demeter and Persephone were worshipped in an important cult at Eleusis, whose rituals were guarded by the initiates with utmost secrecy.

Homeric Hymn to Demeter

Demeter I being to sing, the fair-tressed awesome goddess,
herself and her slim-ankled daughter whom Aidoneus[1]
seized; Zeus gave her, heavy-thundering and mighty-voiced,
gave her, without the consent of Demeter, the bright fruit and golden sword,
as she played with the deep-breasted daughters of Ocean,   5
plucking flowers in the lush meadow—roses, crocuses,
and lovely violets, irises and hyacinth and the narcissus,
which Earth grew as a snare for the flower-faced maiden

Translated by Helene P. Foley.

---

1. Hades, god of the underworld.

in order to gratify by Zeus's design the Host-to-Many,[2]
a flower wondrous and bright, awesome for all to see,   10
for the immortals above and for mortals below.
From its root a hundred fold bloom sprang up and smelled
so sweet that the whole vast heaven above
and the whole earth laughed, and the salty swell of the sea.
The girl marvelled and stretched out both hands at once   15
to take the lovely toy. The earth with its wide ways yawned
over the Nysian plain; the lord host-to-many rose up on her
with his immortal horses, the celebrated son of Kronos;[3]
he snatched the unwilling maid into his golden chariot
and led her off lamenting. She screamed with a shrill voice,   20
calling on her father, the son of Kronos highest and best.
Not one of the immortals or of humankind
heard her voice, nor the olives bright with fruit,
except the daughter of Persaios; tender of heart,
she heard her from her cave. Hekate[4] of the delicate veil.   25
And lord Helios, brilliant son of Hyperion, heard
the maid calling her father the Son of Kronos. But he sat apart
from the gods, aloof in a temple ringing with prayers,
and received choice offerings from humankind.
Against her will Hades took her by the design of Zeus   30
with his immortal horses—her father's brother,
commander and host-to-many, the many-named son of Kronos.
So long as the goddess gazed on earth and starry heaven,
on the sea flowing strong and full of fish,
and on the beams of the sun, she still hoped   35
to see her dear mother and the race of immortal gods.
For so long hope charmed her strong mind despite her distress.
The mountain peaks and the depths of the sea echoed
in response to her divine voice, and her goddess mother heard.
Sharp grief seized her heart, and she tore the veil   40
on her ambrosial hair with her own hands.
She cast a dark cloak on her shoulders
and sped like a bird over dry land and sea,
searching. No one was willing to tell her the truth,
not one of the gods or mortals;   45
no bird of omen came to her as truthful messenger.
Then for nine days divine Deo[5] roamed over the earth,
holding torches ablaze in her hands;
in her grief she did not once taste ambrosia
or nectar sweet-to-drink, nor bathed her skin.   50

---

2. A euphemistic epithet of Hades.
3. Hades, like Zeus, was the son of the Titans
   Kronos and Rheia.

4. A divinity regularly associated with the
   goddess Artemis and with Persephone.
5. Demeter.

But when the tenth Dawn came shining on her,
Hekate met her, holding a torch in her hands,
to give her a message. She spoke as follows:
"Divine Demeter, giver of seasons and glorious gifts,
who of the immortals or mortal men   55
seized Persephone and grieved your heart?
For I heard a voice but did not see with my eyes
who he was. To you I say at once the whole truth."
Thus Hekate spoke. The daughter of fair-tressed Rheia[6]
said not a word, but rushed off at her side   60
holding torches ablaze in her hands.
They came to Helios, the observer of gods and mortals,
and stood before his horses. The most august goddess spoke:
"Helios, respect me as a god does a goddess, if ever
with word or deed I pleased your heart and spirit.   65
The daughter I bore, a sweet sprout noble in form—
I heard her voice throbbing through the barren air
as if she were suffering violence. But I did not see her with my eyes.
With your rays you look down through the bright air
on the whole of the earth and the sea.   70
Tell me the truth about my child. Have you somewhere
seen who of gods or mortal men took her
by force from me against her will and went away?"
Thus she spoke and the son of Hyperion replied:
"Daughter of fair-tressed Rheia, mighty Demeter,   75
you will know. For I greatly revere and pity you
grieving for your slim-ankled daughter. No other
of the gods was to blame but cloud-gathering Zeus,
who gave her to Hades his brother to be called
his fertile wife. With his horses Hades   80
snatched her screaming into the misty gloom.
But, Goddess, give up for good your great lamentation.
You must not nurse in vain insatiable anger.
Among the gods Aidoneus is not an unsuitable bridegroom,
commander-to-many and Zeus' own brother of the same stock.   85
As for honor, he got his third at the world's first division,
and dwells with those whose rule has fallen to his lot."
He spoke and called to his horses. At his rebuke
they bore the swift chariot lightly, like long-winged birds.
A more terrible and brutal grief seized the heart   90
of Demeter, angry now at the son of Kronos with his dark clouds.
Withdrawing from the assembly of the gods and high Olympus
she went among the cities and fertile fields of men,

---

6. The mother of Demeter as well as of Zeus
   and Hades.

disguising her beauty for a long time. No one of men
nor low-girt women recognized her when they looked,   95
until she came to the house of skillful Keleos,
the man then ruler of fragrant Eleusis.
There she sat near the road, grief in her heart,
where citizens drew water from the Maiden's Well
in the shade—an olive bush had grown overhead—   100
like a very old woman cut off from child-bearing
and the gifts of garland-loving Aphrodite.
Such are the nurses to children of law-giving kings
and the keepers of stores in their echoing halls.
The daughters of Keleos, son of Eleusis, saw her   105
as they came to fetch water easy-to-draw and bring it
in bronze vessels to their dear father's halls.
Like four goddesses they were in the flower of youth,
Kallidike, Kleisidike, Demo and fair Kallithoe,
who was the first born in birth of them all.   110
They did not know her—gods are hard for mortals to see.
Standing near her, they spoke winged words.
"Who are you, old woman, of those born long ago?
From where? Why have you gone from the city nor
draw near its homes? Women are there in the shadowy halls   115
of your age as well as others born younger,
who would care for you both in word and in deed."
They spoke, and the most august goddess replied:
"Dear children, whoever of womankind you are,
greetings. I will tell you my tale. For it is not wrong   120
to tell you the truth now you ask."

[Demeter proceeds to fabricate a tale about herself and concludes by appealing successfully
to Celeus' daughters to take her into their household. The old woman (as she appears)
becomes the nurse of their infant brother. Her plan to make him immortal is brought to an
abrupt end, however, when the child's horrified mother disturbs the goddess in the act of
putting the child (who flourishes under this divine ministration) into the fire. Demeter reveals
herself, commands the Eleusinians to build her a temple and promises to teach them her
sacred rites.]

The shrine grew as the goddess decreed.
But once they finished and ceased their toil,
each went off home. Then golden-haired Demeter
remained sitting apart from all the immortals,   125
wasting with desire for her deep-girt daughter.
For mortals she ordained a terrible and brutal year
on the deeply-fertile earth. The ground released
no seed, for bright-crowned Demeter kept it buried.
In vain the oxen dragged many curved plows down   130
the furrows. In vain much white barley fell on the earth.
She would have destroyed the whole mortal race

by cruel famine, and stolen the glorious honor of gifts
and sacrifices from those having homes on Olympus,
if Zeus had not seen and pondered their plight in his heart. 135
First he roused golden-winged Iris to summon
fair-tressed Demeter, so lovely in form.
Zeus spoke and Iris obeying the dark-clouded
son of Kronos, raced swiftly between heaven and earth.
She came to the citadel of fragrant Eleusis 140
and found in her temple dark-robed Demeter.
Addressing her, she spoke winged words:
"Demeter, Zeus the father with his unfailing knowledge
bids you rejoin the tribes of immortal gods.
Go and let Zeus's word not remain unfulfilled." 145
Thus she implored, but Demeter's heart was unmoved.
Then the father sent in turn all the blessed immortals;
one by one they kept coming and pleading
and offered her many glorious gifts and whatever
honors she might choose among the immortal gods. 150
Yet not one could bend the mind and thought
of the raging goddess, who harshly spurned their pleas.
Never, she said, would she mount up to fragrant
Olympus nor release the seed from the earth,
until she saw with her eyes her own fair-faced child. 155
When Zeus, heavy-thundering and mighty-voiced,
heard this, he sent down the Slayer of Argos[7] to Erebos[8]
with his golden staff to wheedle Hades with soft words
and lead back holy Persephone from the misty gloom
into the light to join the gods so that her mother 160
might see her with her eyes and desist from anger.
Hermes did not disobey. At once he left Olympus' height
and plunged swiftly into the depths of the earth.
He met lord Hades inside his dwelling,
reclining on a bed with his shy spouse, strongly reluctant 165
through desire for her mother. [still she, Demeter,
was brooding on revenge for the deeds of the blessed gods].
The strong Slayer of Argos stood near and spoke:
"Dark-haired Hades, ruler of the dead, Father Zeus
bids me lead noble Persephone up from Erebos 170
to join us, so that her mother might see her with her eyes
and cease from anger and dread wrath against the gods.
For she is devising a great scheme to destroy
the helpless race of mortals born on earth,
burying the seed beneath the ground and obliterating 175

---

7. The Slayer of Argos was Hermes, the divine   8. The underworld.
   messenger.

divine honors. Her anger is terrible, nor does she go
among the gods, but sits aloof in her fragrant temple,
keeping to the rocky citadel of Eleusis."
Thus he spoke and Aidoneus, lord of the dead, smiled
with his brows, nor disobeyed king Zeus's commands.   180
At once he urged thoughtful Persephone:
"Go, Persephone, to the side of your dark-robed mother,
keeping the spirit and temper in your breast benign.
Do not be so sad and angry beyond the rest;
in no way among immortals will I be an unsuitable spouse,   185
myself a brother of father Zeus. And when you are here
you will have power over all that lives and moves,
and you will possess the greatest honors among the gods.
There will be punishment forevermore for those wrongdoers
who fail to appease your power with sacrifices,   190
performing proper rites and making due offerings."
Thus he spoke and thoughtful Persephone rejoiced.
Eagerly she leapt up for joy. But he
gave her to eat a honey-sweet pomegranate seed,
stealthily passing it around her, lest she once more stay forever   195
by the side of revered Demeter of the dark robe.
Then Aidoneus commander-to-many yoked
his divine horses before the golden chariot.
She mounted the chariot and at her side the strong
Slayer of Argos took the reins and whip in his hands,   200
and dashed from the halls. The horses flew eagerly;
swiftly they completed the long journey; not sea nor
river waters, not grassy glens nor mountain peaks
slowed the speed of the immortal horses,
slicing the deep air as they flew above these places.   205
He brought them to a halt where rich-crowned Demeter
waited before the fragrant temple. With one look she darted
like a maenad down a mountain shaded with woods.
On her side Persephone, [seeing] her mother's [radiant face],
[left chariot and horses,] and leapt down to run   210
[and fall on her neck in passionate embrace].
[While holding her dear child in her arms], her [heart
suddenly sensed a trick. Fearful, she] drew back
from [her embrace and at once enquired:]
"My child, tell me, you [did not taste] food [while below?]   215
Speak out [and hide nothing, so we both may know.]
[For if not], ascending [from miserable Hades],
you will dwell with me and your father, the
dark-clouded [son of Kronos], honored by all the gods.
But if [you tasted food], returning beneath [the earth]   220
you will stay a third part of the seasons [each year],

but two parts with myself and the other immortals.
When the earth blooms in spring with all kinds
of sweet flowers, then from the misty dark you will
rise again, a great marvel to gods and mortal men.   225
By what guile did the mighty Host to Many deceive you?"
Then radiant Persephone replied to her in turn:
"I will tell you the whole truth exactly, Mother.
The Slayer of Argos came to bring fortunate news
from my father, the son of Kronos, and the other gods   230
and lead me from Erebos so that seeing me with your eyes
you would desist from your anger and dread wrath
at the gods. Then I leapt up for joy, but he stealthily
put in my mouth a food honey-sweet, a pomegranate seed,
and compelled me against my will and by force to taste it.   235
For the rest—how seizing me by the shrewd plan of my father,
Kronos' son, he carried me off into the earth's depths—
I shall tell and elaborate all that you ask.
We were all in the beautiful meadow—
Leukippe, Phrono, Elektra, and Ianthe,   240
Melite, Iache, Rhodies, and Kallirhoe,
Melibosis, Tuche, and flower-faced Okurhoe,
Khryseis, Ianeira, Akaste, Admete,
Rhodope, Plouto, and lovely Kalypso,
Styx, Ourania and fair Galaxaura, Pallas,   245
rouser of battles, and Artemis, sender of arrows—
playing and picking lovely flowers with our hands,
soft crocus mixed with irises and hyacinth,
rose buds and lilies, a marvel to see, and the
narcissus that wide earth bore like a crocus.   250
As I joyously plucked it, the ground gaped from beneath,
and the mighty lord, Host-to-Many, rose from it
and carried me off beneath the earth in his goden chariot
much against my will. And I cried out at the top of my voice.
I speak the whole truth, though I grieve to tell it."   255
Then all day long, their minds at one, they soothed
each other's heart and soul in many ways,
embracing fondly, and their spirits abandoned grief,
as they gave and received joy between them.
Hekate of the delicate veil drew near them   260
and often caressed the daughter of holy Demeter;
from that time this lady served her as chief attendant.
To them Zeus, heavy-thundering and mighty-voiced,
sent as mediator fair-tressed Rheia to summon
dark-robed Demeter to the tribes of gods; he promised   265
to give her what honors she might choose among the gods.
He agreed his daughter would spend one third

of the revolving year in the misty dark, and two thirds
with her mother and the other immortals.
So he spoke and the goddess did not disobey his commands.   270
She darted swiftly down the peaks of Olympus
and arrived where the Rharian plain, once life-giving
udder of earth, now giving no life at all, stretched idle
and utterly leafless. For the white barley was hidden
by the designs of lovely-ankled Demeter. Yet as spring came on   275
the fields would soon ripple with long ears of grain;
and the rich furrows would grow heavy on the ground
with grain to be tied with bands into sheaves.
There she first alighted from the barren air.
Mother and daughter were glad to see each other   280
and rejoiced at heart. Rheia of the delicate veil then said:
"Come, child, Zeus, heavy-thundering and mighty-voiced,
summons you to rejoin the tribes of the gods;
he has offered to give what honors you choose among them.
He agreed that his daughter would spend one third   285
of the revolving year in the misty dark, and two thirds
with her mother and the other immortals.
He guaranteed it would be so with a nod of his head.
So come, my child, obey me; do not rage overmuch
and forever at the dark-clouded son of Kronos.   290
Now make the grain grow fertile for humankind."
So Rheia spoke, and rich-crowned Demeter did not disobey.
At once she sent forth fruit from the fertile fields
and the whole wide earth burgeoned with leaves
and flowers. She went to the kings who administer law,   295
Triptolemos and Diokles, driver of horses, mighty
Eumolpos and Keleos, leader of the people, and revealed
the conduct of her rites and taught her mysteries to all,[9]
holy rites which are not to be transgressed, nor pried into,
nor divulged. For a great awe of the gods stops the voice.   300
Blessed is the mortal on earth who has seen these rites,
but the uninitiate who has no share in them, never
has the same lot once dead in the dreary darkness.
When the great goddess had founded all her rites,
they left for Olympos to join the assembly of the other gods.   305
There they dwell by Zeus delighting-in-thunder, inspiring
awe and reverence. Highly blessed is the mortal
on earth whom they graciously favor with love.

---

9. It is not known just what the Eleusinian
mysteries consisted of, but initiation into
them offered the promise of renewal of
agricultural fertility and the possibility for the
initiate of mitigating, in some form, the grim
finality of death.

For soon they will send to the hearth of his great house
Ploutos, the god giving abundance to mortal men.   310
But come, you goddesses, dwelling in the town of
fragrant Eleusis, and sea-girt Paros, and rocky Antron,
revered Deo, mighty giver of seasons and glorious gifts,
you and your very fair daughter Persephone,
For my song grant gladly a living that warms the heart.   315
And I shall remember you and a new song as well.

ANONYMOUS (c. 1200 B.C.E.)

Ancient Mesopotamia

The *Epic of Gilgamesh* is the longest and greatest literary composition of ancient
Mesopotamia. Gilgamesh was an early king of the Sumerian city-state of Uruk
(today in central Iraq); he lived sometime between 2800 and 2500 B.C.E. Stories
about his adventures began to circulate soon after his death. Sometime between
2000 and 1600 B.C.E., the stories were gathered and linked to form an epic
written in Akkadian, the language of the Babylonian Empire. The epic continued
to evolve, reaching its final form around 1200 B.C.E. An account of the flood that
had been circulating separately was added at this time, and Gilgamesh's search
for fame was re'fashioned into the moving story of his search for the secret of
immortality after the death of his friend Enkidu. To learn the secret, Gilgamesh
journeys to see a survivor of the flood named Utanapishtim. Their encounter,
now the climax of the epic, raises his individual story to a wider context of the life
and death of civilization itself.

The *Epic of Gilgamesh* is the first great reworking of a common pool of stories
of friendship, seduction, adventure, and death into a broad exploration of the
meaning and limits of culture as a whole. The epic assesses culture against the
world of the gods, the world of nature, and the limits of human knowledge and
mortality. Parallels in later literature reflect this common heritage. The snake's role
in the epic finds an echo in the story of Eden in the Bible; the friendship of
Gilgamesh and Enkidu survives in the friendship of Achilles and Patroklus in the
Iliad; the theme of journey and return links the *Epic of Gilgamesh* to such narratives
as the *Odyssey* and the tale of Sindbad from the *Thousand and One Nights*.

The Epic of Gilgamesh

Tablet I

He who has seen everything, I will make known to the lands.
I will teach about him who experienced all things.
Anu granted him the totality of knowledge of all.

Translated by Maureen Gallery Kovacs.

He saw the Secret, discovered the Hidden,
he brought information of the time before the Flood.   5
He went on a distant journey, pushing himself to exhaustion,
but then was brought to peace.
He carved on a stone stela all of his toils,
and built the wall of Uruk-Haven,[1]
the wall of the sacred Eanna Temple, the holy sanctuary.   10
Look at its wall which gleams like copper,
inspect its inner wall, the likes of which no one can equal!
Take hold of the threshold stone—it dates from ancient times!
Go close to the Eanna Temple, the residence of Ishtar,[2]
such as no later king or man ever equaled!   15
Go up on the wall of Uruk and walk around,
examine its foundation, inspect its brickwork thoroughly.
Is not even the core of the brick structure made of kiln-fired brick,
and did not the Seven Sages[3] themselves lay out its plans?
One league city, one league palm gardens, one league lowlands, the open area of   20
     the Ishtar Temple,
three leagues and the open area of Uruk the wall encloses.
Find the copper tablet box,
open the hasp of its lock of bronze,
undo the fastening of its secret opening.
Take and read out from the lapis lazuli tablet   25
how Gilgamesh went through every hardship.

Supreme over other kings, lordly in appearance,
he is the hero, born of Uruk, the goring wild bull.
He walks out in front, the leader,
and walks at the rear, trusted by his companions.   30
Mighty net, protector of his people,
raging flood-wave who destroys even walls of stone!
Offspring of Lugalbanda, Gilgamesh is strong to perfection,
son of the august cow, Rimat-Ninsun, Gilgamesh is awesome to perfection.[4]
It was he who opened the mountain passes,   35
who dug wells on the flank of the mountain.
It was he who crossed the ocean, the vast seas, to the rising sun,
who explored the world regions, seeking life.
It was he who reached by his own sheer strength Utanapishtim, the Faraway,[5]
who restored the sanctuaries that the Flood had destroyed!   40

                                        . . .

---

1. Literally "Uruk-the-Sheepfold."
2. Goddess of love; she shared the Eanna Temple in Uruk with her father Anu.
3. Sent to the Gods to teach the arts of civilization to humanity.
4. Gilgamesh's father Lugalbanda was an ear-

lier king of Uruk; his mother is the divine Ninsun. The motif of the "good cow" who gives birth to kings is well documented in Sumerian literature.
5. Utanapishtim is the hero of the Akkadian version of the Flood story.

[handwritten at top: Counterpart to have Gilgamesh]

Who can compare with him in kingliness?
Who can say like Gilgamesh: "I am King!"?
Whose name, from the day of his birth, was called "Gilgamesh"?
Two-thirds of him is god, one-third of him is human.
The Great Goddess[6] designed(?) the model for his body,   45
she prepared his form,

          . . .

beautiful, handsomest of men.
He walks around in the enclosure of Uruk,
like a wild bull he makes himself mighty, head raised over others.
There is no rival who can raise his weapon against him.
His fellows stand at the alert, attentive to his orders.   50
The men of Uruk become anxious:
Gilgamesh does not leave a son to his father;
Is Gilgamesh the shepherd of Uruk-Haven,

          . . .

bold, eminent, knowing, and wise?
Gilgamesh does not leave a girl to her betrothed(?)!
The daughter of the warrior, the bride of the young man,   55
the gods kept hearing their complaints, so
the gods of the heavens implored Anu, Lord of Uruk:
    "You have indeed brought into being a mighty wild bull, head raised!
    There is no rival who can raise a weapon against him.   60
    His fellows stand (at the alert), attentive to his (orders?),
    Gilgamesh does not leave a son to his father,

          . . .

    Is he the shepherd of Uruk-Haven,

          . . .

    bold, eminent, knowing, and wise?
    Gilgamesh does not leave a girl to her betrothed(?)!"   65
The daughter of the warrior, the bride of the young man,
Anu listened to their complaints,
and (the gods) called out to Aruru:
    "It was you, Aruru, who created this man(?),
    now create a counterpart to him.
    Let him be equal to Gilgamesh's stormy heart,   70
    let them be a match for each other so that Uruk may find peace!"
When Aruru heard this she created within herself the counterpart of Anu.
Aruru washed her hands, she pinched off some clay, and threw it into the
    wilderness.

[handwritten margin notes: "the gods were upset that Gilgamesh did not want to leave an heir." / "Takes sons from their homes to join his army" / "Being the King, he takes a new bride to the bed first, before the husband" / "mother/Goddess"]

---

6. The Mother Goddess, creator of humanity,
    known also as Aruru and Beletili.

Counterpart to tame Gilgamesh

Gilg.
Enkidu

In the wilderness she created valiant Enkidu,   75
born of Silence, endowed with strength by Ninurta.[7]
His whole body was shaggy with hair,
he had a full head of hair like a woman,
his locks billowed in profusion like Ashnan.[8]
He knew neither people nor settled living,   80
but wore a garment like Sumukan.[9]
He ate grasses with the gazelles,
and jostled at the watering hole with the animals;
as with animals, his thirst was slaked with water.

A notorious trapper   85
came face-to-face with him opposite the watering hole.
A first, a second, and a third day
he came face-to-face with him opposite the watering hole.
On seeing him the trapper's face went stark with fear,
and he and his animals drew back home.   90
He was rigid with fear, though stock-still
his heart pounded and his face drained of color.
He was miserable to the core,
and his face looked like one who had made a long journey.
The trapper addressed his father saying: 95
    "Father, a certain fellow has come from the mountains.
He is the mightiest in the land,
his strength is as mighty as the meteorite(?) of Anu!   *the hunter*
He continually goes over the mountains,   *couldn't do*
he continually jostles at the watering place with the animals, *his thing because* 100
he continually plants his feet opposite the watering place. *Enkidu was running*
I was afraid, so I did not go up to him.   *around the*
He filled in the pits that I had dug,   *forest undoing*
wrenched out my traps that I had spread,   *everything.*
released from my grasp the wild animals.   105
He does not let me make my rounds in the wilderness!"
The trapper's father spoke to him saying:
    "My son, there lives in Uruk a certain Gilgamesh.
There is no one stronger than he,
he is as strong as the meteorite(?) of Anu.   110
Go, set off to Uruk,
tell Gilgamesh of this Man of Might.
He will give you the harlot Shamhat, take her with you.
The woman will overcome the fellow as if she were strong.

Tarzan

---

7. God of war.
8. Goddess of grain.

9. God of wild animals.

When the animals are drinking at the watering place   115
have her take off her robe and expose her sex.
When he sees her he will draw near to her,
and his animals, who grew up in his wilderness, will be alien to him."
He heeded his father's advice.
The trapper went off to Uruk,   120
he made the journey, stood inside of Uruk,
and declared to Gilgamesh:
  "There is a certain fellow who has come from the mountains—
he is the mightiest in the land,
his strength is as mighty as the meteorite(?) of Anu!   125
He continually goes over the mountains,
he continually jostles at the watering place with the animals,
he continually plants his feet opposite the watering place.
I was afraid, so I did not go up to him.
He filled in the pits that I had dug,   130
wrenched out my traps that I had spread,
released from my grasp the wild animals.
He does not let me make my rounds in the wilderness!"
Gilgamesh said to the trapper:
  "Go, trapper, bring the harlot, Shamhat, with you.   135
When the animals are drinking at the watering place
have her take off her robe and expose her sex.
When he sees her he will draw near to her,
and his animals, who grew up in his wilderness, will be alien to him."

The trapper went, bringing the harlot, Shamhat, with him.   140
They set off on the journey, making direct way.
On the third day they arrived at the appointed place,
and the trapper and the harlot sat down at their posts(?).
A first day and a second they sat opposite the watering hole.
The animals arrived and drank at the watering hole,   145
the wild beasts arrived and slaked their thirst with water.
Then he, Enkidu, offspring of the mountains,
who eats grasses with the gazelles,
came to drink at the watering hole with the animals,
with the wild beasts he slaked his thirst with water.   150
Then Shamhat saw him—a primitive,
a savage fellow from the depths of the wilderness!
  "That is he, Shamhat! Release your clenched arms,
expose your sex so he can take in your voluptuousness.
Do not be restrained—take his energy!   155
When he sees you he will draw near to you.
Spread out your robe so he can lie upon you,
and perform for this primitive the task of womankind!

His animals, who grew up in his wilderness, will become alien to him,
and his lust will groan over you."   160
Shamhat unclutched her bosom, exposed her sex, and he took in her
     voluptuousness.
She was not restrained, but took his energy.
She spread out her robe and he lay upon her,
she performed for the primitive the task of womankind.
His lust groaned over her;   165
for six days and seven nights Enkidu stayed aroused,
and had intercourse with the harlot
until he was sated with her charms.
But when he turned his attention to his animals,
the gazelles saw Enkidu and darted off,   170
the wild animals distanced themselves from his body.
Enkidu's body was utterly depleted,
his knees that wanted to go off with his animals went rigid;
Enkidu was diminished, his running was not as before.
But then he drew himself up, for his understanding had broadened.   175
Turning around, he sat down at the harlot's feet,
gazing into her face, his ears attentive as the harlot spoke.
The harlot said to Enkidu:
   "You are beautiful, Enkidu, you are become like a god.
   Why do you gallop around the wilderness with the wild beasts?   180
   Come, let me bring you into Uruk-Haven,
   to the Holy Temple, the residence of Anu and Ishtar,
   the place of Gilgamesh, who is wise to perfection,
   but who struts his power over the people like a wild bull."
What she kept saying found favor with him.   185
Becoming aware of himself, he sought a friend.
Enkidu spoke to the harlot:
   "Come, Shamhat, take me away with you
   to the sacred Holy Temple, the residence of Anu and Ishtar,
   the place of Gilgamesh, who is wise to perfection,   190
   but who struts his power over the people like a wild bull.
   I will challenge him.
   Let me shout out in Uruk: 'I am the mighty one!'
   Lead me in and I will change the order of things;
   he whose strength is mightiest is the one born in the wilderness!"   195
   "Come, let us go," (she replied) "so he may see your face.
   I will lead you to Gilgamesh—I know where he will be.
   Look about, Enkidu, inside Uruk-Haven,
   where the people show off in skirted finery,
   where every day is a day for some festival,   200
   where the lyre and drum play continually,
   where harlots stand about prettily,

exuding voluptuousness, full of laughter,
and on the couch of night the sheets are spread.
Enkidu, you who do not know how to live,   205
I will show you Gilgamesh, a man of joy and sorrow.
Look at him, gaze at his face—
he is a handsome youth, with freshness,
his entire body exudes voluptuousness.
He has mightier strength than you,   210
without sleeping day or night!
Enkidu, it is your wrong thoughts you must change!
It is Gilgamesh whom Shamash[10] loves,
and Anu, Enlil,[11] and Ea[12] have enlarged his mind.
Even before you came from the mountain
Gilgamesh in Uruk had dreams about you."   215
Gilgamesh got up and revealed the dream, saying to his mother:
  "Mother, I had a dream last night.
  Stars of the sky appeared,
  and some kind of meteorite(?) of Anu fell next to me.
  I tried to lift it but it was too mighty for me,   220
  I tried to turn it over but I could not budge it.
  The Land of Uruk was standing around it,
  the whole land had assembled about it,
  the populace was thronging around it,
  the Men clustered about it,   225
  and kissed its feet as if it were a little baby.
  I loved it and embraced it as a wife.
  I laid it down at your feet,
  and you made it compete with me."
The mother of Gilgamesh, the wise, all-knowing, said to her Lord;   230
Rimat-Ninsun, the wise, all-knowing, said to Gilgamesh:
  "As for the stars of the sky that appeared
  and the meteorite(?) of Anu which fell next to you,
  which you tried to lift but it was too mighty for you,
  which you tried to turn over but were unable to budge it,   235
  which you laid down at my feet,
  and I made it compete with you,
  and you loved and embraced it as a wife:
  There will come to you a mighty man, a comrade who saves his friend—
  he is the mightiest in the land, he is strongest,   240
  his strength is mighty as the meteorite(?) of Anu!
  You loved him and embraced him as a wife;

---

10. The sun god, Gilgamesh's protector.
11. Chief god in the Sumerian pantheon.

12. God of Wisdom and of the underworld sea.

and it is he who will repeatedly save you.
Your dream is good and propitious!"
A second time Gilgamesh said to his mother: 245
    "Mother, I have had another dream:
    At the gate of my marital chamber there lay an axe,
    and people had collected about it.
    The Land of Uruk was standing around it,
    the whole land had assembled about it,   250
    the populace was thronging around it.
    I laid it down at your feet,
    I loved it and embraced it as a wife,
    and you made it compete with me."
The mother of Gilgamesh, the wise, all-knowing, said to her son;   255
Rimat-Ninsun, the wise, all-knowing, said to Gilgamesh:
    "The axe that you saw is a man,
    whom you love and embrace as a wife,
    but whom I have made compete with you.
    There will come to you a mighty man, a comrade who saves his friend—   260
    he is the mightiest in the land, he is strongest,
    he is as mighty as the meteorite(?) of Anu!"
Gilgamesh spoke to his mother saying:
    "By the command of Enlil, the Great Counselor, so may it come to pass!
    May I have a friend and adviser,   265
    a friend and adviser may I have!
    You have interpreted for me the dreams about him!"
After the harlot recounted the dreams of Gilgamesh to Enkidu
the two of them made love.

Tablet II

Enkidu sits in front of her.[13]
Enkidu knew nothing about eating bread for food,
and of drinking beer he had not been taught.
The harlot spoke to Enkidu, saying:
    "Eat the food, Enkidu, it is the way one lives.   5
    Drink the beer, as is the custom of the land."
Enkidu ate the food until he was sated,
he drank the beer—seven jugs!—and became expansive and sang with joy!
He was elated and his face glowed.
He splashed his shaggy body with water,   10
and rubbed himself with oil, and turned into a human.
Shamhat pulled off her clothing,
and clothed him with one piece

---

13. Thirty-three lines are missing here; the
    next fifteen lines are restored in their place

from parallels in the earlier Old Babylonian
version, as are several later passages.

while she clothed herself with a second.
She took hold of him as gods do
and brought him to the hut of the shepherds.   15

The shepherds gathered all around about him,
they marveled to themselves:
  "How the youth resembles Gilgamesh—
  tall in stature, towering up to the battlements over the wall!   20
  Surely he was born in the mountains;
  his strength is as mighty as the meteorite of Anu!"
They placed food in front of him,
they placed beer in front of him;
Enkidu did not eat or drink, but squinted and stared.   25
Enkidu scattered the wolves, he chased away the lions.
The herders could lie down in peace,
for Enkidu was their watchman.
                                                    . . .
Then he raised his eyes and saw a man.
He said to the harlot: 30
  "Shamhat, have that man go away!
  Why has he come? I will call out his name!"
The harlot called out to the man
and went over to him and spoke with him.
  "Young man, where are you hurrying?   35
  Why this arduous pace?"
The young man spoke, saying to Enkidu:
  "They have invited me to a wedding,
  as is the custom of the people,
  to make the selection of brides.   40
  I have heaped up tasty delights for the wedding on the ceremonial platter.
  For the King of Broad-Marted Uruk,
  open is the veil of the people for choosing a girl.
  For Gilgamesh, the King of Broad-Marted Uruk,
  open is the veil of the people for choosing.
  He will have intercourse with the 'destined wife,'   45
  he first, the husband afterward.
  This is ordered by the counsel of Anu,
  from the severing of his umbilical cord it has been destined for him."
At the young man's speech Enkidu's face flushed with anger.
Enkidu walked in front, and Shamhat after him.[14]   50
He walked down the street of Uruk-Haven, ...
He blocked the way through Uruk the Sheepfold.

---

14. Several lines are missing; Enkidu presumably resolves to go and challenge Gilgamesh.

The land of Uruk stood around him,
the whole land assembled about him,
the populace was thronging around him,
and kissed his feet as if he were a little baby. . . .
For Ishara the bed of marriage is ready,
for Gilgamesh as for a god a counterpart is set up.
Enkidu blocked the entry to the marital chamber,
and would not allow Gilgamesh to be brought in.
They grappled with each other at the entry to the marital chamber,
in the street they attacked each other, the public square of the land.
The doorposts trembled and the wall shook.

at first meeting they fight... [handwritten annotation]

55

60

65

[The next seven lines are from the earlier version.]

Gilgamesh bent his knees, with his other foot on the ground,
his anger abated and he turned his chest away.
After he turned his chest Enkidu said to Gilgamesh:
    "Your mother bore you ever unique,
    the Wild Cow of the Enclosure, Ninsun,
    your head is elevated over other men,
    Enlil has destined for you the kingship over the people."

70

They kissed each other and became friends.[15]

. . .

Enkidu made a declaration to Gilgamesh:

then became best of friends. [handwritten annotation]

[Enkidu speaks to Gilgamesh:]

    "In order to protect the Cedar Forest
    Enlil assigned Humbaba[16] as a terror to human beings—
    Humbaba's roar is a Flood, his mouth is Fire, and his breath is Death!
    He can hear 100 leagues away any rustling in his forest!
    Who would go down into his forest?
    Enlil assigned him as a terror to human beings,
    and whoever goes down into his forest paralysis will strike!"

75

80

Gilgamesh spoke to Enkidu saying:

. . .

    "Who, my Friend, can ascend to the heavens?
    Only the gods can dwell forever with Shamash.
    As for human beings, their days are numbered,
    and whatever they keep trying to achieve is but wind!
    Now you are afraid of death—
    what has become of your bold strength?

85

---

15. A fragmentary passage describes Enkidu's sorrow at the loss of his strength. Gilgamesh proposes journeying to the Cedar Forest to kill its protector Humbaba and

cut down the cedars. Enkidu reacts with fear.

16. A demon, grandson of the sacred Cedar Forest.

I will go in front of you,
and your mouth can call out: 'Go on closer, do not be afraid!'   90
Should I fall, I will have established my fame.
They will say: 'It was Gilgamesh who locked in battle with Humbaba the
    Terrible!'
You were born and raised in the wilderness,
a lion leaped up on you, so you have experienced it all!'

I will undertake it and I will cut down the Cedar.   95
It is I who will establish fame for eternity!
Come, my friend, I will go over to the forge
and have them cast the weapons in our presence!"
Holding each other by the hand they went over to the forge.
The craftsmen sat and discussed with one another.   100

   "The hatchet should be one talent in weight,
   Their swords should be one talent,[17] and their armor as well. . . ."
Gilgamesh said to the men of Uruk:
   "Listen to me, . . . you men of Uruk, . . .
   I want to make myself more mighty, and will go on a distant journey!   105
   I will face fighting such as I have never known,
   I will set out on a road I have never traveled!
   Give me your blessings!
   I will enter the city gate of Uruk, . . .   110
   I will devote myself to the New Year's Festival.
   I will perform the New Year's ceremonies,
   The New Year's Festival will take place, . . .
   They will keep shouting 'Hurrah!'. . ."
Enkidu spoke to the Elders: 115

   "Say to him that he must not go to the Cedar Forest—
   the journey is not to be made!"

The Noble Counselors of Uruk arose and
delivered their advice to Gilgamesh:
   "You are young, Gilgamesh, your heart carries you off—   120
   you do not know what you are talking about!

   Humbaba's roar is a Flood,
   his mouth is Fire, his breath Death!
   He can hear any rustling in his forest 100 leagues away!
   Who would go down into his forest?   125
   Who among even the Igigi gods can confront him?

---

17. A unit of weight, perhaps 0.65 pound.

In order to keep the Cedar safe, Enlil[18] assigned him as a terror to human
   beings."
Gilgamesh listened to the statement of his Noble Counselors.

Tablet III

The Elders spoke to Gilgamesh, saying:
   "Gilgamesh, do not put your trust in your vast strength,
   but keep a sharp eye out, make each blow strike its mark!
      'The one who goes on ahead saves the comrade.'
      'The one who knows the route protects his friend.'   5
   Let Enkidu go ahead of you;
   he knows the road to the Cedar Forest,
   he has seen fighting, has experienced battle.
   Enkidu will protect the friend, will keep the comrade safe.
   Let his body urge him back to the wives."   10
[The Elders speak to Enkidu:]
   "In our Assembly we have entrusted the King to you,
   and on your return you must entrust the King back to us!"
Gilgamesh spoke to Enkidu, saying:
   "Come on, my friend, let us go to the Egalmah Temple,   15
   to Ninsun, the Great Queen;
   Ninsun is wise, all-knowing.
   She will put the advisable path at our feet."
Taking each other by the hand,
Gilgamesh and Enkidu walked to the Egalmah,   20
to Ninsun, the Great Queen.
Gilgamesh arose and went to her.
   "Ninsun, even though I am extraordinarily strong,
   I must now travel a long way to where Humbaba is,
   I must face fighting such as I have not known,   25
   and I must travel on a road that I do not know!
   Until the time that I go and return,
   until I reach the Cedar Forest,
   until I kill Humbaba the Terrible,
   and eradicate from the land something baneful that Shamash hates,   30
   intercede with Shamash on my behalf!
   If I kill Humbaba and cut his Cedar
   let there be rejoicing all over the land,
   and I will erect a monument of the victory before you!"

The words of Gilgamesh, her son,   35
grieving Queen Ninsun heard over and over.
Ninsun went into her living quarters.

---

18. The chief Sumerian god, god of destinies.

She washed herself with the purity plant,
she donned a robe worthy of her body,
she donned jewels worthy of her chest,   40
she donned her sash, and put on her crown.
She sprinkled water from a bowl onto the ground.

                            . . .

She went up to the roof and set incense in front of Shamash,
she offered fragrant cuttings, and raised her arms to Shamash.
   "Why have you imposed—nay, inflicted!—a restless heart on my son,
      Gilgamesh?
   Now you have touched him so that he wants to travel   45
   a long way to where Humbaba is!
   He will face fighting such as he has not known,
   and will travel on a road that he does not know!
   Until he goes away and returns,   50
   until he reaches the Cedar Forest,
   until he kills Humbaba the Terrible,
   and eradicates from the land something baneful that you hate,
   on the day that you see him on the road
   may Aja, the Bride,[19] without fear remind you,   55
   and command also the Watchmen of the Night,
   the stars, and at night your father, Sin."

[Long passage missing.]

She (Ninsun) banked up the incense and uttered the ritual words.
She called to Enkidu and would give him instructions:
   "Enkidu the Mighty, you are not of my womb,   60
   but now I speak to you along with the sacred votaries of Gilgamesh,
   the high priestesses, the holy women, the temple servers."
She laid a pendant on Enkidu's neck, . . . [saying]
   "I have taken Enkidu; Enkidu to Gilgamesh I have taken."[20]   65

                            . . .

[The Elders said:]

   "Enkidu will protect the friend, will keep the comrade safe.
   Let his body urge him back to the wives.
   In our Assembly we have entrusted the King to you,
   and on your return you must entrust the King back to us!"[21]

Tablet IV

At twenty leagues they broke for some food,
at thirty leagues they stopped for the night,

---

19. Wife of the sun god, Shamash.
20. Five lines are missing; Gilgamesh appar-

ently stresses his ability to carry out his
wishes.
21. The rest of their speech is fragmentary.

walking fifty leagues in a whole day,
a walk of a month and a half.
On the third day they drew near to the Lebanon.   5
They dug a well facing Shamash, the setting sun. . . .
Gilgamesh climbed up a mountain peak,
made a libation of flour, and said:
   "Mountain, bring me a dream, a favorable message from Shamash."
Enkidu prepared a sleeping place for him for the night;   10
a violent wind passed through so he attached a covering.
He made him lie down. . . .
While Gilgamesh rested his chin on his knees,
sleep that pours over mankind overtook him.
In the middle of the night his sleep came to an end,   15
so he got up and said to his friend:
   "My friend, did you not call out to me? Why did I wake up?
   Did you not touch me? Why am I so disturbed?
   Did a god pass by? Why are my muscles trembling?
   Enkidu, my friend, I have had a dream—   20
   and the dream I had was deeply disturbing!
   In the mountain gorges, the mountain fell down on me!"

He who was born in the wilderness,
Enkidu, interpreted the dream for his friend:
   "My friend, your dream is favorable,   25
   The dream is extremely important.
   My friend, the mountain which you saw in the dream is Humbaba.
   It means we will capture Humbaba, and kill him
   and throw his corpse into the wasteland.
   In the morning there will be a favorable message from Shamash."   30

At twenty leagues they broke for some food,
at thirty leagues they stopped for the night,
walking fifty leagues in a whole day,   *actually, 3 days*
a walk of a month and a half.
They dug a well facing Shamash; . . .   35
Gilgamesh climbed up a mountain peak,
made a libation of flour, and said:
   "Mountain, bring me a dream, a favorable message from Shamash."
Enkidu prepared a sleeping place for him for the night;
a violent wind passed through so he attached a covering.   40

. . .

While Gilgamesh rested his chin on his knees,
sleep that pours over mankind overtook him.
In the middle of the night his sleep came to an end,
so he got up and said to his friend:

"My friend, did you not call out to me? Why did I wake up?   45
Did you not touch me? Why am I so disturbed?
Did a god pass by? Why are my muscles trembling?
Enkidu, my friend, I have had a dream,
besides my first dream I have had a second.
And the dream I had—so striking, so . . ., so disturbing!   50
I was grappling with a wild bull of the wilderness,
with his bellow he split the ground, a cloud of dust rose to the sky.
I sank to my knees in front of him. . . .
My tongue hung out, My temples throbbed;
he gave me water to drink from his waterskin."   55
"My friend," (Enkidu said) "the god to whom we go
is not the wild bull! He is totally different!
The wild bull that you saw is Shamash, the protector,
in difficulties he holds our hand.
The one who gave you water to drink from his waterskin   60
is your (personal) god, who brings honor to you, Lugalbanda.
We should join together and do one thing,
a deed such as has never before been done in the land."

At twenty leagues they broke for some food,
at thirty leagues they stopped for the night,   65
walking fifty leagues in a whole day,
a walk of a month and a half.
They dug a well facing Shamash; . . .
Gilgamesh climbed up a mountain peak,
made a libation of flour, and said: 70
    "Mountain, bring me a dream, a favorable message from Shamash."
Enkidu prepared a sleeping place for him for the night;
a violent wind passed through so he attached a covering.

                            . . .
While Gilgamesh rested his chin on his knees,
sleep that pours over mankind overtook him.   75
In the middle of the night his sleep came to an end,
so he got up and said to his friend:
    "My friend, did you not call out to me? Why did I wake up?
    Did you not touch me? Why am I so disturbed?
    Did a god pass by? Why are my muscles trembling?   80
    Enkidu, my friend, I have had a third dream,
    and the dream I had was deeply disturbing.
    The heavens roared and the earth rumbled;
    then it became deathly still, and darkness loomed.
    A bolt of lightning cracked and a fire broke out,   85
    and where it kept thickening, there rained death.
    The the white-hot flame dimmed, and the fire went out,

and everything that had been falling around turned to ash.
Let us go down into the plain so we can talk it over."
Enkidu heard the dream that he had presented and said to Gilgamesh:[22]   90

At twenty leagues they broke for some food,
at thirty leagues they stopped for the night,
walking fifty leagues in a whole day,
a walk of a month and a half.
They dug a well facing Shamash; . . .   95
Gilgamesh climbed up a mountain peak,
made a libation of flour, and said:
    "Mountain, bring me a dream, a favorable message from Shamash."
Enkidu prepared a sleeping place for him for the night;
a violent wind passed through so he attached a covering.   100

                                        . . .

While Gilgamesh rested his chin on his knees,
sleep that pours over mankind overtook him.
In the middle of the night his sleep came to an end,
so he got up and said to his friend:
    "My friend, did you not call out to me? Why did I wake up?   105
    Did you not touch me? Why am I so disturbed?
    Did a god pass by? Why are my muscles trembling?
    Enkidu, my friend, I have had a fourth dream,
    and the dream I had was deeply disturbing.[23]

                                        . . .

Enkidu listened to his dream, and said: 110
    "The dream that you had is favorable, it is extremely important!
    My friend, we will achieve victory over him,
    Humbaba, against whom we rage, and triumph over him.
    In the morning there will be a favorable message from Shamash."[24]   115

His tears were running in the presence of Shamash.
    "What you said in Uruk, be mindful of it, stand by me!"
Gilgamesh, the offspring of Uruk-Haven,
Shamash heard what issued from his mouth,   120
and suddenly there resounded a warning sound from the sky.
    "Hurry, stand by him so that Humbaba does not enter the forest,
    and does not go down into the thickets and hide!
    He has not put on his seven coats of armor,
    he is wearing only one, but has taken off six."[25]   125

                                        . . .

---

22. Enkidu's reply is missing.
23. Gilgamesh's dream is missing.
24. A fifth dream follows, now fragmentary.

25. In a fragmentary passage, Enkidu expresses fear.

The text resumes with Gilgamesh appealing to the sun god Shamash.

Gilgamesh spoke to Enkidu, saying:
  "Why, my friend, . . . we have crossed over all the mountains together; . . .
  my friend, you who are so experienced in battle, . . .
  you need not fear death. . . .
  Let your voice bellow forth like the kettledrum,   130
  let the stiffness in your arms depart,
  let the paralysis in your legs go away.
  Take my hand, my friend, we will go on together.
  Your heart should burn to do battle
  —pay no heed to death, do not lose heart!   135
  The one who watches from the side is a careful man,
  but the one who walks in front protects himself and saves his comrade,
  and through their fighting they establish fame!"
As the two of them reached the evergreen forest
  they cut off their talk, and stood still.   140

Tablet V[26]

They stood at the forest's edge,
gazing at the top of the Cedar Tree,
gazing at the entrance to the forest.
Where Humbaba would walk there was a trail,
the roads led straight on, the path was excellent.   5
Then they saw the Cedar Mountain, the Dwelling of the Gods, the throne dais of
    Irnini.[27]
Across the face of the mountain the Cedar brought forth luxurious foliage,
its shade was good, extremely pleasant.
The thornbushes were matted together, the woods were a thicket, . . .
the Forest was surrounded by a ravine two leagues long.[28]   10

Humbaba spoke to Gilgamesh, saying:
  "An idiot and a moron should give advice to each other,
  but you, Gilgamesh, why have you come to me?
  Give advice, Enkidu, you 'son of a fish,' who does not even know his own
      father,
  to the large and small turtles which do not suck their mother's milk!   15
  When you were still young I saw you but did not go over to you; . . .
  Now, you have brought Gilgamesh into my presence,
  Here you stand, an enemy, a stranger. . . .
  I would feed your flesh to the screeching vulture, the eagle, and the vulture!"

---

26. This entire tablet is fragmentary; several
    passages have been restored on the basis
    of Babylonian and Assyrian versions.
27. A name for Ishtar, in her ferocious aspect.

28. Humbaba appears, frightening En-
    kidu anew. Gilgamesh consoles him,
    but in the following lines Humbaba
    mocks his words.

Gilgamesh spoke to Enkidu, saying: 20
   "My Friend, Humbaba's face keeps changing!"[29]
Enkidu spoke to Gilgamesh, saying:
   "Why, my friend, are you whining so pitiably,
   hiding behind your whimpering?
   Now there, my friend, . . . (it is time)   25
   to send the Flood, to crack the Whip.
   Do not snatch your feet away, do not turn your back;
   strike ever harder!"

The ground split open with the heels of their feet,
as they whirled around in circles Mt. Hermon and Lebanon split.   30
The white clouds darkened,
death rained down on them like fog.
Shamash raised up against Humbaba mighty tempests—
Southwind, Northwind, Eastwind, Westwind, Whistling Wind,
Piercing Wind, Blizzard, Bad Wind, Wind of Simurru,   35
Demon Wind, Ice Wind, Storm, Sandstorm—
thirteen winds rose up against him and covered Humbaba's face.
He could not butt through the front, and could not scramble out the back,
so that Gilgamesh's weapons were in reach of Humbaba.
Humbaba begged for his life, saying to Gilgamesh: 40
   "You are young yet, Gilgamesh, your mother gave birth to you,
   and you are the offspring of Rimat-Ninsun
   It was at the instigation of Shamash, Lord of the Mountain,
   that you were roused to this expedition.
   O scion of the heart of Uruk, King Gilgamesh!   45
   . . .
   Gilgamesh, let me go,
   I will dwell with you as your servant.
   As many trees as you command me I will cut down for you,
   I will guard for you myrtle wood, wood fine enough for your palace!"
Enkidu addressed Gilgamesh, saying: 50
   "My friend, do not listen to Humbaba!"
   . . .

[Humbaba spoke to Enkidu:]

"You understand the rules of my forest, . . .
you are aware of all the things 'So ordered by Enlil.'
I should have carried you up, and killed you at the very entrance to the
   branches of my forest.   55
I should have fed your flesh to the screeching vulture, the eagle, and the
   vulture.

---

29. In two missing lines, it is now Gilgamesh
   who expresses fear.

An impression from a neo-Assyrian period seal, depicting the slaying of Humbaba.

[handwritten annotation: Humbaha speaks to he saved through mocking Enkidu]

So now, Enkidu, clemency is up to you.
Speak to Gilgamesh to spare my life!"
Enkidu addressed Gilgamesh, saying:
"My friend, take Humbaba, Guardian of the Cedar Forest,
grind up, kill, pulverize and . . . him!   60
Humbaba, Guardian of the Forest, grind up, kill, pulverize and . . . him!"

[handwritten annotation: Enkidu says "No Mercy"!]

[Long passage fragmentary or deleted.]

[Enkidu speaks again to Gilgamesh:]

"Before the Preeminent God Enlil hears,
and the gods are full of rage at us.
Enlil is in Nippur, Shamash is in Sippar.
Erect an eternal monument proclaiming how Gilgamesh killed Humbaba."   65
Humbaba heard (all this and said,) . . .
"May he not live the longer of the two,
may Enkidu not have any 'shore' more than his friend Gilgamesh!"
Enkidu spoke to Gilgamesh, saying: 70
"My friend, I have been talking to you but you have not been listening to me,
You have been listening to the curse of Humbaba!"[30]

---

30. In forty fragmentary lines, Gilgamesh and Enkidu slay Humbaba; in the only complete line, "they pulled out his insides including his tongue."

They cut through the Cedar
While Gilgamesh cuts down the trees, Enkidu searches through the urmazallu.
Enkidu addressed Gilgamesh, saying: 75
   "My friend, we have cut down the towering Cedar whose top scrapes the sky.
   Make from it a door 72 cubits high, 24 cubits wide,
   one cubit thick, its fixture, its lower and upper pivots will be out of one piece.
   Let them carry it to Nippur, the Euphrates will carry it down, Nippur will
      rejoice.
They tied together a raft, . . . Enkidu steered it,   80
while Gilgamesh held the head of Humbaba.

Tablet VI

(Gilgamesh) washed out his matted hair and cleaned up his equipment,
shaking out his locks down over his back,
throwing off his dirty clothes and putting on clean ones.
He wrapped himself in regal garments and fastened the sash.
When Gilgamesh placed his crown on his head,   5
Princess Ishtar raised her eyes to the beauty of Gilgamesh.
   "Come along, Gilgamesh, be you my husband,
   to me grant your lusciousness.
   Be you my husband, and I will be your wife.
   I will have harnessed for you a chariot of lapis lazuli and gold,   10
   with wheels of gold and 'horns' of electrum.
   It will be harnessed with great storming mountain mules!
   Come into our house, with the fragrance of cedar.
   And when you come into our house the doorpost and throne dais will kiss your
      feet.
   Bowed down beneath you will be kings, lords, and princes.   15
   The Lullubu people will bring you the produce of the mountains and
      countryside as tribute.
   Your she-goats will bear triplets, your ewes twins,
   your donkey under burden will overtake the mule,
   your steed at the chariot will be bristling to gallop,
   your ox at the yoke will have no match."   20
Gilgamesh addressed Princess Ishtar saying:
   "What would I have to give you if I married you?
   Do you need oil or garments for your body?
   Do you lack anything for food or drink?
   I would gladly feed you food fit for a god,   25
   I would gladly give you wine fit for a king,
                                          . . .
   You are an oven who . . . ice,
   a half-door that keeps out neither breeze nor blast,

a palace that crushes down valiant warriors,
an elephant who devours its own covering,
pitch that blackens the hands of its bearer,
a waterskin that soaks its bearer through,
limestone that buckles out the stone wall,
a battering ram that attracts the enemy land,
a shoe that bites its owner's feet!
Where are your bridegrooms that you keep forever?
Where is your 'Little Shepherd' bird that went up over you?
See here now, I will recite the list of your lovers. . . .
Tammuz, the lover of your earliest youth,
for him you have ordained lamentations year upon year!
You loved the colorful 'Little Shepherd' bird
and then hit him, breaking his wing, so
now he stands in the forest crying 'My Wing'!
You loved the supremely mighty lion,
yet you dug for him seven and again seven pits.
You loved the stallion, famed in battle,
yet you ordained for him the whip, the goad, and the lash,
ordained for him to gallop for seven and seven hours,
ordained for him drinking from muddied waters,
you ordained for his mother Sililli to wail continually.
You loved the Shepherd, the Master Herder,
who continually presented you with bread baked in embers,
and who daily slaughtered for you a kid.
Yet you struck him, and turned him into a wolf,
so his own shepherds now chase him
and his own dogs snap at his shins.
You loved Ishullanu, your father's date gardener,
who continually brought you baskets of dates,
and brightened your table daily.
You raised your eyes to him, and you went to him:
'Oh my Ishullanu, let us taste of your strength,
stretch out your hand to me, and touch our "vulva." '[31]
Ishullanu said to you:
'Me? What is it you want from me?
Has my mother not baked, and have I not eaten
that I should now eat food under contempt and curses
and that alfalfa grass should be my only cover against the cold?'

---

31. A pun; "vulva" sounds like "date palm" in
Akkadian.

As you listened to these his words
you struck him, turning him into a dwarf,
and made him live in the middle of his garden of labors.
And now me! It is me you love, and you will ordain for me as for them!" 70

When Ishtar heard this
in a fury she went up to the heavens,
going to Anu, her father, and crying, 75
going to Antum, her mother, and weeping:
"Father, Gilgamesh has insulted me over and over,
Gilgamesh has recounted despicable deeds about me,
despicable deeds and curses!"
Anu addressed Princess Ishtar, saying: 80
"What is the matter? Was it not you who provoked King Gilgamesh?
So Gilgamesh recounted despicable deeds about you,
despicable deeds and curses!"
Ishtar spoke to her father, Anu, saying:
"Father, give me the Bull of Heaven, 85
so he can kill Gilgamesh in his dwelling.
If you do not give me the Bull of Heaven,
I will knock down the Gates of the Netherworld,
I will smash the door posts, and leave the doors flat down,
and will let the dead go up to eat the living! 90
And the dead will outnumber the living!"
Anu addressed Princess Ishtar, saying:
"If you demand the Bull of Heaven from me,
there will be seven years of empty husks for the land of Uruk.
Have you collected grain for the people? 95
Have you made grasses grow for the animals?"
Ishtar addressed Anu, her father, saying:
"I have heaped grain in the granaries for the people,
I made grasses grow for the animals,
in order that they might eat in the seven years of empty husks. 100
I have collected grain for the people,
I have made grasses grow for the animals."

. . .

When Anu heard her words,
he placed the nose-rope of the Bull of Heaven in her hand.
Ishtar led the Bull of Heaven down to the earth. 105
When it reached Uruk, . . . it climbed down to the Euphrates.
At the snort of the Bull of Heaven a hug pit opened up,
and a hundred Young Men of Uruk fell in.
At his second snort a huge pit opened up,
and two hundred Young Men of Uruk fell in. 110
At his third snort a huge pit opened up,

and Enkidu fell in up to his waist.
Then Enkidu jumped out and seized the Bull of Heaven by its horns.
The Bull spewed his spittle in front of him,
with his thick tail he flung his dung behind him. . . .
Enkidu stalked and hunted down the Bull of Heaven.
He grasped it by the thick of its tail
and held onto it with both his hands,
while Gilgamesh, like an expert butcher,
boldly and surely approached the Bull of Heaven.
Between the nape, the horns, . . . he thrust his sword.
After they had killed the Bull of Heaven,
they ripped out its heart and presented it to Shamash.
They withdrew, bowing down humbly to Shamash.
Then the brothers sat down together.
Ishtar went up onto the top of the Wall of Uruk-Haven,
cast herself into the pose of mourning, and hurled her woeful curse:
   "Woe unto Gilgamesh who slandered me and killed the Bull of Heaven!"
When Enkidu heard this pronouncement of Ishtar,
he wrenched off the Bull's hindquarter and flung it in her face:
   "If I could only get at you I would do the same to you!
   I would drape his innards over your arms!"
Ishtar assembled the (cultic women) of lovely-locks, joy-girls, and harlots,
and set them to mourning over the hindquarter of the Bull.
Gilgamesh summoned all the artisans and craftsmen.
All the artisans admired the thickness of its horns,
each fashioned from 30 minas of lapis lazuli!
Two fingers thick is their casing.
Six vats of oil the contents of the two
he gave as ointment to his personal god Lugalbanda.
He brought the horns in and hung them in the bedroom of the family head.
They washed their hands in the Euphrates,
and proceeded hand in hand,
striding through the streets of Uruk.
The men of Uruk gathered together, staring at them.
Gilgamesh said to the palace retainers:
   "Who is the bravest of the men?
   Who is the boldest of the males?
   —Gilgamesh is the bravest of the men,
   the boldest of the males!
   She at whom we flung the hindquarter of the Bull of Heaven in anger,
   Ishtar has no one that pleases her in the street!"

Gilgamesh held a celebration in his palace.
The Young Men dozed off, sleeping on the couches of the night.

Enkidu was sleeping, and had a dream.
He woke up and revealed his dream to his friend.[32]   155

Tablet VII

"My friend, why are the Great Gods in conference?
In my dream Anu, Enlil, and Shamash held a council,
and Anu spoke to Enlil:
   'Because they killed the Bull of Heaven and have also slain Humbaba,
   the one of them who pulled up the Cedar of the Mountain must die!'   5
Enlil said: 'Let Enkidu die, but Gilgamesh must not die!'
But the Sun God of Heaven replied to valiant Enlil:
   'Was it not at my command that they killed the Bull of Heaven and Humbaba?
   Should now innocent Enkidu die?'
Then Enlil became angry at Shamash, saying: 10
   'It is you who are responsible because you traveled daily with them as their
      friend!' "
Enkidu was lying sick in front of Gilgamesh.
His tears flowing like canals, Gilgamesh said:
  "O brother, dear brother, why are they absolving me instead of my brother?"
Then Enkidu said: "So now must I become a ghost,   15
   to sit with the ghosts of the dead, to see my dear brother nevermore?"

Enkidu raised his eyes, and spoke to the door as if it were human:
  "You stupid wooden door,
  with no ability to understand!
  Already at twenty leagues I selected the wood for you, . . .   20
  your wood was without compare in my eyes.
  Seventy-two cubits was your height, 24 cubits your width, one cubit your
     thickness; . . .
  I fashioned you, and I carried you to Nippur.
  Had I known, O door, that this would be your gratitude . . . .
  I would have taken an axe and chopped you up,   25
  and lashed your planks into a raft!

     . . .
  But yet, O door, I fashioned you, and I carried you to Nippur!
  May a king who comes after me reject you, . . .
  may he remove my name and set his own name there!" . . . .
Gilgamesh kept listening to his words, and retorted quickly,   30
Gilgamesh listened to the words of Enkidu, his Friend, and his tears flowed.
Gilgamesh addressed Enkidu, saying:
  "Friend, the gods have given you a mind broad and . . . deep.
  Though it behooves you to be sensible, you keep uttering improper things!

---

32. This account of Enkidu's dream is taken
    from a Hittite fragment.

Why, my Friend, does your mind utter improper things?   35
The dream is important but very frightening,
your lips are buzzing like flies.
Though there is much fear, the dream is very important.
To the living the gods leave sorrow,
to the living the dream leaves pain.   40
I will pray, and beseech the Great Gods,
I will seek . . . and appeal to your god.

What Enlil says . . . cannot go back,
What he has laid down cannot go back. . . ."

Just as dawn began to glow,   45
Enkidu raised his head and cried out to Shamash,
at the first gleam of the sun his tears poured fourth.
    "I appeal to you, O Shamash, on behalf of my precious life,
    because of that notorious trapper
    who did not let me attain the same as my friend.   50
    May the trapper not get enough to feed himself.
    May his profit be slashed, and his wages decrease! . . .

After he had cursed the trapper to his satisfaction,
his heart prompted him to curse the Harlot.
    "Come now, Harlot, I am going to decree your fate,   55
    a fate that will never come to an end for eternity!
    I will curse you with a Great Curse,
    may my curses overwhelm you suddenly, in an instant!
    May you not be able to make a household,
    and not be able to love a child of your own! . . .   60
    May dregs of beer stain your beautiful lap,
    may a drunk soil your festal robe with vomit,

    May you never acquire anything of bright alabaster, . . .
    may shining silver, man's delight, not be cast into your house,
    may a gateway be where you take your pleasure,   65
    may a crossroad be your home,
    may a wasteland be your sleeping place,
    may the shadow of the city wall be your place to stand,
    may the thorns and briars skin your feet,
    may both the drunk and the dry slap you on the cheek,   70

    may the builder not seal the roof of your house,
    may owls nest in the cracks of your walls!"
                              . . .

When Shamash heard what his mouth had uttered,
he suddenly called out to him from the sky:

"Enkidu, why are you cursing the harlot, Shamhat,   75
she who fed you bread fit for a god,
she who gave you wine fit for a king,
she who dressed you in grand garments,
and she who allowed you to make beautiful Gilgamesh your comrade?
Now Gilgamesh is your beloved brother-friend!   80
He will have you lie on a grand couch,
will have you lie on a couch of honor.
He will seat you in the seat of ease, the seat at his left,
so that the princes of the world kiss your feet.
He will have the people of Uruk go into mourning and moaning over you,   85
will fill the happy people with woe over you.
And after you he will let his body bear a filthy mat of hair,
will don the skin of a lion and roam the wilderness."
As soon as Enkidu heard the words of valiant Shamash,
his agitated heart grew calm, his anger abated.   90
Enkidu spoke to the harlot, saying:
"Come, Shamhat, I will decree your fate for you.
Let my mouth which has cursed you, now turn to bless you!
May governors and nobles love you,
May he who is one league away bite his lip in anticipation,   95
may he who is two leagues away shake out his locks in preparation!
May the soldier not refuse you, but undo his buckle for you,
may he give you rock crystal, lapis lazuli, and gold,
may his gift to you be earrings of filigree.
May his supplies be heaped up. . . .   100
May the wife, the mother of seven, be abandoned because of you!"

Enkidu's innards were churning,
lying there so alone.
He spoke everything he felt, saying to his friend:
"Listen, my friend, to the dream that I had last night.   105
The heavens cried out and the earth replied,
and I was standing between them.
There appeared a man of dark visage—
his face resembled the Anzu:
his hands were the paws of a lion,   110
his nails the talons of an eagle!—
he seized me by my hair and overpowered me.
I struck him a blow, but he skipped about like a jump rope,
and then he struck me and capsized me like a raft,
and trampled on me like a wild bull.   115
He encircled my whole body in a clamp.
   'Help me, my friend!' I cried,
but you did not rescue me, you were afraid and did not."

. . .

"Then he turned me into a dove,
so that my arms were feathered like a bird.   120
Seizing me, he led me down to the House of Darkness, the dwelling of Irkalla,
to the House where those who enter do not come out,
along the road of no return,
to the House where those who dwell do without light,
where dirt is their drink, their food is of clay,   125
where, like a bird, they wear garments of feathers,
and light cannot be seen, they dwell in the dark,
and upon the door and bolt lies dust.
On entering the House of Dust,
everywhere I looked there were royal crowns gathered in heaps,   130
everywhere I listened, it was the bearers of crowns who in the past had ruled the
    land,
but who now served Anu and Enlil cooked meats,
served confections, and poured cool water from waterskins.
In the House of Dust that I entered
there sat the high priest and acolyte,   135
there sat the purification priest and ecstatic,
there sat the anointed priests of the Great Gods.
There sat Etana, there sat Sumukan,
there sat Ereshkigal, the Queen of the Netherworld.
Beletseri, the Scribe of the Netherworld, knelt before her,   140
she was holding the tablet (of destinies,) and was reading it out to her.
She raised her head and when she saw me—
    'Who has taken this man?' "[33]
"I who went through every difficulty,
remember me and forget not all that I went through with you."   145
[Gilgamesh replied:]
    "My friend has had a dream that bodes ill."

Enkidu lies down a first day, a second day, . . .
a third day and fourth day, that Enkidu remains in his bed;
a fifth, a sixth, and seventh, that Enkidu remains in his bed;   150
an eighth, a ninth, a tenth, that Enkidu remains in his bed.
Enkidu's illness grew ever worse.
The eleventh and twelfth day his illness grew ever worse.
Enkidu drew up from his bed,
and called out to Gilgamesh.[34]   155

. . .

---

33. Fifty lines are missing. The text resumes
with the conclusion of Enkidu's speech.

34. Thirty fragmentary lines recount Enkidu's last words and his death.

Tablet VIII

Just as day began to dawn
Gilgamesh addressed his friend, saying:
"Enkidu, your mother, the gazelle,
and your father, the wild donkey, engendered you,
four wild asses raised you on their milk,   5
and the herds taught you all the grazing lands.
May the Roads of Enkidu to the Cedar Forest mourn you
and not fall silent night or day.
May the Elders of the broad city of Uruk-Haven mourn you.
May the peoples who gave their blessing after us mourn you.   10
May the men of the mountains and hills mourn you. . . .
May the pasture lands shriek in mourning as if it were your mother.
May the . . . cypress, and the cedar which we destroyed in our anger mourn
    you.
May the bear, hyena, panther, tiger, water buffalo, jackal, lion, wild bull, stag,
    ibex, all the creatures of the plains mourn you.   15
May the holy River Ulaja, along whose banks we grandly used to stroll, mourn
    you.
May the pure Euphrates, to which we would libate water from our waterskins,
    mourn you.
May the men of Uruk-Haven, whom we saw in our battle when we killed the
    Bull of Heaven, mourn you.
May the farmer, who extols your name in his sweet work song, mourn you.   20
May the people of the broad city, who exalted your name, mourn you.
May the herder, who prepared butter and light beer for your mouth, mourn
    you.
May . . ., who put ointments on your back, mourn you.
May . . ., who prepared fine beer for your mouth, mourn you.
May the harlot, with whom you rubbed yourself with oil and felt good, mourn
    you. . . .   25
May the brothers go into mourning over you like sisters;
as for the lamentation priests, may their hair be shorn off on your behalf.
Enkidu, your mother and your father are in the wastelands,
I mourn you.
Hear me, O Elders of Uruk, hear me, O men!   30
I mourn for Enkidu, my friend,
I shriek in anguish like a mourner.
You, axe at my side, so trusty at my hand—
you, sword at my waist, shield in front of me,
you, my festal garment, a sash over my loins—   35
an evil demon appeared and took him away from me!
My friend, the swift mule, fleet wild ass of the mountain, panther of the
    wilderness,

Enkidu, my friend, the swift mule, fleet wild ass of the mountain, panther of the
    wilderness,
after we joined together and went up into the mountain,
fought the Bull of Heaven and killed it,   40
and overwhelmed Humbaba, who lived in the Cedar Forest,
now what is this sleep which has seized you?
You have turned dark and do not hear me!"
But Enkidu's eyes do not move,
he touched his heart, but it beat no longer.   45
He covered his friend's face like a bride,
swooping down over him like an eagle,
and like a lioness deprived of her cubs
he keeps pacing to and fro.
He shears off his curls and heaps them onto the ground,   50
ripping off his finery and casting it away as an abomination.

Just as day began to dawn, Gilgamesh arose
and issued a call to the land:
    "You, blacksmith! You, lapidary! You, coppersmith!
    You, goldsmith! You, jeweler!   55
    Create 'My Friend,' fashion a statue of him.
    . . . he fashioned a statue of his friend.
    I had you recline on the great couch,
    indeed, on the couch of honor I let you recline,
    I had you sit in the position of ease, the seat at the left, so the princes of the
        world kissed your feet.   60
    I had the people of Uruk mourn and moan for you,
    I filled happy people with woe over you,
    and after you died I let a filthy mat of hair grow over my body,
    and donned the skin of a lion and roamed the wilderness."

[Some 160 lines are missing or fragmentary.]

Tablet IX

Over his friend, Enkidu, Gilgamesh cried bitterly, roaming the wilderness.
    "I am going to die!—am I not like Enkidu?!
    Deep sadness penetrates my core,
    I fear death, and now roam the wilderness—
    I will set out to the region of Utanapishtim, son of Ubartutu, and will go with
        utmost dispatch!   5
    When I arrived at mountain passes at nightfall,
    I saw lions, and I was terrified!
    I raised my head in prayer to Sin,
    to the Great Lady of the gods my supplications poured forth, 'Save me from
        them!' "

He was sleeping in the night, but awoke with a start with a dream: 10
A warrior enjoyed his life—
he raised his axe in his hand,
drew the dagger from his sheath,
and fell into their midst like an arrow.
He struck and he scattered them.[35]
When he reached Mount Mashu,   15
which daily guards the rising and setting of the Sun,
above which only the dome of the heavens reaches,
and whose flank reaches as far as the Netherworld below,
there were Scorpion-beings watching over its gate.   20
Trembling terror they inspire, the sight of them is death,
their frightening aura sweeps over the mountains.
At the rising and setting they watch over the Sun.
When Gilgamesh saw them, trembling terror blanketed his face,
but he pulled himself together and drew near to them.   25
The scorpion-being called out to his female:
    "He who comes to us, his body is the flesh of gods!"
The scorpion-being, his female, answered him:
    "Only two-thirds of him is a god, one-third is human."
The male scorpion-being called out, saying to the offspring of the gods: 30
    "Why have you traveled so distant a journey?
    Why have you come here to me,
    over rivers whose crossing is treacherous?"

[Twenty-nine lines are only partially legible.]

[Gilgamesh answered and said:]
    "I have come on account of my ancestor Utanapishtim,   35
    who joined the Assembly of the Gods, and was given eternal life.
    About Death and Life I must ask him!"
The scorpion-being spoke to Gilgamesh, saying:
    "Never has there been, Gilgamesh, a mortal man who could do that.
    No one has crossed through the mountains,   40
    for twelve leagues it is darkness throughout—
    dense is the darkness, and light there is none."[36]
Gilgamesh answered and said:
    "Though it be in deep sadness and pain,
    in cold or heat gasping after breath, I will go on!   45
    Now! Open the Gate!"
The scorpion-being spoke to Gilgamesh, saying:
    "Go on, Gilgamesh, fear not!

---

35. Thirty fragmentary lines describe the beginning of Gilgamesh's journey to find
Utanapishtim.

36. In seventy missing lines, Gilgamesh persuades the scorpion-man to allow him
through.

The Mashu mountains I give to you freely,
the mountains, the ranges, you may traverse.   50
In safety may your feet carry you. . . .

As soon as Gilgamesh heard this
he heeded the utterances of the scorpion-being.
Along the Road of the Sun he journeyed—
one league he traveled . . . , dense was the darkness, light there was none.   55
Neither what lies ahead nor behind does it allow him to see.
Two leagues he traveled, dense was the darkness, light there was none,
neither what lies ahead nor behind does it allow him to see.
Three leagues he traveled, dense was the darkness, light there was none,
neither what lies ahead nor behind does it allow him to see. . . .   60
Four leagues he traveled . . . , dense was the darkness, light there was none,
neither what lies ahead nor behind does it allow him to see.
Five leagues he traveled . . . , dense was the darkness, light there was none,
neither what lies ahead nor behind does it allow him to see.
Six leagues he traveled . . . , dense was the darkness, light there was none,   65
neither what lies ahead nor behind does it allow him to see.
Seven leagues he traveled . . . , dense was the darkness, light there was none,
neither what lies ahead nor behind does it allow him to see.
Eight leagues he traveled and cried out (?),
dense was the darkness, light there was none,   70
neither what lies ahead nor behind does it allow him to see.
Nine leagues he traveled, the North Wind licked at his face,
dense was the darkness, light there was none,
neither what lies ahead nor behind does it allow him to see.
Ten leagues he traveled; the end of the road is near. . . .   75
Eleven leagues he traveled and came out before the sunrise.
Twelve leagues he traveled and it grew brilliant.

Before him there were trees of precious stones,
and he went straight to look at them.
The tree bears carnelian as its fruit,   80
laden with clusters of jewels, dazzling to behold,
—it bears lapis lazuli as foliage,
bearing fruit, a delight to look upon.

[A long description of the jewelled garden here is too illegible to be transcribed.]

Tablet X

The tavern-keeper Siduri who lives by the seashore, . . .
the pot-stand was made for her, the golden fermenting vat was made for her.
She is covered with a veil.

Gilgamesh was roving about, wearing a skin,
having the flesh of the gods in his body,   5
but sadness deep within him,
looking like one who has been traveling a long distance.
The tavern-keeper was gazing off into the distance,
puzzling to herself, she said,
wondering to herself: 10
    "That fellow is surely a murderer! *referring to Gilgamesh.*
    Where is he heading?"
As soon as the tavern-keeper saw him, she bolted her door,
bolted her gate, bolted the lock.
But at her noise Gilgamesh pricked up his ears,   15
lifted his chin to look about and then laid his eyes on her.
Gilgamesh spoke to the tavern-keeper, saying:
    "Tavern-keeper, what have you seen that made you bolt your door,
    bolt your gate, bolt the lock?
    If you do not let me in I will break your door, and smash the lock!   20

Gilgamesh said to the tavern-keeper:
    "I am Gilgamesh, I killed the Guardian!
    I destroyed Humbaba who lived in the Cedar Forest,
    I slew lions in the mountain passes!
    I grappled with the Bull that came down from heaven, and killed him."   25
The tavern-keeper spoke to Gilgamesh, saying:
    "If you are Gilgamesh, who killed the Guardian,
    who destroyed Humbaba who lived in the Cedar Forest,
    who slew lions in the mountain passes,
    who grappled with the Bull that came down from heaven, and killed him,   30
    why are your cheeks emaciated, your expression desolate?
    Why is your heart so wretched, your features so haggard?
    Why is there such sadness deep within you?
    Why do you look like one who has been traveling a long distance
    so that ice and heat have seared your face?   35
    Why do you roam the wilderness?"
Gilgamesh spoke to her, to the tavern-keeper he said:
    "Tavern-keeper, should not my cheeks be emaciated?
    Should my heart not be wretched, my features not haggard?
    Should there not be sadness deep within me?   40
    Should I not look like one who has been traveling a long distance,
    and should ice and heat not have seared my face?
    Should I not roam the wilderness?
    My friend, the wild ass who chased the wild donkey, panther of the wilderness,
    Enkidu, the wild ass who chased the wild donkey, panther of the wilderness,   45
    we joined together, and went up into the mountain.

We grappled with and killed the Bull of Heaven,
we destroyed Humbaba who lived in the Cedar Forest,
we slew lions in the mountain passes!
My friend, whom I love deeply, who went through every hardship with me,   50
Enkidu, whom I love deeply, who went through every hardship with me,
the fate of mankind has overtaken him.
Six days and seven nights I mourned over him
and would not allow him to be buried
until a maggot fell out of his nose.   55
I was terrified by his appearance,
I began to fear death, and so roam the wilderness.
The issue of my friend oppresses me,
so I have been roaming long trails through the wilderness.
The issue of Enkidu, my friend, oppresses me,   60
so I have been roaming long roads through the wilderness.
How can I stay silent, how can I be still?
My friend whom I love has turned to clay.
Am I not like him? Will I lie down, never to get up again?"[37]
Gilgamesh spoke to the tavern-keeper, saying: 65
"So now, tavern-keeper, what is the way to Utanapishtim?
What are its markers? Give them to me! Give me the markers!
If possible, I will cross the sea;
if not, I will roam through the wilderness."
The tavern-keeper spoke to Gilgamesh, saying: 70
"There has never been, Gilgamesh, any passage whatever,
there has never been anyone since days of yore who crossed the sea.
The one who crosses the sea is valiant Shamash, except for him who can cross?
The crossing is difficult, its ways are treacherous—
and in between are the Waters of Death that bar its approaches!   75
And even if, Gilgamesh, you should cross the sea,
when you reach the Waters of Death what would you do?
Gilgamesh, over there is Urshanabi, the ferryman of Utanapishtim.
'The stone things'[38] are with him, he is in the woods picking mint.
Go on, let him see your face.   80
If possible, cross with him;
if not, you should turn back."

When Gilgamesh heard this
he raised the axe in his hand,
drew the dagger from his belt,   85

---

37. The text notably omits a reply by the
tavern-keeper; in the earlier Old Babylonian version, she had urged Gilgamesh

not to worry about death but to be content
with the pleasures of life.
38. No one is sure what they are.

and slipped stealthily away after them.
Like an arrow he fell among the stone things.
From the middle of the woods their noise could be heard.
Urshanabi, the sharp-eyed, saw. . .
When he heard the axe, he ran toward it.[39]   90

Gilgamesh spoke to Urshanabi, saying:
   "Now, Urshanabi! What is the way to Utanapishtim?
   What are its markers? Give them to me! Give me the markers!
   If possible, I will cross the sea;
   if not, I will roam through the wilderness!"   95

Urshanabi spoke to Gilgamesh, saying:
   "It is your hands, Gilgamesh, that prevent the crossing!
   You have smashed 'the stone things,' you have pulled out their retaining ropes.
   'The stone things' have been smashed, their retaining ropes pulled out!
   Gilgamesh, take the axe in your hand, go down into the woods,   100
   and cut down 300 punting poles each 60 cubits in length.
   Strip them, attach caps, and bring them to the boat!"
When Gilgamesh heard this
he took up the axe in his hand, drew the dagger from his belt,
and went down into the woods,   105
and cut 300 punting poles each 60 cubits in length.
He stripped them and attached caps, and brought them to the boat.
Gilgamesh and Urshanabi boarded the boat,
Gilgamesh launched the boat and they sailed away.
By the third day they had traveled a stretch of a month and a half, and   110
Urshanabi arrived at the Waters of Death.
Urshanabi said to Gilgamesh:
   "Hold back, Gilgamesh, take a punting pole,
   but your hand must not pass over the Waters of Death!
   Take a second, Gilgamesh, a third, and a fourth pole,   115
   take a fifth, Gilgamesh, a sixth, and a seventh pole,
   take an eighth, Gilgamesh, a ninth, and a tenth pole,
   take an eleventh, Gilgamesh, and a twelfth pole!"
In twice 60 rods Gilgamesh had used up the punting poles.
Then he loosened his waist-cloth for a sail;   120
Gilgamesh stripped off his garment
and held it up on the mast with his arms.

Utanapishtim was gazing off into the distance,
puzzling to himself he said, wondering to himself:
   "Why are 'the stone things' of the boat smashed to pieces?   125

---

39. In a fragmentary passage, Gilgamesh and
Urshanabi perhaps fight over the stone
things. Urshanabi then asks Gilgamesh
why he has come; he answers by repeating
his speech to the tavern-keeper.

And why is someone not its master sailing on it?
The one who is coming is not a man of mine."[40]

       . . . .

Utanapishtim said to Gilgamesh:
  "Why are your cheeks emaciated, your expression desolate?
  Why is your heart so wretched, your features so haggard?   130
  Why is there such sadness deep within you?
  Why do you look like one who has been traveling a long distance
  so that ice and heat have seared your face?
  Why do you roam the wilderness?"
Gilgamesh spoke to Utanapishtim saying: 135
  "Should not my cheeks be emaciated, my expression desolate?
  Should my heart not be wretched, my features not haggard?
  Should there not be sadness deep within me?
  Should I not look like one who has been traveling a long distance,
  and should ice and heat not have seared my face?   140
  Should I not roam the wilderness?
  My friend who chased wild asses in the mountain, the panther of the
      wilderness,
  Enkidu, my friend, who chased wild asses in the mountain, the panther of the
      wilderness,
  we joined together, and went up into the mountain.
  We grappled with and killed the Bull of Heaven,   145
  we destroyed Humbaba who dwelled in the Cedar Forest,
  we slew lions in the mountain passes!
  My friend, whom I love deeply, who went through every hardship with me,
  Enkidu, my friend, whom I love deeply, who went through every hardship with
      me,
  the fate of mankind has overtaken him.   150
  Six days and seven nights I mourned over him
  and would not allow him to be buried
  until a maggot fell out of his nose.
  I was terrified by his appearance,
  I began to fear death, and so roam the wilderness.   155
  The issue of my friend oppresses me,
  so I have been roaming long trails through the wilderness.
  The issue of Enkidu, my friend, oppresses me,
  so I have been roaming long roads through the wilderness.
  How can I stay silent, how can I be still?   160
  My friend whom I love has turned to clay;
  Enkidu, my friend whom I love, has turned to clay!
  Am I not like him? Will I lie down never to get up again?"
Gilgamesh spoke to Utanapishtim, saying:

---

40. Gilgamesh arrives and meets Utana-
    pishtim.

"That is why I must go on, to see Utanapishtim whom they call 'The Faraway.'   165
I went circling through all the mountains,
I traversed treacherous mountains, and crossed all the seas—
that is why sweet sleep has not mellowed my face,
through sleepless striving I am strained,
my muscles are filled with pain.   170
I had not yet reached the tavern-keeper's area before my clothing gave out.
I killed bear, hyena, lion, panther, tiger, stag, red-stag, and beasts of the
   wilderness;
I ate their meat and wrapped their skins around me.
The gate of grief must be bolted shut, sealed with pitch and bitumen!
Utanapishtim spoke to Gilgamesh, saying: 175
   "Why, Gilgamesh, do you feel such sadness?
You who were created from the flesh of gods and mankind!

[Long but only partially legible passage follows.]

You have toiled without cease, and what have you got?
Through toil you wear yourself out,
you fill your body with grief,
your long lifetime you are bringing near (to a premature end)!   180
Mankind, whose offshoot is snapped off like a reed in a canebreak,

No one can see death,
no one can see the face of death,
no one can hear the voice of death,
yet there is savage death that snaps off mankind.   185
For how long do we build a household?
For how long do we seal a document?
For how long do brothers share the inheritance?
For how long is there to be jealousy in the land?
For how long has the river risen and brought the overflowing waters,   190
so that dragonflies drift down the river?
The face that could gaze upon the face of the Sun
has never existed ever.
How alike are the sleeping and the dead.
The image of Death cannot be depicted. . . .   195
After Enlil had pronounced the blessing,
the Anunnaki, the Great Gods, assembled.
Mammetum, she who fashions destiny, determined destiny with them.
They established Death and Life,   200
but they did not make known 'the days of death.'"

Tablet XI

Gilgamesh spoke to Utanapishtim, the Faraway:
   "I have been looking at you,

but your appearance is not strange—you are like me!
You yourself are not different—you are like me!
My mind was resolved to fight with you,   5
but instead my arm lies useless over you.
Tell me, how is it that you stand in the Assembly of the Gods, and have found
    life?"
Utanapishtim spoke to Gilgamesh, saying:
    "I will reveal to you, Gilgamesh, a thing that is hidden,
    a secret of the gods I will tell you!   10
    Shuruppak, a city that you surely know,
    situated on the banks of the Euphrates,
    that city was very old, and there were gods inside it.
    The hearts of the Great Gods moved them to inflict the Flood.
    Their Father Anu uttered the oath of secrecy,   15
    Valiant Enlil was their Adviser,
    Ninurta was their Chamberlain,
    Ennugi was their Minister of Canals.
    Ea, the Clever Prince, was under oath with them
    so he repeated their talk to the reed house: 20
      'Reed house, reed house! Wall, wall!
      Hear, O reed house! Understand, O wall!
      O man of Shuruppak, son of Ubartutu:
      Tear down the house and build a boat!
      Abandon wealth and seek living beings!   25
      Spurn possessions and keep alive living beings!
      Make all living beings go up into the boat.
      The boat which you are to build,
      its dimensions must measure equal to each other:
      its length must correspond to its width.   30
      Roof it over like the Apsu.'[41]
I understood and spoke to my lord, Ea:
    'My lord, thus is the command which you have uttered
    I will heed and will do it.
    But what shall I answer the city, the populace, and the Elders?'   35
Ea spoke, commanding me, his servant:
    'You, well then, this is what you must say to them:
      "It appears that Enlil is rejecting me
      so I cannot reside in your city,
      nor set foot on Enlil's earth.   40
      I will go down to the Apsu to live with my lord, Ea,
      and upon you he will rain down abundance,
      a profusion of fowl, myriad fishes.
      He will bring to you a harvest of wealth,

---

41. The freshwater sea beneath the earth, the
    domain of the god Ea or Enki.

in the morning he will let loaves of bread shower down,   45
and in the evening a rain of wheat!"'
Just as dawn began to glow
the land assembled around me—
the carpenter carried his hatchet,
the reed worker carried his flattening stone,   50
The child carried the pitch,
the weak brought whatever else was needed.
On the fifth day I laid out her exterior.
It was a field in area,
its walls were each 10 times 12 cubits in height,   55
the sides of its top were of equal length, 10 times 12 cubits each.
I laid out its interior structure and drew a picture of it.
I provided it with six decks,
thus dividing it into seven levels.[42]
The inside of it I divided into nine compartments.   60
I drove plugs to keep out water in its middle part.
I saw to the punting poles and laid in what was necessary.
Three times 3,600 units of raw bitumen I poured into the bitumen kiln,
three times 3,600 units of pitch I put into it,
there were three times 3,600 porters of casks who carried (vegetable) oil,   65
apart from the 3,600 units of oil which they consumed
and two times 3,600 units of oil which the boatman stored away.
I butchered oxen for the meat,
and day upon day I slaughtered sheep.
I gave the workmen ale, beer, oil, and wine, as if it were river water,   70
so they could make a party like the New Year's Festival.

The boat was finished by sunset.
The launching was very difficult.
They had to keep carrying a runway of poles front to back,
until two-thirds of it had gone into the water.   75
Whatever I had I loaded on it:
whatever silver I had I loaded on it,
whatever gold I had I loaded on it.
All the living beings that I had I loaded on it,
I had all my kith and kin go up into the boat,   80
all the beasts and animals of the field and the craftsmen I had go up.
Shamash had set a stated time:
   'In the morning I will let loaves of bread shower down,
   and in the evening a rain of wheat!
   Go inside the boat, seal the entry!'   85

---

42. The boat is described as a cube, rather than an ordinary boat, in a theological allusion to the dimensions of a ziggurat, the Mesopotamian stepped tower with four to seven levels on top of which stood a temple.

That stated time had arrived.
In the morning he let loaves of bread shower down,
and in the evening a rain of wheat.
I watched the appearance of the weather—
the weather was frightful to behold!   90
I went into the boat and sealed the entry.
For the caulking of the boat, to Puzuramurri, the boatman,
I gave the palace together with its contents.
Just as dawn began to glow
there arose from the horizon a black cloud.   95
Adad[43] rumbled inside of it,
before him went Shullat and Hanish,
heralds going over mountain and land.
Erragal pulled out the mooring poles,
forth went Ninurta and made the dikes overflow.   100
The Anunnaki lifted up the torches,
setting the land ablaze with their flare.
Stunned shock over Adad's deeds overtook the heavens,
and turned to blackness all that had been light.
The land shattered like a pot.   105
All day long the South Wind blew,
blowing fast, submerging the mountain in water,
overwhelming the people like an attack.
No one could see his fellow,
they could not recognize each other in the torrent.   110
The gods were frightened by the Flood,
and retreated, ascending to the heaven of Anu.
The gods were cowering like dogs, crouching by the outer wall.
Ishtar shrieked like a woman in childbirth,
the sweet-voiced Mistress of the Gods wailed: 115
  'The olden days have alas turned to clay,
  because I said evil things in the Assembly of the Gods!
  How could I say evil things in the Assembly of the Gods,
  ordering a catastrophe to destroy my people?!
  No sooner have I given birth to my dear people   120
  than they fill the sea like so many fish!'
The gods—those of the Anunnaki—were weeping with her,
the gods humbly sat weeping, sobbing with grief,
their lips burning, parched with thirst.
Six days and seven nights   125
came the wind and flood, the storm flattening the land.
When the seventh day arrived, the storm was pounding,
the flood was a war—struggling with itself like a woman writhing in labor.

---

43. The storm god. Erragal, below, is the god
of death; Ninurta is the god of war. The
Anunnaki are a group of fifty gods, sons of
Anu.

The sea calmed, fell still, the whirlwind and flood stopped up.
I looked around all day long—quiet had set in 130
and all the human beings had turned to clay!
The terrain was as flat as a roof.
I opened a vent and fresh air fell upon the side of my nose.
I fell to my knees and sat weeping,
tears streaming down the side of my nose. 135
I looked around for coastlines in the expanse of the sea,
and at twelve leagues there emerged a region of land.
On Mt. Nimush the boat lodged firm,
Mt. Nimush held the boat, allowing no sway.[44]
One day and a second Mt. Nimush held the boat, allowing no sway. 140
A third day, a fourth, Mt. Nimush held the boat, allowing no sway.
A fifth day, a sixth, Mt. Nimush held the boat, allowing no sway.
When a seventh day arrived
I sent forth a dove and released it.
The dove went off, but came back to me; 145
no perch was visible so it circled back to me.
I sent forth a swallow and released it.
The swallow went off, but came back to me;
no perch was visible so it circled back to me.
I sent forth a raven and released it. 150
The raven went off, and saw the waters slither back.
It eats, it scratches, it bobs, but does not circle back to me.
Then I sent out everything in all directions and sacrificed a sheep.
I offered incense in front of the mountain-ziggurat.
Seven and seven cult vessels I put in place, 155
and into their bowls I poured reeds, cedar, and myrtle.
The gods smelled the savor,
the gods smelled the sweet savor,
and collected like flies over a sacrifice.
Just then Beletili arrived. 160
She lifted up the large flies (beads) which Anu had made for his enjoyment:[45]
  'You gods, as surely as I shall not forget this lapis lazuli around my neck,
  may I be mindful of these days, and never forget them!
  The gods may come to the incense offering,
  but Enlil may not come to the incense offering, 165
  because without considering he brought about the Flood
  and consigned my people to annihilation.'
Just then Enlil arrived.
He saw the boat and became furious,

---

44. This may be a 9,000-foot peak in eastern Iraq.
45. A necklace with beads in the form of flies,

representing the dead offspring of the mother goddess Beletili/Aruru.

he was filled with rage at the Igigi gods:[46]   170
   'Where did a living being escape?
   No man was to survive the annihilation!'
Ninurta spoke to Valiant Enlil, saying:
   'Who else but Ea could devise such a thing?
   It is Ea who knows every machination!'   175
Ea spoke to Valiant Enlil, saying:
   'It is you, O Valiant One, who is the Sage of the Gods.
   How, how could *you* bring about a Flood without consideration?
   Charge the violation to the violator,
   charge the offense to the offender,   180
   but be compassionate lest (mankind) be cut off,
   be patient lest they be killed.
   Instead of your bringing on the Flood,
   would that a lion had appeared to diminish the people!
   Instead of your bringing on the Flood,   185
   would that a wolf had appeared to diminish the people!
   Instead of your bringing on the Flood,
   would that famine had occurred to slay the land!
   Instead of your bringing on the Flood,
   would that Pestilent Erra had appeared to ravage the land!   190
   It was not I who revealed the secret of the Great Gods,
   I only made a dream appear to Atrahasis[47] and (thus) he heard the secret of
     the gods.
   Now then! The deliberation should be about him!'
Enlil went up inside the boat
and, grasping my hand, made me go up.   195
He had my wife go up and kneel by my side.
He touched our forehead and, standing between us, he blessed us:
   'Previously Utanapishtim was a human being.
   But now let Utanapishtim and his wife become like us, the gods!
   Let Utanapishtim reside far away, at the Mouth of the Rivers.'   200
They took us far away and settled us at the Mouth of the Rivers."

"Now then, (Gilgamesh,) who will convene the gods on your behalf,
that you may find the life that you are seeking?
Wait! You must not lie down for six days and seven nights."
As soon as he sat down with his head between his legs   205
sleep, like a fog, blew upon him.
Utanapishtim said to his wife:
   "Look there! The man, the youth who wanted eternal life!
   Sleep, lie a fog, blew over him."

---

46. A group of lesser gods who did manual
    labor for the Anunnaki.
47. Atrahasis, "Exceedingly Wise," is the hero

of an earlier Flood epic, from which this
account draws; here the name is applied
to Utanapishtim.

His wife said to Utanapishtim the Faraway: 210
   "Touch him, let the man awaken.
   Let him return safely by the way he came.
   Let him return to his land by the gate through which he left."
Utanapishtim said to his wife:
   "Mankind is deceptive, and will deceive you.   215
   Come, bake loaves for him and keep setting them by his head
   and draw on the wall each day that he lay down."
She baked his loaves and placed them by his head
and marked on the wall the day that he lay down.
The first loaf was dessicated,   220
the second stale, the third moist, the fourth turned white, . . .
the fifth sprouted gray (mold), the sixth is still fresh.
The seventh—suddenly he touched him and the man awoke.
Gilgamesh said to Utanapishtim:
   "The very moment sleep was pouring over me   225
   you touched me and alerted me!"
Utanapishtim spoke to Gilgamesh, saying:
   "Look over here, Gilgamesh, count your loaves!
   You should be aware of what is marked on the wall!
   Your first loaf is dessicated,   230
   the second stale, the third moist, your fourth turned white, . . .
   the fifth sprouted gray mold, the sixth is still fresh.
   The seventh—at that instant you awoke!"
Gilgamesh said to Utanapishtim the Faraway:
   "O woe! What shall I do, Utanapishtim, where shall I go?   235
   The Snatcher has taken hold of my flesh,
   in my bedroom Death dwells,
   and wherever I set foot there too is Death!"

Utanapishtim said to Urshanabi, the ferryman:
   "May the harbor reject you, may the ferry landing reject you!   240
   May you who used to walk its shores be denied its shores!
   The man in front of whom you walk, matted hair chains his body,
   animal skins have ruined his beautiful skin.
   Take him away, Urshanabi, bring him to the washing place.
   Let him wash his matted hair in water.   245
   Let him cast away his animal skin and have the sea carry it off,
   let his body be moistened with fine oil,
   let the wrap around his head be made new,
   let him wear royal robes worthy of him!
   Until he goes off to his city,
   until he sets off on his way,   250
   let his royal robe not become spotted, let it be perfectly new!"
Urshanabi took him away and brought him to the washing place.
He washed his matted hair with water. . . .

He cast off his animal skin and the sea carried it off.   255
He moistened his body with fine oil,
and made a new wrap for his head.
He put on a royal robe worthy of him.
Until he went away to his city,
until he set off on his way,   260
his royal robe remained unspotted, it was perfectly clean.
Gilgamesh and Urshanabi boarded the boat,
they cast off the boat, and sailed away.

The wife of Utanapishtim the Faraway said to him:
    "Gilgamesh came here exhausted and worn out.   265
    What can you give him so that he can return to his land with honor?"
Then Gilgamesh raised a punting pole
and drew the boat to shore.
Utanapishtim spoke to Gilgamesh, saying:
    "Gilgamesh, you came here exhausted and worn out.   270
    What can I give you so you can return to your land?
    I will disclose to you a thing that is hidden, Gilgamesh,
    a secret I will tell you.
    There is a plant like a boxthorn,
    whose thorns will prick your hand like a rose.   275
    If your hands reach that plant you will become a young man again."
Hearing this, Gilgamesh opened a conduit(?) to the Apsu
and attached heavy stones to his feet.
They dragged him down, to the Apsu they pulled him.
He took the plant, though it pricked his hand,   280
and cut the heavy stones from his feet,
letting the waves throw him onto its shores.
Gilgamesh spoke to Urshanabi, the ferryman, saying:
    "Urshanabi, this plant is a plant against decay
    by which a man can attain his survival.   285
    I will bring it to Uruk-Haven,
    and have an old man eat the plant to test it.
    The plant's name is 'The Old Man Becomes a Young Man.'[48]
    Then I will eat it and return to the condition of my youth."
At twenty leagues they broke for some food,   290
at thirty leagues they stopped for the night.
Seeing a spring and how cool its waters were,
Gilgamesh went down and was bathing in the water.
A snake smelled the fragrance of the plant,

---

48. This is probably the meaning of "Gilgamesh."

silently came up and carried off the plant.   295
While going back it sloughed off its casing.
At that point Gilgamesh sat down, weeping,
his tears streaming over the side of his nose.
　　"Counsel me, O ferryman Urshanabi!
　　For whom have my arms labored, Urshanabi?   300
　　For whom has my heart's blood roiled?
　　I have not secured any good deed for myself,
　　but done a good deed for the 'lion of the ground'!
　　Now the high waters are coursing twenty leagues distant,
　　as I was opening the conduit(?) I turned my equipment over into it.   305
　　What can I find to serve as a marker for me?
　　I will turn back from the journey by sea and leave the boat by the shore!"

At twenty leagues they broke for some food,
at thirty leagues they stopped for the night.
They arrived in Uruk-Haven.   310
Gilgamesh said to Urshanabi, the ferryman:
　　"Go up, Urshanabi, onto the wall of Uruk and walk around.
　　Examine its foundation, inspect its brickwork thoroughly—
　　is not even the core of the brick structure of kiln-fired brick,
　　and did not the Seven Sages themselves lay out its plan?   315
　　One league city, one league palm gardens, one league lowlands, the open area
　　　of the Ishtar Temple,
　　three leagues and the open area of Uruk the wall encloses."

HOMER (EIGHTH CENTURY B.C.E.)
Greece

The *Iliad*'s central themes—friendship and fame, human and divine relations, and a hero's confrontation with his own mortality—will be familiar to readers of the Babylonian *Epic of Gilgamesh*, which may have reached Greece through trading contacts in Asia Minor during the period when the *Iliad* was being shaped. The *Iliad*, whose title means "the story of Ilium" (Troy), was itself the product of a centuries-old oral narrative tradition about the Trojan War, an enduring subject around which a rich and elaborate mythology developed.

　　The events of the *Iliad* are concentrated into a few crucial days in the final year of the ten-year struggle. It begins with the strife between Achilles, preeminent among the Greek heroes, and Agamemnon, king of Mycenae and leader of the Greek forces. Their rift causes Achilles to withdraw from the war, and he returns to it only after his friend Patroclus is killed by Hector, son of Priam, the Trojan king. The final scene in our selection narrates the meeting of

Achilles and Priam in the poem's last book, when each expresses his compassion for the other.

The *Iliad* is thought to have taken the form in which we now have it in the early to mid-eighth century B.C.E., having been preceded by countless oral recreations of its story. Although numerous individuals must have left their mark on it as they sang different versions of the story, Homer is the name that has come down to us from antiquity as the creator of both the *Iliad* and the *Odyssey*. We know nothing whatever of Homer; but by his name we refer to the poet to whose artistic imprint these complex works owe their unmistakable coherence and unforgettable beauty. It is impossible to overstate their influence on later European literature.

from **Iliad**

Book 1 [*The Rage of Achilles*]

Rage—Goddess[1] sing the rage of Peleus' son Achilles,
murderous, doomed, that cost the Achaeans[2] countless losses,
hurling down to the House of Death so many sturdy souls,
great fighters' souls, but made their bodies carrion,
feasts for the dogs and birds,   5
and the will of Zeus was moving toward its end.
Begin, Muse, when the two first broke and clashed,
Agamemnon lord of men and brilliant Achilles.
    What god drove them to fight with such a fury?
Apollo the son of Zeus and Leto. Incensed at the king   10
he swept a fatal plague through the army—men were dying
and all because Agamemnon spurned Apollo's priest.
Yes, Chryses approached the Achaeans' fast ships
to win his daughter back, bringing a priceless ransom
and bearing high in hand, wound on a golden staff,   15
the wreaths of the god, the distant deadly Archer.
He begged the whole Achaean army but most of all[3]
the two supreme commanders, Atreus' two sons,
"Agamemnon, Menelaus—all Argives geared for war!
May the gods who hold the halls of Olympus give you   20
Priam's[4] city to plunder, then safe passage home.

Translated by Robert Fagles.

---

1. The goddess is the Muse, who is also invoked in the opening line of the *Odyssey*. In early Greek poetry the Muse (sometimes in the plural) is represented as the ultimate source of the poet's skill; she is considered to have witnessed the great deeds of the past, which are the subject of epic poetry, and can thus guarantee the authenticity of the poet's song.

2. A Homeric name for the Greek forces, also called Argives (from the city of Argos) and Danaans (referring to their descent from a mythical King Danaus who was said to have been given refuge in Argos).

3. Apollo, the archer god, can inflict disease but is also the god of healing.

4. Priam is king of Troy and father of Hector, the city's chief defender.

Just set my daughter free, my dear one . . . here,
accept these gifts, this ransom. Honor the god
who strikes from worlds away—the son of Zeus, Apollo!"
　　And all ranks of Achaeans cried out their assent:　　　　　　　25
"Respect the priest, accept the shining ransom!"
But it brought no joy to the heart of Agamemnon.
The king dismissed the priest with a brutal order
ringing in his ears: "Never again, old man,
let me catch sight of you by the hollow ships!　　　　　　　　30
Not loitering now, not slinking back tomorrow.
The staff and the wreaths of god will never save you then.
The girl—I won't give up the girl. Long before that,
old age will overtake her in *my* house, in Argos,
far from her fatherland, slaving back and forth　　　　　　　　35
at the loom, forced to share my bed!
　　　　　　　　　　　　　Now go,
don't tempt my wrath—and you may depart alive."
　　The old man was terrified. He obeyed the order,
turning, trailing away in silence down the shore
where the roaring battle lines of breakers crash and drag.　　　40
And moving off to a safe distance, over and over
the old priest prayed to the son of sleek-haired Leto,
lord Apollo, "Hear me, Apollo! God of the silver bow
who strides the walls of Chryse and Cilla[5] sacrosanct—
lord in power of Tenedos—Smintheus,[6] god of the plague!　　45
If I ever roofed a shrine to please your heart,
ever burned the long rich bones of bulls and goats
on your holy altar, now, now bring my prayer to pass.
Pay the Danaans back—your arrows for my tears!"
　　His prayer went up and Phoebus Apollo heard him.　　　　50
Down he strode from Olympus' peaks, storming at heart
with his bow and hooded quiver slung across his shoulders.
The arrows clanged at his back as the god quaked with rage,
the god himself on the march and down he came like night.
Over against the ships he dropped to a knee, let fly a shaft　　55
and a terrifying clash rang out from the great silver bow.
First he went for the mules and circling dogs but then,
launching a piercing shaft at the men themselves,
he cut them down in droves—
and the corpse-fires burned on, night and day, no end in sight.　60
　　Nine days the arrows of god swept through the army.

---

5. Chryse and Cilla are towns to the south of Troy; the priest's name is taken from the town of Chryse. Tenedos is an island off the coast near Troy.

6. This epithet is thought to come from the Cretan word for "mouse" and to refer either to an early stage of worship of the god in animal form or to Apollo as a protector against mice, which destroy the crops.

On the tenth Achilles called all ranks to muster—
the impulse seized him, sent by white-armed Hera[7]
grieving to see Achaean fighters drop and die.
Once they'd gathered, crowding the meeting grounds,   65
the swift runner Achilles rose and spoke among them:
"Son of Atreus, now we are beaten back, I fear,
the long campaign is lost. So home we sail . . .
if we can escape our death—if war and plague
are joining forces now to crush the Argives.   70
But wait: let us question a holy man,
a prophet, even a man skilled with dreams—
dreams as well can come our way from Zeus—
come, someone to tell us why Apollo rages so,
whether he blames us for a vow we failed, or sacrifice.   75
If only the god would share the smoky savor of lambs
and full-grown goats, Apollo might be willing, still,
somehow, to save us from this plague."

                                      So he proposed
and down he sat again as Calchas rose among them,
Thestor's son, the clearest by far of all the seers   80
who scan the flight of birds. He knew all things that are,
all things that are past and all that are to come,
the seer who had led the Argive ships to Troy
with the second sight that god Apollo gave him.
For the armies' good the seer began to speak: 85
"Achilles, dear to Zeus . . .
you order me to explain Apollo's anger,
the distant deadly Archer? I will tell it all.
But strike a pact with me, swear you will defend me
with all your heart, with words and strength of hand.   90
For there is a man I will enrage—I see it now—
a powerful man who lords it over all the Argives,
one the Achaeans must obey . . . A mighty king,
raging against an inferior, is too strong.
Even if he can swallow down his wrath today,   95
still he will nurse the burning in his chest
until, sooner or later, he sends it bursting forth.
Consider it closely, Achilles. Will you save me?"

    And the matchless runner reassured him: "Courage!
Out with it now, Calchas. Reveal the will of god,   100
whatever you may know. And I swear by Apollo
dear to Zeus, the power you pray to, Calchas,
when you reveal god's will to the Argives—no one,
not while I am alive and see the light on earth, no one

---

7. The wife (and sister) of Zeus, patriarch of
   the gods who live on Mt. Olympus.

will lay his heavy hands on you by the hollow ships.   105
None among all the armies. Not even if you mean
Agamemnon here who now claims to be, by far,
the best of the Achaeans."
                   The seer took heart
and this time he spoke out, bravely: "Beware—
he casts no blame for a vow we failed, a sacrifice.   110
The god's enraged because Agamemnon spurned his priest,
he refused to free his daughter, he refused the ransom.
That's why the Archer sends us pains and he will send us more
and never drive this shameful destruction from the Argives,
not till we give back the girl with sparkling eyes   115
to her loving father—no price, no ransom paid—
and carry a sacred hundred bulls to Chryse town.
Then we can calm the god, and only then appease him."
    So he declared and sat down. But among them rose
the fighting son of Atreus, lord of the far-flung kingdoms,   120
Agamemnon—furious, his dark heart filled to the brim,
blazing with anger now, his eyes like searing fire.
With a sudden, killing look he wheeled on Calchas first:
"Seer of misery! Never a word that works to my advantage!
Always misery warms your heart, your prophecies—   125
never a word of profit said or brought to pass.
Now, again, you divine god's will for the armies,
bruit it about, as fact, why the deadly Archer
multiplies our pains: because I, I refused
that glittering price for the young girl Chryseis.   130
Indeed, I prefer *her* by far, the girl herself,
I want her mine in my own house! I rank her higher
than Clytemnestra, my wedded wife—she's nothing less
in build or breeding, in mind or works of hand.
But I am willing to give her back, even so,   135
if that is best for all. What I really want
is to keep my people safe, not see them dying
But fetch me another prize, and straight off too
else I alone of the Argives go without my honor.
That would be a disgrace. You are all witness   140
look—*my* prize is snatched away!"
                     But the swift runner
Achilles answered him at once, "Just how, Agamemnon,
great field marshal . . . most grasping man alive,
how can the generous Argives give you prizes now?
I know of no troves of treasure, piled, lying idle,   145
anywhere. Whatever we dragged from towns we plundered,
all's been portioned out. But collect it, call it back
from the rank and file? *That* would be the disgrace.

So return the girl to the god, at least for now.
We Achaeans will pay you back, three, four times over,   150
if Zeus will grant us the gift, somehow, someday,
to raze Troy's massive ramparts to the ground."
    But King Agamemnon countered, "Not so quickly,
brave as you are, godlike Achilles—trying to cheat *me*.
Oh no, you won't get past me, take me in that way!   155
What do you want? To cling to your own prize
while I sit calmly by—empty-handed here?
Is that why you order me to give her back?
No—if our generous Argives *will* give me a prize,
a match for my desires, equal to what I've lost,   160
well and good. But if they give me nothing
I will take a prize myself—your own, or Ajax'
or Odysseus'[8] prize—I'll commandeer her myself
and let that man I go to visit choke with rage!
Enough. We'll deal with all this later, in due time.   165
Now come, we haul a black ship down to the bright sea,
gather a decent number of oarsmen along her locks
and put aboard a sacrifice, and Chryseis herself,
in all her beauty . . . we embark her too.
Let one of the leading captains take command.   170
Ajax, Idomeneus, trusty Odysseus or you, Achilles,
you—the most violent man alive—so you can perform
the rites for us and calm the god yourself."
                                                    A dark glance
and the headstrong runner answered him in kind: "Shameless—
armored in shamelessness—always shrewd with greed!   175
How could any Argive soldier obey your orders,
freely and gladly do your sailing for you
or fight your enemies, full force? Not I, no.
It wasn't Trojan spearmen who brought me here to fight.
The Trojans never did *me* damage, not in the least,   180
they never stole my cattle or my horses, never
in Phthia where the rich soil breeds strong men
did they lay waste my crops. How could they?
Look at the endless miles that lie between us . . .
shadowy mountain ranges, seas that surge and thunder.   185
No, you colossal, shameless—we all followed you,
to please you, to fight for you, to win your honor
back from the Trojans—Menelaus and you, you dog-face!
What do *you* care? Nothing. You don't look right or left.
And now you threaten to strip me of my prize in person—   190

---

8. Two of the preeminent Achaean warriors.

the one I fought for long and hard, and sons of Achaea
handed her to me.
               My honors never equal yours,
whenever we sack some wealthy Trojan stronghold—
my arms bear the brunt of the raw, savage fighting,
true, but when it comes to dividing up the plunder   195
the lion's share is yours, and back I go to my ships,
clutching some scrap, some pittance that I love,
when I have fought to exhaustion.
                       No more now—
back I go to Phthia.[9] Better that way by far,
to journey home in the beaked ships of war.   200
I have no mind to linger here disgraced,
brimming your cup and piling up your plunder."
    But the lord of men Agamemnon shot back,
"*Desert,* by all means—if the spirit drives you home!
I will never beg you to stay, not on *my* account.   205
Never—others will take my side and do me honor,
Zeus above all, whose wisdom rules the world.
You—I hate you most of all the warlords
loved by the gods. Always dear to your heart,
strife, yes, and battles, the bloody grind of war.   210
What if you are a great soldier? That's just a gift of god.
Go home with your ships and comrades, lord it over your Myrmidons![10]
You *are* nothing to me—you and your overweening anger!
But let this be my warning on your way:
since Apollo insists on taking my Chryseis,[11]   215
I'll send her back in my own ships with *my* crew.
But I, I will be there in person at your tents
to take Briseis in all her beauty, your own prize—
so you can learn just how much greater I am than you
and the next man up may shrink from matching words with me,   220
from hoping to rival Agamemnon strength for strength!"
    He broke off and anguish gripped Achilles.
The heart in his rugged chest was pounding, torn . . .
Should he draw the long sharp sword slung at his hip,
thrust through the ranks and kill Agamemnon now?—   225
or check his rage and beat his fury down?
As his racing spirit veered back and forth,
just as he drew his huge blade from its sheath,

---

9. Achilles' home in Thessaly, in the north of
    mainland Greece.
10. Achilles' warrior companions who came
    with him from Phthia.

11. Her name means simply "daughter of
    Chryseis."

down from the vaulting heavens swept Athena,[12]
the white-armed goddess Hera sped her down: 230
Hera loved both men and cared for both alike.
Rearing behind him Pallas seized his fiery hair—
only Achilles saw her, none of the other fighters—
struck with wonder he spun around, he knew her at once,
Pallas Athena! the terrible blazing of those eyes,   235
and his winged words went flying: "Why, why now?
Child of Zeus with the shield of thunder, why come now?
To witness the outrage Agamemnon just committed?
I tell you this, and so help me it's the truth—
he'll soon pay for his arrogance with his life!"   240
     Her gray eyes clear, the goddess Athena answered,
"Down from the skies I come to check your rage
if only you will yield.
The white-armed goddess Hera sped me down:
she loves you both, she cares for you both alike.   245
Stop this fighting, now. Don't lay hand to sword.
Lash him with threats of the price that he will face.
And I tell you this—and I *know* it is the truth—
one day glittering gifts will lie before you,
three times over to pay for all his outrage.   250
Hold back now. Obey us both."
                              So she urged
and the swift runner complied at once: "I must—
when the two of you hand down commands, Goddess,
a man submits though his heart breaks with fury.
Better for him by far. If a man obeys the gods   255
they're quick to hear his prayers."
                              And with that
Achilles stayed his burly hand on the silver hilt
and slid the huge blade back in its sheath.
He would not fight the orders of Athena.
Soaring home to Olympus, she rejoined the gods   260
aloft in the halls of Zeus whose shield is thunder.
     But Achilles rounded on Agamemnon once again,
lashing out at him, not relaxing his anger for a moment:
"Staggering drunk, with your dog's eyes, your fawn's heart!
Never once did you arm with the troops and go to battle   265
or risk an ambush packed with Achaea's picked men—
you lack the courage, you can see death coming.

---

12. Pallas Athena, Zeus's daughter, and Hera,
his wife, are partisans of the Greek side in
the conflict and perpetually hostile to the
Trojans. Athena is goddess of war as well
as of the civilizing arts.

Safer by far, you find, to foray all through camp,
commandeering the prize of any man who speaks against you.
King who devours his people! Worthless husks, the men you rule—   270
if not, Atrides,[13] this outrage would have been your last.
I tell you this, and I swear a mighty oath upon it . . .
by this, this scepter, look,
that never again will put forth crown and branches,
now it's left its stump on the mountain ridge forever,   275
nor will it sprout new green again, now the brazen ax
has stripped its bark and leaves, and now the sons of Achaea
pass it back and forth as they hand their judgments down,
upholding the honored customs whenever Zeus commands—
This scepter will be the mighty force behind my oath: 280
someday, I swear, a yearning for Achilles will strike
Achaea's sons and all your armies! But then, Atrides,
harrowed as you will be, *nothing* you do can save you—
not when your hordes of fighters drop and die,
cut down by the hands of man-killing Hector![14] Then—   285
then you will tear your heart out, desperate, raging
that you disgraced the best of the Achaeans!"

                             Down on the ground
he dashed the scepter studded bright with golden nails,
then took his seat again.

[After Achilles withdraws from the war, the fighting between Greeks and Trojans resumes. Thanks to the prowess of the warrior Diomedes, the Greeks have considerable success on the battlefield, prompting Hector to return to the city to instruct the Trojans to appeal to the goddess Athena for aid. Before departing again for battle Hector visits his own house, looking for his wife, Andromache, and their infant son.]

Book 6 [Hector Returns to Troy]

A flash of his helmet
and off he strode and quickly reached his sturdy,
well-built house. But white-armed Andromache—
Hector could not find her in the halls.
She and the boy and a servant finely gowned   5
were standing watch on the tower, sobbing, grieving.
When Hector saw no sign of his loyal wife inside
he went to the doorway, stopped and asked the servants,
"Come, please, tell me the truth now, women.
Where's Andromache gone? To my sister's house?   10

---

13. Achilles addresses Agamemnon as "son of Atreus." A warrior will often be referred to, as here, only by his patronymic, which designates him as "son of. . . ."

14. The leading Trojan warrior, son of King Priam.

To my brothers' wives with their long flowing robes?
Or Athena's shrine where the noble Trojan women
gather to win the great grim goddess over?"
A busy, willing servant answered quickly,
"Hector, seeing you want to know the truth,   15
she hasn't gone to your sisters, brothers' wives
or Athena's shrine where the noble Trojan women
gather to win the great grim goddess over.
Up to the huge gate-tower of Troy she's gone
because she heard our men are so hard-pressed,   20
the Achaean fighters coming on in so much force.
She sped to the wall in panic, like a madwoman—
the nurse went with her, carrying your child."
At that, Hector spun and rushed from his house,
back by the same way down the wide, well-paved streets   25
throughout the city until he reached the Scaean Gates,
the last point he would pass to gain the field of battle.
There his warm, generous wife came running up to meet him,
Andromache the daughter of gallant-hearted Eetion
who had lived below Mount Placos[15] rich with timber,   30
in Thebe below the peaks, and ruled Cilicia's people.
His daughter had married Hector helmed in bronze.
She joined him now, and following in her steps
a servant holding the boy against her breast,
in the first flush of life, only a baby,   35
Hector's son, the darling of his eyes
and radiant as a star . . .
Hector would always call the boy Scamandrius,[16]
townsmen called him Astyanax, Lord of the City,
since Hector was the lone defense of Troy.   40
The great man of war breaking into a broad smile,
his gaze fixed on his son, in silence. Andromache,
pressing close beside him and weeping freely now,
clung to his hand, urged him, called him: "Reckless one,
my Hector—your own fiery courage will destroy you!   45
Have you no pity for him, our helpless son? Or me,
and the destiny that weighs me down, your widow,
now so soon. Yes, soon they will kill you off,
all the Achaean forces massed for assault, and then,
bereft of you, better for me to sink beneath the earth.   50
What other warmth, what comfort's left for me,
once you have met your doom? Nothing but torment!

---

15. Andromache's father ruled an area to the
south of Troy, near Mt. Ida.

16. Hector has named his son after the Trojan
river Scamander. Astyanax literally means
"lord of the city."

I have lost my father. Mother's gone as well.
Father . . . the brilliant Achilles laid him low
when he stormed Cilicia's city filled with people,   55
Thebe with her towering gates. He killed Eetion,
not that he stripped his gear—he'd some respect at least—
for he burned his corpse in all his blazoned bronze,
then heaped a grave-mound high above the ashes
and nymphs of the mountain planted elms around it,   60
daughters of Zeus whose shield is storm and thunder.
And the seven brothers I had within our halls . . .
all in the same day went down to the House of Death,
the great godlike runner Achilles butchered them all,
tending their shambling oxen, shining flocks.   65
                                            And mother,
who ruled under the timberline of woody Placos once—
he no sooner haled her here with his other plunder
than he took a priceless ransom, set her free
and home she went to her father's royal halls
where Artemis,[17] showering arrows, shot her down.   70
You, Hector—you are my father now, my noble mother,
a brother too, and you are my husband, young and warm and strong!
Pity me, please! Take your stand on the rampart here,
before you orphan your son and make your wife a widow.
Draw your armies up where the wild fig tree stands,   75
there, where the city lies most open to assault,
the walls lower, easily overrun. Three times
they have tried that point, hoping to storm Troy,
their best fighters led by the Great and Little Ajax,
famous Idomeneus, Atreus' sons, valiant Diomedes.[18]   80
Perhaps a skilled prophet revealed the spot—
or their own fury whips them on to attack."
    And tall Hector nodded, his helmet flashing:
"All this weighs on my mind too, dear woman.
But I would die of shame to face the men of Troy   85
and the Trojan women trailing their long robes
if I would shrink from battle now, a coward.
Nor does the spirit urge me on that way.
I've learned it all too well. To stand up bravely,
always to fight in the front ranks of Trojan soldiers,   90
winning my father great glory, glory for myself.
For in my heart and soul I also know this well:

---

17. The goddess Artemis is Apollo's sister, the
daughter of Zeus and Leto.
18. Andromache names some of the major
Greek warriors; two were named Ajax, so

they were distinguished by the epithets
Great (for the Ajax who takes part in the
embassy to Achilles in Book 9) and Little.

the day will come when sacred Troy must die,
Priam must die and all his people with him,
Priam who hurls the strong ash spear. . .   95
                                         Even so,
it is less the pain of the Trojans still to come
that weighs me down, not even of Hecuba herself
or King Priam, or the thought that my own brothers
in all their numbers, all their gallant courage,
may tumble in the dust, crushed by enemies—   100
That is nothing, nothing beside your agony
when some brazen Argive hales you off in tears,
wrenching away your day of light and freedom!
Then far off in the land of Argos you must live,
laboring at a loom, at another woman's beck and call,   105
fetching water at some spring, Messeis or Hyperia,[19]
resisting it all the way—
the rough yoke of necessity at your neck.
And a man may say, who sees you streaming tears,
'There is the wife of Hector, the bravest fighter   110
they could field, those stallion-breaking Trojans,
long ago when the men fought for Troy.' So he will say
and the fresh grief will swell your heart once more,
widowed, robbed of the one man strong enough
to fight off your day of slavery.   115
                                    No, no,
let the earth come piling over my dead body
before I hear your cries, I hear you dragged away!"
    In the same breath, shining Hector reached down
for his son—but the boy recoiled,
cringing against his nurse's full breast,   120
screaming out at the sight of his own father,
terrified by the flashing bronze, the horsehair crest,
the great ridge of the helmet nodding, bristling terror—
so it struck his eyes. And his loving father laughed,
his mother laughed as well, and glorious Hector,   125
quickly lifting the helmet from his head,
set it down on the ground, fiery in the sunlight,
and raising his son he kissed him, tossed him in his arms,
lifting a prayer to Zeus and the other deathless gods:
"Zeus, all you immortals! Grant this boy, my son,   130
may be like me, first in glory among the Trojans,
strong and brave like me, and rule all Troy in power
and one day let them say, 'He is a better man than his father!'—

---

19. Messeis was a spring in Sparta, Hyperia in
    northern Greece.

when he comes home from battle bearing the bloody gear
of the mortal enemy he has killed in war—   135
a joy to his mother's heart."
                                So Hector prayed
and placed his son in the arms of his loving wife.
Andromache pressed the child to her scented breast,
smiling through her tears. Her husband noticed,
and filled with pity now, Hector stroked her gently,   140
trying to reassure her, repeating her name: "Andromache,
dear one, why so desperate? Why so much grief for me?
No man will hurl me down to Death, against my fate.
And fate? No one alive has ever escaped it,
neither brave man nor coward, I tell you—   145
it's born with us the day that we are born.
So please go home and tend to your own tasks,
the distaff and the loom, and keep the women
working hard as well. As for the fighting,
men will see to that, all who were born in Troy   150
but I most of all."
                                Hector aflash in arms
took up his horsechair-crested helmet once again.
And his loving wife went home, turning, glancing
back again and again and weeping live warm tears.
She quickly reached the sturdy house of Hector,   155
man-killing Hector,
and found her women gathered there inside
and stirred them all to a high pitch of mourning.
So in his house they raised the dirges for the dead,
for Hector still alive, his people were so convinced   160
that never again would he come home from battle,
never escape the Argives' rage and bloody hands.

[As Zeus fulfills the promise he made to Thetis in Book 1. The battle turns against the
Greeks—so much so that the Trojans are able to drive them back to their ships and encamp
in the plain nearby waiting to attack on the following day. The Greek leaders send an
embassy of three warriors—Odysseus, Ajax, and Achilles's old tutor Phoenix—to persuade
Achilles to rejoin the fighting. Odysseus enumerates a long list of gifts Agamemnon has
offered to bestow on Achilles (including marriage to Agamemnon's daughter) if he will return
to battle.]

Book 9 [The Embassy to Achilles]

The famous runner Achilles rose to his challenge:
"Royal son of Laertes, Odysseus, great tactician . . .
I must say what I have to say straight out,
must tell you how I feel and how all this will end—
so you won't crowd around me, one after another,   5
coaxing like a murmuring clutch of doves.

I hate that man like the very Gates of Death
who says one thing but hides another in his heart.
I will say it outright. That seems best to me.
Will Agamemnon win me over? Not for all the world,   10
I swear it—nor will the rest of the Achaeans.
No, what lasting thanks in the long run
for warring with our enemies, on and on, no end?
One and the same lot for the man who hangs back
and the man who battles hard. The same honor waits   15
for the coward and the brave. They both go down to Death,
the fighter who shirks, the one who works to exhaustion.
And what's laid up for me, what pittance? Nothing—
and after suffering hardships, year in, year out,
staking my life on the mortal risks of war.   20
    Like a mother bird hurrying morsels back
to her wingless young ones—whatever she can catch—
but it's all starvation wages for herself.
                        So for me.
Many a sleepless night I've bivouacked in harness,
day after bloody day I've hacked my passage through,   25
fighting other soldiers to win their wives as prizes.
Twelve cities of men I've stormed and sacked from shipboard,
eleven I claim by land, on the fertile earth of Troy.
And from all I dragged off piles of splendid plunder,
hauled it away and always gave the lot to Agamemnon,   30
that son of Atreus—always skulking behind the lines,
safe in his fast ships—and he would take it all,
he'd parcel out some scraps but keep the lion's share.
Some he'd hand to the lords and kings—prizes of honor—
and they, they hold them still. From me alone, Achilles   35
of all Achaeans, he seizes, he keeps the wife I love . . .
Well *let* him bed her now—
enjoy her to the hilt!
                        Why must we battle Trojans,
men of Argos? Why did he muster an army, lead us here,
that son of Atreus? Why, why in the world if not   40
for Helen with her loose and lustrous hair?
Are *they* the only men alive who love their wives,
those sons of Atreus? Never! Any decent man,
a man with sense, loves his own, cares for his own
as deeply as I, I loved that woman with all my heart,   45
though I won her like a trophy with my spear . . .
But now that he's torn my honor from my hands,
robbed me, lied to me—don't let him try me now.
I know *him* too well—he'll never win me over!
                        No, Odysseus,

let him rack his brains with you and the other captains   50
how to fight the raging fire off the ships. Look—
what a mighty piece of work he's done without *me!*
Why, he's erected a rampart, driven a trench around it,
broad, enormous, and planted stakes to guard it. No use!
He still can't block the power of man-killing Hector!   55
No, though as long as I fought on Achaea's lines
Hector had little lust to charge beyond his walls,
never ventured beyond the Scaean Gates and oak tree.
There he stood up to me alone one day—
and barely escaped my onslaught.   60
                      Ah but now,
since I have no desire to battle glorious Hector,
tomorrow at daybreak, once I have sacrificed
to Zeus and all the gods and loaded up my holds
and launched out on the breakers—watch, my friend,
if you'll take the time and care to see me off,   65
and you will see my squadrons sail at dawn,
fanning out on the Hellespont that swarms with fish,
my crews manning the oarlocks, rowing out with a will,
and if the famed god of the earthquake grants us safe passage,
the third day out we raise the dark rich soil of Phthia.   70
There lies my wealth, hoards of it, all I left behind
when I sailed to Troy on this, this insane voyage—
and still more hoards from here: gold, ruddy bronze,
women sashed and lovely, and gleaming gray iron,
and I will haul it home, all I won as plunder.   75
All but my prize of honor . . .
he who gave that prize has snatched it back again—
what outrage! That high and mighty King Agamemnon,
that son of Atreus!
                      Go back and tell him all,
all I say—out in the open too—so other Achaeans   80
can wheel on him in anger if he still hopes—
who knows?—to deceive some other comrade.
                                    Shameless,
inveterate—armored in shamelessness! Dog that he is,
he'd never dare to look me straight in the eyes again.
No, I'll never set heads together with that man—   85
no planning in common, no taking common action.
He cheated me, did me damage, wrong! But never again,
he'll never rob me blind with his twisting words again!
Once is enough for him. Die and be damned for all I care!
Zeus who rules the world has ripped his wits away.   90
His gifts, I loathe his gifts . . .
I wouldn't give you a splinter for that man!

Not if he gave me ten times as much, twenty times over, all
he possesses now, and all that could pour in from the world's end—
not all the wealth that's freighted into Orchomenos,[20] even into Thebes,   95
Egyptian Thebes[21] where the houses overflow with the greatest troves of treasure.
Thebes with the hundred gates and through each gate battalions,
two hundred fighters surge to war with teams and chariots—
no, not if his gifts outnumbered all the grains of sand
and dust in the earth—no, not even then could Agamemnon   100
bring my fighting spirit round until he pays me back,
pays full measure for all his heartbreaking outrage!
   His daughter . . . I will marry no daughter of Agamemnon.
Not if she rivaled Aphrodite in all her golden glory,
not if she matched the crafts of clear-eyed Athena,   105
not even then would I make *her* my wife! No,
let her father pitch on some other Argive—
one who can please *him,* a greater king than I.
If the gods pull me through and I reach home alive,
Peleus needs no help to fetch a bride for me himself.   110
Plenty of Argive women wait in Hellas and in Phthia,
daughters of lords who rule their citadels in power.
Whomever I want I'll make my cherished wife—at home.
Time and again my fiery spirit drove me to win a wife,
a fine partner to please my heart, to enjoy with her   115
the treasures my old father Peleus piled high.
I say no wealth is worth my life! Not all they claim
was stored in the depths of Troy, that city built on riches,
in the old days of peace before the sons of Achaea came—
not all the gold held fast in the Archer's rocky vaults,   120
in Phoebus Apollo's house on Pytho's sheer cliffs!
Cattle and fat sheep can all be had for the raiding,
tripods all for the trading, and tawny-headed stallions.
But a man's life breath cannot come back again—
no raiders in force, no trading brings it back,   125
once it slips through a man's clenched teeth.
                       Mother tells me,
the immortal goddess Thetis with her glistening feet,
that two fates bear me on to the day of death.
If I hold out here and I lay siege to Troy,
my journey home is gone, but my glory never dies.   130
If I voyage back to the fatherland I love,
my pride, my glory dies . . .

---

20. A city in Boeotia in central Greece, famous
for its wealth in the Mycenaean period (c.
1400–1200 B.C.E.), centuries before the
Iliad was sung in its present form.

21. The *Iliad* preserves the ancient memory of
this Egyptian city's prosperity and power,
at their height not later than the 14th
century B.C.E.

true, but the life that's left me will be long,
the stroke of death will not come on me quickly.
    One thing more. To the rest I'd pass on this advice: 135
sail home now! You will never set your eyes
on the day of doom that topples looming Troy.
Thundering Zeus has spread his hands above her—
her armies have taken heart!
                      So you go back
to the great men of Achaea. You report my message—   140
since this is the privilege of senior chiefs—
let *them* work out a better plan of action,
use their imaginations now to save the ships
and Achaea's armies pressed to their hollow hulls.
This maneuver will never work for them, this scheme   145
they hatched for the moment as I raged on and on.

[Agamemnon's lavish offer fails to persuade Achilles to reenter the battle, although the embassy's appeals to him on the basis of friendship have their effect; he will not leave Troy as he had threatened, but he refuses to fight until enemy fire comes to his own ships. The Greeks continue to suffer increasingly drastic reverses, until finally, with many of their major fighters wounded and with the Trojans menacing their ships, Patroclus tries to convince Achilles to rejoin the fighting.]

Book 16 [Patroclus Fights and Dies]

So they fought to the death around that benched beaked ship
as Patroclus reached Achilles, his great commander,
and wept warm tears like a dark spring running down
some desolate rock face, its shaded currents flowing.
And the brilliant runner Achilles saw him coming,   5
filled with pity and spoke out winging words:
"Why in tears, Patroclus?
Like a girl, a baby running after her mother,
begging to be picked up, and she tugs her skirts,
holding her back as she tries to hurry off—all tears,   10
fawning up at her, till she takes her in her arms . . .
That's how you look, Patroclus, streaming live tears.
But why? Some news for the Myrmidons, news for me?
Some message from Phthia that you alone have heard?
They tell me Menoetius,[22] Actor's son, is still alive,   15
and Peleus, Aeacus' son, lives on among his Myrmidons—
if both our fathers had died, we'd have some cause for grief.
Or weeping over the Argives, are you? Seeing them die
against the hollow ships, repaid for their offenses?

---

22. Patroclus's father.

Out with it now! Don't harbor it deep inside you.   20
We must share it all."
                   With a wrenching groan
you answered your friend, Patroclus O my rider:
"Achilles, son of Peleus, greatest of the Achaeans,
spare me your anger, please—
such heavy blows have overwhelmed the troops.   25
Our former champions, all laid up in the ships,
all are hit by arrows or run through by spears.
There's powerful Diomedes brought down by an archer,
Odysseus wounded, and Agamemnon too, the famous spearman,
and Eurypylus took an arrow-shot in the thigh . . .   30
Healers are working over them, using all their drugs,
trying to bind the wounds—
                  But *you* are intractable, Achilles!
Pray god such anger never seizes *me,* such rage you nurse.
Cursed in your own courage! What good will a man,
even one in the next generation, get from you   35
unless you defend the Argives from disaster?
You heart of iron! He was not your father,
the horseman Peleus—Thetis was not your mother.
Never. The salt gray sunless ocean gave you birth
and the towering blank rocks—your temper's so relentless.   40
But still, if down deep some prophecy makes you balk,
some doom your noble mother revealed to you from Zeus,
well and good: at least send *me* into battle, quickly.
Let the whole Myrmidon army follow my command—
I might bring some light of victory to our Argives!   45
And give me your own fine armor to buckle on my back,
so the Trojans might take *me* for you, Achilles, yes,
hold off from attack, and Achaea's fighting sons
get second wind, exhausted as they are . . .
Breathing room in war is all too brief.   50
We're fresh, unbroken. The enemy's battle-weary—
we could roll those broken Trojans back to Troy,
clear of the ships and shelters!"
                  So he pleaded,
lost in his own great innocence . . .
condemned to beg for his own death and brutal doom.   55
And moved now to his depths, the famous runner cried,
"No, no, my prince, Patroclus, what are you saying?
Prophecies? None that touch me. None I know of.
No doom my noble mother revealed to me from Zeus,
just this terrible pain that wounds me to the quick—   60
when one man attempts to plunder a man his equal,
to commandeer a prize, exulting so in his own power.

That's the pain that wounds me, suffering such humiliation.
That girl—the sons of Achaea picked her as my prize,
and I'd sacked a walled city, won her with my spear   65
but right from my grasp he tears her, mighty Agamemnon,
that son of Atreus! Treating me like some vagabond,
some outcast stripped of all my rights . . .
                                        Enough.
Let bygones be bygones now. Done is done.
How on earth can a man rage on forever?   70
Still, by god, I said I would not relax my anger,
not till the cries and carnage reached my own ships.
So you, you strap my splendid armor on your back,
you lead our battle-hungry Myrmidons into action!—
if now, in fact, the black cloud of the Trojans   75
blasts down on the ships with full gale force,
our backs to the breaking surf but clinging still
to a cramped strip of land—the Argives, lost.
The whole city of Troy comes trampling down on us,
daring, wild—why? They cannot see the brow of my helmet   80
flash before their eyes—Oh they'd soon run for their lives
and choke the torrent-beds of the field with all their corpses
if only the mighty Agamemnon met me with respect:
now, as it is, they're fighting round our camp!
No spear rages now in the hand of Diomedes,   85
keen to save the Argives from disaster . . .
I can't even hear the battle cry of Agamemnon
break from his hated skull. But it's man-killing Hector
calling his Trojans on, his war cries crashing round me,
savage cries of his Trojans sweeping the whole plain,   90
victors bringing the Argive armies to their knees.
Even so, Patroclus, fight disaster off the ships,
fling yourself at the Trojans full force—
before they gut our hulls with leaping fire
and tear away the beloved day of our return.   95
But take this command to heart—obey it to the end.
So you can win great honor, great glory for me
in the eyes of all the Argive ranks, and they,
they'll send her back, my lithe and lovely girl,
and top it off with troves of glittering gifts.   100
Once you have whipped the enemy from the fleet
you must come back, Patroclus. Even if Zeus
the thundering lord of Hera lets you seize your glory,
you must not burn for war against these Trojans,
madmen lusting for battle—not without *me*—   105
you will only make *my* glory that much less . . .
You must not, lost in the flush and fire of triumph,

slaughtering Trojans outright, drive your troops to Troy—
what if one of the gods who never die comes down
from Olympus heights to intervene in battle?   110
The deadly Archer loves his Trojans dearly.
No, you must turn back—
soon as you bring the light of victory to the ships.
Let the rest of them cut themselves to pieces on the plain!
Oh would to god—Father Zeus, Athena and lord Apollo—   115
not one of all these Trojans could flee his death, not one,
no Argive either, but we could stride from the slaughter
so we could bring Troy's hallowed crown of towers
toppling down around us—you and I alone!"

But Achilles strode back to his shelter now   120
and opened the lid of the princely inlaid sea chest
that glistening-footed Thetis stowed in his ship to carry,
filled to the brim with war-shirts, windproof cloaks
and heavy fleecy rugs. And there it rested . . .
his handsome, well-wrought cup. No other man   125
would drink the shining wine from its glowing depths,
nor would Achilles pour the wine to any other god,
none but Father Zeus. Lifting it from the chest
he purified it with sulphur crystals first
then rinsed it out with water running clear,   130
washed his hands and filled it bright with wine.
And then, taking a stand before his lodge, he prayed,
pouring the wine to earth and scanning the high skies
and the god who loves the lightning never missed a word:
"King Zeus—Pelasgian Zeus,[23] lord of Dodona's holy shrine, 135
dwelling far away, brooding over Dodona's bitter winters!
Your prophets dwelling round you, Zeus, the Selli
sleeping along the ground with unwashed feet . . .
If you honored me last time and heard my prayer
and rained destruction down on all Achaea's ranks,   140
now, once more, I beg you, bring my prayer to pass!
I myself hold out on shore with the beached ships here
but I send my comrade forth to war with troops of Myrmidons—
Launch glory along with him, high lord of thunder, Zeus!
Fill his heart with courage—so even Hector learns   145
if Patroclus has the skill to fight his wars alone,
my friend-in-arms, or his hands can rage unvanquished
only when *I* go wading in and face the grind of battle.

---

23. Pelasgian is a name used elsewhere in the
poem to denote the region of Achilles's
home in northern Greece; in the west of
that region, in Dodona, was an ancient
oracle of Zeus. The Selloi seem to have
been the priests of Zeus at Dodona.

But once he repels the roaring onslaught from the ships
let him come back to me and our fast fleet—unharmed—   150
with all my armor round him, all our comrades
fighting round my friend!"
                          So Achilles prayed
and Zeus in all his wisdom heard those prayers.
One prayer the Father granted, the other he denied:
Patroclus would drive the onslaught off the ships—   155
that much Zeus granted, true,
but denied him safe and sound return from battle.

[After Achilles agrees to let Patroclus enter the battle wearing Achilles's armor, Patroclus
valiantly manages to turn the battle against the Trojans but is killed by Hector with
assistance from Apollo. Hector strips Achilles's armor from Patroclus's body. Bitter fighting
ensues over the body, and the news of Patroclus's death is brought to Achilles.]

Book 18 [The Shield of Achilles]

So the men fought on like a mass of whirling fire
as swift Antilochus[24] raced the message toward Achilles.
Sheltered under his curving, beaked ships he found him,
foreboding, deep down, all that had come to pass.
Agonizing now he probed his own great heart: 5
"Why, why? Our long-haired Achaeans routed again,
driven in terror off the plain to crowd the ships, but why?
Dear gods, don't bring to pass the grief that haunts my heart—
the prophecy that mother revealed to me one time . . .
she said the best of the Myrmidons—while I lived—   10
would fall at Trojan hands and leave the light of day.
And now he's dead, I know it. Menoetius' gallant son,
my headstrong friend! And I told Patroclus clearly,
'Once you have beaten off the lethal fire, quick,
come back to the ships—you must not battle Hector!'"   15
    As such fears went churning through his mind
the warlord Nestor's son drew near him now,
streaming warm tears, to give the dreaded message:
"Ah son of royal Peleus, what you must hear from me!
What painful news—would to god it had never happened!   20
Patroclus has fallen. They're fighting over his corpse.
He's stripped, naked—Hector with that flashing helmet,
Hector has your arms!"
                          So the captain reported.
A black cloud of grief came shrouding over Achilles.
Both hands clawing the ground for soot and filth,   25

---

24. A Greek warrior, son of Nestor and friend
    of Achilles.

he poured it over his head, fouled his handsome face
and black ashes settled onto his fresh clean war-shirt.
Overpowered in all his power, sprawled in the dust,
Achilles lay there, fallen . . .
tearing his hair, defiling it with his own hands.   30
And the women he and Patroclus carried off as captives
caught the grief in their hearts and keened and wailed,
out of the tents they ran to ring the great Achilles,
all of them beat their breasts with clenched fists,
sank to the ground, each woman's knees gave way.   35
Antilochus kneeling near, weeping uncontrollably,
clutched Achilles' hands as he wept his proud heart out—
for fear he would slash his throat with an iron blade.
Achilles suddenly loosed a terrible, wrenching cry
and his noble mother heard him, seated near her father,   40
the Old Man of the Sea in the salt green depths,
and she cried out in turn. And immortal sea-nymphs
gathered round their sister, all the Nereids[25] dwelling
down the sounding depths, they all came rushing now—
Glitter, blossoming Spray and the swells' Embrace,   45
Fair-Isle and shadowy Cavern, Mist and Spindrift,
ocean nymphs of the glances pooling deep and dark,
Race-with-the-Waves and Headlands' Hope and Safe Haven,
Glimmer of Honey, Suave-and-Soothing, Whirlpool, Brilliance,
Bounty and First Light and Speeder of Ships and buoyant Power,   50
Welcome Home and Bather of Meadows and Master's Lovely Consort,
Gift of the Sea, Eyes of the World and the famous milk-white Calm
and Truth and Never-Wrong and the queen who rules the tides in beauty
and in rushed Glory and Healer of Men and the one who rescues kings
and Sparkler, Down-from-the-Cliffs, sleek-haired Strands of Sand   55
and all the rest of the Nereids dwelling down the depths.
The silver cave was shimmering full of sea-nymphs,
all in one mounting chorus beating their breasts
as Thetis launched the dirge: "Hear me, sisters,
daughters of Nereus, so you all will know it well—   60
listen to all the sorrows welling in my heart!
I am agony—
                    mother of grief and greatness—O my child!
Yes, I gave birth to a flawless, mighty son . . .
the splendor of heroes, and he shot up like a young branch,
like a fine tree I reared him—the orchard's crowning glory—   65
but only to send him off in the beaked ships to Troy
to battle Trojans! Never again will I embrace him

---

25. Thetis's sisters, daughters of the sea-god
    Nereus. Many of their names are etymo-
    logically related to, or descriptive of,
    different aspects of the sea, as the literal
    translation of them here makes clear.

striding home through the doors of Peleus' house.
And long as I have him with me, still alive,
looking into the sunlight, he is racked with anguish.   70
And I, I go to his side—nothing I do can help him.
Nothing. But go I shall, to see my darling boy,
to hear what grief has come to break his heart
while he holds back from battle."
                So Thetis cried
as she left the cave and her sisters swam up with her,   75
all in a tide of tears, and billowing round them now
the ground swell heaved open. And once they reached
the fertile land of Troy they all streamed ashore,
row on row in a long cortege, the sea-nymphs
filing up where the Myrmidon ships lay hauled,   80
clustered closely round the great runner Achilles . . .
As he groaned from the depths his mother rose before him
and sobbing a sharp cry, cradled her son's head in her hands
and her words were all compassion, winging pity: "My child—
why in tears? What sorrow has touched your heart?   85
Tell me, please. Don't harbor it deep inside you.
Zeus has accomplished everything you wanted,
just as you raised your hands and prayed that day.
All the sons of Achaea are pinned against the ships
and all for want of you—they suffer shattering losses."   90
    And groaning deeply the matchless runner answered,
"O dear mother, true! All those burning desires
Olympian Zeus has brought to pass for me—
but what joy to me now? My dear comrade's dead—
Patroclus—the man I loved beyond all other comrades,   95
loved as my own life—I've lost him—Hector's killed him,
stripped the gigantic armor off his back, a marvel to behold—
my burnished gear! Radiant gifts the gods presented Peleus
that day they drove you into a mortal's marriage bed . . .
I wish you'd lingered deep with the deathless sea-nymphs,   100
lived at ease, and Peleus carried home a mortal bride.
But now, as it is, sorrows, unending sorrows must surge
within your heart as well—for your own son's death.
Never again will you embrace him striding home.
My spirit rebels—I've lost the will to live,   105
to take my stand in the world of men—unless,
before all else, Hector's battered down by my spear
and gasps away his life, the blood-price for Patroclus,
Menoetius' gallant son he's killed and stripped!"
    But Thetis answered, warning through her tears,   110
"You're doomed to a short life, my son, from all you say!
For hard on the heels of Hector's death your death

must come at once—"
                    "Then let me die at once"—
Achilles burst out, despairing—"since it was not my fate
to save my dearest comrade from his death! Look,   115
a world away from his fatherland he's perished,
lacking me, my fighting strength, to defend him.
But now, since I shall not return to my fatherland . . .
nor did I bring one ray of hope to my Patroclus,
nor to the rest of all my steadfast comrades,   120
countless ranks struck down by mighty Hector—
No, no, here I sit by the ships . . .
a useless, dead weight on the good green earth—
I, no man my equal among the bronze-armed Achaeans,
not in battle, only in wars of words that others win.   125
If only strife could die from the lives of gods and men
and anger that drives the sanest man to flare in outrage—
bitter gall, sweeter than dripping streams of honey,
that swarms in people's chests and blinds like smoke—
just like the anger Agamemnon king of men   130
has roused within me now . . .
                    Enough.
Let bygones be bygones. Done is done.
Despite my anguish I will beat it down,
the fury mounting inside me, down by force.
But now I'll go and meet that murderer head-on,   135
that Hector who destroyed the dearest life I know.
For my own death, I'll meet it freely—whenever Zeus
and the other deathless gods would like to bring it on!
Not even Heracles fled his death, for all his power,
favorite son as he was to Father Zeus the King.   140
Fate crushed him, and Hera's savage anger.[26]
And I too, if the same fate waits for me . . .
I'll lie in peace, once I've gone down to death.
But now, for the moment, let me seize great glory!—
and drive some woman of Troy or deep-breasted Dardan[27]   145
to claw with both hands at her tender cheeks and wipe away
her burning tears as the sobs come choking from her throat—
they'll learn that I refrained from war a good long time!
Don't try to hold me back from the fighting, mother,
love me as you do. You can't persuade me now."   150

[Thetis travels to Olympus to ask the divine craftsman Hephaestus to make armor for
Achilles, to replace that worn by Patroclus and stripped from his body by Hector.]

---

26. Hera hated Zeus's son Heracles because he
    was born to a mortal woman, Alcmene,
    whom Zeus had seduced.

27. The Dardanians were neighbors and allies
    of the Trojans, related to them through
    their ancestor Dardanus.

. . . Thetis burst into tears, her voice welling:
"Oh Hephaestus—who of all the goddesses on Olympus,
who has borne such withering sorrows in her heart?
Such pain as Zeus has given me, above all others!
Me out of all the daughters of the sea he chose   5
to yoke to a mortal man, Peleus, son of Aeacus,
and I endured his bed, a mortal's bed, resisting
with all my will. And now he lies in the halls,
broken with grisly age, but now my griefs are worse.
Remember? Zeus also gave me a son to bear and breed,   10
the splendor of heroes, and he shot up like a young branch,
like a fine tree I reared him—the orchard's crowning glory—
but only to send him off in the beaked ships to Troy
to battle Trojans! Never again will I embrace him
striding home through the doors of Peleus' house.   15
And long as I have him with me, still alive,
looking into the sunlight, he is racked with anguish.
I go to his side—nothing I do can help him. Nothing.
That girl the sons of Achaea picked out for his prize—
right from his grasp the mighty Agamemnon tore her,   20
and grief for her has been gnawing at his heart.
But then the Trojans pinned the Achaeans tight
against their sterns, they gave them no way out,
and the Argive warlords begged my son to help,
they named in full the troves of glittering gifts   25
they'd send his way. But at that point he refused
to beat disaster off—refused himself, that is—
but he buckled his own armor round Patroclus,
sent him into battle with an army at his back.
And all day long they fought at the Scaean Gates,   30
that very day they would have stormed the city too,
if Apollo had not killed Menoetius' gallant son
as he laid the Trojans low—Apollo cut him down
among the champions there and handed Hector glory.
So now I come, I throw myself at your knees,   35
please help me! Give my son—he won't live long—
a shield and helmet and tooled greaves with ankle-straps
and armor for his chest. All that he had was lost,
lost when the Trojans killed his steadfast friend.
Now he lies on the ground—his heart is breaking."   40

And the famous crippled Smith[28] replied, "Courage!
Anguish for all that armor—sweep it from your mind.

---

28. Different myths give differing accounts of
the lameness of Hephaestus, god of the
forge; either he was lame from birth or as
a result of having been thrown from
Olympus by Zeus or Hera.

If only I could hide him away from pain and death,
that day his grim destiny comes to take Achilles,
as surely as glorious armor shall be his, armor   45
that any man in the world of men will marvel at
through all the years to come—whoever sees its splendor."

  With that he left her there and made for his bellows,
turning them on the fire, commanding, "Work—to work!"
And the bellows, all twenty, blew on the crucibles,   50
breathing with all degrees of shooting, fiery heat
as the god hurried on—a blast for the heavy work,
a quick breath for the light, all precisely gauged
to the god of fire's wish and the pace of the work in hand.
Bronze he flung in the blaze, tough, durable bronze   55
and tin and priceless gold and silver, and then,
planting the huge anvil upon its block, he gripped
his mighty hammer in one hand, the other gripped his tongs.
  And first Hephaestus makes a great and massive shield,
blazoning well-wrought emblems all across its surface,   60
raising a rim around it, glittering, triple-ply
with a silver shield-strap run from edge to edge
and five layers of metal to build the shield itself,
and across its vast expanse with all his craft and cunning
the god creates a world of gorgeous immortal work.   65
  There he made the earth and there the sky and the sea
and the inexhaustible blazing sun and the moon rounding full
and there the constellations, all that crown the heavens,
the Pleiades and the Hyades, Orion in all his power too
and the Great Bear[29] that mankind also calls the Wagon: 70
she wheels on her axis always fixed, watching Orion,
and she alone is denied a plunge in the Ocean's baths.
  And he forged on the shield two noble cities filled
with mortal men. With weddings and wedding feasts in one
and under glowing torches they brought forth the brides   75
from the women's chambers, marching through the streets
while choir on choir the wedding song rose high
and the young men came dancing, whirling round in rings
and among them the flutes and harps kept up their stirring call—
women rushed to the doors and each stood moved with wonder.   80
And the people massed, streaming into the marketplace
where a quarrel had broken out and two men struggled
over the blood-price for a kinsman just murdered.
One declaimed in public, vowing payment in full—
the other spurned him, he would not take a thing—   85
so both men pressed for a judge to cut the knot.

---

29. The "Big Dipper."

The crowd cheered on both, they took both sides,
but heralds held them back as the city elders sat
on polished stone benches, forming the sacred circle,
grasping in hand the staffs of clear-voiced heralds,   90
and each leapt to his feet to plead the case in turn.
Two bars of solid gold shone on the ground before them;
a prize for the judge who'd speak the straightest verdict.
     But circling the other city camped a divided army
gleaming in battle-gear, and two plans split their ranks: 95
to plunder the city or share the riches with its people,
hoards the handsome citadel stored within its depths.
But the people were not surrendering, not at all.
They armed for a raid, hoping to break the siege—
loving wives and innocent children standing guard   100
on the ramparts, flanked by elders bent with age
as men marched out to war. Ares[30] and Pallas led them,
both burnished gold, gold the attire they donned, and great,
magnificent in their armor—gods for all the world,
looming up in their brillance, towering over troops.   105
And once they reached the perfect spot for attack,
a watering place where all the herds collected,
there they crouched, wrapped in glowing bronze.
Detached from the ranks, two scouts took up their posts,
the eyes of the army waiting to spot a convoy,   110
the enemy's flocks and crook-horned cattle coming . . .
Come they did, quickly, two shepherds behind them,
playing their hearts out on their pipes—treachery
never crossed their minds. But the soldiers saw them,
rushed them, cut off at a stroke the herds of oxen   115
and sleek sheep-flocks glistening silver-gray
and killed the herdsmen too. Now the besiegers,
soon as they heard the uproar burst from the cattle
as they debated, huddled in council, mounted at once
behind their racing teams, rode hard to the rescue,   120
arrived at once, and lining up for assault
both armies battled it out along he river banks—
they raked each other with hurtling bronze-tipped spears.
And Strife and Havoc plunged in the fight, and violent Death—
now seizing a man alive with fresh wounds, now one unhurt,   125
now hauling a dead man through the slaughter by the heels,
the cloak on her back stained red with human blood.
So they clashed and fought like living, breathing men
grappling each other's corpses, dragging off the dead.
     And he forged a fallow field, broad rich plowland   130

---

30. The god of war.

tilled for the third time, and across it crews of plowmen
wheeled their teams, driving them up and back and soon
as they'd reach the end-strip, moving into the turn,
a man would run up quickly
and hand them a cup of honeyed, mellow wine   135
as the crews would turn back down along the furrows,
pressing again to reach the end of the deep fallow field
and the earth churned black behind them, like earth churning,
solid gold as it was—that was the wonder of Hephaestus' work.

   And he forged a king's estate where harvesters labored,   140
reaping the ripe grain, swinging their whetted scythes.
Some stalks fell in line with the reapers, row on row,
and others the sheaf-binders girded round with ropes,
three binders standing over the sheaves, behind them
boys gathering up the cut swaths, filling their arms,   145
supplying grain to the binders, endless bundles.
And there in the midst the king,
scepter in hand at the head of the reaping-rows,
stood tall in silence, rejoicing in his heart.
And off to the side, beneath a spreading oak,   150
the heralds were setting out the harvest feast,
they were dressing a great ox they had slaughtered,
while attendant women poured out barley, generous,
glistening handfuls strewn for the reapers' midday meal.

   And he forged a thriving vineyard loaded with clusters,   155
bunches of lustrous grapes in gold, ripening deep purple
and climbing vines shot up on silver vine-poles.
And round it he cut a ditch in dark blue enamel
and round the ditch he staked a fence in tin.
And one lone footpath led toward the vineyard   160
and down it the pickers ran
whenever they went to strip the grapes at vintage—
girls and boys, their hearts leaping in innocence,
bearing away the sweet ripe fruit in wicker baskets.
And there among them a young boy plucked his lyre,   165
so clear it could break the heart with longing,
and what he sang was a dirge for the dying year,
lovely . . . his fine voice rising and falling low
as the rest followed, all together, frisking, singing,
shouting, their dancing footsteps beating out the time.   170

   And he forged on the shield a herd of longhorn cattle,
working the bulls in beaten gold and tin, lowing loud
and rumbling out of the farmyard dung to pasture
along a rippling stream, along the swaying reeds.
And the golden drovers kept the herd in line,   175
four in all, with nine dogs at their heels,

their paws flickering quickly—a savage roar!—
a crashing attack—and a pair of ramping lions
had seized a bull from the cattle's front ranks—
he bellowed out as they dragged him off in agony.   180
Packs of dogs and the young herdsmen rushed to help
but the lions ripping open the hide of the huge bull
were gulping down the guts and the black pooling blood
while the herdsmen yelled the fast pack on—no use.
The hounds shrank from sinking teeth in the lions,   185
they balked, hunching close, barking, cringing away.
    And the famous crippled Smith forged a meadow
deep in a shaded glen for shimmering flocks to graze,
with shepherds' steadings, well-roofed huts and sheepfolds.
    And the crippled Smith brought all his art to bear   190
on a dancing circle, broad as the circle Daedalus[31]
once laid out on Cnossos spacious fields
for Ariadne the girl with lustrous hair.
Here young boys and girls, beauties courted
with costly gifts of oxen, danced and danced,   195
linking their arms, gripping each other's wrists.
And the girls wore robes of linen light and flowing,
the boys wore finespun tunics rubbed with a gloss of oil,
the girls were crowned with a bloom of fresh garlands,
the boys swung golden daggers hung on silver belts.   200
And now they would run in rings on their skilled feet,
nimbly, quick as a crouching potter spins his wheel,
palming it smoothly, giving it practice twirls
to see it run, and now they would run in rows,
in rows crisscrossing rows—rapturous dancing.   205
A breathless crowd stood round them struck with joy
and through them a pair of tumblers dashed and sprang,
whirling in leaping handsprings, leading out the dance.
    And he forged the Ocean River's mighty power girdling
round the outmost rim of the welded indestructible shield.   210
    And once the god had made that great and massive shield
he made Achilles a breastplate brighter than gleaming fire,
he made him a sturdy helmet to fit the fighter's temples,
beautiful, burnished work, and raised its golden crest
and made him greaves of flexing, pliant tin.   215
                                    Now,
when the famous crippled Smith had finished off
that grand array of armor, lifting it in his arms
he laid it all at the feet of Achilles' mother Thetis—

---

31. Master craftsman, famous in myth for his
    elaborate constructions designed for the
    family of King Minos of Crete, Ariadne's
    father, in the chief Cretan city, Cnossos.

and down she flashed like a hawk from snowy Mount Olympus
bearing the brilliant gear, the god of fire's gift.   220

[Armed with the weapons forged for him by Hephaestus, Achilles returns to battle,
slaughtering numerous Trojans in revenge for the killing of Patroclus. Apollo, always a Trojan
partisan, diverts Achilles's relentless pursuit by taking the form of a Trojan warrior in order
to draw Achilles away from the rest of the retreating Trojans, all of whom flee into the
city—except Hector, who remains outside the walls.]

Book 22 [The Death of Hector]

So all through Troy the men who had fled like panicked fawns
were wiping off their sweat, drinking away their thirst,
leaning along the city's massive ramparts now
while Achaean troops, sloping shields to shoulders,
closed against the walls. But there stood Hector,   5
shackled fast by his deadly fate, holding his ground,
exposed in front of Troy and the Scaean Gates.
And now Apollo turned to taunt Achilles:
"Why are you chasing *me*? Why waste your speed?—
son of Peleus, you a mortal and I a deathless god.   10
You still don't know that I am immortal, do you?—
straining to catch me in your fury! Have you forgotten?
There's a war to fight with the Trojans you stampeded,
look, they're packed inside their city walls, but you,
you've slipped away out here. You can't kill *me*—   15
I can never die—it's not my fate!"
                                   Enraged at that,
Achilles shouted in mid-stride, "You've blocked my way,
you distant, deadly Archer, deadliest god of all—
you made me swerve away from the rampart there.
Else what a mighty Trojan army had gnawed the dust   20
before they could ever straggle through their gates!
Now you've robbed me of great glory, saved their lives
with all your deathless ease. Nothing for you to fear,
no punishment to come. Oh I'd pay you back
if I only had the power at my command!"   25
    No more words—he dashed toward the city,
heart racing for some great exploit, rushing on
like a champion stallion drawing a chariot full tilt,
sweeping across the plain in easy, tearing strides—
so Achilles hurtled on, driving legs and knees.   30
    And old King Priam was first to see him coming,
surging over the plain, blazing like the star
that rears at harvest, flaming up in its brilliance,—
far outshining the countless stars in the night sky,

that star they call Orion's Dog[32]—brightest of all
but a fatal sign emblazoned on the heavens,
it brings such killing fever down on wretched men.
So the bronze flared on his chest as on he raced—
and the old man moaned, flinging both hands high,
beating his head and groaning deep he called,   40
begging his dear son who stood before the gates,
unshakable, furious to fight Achilles to the death.
The old man cried, pitifully, hands reaching out to him,
"Oh Hector! Don't just stand there, don't, dear child,
waiting that man's attack—alone, cut off from friends!   45
You'll meet your doom at once, beaten down by Achilles,
so much stronger than you—that hard, headlong man.
Oh if only the gods loved him as much as I do . . .
dogs and vultures would eat his fallen corpse at once!—
with what a load of misery lifted from my spirit.   50
That man who robbed me of many sons, brave boys,
cutting them down or selling them off as slaves,
shipped to islands half the world away . . . .
Even now there are two, Lycaon and Polydorus[33]—
I cannot find them among the soldiers crowding Troy,   55
those sons Laothoë bore me, Laothoë queen of women.
But if they are still alive in the enemy's camp,
then we'll ransom them back with bronze and gold.
We have hoards inside the walls, the rich dowry
old and famous Altes presented with his daughter.   60
But if they're dead already, gone to the House of Death,
what grief to their mother's heart and mine—we gave them life.
For the rest of Troy, though, just a moment's grief
unless you too are battered down by Achilles.
Back, come back! Inside the walls, my boy!   65
Rescue the men of Troy and the Trojan women—
don't hand the great glory to Peleus' son,
bereft of your own sweet life yourself.
                                    Pity me too!—
still in my senses, true, but a harrowed, broken man
marked out by doom—past the threshold of old age   70
and Father Zeus will waste me with a hideous fate,
and after I've lived to look on so much horror!
My sons laid low, my daughters dragged away
and the treasure-chambers looted, helpless babies
hurled to the earth in the red barbarity of war . . .   75

---

32. Also called Sirius, the brightest star in the late summer sky.
33. These sons of Priam were killed by Achilles, Polydorus in Book 20 and Lycaon in Book 21.

my sons' wives hauled off by the Argives' bloody hands!
And I, I last of all—the dog before my doors
will eat me raw, once some enemy brings me down
with his sharp bronze sword or spits me with a spear,
wrenching the life out of my body, yes, the very dogs   80
I bred in my own halls to share my table, guard my gates—
mad, rabid at heart they'll lap their master's blood
and loll before my doors.
                         Ah for a young man
all looks fine and noble if he goes down in war,
hacked to pieces under a slashing bronze blade—   85
he lies there dead . . . but whatever death lays bare,
all wounds are marks of glory. When an old man's killed
and the dogs go at the gray head and the gray beard
and mutilate the genitals—that is the cruelest sight
in all our wretched lives!"   90
                       So the old man groaned
and seizing his gray hair tore it out by the roots
but he could not shake the fixed resolve of Hector.
And his mother wailed now, standing beside Priam,
weeping freely, loosing her robes with one hand
and holding out her bare breast with the other,   95
her words pouring forth in a flight of grief and tears:
"Hector, my child! Look—have some respect for *this*!
Pity your mother too, if I ever gave you the breast
to soothe your troubles, remember it now, dear boy—
beat back that savage man from safe inside the walls!   100
Don't go forth, a champion pitted against him—
merciless, brutal man. If he kills you now,
how can I ever mourn you on your deathbed?—
dear branch in bloom, dear child I brought to birth!—
Neither I nor your wife, that warm, generous woman . . .   105
Now far beyond our reach, now by the Argive ships
the rushing dogs will tear you, bolt your flesh!"

    So they wept, the two of them crying out
to their dear son, both pleading time and again
but they could not shake the fixed resolve of Hector.   110
No, he waited Achilles, coming on, gigantic in power.
As a snake in the hills, guarding his hole, awaits a man—
bloated with poison, deadly hatred seething inside him,
glances flashing fire as he coils round his lair . . .
so Hector, nursing his quenchless fury, gave no ground,   115
leaning his burnished shield against a jutting wall,
but harried still, he probed his own brave heart:
"No way out. If I slip inside the gates and walls,

Polydamas will be first to heap disgrace on me—
he was the one who urged me to lead our Trojans
back to Ilium just last night, the disastrous night   120
Achilles rose in arms like a god. But did I give way?
Not at all. And how much better it would have been!
Now my army's ruined, thanks to my own reckless pride,
I would die of shame to face the men of Troy   125
and the Trojan women trailing their long robes . . .
Someone less of a man than I will say, 'Our Hector—
staking all on his own strength, he destroyed his army!'
So they will mutter. So now, better by far for me
to stand up to Achilles, kill him, come home alive   130
or die at his hands in glory out before the walls.
But wait—what if I put down my studded shield
and heavy helmet, prop my spear on the rampart
and go forth, just as I am, to meet Achilles,
noble Prince Achilles . . .   135
why, I could promise to give back Helen, yes,
and all her treasures with her, all those riches
Paris once hauled home to Troy in the hollow ships—
and they were the cause of all our endless fighting—
Yes, yes, return it all to the sons of Atreus now   140
to haul away, and then, at the same time, divide
the rest with all the Argives, all the city holds,
and then I'd take an oath for the Trojan royal council
that we will hide nothing! Share and share alike the hoards
our handsome citadel stores within its depths and—   145
Why debate, my friend? Why thrash things out?
I must not go and implore him. He'll show no mercy,
no respect for me, my rights—he'll cut me down
straight off—stripped of defenses like a woman
once I have loosed the armor off my body.   150
No way to parley with that man—not now—
not from behind some oak or rock to whisper,
like a boy and a young girl, lovers' secrets
a boy and girl might whisper to each other . . .
Better to clash in battle, now, at once—   155
see which fighter Zeus awards the glory!"
                                    So he wavered,
waiting there, but Achilles was closing on him now
like the god of war, the fighter's helmet flashing,
over his right shoulder shaking the Pelian[34] ash spear,

---

34. Achilles's spear, made of wood from Mt.
Pelion, had been given to him by his
father.

that terror, and the bronze around his body flared 160
like a raging fire or the rising, blazing sun.
Hector looked up, saw him, started to tremble,
nerve gone, he could hold his ground no longer,
he left the gates behind and away he fled in fear—
and Achilles went for him, fast, sure of his speed 165
as the wild mountain hawk, the quickest thing on wings,
launching smoothly, swooping down on a cringing dove
and the dove flits out from under, the hawk screaming
over the quarry, plunging over and over, his fury
driving him down to beak and tear his kill— 170
so Achilles flew at him, breakneck on in fury
with Hector fleeing along the walls of Troy,
fast as his legs would go. On and on they raced,
passing the lookout point, passing the wild fig tree
tossed by the wind, always out from under the ramparts 175
down the wagon trail they careered until they reached
the clear running springs where whirling Scamander[35]
rises up from its double wellsprings bubbling strong—
and one runs hot and the steam goes up around it,
drifting thick as if fire burned at its core 180
but the other even in summer gushes cold
as hail or freezing snow or water chilled to ice . . .
And here, close to the springs, lie washing-pools
scooped out in the hollow rocks and broad and smooth
where the wives of Troy and all their lovely daughters 185
would wash their glistening robes in the old days,
the days of peace before the sons of Achaea came . . .
Past these they raced, one escaping, one in pursuit
and the one who fled was great but the one pursuing
greater, even greater—their pace mounting in speed 190
since both men strove, not for a sacrificial beast
or oxhide trophy, prizes runners fight for, no,
they raced for the life of Hector breaker of horses.
Like powerful stallions sweeping round the post for trophies,
galloping full stretch with some fine prize at stake, 195
a tripod, say, or woman offered up at funeral games
for some brave hero fallen—so the two of them
whirled three times around the city of Priam,
sprinting at top speed while all the gods gazed down,
and the father of men and gods broke forth among them now: 200
"Unbearable—a man I love, hunted round his own city walls

---

35. The Trojan river, after which Hector's son
is named.

and right before my eyes. My heart grieves for Hector.
Hector who burned so many oxen in my honor, rich cuts,
now on the rugged crests of Ida, now on Ilium's heights.
But now, look, brilliant Achilles courses him round   205
the city of Priam in all his savage, lethal speed.
Come, you immortals, think this through. Decide.
Either we pluck the man from death and save his life
or strike him down at last, here at Achilles' hands—
for all his fighting heart."
                  But immortal Athena,   210
her gray eyes wide, protested strongly: "Father!
Lord of the lightning, king of the black cloud,
what are you saying? A man, a mere mortal,
his doom sealed long ago? You'd set him free
from all the pains of death?
                  Do as you please—   215
but none of the deathless gods will ever praise you."
    And Zeus who marshals the thunderheads replied,
"Courage, Athena, third-born of the gods, dear child.
Nothing I said was meant in earnest, trust me,
I mean you all the good will in the world. Go.   220
Do as your own impulse bids you. Hold back no more."
    So he launched Athena already poised for action—
down the goddess swept from Olympus' craggy peaks.
    And swift Achilles kept on coursing Hector, nonstop
as a hound in the mountains starts a fawn from its lair,   225
hunting him down the gorges, down the narrow glens
and the fawn goes to ground, hiding deep in brush
but the hound comes racing fast, nosing him out
until he lands his kill. So Hector could never throw
Achilles off his trail, the swift racer Achilles—   230
time and again he'd make a dash for the Dardan Gates,
trying to rush beneath the rock-built ramparts, hoping
men on the heights might save him, somehow, raining spears
but time and again Achilles would intercept him quickly,
heading him off, forcing him out across the plain   235
and always sprinting along the city side himself—
endless as in a dream . . .
when a man can't catch another fleeing on ahead
and he can never escape nor his rival overtake him—
so the one could never run the other down in his speed   240
nor the other spring away. And how could Hector have fled
the fates of death so long? How unless one last time,
one final time Apollo had swept in close beside him,
driving strength in his legs and knees to race the wind?
And brilliant Achilles shook his head at the armies,   245

never letting them hurl their sharp spears at Hector—
someone might snatch the glory, Achilles come in second.
But once they reached the springs for the fourth time,
then Father Zeus held out his sacred golden scales:
in them he placed two fates of death that lays men low—   250
one for Achilles, one for Hector breaker of horses—
and gripping the beam mid-haft the Father raised it high
and down went Hector's day of doom, dragging him down
to the strong House of Death—and god Apollo left him.
Athena rushed to Achilles, her bright eyes gleaming,   255
standing shoulder-to-shoulder, winging orders now:
"At last our hopes run high, my brilliant Achilles—
Father Zeus must love you—
we'll sweep great glory back to Achaea's fleet,
we'll kill this Hector, mad as he is for battle!   260
No way for him to escape us now, no longer—
not even if Phoebus the distant deadly Archer
goes through torments, pleading for Hector's life,
groveling over and over before our storming Father Zeus.
But you, you hold your ground and catch your breath   265
while I run Hector down and persuade the man
to fight you face-to-face."
                              So Athena commanded
and he obeyed, rejoicing at heart—Achilles stopped,
leaning against his ashen spearshaft barbed in bronze.
And Athena left him there, caught up with Hector at once.   270
and taking the build and vibrant voice of Deiphobus
stood shoulder-to-shoulder with him, winging orders:
"Dear brother, how brutally swift Achilles hunts you—
coursing you round the city of Priam in all his lethal speed!
Come, let us stand our ground together—beat him back."   275
    "Deiphobus!"—Hector, his helmet flashing, called out to her—
"dearest of all my brothers, all these warring years,
of all the sons that Priam and Hecuba produced!
Now I'm determined to praise you all the more,
you who dared—seeing me in these straits—   280
to venture out from the walls, all for *my* sake,
while the others stay inside and cling to safety."
    The goddess answered quickly, her eyes blazing,
"True, dear brother—how your father and mother both
implored me, time and again, clutching my knees,   285
and the comrades round me begging me to stay!
Such was the fear that broke them, man for man,
but the heart within me broke with grief for you.
Now headlong on and fight! No letup, no lance spared!
So now, now we'll *see* if Achilles kills us both   290

and hauls our bloody armor back to the beaked ships
or he goes down in pain beneath your spear."
    Athena luring him on with all her immortal cunning—
and now, at last, as the two came closing for the kill
it was tall Hector, helmet flashing, who led off: 295
"No more running from you in fear, Achilles!
Not as before. Three times I fled around
the great city of Priam—I lacked courage then
to stand your onslaught. Now my spirit stirs me
to meet you face-to-face. Now kill or be killed!   300
Come, we'll swear to the gods, the highest witnesses—
the gods will oversee our binding pacts. I swear
I will never mutilate you—merciless as you are—
if Zeus allows me to last it out and tear your life away.
But once I've stripped your glorious armor, Achilles,   305
I will give your body back to your loyal comrades.
Swear you'll do the same."
                        A swift dark glance
and the headstrong runner answered, "Hector, stop!
You unforgivable, you . . . don't talk to me of pacts.
There are no binding oaths between men and lions—   310
wolves and lambs can enjoy no meeting of the minds—
they are all bent on hating each other to the death.
So with you and me. No love between us. No truce
till one or the other falls and gluts with blood
Ares who hacks at men behind his rawhide shield.   315
Come, call up whatever courage you can muster.
Life or death—now prove yourself a spearman,
a daring man of war! No more escape for you—
Athena will kill you with my spear in just a moment.
Now you'll pay at a stroke for all my comrades' grief,   320
all you killed in the fury of your spear!"
                               With that,
shaft poised, he hurled and his spear's long shadow flew
but seeing it coming glorious Hector ducked away,
crouching down, watching the bronze tip fly past
and stab the earth—but Athena snatched it up   325
and passed it back to Achilles
and Hector the gallant captain never saw her.
He sounded out a challenge to Peleus' princely son:
"You missed, look—the great godlike Achilles!
So you knew nothing at all from Zeus about my death—   330
and yet how sure you were! All bluff, cunning with words,
that's all you are—trying to make me fear you,
lose my nerve, forget my fighting strength.
Well, you'll never plant your lance in my back

as I flee *you* in fear—plunge it through my chest   335
as I come charging in, if a god gives you the chance!
But now it's for you to dodge *my* brazen spear—
I wish you'd bury it in your body to the hilt.
How much lighter the war would be for Trojans then
if you, their greatest scourge, were dead and gone!"   340
    Shaft poised, he hurled and his spear's long shadow flew
and it struck Achilles' shield—a dead-center hit—
but off and away it glanced and Hector seethed,
his hurtling spear, his whole arm's power poured
in a wasted shot. He stood there, cast down . . .   345
he had no spear in reserve. So Hector shouted out
to Deiphobus bearing his white shield—with a ringing shout
he called for a heavy lance—
                              but the man was nowhere near him,
vanished—
                   yes and Hector knew the truth in his heart
and the fighter cried aloud, "My time has come!   350
At last the gods have called me down to death.
I thought he was at my side, the hero Deiphobus—
he's safe inside the walls, Athena's tricked me blind.
And now death, grim death is looming up beside me,
no longer far away. No way to escape it now. This,   355
this was their pleasure after all, sealed long ago—
Zeus and the son of Zeus, the distant deadly Archer—
though often before now they rushed to my defense.
So now I meet my doom. Well let me die—
but not without struggle, not without glory, no,   360
in some great clash of arms that even men to come
will hear of down the years!"
                                And on that resolve
he drew the whetted sword that hung at his side,
tempered, massive, and gathering all his force
he swooped like a soaring eagle   365
launching down from the dark clouds to earth
to snatch some helpless lamb or trembling hare.
So Hector swooped now, swinging his whetted sword
and Achilles charged too, bursting with rage, barbaric,
guarding his chest with the well-wrought blazoned shield,   370
head tossing his gleaming helmet, four horns strong
and the golden plumes shook that the god of fire
drove in bristling thick along its ridge.
Bright as that star amid the stars in the night sky,
star of the evening, brightest star that rides the heavens,   375
so fire flared from the sharp point of the spear Achilles
brandished high in his right hand, bent on Hector's death,

scanning his splendid body—where to pierce it best?
The rest of his flesh seemed all encased in armor,
burnished, brazen—*Achilles'* armor that Hector stripped   380
from strong Patroclus when he killed him—true,
but one spot lay exposed,
where collarbones lift the neckbone off the shoulders,
the open throat, where the end of life comes quickest—*there*
as Hector charged in fury brilliant Achilles drove his spear   385
and the point went stabbing clean through the tender neck
but the heavy bronze weapon failed to slash the windpipe—
Hector could still gasp out some words, some last reply . . . .
he crashed in the dust—
                                    godlike Achilles gloried over him:
"Hector—surely you thought when you stripped Patroclus' armor   390
that you, you would be safe! Never a fear of me—
far from the fighting as I was—you fool!
Left behind there, down by the beaked ships
his great avenger waited, a greater man by far—
that man was I, and I smashed your strength! And you—   395
the dogs and birds will maul you, shame your corpse
while Achaeans bury my dear friend in glory!"
     Struggling for breath, Hector, his helmet flashing,
said, "I beg you, beg you by your life, your parents—
don't let the dogs devour me by the Argive ships!   400
Wait, take the princely ransom of bronze and gold,
the gifts my father and noble mother will give you—
but give my body to friends to carry home again,
so Trojan men and Trojan women can do me honor
with fitting rites of fire once I am dead."   405
     Staring grimly, the proud runner Achilles answered,
"Beg no more, you fawning dog—begging me by my parents!
Would to god my rage, my fury would drive me now
to hack your flesh away and eat you raw—
such agonies you have caused me! Ransom?   410
No man alive could keep the dog-packs off you,
not if they haul in ten, twenty times that ransom
and pile it here before me and promise fortunes more—
no, not given if Dardan Priam should offer to weigh out
your bulk in gold! Not even then will your noble mother   415
lay you on your deathbed, mourn the son she bore . . . .
The dogs and birds will rend you—blood and bone!"
     At the point of death, Hector, his helmet flashing,
said, "I know you well—I see my fate before me.
Never a chance that I could win you over   420
Iron inside your chest, that heart of yours.
But now beware, or my curse will draw god's wrath

upon your head, that day when Paris[36] and lord Apollo—
for all your fighting heart—destroy you at the Scaean Gates!"
    Death cut him short. The end closed in around him.   425
Flying free of his limbs
his soul went winging down to the House of Death,
wailing his fate, leaving his manhood far behind,
his young and supple strength. But brilliant Achilles
taunted Hector's body, dead as he was, "Die, die!   430
For my own death, I'll meet it freely—whenever Zeus
and the other deathless gods would like to bring it on!"
    With that he wrenched his bronze spear from the corpse,
laid it aside and ripped the bloody armor off the back.
And the other sons of Achaea, running up around him,   435
crowded closer, all of them gazing wonder-struck
at the build and marvelous, lithe beauty of Hector.
And not a man came forward who did not stab his body,
glancing toward a comrade, laughing: "Ah, look here—
how much softer he is to handle now, this Hector,   440
than when he gutted our ships with roaring fire!"
    Standing over him, so they'd gloat and stab his body.
But once he had stripped the corpse the proud runner Achilles
took his stand in the midst of all the Argive troops
and urged them on with a flight of winging orders: 445
"Friends—lords of the Argives, O my captains!
Now that the gods have let me kill this man
who caused us agonies, loss on crushing loss—
more than the rest of all their men combined—
come, let us ring their walls in armor, test them,   450
see what recourse the Trojans still may have in mind.
Will they abandon the city heights with this man fallen?
Or brace for a last, dying stand though Hector's gone?
But wait—what am I saying? Why this deep debate?
Down by the ships a body lies unwept, unburied—   455
Patroclus . . . I will never forget him,
not as long as I'm still among the living
and my springing knees will lift and drive me on.
Though the dead forget their dead in the House of Death,
I will remember, even there, my dear companion.   460
                                                        Now,
come, you sons of Achaea, raise a song of triumph!
Down to the ships we march and bear this corpse on high—
we have won ourselves great glory. We have brought

---

36. Hector's brother, whose seduction of
     Menelaos' wife Helen was the cause of the
     war.

magnificent Hector down, that man the Trojans
glorified in their city like a god!"
                                    So he triumphed   465
and now he was bent on outrage, on shaming noble Hector.
Piercing the tendons, ankle to heel behind both feet,
he knotted straps of rawhide through them both,
lashed them to his chariot, left the head to drag
and mounting the car, hoisting the famous arms aboard,   470
he whipped his team to a run and breakneck on they flew,
holding nothing back. And a thick cloud of dust rose up
from the man they dragged, his dark hair swirling round
that head so handsome once, all tumbled low in the dust—
since Zeus had given him over to his enemies now   475
to be defiled in the land of his own fathers.
    So his whole head was dragged down in the dust.
And now his mother began to tear her hair . . .
she flung her shining veil to the ground and raised
a high, shattering scream, looking down at her son.   480
Pitifully his loving father groaned and round the king
his people cried with grief and wailing seized the city—
for all the world as if all Troy were torched and smoldering
down from the looming brows of the citadel to her roots.
Priam's people could hardly hold the old man back,   485
frantic, mad to go rushing out the Dardan Gates.
He begged them all, groveling in the filth,
crying out to them, calling each man by name,
"Let go, my friends! Much as you care for me,
let me hurry out of the city, make my way,   490
all on my own, to Achaea's waiting ships!
I must implore that terrible, violent man . . .
Perhaps—who knows?—he may respect my age,
may pity an old man. He has a father too,
as old as I am—Peleus sired him once,   495
Peleus reared him to be the scourge of Troy
but most of all to me—he made my life a hell.
So many sons he slaughtered, just coming into bloom . . .
but grieving for all the rest, one breaks my heart the most
and stabbing grief for him will take me down to Death—   500
my Hector—would to god he had perished in my arms!
Then his mother who bore him—oh so doomed,
she and I could glut ourselves with grief."
    So the voice of the king rang out in tears,
the citizens wailed in answer, and noble Hecuba[37]   505
led the wives of Troy in a throbbing chant of sorrow:

---

37. Hector's mother.

"O my child—my desolation! How can I go on living?
What agonies must I suffer now, now *you* are dead and gone?
You were my pride throughout the city night and day—
a blessing to us all, the men and women of Troy: 510
throughout the city they saluted you like a god.
You, you were their greatest glory while you lived—
now death and fate have seized you, dragged you down!"
     Her voice rang out in tears, but the wife of Hector
had not heard a thing. No messenger brought the truth   515
of how her husband made his stand outside the gates.
She was weaving at her loom, deep in the high halls,
working flowered braiding into a dark red folding robe.
And she called her well-kempt women through the house
to set a large three-legged cauldron over the fire   520
so Hector could have his steaming hot bath
when he came home from battle—poor woman,
she never dreamed how far he was from bathing,
struck down at Achilles' hands by blazing-eyed Athena.
But she heard the groans and wails of grief from the rampart now   525
and her body shook, her shuttle dropped to the ground,
she called out to her lovely waiting women, "Quickly—
two of you follow me—I must see what's happened.
That cry—that was Hector's honored mother I heard!
My heart's pounding, leaping up in my throat,   530
the knees beneath me paralyzed—Oh I know it . . .
something terrible's coming down on Priam's children.
Pray god the news will never reach my ears!
Yes but I dread it so—what if great Achilles
has cut my Hector off from the city, daring Hector,   535
and driven him out across the plain, and all alone?—
He may have put an end to that fatal headstrong pride
that always seized my Hector—never hanging back
with the main force of men, always charging ahead,
giving ground to no man in his fury!"
                                        So she cried,   540
dashing out of the royal halls like a madwoman,
her heart racing hard, her women close behind her.
But once she reached the tower where soldiers massed
she stopped on the rampart, looked down and saw it all—
saw him dragged before the city, stallions galloping,   545
dragging Hector back to Achaea's beaked warships—
ruthless work. The world went black as night
before her eyes, she fainted, falling backward.
gasping away her life breath . . .
She flung to the winds her glittering headdress,   550
the cap and the coronet, braided band and veil,

all the regalia golden Aphrodite gave her once,
the day that Hector, helmet aflash in sunlight,
led her home to Troy from her father's house
with countless wedding gifts to win her heart.   560

[After Hector is killed, Achilles holds Patroclus's funeral, followed by the customary athletic games in celebration and commemoration of the dead hero. Meanwhile, Hector's body remains unburied. Priam, at Zeus's prompting and despite Hecuba's efforts to dissuade him, makes his way across the battlefield at night to Achilles's tent to offer him ransom for the body of Hector.]

Book 24 [Achilles and Priam]

The majestic king of Troy slipped past the rest
and kneeling down beside Achilles, clasped his knees
and kissed his hands, those terrible, man-killing hands
that had slaughtered Priam's many sons in battle.
Awesome—as when the grip of madness seizes one   5
who murders a man in his own fatherland and flees
abroad to foreign shores, to a wealthy, noble host,
and a sense of marvel runs through all who see him—
so Achilles marveled, beholding majestic Priam.
His men marveled too, trading startled glances.   10
But Priam prayed his heart out to Achilles:
"Remember your own father, great godlike Achilles—
as old as I am, past the threshold of deadly old age!
No doubt the countrymen round about him plague him now,
with no one there to defend him, beat away disaster.   15
No one—but at least he hears you're still alive
and his old heart rejoices, hopes rising, day by day,
to see his beloved son come sailing home from Troy.
But I—dear god, my life so cursed by fate . . .
I fathered hero sons in the wide realm of Troy   20
and now not a single one is left, I tell you.
Fifty sons I had when the sons of Achaea came,
nineteen born to me from a single mother's womb
and the rest by other women in the palace. Many,
most of them violent Ares cut the knees from under.   25
But one, one was left me, to guard my walls, my people—
the one you killed the other day, defending his fatherland,
my Hector! It's all for him I've come to the ships now,
to win him back from you—I bring a priceless ransom.
Revere the gods, Achilles! Pity me in my own right,   30
remember your own father! I deserve more pity . . .
I have endured what no one on earth has ever done before—
I put to my lips the hands of the man who killed my son."

   Those words stirred within Achilles a deep desire
to grieve for his own father. Taking the old man's hand   35
he gently moved him back. And overpowered by memory
both men gave way to grief. Priam wept freely
for man-killing Hector, throbbing, crouching
before Achilles' feet as Achilles wept himself,
now for his father, now for Patroclus once again,   40
and their sobbing rose and fell throughout the house.
Then, when brilliant Achilles had had his fill of tears
and the longing for it had left his mind and body,
he rose from his seat, raised the old man by the hand
and filled with pity now for his gray head and gray beard,   45
he spoke out winging words, flying straight to the heart:
"Poor man, how much you've borne—pain to break the spirit!
What daring brought you down to the ships, all alone,
to face the glance of the man who killed your sons,
so many fine brave boys? You have a heart of iron.   50
Come, please, sit down on this chair here . . .
Let us put our griefs to rest in our own hearts,
rake them up no more, raw as we are with mourning.
What good's to be won from tears that chill the spirit?
So the immortals spun our lives that we, we wretched men   55
live on to bear such torments—the gods live free of sorrows.
There are two great jars that stand on the floor of Zeus's halls
and hold his gifts, our miseries one, the other blessings.
When Zeus who loves the lightning mixes gifts for a man,
now he meets with misfortune, now good times in turn.   60
When Zeus dispenses gifts from the jar of sorrows only,
he makes a man an outcast—brutal, ravenous hunger
drives him down the face of the shining earth,
stalking far and wide, cursed by gods and men.
So with my father, Peleus: What glittering gifts   65
the gods rained down from the day that he was born!
He excelled all men in wealth and pride of place,
he lorded the Myrmidons, and mortal that he was,
they gave the man an immortal goddess for a wife.
Yes, but even on him the Father piled hardships,   70
no powerful race of princes born in his royal halls,
only a single son he fathered, doomed at birth,
cut off in the spring of life—
and I, I give the man no care as he grows old
since here I sit in Troy, far from my fatherland,   75
a grief to you, a grief to all your children . . .
And you too, old man, we hear you prospered once:
as far as Lesbos, Macar's kingdom, bounds to seaward,

Phrygia east and upland, the Hellespont vast and north—
that entire realm, they say, you lorded over once,   80
you excelled all men, old king, in sons and wealth.
But then the gods of heaven brought this agony on you—
ceaseless battles round your walls, your armies slaughtered.
You must bear up now. Enough of endless tears,
the pain that breaks the spirit.   85
Grief for your son will do no good at all.
You will never bring him back to life—
sooner you must suffer something worse."

[Achilles returns Hector's body to Priam and offers to delay the fighting until the Trojans have performed Hector's funeral rites. Priam brings his son's body back to Troy and the poem ends with with grief-stricken Trojans mourning their fallen defender.]

HOMER (EIGHTH CENTURY B.C.E.)
Greece

The subject of the *Odyssey* is the ten-year-long return of the Greek hero Odysseus, after the fall of Troy, to his home on the island of Ithaca. In four of the poem's twenty-four books, Odysseus is the first-person narrator of his voyage through uncharted territories. He relates his travels (beginning with our Book 9 selection) to the Phaeacians on the island of Scheria, where he has taken refuge after being shipwrecked in a storm brought on by Poseidon, ruling divinity of the sea.

Odysseus' encounters with unfamiliar beings and their customs serve to delineate the contrast between civilized and noncivilized existence, bringing to the fore the idea of culture itself. In Book Nine, Polyphemos, one of the Cyclopes—a group of giants living without agriculture or social organization, so that each family is literally a "law unto itself"—makes a mockery of the fundamental norms of social relations in early Greece in a grisly perversion of the inviolable code of hospitality. The episode establishes Odysseus as a master strategist who through sheer intelligence and perspicacity outwits his vastly more powerful adversary—an aspect of heroism less evident in the *Iliad*. In this poem's second half, Odysseus' wife, Penelope, is depicted as sharing these same qualities. Together, they bring about the defeat of Penelope's corrupt suitors, who in Odysseus' absence have overrun and exploited his entire household.

The *Odyssey* is generally thought (on linguistic grounds) to have reached its present form at a slightly later date than the *Iliad*. In its description (in Book 8) of a bard accompanying himself on the lyre and responding to the requests of an attentive audience, it gives us our earliest picture of how an epic may originally have been composed and sung.

from *Odyssey*

Book 1 [Invocation]

Tell me, Muse, of the man of many ways, who was driven
far journeys, after he had sacked Troy's sacred citadel.
Many were they whose cities he saw, whose minds he learned of,
many the pains he suffered in his spirit on the wide sea,
struggling for his own life and the homecoming of his companions.   5
Even so he could not save his companions, hard though
he strove to; they were destroyed by their own wild recklessness,
fools, who devoured the oxen of Helios, the Sun God,
and he took away the day of their homecoming. From some point
here, goddess, daughter of Zeus, speak, and begin our story.   10
 Then all the others, as many as fled sheer destruction,
were at home now, having escaped the sea and the fighting.
This one alone, longing for his wife and his homecoming,
was detained by the queenly nymph Kalypso, bright among goddesses,
in her hollowed caverns, desiring that he should be her husband.   15
But when in the circling of the years that very year came
in which the gods had spun for him his time of homecoming
to Ithaka, not even then was he free of his trials
nor among his own people. But all the gods pitied him
except Poseidon; he remained relentlessly angry   20
with godlike Odysseus, until his return to his own country.

[Odysseus, after being shipwrecked on his voyage homeward in a storm brought on by the
sea-god Poseidon, manages to swim to shore on the island of Scheria, where, although his
identity is unknown, he is given shelter by the king and queen of the Phaeacians. They
entertain him at a feast in which a singer sings about the Trojan War, including Odysseus's
own exploits. Observing his guest weeping at the songs, King Alkinoos asks Odysseus to
reveal his name and to explain the cause of his grief.]

Book 9 [The Wanderings of Odysseus]

Then resourceful Odysseus spoke in turn and answered him:
'O great Alkinoos, pre-eminent among all people,
surely indeed it is a good thing to listen to a singer
such as this one before us, who is like the gods in his singing;
for I think there is no occasion accomplished that is more pleasant   5
than when festivity holds sway among all the populace,
and the feasters up and down the houses are sitting in order
and listening to the singer, and beside them the tables are loaded

Translated by Richmond Lattimore.

with bread and meats, and from the mixing bowl the wine steward
draws the wine and carries it about and fills the cups. This   10
seems to my own mind to be the best of occasions.
But now your wish was inclined to ask me about my mournful
sufferings, so that I must mourn and grieve even more. What then
shall I recite to you first of all, what leave till later?
Many are the sorrows the gods of the sky have given me.   15
Now first I will tell you my name, so that all of you
may know me, and I hereafter, escaping the day without pity,
be your friend and guest, though the home where I live is far away from you.
I am Odysseus son of Laertes, known before all men
for the study of crafty designs, and my fame goes up to the heavens.   20
I am at home in sunny Ithaka. There is a mountain
there that stands tall, leaf-trembling Neritos, and there are islands
settled around it, lying one very close to another.
There is Doulichion and Same, wooded Zakynthos,
but my island lies low and away, last of all on the water   25
toward the dark, with the rest below facing east and sunshine,
a rugged place, but a good nurse of men; for my part
I cannot think of any place sweeter on earth to look at.
For in truth Kalypso,[1] shining among divinities, kept me
with her in her hollow caverns desiring me for her husband,   30
and so likewise Aiaian Circe[2] the guileful detained me
beside her in her halls, desiring me for her husband,
but never could she persuade the heart within me. So it is
that nothing is more sweet in the end than country and parents
ever, even when far away one lives in a fertile   35
place, when it is in alien country, far from his parents.
But come, I will tell you of my voyage home with its many
troubles, which Zeus inflicted on me as I came from Troy land.

'From Ilion the wind took me and drove me ashore at Ismaros
by the Kikonians. I sacked their city and killed their people,   40
and out of their city taking their wives and many possessions
we shared them out, so none might go cheated of his proper
portion. There I was for the light foot and escaping,
and urged it, but they were greatly foolish and would not listen,
and then and there much wine was being drunk, and they slaughtered   45
many sheep on the beach, and lumbering horn-curved cattle.
But meanwhile the Kikonians went and summoned the other

---

1. The nymph Kalypso (whose name means
"the one who conceals"), on whose island
Odysseus took refuge after an earlier shipwreck in which all his companions were
lost, kept him with her for seven years, until
Zeus obliged her to let Odysseus continue
his journey home.

2. On his return from Troy, before reaching
Kalypso's island, Odysseus and his companions on the one remaining ship reach
Circe's island of Aiaia, where they stay for a
year before setting out for Ithaca again.

Kikonians, who were their neighbors living in the inland country,
more numerous and better men, well skilled in fighting
men with horses, but knowing too at need the battle   50
on foot. They came at early morning, like flowers in season
or leaves, and the luck that came our way from Zeus was evil,
to make us unfortunate, so we must have hard pains to suffer.
Both sides stood and fought their battle there by the running
ships, and with bronze-headed spears they cast at each other,   55
and as long as it was early and the sacred daylight increasing,
so long we stood fast and fought them off, though there were more of them;
but when the sun had gone to the time for unyoking of cattle,
then at last the Kikonians turned the Achaians back and beat them,
and out of each ship six of my strong-greaved companions   60
were killed, but the rest of us fled away from death and destruction.
   'From there we sailed on further along, glad to have escaped death,
but grieving still at heart for the loss of our dear companions.
Even then I would not suffer the flight of my oarswept vessels
until a cry had been made three times for each of my wretched   65
companions, who died there in the plain, killed by the Kikonians.
Cloud-gathering Zeus drove the North Wind against our vessels
in a supernatural storm, and huddled under the cloud scuds
land alike and the great water. Night sprang from heaven.
The ships were swept along yawing down the current; the violence   70
of the wind ripped our sails into three and four pieces. These then,
in fear of destruction, we took down and stowed in the ships' hulls,
and rowed them on ourselves until we had made the mainland.
There for two nights and two days together we lay up,
for pain and weariness together eating our hearts out.   75
But when the fair-haired Dawn in her rounds brought on the third day,
we, setting the masts upright, and hoisting the white sails on them,
sat still, and let the wind and the steersmen hold them steady.
And now I would have come home unscathed to the land of my fathers,
but as I turned the hook of Maleia,[3] the sea and current   80
and the North Wind beat me off course, and drove me on past Kythera.
   'Nine days then I was swept along by the force of the hostile
winds on the fishy sea, but on the tenth day we landed
in the country of the Lotus-Eaters, who live on a flowering
food, and there we set foot on the mainland, and fetched water,   85
and my companions soon took their supper there by the fast ships.
But after we had tasted of food and drink, then I sent
some of my companions ahead, telling them to find out
what men, eaters of bread, might live here in this country.
I chose two men, and sent a third with them, as a herald.   90
My men went on and presently met the Lotus-Eaters,

---

3. The southernmost tip of the Peloponnesus.

nor did these Lotus-Eaters have any thoughts of destroying
our companions, but they only gave them lotus to taste of.
But any of them who ate the honey-sweet fruit of lotus
was unwilling to take any message back, or to go   95
away, but they wanted to stay there with the lotus-eating
people, feeding on lotus, and forget the way home. I myself
took these men back weeping, by force, to where the ships were,
and put them aboard under the rowing benches and tied them
fast, then gave the order to the rest of my eager   100
companions to embark on the ships in haste, for fear
someone else might taste of the lotus and forget the way home,
and the men quickly went aboard and sat to the oarlocks,
and sitting well in order dashed the oars in the gray sea.
    'From there, grieving still at heart, we sailed on further   105
along, and reached the country of the lawless outrageous
Cyclopes who, putting all their trust in the immortal
gods, neither plow with their hands nor plant anything,
but all grows for them without seed planting, without cultivation,
wheat and barley and also the grapevines, which yield for them   110
wine of strength, and it is Zeus' rain that waters it for them.
These people have no institutions, no meetings for counsels;
rather they make their habitations in caverns hollowed
among the peaks of the high mountains, and each one is the law
for his own wives and children, and cares nothing about the others.   115
    'There is a wooded island that spreads, away from the harbor,
neither close in to the land of the Cyclopes nor far out
from it; forested; wild goats beyond number breed there,
for there is no coming and going of human kind to disturb them,
nor are they visited by hunters, who in the forest   120
suffer hardships as they haunt the peaks of the mountains,
neither again is it held by herded flocks, nor farmers,
but all its days, never plowed up and never planted,
it goes without people and supports the bleating wild goats.
For the Cyclopes have no ships with cheeks of vermilion,   125
nor have they builders of ships among them, who could have made the
strong-benched vessels, and these if made could have run them sailing
to all the various cities of men, in the way that people
cross the sea by means of ships and visit each other,
and they could have made this island a strong settlement for them.   130
For it is not a bad place at all, it could bear all crops
in season, and there are meadow lands near the shores of the gray sea,
well watered and soft; there could be grapes grown there endlessly,
and there is smooth land for plowing, men could reap a full harvest
always in season, since there is very rich subsoil. Also   135
there is an easy harbor, with no need for a hawser
nor anchor stones to be thrown ashore nor cables to make fast;

one could just run ashore and wait for the time when the sailors'
desire stirred them to go and the right winds were blowing.
Also at the head of the harbor there runs bright water,   140
spring beneath rock, and there are black poplars growing around it.
There we sailed ashore, and there was some god guiding
us in through the gloom of the night, nothing showed to look at,
for there was a deep mist around the ships, nor was there any moon
showing in the sky, but she was under the clouds and hidden.   145
There was none of us there whose eyes had spied out the island,
and we never saw any long waves rolling in and breaking
on the shore, but the first thing was when we beached the well-benched vessels.
Then after we had beached the ships we took all the sails down,
and we ourselves stepped out onto the break of the sea beach,   150
and there we fell asleep and waited for the divine Dawn.
    'But when the young Dawn showed again with her rosy fingers,
we made a tour about the island, admiring everything
there, and the nymphs, daughters of Zeus of the aegis,[4] started
the hill-roving goats our way for my companions to feast on.   155
At once we went and took from the ships curved bows and javelins
with long sockets, and arranging ourselves in three divisions
cast about, and the god granted us the game we longed for.
Now there were twelve ships that went with me, and for each one nine goats
were portioned out, but I alone had ten for my portion.   160
So for the whole length of the day until the sun's setting,
we sat there feasting on unlimited meat and sweet wine;
for the red wine had not yet given out in the ships, there was
some still left, for we all had taken away a great deal
in storing jars when we stormed the Kikonians' sacred citadel.   165
We looked across at the land of the Cyclopes, and they were
near by, and we saw their smoke and heard sheep and goats bleating.
But when the sun went down and the sacred darkness came over,
then we lay down to sleep along the break of the seashore;
but when the young Dawn showed again with her rosy fingers,   170
then I held an assembly and spoke forth before all:
"The rest of you, who are my eager companions, wait here,
while I, with my own ship and companions that are in it,
go and find out about these people, and learn what they are,
whether they are savage and violent, and without justice,   175
or hospitable to strangers and with minds that are godly."
    'So speaking I went aboard the ship and told my companions
also to go aboard, and to cast off the stern cables,
and quickly they went aboard the ship and sat to the oarlocks,
and sitting well in order dashed the oars in the gray sea.   180
But when we had arrived at the place, which was nearby, there

---

4. The aegis is Zeus's shield.

at the edge of the land we saw the cave, close to the water,
high, and overgrown with laurels, and in it were stabled
great flocks, sheep and goats alike, and there was a fenced yard
built around it with a high wall of grubbed-out boulders   185
and tall pines and oaks with lofty foliage. Inside
there lodged a monster of a man, who now was herding
the flocks at a distance away, alone, for he did not range with
others, but stayed away by himself; his mind was lawless,
and in truth he was a monstrous wonder made to behold, not   190
like a man, an eater of bread, but more like a wooded
peak of the high mountains seen standing away from the others.
    'At that time I told the rest of my eager companions
to stay where they were beside the ship and guard it. Meanwhile
I, choosing out the twelve best men among my companions,   195
went on, but I had with me a goatskin bottle of black wine,
sweet wine, given me by Maron, son of Euanthes
and priest of Apollo, who bestrides Ismaros; he gave it
because, respecting him with his wife and child, we saved them
from harm. He made his dwelling among the trees of the sacred   200
grove of Phoibos Apollo, and he gave me glorious presents.
He gave me seven talents of well-wrought gold, and he gave me
a mixing bowl made all of silver, and gave along with it
wine, drawing it off in storing jars, twelve in all. This was
a sweet wine, unmixed, a divine drink. No one of his servants   205
or thralls that were in his household knew anything about it,
but only himself and his dear wife and a single housekeeper.
Whenever he drank this honey-sweet red wine, he would pour out
enough to fill one cup, then twenty measures of water
were added, and the mixing bowl gave off a sweet smell;   210
magical; then would be no pleasure in holding off. Of this
wine I filled a great wineskin full, and took too provisions
in a bag, for my proud heart had an idea that presently
I would encounter a man who was endowed with great strength,
and wild, with no true knowledge of laws or any good customs.   215
    'Lightly we made our way to the cave, but we did not find him
there, he was off herding on the range with his fat flocks.
We went inside the cave and admired everything inside it.
Baskets were there, heavy with cheeses, and the pens crowded
with lambs and kids. They had all been divided into separate   220
groups, the firstlings in one place, and then the middle ones,
the babies again by themselves. And all his vessels, milk pails
and pans that he used for milking into, were running over
with whey. From the start my companions spoke to me and begged me
to take some of the cheeses, come back again, and the next time   225
to drive the lambs and kids from their pens, and get back quickly
to the ship again, and go sailing off across the salt water;

but I would not listen to them, it would have been better their way,
not until I could see him, see if he would give me presents.
My friends were to find the sight of him in no way lovely.   230
    'There we built a fire and made sacrifice, and helping
ourselves to the cheeses we ate and sat waiting for him
inside, until he came home from his herding. He carried a heavy
load of dried-out wood, to make a fire for his dinner,
and threw it down inside the cave, making a terrible   235
crash, so in fear we scuttled away into the cave's corners.
Next he drove into the wide cavern all from the fat flocks
that he would milk, but he left all the male animals, billygoats
and rams, outside in his yard with the deep fences. Next thing,
he heaved up and set into position the huge door stop,   240
a massive thing; no twenty-two of the best four-wheeled
wagons could have taken that weight off the ground and carried it,
such a piece of sky-towering cliff that was he set over
his gateway. Next he sat down and milked his sheep and his bleating
goats, each of them in order, and put lamb or kid under each one   245
to suck, and then drew off half of the white milk and put it
by in baskets made of wickerwork, stored for cheeses,
but let the other half stand in the milk pails so as to have it
to help himself to and drink from, and it would serve for his supper.
But after he had briskly done all his chores and finished,   250
at last he lit the fire, and saw us, and asked us a question:
"Strangers, who are you? From where do you come sailing over the watery
ways? Is it on some business, or are you recklessly roving
as pirates do, when they sail on the salt sea and venture
their lives as they wander, bringing evil to alien people?"[5]   255
    'So he spoke, and the inward heart in us was broken
in terror of the deep voice and for seeing him so monstrous;
but even so I had words for an answer, and I said to him:
"We are Achaians coming from Troy, beaten off our true course
by winds from every direction across the great gulf of the open   260
sea, making for home, by the wrong way, on the wrong courses.
So we have come. So it has pleased Zeus to arrange it.
We claim we are of the following of the son of Atreus,
Agamemnon, whose fame now is the greatest thing under heaven,
such a city was that he sacked and destroyed so many   265
people; but now in turn we come to you and are suppliants
at your knees, if you might give us a guest present or otherwise
some gift of grace, for such is the right of strangers. Therefore
respect the gods, O best of men. We are your suppliants,

---

5. The code of hospitality required a host to offer a visitor food, shelter, and gifts for his journey before asking him to identify himself; the Cyclops's ominous greeting itself thus violates established practice, even before he takes any further action.

and Zeus the guest god, who stands behind all strangers with honor   270
due them, avenges any wrong toward strangers and suppliants."
  'So I spoke, but he answered me in pitiless spirit:
"Stranger, you are a simple fool, or come from far off,
when you tell me to avoid the wrath of the gods or fear them.
The Cyclopes do not concern themselves over Zeus of the aegis,   275
nor any of the rest of the blessed gods, since we are far better
than they, and for fear of the hate of Zeus I would not spare
you or your companions either, if the fancy took me
otherwise. But tell me, so I may know: where did you
put your well-made ship when you came? Nearby or far off?"   280
  'So he spoke, trying me out, but I knew too much and was not
deceived, but answered him in turn, and my words were crafty:
"Poseidon, Shaker of the Earth, has shattered my vessel.
He drove it against the rocks on the outer coast of your country,
cracked on a cliff, it is gone, the wind on the sea took it;   285
but I, with these you see, got away from sudden destruction."
  'So I spoke, but he in pitiless spirit answered
nothing, but sprang up and reached for my companions,
caught up two together and slapped them, like killing puppies,
against the ground, and the brains ran all over the floor, soaking   290
the ground. Then he cut them up limb by limb and got supper ready,
and like a lion reared in the hills, without leaving anything,
ate them, entrails, flesh and the marrowy bones alike. We
cried out aloud and held our hands up to Zeus, seeing
the cruelty of what he did, but our hearts were helpless.   295
But when the Cyclops had filled his enormous stomach, feeding
on human flesh and drinking down milk unmixed with water,
he lay down to sleep in the cave sprawled out through his sheep. Then I
took counsel with myself in my great-hearted spirit
to go up close, drawing from beside my thigh the sharp sword,   300
and stab him in the chest, where the midriff joins on the liver,
feeling for the place with my hand; but the second thought stayed me;
for there we too would have perished away in sheer destruction,
seeing that our hands could never have pushed from the lofty
gate of the cave the ponderous boulder he had propped there.   305
So mourning we waited, just as we were, for the divine Dawn.
  'But when the young Dawn showed again with her rosy fingers,
he lit his fire, and then set about milking his glorious
flocks, each of them in order, and put lamb or kid under each one.
But after he had briskly done all his chores and finished,   310
again he snatched up two men, and prepared them for dinner,
and when he had dined, drove his fat flocks out of the cavern,
easily lifting off the great doorstone, but then he put it
back again, like a man closing the lid on a quiver.
And so the Cyclops, whistling loudly, guided his fat flocks   315

to the hills, leaving me there in the cave mumbling my black thoughts
of how I might punish him, how Athene might give me that glory.
And as I thought, this was the plan that seemed best to me.
The Cyclops had lying there beside the pen a great bludgeon
of olive wood, still green. He had cut it so that when it dried out   320
he could carry it about, and we looking at it considered
it to be about the size for the mast of a cargo-carrying
broad black ship of twenty oars which crosses the open
sea; such was the length of it, such the thickness, to judge by
looking. I went up and chopped a length of about a fathom,   325
and handed it over to my companions and told them to shave it
down, and they made it smooth, while I standing by them sharpened
the point, then put it over the blaze of the fire to harden.
Then I put it well away and hid it under the ordure
which was all over the floor of the cave, much stuff lying   330
about. Next I told the rest of the men to cast lots, to find out
which of them must endure with me to take up the great beam
and spin it in Cyclops' eye when sweet sleep had come over him.
The ones drew it whom I myself would have wanted chosen,
four men, and I myself was the fifth, and allotted with them.   335
With the evening he came back again, herding his fleecy
flocks, but drove all his fat flocks inside the wide cave
at once, and did not leave any outside in the yard with the deep fence,
whether he had some idea, or whether a god so urged him.
When he had heaved up and set in position the huge door stop,   340
next he sat down and started milking his sheep and his bleating
goats, each of them in order, and put lamb or kid under each one.
But after he had briskly done all his chores and finished,
again he snatched up two men and prepared them for dinner.
Then at last I, holding in my hands an ivy bowl   345
full of the black wine, stood close up to the Cyclops and spoke out:
"Here, Cyclops, have a drink of wine, now you have fed on
human flesh, and see what kind of drink our ship carried
inside her. I brought it for you, and it would have been your libation
had you taken pity and sent me home, but I cannot suffer   350
your rages. Cruel, how can any man come and visit
you ever again, now you have done what has no sanction?"

   'So I spoke, and he took it and drank it off, and was terribly
pleased with the wine he drank and questioned me again, saying:
"Give me still more, freely, and tell me your name straightway   355
now, so I can give you a guest present to make you happy.
For the grain-giving land of the Cyclopes also yields them
wine of strength, and it is Zeus' rain that waters it for them;
but this comes from where ambrosia and nectar flow in abundance."

   'So he spoke, and I gave him the gleaming wine again. Three times   360
I brought it to him and gave it to him, three times he recklessly

drained it, but when the wine had got into the brains of the Cyclops,
then I spoke to him, and my words were full of beguilement:
"Cyclops, you ask me for my famous name. I will tell you
then, but you must give me a guest gift as you have promised.   365
Nobody is my name. My father and mother call me
Nobody, as do all the others who are my companions."
    'So I spoke, and he answered me in pitiless spirit:
"Then I will eat Nobody after his friends, and the others
I will eat first, and that shall be my guest present to you."   370
    'He spoke and slumped away and fell on his back, and lay there
with his thick neck crooked over on one side, and sleep who subdues all
came on and captured him, and the wine gurgled up from his gullet
with gobs of human meat. This was his drunken vomiting.
Then I shoved the beam underneath a deep bed of cinders,   375
waiting for it to heat, and I spoke to all my companions
in words of courage, so none should be in a panic, and back out;
but when the beam of olive, green as it was, was nearly
at the point of catching fire and glowed, terribly incandescent,
then I brought it close up from the fire and my friends about me   380
stood fast. Some great divinity breathed courage into us.
They seized the beam of olive, sharp at the end, and leaned on it
into the eye, while I from above leaning my weight on it
twirled it, like a man with a brace-and-bit who bores into
a ship timber, and his men from underneath, grasping   385
the strap on either side whirl it, and it bites resolutely deeper.
So seizing the fire-point-hardened timber we twirled it
in his eye, and the blood boiled around the hot point, so that
the blast and scorch of the burning ball singed all his eyebrows
and eyelids, and the fire made the roots of his eye crackle.   390
As when a man who works as a blacksmith plunges a screaming
great ax blade or plane into cold water, treating it
for temper, since this is the way steel is made strong, even
so Cyclops' eye sizzled about the beam of the olive.
He gave a giant horrible cry and the rocks rattled   395
to the sound, and we scuttled away in fear. He pulled the timber
out of his eye, and it blubbered with plenty of blood, then
when he had frantically taken it in his hands and thrown it
away, he cried aloud to the other Cyclopes, who live
around him in their own caves along the windy pinnacles.   400
They hearing him came swarming up from their various places,
and stood around the cave and asked him what was his trouble:
"Why, Polyphemos, what do you want with all this outcry
through the immortal night and have made us all thus sleepless?
Surely no mortal against your will can be driving your sheep off?   405
Surely none can be killing you by force or treachery?"

'Then from inside the cave strong Polyphemos answered:
"Good friends, Nobody is killing me by force or treachery."[6]
  'So then the others speaking in winged words gave him an answer:
"If alone as you are none uses violence on you,   410
why, there is no avoiding the sickness sent by great Zeus;
so you had better pray to your father, the lord Poseidon."
  'So they spoke as they went away, and the heart within me
laughed over how my name and my perfect planning had fooled him.
But the Cyclops, groaning aloud and in the pain of his agony,   415
felt with his hands, and took the boulder out of the doorway,
and sat down in the entrance himself, spreading his arms wide,
to catch anyone who tried to get out with the sheep, hoping
that I would be so guileless in my heart as to try this;
but I was planning so that things would come out the best way,   420
and trying to find some release from death, for my companions
and myself too, combining all my resource and treacheries,
as with life at stake, for the great evil was very close to us.
And as I thought, this was the plan that seemed best to me.
There were some male sheep, rams, well nourished, thick and fleecy,   425
handsome and large, with a dark depth of wool. Silently
I caught these and lashed them together with pliant willow
withes, where the monstrous Cyclops lawless of mind had used to
sleep. I had them in threes, and the one in the middle carried
a man, while the other two went on each side, so guarding   430
my friends. Three rams carried each man, but as for myself,
there was one ram, far the finest of all the flock. This one
I clasped around the back, snuggled under the wool of the belly,
and stayed there still, and with a firm twist of the hands and enduring
spirit clung fast to the glory of this fleece, unrelenting.   435
So we grieved for the time and waited for the divine Dawn.
  'But when the young Dawn showed again with her rosy fingers,
then the male sheep hastened out of the cave, toward pasture,
but the ewes were bleating all through the pens unmilked, their udders
ready to burst. Meanwhile their master, suffering and in   440
bitter pain, felt over the backs of all his sheep, standing
up as they were, but in his guilelessness did not notice
how my men were fastened under the breasts of his fleecy
sheep. Last of all the flock the ram went out of the doorway,
loaded with his own fleece, and with me, and my close counsels.   445
Then, feeling him, powerful Polyphemos spoke a word to him:
"My dear old ram, why are you thus leaving the cave last of
the sheep? Never in the old days were you left behind by

---

6. There is an aural pun in the Greek here. The word for "Nobody" in Polyphemos's answer about his adversary sounds virtually exactly like the word for "intelligence."

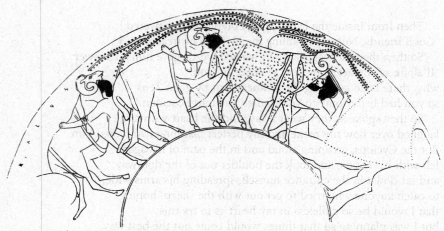

A vase painting showing Odysseus and his followers escaping the cave of Polyphemos. 480–460 B.C.E.

the flock, but long-striding, far ahead of the rest would pasture
on the tender bloom of the grass, be first at running rivers,   450
and be eager always to lead the way first back to the sheepfold
at evening. Now you are last of all. Perhaps you are grieving
for your master's eye, which a bad man with his wicked companions
put out, after he had made my brain helpless with wine, this
Nobody, who I think has not yet got clear of destruction.   455
If only you could think like us and only be given
a voice, to tell me where he is skulking away from my anger,
then surely he would be smashed against the floor and his brains go
spattering all over the cave to make my heart lighter
from the burden of all the evils this niddering Nobody gave me."   460
    'So he spoke, and sent the ram along from him, outdoors,
and when we had got a little way from the yard and the cavern,
first I got myself loose from my ram, then set my companions
free, and rapidly then, and with many a backward glance, we
drove the long-striding sheep, rich with fat, until we reached   465
our ship, and the sight of us who had escaped death was welcome
to our companions, but they began to mourn for the others;
only I would not let them cry out, but with my brows nodded
to each man, and told them to be quick and to load the fleecy
sheep on board our vessel and sail out on the salt water.   470
Quickly they went aboard the ship and sat to the oarlocks,
and sitting well in order dashed the oars in the gray sea.
But when I was as far from the land as a voice shouting
carries, I called out aloud to the Cyclops, taunting him:
"Cyclops, in the end it was no weak man's companions   475

you were to eat by violence and force in your hollow
cave, and your evil deeds were to catch up with you, and be
too strong for you, hard one, who dared to eat your own guests
in your own house, so Zeus and the rest of the gods have punished you."
  'So I spoke, and still more the heart in him was angered.   480
He broke away the peak of a great mountain and let it
fly, and threw it in front of the dark-prowed ship by only
a little, it just failed to graze the steering oar's edge,
but the sea washed up in the splash as the stone went under, the tidal
wave it made swept us suddenly back from the open   485
sea to the mainland again, and forced us on shore. Then I
caught up in my hands the very long pole and pushed her
clear again, and urged my companions with words, and nodding
with my head, to throw their weight on the oars and bring us
out of the threatening evil, and they leaned on and rowed hard.   490
But when we had cut through the sea to twice the previous distance
again I started to call to Cyclops, but my friends about me
checked me, first one then another speaking, trying to soothe me:
"Hard one, why are you trying once more to stir up this savage
man, who just now threw his missile in the sea, forcing   495
our ship to the land again, and we thought once more we were finished
and if he had heard a voice or any one of us speaking,
he would have broken all our heads and our ship's timbers
with a cast of a great jagged stone, so strong is his throwing."
  'So they spoke, but could not persuade the great heart in me,   500
but once again in the anger of my heart I cried to him:
"Cyclops, if any mortal man ever asks you who it was
that inflicted upon your eye this shameful blinding,
tell him that you were blinded by Odysseus, sacker of cities.
Laertes is his father, and he makes his home in Ithaka."   505
  'So I spoke, and he groaned aloud and answered me, saying:
"Ah now, a prophecy spoken of old is come to completion.
There used to be a man here, great and strong, and a prophet,
Telemos, Eurymos' son, who for prophecy was pre-eminent
and grew old as a prophet among the Cyclopes. This man told me   510
how all this that has happened now must someday be accomplished,
and how I must lose the sight of my eye at the hands of Odysseus.
But always I was on the lookout for a man handsome
and tall, with great endowment of strength on him, to come here;
but now the end of it is that a little man, niddering, feeble,   515
has taken away the sight of my eye, first making me helpless
with wine. So come here, Odysseus, let me give you a guest gift
and urge the glorious Shaker of the Earth to grant you conveyance
home. For I am his son, he announces himself as my father.
He himself will heal me, if he will, but not any other   520
one of the blessed gods, nor any man who is mortal."

'So he spoke, but I answered him again and said to him:
"I only wish it were certain I could make you reft of spirit
and life, and send you to the house of Hades, as it is certain
that not even the Shaker of the Earth will ever heal your eye for you." 525
'So I spoke, but he then called to the lord Poseidon
in prayer, reaching both arms up toward the starry heaven:
"Hear me, Poseidon who circle the earth, dark-haired. If truly
I am your son, and you acknowledge yourself as my father,
grant that Odysseus, sacker of cities, son of Laertes, 530
who makes his home in Ithaka, may never reach that home;
but if it is decided that he shall see his own people,
and come home to his strong-founded house and to his own country,
let him come late, in bad case, with the loss of all his companions,
in someone else's ship, and find troubles in his household." 535
'So he spoke in prayer, and the dark-haired god heard him.
Then for the second time lifting a stone far greater
he whirled it and threw, leaning into the cast his strength beyond measure,
and the stone fell behind the dark-prowed ship by only
a little, it just failed to graze the steering oar's edge, 540
and the sea washed up in the splash as the stone went under; the tidal
wave drove us along forward and forced us onto the island.
But after we had so made the island, where all the rest of
our strong-benched ships were waiting together, and our companions
were sitting about them grieving, having waited so long for us, 545
making this point we ran our ship on the sand and beached her,
and we ourselves stepped out onto the break of the sea beach,
and from the hollow ships bringing out the flocks of the Cyclops
we shared them out so none might go cheated of his proper
portion; but for me alone my strong-greaved companions 550
excepted the ram when the sheep were shared, and I sacrificed him
on the sands to Zeus, dark-clouded son of Kronos, lord over
all, and burned him the thighs; but he was not moved by my offerings,
but still was pondering on a way how all my strong-benched
ships should be destroyed and all my eager companions. 555
So for the whole length of the day until the sun's setting,
we sat there feasting on unlimited meat and sweet wine.
But when the sun went down and the sacred darkness came over,
then we lay down to sleep along the break of the seashore;
but when the young Dawn showed again with her rosy fingers, 560
then I urged on the rest of my companions and told them
to go aboard their ships and to cast off the stern cables,
and quickly they went aboard the ships and sat to the oarlocks,
and sitting well in order dashed their oars in the gray sea.
From there we sailed on further along, glad to have escaped death, 565
but grieving still at heart for the loss of our dear companions.

KABTI-ILANI-MARDUK

(EARLY EIGHTH CENTURY B.C.E.)

Babylon

This extraordinary poem was written, as its closing lines inform us, by Kabti-ilani-Marduk, a priest of Marduk, the patron god of Babylon. The poem depicts a time of troubles, characterized both by civil unrest and by incursions of nomadic invaders, during which Marduk's temple was sacked. Kabti-ilani-Marduk, who probably lived in the first half of the eighth century B.C.E. seeks to explore the roots of the disorder, and especially to explain how Marduk could have allowed his own temple to be overrun. The poet wants to show that Marduk himself was not defeated by hostile forces and that he did not simply desert his own people; in particular, the poem exonerates the priesthood of Marduk from accusations of neglect of their duties.

More generally, the poet outlines the nature of responsible and irresponsible government, implicitly admonishing the rulers of Babylon through his story of the consequences of power politics among the gods. Erra, the god of pestilence, persuades Marduk to journey away from Babylon and then usurps his place. He is moved to hatch this plot not from some pure, mythic love of violence but at the behest of his seven disease demons. Normally mere henchmen, here they are shown as a kind of military-pestilential complex, fomenting a war so as to keep their own weapons and tactics in good order; they argue that a spectacular first strike against a weaker opponent will improve Erra's standing at home. Erra, for his part, approves their plan because he realizes that he can use the ensuing disorder to dominate his fellow gods. His depredations end only when his counselor Ishum manages to calm him down. The poem is a striking instance of mythic material used for acute social and political analysis, all presented with vivid dialogue and moving descriptions of the war and its effects.

The Erra Epic

Tablet I

I sing of the son of the lord of the inhabited lands, creator of the universe,
of Hendursanga, Enlil's first-born son,[1] governor of the world,
bearer of the august scepter, guardian of the dark-headed ones, shepherd of
      humanity:
Ishum, glorious warrior whose hands are made to brandish his furious weapons,

Translated by David Damrosch.

Note on translation: This translation is based on the edition and Italian translation by Luigi Cagni; the translator also adopted a number of readings from translations by René Labat and by Stephanie Dalley.

1. Enlil is the chief Sumerian deity; Hendur-sanga is a name for his son Ishum, war leader of the gods, herald and adviser to Erra.

at the flash of whose impetuous spear Erra himself, most valiant of the gods,
   trembles on his throne!   5
When Erra's heart urges him on to battle,
he says to his weapons, "Spread on yourselves the poison of death!"
and to the Seven,[2] heroes unequalled, "Strap your weapons on!"
To you, Ishum, he says, "I am ready to march;
you are the torch, we see by your light;   10
you are the herald, the gods follow your lead;
you are the blade, it is you who will slay."

"Then let us go, Erra!" Ishum replies. "To lay waste the lands,
how it refreshes your spirit, how it gladdens your heart!"
Yet Erra's arms are heavy, as of one who needs sleep.   15
He says to himself, "Should I arise? Should I lie down some more?"
He says to his weapons: "Remain in the corner!"
He says to the Seven, heroes unequalled, "Go back to your homes!"
Until you wake him, Ishum, he stays in his bed,
given over to pleasure with Mami, his wife.   20
O Engidudu,[3] lord who prowls at night, the prince's vigilant guardian,
he watches over the youths and the maidens and makes them shine like day.

But as for the Seven, heroes unequalled, their nature is different indeed.
Their origin is strange, they are replete with terrors,
whoever sees them is horror-struck; their breath is fatal.   25
Mortals tremble, they dare not approach them;
Ishum is their bulwark, a door closed before them.
When Anu, king of the gods, impregnated the Earth,
she bore him seven gods, and he called them the Seven.
They stood before him, and he fixed their destinies.   30
He called the first to give him this order:
"Wherever you spread terror, may you have no rival!"
He said to the second, "Burn like fire, and scorch like flame!"
He said to the third, "Take the features of a lion: those who see you will return to
   nothingness!"
He said to the fourth, "When you raise your furious weapons, the mountains will
   crumble!"   35
He said to the fifth, "Howl like the wind, and search across the sphere of the
   universe!"
He ordered the sixth, "Go from the heights to the depths, and let no one be
   spared!"
He charged the seventh with viper's venom, saying, "Destroy the living!"
After Anu had fixed the destinies of all of the Seven,
he gave them to Erra, champion of the gods, saying, "These will march at your
   side.   40

---

2. The seven disease demons, Erra's lieutenants.

3. A name for Erra.

If the tumult of the inhabited lands becomes distressing to you,
and your heart is moved to wreak destruction,
to kill the dark-headed ones and slaughter the cattle of Shakkan,[4]
then let these be your furious weapons, may they march by your side!"

And now they brandish their arms in rage,   45
saying to Erra: "Get up! Go to it!
Why do you stay in the city, like a feeble old man,
why do you stay at home, like a weak little child?
Like those who do not take the field, should we eat women's bread?
As though we did not know battle, should we tremble, full of fear?   50
For young men, going to war is like going to a feast!
Even a prince who stays in town cannot eat his bread in peace;
he is mocked by his people, and his person is despised.
How can he measure up against those who take the field?
The one who stays in town, however great his strength,   55
in what can he prevail over one who takes the field?
City bread in plenty cannot compare to flat loaves baked in embers,
the sweetest beer cannot compare to water from a goatskin,
nor can a terraced palace be compared to a hut in the field.
Valiant Erra, go into the field, and let your arms resound!   60
Launch your battle-cry so strongly that all who hear will tremble;
that the Igigi,[5] hearing it, may magnify your name;
that the Anunnaki,[6] hearing it, may tremble at your name;
that all the gods, hearing it, may bow beneath your yoke;
that kings, hearing it, may fall down at your feet;   65
that the nations, hearing it, may bring their tribute to you;
that the demons, hearing it, may hide themselves away;
that the powerful, hearing it, may bite their lips in fear;
that the high mountains, hearing it, may shudder and bow their heads;
that the oceans, hearing it, may surge and drown all they produce;   70
that in the ancient forest, the tree-trunks may be shattered;
that in the densest cane-field, the reeds may all be broken;
that the humans may be filled with fear, and quiet their tumult down;
that the beasts be filled with panic, and all return to clay;
seeing all this, may the gods your fathers glorify your valor!   75
Valiant Erra, why have you shunned the field, to rest within the city?
Even the cattle of Shakkan and the other animals scorn us.
O valiant Erra, to you we speak, may our words not displease you!
Before the entire human land becomes too strong for us,
may you take our words to heart!   80
For the Anunnaki, who love silence, you should do a good deed—
the Anunnaki, troubled by the humans' noise, no longer can sleep.

---

4. God of cattle and herdsmen.
5. A group of gods.

6. A group of fifty gods, sons of Anu, judges of
the underworld.

The cattle are trampling down the pastures, the life of the land,
the laborer in his fields is weeping bitterly;
the lion and the wolf are carrying off the cattle of Shakkan,   85
and the shepherd, concerned for his flock, has no rest day or night: it is you he
    implores!
And we, who knew the mountain passes, have completely forgotten the way.
Across our weapons of war the spider has stretched her webs;
our trusty bow, rebelling, has become too strong for us,
the sharp edge of our arrow has been blunted,   90
and our sword is covered with rust instead of blood!"

The valiant Erra heard them;
the words of the Seven pleased him like fine oil.
He opened his mouth and said to Ishum,
"Why, having heard this, do you sit silent and still?   95
Open the way, I would take the path of war!
The Seven, heroes unequalled, are to accompany me;
let my valiant weapons march at my sides,
and as for you, march before me and behind me!"

When Ishum heard these words,   100
he opened his mouth and replied to valiant Erra,
"Lord Erra, why do you plan evil against the gods?
Why do you plan evil, to lay waste the lands and exterminate their people?"

Erra opened his mouth and spoke; to Ishum, his herald, he replied:
"Attend, Ishum, and hear what I have to say!   105
As for the inhabitants of the lands, whom you ask me to spare,
O herald of the gods, wise Ishum, whose counsel is good,
in heaven I am a wild bull, on earth I am a lion!
Among the nations I am the king, among the gods the ferocious one.
Among the Igigi I am the most valiant, among the Anunnaki the most powerful.   110
Among the cattle I am the butcher, among the mountains the wild ram.
In the cane-field, I am the fire; in the forest, the battle-axe.
On the path of war, I am the standard.
I howl like the wind, I thunder like Adad,[7]
like Shamash[8] I survey the entire sphere of the universe.   115
When I go into the field, I am at home like a wild sheep,
when I go up to heaven, I make my home there too.
All of the gods dread battle with me,
but the humans, the dark-headed ones, hold me in contempt!
And so I—since they fear my name no longer,   120
and since they follow their own inclination, rejecting the word of Marduk[9]—
I will stir lord Marduk to anger: I will cause him to leave his throne;
I will destroy the human race!"

---

7. God of storms.
8. God of the sun.

9. Patron god of Babylon, hero of *Enuma Elish*.

Then valiant Erra turned his face toward Shuanna,[10] city of the king of the gods;
he entered Esagil,[11] palace of heaven and earth, and came before Marduk's
    presence.   125
He opened his mouth and spoke to the king of the gods:
"How could it be that your regalia, insignia of your sovereignty, are blemished,
though they should be full of splendor like the stars of heaven?
How could it be that the appearance of your royal crown is dimmed,
though it should illuminate the temple Ehalanki like your tower Etemenanki?"[12] 130

The king of the gods opened his mouth and spoke;
to Erra, champion of the gods, he returned these words:
"Valiant Erra, as for this task you urge me to undertake,
long ago I stirred myself to anger; I left my throne, and I brought about the Flood;
I left my throne, and the bonds of heaven and earth were untied,   135
And then the heavens trembled; the stars were shaken, and did not return to their
    place;
the underworld was stirred up, and the fruit of the furrows grew scarce: a tribute
    imposed forever.
When I had untied the bonds of heaven and earth, the deep waters dried up, and
    the floods ebbed away.
I returned and saw this: it was hard to bring the waters back!
The fertility of living things had diminished, and I could not return them to their
    former state,   140
until, like a farm laborer, I had taken their seed in my own hands,
and until I had built a house and installed myself within.
The appearance of my regalia, tarnished by the deluge, was darkened.
I assigned to Girru[13] the task of renewing the splendor of my features, and
    purifying my vestments.
After he had restored the splendor of my regalia, and had completed this work for
    me,   145
and I had put back on the crown of my sovereignty and had resumed my place,
my features expressed haughtiness, and my look was awesome.
As for the humans who survived the flood and witnessed this work,
should I now wield my arms and destroy the rest?
As for the wise craftsmen, I had sent them into the Abyss, and I did not ordain
    their return.   150
And as for the materials, the rosewood and rock crystal, I had changed their
    location and revealed it to no one.
And so, for the work you propose, O valiant Erra,
where can be found the rosewood, flesh of the gods, insignia of the king of the
    universe?
It is the pure wood, the august youth, fitted for sovereignty,

---

10. A name for Babylon.
11. Marduk's temple.
12. Ehelanki is a shrine in Babylon; Etemenanki is the great ziggurat tower of Marduk.
13. God of fire.

whose root, reaching a hundred leagues into the waters of the great ocean, attains
    the foundations of the nether world;   155

whose root stretches up to the height of the heaven of Anu.
Where is the translucent sapphire, which I had set aside?
Where is Ninildu, great carpenter of my divinity,
who carries the golden adze, and who knows all timbers,
who makes his work shine like day, and who bows before me?   160
Where is Gushkinbanda, creator of god and of man, whose hands are pure?
Where is Ninagal, bearer of the hammer and anvil,
who cuts hard copper as if it were leather, and who makes the needed tools?
Where are the precious stones to be found, product of the vast ocean, ornaments
    of my crown?
Where are now the Seven Sages of the Abyss, the holy carp,   165
filled like their father Ea with sublime understanding, adept at purifying my
    body?"[14]

Hearing him, valiant Erra stepped forward; he opened his mouth and spoke to
    lord Marduk.
"I, Marduk, I will retrieve the rock crystal that you desire,
I will bring back the pure rosewood that you desire."
Hearing this, Marduk opened his mouth and spoke to valiant Erra: 170
"If I should leave my throne again, the bonds of heaven and earth would be
    untied,
the waters would rise up and flood the land.
Bright day would change to darkness,
the tempest would arise and cover the stars;
the evil wind would blow and block the sight of mankind, the progeny of the
    living;   175
demons would ascend from the nether world, and death would seize the living;
until I had resumed my arms, who would repel them?"

Hearing this, Erra opened his mouth and spoke to lord Marduk:
"O prince Marduk, until you have returned to your home, vestments purified by
    Girru,
until you have returned to your place, until that very moment,   180
I myself will take your place, and I will make fast the bonds of heaven and earth!
I will go up to heaven and give the Igigi their orders,
I will descend to the Abyss and assign the Anunnaki's tasks.
I will chase the savage demons to the Land of No Return;
I will unleash my furious weapons against them.   185
As for the evil wind, I will tie up its wings like a bird,
and at that house which you enter, O prince Marduk,
to the right and the left of your door, like guardian bulls,

---

14. Ea, god of freshwater and wisdom, sent
    the Seven Sages in the form of fish to teach
    humanity the arts of civilization.

I will cause the divine Anu and Enlil to lie!"
Lord Marduk heard him out; he was pleased by the words Erra said. 190
He arose from his inaccessible throne, and turned his face toward the Anunnaki's
    dwelling.

Tablet II [15]

Erra entered Emeslam and occupied the throne.
He consulted with himself about what he should do,
but his heart was raging and gave him no reply.
To Ishum he repeated his commands:
"Make the way open: I wish to take the path of war! 5
The day is over, the term is at an end.
I say: Let the splendor of the rays of Shamash be dimmed!
I will cover the face of the Moon at night!
To Adad I will say: 'Hold back your well-springs,
withdraw your clouds, and stop the snow and the rain!' 10
To Marduk and to Ea I will carry this news:
The one who has flourished in times of abundance will be buried in times of
    distress;
the one who has travelled on well-watered roads will return on a pathway of dust!
To the king of the gods I will say: 'Reside in Esagil;
the words you have spoken will be carried out, your orders will be fulfilled; 15
but if the dark-headed ones cry out to you, do not grant their prayers!'
I will destroy the nations and reduce them to heaps of debris.
I will lay the cities low and reduce them all to desert.
I will shatter the mountains and slaughter the cattle on them;
I will stir up the oceans and destroy the things they produce; 20
I will devastate cane-field and forest, burning them up like fire;
I will slaughter the people, leaving no soul alive.
I will not spare a single one, that they could multiply;
I will not let the cattle of Shakkan or any animal escape.
I will take charge over one city after another: 25
The son will no longer think of the health of his father, nor the father care for the
    son.
The mother will plot her daughter's misfortune in the midst of the joys of love.
Into the dwelling of the gods, forbidden to the wicked, I will cause the wicked to
    enter;
into the dwelling of princes I will introduce the scoundrel.
I will cause beasts to enter the city, 30
and I will empty it of people.
I will cause them to strike at the hearts of the mountains;

---

15. The first seventy-five lines of this tablet are fragmentary; the predicted natural disasters occur after Marduk departs. When the text resumes, Erra is taking advantage of the chaos to seize power.

wherever they set their foot, I will devastate that place;
I will cause wild beasts of the steppe to roam about the city.
I will render omens evil; I will devastate the holy precincts.   35
Into the dwellings of the gods I will bring the demon Saghulhaga;
the palace of kings I will bring to ruin.
I will silence the cry of humanity, and deprive them of every joy!"

Tablet III

Erra, in his rage, listens to no one;
he ignores the counsel he is given,
a lion in appearance and in voice.
Then to Ishum, who marches before him, he says these words:
"I will change the sunlight into darkness!   5
I will take the wise man in his house, and I will cut short his days!
As for the just man, the good intercessor, I will cut off his life,
and in his place I will put the wicked man, the cut-throat.
I will alter the human heart: the father will not heed his son,
and the daughter will speak hatefully to her mother.   10
I will render their speech evil: they will forget their god,
and against their goddess they will speak vile insults.
I will raise up brigands to block the roads,
and within the cities, neighbors will steal each other's goods,
while the lion and the wolf attack the cattle of Shakkan.   15
I will enrage the goddess of creation and she will put an end to childbirth;
I will deprive the wet-nurse of the crying of infants and of children.
I will disrupt the song of the workers in the fields;
shepherd and herdsman will forget the shelter of their hut.
I will strip the clothing from the human body: 20
the young will creep naked through their cities,
and I will make them, naked, descend to the nether world.
They will lack the sacrificial sheep to save their life;
even for the prince the lamb needed for the oracles of Shamash will be rare,
and one who is ill will long in vain for the roasted meat for his offering!"[16]   25

Ishum was filled with pity, and said to himself,
"Alas for my people, against whom Erra is enraged!
They have aroused the vengeance of valiant Nergal; now, as in days of combat,
when he killed the conquered Asakku, his arms do not tire;
as if to bind the wicked Anzu, he stretches out his net!"[17]   30
Then Ishum opened his mouth and spoke; to valiant Erra he said these words:
"Why have you had evil thoughts against god and humankind?
Why these endless evil thoughts against the humans, the dark-headed ones?"

---

16. Several dozen fragmentary lines detail
    Erra's depredations and the gods' distress.
    When the text resumes, Ishum responds.

17. The Asakku were a group of demons;
    Anzu was a lion-headed eagle.

Erra opened his mouth and spoke; to Ishum, his herald, he said these words:
"You know the decrees of the Igigi, and the Anunnakis' counsel;   35
you give orders to humanity, the dark-headed ones, and open their
    understanding:
why then do you speak as one who knows nothing?
Why do you counsel me as though you did not know what Marduk has said?
The king of the gods has abandoned his throne—
how could the nations remain stable?   40
He has put aside the crown of his sovereignty:
kings and princes, like slaves, forget their duties.
He has loosened the buckle of his belt,
and the chain linking god and mortals is unfastened: it is hard to retie!
The terrible Girru has made Marduk's precious regalia shine like day, has raised
    up again his divine splendor.   45
His right hand has seized the mace, his great weapon,
and the glance of lord Marduk is fearsome.
O herald of the gods, wise Ishum, whose counsel is benevolent,
why do the words of Marduk displease you?"   50

Ishum opened his mouth and spoke to valiant Erra:
"Warrior Erra, you grasp the reins of heaven,
you are lord of all the earth, you are master of the nations;
you stir up the oceans, you lay the mountains low;
you govern humanity, you give the cattle pasture;   55
Esharra is at your disposal, Engurra is in your hands;
you control Shuanna, you give orders for Esagil;
you gather together all the sacred ordinances: the gods fear you,
the Igigi revere you, the Anunnaki tremble before you.
If you render a decision, even Anu heeds you,   60
even Enlil obeys you. Without you, would there be hostilities,
and without you, would there be battle?
A breastplate of battle is your robe!
And yet you say in your heart: 'They have despised me!'

Tablet IV

"Valiant Erra, you have not feared the name of Marduk;
of the city of the king of the gods, Dimkurkurra, "Bond of the Nations," you have
    broken the bond.
You have altered your divine nature and taken the form of a man;
you have put on your weapons and entered inside the city;
in Babylon, you have spoken as a master, like one who has conquered a city.   5
The people of Babylon, used to growing freely like the reeds of the canals, are all
    clustered around you.
The one who knew no weapons, has his sword unsheathed;
the one who knew no arrow, now his bow is bent;
he who knew no combat, his battle is engaged;

he who knew no haste, flies like a bird;   10
the slow one passes the swift, the feeble surpasses the strong.
Against the governor, provider of their holy city, great insults are spoken;
the gate of Babylon, canal of their abundance, the people themselves have blocked
    up;
they have put the sanctuary of Babylon to fire, as if they were their own
    conquerors!
And you, you marched before them as their herald!   15
You struck with an arrow the great wall Imgur-Enlil—'Ah, my heart!' it exclaimed.
The throne of Muhra, custodian of the entry, you drowned in the blood of
    children.
The inhabitants of Babylon are birds, and you the decoy—
you led them into the net, to be captured and destroyed, O valiant Erra!
Then you left the city, and you went yet further: 20
You assumed the features of a lion and entered into the palace.
Seeing you, the troops put on their arms,
and the heart of the governor, Babylon's protector, became enraged.
He ordered his army to pillage like enemy looters,
and the captain of the guard he incited to evil: 25
'When I send you into the city, my brave one,
fear no god and dread no mortal;
young and old together, put them all to death,
do not spare a single babe or suckling!
Strip off Babylon's riches as your plunder!'   30
The king's army assembled and entered the city;
the arrow blazes, the sword is thrust!
The free man, protected by the holiness of Anu and of Dagan, you have called to
    arms;
you have spilled their blood like water down the city's drains,
you have opened their veins, and made the river flow in blood!   35

"The great lord Marduk has seen this and exclaimed 'Alas!'
His heart was seized, an inexpiable curse was on his lips.
He swore that he would never again drink the river's water;
he shunned their blood and refused to enter Esagil.
'Alas, Babylon,' he cried, 'whose head I ripened like a palm tree, now withered by
    the wind!   40
Alas, Babylon, which I filled with seeds like a pine-cone, whose fullness I cannot
    enjoy!
Alas, Babylon, which I planted like a lush garden, whose fruits I cannot taste!
Alas, Babylon, which like a crystal seal I set at the throat of Anu!
Alas, Babylon, which I held in my hands like the tablet of destiny, and entrusted
    to no one else!'
Thus spoke lord Marduk: 45
'Let the river routes dry up, till they are passable on foot!
May the wells lose thirty fathoms of water, that no one may survive!

May they need to haul the sailor's boat a hundred leagues to reach the waters of
the sea!'

"As for Sippar, primeval city, which the Lord of the Lands did not let the Deluge
drown, for it was dear in his sight,
against the will of Shamash you have destroyed its wall, you have felled its
rampart.
And in Uruk, seat of Anu and of Ishtar—city of courtesans, of temple slaves and
prostitutes,
all those whom Ishtar has deprived of husbands, devoting them to her service—
there the cries of Sutean men and women now ring out![18]
They rouse within Esagil eunuchs and transvestites,
whose masculinity Ishtar, to inspire the people with awe, had changed to
femininity,
bearers of rapiers, of knives, of pruning knives and knives of flint,
those who, to rejoice the heart of Ishtar, give themselves over to abominations;
over these you have placed a cruel and pitiless governor,
who oppresses the people and transgresses their rites.
Ishtar herself, seized with rage, is angered at Uruk as well:
she raises an enemy who sweeps away the people like grain before onrushing
water.
The citizens of Daksa lament without respite the loss of E'ugal,[19] committed to
ruins.
The enemy you have raised up does not know when to stop!

"Ishtaran, god of Der, says these words:
'You have made a desert of my city;
you have broken those inside it like reeds,
and swept their cry away like foam upon the water!
Even me you have not left free: you have delivered me to the Suteans.
And so, on account of Der, my city,
no longer will I render judgments, I will not hand down decisions for the land,
I will give no more orders, nor make my wishes known!' "

(Erra answered thus:)[20] "Since the people have forsaken equity, embracing
violence instead,
since they have abandoned what is just and have turned to plotting evil,
therefore I have unleashed the seven winds against this single country!
Whoever does not die in battle will perish from the plague;
whoever does not die of plague, the enemy will plunder;
whoever the enemy does not plunder will be robbed by the thief;
whoever the thief does not rob will be raked by the weapons of the king;

---

18. The Suteans were semitic nomads, traditional enemies of the settled Akkadians.
19. A major temple of Enlil.
20. The speaker of the following lines is not
identified and may still be Ishtaran,
though Erra seems more likely. Similarly,
the next speech is unattributed but appears to be Ishum's reply to Erra.

whoever is not raked by the weapons of the king will be struck down by the prince;
whoever the prince does not strike down, will be drowned by the storms of Adad;   80
whoever is not drowned by Adad, will be carried off by Shamash;
whoever escapes into the open will be smitten by the wind;
whoever goes into his own house will be struck down by a demon;
whoever climbs to a high place will perish of thirst;
whoever descends into a valley, will perish from the waters;   85
heights and valleys alike will all be fatal!
The governor of the city will speak to his mother thus:
'If only, on the day you bore me, I had been blocked within your womb!
If only you had died in childbirth, and our lives had ended then!
You delivered me into a city whose wall has collapsed;   90
its people become like cattle, and the butcher is their god!'
The net is tightly woven, there is none who can escape.
Whoever sires a son and exclaims: 'Behold my son,
whom I have raised: he will avenge me!'—
that son I will give over to death, and his father must inter him;   95
and then I will give the father to death, and there will be none to dig his grave.
Whoever has built a house, and exclaims: 'This is my dwelling,
this is what I have made, and within it I shall take my rest:
on the day my destiny claims my life, here I will find my resting-place'—
him will I give over to death, and I will have his dwelling plundered;   100
and once it has been sacked, I will give the house to another."

"O valiant Erra," (Ishum responded), "you have slain the just,
and you have slain the unjust alike!
You have slain the one who offended you,
and you have slain the one who has not offended you.   105
You have slain the priest zealous in bringing offerings to his god,
and you have slain the palace attendant, servant of his king.
You have slain the elders in their rooms,
and you have slain the young maiden in her bed.
Yet none of this has calmed you in the least!   110
You say within your heart: 'They have held me in contempt!'
As you say within your heart, O valiant Erra:
'I wish to fell the strong and terrify the weak;
I wish to kill the commander, and scatter his troops in flight;
I wish to shatter the chamber of the sanctuary and the parapet of the wall,
    destroying the city's vital strength;   115
I wish to tear apart the mooring-post, that the boat be pulled away by the current;
I wish to shatter the rudder, that the ship not be able to land;
I wish to shiver the mainmast, and tear its rigging off!
I wish to dry up the mother's breast, that her infant not survive;
I wish to dam the springs, that the rivers lose their water;   120
I wish to send earthquakes through the nether world, that even the heavens may
    shake;

I wish to extinguish the splendor of Shulpae's rays,[21] and cast aside the stars;
I wish to sever the roots of trees, that their buds may not unfold;
I wish to undermine the walls, that their pinnacles may totter,
and I will go to the throne of the king of the gods, that his counsel no longer
   hold!' "   125

When valiant Erra heard Ishum's words, they pleased him like fine oil.
Then valiant Erra spoke thus:
"The sea-folk, the sea-folk; the Subartean, the Subartean; the Assyrian, the
   Assyrian;
the Elamite, the Elamite; the Kassite, the Kassite;
the Sutean, the Sutean; the Gutean, the Gutean; the Lullubean, the Lullubean;[22]   130
one country, another country; one city, another city; one house, another house;
one man, another man; one brother, his brother, without mercy:
May they all kill each other!
Only then may Akkad arise again, destroy them all and rule over them!"

Then valiant Erra said these words to his herald Ishum: 135
"Go, Ishum! Satisfy the longing of your heart to do all that you've said!"
Ishum turned his face toward mount Hihi,[23]
the Seven, heroes unequalled, pressing on behind him.
The hero reached mount Hihi:
he raised his hand and destroyed the mountain,   140
razing mount Hihi to the ground,
and he uprooted the trunks of the forest of cypress.
Once the royal road was cleared, Erra followed after Ishum.
He annihilated the cities and reduced them to desert,
he destroyed the mountains and slaughtered their cattle,   145
he stirred the oceans up and did not spare their produce,
he devastated cane and reed fields, and burned them up like fire,
he cursed the cattle and reduced them all to clay.

Tablet V

When Erra had calmed himself and returned to his throne,
all the gods looked toward his face.
Igigi and Anunnaki alike were full of fear.
Erra opened his mouth, and spoke to all the gods:
"Listen well, all of you! Pay attention to my words!   5
Truly, in this time of fault now past, I plotted wickedness;
my heart burned with rage, and I wished to slaughter the human race.
Like a mercenary shepherd, I stole the leader of the flock;
like one who knows no husbandry, I cut the orchard down;

---

21. A major Sumerian god, identified with the
   planet Jupiter.
22. Erra names various groups both within

southern Mesopotamia and to the north,
east, and west.
23. A mythical mountain, birthplace of Anzu.

like one who lays a country waste, I treated good and evil alike: I killed them all!   10
Yet one cannot pull a corpse from the mouth of a raging lion,
and where one is in a rage, another cannot give counsel!
Without Ishum, my herald, what more might have happened?
Where would your temple supplies be, where would your high priest be?
Where would your food offerings be? No longer would you smell incense!"   15

Ishum opened his mouth and spoke; to valiant Erra he addressed these words:
"Valiant one, listen well! Pay attention to my words!
Very well then, may you now be calm! We wish to be at your service;
in the day of your wrath, who can affront you?"

Erra heard this, and his visage cleared;   20
His radiant features shone like a sunlit day.
He entered Emeslam and occupied his throne,
while Ishum gave orders concerning the ruined people of Akkad:
"Let the remnant of the people begin to multiply again!
May little ones walk the roads with their elders once again.   25
May the weakened Akkadian overcome the mighty Sutean,
may each of you lead seven in tow, as though they were sheep!
May you reduce their cities to ruin, and their grazing lands to desert,
and bring their massive booty into Shuanna!
You will return the gods of your land, no longer angry, to their thrones in safety;   30
you will cause Shakkan and Nisaba[24] to descend to their land again.
The steppe will again produce its riches, and the sea will provide its tribute;
you will make the fields, laid waste, productive once again.
The governors of all the cities will bear their massive tribute into Shuanna.
May the temples now in ruins raise their heads like the rising sun,   35
may the Tigris and Euphrates flow with water in abundance;
let all governors bring supplies to the providers for Esagil and for Babylon.
For years without number, may you praise the great lord Nergal[25] and valiant
     Ishum:
be it said that Erra, consumed with anger, planned to destroy the lands and their
     people,
but Ishum, his counselor, calmed him down and saved a remnant!   40
To Kabti-ilani-Marduk, son of Dabibi, composer of these tablets,
I revealed these verses at night; when he recited them in the morning,
he did not omit a single line, nor did he add a line."

Erra heard this and expressed his approbation;
he was pleased with Ishum, his herald, and the gods all joined in his praise.   45
And then spoke valiant Erra thus:
"As for the god who esteems this song, may his sanctuary grow in wealth,
but the god who rejects it, may he never more smell incense!

---

24. Goddess of grain.

25. The god of death, here identified with
     Erra.

The king who magnifies my name will have lordship over the world,
the prince who proclaims the praise of my valor, he will have no rival!   50
The singer who chants this song will not perish from the plague,
but his words will please both king and prince alike!
The scribe who commits it to memory will escape the land of the enemy, and will
    be honored in his own land;
In the sanctuary of the wise, where they will continually proclaim my name, I will
    give wisdom to them.
In the house where these tablets are placed, should Erra become enraged, should
    the Seven turn murderous again,   55
the sword of destruction will not approach them, but safety will lie upon them.
May this song endure forever, may it last throughout all time!
May all the lands hear it and celebrate my valor,
may all people come to know it, and magnify my name!"

[Postscript to the copy from Assur.]

I, Assurbanipal, great king, mighty king, king of the world, king of Assyria, son of   60
Esarhaddon king of Assyria, son of Sennacherib king of Assyria, wrote,
checked, and collated this tablet in the company of scholars in accordance
with clay tablets and wooden writing boards, exemplars from Assyria, Sumer
and Akkad, and put it in my palace for royal reading. Whoever erases my
written name and writes his own name, may Nabu,[26] the scribe of all, erase
his name.   65

HESIOD (EIGHTH CENTURY B.C.E.)
Greece

Hesiod's *Theogony* chronicles the struggles on Olympus that establish Zeus's
indisputable supremacy. In *Works and Days,* it is justice, given to human beings
by Zeus, that (the poem tells us) distinguishes humankind from wild beasts. The
occasion for *Works and Days*—and for the poet's invoking the justice of
Zeus—purports to be a quarrel between Hesiod and his brother Perses, whom he
accuses of unjustly trying to claim a larger portion of the land that the two have
inherited from their father.

    The dispute gives rise to Hesiod's complaints against corrupt authority
(especially, we can presume, those judges who let Perses get away with his
grab) and to his reflections on the rigors and sorrows of human existence in

Translated by Dorothea Wender.

---

26. God of writing and wisdom.

his contemporary world. The myth about the creation of woman (in the form of Pandora) accounts in part for the suffering intrinsic to the human condition, while the myth of the five generations describes the collective decline of the human race from its earliest stage of equality with the gods, to its present state, characterized by endless labor and pain. Hesiod's exhortations to overcome idleness and restrain greed by means of honest toil (now that work is unavoidably the human lot) are combined in the last half of the poem with practical instructions on how the industrious peasant should spend his day, according to the season, interspersed with ethical precepts designed to ensure him stable prosperity. Literary works of instruction and exhortation known as "wisdom texts" existed in the Near East as early as the middle of the third millenium B.C.E.; Hesiod's poem shows their influence in form as well as content.

from *Works and Days*

[O Perses, store this in your heart]

O Perses, store this in your heart; do not
Let Wicked Strife persuade you, skipping work,
To gape at politicians and give ear
To all the quarrels of the market place.
He has n time for courts and public life   5
Who has not stored up one full year's supply
Of corn, Demeter's gift,[1] got from the earth.
When you have grain piled high, you may dispute
And fight about the goods of other men.
But *you* will never get this chance again: 10
Come, let us settle our dispute at once,
And let our judge be Zeus, whose laws are just.
We split our property in half, but you
Grabbed at the larger part and praised to heaven
The lords who love to try a case like that,   15
Eaters of bribes. The fools! They do not know
That half may be worth more by far than whole,
Nor how much profit lies in poor man's bread.

The gods desire to keep the stuff of life
Hidden from us. If they did not, you could   20
Work for a day and earn a year's supplies;
You'd pack away your rudder, and retire
The oxen and the labouring mules. But Zeus
Concealed the secret, angry in his heart
At being hoodwinked by Prometheus,[2]   25

---

1. Demeter is goddess of agricultural crops and presides over the harvest.

2. The story of how the Titan Prometheus tricked Zeus is told in the *Theogony*.

And so he thought of painful cares for men.
First he hid fire. But the son of Iapetos
Stole it from Zeus the Wise, concealed the flame
In a fennel stalk, and fooled the Thunderer.

Then, raging, spoke the Gatherer of Clouds:[3]   30
'Prometheus, most crafty god of all,
You stole the fire and tricked me, happily,
You, plague on all mankind and on yourself.
They'll pay for fire: I'll give another gift
To men, an evil thing for their delight,   35
And all will love this ruin in their hearts.
So spoke the father of men and gods, and laughed.

He told Hephaistos[4] quickly to mix earth
And water, and to put in it a voice
And human power to move, to make a face   40
Like an immortal goddess, and to shape
The lovely figure of a virgin girl.
Athene was to teach the girl to weave,
And golden Aphrodite[5] to pour charm
Upon her head, and painful, strong desire,   45
And body-shattering cares. Zeus ordered, then,
The killer of Argos, Hermes,[6] put in
Sly manners, and the morals of a bitch.
The son of Kronos spoke, and was obeyed.
The Lame God moulded earth as Zeus decreed   50
Into the image of a modest girl,
Grey-eyed Athene made her robes and belt,
Divine Seduction and the Graces gave
Her golden necklaces, and for her head
The Seasons wove spring flowers into a crown.   55
Hermes the Messenger put in her breast
Lies and persuasive words and cunning ways;
The herald of the gods then named the girl
Pandora[7] for the gifts which all the gods
Had given her, this ruin of mankind.   60

The deep and total trap was now complete;
The Father sent the gods' fast messenger

---

3. An epithet of Zeus, whose dominion is the sky.
4. The divine craftsman.
5. Goddess of love and sexuality.
6. Hermes, the divine messenger, is also a renowned thief and the patron deity of thieves.
7. The name means "all gifts." Woman in this account is viewed as a construction, fabricated by joining together disconnected elements, rather than as an integrated being.

To bring the gift to Epimetheus.[8]
And Epimetheus forgot the words
His brother said, to take no gift from Zeus,   65
But send it back, lest it should injure men.
He took the gift, and understood, too late.

Before this time men lived upon the earth
Apart from sorrow and from painful work,
Free from disease, which brings the Death-gods in.   70
But now the woman opened up the cask,
And scattered pains and evils among men.
Inside the cask's hard walls remained one thing,
Hope, only, which did not fly through the door.
The lid stopped her, but all the others flew,   75
Thousands of troubles, wandering the earth.
The earth is full of evils, and the sea.
Diseases come to visit men by day
And, uninvited, come again at night
Bringing their pains in silence, for they were   80
Deprived of speech by Zeus the Wise. And so
There is no way to flee the mind of Zeus.

And now with art and skill I'll summarize
Another tale, which you should take to heart,
Of how both gods and men began the same.   85
The gods, who live on Mount Olympus, first
Fashioned a golden race of mortal men;
These lived in the reign of Kronos, king of heaven,[9]
And like the gods they lived with happy hearts
Untouched by work or sorrow. Vile old age   90
Never appeared, but always lively-limbed,
Far from all ills, they feasted happily.
Death came to them as sleep, and all good things
Were theirs; ungrudgingly, the fertile land
Gave up her fruits unasked. Happy to be   95
At peace, they lived with every want supplied,
[Rich in their flocks, dear to the blessed gods.]

And then this race was hidden in the ground.
But still they live as spirits of the earth,
Holy and good, guardians who keep off harm,   100

---

8. Brother of Prometheus.
9. Father of Zeus and the other Olympian gods. His reign was thought of as a golden age of simplicity and plenty, subsequent to which men's lives underwent progressive hardships and physical and moral degener-ation. The myth of the deteriorating ages of man represented by successively inferior metals has parallels in Babylonian and Persian mythology, as well as in the Book of Daniel.

Givers of wealth: this kingly right is theirs.
The gods, who live on Mount Olympus, next
Fashioned a lesser, silver race of men:
Unlike the gold in stature or in mind.
A child was raised at home a hundred years   105
And played, huge baby, by his mother's side.
When they were grown and reached their prime, they lived
Brief, anguished lives, from foolishness, for they
Could not control themselves, but recklessly
Injured each other and forsook the gods;   110
They did not sacrifice, as all tribes must, but left
The holy altars bare. And, angry, Zeus
The son of Kronos, hid this race away,
For they dishonoured the Olympian gods.

The earth then hid this second race, and they   115
Are called the spirits of the underworld,
Inferior to the gold, but honoured, too.
And Zeus the father made a race of bronze,
Sprung from the ash tree, worse than the silver race,
But strange and full of power. And they loved   120
The groans and violence of war; they ate
No bread; their hearts were flinty-hard; they were
Terrible men; their strength was great, their arms
And shoulders and their limbs invincible.
Their weapons were of bronze, their houses bronze;   125
Their tools were bronze: black iron was not known.
They died by their own hands, and nameless, went
To Hades' chilly house. Although they were
Great soldiers, they were captured by black Death,
And left the shining brightness of the sun.   130

But when this race was covered by the earth,
The son of Kronos made another, fourth,
Upon the fruitful land, more just and good,
A godlike race of heroes, who are called
The demi-gods—the race before our own.   135
Foul wars and dreadful battles ruined some;
Some sought the flocks of Oedipus,[10] and died
In Cadmus' land, at seven-gated Thebes;
And some, who crossed the open sea in ships,
For fair-haired Helen's sake, were killed at Troy.   140
These men were covered up in death, but Zeus

---

10. A reference to the struggle between the
    sons of Oedipus for power in the city of
    Thebes. (See Sophocles's *Antigone*.)

The son of Kronos gave the others life
And homes apart from mortals, at Earth's edge.
And there they live a carefree life, beside
The whirling Ocean, on the Blessed Isles.   145
Three times a year the blooming, fertile earth
Bears honeyed fruits for them, the happy ones.
And Kronos is their king, far from the gods,
For Zeus released him from his bonds, and these,
The race of heroes, will deserve their fame.   150

Far-seeing Zeus then made another race,
The fifth, who live now on the fertile earth.
I wish I were not of this race, that I
had died before, or had not yet been born.
This is the race of iron. Now, by day,   155
Men work and grieve unceasingly; by night,
They waste away and die. The gods will give
Harsh burdens, but will mingle in some good;
Zeus will destroy this race of mortal men,
When babies shall be born with greying hair.   160
Father will have no common bond with son,
Neither will guest with host, nor friend with friend;
The brother-love of past days will be gone.
Men will dishonour parents, who grow old
Too quickly, and will blame and criticize   165
With cruel words. Wretched and godless, they
Refusing to repay their bringing up,
Will cheat their aged parents of their due.
Men will destroy the towns of other men.
The just, the good, the man who keeps his word   170
Will be despised, but men will praise the bad
And insolent. Might will be Right, and shame
Will cease to be. Men will do injury
To better men by speaking crooked words
And adding lying oaths;   175

. . .

O Perses, follow right; control your pride.
For pride is evil in a common man.
Even a noble finds it hard to bear;
It weighs him down and leads him to disgrace.
The road to justice is the better way,   180
For Justice in the end will win the race
And Pride will lose: the simpleton must learn
This fact through suffering. The god of Oaths
Runs faster than a crooked verdict; when
Justice is dragged out of the way by men   185

Who judge dishonestly and swallow bribes,
A struggling sound is heard; then she returns
Back to the city and the homes of men,
Wrapped in a mist and weeping, and she brings
Harm to the crooked men who drove her out.   190
But when the judges of a town are fair
To foreigner and citizen alike,
Their city prospers and her people bloom;
Since Peace is in the land, her children thrive;
Zeus never marks them out for cruel war.   195
Famine and blight do not beset the just,
Who till their well-worked fields and feast. The earth
Supports them lavishly; and on the hills
The oak bears acorns for them at the top
And honey-bees below; their woolly sheep   200
Bear heavy fleeces, and their wives bear sons
Just like their fathers. Since they always thrive,
They have no need to go on ships, because
The plenty-bringing land gives them her fruit.

But there are some who till the fields of pride   205
And work at evil deeds; Zeus marks them out,
And often, all the city suffers for
Their wicked schemes, and on these men, from heaven
The son of Kronos sends great punishments,
Both plague and famine, and the people die.   210
Their wives are barren, and their villages
Dwindle, according to the plan of Zeus.
At other times the son of Kronos will
Destroy their army, or will snatch away
Their city wall, or all their ships at sea.   215
You lords, take notice of his punishment.
The deathless gods are never far away;
They mark the crooked judges who grind down
Their fellow-men and do not fear the gods.
Three times ten thousand watchers-over-men,   220
Immortal, roam the fertile earth for Zeus.
Clothed in a mist, they visit every land
And keep a watch on law-suits and on crimes.
One of them is the virgin, born of Zeus,
Justice, revered by all the Olympian gods.   225
Whenever she is hurt by perjurers,
Straightway she sits beside her father Zeus,
And tells him of the unjust hearts of men,
Until the city suffers for its lords
Who recklessly, with mischief in their minds,   230

Pervert their judgments crookedly. Beware,
You lords who swallow bribes, and try to judge
Uprightly, clear your minds of crookedness.
He hurts himself who hurts another man,
And evil planning harms the planner most.   235

The eye of Zeus sees all, and understands,
And when he wishes, marks and does not miss
How just a city is, inside. And I
Would not myself be just, nor have my son
Be just among bad men: for it is bad   240
To be an honest man where felons rule;
I trust wise Zeus to save me from this pass.
But you, O Perses, think about these things;
Follow the just, avoiding violence.
The son of Kronos made this law for men: 245
That animals and fish and winged birds
Should eat each other, for they have no law.
But mankind has the law of Right from him,
Which is the better way. And if one knows
The law of Justice and proclaims it, Zeus   250
Far-seeing gives one great prosperity.
But if a man, with knowledge, swears an oath
Committing perjury and harming right
Beyond repair, his family will be cursed
In after times, and come to nothing. He   255
Who keeps his oath will benefit his house.

I say important things for you to hear,
O foolish Perses: Badness can be caught
In great abundance, easily; the road
To her is level, and she lives near by.   260
But Good is harder, for the gods have placed
In front of her much sweat; the road is steep
And long and rocky at the first, but when
You reach the top, she is not hard to find.

That man is best who reasons for himself,   265
Considering the future. Also good
Is he who takes another's good advice.
But he who neither thinks himself nor learns
From others, is a failure as a man.

O noble Perses, keep my words in mind,   270
And work till Hunger is your enemy
And till Demeter, awesome, garlanded,
Becomes your friend and fills your granary.
For Hunger always loves a lazy man;

Both gods and men despise him, for he is   275
Much like the stingless drone, who does not work
But eats, and wastes the effort of the bees.
But you must learn to organize your work
So you may have full barns at harvest time.
From working, men grow rich in flocks and gold   280
And dearer to the deathless gods. In work
There is no shame; shame is in idleness.
And if you work, the lazy man will soon
Envy your wealth: a rich man can become
Famous and good. No matter what your luck,   285
To work is better; turn your foolish mind
From other men's possessions to your own,
And earn your living, as I tell you to.
A cringing humbleness accompanies
The needy man, a humbleness which may   290
Destroy or profit him. The humble are
The poor men, while the rich are self-assured.
Money should not be seized; that gold which is
God's gift is better. If a man gets wealth
By force of hands or through his lying tongue,   295
As often happens, when greed clouds his mind
And shame is pushed aside by shamelessness,
Then the gods blot him out and blast his house
And soon his wealth deserts him. Also, he
Who harms a guest or suppliant, or acts   300
Unseemly, sleeping with his brother's wife,
Or in his folly, hurts an orphan child,
Or he who picks rough quarrels, and attacks
His father at the threshold of old age,
He angers Zeus himself, and in the end   305
He pays harsh penalties for all his sins.

Now, shut your foolish heart against these things
And sacrifice to the immortal gods
With reverence and ritual cleanliness,
And burn the glorious thigh-bones; please the gods   310
With incense and libations, when you go
To bed, and when the holy light returns,
That they may favour you, with gracious hearts
And spirits, so that you may buy the lands
Of other men, and they may not buy yours.   315

Invite your friend, but not your enemy,
To dine; especially, be cordial to
Your neighbour, for if trouble comes at home,
A neighbour's there, at hand; while kinsmen take

Some time to arm themselves. It is a curse
To have a worthless neighbour; equally,
A good one is a blessing; he who is
So blest possesses something of great worth.
No cow of yours will stray away if you
Have watchful neighbours. Measure carefully
When you must borrow from your neighbour, then,
pay back the same, or more, if possible,
And you will have a friend in time of need.

Shun evil profit, for dishonest gain
Is just the same as failure. Love your friends.

320
325
330

ARCHILOCHUS
(SEVENTH CENTURY B.C.E.)
TYRTAEUS (SEVENTH CENTURY B.C.E.)
SOLON (c. 640–558 B.C.E.)
Greece

As increasingly complex forms of political and social organization developed throughout Greece in the seventh century B.C.E., the experience of belonging to a community, with all the entailed responsibilities and benefits, became a subject for reflection. A number of poetic forms lent themselves to the expression of community-centered concerns at this period (literary prose came only much later); among them was the elegy. Ancient critics made a formal distinction between elegiac and lyric poetry, the elegy being accompanied by the flute, the lyric being sung to a stringed instrument called the lyre. In addition, the elegy's distinctive meter, consisting of two-line sequences, set it apart from the stanzaic structure of lyric verse. In later periods the term elegy came exclusively to denote poetry of mourning, but in early Greece elegiac meter was used for poetry on a wide variety of subjects, notably that of political address as well as private reflection. All of the poems in this selection, with the exception of Archilochus's "Heart, my heart" and "I don't like a tall general, swaggering" are elegies.

Archilochus, who lived in the mid-seventh century B.C.E. and came from the island of Paros, is the first practitioner of elegy whose work survives to us (although he wrote in other verse forms as well). In a striking departure from the way in which Homer and even Hesiod present themselves in their poetry, Archilochus represents himself as a citizen, a member of a political entity, deeply affected by the loss of his fellow citizens.

Tyrtaeus, Archilochus's younger contemporary from Sparta, returns us to an image of battle reminiscent of the *Iliad* (and clearly influenced by it). Here, however, the call to valor is a call to patriotism; the context for Tyrtaeus was his city's war with a neighboring territory, and he exhorts his fellow Spartans to brave action on the battlefield by reminding them of each individual's dependence on the city for which he fights.

Solon was both a poet and a crucial figure in Athenian political history who was responsible for far-reaching constitutional reforms. The broad civic (rather than simply military) obligation of citizens to the community that sustains them is a major theme of Solon's poetry. His emphasis on justice and individual righteous behavior recalls Hesiod's *Works and Days,* while his unshakable commitment to the city—Athens—as the environment that best allows the individual to flourish, has much in common with Thucydides in his *Funeral Oration.*

ARCHILOCHUS

[I am a servant of the War Lord]

I am a servant of the War Lord
and of the Muses, knowing their desirable gift.

[I don't like a tall general, swaggering]

I don't like a tall general, swaggering,
proud of his curls, with a fancy shave.
I'd rather have a short man, who looks
bow-legged, with a firm stride, full of heart.

[Some Thracian exults in an excellent shield]

Some Thracian exults in an excellent shield,
which I left—not willingly—by a bush.
I saved myself. What do I care for that shield?
To hell with it. I'll buy one again, no worse.

[Heart, my heart churning with fathomless cares]

Heart, my heart churning with fathomless cares,
get up! Fight! Heave your chest against the foe,
standing firm near the enemy's shafts.
And don't exult openly in victory,

Poems by Archilochus are translated by Diane J. Rayor.

nor in defeat collapse at home and weep.   5
But rejoice in joys and chafe at evils—
not too much. Recognize what rhythm holds men.

[No townsman, Perikles, will blame us]

No townsman, Perikles,[1] will blame us for groaning
with cares, nor will the city celebrate feasts:
Such men the waves of the thundering sea
washed under, that our lungs are swollen
with sorrow. But for incurable ills, my friend,   5
the gods created powerful endurance
as a drug. Pain strikes one, then another.
Now it turns to us and we groan over a bloody
wound; next it'll turn to someone else. So now
endure, driving back womanly grief.   10

TYRTAEUS

[I would not say anything for a man nor take account of him]

I would not say anything for a man nor take account of him
    for any speed of his feet or wrestling skill he might have,
not if he had the size of a Cyclops and strength to go with it,
    not if he could outrun Bóreas, the North Wind of Thrace,
not if he were more handsome and gracefully formed than Tithónos,[1]   5
    or had more riches than Midas[2] had, or Kínyras[3] too,
not if he were more of a king than Tantalid Pelops,[4]
    or had the power of speech and persuasion Adrastos[5] had,
not if he had all splendors except for a fighting spirit.
    For no man ever proves himself a good man in war   10
unless he can endure to face the blood and the slaughter,
    go close against the enemy and fight with his hands.
Here is courage, mankind's finest possession, here is
    the noblest prize that a young man can endeavor to win,

Poems by Tyrtaeus and Solon are translated by Richmond Lattimore.

Archilochus
1. One of Archilochus's friends, otherwise unknown.
Tyrtaeus
1. The lover of the Dawn goddess; legendary as a young man, for his beauty.
2. A mythical Phrygian king whose touch turned things to gold.

3. A legendary king of Cyprus, famous for his wealth.
4. A mythical king for whom the Peloponnese, where he ruled, was named; the grandfather of Agamemnon and Menelaus (see Selection 8).
5. A king of Argos, in the Peloponnese.

and it is a good thing his city and all the people share with him   15
    when a man plants his feet and stands in the foremost spears
relentlessly, all thought of foul flight completely forgotten,
    and has well trained his heart to be steadfast and to endure,
and with words encourages the man who is stationed beside him.
    Here is man who proves himself to be valiant in war.   20
With a sudden rush he turns to flight the rugged battalions
    of the enemy, and sustains the beating waves of assault.
And he who so falls among the champions and loses his sweet life,
    so blessing with honor his city, his father, and all his people,
with wounds in his chest, where the spear that he was facing has transfixed   25
    that massive guard of his shield, and gone through his breastplate as well,
why, such a man is lamented alike by the young and the elders,
    and all his city goes into mourning and grieves for his loss.
His tomb is pointed to with pride, and so are his children,
    and his children's children, and afterward all the race that is his.   30
His shining glory is never forgotten, his name is remembered,
    and he becomes an immortal, though he lies under the ground,
when one who was a brave man has been killed by the furious War God
    standing his ground and fighting hard for his children and land.
But if he escapes the doom of death, the destroyer of bodies,   35
    and wins his battle, and bright renown for the work of his spear,
all men give place to him alike, the youth and the elders,
    and much joy comes his way before he goes down to the dead.
Aging, he has reputation among his citizens. No one
    tries to interfere with his honors or all he deserves;   40
all men withdraw before his presence, and yield their seats to him,
    the youth, and the men his age, and even those older than he.
Thus a man should endeavor to reach this high place of courage
    with all his heart, and, so trying, never be backward in war.

SOLON

[This city of ours will never be destroyed]

This city of ours[1] will never be destroyed by the planning
    of Zeus, nor according to the wish of the immortal gods;
such is she who, great hearted, mightily fathered, protects us,
    Pallas Athene, whose hands are stretched out over our heads.

Solon
1. Athens.

But the citizens themselves in their wildness are bent on destruction   5
  of their great city, and money is the compulsive cause.
The leaders of the people are evil-minded. The next stage
  will be great suffering, recompense for their violent acts,
for they do not know enough to restrain their greed and apportion
  orderly shares for all as if at a decorous feast.   10

  they are tempted into unrighteous acts and grow rich.

  sparing the property neither of the public nor of the gods,
they go on stealing, by force or deception, each from the other,
  nor do the solemn commitments of Justice keep them in check;
but she knows well, though silent, what happens and what has been happening,
  and in her time she returns to extract a full revenge;   15
for it comes upon the entire city as a wound beyond healing,
  and quickly it happens that foul slavery is the result,
and slavery wakens internal strife, and sleeping warfare,
  and this again destroys many in the pride of their youth,
for from enemies' devising our much-adored city is afflicted   20
  before long by conspiracies so dear to wicked men.
Such evils are churning in the home country, but, of the impoverished,
  many have made their way abroad on to alien soil,
sold away, and shamefully going in chains of slavery.

Thus the public Ruin invades the house of each citizen,   25
  and the courtyard doors no longer have strength to keep it away,
but it overleaps the lofty wall, and though a man runs in
  and tries to hide in chamber or closet, it ferrets him out.
So my spirit dictates to me: I must tell the Athenians
  how many evils a city suffers from Bad Government,   30
and how Good Government displays all neatness and order,
  and many times she must put shackles on the breakers of laws.
She levels rough places, stops Glut and Greed, takes the force from Violence;
  she dries up the growing flowers of Despair as they grow;
she straightens out crooked judgments given, gentles the swollen   35
  ambitions, and puts an end to acts of divisional strife;
she stills the gall of wearisome Hate, and under her influence
  all life among mankind is harmonious and does well.

[I gave the people as much privilege as they have a right to]

I gave the people as much privilege as they have a right to:
  I neither degraded them from rank nor gave them free hand;
and for those who already held the power and were envied for money,

   I worked it out that they also should have no cause for complaint.
I stood there holding my sturdy shield over both the parties;   5
   I would not let either side win a victory that was wrong.

                                   . . .

Thus would the people be best off, with the leaders they follow:
   neither given excessive freedom nor put to restraint;
for Glut gives birth to Greed, when great prosperity suddenly
   befalls those people who do not have an orderly mind.   10

   Acting where issues are great, it is hard to please all.

[My purpose was to bring my scattered people back]

My purpose was to bring my scattered people back
together. Where did I fall short of my design?
I call to witness at the judgment seat of time
one who is noblest, mother of Olympian
divinities, and greatest of them all, Black Earth.   5
I took away the mortgage stones[1] stuck in her breast,
and she, who went a slave before, is now set free.
Into this sacred land, our Athens, I brought back
a throng of those who had been sold, some by due law,
though others wrongly; some by hardship pressed to escape   10
the debts they owed; and some of these no longer spoke
Attic, since they had drifted wide around the world,
while those in the country had the shame of slavery
upon them, and they served their masters' moods in fear.
These I set free; and I did this by strength of hand,   15
welding right law with violence to a single whole.
So have I done, and carried through all that I pledged.
I have made laws, for the good man and the bad alike,
and shaped a rule to suit each case, and set it down.
Had someone else not like myself taken the reins,   20
some ill-advised or greedy person, he would not
have held the people in. Had I agreed to do
what pleased their adversaries at that time, or what
they themselves planned to do against their enemies,
our city would have been widowed of her men. Therefore,   25
I put myself on guard at every side, and turned
among them like a wolf inside a pack of dogs.

[My purpose was to bring]
1. Among Solon's democratic reforms was his
abolition of serfdom, including the cancel-
lation of all existing debts and mortgages.

SOPHOCLES (496–406 B.C.E.)
Greece

Tragic drama in Greece was closely associated with the city of Athens. It was regarded in antiquity as originating there, and it was certainly in the hands of Athenian playwrights that it flourished with the support and participation of Athenian citizens. In the sixth century B.C.E., Athens established a competition in tragedy, held at an annual civic and religious festival honoring the god Dionysus. An individual was chosen by lot from the community at large to be in charge of the festival. It was that person's responsibility to select the major participants: three competing playwrights, each of whom would produce four plays for the occasion; the financial sponsors, who as a service to the city provided money for the staging of the plays; the chorus members; and the judges, who awarded the prizes. Audiences were huge, by modern standards: the Theater of Dionysus where the tragedies were performed, located just below the Acropolis in Athens, held 14,000 people.

The fifth century B.C.E. was especially rich in tragic drama, including the plays of Aeschylus, Sophocles, and Euripides, among others. Over a lifetime that practically spanned the century, Sophocles wrote 123 plays, many of which took first prize in the competition; he also held, at different times, important military, political, and religious offices in Athens.

The myth of Oedipus provided the subject for tragedies by Aeschylus and Euripides as well as for three of Sophocles' seven surviving plays. Although one

Sophocles. Roman copy of bronze original erected in the Theater of Dionysus, Athens.

play (by Aeschylus) on a historical subject is extant, and we know of others, most tragedies were based on episodes from mythology familiar to their audience; through them the poets explored issues fundamental to the political, moral, and intellectual concerns of their city, as *Antigone* powerfully demonstrates.

Antigone

Characters

ANTIGONE	HAEMON
ISMENE	TEIRESIAS
CHORUS OF THEBAN ELDERS	A MESSENGER
CREON	EURYDICE
A GUARD	

[When Oedipus, the father of Antigone and Ismene, was exiled from Thebes, after the discovery that he had unknowingly murdered his father and married his mother, his sons Eteocles and Polyneices became rivals for their father's throne. Despite his equal claim, Polyneices was expelled from Thebes by his brother. Polyneices thereupon raised an army captained by himself and six leading Argive warriors, and marched against Thebes. The attacking army was defeated and the two brothers died at each other's hands, leaving Creon, the brother of Oedipus's wife (and mother) Jocasta, as the city's new ruler.]

Scene

Thebes, before the royal palace. Antigone and Ismene emerge from its great central door.

ANTIGONE: My sister, my Ismene, do you know
    of any suffering from our father sprung
    that Zeus does not achieve for us survivors?
    There's nothing grievous, nothing free from doom,
    not shameful, not dishonored, I've not seen.   5
    Your sufferings and mine.
    And now, what of this edict which they say
    the commander has proclaimed to the whole people?
    Have you heard anything? Or don't you know
    that the foes' trouble comes upon our friends?   10
ISMENE: I've heard no word, Antigone, of our friends.
    Not sweet nor bitter, since that single moment
    when we two lost two brothers
    who died on one day by a double blow.
    And since the Argive army went away   15
    this very night, I have no further news
    of fortune or disaster for myself.
ANTIGONE: I knew it well, and brought you from the house
    for just this reason, that you alone may hear.
ISMENE: What is it? Clearly some news has clouded you.   20

Translated by Elizabeth Wyckoff.

ANTIGONE: It has indeed. Creon will give the one
    of our two brothers honor in the tomb;
    the other none.
    Eteocles, with just entreatment treated,
    as law provides he has hidden under earth   25
    to have full honor with the dead below.
    But Polyneices' corpse who died in pain,
    they say he has proclaimed to the whole town
    that none may bury him and none bewail,
    but leave him unwept, untombed, a rich sweet sight   30
    for the hungry birds' beholding.
    Such orders they say the worthy Creon gives
    to you and me—yes, yes I say to *me*—
    and that he's coming to proclaim it clear
    to those who know it not.   35
    Further: he has the matter so at heart
    that anyone who dares attempt the act
    will die by public stoning in the town.
    So there you have it and you soon will show
    if you are noble, or fallen from your descent.
ISMENE: If things have reached this stage, what can I do,
    poor sister, that will help to make or mend?   40
ANTIGONE: Think will you share my labor and my act.
ISMENE: What will you risk? And where is your intent?
ANTIGONE: Will you take up that corpse along with me?
ISMENE: To bury him you mean, when it's forbidden?
ANTIGONE: My brother, and yours, though you may wish he were not. 45
    I never shall be found to be his traitor.
ISMENE: O hard of mind! When Creon spoke against it!
ANTIGONE: It's not for him to keep me from my own.
ISMENE: Alas, Remember, sister, how our father
    perished abhorred, ill famed.   50
    Himself with his own hand, through his own curse
    destroyed both eyes.
    Remember next his mother and his wife
    finishing life in the shame of the twisted strings.
    And third two brothers on a single day,   55
    poor creatures, murdering, a common doom
    each with his arm accomplished on the other.
    And now look at the two of us alone.
    We'll perish terribly if we force law
    and try to cross the royal vote and power.   60
    We must remember that we two are women
    so not to fight with men.
    And that since we are subject to strong power
    we must hear these orders, or any that may be worse.

So I shall ask of them beneath the earth   65
forgiveness, for in these things I am forced,
and shall obey the men in power. I know
that wild and futile action makes no sense.

ANTIGONE: I wouldn't urge it. And if now you wished
to act, you wouldn't please me as a partner.   70
Be what you want to; but that man shall I
bury. For me, the doer, death is best.
Friend shall I lie with him, yes friend with friend,
when I have dared the crime of piety.
Longer the time in which to please the dead   75
than that for those up here.
There shall I lie forever. You may see fit
to keep from honor what the gods have honored.

ISMENE: I shall do no dishonor, But to act
against the citizens. I cannot.

ANTIGONE: That's your protection. Now I go, to pile   80
the burial-mound for him, my dearest brother.

ISMENE: Oh my poor sister. How I fear for you!

ANTIGONE: For me, don't borrow trouble. Clear your fate.

ISMENE: At least give no one warning of this act;
you keep it hidden, and I'll do the same.   85

ANTIGONE: Dear God! Denounce me. I shall hate you more
if silent, not proclaiming this to all.

ISMENE: You have a hot mind over chilly things.

ANTIGONE: I know I please those whom I most should please.

ISMENE: If but you can. You crave what can't be done.   90

ANTIGONE: And so, when strength runs out, I shall give over.

ISMENE: Wrong from the start, to chase what cannot be.

ANTIGONE: If that's your saying, I shall hate you first,
and next the dead will hate you in all justice.
But let me and my own ill-counselling   95
suffer this terror. I shall suffer nothing
as great as dying with a lack of grace.

ISMENE: Go, since you want to. But know this: you go
senseless indeed, but loved by those who love you.

[Ismene returns to the palace; Antigone leaves by one of the side entrances.
The Chorus now enters from the other side.]

CHORUS: Sun's own radiance, fairest light ever shone on the gates of Thebes,   100
then did you shine, O golden day's
eye, coming over Dirce's[1] stream,

---

1. A river on the western side of Thebes.

on the Man who had come from Argos[2] with all his armor
running now in headlong fear as you shook his bridle free.

He was stirred by the dubious quarrel of Polyneices.   105
So, screaming shrill,
like an eagle over the land he flew,
covered with white-snow wing,
with many weapons,
with horse-hair crested helms.   110

He who had stood above our halls, gaping about our seven gates,
with that circle of thirsting spears.
Gone, without our blood in his jaws,   115
before the torch took hold on our tower-crown.
Rattle of war at his back; hard the fight for the dragon's foe.

The boasts of a proud tongue are for Zeus to hate.
So seeing them streaming on
in insolent clangor of gold,   120
he struck with hurling fire him who rushed
for the high wall's top,
to cry conquest abroad.

Swinging, striking the earth he fell
fire in hand, who in mad attack,   125
had raged against us with blasts of hate.
He failed. He failed of his aim.
For the rest great Ares[3] dealt his blows about,
first in the war-team.   130

The captains stationed at seven gates
fought with seven and left behind
their brazen arms as an offering
to Zeus who is turner of battle.
All but those wretches, sons of one man,   135
one mother's sons, who sent their spears
each against each and found the share
of a common death together.

Great-named Victory comes to us
answering Thebe's warrior-joy.   140
Let us forget the wars just done
and visit the shrines of the gods.
All, with night-long dance which Bacchus[4] will lead,
who shakes Thebe's acres.

---

2. This refers collectively to the invading army   4. The god Dionysus, closely associated with
   raised by Polyneices in Argos.   the city of Thebes. [See Euripides' *Bacchae*]
3. The god of war.

[Creon enters from the palace.]

Now here he comes, the king of the land,   145
Creon, Menoeceus' son,
newly named by the gods' new fate.
What plan that beats about his mind
has made him call this council-session,
sending his summons to all?   150

CREON: My friends, the very gods who shook the state
with mighty surge have set it straight again.
So now I sent for you, chosen from all,
first that I knew you constant in respect
to Laius' royal power; and again   155
when Oedipus had set the state to rights,
and when he perished, you were faithful still
in mind to the descendants of the dead.
When they two perished by a doubt fate,
on one day struck and striking and defiled   160
each by his own hand, now it comes that I
hold all the power and the royal throne
through close connection with the perished men.
You cannot learn of any man the soul,
the mind, and the intent until he shows   165
his practice of the government and law.
For I believe that who controls the state
and does not hold to the best plans of all,
but locks his tongue up through some kind of fear,
that he is worst of all who are or were.   170
And he who counts another greater friend
than his own fatherland, I put him nowhere.
So I—may Zeus all-seeing always know it—
could not keep silent as disaster crept
upon the town, destroying hope of safety.   175
Nor could I count the enemy of the land
friend to myself, not I who know so well
that she it is who saves us, sailing straight,
and only so can we have friends at all.
With such good rules shall I enlarge our state.   180
And now I have proclaimed their brother-edict.
In the matter of the sons of Oedipus,
citizens, know: Eteocles who died,
defending this our town with champion spear,
is to be covered in the grave and granted   185
all holy rites we give the noble dead.
But his brother Polyneices whom I name
the exile who came back and sought to burn

his fatherland, the gods who were his kin,
who tried to gorge on blood he shared, and lead 190
the rest of us as slaves—
it is announced that no one in this town
may give him burial or mourn for him.
Leave him unburied, leave his corpse disgraced,
a dinner for the birds and for the dogs. 195
Such is my mind. Never shall I, myself,
honor the wicked and reject the just.
The man who is well-minded to the state
from me in death and life shall have his honor.

CHORUS: This resolution, Creon, is your own,
in the matter of the traitor and the true. 200
For you can make such rulings as you will
about the living and about the dead.

CREON: Now you be sentinels of the decree.

CHORUS: Order some younger man to take this on.

CREON: Already there are watchers of the corpse. 205

CHORUS: What other order would you give us, then?

CREON: Not to take sides with any who disobey.

CHORUS: No fool is fool as far as loving death.

CREON: Death is the price. But often we have known
men to be ruined by the hope of profit. 210

[Enter, from the side, a guard.]

GUARD: Lord, I can't claim that I am out of breath
from rushing here with light and hasty step,
for I had many haltings in my thought
making me double back upon my road.
My mind kept saying many things to me: 215
"Why go where you will surely pay the price?"
"Fool, are you halting? And if Creon learns
from someone else, how shall you not be hurt?"
Turning this over, on I dilly-dallied.
And so a short trip turns itself to long. 220
Finally, though, my coming here won out.
If what I say is nothing, still I'll say it.
For I come clutching to one single hope
that I can't suffer what is not my fate.

CREON: What is it that brings on this gloom of yours? 225

GUARD: I want to tell you first about myself.
I didn't do it, didn't see who did it.
It isn't right for me to get in trouble.

CREON: Your aim is good. You fence the fact around.
It's clear you have some shocking news to tell. 230

GUARD: Terrible tidings make for long delays.

CREON: Speak out the story, and then get away.
GUARD: I'll tell you. Someone left the corpse just now,
    burial all accomplished, thirsty dust
    strewn on the flesh, the ritual complete.   235
CREON: What are you saying? What man has dared to do it?
GUARD: I wouldn't know. There were no marks of picks,
    no grubbed-out earth. The ground was dry and hard,
    no trace of wheels. The door left no sign.
    When the first fellow on the day-shift showed us,   240
    we all were sick with wonder.
    For he was hidden, not inside a tomb,
    light dust upon him, enough to turn the curse,
    no wild beast's track, nor track of any hound
    having been near, nor was the body torn.   245
    We roared bad words about, guard against guard,
    and came to blows. No one was there to stop us.
    Each man had done it, nobody had done it
    so as to prove it on him—we couldn't tell.
    We were prepared to hold to red-hot iron,   250
    to walk through fire, to swear before the gods
    we hadn't done it, hadn't shared the plan,
    when it was plotted or when it was done.
    And last, when all our sleuthing came out nowhere,
    one fellow spoke, who made our heads to droop   255
    low toward the ground. We couldn't disagree.
    We couldn't see a chance of getting off.
    He said we had to tell you all about it.
    We couldn't hide the fact.
    So he won out. The lot chose poor old me   260
    to win the prize. So here I am unwilling,
    quite sure you people hardly want to see me.
    Nobody likes the bringer of bad news.
CHORUS: Lord, while he spoke, my mind kept on debating.
    Isn't this action possibly a god's?   265
CREON: Stop now, before you fill me up with rage,
    or you'll prove yourself insane as well as old.
    Unbearable, your saying that the gods
    take any kindly forethought for this corpse.
    Would it be they had hidden him away,   270
    honoring his good service, his who came
    to burn their pillared temples and their wealth,
    even their land, and break apart their laws?
    Or have you seen them honor wicked men?
    It isn't so.   275
    No, from the first there were some men in town
    who took the edict hard, and growled against me,

who hid the fact that they were rearing back,
not rightly in the yoke, no way my friends.
These are the people—oh it's clear to me—   280
who have bribed these men and brought about the deed.
No current custom among men as bad
as silver currency. This destroys the state;
this drives men from their homes; this wicked teacher
drives solid citizens to acts of shame.   285
It shows men how to practise infamy
and know the deeds of all unholiness.
Every least hireling who helped in this
brought about then the sentence he shall have.
But further, as I still revere great Zeus,   290
understand this, I tell you under oath,
if you don't find the very man whose hands
buried the corpse, bring him for me to see,
not death alone shall be enough for you
till living, hanging, you make clear the crime.   295
For any future grabbings you'll have learned
where to get pay, and that it doesn't pay
to squeeze a profit out of every source.
For you'll have felt that more men come to doom
through dirty profits than are kept by them.   300

GUARD: May I say something? Or just turn and go?
CREON: Aren't you aware your speech is most unwelcome?
GUARD: Does it annoy your hearing or your mind?
CREON: Why are you out to allocate my pain?
GUARD: The doer hurts your mind. I hurt your ears.   305
CREON: You are a quibbling rascal through and through.
GUARD: But anyhow I never did the deed.
CREON: And you the man who sold your mind for money!
GUARD: Oh!
        How terrible to guess, and guess at lies!
CREON: Go pretty up your guesswork. If you don't   310
        show me the doers you will have to say
        that wicked payments work their own revenge.
GUARD: Indeed, I pray he's found, but yes or no,
        taken or not as luck may settle it,
        you won't see me returning to this place.   315
        Saved when I neither hoped nor thought to be,
        I owe the gods a mighty debt of thanks.

[Creon enters the palace. The Guard leaves by the way he came.]

CHORUS: Many the wonders but nothing walks stranger than man.
         This thing[5] crosses the sea in the winter's storm,

---

5. This remarkable creature, man.

making his path through the roaring waves.   320
And she, the greatest of gods, the earth—
ageless she is, and unwearied—he wears her away
as the ploughs go up and down from year to year
and his mules turn up the soil.

Gay nations of birds he snares and leads,   325
wild beast tribes and the salty brood of the sea,
with the twisted mesh of his nets, this clever man.
He controls with craft the beasts of the open air,
walkers on hills. The horse with his shaggy mane
he holds and harnesses, yoked about the neck,   330
and the strong bull of the mountain.

Language, and thought like the wind
and the feelings that make the town,
he has taught himself, and shelter against the cold,
refuge from rain. He can always help himself.   335
He faces no future helpless. There's only death
that he cannot find an escape from. He has contrived
refuge from illnesses once beyond all cure.

Clever beyond all dreams
the inventive craft that he has   340
which may drive him one time or another to well or ill.
When he honors the laws of the land and the gods' sworn right
high indeed is his city; but stateless the man
who dares to dwell with dishonor. Not by my fire,
never to share my thoughts, who does these things.   345

[*The Guard enters with Antigone.*]

My mind is split at this awful sight.
I know her. I cannot deny
Antigone is here.
Alas, the unhappy girl,
her unhappy father's child.   350
Oh what is the meaning of this?
It cannot be you that they bring
for breaking the royal law,
caught in open shame.

GUARD: This is the woman who has done the deed.   355
        We caught her at the burying. Where's the king?

        [*Creon enters.*]

CHORUS: Back from the house again just when he's needed.
CREON: What must I measure up to? What has happened?
GUARD: Lord, one should never swear off anything.

Afterthought makes the first resolve a liar.   360
I could have vowed I wouldn't come back here
after your threats, after the storm I faced.
But joy that comes beyond the wildest hope
is bigger than all other pleasure known.
I'm here, though I swore not to be, and bring   365
this girl. We caught her burying the dead.
This time we didn't need to shake the lots;
mine was the luck, all mine.
So now, lord, take her, you, and question her
and prove her as you will. But I am free.   370
And I deserve full clearance on this charge.

CREON: Explain the circumstance of the arrest.

GUARD: She was burying the man. You have it all.

CREON: Is this the truth? And do you grasp its meaning?

GUARD: I saw her burying the very corpse   375
      you had forbidden. Is this adequate?

CREON: How was she caught and taken in the act?

GUARD: It was like this: when we got back again
      struck with those dreadful threatenings of yours,
      we swept away the dust that hid the corpse.   380
      We stripped it back to slimy nakedness.
      And then we sat to windward on the hill
      so as to dodge the smell.
      We poked each other up with growling threats
      if anyone was careless of his work.   385
      For some time this went on, till it was noon.
      The sun was high and hot. Then from the earth
      up rose a dusty whirlwind to the sky,
      filling the plain, smearing the forest-leaves,
      clogging the upper air. We shut our eyes,   390
      sat and endured the plague the gods had sent.
      So the storm left us after a long time.
      We saw the girl. She cried the sharp and shrill
      cry of a bitter bird which sees the nest
      bare where the young birds lay.   395
      So this same girl, seeing the body stripped,
      cried with great groanings, cried a dreadful curse
      upon the people who had done the deed.
      Soon in her hands she brought the thirsty dust,
      and holding high a pitcher of wrought bronze   400
      she poured the three libations for the dead.
      We saw this and surged down. We trapped her fast;
      and she was calm. We taxed her with the deeds
      both past and present. Nothing was denied.
      And I was glad, and yet I took it hard.   405

One's own escape from trouble makes one glad;
but bringing friends to trouble is hard grief.
Still, I care less for all these second thoughts
than for the fact that I myself am safe.

CREON: You there, whose head is drooping to the ground,   410
    do you admit this, or deny you did it?

ANTIGONE: I say I did it and I don't deny it.

CREON (TO THE GUARD): Take yourself off wherever you wish to go
    free of a heavy charge.

CREON (TO ANTIGONE): You—tell me not at length but in a word.   415
    You knew the order not to do this thing?

ANTIGONE: I knew, of course I knew. The word was plain.

CREON: And still you dared to overstep these laws?

ANTIGONE: For me it was not Zeus who made that order.
    Nor did that Justice who lives with the gods below   420
    mark out such laws to hold among mankind.
    Nor did I think your orders were so strong
    that you, a mortal man, could over-run
    the gods' unwritten and unfailing laws.
    Not now, nor yesterday's, they always live,   425
    and no one knows their origin in time.
    So not through fear of any man's proud spirit
    would I be likely to neglect these laws,
    draw on myself the gods' sure punishment.
    I knew that I must die; how could I not?   430
    even without your warning. If I die
    before my time, I say it is a gain.
    Who lives in sorrows many as are mine
    how shall he not be glad to gain his death?
    And so, for me to meet this fate, no grief.   435
    But if I left that corpse, my mother's son,
    dead and unburied I'd have cause to grieve
    as now I grieve not.
    And if you think my acts are foolishness
    the foolishness may be in a fool's eye.   440

CHORUS: The girl is bitter. She's her father's child.
    She cannot yield to trouble; nor could he.

CREON: These rigid spirits are the first to fall.
    The strongest iron, hardened in the fire,
    most often ends in scraps and shatterings.   445
    Small curbs bring raging horses back to terms.
    Slave to his neighbor, who can think of pride?
    This girl was expert in her insolence
    when she broke bounds beyond established law.
    Once she had done it, insolence the second,   450
    to boast her doing, and to laugh in it.

I am no man and she the man instead
if she can have this conquest without pain.
She is my sister's child, but were she child
of closer kin than any at my hearth,   455
she and her sister should not so escape
their death and doom. I charge Ismene too.
She shared the planning of this burial.
Call her outside. I saw her in the house,
maddened, no longer mistress of herself.   460
The sly intent betrays itself sometimes
before the secret plotters work their wrong.
I hate it too when someone caught in crime
then wants to make it seem a lovely thing.

ANTIGONE: Do you want more than my arrest and death?   465

CREON: No more than that. For that is all I need.

ANTIGONE: Why are you waiting? Nothing that you say
fits with my thought. I pray it never will.
Nor will you ever like to hear my words.
And yet what greater glory could I find   470
than giving my own brother funeral?
All these would say that they approved my act
did fear not mute them.
(A king is fortunate in many ways,
and most, that he can act and speak at will.)   475

CREON: None of these others see the case this way.

ANTIGONE: They see, and do not say. You have them cowed.

CREON: And you are not ashamed to think alone?

ANTIGONE: No, I am not ashamed. When was it shame
to serve the children of my mother's womb?

CREON: It was not your brother who died against him, then?

ANTIGONE: Full brother, on both sides, my parents' child.

CREON: Your act of grace, in his regard, is crime.

ANTIGONE: The corpse below would never say it was.

CREON: When you honor him and the criminal just alike?   485

ANTIGONE: It was a brother, not a slave, who died.

CREON: Died to destroy this land the other guarded.

ANTIGONE: Death yearns for equal law for all the dead.

CREON: Not that the good and bad draw equal shares.

ANTIGONE: Who knows that this is holiness below?   490

CREON: Never the enemy, even in death, a friend.

ANTIGONE: I cannot share in hatred, but in love.

CREON: Then go down there, if you must love, and love
the dead. No woman rules me while I live.

[Ismene is brought from the palace under guard.]

CHORUS: Look there! Ismene is coming out.   495
              She loves her sister and mourns,
              with clouded brow and bloodied cheeks,
              tears on her lovely face.
CREON: You, lurking like a viper in the house,
              who sucked me dry. I looked the other way   500
              while twin destruction planned against the throne.
              Now tell me, do you say you shared this deed?
              Or will you swear you didn't even know?
ISMENE: I did the deed, if she agrees I did.
              I am accessory and share the blame.   505
ANTIGONE: Justice will not allow this. You did not
              wish for a part, nor did I give you one.
ISMENE: You are in trouble, and I'm not ashamed
              to sail beside you into suffering.
ANTIGONE: Death and the dead, they know whose act it was.   510
              I cannot love a friend whose love is words.
ISMENE: Sister, I pray, don't fence me out from honor,
              from death with you, and honor done the dead.
ANTIGONE: Don't die along with me, nor make your own
              that which you did not do. My death's enough.   515
ISMENE: When you are gone what life can be my friend?
ANTIGONE: Love Creon. He's your kinsman and your care.
ISMENE: Why hurt me, when it does yourself no good?
ANTIGONE: I also suffer, when I laugh at you.
ISMENE: What further service can I do you now?   520
ANTIGONE: To save yourself. I shall not envy you.
ISMENE: Alas for me. Am I outside your fate?
ANTIGONE: Yes. For you chose to live when I chose death.
ISMENE: At least I was not silent. You were warned.
ANTIGONE: Some will have thought you wiser. Some will not.   525
ISMENE: And yet the blame is equal for us both.
ANTIGONE: Take heart. You live. My life died long ago.
              And that has made me fit to help the dead.
CREON: One of these girls has shown her lack of sense
              just now. The other had it from her birth.   530
ISMENE: Yes, lord. When people fall in deep distress
              their native sense departs, and will not stay.
CREON: You chose your mind's distraction when you chose
              to work out wickedness with this wicked girl.
ISMENE: What life is there for me to live without her?   535
CREON: Don't speak of her. For she is here no more.
ISMENE: But will you kill your own son's promised bride?[6]

---

6. Antigone is to marry Creon's son Haemon.

CREON: Oh, there are other furrows for his plough.
ISMENE: But where the closeness that has bound these two?
CREON: Not for my sons will I choose wicked wives.
ISMENE: Dear Haemon, your father robs you of your rights.
CREON: You and your marriage trouble me too much.
ISMENE: You will take away his bride from your own son?
CREON: Yes. Death will help me break this marriage off.
CHORUS: It seems determined that the girl must die.   545
CREON: You helped determine it. Now, no delay!
          Slaves, take them in. They must be women now.
          No more free running.
          Even the bold will fly when they see Death
          drawing in close enough to end their life.   550

[Antigone and Ismene are taken inside.]

CHORUS: Fortunate they whose lives have no taste of pain.
          For those whose house is shaken by the gods
          escape no kind of doom. It extends to all the kin
          like the wave that comes when the winds of Thrace[7]
          run over the dark of the sea.   555
          The black sand of the bottom is brought from the depth;
          the beaten capes sound back with a hollow cry.

          Ancient the sorrow of Labdacus'[8] house, I know.
          Dead men's grief comes back, and falls on grief.
          No generation can free the next.   560
          One of the gods will strike. There is no escape.
          So now the light goes out
          for the house of Oedipus, while the bloody knife
          cuts the remaining root. Folly and Fury have done this.

          What madness of man, O Zeus, can bind your power?   565
          Not sleep can destroy it who ages all,
          nor the weariless months the gods have set. Unaged in time
          monarch you rule of Olympus' gleaming light.
          Near time, far future, and the past,
          one law controls them all: 570
          any greatness in human life brings doom.

          Wandering hope brings help to many men.
          But others she tricks from their giddy loves,
          and her quarry knows nothing until he has walked into flame.
          Word of wisdom it was when someone said,   575
          "The bad becomes the good

---

7. A region in northern Greece, believed to be the home of the north wind, Boreas.

8. The grandfather of Oedipus and great-grandfather of Antigone.

to him a god would doom."
Only briefly is that one from under doom.

[*Haemon enters from the side.*]

Here is your one surviving son.
Does he come in grief at the fate of his bride,   580
in pain that he's tricked of his wedding?
CREON: Soon we shall know more than a seer could tell us.
Son, have you heard the vote condemned your bride?
And are you here, maddened against your father,
or are we friends, whatever I may do?   585
HAEMON: My father, I am yours. You keep me straight
with your good judgment, which I shall ever follow.
Nor shall a marriage count for more with me
than your kind leading.
CREON: There's my good boy. So should you hold at heart   590
and stand behind your father all the way.
It is for this men pray they may beget
households of dutiful obedient sons,
who share alike in punishing enemies,
and give due honor to their father's friends.   595
Whoever breeds a child that will not help
what has he sown but trouble for himself,
and for his enemies laughter full and free?
Son, do not let your lust mislead your mind,
all for a woman's sake, for well you know   600
how cold the thing he takes into his arms
who has a wicked woman for his wife.
What deeper wounding than a friend no friend?
Oh spit her forth forever, as your foe.
Let the girl marry somebody in Hades.   605
Since I have caught her in the open act,
the only one in town who disobeyed,
I shall not now proclaim myself a liar,
but kill her. Let her sing her song of Zeus
who guards the kindred.   610
If I allow disorder in my house
I'd surely have to licence it abroad.
A man who deals in fairness with his own,
he can make manifest justice in the state.
But he who crosses law, or forces it,   615
or hopes to bring the rulers under him,
shall never have a word of praise from me.
The man the state has put in place must have
obedient hearing to his least command
when it is right, and even when it's not.   620

He who accepts this teaching I can trust,
ruler, or ruled, to function in his place,
to stand his ground even in the storm of spears,
a mate to trust in battle at one's side.
There is no greater wrong than disobedience.   625
This ruins cities, this tears down our homes,
this breaks the battle-front in panic-rout.
If men live decently it is because
discipline saves their very lives for them.
So I must guard the men who yield to order,   630
not let myself be beaten by a woman.
Better, if it must happen, that a man
should overset me.
I won't be called weaker than womankind.
CHORUS: We think—unless our age is cheating us—   635
that what you say is sensible and right.
HAEMON: Father, the gods have given men good sense,
the only sure possession that we have.
I couldn't find the words in which to claim
that there was error in your late remarks.   640
Yet someone else might bring some further light.
Because I am your son I must keep watch
on all men's doing where it touches you,
their speech, and most of all, their discontents.
Your presence frightens any common man   645
from saying things you would not care to hear.
But in dark corners I have heard them say
how the whole town is grieving for this girl,
unjustly doomed, if ever woman was,
to die in shame for glorious action done.   650
She would not leave her fallen, slaughtered brother
there, as he lay, unburied, for the birds
and hungry dogs to make an end of him.
Isn't her real desert a golden prize?
This is the undercover speech in town.   655
Father, your welfare is my greatest good.
What loveliness in life for any child
outweighs a father's fortune and good fame?
And so a father feels his children's faring.
Then, do not have one mind, and one alone   660
that only your opinion can be right.
Whoever thinks that he alone is wise,
his eloquence, his mind, above the rest,
come the unfolding, shows his emptiness.
A man, though wise, should never be ashamed   670
of learning more, and must unbend his mind.

Have you not seen the trees beside the torrent,
the ones that bend them saving every leaf,
while the resistant perish root and branch?
And so the ship that will not slacken sail,   675
the sheet drawn tight, unyielding, overturns.
She ends the voyage with her keel on top.
No, yield your wrath, allow a change of stand.
Young as I am, if I may give advice,
I'd say it would be best if men were born   680
perfect in wisdom, but that failing this
(which often fails) it can be no dishonor
to learn from others when they speak good sense.

CHORUS: Lord, if your son has spoken to the point
    you should take his lesson. He should do the same.   685
    Both sides have spoken well.

CREON: At my age I'm to school my mind by his?
    This boy instructor is my master, then?

HAEMON: I urge no wrong. I'm young, but you should watch
    my actions, not my years, to judge of me.   690

CREON: A loyal action, to respect disorder?

HAEMON: I wouldn't urge respect for wickedness.

CREON: You don't think she is sick with that disease?

HAEMON: Your fellow-citizens maintain she's not.

CREON: Is the town to tell me how I ought to rule?   695

HAEMON: Now there you speak just like a boy yourself.

CREON: Am I to rule by other mind than mine?

HAEMON: No city is property of a single man.

CREON: But custom gives possession to the ruler.

HAEMON: You'd rule a desert beautifully alone.   700

CREON (TO THE CHORUS): It seems he's firmly on the woman's side.

HAEMON: If you're a woman. It is you I care for.

CREON: Wicked, to try conclusions with your father.

HAEMON: When you conclude unjustly, so I must.

CREON: An I unjust, when I respect my office?   705

HAEMON: You tread down the gods' due. Respect is gone.

CREON: Your mind is poisoned. Weaker than a woman!

HAEMON: At least you'll never see me yield to shame.

CREON: Your whole long argument is but for her.

HAEMON: And you, and me, and for the gods below.   710

CREON: You shall not marry her while she's alive.

HAEMON: Then she shall die. Her death will bring another.

CREON: Your boldness has made progress. Threats, indeed!

HAEMON: No threat, to speak against your empty plan.

CREON: Past due, sharp lessons for your empty brain.   715

HAEMON: If you weren't father, I should call you mad.

CREON: Don't flatter me with "father," you woman's slave.

HAEMON: You wish to speak but never wish to hear.
CREON: You think so? By Olympus, you shall not
    revile me with these tauntings and go free.   720
    Bring out the hateful creature; she shall die
    full in his sight, close at her bridegroom's side.
HAEMON: Not at my side her death, and you will not
    ever lay eyes upon my face again.
    Find other friends to rave with after this.   725

[Haemon leaves, by one of the side entrances.]

CHORUS: Lord, he has gone with all the speed of rage.
    When such a man is grieved his mind is hard.
CREON: Oh, let him go, plan superhuman action.
    In any case the girls shall not escape.
CHORUS: You plan for both the punishment of death?   730
CREON: Not her who did not do it. You are right.
CHORUS: And what death have you chosen for the other?
CREON: To take her where the foot of man comes not.
    There shall I hide her in a hollowed cave
    living, and leave her just so much to eat   735
    as clears the city from the guilt of death.
    There, if she prays to Death, the only god
    of her respect, she may manage not to die.
    Or she may learn at last and even then
    how much too much her labor for the dead.   740

[Creon returns to the palace.]

CHORUS: Love unconquered in fight, love who falls on our havings.
    You rest in the bloom of a girl's unwithered face.
    You cross the sea, you are known in the wildest lairs.
    Not the immortal gods can fly,
    nor men of a day. Who has you within him is mad.   745
    You twist the minds of the just. Wrong they pursue and are ruined.
    You made this quarrel of kindred before us now.
    Desire looks clear from the eyes of a lovely bride:
    power as strong as the founded world.
    For there is the goddess at play with whom no man can fight.   750

[Antigone is brought from the palace under guard.]

Now I am carried beyond all bounds.
My tears will not be checked.
I see Antigone depart
to the chamber where all men sleep.
ANTIGONE: Men of my fathers' land, you see me go   755
    my last journey. My last sight of the sun,
    then never again. Death who brings all to sleep

takes me alive to the shore
of the river underground.
Not for me was the marriage-hymn, nor will anyone start the song   760
at a wedding of mine. Acheron[9] is my mate.

CHORUS: With praise as your portion you go
in fame to the vault of the dead.
Untouched by wasting disease,
not paying the price of the sword,   765
of your own motion you go.
Alone among mortals will you descend
in life to the house of Death.

ANTIGONE: Pitiful was the death that stranger died,
our queen once, Tantalus' daughter[10]. The rock   770
it covered her over, like stubborn ivy it grew.
Still, as she wastes, the rain
and snow companion her.
Pouring down from her mourning eyes comes the water that soaks the
    stone.   775.
My own putting to sleep a god has planned like hers.

CHORUS: God's child and god she was.
We are born to death.
Yet even in death you will have your fame,
to have gone like a god to your fate,   780
in living and dying alike.

ANTIGONE: Laughter against me now. In the name of our fathers' gods,
could you not wait till I went? Must affront be thrown in my face?
O city of wealthy men.
I call upon Dirce's spring.   785
I call upon Thebe's grove in the armored plain,
to be my witnesses, how with no friend's mourning,
by what decree I go to the fresh-made prison-tomb.
Alive to the place of corpses, an alien still,
never at home with the living nor with the dead.   790

CHORUS: You went to the furthest verge
of daring, but there you found
the high foundation of justice, and fell.
Perhaps you are paying your father's pain.

---

9. A river believed to be at the boundary
between the upper world and Hades. The
name Acheron was sometimes used to
refer generally to the Underworld as a
whole. Young women who died before
marriage were said to be the brides of
Hades.

10. Tantalus's daughter is Niobe, who was
supposed to have compared herself favorably to the goddess Leto, because she had

numerous children while Leto had only
two. Leto's children, however, were the
gods Apollo and Artemis, who avenged
the slight to their mother's reputation by
killing the children of Niobe. Niobe herself was said to have been turned into a
figure of stone on Mt. Sipylus in Lydia, the
water that ran perpetually down the face
of the rock being her ceaseless tears.

ANTIGONE: You speak of my darkest thought, my pitiful father's fame,   795
spread through all the world, and the doom that haunts our house,
the royal house of Thebes.
My mother's marriage-bed.
Destruction where she lay with her husband-son,
my father. These are my parents and I their child.   800
I go to stay with them. My curse is to die unwed.
My brother, you found your fate when you found your bride,
found it for me as well. Dead, you destroy my life.

CHORUS: You showed respect for the dead.
So we for you: but power   805
is not to be thwarted so.
Your self-sufficiency has brought you down.

ANTIGONE: Unwept, no wedding-song, unfriended, now I go
the road laid down for me.
No longer shall I see this holy light of the sun.   810
No friend to bewail my fate.

[Creon enters from the palace.]

CREON: When people sing the dirge for their own deaths
ahead of time, nothing will break them off
if they can hope that this will buy delay.
Take her away at once, and open up   815
the tomb I spoke of. Leave her there alone.
There let her choose: death, or a buried life.
No stain of guilt upon us in this case,
but she is exiled from our life on earth.

ANTIGONE: O tomb, O marriage-chamber, hollowed out   820
house that will watch forever, where I go.
To my own people, who are mostly there;
Persephone has taken them to her.
Last of them all, ill-fated past the rest,
shall I descend, before my course is run.   825
Still when I get there I may hope to find
I come as a dear friend to my dear father,
to you, my mother, and my brother too.
All three of you have known my hand in death.
I washed your bodies, dressed them for the grave,   830
poured out the last libation at the tomb.
Last, Polyneices knows the price I pay
for doing final service to his corpse.
And yet the wise will know my choice was right.
Had I had children or their father dead,   835
I'd let them moulder. I should not have chosen
in such a case to cross the state's decree.
What is the law that lies behind these words?

One husband gone, I might have found another,
or a child from a new man in first child's place,   840
but with my parents hid away in death,
no brother, ever, could spring up for me.
Such was the law by which I honored you.
But Creon thought the doing was a crime,
a dreadful daring, brother of my heart.   845
So now he takes and leads me out by force.
No marriage-bed, no marriage-song for me,
and since no wedding, so no child to rear.
I go, without a friend, struck down by fate,
live to the hollow chambers of the dead.   850
What divine justice have I disobeyed?
Why, in my misery, look to the gods for help?
Can I call any of them my ally?
I stand convicted of impiety,
the evidence my pious duty done.   855
Should the gods think that this is righteousness,
in suffering I'll see my error clear.
But if it is the others who are wrong
I wish them no greater punishment than mine.

CHORUS: The same tempest of mind   860
    as ever, controls the girl.

CREON: Therefore her guards shall regret
    the slowness with which they move.

ANTIGONE: That word comes close to death.

CREON: You are perfectly right in that.   865

ANTIGONE: O town of my fathers in Thebe's land,
    O gods of our house.
    I am led away at last.
    Look, leaders of Thebes,
    I am last of your royal line.   870
    Look what I suffer, at whose command,
    because I respected the right.

[Antigone is led away. The slow procession should begin during the preceding passage.]

CHORUS: Danaë[11] suffered too.
    She went from the light to the brass-built room,
    chamber and tomb together. Like you, poor child,   875
    she was of great descent, and more, she held and kept

---

11. Danaë was a virgin imprisoned by her father, who feared a prediction that he would be killed at the hands of a child that would someday be born to her; Zeus entered the prison room in the form of a shower of golden rain and impregnated Danae.

the seed of the golden rain which was Zeus.
Fate was terrible power.
You cannot escape it by wealth or war.
No fort will keep it out, no ships outrun it.   880

Remember the angry king,
son of Dryas,[12] who raged at the god and paid,
pent in a rock-walled prison. His bursting wrath
slowly went down. As the terror of madness went,
he learned of his frenzied attack on the god.   885
Fool, he had tried to stop
the dancing women possessed of god,
the fire of Dionysus, the songs and flutes.

Where the dark rocks divide
sea from sea in Thrace   890
is Salmydessus whose savage god
beheld the terrible blinding wounds
dealt to Phineus' sons by their father's wife.[13]
Dark the eyes that looked to avenge their mother.
Sharp with her shuttle she struck, and blooded her hands.   895

Wasting they wept their fate,
settled when they were born
to Cleopatra, unhappy queen.
She was a princess too, of an ancient house,
reared in the cave of the wild north wind, her father.   900
Half a goddess but, child, she suffered like you.

[Enter, from the side Teiresias, the blind prophet, led by a boy attendant.]

TEIRESIAS: Elders of Thebes, we two have come one road,
         two of us looking through one pair of eyes.
         This is the way of walking for the blind.
CREON: Teiresias, what news has brought you here?   905
TEIRESIAS: I'll tell you. You in turn must trust the prophet.
CREON: I've always been attentive to your counsel.
TEIRESIAS: And therefore you have steered this city straight.
CREON: So I can say how helpful you have been.
TEIRESIAS: But now you are balanced on a razor's edge.   910
CREON: What is it? How I shudder at your words!
TEIRESIAS: You'll know, when you hear the signs that I have marked

---

12. Lycurgus, a king of Thrace who was said
   to have attacked Dionysus and his followers. Dionysus drove him mad, so that he
   was eventually imprisoned by his own
   people.
13. Cleopatra, in mythology the daughter of

the north wind, Boreas. She married
Phineus, king of the Thracian city of Salmydessus, to whom she bore two sons.
Phineus later imprisoned her and remar-
ried; his second wife persecuted both Cleopatra and her sons, blinding the two boys.

I sat where every bird of heaven comes
in my old place of augury, and heard
bird-cries I'd never known. They screeched about   915
goaded by madness, inarticulate.
I marked that they were tearing one another
with claws of murder. I could hear the wing-beats.
I was afraid, so straight away I tried
burnt sacrifice upon the flaming altar.   920
No fire caught my offerings. Slimy ooze
dripped on the ashes, smoked and sputtered there.
Gall burst its bladder, vanished into vapor;
the fat dripped from the bones and would not burn.
These are the omens of the rites that failed,   925
as my boy here has told me. He's my guide
as I am guide to others.
Why has this sickness struck against the state?
Through your decision.
All of the altars of the town are choked   930
with leavings of the dogs and birds; their feast
was on that fated, fallen Polyneices.
So the gods will have no offering from us,
not prayer, nor flame of sacrifice. The birds
will not cry out a sound I can distinguish,   935
gorged with the greasy blood of that dead man.
Think of these things, my son. All men may err
but error once committed, he's no fool
nor yet unfortunate, who gives up his stiffness
and cures the trouble he has fallen in.   940
Stubbornness and stupidity are twins.
Yield to the dead. Why goad him where he lies?
What use to kill the dead a second time?
I speak for your own good. And I am right.
Learning from a wise counsellor is not pain   945
if what he speaks are profitable words.

CREON: Old man, you all, like bowmen at a mark,
have bent your bows at me. I've had my share
of seers. I've been an item in your accounts.
Make profit, trade in Lydian silver-gold,   950
pure gold of India; that's your chief desire.
But you will never cover up that corpse.
Not if the very eagles tear their food
from him, and leave it at the throne of Zeus.
I wouldn't give him up for burial   955
in fear of that pollution. For I know
no mortal being can pollute the gods.
O old Teiresias, human beings fall;

the clever ones the furthest, when they plead
a shameful case so well in hope of profit.   960
TEIRESIAS: Alas!
          What man can tell me, has he thought at all . . .
CREON: What hackneyed saw is coming from your lips?
TEIRESIAS: How better than all wealth is sound good counsel.
CREON: And so is folly worse than anything.   965
TEIRESIAS: And you're infected with that same disease.
CREON: I'm reluctant to be uncivil to a seer . . .
TEIRESIAS: You're that already. You have said I lie.
CREON: Well, the whole crew of seers are money-mad.
TEIRESIAS: And the whole tribe of tyrants grab at gain.   970
CREON: Do you realize you are talking to a king?
TEIRESIAS: I know. Who helped you save this town you hold?
CREON: You're a wise seer, but you love wickedness.
TEIRESIAS: You'll bring me to speak the unspeakable, very soon.
CREON: Well, speak it out. But do not speak for profit.   975
TEIRESIAS: No, there's no profit in my words for you.
CREON: You'd better realise that you can't deliver
          my mind, if you should sell it, to the buyer.
TEIRESIAS: Know well, the sun will not have rolled its course
          many more days, before you come to give   980
          corpse for these corpses, child of your own loins.
          For you've confused the upper and lower worlds.
          You sent a life to settle in a tomb;
          you keep up here that which belongs below
          the corpse unburied, robbed of its release.   985
          Not you, nor any god that rules on high
          can claim him now.
          You rob the nether gods of what is theirs.
          So the pursuing horrors lie in wait
          to track you down. The Furies sent by Hades   990
          and by all gods will even you with your victims.
          Now say that I am bribed! At no far time
          shall men and women wail within your house.
          And all the cities that you fought in war
          whose sons had burial from wild beasts, or dogs,   995
          or birds that brought the stench of your great wrong
          back to each hearth, they move against you now.
          A bowman, as you said, I send my shafts,
          now you have moved me, straight. You'll feel the wound.
          Boy, take me home now. Let him spend his rage   1000
          on younger men, and learn to calm his tongue,
          and keep a better mind than now he does.

          [Exit.]

CHORUS: Lord, he has gone. Terrible prophecies!
    And since the time when I first grew grey hair
    his sayings to the city have been true.   1005
CREON: I also know this. And my mind is torn.
    To yield is dreadful. But to stand against him.
    Dreadful to strike my spirit to destruction.
CHORUS: Now you must come to counsel, and take advice.
CREON: What must I do? Speak, and I shall obey.   1010
CHORUS: Go free the maiden from that rocky house.
    Bury the dead who lies in readiness.
CREON: This is your counsel? You would have me yield?
CHORUS: Quick as you can. The gods move very fast
    when they bring ruin on misguided men.   1015
CREON: How hard, abandonment of my desire.
    But I can fight necessity no more.
CHORUS: Do it yourself. Leave it to no one else.
CREON: I'll go at once. Come, followers, to your work.
    You that are here round up the other fellows.   1020
    Take axes with you, hurry to that place
    that overlooks us.
    Now my decision has been overturned
    shall I, who bound her, set her free myself.
    I've come to fear it's best to hold the laws   1025
    of old tradition to the end of life.

    [Exit.]

CHORUS: God of the many names, Semele's golden child,
    child of Olympian thunder, Italy's lord.[14]
    Lord of Eleusis, where all men come
    to mother Demeter's plain.   1030
    Bacchus, who dwell in Thebes,
    by Ismenus' running water,
    where wild Bacchic women are at home,
    on the soil of the dragon seed.

    Seen in the glaring flame, high on the double mount,   1035
    with the nymphs of Parnassus[15] at play on the hill,
    seen by Kastalia's flowing stream.
    You come from the ivied heights,
    from green Euboea's shore.
    In immortal words we cry   1040
    your name, lord, who watch the ways,
    the many ways of Thebes.

---

14. Dionysus.   **15.** The mountain below which is the site
                           of Apollo's oracle at Delphi.

This is your city, honored beyond the rest,
the town of your mother's miracle-death.
Now, as we wrestle our grim disease,   1045
come with healing step from Parnassus' slope
or over the moaning sea.

Leader in dance of the fire-pulsing stars,
overseer of the voices of night,
child of Zeus, be manifest,   1050
with due companionship of Maenad maids[16]
whose cry is but your name.

[Enter one of those who left with Creon, as messenger.]

MESSENGER: Neighbors of Cadmus, and Amphion's[17] house,
there is no kind of state in human life
which I now dare to envy or to blame.   1055
Luck sets it straight, and luck she overturns
the happy or unhappy day by day.
No prophecy can deal with men's affairs.
Creon was envied once, as I believe,
for having saved this city from its foes   1060
and having got full power in this land.
He steered it well. And he had noble sons.
Now everything is gone.
Yes, when a man has lost all happiness,
he's not alive. Call him a breathing corpse.   1065
Be very rich at home. Live as a king.
But once your joy has gone, though these are left
they are smoke's shadow to lost happiness.
CHORUS: What is the grief of princes that you bring?
MESSENGER: They're dead. The living are responsible.   1070
CHORUS: Who died? Who did the murder? Tell us now.
MESSENGER: Haemon is gone. One of his kin drew blood.
CHORUS: But whose arm struck? His father's or his own?
MESSENGER: He killed himself. His blood is on his father.
CHORUS: Seer, all too true the prophecy you told!   1075
MESSENGER: This is the state of things. Now make your plans.

[Enter, from the palace, Eurydice.]

CHORUS: Eurydice is with us now, I see.
Creon's poor wife. She may have come by chance.
She may have heard something about her son.
EURYDICE: I heard your talk as I was coming out   1080

---

16. Dionysus's followers.   17. A mythical king of Thebes, husband
                                                 of Niobe.

to greet the goddess Pallas with my prayer.
And as I moved the bolts that held the door
I heard of my own sorrow.
I fell back fainting in my women's arms.
But say again just what the news you bring. 1085
I, whom you speak to, have known grief before.

MESSENGER: Dear lady, I was there, and I shall tell,
leaving out nothing of the true account.
Why should I make it soft for you with tales
to prove myself a liar? Truth is right. 1090
I followed your husband to the plain's far edge,
where Polyneices' corpse was lying still
unpitied. The dogs had torn him all apart.
We prayed the goddess of all journeyings,
and Pluto, that they turn their wrath to kindness, 1095
we gave the final purifying bath,
then burned the poor remains on new-cut boughs,
and heaped a high mound of his native earth.
Then turned we to the maiden's rocky bed,
death's hollow marriage-chamber. 1100
But, still far off, one of us heard a voice
in keen lament by that unblest abode.
He ran and told the master. As Creon came
he heard confusion crying. He groaned and spoke:
"Am I a prophet now, and do I tread 1105
the saddest of all roads I ever trod?
My son's voice crying! Servants, run up close,
stand by the tomb and look, push through the crevice
where we built the pile of rock, right to the entry.
Find out if that is Haemon's voice I hear 1110
or if the gods are tricking me indeed."
We obeyed the order of our mournful master.
In the far corner of the tomb we saw
her, hanging by the neck, caught in a noose
of her own linen veiling. 1115
Haemon embraced her as she hung, and mourned
his bride's destruction, dead and gone below,
his father's actions, the unfated marriage.
When Creon saw him, he groaned terribly,
and went toward him, and called him with lament: 1120
"What have you done, what plan have you caught up,
what sort of suffering is killing you?
Come out, my child, I do beseech you, come!"
The boy looked at him with his angry eyes,
spat in his face and spoke no further word. 1125
He drew his sword, but as his father ran,

he missed his aim. Then the unhappy boy,
in anger at himself, leant on the blade.
It entered, half its length, into his side.
While he was conscious he embraced the maiden,   1130
holding her gently. Last, he gasped out blood,
red blood on her white cheek.
Corpse on a corpse he lies. He found his marriage.
Its celebration in the halls of Hades.
So he as made it very clear to men   1135
that to reject good counsel is a crime.

[Eurydice returns to the house.]

CHORUS: What do you make of this? The queen has gone
    in silence. We know nothing of her mind.
MESSENGER: I wonder at her, too. But we can hope
    that she has gone to mourn her son within   1140
    with her own women, not before the town.
    She knows discretion. She will do no wrong.
CHORUS: I am not sure. This muteness may portend
    as great disaster as a loud lament.
MESSENGER: I will go in and see if some deep plan   1145
    hides in her heart's wild pain. You may be right.
    There can be heavy danger in mute grief.

*[The messenger goes into the house. Creon enters with his followers. They are
carrying Haemon's body on a bier.]*

CHORUS: But look, the king draws near.
    His own hand brings
    the witness of his crime,   1150
    the doom he brought on himself.
CREON: O crimes of my wicked heart,
    harshness bringing death.
    You see the killer, you see the kin he killed.
    My planning was all unblest.   1155
    Son, you have died too soon.
    Oh, you have gone away
    through my fault, not your own.
CHORUS: You have learned justice, though it comes too late.
CREON: Yes, I have learned in sorrow. It was a god who struck,   1160
    who has weighted my head with disaster; he drove me to wild strange
        ways,
    his heavy heel on my joy.
    Oh sorrows, sorrows of men.

[Re-enter the messenger, from a side door of the palace.]

MESSENGER: Master you hold one sorrow in your hands
　　　　　but you have more, stored up inside the house.　　　　　1165.
CREON: What further suffering can come on me?
MESSENGER: Your wife has died. The dead man's mother in deed,
　　　　　poor soul, her wounds are fresh.
CREON: Hades, harbor of all,
　　　　you have destroyed me now.　　　　　1170
　　　　Terrible news to hear, horror the tale you tell.
　　　　I was dead, and you kill me again.
　　　　Boy, did I hear you right?
　　　　Did you say the queen was dead,
　　　　slaughter on slaughter heaped?　　　　　1175

[The central doors of the palace begin to open.]

CHORUS: Now you can see. Concealment is all over.

[The doors are open, and the corpse of Eurydice is revealed.]

CREON: My second sorrow is here. Surely no fate remains
　　　　which can strike me again. Just now, I held my son in my arms.
　　　　And now I see her dead.　　　　　1180
　　　　Woe for the mother and son.
MESSENGER: There, by the altar, dying on the sword,
　　　　her eyes fell shut. She wept her older son
　　　　who died before, and this one. Last of all
　　　　she cursed you as the killer of her children.
CREON: I am mad with fear. Will no one strike　　　　　1185
　　　　and kill me with cutting sword?
　　　　Sorrowful, soaked in sorrow to the bone!
MESSENGER: Yes, for she held you guilty in the death
　　　　of him before you, and the elder dead.
CREON: How did she die?　　　　　1190
MESSENGER: Struck home at her own heart
　　　　when she had heard of Haemon's suffering.
CREON: This is my guilt, all mine. I killed you, I say it clear.
　　　　Servants, take me away, out of the sight of men.
　　　　I who am nothing more than nothing now.　　　　　1195
CHORUS: Your plan is good—if any good is left.
　　　　Best to cut short our sorrow.
CREON: Let me go, let me go. May death come quick,
　　　　bringing my final day.
　　　　O let me never see tomorrow's dawn.　　　　　1200
CHORUS: That is the future's. We must look to now.
　　　　What will be is in other hands than ours.
CREON: All my desire was in that prayer of mine.
CHORUS: Pray not again. No mortal can escape
　　　　the doom prepared for him.　　　　　1205

CREON: Take me away at once, the frantic man who killed
my son, against my meaning. I cannot rest.
My life is warped past cure. My fate has struck me down.

[Creon and his attendants enter the house.]

CHORUS: Our happiness depends
on wisdom all the way.   1210
The gods must have their due.
Great words by men of pride
bring greater blows upon them.
So wisdom comes to the old.

THUCYDIDES (c. 460–400 B.C.E.)
Greece

Thucydides, an Athenian, was not simply an observer of the Peloponnesian War
but a participant in it; he was for a time a general in that protracted conflict
between Athens and Sparta, which convulsed the entire Greek world, as almost
every city-state was drawn in—willingly or not—in support of one side or the
other. He described the war, accurately enough, as being unprecedented in the
Greek world in its magnitude and severity; it lasted from 431 to 404 B.C.E., was
fought all across the map of Greece, and involved enormous numbers of people
and resources.

Thucydides' account of this struggle, written in eight books, set a standard
of accuracy and objectivity for later historical writing. His purpose, he stated in
the opening chapters, was to identify not the superficial pretexts but the
underlying causes of the conflict, the fundamental social forces that were
responsible for it, so that future generations could recognize them when they
recurred, as he believed was inevitable—"human nature," as he wrote "being
always the same."

Among the striking features of Thucydides' history are the numerous
speeches he reports; some he heard himself, others he reconstructed. Pericles, by
far the most important and influential Athenian statesman during the middle
decades of the fifth century B.C.E., delivered the *Funeral Oration* (at which
Thucydides may well have been present) as a memorial to the men who fell in
battle in the first year of the war. His representation of the humane, participatory
Athenian democracy of this period—attentive to "unwritten" moral laws reminiscent of those invoked by Antigone in Sophocles' play—contrasts dramatically
with the imperialist doctrine of power and expediency later endorsed by the
Athenians in the "Melian Dialogue."

from The History of the Peloponnesian War

Pericles' Funeral Oration

In the same winter[1] the Athenians, following their annual custom, gave a public funeral for those who had been the first to die in the war. These funerals are held in the following way: two days before the ceremony the bones of the fallen are brought and put in a tent which has been erected, and people make whatever offerings they wish to their own dead. Then there is a funeral procession in which coffins of cypress wood are carried on wagons. There is one coffin for each tribe, which contains the bones of members of that tribe. One empty bier is decorated and carried in the procession: this is for the missing, whose bodies could not be recovered. Everyone who wishes to, both citizens and foreigners, can join in the procession, and the women who are related to the dead are there to make their laments at the tomb. The bones are laid in the public burial-place, which is in the most beautiful quarter outside the city walls. Here the Athenians always bury those who have fallen in war. The only exception is those who died at Marathon,[2] who, because their achievement was considered absolutely outstanding, were buried on the battlefield itself.

When the bones have been laid in the earth, a man chosen by the city for his intellectual gifts and for his general reputation makes an appropriate speech in praise of the dead, and after the speech all depart. This is the procedure at these burials, and all through the war, when the time came to do so, the Athenians followed this ancient custom. Now, at the burial of those who were the first to fall in the war Pericles, the son of Xanthippus, was chosen to make the speech. When the moment arrived, he came forward from the tomb and, standing on a high platform, so that he might be heard by as many people as possible in the crowd, he spoke as follows:

'Many of those who have spoken here in the past have praised the institution of this speech at the close of our ceremony. It seemed to them a mark of honour to our soldiers who have fallen in war that a speech should be made over them. I do not agree. These men have shown themselves valiant in action, and it would be enough, I think, for their glories to be proclaimed in action, as you have just seen it done at this funeral organized by the state. Our belief in the courage and manliness of so many should not be hazarded on the goodness or badness of one man's speech. Then it is not easy to speak with a proper sense of balance, when a man's listeners find it difficult to believe in the truth of what one is saying. The man who knows the facts and loves the dead may well think that an oration tells less than what he knows and what he would like to hear: others who do not know so much may feel envy for the dead, and think the orator over-praises them, when he speaks of exploits that are

Translated by Rex Warner.

---

1. The ceremony was held to commemorate those who had died in the first year of the war, 431 B.C.E.
2. The site of the Persian invasion of 490 B.C.E., where Athens won a remarkable victory, despite the Persians' vastly greater numbers.

beyond their own capacities. Praise of other people is tolerable only up to a certain point, the point where one still believes that one could do oneself some of the things one is hearing about. Once you get beyond this point, you will find people becoming jealous and incredulous. However, the fact is that this institution was set up and approved by our forefathers, and it is my duty to follow the tradition and do my best to meet the wishes and the expectations of every one of you.

'I shall begin by speaking about our ancestors, since it is only right and proper on such an occasion to pay them the honour of recalling what they did. In this land of ours there have always been the same people living from generation to generation up till now, and they, by their courage and their virtues, have handed it on to us, a free country. They certainly deserve our praise. Even more so do our fathers deserve it. For to the inheritance they had received they added all the empire we have now, and it was not without blood and toil that they handed it down to us of the present generation. And then we ourselves, assembled here today, who are mostly in the prime of life, have, in most directions, added to the power of our empire and have organized our State in such a way that it is perfectly well able to look after itself both in peace and in war.

'I have no wish to make a long speech on subjects familiar to you all: so I shall say nothing about the warlike deeds by which we acquired our power or the battles in which we or our fathers gallantly resisted our enemies, Greek or foreign. What I want to do is, in the first place, to discuss the spirit in which we faced our trials and also our constitution and the way of life which has made us great. After that I shall speak in praise of the dead, believing that this kind of speech is not inappropriate to the present occasion, and that this whole assembly, of citizens and foreigners, may listen to it with advantage.

'Let me say that our system of government does not copy the institutions of our neighbours. It is more the case of our being a model to others, than of our imitating anyone else. Our constitution is called a democracy because power is in the hands not of a minority but of the whole people. When it is a question of settling private disputes, everyone is equal before the law; when it is a question of putting one person before another in positions of public responsibility, what counts is not membership of a particular class, but the actual ability which the man possesses. No one, so long as he has it in him to be of service to the state, is kept in political obscurity because of poverty. And, just as our political life is free and open, so is our day-to-day life in our relations with each other. We do not get into a state with our next-door neighbour if he enjoys himself in his own way, nor do we give him the kind of black looks which, though they do no real harm, still do hurt people's feelings. We are free and tolerant in our private lives; but in public affairs we keep to the law. This is because it commands our deep respect.

'We give our obedience to those whom we put in positions of authority, and we obey the laws themselves, especially those which are for the protection of the oppressed, and those unwritten laws which it is an acknowledged shame to break.

'And here is another point. When our work is over, we are in a position to enjoy all kinds of recreation for our spirits. There are various kinds of contests and sacrifices regularly throughout the year; in our own homes we find a beauty and a good taste which delight us every day and which drive away our cares. Then the greatness of our city brings it about that all the good things from all over the world flow in to us, so that to us it seems just as natural to enjoy foreign goods as our own local products.

'Then there is a great difference between us and our opponents, in our attitude towards military security. Here are some examples: Our city is open to the world, and we have no periodical deportations in order to prevent people observing or finding out secrets which might be of military advantage to the enemy. This is because we rely, not on secret weapons, but on our own real courage and loyalty. There is a difference, too, in our educational systems. The Spartans, from their earliest boyhood, are submitted to the most laborious training in courage; we pass our lives without all these restrictions, and yet are just as ready to face the same dangers as they are. Here is a proof of this: When the Spartans invade our land, they do not come by themselves, but bring all their allies with them; whereas we, when we launch an attack abroad, do the job by ourselves, and, though fighting on foreign soil, do not often fail to defeat opponents who are fighting for their own hearths and homes. As a matter of fact none of our enemies has ever yet been confronted with our total strength, because we have to divide our attention between our navy and the many missions on which our troops are sent on land. Yet, if our enemies engage a detachment of our forces and defeat it, they give themselves credit for having thrown back our entire army; or, if they lose, they claim that they were beaten by us in full strength. There are certain advantages, I think, in our way of meeting danger voluntarily, with an easy mind, instead of with a laborious training, with natural rather than with state-induced courage. We do not have to spend our time practising to meet sufferings which are still in the future; and when they are actually upon us we show ourselves just as brave as these others who are always in strict training. This is one point in which, I think, our city deserves to be admired. There are also others:

'Our love of what is beautiful does not lead to extravagance; our love of the things of the mind does not make us soft. We regard wealth as something to be properly used, rather than as something to boast about. As for poverty, no one need be ashamed to admit it: the real shame is in not taking practical measures to escape from it. Here each individual is interested not only in his own affairs but in the affairs of the state as well: even those who are mostly occupied with their own business are extremely well-informed on general politics—this is a peculiarity of ours: we do not say that a man who takes no interest in politics is a man who minds his own business; we say that he has no business here at all. We Athenians, in our own persons, take our decisions on policy or submit them to proper discussions: for we do not think that there is an incompatibility between words and deeds; the worst thing is to rush into action before the consequences have been properly debated. And this is another point where we differ from other people. We are capable at the same time of taking risks and of estimating them beforehand. Others are brave out of ignorance; and, when they stop to think, they begin to fear. But the man who can most truly be accounted brave is he who best knows the meaning of what is sweet in life and of what is terrible, and then goes out undeterred to meet what is to come.

'Again, in questions of general good feeling there is a great contrast between us and most other people. We make friends by doing good to others, not by receiving good from them. This makes our friendship all the more reliable, since we want to keep alive the gratitude of those who are in our debt by showing continued goodwill to them: whereas the feelings of one who owes us something lack the same enthusiasm, since he knows that, when he repays our kindness, it will be more like paying back a debt than giving something spontaneously. We are unique in this. When we do kindnesses to others, we do not do them out of any calculations of profit or loss: we do them without afterthought, relying on our free liberality. Taking everything together then, I declare that our city is an education to Greece, and I declare that in my opinion each single one of our citizens, in all the manifold aspects of life, is able to show himself the rightful lord and owner of his own person, and do this, moreover, with exceptional grace and exceptional versatility. And to show that this is no empty boasting for the present occasion, but real tangible fact, you have only to consider the power which our city possesses and which has been won by those very qualities which I have mentioned. Athens, alone of the states we know, comes to her testing time in a greatness that surpasses what was imaged of her. In her case, and in her case alone, no invading enemy is ashamed at being defeated, and no subject can complain of being governed by people unfit for their responsibilities. Mighty indeed are the marks and monuments of our empire which we have left. Future ages will wonder at us, as the present age wonders at us now. We do not need the praises of a Homer, or of anyone else whose words may delight us for the moment, but whose estimation of facts will fall short of what is really true. For our adventurous spirit has forced an entry into every sea and into every land; and everywhere we have left behind us everlasting memorials of good done to our friends or suffering inflicted on our enemies.

'This, then, is the kind of city for which these men, who could not bear the thought of losing her, nobly fought and nobly died. It is only natural that every one of us who survive them should be willing to undergo hardships in her service. And it was for this reason that I have spoken at such length about out city, because I wanted to make it clear that for us there is more at stake than there is for others who lack our advantages; also I wanted my words of praise for the dead to be set in the bright light of evidence. And now the most important of these words has been spoken. I have sung the praises of our city; but it was the courage and gallantry of these men, and of people like them, which made her splendid. Nor would you find it true in the case of many of the Greeks, as it is true of them, that no words can do more than justice to their deeds.

'To me it seems that the consummation which has overtaken these men shows us the meaning of manliness in its first revelation and in its final proof. Some of them, no doubt, had their faults; but what we ought to remember first is their gallant conduct against the enemy in defence of their native land. They have blotted out evil with good, and done more service to the commonwealth than they ever did harm in their private lives. No one of these men weakened because he wanted to go on enjoying his wealth: no one put off the awful day in the hope that he might live to escape his poverty and grow rich. More to be desired than such things, they chose to check the enemy's pride. This, to them, was a risk most glorious, and they accepted it, willing to strike down the enemy and relinquish everything else. As for success or failure, they left that in the doubtful hands of Hope, and when the reality of battle was before their faces, they put their trust in their own selves. In the fighting, they thought it more honourable to stand their ground and suffer death than to give in and save their lives. So they fled from the reproaches of men, abiding with life and limb the brunt of battle; and, in a small moment of time, the climax of their lives, a culmination of glory, not of fear, were swept away from us.

'So and such they were, these men—worthy of their city. We who remain behind may hope to be spared their fate, but must resolve to keep the same daring spirit against the foe. It is not simply a question of estimating the advantages in theory. I could tell you a long story (and you know it as well as I do) about what is to be gained by beating the enemy back. What I would prefer is that you should fix your eyes every day on the greatness of Athens as she really is, and should fall in love with her. When you realize her greatness, then reflect that what made her great was men with a spirit of adventure, men who knew their duty, men who were ashamed to fall below a certain standard. If they ever failed in an enterprise, they made up their minds that at any rate the city should not find their courage lacking to her, and they gave to her the best contribution that they could. They gave her their lives, to her and to all of us, and for their own selves they won praises that never grow old, the most splendid of sepulchres—not the sepulchre in which their bodies are laid, but where their glory remains eternal in men's minds, always there on the right occasion to stir others to speech or to action. For famous men have the whole earth as their memorial: it is not only the inscriptions on their graves in their own country that mark them out; no, in foreign lands also, not in any visible form but in people's hearts, their memory abides and grows. It is for you to try to be like them. Make up your minds that happiness depends on being free, and freedom depends on being courageous. Let there be no relaxation in face of the perils of the war. The people who have most excuse for despising death are not the wretched and unfortunate, who have no hope of doing well for themselves, but those who run the risk of a complete reversal in their lives, and who would feel the difference most intensely, if things went wrong for them. Any intelligent man would find a humiliation caused by his own slackness more painful to bear than death, when death comes to him unperceived, in battle, and in the confidence of his patriotism.

'For these reasons I shall not commiserate with those parents of the dead, who are present here. Instead I shall try to comfort them. They are well aware that they have grown up in a world where there are many changes and chances. But this is good fortune—for men to end their lives with honour, as these have done, and for you honourably to lament them: their life was set to a measure where death and happiness went hand in hand. I know that it is difficult to convince you of this. When you see other people happy you will often be reminded of what used to make you happy too. One does not feel sad at not having some good thing which is outside one's experience: real grief is felt at the loss of something which one is used to. All the same, those of you who are of the right age must bear up and take comfort in the thought of having more children. In your own homes these new children will prevent you from brooding over those who are no more, and they will be a help to the city, too, both in filling the empty places, and in assuring her security. For it is impossible for a man to put forward fair and honest views about our affairs if he has not, like everyone else, children whose lives may be at stake. As for those of you who are now too old to have children, I would ask you to count as gain the greater part of your life, in which you have been happy, and remember that what remains is not long, and let your hearts be lifted up at the thought of the fair fame of the dead. One's sense of honour is the only thing that does not grow old, and the last pleasure, when one is worn out with age, is not, as the poet said, making money, but having the respect of one's fellow men.

'As for those of you here who are sons or brothers of the dead, I can see a hard struggle in front of you. Everyone always speaks well of the dead, and, even if you rise to the greatest heights of heroism, it will be a hard thing for you to get the reputation of having come near, let alone equalled, their standard. When one is alive, one is always liable to the jealousy of one's competitors, but when one is out of the way, the honour one receives is sincere and unchallenged.

'Perhaps I should say a word or two on the duties of women to those among you who are now widowed. I can say all I have to say in a short word of advice. Your great glory is not to be inferior to what God has made you, and the greatest glory of a woman is to be least talked about by men, whether they are praising you or criticizing you. I have now, as the law demanded, said what I had to say. For the time being our offerings to the dead have been made, and for the future their children will be supported at the public expense by the city, until they come of age. This is the crown and prize which she offers, both to the dead and to their children, for the ordeals which they have faced. Where the rewards of valour are the greatest, there you will find also the best and bravest spirits among the people. And now, when you have mourned for your dear ones, you must depart.'

PLATO (427–348 B.C.E.)
Greece

Plato's *Apology* purports to be the speech Socrates delivered in his own defense at his trial in 399 B.C.E., when he was seventy years old. (The word *apologia* in the Greek title of this work simply means "defense;" it has none of the connotations of regret or retraction associated with the English word *apology*.) Our knowledge of Socrates' life and thought comes from the writings of a few of his younger contemporaries, most notably, Plato. Socrates himself left no written record of his ideas or activities; his chosen vehicle for philosophical inquiry was oral discourse with his fellow Athenians. It was Plato who gave these conversations their literary form: in a set of works structured as dialogues, he reproduces Socrates' manner of questioning and eliciting responses, of turning each discussion into a process of intellectual discovery in the course of which the rational basis of belief is tested and the overriding value of moral goodness is affirmed. In the *Apology* (which for the most part describes, rather than reproduces, Socrates' approach as an interlocutor), Socrates says that he considers it a moral obligation and a service to Athens to be the conscience of the city—exposing ignorance, shallowness, and hypocrisy where he finds it—although he is aware that in doing so he incurs the animosity of many Athenians. Perhaps because his youthful followers learned from him to question conventional attitudes and to reject the pretensions of many of those in authority, Socrates was brought to trial on charges of impiety and of corrupting the youth. Such was the resentment against him that, despite the inability of his prosecutors to substantiate their accusations, he was convicted and condemned to death.

from *The Apology*

[*The Trial of Socrates*]

I do not know, gentlemen of the jury, how my accusers affected you; as for me, I was almost carried away in spite of myself, so persuasively did they speak. And yet, hardly anything of what they said is true. Of the many lies they told, one in particular surprised me, namely that you should be careful not to be deceived by an accomplished speaker like me. That they are not ashamed to be immediately proved wrong by the facts, when I show myself not to be an accomplished speaker at all, that I think is most shameless on their part—unless indeed they call an accomplished speaker the man who speaks the truth. If they mean that, I would agree that I am an orator, but not after their manner, for indeed, as I say, practically nothing they said was true. From me you will hear the whole truth, though not, by Zeus, gentlemen, expressed in embroidered and stylized phrases like theirs, but things spoken at random and expressed in the first words that come to mind, for I put my trust in the justice of what I say, and let none of you expect anything else. It would not be fitting at my age, as it might be for a young man, to toy with words when I appear before you.

One thing I do ask and beg of you, gentlemen: if you hear me making my defence in the same kind of language as I am accustomed to use in the market place by the bankers' tables, where many of you have heard me, and elsewhere, do not be surprised or create a disturbance on that account. The position is this: this is my first appearance in a lawcourt, at the age of seventy; I am therefore simply a stranger to the manner of speaking here. Just as if I were really a stranger, you would certainly excuse me if I spoke in that dialect and manner in which I had been brought up, so too my present request seems a just one, for you to pay no attention to my manner of speech—be it better or worse—but to concentrate your attention on whether what I say is just or not, for the excellence of a judge lies in this, as that of a speaker, in telling the truth.

It is right for me, gentlemen, to defend myself first against the first lying

Translated by G. M. A. Grube.

accusations made against me and my first accusers, and then against the later accusations and the later accusers. There have been many who have accused me to you for many years now, and none of their accusations are true. These I fear much more than I fear Anytus and his friends, though they too are formidable. These earlier ones, however, are more so, gentlemen; they got hold of most of you from childhood, persuaded you and accused me quite falsely, saying that there is a man called Socrates, a wise man, a student of all things in the sky and below the earth, who makes the worse argument the stronger. Those who spread that rumour, gentlemen, are my dangerous accusers, for their hearers believe that those who study these things do not even believe in the gods. Moreover, these accusers were numerous, they have been at it a long time; also, they spoke to you at an age when you would most readily believe them, some of you being children and adolescents, and they won their case by default, as there was no defence.

What is most absurd in all this is that one cannot even know or mention their names unless one of them is a writer of comedies.[1] Those who maliciously and slanderously persuaded you, those too, who, when persuaded themselves then persuaded others, all those are most difficult to deal with: one cannot bring one of them into court or refute him; one is simply fighting with shadows in making one's defence, and cross-examining when no one answers. I want you to realize too that my accusers are of two kinds: those who have accused me recently, and the old ones I mention; and to think that I must first defend myself against the latter, for you have also heard their accusations first, and to a much greater extent than the more recent.

Very well then. I must surely defend myself and attempt to uproot from your minds in so short a time the slander that has resided there so long. I wish this may happen, if it is in any way better for you and me, and that my defence may be successful, but I think this is very difficult and I am fully aware of how difficult it is. Even so, let the matter proceed as the gods may wish, but I must obey the law and make by defence.

Let us then take up the case from its beginning. What is the accusation from which arose the slander in which Meletus trusted when he wrote out the charge against me? What did they say when they slandered me? I must, as if they were my actual prosecutors, read the affidavit they would have sworn. It goes something like this: Socrates is guilty of wrongdoing in that he busies himself studying things in the sky and below the earth; he makes the worse into the stronger argument, and he teaches these same things to others.[2] You have seen this yourselves in the comedy of Aristophanes, a Socrates swinging about there, saying he was walking on air and talking a lot of other nonsense about things of which I know nothing at all. I do not speak in contempt of such knowledge, if someone is wise in these

---

1. Aristophanes had parodied (and misrepresented) Socrates in his comedy the *Clouds*, produced in 423 B.C.E.
2. "Making the worse argument into the stronger" was the practice of the Sophists, professional teachers of rhetoric, who—for a substantial fee—taught their students to ar-

gue effectively without regard to the moral implications of their arguments. Socrates's accusers conveniently confused Socrates with the Sophists, although his attempt to guide people to reason and to live ethically on the basis of rationality had nothing in common with Sophistic teaching.

things—lest Meletus bring more cases against me—but, gentlemen, I have no part in it, and on this point I call upon the majority of you as witnesses. I think it right that all those of you who have heard me conversing, and many of you have, should tell each other if anyone of you has ever heard me discussing such subjects to any extent at all. From this you will learn that the other things said about me by the majority are of the same kind. Not one of them is true.

One of you might perhaps interrupt me and say: "But Socrates, what is your occupation? From where have these slanders come? For surely if you did not busy yourself with something out of the common, all these rumours and talk would not have arisen unless you did something other than most people. Tell us what it is, that we may not speak inadvisedly about you." Anyone who says that seems to be right, and I will try to show you what has caused this reputation and slander. Listen then. Perhaps some of you will think I am jesting, but be sure that all that I shall say is true. What has caused my reputation is none other than a certain kind of wisdom. What kind of wisdom? Human wisdom, perhaps. It may be that I really possess this, while those whom I mentioned just now are wise with a wisdom more than human: else I cannot explain it, for I certainly do not possess it, and whoever says I do is lying and speaks to slander me. Do not create a disturbance, gentlemen, even if you think I am boasting, for the story I shall tell does not originate with me, but I will refer you to a trustworthy source. I shall call upon the god at Delphi[3] as witness to the existence and nature of my wisdom, if it be such. You know Chairephon. He was my friend from youth, and the friend of most of you, as he shared your exile and your return.[4] You surely know the kind of man he was, how impulsive in any course of action. He went to Delphi at one time and ventured to ask the oracle—as I say, gentlemen, do not create a disturbance—he asked if any man was wiser than I, and the Pythian replied that no one was wiser. Chairephon is dead, but his brother will testify to you about this.

Consider that I tell you this because I would inform you about the origin of the slander. When I heard of this reply I asked myself: "Whatever does the god mean? What is his riddle? I am very conscious that I am not wise at all: what then does he mean by saying that I am the wisest? For surely he does not lie: it is not legitimate for him to do so." For a long time I was at a loss: then I very reluctantly turned to some such investigation as this: I went to one of those reputed wise, thinking that there, if anywhere, I could refute the oracle and say to it: "This man is wiser than I, but you said I was." Then, when I examined this man—there is no need for me to tell you his name, he was one of our public men—my experience was something like this: I thought that he appeared wise to many people and especially to himself, but he was not. I then tried to show him that he thought himself wise, but that he was not. As a result he came to dislike me, and so did

---

3. Apollo, whose oracle was located at Delphi.
4. In 404 B.C.E., an oligarchic coup (supported by the Spartan leadership) overthrew the democratic government in Athens. The oligarchs, who came to be known as the Thirty Tyrants, terrorized Athens with their brutality and corruption for the better part of a year; many prominent democrats fled into exile until the restoration of the democracy in 403.

many of the bystanders. So I withdrew and thought to myself: "I am wiser than this man; it is likely that neither of us knows anything worthwhile, but he thinks he knows something when he does not, whereas when I do not know, neither do I think I know; so I am likely to be wiser to this small extent, that I do not think I know what I do not know." After this I approached another man, one of those thought to be wiser than he, and I thought the same thing, and so I came to be disliked both by him and by many others.

After that I proceeded systematically. I realized, to my sorrow and alarm, that I was getting unpopular, but I thought that I must attach the greatest importance to the god's oracle, so I must go to all those who had any reputation for knowledge to examine its meaning. And by the dog,[5] gentlemen of the jury—for I must tell you the truth—I experienced something like this: in my investigation in the service of the god I found that those who had the highest reputation were nearly the most deficient, while those who were thought to be inferior were more knowledgeable. I must give you an account of my journeyings as if they were labours I had undertaken to prove the oracle irrefutable. After the politicians, I went to the poets, the writers of tragedies and dithyrambs[6] and the others, intending in their case to catch myself being more ignorant then they. So I took up those poems with which they seemed to have taken most trouble and asked them what they meant, in order that I might at the same time learn something from them. I am ashamed to tell you the truth, gentlemen, but I must. Almost all the bystanders explained the poems better than their authors could. I soon realized that poets do not compose their poems with knowledge, but by some inborn talent and by inspiration, like seers and prophets who also say many fine things without any understanding of what they say. The poets seemed to me to have had a similar experience. At the same time I saw that, because of their poetry, they thought themselves very wise men in other respects, which they were not. So there again I withdrew, thinking that I had the same advantage over them as I had over the politicians.

Finally I went to the craftsmen, for I was conscious of knowing practically nothing, and I knew that I would find that they had knowledge of many fine things. In this I was not mistaken; they knew things I did not know, and to that extent they were wiser than I. But, gentlemen of the jury, the good craftsmen seemed to me to have the same fault as the poets: each of them, because of his success at his craft, thought himself very wise in other most important pursuits, and this error of theirs overshadowed the wisdom they had, so that I asked myself, on behalf of the oracle, whether I should prefer to be as I am, with neither their wisdom nor their ignorance, or to have both. The answer I gave myself and the oracle was that it was to my advantage to be as I am.

As a result of this investigation, gentlemen of the jury, I acquired much unpopularity, of a kind that is hard to deal with and is a heavy burden; many slanders came from these people and a reputation for wisdom, for in each case the bystanders thought that I myself possessed the wisdom that I proved that my

---

5. An oath occasionally used by Socrates, un-
known elsewhere.

6. A form of choral poetry, written for public
performance.

interlocutor did not have. What is probable, gentlemen, is that in fact that god is wise and that his oracular response meant that human wisdom is worth little or nothing, and that when he says this man, Socrates, he is using my name as an example, as if he said: "This man among you, mortals, is wisest who, like Socrates, understands that this wisdom is worthless." So even now I continue this investigation as the gods bade me—and I go around seeking out anyone, citizen or stranger, whom I think wise. Then if I do not think he is, I come to the assistance of the god and show him that he is not wise. Because of this occupation, I do not have the leisure to engage in public affairs to any extent, nor indeed to look after my own, but I live in great poverty because of my service to the god.

Furthermore, the young men who follow me around of their own free will, those who have most leisure, the sons of the very rich, take pleasure in hearing people questioned; they themselves often imitate me and try to question others. I think they find an abundance of men who believe they have some knowledge but know little or nothing. The result is that those whom they question are angry, not with themselves but with me. They say: "That man Socrates is a pestilential fellow who corrupts the young." If one asks them what he does and what he teaches to corrupt them, they are silent, as they do not know, but, so as not to appear at a loss, they mention those accusations that are available against all philosophers, about "things in the sky and things below the earth," about "not believing in the gods" and "making the worse the stronger argument;" they would not want to tell the truth, that they have been proved to lay claim to knowledge when they know nothing. These people are ambitious, violent and numerous; they are continually and convincingly talking about me; they have been filling your ears for a long time with vehement slanders against me. From them Meletus[7] attacked me, and Anytus and Lycon, Meletus being vexed on behalf of the poets, Anytus on behalf of the craftsmen and the politicians, Lycon on behalf of the orators, so that, as I started out by saying, I should be surprised if I could rid you of so much slander in so short a time. That, gentlemen of the jury, is the truth for you. I have hidden or omitted nothing. I know well enough that this very conduct makes me unpopular, and this is proof that what I say is true, that such is the slander against me, and that such are its causes. If you look into this either now or later, this is what you will find.

Let this suffice as a defence against the charges of my earlier accusers. After this I shall try to defend myself against Meletus, that good and patriotic man, as he says he is, and my later accusers. As these are a different lot of accusers, let us again take up their sworn deposition. It goes something like this: Socrates is guilty of corrupting the young and of not believing in the gods in whom the city believes, but in other new divinities. Such is their charge. Let us examine it point by point.

He says that I am guilty of corrupting the young, but I say that Meletus is guilty of dealing frivolously with serious matters, of irresponsibly bringing people into court, and of professing to be seriously concerned with things about none of

---

7. Meletus was Socrates' chief accuser, although Anytus, the wealthiest, was probably the most influential.

which he has ever cared, and I shall try to prove that this is so. Come here and tell me, Meletus. Surely you consider it of the greatest importance that our young men be as good as possible?—Indeed I do.

Come then, tell the jury who improves them. You obviously know, in view of your concern. You say you have discovered the one who corrupts them, namely me, and you bring me here and accuse me to the jury. Come, inform the jury and tell them who it is. You see, Meletus, that you are silent and know not what to say. Does this not seem shameful to you and a sufficient proof of what I say, that you have not been concerned with any of this. Tell me, my good sir, who improves our young men?—The laws.

That is not what I am asking, but what person, who has previously acquired knowledge of the laws?—These jurymen,[8] Socrates.

How do you mean, Meletus? Are these able to educate the young and improve them?—Certainly.

All of them, or some but not others?—All of them.

Very good, by Hera. You mention a great abundance of benefactors. But what about the audience? Do they improve the young or not?—They do, too.

What about the members of Council?[9] The Councillors, also.

But, Meletus, what about the assembly? Do members of the assembly corrupt the young, or do they all improve them?—They improve them.

All the Athenians, it seems, make the young into fine good men, except me, and I alone corrupt them. Is that what you mean?—That is most definitely what I mean.

You condemn me to a great misfortune. Does this also apply to horses do you think? That all men improve them and one individual corrupts them. Or is quite the contrary true, one individual is able to improve them, or very few, namely the horse breeders, whereas the majority, if they have horses and use them, corrupt them. Is that not the case, Meletus, both with horses and all other animals? Of course it is, whether you and Anytus say so or not. It would be a very happy state of affairs if only one person corrupted our youth, while the others improved them.

You have made it sufficiently obvious, Meletus, that you have never had any concern for our youth; you show your indifference clearly; that you have given no thought to the subjects about which you bring me to trial.

And by Zeus, Meletus, tell us also whether it is better for a man to live among good or wicked fellow-citizens. Answer, my good man, for I am not asking a difficult question. Do not the wicked always do some harm to their nearest neighbours, whereas good people benefit them?—Certainly.

And does the man exist who would rather be harmed than benefited by his associates? Answer, my good sir, for the law orders you to answer. Is there any man who wants to be harmed?—Of course not.

Come now, do you accuse me here of corrupting the young and making them

---

8. Athenian juries were huge, consisting of as many as 500 men for this trial; there was no judge.
9. The deliberative body of 500 men who

prepared the agenda for the assembly, which was the chief decision-making body in Athens and open to the participation of all adult males—perhaps some 40,000 people.

worse deliberately or unwillingly?—Deliberately.

What follows, Meletus? Are you so much wiser at your age than I am at mine that you understand that wicked people always do some harm to their closest neighbours while good people do them good, but I have reached such a pitch of ignorance that I do not realize this, namely that if I make one of my associates wicked I run the risk of being harmed by him so that I do such a great evil deliberately, as you say. I do not believe you, Meletus, and I do not think anyone else will. Either I do not corrupt the young or, if I do, it is unwillingly, and you are lying in either case. Now if I corrupt them unwillingly, the law does not require you to bring people to court for such unwilling wrongdoings, but to get hold of them privately, to instruct them and exhort them; for clearly, if I learn better, I shall cease to do what I am doing unwillingly. You, however, have avoided my company and were unwilling to instruct me, but you bring me here, where the law requires one to bring those who are in need of punishment, not of instruction.

[Socrates, by questioning Meletus and exposing the logical fallacies in his argument about Socrates' irreligiosity, quickly disposes of that charge.]

I do not think, gentlemen of the jury, that it requires a prolonged defence to prove that I am not guilty of the charges in Meletus' deposition, but this is sufficient. On the other hand, you know that what I said earlier is true, that I am very unpopular with many people. This will be my undoing, if I am undone, not Meletus or Anytus but the slanders and envy of many people. This has destroyed many and will, I think, continue to do so. There is no danger that it will stop at me.

Someone might say: "Are you not ashamed, Socrates, to have followed the kind of occupation that has led to your being now in danger of death?" However, I should be right to reply to him: "You are wrong, sir, if you think that a man who is any good at all should take into account the risk of life or death; he should look to this only in his actions, whether what he does is right or wrong, whether he is acting like a good or a bad man." According to your view, all the heroes who died at Troy were inferior people, especially the son of Thetis who was so contemptuous of danger compared with disgrace.[10] When he was eager to kill Hector, his goddess mother warned him, as I believe, in some such words as these: "My child, if you avenge the death of your comrade, Patroclus, and you kill Hector, you will die yourself, for your death is to follow immediately after Hector's." Hearing this, he despised death and danger and was much more afraid to live a coward who did not avenge his friends. "Let me die at once," he said, after attacking his killer, "rather than remain here, a laughingstock by the curved ships, a burden upon the earth." Do you think he gave thought to death and danger?

This is the truth of the matter, gentlemen of the jury: wherever a man has taken a position that he believes to be best, or has been placed by his commander, there he must I think remain and face danger, without a thought for death or

---

10. Achilles, in Book 18 of the *Iliad*, risks his life to avenge the death of Patroclus. (See the *Iliad*, Book 18.)

anything else, rather than disgrace. It would have been a dreadful way to behave, gentlemen of the jury, if, at Potidaea[11] Amphipolis and Delium, I had, at the risk of death, like anyone else, remained at my post where those you had elected to command had ordered me, and then, when the god ordered me, as I thought and believed, to live the life of a philosopher, to examine myself and others, I had abandoned my post for fear of death or anything else. That would have been a dreadful thing, and then I might truly have justly been brought here for not believing in the gods, disobeying the oracle, fearing death, and thinking I was wise when I was not. To fear death, gentlemen, is no other than to think oneself wise when one is not, to think one knows what one does not know. No one knows whether death may not be the greatest of all blessings for a man, yet men fear it as if they knew that it is the greatest of evils. And surely it is the most blameworthy ignorance to believe that one knows what one does not know. It is perhaps on this point and in this respect, gentlemen, that I differ from the majority of men, and if I were to claim that I am wiser than anyone in anything, it would be in this, that, as I have no adequate knowledge of things in the underworld, so I do not think I have. I do know, however, that it is wicked and shameful to do wrong, to disobey one's superior, be he god or man. I shall never fear or avoid things of which I do not know, whether they may not be good rather than things that I know to be bad. Even if you acquitted me now and did not believe Anytus, who said to you that either I should not have been brought here in the first place, or that now I am here, you cannot avoid executing me, for if I should be acquitted, your sons would practice the teachings of Socrates and all be thoroughly corrupted. If you said to me in this regard: "Socrates, we do not believe Anytus now; we acquit you, but only on condition that you spend no more time on this investigation and do not practise philosophy, and if you are caught doing so you will die;" if, as I say, you were to acquit me on those terms, I would say to you: "Gentlemen of the jury, I am grateful and I am your friend, but I will obey the god rather than you, and as long as I draw breath and am able, I shall not cease to practise philosophy, to exhort you and to point out to anyone of you whom I happen to meet: Good Sir, you are an Athenian, a citizen of the greatest city with the greatest reputation for both wisdom and power; are you not ashamed of your eagerness to possess as much wealth, reputation and honours as possible, while you do not care for nor give thought to wisdom or truth, or the best possible state of your soul?" Then, if one of you disputes this and says he does care, I shall not let him go at once or leave him, but I shall question him, examine him and test him, and if I do not think he has attained the goodness that he says he has, I shall reproach him because he attaches little importance to the most important things and greater importance to inferior things. I shall treat in this way anyone I happen to meet, young and old, citizen and stranger, and more so the citizens because you are more kindred to me. Be sure that this is what the god orders me to do, and I think there is no greater blessing for the city than my service to the god. For I go around

---

11. Potidaea, Amphipolis, and Delium were
the locations of battles in the Peloponnesian war, where Socrates had fought.

doing nothing but persuading both young and old among you not to care for your body or your wealth in preference to or as strongly as for the best possible state of your soul, as I say to you: "Wealth does not bring about excellence, but excellence brings about wealth and all other public and private blessings for men."

Now if by saying this I corrupt the young, this advice must be harmful, but if anyone says that I give different advice, he is talking nonsense. On this point I would say to you, gentlemen of the jury: "Whether you believe Anytus or not, whether you acquit me or not, do so on the understanding that this is my course of action, even if I am to face death many times. Do not create a disturbance, gentlemen, but abide by my request not to cry out at what I say but to listen, for I think it will be to your advantage to listen, and I am about to say other things at which you will perhaps cry out. By no means do this. Be sure that if you kill the sort of man I say I am, you will not harm me more than yourselves. Neither Meletus nor Anytus can harm me in any way, he could not harm me, for I do not think it is permitted that a better man be harmed by a worse; certainly he might kill me, or perhaps banish or disfranchise me, which he and maybe others think to be great harm, but I do not think so. I think he is doing himself much greater harm doing what he is doing now, attempting to have a man executed unjustly. Indeed, gentlemen of the jury. I am far from making a defence now on my own behalf, as might be thought, but on yours, to prevent you from wrongdoing by mistreating the god's gift to you by condemning me; for if you kill me you will not easily find another like me. I was attached to this city by the god—though it seems a ridiculous thing to say—as upon a great and noble horse which was somewhat sluggish because of its size and needed to be stirred up by a kind of gadfly. It is to fulfill some such function that the god has placed me in the city. I never cease to rouse everyone of you, to persuade and reproach you all day long and everywhere I find myself in your company.

Another such man will not easily come to be among you, gentlemen, and if you believe me you will spare me. You might easily strike out at me as people do when they are aroused from a doze; if convinced by Anytus you could easily kill me, and then you could sleep on for the rest of your days, unless the god, in his care for you, sent you someone else. That I am the kind of person to be a gift of the god to the city you might realize from the fact that it does not seem like human nature for me to have neglected all my own affairs and to have tolerated this neglect now for so many years while I was always concerned with you, approaching each one of you like a father or an elder brother to persuade you to care for virtue. Now if I profited from this by charging a fee for my advice, there would be some sense to it, but you can see for yourselves that, for all their shameless accusations, my accusers have not been able in their impudence to bring forward a witness to say that I have ever received a fee or ever asked for one. I, on the other hand, have a convincing witness that I speak the truth, my poverty.

It may seem strange that while I go around and give this advice privately and interfere in private affairs, I do not venture to go to the assembly and there advise the city. You have heard me give the reason for this in many places. I have a divine sign from the god which Meletus has ridiculed in his deposition. This began when I was a child. It is a voice, and whenever it speaks it turns me away from something I am about to do, but it never encourages me to do anything. This is what has prevented me from taking part in public affairs, and I think it was quite right to prevent me. Be sure, gentlemen of the jury, that if I had long ago attempted to take part in politics, I should have died long ago, and benefitted neither you nor myself. Do not be angry with me for speaking the truth; no man will survive who genuinely opposes you or any other crowd and prevents the occurrence of many unjust and illegal happenings in the city. A man who really fights for justice must lead a private, not a public, life if he is to survive for even a short time.

> [Socrates describes two incidents of civil disobedience on his part, in which he disobeyed official directives—one under the democratic government and one under the oligarchy— that he believed to be illegal.]

Very well, gentlemen of the jury. This, and maybe other similar things, is what I have to say in my defence. Perhaps one of you might be angry as he recalls that when he himself stood trial on a less dangerous charge, he begged and implored the jury with many tears, that he brought his children and many of his friends and family into court to arouse as much pity as he could, but that I do none of these things, even though I may seem to be running the ultimate risk. Thinking of this, he might feel resentful and angry and cast his vote in anger. If there is such a one among you—I do not deem there is, but if there is—I think it would be right to say in reply: "My good sir, I too have a household and, in Homer's phrase, I am not born from oak or rock but from men, so that I have a family, indeed three sons, gentlemen of the jury, of whom one is an adolescent while two are children. Nevertheless, I will not beg you to acquit me by bringing them here. Why do I do none of these things? Not through arrogance, gentlemen, nor through lack of respect for you. Whether I am brave in the face of death is another matter, but with regard to my reputation and yours and that of the whole city, it does not seem right to me to do these things, especially at my age and with my reputation. For it is generally believed, whether it be true or false, that in certain respects Socrates is superior to the majority of men. Now if those of you who are considered superior, be it in wisdom or courage or whatever other virtue makes them so, are seen behaving like that, it would be a disgrace. Yet I have often seen them do this sort of thing when standing trial, men who are thought to be somebody, doing amazing things as if they thought it a terrible thing to die, and as if they were to be immortal if you did not execute them. I think these men bring shame upon the city so that a stranger, too, would assume that those who are outstanding in virtue among the Athenians, whom they themselves select from themselves to fill offices of state and receive other honours, are in no way better than women. You should not act like that, gentlemen of the jury, those of you who have any reputation at all, and if we do, you should not allow it. You should make it very clear that you will more readily convict a man who performs these pitiful dramatics in court and so makes the city a laughingstock, than a man who keeps quiet.

Quite apart from the question of reputation, gentlemen, I do not think it right to supplicate the jury and to be acquitted because of this. It is not the purpose of a juryman's office to give justice as a favour to whomever seems good to him, but to judge according to law, and this he has sworn to do. We should not accustom you to perjure yourselves, nor should you make a habit of it. This is irreverent conduct for either of us.

Do not deem it right for me, gentlemen of the jury, that I should act towards you in a way that I do not consider to be good or just or pious, especially, by Zeus, as I am being prosecuted by Meletus here for impiety; clearly, if I convinced you by my supplication to do violence to your oath of office, I would be teaching you not to believe in the gods, and my defence would convict me of not believing in them, as my accusers do now, gentlemen of the jury. This is far from being the case, gentlemen, for I do believe in them as none of my accusers do. I leave it to you and the god to judge me in the way that will be best for me and for you.

[The jury now gives its verdict of guilty, and Meletus asks for the penalty of death.]

There are many other reasons for my not being angry with you for convicting me, gentlemen of the jury, and what happened was not unexpected. I am much more surprised at the number of votes cast on each side, for I did not think the decision would be by so few votes but by a great many. As it is, a switch of only thirty votes would have acquitted me.[12] I think myself that I have been cleared on Meletus' charges, and it is clear to all that, if Anytus and Lycon had not joined him in accusing me, he would have been fined a thousand drachmas for not receiving a fifth of the votes.

He assesses the penalty at death. What counter-assessment should I propose to you, gentlemen of the jury?[13] Clearly it should be a penalty I deserve, and what do I deserve to suffer or to pay because I have deliberately not led a quiet life but have neglected what occupies most people: wealth, household affairs, the position of general or public orator or the other offices, the political clubs and factions that exist in the city? I thought myself too honest to survive if I occupied myself with those things. I did not follow that path that would have made me of no use either to you or to myself, but I went to each of you privately and conferred upon him what I say is the greatest benefit, by persuading him not to care for any of his belongings before caring that he himself should be as good and as wise as possible, not to care for the city's possessions more than for the city itself, and to care for other things in the same way. What do I deserve for being such a man? Some good, gentlemen of the jury, if I must truly make an assessment according to my deserts, and something suitable. What is suitable for a benefactor who needs leisure to exhort you? Nothing is more suitable, gentlemen, than for such a man to be fed in the Prytaneum,[14] much more suitable for him than for anyone of you who has won a victory at Olympia with a pair or a team of horses. The Olympian victor makes you think yourself happy, I make you be happy. Besides, he does not

---

12. The vote seems to have been 280 to 220. A tie vote would have been equivalent to acquittal. In order to discourage frivolous lawsuits, prosecutors who did not obtain a fifth of the votes were subject to a fine; Socrates humorously suggests that had he had only one accuser instead of three, that accuser would have fallen short of the requisite fifth of the total votes.

13. The defendant was legally entitled to propose a counterpenalty, such as exile.

14. A kind of town hall, where visiting dignitaries and Olympic victors were entertained.

need food, but I do. So if I must make a just assessment of what I deserve, I assess it at this: free meals in the Prytaneum.

When I say this you may think, as when I spoke of appeals to pity and entreaties, that I speak arrogantly, but that is not the case, gentlemen of the jury, rather it is like this: I am convinced that no man willingly does wrong, but I am not convincing you of this, for we have talked together but a short time. If it were the law with us, as it is elsewhere, that a trial for life should not last one but many days, you would be convinced, but now it is not easy to dispel great slanders in a short time. Since I am convinced that I wrong no one, I am not likely to wrong myself, to say that I deserve some evil and to make some such assessment against myself. What should I fear? That I should suffer the penalty Meletus has assessed against me, of which I say I do not know whether it is good or bad? Am I then to choose in preference to this something that I know very well to be an evil and assess the penalty at that? Imprisonment? Why should I live in prison, always subjected to the ruling magistrates? A fine, and imprisonment until I pay it? That would be the same thing for me, as I have no money. Exile? for perhaps you might accept that assessment.

I should have to be inordinately fond of life, gentlemen of the jury, to be so unreasonable as to suppose that other men will easily tolerate my company and conversation when you, my fellow citizens, have been unable to endure them, but found them a burden and resented them so that you are now seeking to get rid of them. Far from it, gentlemen. It would be a fine life at my age to be driven out of one city after another, for I know very well that wherever I go the young men will listen to my talk as they do here. If I drive them away, they will themselves persuade their elders to drive me out; if I do not drive them away, their fathers and relations will drive me out on their behalf.

Perhaps someone might say: But Socrates, if you leave us will you not be able to live quietly, without talking? Now this is the most difficult point on which to convince some of you. If I say that it is impossible for me to keep quiet because that means disobeying the god, you will not believe me and will think I am being ironical. On the other hand, if I say that it is the greatest good for a man to discuss virtue every day and those other things about which you hear me conversing and testing myself and others, for the unexamined life is not worth living for man, you will believe me even less.

[Socrates says that his friends (including Plato) have urged him to propose a fine; he proposes an absurdly small one. The jury now votes again and sentences Socrates to death.]

It is for the sake of a short time, gentlemen of the jury, that you will acquire the reputation and the guilt, in the eyes of those who want to denigrate the city, of having killed Socrates, a wise man, for they will say that I am wise even if I am not. If you had waited but a little while, this would have happened of its own accord. You see my age, that I am already advanced in years and close to death. I am saying this not to all of you but to those who condemned me to death, and to these same jurors I say: Perhaps you think that I was convicted for lack of such words as might have convinced you, if I thought I should say or do all I could to avoid my sentence. Far from it. I was convicted because I lacked not words but boldness and shamelessness and the willingness to say to you what you would most gladly have heard from me, lamentations and tears and my saying and doing many things that I say are unworthy of me but that you are accustomed to hear from others. I did not think then that the danger I ran should make me do anything mean, nor do I now regret the nature of my defence. I would much rather die after this kind of defence than live after making the other kind. Neither I nor any other man should, on trial or in war, contrive to avoid death at any cost. Indeed it is often obvious in battle that one could escape death by throwing away one's weapons and by turning to supplicate one's pursuers, and there are many ways to avoid death in every kind of danger if one will venture to do or say anything to avoid it. It is not difficult to avoid death, gentlemen of the jury, it is much more difficult to avoid wickedness, for it runs faster than death. Slow and elderly as I am, I have been caught by the slower pursuer, whereas my accusers, being clever and sharp, have been caught by the quicker, wickedness. I leave you now, condemned to death by you, but they are condemned by truth to wickedness and injustice. So I maintain my assessment, and they maintain theirs. This perhaps had to happen, and I think it is as it should be.

Now I want to prophesy to those who convicted me, for I am at the point when men prophesy most, when they are about to die. I say gentlemen, to those who voted to kill me, that vengeance will come upon you immediately after my death, a vengeance much harder to bear than that which you took in killing me. You did this in the belief that you would avoid giving an account of your life, but I maintain that quite the opposite will happen to you. There will be more people to test you, whom I now held back, but you did not notice it. They will be more difficult to deal with as they will be younger and you will resent them more. You are wrong if you believe that by killing people you will prevent anyone from reproaching you for not living in the right way. To escape such tests is neither possible nor good, but it is best and easiest not to discredit others but to prepare oneself to be as good as possible. With this prophecy to you who convicted me, I part from you.

I should be glad to discuss what has happened with those who voted for my acquittal during the time that the officers of the court are busy and I do not yet have to depart to my death. So, gentlemen, stay with me awhile, for nothing prevents us from talking to each other while it is allowed. To you, as being my friends, I want to show the meaning of what has occurred. A surprising thing has happened to me, judges—you I would rightly call judges. At all previous times my usual mantic sign frequently opposed me, even in small matters, when I was about to do something wrong, but now that, as you can see for yourselves, I was faced with what one might think, and what is generally thought to be, the worst of evils, my divine sign has not opposed me, either when I left home at dawn, or when I came into court, or at any time that I was about to say something during my speech. Yet in other talks if often held me back in the middle of my speaking, but now it has opposed no word or deed of mine. What do I think is the reason for this? I will tell you. What has happened to me may well be a good thing, and those of us who believe death to be an evil are certainly mistaken. I have convincing proof of this, for it is impossible that my customary sign did not oppose me if I was not about to do what was right.

Let us reflect that there is good hope that death is a blessing, for it is one of two things: either the dead are nothing and have no perception of anything, or it is, as we are told, a change for the soul from here to another place. If it is complete lack of perception, like a dreamless sleep, then death would be a great advantage. For I think that if one had to pick out that night during which a man slept soundly and did not dream, put beside it the other nights and days of his life, and then see how many days and nights had been better and more pleasant than that night, not only a private person but the great king would find them easy to count compared with the other days and nights. If death is like this I say it is an advantage, for all eternity would then seem to be no more than a single night. If, on the other hand, death is a change from here to another place, and what we are told is true and all who have died are there, what greater blessing could there be, gentlemen of the jury? If anyone arriving in Hades will have escaped from those who call themselves judges here, and will find those true judges who are said to sit in judgement there, Minos[15] and Radamanthus and Aeacus and Triptolemus and the other demi-gods who have been upright in their own life, would that be a poor kind of change? Again, what would one of you give to keep company with Orpheus[16] and Musaeus, Hesiod and Homer? I am willing to die many times if that is true. It would be a wonderful way for me to spend my time whenever I met Palamedes and Ajax, the son of Telamon, and any other of the men of old who died through an unjust conviction, to compare my experience with theirs. I think it would be pleasant. Most important, I could spend my time testing and examining people there, as I do here, as to who among them is wise, and who thinks he is, but is not.

You too must be of good hope as regards death, gentlemen of the jury, and keep this one truth in mind, that a good man cannot be harmed either in life or in death, and that his affairs are not neglected by the gods. What has happened to me now has not happened of itself, but it is clear to me that it was better for me to die now and to escape from trouble. That is why my divine sign did not oppose me at any point. So I am certainly not angry with those who convicted me, or with my accusers. Of course that was not their purpose when they accused and convicted me, but they thought they were hurting me, and for this they deserve blame. This much I ask from them: when my sons grow up, avenge yourselves by causing them the same kind of grief that I caused you, if you think they care for money or anything else more than they care for virtue, or if they think they are somebody when they are nobody. Reproach them as I reproach you, that they do not care for the right things and think they are worthy when they are not worthy of anything. If you do this, I shall have been justly treated by you, and my sons also.

Now the hour to part has come. I go to die, you go to live. Which of us goes to the better lot is known to no one, except the god.

---

15. Minos, Radamanthus, and Aeacus were famous in myth as just men who became judges of the dead in the underworld. Triptolemus, an Eleusinian to whom

Demeter taught both agriculture and the rites of her worship, is not elsewhere associated with the underworld.

16. Orpheus and Musaeus are legendary poets.

LUCRETIUS (98?–55 B.C.E.)
Rome

Lucretius's poem *On the Nature of Things* has its antecedents in such didactic poems as Hesiod's *Works and Days,* with its emphatic moral lessons (and its connections to Near Eastern wisdom literature). The stated purpose of Lucretius's poem is to challenge and dispel the superstitions of his contemporaries, including those about divine intervention in human life and, most especially, those about the terrors of death. To counter these fears, Lucretius expounded the teachings of Epicurus, a Greek philosopher of the early third century B.C.E., whose theory of the material nature of the universe, through its combination of physics and ethical precepts, proposed ways to achieve peace of mind and freedom from irrational anxiety. Epicurus depicted the entire universe as a combination of perpetually moving atoms: human beings are formed of them, as everything else in the world must also be, including the gods. When a person dies, the soul's atoms cease to coalesce, so that death is final; fears of punishment in the underworld are groundless and therefore foolish. Nominally addressing his friend Memmius, Lucretius set forth the philosophical doctrine of Epicurus in clear and forceful language that a wide audience might understand and learn from.

from *On the Nature of Things [De Rerum Natura]*

[Mother of all the Romans]

Mother of all the Romans, delight of men and gods,
life-giving Venus,[1] who under the gliding constellations
fill with teeming life the sea that bears our ships
and land that bears our crops—through you each living creature
is conceived and issues forth to look upon the sunlight;   5
at your coming, O goddess, the winds and clouds of heaven
are put to flight; for you the skillful earth brings forth
her sweetest flowers; for you the ocean levels smile;
and heaven, now grown calm, pours forth its gentle light.
For when the day puts on her lovely dress of spring   10
and the life-bringing West Wind blows with all his force,
then first the birds of heaven herald your approach,
for it is your power, goddess, that strikes them to the heart.
And cattle all run wild and prance through the rich pastures
and swim the rapid rivers: they are enthralled by your charm   15
and follow wherever you lead them with a keen desire.

Translated by James H. Mantinband.

1. The Roman goddess of love and fertility,
   identified with the Greek goddess Aphrodite; mother of Aeneas [see the
   Aeneid in this section].

And through the seas and mountains and the rushing rivers,
the leafy dwellings of the birds, and the verdant meadows,
their hearts are all inspired by you with gentle passion,
so that they long to reproduce their several species.   20
Since you alone, O goddess, are the Queen of Nature,
and since without you, nothing comes into the daylight,
nothing happy, nothing beautiful is created,
I crave your help in writing these verses, which I am trying
to fashion on the Nature of the Universe   25
for Memmius, my good friend, the man whom you have wished
always to excel, endowed with every gift.
Therefore, goddess, grant a lasting grace to my words,
and meanwhile cause the brutal works of war to cease,
to sleep and to be still, on every land and sea.   30
For you alone can bless mankind with tranquil peace,
since it is mighty Mars who is the Lord of War
and all its brutal works, and he often lies in your lap,
entirely conquered by the eternal wound of love,
and looking upward with his shapely neck bent back,   35
he feasts his avid eyes upon you, hungry for love;
his breath is hanging upon your lips as he reclines.
And you, O goddess, bend over him as he lies there
upon your holy body, and shed your honeyed words,
and for your Romans, glorious goddess, seek placid peace.   40
For in such troubled times, I cannot do my work
with quiet mind, nor can the noble Memmius
at such a time be wanting to the common safety.

It now remains for you to devote receptive ears
and a keen mind, removed from cares, to the True Reason,   45
lest my gifts, set forth for you with faithful zeal,
be scornfully cast aside before they are understood.
For I am about to disclose to you the laws of heaven
and of the gods; I shall unfold the beginnings of things
whence Nature creates all things, increases and fosters them,   50
and whither this same Nature dissolves and reduces them,
—which we shall designate by some such names as Matter,
and Generative Bodies, and the Seeds of Things,
and likewise call them by the name of First Bodies,
because from these First Elements all things are made.   55

[Therefore death is nothing to us]

Therefore death is nothing to us, for it matters not,
since the nature of the mind is known to be mortal;

and just as, in the days of old, we felt no distress
when Carthaginians[2] were pouring in to do battle,
and when the entire world, shaken by war's dread tumult,   5
reeled and trembled under the lofty vault of heaven,
and all men were in doubt, not knowing to which empire
all humanity on land and sea would be subject:—
so, when we shall be no more, when body and spirit,
by whose union we exist, have been separated,   10
nothing more will be able to touch us, who shall not be,
nothing at all will be able to affect our senses,
not though earth were fused with sea or sea with sky.
And even granted that the nature of mind and spirit
still had the power to feel, when torn away from the body,   15
that is nothing to us, who are brought into existence
by the wedlock of body and spirit, joined and made one.
And even if the atoms that compose our body
were reassembled by time and brought to their present arrangement,
and to this arrangement the light of life were given—   20
even that would not be any concern of ours,
once the chain of memory had been snapped and broken.
We, who are now, are not concerned with ourselves that were
in any previous time, nor touched by former sufferings.
For when you look back at all the tremendous expanse   25
of unmeasured time, and think how many and varied
are the atoms' movements, then you might believe with ease
that these same atoms that now compose us, have been arranged
many times before in the same combinations.
But our mind cannot recall or remember this: 30
for a break in life has intervened, and the atoms' motions
all have wandered far astray from any sensation.
For if the future holds misery and woe for a man,
then he himself will have to exist in that future time
in order to suffer. But death removes us from this fate,   35
denying existence to the self that would suffer thus;
so we may be sure we have nothing to fear in death:
one who no longer is, cannot be miserable,
or differ at all from one who never has been born,
when immortal death has taken mortal life away.   40

And therefore when you see a man resenting his lot,
that after death his corpse will molder in the tomb,
or be destroyed by fire or the jaws of beasts,
you may be certain that his words do not ring true,

---

2. Rome and Carthage, in north Africa, were
embroiled in a series of wars fought at long
intervals, beginning in the mid-third century B.C.E. and ending with Roman victory
and domination more than a century later.

that deep in his heart there lurks some secret pang, although   45
he may deny the belief in sensation after death.
I think he does not admit what he professes, and why;
and he does not completely remove himself from life,
but unconsciously makes something of himself survive.
For when a living man anticipates the thought   50
that after death the birds and beasts will rend his body,
he pities himself: he does not distinguish between himself
and the outcast corpse; but imagines himself to be that object,
and, standing there, he projects his own feelings into it.
And so he resents having been born mortal: he does not see   55
that in real death there will not be another self
to mourn his own departure or to stand by and suffer
with the agony of being mangled or cremated.
For if it is a bad thing after death to be mauled
by wild beasts' jaws, why should it not be just as painful   60
to be roasted in the blazing flames on a funeral pyre,
or to lie embalmed in honey, suffocated
and stiff with cold upon a slab of chilly marble,
or to be crushed beneath a heavy load of earth?
    "No longer now your happy home and your good wife   65
shall welcome you, nor your sweet children come a-running
to win the first kiss, touching your heart with silent joy!
No more prosperity, no protection for your family.
Alas, unhappy wretch!" men say, "one fatal day
has cheated you of all the blessings of this life!"   70
But they do not go on to add: "And now no yearning
for all these lost delights can touch you any more."
If they could clearly see, and spoke accordingly,
they would rid their hearts of weighty fears and torments!
"Yes, you are now at peace in the quiet sleep of death   75
and will remain so forever, free of pain and grief;
but we, beside you as you burn on the dreadful pyre,
we have wept insatiably for you, and no day
shall ever come to lift the load of grief from our hearts."
Of such a man we should ask, why all this bitterness,   80
if a body returns to sleep and peaceful repose,
what reason to pine and weep with everlasting sorrow?
    Thus, again, men speak, when they recline at the banquet
with goblets in their hands and garlands on their brows—
they say in their hearts: "How short the enjoyment for us poor mortals!   85
Soon it will be gone and it can never return!"
As if in death the chief calamity for them
will be that they are parched and shrivelled by burning thirst,
or tormented by the longing for anything.
For no one misses himself, nor does he long for life,   90

when mind and body alike are peacefully asleep.
And even if that sleep should be made everlasting,
no longing for ourselves would torment us at all.
And yet the vital atoms dispersed throughout the body
are not wandering far away from the sensory motions,   95
when a man wakes up from sleep and collects his wits.
Death, then, must be thought to be even less than sleep,
if anything can be less than what we see to be nothing:
for there is a greater dispersion of the disturbed matter
once we are dead, nor can anyone awake and arise   100
whom once the chilly end of life has overtaken.
    Suppose that Nature herself should suddenly find a voice
and reprimand some one of us in such words as these:
"What grieves you, mortal, making you indulge yourself
in all these lamentations? Why weep and wail at death?   105
For if your life until this moment has been pleasant,
if all your blessings have not flowed away like water
in a leaky vase, and been wasted and unenjoyed,
why not, O foolish man, retire, as a dinner guest
who has had his fill, and take your rest in peace and quiet?   110
But if all your blessings have been spilt and lost,
if life is odious to you, why seek to prolong it,
when you will only be a prey to future misfortunes?
Why not rather make an end of life and affliction?
For I have no new invention or contrivance   115
that can please you: everything remains the same.
If your body is not already worn out with years
and your limbs decrepit, still nothing new can happen,
even though you should outlive all generations,
even though you never were to die at all."   120
What could we answer Nature, except that she is right,
and the argument she sets forth is a valid one?
But suppose some aged person should complain
—some miserable man bewailing imminent doom—
would she not be right to scold him all the more: 125
"Away with tears, you villain! Cease your lamentations!
Before you withered, you tasted all the joys of life;
but since you always want what you haven't and scorn what you have,
your life has slipped away unblessed and unfulfilled.
And death is standing by your head, without your knowledge,   130
before you can retire, sated, from the banquet.
But come now, and dismiss what is not meet for your years.
Depart: make room for your children, since you have no choice."
She would be right, in my opinion, thus to reproach.
For the old is always thrust aside to make a place   135
for the new; one thing is built from the wreckage of another.

But there is no black pit of Hell awaiting us:
atoms are needed for future generations' growth,
and when they have lived their lives they will follow you.
Earlier generations have gone, and future ones   140
will do the same: one thing will always grow from another.
No man has life in freehold: we all are merely tenants.
Look back at all the ages that passed before our birth
and see how utterly they count to us as nothing.
This is the mirror Nature is holding up for us   145
to see the time that is to come when we are dead.
Is this so terrible? Is it so very depressing?
Is it not more tranquil than the deepest sleep?

And as for all the tortures that are said to exist
in Hell, they all exist for us here in this life.   150
There is no fabled Tantalus,[3] trembling with vain fears,
at the mighty rock poised in the air above him;
but rather, in this life, it is groundless superstition
oppressing mortals, who fear any fate that may befall.
No Tityos[4] lies in Hell, torn by ravening birds—   155
indeed, how could they ever find enough sustenance
in that mighty chest for all eternity?
It would not matter how huge his Titanic body is,
covering not only nine acres with outstretched limbs,
but the entire globe of the earth—yet even so   160
he will not be able to suffer everlasting pain,
nor furnish everlasting food from his own body.
But our Tityos is here, prostrated by passion;
the ravening birds that tear him apart are his own emotions—
anxieties and lusts and gnawing jealousies.   165
Sisyphus[5] too is here in this life, before our eyes,
thirsting for official insignia, lictor's rods,
and cruel axes, a bitter and frustrated man.
For to strive for empty, unattainable power,
and to endure toils and labors because of this,   170
is just like pushing a boulder up the steepest hill,
laboriously, and when it reaches the very top,
it rolls down again, headlong, to the level of the plain.
Again, to be always feeding an ungrateful mind,

---

3. In the myth of Tantalus, which Lucretius
discredits, he was punished for a hideous
crime against his own son by being consigned to a perpetual punishment in Hades,
whereby (among other things) a stone was
suspended over his head, threatening at
every moment to crush him.

4. The subject of another myth about punish-

ment after death, Tityos was stretched on
the ground in the underworld while vultures ate his liver.

5. A further example of the purported miseries
of the underworld. Sisyphus was obliged
forever to push a boulder uphill, which,
when it approached the top of the hill,
always rolled back down to the bottom.

never able to satisfy it with life's blessings,   175
just as the seasons of the year do with mankind
when they come circling round with fruits and varied delights,
yet we are never surfeited with the fruits of life—
this, I think, is what is meant by the tale of maidens
young and lovely, carrying water in leaky vessels,[6]   180
which, no matter how they try, can never be filled.
Cerberus and the Furies and the pitch-black darkness

the jaws of Tartarus belching forth their hideous fires,
all these do not and cannot exist anywhere,
but in this life we fear retribution for our sins,   185
and the fear is in proportion to the crime,
punishments, prison, being cast from the terrible Rock,
the lash, the hangman, pitch and torches and branding-irons—
and even if these are absent, still the guilty conscience
in frightened anticipation, torments itself with whips,   190
and does not see what end there can be to its misery,
or what is the final limit of the punishments,
fearing that these will be even greater after death.
So foolish men make for themselves a Hell on earth.
    This is something you can tell yourself at times: 195
"Even good King Ancus[7] looked his last at the light,
and he was a far, far better man than you, you scoundrel!
And many other kings and potentates have died,
men who were mighty monarchs and ruled over great kingdoms.
Even the Great King[8] who built a road across the sea   200
and gave his soldiers a road to take them over the water,
teaching them to march on foot across the brine,
and scorning the ocean's roar with charging cavalry—
even he was robbed of the light and poured out his spirit.
Scipio,[9] thunderbolt of war and terror of Carthage,   205
gave his bones to the earth the same as the meanest slave.
Add to these the discoverers of knowledge and beauty,
add the companions of the Muses, Homer among them,
their only king—yes, even he was laid to rest.
Democritus,[10] when ripe old age reminded him   210
that his mind and intellect were beginning to fail,

---

6. The daughters of the mythical king Danaus
   were punished for a crime they had committed by being made to draw water perpetually in leaky jars.
7. One of the early kings of Rome.
8. The fifth-century Persian king Xerxes I,
   against whom the Greeks fought the Persian wars; his army and fleet of ships were

so vast that he bridged the Hellespont
with them.
9. Roman statesman and general who conquered and destroyed Carthage in 146
   B.C.E.
10. A Greek philosopher of the mid-fifth cen-
    tury B.C.E.

of his own free will offered his head to death.
Epicurus himself, when his life had run its course,
died: he whose genius surpassed the entire race of men,
who outshone other men as the sun outshines the stars.   215
Will you, then flinch and hesitate to meet your death?
You whose life is all but dead, though you live and see,
you who squander the greater part of your time in sleep,
and even when awake are snoring still and dreaming!
You whose mind is terrified by groundless fears,   220
who cannot even discover what it is that ails you,
when you are hounded by your troubles, you drunken wretch,
drifting on the wandering waves of fantasy!"
      Men clearly feel that there is a burden on their minds
whose weight oppresses them; but if they could recognize   225
what are the reasons for this oppression, if they could see
whence comes this burden of misery into their hearts,
they would not live their lives as we now see they do,
with no one knowing what he wants, but always seeking
to escape, as if by moving he could throw off the burden.   230
The owner of a stately mansion will venture forth,
utterly bored at home, then suddenly return
because he feels no better off when out of doors.
So off he drives to his country house at breakneck speed,
as if he were in a hurry to save a house on fire.   235
But when he reaches the threshold he begins to yawn,
or falls into the deepest sleep of oblivion,
or else he rushes all the way back to the city again.
So each man flees himself, but, as you can plainly see,
the self he cannot escape clings to him against his will.   240
He hates himself because he is sick, not knowing the cause;
if only he knew this, he would throw everything aside
and he would devote himself to studying Nature,
since what is at stake is not the passing hour,
but all the time to come—the lot for all mankind   245
through the eternal lapse of time after our death.
      What is this evil lust for life that holds us in fear
and makes us slaves to such anxiety and danger?
There is a definite end of life for mortal men.
Death cannot be avoided: everyone must die.   250
Besides, we live our lives the same from day to day;
nor can we create new pleasures by living longer;
as long as we lack what we desire, it seems more precious
than anything else; but when we have it, we want something different.
One long unchanging thirst for life keeps us always gasping.   255
We never know what fortune the years to come will bring,
what lies in store for us, or what the end will be.

By prolonging life we do not take away one bit
from the duration of our death; we cannot diminish
the time we shall be dead after we leave the earth.   260
However many generations you may live,
the same eternal death will still be waiting for you.
The time of Non-existence will be no less for him
who made an end of life at sunset yesterday,
than for him who perished many months and years before.   265

ANONYMOUS (THIRD MILLENNIUM B.C.E.)
Sumer

These Sumerian compositions of the third millennium B.C.E. reveal how stories of
the gods were used as the basis for the continuance of society. In the first poem,
Inanna, the goddess of love, celebrates her seduction by Dumuzi. Because it was
believed that their periodic union gave rise to seasonal fertility, this poem was
performed at annual agricultural festivals. For all its mythic resonance, the poem
is notable for the very human concern that Inanna (Ishtar) shows: What will she
tell her mother that she has been doing?

The second poem formed part of a sacred marriage ceremony in which the
king would renew his intimate connection to the gods by having intercourse with

Alabaster vase from Uruk,
possibly representing the sacred
marriage of Inanna (Ishtar). Early
Sumerian period, third quarter of
the fourth millennium B.C.E..

a priestess playing the role of Inanna. This ceremony, too, would have been carried out annually. Political and agricultural stability were both expected to follow from this earthly translation of the union of Inanna and Dumuzi.

from *Sacred Marriage Texts of Sumer*

The Ecstasy of Love

Last night, as I, the queen, was shining bright,
Last night, as I, the queen of heaven, was shining bright,
As I was shining bright, as I was dancing about,
As I was uttering a song at the brightening of the oncoming night,
He met me, he met me,   5
The Lord Kuli-Anna[1] met me,
The lord put his hand into my hand,
Ushumgalanna embraced me.

"Come now, wild bull, set me free, I must go home,
Kuli-Enlil, set me free, I must go home,   10
What shall I say to deceive my mother!
What shall I say to deceive my mother Ningal!"

"Let me inform you, let me inform you.
Inanna, most deceitful of women, let me inform you:
'My girl friend took me with her to the public square,   15
She entertained me there with music and dancing,
Her chant, the sweet, she sang for me.
In sweet rejoicing I whiled away the time there—
Thus deceitfully stand up to your mother,
While we by the moonlight indulge our passion,   20
I will prepare for you a bed pure, sweet, and noble,
Will while away the sweet time with you in joyful fulfillment."

I have come to our mother's gate,   25
I, in joy I walk,
I have come to Ningal's gate,
I, in joy I walk.
To my mother he will say the word,
He will sprinkle cypress oil on the ground,   30
To my mother Ningal he will say the word,
He will sprinkle cypress oil on the ground,

Translated by S. N. Kramer.

---

1. Kuli-Anna is a name for Dumuzi, as are
   Ushumgalanna, Kuli-Enlil, and
   Amaushumgalanna.

He whose dwelling is fragrant,
Whose word brings deep joy.

My lord is seemly for the holy lap,   35
Amaushumgalanna, the son-in-law of Sin,[2]
The lord Dumuzi is seemly for the holy lap,
Amaushumgalanna, the son-in-law of Sin.
My lord, sweet is your increase,
Tasty your plants and herbs in the plain,   40
Amaushumgalanna, sweet is your increase,
Tasty your plants and herbs in the plain.

Blessing on the Wedding Night

"Guidance of the house of Eridu,[3]
radiance of the house of Sin,
habitation of the Eanna[4]:
this house has been presented to you.
In my enduring house which floats like a cloud,   5
Whose name in truth, is a goodly vision,
Where a fruitful bed, lapis-bedecked,
Gibil[5] had purified for you in the great shrine,
He who is well-suited for 'queenship,'
The lord has erected his altar,   10
In his reed-filled house which he has purified for you, he performs your rites.

The sun has gone to sleep, the day has passed,
As in bed you gaze lovingly upon him,
As you caress the lord,
Give life unto the lord,   15
Give the staff and crook unto the lord."
She craves it, she craves it, she craves the bed,
She craves the bed of the rejoicing heart, she craves the bed,
She craves the bed of the sweet lap, she craves the bed,
She craves the bed of kingship, she craves the bed,   20
She craves the bed of queenship, she craves the bed.
By his sweet, by his sweet, by his sweet bed,
By his sweet bed of the rejoicing heart, by his sweet bed,
By his sweet bed of the sweet lap, by his sweet bed,
By his sweet bed of kingship, by his sweet bed,   25

---

2. God of the moon.
3. Eridu was a founder of the royal line of
   Sumer. As the poem begins, the poet, or a
   god, is addressing Inanna.

4. The name of the temple where the ritual is
   taking place.
5. Gibil is a divine craftsman.

By his sweet bed of queenship, by his sweet bed,
He covers the bed for her, covers the bed for her,
He covers the bed for her, covers the bed for her.

The beloved speaks to the king on his sweet bed,
Speaks to him words of life, words of long days.   30

Ninshubur, the trustworthy vizier of the Eanna,
Took him by his right forearm,
Brought him blissfully to the lap of Inanna:
"May the lord whom you have called to your heart,
The king, your beloved husband, enjoy long days at your holy lap, the sweet,   35
Give him a reign favorable and glorious,
Give him the throne of kingship on its enduring foundation,
Give him the people-directing scepter, the staff and the crook,
Give him an enduring crown, a diadem which ennobles the head,
From where the sun rises, to where the sun sets,   40
From south to north,
From the Upper Sea to the Lower Sea,
From where the halub tree grows to where the cedar grows,
Over all Sumer and Akkad give him the staff and the crook,
May he exercise the shepherdship of the dark-headed people wherever they
    dwell,   45
May he like the farmer make productive the fields.
May he multiply the sheepfolds like a trustworthy shepherd.

Under his reign may there be plants, may there be grain,
At the river, may there be overflow,
In the field may there be late-grain,   50
In the marshland may the fish and birds make much chatter,
In the canebrake may the old reeds, the young reeds grow high,
In the steppe may the trees grow high,
In the forests may the deer and the wild goats multiply,
May the watered garden produce honey and wine,   55
In the trenches may the lettuce and cress grow high,
In the palace may there be long life,
Into the Tigris and Euphrates may flood water be brought,
On their banks may the grass grow high, may the meadows be covered,
May the holy queen of vegetation pile high the grain heaps and mounds,   60
Oh my queen, queen of the universe, the queen who encompasses the universe,
May he enjoy long days at your holy lap."

The king goes with lifted head to the holy lap,
He goes with lifted head to the holy lap of Inanna,
The king going with lifted head,   65
Going to my queen with lifted head,
Embraces the priestess.

ANONYMOUS

(MID-SECOND MILLENNIUM B.C.E.)

Egypt

These delightful, anonymous poems survive on scraps of pottery and on several scrolls—compilations with names like "Songs of Excellent Enjoyment"—placed in tombs for the pleasure of the deceased. During the course of the New Kingdom (1570–1090 B.C.E.), and probably before that as well, the living performed them at parties and sang them in the fields. More than fifty such poems survive, forming the most extensive body of ancient Near Eastern love poetry known to us. Motifs from the poems recur in The Song of Songs and in the poetry of Greece, Rome, and India.

from *Love Poems from Egypt*

[If I am not with you, where will you set your heart?]

If I am not with you, where will you set your heart?
If you do not embrace me, where will you go?
If good fortune comes your way, you still cannot find happiness.
But if you try to touch my thighs and breasts,
Then you'll be satisfied.   5

Because you remember you are hungry
    would you then leave?
Are you a man thinking only of his stomach?
Would you walk off from me
    concerned with your stylish clothes
and leave me the sheet?

Because of hunger
    would you then leave me?   10
Take then my breast:
    for you its gift overflows.
Better indeed is one day in your arms
    than a hundred thousand anywhere on earth.

[Distracting is the foliage of my pasture]

Distracting is the foliage of my pasture:
the mouth of my girl is a lotus bud,
her breasts are mandrake apples,

All poems in this selection are translated by William Kelly Simpson.

her arms are vines,
her eyes are fixed like berries,   5
her brow a snare of willow,
and I the wild goose!
My beak snips her hair for bait,
as worms for bait in the trap.

[My heart is not yet happy with your love]

My heart is not yet happy with your love,
my wolf cub, so be lascivious unto drunkenness.

Yet I will not leave it unless sticks beat me off
to dally in the Delta marshes
or driven to the land of Khor with cudgels and maces   5
to the land of Kush[1] with palm switches
to the highground with staves
to the lowland with rushes.

So I'll not heed their arguments
to leave off needing you.   10

[The voice of the turtledove speaks out]

The voice of the turtledove speaks out. It says:
day breaks, which way are you going?
Lay off, little bird,
must you so scold me?

I found my lover on his bed,
and my heart was sweet to excess.   5

We said:

I shall never be far away from you
while my hand is in your hand,
and I shall stroll with you
in every favorite place.   10

He set me as first of the girls
and he does not break my heart.

[My heart remembers well your love]

My heart remembers well your love.
One half of my temple was combed,

My heart is not yet

1. Khor is the region of Syria and Palestine;
   Kush is Nubia, in the far south.

I came rushing to see you,
and I forgot my hair.

[I embrace her]

I embrace her,
and her arms open wide,
I am like a man in Punt,[1]
like someone overwhelmed with drugs.

I kiss her,
her lips open,
and I am drunk
without a beer.

[How well the lady knows to cast the noose]

How well the lady knows to cast the noose
yet still escape the cattle tax.

With her hair she throws lassoes at me,
with her eyes she catches me,
with her necklace entangles me
and with her seal ring brands me.

[Why need you hold converse with your heart?]

Why need you hold converse with your heart?
To embrace her is all my desire.
As Amun[1] lives, I come to you,
my loin cloth on my shoulder.

[I found the lover at the ford]

I found the lover at the ford,
His feet set in the water;
he builds a table there for feasts
and sets it out with beer.

He brings a blush to my skin,
for he is tall and lean.

I embrace her   *Why need you*
1. Source of exotic spices and produce.   **1.** God of the sun, also called Amun-Re or Re.

[I passed by her house in the dark]

I passed by her house in the dark,
I knocked and no one opened.
What a beautiful night for our doorkeeper!

Open, door bolts!
Door leaves you are my fate, you are my genie.   5
Our ox will be slaughtered for you inside.
Door leaves do not use your strength.

A long-horned bull will be slaughtered to the bolt,
a short-horned bull to the door pin,
a wild fowl to the threshold,   10
and its fat to the key.

But all the best parts of our ox
shall go to the carpenter's boy,
so he'll make us a door of grass
and a door bolt of reeds,   15

And any time when the lover comes
he'll find her house open,
he'll find beds made with linen sheets
and in them a lovely girl.

And the girl will say to me: 20
this place belongs to the captain's boy!

THE BIBLE

(MID- TO LATE FIRST MILLENNIUM B.C.E.)
Israel

A loosely ordered collection of lyrics, the Song of Songs is presented in the Bible
as a cycle of wedding songs from the time of King Solomon. The poems
undoubtedly circulated in various forms for several centuries before the final
compilation was made, probably in the third century B.C.E. Although there is no
consistent formal structure to the poems, the speakers throughout are a bride,
her groom, and a chorus of attendants or friends.

The Song has no overt religious content, and justification for its inclusion in
the Bible was a matter of early rabbinical debate. The decision in favor (c. 100
B.C.E.) was partly based on precedent: Hebrew prophets such as Hosea and Isaiah
had used imagery from love poetry to describe the relations between God and
Israel. It was thus possible to interpret the Song allegorically along similar lines.

Modern scholarship tends to stress instead the Song's thematic links to older fertility myths. However, we can also think of the poems as infusing theology back into daily life, for they endow their lovers with elements of mystery not found in the earlier Egyptian love poems.

from **The Bible**

THE SONG OF SONGS

[Let him kiss me with the kisses of his mouth]

The Song of Songs, which is Solomon's.

Let him kiss me with the kisses of his mouth.
Your love is more delightful than wine;
delicate is the fragrance of your perfume,
your name is an oil poured out,
and that is why the maidens love you.   5
Draw me in your footsteps, let us run.
The King has brought me into his rooms;
you will be our joy and our gladness.
We shall praise your love above wine;   10
how right it is to love you.

[I am black but lovely, daughters of Jerusalem]

I am black but lovely, daughters of Jerusalem,
like the tents of Kedar,
like the pavilions of Salmah.[1]
Take no notice of my swarthiness,
it is the sun that has burnt me.   5
My mother's sons turned their anger on me,
they made me look after the vineyards.
Had I only looked after my own!

                              . . .

—How beautiful you are, my love,
how beautiful you are!   10
Your eyes are doves.
—How beautiful you are, my Beloved,
and how delightful!
All green is our bed.
—The beams of our house are of cedar,   15
the panelling of cypress.

Jerusalem Bible translation.

---

1. Or Solomon.

—I am the rose of Sharon,[2]
the lily of the valleys.
—As a lily among the thistles,
so is my love among the maidens.
—As an apple tree among the trees of the orchard,   20
so is my Beloved among the young men.
In his longed-for shade I am seated
and his fruit is sweet to my taste.
He has taken me to his banquet hall,
and the banner he raises over me is love.   25
Feed me with raisin cakes,
restore me with apples,
for I am sick with love.
His left arm is under my head,
his right embraces me.   30
—I charge you,
daughters of Jerusalem,
by the gazelles, by the hinds of the field,
not to stir my love, nor rouse it,
until it please to awake.   35

[See where he stands]

See where he stands
behind our wall.
He looks in at the window,
he peers through the lattice.
My Beloved lifts up his voice,   5
he says to me,
'Come then, my love,
my lovely one, come.
For see, winter is past,
the rains are over and gone.   10
The flowers appear on the earth.
The season of glad songs has come,
the cooing of the turtledove is heard in our land.
The fig tree is forming its first figs
and the blossoming vines give out their fragrance.   15
Come then, my love,
my lovely one, come.
My dove, hiding in the clefts of the rock,
in the coverts of the cliff,
show me your face,   20

---

2. A rich plain along the Mediterranean coast.

let me hear your voice;
for your voice is sweet
and your face is beautiful.

. . .

On my bed, at night, I sought him
whom my heart loves.
I sought but did not find him.
So I will rise and go through the City;
in the streets and the squares
I will seek him whom my heart loves.
The watchmen came upon me
on their rounds in the City:
'Have you seen him whom my heart loves?'
Scarcely had I passed them
than I found him whom my heart loves.
I held him fast, nor would I let him go
till I had brought him
into my mother's house,
into the room of her who conceived me.

[How beautiful you are, my love]

How beautiful you are, my love,[3]
how beautiful you are!
Your eyes, behind your veil,
are doves;
your hair is like a flock of goats
frisking down the slopes of Gilead.
Your teeth are like a flock of shorn ewes
as they come up from the washing.
Each one has its twin,
not one unpaired with another.
Your lips are a scarlet thread
and your words enchanting.
Your cheeks, behind your veil,
are halves of pomegranate.
Your neck is the tower of David
built as a fortress,
hung round with a thousand bucklers,
and each the shield of a hero.
Your two breasts are two fawns,
twins of a gazelle,
that feed among the lilies.

---

3. This poem is spoken by the groom.

Before the dawn-wind rises,
before the shadows flee,
I will go to the mountain of myrrh,
to the hill of frankincense.
You are wholly beautiful, my love,   25
and without a blemish.
Come from Lebanon, my promised bride,
come from Lebanon, come on your way.
Lower your gaze, from the heights of Amana,   30
from the crests of Senir and Hermon,[4]
the haunt of lions,
the mountains of leopards.
You ravish my heart,
my sister, my promised bride,   35
you ravish my heart
with a single one of your glances,
with one single pearl of your necklace.
What spells lie in your love,
my sister, my promised bride!   40

[I sleep, but my heart is awake]

I sleep, but my heart is awake.
I hear my Beloved knocking.
'Open to me, my sister, my love,
my dove, my perfect one,
for my head is covered with dew,   5
my locks with the drops of night.'
—'I have taken off my tunic,
am I to put it on again?
I have washed my feet,
am I to dirty them again?'   10
My Beloved thrust his hand
through the hole in the door;
I trembled to the core of my being.
Then I rose to open to my Beloved,
myrrh ran off my hands,   15
pure myrrh off my fingers,
on to the handle of the bolt.
I opened to my Beloved,
but he had turned his back and gone!
My soul failed at his flight.   20
I sought him but I did not find him,

---

4. The mountain home of the Syrian goddess
of fertility.

I called to him but he did not answer.
The watchmen came upon me
as they made their rounds in the City.
They beat me, they wounded me,   25
they took away my cloak,
they who guard the ramparts.
I charge you, daughters of Jerusalem,
if you should find my Beloved,
what must you tell him?   30
That I am sick with love.
What makes your Beloved better than other lovers,
O loveliest of women?
What makes your Beloved better than other lovers,
to give us a charge like this?   35
My Beloved is fresh and ruddy,
to be known among ten thousand.
His head is golden, purest gold,
his locks are palm fronds
and black as the raven.   40
His eyes are doves
at a pool of water,
bathed in milk,
at rest on a pool.
His cheeks are beds of spices,   45
banks sweetly scented.
His lips are lilies,
distilling pure myrrh.
His hands are golden, rounded,
set with jewels of Tarshish.   50
His belly a block of ivory
covered with sapphires.
His legs are alabaster columns
set in sockets of pure gold.
His appearance is that of Lebanon,   55
unrivalled as the cedars.
His conversation is sweetness itself,
he is altogether lovable.
Such is my Beloved, such is my friend,
O daughters of Jerusalem.   60

[You are beautiful as Tirzah, my love]

You are beautiful as Tirzah,[5] my love,
fair as Jerusalem.

---

5. Former capital of Israel.

Turn your eyes away,
for they hold me captive.

The maidens saw her, and proclaimed her blessed,   5
queens and concubines sang her praises:
'Who is this arising like the dawn,
fair as the moon,
resplendent as the sun,
terrible as an army with banners?'   10

How beautiful are your feet in their sandals,
O prince's daughter!
The curve of your thighs is like the curve of a necklace,
work of a master hand.
Your navel is a bowl well rounded   15
with no lack of wine,
your belly a heap of wheat
surrounded with lilies.
Your two breasts are two fawns,
twins of a gazelle.   20
Your neck is an ivory tower.
Your eyes, the pools of Heshbon,
by the gate of Bath-rabbim.
Your nose, the Tower of Lebanon,
sentinel facing Damascus.   25
Your head is held high like Carmel,[6]
and its plaits are as dark as purple;
a king is held captive in your tresses.
How beautiful you are, how charming,
my love, my delight!   30
In stature like the palm tree,
its fruit-clusters your breasts.
'I will climb the palm tree,' I resolved,
'I will seize its clusters of dates.'
May your breasts be clusters of grapes,   35
your breath sweet-scented as apples,
your speaking, superlative wine.

Wine flowing straight to my Beloved,
as it runs on the lips of those who sleep.
I am my Beloved's, and his desire is for me.   40

---

6. A prominent mountain on the Mediterranean coast.

Come, my Beloved, let us go to the fields.
We will spend the night in the villages,
and in the morning we will go to the vineyards.
We will see if the vines are budding,
if their blossoms are opening,   45
if the pomegranate trees are in flower.
Then I shall give you the gift of my love.
The mandrakes yield their fragrance,
the rarest fruits are at our doors;
the new as well as the old,   50
I have stored them for you, my Beloved.
Ah, why are you not my brother,
nursed at my mother's breast!
Then if I met you out of doors, I could kiss you
without people thinking ill of me.   55
I should lead you, I should take you
into my mother's house, and you would teach me!
I should give you spiced wine to drink,
juice of my pomegranates.
His left arm is under my head   60
and his right embraces me.
I charge you,
daughters of Jerusalem,
not to stir my love, nor rouse it,
until it please to awake.   65

[Who is this coming up from the desert/leaning on her Beloved?]

Who is this coming up from the desert
leaning on her Beloved?
I awakened you under the apple tree,
there where your mother conceived you,
there where she who gave birth to you conceived you.   5
Set me like a seal on your heart,
like a seal on your arm.
For love is strong as Death,
jealousy relentless as Sheol.[7]
The flash of it is a flash of fire,   10
a flame of Yahweh himself.
Love no flood can quench,
no torrents drown.

---

7. The underworld.

ALCAEUS (MID-SEVENTH TO EARLY SIXTH CENTURY B.C.E.)

SAPPHO (MID-SEVENTH TO EARLY SIXTH CENTURY B.C.E.)

Greece

Lyric poetry in Greece—composed in stanzas, sung by performers accompanying themselves on the lyre—flourished vigorously in the Aegean islands in the seventh and sixth centuries B.C.E. Like elegiac poetry (from which it differed musically and metrically), and unlike the epic, the lyric poetry of this period lent itself especially to the expression of intense personal emotion and to statements of the individual's values; most often lyric themes were those of private rather than public experience, and presupposed an audience closely associated with the poet.

Sappho and Alcaeus were contemporaries (born c. 630 B.C.E.) from the island of Lesbos at a time when it was torn by civil conflict. Of all the lyricists, Alcaeus is the one whose poetry most explicitly reflects the political conditions of the day. He was equally influential, however, for his poems celebrating the pleasures of camaraderie in a convivial setting, in which wine is a prominent feature; there is evidence that most of Alcaeus's verse may have been composed to be sung at symposia (drinking parties) among friends and political allies.

As with Alcaeus, what remains to us of Sappho's poetry is largely fragmentary: only the first poem we give has been preserved in its entirety. Sappho is the earliest of the very few female poets of antiquity whose work has survived in any form, providing us with an irreplaceable alternative to the male perspective that prevails throughout this entire section. Her audience, too, seems to have been a circle of intimate friends; their companionship—valued for its own sake rather than as an expression of political solidarity, as is often the case in Alcaeus's writings—is the focus of much of her surviving verse. In poems like "Some say . . . ," she asserts the primacy of private affections, claiming for them a heroic stature to rival epic subject matter.

ALCAEUS

[Zeus rains upon us]

Zeus rains upon us, and from the sky comes down
enormous winter. Rivers have turned to ice.

. . .

Dash down the winter. Throw a log on the fire
and mix the flattering wine (do not water it too much) and bind on round our
    foreheads soft ceremonial wreaths of spun fleece.   5

Poems by Alcaeus are translated by Richmond Lattimore.

We must not let our spirits give way to grief.
By being sorry we get no further on, my Bukchis.[1] Best of all defenses is to mix
    plenty of wine, and drink it.

[Wet your whistle with wine now]

Wet your whistle with wine now, for the dog star, wheeling up the sky,
brings back summer, the time all things are parched under the searing heat.
Now the cicada's cry, sweet in the leaves, shrills from beneath his wings.
Now the artichoke flowers, women are lush, ask too much of their men,
who grow lank, for the star burning above withers their brains and knees.   5

SAPPHO

[On the throne of many hues, Immortal Aphrodite]

On the throne of many hues, Immortal Aphrodite,
child of Zeus, weaving wiles—I beg you
not to subdue my spirit, Queen,
with pain or sorrow

but come—if ever before   5
having heard my voice from far away
you listened, and leaving your father's
golden home you came

in your chariot yoked with swift, lovely
sparrows bringing you over the dark earth   10
thick-feathered wings swirling down
from the sky through mid-air

arriving quickly—you, Blessed One,
with a smile on your unaging face
asking again what have I suffered   15
and why am I calling again

and in my wild heart what did I most wish
to happen to me: "Again whom must I persuade
back into the harness of your love?
Sappho, who wrongs you?   20

For if she flees, soon she'll pursue,
she doesn't accept gifts, but she'll give,

Poems by Sappho are translated by Diane J. Rayor.

Zeus rains

1. The name of one of Alcaeus's friends.

if not now loving, soon she'll love
even against her will."

Come to me now again, release me from
this pain, everything my spirit longs
to have fulfilled, fulfill, and you
be my ally.

[Some say an army of horsemen]

Some say an army of horsemen, others
say foot-soldiers, still others, a fleet,
is the fairest thing on the dark earth:
I say it is whatever one loves.

Everyone can understand this—
consider that Helen,[1] far surpassing
the beauty of mortals, leaving behind
the best man of all,

sailed away to Troy. She had no
memory of her child or dear parents,
since she was led astray
[by Kypris][2]

              . . .
          . . . lightly

. . . reminding me now of Anaktoria[3]
being gone,

I would rather see her lovely step
and the radiant sparkle of her face
than all the war-chariots in Lydia[4]
and soldiers battling in shining bronze.

[To me it seems]

To me it seems
that man has the fortune of gods,
whoever sits beside you, and close,

Some say

1. Helen left her husband Menelaos to follow
   the Trojan prince Paris to Troy.
2. Aphrodite, the goddess of love. There is a
   gap in the text at this point.

3. One of Sappho's friends.
4. A country in western Asia Minor that
   was prosperous and powerful in this
   period.

who listens to you sweetly speaking
and laughing temptingly;   5
my heart flutters in my breast,
whenever I look quickly, for a moment—
I say nothing, my tongue broken,
a delicate fire runs under my skin,
my eyes see nothing, my ears roar,   10
cold sweat rushes down me,
trembling seizes me,
I am greener than grass,
to myself I seem
needing but little to die.   15

But all must be endured, since . . .

[Evening Star who gathers everything]

Evening Star who gathers everything
shining dawn scattered—
you bring the sheep and the goats,
you bring the child back to its mother.

[The sweet apple reddens on a high branch]

The sweet apple reddens on a high branch
high upon highest, missed by the applepickers:
no, they didn't miss, so much as couldn't touch.

IBYCUS (MID-SIXTH CENTURY B.C.E.)
ANACREON (c. 582–c. 485 B.C.E.)
Greece

Ibycus and Anacreon were mid-sixth century B.C.E. contemporaries born at
opposite ends of the Greek map (Ibycus in the west and Anacreon on the Ionian
coast). Both poets came to live and write at the court of the island of Samos under
the patronage of its ruler. Ibycus composed primarily for choral performance,
while Anacreon's love songs, like Alcaeus's, suited individual performance in the
setting of the symposium; both enlarged the lyric repertory of erotic imagery.

IBYCUS

[In Spring, quince trees]

In Spring, quince trees
irrigated with streams
from rivers, in the Virgins'
inviolate garden, and vinebuds
growing beneath shady shoots   5
of vinetwigs bloom. But for me
Love rests for no season:
blazing with lightning
Thracian Boreas,
darting from Kypris, dark   10
with parching madness, shameless,
violently shakes
my senses from the depth.

[Again Love]

Again Love, glancing meltingly
beneath royal blue eyelids,
with myriad enchantments throws me
into the infinite nets of Kypris.
Yes, I tremble at his approach,   5
as a yoke-bearing horse,
    a prizewinner near old age,
goes to the contest unwillingly
    with the swift chariots.

ANACREON

[Lad, glancing like a virgin]

Lad, glancing like a virgin,
I seek you, but you don't hear,
not knowing that you
are my soul's charioteer.

[The dice of Love]

The dice of Love are
madness and turmoil.

All poems in this selection are translated by Diane J. Rayor.

[Again Love struck me]

Again Love struck me like a smith with a giant
hammer, and washed me in a wintry torrent.

[Thracian filly]

Thracian filly, why do you
look with eyes askance
and stubbornly flee me, and why
do you think I've no skill?
Understand this: I could well　　　　　　　　　　　　　5
throw a bridle on you,
and holding the reins I could turn
you round the goal of the track.
But now you graze the meadows
and, frisking nimbly, play,　　　　　　　　　　　　　10
since you've no dextrous horseman,
no easy rider.

CATULLUS (84?–54? B.C.E.)
Rome

The Rome to which Gaius Valerius Catullus moved from his native Verona was
the political as well as the intellectual center of Italy under the republic in the first
century B.C.E. In the more than one hundred highly varied poems by Catullus that
survive, however, politics is never his subject (although he pokes fun at a number
of public figures). His poems are primarily concerned with love—for men as well
as women—with friendship, and with poetry itself. They are frequently colloquial in tone and for the most part clearly set in Rome, allowing us valuable
glimpses of contemporary social behavior in that city; their intended initial
audience was probably the poet's close circle of literary friends.

　　Together with Horace, Catullus is the heir to the poetic forms and themes
of the Greek lyric poets, although unlike their poetry, his works and Horace's
were written to be recited rather than sung. He shows special affinity for
Sappho, directly imitating her poetry on occasion. A number of poems addressed to a woman he calls Lesbia (in an allusion to his literary forebears,
Sappho and Alcaeus, who were from the Aegean island of Lesbos) chart the
course of an ardent love affair that ultimately ends in anguished disillusionment. We do not know whether the passionate narrative presented in these
poems was real or fictive, but our uncertainty does nothing to diminish their
power.

[My Lesbia, let us live and love]*

My Lesbia, let us live and love
And not care tuppence for old men
Who sermonise and disapprove.
Suns when they sink can rise again,
But we, when our brief light has shone,   5
Must sleep the long night on and on.
Kiss me: a thousand kisses, then
A hundred more, and now a second
Thousand and hundred, and now still
Hundreds and thousands more, until   10
The thousand thousands can't be reckoned
And we've lost track of the amount
And nobody can work us ill
With the evil eye by keeping count.

[How many kisses satisfy]*

How many kisses satisfy,
How many are enough and more,
You ask me, Lesbia. I reply,
As many as the Libyan sands
Sprinkling the Cyrenaic[1] shore   5
Where silphium grows, between the places
Where old King Battus's tomb stands
And Jupiter Ammon has his shrine
In Siwa's sweltering oasis;
As many as the stars above   10
That in the dead of midnight shine
Upon men's secrecies of love.
When he has all those kisses, mad-
Hungry Catullus will have had
Enough to slake his appetite—   15
So many that sharp eyes can't tell
The number, and the tongues of spite
Are too confused to form a spell.

[Enough, Catullus, of this silly whining]*

Enough, Catullus, of this silly whining;
What you can see is lost, write off as lost.

*Translated by James Michie.

How many kisses satisfy
1. Cyrene was a city in Libya, thought to have been founded by a Greek named Battus in the seventh century B.C.E.

Not long ago the sun was always shining,
And, loved as no girl ever will be loved,
She led the way and you went dancing after.   5
Those were the days of lovers' games and laughter
When anything you wanted she approved;
That was a time when the sun really shone.
But now she's cold, you too must learn to cool;
Weak though you are, stop groping for what's gone,   10
Stop whimpering, and be stoically resigned.
Goodbye, my girl. Catullus from now on
Is adamant: he has made up his mind:
He won't beg for your favour like a bone.
You'll feel the cold, though, you damned bitch, when men   15
Leave *you* alone. What life will you have then?
Who'll visit you? Who'll think you beautiful? Who'll
Be loved by you? Parade you as his own?
Whom will you kiss and nibble then?
                              Oh fool,
Catullus, stop this, stand firm, become stone.   20

[Furius and Aurelius, loyal comrades]*

Furius and Aurelius, loyal comrades,
Who'd travel with me to remotest India,
Where the beaches pounded by the Eastern Ocean
    Boom to the rollers' thud,

Into Hyrcania,[1] languorous Arabia,   5
Among the Scythians or the archer Parthians,
Or to the plains which Nile, the seven-tongued river,
    Darkens with churned-up mud,

Who'd march on foot across the Alpine passes
To view the trophy-sites of mighty Caesar,[2]   10
The Rhine in Gaul, or the outlandish Britons
    Fenced by their sullen strait—

Staunch friends, ready to share all hazards with me,
Anything that the will of heaven proposes,
Please take this message to my girl, a few short   15
    Words to express my hate:

Good luck to her, let her enjoy her lovers,
The whole three hundred that she hugs together,

Furius and Aurelius, loyal comrades
1. A territory on the Caspian Sea.

2. Julius Caesar; the first invasion of Britain took place in 55 B.C.E..

Loving none truly, by grim repetition
    Wringing them all sperm-dry.   20

Let her not look to find my love unaltered;
Through her own fault it lies in ruins, fallen
Like a wildflower at a field's edge that the ploughshare
    Touches and passes by.

[She swears she'd rather marry me]*

She swears she'd rather marry me
Than anyone—even Jupiter,[1]
Supposing he were courting her.
She swears; but what a girl will swear
To the man who loves her ought to be   5
Scribbled on water, scrawled on air.

[I can remember, Lesbia, when you swore]*

I can remember, Lesbia, when you swore
You were mine and mine only, called me more
Desirable than Jove.[1] I loved you then,
And not just in the way that other men
Love mistresses, but as a father cares   5
For his own sons and daughters, for his heirs.
Now that I know you, you're much cheaper, lighter,
And yet desire in me flares even brighter.
'How can that be?' you say. In love deceit
Freezes affection, though it stokes up heat.   10

[If in recalling former kindnesses]†

If in recalling former kindnesses there's pleasure
    When a man reflects that he has been true
Nor broken solemn promise nor in any pact
    Abused the Gods' goodwill to fool his fellow men,
Then many joys remain in store for you, Catullus,   5
    Through a long lifetime from this ungrateful love.
For whatever kind things men can say or
    do
    To anyone, these you have said and done,

†*Translated by Guy Lee.*

She swears

1. The supreme deity of the Romans, identified with the Greek god Zeus.

I can remember

1. Another name for Jupiter.

But credited to ingratitude they have all been wasted.
    So now why torture yourself any more? 10
Why not harden your heart and tear yourself away
    And stop being wretched against the Gods' will?
It's difficult to break with long love suddenly.
    It's difficult, but this you must somehow do.
This is your only chance. You must win through to this. 15
    Possible or not, this you must achieve.
O Gods, if you can pity or have ever brought
    Help at last to any on the point of death,
Look on my wretchedness and if I have led a decent life
    Take away from me this deadly disease, 20
Which like a paralysis creeping into my inmost being
    Has driven from my heart every happiness.
I do not ask now that she love me in return
    Or, what's impossible, that she be chaste.
I pray for my own health, to be rid of this foul sickness. 25
    O Gods, grant me this for my true dealing.

[Travelling through many nations]†

Travelling through many nations and through many seas[1]
    I have come, brother, for these poor funeral rites,
That I might render you the last dues of the dead
    And vainly comfort your dumb ashes,
Because Fortune has robbed me of your self, alas, 5
    Poor brother, unfairly taken from me.
But now, meanwhile, accept these gifts which by old custom
    Of the ancestors are offered in sad duty
At funeral rites, gifts drenched in a brother's tears,
    And forever, brother, greetings and farewell. 10

HORACE (65–8 B.C.E.)
Rome

A writer of great versatility, Horace (whose Latin name was Quintus Horatius
Flaccus) produced a substantial and varied body of poetry. In addition to a
collection of lyric poems organized into four books—the Odes, from which our

---

Travelling through many nations
1. Catullus's brother died in the region of Asia
Minor called the Troad, after its principal
city, Troy.

selection is drawn—his writings include literary criticism and philosophical meditations (often combined) in the form of satires and epistles in verse. From these latter groups of poems we learn a considerable number of biographical details. Horace's father was a slave who had been freed; he saw to Horace's education, sending him to Athens to study philosophy. There Horace grew to know the poetic traditions of Greece and was profoundly influenced by Archilochus, Sappho, and Alcaeus, as many of his odes attest. (Compare his Ode "You see how deep . . ." with Alcaeus's "Zeus rains upon us," presented earlier in this section.) Although not an innovator of formal poetic features, Horace brilliantly synthesized traditional elements from earlier Greek and Roman writers and deservedly claimed for himself the remarkable achievement of having successfully adapted to the Latin language the extraordinarily complex rhythms of Greek lyric poetry.

Through the poet Vergil, Horace met Maecenas, the preeminent literary patron of the time and a powerful friend of the emperor Augustus. From within the elite circle around Maecenas, Horace wrote a number of poems on Roman civic themes. Most frequently, however, his lyrics, like those of his Greek predecessors, represent private emotions and sensibilities, within which an appreciation of the transience of all things mortal is often central. In many of his poems Horace's perspective is framed by images of the natural world, and in others by those of the impersonal life of the city.

[Winter's fists unclench at the touch of spring]*

Winter's fists unclench at the touch of spring and western breezes,
   dried-out keels are drawn down to the waves,
flocks are no longer at ease in stables, farmers at firesides,
   meadows are no longer white with frost.

Under a hovering moon come dancers led by white Aphrodite,   5
   the slender Graces join hands with the nymphs
lightly to waltz on the grass, as Cyclops[1] under sweltering Vulcan
   forge bolts of lightning for the storms to come.

Now is the time to garland glistening hair with green myrtle
   or flowers, as the freed earth rejoices in birth;   10
now a gift to Faunus[2] is proper, in shadowy groves a victim,
   whatever is to his taste, ewe lamb or kid.

Death with his drained-out face will drum at destitute cottage
   and royal castle. You have been lucky, Sestius:[3]

---

*Translated by Joseph P. Clancy.

Winter's fists

1. According to some mythological traditions, the Cyclopes were assistants to the god Hephaestus [see *Iliad*, Book 18], with whom Vulcan, the Roman god of fire and of the forge, was identified.

2. A deity who protects flocks, herds, and agriculture in general.

3. Sestius, Horace's friend, was a prominent figure in Roman political life in the middle of the 1st century B.C.E.

all of life is only a little, no long-term plans are allowed.
    Soon night and half-remembered shapes and drab   15

Pluto's[4] walls will be closing in; enter his halls and you're done with
    tosses of dice that crown you toastmaster,
marveling glances at slim young Lycidas, for whom all the boys are
    now burning, and the girls will soon catch fire.   20

[What slim youth, Pyrrha]†

What slim youth, Pyrrha, drenched in perfumed oils,
Lying in an easy grotto among roses, roses,
    Now woos, and watches you
    Gathering back your golden hair,

With artless elegance? How many a time   5
Will he cry out, seeing all changed, the gods, your promise,
    And stare in wondering shock
    At winds gone wild on blackening seas!

Now fondling you, his hope, his perfect gold,
He leans on love's inviolable constancy, not dreaming   10
    How false the breeze can blow.
    Ah, pity all those who have not found

Your glossy sweetness out! My shipwreck's tale
Hangs, told in colors, on Neptune's temple wall,[1] a votive
    Plaque, with salvaged clothes   15
    Still damp, vowed to the sea's rough lord.

[You see how deep Soracte stands in snow]†

You see how deep Soracte[1] stands in snow,
A hoary blaze, the laboring forests cringing
    Under the load, the rivers standing
    Pinned in their course by piercing ice.

Heap logs in plenty on the grate, melt off   5
The cold, and tilt the crock up by both handles,

---

†Translated by Cedric Whitman.

4. Pluto is one of the names of the god of the underworld.

What slim youth

1. The Roman god of the sea, identified with the Greek Poseidon. Sailors who had survived shipwreck would often dedicate to Neptune a tablet or picture to commemorate the event, along with the clothes they had worn at sea.

You see how deep

1. A mountain north of Rome, which was visible from the city.

Good revel master, pour the four year
Vintage out with freer hand.

Leave all the rest to the gods; once they have laid
Asleep these winds that now go brawling over   10
    The boiling sea, no more will cypress
    Shiver and flail, nor aged ash.

Let be what comes tomorrow, reckoning
Pure gain whatever gift of days your fortune
    Yields, and in youth be not disdainful   15
    Of love in all its sweetness; dance,

While yet no sorry white head nods upon
Your springtime shoulders; look to the piazza,
    The pleasure walks, the hushed whisper
    By nightfall at the trysting hour;   20

When a girl's laughter happily betrays
Her hiding place, lurked in a secret corner;
    Then plunder a trinket from her finger,
    Or languidly protesting arm.

[Don't ask, Leuconoë, the forbidden question]*

Don't ask, Leuconoë, the forbidden question, how long
the gods have given to you and to me: don't imagine
fortunetellers know. Better to take what is coming,
whether Jove allows us more winters, or this that now
wearies the Etruscan sea as it beats on the cliffs   5
is the last. Be sensible: strain the wine: in a little life,
take no long looks ahead. As we talk, time spites us
and runs: reap today: save no hopes for tomorrow.

[Those wars, Venus, are long over]*

Those wars, Venus, are long over,
    and now you provoke them again. Please, please, spare me.
I am not what I was when dear
    Cinara ruled me. Put an end to your efforts,

cruel mother of sweet Cupids,   5
    to soften the stiffness of a man now fifty
by your gentle orders: go where
    the young men invite you with flattering prayers.

This is a better time for you
    to bring, drawn by your swans' glowing wings, your joy to   10
the home of Paulus Maximus,[1]
    if you're looking for the kind of heart to catch fire.

For he is noble and handsome,
    and speaks well in defending his troubled clients,
a young man of many talents   15
    who will carry the banner of your service far;

and whenever he is happy
    to have conquered the gifts of a spendthrift rival,
he will set your marble statue
    under a cedar roof, beside the Alban lakes.   20

There you will breathe in plentiful
    incense, and you will find delight in the music
of the Berecyntian[2] flute
    mingled with the strings, with the pipe not forgotten;

there, twice every day, the boys   25
    and delicate virgins will chant the praises of
your divinity, their white feet
    beating the ground in tripletime Salian[3] dance.

As for me, not woman nor boy
    nor the hope that believes its feelings are returned   30
pleases me now, nor drinking bouts,
    nor having fresh flowers wound about my forehead.

But why, ah Ligurinus,[4] why
    does a tear now and then run trickling down my cheek?
Why does my tongue, once eloquent,   35
    fall, as I'm talking, into ungracious silence?

At night I see you in my dreams,
    now caught, and I hold you, now I follow as you
run away, over the grassy
    Field of Mars,[5] over flowing streams, with your hard heart.   40

Those wars

1. A prominent member of Roman society
who was a friend of the emperor Augustus.
2. An instrument used in the worship of several Roman deities, notably the
god Bacchus.

3. The Salians were legendary dancers.
4. The addressee of this poem is unknown;
the name may be imaginary.
5. A public area near the Tiber, popular with
the Romans as a place for exercise and
entertainment.

Akhnaten and Nefertiti offering libations to
the Aten. Fragment from a balustrade from
the Great Palace, Amarna. Egyptian,
Eighteenth Dynasty (fourteenth century
B.C.E.).

ANONYMOUS (c. 1300 B.C.E.)
Egypt

For most of its history, ancient Egypt was a thoroughly polytheistic society. But
King Akhnaten, who ruled from 1350 to 1334 B.C.E., espoused the worship of a
single god, the sun disk, or Aten. Akhnaten emphasized the international
supremacy of the Aten by pointing out that the sun shines on all peoples equally.
He presented himself as the Aten's son, the chief intermediary between the Aten
and humanity. The worship of the Aten may not have been true monotheism,
especially given the king's own quasi-divine role. Nevertheless, the cults of the
old gods were systematically repressed, and even their names were removed from
public inscriptions. Artistic reforms were undertaken as well, with a new realism
emerging in portaiture.

This hymn was found inscribed on a wall of the tomb of Ay, a high official
in Akhnaten's court. It gives an almost anthropological view of the different races
and emphasizes the Aten's tender care for his whole creation. The worship of the
Aten was a remarkable episode in Egyptian history. It is almost as though the
Egyptians were trying to see the world whole for the first time, uniting the many
peoples of their cosmopolitan empire under the Aten while accepting their great
diversity. The moment did not last long, however. After Akhnaten's death, the
older gods were reestablished and his own name was supressed in turn.

The Great Hymn to the Aten

Adoration of Re-Harakhti-who-rejoices-in-the horizon In-his-name-Shu-who-is-Aten, living forever; the great living Aten who is in jubilee, the lord of all that the Disk encircles, lord of sky, lord of earth, lord of the house-of-Aten in Akhet-Aten; and of the King of Upper and Lower Egypt, who lives by Maat,[1] the Lord of the Two Lands,[2] Neferkheprure, Sole-one-of-Re; the Son of Re who lives by Maat, the Lord of Crowns, Akhenaten, great in his lifetime; and his beloved great Queen, the Lady of the Two Lands, Nefer-nefru-Aten Nefertiti, who lives in health and youth forever. The Vizier, the Fanbearer on the right of the King, Ay; he says:

Splendid you rise in heaven's horizon,
O living Aten, creator of life!
When you have dawned in the eastern horizon,
You fill every land with your beauty.
You are beauteous, great, radiant,   5
High over every land;
Your rays embrace the lands,
To the limit of all that you made.
Being Re, you reach their limits,
You bend them for the son whom you love;   10
Though you are far, your rays are on earth,
Though one sees you, your strides are unseen.

When you set in the western horizon,
Earth is in darkness as if in death;
One sleeps in chambers, heads covered,   15
One eye does not see another.
Were they robbed of their goods,
That are under their heads,
People would not remark it.
Every lion comes from its den,   20
All the serpents bite;
Darkness hovers, earth is silent,
As their maker rests in the horizon.

Earth brightens when you dawn in the horizon,
When you shine as Aten of daytime;   25
As you dispel the dark,
As you cast your rays,
The Two Lands are in festivity.
Awake they stand on their feet,
You have roused them;   30

Translated by Miriam Lichtheim.

1. *Maat* means "truth."   2. Upper and Lower Egypt, united by the first pharaoh.

Bodies cleansed, clothed,
Their arms adore your appearance.
The entire land sets out to work,
All beasts browse on their herbs;
Trees, herbs are sprouting,   35
Birds fly from their nests,
Their wings greeting your spirit.
All flocks frisk on their feet,
All that fly up and alight,
They live when you dawn for them.   40
Ships fare north, fare south as well,
Roads lie open when you rise;
The fish in the river dart before you,
Your rays are in the midst of the sea.

Who makes seed grow in women,   45
Who creates people from sperm;
Who feeds the son in his mother's womb,
Who soothes him to still his tears.
Nurse in the womb,
Giver of breath,   50
To nourish all that he made.
When he comes from the womb to breathe,
On the day of his birth,
You open wide his mouth,
You supply his needs.   55
When the chick in the egg speaks in the shell,
You give him breath within to sustain him;
When you have made him complete,
To break out from the egg,
He comes out from the egg,   60
To announce his completion,
Walking on his legs he comes from it.

How many are your deeds,
Though hidden from sight,
O Sole God beside whom there is none!   65
You made the earth as you wished, you alone,
All peoples, herds, and flocks;
All upon earth that walk on legs,
All on high that fly on wings,
The lands of Khor and Kush,   70
The land of Egypt.
You set every man in his place,
You supply their needs;
Everyone has his food,

His lifetime is counted.   75
Their tongues differ in speech,
Their characters likewise;
Their skins are distinct,
For you distinguished the peoples.

You made Hapy[3] in the underworld;   80
You bring him when you will,
To nourish the people,
For you made them for yourself.
Lord of all who toils for them,
Lord of all lands who shines for them,   85
Aten of daytime, great in glory!
All distant lands, you make them live,
You made a heavenly Hapy descend for them;
He makes waves on the mountains like the sea,
To drench their fields and their towns.   90
How excellent are your ways, O Lord of eternity!
A Hapy from heaven for foreign peoples,
And all lands' creatures that walk on legs,
For Egypt the Hapy who comes from the underworld.

Your rays nurse all fields,   95
When you shine they live, they grow for you;
You made the seasons to foster all that you made,
Winter to cool them, heat that they taste you.
You made the far sky to shine therein,
To behold all that you made;   100
You alone, shining in your form of living Aten,
Risen, radiant, distant, near.
You made millions of forms from yourself alone,
Towns, villages, fields, the river's course;
All eyes observe you upon them,   105
For you are the Aten of daytime on high.

You are in my heart,
There is no other who knows you,
Only your son, Neferkheprure, Sole-one-of-Re,
Whom you have taught your ways and your might.   110
Those on earth come from your hand as you made them,
When you have dawned they live,
When you set they die;
You yourself are lifetime, one lives by you.

---

3. Hapy is the god who controls the Nile's
annual inundation.

All eyes are on your beauty until you set,   115
All labor ceases when you rest in the west;
When you rise you stir everyone for the King,
Every leg is on the move since you founded the earth.
You rouse them for your son who came from your body,
The King who lives by Maat, the Lord of the Two Lands,   120
Neferkheprure, Sole-one-of-Re,
The Son of Re who lives by Maat, the Lord of crowns,
Akhenaten, great in his lifetime;
And the great Queen whom he loves, the Lady of the Two Lands,
Nefer-nefru-Aten Nefertiti, living forever.   125

ANONYMOUS (c. 1900 B.C.E.)
Egypt

This remarkable autobiography begins with the death of the first king of the
Twelfth Dynasty, Amenemhet I, in 1961 B.C.E. Upon hearing the news, the
courtier Sinuhe flees Egypt, apparently fearing that the new dynasty will not
survive its founder's death. The ensuing story describes Sinuhe's survival and
eventual prosperity in Syria and Palestine. He returns in old age to the court of
Amenemhet's successor, Sesostris I, where he is received with honor and, most
importantly, granted a traditional burial and funerary rites.

The story survives in various manuscripts from the Twelfth Dynasty
onward. It is usually supposed that it was copied from an inscription in Sinuhe's
tomb, although neither a tomb nor any other record of Sinuhe has ever been
discovered. Almost four thousand years old, the "Story of Sinuhe" is a masterpiece of realistic narration.

The Story of Sinuhe

The Prince, Count, Governor of the domains of the sovereign in the lands of the
Asiatics, true and beloved Friend of the King, the Attendant Sinuhe, says:

I was an attendant who attended his lord, a servant of the royal harem,
waiting on the Princess, the highly praised Royal Wife of King Sesostris in
Khenemsut, the daughter of King Amenemhet in Kanefru, Nefru, the revered.[1]

Year 30, third month of the inundation, day 7: the god ascended to his
horizon. The King of Upper and Lower Egypt, Sehetepibre, flew to heaven and

Translated by Miriam Lichtheim.

---

1. Sinuhe is an official of Princess Nefru,   are the pyramid towns of Sesostris and his
   daughter of Amenemhet and wife of her   father.
   brother Sesostris I. Khenemsut and Kanefru

united with the sun-disk, the divine body merging with its maker. Then the residence was hushed; hearts grieved; the great portals were shut; the courtiers were head-on-knee; the people moaned.

His majesty, however, had despatched an army to the land of the Tjemeh, with his eldest son as its commander, the good god Sesostris. He had been sent to smite the foreign lands and to punish those of Tjehenu.[2] Now he was returning, bringing captives of the Tjehenu and cattle of all kinds beyond number. The officials of the palace sent to the western border to let the king's son know the event that had occurred at the court. The messengers met him on the road, reaching him at night. Not a moment did he delay. The falcon flew with his attendants, without letting his army know it.

But the royal sons who had been with him on this expedition had also been sent for. One of them was summoned while I was standing there. I heard his voice, as he spoke, while I was in the near distance. My heart fluttered, my arms spread out, a trembling befell all my limbs. I removed myself in leaps, to seek a hiding place. I put myself between two bushes, so as to leave the road to its traveler.

I set out southward. I did not plan to go to the residence. I believed there would be turmoil and did not expect to survive it. I crossed Maaty near Sycamore; I reached Isle-of-Snefru. I spent the day there at the edge of the cultivation. Departing at dawn I encountered a man who stood on the road. He saluted me while I was afraid of him. At dinner time I reached "Cattle-Quay." I crossed in a barge without a rudder, by the force of the westwind. I passed to the east of the quarry, at the height of "Mistress of the Red Mountain." Then I made my way northward.[3] I reached the "Walls of the Ruler," which were made to repel the Asiatics and to crush the Sand-farers. I crouched in a bush for fear of being seen by the guard on duty upon the wall.

I set out at night. At dawn I reached Peten. I halted at "Isle-of-Kem-Wer." An attack of thirst overtook me; I was parched, my throat burned. I said, "This is the taste of death." I raised my heart and collected myself when I heard the lowing sound of cattle and saw Asiatics. One of their leaders, who had been in Egypt, recognized me. He gave me water and boiled milk for me. I went with him to his tribe. What they did for me was good.

Land gave me to land. I traveled to Byblos; I returned to Qedem. I spent a year and a half there. Then Ammunenshi, the ruler of Upper Retenu,[4] took me to him, saying to me: "You will be happy with me; you will hear the language of Egypt." He said this because he knew my character and had heard of my skill, Egyptians who were with him having borne witness for me. He said to me: "Why have you come here? Has something happened at the residence?" I said to him: "King Sehetepibre departed to the horizon, and one did not know the circumstances." But I spoke in half-truths: "When I returned from the expedition to the land of the Tjemeh, it was reported to me and my heart grew faint. It carried me away on the

---

2. Tjemeh and Tjehenu are names of two Libyan peoples.
3. Sinuhe began by traveling south. He turns northward upon crossing the Nile, perhaps

inspired by the downstream (northward) drift of his rudderless boat.
4. A region in parts of Palestine and Syria.

path of flight, though I had not been talked about; no one had spat in my face; I had not heard a reproach; my name had not been heard in the mouth of the herald. I do not know what brought me to this country; it is as if planned by god. As if a Delta-man saw himself in Yebu, a marsh-man in Nubia."[5]

Then he said to me: "How then is that land without that excellent god, fear of whom was throughout the lands like Sakhmet[6] in a year of plague?" I said to him in reply: "Of course his son has entered into the palace, having taken his father's heritage.

> He is a god without peer,
> No other comes before him;
> He is lord of knowledge, wise planner, skilled leader,
> One goes and comes by his will.
>
> He was the smiter of foreign lands,
> While his father stayed in the palace,
> He reported to him on commands carried out.
>
> He is a champion who acts with his arm,
> A fighter who has no equal,
> When seen engaged in archery,
> When joining the melee.
>
> Horn-curber who makes hands turn weak,
> His foes can not close ranks;
> Keen-sighted he smashes foreheads,
> None can withstand his presence.
>
> Wide-striding he smites the fleeing,
> No retreat for him who turns him his back;
> Steadfast in time of attack,
> He makes turn back and turns not his back.
>
> Stouthearted when he sees the mass,
> He lets not slackness fill his heart;
> Eager at the sight of combat,
> Joyful when he works his bow.
>
> Clasping his shield he treads under foot,
> No second blow needed to kill;
> None can escape his arrow,
> None turn aside his bow.
>
> The Bowmen flee before him,
> As before the might of the goddess;
> As he fights he plans the goal,
> Unconcerned about all else.
>
> Lord of grace, rich in kindness,
> He has conquered through affection;

---

5. I.e., at the opposite end of the country.   6. Goddess of war.

His city loves him more than itself,
Acclaims him more than its own god.

Men outdo women in hailing him,
Now that he is king;
Victor while yet in the egg,
Set to be ruler since his birth.

Augmenter of those born with him,
He is unique, god-given;
Happy the land that he rules!

Enlarger of frontiers,
He will conquer southern lands,
While ignoring northern lands,
Though made to smite Asiatics and tread on Sand-farers!

"Send to him! Let him know your name as one who inquires while being far from his majesty. He will not fail to do good to a land that will be loyal to him."

He said to me: "Well then, Egypt is happy knowing that he is strong. But you are here. You shall stay with me. What I shall do for you is good."

He set me at the head of his children. He married me to his eldest daughter. He let me choose for myself of his land, of the best that was his, on his border with another land. It was a good land called Yaa. Figs were in it and grapes. It had more wine than water. Abundant was its honey, plentiful its oil. All kinds of fruit were on its trees. Barley was there and emmer, and no end of cattle of all kinds. Much also came to me because of the love of me; for he had made me chief of a tribe in the best part of his land. Loaves were made for me daily, and wine as daily fare, cooked meat, roast fowl, as well as desert game. For they snared for me and laid it before me, in addition to the catch of my hounds. Many sweets were made for me, and milk dishes of all kinds.

I passed many years, my children becoming strong men, each a master of his tribe. The envoy who came north or went south to the residence stayed with me. I let everyone stay with me. I gave water to the thirsty; I showed the way to him who had strayed; I rescued him who had been robbed. When Asiatics conspired to attack the Rulers of Hill-Countries, I opposed their movements. For this ruler of Retenu made me carry out numerous missions as commander of his troops. Every hill tribe against which I marched I vanquished, so that it was driven from the pasture of its wells. I plundered its cattle, carried off its families, seized their food, and killed people by my strong arm, by my bow, by my movements and my skillful plans. I won his heart and he loved me, for he recognized my valor. He set me at the head of his children, for he saw the strength of my arms.

There came a hero of Retenu,
To challenge me in my tent.
A champion was he without peer,
He had subdued it all.
He said he would fight with me,
He planned to plunder me,

He meant to seize my cattle
At the behest of his tribe.

The ruler conferred with me and I said: "I do not know him; I am not his ally, that I could walk about in his camp. Have I ever opened his back rooms or climbed over his fence? It is envy, because he sees me doing your commissions. I am indeed like a stray bull in a strange herd, whom the bull of the herd charges, whom the longhorn attacks. Is an inferior beloved when he becomes a superior? No Asiatic makes friends with a Delta-man. And what would make papyrus cleave to the mountain?[7] If a bull loves combat, should a champion bull retreat for fear of being equaled? If he wishes to fight, let him declare his wish. Is there a god who does not know what he has ordained, and a man who knows how it will be?"

At night I strung my bow, sorted my arrows, practiced with my dagger, polished my weapons. When it dawned Retenu came. It had assembled its tribes; it had gathered its neighboring peoples; it was intent on this combat.

He came toward me while I waited, having placed myself near him. Every heart burned for me; the women jabbered. All hearts ached for me thinking: "Is there another champion who could fight him?" He raised his battle-axe and shield, while his armful of missiles fell toward me. When I had made his weapons attack me, I let his arrows pass me by without effect, one following the other. Then, when he charged me, I shot him, my arrow sticking in his neck. He screamed; he fell on his nose; I slew him with his axe. I raised my war cry over his back, while every Asiatic shouted. I gave praise to Mont,[8] while his people mourned him. The ruler Ammunenshi took me in his arms.

Then I carried off his goods; I plundered his cattle. What he had meant to do to me I did to him. I took what was in his tent; I stripped his camp. Thus I became great, wealthy in goods, rich in herds. It was the god who acted, so as to show mercy to one with whom he had been angry, whom he had made stray abroad. For today his heart is appeased.

A fugitive fled his surroundings
    I am famed at home.
A laggard lagged from hunger—
    I give bread to my neighbor.
A man left his land in nakedness—
    I have bright clothes, fine linen.
A man ran for lack of one to send—
    I am rich in servants.
My house is fine, my dwelling spacious—
    My thoughts are at the palace!

Whichever god decreed this flight, have mercy, bring me home! Surely you will let me see the place in which my heart dwells! What is more important than that my corpse be buried in the land in which I was born! Come to my aid! What

---

7. Papyrus grows in fertile lowland like Sinuhe's native Nile Delta; the mountains are dry and implicitly less cultivated (in both senses).

8. Patron god of warriors.

if the happy event should occur![9] May god pity me! May he act so as to make happy the end of one whom he punished! May his heart ache for one whom he forced to live abroad! If he is truly appeased today, may he hearken to the prayer of one far away! May he return one whom he made roam the earth to the place from which he carried him off!

May Egypt's king have mercy on me, that I may live by his mercy! May I greet the mistress of the land who is in the palace! May I hear the commands of her children! Would that my body were young again! For old age has come; feebleness has overtaken me. My eyes are heavy, my arms weak; my legs fail to follow. The heart is weary; death is near. May I be conducted to the city of eternity! May I serve the Mistress of All![10] May she speak well of me to her children; may she spend eternity above me!

Now when the majesty of King Kheperkare was told of the condition in which I was, his majesty sent word to me with royal gifts, in order to gladden the heart of this servant like that of a foreign ruler. And the royal children who were in his palace sent me their messages. Copy of the decree brought to this servant concerning his return to Egypt:

Horus: Living in Births; the Two Ladies: Living in Births; the King of Upper and Lower Egypt: Kheperkare; the Son of Re: Sesostris, who lives forever. Royal decree to the Attendant Sinuhe:

This decree of the King is brought to you to let you know: That you circled the foreign countries, going from Qedem to Retenu, land giving you to land, was the counsel of your own heart. What had you done that one should act against you? You had not cursed, so that your speech would be reproved. You had not spoken against the counsel of the nobles, that your words should have been rejected. This matter—it carried away your heart. It was not in my heart against you. This your heaven in the palace lives and prospers to this day.[11] Her head is adorned with the kingship of the land; her children are in the palace. You will store riches which they give you; you will live on their bounty. Come back to Egypt! See the residence in which you lived! Kiss the ground at the great portals, mingle with the courtiers! For today you have begun to age. You have lost a man's strength. Think of the day of burial, the passing into reveredness.

A night is made for you with ointments and wrappings from the hand of Tait.[12] A funeral procession is made for you on the day of burial; the mummy case is of gold, its head of lapis lazuli. The sky is above you as you lie in the hearse, oxen drawing you, musicians going before you. The dance of the funerary dancers is done at the door of your tomb; the offering-list is read to you; sacrifice is made before your offering-stone. Your tomb-pillars, made of white stone, are among those of the royal children. You shall not die abroad! Nor shall Asiatics inter you. You shall not be wrapped in the skin of a ram to serve as your coffin. Too long a roaming of the earth! Think of your corpse, come back!

---

9. I.e., death.
10. Sinuhe identifies the queen with the sky goddess, who shields souls in the underworld.
11. I.e., Princess Nefru is secure as the new queen.
12. Goddess of weaving, including mummy-wrappings.

This decree reached me while I was standing in the midst of my tribe. When it had been read to me, I threw myself on my belly. Having touched the soil, I spread it on my chest. I strode around my camp shouting: "What compares with this which is done to a servant whom his heart led astray to alien lands? Truly good is the kindness that saves me from death! Your spirit will grant me to reach my end, my body being at home!"

Copy of the reply to this decree:

The servant of the Palace, Sinuhe, says: In very good peace! Regarding the matter of this flight which this servant did in his ignorance. It is your spirit, O good god, lord of the Two Lands, which Re loves and which Mont lord of Thebes favors; and Amun lord of Thrones-of-the-Two-Lands, and Sobk-Re lord of Sumenu, and Horus, Hathor, Atum with his Ennead, and Sopdu-Neferbau-Semseru the Eastern Horus, and the Lady of Yemet—many she enfold your head—and the conclave upon the flood, and Min-Horus of the hill-countries, and Wereret lady of Punt, Nut, Haroeris-Re, and all the gods of Egypt and the isles of the sea—may they give life and joy to your nostrils, may they endue you with their bounty, may they give you eternity without limit, infinity without bounds! May the fear of you resound in lowlands and highlands, for you have subdued all that the sun encircles! This is the prayer of this servant for his lord who saves from the West.

The lord of knowledge who knows people knew in the majesty of the palace that this servant was afraid to say it. It is like a thing too great to repeat. The great god, the peer of Re, knows the heart of one who has served him willingly. This servant is in the hand of one who thinks about him. He is placed under his care. Your Majesty is the conquering Horus; your arms vanquish all lands. May then your Majesty command to have brought to you the prince of Meki from Qedem, the mountain chiefs from Keshu, and the prince of Menus from the lands of the Fenkhu. They are rulers of renown who have grown up in the love of you. I do not mention Retenu—it belongs to you like your hounds.

Lo, this flight which the servant made—I did not plan it. It was not in my heart; I did not devise it. I do not know what removed me from my place. It was like a dream. As if a Delta-man saw himself in Yebu, a marsh-man in Nubia. I was not afraid; no one ran after me. I had not heard a reproach; my name was not heard in the mouth of the herald. Yet my flesh crept, my feet hurried, my heart drove me; the god who had willed this flight dragged me away. Nor am I a haughty man. He who knows his land respects men. Re has set the fear of you throughout the land, the dread of you in every foreign country. Whether I am at the residence, whether I am in this place, it is you who covers this horizon. The sun rises at your pleasure. The water in the river is drunk when you wish. The air of heaven is breathed at your bidding. This servant will hand over his possessions to the brood which this servant begot in this place. This servant has been sent for! Your Majesty will do as he wishes! One lives by the breath which you give. As Re, Horus, and Hathor love your august nose,[13] may Mont lord of Thebes wish it to live forever!

---

13. The nose, associated with the breath of life, was seen as a center of sensation and emotion.

I was allowed to spend one more day in Yaa, handing over my possessions to my children, my eldest son taking charge of my tribe; all my possessions became his—my serfs, my herds, my fruit, my fruit trees. This servant departed southward. I halted at Horusways. The commander in charge of the garrison sent a message to the residence to let it be known. Then his majesty sent a trusted overseer of the royal domains with whom were loaded ships, bearing royal gifts for the Asiatics who had come with me to escort me to Horusways. I called each one by his name, while every butler was at his task. When I had started and set sail, there was kneading and straining beside me, until I reached the city of Itj-tawy.

When it dawned, very early, they came to summon me. Ten men came and ten men went to usher me into the palace. My forehead touched the ground between the sphinxes, and the royal children stood in the gateway to meet me. The courtiers who usher through the forecourt set me on the way to the audience-hall. I found his majesty on the great throne in a kiosk of gold. Stretched out on my belly, I did not know myself before him, while this god greeted me pleasantly. I was like a man seized by darkness. My soul was gone, my limbs trembled; my heart was not in my body, I did not know life from death.

His majesty said to one of the courtiers: "Lift him up, let him speak to me." Then his majesty said: "Now you have come, after having roamed foreign lands. Flight has taken its toll of you. You have aged, have reached old age. It is no small matter that your corpse will be interred without being escorted by Bowmen.[14] But don't act thus, don't act thus, speechless though your name was called!" Fearful of punishment I answered with the answer of a frightened man: "What has my lord said to me, that I might answer it? It is not disrespect to the god! It is the terror which is in my body, like that which caused the fateful flight! Here I am before you. Life is yours. May your Majesty do as he wishes!"

Then the royal daughters were brought in, and his majesty said to the queen: "Here is Sinuhe, come as an Asiatic, a product of nomads!" She uttered a very great cry, and the royal daughters shrieked all together. They said to his majesty: "Is it really he, O king, our lord?" Said his majesty: "It is really he!" Now having brought with them their necklaces, rattles, and sistra, they held them out to his majesty:

> Your hands upon the radiance, eternal king,
> Jewels of heaven's mistress!
> The Golden One gives life to your nostrils,
> The Lady of Stars enfolds you!
>
> Southcrown fared north, northcrown south,
> Joined, united by your majesty's word.
> While the Cobra decks your brow,
> You deliver the poor from harm.
> Peace to you from Re, Lord of Lands!
> Hail to you and the Mistress of All!
>
> Slacken your bow, lay down your arrow,
> Give breath to him who gasps for breath!

---

14. I.e., by the rough nomads.

Give us our good gift on this good day,
Grant us the son of northwind, Bowman born in Egypt!

He made the flight in fear of you,
He left the land in dread of you!
A face that sees you shall not pale,
Eyes that see you shall not fear!

His majesty said: "He shall not fear, he shall not dread!" He shall be a
Companion among the nobles. He shall be among the courtiers. Proceed to the
robing-room to wait on him!"

I left the audience-hall, the royal daughters giving me their hands. We went
through the great portals, and I was put in the house of a prince. In it were
luxuries: a bathroom and mirrors. In it were riches from the treasury; clothes of
royal linen, myrrh, and the choice perfume of the king and of his favorite courtiers
were in every room. Every servant was at his task. Years were removed from my
body. I was shaved; my hair was combed. Thus was my squalor returned to the
foreign land, my dress to the Sand-farers. I was clothed in fine linen; I was
anointed with fine oil. I slept on a bed. I had returned the sand to those who dwell
in it, the tree-oil to those who grease themselves with it.

I was given a house and garden that had belonged to a courtier. Many
craftsmen rebuilt it, and all its woodwork was made anew. Meals were brought to
me from the palace three times, four times a day, apart from what the royal
children gave without a moment's pause.

A stone pyramid was built for me in the midst of the pyramids. The masons
who build tombs constructed it. A master draughtsman designed in it. A master
sculptor carved in it. The overseers of construction in the necropolis busied
themselves with it. All the equipment that is placed in a tomb-shaft was supplied.
Mortuary priests were given me. A funerary domain was made for me. It had fields
and a garden in the right place, as is done for a Companion of the first rank. My
statue was overlaid with gold, its skirt with electrum. It was his majesty who
ordered it made. There is no commoner for whom the like has been done. I was
in the favor of the king, until the day of landing[15] came.

Colophon   It is done from beginning to end as it was found in writing.

ANONYMOUS (c. 1200 B.C.E.)
Egypt

This mysterious story was found on a papyrus copied—or written—by an
Egyptian scribe named Ennana, who lived around 1200 B.C.E. Its protagonists

---

15. I.e., death.

bear the names of two gods: Anubis was god of the dead and embalming; Bata was a pastoral god, often pictured as a ram or as a bull. Whether or not they are divine in this story is unclear. They may be gods, or they may be essentially human characters who share some traits with divine namesakes. In either case, the story mixes magical and earthly realism with a full presentation of familial and psychological conflict.

The Two Brothers

It is said, there were two brothers, of the same mother and the same father. Anubis was the name of the elder, and Bata the name of the younger. As for Anubis, he had a house and a wife; and his young brother was with him as if he were a son. He was the one who made clothes for him, and he went behind his cattle to the fields. He was the one who did the plowing, and he harvested for him. He was the one who did for him all kinds of labor in the fields. Indeed, his young brother was an excellent man. There was none like him in the whole land, for a god's strength was in him.

Now when many days had passed, his young brother was tending his cattle according to his daily custom. And he returned to his house in the evening, laden with all kinds of field plants, and with milk, with wood, and with every good thing of the field. He placed them before his elder brother, as he was sitting with his wife. Then he drank and ate and [went to sleep in] his stable among his cattle.

Now when it had dawned and another day had come, he took foods that were cooked and placed them before his elder brother. Then he took bread for himself for the fields, and he drove his cattle to let them eat in the fields. He walked behind his cattle, and they would say to him: "The grass is good in such-and-such a place." And he heard all they said and took them to the place of good grass that they desired. Thus the cattle he tended became exceedingly fine, and they increased their offspring very much.

Now at plowing time his elder brother said to him: "Have a team of oxen made ready for us for plowing, for the soil has emerged and is right for plowing. Also, come to the field with seed, for we shall start plowing tomorrow." So he said to him. Then the young brother made all the preparations that his elder brother had told him to make.

Now when it had dawned and another day had come, they went to the field with their seed and began to plow. And their hearts were very pleased with this work they had undertaken. And many days later, when they were in the field, they had need of seed. Then he sent his young brother, saying: "Hurry, fetch us seed from the village." His young brother found the wife of his elder brother seated braiding her hair. He said to her: "Get up, give me seed, so that I may hurry to the field, for my elder brother is waiting for me. Don't delay." She said to him: "Go, open the storeroom and fetch what you want. Don't make me leave my hairdo unfinished."

Then the youth entered his stable and fetched a large vessel, for he wished to take a great quantity of seed. He loaded himself with barley and emmer and came out with it. Thereupon she said to him: "How much is what you have on your

Translated by Miriam Lichtheim.

shoulder?" He said to her: "Three sacks of emmer and two sacks of barley, five in all, are on my shoulder." So he said to her. Then she spoke to him saying: "There is great strength in you. I see your vigor daily." And she desired to know him as a man. She got up, took hold of him, and said to him: "Come, let us spend an hour lying together. It will be good for you. And I will make fine clothes for you."

Then the youth became like a leopard in his anger over the wicked speech she had made to him; and she became very frightened. He rebuked her, saying: "Look, you are like a mother to me; and your husband is like a father to me. He who is older than I has raised me. What is this great wrong you said to me? Do not say it to me again! But I will not tell it to anyone. I will not let it come from my mouth to any man." He picked up his load; he went off to the field. He reached his elder brother, and they began to work at their task. When evening had come, his elder brother returned to his house. And his young brother tended his cattle, loaded himself with all things of the field, and drove his cattle before him to let them sleep in their stable in the village.

Now the wife of his elder brother was afraid on account of the speech she had made. So she took fat and grease and made herself appear as if she had been beaten, in order to tell her husband, "It was your young brother who beat me." Her husband returned in the evening according to his daily custom. He reached his house and found his wife lying down and seeming ill. She did not pour water over his hands in the usual manner; nor had she lit a fire for him. His house was in darkness, and she lay vomiting.

Her husband said to her: "Who has had words with you?" She said to him: "No one has had words with me except your young brother. When he came to take seed to you, he found me sitting alone. He said to me: 'Come, let us spend an hour lying together; loosen your braids.' So he said to me. But I would not listen to him. 'Am I not your mother? Is your elder brother not like a father to you?' So I said to him. He became frightened and he beat me, so as to prevent me from telling you. Now if you let him live, I shall die! Look, when he returns, do not let him live! For I am ill from this evil design which he was about to carry out in the morning."

Then his elder brother became like a leopard. He sharpened his spear and took it in his hand. Then his elder brother stood behind the door of his stable, in order to kill his younger brother when he came in the evening to let his cattle enter the stable. Now when the sun had set he loaded himself with all the plants of the field according to his daily custom. He returned, and as the lead cow was about to enter the stable she said to her herdsman: "Here is your elder brother waiting for you with his spear in order to kill you. Run away from him." He heard what his lead cow said, and when another went in she said the same. He looked under the door of his stable and saw the feet of his elder brother as he stood behind the door with his spear in his hand. He set his load on the ground and took off at a run so as to flee. And his elder brother went after him with his spear.

Then his young brother prayed to Pre-Harakhti,[1] saying: "My good lord! It is you who judge between the wicked and the just!" And Pre heard all his plea; and Pre made a great body of water appear between him and his elder brother, and it

---

1. A name for the sun god Re or Ra.

was full of crocodiles. Thus one came to be on the one side, and the other on the other side. And his elder brother struck his own hand twice, because he had failed to kill him. Then his young brother called to him on this side, saying: "Wait here until dawn! When the Aten[2] has risen, I shall contend with you before him; and he will hand over the wicked to the just! For I shall not be with you any more. I shall not be in the place in which you are. I shall go to the Valley of the Pine."

Now when it dawned and another day had come, and Pre-Harakhti had risen, one gazed at the other. Then the youth rebuked his elder brother, saying: "What is your coming after me to kill me wrongfully, without having listened to my words? For I am yet your young brother, and you are like a father to me, and your wife is like a mother to me. Is it not so that when I was sent to fetch seed for us your wife said to me: 'Come, let us spend an hour lying together'? But look, it has been turned about for you into another thing." Then he let him know all that had happened between him and his wife. And he swore by Pre-Harakhti, saying: "As to your coming to kill me wrongfully, you carried your spear on the testimony of a filthy whore!" Then he took a reed knife, cut off his phallus, and threw it into the water; and the catfish swallowed it. And he grew weak and became feeble. And his elder brother became very sick at heart and stood weeping for him loudly. He could not cross over to where his young brother was on account of the crocodiles.

Then his young brother called to him, saying: "If you recall something evil, will you not also recall something good, or something that I have done for you? Go back to your home and tend your cattle, for I shall not stay in the place where you are. I shall go to the Valley of the Pine. But what you shall do for me is to come and look after me, when you learn that something has happened to me. I shall take out my heart and place it on top of the blossom of the pine. If the pine is cut down and falls to the ground, you shall come to search for it. If you spend seven years searching for it, let your heart not be disgusted. And when you find it and place it in a bowl of cool water, I shall live to take revenge on him who wronged me. You will know that something has happened to me when one puts a jug of beer in your hand and it ferments. Do not delay at all when this happens to you."

Then he went away to the Valley of the Pine; and his elder brother went to his home, his hand on his head and smeared with dirt.[3] When he reached his house, he killed his wife, cast her to the dogs, and sat mourning for his young brother.

Now many days after this, his young brother was in the Valley of the Pine. There was no one with him, and he spent the days hunting desert game. In the evening he returned to sleep under the pine on top of whose blossom his heart was. And after many days he built a mansion for himself with his own hand in the Valley of the Pine, filled with all good things, for he wanted to set up a household.

Coming out of his mansion, he encountered the Ennead[4] as they walked about administering the entire land. Then the Ennead addressed him in unison, saying: "O Bata, Bull of the Ennead, are you alone here, having left your town on account of the wife of Anubis, your elder brother? He has killed his wife and you are avenged of all the wrong done to you." And as they felt very sorry for him,

---

2. The disk of the sun.   4. The council of nine major gods.
3. Signs of mourning.

Pre-Harakhti said to Khnum[5]: "Fashion a wife for Bata, that he not live alone!" Then Khnum made a companion for him who was more beautiful in body than any woman in the whole land, for the fluid of every god was in her. Then the seven Hathors[6] came to see her, and they said with one voice: "She will die by the knife."

He desired her very much. She sat in his house while he spent the day hunting desert game, bringing it and putting it before her. He said to her: "Do not go outdoors, lest the sea snatch you. I cannot rescue you from it, because I am a woman like you. And my heart lies on top of the blossom of the pine. But if another finds it, I shall fight with him." Then he revealed to her all his thoughts.

Now many days after this, when Bata had gone hunting according to his daily custom, the young girl went out to stroll under the pine which was next to her house. Then she saw the sea surging behind her, and she started to run before it and entered her house. Thereupon the sea called to the pine, saying: "Catch her for me!" And the pine took away a lock of her hair. Then the sea brought it to Egypt and laid it in the place of the washermen of Pharaoh. Thereafter the scent of the lock of hair got into the clothes of Pharaoh. And the king quarreled with the royal washermen, saying: "A scent of ointment is in the clothes of Pharaoh!" He quarreled with them every day, and they did not know what to do.

The chief of the royal washermen went to the shore, his heart very sore on account of the daily quarrel with him. Then he realized that he was standing on the shore opposite the lock of hair which was in the water. He had someone go down, and it was brought to him. Its scent was found to be very sweet, and he took it to Pharaoh.

Then the learned scribes of Pharaoh were summoned, and they said to Pharaoh: "As for this lock of hair, it belongs to a daughter of Pre-Harakhti in whom there is the fluid of every god. It is a greeting to you from another country. Let envoys go to every foreign land to search for her. As for the envoy who goes to the Valley of the Pine, let many men go with him to fetch her." His majesty said: "What you have said is very good." And they were sent.

Now many days after this, the men who had gone abroad returned to report to his majesty. But those who had gone to the Valley of the Pine did not return, for Bata had killed them, leaving only one of them to report to his majesty. Then his majesty sent many soldiers and charioteers to bring her back, and with them was a woman into whose hand one had given all kinds of beautiful ladies' jewelry. The woman returned to Egypt with her, and there was jubilation for her in the entire land. His majesty loved her very very much, and he gave her the rank of Great Lady. He spoke with her in order to make her tell about her husband, and she said to his majesty: "Have the pine felled and cut up." The king sent soldiers with their tools to fell the pine. They reached the pine, they felled the blossom on which was Bata's heart, and he fell dead at that moment.

When it had dawned and the next day had come, and the pine had been felled, Anubis, the elder brother of Bata, entered his house. He sat down to wash his hands. He was given a jug of beer, and it fermented. He was given another of

---

5. The potter god who shapes bodies.

6. Manifestations of the sky goddess Hathor, who foretell a child's fate at birth.

wine, and it turned bad. Then he took his staff and his sandals, as well as his clothes and his weapons, and he started to journey to the Valley of the Pine. He entered the mansion of his young brother and found his young brother lying dead on his bed. He wept when he saw his young brother lying dead. He went to search for the heart of his young brother beneath the pine under which his young brother had slept in the evening. He spent three years searching for it without finding it.

When he began the fourth year, his heart longed to return to Egypt, and he said: "I shall depart tomorrow." So he said in his heart. When it had dawned and another day had come, he went to walk under the pine and spent the day searching for it. When he turned back in the evening, he looked once again in search of it and he found a fruit. He came back with it, and it was the heart of his young brother! He fetched a bowl of cool water, placed it in it, and sat down according to his daily custom.

When night had come, his heart swallowed the water, and Bata twitched in all his body. He began to look at his elder brother while his heart was in the bowl. Then Anubis, his elder brother, took the bowl of cool water in which was the heart of his young brother and let him drink it. Then his heart stood in its place, and he became as he had been. Thereupon they embraced each other, and they talked to one another.

Then Bata said to his elder brother: "Look, I shall change myself into a great bull of beautiful color, of a kind unknown to man, and you shall sit on my back. By the time the sun has risen, we shall be where my wife is, that I may avenge myself. You shall take me to where the king is, for he will do for you everything good. You shall be rewarded with silver and gold for taking me to Pharaoh. For I shall be a great marvel, and they will jubilate over me in the whole land. Then you shall depart to your village."

When it had dawned and the next day had come, Bata assumed the form which he had told his elder brother. Then Anubis, his elder brother, sat on his back. At dawn he reached the place where the king was. His majesty was informed about him; he saw him and rejoiced over him very much. He made a great offering for him, saying: "It is a great marvel." And there was jubilation over him in the entire land. Then the king rewarded his elder brother with silver and gold, and he dwelled in his village. The king gave him many people and many things, for Pharaoh loved him very much, more than anyone else in the whole land.

Now when many days had passed, Bata entered the kitchen, stood where the Lady was, and began to speak to her, saying: "Look, I am yet alive!" She said to him: "Who are you?" He said to her: "I am Bata. I know that when you had the pine felled for Pharaoh, it was on account of me, so that I should not live. Look, I am yet alive! I am a bull." The Lady became very frightened because of the speech her husband had made to her. Then he left the kitchen.

His majesty sat down to a day of feasting with her. She poured drink for his majesty, and he was very happy with her. Then she said to his majesty: "Swear to me by God, saying: 'Whatever she will say, I will listen to it!' " He listened to all that she said: "Let me eat of the liver of this bull; for he is good for nothing." So she said to him. He became very vexed over what she had said, and the heart of Pharaoh was very sore.

When it had dawned and another day had come, the king proclaimed a great offering, namely, the sacrifice of the bull. He sent one of the chief royal slaughterers to sacrifice the bull. And when he had been sacrificed and was carried on the shoulders of the men, he shook his neck and let fall two drops of blood beside the two doorposts of his majesty, one on the one side of the great portal of Pharaoh, and the other on the other side. They grew into two big Persea trees, each of them outstanding. Then one went to tell his majesty: "Two big Persea trees have grown this night—a great marvel for his majesty—beside the great portal of his majesty." There was jubilation over them in the whole land, and the king made an offering to them.

Many days after this, his majesty appeared at the audience window of lapis lazuli with a wreath of all kinds of flowers on his neck. Then he mounted a golden chariot and came out of the palace to view the Persea trees. Then the Lady came out on a team behind Pharaoh. His majesty sat down under one Persea tree and the Lady under the other. Then Bata spoke to his wife: "Ha, you false one! I am Bata! I am alive in spite of you. I know that when you had the pine felled for Pharaoh, it was on account of me. And when I became a bull, you had me killed."

Many days after this, the Lady stood pouring drink for his majesty, and he was happy with her. Then she said to his majesty: "Swear to me by God, saying: 'Whatever she will say, I will listen to it!' So you shall say." He listened to all that she said. She said: "Have the two Persea trees felled and made into fine furniture." The king listened to all that she said. After a short while his majesty sent skilled craftsmen. They felled the Persea trees of Pharaoh, and the Queen, the Lady, stood watching it. Then a splinter flew and entered the mouth of the Lady. She swallowed it, and in a moment she became pregnant. The king ordered made of the trees whatever she desired.

Many days after this, she gave birth to a son. One went to tell his majesty: "A son has been born to you." He was fetched, and a nurse and maids were assigned to him. And there was jubilation over him in the whole land. The king sat down to a feastday and held him on his lap. From that hour his majesty loved him very much, and he designated him as Viceroy of Kush. And many days after this, his majesty made him crown prince of the whole land.

Now many days after this, when he had spent many years as crown prince of the whole land, his majesty flew up to heaven.[7] Then the king[8] said: "Let my great royal officials be brought to me, that I may let them know all that has happened to me." Then his wife was brought to him. He judged her in their presence, and they gave their assent. His elder brother was brought to him, and he made him crown prince of the whole land. He spent thirty years as king of Egypt. He departed from life; and his elder brother stood in his place on the day of death.

Colophon   It has come to a good end under the scribe of the treasury, Kagab, and the scribes of the treasury, Hori and Meremope. Written by the scribe Ennana, the owner of this book. Whoever maligns this book, Thoth[9] will contend with him.

---

7. I.e., died.
8. Now Bata.

9. The gods' messenger, patron of wisdom and writing.

THE BIBLE (c. 900 B.C.E.)
Israel

One of the masterpieces of biblical narrative, the story of Joseph forms the final third of the Book of Genesis. It serves as a bridge between the history of the patriarchs and matriarchs of Israel (Genesis 12–36) and the story of Moses and the flight from Egypt in the ensuing Book of Exodus. The story may have been written in the cosmopolitan court of Solomon in the late tenth century B.C.E., or it may be of later date.

The narrative shows great psychological depth in its portrayal of the tensions in Joseph's family and their gradual resolution. It also provides an extended look at how the clan-based Hebrews viewed imperial Egyptian society. As the tale of a person from Palestine making good in Egypt, "The Joseph Story" is especially fascinating to read in juxtaposition with the "Story of Sinuhe," in which the narrator flees Egypt and establishes himself in Palestine. The story also invites comparisons with parallel motifs in earlier literature—the use of dream in Gilgamesh, the adulterous wife in "The Two Brothers." Centuries later, the same material was reworked for inclusion in the Qur'an, the holy book of Islam.

from *The Bible*

Genesis 37–50

The Joseph Story

37

This is the story of Joseph.

Joseph was seventeen years old. As he was still young, he was shepherding the flock with his brothers, with the sons of Bilhah and Zilpah his father's wives. Joseph informed their father of the evil spoken about them.

Israel[1] loved Joseph more than all his other sons, for he was the son of his old age, and he had a coat with long sleeves made for him. But his brothers, seeing how his father loved him more than all his other sons, came to hate him so much that they could not say a civil word to him.

Now Joseph had a dream, and he repeated it to his brothers. "Listen," he said, "to this dream I have had. We were binding sheaves in the countryside; and my sheaf, it seemed, rose up and stood upright; then I saw your sheaves gather round and bow to my sheaf." "So you want to be king over us," his brothers retorted, "or

---

New International Version translation.

1. Jacob received the name Israel ("He who wrestles with God") after struggling all night with an angel who tried to kill him (Genesis 32).

to lord it over us?" And they hated him still more, on account of his dreams and of what he said. He had another dream which he told to his brothers.

"Look, I have had another dream," he said. "I thought I saw the sun, the moon and eleven stars, bowing to me." He told his father and brothers, and his father scolded him. "A fine dream to have!" he said to him. "Are all of us then, myself, your mother and your brothers, to come and bow to the ground before you?" His brothers were jealous of him, but his father kept the thing in mind.

His brothers went to pasture their father's flock at Shechem. Then Israel said to Joseph, "Are not your brothers with the flock at Shechem? Come, I am going to send you to them." "I am ready," he replied. He said to him, "Go and see how your brothers and the flock are doing, and bring me word." He sent him from the valley of Hebron, and Joseph arrived at Shechem.

A man found him wandering in the countryside and the man asked him, "What are you looking for?" "I am looking for my brothers," he replied. "Please tell me where they are pasturing their flock." The man answered, "They have moved on from here; indeed I heard them say, 'Let us go to Dothan.' " So Joseph went after his brothers and found them at Dothan.

They saw him in the distance, and before he reached them they made a plot among themselves to put him to death. "Here comes the man of dreams," they said to one another. "Come on, let us kill him and throw him into some well; we can say that a wild beast devoured him. Then we shall see what becomes of his dreams."

But Reuben[2] heard, and he saved him from their violence. "We must not take his life," he said. "Shed no blood," said Reuben to them, "throw him into this well in the wilderness, but do not lay violent hands on him"—intending to save him from them and to restore him to his father. So, when Joseph reached his brothers, they pulled off his coat, the coat with long sleeves that he was wearing, and catching hold of him they threw him into the well, an empty well with no water in it. They then sat down to eat.

Looking up they saw a group of Ishmaelites who were coming from Gilead, their camels laden with gum, tragacanth, balsam and resin, which they were taking down into Egypt. Then Judah said to his brothers, "What do we gain by killing our brother and covering up his blood? Come, let us sell him to the Ishmaelites, but let us not do any harm to him. After all, he is our brother, and our own flesh." His brothers agreed.

Now some Midianite merchants were passing, and they drew Joseph up out of the well. They sold Joseph to the Ishmaelites for twenty silver pieces, and these men took Joseph to Egypt.[3] When Reuben went back to the well there was no sign of Joseph. Tearing his clothes, he went back to his brothers. "The boy has disappeared," he said. "What am I going to do?"

They took Joseph's coat and, slaughtering a goat, they dipped the coat in the blood. Then they sent back the coat with long sleeves and had it taken to their

---

2. Joseph's oldest brother.

3. Two traditions appear to have been combined here; in one version, the brothers sell Joseph to Ishmaelite traders; in the other, Reuben discovers that Joseph has been kidnapped from the pit by Midianites.

father, with the message, "This is what we have found. Examine it and see whether or not it is your son's coat." He examined it and exclaimed, "It is my son's coat! A wild beast has devoured him. Joseph has been the prey of some animal and has been torn to pieces." Jacob, tearing his clothes and putting on a loin-cloth of sackcloth, mourned his son for a long time. All his sons and daughters came to comfort him, but he refused to be comforted. "No," he said, "I will go down in mourning to Sheol, beside my son." And his father wept for him.

Meanwhile the Midianites had sold him in Egypt to Potiphar, one of Pharaoh's officials and commander of the guard.

38

It happened at that time that Judah left his brothers, to go down and stay with an Adullamite called Hirah. There Judah saw the daughter of a Canaanite called Shua.[4] He made her his wife and slept with her. She conceived and gave birth to a son whom she named Er. She conceived again and gave birth to a son whom she named Onan. Yet again she gave birth to a son whom she named Shelah. She was at Chezib when she gave birth to him.

Judah took a wife for his first-born Er, and her name was Tamar. But Er, Judah's first-born, offended Yahweh greatly, so Yahweh brought about his death. Then Judah said to Onan, "Take your brother's wife, and do your duty as her brother-in-law, to produce a child for your brother." But Onan, knowing the child would not be his, spilt his seed on the ground every time he slept with his brother's wife, to avoid providing a child for his brother. What he did was offensive to Yahweh, so he brought about his death also. Then Judah said to his daughter-in-law Tamar, "Return home as a widow to your father, and wait for my son Shelah to grow up," for he was thinking, "He must not die like his brothers." So Tamar went back home to her father.

A long time passed, and then Shua's daughter, the wife of Judah, died. After Judah had been comforted[5] he went up to Timnah to the men who sheared his sheep, himself and Hirah, his Adullamite friend. This was reported to Tamar, "Listen, your father-in-law is going up to Timnah for the shearing of his sheep." She therefore changed her widow's clothes, wrapped a veil around her, and sat down, heavily swathed, where the road to Enaim branches off the road to Timnah. Shelah had now grown up, as she saw, and yet she had not been given to him as his wife.

Judah, seeing her, took her for a prostitute, since her face was veiled. Going up to her on the road, he said, "Come, let me sleep with you." He did not know that she was his daughter-in-law. "What will you give me to sleep with me?" she asked. "I will send you a kid from the flock," he answered. "Agreed, if you give me a pledge until you send it," she answered. "What pledge shall I give you?" he asked. "Your seal, your cord and the stick you are holding," she answered. He gave them to her and slept with her, and she conceived by him. Then she rose and left him, and taking off her veil she put on her widow's weeds.

---

4. Judah is marrying a non-Hebrew wife, always a problem in Genesis.

5. I.e., when the period of mourning had ended.

Judah sent the kid by his Adullamite friend to recover the pledge from the woman. But he did not find her. He inquired from the men of the place, "Where is the prostitute who was by the roadside at Enaim?" "There has been no prostitute there," they answered. So returning to Judah he said, "I did not find her. What is more, the men of the place told me there had been no prostitute there." "Let her keep what she has," Judah replied, "or we shall become a laughing-stock. At least I sent her this kid, even though you did not find her."

About three months later it was reported to Judah, "Your daughter-in-law has played the harlot; furthermore, she is pregnant, as a result of her misconduct." "Take her outside and burn her," said Judah. But as she was being led off she sent this message to her father-in-law, "It was the man to whom these things belong who made me pregnant. Look at them," she said, "and see whose seal and cord and stick these are." Judah examined them and then said, "She is in the right, rather than I. This comes of my not giving her to my son Shelah to be his wife." He had no further intercourse with her.

When the time for her confinement came she was found to have twins in her womb. During the delivery one of them put out a hand, and the midwife caught it and tied a scarlet thread to it, saying, "This is the first to arrive." But he drew his hand back, and it was his brother who came out first. Then she said, "What a breach you have opened for yourself!" So he was named Perez.[6] The his brother came out with the scarlet thread on his hand, so he was named Zerah.[7]

39

Now Joseph had been taken down into Egypt. Potiphar the Egyptian, one of Pharaoh's officials and commander of the guard, bought him from the Ishmaelites who had brought him down there. Yahweh was with Joseph, and everything went well with him. He lodged in the house of his Egyptian master, and when his master saw how Yahweh was with him and how Yahweh made everything succeed that he turned his hand to, he was pleased with Joseph and made him his personal attendant; and his master put him in charge of his household, entrusting everything to him. And from the time he put him in charge of his household and all his possessions, Yahweh blessed the Egyptian's household out of consideration for Joseph; Yahweh's blessing extended to all his possessions, both household and estate. So he left Joseph to handle all his possessions, and with him at hand, concerned himself with nothing beyond the food he ate.

Now Joseph was well built and handsome, and it happened some time later that his master's wife looked desirously at him and said, "Sleep with me." But he refused, and answered his master's wife, "Because of me, my master does not concern himself with what happens in the house; he has handed over all his possessions to me. He is no more master in this house than I am. He has withheld nothing from me except yourself, because you are his wife. How could I do anything so wicked, and sin against God?" Although she spoke to Joseph day after day he would not agree to sleep with her and surrender to her.

---

6. Perez means "breaking out."

7. Zerah can mean "scarlet" or "brightness."

But one day Joseph in the course of his duties came to the house, and there was not a servant there indoors. The woman caught hold of him by his tunic and said, "Sleep with me." But he left the tunic in her hand and ran out of the house. Seeing he had left the tunic in her hand and left the house, she called her servants and said to them, "Look at this! He has brought us a Hebrew to insult us. He came to me to sleep with me, but I screamed, and when he heard me scream and shout he left his tunic beside me and ran out of the house."

She put the tunic down by her side until the master came home. Then she told him the same tale, "The Hebrew slave you bought us came to insult me. But when I screamed and called out he left his garment by my side and made his escape." When the master heard his wife say, "This is how your slave treated me," he was furious. Joseph's master had him arrested and committed to the jail where the king's prisoners were kept.

And there in jail he stayed. But Yahweh was with Joseph. He was kind to him and made him popular with the chief jailer. The chief jailer put Joseph in charge of all the prisoners in the jail, making him responsible for everything done there. The chief jailer did not need to interfere with Joseph's administration, for Yahweh was with him, and Yahweh made everything he undertook successful.

40

It happened some time later that the king of Egypt's cupbearer and his baker offended their master the king of Egypt. Pharaoh was angry with his two officials, the chief cupbearer and the chief baker, and put them under arrest in the house of the commander of the guard, in the jail where Joseph was a prisoner. The commander of the guard assigned Joseph to them to attend to their wants, and they remained under arrest for some time.

Now both of them had dreams on the same night, each with its own meaning for the cupbearer and the baker of the king of Egypt, who were prisoners in the jail. When Joseph came to them in the morning, he saw that they looked gloomy, and he asked the two officials who were with him under arrest in his master's house, "Why these black looks today?" They answered him, "We have had a dream, but there is no one to interpret it." "Are not interpretations God's business?" Joseph asked them. "Come, tell me."

So the chief cupbearer described his dream to Joseph, telling him, "In my dream I saw a vine in front of me. On the vine were three branches; no sooner had it budded than it blossomed, and its clusters became ripe grapes. I had Pharaoh's cup in my hand; I picked the grapes and squeezed them into Pharaoh's cup, and put the cup into Pharaoh's hand." "Here is the interpretation of it," Joseph told him. "The three branches are three days. In another three days Pharaoh will release you and restore you to your place. Then you will hand Pharaoh his cup, as you did before, when you were his cupbearer. But be sure to remember me when things go well with you, and do me the kindness of reminding Pharaoh about me, to get me out of this house. I was kidnaped from the land of the Hebrews in the first place, and even here I have done nothing to warrant imprisonment."

The chief baker, seeing that the interpretation had been favorable, said to

Joseph, "I too had a dream; there were three trays of cakes on my head. In the top tray there were all kinds of Pharaoh's favorite cakes, but the birds ate them off the tray on my head." Joseph gave him this answer. "Here is the interpretation of it: the three trays are three days. In another three days Pharaoh will release you and hang you on a gallows, and the birds will eat the flesh off your bones."

And so it happened; the third day was Pharaoh's birthday and he gave a banquet for all his officials, and he released the chief cupbearer and the chief baker in the presence of his officials. The chief cupbearer he restored to his position as cupbearer, to hand Pharaoh his cup; the chief baker he hanged. It was as Joseph had said in his interpretation. But the chief cupbearer did not remember Joseph: he forgot him.

41

Two years later it happened that Pharaoh had a dream: he was standing by the Nile, and there, coming up from the Nile, were seven cows, sleek and fat, and they began to feed among the rushes. And seven other cows, ugly and lean, came up from the Nile after them; and these went over and stood beside the other cows on the bank of the Nile. The ugly and lean cows ate the seven sleek and fat cows. Then Pharaoh awoke.

He fell asleep and dreamed a second time: there, growing on one stalk, were seven ears of corn full and ripe. And sprouting up after them came seven ears of corn, meager and scorched by the east wind. The scanty ears of corn swallowed the seven full and ripe ears of corn. Then Pharaoh awoke; it was a dream.

In the morning Pharaoh, feeling disturbed, had all the magicians and wise men of Egypt summoned to him. Pharaoh told them his dream, but no one could interpret it for Pharaoh. Then the chief cupbearer addressed Pharaoh, "Today I must recall my offenses. Pharaoh was angry with his servants and put myself and the chief baker under arrest in the house of the commander of the guard. We had a dream on the same night, he and I, and each man's dream had a meaning for himself. There was a young Hebrew with us, one of the slaves belonging to the commander of the guard. We told our dreams to him and he interpreted them, giving each of us the interpretation of his dream. It turned out just as he interpreted for us: I was restored to my place, but the other man was hanged."

Then Pharaoh had Joseph summoned, and they hurried him from prison. He shaved and changed his clothes, and came into Pharaoh's presence. Pharaoh said to Joseph, "I have had a dream which no one can interpret. But I have heard it said of you that when you hear a dream you can interpret it." Joseph answered Pharaoh, "I do not count. It is God who will give Pharaoh a favorable answer."

So Pharaoh told Joseph, "In my dream I was standing on the bank of the Nile. And there were seven cows, fat and sleek, coming up out of the Nile, and they began to feed among the rushes. And seven other cows came up after them, starved, ugly and lean; I have never seen such poor cows in all the land of Egypt. The lean and ugly cows ate up the seven fat cows. But when they had eaten them up, it was impossible to tell they had eaten them, for they remained as lean as before. Then I woke up. And then again in my dream, there, growing on one stalk, were seven ears of corn, beautifully ripe; but sprouting up after them came seven ears of corn, withered, meager and scorched by the east wind. The shriveled ears of corn swallowed the seven ripe ears of corn. I told the magicians this, but no one could tell me the meaning."

Joseph told Pharaoh, "Pharaoh's dreams are one and the same: God has revealed to Pharaoh what he is going to do. The seven fine cows are seven years and the seven ripe ears of corn are seven years; it is one and the same dream. The seven gaunt and lean cows coming up after them are seven years, as are the seven shriveled ears of corn scorched by the east wind: there will be seven years of famine. It is as I have told Pharaoh: God has revealed to Pharaoh what he is going to do. Seven years are coming, bringing great plenty to the whole land of Egypt, but seven years of famine will follow them, when all the plenty in the land of Egypt will be forgotten, and famine will exhaust the land. The famine that is to follow will be so very severe that no one will remember what plenty the country enjoyed. The reason why the dream came to Pharaoh twice is because the event is already determined by God, and God is impatient to bring it about.

"Pharaoh should now choose a man who is intelligent and wise to govern the land of Egypt. Pharaoh should take action and appoint supervisors over the land, and impose a tax of one fifth on the land of Egypt during the seven years of plenty. They will collect all food produced during these good years that are coming. They will store the corn in Pharaoh's name, and place the food in the towns and hold it there. This food will serve as a reserve for the land during the seven years of famine that will afflict the land of Egypt. And so the land will not be destroyed by the famine."

Pharaoh and all his ministers approved of what he had said. Then Pharaoh asked his ministers, "Can we find any other man like this, possessing the spirit of God?" So Pharaoh said to Joseph, "Seeing that God has given you knowledge of all this, there can be no one as intelligent and wise as you. You shall be my chancellor, and all my people shall respect your orders; only this throne shall set me above you." Pharaoh said to Joseph, "I hereby make you governor of the whole land of Egypt." Pharaoh took the ring from his hand and put it on Joseph's. He clothed him in fine linen and put a gold chain around his neck. He made him ride in the best chariot he had after his own, and they cried before him "Make way!" This is the way he was made governor of the whole land of Egypt.

Pharaoh said to Joseph, "I am Pharaoh: without your permission no one is to move hand or foot throughout the whole land of Egypt." Pharaoh named Joseph Zaphenath-paneah, and gave him Asenath the daughter of Potiphera, priest of On, for his wife.[8] Joseph traveled through the land of Egypt.

Joseph was thirty years old when he appeared before Pharaoh king of Egypt. After leaving Pharaoh's presence Joseph went through the whole land of Egypt. During the seven years of plenty, the soil yielded generously. He collected all the food of the seven years when there was an abundance in the land of Egypt, and

---

8. Joseph's assimilation into Egyptian society is to be sealed with the bestowal of an Egyptian name and a wife from a prominent priestly family.

allotted food to the towns, placing in each the food from the surrounding countryside. Joseph stored the corn like the sand of the sea, so much that they stopped reckoning, since it was beyond all estimating.

Before the year of famine came, two sons were born to Joseph: Asenath, the daughter of Potiphera priest of On, bore him these. Joseph named the first-born Manasseh, "Because," he said, "God has made me forget all my suffering and all my father's household."[9] He named the second Ephraim, "Because," he said, "God has made me fruitful in the country of my misfortune."[10]

Then the seven years of plenty that there had been in the land of Egypt came to an end. The seven years of famine began to come as Joseph had said. There was famine in every country, but there was bread to be had throughout the land of Egypt. When the whole country began to feel the famine, the people cried out to Pharaoh for bread. But Pharaoh told all the Egyptians, "Go to Joseph and do what he tells you."—There was famine all over the world.—Then Joseph opened all the granaries and sold grain to the Egyptians. The famine grew worse in the land of Egypt. People came to Egypt from all over the world to buy grain from Joseph, for the famine had grown severe throughout the world.

42   *Sold grain back during famine*

Jacob, seeing that there was grain for sale in Egypt, said to his sons, "Why do you stand looking at one another? I hear," he said, "that there is grain for sale in Egypt. Go down and buy grain for us there, that we may survive and not die." So ten of Joseph's brothers went down to buy grain in Egypt. But Jacob did not send Joseph's brother Benjamin with his brothers. "Nothing must happen to him," he said.[11]

Israel's sons with others making the same journey went to buy grain, for there was famine in the land of Canaan. It was Joseph, as the man in authority over the country, who sold the grain to all comers. So Joseph's brothers went and bowed down before him, their faces touching the ground. When Joseph saw his brothers he recognized them. But he did not make himself known to them, and he spoke harshly to them. "Where have you come from?" he asked. "From the land of Canaan to buy food," they replied.

So Joseph recognized his brothers, but they did not recognize him. Joseph, remembering the dreams he had had about them, said to them, "You are spies. You have come to discover the country's weak points." "No, my lord," they told him, "your servants have come to buy food. We are all sons of the same man. We are honest men, your servants are not spies." "Not so!" he replied. "It is the country's weak points you have come to discover." "Your servants are twelve brothers," they said, "sons of the same man, from the land of Canaan. The youngest, we should explain, is at present with our father, and the other one is no more." Joseph answered them, "It is as I said, you are spies. This is the test you are to undergo: as sure as Pharaoh lives you shall not leave unless your youngest

---

9. Manasseh sounds like the Hebrew for "forget."
10. Ephraim sounds like the Hebrew for "twice fruitful."

11. Benjamin, Jacob's youngest son, is Joseph's only full brother.

brother comes here. Send one of your number to fetch your brother; you others will remain under arrest, so that your statements can be tested to see whether or not you are honest. If not, then as sure as Pharaoh lives you are spies." Then he kept them all in custody for three days.

On the third day Joseph said to them, "Do this and you shall keep your lives, for I am a man who fears God. If you are honest men let one of your brothers be kept in the place of your detention; as for you, go and take grain to relieve the famine of your families. You shall bring me your youngest brother; this way your words will be proved true, and you will not have to die!" This they did. They said to one another, "Truly we are being called to account for our brother. We saw his misery of soul when he begged our mercy, but we did not listen to him and now this misery has come home to us." Reuben answered them, "Did I not tell you not to wrong the boy? But you did not listen, and now we are brought to account for his blood." They did not know that Joseph understood, because there was an interpreter between them. He left them and wept. Then he went back to them and spoke to them. Of their number he took Simeon and had him bound while they looked on.

Joseph gave the order to fill their panniers with corn, to put back each man's money in his sack, and to give them provisions for the journey. This was done for them. They loaded the grain on their donkeys and went away. But when they camped for the night one of them opened his corn sack to give fodder to his donkey and saw his money in the mouth of his sack. He said to his brothers, "My money has been put back; here it is in my corn sack." Their hearts sank, and they looked at one another in panic, saying, "What is this that God has done to us?"

Returning to their father Jacob in the land of Canaan, they gave him a full report of what had happened to them. "The man who is lord of the land spoke harshly to us, taking us for men spying on the country. We told him, 'We are honest men, we are not spies. We are twelve brothers, sons of the same father. One of us is no more, and the youngest is at present with our father in the land of Canaan.' But the man who is lord of the land said to us, 'This is how I shall know if you are honest: leave one of your brothers with me. Take the grain your families stand in need of, and go. But bring me back your youngest brother and then I shall know that you are not spies but honest men. Then I will hand over your brother to you, and you can trade in the country.'"

As they emptied their sacks, each discovered his bag of money in his sack. On seeing their bags of money they were afraid, and so was their father. Then their father Jacob said to them, "You are robbing me of my children; Joseph is no more; Simeon is no more; and now you want to take Benjamin. All this I must bear."

Then Reuben said to his father, "You may put my two sons to death if I do not bring him back to you. Put him in my care and I will bring him back to you." But he replied, "My son is not going down with you, for now his brother is dead he is the only one left. If any harm came to him on the journey you are to undertake, you would send me down to Sheol with my white head bowed in grief."

43

But the country was hard pressed by famine, and when they had finished eating the grain they had brought from Egypt their father said to them, "Go back and buy us a little food." "But the man expressly warned us," Judah told him. "He said, 'You will not be admitted to my presence unless your brother is with you.' If you are ready to send our brother with us, we are willing to go down and buy food for you. But if you are not ready to send him we will not go down, for the man told us, 'You will not be admitted to my presence unless your brother is with you.' " Then Israel said, "Why did you bring this misery on me by telling the man you had another brother?" They replied, "He kept questioning us about ourselves and our kinsfolk, 'Is your father still alive?' and, 'Have you a brother?' That is why we told him. How could we know he was going to say, 'Bring your brother down here?' " Judah said to his father Israel, "Send the boy with me. Let us start off and go, so that we may save our lives and not die, we, you, and our dependents. I will go surety for him, and you can hold me responsible for him. If I do not bring him back to you and set him before you, let me bear the blame all my life. Indeed, if we had not wasted so much time we should have been back again by now!"

Then their father Israel said to them, "If it must be so, then do this: take some of the land's finest products in your panniers, and carry them down to the man as a gift, a little balsam, a little honey, gum, tragacanth, resin, pistachio nuts and almonds. Take double the amount of money with you and return the money put back in the mouths of your sacks; it may have been a mistake. Take your brother, and go back to the man. May El Shaddai move the man to be kind to you, and allow you to bring back your other brother and Benjamin. As for me, if I must be bereaved, bereaved I must be."

The men took this gift; they took double the amount of money with them, and Benjamin. They started off and went down to Egypt. They presented themselves to Joseph. When Joseph saw Benjamin with them he said to his chamberlain, "Take these men to the house. Slaughter a beast and prepare it, for these men are to eat with me at midday." The man did as Joseph had ordered, and took the men to Joseph's house.

The men were afraid at being taken to Joseph's house, thinking, "We are being taken there because of the money replaced in our corn sacks the first time. They will set on us; they will fall on us and make slaves of us, and take our donkeys too." So they went up to Joseph's chamberlain and spoke to him at the entrance to the house. "By your leave, sir," they said, "we came down once before to buy food, and when we reached camp and opened our corn sacks, there was each man's money in the mouth of his sack, to its full amount. But we have brought it back with us, and we have brought more money with us to buy food. We do not know who put the money in our corn sacks." "Peace to you," he replied, "do not be afraid. Your God and your father's God has put a treasure in your corn sacks. Your money reached me safely." And he brought Simeon out to them.

The man took the men into Joseph's house. He offered them water to wash their feet, and gave their donkeys fodder. They arranged their gift while they waited for Joseph to come at midday, for they had heard they were to dine there.

When Joseph arrived at the house they offered him the gift they had with them, and bowed before him to the ground. But he greeted them kindly, asking, "Is your father well, the old man you told me of? Is he still alive?" "Your servant our father is well," they replied, "he is still alive," and they bowed low in homage.

Looking up he saw his brother Benjamin, his mother's son. "Is this your youngest brother," he asked, "of whom you told me?" Then he said to him, "God be good to you, my son." Joseph hurried out, for his heart was moved at the sight of his brother and he was near to weeping. He went into his room, and there he wept. After bathing his face he returned and, controlling himself, gave the order: "Serve the meal." He was served separately; so were they, and so were the Egyptians who ate in his household, for Egyptians cannot take food with Hebrews: they have a horror of it. They were placed opposite him each according to his rank, from the eldest to the youngest, and the men looked at one another in amazement. He had portions carried to them from his own dish, the portion for Benjamin being five times larger than any of the others. They drank with him and were happy.

44

Joseph gave this order to his chamberlain: "Fill these men's sacks with as much food as they can carry, and put each man's money in the mouth of his sack. And put my cup, the silver one, in the mouth of the youngest one's sack as well as the money for his grain." He carried out the instructions Joseph had given.

When morning came and it was light, the men were sent off with their donkeys. They had scarcely left the city, and had not gone far before Joseph said to his chamberlain, "Away now and follow those men. When you catch up with them say to them, 'Why did you reward good with evil? Is this not the one my lord uses for drinking and also for reading omens? What you have done is wrong.'"

So when he caught up with them he repeated these words. They asked him, "What does my lord mean? Your servants would never think of doing such a thing. Look, the money we found in the mouths of our corn sacks we brought back to you from the land of Canaan. Are we likely to have stolen the silver or gold from your master's house? Whichever of your servants is found to have it shall die, and we ourselves shall be slaves of my lord." "Very well, then," he replied, "it shall be as you say. The one on whom it is found shall become my slave, but the rest of you can go free." Each of them quickly lifted his corn sack to the ground, and each opened his own. He searched them, beginning with the eldest and ending with the youngest, and found the cup in Benjamin's sack. Then they tore their clothes, and when each man had reloaded his ass they returned to the city.

When Judah and his brothers arrived at Joseph's house he was still there, so they fell on the ground in front of him. "What is this deed you have done?" Joseph asked them. "Did you not know that a man such as I am is a reader of omens?" "What can we answer my lord?" Judah replied. "What can we say? How can we clear ourselves? God himself has uncovered your servants' guilt. Here we are then, my lord's slaves, we no less than the one in whose possession the cup was found." "I could not think of doing such a thing," he replied. "The man in whose possession the cup was found shall be my slave, but you can go back safe and sound to your father."

Then Judah went up to him and said, "May it please my lord, let your servant have a word privately with my lord. Do not be angry with your servant, for you are like Pharaoh himself. My lord questioned his servants, 'Have you father or brother?' And we said to my lord, 'We have an old father, and a younger brother born of his old age. His brother is dead, so he is the only one left of his mother, and his father loves him.' Then you said to your servants, 'Bring him down to me that my eyes may look on him.' We replied to my lord, 'The boy cannot leave his father. If he leaves him, his father will die.' But you said to your servants, 'If your youngest brother does not come down with you, you will not be admitted to my presence again.' When we went back to your servant my father, we repeated to him what my lord had said. So when our father said, 'Go back and buy us a little food,' we said, 'We cannot go down. If our youngest brother is with us, we will go down, for we cannot be admitted to the man's presence unless our youngest brother is with us.' So your servant our father said to us, 'You know that my wife bore me two children. When one left me, I said that he must have been torn to pieces. And I have not seen him to this day. If you take this one from me too and any harm comes to him, you will send me down to Sheol with my white head bowed in misery.' If I go to your servant my father now, and we have not the boy with us, he will die as soon as he sees the boy is not with us, for his heart is bound up with him. Then your servants will have sent your servant our father down to Sheol with his white head bowed in grief. Now your servant went surety to my father for the boy. I said: If I do not bring him back to you, let me bear the blame before my father all my life. Let your servant stay, then, as my lord's slave in place of the boy, I implore you, let the boy go back with his brothers. How indeed could I go back to my father and not have the boy with me? I could not bear to see the misery that would overwhelm my father."

45

Then Joseph could not control his feelings in front of all his retainers, and he exclaimed, "Let everyone leave me." No one therefore was present with him while Joseph made himself known to his brothers, but he wept so loudly that all the Egyptians heard, and the news reached Pharaoh's palace.

Joseph said to his brothers, "I am Joseph. Is my father really still alive?" His brothers could not answer him, they were so dismayed at the sight of him. Then Joseph said to his brothers, "Come closer to me." When they had come closer to him he said, "I am your brother Joseph whom you sold into Egypt. But now, do not grieve, do not reproach yourselves for having sold me here, since God sent me before you to preserve your lives. For this is the second year there has been famine in the country, and there are still five years to come of no plowing or reaping. God sent me before you to make sure that your race would have survivors in the land and to save your lives, many lives at that. So it was not you who sent me here but God, and he has made me father to Pharaoh, lord of all his household and administrator of the whole land of Egypt.

"Return quickly to your father and tell him, 'Your son Joseph says this: God has made me lord of all Egypt. Come down to me at once. You shall live in the country of Goshen[12] where you will be near me, you, your children and your

---

12. An area of grazing land in the Nile delta.

grandchildren, your flocks, your cattle and all your possessions. I will provide for you there, for there are still five years of famine, and I do not want you to be in need, you and your household and all you have.' You can see with your own eyes, and my brother Benjamin can see too that it is my own mouth speaking to you. Give my father a full report of all the honor I enjoy in Egypt, and of all you have seen. Then hurry and bring my father down here."

Then throwing his arms around the neck of his brother Benjamin he wept; and Benjamin wept on his shoulder. He kissed all his brothers, weeping over them. After which his brothers talked with him.

News reached Pharaoh's palace that Joseph's brothers had come, and Pharaoh was pleased to hear it, as were his servants. Pharaoh told Joseph, "Say to your brothers, 'Do this: load your beasts and go off to the land of Canaan. Fetch your father and families, and come back to me. I will give you the best the land of Egypt offers, and you shall feed on the fat of the land.' And you, for your part, give them this command: 'Do this: take wagons from the land of Egypt, for your little ones and your wives. Get your father and come. Never mind about your property, for the best that the land of Egypt offers is yours.'"

Israel's sons did as they were told. Joseph gave them wagons as Pharaoh had ordered, and he gave them provisions for the journey. To each and every one he gave a festal garment, and to Benjamin three hundred shekels of silver and five festal garments. And he sent his father ten donkeys laden with the best that Egypt offered, and ten she-donkeys laden with grain, bread and food for his father's journey. Then he sent his brothers on their way. His final words to them were, "Do not be upset on the journey."

And so they left Egypt. When they reached the land of Canaan and their father Jacob, they gave him this report, "Joseph is still alive. Indeed it is he who is administrator of the whole land of Egypt." But he was as one stunned, for he did not believe them. However, when they told him all Joseph had said to them, and when he saw the wagons that Joseph had sent to fetch him, the spirit of their father Jacob revived, and Israel said, "That is enough! My son Joseph is still alive. I must go and see him before I die."

46

Israel left with his possessions, and reached Beersheba. There he offered sacrifices to the God of his father Isaac. God spoke to Israel in a vision at night, "Jacob, Jacob," he said. "I am here," he replied. "I am God, the God of your father," he continued. "Do not be afraid of going down to Egypt, for I will make you a great nation there. I myself will go down to Egypt with you. I myself will bring you back again, and Joseph's hand shall close your eyes." Then Jacob left Beersheba. Israel's sons conveyed their father Jacob, their little children and their wives in the wagons Pharaoh had sent to fetch him.

Taking their livestock and all that they had acquired in the land of Canaan, they went to Egypt, Jacob and all his family with him: his sons and his grandsons, his daughters and his granddaughters, in a word, all his children he took with him to Egypt.

These are the names of Israel's sons who came to Egypt,[13] Reuben, Jacob's first-born, and the sons of Reuben: Hanoch, Pallu, Hezron, Carmi. The sons of Simeon: Jemuel, Jamin, Ohad, Jachin, Zohar, and Shaul the son of the Canaanite woman. The sons of Levi: Gershon, Kohath, Merari. The sons of Judah: Er, Onan, Shelah, Perez, and Zerah (though Er and Onan died in the land of Canaan), and Hezron and Hamul, sons of Perez. The sons of Issachar: Tola, Puvah, Jashub and Shimron. The sons of Zebulun: Sered, Elon, Jahleel. These are the sons that Leah had born to Jacob in Paddan-aram, besides his daughter Dinah; in all, his sons and daughters numbered thirty-three.

The sons of Gad: Ziphion, Haggi, Shuni, Ezbon, Eri, Arodi, and Areli. The sons of Asher: Imnah, Ishvah, Ishvi, Beriah, with their sister Serah; the sons of Beriah: Heber and Malchiel. These are the sons of Zilpah whom Laban gave to his daughter Leah; she bore these to Jacob—sixteen persons.

The sons of Rachel, wife of Jacob: Joseph and Benjamin. Born to Joseph in Egypt were: Manasseh and Ephraim, children of Asenath, the daughter of Potiphera priest of On. The sons of Benjamin: Bela, Becher, Ashbel, Gera, Naaman, Ehi, Rosh, Muppim, Huppim and Ard. These are the sons that Rachel bore to Jacob—fourteen persons in all.

The sons of Dan: Hushim. The sons of Naphtali: Jahzeel, Guni, Jezer and Shillem. These are the sons of Bilhah whom Laban gave to his daughter Rachel; she bore these to Jacob—seven persons in all.

The people who went to Egypt with Jacob, of his own blood and not counting the wives of Jacob's sons, numbered sixty-six all told. Joseph's sons born to him in Egypt were two in number. The members of the family of Jacob who went to Egypt totaled seventy.

Israel sent Judah ahead to Joseph, so that the latter might present himself to him in Goshen. When they arrived in the land of Goshen, Joseph had his chariot made ready and went up to meet his father Israel in Goshen. As soon as he appeared he threw his arms around his neck and for a long time wept on his shoulder. Israel said to Joseph, "Now I can die, now that I have seen you again, and seen you still alive."

Then Joseph said to his brothers and his father's family, "I will go up and break the news to Pharaoh. I will tell him, 'My brothers and my father's family who were in the land of Canaan have come to me. The men are shepherds and look after livestock, and they have brought their flocks and cattle and all their possessions.' Thus, when Pharaoh summons you and asks, 'What is your occupation?', you are to say, 'Ever since our boyhood your servants have looked after livestock, we and our fathers before us.' And so you will be able to stay in the land of Goshen." For the Egyptians have a horror of all shepherds.

---

13. The text lists all the children of Joseph and
his brothers—the founders of the twelve
tribes of Israel.

47

So Joseph went and told Pharaoh, "My father and brothers, along with their flocks and cattle and all their possessions, have come from the land of Canaan and are now in the land of Goshen." He had taken five of his brothers, and he now presented them to Pharaoh. Pharaoh asked his brothers, "What is your occupation?" and they gave Pharaoh the answer, "Your servants are shepherds, like our fathers before us." They went on to tell Pharaoh, "We have come to stay for the present in this land, for there is no pasture for your servants' flocks, the land of Canaan is hard pressed by famine. Now give your servants leave to stay in the land of Goshen." Then Pharaoh said to Joseph, "They may stay in the land of Goshen, and if you know of any capable men among them, put them in charge of my own livestock."

Jacob and his sons went to Egypt where Joseph was. Pharaoh, king of Egypt, heard of this and said to Joseph, "Your father and brothers have come to you. The country of Egypt is open to you: settle your father and brothers in the best region." Joseph brought his father and presented him to Pharaoh. Jacob blessed Pharaoh. Pharaoh asked Jacob, "How many years of life can you reckon?" "My life of wandering has lasted one hundred and thirty years," Jacob told Pharaoh, "few years and unhappy, falling short of the years of my fathers in their life of wandering." Jacob blessed Pharaoh and left Pharaoh's presence. Joseph settled his father and brothers, giving them a holding in the land of Egypt, and in the best region of the land, namely the land of Rameses, according to Pharaoh's command.

Joseph provided his father, brothers and all his father's family with food according to the number of their dependents.

There was no bread in the whole land, for the famine had grown so severe that the land of Egypt and the land of Canaan were weakened with hunger. Joseph accumulated all the money there was to be found in the land of Egypt and in the land of Canaan, in return for the grain which men were buying, and he brought the money to Pharaoh's palace.

When all the money in the land of Egypt and in the land of Canaan had run out, the Egyptians all came to Joseph: "Give us bread," they said. "Have we to perish before your eyes? For our money has come to an end." Joseph answered, "Hand over your livestock; I am willing to give you bread in exchange for your livestock, if your money has come to an end." So they brought their livestock to Joseph, and Joseph gave them bread, in exchange for horses and livestock, whether sheep or cattle, and for donkeys. Thus he fed them that year with bread, in exchange for all their livestock.

When that year was over, they came to him the next year, and said to him, "We cannot hide it from my lord: the truth is, our money has run out and the livestock is in my lord's possession. There is nothing left for my lord except our bodies and our land. Have we to perish before your eyes, we and our land? Buy us and our land in exchange for bread; we with our land will be Pharaoh's serfs. But give us something to sow, that we may keep our lives and not die and the land may not become desolate."

Thus Joseph acquired all the land in Egypt for Pharaoh, since one by one the Egyptians sold their estates, so hard pressed were they by the famine, and the whole country passed into Pharaoh's possession.[14] As for the people, he reduced them to serfdom from one end of Egypt to the other. The only land he did not acquire belonged to the priests, for the priests received an allowance from Pharaoh and lived on the allowance that Pharaoh gave them. Therefore they did not have to sell their land.

Then Joseph said to the people, "This is how we stand: I have bought you out, with your land, on Pharaoh's behalf. Here is seed for you so that you can sow the land. But when harvest comes you must give a fifth to Pharaoh. The other four fifths you can have for sowing your fields, to provide food for yourselves and your households, and food for your dependents." "You have saved our lives," they replied. "If we may enjoy my lord's favor, we will be Pharaoh's serfs." So Joseph made a statute, still in force today, concerning the soil of Egypt: a fifth goes to Pharaoh. The land of the priests alone did not go to Pharaoh.

The Israelites stayed in the land of Egypt, in the country of Goshen. They acquired property there; they were fruitful and increased in numbers greatly. Jacob lived seventeen years in the land of Egypt, and the length of his life was a hundred and forty-seven years. When Israel's time to die drew near he called his son Joseph and said to him, "If I enjoy your favor, place your hand under my thigh and promise to be kind and good to me, do not bury me in Egypt. When I sleep with my fathers, carry me out of Egypt and bury me in their tomb." "I will do as you say," he replied. "Swear to me," he insisted. So he swore to him, and Israel sank back on the pillow.

48

Some time later it was reported to Joseph, "Your father has been taken ill." So he took with him his two sons Manasseh and Ephraim. When Jacob was told, "Look, your son Joseph has come to you," Israel, summoning his strength, sat up in bed. "El Shaddai appeared to me at Luz in the country of Canaan," Jacob told Joseph, "and he blessed me, saying to me, 'I will make you fruitful and increase you in numbers. I will make you a group of peoples and give this country to your descendants after you, to own in perpetuity.' Now your two sons, born to you in the land of Egypt before I came to you in Egypt, shall be mine; Ephraim and Manasseh shall be as much mine as Reuben and Simeon. But with regard to the children you have had since them, they shall be yours, and they shall be known by their brothers' names for the purpose of their inheritance.

"When I was on my way from Paddan,[15] to my sorrow death took your mother Rachel[16] from me, in the land of Canaan, on the journey while we were

---

14. The writer uses the story of the famine to account for the fact that, in the feudal Egyptian system, all land except for religious property was considered to be owned by the king.

15. Northwest Mesopotamia.
16. Mother of Joseph and Benjamin.

still some distance from Ephrath. I buried her there on the road to Ephrath at Bethlehem."

When Israel saw Joseph's two sons, he asked, "Who are these?" "They are my sons, whom God has given me here," Joseph told his father. "Then bring them to me," he said, "that I may bless them." Israel's sight was failing because of his great age, and so he could not see. Joseph therefore made them come closer to him and he kissed and embraced them. Then Israel said Joseph, "I did not think that I should see you again, but God has let me see your family as well." Joseph took them from his lap and bowed to the ground.

Joseph took hold of the two of them, Ephraim with his right hand so that he should be on Israel's left, and Manasseh with his left hand, so that he should be on Israel's right, and brought them close to him. But Israel held out his right hand and laid it on the head of Ephraim, the younger, and his left on the head of Manasseh, crossing his hands—Manasseh was, in fact, the elder.[17] Then he blessed Joseph saying:

> "May God in whose presence my fathers Abraham and Isaac walked,
> may God who has been my shepherd from my birth until this day,
> may the angel who has been my savior from all harm, bless these boys,
> may my name live on in them, and the names of my fathers Abraham and Isaac.
> May they grow and increase on the earth."

Joseph saw that his father was laying his right hand on the head of Ephraim, and this upset him. He took his father's hand and tried to shift it from the head of Ephraim to the head of Manasseh. Joseph protested to his father, "Not like that, father! This one is the elder; put your right hand on his head." But his father refused. "I know, my son, I know," he said. "He too shall become a people; he too shall be great. Yet his younger brother shall be greater than he, and his descendants shall become a multitude of nations."

So he blessed them that day saying:

> "May you be a blessing in Israel; may they say,
> 'God make you like Ephraim and Manasseh!' "

In this way he put Ephraim before Manasseh.

Then Israel said to Joseph, "Now I am about to die. But God will be with you and take you back to the country of your fathers. As for me, I give you a Shechem more than your brothers, the one I took from the Amorites with my sword and my bow."

49

Jacob called his sons and said, "Gather together that I may declare to you what lies before you in time to come.

---

17. This scene recalls an earlier episode in which Jacob himself tricked his blind father Isaac into giving him the blessing meant for his brother Esau (Genesis 27).

[The body of Chapter 49, omitted here, is an independent account of Jacob's final words to his sons, characterizing the natures of the different tribes of Israel.]

He blessed them, giving to each one an appropriate blessing.

Then he gave them these instructions, "I am about to be gathered to my people. Bury me near my fathers, in the cave that is in the field of Ephron the Hittite, in the cave in the field at Machpelah, opposite Mamre, in the land of Canaan, which Abraham bought from Ephron the Hittite as a burial plot. There Abraham was buried and his wife Sarah. There Isaac was buried and his wife Rebekah. There I buried Leah.[18] I mean the field and the cave in it that were bought from the sons of Heth."

When Jacob had finished giving his instructions to his sons, he drew his feet up into the bed, and breathing his last was gathered to his people.

50

At this, Joseph threw himself on his father, covering his face with tears and kissing him. Then Joseph ordered the doctors in his service to embalm his father. The doctors embalmed Israel, and it took them forty days, for embalming takes forty days to complete.

The Egyptians mourned him for seventy days. When the period of mourning for him was over, Joseph said to Pharaoh's household, "If I may presume to enjoy your favor, please see that this message reaches Pharaoh's ears, 'My father made me swear an oath: I am about to die, he said, I have a tomb which I dug for myself in the land of Canaan, and there you must bury me. So now I seek leave to go up and bury my father, and then I shall come back.'" Pharaoh replied, "Go up and bury your father, in accordance with the oath he made you swear."

Joseph went up to bury his father, all Pharaoh's servants and the palace dignitaries going up with him, joined by all the dignitaries of the land of Egypt, as well as all Joseph's family and his brothers, along with his father's family. They left no one in the land of Goshen but their dependents, with their flocks and their cattle. Chariots also and horsemen went up with them; it was a very large retinue. On arriving at Goren-ha-atad, which is across the Jordan, they performed there a long and solemn lamentation, and Joseph observed three days' mourning for his father. When the Canaanites, the inhabitants of the land, witnessed the mourning at Goren-ha-atad they exclaimed, "This is a solemn act of mourning for the Egyptians." For this reason they call this place Abel-mizraim[19]—it is across the Jordan.

His sons did what he had ordered them to do for him. His sons carried him to the land of Canaan and buried him in the cave in the field at Machpelah opposite Mamre, which Abraham had bought from Ephron the Hittite as a burial plot.

Then Joseph returned to Egypt, he and his brothers, along with all those who had come up with him for his father's burial.

Seeing that their father was dead, Joseph's brothers said, "What if Joseph

---

18. Jacob's first wife, Rachel's older sister.   19. "Mourning for the Egyptians."

intends to treat us as enemies and repay us in full for all the wrong we did him?"
So they sent this message to Joseph: "Before your father died he gave us this order:
'You must say to Joseph: Oh forgive your brothers their crime and their sin and all
the wrong they did you.' Now therefore, we beg you, forgive the crime of the
servants of your father's God." Joseph wept at the message they sent to him.

His brothers came themselves and fell down before him. "We present
ourselves before you," they said, "as your slaves." But Joseph answered them, "Do
not be afraid; is it for me to put myself in God's place? The evil you planned to do
me has by God's design been turned to good, that he might bring about, as indeed
he has, the deliverance of a numerous people. So you need not be afraid; I myself
will provide for you and your dependents." In this way he reassured them with
words that touched their hearts.

So Joseph stayed in Egypt with his father's family; and Joseph lived a hundred
and ten years. Joseph saw the third generation of Ephraim's children, as also the
children of Machir, Manasseh's son, who were born on Joseph's lap. At length
Joseph said to his brothers, "I am about to die; but God will be sure to remember
you kindly and take you back from this country to the land that he promised on
oath to Abraham, Isaac and Jacob." And Joseph made Israel's sons swear an oath,
"When God remembers you with kindness be sure to take my bones from here."

Joseph died at the age of a hundred and ten; they embalmed him and laid him
in his coffin in Egypt.

HERODOTUS (c. 485–c. 425 B.C.E.)
Greece

Ancient historiography originates with Herodotus's account of the wars between
Persia and Greece. In his introduction, Herodotus describes the history he has
written as the "exposition of his researches" in order to emphasize that, in
gathering information, he has relied above all on empirical observation and that
his historical method, unlike that of the mythologizing chronicles of his
predecessors, is based on the critical evaluation of evidence. In the course of his
investigations into the causes of Persian imperialism, Herodotus traveled widely
to (among other places) Egypt, Phoenicia, Mesopotamia, and Scythia, including
in his work detailed ethnographic reports on many nations with whom the
Persians had contact,—from Lydia and Babylon to Egypt, India and others. His
account serves to document at the same time the pervasive and profound
influences of the Eastern world on Greek life and thought.

Fundamental to Herodotus's narrative is his belief in a continuous cycle in
human affairs, in which prosperity and decline alternate perpetually through
every nation's history. This cycle, as Herodotus sees it, is an expression of divine
justice, which exacts retribution for the unjust acquisition of power. As in the
case of Croesus—whose eventual downfall was traced back five generations to an
ancestor who usurped the Lydian throne by killing the king—retribution may

come late, but it comes inevitably. Herodotus recounts that, years after the meeting described in this selection, Croesus was disastrously defeated and captured by the Persian king Cyrus; as he was about to be put to death, Croesus called out the name of Solon, remembering his wise words about the transience of happiness.

from *The Histories*

The Story of Solon and Croesus

When all these nations had been added to the Lydian empire,[1] and Sardis[2] was at the height of her wealth and prosperity, all the great Greek teachers of that epoch, one after another, paid visits to the capital. Much the most distinguished of them was Solon the Athenian,[3] the man who at the request if his countrymen had made a code of laws for Athens. He was on his travels at the time, intending to be away ten years, in order to avoid the necessity of repealing any of the laws he had made. That, at any rate, was the real reason of his absence, though he gave it out that what he wanted was just to see the world. The Athenians could not alter any of Solon's laws without him, because they had solemnly sworn to give them a ten years' trial.

For this reason, then—and also no doubt for the pleasure of foreign travel—Solon left home and, after a visit to the court of Amasis[4] in Egypt, went to Sardis to see Croesus.

Croesus entertained him hospitably in the palace, and three or four days after his arrival instructed some servants to take him on a tour of the royal treasuries and point out the richness and magnificence of everything. When Solon had made as thorough an inspection as opportunity allowed, Croesus said: " 'Well, my Athenian friend, I have heard a great deal about your wisdom, and how widely you have travelled in the pursuit of knowledge. I cannot resist my desire to ask you a question: who is the happiest man you have ever seen?' "

The point of the question was that Croesus supposed himself to be the happiest of men. Solon, however, refused to flatter, and answered in strict accordance with his view of the truth. "An Athenian," he said, "called Tellus."[5]

Croesus was taken aback. "And what," he asked sharply, "is your reason for this choice?"

"There are two good reasons," said Solon, "first, his city was prosperous, and he had fine sons, and lived to see children born to each of them, and all these

Translated by Aubrey de Selincourt.

1. Lydia, under the rule of Croesus in the mid-sixth century B.C.E., was the most powerful kingdom in Asia Minor until its defeat by Persia in 546 B.C.E.
2. Sardis was the capital city of Lydia.
3. The Athenian lawgiver (born c. 640 B.C.E.), whose poetry is presented earlier in this section. It is unlikely, for reasons of chronology, that Solon and Croesus ever actually met, but both were so renowned that Herodotus could use the contrast between them to illustrate an ethical point.
4. King of Egypt.
5. Solon uses the name of a typical Athenian citizen.

children surviving; and, secondly, after a life which by our standards was a good one, he had a glorious death. In a battle with the neighbouring town of Eleusis, he fought for his countrymen, routed the enemy, and died like a soldier; and the Athenians paid him the high honour of a public funeral on the spot where he fell."

All these details about the happiness of Tellus, Solon doubtless intended as a moral lesson for the king; Croesus, however, thinking he would at least be awarded second prize, asked who was the next happiest person whom Solon had seen.

"Two young men of Argos," was the reply; "Cleobis and Biton. They had enough to live on comfortably; and their physical strength is proved not merely by their success in athletics, but much more by the following incident. The Argives were celebrating the festival of Hera, and it was most important that the mother of the two young men should drive to the temple in her ox-cart; but it so happened that the oxen were late in coming back from the fields. Her two sons therefore, as there was no time to lose, harnessed themselves to the cart and dragged it along, with their mother inside, for a distance of nearly six miles, until they reached the temple. After this exploit, which was witnessed by the assembled crowd, they had a most enviable death—a heaven-sent proof of how much better it is to be dead than alive. Men kept crowding round them and congratulating them on their strength, and women kept telling the mother how lucky she was to have such sons, when, in sheer pleasure at this public recognition of her sons' act, she prayed the goddess Hera, before whose shrine she stood, to grant Cleobis and Biton, who had brought her such honour, the greatest blessing that can fall to mortal man.

"After her prayer came the ceremonies of sacrifice and feasting; and the two lads, when all was over, fell asleep in the temple—and that was the end of them, for they never woke again.

"The Argives had statues made of them, which they sent to Delphi[6] as a mark of their particular respect."

Croesus was vexed with Solon for giving the second prize for happiness to the two young Argives, and snapped out: "That's all very well, my Athenian friend; but what of my own happiness? Is it so utterly contemptible that you won't even compare me with mere common folk like those you have mentioned?"

"My lord," replied Solon, "I know God is envious of human prosperity and likes to trouble us; and you question me about the lot of man. Listen then: as the years lengthen out, there is much both to see and to suffer which one would wish otherwise. Take seventy years as the span of a man's life: those seventy years contain 25,200 days, without counting intercalary months. Add a month every other year, to make the seasons come round with proper regularity, and you will have thirty-five additional months, which will make 1,050 additional days. Thus the total of days for your seventy years is 26,250, and not a single one of them is like the next in what it brings. You can see from that, Croesus, what a chancy thing

---

6. Delphi was the most important religious
   site in Greece, located on the mainland
   above the Gulf of Corinth.

life is. You are very rich, and you rule a numerous people; but the question you asked me I will not answer, until I know that you have died happily. Great wealth can make a man no happier than moderate means, unless he has the luck to continue in prosperity to the end. Many very rich men have been unfortunate, and many with a modest competence have had good luck. The former are better off than the latter in two respects only, whereas the poor but lucky man has the advantage in many ways; for though the rich have the means to satisfy their appetites and to bear calamities, and the poor have not, the poor, if they are lucky, are more likely to keep clear of trouble, and will have besides the blessings of a sound body, health, freedom from trouble, fine children, and good looks.

"Now if a man thus favoured dies as he has lived, he will be just the one you are looking for: the only sort of person who deserves to be called happy. But mark this: until he is dead, keep the word 'happy' in reserve. Till then, he is not happy, but only lucky.

"Nobody of course can have all these advantages, any more than a country can produce everything it needs: whatever it has, it is bound to lack something. The best country is the one which has most. It is the same with people: no man is ever self-sufficient—there is sure to be something missing. But whoever has the greatest number of the good things I have mentioned, and keeps them to the end, and dies a peaceful death, that man, my lord Croesus, deserves in my opinion to be called happy.

"Look to the end, no matter what it is you are considering. Often enough God gives a man a glimpse of happiness, and then utterly ruins him."

These sentiments were not of the sort to give Croesus any pleasure; he let Solon go with cold indifference, firmly convinced that he was a fool. For what could be more stupid than to keep telling him to look at the "end" of everything, without any regard to present prosperity?

After Solon's departure Croesus was dreadfully punished, presumably because God was angry with him for supposing himself the happiest of men.

[Croesus lived to witness his country's defeat and the capture of Sardis by the Persians under their king, Cyrus, in 546 B.C.E. As he was on the point of being put to death, he invoked the name of Solon. Upon explaining to Cyrus the lesson that Solon had tried to teach him, Croesus was pardoned by Cyrus and his life spared.]

THE BIBLE (AFTER 538 B.C.E.)
Palestine

The biblical Book of Ruth is set in the days of Judges, an era that preceded the establishment of the Hebrew monarchy in the late eleventh century B.C.E. It was probably composed much later, however, most likely after the Israelites returned from exile in Babylon around 538 B.C.E.

On the death of her husband, Ruth chooses to return to Bethlehem in Judah with her Hebrew mother-in-law, Naomi; she will share the fortunes of her new family rather than stay with her own people in the land of Moab. The relationship between Ruth and Naomi is one of the most beautiful in biblical literature. The sympathetic portrayal of the Moabite Ruth suggests that the story may have been meant to combat fifth- and fourth-century decrees requiring Hebrew men to divorce their foreign wives and marry only within the covenant community.

from *The Bible*

The Book of Ruth

In the days when the judges ruled, there was a famine in the land, and a man from Bethlehem in Judah, together with his wife and two sons, went to live for a while in the country of Moab.[1] The man's name was Elimelech, his wife's name Naomi, and the names of his two sons were Mahlon and Kilion. They were Ephrathites from Bethlehem in Judah. And they went to Moab and lived there.

Now Elimelech, Naomi's husband, died, and she was left with her two sons. They married Moabite women, one named Orpah and the other Ruth. After they had lived there about ten years, both Mahlon and Kilion also died, and Naomi was left without her two sons and her husband.

When she heard in Moab that the LORD had come to the aid of his people by providing food for them, Naomi and her daughters-in-law prepared to return home from there. With her two daughters-in-law she left the place where she had been living and set out on the road that would take them back to the land of Judah.

Then Naomi said to her two daughters-in-law, "Go back, each of you, to your mother's home. May the LORD show kindness to you, as you have shown to your dead and to me. May the LORD grant that each of you will find rest in the home of another husband."

Then she kissed them and they wept aloud and said to her, "We will go back with you to your people."

But Naomi said, "Return home, my daughters. Why would you come with me? Am I going to have any more sons, who could become your husbands? Return home, my daughters; I am too old to have another husband. Even if I thought there was still hope for me—even if I had a husband tonight and then gave birth to sons—would you wait until they grew up? Would you remain unmarried for them? No, my daughters. It is more bitter for me than for you, because the LORD's hand has gone out against me!"

At this they wept again. Then Orpah kissed her mother-in-law good-by, but Ruth clung to her.

New International Version translation.

---

1. The Moabites, east of the Dead Sea, were often enemies of the Israelites.

"Look," said Naomi, "your sister-in-law is going back to her people and her gods. Go back with her."

But Ruth replied, "Don't urge me to leave you or to turn back from you. Where you go I will go, and where you stay I will stay. Your people will be my people and your God my God. Where you die I will die, and there I will be buried. May the LORD deal with me, be it ever so severely, if anything but death separates you and me." When Naomi realized that Ruth was determined to go with her, she stopped urging her.

So the two of them went on until they came to Bethlehem. When they arrived in Bethlehem, the whole town was stirred because of them, and the women exclaimed, "Can this be Naomi?"

"Don't call me Naomi," she told them. "Call me Mara,[2] because the Almighty has made my life very bitter. I went away full, but the LORD has brought me back empty. Why call me Naomi? The LORD has afflicted me; the Almighty has brought misfortune upon me."

So Naomi returned from Moab accompanied by Ruth the Moabitess, her daughter-in-law, arriving in Bethlehem as the barley harvest was beginning.

Now Naomi had a relative on her husband's side, from the clan of Elimelech, a man of standing, whose name was Boaz.

And Ruth the Moabitess said to Naomi, "Let me go to the fields and pick up the leftover grain behind anyone in whose eyes I find favor."

Naomi said to her, "Go ahead, my daughter." So she went out and began to glean in the fields behind the harvesters. As it turned out, she found herself working in a field belonging to Boaz, who was from the clan of Elimelech.

Just then Boaz arrived from Bethlehem and greeted the harvesters, "The LORD be with you!"

"The LORD bless you!" they called back.

Boaz asked the foreman of his harvesters, "Whose young woman is that?"

The foreman replied, "She is the Moabitess who came back from Moab with Naomi. She said, 'Please let me glean and gather among the sheaves behind the harvesters.' She went into the field and has worked steadily from morning till now, except for a short rest in the shelter."

So Boaz said to Ruth, "My daughter, listen to me. Don't go and glean in another field and don't go away from here. Stay here with my servant girls. Watch the field where the men are harvesting, and follow along after the girls. I have told the men not to touch you. And whenever you are thirsty, go and get a drink from the water jars the men have filled."

At this, she bowed down with her face to the ground. She exclaimed, "Why have I found such favor in your eyes that you notice me—a foreigner?"

Boaz replied, "I've been told all about what you have done for your mother-in-law since the death of your husband—how you left your father and mother and your homeland and came to live with a people you did not know

---

2. "Bitter."

before May the LORD repay you for what you have done. May you be richly rewarded by the LORD, the God of Israel, under whose wings you have come to take refuge."

"May I continue to find favor in your eyes, my lord," she said. "You have given me comfort and have spoken kindly to your servant—though I do not have the standing of one of your servant girls."

At mealtime Boaz said to her, "Come over here. Have some bread and dip it in the wine vinegar."

When she sat down with the harvesters, he offered her some roasted grain. She ate all she wanted and had some left over. As she got up to glean, Boaz gave orders to his men, "Even if she gathers among the sheaves, don't embarrass her. Rather, pull out some stalks for her from the bundles and leave them for her to pick up, and don't rebuke her."

So Ruth gleaned in the field until evening. Then she threshed the barley she had gathered, and it amounted to about half a bushel. She carried it back to town, and her mother-in-law saw how much she had gathered. Ruth also brought out and gave her what she had left over after she had eaten enough.

Her mother-in-law asked her, "Where did you glean today? Where did you work? Blessed be the man who took notice of you!"

Then Ruth told her mother-in-law about the one at whose place she had been working. "The name of the man I worked with today is Boaz," she said.

"The LORD bless him," Naomi said to her daughter-in-law. "The LORD has not stopped showing his kindness to the living and the dead." She added, "That man is our close relative; he is one of our next of kin."

Then Ruth the Moabitess said, "He even said to me, 'Stay with my workers until they finish harvesting all my grain.'"

Naomi said to Ruth her daughter-in-law, "It will be good for you, my daughter, to go with his girls, because in someone else's field you might be harmed."

So Ruth stayed close to the servant girls of Boaz to glean until the barley and wheat harvests were finished. And she lived with her mother-in-law.

One day Naomi her mother-in-law said to her, "My daughter, should I not try to find a home for you, where you will be well provided for? Is not Boaz, with whose servant girls you have been, a kinsman of ours? Tonight he will be winnowing barley on the threshing floor. Wash and perfume yourself, and put on your best clothes. Then go down to the threshing floor, but don't let him know you are there until he has finished eating and drinking. When he lies down, note the place where he is lying. Then go and uncover his feet and lie down. He will tell you what to do."

"I will do whatever you say," Ruth answered. So she went down to the threshing floor and did everything her mother-in-law told her to do.

When Boaz had finished eating and drinking and was in good spirits, he went over to lie down at the far end of the grain pile. Ruth approached quietly, uncovered his feet and lay down. In the middle of the night something startled the man, and he turned and discovered a woman lying at his feet.

"Who are you?" he asked.

"I am your servant Ruth," she said. "Spread the corner of your garment over me, since you are my next of kin."[3]

"The LORD bless you, my daughter," he replied. "This kindness is greater than that which you showed earlier. You have not run after the younger men, whether rich or poor. And now, my daughter, don't be afraid. I will do for you all you ask. All my fellow townsmen know that you are a woman of noble character. Although it is true that I am near of kin, there is a kinsman nearer than I. Stay here for the night, and in the morning if he wants to redeem, good; let him redeem. But if he is not willing, I vow that, as surely as the LORD lives, I will do it. Lie here until morning."

So she lay at his feet until morning, but got up before anyone could be recognized; and he said, "Don't let it be known that a woman came to the threshing floor."

He also said, "Bring me the shawl you are wearing and hold it out." When she did so, he poured into it six measures of barley and put it on her. Then he went back to town.

When Ruth came to her mother-in-law, Naomi asked, "How did it go, my daughter?"

Then she told her everything Boaz had done for her and added, "He gave me these six measures of barley, saying, 'Don't go back to your mother-in-law empty-handed.' "

Then Naomi said, "Wait, my daughter, until you find out what happens. For the man will not rest until the matter is settled today."

Meanwhile Boaz went up to the town gate and sat there. When the kinsman he had mentioned came along, Boaz said, "Come over here, my friend, and sit down." So he went over and sat down.

Boaz took ten of the elders of the town and said, "Sit here," and they did so. Then he said to the kinsman, "Naomi, who has come back from Moab, is selling the piece of land that belonged to our brother Elimelech. I thought I should bring the matter to your attention and suggest that you buy it in the presence of these seated here and in the presence of the elders of my people. If you will redeem it, do so. But if you will not, tell me, so I will know. For no one has the right to do it except you, and I am next in line."

"I will redeem it," he said.

Then Boaz said, "On the day you buy the land from Naomi and from Ruth the Moabitess, you acquire the dead man's widow, in order to maintain the name of the dead with his property."

At this, the kinsman said, "Then I cannot redeem it because I might endanger my own estate. You redeem it yourself. I cannot do it."

(Now in earlier times in Israel, for the redemption and transfer of property to

---

3. To spread his garment over her would mean to take her as his wife; as her next of kin, it would be Boaz's responsibility to protect the widow and maintain her de-ceased husband's family line (an exception to the ordinary prohibition of marriage of brother and sister-in-law).

become final, one party took off his sandal and gave it to the other. This was the method of legalizing transactions in Israel.)

So the kinsman said to Boaz, "Buy it yourself." And he removed his sandal.

Then Boaz announced to the elders and all the people. "Today you are witnesses that I have bought from Naomi all the property of Elimelech, Kilion and Mahlon. I have also acquired Ruth the Moabitess, Mahlon's widow, as my wife, in order to maintain the name of the dead with his property, so that his name will not disappear from among his family or from the town records. Today you are witnesses!"

Then the elders and all those at the gate said, "We are witnesses. May the LORD make the woman who is coming into your home like Rachel and Leah[4] who together built up the house of Israel. May you have standing in Ephrathah and be famous in Bethlehem. Through the offspring the LORD gives you by this young woman, may your family be like that of Perez, whom Tamar bore to Judah."[5]

So Boaz took Ruth and she became his wife. And the LORD enabled her to conceive, and she gave birth to a son. The women said to Naomi: "Praise be to the LORD, who this day has not left you without a kinsman. May he become famous throughout Israel! He will renew your life and sustain you in your old age. For your daughter-in-law, who loves you and who is better to you than seven sons, has given him birth."

Then Naomi took the child, laid him in her lap and cared for him. The women living there said, "Naomi has a son." And they named him Obed. He was the father of Jesse, the father of David.[6]

This, then, is the family line of Perez:

Perez was the father of Hezron, Hezron the father of Ram, Ram the father of Amminadab, Amminadab the father of Nahshon, Nahshon the father of Salmon, Salmon the father of Boaz, Boaz the father of Obed, Obed the father of Jesse, and Jesse the father of David.

THUCYDIDES (c. 460–c. 400 B.C.E.)
Greece

Early in the fifth century B.C.E., Persia, under King Darius and his son Xerxes, was largely successful in gaining political control of the nearby Greek cities in Asia Minor and finally invaded Greece itself in 490 B.C.E. and again in 480. Athens played a decisive role in the defense of Greece at the battle of Marathon in 490 and in the Persian defeat at Salamis in 480. As a result, it was under Athenian

---

4. The sisters who were the wives of the patriarch Isaac.
5. See Genesis 38.

6. Thus Naomi, Ruth, and Boaz become progenitors of Israel's greatest king.

hegemony that the Greek cities were subsequently organized into a defensive league to protect themselves against further potential aggression by Persia; the cities contributed money to Athens, which maintained a fleet for the general protection. Athenian domination over the league grew increasingly inflexible in the middle decades of the century, as Athens made tribute payments compulsory and refused to allow member cities to withdraw from the league, forcibly punishing efforts to do so. Thucydides' history of the Peloponnesian War [See the introductory headnote to Pericles' Funeral Oration] is thus a history of the growth—and ultimate dissolution—of the Athenian empire, and of the reactions of the rest of Greece. "What made war inevitable," Thucydides writes, "was the growth of Athenian power and the fear which this caused in Sparta."

The small Aegean island of Melos was one of the few to have remained independent of both the Athenian league and the Spartan alliance. In 416 B.C.E., with a view to increasing its resources, Athens sent a naval expedition to coerce the unwilling Melians into the empire as tribute-paying league members. Thucydides reports a dialogue between the Athenian generals and the Melian leaders in which the brutality and amoral cynicism of imperial power in action is fully revealed.

from *The History of the Peloponnesian War*

[The Melian Dialogue]

The Athenians also made an expedition against the island of Melos. They had thirty of their own ships, six from Chios[1] and two from Lesbos; 1,200 hoplites,[2] 300 archers, and twenty mounted archers, all from Athens; and about 1,500 hoplites from the allies and the islanders.

The Melians are a colony from Sparta. They had refused to join the Athenian empire like the other islanders, and at first had remained neutral without helping either side; but afterwards, when the Athenians had brought force to bear on them by laying waste their land, they had become open enemies of Athens.

Now the generals Cleomedes, the son of Lycomedes, and Tisias, the son of Tisimachus, encamped with the above force in Melian territory and, before doing any harm to the land, first of all sent representatives to negotiate. The Melians did not invite these representatives to speak before the people, but asked them to make the statement for which they had come in front of the governing body and the few.[3] The Athenian representatives then spoke as follows:

'So we are not to speak before the people, no doubt in case the mass of the people should hear once and for all and without interruption an argument from us which is both persuasive and incontrovertible, and should so be led astray. This, we realize, is your motive in bringing us here to speak before the few. Now suppose that you who sit here should make assurance doubly sure. Suppose that

Translated by Rex Warner.

1. Chios and Lesbos, islands in the eastern Aegean off the coast of Asia Minor, were under Athenian domination at this time.
2. Heavily armed infantrymen.
3. Leaders of the Melian oligarchy governing the island.

you, too, should refrain from dealing with every point in detail in a set speech, and should instead interrupt us whenever we say something controversial and deal with that before going on to the next point? Tell us first whether you approve of this suggestion of ours.'

The Council of the Melians replied as follows:

'No one can object to each of us putting forward our own views in a calm atmosphere. That is perfectly reasonable. What is scarcely consistent with such a proposal is the present threat, indeed the certainty, of your making war on us. We see that you have come prepared to judge the argument yourselves, and that the likely end of it all will be either war, if we prove that we are in the right, and so refuse to surrender, or else slavery.'

ATHENIANS: If you are going to spend the time in enumerating your suspicions about the future, or if you have met here for any other reason except to look the facts in the face and on the basis of these facts to consider how you can save your city from destruction, there is no point in our going on with this discussion. If, however, you will do as we suggest, then we will speak on.

MELIANS: It is natural and understandable that people who are placed as we are should have recourse to all kinds of arguments and different points of view. However, you are right in saying that we are met together here to discuss the safety of our country and, if you will have it so, the discussion shall proceed on the lines that you have laid down.

ATHENIANS: Then we on our side will use no fine phrases saying, for example, that we have a right to our empire because we defeated the Persians, or that we have come against you now because of the injuries you have done us—a great mass of words that nobody would believe. And we ask you on your side not to imagine that you will influence us by saying that you, though a colony of Sparta, have not joined Sparta in the war, or that you have never done us any harm. Instead we recommend that you should try to get what it is possible for you to get, taking into consideration what we both really do think; since you know as well as we do that, when these matters are discussed by practical people, the standard of justice depends on the equality of power to compel and that in fact the strong do what they have the power to do and the weak accept what they have to accept.

MELIANS: Then in our view (since you force us to leave justice out of account and to confine ourselves to self-interest)—in our view it is at any rate useful that you should not destroy a principle that is to the general good of all men—namely, that in the case of all who fall into danger there should be such a thing as fair play and just dealing, and that such people should be allowed to use and to profit by arguments that fall short of a mathematical accuracy. And this is a principle which affects you as much as anybody, since your own fall would be visited by the most terrible vengeance and would be an example to the world.

ATHENIANS: As for us, even assuming that our empire does come to an end, we are not despondent about what would happen next. One is not so much frightened of being conquered by a power which rules over others, as Sparta does (not that we are concerned with Sparta now), as of what would happen if a ruling power is attacked and defeated by its own subjects. So far as this point is concerned, you can leave it to us to face the risks involved. What we shall do now is to show you that it is for the good of our own empire that we are here and that it is for the preservation of your city that we shall say what we are going to say. We do not want any trouble in bringing you into our empire, and we want you to be spared for the good both of yourselves and of ourselves.

MELIANS: And how could it be just as good for us to be the slaves as for you to be the masters?

ATHENIANS: You, by giving in, would save yourselves from disaster; we, by not destroying you, would be able to profit from you.

MELIANS: So you would not agree to our being neutral, friends instead of enemies, but allies of neither side?

ATHENIANS: No, because it is not so much your hostility that injures us; it is rather the case that, if we were on friendly terms with you, our subjects would regard that as a sign of weakness in us, whereas your hatred is evidence of our power.

MELIANS: Is that your subjects' idea of fair play—that no distinction should be made between people who are quite unconnected with you and people who are mostly your own colonists or else rebels whom you have conquered?

ATHENIANS: So far as right and wrong are concerned they think that there is no difference between the two, that those who still preserve their independence do so because they are strong, and that if we fail to attack them it is because we are afraid. So that by conquering you we shall increase not only the size but the security of our empire. We rule the sea and you are islanders, and weaker islanders too than the others; it is therefore particularly important that you should not escape.

MELIANS: But do you think there is no security for you in what we suggest? For here again, since you will not let us mention justice, but tell us to give in to your interests, we, too, must tell you what our interests are and, if yours and ours happen to coincide, we must try to persuade you of the fact. Is it not certain that you will make enemies of all states who are at present neutral, when they see what is happening here and naturally conclude that in course of time you will attack them too? Does not this mean that you are strengthening the enemies you have already and are forcing others to become your enemies even against their intentions and their inclinations?

ATHENIANS: As a matter of fact we are not so much frightened of states on the continent. They have their liberty, and this means that it will be a long time before they begin to take precautions against us. We are more concerned about islanders like yourselves, who are still unsubdued, or subjects who have already become embittered by the constraint which our empire imposes on them. These are the people who are most likely to act in a reckless manner and to bring themselves and us, too, into the most obvious danger.

MELIANS: Then surely, if such hazards are taken by you to keep your empire and by your subjects to escape from it, we who are still free would show ourselves great cowards and weaklings if we failed to face everything that comes rather than submit to slavery.

ATHENIANS: No, not if you are sensible. This is no fair fight, with honour on one side and shame on the other. It is rather a question of saving your lives and not resisting those who are far too strong for you.

MELIANS: Yet we know that in war fortune sometimes makes the odds more level than could be expected from the difference in numbers of the two sides. And if we surrender, then all our hope is lost at once, whereas, so long as we remain in action, there is still a hope that we may yet stand upright.

ATHENIANS: Hope, that comforter in danger! If one already has solid advantages to fall back upon, one can indulge in hope. It may do harm, but will not destroy one.

But hope is by nature an expensive commodity, and those who are risking their all on one cast find out what it means only when they are already ruined; it never fails them in the period when such a knowledge would enable them to take precautions. Do not let this happen to you, you who are weak and whose fate depends on a single movement of the scale. And do not be like those people who, as so commonly happens, miss the chance of saving themselves in a human and practical way, and, when every clear and distinct hope has left them in their adversity, turn to what is blind and vague, to prophecies and oracles and such things which by encouraging hope lead men to ruin.

MELIANS: It is difficult, and you may be sure that we know it, for us to oppose your power and fortune, unless the terms be equal. Nevertheless we trust that the gods will give us fortune as good as yours, because we are standing for what is right against what is wrong; and as for what we lack in power, we trust that it will be made up for by our alliance with the Spartans, who are bound, if for no other reason, then for honour's sake, and because we are their kinsmen, to come to our help. Our confidence, therefore, is not so entirely irrational as you think.

ATHENIANS: So far as the favour of the gods is concerned, we think we have as much right to that as you have. Our aims and our actions are perfectly consistent with the beliefs men hold about the gods and with the principles which govern their own conduct. Our opinion of the gods and our knowledge of men lead us to conclude that it is a general and necessary law of nature to rule whatever one can. This is not a law that we made ourselves, nor were we the first to act upon it when it was made. We found it already in existence, and we shall leave it to exist for ever among those who come after us. We are merely acting in accordance with it, and we know that you or anybody else with the same power as ours would be acting in precisely the same way. And therefore, so far as the gods are concerned, we see no good reason why we should fear to be at a disadvantage. But with regard to your views about Sparta and your confidence that she, out of a sense of honour, will come to your aid, we must say that we congratulate you on your simplicity but do not envy you your folly. In matters that concern themselves or their own constitution the Spartans are quite remarkably good; as for their relations with others, that is a long story, but it can be expressed shortly and clearly by saying that of all people we know the Spartans are most conspicuous for believing that what they like doing is honourable and what suits their interests is just. And this kind of attitude is not going to be of much help to you in your absurd quest for safety at the moment.

MELIANS: But this is the very point where we can feel most sure. Their own self-interest will make them refuse to betray their own colonists, the Melians, for that would mean losing the confidence of their friends among the Hellenes[4] and doing good to their enemies.

ATHENIANS: You seem to forget that if one follows one's self-interest one wants to be safe, whereas the path of justice and honour involves one in danger. And, where danger is concerned, the Spartans are not, as a rule, very venturesome.

MELIANS: But we think that they would even endanger themselves for our sake and count the risk more worth taking than in the case of others, because we are so close to the Peloponnese that they could operate more easily, and because they

---

4. Greeks.

can depend on us more than on others, since we are of the same race and share the same feelings.

ATHENIANS: Goodwill shown by the party that is asking for help does not mean security for the prospective ally. What is looked for is a positive preponderance of power in action. And the Spartans pay attention to this point even more than others do. Certainly they distrust their own native resources so much that when they attack a neighbour they bring a great army of allies with them. It is hardly likely therefore that, while we are in control of the sea, they will cross over to an island.

MELIANS: But they still might send others. The Cretan sea[5] is a wide one, and it is harder for those who control it to intercept others than for those who want to slip through to do so safely. And even if they were to fail in this, they would turn against your own land and against those of your allies left unvisited by Brasidas.[6] So, instead of troubling about a country which has nothing to do with you, you will find trouble nearer home, among your allies, and in your own country.

ATHENIANS: It is a possibility, something that has in fact happened before. It may happen in your case, but you are well aware that the Athenians have never yet relinquished a single siege operation through fear of others. But we are somewhat shocked to find that, though you announced your intention of discussing how you could preserve yourselves, in all this talk you have said absolutely nothing which could justify a man in thinking that he could be preserved. Your chief points are concerned with what you hope may happen in the future, while your actual resources are too scanty to give you a chance of survival against the forces that are opposed to you at this moment. You will therefore be showing an extraordinary lack of common sense if, after you have asked us to retire from this meeting, you still fail to reach a conclusion wiser than anything you have mentioned so far. Do not be led astray by a false sense of honour—a thing which often brings men to ruin when they are faced with an obvious danger that somehow affects their pride. For in many cases men have still been able to see the dangers ahead of them, but this thing called dishonour, this word, by its own force of seduction, has drawn them into a state where they have surrendered to an idea, while in fact they have fallen voluntarily into irrevocable disaster, in dishonour that is all the more dishonourable because it has come to them from their own folly rather than their misfortune. You, if you take the right view, will be careful to avoid this. You will see that there is nothing disgraceful in giving way to the greatest city in Hellas when she is offering you such reasonable terms—alliance on a tribute-paying basis and liberty to enjoy your own property. And, when you are allowed to choose between war and safety, you will not be so insensitively arrogant as to make the wrong choice. This is the safe rule—to stand up to one's equals, to behave with deference towards one's superiors, and to treat one's inferiors with moderation. Think it over again, then, when we have withdrawn from the meeting, and let this be a point that constantly recurs to your minds—that you are discussing the fate of your country, that you have only one country, and that its future for good or ill depends on this one single decision which you are going to make.

---

5. The part of the Aegean around the island of Crete, south of Melos.

6. A Spartan general.

The Athenians then withdrew from the discussion. The Melians, left to themselves, reached a conclusion which was much the same as they had indicated in their previous replies. Their answer was as follows:

'Our decision, Athenians, is just the same as it was at first. We are not prepared to give up in a short moment the liberty which our city has enjoyed from its foundation for 700 years. We put our trust in the fortune that the gods will send and which has saved us up to now, and in the help of men—that is, of the Spartans; and so we shall try to save ourselves. But we invite you to allow us to be friends of yours and enemies to neither side, to make a treaty which shall be agreeable to both you and us, and so to leave our country.'

The Melians made this reply, and the Athenians, just as they were breaking off the discussion, said:

'Well, at any rate, judging from this decision of yours, you seem to us quite unique in your ability to consider the future as something more certain than what is before your eyes, and to see uncertainties as realities, simply because you would like them to be so. As you have staked most on and trusted most in Spartans, luck, and hopes, so in all these you will find yourselves most completely deluded.'

The Athenian representatives then went back to the army, and the Athenian generals, finding that the Melians would not submit, immediately commenced hostilities and built a wall completely round the city of Melos, dividing the work out among the various states. Later they left behind a garrison of some of their own and some allied troops to blockade the place by land and sea, and with the greater part of their army returned home. The force left behind stayed on and continued with the siege.

. . .

Meanwhile the Melians made a night attack and captured the part of the Athenian lines opposite the market-place. They killed some of the troops, and then, after bringing in corn and everything else useful that they could lay their hands on, retired again and made no further move, while the Athenians took measures to make their blockade more efficient in future. So the summer came to an end.

In the following winter the Spartans planned to invade the territory of Argos, but when the sacrifices for crossing the frontier turned out unfavourably, they gave up the expedition. The fact that they had intended to invade made the Argives suspect certain people in their city, some of whom they arrested, though others succeeded in escaping.

About this same time the Melians again captured another part of the Athenian lines where there were only a few of the garrison on guard. As a result of this, another force came out afterwards from Athens under the command of Philocrates, the son of Demeas. Siege operations were now carried on vigorously and, as there was also some treachery from inside, the Melians surrendered unconditionally to the Athenians, who put to death all the men of military age whom they took, and sold the women and children as slaves. Melos itself they took over for themselves, sending out later a colony of 500 men.

EURIPIDES (480? B.C.E.–406 B.C.E.)
Greece

Together with Aeschylus and Sophocles, the two other major Athenian tragedians of the fifth century B.C.E., Euripides shaped the future of tragic drama as a genre. His innovative writings were controversial, and largely unpopular, in his lifetime—he won first prize only four times out of twenty-two entries in the annual competition at the festival known as the City Dionysia, and he was often the subject of parody in contemporary comedies. His works were greatly prized, however, in the century after his death and thereafter, especially for the psychological depth of their characters. Aristotle called him the "most tragic" of the playwrights.

The *Bacchae* is concerned with the baffling, enigmatic nature of the god Dionysus, the very god at whose festival (and, according to the Athenians, in whose presence) the drama was performed. Dionysus seems to be both an exotic visitor from the East and a native Theban son; at once the liberating source of pleasure and release for human beings and the overpowering manipulator of their actions and responses; the benign promoter of fertility as well as a violent force of calamitous destruction. All these aspects are evident in the *Bacchae*, which in its representation of the god's female worshippers reflects several historically documented cult practices. Euripides, remarkably, makes the god himself the protagonist of the tragedy. Within the play, Dionysus, the patron deity of drama, both directs the action and is himself an actor, taking the part of a stranger devoted to the worship of Dionysus. Even Euripides' contemporaries recognized the extraordinary qualities of the *Bacchae*, his last play: Performed posthumously in 406, it won one of his rare first prizes.

Bacchae

Characters

DIONYSUS, *the son of the god Zeus and the mortal Semele*

PENTHEUS (*pronounced as two syllables, PEN-theus*), *the king of Thebes, whose crown has been bestowed on him by his grandfather Cadmus*

CADMUS, *the grandfather of Pentheus, and of Dionysus*

TIRESIAS, *the blind seer*

AGAVE, *Pentheus' mother, the daughter of Cadmus*

THE CHORUS, *the adepts of Dionysus, who have followed him from Asia, and who are thus strangers in Thebes. They are the Bacchae, also known as Bacchants, or Maenads, who are entirely dedicated to the ecstatic worship of the god*

There are two messengers—one a cowherd and one who goes with Pentheus on his journey to Cithaeron—and a guard.

Translated by C.K. Williams.

The royal palace of Thebes. To one side, a tomb covered with vines, and the rubble of a house, with smoke rising from it.

[Enter Dionysus.] *God of Wine*

DIONYSUS: I am Dionysus.[1] I am Bacchus.
Bromius[2] and Iacchus.
Dithyrambus and Evius.
I am a god, the son of Zeus,
but I have assumed the semblance of a mortal,   5
and come to Thebes, where my mother, Semele,
the daughter of King Cadmus, gave birth to me.
Her midwife was the lightning bolt that killed her.
There is the river Dirce,[3] and there the stream
Ismenus. Over there, near the palace,   10
is my mother's tomb, and her ruined house,
still smoldering with the living flame of Zeus,
Hera's unrelenting hatred towards her.
I praise Cadmus. He made the ruins hallowed ground,
dedicated to his daughter. I myself   15
caused these vines to grow so thickly on them.

I was in Phrygia[4] before I came here,
and Lydia, where the earth flows gold. I passed
the broiling plains of Persia, and Bactria's[5]
walled towns. The Medes[6] then, their freezing winters,   20
then opulent Arabia and down
along the bitter, salt-sea coast of Asia
where Hellenes[7] and barbarians mingle
in teeming, beautifully towered cities.
When I had taught my dances there, established   25
the rituals of my mystery, making
my divinity manifest to mortals,

---

1. Son of Zeus and a mortal woman, Semele—
the daughter of King Cadmus of Thebes, a
city in central Greece—Dionysus (also
called Bacchus) is the god of burgeoning
vegetation, especially of the grapevine, and
of wine. Zeus visited Semele in disguise,
whereupon his jealous wife Hera persuaded
Semele to extract from him a promise Hera
knew would result in Semele's death: that
Zeus should appear before her in his true
form. Zeus was obliged to fulfill the promise and Semele, pregnant with Dionysus,
was killed by fire from his thunderbolt.
Zeus rescued his unborn child, whom he
put in his thigh and removed after a full
term of gestation.
2. Bromius, Iacchus, Dithyrambus, and Evius

are all titles of Dionysus. Bromius, used
frequently throughout the play, means the
"roarer" or "thunderer"; it may refer to the
bellowing of a bull—a form in which Dionysus sometimes manifested himself.
3. Dirce, a spring on Mount Cithaeron, near
Thebes, is named for a mythical Theban
queen who had been a follower of Dionysus.
4. Phrygia, a country in western Asia Minor,
was bordered on the west by the kingdom
of Lydia.
5. Bactria was a province of Persia.
6. The Medes were inhabitants of a territory to
the southwest of the Caspian Sea.
7. The Greek name for Greek-speaking peoples.

I came to Greece, to Thebes, the first Greek city
I've caused to shriek in ecstasy for me,
the first whose women I've clothed in fawnskin and in   30
whose hands I've placed my ivy spear, the thyrsus.[8]
Why did I choose Thebes? Because my mother's sisters,
who should have been the last to even *think*
of saying such a thing, started rumors:
that Dionysus was *not* the son of Zeus,   35
that Semele's lover had been a mortal
and she'd imputed the disgrace to Zeus, a fraud
Cadmus had contrived. They kept whispering
that Zeus destroyed her because she'd lied and said
he was her lover. Therefore I've stung them   40
with madness, and goaded them raving from their houses.
They're living on the mountain now, delirious,
dressed, as I've compelled them to be dressed,
in the garments of my rituals.
And all the rest, the whole female seed of Thebes,   45
I've driven frenzied out of house and home.
They're with the daughters of King Cadmus now,
huddled on bare rocks beneath the pines.
This city must learn, and know, against its will or not,
that it is uninitiated in my mysteries.   50
As for Semele, her memory
will be vindicated when I appear
to mortal eyes as the power she bore Zeus.
Cadmus has abdicated now to Pentheus,
the son of Agave, another of his daughters,   55
and Pentheus is warring with divinity
by excluding me from rituals
and not invoking my name in prayers.

Because of this, I'm going to demonstrate to him
and to all Thebes the god I really am.   60
When order is established, I'll go on,
revealing my identity in other lands.
But if, by rage and force of arms, the citizens
of Thebes drive the Bacchae from the mountain,
then I lead the army of my Maenads[9] into war.   65
This is why I have assumed a mortal shape,
shedding my divine form for a human's.

[*Dionysus calls to the Chorus.*]

---

8. The thyrsus was a wand that was wound
   around with ivy and carried by the followers of Dionysus.

9. Maenads were female worshippers of Dionysus who followed him as he journeyed
   through different lands.

Now, women, come: all you who left the ramparts
of Tmolus,[10] who left Lydia, left barbarian lands
to follow me and worship me, my women: come.   70
Bring the drum we brought from Phrygia,
the drum that pulses with the beat of Mother Earth.
Surround the royal walls of Pentheus with thunder:
let the city of King Cadmus see!

I am going to the gorges of Cithaeron now;   75
I am going to the Bacchae, to their dances.

[Enter Chorus. Exit Dionysus.]   women followers

CHORUS: Down
         from Asia, down
             from sacred Tmolus
     I have soared and
         soar, still, for
             Bromius, in
     the labor, difficult,
         difficult
             and sweet, the   85
     sweet, exacting labor
         of exalting
             him, of crying
     out
         for him, *Bacchus,*
             holy Bacchus!   90

     Who is in
         the road,
             who
     is in
         the
             streets and who   95
     is in
         the palace, in
             its chambers?
     Be here,
         now, be   100
             here, anyone,
     anywhere, be
         here, lips
             dedicated,   105
     pious, purified, be

---

10. A mountain in Lydia.

here, now, as
    I, as all, all
sing the
    ancient
        blessings, the
ancient, hallowed
    blessings
        of Dionysus!

Blessed, blessed
    and happy,
        blessed and
blessed again
    are they who,
        in the holy
rituals,
    consecrate themselves,
        who
know the
    mysteries.
        Blessed
in spirit, blessed
    spirit fused,
        fused
with and consecrated
    to the holy
        bands upon
the mountains,
    the bands
        of Bacchus praying
in the mountains,
    blessing, praising
        Bacchus, holy
Bacchus,
    blessed
        with purity and
blessed
    with prayer. And
        the rituals
of our great mother
    Cybele,[11] and
        the rituals

---

11. A fertility goddess in Lydia and Phrygia whose cult was introduced into Greece in the fifth century, and who in turn was closely connected with Dionysus and his worship.

of the ivy-covered
    thyrsus and the ritual
        of its rattling,   150
of the rattling of
    the ivy of
        the holy wand,
holy   155
    thyrsus, and
        the ritual
of the holy, ivy-
    covered crown of
        Bacchus.   160

Plummet
    down, now,
        Bacchants, plummet
down,
    hover,
        Bacchants, down,   165
down from
    Phrygia, down
        its mountains,
down   170
    to here, the
        broad
ways here, lead
    Bromius down,
        Bromius,   175
Dionysus, god, son
    of god and
        god, lead
him down!
    Bromius! Roarer!   180
    Roarer!
Once, she,
    his
        mother, of
whom, in   185
    agony, and in
        a blast
of fire from
    Zeus, he
        was born;   190
once,
    his mother, from
        whom he

was torn out
  by Zeus's lightning . . .
    And
she died with
  it, and he,
    then,
by his father,   200
  Zeus, son
    of Cronos,
was caught,
  uplifted, and,
    that
instant, pinned,
  with golden
    clips,
into his holy
  thigh, and   210
    he kept
him there, a
  secret
    from his wife,
a gold-   215
  bound secret
    from Hera,
wife of
  Zeus . . .
    And it was   220
Zeus who,
  when the
    time
the fates deemed
  proper   225
    came,
it was
  Zeus who
    brought him
forth again, to   230
  his birth
    again,
a god,
  though, now,
    horned,   235
horns rising
  like
    a bull's
now, horns

195

flourished, garlanded
  with
beast-nourished
  serpents, and
    his Maenads,
too, in their
  tresses, too,
    weave
serpents, all
  his holy
    Maenads.
Thebes, O
  Thebes, who nurtured
    her, Semele,
garland now
  yourself, Thebes, with
    ivy garlands
now and
  with myrtle, luscious
    myrtle, crown
yourself and
  with oak and
    fir-twigs; be the
Bacchant now,
  yourself, and
    dappled fawnskins
wrap
  upon yourself,
    and
white curls of
  braided wool,
    take unto
yourself the wild
  thyrsus now,
    behold, now,
yourself, behold,
  holy now,
    all the land,
yourself and all
  the land, shall
    dance now,
dance
  again, when
    Bromius leads
the dance
  onto the

240

245

250

255

260

265

270

275

280

285

    holy
mountain!
    Bromius
      calls
his band and
    leads them
      where, already,   290
one band
    waits, the band
      of women
waits, driven   295
    from their
      looms, driven
from
    their shuttles,   300
      stung,
stung by
    Dionysus, from
      themselves!

Oh, and   305
    you, the
      holy
caves of
    Crete, the
      dens   310
of the Curetes,[12]
    the
      caves where
Zeus was
    born and where   315
      the drum,
too, was
    born, was given
      by you, you
who wear   320
    three helmets,
      you,
Corybants, you
    who made my
      leather drum for   325
me and
    danced for

---

12. In myth, the Curetes were votaries of Rhea, the Cretan mother goddess. They were often identified with Cybele's attendants, the Corybantes.

me, and who,
dancing out
  the Bacchic rites,
    mixed
the drumbeat
  into the wild,
    ecstatic dances
with the sharp,
  sweet calling
    crying
of the flute, and
  handed
    it, my
drum, to her, Mother
  Rhea, so
    that she
could hand it
  to the Satyrs, who
    were wild with
dancing, too,
  and
    brought
it to the dances
  now
    in which
Dionysus, in
  his gigantic
    year,[13] in
his festival
  exults—
    Holy Dionysus!

Delectable he
  is, delectable,
    upon
the mountain and he
  falls out of
    the holy bands, onto
the ground; delectable
  he is, in the
    holy

330

335

340

345

350

355

360

365

---

13. One of the rites practiced by women and sacred to Dionysus took place in alternate years; the ritual included dancing on a mountainside and, in at least some Dionysiac cults, it was documented as involving the practice of tearing an animal to pieces and eating it raw.

fawnskin, and he
　joyfully
　　devours the living
flesh of new-
　ly slaughtered goats and
　　on the mountain   370
now, again,
　in Phrygia,
　in Lydia, and   375
always, rushing
　everywhere
　　before
us, sweetly calling,   380
　is
　　Bromius!
And the earth
　flows, flows
　　beneath us, then   385
milk
　flows, and wine
　　flows,
and nectar
　flows, like   390
　　flame,
like the fire
　from Syria, from
　　the frankincense,
delectable, the   395
　flame that
　　flows, now,
from
　his torch, and rushes,
　　flowing now,   400
from his thyrsus
　as he whirls
　　it, runs
with it, rushes,
　driving on his   405
　　dancers with
it, roaring
　on
　　with it, and
his locks   410
　flow thickly and
　　his locks dance
and *Onwards,*

Bacchae, he

   is roaring, *Onwards,*

Bacchae,

  blazing with

   the gold of

golden Tmolus,

   Evohe! he

    roars, *Evohe!* he

calls, *Sing*

  to Dionysus,

   Sing!

And make

  the drums, make

   the

drums

  roar, let the drums

   honor

Bacchus, let

  the flute shriek, and

   the holy

shriekings

  and delectable and

   holy and now

shriek again, it

  is woven

   now, together,

the holy flute,

  the way up

   to the

mountain,

  holiness and

   mountain!

And the

  Bacchant

   then, as

joyful

  as a foal

   near

its mother,

  grazing, leaps

   cavorts,

prances, so

  she dances

   now,

the Bacchant,

  and she

415

420

425

430

435

440

445

450

455

soars
now, being,
  now,   460
    joy-
fully, playfully,
  the   465
    Bacchant.

[Enter Tiresias.]

TIRESIAS: Who is at the gates? Call Cadmus from the house:
the son of Agenor, who came from Sidon
to build the walls and towers of Thebes.
Tell him Tiresias is here. He'll know why.   470
He and I, ancient and more ancient, have made vows:
to adorn ourselves with fawnskins, with Bacchic wands,
and to wreathe shoots of ivy in our hair.

[Enter Cadmus.]

CADMUS: I knew it was you, old friend. I was in the palace,
but I recognized that wise old voice of yours.   475
You always know a voice like that, the wisdom in it.
Here I am, in the god's equipment, all prepared.
He's my daughter's son. We have to lift him high,
as high as possible—Dionysus,
who's revealed himself to mortals as a god.   480
Now, where will the dancing be? Show me
where my feet should go: they'll dance; we'll toss
these old white manes of ours. Explain where,
Tiresias, old man to old man: you're wise.
I'll dance all day and night and not get tired,   485
beating my thyrsus on the ground. In our joy,
we've even forgotten how we've gotten on.
TIRESIAS: That's it, that's how I feel, young, too.
I'll dance, I'll take my chances.
CADMUS: Shall we ride in a chariot to the mountain?   490
TIRESIAS: No, we'll walk, it will show more reverence.
CADMUS: We're both old, but shall I lead you?
TIRESIAS: The god will lead us without our trying.
CADMUS: Are we the only men who'll dance for Dionysus?
TIRESIAS: Only we can see. The rest of them are mad.   495
CADMUS: Let's not waste time. Let me lead you there.
TIRESIAS: Here, take my hand in yours.
CADMUS: I'm only human: I won't despise the gods.
TIRESIAS: Compared with their wisdom, ours is nothing.
What comes down to us, from our fathers,   500
out of ancient time, no argument's more powerful

than that: the wisest mind can't theorize past that.
When I put on my ivy now, and go to dance,
they'll say, "Old fool, shameless fool,"
but the god makes no distinction, old or young: 505
he wants us all to honor him, he wants
us united in his exaltation.

CADMUS: Since you can't see this sight, Tiresias,
let me tell you what's about to happen.
Pentheus, the son of Echion,   510
to whom I've resigned my powers as king,
is rushing towards the palace. He seems agitated.

[Enter Pentheus.]

PENTHEUS: I happened to be gone from Thebes, now I hear
awful evils have erupted in the city.
Our women have deserted home to perpetrate   515
false Bacchic mysteries in the dark woods
on the mountain, dancing to celebrate their upstart
deity, Dionysus . . . whoever Dionysus is.
They fill great bowls of wine, then they creep
into the bushes and lie down for lusting men.   520
Priestesses, they say they are, Maenads,
sworn to Bacchus. I say if it's anyone
they're dedicated to, it's Aphrodite.
Some of them I've had trapped: they're in prison,
chained. The rest are in the hills.   525
I'll track them down, all of them, even Agave,
my mother, and her sisters, Ino,[14]
and Autonoe, the mother of Actaeon.
I'll have them all in cages.
I'll stamp out these obscene orgies.   530
There's an intruder, too, I hear, a foreigner,
a sorcerer, a charlatan, from Lydia.
Long, scented yellow hair, they say, cheeks like wine,
with Aphrodite's[15] love charms in his eyes.
Day and night he mixes with young girls,   535
holding his mysteries up for them to admire.
Once I get him here, though, inside the walls,
he won't be tossing his locks or beating the ground
with his famous thyrsus. Not when I have his head.
He's the one who claims Dionysus is a god,   540
that he was stitched into the thigh of Zeus,

[handwritten margin note: Dionyses in human form.]

---

14. Agave, Ino, and Autonoe were the sisters
of Semele. Actaeon, Autonoe's son, was
turned into a stag for an offense against

the goddess Artemis and was devoured by
his own hunting dogs.
15. Aphrodite was the goddess of erotic love.

when really the child and the mother were both
consumed by lightning, because she'd lied
and said that Zeus had been her lover.
I don't know who this stranger is,   545
but doesn't such insulting outrage deserve hanging?

[He sees Cadmus and Tiresias.]

Not another miracle! Look: the seer,
rigged up in dappled fawnskin—Tiresias himself.
And my mother's father, you, too, decked out
like a Bacchant with your thyrsus. Ridiculous!   550
Are you both senile? I'm ashamed, Grandfather.
Shake that ivy off, right away;
let go of that thyrsus. Tiresias,
you instigated this! One more imported deity,
more flocks of birds for you to read,   555
more burnt offerings to get fees for!
You're fortunate you're old, that's why
you're not shackled with the Bacchae
for having brought these wretched rites to Thebes.
Whenever wine gleams at a women's feast,   560
I say nothing's healthy in those mysteries.

CHORUS LEADER: This is impiety! Stranger, do you offer reverence
neither to the gods, nor to Cadmus,
who sowed the crop of those born of the earth?[16]
You, the son of Echion, will you deny your race?   565

TIRESIAS: If a wise man finds an honest case to argue,
being eloquent is hardly difficult.
As for you, though your glibness gives you the air
of being sane, there's nothing rational about you.
A man who influences others with overbearing   570
is dangerous for his city: he lacks reason.
This new god you're subjecting to ridicule,
I can't tell you how great he'll be
throughout Greece.
                          There are, young man,
two principles for humankind: first, the goddess   575
Demeter—you can call her that, or Earth—
who nourishes us with solid food. Then comes
the son of Semele, equal in power, who invented
and introduced to mortals the liquid of the grape,

---

16. One of the myths about Thebes was that   snake he had killed; from the sown teeth
    Cadmus had populated the city by sowing   armed men sprang up.
    in plowed furrows the teeth of a sacred

which gives weak humans surcease from pain,   580
when they're glutted with the liquor of the vine,
and gives us sleep, to forget the evils of our days.
There is no other remedy for our affliction.
He, a god himself, is poured as a libation to the gods,
it's thanks to him men have these blessings.   585

You sneer at him being sewn into the thigh
of Zeus? I'll teach you what that really means.
When Zeus snatched the newborn from the lightning
and carried him up onto Olympus as a god,
Hera wanted to throw the child from heaven,   590
but Zeus, in his godly wisdom, countered her.
Breaking off a fragment of the ether
the world floats in, he made a doll, a Dionysus-
doll, that he showed Hera. But men confused
the words: they garbled "showed" to "sewed" and made   595
the story up about his having "sewed"
the god in his thigh to hide him from Hera.

And this god is a prophet, too: the Bacchic
frenzy gives the power of foresight; when
Bacchus fully infiltrates the body   600
of whoever is possessed, they foretell the future.
Dionysus even has a share
of the god of war: an army will be ranged
with arms for battle—before a lance is lifted,
a panic suddenly takes them and they flee.   605
This dementia also comes from Dionysus.
Someday you'll see him soaring on the rocks
at Delphi, leaping with pine torches
on the double cliffs, his Bacchic thyrsus
whirling, lashing, great in all Greece.   610
Pentheus, listen: don't believe that power
dominates in human life, and though
your sick imagination makes you think it,
don't believe you're sane. Welcome the god,
offer him libations, be a Bacchant, wear garlands.   615
It's not Dionysus who'll compel
a woman to be virtuous: chastity
is a part of one's nature or it's not;
even plunged in the deliriums of ritual,
a woman who is truly chaste won't be corrupted.   620

You know you're proud when your name is glorified,
when the multitude cries "Pentheus!" from the towers.
I believe the god is pleased by homage, too.

Therefore both Cadmus and I, the butt of your jokes,
will wreathe our heads with ivy and we'll dance: 625
gray-haired or not, both of us will dance.
You won't persuade me to fight the god.
You're mad, and there are no drugs to heal you,
because you must be drugged to be this painfully mad.

CHORUS LEADER: Old man, Apollo would approve your words.   630
Honoring the great god Bromius proves your wisdom.

CADMUS: My boy, the advice Tiresias is offering is good.
Believe him. Live with us. Don't break tradition.
For the moment, you're distracted, deluded.
But besides, even if the god isn't a god,   635
say he is: it's a pious lie. Semele,
the mother of a god: consider the honor
it brings our family and remember Actaeon:
his death, how horrible it was; the hounds
he'd raised with meat from his own hands,   640
tearing him to pieces on the mountain,
because he bragged he could outhunt Artemis.
Don't let that be you. Here, I'll crown you
with ivy: stay with us, offer homage to the god.

PENTHEUS: Don't touch me! Go play with your Bacchus,   645
but don't wipe your madness off on me.
And Tiresias, the instructor of your foolishness,
will pay for this.

[Enter guards.]

        Someone, quickly, go,
now, to the place where he observes his birds.
Take a lever, turn the whole thing over, demolish it,   650
throw his sacred garlands to the storming winds.
There's no way I can hurt him more than that.
The rest of you, patrol the city.
That girlish stranger who's introduced this new plague
and fouled our beds—I want him. Track him down   655
and when you find him, tie him up, bring him here,
so he can get what he deserves, death by stoning.
He'll rue the Bacchic orgies he'll find in Thebes.

[Exit guards.]

TIRESIAS: You poor fool. You don't know the meaning
of your own words. Before, you were insane,   660
now you're raving. Come, Cadmus, we'll pray for him.
May the god have pity on the wild man and may
he not inflict reprisals on the city.
Come, we'll support one another.

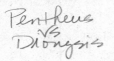

Pentheus
vs
Dionysis

Hold your thyrsus. Two old men,   665
we mustn't fall, we would be disgraced.
We must serve Bacchus, son of Zeus, and so we will.
Cadmus, beware that Pentheus doesn't make your house
repent. This isn't prophecy, but fact:
the fool speaks foolishness.   670

[Exit Pentheus to the palace. Exit Cadmus and Tiresias to Cithaeron.]

honor Dionysis

CHORUS: Holiness, queen
            of all the
               gods, Holiness,
         who to
            the earth
               hovers
         down, on
            gold
               wings, down   675
         to us: do
            you hear
               him? Do you   680
         hear this
            Pentheus, his
               unholy,
         raging insolence
            against the   685
               god? Against
         Bromius, son of
            Semele, most
               blessed, most   690
         holy, of the
            divine, who,
               at the god's
         lovely garlanded
            celebration, has   695
               this gift, to
         dance, to bring men,
            to bring men
               together in   700
         the dance, and
            this,
               when the
         flute shrieks, to
            laugh, and   705
               this, to
         stop cares, to
            stop

                woe, and
    when the glistening   710
        wine
            into the holy,
    ivy-bearing
        god-feast comes,
            to banish   715
    everything, to wrap
        us all
            in sleep.

    Tongues
        without bits;   720
            defiance
    without law:
        together
            they create
    disaster.   725
        But this, the
            life
    of calm, the
        life of rational
            tranquillity, this   730
    sustains us, this
        holds our house
            together.

    The gods
        are far from   735
            us: how far
    in their azure
        are they, how
            far they
    are, in their   740
        eons: but still
            they
    watch us,
        see us, see
            our actions,   745
    watch
        our
            goings on.

    Knowledge
        is not wisdom: 750
            cleverness

is not, not
  without
    awareness
of our   755
  death,
    not
without recalling
  just how
    brief   760
our flare
  is. He
    who overreaches
will, in his
  overreaching, lose   765
    what
he possesses,
  betray
    what
he has   770
  now. That
    which is
beyond us,
  which is
    greater   775
than
  the human, the
    unattainably
great, is
  for   780
    the mad, or
for those
  who listen
    to
the mad, and then   785
  believe
    them.

Oh, let me, let
  me go, let
    me go   790
to Cyprus,
  Aphrodite's
    island, where
the heart's
  beguilers,   795
    tempters

of men's
    hearts
        live.

Oh, there at   800
    Paphos,[17]
        where, with
no rain,
    the river
        with a hundred   805
mouths
    brings forth gigantic
        harvests.
There, or
    Pieria, lovely
        Pieria, where   810
Olympus
    is, where
        the muses
have their holy   815
    place; take me
        there,
Master, O
    Bromius, there
        the Graces
are, there   820
    Desire, and there
        the Bacchants
can lawfully
    enact their holy   825
        rites.
The god, the
    son of
        Zeus, finds
rituals
    joyful! He   830
        cherishes
peace, and peace
    cherishes
        the
young. He   835
    brings goodness to

---

17. A city on the southwest coast of Cyprus; a
center of the worship of Aphrodite.

both
rich and
  lesser mortals,
    offering
all, all
  happiness, all
    wine,   840
all
  painlessness
    and pleasure.
They, though,
  who
    will not take   850
these
  gifts, who
    refuse
the happiness of
  those
    who choose to   855
live a life
  rich by
    day and
blessed at night, those   860
  he detests! He
    detests excess,
detests
  insatiable, excessive
    men!   865
And so, what
  the common man
    thinks, what
the simple
  man believes, the   870
    most
humble, that
  I, too,
    will
take   875
  as my
    example.

[*Enter guards, leading Dionysus, bound. Enter Pentheus.*]

GUARD: Pentheus, here we are: we've hunted down
        the prey you wanted. Except . . .
        the animal was tame: he didn't try to run,   880
        he never lost the flushed wine color in his cheeks.

[handwritten margin note:] Pentheus has sent guards after Dionysus

He just smiled, gave us his hands, told us
we'd better tie him. I felt ashamed. "Stranger,"
I said, "I'm doing this against my will:
it's Pentheus who gave the order." 885
And those women you had chained, locked
in the dungeon? Well, they're gone now.
They're off in the meadows, dancing,
calling on their god Bromius. The chains around
their legs just snapped, the barred doors 890
came open by themselves: no mortal did all that.
This person who's come to Thebes is full of miracles.
But all this is your responsibility.
PENTHEUS: Untie his hands, he's in my net,
he won't be dancing out of this. 895
Well, you're not impossible to look at, are you?
Women wouldn't think so, anyway. Not in Thebes,
they wouldn't, which is why you're here, of course.
What a mane of hair you have: very seductive.
Look at it falling down your cheeks. 900
Good hand holds for a wrestler.
And how white your skin is: you must be careful
about staying out of the sun.
Oh, yes, handsome you, in the shade,
hunting with Aphrodite. All right, who are you? 905
DIONYSUS: I'll tell you, I have no secrets.
You've heard of Tmolus of the thousand flowers?
PENTHEUS: I know it, it flanks the town of Sardis.
DIONYSUS: I come from there, my country is Lydia.
PENTHEUS: Why have you brought these rituals to Greece? 910
DIONYSUS: By command of Dionysus, son of Zeus.
PENTHEUS: Is there a Zeus in Lydia spawning new gods?
DIONYSUS: No, it's your Zeus, who married Semele.
PENTHEUS: He commanded you . . . Face to face, or in a dream?
DIONYSUS: He revealed his mysteries face to face. 915
PENTHEUS: And these mysteries: what are they?
DIONYSUS: They are forbidden, unutterable to unbelievers.
PENTHEUS: What do they confer on those who sacrifice?
DIONYSUS: It would be sacrilege to tell, but there's great good.
PENTHEUS: You're clever. You want to make me curious. 920
DIONYSUS: The mysteries detest an impious man.
PENTHEUS: You say you saw the god: what form did he take?
DIONYSUS: Any form he wanted to—it wasn't my doing.
PENTHEUS: Another evasion. You make no sense.
DIONYSUS: Sense *is* nonsense, for a fool. 925
PENTHEUS: Is Thebes the first stop on your god's itinerary?
DIONYSUS: No, foreigners everywhere dance to him.

PENTHEUS: Foreigners are less intelligent than Greeks.

DIONYSUS: In this, more intelligent: customs vary.

PENTHEUS: Do you perform your mysteries by day, or at night? 930

DIONYSUS: Usually at night: there's more awe in darkness.

PENTHEUS: And for women, more treachery and corruption.

DIONYSUS: There's corruption in broad daylight, too.

PENTHEUS: Cheap sophistries! You'll pay for them.

DIONYSUS: *You'll* pay, for your impiety and stubbornness. 935

PENTHEUS: Well, Bacchic backtalk. You wrestle well, with words.

DIONYSUS: Tell me, how do you propose to punish me?

PENTHEUS: First I'll shear those lovely locks of yours.

DIONYSUS: My hair is holy: I've grown it for the god.

PENTHEUS: Now your thyrsus, you'll hand that over. 940

DIONYSUS: You'll have to take it: it belongs to Dionysus.

PENTHEUS: Now I'll put you in chains, in prison.

DIONYSUS: The god will free me, when I want him to.

PENTHEUS: Call him all you like, you and your Bacchae.

DIONYSUS: He's here now, seeing what I'm suffering. 945

PENTHEUS: Where is he? I don't see anything.

DIONYSUS: He's with me. You're unholy. You can't see.

PENTHEUS: Tie him up! He's scorning Thebes and me!

DIONYSUS: I am sane. I won't be bound by the insane.

PENTHEUS: I say bind him! I'm the power here, not you! 950

DIONYSUS: Your power is mortal, you don't know what
    you're doing: you don't even know who you are.

PENTHEUS: I am Pentheus. Son of Echion. Son of Agave.

DIONYSUS: Pentheus, Pentheus, you'll repent that name.[18]

PENTHEUS: Take him. Lock him up. Put him in the stable. 955
    If it's dark he wants, give him darkness.
    Go dance there. And your women,
    your accomplices, I'll sell them as slaves,
    or keep them in my house, laboring at looms,
    instead of beating on their maddening drums. 960

DIONYSUS: Take me. What isn't to be suffered won't be.
    But you: Dionysus, whom you've offered outrage to,
    whose very being you deny, will punish you.
    Wrong us, it's him you bind in chains.

[The guards lead Dionysus off. Pentheus follows.]

CHORUS: Queen 965
    Dirce, you are
      the daughter

---

18. The name "Pentheus" sounds like the
    Greek word for "grief," *penthos.*

of Achelous;[19]
  holy
    Dirce, more
than holy, for
  to you Zeus
    once
touched his
  child, touched him
    to your waters
as he tore
  him from the unrelenting
    fire
and placed him
  in his thigh and
    roared:
You
  are Dithyrambus!
    Into my male
womb, come!
  You
    are Bacchus!
Come, I will
  reveal you to
    Thebes!
You
  are Bacchus!
    They
shall call
  you
    Bacchus!
But you, Dirce,
  blessed
    river, you
thrust me from
  you, you thrust the
    garlanded
bands who dance
  near you. Why
    thrust me from
you this way? Why
  shun me
    so? Soon,
though, by

970

975

980

985

990

995

1000

1005

1010

---

19. A river in the southwest part of mainland
Greece.

the luscious grapes
    of Dionysus'
vines, I swear
    soon the name
        Bromius
will have   1015
    a meaning for
        you, too.

Rage, and
    rage and rage   1020
        is what
he, this
    earth-child,
        this
Pentheus,   1025
    dragon's
        seed, this
monstrous
    son
        of Echion,[20]   1030
reveals, an earth-
    child, just
        as the monstrous
giants are,
    children of   1035
        the earth, as
they, gory, wild-
    faced, rage, so
        he, daring,
daring to dare   1040
    gods, rages, and
        will
dare, soon,
    too, to
        threaten   1045
me, with
    chains, and who
        already, in
his house, in
    the darkness of   1050
        his prison,
has

---

20. One of the armed men who sprang up
from the earth when Cadmus sowed the
dragon's teeth. He married Cadmus's
daughter Agave; Pentheus was his son.

my dancing
   comrade.

Do
   you see us?
      Do you
see these
   things, son
      of Zeus?
Dionysus,
   do you see
      our battle,
our suffering
   in
      oppression?
Come, be
   with us, come
      down from
Olympus,
   come whirl
      your thyrsus with
its golden
   face
      quell
this vile person's
insolence
      and violence!

Are you on
   Nysa[21] now, which
      nurtures
beasts, or are
   you now,
      Dionysus,
guiding with your
   wand bands
      of dancers in
the mountains of
   Corycia?
      Or on

1055

1060

1065

1070

1075

1080

1085

1090

---

21. According to some versions of the myth,
the child Dionysus was raised by nymphs
on a mountain called Nysa. The chorus
refers here to several mountainous areas
frequented by Dionysus: Corycia is part of
Mount Parnassus, while Pieria is on the
northern side of Mount Olympus in Thessaly, in the northern part of mainland
Greece.

Olympus, in
   the forest
      where
Orpheus played
   his lyre and brought,   1095
      with his
muse, the
   trees
      to him and
the ferocious
   beasts to   1100
      him, are
you there? Oh,
   Pieria,
      blessed,   1105
honors you and with
   your own cries,
      Evius, honors
you, and he
   will come   1110
      dance
in Bacchic
   celebrations, and
      over the
roaring river   1115
   Axios[22] will
      spin
his Maenads, and
   over the
      rich   1120
waters of
   Lydias
      spin them,
Lydias,
   bliss-giver,   1125
      father, whose lovely
waters make that
   land of horses
      gleam.

[Dionysus' voice is heard from offstage.]

DIONYSUS: Listen!
   Listen to me, Bacchae!   1130

followers, worshipers [handwritten annotation]

---

22. Axios and Lydias are Macedonian rivers.

I am calling! Listen, Bacchae, listen to me!

CHORUS: Who? To
     whom
       listen?   1135
Whose
     call? Whose
       call, O
Evius, where
     are you to listen   1140
       to, Evius?

DIONYSUS: Again! Listen! I call again!
The son of Zeus, the son of Semele, calls again!

CHORUS: *Bromius!*
     Roarer!   1145
       You!
Lord! You
     come to us, oh,
       be here, lord!

DIONYSUS: *Earthquake! Be here! Shake the world!*   1150
Come, shudder the foundations of the world!

CHORUS: Look, the
     palace, Pentheus,
       his palace, look,
it shudders, the   1155
     whole palace trembles, now
       it falls!
Dionysus!
     Look! Dionysus!
       Loved one!   1160
Dionysus now is in
     the palace! Love him,
       oh, we adore
him! Look, the lintels
     craze, and   1165
       look, the stones
craze! Over
     the pillars, crazing,
       the stone shatters!
Listen, now: Bromius!   1170
     Bromius roars! He roars
       now, Bromius!

DIONYSUS: *Roar, lightning! Roar, bolt! Fire!*
Let the fire consume! Consume and roar!

CHORUS: Look!   1175
     The fire, look,
       it roars

    upon
      the tomb
        of Semele! Look!   1180
    The fire-
      bolt, Zeus's
      fire,
    it falls upon
      the fire of   1185
        Semele!
    Fall,
      Maenads!
      Fall!
    There, the   1190
      ground, fall
        to it!
    Tremble! Look!
      Our lord, the
        son   1195
    of Zeus, has
      brought these
        high
    halls
      down to   1200
      ruin.

[Enter Dionysus.]

DIONYSUS: Ah, my Oriental women: did you fall?
    Why? Was it fear that made you fall?
    You saw the house of Pentheus, when Dionysus
    made it shake, and you were shaken, too, by fear.   1205
    Come, no fear now, no fall: rise.
CHORUS LEADER: O Light, without you there was no dance,
    I was lost without you, Light.
DIONYSUS: Were you lost when I was locked in there?
    In the dark there, in the net of Pentheus?   1210
    Did you think that I was lost?
CHORUS LEADER: I was lost. What else, without you, but lost?
    The man who has no god had you. How are you free?
DIONYSUS: I saved myself. It took no effort.
CHORUS LEADER: But he'd bound your hands in knots!   1215
DIONYSUS: That was how I took my vengeance on him,
    how I humiliated him: he tried to bind me,
    his hands, though, never touched me;
    he fed on his desires. A bull was in there,
    by its stall—my jail, he thought. He took his ropes   1220
    and bent to wind them on its knees and hooves.

He was panting: *rage!* He was sweating, dripping,
biting at his lips. I was right there next to him.
I watched him. I was quiet. Then Bromius
revealed himself. The house shook! The grave
of Semele shot flames! Pentheus cried out.   1225
He thought the palace was in flames.
Where are all my slaves? he cried. He ran.
The slaves ran. *Water!* he shouted, *from the river,
from Achelous,* but all their work was futile.   1230
Then he stopped. He thought of me: I might escape.
He drew a pitch-black sword and ran into the palace.
But it seems Bromius must have made a shape,
in the courtyard: Pentheus stabbed at it,
at the gleaming air, as though it were me.   1235
Bacchus wasn't finished, though, humiliating him.
The palace crashes down, everything is shattered.
Now Pentheus can see the bitterness my chains
have brought him. His sword falls. He's exhausted.
A man, a mortal, dares to struggle with a god!   1240
I left him there. I walked out quietly to you.
Pentheus! What is he to me? I imagine he'll be coming.
Listen to him tramping through the courtyard.
I'll be patient: let him rage. Wise men
know how to practice self-control.   1245

[Enter Pentheus and guards.]

PENTHEUS: Terrible: that stranger, that man I had in chains . . .
    he's escaped . . . You!
    What are you doing here, at the gate?
    How did you get out?
DIONYSUS: Step calmly with your anger.   1250
PENTHEUS: How did you escape your bonds?
DIONYSUS: Weren't you listening when I told you
    someone would be here to free me?
PENTHEUS: Someone? You keep making riddles.
DIONYSUS: Someone who makes grapevines grow for human beings.   1255
PENTHEUS: The gift of wine! You reproach this god yourself!
    I want the tower gates all closed.
DIONYSUS: Can't gods leap over walls?
PENTHEUS: You're very wise. Except when you should be wise.
DIONYSUS: Wisest of all when I have to be.   1260
    Wait, though, someone's running towards us.
    He's coming from the mountain with a message.
    We'll wait, we won't try to run away.

[Enter Messenger.]

MESSENGER: Pentheus. King of Thebes.
    I come from Cithaeron, 1265
    where the white snow gleams
    and falls and never falters . . .

PENTHEUS: Is this news urgent?

MESSENGER: I've seen the holy Bacchae, the women from Thebes,
    who shot bare-legged out of the city like arrows. 1270
    I want to tell it to you, lord,
    to the entire city. It's astonishing,
    a miracle . . . May I speak freely, though?
    You have a temper, lord. I'm afraid
    of you, of your royal rage. 1275

PENTHEUS: Speak, I won't hurt you. Tell me everything.
    Being angry with an honest man is wrong.
    The more scandalous the things you tell about
    the Bacchae, though, the more the man who gave
    the women those ideas is going to suffer. 1280

MESSENGER: Our cattle were just coming up
    the last ridge to the high meadow.
    The sun was barely in the sky,
    just starting to warm the ground,
    when I saw them, the dancers, all three 1285
    troops of them, with their leaders.
    Autonoe first, then Agave, your mother,
    and finally, Ino.
    All of them were sound asleep, some
    stretched out on pine boughs, 1290
    others lying modestly here and there
    among the oak leaves, their heads on the ground.
    They were drunk with wine, but not
    the way you say, intoxicated with shrieking
    flutes and driven into ecstasies 1295
    tracking Aphrodite in the bushes.
    But then your mother, hearing
    the lowing of our stock, was on her feet,
    letting out a ritual scream, and then
    the rest of the Bacchae, in one bound, 1300
    as though with a single mind, woke,
    too, rubbing their eyes like children.
    There were old women and young,
    and unmarried girls: all wonderfully
    well disciplined. They shook their long hair 1305
    out over their shoulders. The ones whose
    fawnskin robes had slipped refastened them
    with living snakes, whose tongues
    flickered over the women's cheeks.

I saw mothers who'd abandoned babies;   1310
their breasts gorged with milk, they held
wolf cubs in their arms, or young
gazelles, and were suckling them.
Now they all put garlands on their heads,
flowering myrtle and oak leaves.   1315
Now one, with her thyrsus, strikes
a rock: living water fountains up.
Another drives her wand into the ground:
the god jets up a spring of wine.
If they wanted milk to drink,   1320
they scratched at the earth with their nails
and milk streamed for them, and pure honey
spurted from the tips of their wands.
If you had been there, sire,
if you had seen these miracles,   1325
believe me, the god whom you abuse now
you'd supplicate with prayers.

We, the shepherds and cow-tenders,
all of us there watching, were all
talking at once by then, trying   1330
to explain to one another the wonderful
and awful things they were doing.
Then someone, a wanderer, who'd spent
time in town and had a way
with words, said to us: "Listen,   1335
all of you who live up here
on the holy highlands
of the mountains, don't you want
to curry favor with the king?
Let's hunt down Agave for him   1340
and drag her from those dances."
We let him talk us into it.
We set up ambush in the brush,
camouflaged with leaves. The women,
when the time came, started dancing.   1345
Suddenly their wands were whirling,
then the women, whirling, spinning,
were crying out, "O Iacchus,
O Bromius, O son of Zeus,
O Lord of Cries,"   1350
then everything, all of them,
the whole mountain, all the wild
animals, went Bacchic, too,

nothing was unmoved; the women ran,
and it all ran with them.   1355

Agave came leaping past my hiding
place and I leaped out
to try to capture her,
but she was howling now: "Bitches,
dogs who hunt with me, it's *us*   1360
these men are hunting! Look! Follow
me! Arm yourself with thyrsi!"
Then it was we who had to run,
to keep from being torn apart.
They swooped down on our grazing   1365
cattle: bare-handed, they attacked.
Watch: a bellowing heifer, udders
gorged—a woman picks it bodily up,
and tears it limb from limb.
Watch now: full-grown cows,   1370
dismembered. Ribs,
hooves, flying this way, that way,
catching on the pine boughs,
hanging there, dribbling gore.
Even bulls, all power and arrogance,   1375
rage rising in their horns:
soft, young hands wrestle them
to the earth and flay them, faster
than your royal eyes could blink.
Then the women, like a flock of birds,   1380
soared out across the lowlands,
along the river Asopus, where the rich
cornfields of the Thebans are.
Now, at the foot of Cithaeron,
the two hamlets, Hysiae   1385
and Eurythrae, are invaded,
the women are attacking,
plundering. They tear children
from their houses, and whatever they put
on their backs stays there,   1390
without straps, even bronze and iron.
They carried fire on their hair
and weren't scorched. Now the men
had had enough: in rage, they rose,
took up their weapons. What we see   1395
next is dreadful, lord.
The men throw their spears, and draw

no blood; the women, though, let loose
their *wands,* and *wound* the men and
the men run! . . . Women defeating men! 1400
Certainly a god was in it.
The women went back then
to the springs the god had gushed
out of the earth, and washed away
the blood, the snakes licked the drops 1405
from their cheeks.
                    Master,
this god, whoever he may be,
I don't know, but welcome him to Thebes.
He's great in other ways as well, 1410
but beyond all that, they say
it's he who gave mortals wine,
which eases our suffering.
If we didn't have our wine, there
wouldn't be sexual love: what pleasure 1415
would there be for humans then?

[Exit Messenger.]

CHORUS LEADER: I don't know how to speak freely
to a king: I'm afraid, but I will say it,
I will cry it out: Dionysus is divine!
Dionysus cedes nothing to the other gods! 1420
PENTHEUS: Everything is roaring closer, like a fire.
This outrage of the Bacchae:
humiliation for all Greece!
To the gates. No time to lose.
I want all the horses, all the shields; 1425
every soldier who can snap a bowstring,
every trooper who can lift a lance.
We march on the Bacchae!
This is beyond endurance.
To have to suffer this from women! 1430
DIONYSUS: You pretend to listen, Pentheus,
but you don't pay attention.
You wronged me, but still, I'll tell you again:
don't war against a god. Stay at peace.
Bromius won't allow his Bacchae to be driven 1435
from where the mountain cries in ecstasy.
PENTHEUS: Don't preach at me. You were chained, you escaped.
Keep your freedom. Shall I punish you again?
DIONYSUS: In your place, I'd offer sacrifice to him,
instead of sacrilege and fighting the bit. 1440
You're mortal, he's a god.

PENTHEUS: I'll make sacrifice. Women's blood,
              pouring down the flanks of Cithaeron. As they deserve.
DIONYSUS: You'll be routed, shamed, disgraced.
              They'll lift their ivied wands,   1445
              your bronze shields will wilt.
PENTHEUS: There's no way to pin this stranger, is there?
              Chain him or unchain him, he still won't be quiet.
DIONYSUS: Listen, friend! We still can make this turn out well.
PENTHEUS: By doing what, obeying my own slaves?   1450
DIONYSUS: I'll bring the women here, with no recourse to arms.
PENTHEUS: Another of your traps.
DIONYSUS: I'll use my powers to save you: is that a trap?
PENTHEUS: You and these powers conspire to save your rituals.
DIONYSUS: I have conspired, but with the god.   1455
PENTHEUS: Bring my weapons. You: not another word.
DIONYSUS: Wait! Wouldn't you like to see them on the mountain?
PENTHEUS: See? Yes, I'd give gold to see that.
DIONYSUS: That? Why such a wild craving to see that?
PENTHEUS: I'd hate to see them drunk, if they were drunk.   1460
DIONYSUS: Even if you hate it, though, you'd like to see?
PENTHEUS: I could hide. Under the pines, and watch quietly.
DIONYSUS: Hide or not, they might sniff you out.
PENTHEUS: Yes. Let them behold me openly.
DIONYSUS: Are you ready now? Shall I take you there?   1465
PENTHEUS: Take me there. Let's not waste time.
DIONYSUS: First, put on a dress, a long, linen dress.
PENTHEUS: A dress? Do I have to be demoted to a woman?
DIONYSUS: If they see you as a man, they'll kill you.
PENTHEUS: You're right. Again. You always seem to know.   1470
DIONYSUS: Dionysus taught me what to know.
PENTHEUS: What is it you know next?
DIONYSUS: We'll go inside. I'll put you in your dress.
PENTHEUS: The dress? Still? A woman's dress? Shame.
DIONYSUS: Don't you want to see the Maenads?   1475
PENTHEUS: What sort of costume will you dress me in?
DIONYSUS: I'll put you in a wig. You'll have long curls.
PENTHEUS: Put me in a wig? . . . with long curls?
DIONYSUS: The long dress, and a net for the long curls
PENTHEUS: Long dress . . . a net for the long curls.   1480
DIONYSUS: Then a thyrsus for your hand; and a fawnskin.
PENTHEUS: A woman's costume? No, I won't; I can't.
DIONYSUS: Blood will flow if you battle the Bacchae.
PENTHEUS: Yes, first we have to scout them out.
DIONYSUS: Better than hunting one evil with another.   1485
PENTHEUS: How get through the city, though, and not be seen?
DIONYSUS: We'll take the alleys and back ways: I'll lead you.

PENTHEUS: Just so the Bacchae can't mock me.
Come inside now. I'll make up my mind.

DIONYSUS: As you please, you make up your mind.   1490

PENTHEUS: I'll go in, then either I'll come out in arms
or go with you, and follow your advice.

[Exit Pentheus into the palace.]

DIONYSUS: He's in the net now, women. He'll get to see
his Bacchae. He'll get what he deserves . . . to die.
Dionysus, you are near now; your task,   1495
too, is near: your revenge, our vengeance.
Make him insane. Give him ecstasy, and madness.
In his right mind, he'd never wear that woman's dress,
but driven from his sense, he'll slide right into it.
I want him to be the laughingstock of Thebes,   1500
led through the streets, costumed as a woman,
after all the bragging that made him seem so fearsome.
I'll go in now, I'll put him in his dress:
he'll take it to Hades with him
when his mother slaughters him.   1505
                          Then, at last,
he'll know; Dionysus is a god.
Dionysus is the son of Zeus.
Dionysus is, for humans, fiercest and most sweet.

[Exit Dionysus into the palace.]

CHORUS: Oh, will I, some-
      time, in the all-
            night dances, dance   1510
again, bare-
      foot, rapt,
            again, in
Bacchus, all
      in Bacchus,   1515
            again?

Will I
      throw my bared
            throat
back, to the cool   1520
      night back, the
            way,
oh, in the green joys
      of the meadow, the
            way   1525
a fawn

frisks, leaps,
   throws itself
as it finds itself
   safely past
      the frightening
hunters, past the
   nets, the
      houndsmen
urging on
   their straining
      hounds, free
now, leaping, tasting
   free wind now,
      being wind
now as it leaps
   the plain, the
      stream
and river, out
   at last, out from
      the human,
free, back
   into the
      green,
rich, dapple-
   shadowed tresses of the
      forest.

What is
   wisdom?
      What
the fairest
   gift the gods
      can offer
us
   below?
      What
is nobler
   than
      to hold
a dominating
   hand
      above
the bent
   head of
      the enemy?
The fair, the

1530

1535

1540

1545

1550

1555

1560

1565

1570

noble, how
we
cherish, how
we welcome
them.

Hardly
stirring, hardly
seeming
to happen, it
happens sometimes
so
slowly, the power
of the gods, but
it does, then,
stir, does
come
to pass, and,
inexorably, comes
to punish
humans,
who honor first
self-pride, and
turn,
their judgment
torn, their reason
torn,
demented, from
the
holy.

The first step
of the gods, it
hardly, in
its great
time, seems
to stir, the
first step
of the godly hunt
of
the unholy, first
step
of the revenge
on those who
put themselves

beyond
and
   over
    law.

So little
   does
    it cost   1620
to understand
   that *this*
    has power, whatever   1625
is divine; so
   little
    cost
to comprehend
   that what has   1630
    long
been lawful,
   over
    centuries,
comes forever   1635
   out
    of Nature.

What is
   wisdom?
    What   1640
the fairest
   gift the gods
    can offer
us
   below?   1645
    What
is nobler
   than
    to hold
a dominating   1650
   hand
    above
the bent
   head of
    the enemy?   1655
The fair, the
   noble, how
    we

cherish, how
  we welcome
    them.   1660

He
  is happy who,
    from the
storm, from
  the   1665
    ocean,
reaches
  harbor, and he,
    he   1670
is happy who,
  out of
    labor, out
of toil,
  has   1675
    risen. And
the one
  with wealth, and
    the one with
power surpassing   1680
  others: he
    is happy.

And hope: there
  are
    countless hopes.   1685
Hopes
  come one
    by one, some
end well and
  others   1690
    merely end.
But he who
  lives,
    day by
single day,   1695
  in
    happiness, he,
and only he,
  will I name
    blessed.   1700

[Enter Dionysus from the palace. He turns and calls back to Pentheus.]

DIONYSUS: If you still want to see what you shouldn't see,
 if you desire what shouldn't be desired, come out.
 Pentheus, come out here, let me see you.
 Maenad, Bacchant, woman: show us your long dress,
 show us how you'll scout your mother and her troop. 1705

[Enter Pentheus, dressed as a Bacchant.]

 Why, you look like one of the daughters of Cadmus.
PENTHEUS: Look! What I see! I think I see two suns
 and Thebes, too, twice: the seven-gated fortress, twice.
 And you, you seem to be a bull, out there before me,
 the double horns sprouting on your forehead: 1710
 were you an animal before, the way now you're a bull?
DIONYSUS: The god is with us now. He's not angry now.
 He's made peace. You see now what you ought to see.
PENTHEUS: What do I look like now?
 Do I stand like Ino or my mother? 1715
DIONYSUS: When I see you, I might be seeing them.
 Wait, a curl has come loose.
 I'll tuck it in its net; it must have fallen.
PENTHEUS: It must have fallen, I was in there dancing
 Bacchic dances, shaking my head backwards and forwards . . . 1720
DIONYSUS: Hold your head still now. I'll be your maid.
 I'll put the curl back, like this.
PENTHEUS: You'll put it back. Yes, I'm in your hands.
DIONYSUS: But wait, your sash has slipped. The pleats
 are disarrayed; the hem is too low. 1725
PENTHEUS: Not on the right too low; on the left, though . . .
 Watch, when I lift my left leg, this way . . .
DIONYSUS: You're going to think that I'm your closest friend,
 when you see how surprisingly chaste the Bacchae are.
PENTHEUS: Would a good Bacchant hold her thyrsus this way, 1730
 in her right hand, or like this, in her left?
DIONYSUS: The right hand, yes. Now the right leg, lift that.
 I commend your change of mind.
PENTHEUS: Tell me, could I lift Cithaeron now—
 Bacchae, cliffs, all of it: could I? 1735
DIONYSUS: You could, if you wanted to. Your mind before
 wasn't healthy, now you have the mind you should.
PENTHEUS: Will I need levers, or shall I tear the cliffs up
 with my hands and put them on my shoulders?
DIONYSUS: Now wait: don't destroy the Nymphs' groves, 1740
 the sacred places where Pan plays his flute.
PENTHEUS: You're right. One shouldn't need brute force
 to conquer women. I'll stay out of sight in the pines.

DIONYSUS: You'll have the proper hiding place to hide;
    then, when you're hidden, you'll spy on the Maenads.   1745

PENTHEUS: Yes, I can see them now, in the bushes,
    little birds, trapped in the toils of love.

DIONYSUS: That's your mission, isn't it? To keep an eye on them?
    You might catch them at it, unless they catch you . . .

PENTHEUS: Take me through Thebes now. Let all Thebes see   1750
    the single person man enough to dare all this.

DIONYSUS: You and only you will suffer for this city.
    Ordeals await you, they are fated for you.
    Come, I'll lead you there safely.
    You'll return with someone else.   1755

PENTHEUS: My mother . . .

DIONYSUS: . . . a model for all men . . .

PENTHEUS: That's my purpose.

DIONYSUS: You'll be carried home . . .

PENTHEUS: You're spoiling me!   1760

DIONYSUS: . . . in your mother's arms.

PENTHEUS: . . . No, you're *spoiling* me

DIONYSUS: Yes, I *want* to spoil you, in my way.

PENTHEUS: I'll have what I deserve.

DIONYSUS: You'll have the outcome you deserve.   1765
    You are awe-inspiring.
    Your outcome will inspire awe.
    Your fame will reach the heavens.

[Exit Pentheus towards Cithaeron.]

    Agave! Listen to me! Listen to me, daughters
    of Cadmus! I am calling! Hold out your hands!   1770
    I lead this young man to his ordeal.
    The victory will be for me, and for Bromius.
    The rest will be revealed.

[Exit Dionysus.]

CHORUS: Now, hounds,
    now,
        quickly, hounds   1775
  of madness, quickly
    to the mountain,
        quickly
  to the bands   1780
    of Cadmus' daughters—
        sting
  them, goad
    them on,
        lead   1785

them to the man
  costumed
    as a woman, to
the frenzied
  spy, goad
    them. First his
mother will
  see him, on
    the smooth
stone cliff, or
  on his tree, will
    see him
watching, and
  will call
    the others
to her, the other
  Maenads to
    be with her.
"Who is
  this?" she'll
    call. "Who
is this who
  searches for
    the
daughters of
  Cadmus in the
    mountain,
on our
  mountain?
    Bacchae,"
she'll
  call, "*Bacchae,*
    was he
from woman
  born? *Who*
    dared
spill blood to
  bear him? Surely
    not a
woman, surely
  a
    lioness, yes,
not a
  woman but some
    monstrous
Gorgon, from

1790

1795

1800

1805

1810

1815

1820

1825

1830

Lydia, a
   monster."

Justice
   now! Let justice
      go   1835
forth clearly
   now! Justice
      goes
forth with   1840
   her sword
      now!
Justice thrusts
   through
      the throat   1845
now of the
   godless, lawless
      unjust son
of Echion, earth-
   born offspring   1850
      of the snake.

No justice and no
   judgment and
      no
law has he, to   1855
   rise against
      you, Bacchic
one, against your
   secret worship
      and your   1860
mother's; with
   force, insanity,
      frenzy,
did he
   rise as   1865
      though
to conquer the
   unconquerable
      with his frenzy and
his force.   1870
   Death,
      though,
death will
   temper him and
      tame him; implacable   1875

death chastises
  minds which
    do
not understand the
  things
    of gods.   1880

To understand
  that we
    are mortal
is to live   1885
  without insufferable
    pain.

I hardly envy
  wisdom; my
    joy,   1890
instead, is
  hunting down
    those other
values, great
  and clear, that   1895
    lead
life towards
  the
    good:
to be, day-   1900
  long, night-
    long,
reverent,
  pure, and
    to   1905
give my
  honor to
    the gods
by casting
  out   1910
    those customs
which
  are outside
    justice.

Justice   1915
  now! Justice
    goes
forth clearly

now! Justice
  goes
forth with
  her sword
    now!
Justice thrusts
  through
    the throat
now of the
  godless, lawless,
    unjust son
of Echion, earth-
  born offspring
    of the snake.

A bull be,
  Bacchus, or a
    serpent, many-
headed, be,
  or a lion,
    like a flame
be. Hunt
  the hunter,
    Bacchus, hunt
him, be the
  fighter, Bacchus, now,
    throw the net
now, laughing, lethal,
  pull him
    down now, let
him fall,
  beneath
    the herd
of Maenads, let
  him fall
    now.

[Enter Messenger.]

MESSENGER: O house, O famous house:
all Greece once thought you fortunate.
Cadmus came from Sidon, sowing the earth-
born dragon's harvests in the serpent's land.
Now I, a slave, mourn for you.
CHORUS: What? What news from the Bacchae?
MESSENGER: The son of Echion, Pentheus, is dead.

CHORUS: King Bromius! You
      reveal your
        greatness!

MESSENGER: What are you saying? What do these words mean?
      Does my master's anguish give you joy?   1965

CHORUS: Ecstasy, for
      us, the Asian
        strangers: no
    chains, no
      terror   1970
        now!

MESSENGER: Do you think no men are left in Thebes?

CHORUS: Dionysus now! Not
    Thebes!
      Dionysus   1975
  has power
      over
      me!

MESSENGER: I can pardon what you feel—still, women:
      rejoicing in misfortune isn't right.   1980

CHORUS: What doom, tell
    me, did he
      die,
  the tyrant, the
    man of unjust   1985
    accomplishments?

MESSENGER: When we'd marched out of Thebes, past
  the last farms, then the river Asopus, we headed
  into the hills of Cithaeron, Pentheus and I—
  I was accompanying my master—and the stranger   1990
  who was the escort for our spying mission.
  After a while we stopped: grass, a valley.
  Stay down, be quiet, watch your step—
  we want to see, not be seen. Ahead of us,
  the hills move in: cliffs, a cut,   1995
  water wandering through, pines and shade,
  and there they are, sitting quietly, the Maenads,
  peacefully working with their hands.
  A few were wreathing tendrils of ivy on a tattered
  thyrsus, some were chanting Bacchic songs   2000
  to one another, like fillies when their harnesses
  are taken off at night. Pentheus,
  though, poor Pentheus, couldn't see the women.
  "Stranger," he said, "from where we are—
  I can't make them out, the imposter Maenads.   2005

If I could climb a high pine on the cliff,
I could see their shameless orgies."

Suddenly, the stranger now: a miracle.
He reaches into the sky, and, seizing the topmost
branch of a pine tree, he drags it down,   2010
down and down, until it touches the black earth,
until it's bent, curved, the way a bow is curved,
the way a wooden rim is curved on pegs to form a wheel.

With his two hands the stranger bent it, tough
mountain pine: this wasn't mortal's work.   2015
Now, taking Pentheus, he puts him on the branches
of the pine and, sliding the trunk through his hands,
he lets it rise . . . gently, though, so it wouldn't
throw its rider. Pentheus wasn't thrown,
he rode it up until it towered   2020
into the towering air, and the Maenads
saw him . . . He didn't see them, though.

Now, suddenly, as Pentheus appeared in the sky,
the stranger vanished and a voice was in the sky—
it had to have been Dionysus—crying: 2025
"Women! I've brought the man who mocks us:
you, me, my mysteries—take revenge!"

As he cried, a light of sacred fire formed,
linking earth and heaven: the high air
suddenly went still, and everything, sky, forest,   2030
leaf and creature, everything was still.

The women, too, not sure what they had heard,
stood still, looking around them. Then the voice
again, his command, clearer now, and they heard it
now, the daughters of Cadmus; Agave, the mother   2035
of Pentheus, her sisters, all the Bacchae
heard him now, and understood, and ran,
flew, like darting doves, through the glade,
over the boiling stream, over the jagged stones.
They were soaring now, the god's breath maddening them.   2040
Finally they saw him, Pentheus, in his tree.
Scaling a cliff that towered across from him,
they pitched stones at their pitiful target,
and branches, and some even threw their thyrsi.
He was out of reach of their passion,   2045
but he was helpless, wretched, treed.
They sheared limbs from oaks then, and there they were,
with wooden levers, prying at the roots.

Again they failed. Then Agave shouted:
"Maenads, here! Circle the tree! Hold on to it!   2050
We have to catch the animal who's mounted there.
He'll reveal the secrets of the dances of the god!"
How many hands were on that tree!
They wrenched it from the ground. And he,
he fell . . . So high he was, and he was falling,   2055
moaning: he'd begun to understand his doom.

The first one at him was the priestess of the slaughter,
his own mother. She fell upon him, and he,
that she, poor Agave, might recognize him, tore
his headband off and, touching her cheek, shrieked   2060
at her: "*Me!* It's me! It's Pentheus, Mother.
Your son! You are my *mother*! Look at me!
I've made mistakes, but I'm your son: don't kill me!"

Agave was foaming at the mouth, though.
Her eyes were rolling, wild; she was mad,   2065
utterly possessed by Bacchus: what Pentheus said
was nothing to her. She took him by the arm,
the left arm, under the elbow, then she planted
a foot against his ribs and tore his arm off.
Not by herself: it was the power of the god   2070
that put so much force into her hands.

Ino was working at his other side,
clawing at the flesh. And Autonoe
and the rest of them, the whole horde of them,
were swarming over him and everything   2075
by then was one horrifying scream:
he, groaning with the little breath left in him,
they, howling in triumph. One had a forearm,
one had one of his feet, still warm in its sandal.
His ribs were stripped of flesh, and all the women,   2080
all those bloody hands, were throwing pieces of him
back and forth between them as though it were a game.

Now the body is scattered. Parts at the base
of the cliff, parts hidden in the undergrowth.
His pitiful head his mother happened on;   2085
she took it in her hands, impaled it,
like a mountain lion's, on her thyrsus,
and now she's carrying it home across Cithaeron,
leaving her sisters in the dances of the Maenads.
She's here now, in Thebes, carrying her hideous   2090
trophy, exulting, calling on her Bacchus,
her partner in the hunt, comrade in the capture—

but all her crown of victory will really be
is tears. I want away from this calamity.
I'm leaving now, before Agave reaches the palace.   2095
To know your human limits, to revere the gods,
is the noblest and I think the wisest course
that mortal men can follow.

[Exit Messenger.]

CHORUS: Dance
         now! Exult   2100
            and dance
      now, Bacchae!
         Exult and dance the
            misery of
      Pentheus, offspring   2105
         of
            the Snake, who
      took a woman's
         dress, took
            the   2110
      holy
         thyrsus and
            took with it the
      road marked out
         by the Bull, to   2115
            Hades. (hell)

      O Theban
         Bacchae! What
            a song of
      victory have you   2120
         wailed, what
            triumph wailed,
      a victory of tears
         and
            mourning. How   2125
      lovely is
         the conflict, how
            lovely,
      with one's bloody
         hand   2130
            embracing,
      lovely, one's
         own
            child!
But here is Agave, here is the mother of Pentheus.   2135

Her eyes are wild. Welcome now the joyous
dancers of the God of Evohe!

[Enter Agave. She carries the head of Pentheus.]

AGAVE: Bacchae! Asians!
CHORUS: What do you
   want of
     us?   2140
AGAVE: Look what we
   have! What we
     bring home!
CHORUS: We can   2145
   see it. I welcome you,
     fellow dancer.
AGAVE: I caught it by
   myself,
     this offspring
of a savage   2150
   lion, and with no
     net: look!
CHORUS: In what
   wilderness?   2155
AGAVE: Cithaeron . . .
CHORUS: Cithaeron? . . .
AGAVE: . . . butchered him.
CHORUS: Who
   struck him
     first?   2160
AGAVE: I
   had the honor first.
CHORUS: Blessed
   Agave!
AGAVE: So I'm called   2165
   among my
     pack!
CHORUS: No
   one else? . . .
AGAVE: Cadmus . . .   2170
CHORUS: Cadmus?
AGAVE: His daughters,
   after me,
   after I
     had touched,   2175
     touched,
   too, the
     beast. Blessed

                    hunting!   2180
          Now take part
                    in
                    the feast!
CHORUS: Take
          part? Pitiful   2185
                    woman!
AGAVE: Look, though,
          the bull
                    is
          young, look,   2190
          his mane
                    is soft, his
          cheeks
          are barely
                    downed.   2195
CHORUS: At least he
          seems, yes,
                    with
          his mane, to be
          a savage   2200
                    animal.
AGAVE: Our god, Bacchus,
          hunter,
                    whipped,
          cunningly, his pack   2205
          of women on
                    the beast!
CHORUS: Our lord god,
          yes, is a
                    hunter.   2210
AGAVE: Do you praise
          me?
CHORUS: I
          praise
          you.   2215
AGAVE: And
          the Cadmeans,
          soon? . . .
CHORUS: . . . and
          your son, Pentheus . . .   2220
AGAVE: . . . will praise his
          mother for . . .
CHORUS: . . . her savage . . .
AGAVE: . . . catch, lion . . .

CHORUS: . . . born, prod-   2225
      igious . . .

AGAVE: . . . catch . . .

CHORUS: . . . caught
      prodigiously.

AGAVE: Prodigious   2230
      catch.

CHORUS: Do you
      exult?

AGAVE: I
      exult!   2235
      Greatness have
       I
      accomplished, great
       the deeds, great
       and shining!   2240

CHORUS LEADER: Show it now, poor woman. Show your blessed trophy
      to the people. Let them behold your victory.

AGAVE: Thebans! Citizens!
      Everyone who lives beneath these high towers,
      look! Come see the beast the daughters of Cadmus   2245
      hunted down, not with nets, not with spears,
      but with the white nails of our hands.
      Who is the hunter, armed with useless spears,
      who'll dare boast now, when all needed
      were our hands to bring the creature down   2250
      and tear it completely to pieces?

      Where's my father?
      Old, good Cadmus, he should be here.
      And my child, Pentheus, find him for me, too.
      Have him bring a ladder; have him stand it   2255
      here to nail the lion's head to the cornice.
      I captured it myself, and brought it here.

*[Enter Cadmus, with attendants carrying a litter with the remains of
Pentheus.]*

CADMUS: Come this way, please . . . Put the dreadful burden
      which was Pentheus here, before the palace.
      I've brought the body back: I searched forever.   2260
      It was in the folds of Cithaeron, torn to shreds,
      scattered through the impenetrable forest,
      no two parts of him in any single spot.
      When they described the atrocity my daughters
      had committed, I'd returned to the walls of the town   2265
      with old Tiresias: we'd been with the Bacchae.

I turned back again, up to the mountain,
where I gathered the body of this boy,
murdered by the Maenads. I saw Autonoe there,
Aristaeus' wife, the mother of poor Actaeon,   2270
and I saw Ino, both of them, still in the thickets,
pitiful women, still stung with frenzy, still insane.
Now someone has told me that Agave,
still possessed by the god, has come to Thebes . . .
And they were right, I see her,   2275
a dismal sight to have to behold.

AGAVE: Father, you can boast now; the daughters you sired
are more noble than any other mortal's.
I speak of all of us, but especially me,
who have left the loom and shuttle and risen   2280
to greatness: hunting wild creatures with my hands.

Look what I have here in my arms:
a trophy for the palace. Here, Father,
take it in your hands, glory in my kill.
Invite your friends to feast, for you   2285
are blessed, blessed by our accomplishments.

CADMUS: I cannot watch this. This is grief that has no measure.
What your poor hands accomplished was butchery.
A lovely victim you have murdered for the gods,
whom you call for Thebes and me to celebrate.   2290
Anguish for you, anguish, too, for me.
With justice, but with too much severity,
Lord Bromius, our own blood, has ruined us.

AGAVE: Complaining, scowling: old age makes men sour!
Would my son at least could be a happy hunter,   2295
like his mother, when he goes out on the chase
with his young friends from Thebes.
But all he does is struggle with the god.
Father, he needs talking to, by you.
Someone call him, let me see him.   2300
Let him see his mother, Agave the blessed.

CADMUS: Child, if consciousness should come to you
of what you've done, how grievously you'll suffer.
If you could pass your life in your present mind,
we'd never call you happy but at least   2305
you wouldn't know how miserable you are.

AGAVE: But this is wonderful! What could cause pain here?

CADMUS: First, turn your eyes upwards, towards the sky.

AGAVE: There. Why should I look into the sky, though?

CADMUS: Does the sky look the same? Might it be changing?   2310

AGAVE: Yes, it is; it's more transparent, clearer.

CADMUS: And do you still feel flurries of excitement in you?

AGAVE: I don't know what you mean . . . No . . . Yes . . .
    Yes, something is changing, my mind is calmer.

CADMUS: Can you hear me? Can you answer clearly?   2315

AGAVE: What were we saying, Father? I've forgotten.

CADMUS: In whose household did you marry?

AGAVE: You gave me to Echion, the sown-man they called him.

CADMUS: And what child did you bear your husband there?

AGAVE: Pentheus was the outcome of our marriage.   2320

CADMUS: Now, whose head are you holding in your arms?

AGAVE: A lion's . . . The huntresses . . . They told me . . .

CADMUS: Look right at it. One look will be enough.

AGAVE: What? What am I seeing? What is in my hands?

CADMUS: Look carefully. Study it more closely.   2325

AGAVE: I see horror. I see suffering. I see grief.

CADMUS: Does it still look like a lion?

AGAVE: No, Pentheus: I am holding his head.

CADMUS: Yes, now you know, I mourn Pentheus.

AGAVE: Who killed him? Why is he in *my* hands?   2330

CADMUS: Savage truth, how long you took to come to light.

AGAVE: Tell me, my heart is trembling with it.

CADMUS: You killed him. With your sisters.

AGAVE: Where did it happen? At home? Where?

CADMUS: Where Actaeon was dismembered by his hounds.   2335

AGAVE: On Cithaeron? Why was my poor Pentheus there?

CADMUS: He went to mock the gods, and your rituals.

AGAVE: But we, why were we there?

CADMUS: You were mad. The city was possessed by Dionysus.

AGAVE: I see now. Dionysus has destroyed us.   2340

CADMUS: You enraged him. You denied he was god.

AGAVE: My son's beloved body, where is it, Father?

CADMUS: There he is, what I could find of him.

AGAVE: Is he decently put back together?
    Why did Pentheus have to suffer for my madness?   2345

CADMUS: He, too, refused the god, and the god,
    for this, has ruined us all—
    you, this boy: our whole house is ruined.
    And I, with no male heirs, have to see him now,
    this branching of your womb, the new light   2350
    of our house, shamefully destroyed.

    O child, you held our house together, you,
    my daughter's son, how the city was in awe of you.
    No one looking at your face would dare affront my age—
    you'd have punished them as they deserved.   2355
    Now I'll be exiled, my honors stripped from me.

I, the great Cadmus, sower of the race of Thebes,
who harvested the most lovely of harvests.
O dearest of men, you are no longer living
but you are still, child, among those I love   2360
beyond all else. Who will stroke my beard now?
Who embrace me, call me Grandfather, ask me,
"Has anyone offended you, old man, not shown you
adequate respect? Disturbed, dishonored you?
Tell me who it was, Grandfather, I'll punish him."   2365
Now I am nothing. You, a ruin. Your mother
only to be pitied, and her unhappy sisters, too.
Is there anyone who scorns the gods? Look now
at this murdered boy: now, believe!

CHORUS LEADER: I grieve with you, Cadmus: your daughter's son   2370
has justice now, but so much grief for you.

AGAVE: Father, look at me, how my destiny has turned.

[She kneels to the body of Pentheus.]

Who is this person? Who is this corpse?
Who am I? How can I, in all reverence,
knowing that my hands dismembered him   2375
and are polluted with his blood,
dare to touch him, dare take him
to my breast, dare sing his dirge to him?
But how can I not? What other hands
can care for you, my child?   2380

O old man, come help me, help me
touch this wretched boy. Show me
where to lay his head, show me how
to put his body back together.

Look, his arms are so well muscled,   2385
his legs so strong, but his face, oh,
dearest face, its cheek is barely feathered.
This flesh I nurtured once, I kiss.
The fragments of this body I loved
once, I lay in place.   2390

How am I doing this? How can I touch
my crime with my polluted hands?
With what robes shall I veil you, child?
Here: I'll give you mine. I'll hide your head.
Here, hide your shattered, bloodstained body. 2395

[She covers the body with her veil. Dionysus appears, as himself, above.]

DIONYSUS: I am Dionysus. I am Bacchus.
Bromius and Iacchus.
Dithyrambus and Evius.
I am the son of Zeus.
I have come to the country of the Thebans,   2400
where Semele, the daughter of King Cadmus,
bore me in a blaze of lightning.
When I arrived in Thebes, there was blasphemy.
"He was born of mortals," they were saying.
Slander. Irreverence. Impiety.   2405
I offered these people everything.
How did they repay my generosity?
With malice, ingratitude, and lies.

Now I shall recite your future for you.
First, your future will be suffering.   2410
Then your future will be suffering again.
Banishment and slavery and pain.
You will be driven from this city.
You will be hounded into other lands.
Captives in a war.   2415
Chains. Slavery. Toil.
Your lives will wear away like sand.

Behold our Pentheus. He found the death
he deserved: torn to pieces.

You beheld him. You beheld his lies.   2420
His impudence. You beheld him
when he tried to chain me and abused me
and tried—and *dared* to try—
to punish me.
I am Dionysus! Behold me!   2425

The hands that should have been the last
to do this to him were the very hands
that did it. Why? Because he did
what he should not have done.

And now your doom, Agave, is this: 2430
for you and for your sisters—exile.
You must expiate your crime.
You are polluted, you cannot stay
in the precincts of these graves.

And Cadmus: there are ordeals for you.   2435
You will be transfigured into a snake.
And Harmonia, the daughter of Ares, whom you won

as wife despite your being mortal,
she, too, will be a beast, a snake.
Then both of you, drawn by oxen in a cart,   2440
will, according to the oracle of Zeus,
lead an innumerable barbarian horde
to lay waste cities, to ravage and destroy.
And when the shrine of Apollo is sacked,
the hordes will turn, and the turning   2445
and the coming back, will be tragic.

Ares, in the end, will save you and save
Harmonia and bring your lives
into the country of the blessed.

This is the decree of Dionysus,   2450
the son not of a human but of Zeus.
If you had understood your mortal natures
when you refused to understand them,
the son of Zeus would have been your ally.
You would now be in blessedness.   2455

CADMUS: Dionysus, we implore you, we have offended.

DIONYSUS: You learned too late to know me.
When you had time, you did not know me.

CADMUS: We confess that, but your punishment is harsh.

DIONYSUS: I am a god! You outraged my divinity.   2460

CADMUS: Gods should not resemble mortals in anger.

DIONYSUS: Long ago, my father, Zeus, ordained all this.

AGAVE: Father, the sentence is decreed: banishment.

DIONYSUS: Why do you delay your doom?

CADMUS: Oh, my child, to what a terrible fate   2465
have we been reduced.
You, your pitiful sisters, and myself, all wretched.
An old man, to have to live a stranger among strangers.
There is an oracle as well that I will lead
a ragged barbarian army against Hellas. My wife,   2470
Harmonia, the daughter of Ares, will be a savage snake,
and I, too, will be a snake, and against the altars
and the graves of Greece will lead those spears.
And no respite. I will cross the river Acheron,[23]
as it plunges down, and have, still, no peace.   2475

AGAVE: And me, O Father, banishment!
To be torn from you!

---

23. The Acheron River was said to form one of
the boundaries of the underworld.

CADMUS: My poor child, why put your arms around me?
　A white swan sheltering its hoary, helpless father.

AGAVE: Tell me, where shall I go, outcast from my country? 2480

CADMUS: I don't know, child. Your father is no help.

AGAVE: Farewell, my house; farewell,
　my country. Banished from my home,
　exiled from everything I love.
　What is left for me? 2485

CADMUS: Poor daughter: go to Aristaeus, Actaeon's father.

AGAVE: I am mourning for you, Father.

CADMUS: And I, daughter, these tears are for you,
　and for your sisters.

AGAVE: How terrible the blows Dionysus 2490
　struck against your house.

DIONYSUS: I suffered terribly,
　my name, in Thebes, deprived of honor.

AGAVE: Goodbye, Father.

CADMUS: Child, poor child, farewell. 2495
　Faring well, though, will be hard for you.

AGAVE: Take me away from here, to my sisters,
　the sisters of my endless exile.
　Let awful Cithaeron never see me again.
　Let me never set my eyes on Cithaeron again, 2500
　and let me never see another thyrsus,
　to bring this back to me again.

　All of that I leave, all
　of it, to other Bacchae.

　[Exit Agave.]

CHORUS: Many forms are 2505
　there of the
　　divine.
　Many things the
　　gods accomplish
　　　unexpectedly.
　What we waited 2510
　for does not
　　come to pass, while
　for what remained
　　undreamed the god 2515
　　　finds ways.
　Just such
　　doing was this
　　　doing.

　[Exit all.]

VERGIL (70–19 B.C.E.)
Rome

Vergil (Latin name Publius Vergilius Maro) channeled his genius and ambition exclusively through traditional Greek genres, but his poems reinvent the themes and forms they inherit in the service of Roman politics, culture, and ideology. The *Aeneid,* Vergil's last monumental work and the labor of a decade, is inspired simultaneously by the *Iliad* and the *Odyssey* and composed in dactylic hexameter. In twelve books, Vergil follows his eponymous hero from the smoking ruins of Troy to the shores of Italy, where Aeneas becomes the living link between the legendary Homeric age and the Rome in which Vergil lived and wrote, then at the crucial moment of its transition to empire.

Like Odysseus, (and Gilgamesh before him), Aeneas must voyage and endure; like Achilles, his half-human, half-divine nature meets its greatest challenges in combat and the clash of arms. But while the self-awareness of the Homeric heroes exalts them, Aeneas displays a far more modern consciousness. Both a maker and an agent of history, Aeneas is burdened by the fate that selects him as Rome's glorious progenitor. Caught between obligations to the past and to the future, Aeneas puts collective values before personal goals, accepting responsibility for ends that he can neither control nor wholly envision. Nowhere is this more evident than in Book 4, where Aeneas must choose between his love for Dido, queen of Carthage, and his destiny. Vergil's orchestration of Trojan past, Roman future, and vivid psychological present created an imperial mythology for Augustus Caesar, Vergil's patron and the first Roman emperor. Yet Vergil's celebration of Roman triumph is also suffused with a sense of its price: above all, of the pity of war. The profundity and virtuosity of Vergil's epic, combined with the longevity of Roman influence and the Latin language in European civilization, make the *Aeneid* the most influential single poem in Western literature.

from *Aeneid*

Book 4 [The Passion of the Queen[1]]

The queen, for her part, all that evening ached[1]
With longing that her heart's blood fed, a wound
Or inward fire eating her away.

Translated by Robert Fitzgerald.

---

1. Aeneas, son of Aphrodite and the Trojan Anchises (see the *Homeric Hymn to Aphrodite*), escapes the sack of Troy and, at the gods' urging, sails for Italy with a group of comrades in order to build a new settlement of Trojan descendants there. Driven by stormwinds to the coast of North Africa, the fleet lands at Carthage, a city recently founded by Queen Dido, a daughter of the ruling family of Tyre in Phoenicia. Dido has recently fled her native city after her brother's treacherous murder of her husband, and, sympathetic to the distress of the homeless Trojans, receives them hospitably. Aeneas recounts to her the destruction of Troy and the subsequent wanderings of his band of survivors until their arrival in Carthage.

The manhood of the man, his pride of birth,
Came home to her time and again; his looks,   5
His words remained with her to haunt her mind,
And desire for him gave her no rest.
                                        When Dawn
Swept earth with Phoebus' torch and burned away
Night-gloom and damp, this queen, far gone and ill,
Confided to the sister of her heart: 10
"My sister Anna, quandaries and dreams
Have come to frighten me—such dreams!
                                    Think what a stranger

Yesterday found lodging in our house:
How princely, how courageous, what a soldier.
I can believe him in the line of gods,   15
And this is no delusion. Tell-tale fear
Betrays inferior souls. What scenes of war
Fought to the bitter end he pictured for us!
What buffetings awaited him at sea!
Had I not set my face against remarriage   20
After my first love died and failed me, left me
Barren and bereaved—and sick to death
At the mere thought of torch and bridal bed—
I could perhaps give way in this one case
To frailty. I shall say it: since that time   25
Sychaeus, my poor husband, met his fate,
And blood my brother shed stained our hearth gods,
This man alone has wrought upon me so
And moved my soul to yield. I recognize
The signs of the old flame, of old desire.   30
But O chaste life, before I break your laws,
I pray that Earth may open, gape for me
Down to its depth, or the omnipotent
With one stroke blast me to the shades, pale shades
Of Erebus[2] and the deep world of night!   35
That man who took me to himself in youth
Has taken all my love; may that man keep it,
Hold it forever with him in the tomb."
At this she wept and wet her breast with tears.
But Anna answered:
                            "Dearer to your sister   40
Than daylight is, will you wear out your life,
Young as you are, in solitary mourning,
Never to know sweet children, or the crown
Of joy that Venus brings? Do you believe

---

2. The underworld.

This matters to the dust, to ghosts in tombs?   45
Granted no suitors up to now have moved you,
Neither in Libya nor before, in Tyre—
Iarbas[3] you rejected, and the others,
Chieftains bred by the land of Africa
Their triumphs have enriched—will you contend   50
Even against a welcome love? Have you
Considered in whose lands you settled here?
On one frontier the Gaetulans,[4] their cities,
People invincible in war—with wild
Numidian horsemen, and the offshore banks,   55
The Syrtës; on the other, desert sands,
Bone-dry, where fierce Barcaean nomads range.
Or need I speak of future wars brought on
From Tyre, and the menace of your brother?
Surely by dispensation of the gods   60
And backed by Juno's will, the ships from Ilium[5]
Held their course this way on the wind.
                                                    Sister,
What a great city you'll see rising here,
And what a kingdom, from this royal match!
With Trojan soldiers as companions in arms   65
By what exploits will Punic[6] glory grow!
Only ask the indulgence of the gods,
Win them with offerings, give your guests ease,
And contrive reasons for delay, while winter
Gales rage, drenched Orion storms at sea,   70
And their ships, damaged still, face iron skies."
This counsel fanned the flame, already kindled,
Giving her hesitant sister hope, and set her
Free of scruple. Visiting the shrines
They begged for grace at every altar first,   75
Then put choice rams and ewes to ritual death
For Ceres Giver of Laws,[7] Father Lyaeus,
Phoebus, and for Juno most of all
Who has the bonds of marriage in her keeping.
Dido herself, splendidly beautiful,   80
Holding a shallow cup, tips out the wine

---

3. Iarbas was a North African king and an
   unsuccessful suitor of the widowed Queen
   Dido.
4. The people of Iarbas's kingdom.
5. Troy.
6. Phoenician.
7. Ceres was the Roman goddess of agricultural fertility. She was called "lawgiver"

presumably because of her regulation of the
processes of agriculture. Lyaeus is an epithet of Dionysus, or Bacchus, also a deity
associated with fertility (see Euripides' Bacchae in this section). Juno, daughter of
Saturn and wife of the supreme deity, Jupiter, is especially associated with marriage
and domesticity.

On a white shining heifer, between the horns,
Or gravely in the shadow of the gods
Approaches opulent altars. Through the day
She brings new gifts, and when the breasts are opened   85
Pores over organs, living still, for signs.
Alas, what darkened minds have soothsayers!
What good are shrines and vows to maddened lovers?
The inward fire eats the soft marrow away,
And the internal wound bleeds on in silence.   90
Unlucky Dido, burning, in her madness
Roamed through all the city, like a doe
Hit by an arrow shot from far away
By a shepherd hunting in the Cretan woods—
Hit by surprise, nor could the hunter see   95
His flying steel had fixed itself in her;
But though she runs for life through copse and glade
The fatal shaft clings to her side.
                           Now Dido
Took Aeneas with her among her buildings,
Showed her Sidonian wealth, her walls prepared,   100
And tried to speak, but in mid-speech grew still.
When the day waned she wanted to repeat
The banquet as before, to hear once more
In her wild need the throes of Ilium,
And once more hung on the narrator's words.   105
Afterward, when all the guests were gone,
And the dim moon in turn had quenched her light,
And setting stars weighed weariness to sleep,
Alone she mourned in the great empty hall
And pressed her body on the couch he left: 110
She heard him still, though absent—heard and saw him.
Or she would hold Ascanius[8] in her lap,
Enthralled by him, the image of his father,
As though by this ruse to appease a love
Beyond all telling.
                        Towers, half-built, rose   115
No farther; men no longer trained in arms
Or toiled to make harbors and battlements
Impregnable. Projects were broken off,
Laid over, and the menacing huge walls
With cranes unmoving stood against the sky.   120
As soon as Jove's[9] dear consort saw the lady
Prey to such illness, and her reputation

---

8. Aeneas' son, also called Iulus; his mother
Creusa died in the sack of Troy.

9. Jupiter, supreme deity of the Roman pantheon.

Standing no longer in the way of passion,
Saturn's daughter said to Venus:
                              "Wondrous!
Covered yourself with glory, have you not,   125
You and your boy, and won such prizes, too.
Divine power is something to remember
If by collusion of two gods one mortal
Woman is brought low.
                              I am not blind.
Your fear of our new walls has not escaped me,   130
Fear and mistrust of Carthage at her height,
But how far will it go? What do you hope for,
Being so contentious? Why do we not
Arrange eternal peace and formal marriage?
You have your heart's desire: Dido in love,   135
Dido consumed with passion to her core.
Why not, then, rule this people side by side
With equal authority? And let the queen
Wait on her Phrygian[10] lord, let her consign
Into your hand her Tyrians as a dowry."   140
Now Venus knew this talk was all pretence,
All to divert the future power from Italy
To Libya; and she answered:
                              "Who would be
So mad, so foolish as to shun that prospect
Or prefer war with you? That is, provided   145
Fortune is on the side of your proposal.
The fates here are perplexing: would one city
Satisfy Jupiter's will for Tyrians
And Trojan exiles? Does he approve
A union and a mingling of these races?   150
You are his consort: you have every right
To sound him out. Go on, and I'll come, too."
But regal Juno pointedly replied:
"That task will rest with me. Just now, as to
The need of the moment and the way to meet it,   155
Listen, and I'll explain in a few words.
Aeneas and Dido in her misery
Plan hunting in the forest, when the Titan
Sun comes up with rays to light the world.
While beaters in excitement ring the glens   160
My gift will be a black raincloud, and hail,

---

10. Troy was situated in Phrygia, a large terri-
    tory in Anatolia, in northwestern Asia
    Minor.

A downpour, and I'll shake heaven with thunder.
The company will scatter, lost in gloom,
As Dido and the Trojan captain come
To one same cavern. I shall be on hand,   165
And if I can be certain you are willing,
There I shall marry them and call her his.
A wedding, this will be."
                          Then Cytherea,[11]
Not disinclined, nodded to Juno's plea,
And smiled at the stratagem now given away.   170
Dawn came up meanwhile from the Ocean stream,
And in the early sunshine from the gates
Picked huntsmen issued: wide-meshed nets and snares,
Broad spearheads for big game, Massylian horsemen
Trooping with hounds in packs keen on the scent.   175
But Dido lingered in her hall, as Punic
Nobles waited, and her mettlesome hunter
Stood nearby, cavorting in gold and scarlet,
Champing his foam-flecked bridle. At long last
The queen appeared with courtiers in a crowd,   180
A short Sidonian cloak edged in embroidery
Caught about her, at her back a quiver
Sheathed in gold, her hair tied up in gold,
And a brooch of gold pinning her scarlet dress.
Phrygians came in her company as well,   185
And Iulus, joyous at the scene. Resplendent
Above the rest, Aeneas walked to meet her,
To join his retinue with hers. He seemed—
Think of the lord Apollo in the spring
When he leaves wintering in Lycia   190
By Xanthus'[12] torrent, for his mother's isle
Of Delos, to renew the festival;
Around his altars Cretans, Dryopës,
And painted Agathyrsans raise a shout,
But the god walks the Cynthian ridge alone   195
And smooths his hair, binds it in fronded laurel,
Braids it in gold; and shafts ring on his shoulders.
So elated and swift, Aeneas walked
With sunlit grace upon him.
                          Soon the hunters,
Riding in company to high pathless hills,
Saw mountain goats shoot down from a rocky peak   200

---

11. An epithet of Venus, who was especially
    associated with the island of Cythera (see
    the *Homeric Hymn to Aphrodite*).

12. A river in the Trojan plain.

And scamper on the ridges; toward the plain
Deer left the slopes, herding in clouds of dust
In flight across the open lands. Alone,
The boy Ascanius, delightedly riding   205
His eager horse amid the lowland vales,
Outran both goats and deer. Could he only meet
Amid the harmless game some foaming boar,
Or a tawny lion down from the mountainside!
Meanwhile in heaven began a rolling thunder,   210
And soon the storm broke, pouring rain and hail.
Then Tyrians and Trojans in alarm—
With Venus' Dardan grandson[13]—ran for cover
Here and there in the wilderness, as freshets
Coursed from the high hills.
                         Now to the self-same cave   215
Came Dido and the captain of the Trojans.
Primal Earth herself and Nuptial Juno
Opened the ritual, torches of lightning blazed,
High Heaven became witness to the marriage,
And nymphs cried out wild hymns from a mountain top.   220
That day was the first cause of death, and first
Of sorrow. Dido had no further qualms
As to impressions given and set abroad;
She thought no longer of a secret love
But called it marriage. Thus, under that name,   225
She hid her fault.
                    Now in no time at all
Through all the African cities Rumor goes—
Nimble as quicksilver among evils.

In those days Rumor took an evil joy
At filling countrysides with whispers, whispers,   230
Gossip of what was done, and never done:
How this Aeneas landed, Trojan born,
How Dido in her beauty graced his company,
Then how they reveled all the winter long
Unmindful of the realm, prisoners of lust.   235
These tales the scabrous goddess put about
On men's lips everywhere. Her twisting course
Took her to King Iarbas, whom she set
Ablaze with anger piled on top of anger.

---

13. Ascanius, whose grandfather Anchises was
   a Dardanian prince.

. . . Before his altars   240
King Iarbas, crazed by the raw story,
Stood, they say, amid the Presences,
With supplicating hands, pouring out prayer:
"All powerful Jove, to whom the feasting Moors
At ease on colored couches tip their wine,   245
Do you see this? Are we then fools to fear you
Throwing down your bolts? Those dazzling fires
Of lightning, are they aimless in the clouds
And rumbling thunder meaningless? This woman
Who turned up in our country and laid down   250
A tiny city at a price, to whom
I gave a beach to plow—and on my terms—
After refusing to marry me has taken
Aeneas to be master in her realm.
And now Sir Paris[14] with his men, half-men,   255
His chin and perfumed hair tied up
In a Maeonian[15] bonnet, takes possession.
As for ourselves, here we are bringing gifts
Into these shrines—supposedly your shrines—
Hugging that empty fable."

                               Pleas like this   260
From the man clinging to his altars reached
The ears of the Almighty. Now he turned
His eyes upon the queen's town and the lovers
Careless of their good name; then spoke to Mercury,[16]
Assigning him a mission:

                             "Son, bestir yourself,   265
Call up the Zephyrs, take to your wings and glide.
Approach the Dardan captain where he tarries
Rapt in Tyrian Carthage, losing sight
Of future towns the fates ordain. Correct him,
Carry my speech to him on the running winds: 270
No son like this did his enchanting mother
Promise to us, nor such did she deliver
Twice from peril at the hands of Greeks.
He was to be the ruler of Italy,
Potential empire, armorer of war;   275
To father men from Teucer's noble blood[17]
And bring the whole world under law's dominion.
If glories to be won by deeds like these

---

14. Iarbas identifies Aeneas with his Trojan
    relative Paris, whose seduction of his host
    Menelaos's wife Helen started the Trojan
    War.

15. Phrygian.
16. Mercury was known as the divine
    messenger.
17. Teucer was the first Trojan king.

Cannot arouse him, if he will not strive
For his own honor, does he begrudge his son, 280
Ascanius, the high strongholds of Rome?
What has he in mind? What hope, to make him stay
Amid a hostile race and lose from view
Ausonian progeny,[18] Lavinian lands?
The man should sail: that is the whole point. 285
Let this be what you tell him, as from me."
He finished and fell silent. Mercury
Made ready to obey the great command
Of his great father, and he first tied on
The golden sandals, winged, that high in air 290
Transport him over seas or over land
Abreast of gale winds; then he took the wand
With which he summons pale souls out of Orcus[19]
And ushers others to the undergloom,
Lulls men to slumber or awakens them, 295
And open dead men's eyes.

Alighting tiptoe
On the first hutments, there he found Aeneas
Laying foundations for new towers and homes.
He noted well the swordhilt the man wore,
Adorned with yellow jasper; and the cloak 300
Aglow with Tyrian dye upon his shoulders—
Gifts of the wealthy queen, who had inwoven
Gold thread in the fabric. Mercury
Took him to task at once:
                                   "Is it for you
To lay the stones for Carthage's high walls, 305
Tame husband that you are, and build their city?
Oblivious of your own world, your own kingdom!
From bright Olympus he that rules the gods
And turns the earth and heaven by his power—
He and no other sent me to you, told me 310
To bring this message on the running winds:
What have you in mind? What hope, wasting your days
In Libya? If future history's glories
Do not affect you, if you will not strive
For your own honor, think of Ascanius, 315
Think of the expectations of your heir,
Iulus, to whom the Italian realm, the land

---

18. The Ausonians were early inhabitants of southern Italy; Ausonia refers to Italy in general.

19. Like Erebus, Orcus was one of the names for the underworld.

Of Rome, are due."

                 And Mercury, as he spoke,
Departed from the visual field of mortals
To a great distance, ebbed in subtle air.   320
Amazed, and shocked to the bottom of his soul
By what his eyes had seen, Aeneas felt
His hackles rise, his voice choke in his throat.
As the sharp admonition and command
From heaven had shaken him awake, he now   325
Burned only to be gone, to leave that land
Of the sweet life behind. What can he do? How tell
The impassioned queen and hope to win her over?
What opening shall he choose? This way and that
He let his mind dart, testing alternatives,   330
Running through every one. And as he pondered
This seemed the better tactic: he called in
Mnestheus, Sergestus and stalwart Serestus,
Telling them:
              "Get the fleet ready for sea,
But quietly, and collect the men on shore.   335
Lay in ship stores and gear."
      As to the cause
For a change of plan, they were to keep it secret,
Seeing the excellent Dido had no notion,
No warning that such love could be cut short;
He would himself look for the right occasion,   340
The easiest time to speak, the way to do it.
The Trojans to a man gladly obeyed.
The queen, for her part, felt some plot afoot
Quite soon—for who deceives a woman in love?
She caught wind of a change, being in fear   345
Of what had seemed her safety. Evil Rumor,
Shameless as before, brought word to her
In her distracted state of ships being rigged
In trim for sailing. Furious, at her wits' end,
She traversed the whole city, all aflame   350
With rage, like a Bacchantë driven wild[20]
By emblems shaken, when the mountain revels
Of the odd year possess her, when the cry
Of Bacchus rises and Cithaeron calls
All through the shouting night. Thus it turned out   355
She was the first to speak and charge Aeneas:

---

20. Bacchantes were worshippers of the god
    Bacchus.

"You even hoped to keep me in the dark
As to this outrage, did you, two-faced man,
And slip away in silence? Can our love
Not hold you, can the pledge we gave not hold you,   360
Can Dido not, now sure to die in pain?
Even in winter weather must you toil
With ships, and fret to launch against high winds
For the open sea? Oh, heartless!

                    Tell me now,
If you were not in search of alien lands   365
And new strange homes, if ancient Troy remained,
Would ships put out for Troy on these big seas?
Do you go to get away from me? I beg you,
By these tears, by your own right hand, since I
Have left my wretched self nothing but that—   370
Yes, by the marriage that we entered on,
If ever I did well and you were grateful
Or found some sweetness in a gift from me,
Have pity now on a declining house!
Put this plan by, I beg you, if a prayer   375
Is not yet out of place.
Because of you, Libyans and nomad kings
Detest me, my own Tyrians are hostile;
Because of you, I lost my integrity
And that admired name by which alone   380
I made my way once toward the stars.

                    To whom
Do you abandon me, a dying woman,
Guest that you are—the only name now left
From that of husband? Why do I live on?
Shall I, until my brother Pygmalion comes   385
To pull my walls down? Or the Gaetulan
Iarbas leads me captive? If at least
There were a child by you for me to care for,
A little one to play in my courtyard
And give me back Aeneas, in spite of all,   390
I should not feel so utterly defeated,
Utterly bereft."

                  She ended there.
The man by Jove's command held fast his eyes
And fought down the emotion in his heart.
At length he answered:

                    "As for myself, be sure   395
I never shall deny all you can say,
Your majesty, of what you meant to me.

Never will the memory of Elissa[21]
Stale for me, while I can still remember
My own life, and the spirit rules my body.   400
As to the event, a few words. Do not think
I meant to be deceitful and slip away.
I never held the torches of a bridegroom,
Never entered upon the pact of marriage.
If Fate permitted me to spend my days   405
By my own lights, and make the best of things
According to my wishes, first of all
I should look after Troy and the loved relics
Left me of my people. Priam's great hall
Should stand again; I should have restored the tower   410
Of Pergamum[22] for Trojans in defeat.
But now it is the rich Italian land
Apollo tells me I must make for: Italy,
Named by his oracles. There is my love;   415
There is my country. If, as a Phoenician,
You are so given to the charms of Carthage,
Libyan city that it is, then tell me,
Why begrudge the Teucrians new lands
For homesteads in Ausonia? Are we not   420
Entitled, too, to look for realms abroad?
Night never veils the earth in damp and darkness,
Fiery stars never ascend the east,
But in my dreams my father's troubled ghost[23]
Admonishes and frightens me. Then, too,   425
Each night thoughts come of young Ascanius,
My dear boy wronged, defrauded of his kingdom,
Hesperian lands of destiny. And now
The gods' interpreter, sent by Jove himself—
I swear it by your head and mine—has brought   430
Commands down through the racing winds! I say
With my own eyes in full daylight I saw him
Entering the building! With my very ears
I drank his message in! So please, no more
Of these appeals that set us both afire.   435
I sail for Italy not of my own free will."
During all this she had been watching him
With face averted, looking him up and down

---

21. Another name for Dido.
22. An important citadel in northwest Asia
Minor near Troy and, in myth, allied with
the Trojan cause.

23. Aeneas's father Anchises died during
their early wanderings, after they escaped the sack of Troy.

In silence, and she burst out raging now:
"No goddess was your mother. Dardanus   440
Was not the founder of your family.
Liar and cheat! Some rough Caucasian cliff
Begot you on flint. Hyrcanian tigresses
Tendered their teats to you. Why should I palter?
Why still hold back for more indignity?   445
Sigh, did he, while I wept? Or look at me?
Or yield a tear, or pity her who loved him?
What shall I say first, with so much to say?
The time is past when either supreme Juno
Or the Saturnian father[24] viewed these things   450
With justice. Faith can never be secure.
I took the man in, thrown up on this coast
In dire need, and in my madness then
Contrived a place for him in my domain,
Rescued his lost fleet, saved his shipmates' lives.   455
Oh, I am swept away burning by furies!
Now the prophet Apollo, now his oracles,
Now the gods' interpreter, if you please,
Sent down by Jove himself, brings through the air
His formidable commands! What fit employment   460
For heaven's high powers! What anxieties
To plague serene immortals! I shall not
Detain you or dispute your story. Go,
Go after Italy on the sailing winds,
Look for your kingdom, cross the deepsea swell!   465
If divine justice counts for anything,
I hope and pray that on some grinding reef
Midway at sea you'll drink your punishment
And call and call on Dido's name!
From far away I shall come after you   470
With my black fires, and when cold death has parted
Body from soul I shall be everywhere
A shade to haunt you! You will pay for this,
Unconscionable! I shall hear! The news will reach me
Even among the lowest of the dead!"   475
At this abruptly she broke off and ran
In sickness from his sight and the light of day,
Leaving him at a loss, alarmed, and mute
With all he meant to say. The maids in waiting

---

24. Jupiter, son of Saturn.

Caught her as she swooned and carried her   480
To bed in her marble chamber.

                          Duty-bound,
Aeneas, though he struggled with desire
To calm and comfort her in all her pain,
To speak to her and turn her mind from grief,   485
And though he sighed his heart out, shaken still
With love of her, yet took the course heaven gave him
And went back to the fleet. Then with a will
The Teucrians fell to work and launched the ships
Along the whole shore: slick with tar each hull   490
Took to the water. Eager to get away,
The sailors brought oar-boughs out of the woods
With leaves still on, and oaken logs unhewn.
Now you could see them issuing from the town
To the water's edge in streams, as when, aware   495
Of winter, ants will pillage a mound of spelt
To store it in their granary; over fields
The black battalion moves, and through the grass
On a narrow trail they carry off the spoil;
Some put their shoulders to the enormous weight   500
Of a trundled grain, while some pull stragglers in
And castigate delay; their to-and-fro
Of labor makes the whole track come alive.
At that sight, what were your emotions, Dido?
Sighing how deeply, looking out and down   505
From your high tower on the seething shore
Where all the harbor filled before your eyes
With bustle and shouts! Unconscionable Love,
To what extremes will you not drive our hearts!
She now felt driven to weep again, again   510
To move him, if she could, by supplication,
Humbling her pride before her love—to leave
Nothing untried, not to die needlessly.
"Anna, you see the arc of waterfront
All in commotion: they come crowding in   515
From everywhere. Spread canvas calls for wind,
The happy crews have garlanded the sterns.
If I could brace myself for this great sorrow,
Sister, I can endure it, too. One favor,
Even so, you may perform for me.   520
Since that deserter chose you for his friend
And trusted you, even with private thoughts,
Since you alone know when he may be reached,
Go, intercede with our proud enemy.

Remind him that I took no oath at Aulis[25]   525
With Danaans to destroy the Trojan race;
I sent no ship to Pergamum. Never did I
Profane his father Anchisës' dust and shade.
Why will he not allow my prayers to fall
On his unpitying ears? Where is he racing?   530
Let him bestow one last gift on his mistress:
This, to await fair winds and easier flight.
Now I no longer plead the bond he broke
Of our old marriage, nor do I ask that he
Should live without his dear love, Latium,[26]   535
Or yield his kingdom. Time is all I beg,
Mere time, a respite and a breathing space
For madness to subside in, while my fortune
Teaches me how to take defeat and grieve.
Pity your sister. This is the end, this favor—   540
To be repaid with interest when I die."
She pleaded in such terms, and such, in tears,
Her sorrowing sister brought him, time and again.
But no tears moved him, no one's voice would he
Attend to tractably. The fates opposed it;   545
God's will blocked the man's once kindly ears.
And just as when the north winds from the Alps
This way and that contend among themselves
To tear away an oaktree hale with age,
The wind and tree cry, and the buffeted trunk   550
Showers high foliage to earth, but holds
On bedrock, for the roots go down as far
Into the underworld as cresting boughs
Go up in heaven's air: just so this captain,
Buffeted by a gale of pleas
This way and that way, dinned all the day long,   555
Felt their moving power in his great heart,
And yet his will stood fast; tears fell in vain.
On Dido in her desolation now
Terror grew at her fate. She prayed for death,
Being heartsick at the mere sight of heaven.   560
That she more surely would perform the act
And leave the daylight, now she saw before her
A thing one shudders to recall: on altars
Fuming with incense where she placed her gifts,   565

---

25. At aulis, where Agamemnon marshalled
    the Greek expedition against Troy, the
    chieftains swore an oath of loyalty to his

effort to avenge the abduction of Helen by
sacking Troy.
26. The region of Italy around and to the
    south of Rome.

The holy water blackened, the spilt wine
Turned into blood and mire. Of this she spoke
To no one, not to her sister even. Then, too,
Within the palace was a marble shrine
Devoted to her onetime lord, a place   570
She held in wondrous honor, all festooned
With snowy fleeces and green festive boughs.
From this she now thought voices could be heard
And words could be made out, her husband's words,
Calling her, when midnight hushed the earth;   575
And lonely on the rooftops the night owl
Seemed to lament, in melancholy notes,
Prolonged to a doleful cry. And then, besides,
The riddling words of seers in ancient days,
Foreboding sayings, made her thrill with fear.   580
In nightmare, fevered, she was hunted down
By pitiless Aeneas, and she seemed
Deserted always, uncompanioned always,
On a long journey, looking for her Tyrians
In desolate landscapes—   585

           as Pentheus[27] gone mad
Sees the oncoming Eumenidës and sees
A double sun and double Thebes appear,
Or as when, hounded on the stage, Orestës
Runs from a mother armed with burning brands,   590
With serpents hellish black,
And in the doorway squat the Avenging Ones.
So broken in mind by suffering, Dido caught
Her fatal madness and resolved to die.
She pondered time and means, then visiting   595
Her mournful sister, covered up her plan
With a calm look, a clear and hopeful brow.
"Sister, be glad for me! I've found a way
To bring him back or free me of desire.
Near to the Ocean boundary, near sundown,   600
The Aethiops' farthest territory lies,
Where giant Atlas turns the sphere of heaven
Studded with burning stars. From there
A priestess of Massylian stock has come;
She had been pointed out to me: custodian   605
Of that shrine named for daughters of the west,
Hesperidës; and it is she who fed

---

27. The Theban king whose hostility to the
    god Dionysus resulted in his destruction,
    as dramatized by Euripides in the *Bacchae*.

The dragon, guarding well the holy boughs
With honey dripping slow and drowsy poppy.
Chanting her spells she undertakes to free   610
What hearts she wills, but to inflict on others
Duress of sad desires; to arrest
The flow of rivers, make the stars move backward,
Call up the spirits of deep Night. You'll see
Earth shift and rumble underfoot and ash trees   615
Walk down mountainsides. Dearest, I swear
Before the gods and by your own sweet self,
It is against my will that I resort
For weaponry to magic powers. In secret
Build up a pyre in the inner court   620
Under the open sky, and place upon it
The arms that faithless man left in my chamber,
All his clothing, and the marriage bed
On which I came to grief—solace for me
To annihilate all vestige of the man,   625
Vile as he is: my priestess shows me this."
While she was speaking, cheek and brow grew pale.
But Anna could not think her sister cloaked
A suicide in these unheard-of rites;
She failed to see how great her madness was   630
And feared no consequence more grave
Than at Sychaeus' death. So, as commanded,
She made the preparations. For her part,
The queen, seeing the pyre in her inmost court
Erected huge with pitch-pine and sawn ilex,   635
Hung all the place under the sky with wreaths
And crowned it with funereal cypress boughs.
On the pyre's top she put a sword he left
With clothing, and an effigy on a couch,
Her mind fixed now ahead on what would come.   640
Around the pyre stood altars, and the priestess,
Hair unbound, called in a voice of thunder
Upon three hundred gods, on Erebus,
On Chaos, and on triple Hecatë,[28]
Three-faced Diana. Then she sprinkled drops   645
Purportedly from the fountain of Avernus.[29]
Rare herbs were brought out, reaped at the new moon
By scythes of bronze, and juicy with a milk

---

28. Hecate was a divinity associated with Persephone, queen of the underworld, as well
as with the goddess Diana; she is often
represented as a woman with three bodies.

29. A lake near Naples, thought to be an entrance
to the underworld.

Of dusky venom; then the rare love-charm
Or caul torn from the brow of a birthing foal   650
And snatched away before the mother found it.
Dido herself with consecrated grain
In her pure hands, as she went near the altars,
Freed one foot from sandal straps, let fall
Her dress ungirdled, and, now sworn to death,   655
Called on the gods and stars that knew her fate.
She prayed then to whatever power may care
In comprehending justice for the grief
Of lovers bound unequally by love.
The night had come, and weary in every land   660
Men's bodies took the boon of peaceful sleep.
The woods and the wild seas had quieted
At that hour when the stars are in mid-course
And every field is still; cattle and birds
With vivid wings that haunt the limpid lakes   665
Or nest in thickets in the country places
All were asleep under the silent night.
Not, though, the agonized Phoenician queen:
She never slackened into sleep and never
Allowed the tranquil night to rest   670
Upon her eyelids or within her heart.
Her pain redoubled; love came on again,
Devouring her, and on her bed she tossed
In a great surge of anger.
                          So awake,   675
She pressed these questions, musing to herself:
"Look now, what can I do? Turn once again
To the old suitors, only to be laughed at—
Begging a marriage with Numidians
Whom I disdained so often? Then what? Trail   680
The Ilian ships and follow like a slave
Commands of Trojans? Seeing them so agreeable,
In view of past assistance and relief,
So thoughtful their unshaken gratitude?
Suppose I wished it, who permits or takes   685
Aboard their proud ships one they so dislike?
Poor lost soul, do you not yet grasp or feel
The treachery of the line of Laömedon?[30]
What then? Am I to go alone, companion
Of the exultant sailors in their flight?   690
Or shall I set out in their wake, with Tyrians,
With all my crew close at my side, and send

---

30. A king of Troy.

The men I barely tore away from Tyre
To sea again, making them hoist their sails
To more sea-winds? No: die as you deserve,   695
Give pain quietus with a steel blade.

                             Sister,
You are the one who gave way to my tears
In the beginning, burdened a mad queen
With sufferings, and thrust me on my enemy.   700
It was not given me to lead my life
Without new passion, innocently, the way
Wild creatures live, and not to touch these depths.
The vow I took to the ashes of Sychaeus
Was not kept."   705

                   So she broke out afresh
In bitter mourning. On his high stern deck
Aeneas, now quite certain of departure,
Everything ready, took the boon of sleep.
In dream the figure of the god returned   710
With looks reproachful as before: he seemed
Again to warn him, being like Mercury
In every way, in voice, in golden hair,
And in the bloom of youth.

                      "Son of the goddess,   715
Sleep away this crisis, can you still?
Do you not see the dangers growing round you,
Madman, from now on? Can you not hear
The offshore westwind blow? The woman hatches
Plots and drastic actions in her heart,   720
Resolved on death now, whipping herself on
To heights of anger. Will you not be gone
In flight, while flight is still within your power?
Soon you will see the offing boil with ships
And glare with torches; soon again   725
The waterfront will be alive with fires,
If Dawn comes while you linger in this country.
Ha! Come, break the spell! Woman's a thing
Forever fitful and forever changing."
At this he merged into the darkness. Then   730
As the abrupt phantom filled him with fear,
Aeneas broke from sleep and roused his crewmen:
"Up, turn out now! Oarsmen, take your thwarts!
Shake out sail! Look here, for the second time
A god from heaven's high air is goading me   735
To hasten our break away, to cut the cables.
Holy one, whatever god you are,
We go with you, we act on your command

Most happily! Be near, graciously help us,
Make the stars in heaven propitious ones!"   740
He pulled his sword aflash out of its sheath
And struck at the stern hawser. All the men
Were gripped by his excitement to be gone,
And hauled and hustled. Ships cast off their moorings,
And an array of hulls hid inshore water   745
As oarsmen churned up foam and swept to sea.
Soon early Dawn, quitting the saffron bed
Of old Tithonus, cast new light on earth,
And as air grew transparent, from her tower
The queen caught sight of ships on the seaward reach   750
With sails full and the wind astern. She knew
The waterfront now empty, bare of oarsmen.
Beating her lovely breast three times, four times,
And tearing her golden hair,
                        "O Jupiter,"   755
She said, "will this man go, will he have mocked
My kingdom, stranger that he was and is?
Will they not snatch up arms and follow him
From every quarter of the town? and dockhands
Tear our ships from moorings? On! Be quick   760
With torches! Give out arms! Unship the oars!
What am I saying? Where am I? What madness
Takes me out of myself? Dido, poor soul,
Your evil doing has come home to you.
Then was the right time, when you offered him   765
A royal scepter. See the good faith and honor
But rise up from my bones, avenging spirit!
Harry with fire and sword the Dardan countrymen
Now, or hereafter, at whatever time
The strength will be afforded. Coast with coast   770
In conflict, I implore, and sea with sea,
And arms with arms: may they contend in war,
Themselves and all the children of their children!"
Now she took thought of one way or another,
At the first chance, to end her hated life,   775
And briefly spoke to Barcë, who had been
Sychaeus' nurse; her own an urn of ash
Long held in her ancient fatherland.
                        "Dear nurse,
Tell Sister Anna to come here, and have her   780
Quickly bedew herself with running water
Before she brings our victims for atonement.
Let her come that way. And you, too, put on
Pure wool around your brows. I have a mind

To carry out that rite to Stygian Jove[31]   785
That I have readied here, and put an end
To my distress, committing to the flames
The pyre of that miserable Dardan."
At this with an old woman's eagerness
Barcë hurried away. And Dido's heart   790
Beat wildly at the enormous thing afoot.
She rolled her bloodshot eyes, her quivering cheeks
Were flecked with red as her sick pallor grew
Before her coming death. Into the court
She burst her way, then at her passion's height   795
She climbed the pyre and bared the Dardan sword—
A gift desired once, for no such need.
Her eyes now on the Trojan clothing there
And the familiar bed, she paused a little,
Weeping a little, mindful, then lay down   800
And spoke her last words:
                          "Remnants dear to me
While god and fate allowed it, take this breath
And give me respite from these agonies.
I lived my life out to the very end   805
And passed the stages Fortune had appointed.
Now my tall shade goes to the under world.
I built a famous town, saw my great walls,
Avenged my husband, made my hostile brother
Pay for his crime. Happy, alas, too happy,   810
If only the Dardanian keels had never
Beached on our coast." And here she kissed the bed.
"I die unavenged," she said, "but let me die.
This way, this way, a blessed relief to go
Into the undergloom. Let the cold Trojan,   815
Far at sea, drink in this conflagration
And take with him the omen of my death!"
Amid these words her household people saw her
Crumpled over the steel blade, and the blade
Aflush with red blood, drenched her hands. A scream   820
Pierced the high chambers. Now through the shocked city
Rumor went rioting, as wails and sobs
With women's outcry echoed in the palace
And heaven's high air gave back the beating din,
As though all Carthage or old Tyre fell   825
To storming enemies, and, out of hand,
Flames billowed on the roofs of men and gods.

---

31. The mythical Styx was the principal river
    of the underworld.

Her sister heard and trembling, faint with terror,
Lacerating her face, beating her breast,
Ran through the crowd to call the dying queen: 830
"It came to this, then, sister? You deceived me?
The pyre meant this, altars and fires meant this?
What shall I mourn first, being abandoned? Did you
Scorn your sister's company in death?
You should have called me out to the same fate!   835
The same blade's edge and hurt, at the same hour,
Should have taken us off. With my own hands
Had I to build this pyre, and had I to call
Upon our country's gods, that in the end
With you placed on it there, O heartless one,   840
I should be absent? You have put to death
Yourself and me, the people and the fathers
Bred in Sidon, and your own new city.
Give me fresh water, let me bathe her wound
And catch upon my lips any last breath   845
Hovering over hers."

              Now she had climbed
The topmost steps and took her dying sister
Into her arms to cherish, with a sob,
Using her dress to stanch the dark blood flow.   850
But Dido trying to lift her heavy eyes
Fainted again. Her chest-wound whistled air.
Three times she struggled up on one elbow
And each time fell back on the bed. Her gaze
Went wavering as she looked for heaven's light   855
And groaned at finding it. Almighty Juno,
Filled with pity for this long ordeal
And difficult passage, now sent Iris down
Out of Olympus to set free
The wrestling spirit from the body's hold.   860
For since she died, not at her fated span
Nor as she merited, but before her time
Enflamed and driven mad, Proserpina[32]
Had not yet plucked from her the golden hair,
Delivering her to Orcus of the Styx.   865
So humid Iris through bright heaven flew
On saffron-yellow wings, and in her train
A thousand hues shimmered before the sun.
At Dido's head she came to rest.

                       "This token   870

---

32. Persephone, wife of Hades, lord of the
   underworld.

Sacred to Dis[33] I bear away as bidden
And free you from your body."

Saying this,

She cut a lock of hair. Along with it
Her body's warmth fell into dissolution,
And out into the winds her life withdrew.

875

THE BIBLE (LATE FIRST CENTURY C.E.)
Palestine or Greece (?)

The Gospel According to Luke and the Acts of the Apostles, together comprise a two-volume work describing the life and teachings of Jesus and the early history of the church. Their authorship is unknown, but they were traditionally attributed to Luke the Physician, a Gentile convert and friend of the apostle Paul. Written in Greek, his works date from the late first century C.E. Much of Luke's gospel is based on the earlier gospel of Mark, with substantial information added from oral tradition and from other written sources now lost. The selections presented here are the opening five gospel chapters—describing the birth of Jesus, his childhood, and his early ministry; the final three gospel chapters, describing Jesus' betrayal, trial, crucifixion, death, and resurrection—and the opening two chapters of Acts, recounting the beginnings of the church up through Pentecost.

Throughout his account, Luke interweaves events and teachings, setting the Hebrew tradition in counterpoint against the wider world of the Roman empire, of which Palestine was then a part. Although the imperial culture posed a threat to the preservation of local ethnic identity, it also provided the means to spread the universalist message of the gospels. This is vividly dramatized in the miraculous ability of the apostles to be understood by all peoples at Pentecost.

The Gospel According to Luke 1–5, 22–24

1

Inasmuch as many have undertaken to compile a narrative of the things which have been accomplished among us, just as they were delivered to us by those who from the beginning were eyewitnesses and ministers of the word, it seemed good to me also, having followed all things closely for some time past, to write an

---

Revised Standard Version translation.

---

33. One of the names of Hades.

orderly account for you, most excellent Theophilus, that you may know the truth concerning the things of which you have been informed.

In the days of Herod,[1] king of Judea, there was a priest named Zechariah, of the division of Abijah; and he had a wife of the daughters of Aaron, and her name was Elizabeth. And they were both righteous before God, walking in all the commandments and ordinances of the Lord blameless.

But they had no child, because Elizabeth was barren, and both were advanced in years.

Now while he was serving as priest before God when his division was on duty, according to the custom of the priesthood, it fell to him by lot to enter the temple of the Lord and burn incense. And the whole multitude of the people were praying outside at the hour of incense. And there appeared to him an angel of the Lord standing on the right side of the altar of incense. And Zechariah was troubled when he saw him, and fear fell upon him. But the angel said to him, "Do not be afraid, Zechariah, for your prayer is heard, and your wife Elizabeth will bear you a son, and you shall call his name John.

> And you will have joy and gladness,
> and many will rejoice at his birth;
> for he will be great before the Lord,
> and he shall drink no wine nor strong drink,
> and he will be filled with the Holy Spirit,
> even from his mother's womb.
> And he will turn many of the sons of Israel to the Lord their God,
> And he will go before him in the spirit and power of Elijah,[2]
> to turn the hearts of the fathers to the children,
> and the disobedient to the wisdom of the just,
> to make ready for the Lord a people prepared."

And Zechariah said to the angel, "How shall I know this? For I am an old man, and my wife is advanced in years." And the angel answered him, "I am Gabriel, who stand in the presence of God; and I was sent to speak to you, and to bring you this good news. And behold, you will be silent and unable to speak until the day that these things come to pass, because you did not believe my words, which will be fulfilled in their time." And the people were waiting for Zechariah, and they wondered at his delay in the temple. And when he came out, he could not speak to them, and they perceived that he had seen a vision in the temple; and he made signs to them and remained dumb. And when his time of service was ended, he went to his home.

After these days his wife Elizabeth conceived, and for five months she hid herself, saying, "Thus the Lord has done to me in the days when he looked on me, to take away my reproach among men."

In the sixth month the angel Gabriel was sent from God to a city of Galilee

---

1. Herod the Great ruled Palestine under Roman control from 37 to 4 B.C.E.
2. In the biblical book of Malachi, the great prophet Elijah is described as returning as God's messenger before the final days of the world.

named Nazareth, to a virgin betrothed to a man whose name was Joseph, of the house of David; and the virgin's name was Mary. And he came to her and said, "Hail, O favored one, the Lord is with you!" But she was greatly troubled at the saying, and considered in her mind what sort of greeting this might be. And the angel said to her, "Do not be afraid, Mary, for you have found favor with God. And behold, you will conceive in your womb and bear a son, and you shall call his name Jesus.

> He will be great, and will be called the Son of the Most High;
> and the Lord God will give to him the throne of his father David,[3]
> and he will reign over the house of Jacob[4] for ever;
> and of his kingdom there will be no end."

And Mary said to the angel, "How can this be, since I have no husband?"

> And the angel said to her,
> "The Holy Spirit will come upon you,
> and the power of the Most High will overshadow you;
> therefore the child to be born will be called holy,
> the Son of God.

And behold, your kinswoman Elizabeth in her old age has also conceived a son; and this is the sixth month with her who was called barren. For with God nothing will be impossible." And Mary said, "Behold, I am the handmaid of the Lord; let it be to me according to your word." And the angel departed from her.

In those days Mary arose and went with haste into the hill country, to a city of Judah, and she entered the house of Zechariah and greeted Elizabeth. And when Elizabeth heard the greeting of Mary, the babe leaped in her womb; and Elizabeth was filled with the Holy Spirit and she exclaimed with a loud cry, "Blessed are you among women, and blessed is the fruit of your womb! And why is this granted me, that the mother of my Lord should come to me? For behold, when the voice of your greeting came to my ears, the babe in my womb leaped for joy. And blessed is she who believed that there would be fulfillment of what was spoken to her from the Lord."

> And Mary said,
> "My soul magnifies the Lord,
> and my spirit rejoices in God my Savior,
> for he has regarded the low estate of his handmaiden.
> For behold, henceforth all generations will call me blessed;
> for he who is mighty has done great things for me,
> and holy is his name.
> And his mercy is on those who fear him
> from generation to generation.
> He has shown strength with his arm,

---

3. David (reigned c. 1000 to 965 B.C.E.), second king of Israel.

4. Jacob was the legendary patriarch whose twelve sons founded the twelve tribes of Israel.

> he has scattered the proud in the imagination of their hearts,
> he has put down the mighty from their thrones,
> and exalted those of low degree;
> he has filled the hungry with good things,
> and the rich he has sent empty away.
> He has helped his servant Israel,
> in remembrance of his mercy,
> as he spoke to our fathers,
> to Abraham and to his posterity for ever."

And Mary remained with her about three months, and returned to her home.

Now the time came for Elizabeth to be delivered, and she gave birth to a son. And her neighbors and kinsfolk heard that the Lord had shown great mercy to her, and they rejoiced with her. And on the eighth day they came to circumcise the child; and they would have named him Zechariah after his father, but his mother said, "Not so; he shall be called John." And they said to her, "None of your kindred is called by this name." And they made signs to his father, inquiring what he would have him called. And he asked for a writing tablet, and wrote, "His name is John." And they all marveled. And immediately his mouth was opened and his tongue loosed, and he spoke, blessing God. And fear came on all their neighbors. And all these things were talked about through all the hill country of Judea; and all who heard them laid them up in their hearts, saying, "What then will this child be?" For the hand of the Lord was with him.

And his father Zechariah was filled with the Holy Spirit, and prophesied, saying,

> "Blessed be the Lord God of Israel,
> for he was visited and redeemed his people,
> and has raised up a horn of salvation for us
> in the house of his servant David,
> as he spoke by the mouth of his holy prophets from of old,
> that we should be saved from our enemies,
> and from the hand of all who hate us;
> to perform the mercy promised to our fathers,
> and to remember his holy covenant,
> the oath which he swore to our father Abraham, to grant us
> that we, being delivered from the hand of our enemies,
> might serve him without fear,
> in holiness and righteousness before him all the days of our life.
> And you, child, will be called the prophet of the Most High;
> for you will go before the Lord to prepare his ways,
> to give knowledge of salvation to his people
> in the forgiveness of their sins,
> through the tender mercy of our God,
> when the day shall dawn upon us from on high
> to give light to those who sit in darkness and in the shadow of death,
> to guide our feet into the way of peace."

And the child grew and became strong in spirit, and he was in the wilderness till the day of his manifestation to Israel.

2

In those days a decree went out from Caesar Augustus[5] that all the world should be enrolled. This was the first enrollment, when Quirinius was governor of Syria. And all went to be enrolled, each to his own city. And Joseph also went up from Galilee, from the city of Nazareth, to Judea, to the city of David, which is called Bethlehem, because he was of the house and lineage of David, to be enrolled with Mary his betrothed, who was with child. And while they were there, the time came for her to be delivered. And she gave birth to her first-born son and wrapped him in swaddling cloths, and laid him in a manger, because there was no place for them in the inn.

And in that region there were shepherds out in the field, keeping watch over their flock by night. And an angel of the Lord appeared to them, and the glory of the Lord shone around them, and they were filled with fear. And the angel said to them, "Be not afraid; for behold, I bring you good news of a great joy which will come to all the people; for to you is born this day in the city of David a Savior, who is Christ the Lord. And this will be a sign for you: you will find a babe wrapped in swaddling cloths and lying in a manger." And suddenly there was with the angel a multitude of the heavenly host praising God and saying,

"Glory to God in the highest,
and on earth peace among men with whom he is pleased!"

When the angels went away from them into heaven, the shepherds said to one another, "Let us go over to Bethlehem and see this thing that has happened, which the Lord has made known to us." And they went with haste, and found Mary and Joseph, and the babe lying in a manger. And when they saw it they made known the saying which had been told them concerning this child; and all who heard it wondered at what the shepherds told them. But Mary kept all these things, pondering them in her heart. And the shepherds returned, glorifying and praising God for all they had heard and seen, as it had been told them.

And at the end of eight days, when he was circumcised, he was called Jesus, the name given by the angel before he was conceived in the womb.

And when the time came for their purification according to the law of Moses, they brought him up to Jerusalem to present him to the Lord (as it is written in the law of the Lord, "Every male that opens the womb shall be called holy to the Lord") and to offer a sacrifice according to what is said in the law of the Lord, "a pair of turtledoves, or two young pigeons." Now there was a man in Jerusalem, whose name was Simeon, and this man was righteous and devout, looking for the consolation of Israel, and the Holy Spirit was upon him. And it had been revealed to him by the Holy Spirit that he should not see death before he had seen the Lord's Christ.[6] And inspired by the Spirit he came into the temple; and when the parents brought in the child Jesus, to do for him according to the custom of the law, he took him up in his arms and blessed God and said,

---

5. Augustus was Roman emperor from 27 B.C.E. to 14 C.E.; the census was taken in 7 to 6 B.C.E.

6. "Christ" is a translation of the Hebrew "Messiah," "the anointed one."

"Lord, now lettest thou thy servant depart in peace,
according to thy word;
for mine eyes have seen thy salvation
which thou hast prepared in the presence of all peoples,
a light for revelation to the Gentiles,
and for glory to thy people Israel."
And his father and his mother marveled at what was said about him; and Simeon
    blessed them and said to Mary his mother,
"Behold, this child is set for the fall and rising of many in Israel,
and for a sign that is spoken against
(and a sword will pierce through your own soul also),
that thoughts out of many hearts may be revealed."

And there was a prophetess, Anna, the daughter of Phanuel, of the tribe of Asher; she was of a great age, having lived with her husband seven years from her virginity, and as a widow till she was eighty-four. She did not depart from the temple, worshiping with fasting and prayer night and day. And coming up at that very hour she gave thanks to God, and spoke of him to all who were looking for the redemption of Jerusalem.

And when they had performed everything according to the law of the Lord, they returned into Galilee, to their own city, Nazareth. And the child grew and became strong, filled with wisdom; and the favor of God was upon him.

Now his parents went to Jerusalem every year at the feast of the Passover. And when he was twelve years old, they went up according to custom; and when the feast was ended, as they were returning, the boy Jesus stayed behind in Jerusalem. His parents did not know it, but supposing him to be in the company they went a day's journey, and they sought him among their kinsfolk and acquaintances; and when they did not find him, they returned to Jerusalem, seeking him. After three days they found him in the temple, sitting among the teachers, listening to them and asking them questions; and all who heard him were amazed at his understanding and his answers. And when they saw him they were astonished; and his mother said to him, "Son, why have you treated us so? Behold, your father and I have been looking for you anxiously." And he said to them, "How is it that you sought me? Did you not know that I must be in my Father's house?" And they did not understand the saying which he spoke to them. And he went down with them and came to Nazareth, and was obedient to them; and his mother kept all these things in her heart.

And Jesus increased in wisdom and in stature, and in favor with God and man.

3

In the fifteenth year of the reign of Tiberius Caesar,[7] Pontius Pilate being governor of Judea, and Herod being tetrarch of Galilee, and his brother Philip tetrarch of the region of Ituraea and Trachonitis,[8] and Lysanias tetrarch of Abilene, in the

---

7. 26 or 27 C.E.
8. The Roman governor Pilate now ruled Judea directly; the remainder of the kingdom of Herod the Great was divided between his sons Herod Antipas and Philip, as tetrarchs (rulers of a subordinate territory).

high-priesthood of Annas and Caiaphas, the word of God came to John the son of Zechariah in the wilderness; and he went into all the region about the Jordan, preaching a baptism of repentance for the forgiveness of sins. As it is written in the book of the words of Isaiah the prophet,

> "The voice of one crying in the wilderness:
> Prepare the way of the Lord,
> make his paths straight.
> Every valley shall be filled,
> and every mountain and hill shall be brought low,
> and the crooked shall be made straight,
> and the rough ways shall be made smooth;
> and all flesh shall see the salvation of God."

He said therefore to the multitudes that came out to be baptized by him, "You brood of vipers! Who warned you to flee from the wrath to come? Bear fruits that befit repentance, and do not begin to say to yourselves, 'We have Abraham as our father'; for I tell you, God is able from these stones to raise up children to Abraham. Even now the axe is laid to the root of the trees; every tree therefore that does not bear good fruit is cut down and thrown into the fire."

And the multitudes asked him, "What then shall we do?" And he answered them, "He who has two coats, let him share with him who has none; and he who has food, let him do likewise." Tax collectors also came to be baptized, and said to him, "Teacher, what shall we do?" And he said to them, "Collect no more than is appointed you." Soldiers also asked him, "And we, what shall we do?" And he said to them, "Rob no one by violence or by false accusation, and be content with your wages."

As the people were in expectation, and all men questioned in their hearts concerning John, whether perhaps he were the Christ, John answered them all, "I baptize you with water; but he who is mightier than I is coming, the thong of whose sandals I am not worthy to untie; he will baptize you with the Holy Spirit and with fire. His winnowing fork is in his hand, to clear his threshing floor, and to gather the wheat into his granary, but the chaff he will burn with unquenchable fire."

So, with many other exhortations, he preached good news to the people. But Herod the tetrarch, who had been reproved by him for Herodias, his brother's wife,[9] and for all the evil things that Herod had done, added this to them all, that he shut up John in prison.

Now when all the people were baptized, and when Jesus also had been baptized and was praying, the heaven was opened, and the Holy Spirit descended upon him in bodily form, as a dove, and a voice came from heaven, "Thou art my beloved Son; with thee I am well pleased."

Jesus, when he began his ministry, was about thirty years of age, being the son (as was supposed) of Joseph, the son of Heli, the son of Matthat, the son of Levi,

---

9. Herod had married his brother's wife, in
   violation of Jewish law.

the son of Melchi, the son of Jannai, the son of Joseph, the son of Mattathias, the son of Amos, the son of Nahum, the son of Esli, the son of Naggai, the son of Maath, the son of Mattathias, the son of Semein, the son of Josech, the son of Joda, the son of Joanan, the son of Rhesa, the son of Zerubbabel, the son of Shealtiel, the son of Neri, the son of Melchi, the son of Addi, the son of Cosam, the son of Elmadam, the son of Er, the son of Joshua, the son of Eliezer, the son of Jorim, the son of Matthat, the son of Levi, the son of Simeon, the son of Judah, the son of Joseph, the son of Jonam, the son of Eliakim, the son of Melea, the son of Menna, the son of Mattatha, the son of Nathan, the son of David, the son of Jesse, the son of Obed, the son of Boaz, the son of Sala, the son of Nahshon, the son of Amminadab, the son of Admin, the son of Arni, the son of Hezron, the son of Perez, the son of Judah, the son of Jacob, the son of Isaac, the son of Abraham, the son of Terah, the son of Nahor, the son of Serug, the son of Reu, the son of Peleg, the son of Eber, the son of Shelah, the son of Cainan, the son of Arphaxad, the son of Shem, the son of Noah, the son of Lamech, the son of Methuselah, the son of Enoch, the son of Jared, the son of Mahalaleel, the son of Cainan, the son of Enos, the son of Seth, the son of Adam, the son of God.[10]

4

And Jesus, full of the Holy Spirit, returned from the Jordan, and was led by the Spirit for forty days in the wilderness, tempted by the devil. And he ate nothing in those days; and when they were ended, he was hungry. The devil said to him, "If you are the Son of God, command this stone to become bread." And Jesus answered him, "It is written, 'Man shall not live by bread alone.' " And the devil took him up, and showed him all the kingdoms of the world in a moment of time, and said to him, "To you I will give all this authority and their glory; for it has been delivered to me, and I give it to whom I will. If you, then, will worship me, it shall all be yours." And Jesus answered him, "It is written,

'You shall worship the Lord your God,
and him only shall you serve.' "

And he took him to Jerusalem, and set him on the pinnacle of the temple, and said to him, "If you are the Son of God, throw yourself down from here; for it is written,

'He will give his angels charge of you, to guard you,'
and
'On their hands they will bear you up,
lest you strike your foot against a stone,' "

And Jesus answered him, "It is said, 'You shall not tempt the Lord your God.' " And when the devil had ended every temptation, he departed from him until an opportune time.

---

10. Whereas Matthew's gospel traces Jesus's lineage back to Abraham, Luke makes a point of extending his ancestry to the founder of the entire human race.

And Jesus returned in the power of the Spirit into Galilee, and a report concerning him went out through all the surrounding country. And he taught in their synagogues, being glorified by all.

And he came to Nazareth, where he had been brought up; and he went to the synagogue, as his custom was, on the sabbath day. And he stood up to read; and there was given to him the book of the prophet Isaiah. He opened the book and found the place where it was written,

> "The Spirit of the Lord is upon me,
> because he has anointed me to preach good news to the poor.
> He has sent me to proclaim release to the captives
> and recovering of sight to the blind,
> to set at liberty those who are oppressed,
> to proclaim the acceptable year of the Lord."

And he closed the book, and gave it back to the attendant, and sat down; and the eyes of all in the synagogue were fixed on him. And he began to say to them, "Today this scripture has been fulfilled in your hearing." And all spoke well of him, and wondered at the gracious words which proceeded out of his mouth; and they said, "Is not this Joseph's son?" And he said to them, "Doubtless you will quote to me this proverb, 'Physician, heal yourself; what we have heard you did at Capernaum, do here also in your own country.' " And he said, "Truly, I say to you, no prophet is acceptable in his own country. But in truth, I tell you, there were many widows in Israel in the days of Elijah, when the heaven was shut up three years and six months, when there came a great famine over all the land; and Elijah was sent to none of them but only to Zarephath, in the land of Sidon, to a woman who was a widow. And there were many lepers in Israel in the time of the prophet Elisha; and none of them was cleansed, but only Naaman the Syrian." When they heard this, all in the synagogue were filled with wrath. And they rose up and put him out of the city, and led him to the brow of the hill on which their city was built, that they might throw him down headlong. But passing through the midst of them he went away.

And he went down to Capernaum, a city of Galilee. And he was teaching them on the sabbath; and they were astonished at his teaching, for his word was with authority.[11] And in the synagogue there was a man who had the spirit of an unclean demon; and he cried out with a loud voice, "Ah! What have you to do with us, Jesus of Nazareth? Have you come to destroy us? I know who you are, the Holy One of God." But Jesus rebuked him, saying, "Be silent, and come out of him!" And when the demon had thrown him down in the midst, he came out of him, having done him no harm. And they were all amazed and said to one another, "What is this word? For with authority and power he commands the unclean spirits, and they come out." And reports of him went out into every place in the surrounding region.

And he arose and left the synagogue, and entered Simon's house. Now

---

11. Rabbis usually taught in the name of their
    teachers rather than on their own authority.

Simon's mother-in-law was ill with a high fever, and they besought him for her. And he stood over her and rebuked the fever, and it left her; and immediately she rose and served them.

Now when the sun was setting, all those who had any that were sick with various diseases brought them to him; and he laid his hands on every one of them and healed them. And demons also came out of many, crying, "You are the Son of God!" But he rebuked them, and would not allow them to speak, because they knew that he was the Christ.

And when it was day he departed and went into a lonely place. And the people sought him and came to him, and would have kept him from leaving them; but he said to them, "I must preach the good news of the kingdom of God to the other cities also; for I was sent for this purpose." And he was preaching in the synagogues of Judea.

5

While the people pressed upon him to hear the word of God, he was standing by the lake of Gennesaret. And he saw two boats by the lake; but the fishermen had gone out of them and were washing their nets. Getting into one of the boats, which was Simon's, he asked him to put out a little from the land. And he sat down and taught the people from the boat. And when he had ceased speaking, he said to Simon, "Put out into the deep and let down your nets for a catch." And Simon answered, "Master, we toiled all night and took nothing! But at your word I will let down the nets." And when they had done this, they enclosed a great shoal of fish; and as their nets were breaking, they beckoned to their partners in the other boat to come and help them. And they came and filled both the boats, so that they began to sink. But when Simon Peter saw it, he fell down at Jesus' knees, saying, "Depart from me, for I am a sinful man, O Lord." For he was astonished, and all that were with him, at the catch of fish which they had taken; and so also were James and John, sons of Zebedee, who were partners with Simon. And Jesus said to Simon, "Do not be afraid; henceforth you will be catching men." And when they had brought their boats to land, they left everything and followed him.

While he was in one of the cities, there came a man full of leprosy; and when he saw Jesus, he fell on his face and besought him, "Lord, if you will, you can make me clean." And he stretched out his hand, and touched him, saying, "I will; be clean." And immediately the leprosy left him. And he charged him to tell no one; but "go and show yourself to the priest, and make an offering for your cleansing, as Moses commanded, for a proof to the people." But so much the more the report went abroad concerning him; and great multitudes gathered to hear and to be healed of their infirmities. But he withdrew to the wilderness and prayed.

On one of those days, as he was teaching, there were Pharisees[12] and teachers of the law sitting by, who had come from every village of Galilee and Judea and from Jerusalem; and the power of the Lord was with him to heal. And behold, men were bringing on a bed a man who was paralyzed, and they sought to bring him

---

12. A group of strict observers of Jewish law.

in and lay him before Jesus; but finding no way to bring him in, because of the crowd, they went up on the roof and let him down with his bed through the tiles into the midst before Jesus. And when he saw their faith he said, "Man, your sins are forgiven you." And the scribes and the Pharisees began to question, saying, "Who is this that speaks blasphemies? Who can forgive sins but God only?" When Jesus perceived their questionings, he answered them, "Why do you question in your hearts? Which is easier, to say, 'Your sins are forgiven you,' or to say, 'Rise and walk'? But that you may know that the Son of man has authority on earth to forgive sins"—he said to the man who was paralyzed—"I say to you, rise, take up your bed and go home." And immediately he rose before them, and took up that on which he lay, and went home, glorifying God. And amazement seized them all, and they glorified God and were filled with awe, saying, "We have seen strange things today."

After this he went out, and saw a tax collector, named Levi, sitting at the tax office; and he said to him, "Follow me." And he left everything, and rose and followed him.

And Levi made him a great feast in his house; and there was a large company of tax collectors and others sitting at table with them. And the Pharisees and their scribes murmured against his disciples, saying, "Why do you eat and drink with tax collectors and sinners?"[13] And Jesus answered them, "Those who are well have no need of a physician, but those who are sick; I have not come to call the righteous, but sinners to repentance.

And they said to him, "The disciples of John fast often and offer prayers, so do the disciples of the Pharisees, but yours eat and drink." And Jesus said to them, "Can you make wedding guests fast while the bridegroom is with them? The days will come, when the bridegroom is taken away from them, and then they will fast in those days." He told them a parable also: "No one tears a piece from a new garment and puts it upon an old garment; if he does, he will tear the new, and the piece from the new will not match the old. And no one puts new wine into old wineskins; if he does, the new wine will burst the skins and it will be spilled and the skins will be destroyed. But new wine must be put into fresh wineskins. And no one after drinking old wine desires new; for he says, 'The old is good.' "[14]

. . .

22

Now the feast of Unleavened Bread drew near, which is called the Passover. And the chief priests and the scribes were seeking how to put him to death; for they feared the people.

Then Satan entered into Judas called Iscariot, who was of the number of the twelve; he went away and conferred with the chief priests and captains how he

13. Tax collectors were despised both because they typically extorted all they could and because they were agents of the Roman occupation.

14. In Chapters 6–21, Jesus chooses the rest of his twelve disciples and continues to teach and perform miracles, arousing increasing hostility from the religious authorities.

might betray him to them. And they were glad, and engaged to give him money. So he agreed, and sought an opportunity to betray him to them in the absence of the multitude.

Then came the day of Unleavened Bread, on which the passover lamb had to be sacrificed.[15] So Jesus sent Peter and John, saying, "Go and prepare the passover for us, that we may eat it." They said to him, "Where will you have us prepare it?" He said to them, "Behold, when you have entered the city, a man carrying a jar of water will meet you: follow him into the house which he enters, and tell the householder, 'The Teacher says to you, Where is the guest room, where I am to eat the passover with my disciples?' And he will show you a large upper room furnished; there make ready." And they went, and found it as he had told them; and they prepared the passover.

And when the hour came, he sat at table, and the apostles with him. And he said to them, "I have earnestly desired to eat this passover with you before I suffer; for I tell you I shall not eat it until it is fulfilled in the kingdom of God." And he took a cup, and when he had given thanks he said, "Take this, and divide it among yourselves; for I tell you that from now on I shall not drink of the fruit of the vine until the kingdom of God comes." And he took bread, and when he had given thanks he broke it and gave it to them, saying, "This is my body which is given for you. Do this in remembrance of me." And likewise the cup after supper, saying, "This cup which is poured out for you is the new covenant in my blood. But behold the hand of him who betrays me is with me on the table. For the Son of man goes as it has been determined; but woe to that man by whom he is betrayed!" And they began to question one another, which of them it was that would do this.

A dispute also arose among them, which of them was to be regarded as the greatest. And he said to them, "The kings of the Gentiles exercise lordship over them; and those in authority over them are called benefactors. But not so with you; rather let the greatest among you become as the youngest, and the leader as one who serves. For which is the greater, one who sits at table, or one who serves? Is it not the one who sits at table? But I am among you as one who serves.

"You are those who have continued with me in my trials; and I assign to you, as my Father assigned to me, a kingdom, that you may eat and drink at my table in my kingdom, and sit on thrones judging the twelve tribes of Israel.

"Simon, Simon, behold, Satan demanded to have you, that he might sift you like wheat, but I have prayed for you that your faith may not fail; and when you have turned again, strengthen your brethren." And he said to him, "Lord, I am ready to go with you to prison and to death." He said, "I tell you, Peter, the cock will not crow this day, until you three times deny that you know me."

And he said to them, "When I sent you out with no purse or bag or sandals, did you lack anything?" They said, "Nothing." He said to them, "But now, let him who has a purse take it, and likewise a bag. And let him who has no sword sell his mantle and buy one. For I tell you that this scripture must be fulfilled in me, 'And

---

15. Passover commemorates God's deliverance of the Israelites from slavery in Egypt; as they fled, the Hebrews had to eat unleavened bread, lacking time for baking.

he was reckoned with transgressors'; for what is written about me has its fulfillment." And they said, "Look, Lord, here are two swords." And he said to them, "It is enough."

And he came out, and went, as was his custom, to the Mount of Olives; and the disciples followed him. And when he came to the place he said to them, "Pray that you may not enter into temptation." And he withdrew from them about a stone's throw, and knelt down and prayed, "Father, if thou art willing, remove this cup from me; nevertheless not my will, but thine, be done." And when he rose from prayer, he came to the disciples and found them sleeping for sorrow, and he said to them, "Why do you sleep? Rise and pray that you may not enter into temptation."

While he was still speaking, there came a crowd, and the man called Judas, one of the twelve, was leading them. He drew near to Jesus to kiss him; but Jesus said to him, "Judas, would you betray the Son of man with a kiss?" And when those who were about him saw what would follow, they said, "Lord, shall we strike with the sword?" And one of them struck the slave of the high priest and cut off his right ear. But Jesus said, "No more of this!" And he touched his ear and healed him. Then Jesus said to the chief priests and officers of the temple and elders, who had come out against him, "Have you come out as against a robber, with swords and clubs? When I was with you day after day in the temple, you did not lay hands on me. But this is your hour, and the power of darkness."

Then they seized him and led him away, bringing him into the high priest's house. Peter followed at a distance; and when they had kindled a fire in the middle of the courtyard and sat down together, Peter sat among them. Then a maid, seeing him as he sat in the light and gazing at him, said, "This man also was with him." But he denied it, saying, "Woman, I do not know him." And a little later some one else saw him and said, "You also are one of them." But Peter said, "Man, I am not." And after an interval of about an hour still another insisted, saying, "Certainly this man also was with him; for he is a Galilean." But Peter said, "Man, I do not know what you are saying." And immediately, while he was still speaking, the cock crowed. And the Lord turned and looked at Peter. And Peter remembered the word of the Lord, how he had said to him, "Before the cock crows today, you will deny me three times." And he went out and wept bitterly.

Now the men who were holding Jesus mocked him and beat him; they also blindfolded him and asked him, "Prophesy! Who is that struck you?" And they spoke many other words against him, reviling him.

When day came, the assembly of the elders of the people gathered together, both chief priests and scribes; and they led him away to their council, and they said, "If you are the Christ, tell us." But he said to them, "If I tell you, you will not believe; and if I ask you, you will not answer. But from now on the Son of man shall be seated at the right hand of the power of God." And they all said, "Are you the Son of God, then?" And he said to them, "You say that I am." And they said, "What further testimony do we need? We have heard it ourselves from his own lips."

23

Then the whole company of them arose, and brought him before Pilate. And they began to accuse him, saying, "We found this man perverting our nation, and forbidding us to give tribute to Caesar, and saying that he himself is Christ a king." And Pilate asked him, "Are you the King of the Jews?" And he answered him, "You have said so." And Pilate said to the chief priests and the multitudes, "I find no crime in this man." But they were urgent, saying, "He stirs up the people, teaching throughout all Judea, from Galilee even to this place."

When Pilate heard this, he asked whether the man was a Galilean. And when he learned that he belonged to Herod's jurisdiction, he sent him over to Herod, who was himself in Jerusalem at that time. When Herod saw Jesus, he was very glad, for had long desired to see him, because he had heard about him, and he was hoping to see some sign done by him. So he questioned him at some length; but he made no answer. The chief priests and the scribes stood by, vehemently accusing him. And Herod with his soldiers treated him with contempt and mocked him; then, arraying him in gorgeous apparel, he sent him back to Pilate. And Herod and Pilate became friends with each other that very day, for before this they had been at enmity with each other.

Pilate then called together the chief priests and the rulers and the people, and said to them, "You brought me this man as one who was perverting the people; and after examining him before you, behold, I did not find this man guilty of any of your charges against him; neither did Herod, for he sent him back to us. Behold, nothing deserving death has been done by him; I will therefore chastise him and release him.

But they all cried out together, "Away with this man, and release to us Barabbas"—a man who had been thrown into prison for an insurrection started in the city, and for murder. Pilate addressed them once more, desiring to release Jesus; but they shouted out, "Crucify, crucify him!" A third time he said to them, "Why, what evil has he done? I have found in him no crime deserving death; I will therefore chastise him and release him." But they were urgent, demanding with loud cries that he should be crucified. And their voices prevailed. So Pilate gave sentence that their demand should be granted. He released the man who had been thrown into prison for insurrection and murder, whom they asked for; but Jesus he delivered up to their will.

And as they led him away, the seized one Simon of Cyrene, who was coming in from the country, and laid on him the cross, to carry it behind Jesus. And there followed him a great multitude of the people, and of women who bewailed and lamented him. But Jesus turning to them said, "Daughters of Jerusalem, do not weep for me, but weep for yourselves and for your children. For behold, the days are coming when they will say, 'Blessed are the barren, and the wombs that never bore, and the breasts that never gave suck!' Then they will begin to say to the mountains, 'Fall on us'; and to the hills, 'Cover us.' For if they do this when the wood is green, what will happen when it is dry?"[16]

Two others also, who were criminals, were led away to be put to death with him. And when they came to the place which is called The Skull, there they

---

16. I.e., if the innocent Jesus meets such a fate, what will become of guilty Jerusalem as a whole?

crucified him, and the criminals, one on the right and one on the left. And Jesus said, "Father, forgive them; for they know not what they do." And they cast lots to divide his garments. And the people stood by, watching; but the rulers scoffed at him, saying, "He saved others; let him save himself, if he is the Christ of God, his Chosen One!" The soldiers also mocked him, coming up and offering him vinegar, and saying, "If you are the King of the Jews, save yourself!" There was also an inscription over him, "This is the King of the Jews."

One of the criminals who were hanged railed at him, saying, "Are you not the Christ? Save yourself and us!" But the other rebuked him, saying, "Do you not fear God, since you are under the same sentence of condemnation? And we indeed justly; for we are receiving the due reward of our deeds; but this man has done nothing wrong." And he said, "Jesus, remember me when you come in your kingly power." And he said to him, "Truly, I say to you, today you will be with me in Paradise."

It was now about the sixth hour, and there was darkness over the whole land until the ninth hour,[17] while the sun's light failed; and the curtain of the temple was torn in two. Then Jesus, crying with a loud voice, said, "Father, into thy hands I commit my spirit!" And having said this he breathed his last. Now when the centurion saw what had taken place, he praised God, and said, "Certainly this man was innocent!" And all the multitudes who assembled to see the sight, when they saw what had taken place, returned home beating their breasts. And all his acquaintances and the women who had followed him from Galilee stood at a distance and saw these things.

Now there was a man named Joseph from the Jewish town of Arimathea. He was a member of the council, a good and righteous man, who had not consented to their purpose and deed, and he was looking for the kingdom of God. This man went to Pilate and asked for the body of Jesus. Then he took it down and wrapped it in a linen shroud, and laid him in a rock-hewn tomb, where no one had ever yet been laid. It was the day of Preparation, and the sabbath was beginning. The women who had come with him from Galilee followed, and saw the tomb, and how his body was laid; then they returned, and prepared spices and ointments.

On the sabbath they rested according to the commandment.

24

But on the first day of the week, at early dawn, they went to the tomb, taking the spices which they had prepared. And they found the stone rolled away from the tomb, but when they went in they did not find the body. While they were perplexed about this, behold, two men stood by them in dazzling apparel; and as they were frightened and bowed their faces to the ground, the men said to them, "Why do you seek the living among the dead? Remember how he told you, while he was still in Galilee, that the Son of man must be delivered into the hands of sinful men, and be crucified, and on the third day rise." And they remembered his words, and returning from the tomb they told all this to the eleven and to all the

---

17. From noon to 3 P.M.

rest. Now it was Mary Magdalene and Joanna and Mary the mother of James and the other women with them who told this to the apostles; but these words seemed to them an idle tale, and they did not believe them.

That very day two of them were going to a village named Emmaus, about seven miles from Jerusalem, and talking with each other about all these things that had happened. While they were talking and discussing together, Jesus himself drew near and went with them. But their eyes were kept from recognizing him. And he said to them, "What is this conversation which you are holding with each other as you walk?" And they stood still, looking sad. Then one of them, named Cleopas, answered him, "Are you the only visitor to Jerusalem who does not know the things that have happened there in these days?" And he said to them, "What things?" And they said to him, "Concerning Jesus of Nazareth, who was a prophet mighty in deed and word before God and all the people, and how our chief priests and rulers delivered him up to be condemned to death, and crucified him. But we had hoped that he was the one to redeem Israel. Yes, and besides all this, it is now the third day since this happened. Moreover, some women of our company amazed us. They were at the tomb early in the morning and did not find his body; and they came back saying that they had even seen a vision of angels, who said that he was alive. Some of those who were with us went to the tomb, and found it just as the women had said; but him they did not see." And he said to them, "O foolish men, and slow of heart to believe all that the prophets have spoken! Was it not necessary that the Christ should suffer these things and enter into his glory?" And beginning with Moses and all the prophets, he interpreted to them in all the scriptures the things concerning himself.

So they drew near to the village to which they were going. He appeared to be going further, but they constrained him, saying, "Stay with us, for it is toward evening and the day is now far spent." So he went in to stay with them. When he was at table with them, he took the bread and blessed, and broke it, and gave it to them. And their eyes were opened and they recognized him: and he vanished out of their sight. They said to each other, "Did not our hearts burn within us while he talked to us on the road, while he opened to us the scriptures?" And they rose that same hour and returned to Jerusalem; and they found the eleven gathered together and those who were with them, who said, "The Lord has risen indeed, and has appeared to Simon!" Then they told what had happened on the road, and how he was known to them in the breaking of the bread.

As they were saying this, Jesus himself stood among them. But they were startled and frightened, and supposed that they saw a spirit. And he said to them, "Why are you troubled, and why do questionings rise in your hearts? See my hands and my feet, that it is I myself; handle me, and see; for a spirit has not flesh and bones as you see that I have." And while they still disbelieved for joy, and wondered, he said to them, "Have you anything here to eat?" They gave him a piece of broiled fish, and he took it and ate before them.

Then he said to them, "These are my words which I spoke to you, while I was still with you, that everything written about me in the law of Moses and the prophets and the psalms must be fulfilled." Then he opened their minds to understand the scriptures, and said to them, "Thus it is written, that the Christ should suffer and on the third day rise from the dead, and that repentance and forgiveness of sins should be preached in his name to all nations, beginning from Jerusalem. You are witnesses of these things. And behold, I send the promise of my Father upon you; but stay in the city, until you are clothed with power from on high."

Then he led them out as far as Bethany, and lifting up his hands he blessed them. While he blessed them, he parted from them. And they returned to Jerusalem with great joy, and were continually in the temple blessing God.

Acts of the Apostles 1, 2

1

In the first book, O Theophilus, I have dealt with all that Jesus began to do and teach, until the day when he was taken up, after he had given commandment through the Holy Spirit to the apostles whom he had chosen. To them he presented himself alive after his passion by many proofs, appearing to them during forty days, and speaking of the kingdom of God. And while staying with them he charged them not to depart from Jerusalem, but to wait for the promise of the Father, which, he said, "you heard from me, for John baptized with water, but before many days you shall be baptized with the Holy Spirit."

So when they had come together, they asked him, "Lord, will you at this time restore the kingdom to Israel?" He said to them, "It is not for you to know times or seasons which the Father has fixed by his own authority. But you shall receive power when the Holy Spirit has come upon you; and you shall be my witnesses in Jerusalem and in all Judea and Samaria and to the end of the earth." And when he had said this, as they were looking on, he was lifted up, and a cloud took him out of their sight. And while they were gazing into heaven as he went, behold, two men stood by them in white robes, and said, "Men of Galilee, why do you stand looking into heaven? This Jesus, who was taken up from you into heaven, will come in the same way as you saw him go into heaven."

Then they returned to Jerusalem from the mount called Olivet, which is near Jerusalem, a sabbath day's journey away; and when they had entered, they went up to the upper room, where they were staying, Peter and John and James and Andrew, Philip and Thomas, Bartholomew and Matthew, James the son of Alphaeus and Simon the Zealot and Judas the son of James. All these with one accord devoted themselves to prayer, together with the women and Mary the mother of Jesus, and with his brothers.

In those days Peter stood up among the brethren (the company of persons was in all about a hundred and twenty), and said, "Brethren, the scripture had to be fulfilled, which the Holy Spirit spoke beforehand by the mouth of David, concerning Judas who was guide to those who arrested Jesus. For he was numbered among us, and was allotted his share in this ministry. (Now this man bought a field with the reward of his wickedness; and falling headlong he burst

Revised Standard Version translation.

open in the middle and all his bowels gushed out. And it became known to all the inhabitants of Jerusalem, so that the field was called in their language Akeldama, that is, Field of Blood.) For it is written in the book of Psalms.

> 'Let his habitation become desolate, and let there be no one to live in it';
> and
>   'His office let another take.'

So one of the men who have accompanied us during all the time that the Lord Jesus went in and out among us, beginning from the baptism of John until the day when he was taken up from us—one of these men must become with us a witness to his resurrection." And they put forward two, Joseph called Barsabbas, who was surnamed Justus, and Matthias. And they prayed and said, "Lord, who knowest the hearts of all men, show which one of these two thou hast chosen to take the place in this ministry and apostleship from which Judas turned aside, to go to his own place." And they cast lots for them, and the lot fell on Matthias; and he was enrolled with the eleven apostles.

2

When the day of Pentecost had come, they were all together in one place. And suddenly a sound came from heaven like the rush of a mighty wind, and it filled all the house where they were sitting. And there appeared to them tongues as of fire, distributed and resting on each one of them. And they were all filled with the Holy Spirit and began to speak in other tongues, as the Spirit gave them utterance.

Now there were dwelling in Jerusalem Jews, devout men from every nation under heaven. And at this sound the multitude came together, and they were bewildered, because each one heard them speaking in his own language.[1] And they were amazed and wondered, saying, "Are not all these who are speaking Galileans? And how is it that we hear, each of us in his own native language? Parthians and Medes and Elamites and residents of Mesopotamia, Judea and Cappadocia, Pontus and Asia, Phrygia and Pamphylia, Egypt and the parts of Libya belonging to Cyrene, and visitors from Rome, both Jews and proselytes, Cretans and Arabians, we hear them telling in our own tongues the mighty works of God." And all were amazed and perplexed, saying to one another, "What does this mean?" But others mocking said, "They are filled with new wine."

But Peter, standing with the eleven, lifted up his voice and addressed them, "Men of Judea and all who dwell in Jerusalem, let this be known to you, and give ear to my words. For these men are not drunk, as you suppose, since it is only the third hour of the day;[2] but this is what was spoken by the prophet Joel:

> 'And in the last days it shall be, God declares,
> that I will pour out my Spirit upon all flesh,
> and your sons and your daughters shall prophesy,
> and your young men shall see visions,

---

1. An inversion of the splintering of languages at the Tower of Babel (Genesis 11).   2. 9 A.M.

and your old men shall dream dreams;
yea, and on my menservants and my maidservants in those days
I will pour out my Spirit; and they shall prophesy.
And I will show wonders in the heaven above
and signs on the earth beneath,
blood, and fire, and vapor of smoke;
the sun shall be turned into darkness
and the moon into blood,
before the day of the Lord comes,
the great and manifest day.
And it shall be that whoever calls on the name of the Lord shall be saved.'

"Men of Israel, hear these words: Jesus of Nazareth, a man attested to you by God with mighty works and wonders and signs which God did through him in your midst, as you yourselves know—this Jesus, delivered up according to the definite plan and foreknowledge of God, you crucified and killed by the hands of lawless men. But God raised him up, having loosed the pangs of death, because it was not possible for him to be held by it. For David says concerning him,

'I saw the Lord always before me,
for he is at my right hand that I may not be shaken;
therefore my heart was glad, and my tongue rejoiced;
moreover my flesh will dwell in hope.
For thou wilt not abandon my soul to Hades,
nor let thy Holy One see corruption.
Thou hast made known to me the ways of life;
thou wilt make me full of gladness with thy presence.'

"Brethren, I may say to you confidently of the patriarch David that he both died and was buried, and his tomb is with us to this day. Being therefore a prophet, and knowing that God had sworn with an oath to him that he would set one of his descendants upon his throne, he foresaw and spoke of the resurrection of the Christ, that he was not abandoned to Hades, nor did his flesh see corruption. This Jesus God raised up, and of that we all are witnesses. Being therefore exalted at the right hand of God, and having received from the Father the promise of the Holy Spirit, he has poured out this which you see and hear. For David did not ascend into the heavens; but he himself says,

'The Lord said to my Lord, Sit at my right hand,
till I make thy enemies a stool for thy feet.'

Let all the house of Israel therefore know assuredly that God has made him both Lord and Christ, this Jesus whom you crucified."

Now when they heard this they were cut to the heart, and said to Peter and the rest of the apostles, "Brethren, what shall we do?" And Peter said to them, "Repent, and be baptized every one of you in the name of Jesus Christ for the forgiveness of your sins; and you shall receive the gift of the Holy Spirit. For the promise is to you and to your children and to all that are far off, every one whom the Lord our God calls to him." And he testified with many other words and exhorted them, saying, "Save yourselves from this crooked generation." So those who received his word were baptized, and there were added that day about three thousand souls. And they devoted themselves to the apostles' teaching and fellowship, to the breaking of bread and the prayers.

And fear came upon every soul; and many wonders and signs were done through the apostles. And all who believed were together and had all things in common; and they sold their possessions and goods and distributed them to all, as any had need. And day by day, attending the temple together and breaking bread in their homes, they partook of food with glad and generous hearts, praising God and having favor with all the people. And the Lord added to their number day by day those who were being saved.

OVID (43 B.C.E.–17 C.E.)
Rome

Ovid's earliest work—the three volumes of *Amores*—represents the transformation elegiac poetry underwent in the hands of the Roman poets of the first century B.C.E. In contrast to the wide range of subject matter that characterizes Greek elegy, in the writings of the Roman elegists—of whom Ovid (Publius Ovidius Naso) was the last—erotic themes predominate, developing into what amounts to a new and distinctive genre. Although in Ovid's work (as in that of Tibullus and Propertius, contemporary writers of amatory elegy) love does not have the tragic dimensions with which Vergil endows it in his *Aeneid* (See *Aeneid* Book 4, in this section)—and although Ovid explicitly draws a contrast between the grandeur of epic themes and the more modest aims of his chronicle of the everyday vicissitudes of his love affair with a woman (probably fictive) he calls Corinna—the poet often humorously compares the arduous course of love with the rigors and perils of war. Despite his ironic self-deprecation, Ovid expended great care on his elegies, revising them into an edition of three books from an original five, as the epigram to the whole collection indicates.

Some years later Ovid did attempt an epic poem, the *Metamorphoses,* which takes as its subject the phenomenon of *change:* beginning with the transition from chaos to order that created the world, it narrates and gives coherence to numerous Greek and Roman legends about how gods and mortals altered their physical forms—often to pursue or evade each other, sometimes as a truer reflection of their natures.

A virtual archive of mythology, the *Metamorphoses* was an endlessly valuable resource for artists, both literary and visual, of later centuries; in the early modern period, the poem's depictions of the amorous adventures of the gods were often drawn upon to allegorize the activities of a contemporary aristocracy. Ovid never completed his epic. For reasons not clearly known (but sometimes thought to be connected with his publication of a long erotic elegy, the *Ars Amatoria,* or *Art of Love*), Ovid was abruptly banished by the emperor Augustus to a frontier outpost on the Black Sea, where he died after ten years in exile.

from Amores

Epigram by the Poet

We are our author's book. Before, we comprised five sections,
  Now we're cut down to three. The decision was his.
You still may derive no pleasure from reading us—but remember,
  With two of us gone, your labour is that much less.

[Every lover's on active service]

Every lover's on active service, my friend, active service, believe me,
  And Cupid has his headquarters in the field.
Fighting and love-making belong to the same age-group—
  In bed as in war, old men are out of place.
A commander looks to his troops for gallant conduct,   5
  A mistress expects no less.
Soldier and lover both keep night-long vigil,
    Lying rough outside their captain's (or lady's) door.
The military life brings long route-marches—but just let his mistress
  Be somewhere ahead, and the lover too   10
Will trudge on for ever, scale mountains, ford swollen rivers,
  Thrust his way through deep snow.
Come embarkation-time *he* won't talk of 'strong north-easters',
  Or say it's 'too late in the season' to put to sea.
Who but a soldier or lover would put up with freezing   15
  Nights—rain, snow, sleet? The first
Goes out on patrol to observe the enemy's movements,
  The other watches his rival, an equal foe.
A soldier lays siege to cities, a lover to girls' houses,
  The one assaults city gates, the other front doors.   20
Night attacks are a great thing. Catch your opponents sleeping
  And unarmed. Just slaughter them where they lie.
That's how the Greeks dealt with Rhesus[1] and his wild Thracians
  While rustling those famous mares.
Lovers, too, will take advantage of slumber (her husband's),   25
  Strike home while the enemy sleeps: getting past
Night patrols and eluding sentries are games both soldiers
  And lovers need to learn.
Love, like war, is a toss-up. The defeated can recover,
  While some you might think invincible collapse;   30
So if you've got love written off as an easy option

Translated by Peter Green.

---

1. In a grisly episode of the Trojan War narrated in Book 10 of the *Iliad*, the Greek warriors Odysseus and Diomedes killed the Trojan ally Rhesus and his fellow Thracians at night as they slept, and drove the slain Rhesus's prized horses back to the Greek camp.

You'd better think twice. Love calls
For guts and initiative. Great Achilles sulks for Briseis[2]—
  Quick, Trojans, smash through the Argive wall!
Hector went into battle from Andromache's embraces   35
  Helmeted by his wife.
Agamemnon[3] himself, the Supremo, was struck into raptures
  At the sight of Cassandra's tumbled hair;
Even Mars[4] was caught on the job, felt the blacksmith's meshes—
  Heaven's best scandal in years. Then take   40
My own case. I was idle, born to leisure *en déshabillé,*
  Mind softened by lazy scribbling in the shade.
But love for a pretty girl soon drove the sluggard
  To action, made him join up.
And just look at me now—fighting fit, dead keen on night exercises: 45
  If you want a cure for slackness, fall in love!

[A second batch of verses by that naughty provincial poet]

A second batch of verses[5] by that naughty provincial poet,
  Naso, the chronicler of his own
Wanton frivolities; another of Love's commissions (warning
  To puritans: *This volume is not for you).*
I want my works to be read by the far-from-frigid virgin   5
  On fire for her sweetheart, by the boy
In love for the very first time. May some fellow-sufferer,
  Perusing my anatomy of desire,
See his own passion reflected there, cry in amazement:
  'Who told this scribbler about my private affairs?'   10
One time, I recall, I got started on an inflated epic
  About War in Heaven,[6] with all
Those hundred-handed monsters, and Earth's fell vengeance, and towering
  Ossa piled on Olympus (plus Pelion too).

Every lover's on active service

2. The personages (and themes) of Greek mythology, exalted in epic poetry, are frequently subjected to a humorously ironic—and deflating—treatment by the Roman elegists. Here Achilles' devastating wrath over the loss of Briseis and his withdrawal from the Trojan War, which propel the plot of the *Iliad,* are pictured as a case of mere ill humor.
3. The commander of the Greek army brought the Trojan princess and seer Cassandra, King Priam's daughter, home to Argos as a prize of war.
4. Book 8 of the *Odyssey* recounts the adulterous love affair of Ares (identified with Mars, in Roman mythology) and Aphrodite (Venus). Aphrodite's husband Hephaestus, the divine blacksmith, trapped the lovers by constructing a mesh of delicate golden filaments that pinned them, unaware, to the bed as they made love.

A second batch of verses

5. This is the opening poem of the second book of the *Amores.*
6. Invoking a traditional epic subject—the struggle for supremacy in heaven, such as the version narrated by Hesiod in his *Theogony*—Ovid alludes to an episode in which a pair of giants tried to pile two mountains on top of a third, so as to scale them and lay siege to heaven.

But while I was setting up Jove[7]—stormclouds and thunderbolts gathered   15
    Ready to hand, a superb defensive barrage—
My mistress staged a lock-out. I dropped Jupiter and his lightnings
    That instant, didn't give him another thought.
Forgive me, good Lord, if I found your armoury useless—
    Her shut door ran to larger bolts   20
Than any *you* wielded. I went back to verses and compliments,
    My natural weapons. Soft words
Remove harsh door-chains. There's magic in poetry, its power
    Can pull down the bloody moon,
Turn back the sun, make serpents burst asunder   25
    Or rivers flow upstream.
Doors are no match for such spellbinding, the toughest
    Locks can be open-sesamed by its charms.
But epic's a dead loss for me. I'll get nowhere with swift-footed
    Achilles, or with either of Atreus' sons.[8]   30
Old what's-his-name[9] wasting twenty years on war and travel,
    Poor Hector dragged in the dust—
No good. But lavish fine words on some young girl's profile
    And sooner or later she'll tender herself as the fee,
An ample reward for your labours. So farewell, heroic   35
    Figures of legend—the *quid*
Pro quo you offer won't tempt me. A bevy of beauties
    All swooning over my love-songs—that's what *I* want.

[A hot afternoon: siesta-time]

A hot afternoon: siesta-time. Exhausted,
    I lay sprawled across my bed.
One window-shutter was closed, the other stood half-open,
    And the light came sifting through
As it does in a wood. It recalled that crepuscular glow at sunset   5
    Or the trembling moment between darkness and dawn,
Just right for a modest girl whose delicate bashfulness
    Needs some camouflage. And then—
In stole Corinna, long hair tumbled about her
    Soft white throat, a rustle of summer skirts,   10
Like some fabulous Eastern queen *en route* to her bridal-chamber—
    Or a top-line city call-girl, out on the job.
I tore the dress off her—not that it really hid much,
    But all the same she struggled to keep it on:
Yet her efforts were unconvincing, she seemed half-hearted—   15
    Inner self-betrayal made her give up.

A second batch of verses

7. Another name for Jupiter, the supreme deity of the Roman pantheon.

8. Agamemnon and Menelaus.
9. Odysseus.

When at last she stood naked before me, not a stitch of clothing,
    I couldn't fault her body at any point.
Smooth shoulders, delectable arms (I saw, I touched them),
    Nipples inviting caresses, the flat   20
Belly outlined beneath that flawless bosom,
    Exquisite curve of a hip, firm youthful thighs.
But why catalogue details? Nothing came short of perfection,
    And I clasped her naked body close to mine.
Fill in the rest for yourselves! Tired at last, we lay sleeping.   25
    May my siestas often turn out that way!

LUCIUS APULEIUS (SECOND CENTURY C.E.)
Roman North Africa

Lucius Apuleius was born in the Roman province of Africa around 125 C.E. He
studied in Carthage (a city in North Africa near today's Tunis) and Athens, visited
Rome, then probably settled back in Carthage. Apuleius produced poems, orations,
and philosophical works, but he is best known for his satiric masterpiece, originally
titled *Metamorphoses* but later known as *Asinus Aureus—The Golden Ass*.

Consumed with insatiable curiosity (among other appetites), Lucius, the
story's hero, dabbles in magic and finds himself accidentally transformed into the
shape of a donkey. He wanders in search of release, a sort of comic Odysseus,
providing the author with an opportunity to paint a vivid and darkly comic
portrait of life in the cosmopolitan Roman Empire, mixing the magical and the
marvelous with the debased and the depraved. Lucius's bodily transformation is
paralleled by confusions of languages and cultures, and the adventure culminates
with conversion to the worship of Isis, the Egyptian goddess of the moon and
ruler of change itself.

from *The Golden Ass*

Prologue

But[1] I would like to tie together different sorts of tales for you in that Milesian style
of yours,[2] and to caress your ears into approval with a pretty whisper, if only you
will not begrudge looking at Egyptian papyrus inscribed with the sharpness of a
reed from the Nile, so that you may be amazed at men's forms and fortunes

Translated by J. Arthur Hanson.

1. The narrator begins as if in mid-conversation.

2. Stories in the style of the florid erotic tales of a Greek writer, Aristides of Miletus.

transformed into other shapes and then restored again in an interwoven knot. I begin my prologue. Who am I? I will tell you briefly. Attic Hymettos and Ephyrean Isthmos and Spartan Taenaros, fruitful lands preserved for ever in even more fruitful books, form my ancient stock.[3] There I served my stint with the Attic tongue in the first campaigns of childhood. Soon afterwards, in the city of the Latins, as a newcomer to Roman studies I attacked and cultivated their native speech with laborious difficulty and no teacher to guide me. So, please, I beg your pardon in advance if as a raw speaker of this foreign tongue of the Forum I commit any blunders. Now in fact this very changing of language corresponds to the type of writing we have undertaken, which is like the skill of a rider jumping from one horse to another. We are about to begin a Greekish story. Pay attention, reader, and you will find delight.

[Lucius, our hero, is travelling on business through Thessaly in northern Greece. After hearing various marvelous stories from fellow travellers, he finds lodging in a strange city. His hosts are Milo, a miser; Pamphile, his wife; and Fotis, their seductive servant. Lucius goes looking for excitement in town.]

[Seduction in the Enchanted Land of Thessaly]

As soon as night had been scattered and a new sun brought day, I emerged from sleep and bed alike. With my anxiety and my excessive passion to learn the rare and the marvellous, considering that I was staying in the middle of Thessaly, the native land of those spells of the magic art which are unanimously praised throughout the entire world, and recalling that the story told by my excellent comrade Aristomenes had originated at the site of this very city, I was on tenterhooks of desire and impatience alike, and I began to examine each and every object with curiosity. Nothing I looked at in that city seemed to me to be what it was; but I believed that absolutely everything had been transformed into another shape by some deadly mumbo-jumbo: the rocks I hit upon were petrified human beings, the birds I heard were feathered humans, the trees that surrounded the city wall were humans with leaves, and the liquid in the fountains had flowed from human bodies. Soon the statues and pictures would begin to walk, the walls to speak, the oxen and other animals of that sort to prophesy; and from the sky itself and the sun's orb there would suddenly come an oracle.

I was in such a state of shock, or rather so dumbfounded by my torturous longing, that, although I found no trace or vestige whatever of what I longed to see, I continued to circulate anyway.

[Lucius meets a relation, who warns him to beware of his hostess, who is a sorceress. He returns home determined to see her in action. He decides to enlist the aid of Fotis, whom he finds in the kitchen.]

---

3. The narrator claims descent from several different regions in Greece: Athens, Corinth, and Sparta.

She herself was neatly dressed in a linen tunic and had a dainty, bright red band tied up under her breasts. She was turning the cooking pot round and round with her flower-like hands, and she kept shaking it with a circular motion, at the same time smoothly sliding her own body, gently wiggling her hips, softly shaking her supple spine, beautifully rippling. I was transfixed by the sight, utterly stunned. I stood in amazement, as did a part of me which had been lying limp before. Finally I spoke. "How gorgeously, my Photis," I said, "and how delightfully you twist your little pot with your buttocks! What a delicious stew you are cooking! A man would be lucky—surely even blessed—if you would let him dip his finger in there."

Then she, with her wit and her ready tongue, retorted: "Get away, poor boy; get as far away as you can from my oven, because if my little flame should blow against you even slightly, you will burn deep inside and no one will be able to extinguish your fire except me. I can season things deliciously, and I know how to shake a pot and a bed to your equal delight."

As she spoke she looked around at me and laughed. But I did not move away until I had carefully scrutinised every aspect of her appearance. Yet why should I mention anything else, since my exclusive concern has always been with a person's head and hair, to examine it intently first in public and enjoy it later at home? The reasoning behind this preference of mine is deliberate and well-considered: namely, as the dominant part of the body openly located for clear visibility, it is the first thing to meet our eyes. Secondly, what the cheerful colour of flowery clothing does for the rest of the body, its own natural lustre does for the head. Finally, when most women want to prove their own real loveliness, they take off all their garments, remove their clothes: they wish to show their beauty naked, knowing that they will be better liked for the rosy blush of their skin than for the golden colour of their dress. However—though it is forbidden to mention this and I hope that such a horrible illustration of this point will never occur—if you were to strip the hair from the head of the most extraordinary and beautiful woman and rob her face of its natural decoration, even if she were descended from heaven, born out of the sea, and raised by the waves, even, I say, if she were Venus herself, surrounded by the whole chorus of Graces and accompanied by the entire throng of Cupids, wearing her famous girdle, breathing cinnamon, and sprinkling balsam—if she came forth bald she could not attract even her husband Vulcan.

But think what it is like when hair shines with its own lovely colour and brilliant light, and when it flashes lively against the sunbeams or gently reflects them; or when it shifts its appearance to produce opposite charms, now glistening gold compressed into the smooth shadows of honey, now with raven-blackness imitating the dark blue flowerets on pigeons' necks; or when it is anointed with Arabian oils and parted with a sharp comb's fine tooth and gathered at the back so as to meet the lover's eyes and, like a mirror, reflect an image more pleasing than reality; or when, compact with all its tresses, it crowns the top of her head or, let out in a long train, it flows down over her back. In short, the significance of a woman's coiffure is so great that, no matter how finely attired she may be when she steps out in her gold, robes, jewels, and all her other finery, unless she has embellished her hair she cannot be called well-dressed.

In my Photis' case, her coiffure was not elaborate, but its casualness gave her added charm. Her luxuriant tresses were softly loosened to hang down over her neck, then they spread over her shoulders and momentarily rested upon the slightly curved border of her tunic; they were then gathered in a mass at the end and fastened in a knot to the crown of her head.

I could no longer endure the excruciating torture of such intense pleasure, but rushed toward her and planted that most delicious of kisses on the spot where her hair rose toward the top of her head. Then she twisted her neck and turned toward me with a sidelong glance of those biting eyes. "Well, well, my schoolboy," she said, "that is a bittersweet appetiser you are sampling. Be careful not to catch a chronic case of bitter indigestion from eating too sweet honey."

"How so, my merry one?" I replied. "I am prepared, if you will revive me now with one little kiss, to be stretched out over your fire and barbecued." And with that I held her tight and began to kiss her. Her ardour now began to rival my own, and she grew with me to an equal intensity of passion. Her mouth was open now, her breath like cinnamon and her tongue darting against mine with a touch like nectar, her passion unrestrained in her desire for me.

"I am dying," I said. "No, I am already dead unless you have mercy."

After another long kiss she answered, "Cheer up! Because I want what you want, I have become your slave, and our pleasure will not be postponed much longer. When the first lights are lit I will come to your bedroom. So go away now and prepare your forces, because all night long I will make war on you bravely and with all my heart."

After this bantering conversation we separated.

[Fotis becomes Lucius's lover, and enables him to spy on Pamphile as she changes herself into an owl. Lucius persuades Fotis to steal the sorceress's magic ointment for him, but she brings Lucius the wrong box: instead of an owl, he becomes a donkey, a form he will be trapped in until he manages to find some rose blossoms to eat. The bulk of the book describes Lucius's adventures among scoundrels, swindlers and thieves. All the while, he hears strange stories, and sharply observes the world around him, even when he is set to hard labor at a baker's millstone.]

[The Degradation of Lucius and His Fellow Slaves]

After most of the day was past and I was worn out, they took off my rope-collar, disconnected me from the machine, and fastened me to the manger. Although I was exceedingly exhausted, desperately in need of repairing my strength, and really dead from hunger, yet my habitual curiosity held me spellbound and made me quite anxious. So I postponed the plentiful dinner at hand and took a certain pleasure in carefully observing the routine of this undesirable workshop.

Good gods, what stunted little men they were! The whole surface of their skin was painted with livid welts. Their striped backs were merely shaded, not covered, by the tattered patchwork they wore: some had thrown on a tiny cloth that just covered their loins, but all were clad in such a way that you could discern them clearly through their rags. Their foreheads were branded, their heads half-shaved, and their feet chained. They were hideously sallow too, and their eyelids were eaten away by the smoky darkness of scorching murk until they were quite weak-sighted; like boxers who fight sprinkled with dust, they were dirtily white-washed with a floury ash.

As for my comrades, the animals, what can I say? How can I describe their condition? What a sight! Those old mules and feeble geldings stood round the manger with their heads sunk down, munching through piles of chaff; their necks sagged from the rotting decay of sores; their flabby nostrils were distended from constant coughing; their chests were ulcerated from the continual rubbing of the rope harnesses; their flanks were bare to the bone from everlasting whipping, their hoofs stretched out to abnormal dimensions from their multiple circling, and their entire hide rough with decay and mangy starvation.

The funereal example of my fellow-slaves made me fear for myself. Recalling the happy Lucius I once was, now driven to the utmost degradation, I lowered my head and grieved. Nowhere was there any consolation for my tortured existence, except one: I was revived by my innate curiosity, since everyone now took little account of my presence and freely did and said whatever they wished. That divine inventor of ancient poetry among the Greeks, desiring to portray a hero of the highest intelligence, was quite right to sing of a man who acquired the highest excellence by visiting many cities and learning to know various peoples.[4] In fact, I now remember the ass that I was with thankful gratitude because, while I was concealed under his cover and schooled in a variety of fortunes, he made me better-informed, if less intelligent. And so here is a story, better than all the others and delightfully elegant, which I have decided to bring to your ears. So here goes.

The baker who bought me was a good man in general and extremely temperate, but he had drawn as mate the worst and by far the most depraved woman in the world, who brought such dishonour to his bed and hearth that even I, by Hercules, often groaned silently for his sake. That vile woman lacked not a single fault. Her soul was like some muddy latrine into which absolutely every vice had flowed. She was cruel and perverse, crazy for men and wine, headstrong and obstinate, grasping in her mean thefts and a spendthrift in her loathsome extravagances, an enemy of fidelity and a foe to chastity. Furthermore she scorned and spurned all the gods in heaven, and, instead of holding a definite faith, she used the false sacrilegious presumption of a god, whom she would call "one and only",[5] to invent meaningless rites to cheat everyone and deceive her wretched husband, having sold her body to drink from dawn and to debauchery the whole day.

Such being the kind of woman she was, she persecuted me with extraordinary hatred. Even before dawn, while she was still in bed, she would shout out for the apprentice-ass to be yoked to the mill-wheel. Then the very moment she came out of her room she would insistently order me to be whipped over and over again while she watched. And although all the other animals were released for dinner on time, she had me put to the manger much later. This cruelty very greatly increased my natural curiosity about her behaviour. You see, I had heard a young man regularly visiting her bedroom, and I longed with all my heart to see his face, if

---

4. A reference to Homer's opening words about Odysseus.

5. Apparently an allusion to Christianity.

only the covering over my head had allowed my eyes any freedom. My ingenuity would not have failed, one way or another, to expose that terrible woman's scandalous affairs.

[In due course, the wife is entertaining her lover, a handsome young priest, when the baker returns home unexpectedly. She hides her lover under a wooden bin, but Lucius exposes him by treading on his hand.]

The baker, however, was not particularly moved at this damage to his honour. His face was calm and his expression kind as he began to speak caressingly to the bloodlessly pale and trembling boy.

"You have nothing harsh to fear from me, son," he said. "I am not barbarous, and I do not share the boorishness of rustic morality. I will not model myself on the fuller's savagery and kill you with lethal sulphur fumes, and I will not even invoke the strictness of the law to try you on capital charges under the statutes against adultery. You are such a charming and pretty boy: I will treat you as the joint property of my wife and me. Instead of a probate to split an estate, I will institute a suit to share common assets, contending that without controversy or dissension we three should enter into contract in the matter of one bed. You see, I have always lived in such harmony with my spouse that, in accordance with the teachings of the wise, we both have the same tastes. But the principle of equity does not permit a wife to have greater right of ownership than her husband."

When he had finished mocking the boy with the gentleness of this speech, he led him off to bed. Reluctantly the boy followed; and the miller, locking up his virtuous wife in another room, lay alone with the boy and enjoyed the most gratifying revenge for his ruined marriage. But when first the Sun's bright wheel gave birth to day, he summoned the two strongest slaves in the house, ordered them to lift the boy up as high as they could, and then flogged his buttocks with a rod.

[Lucius's misadventures culminate when he is exhibited as a tourist attraction and comes to the attention of a wealthy woman with unusual tastes.]

Among the crowds was a certain influential and wealthy lady, who, after paying for a look at me just like everyone else and enjoying my various tricks, out of her constant wonder at me gradually conceived a wondrous desire for me. She took no remedy for her insane passion but, like some asinine Pasiphae,[6] ardently yearned for my embraces. She therefore bargained with my keeper, offering him a large price to lie with me for one night; and he agreed, not the least concerned whether anything pleasant could result for me, but content only with his own gain.

We had just finished supper and left my owner's dining room when we met the lady, who had already been waiting for a long time in my room. Good gods, what luxurious and splendid fittings! Four eunuchs were hastily making a bed for

---

6. The wife of king Minos of Crete, who mated with a bull and gave birth to the Minotaur, half man and half bull.

us on the ground out of a large number of pillows airily puffed out with soft feathers. Over these they carefully laid covers coloured with gold cloth and Tyrian purple, and on top they scattered some other pillows, small but quite numerous, the kind that refined women use to support their chins and necks. They did not delay their mistress's pleasure by their continued presence, but closed the bedroom door and went away. Inside wax candles sparkled with brilliant light and whitened the night's darkness for us.

Then she stripped herself of all her clothes, including the band with which she had bound her lovely breasts. Standing next to the light, she anointed herself all over with oil of balsam from a pewter jar, and lavishly rubbed me down with the same, but with much greater eagerness. She even moistened my nostrils with frankincense. Then she kissed me intimately—not the sort of kisses tossed about in a whorehouse, the money-begging kisses of prostitutes or the money-refusing kisses of customers, but pure and uncorrupted. And she spoke to me with tender affection, saying "I desire you," "I want you," "It is you alone I love," "I can not live without you," and all the other expressions women use to stimulate their lovers and to declare their own feelings. Next she took me by my halter and made me lie down, as I had learned to do. I obeyed readily, because I did not think my task would be anything new or difficult, and especially since for the first time in a long while I was about to enjoy the passionate embraces of a very beautiful woman. Furthermore I had saturated myself with a generous quantity of the finest wine and aroused my desire for sex with the heady fragrance of the ointment.

I was distressed, however, and not a little frightened as I wondered how I, with so many and such large legs, could mount such a delicate lady; or how I could embrace such a soft, translucent body, all compact of milk and honey, with my hard hoofs; or how I could kiss those fine lips reddened by ambrosial dew with my great monstrous misshapen mouth with its stone-sized teeth. Finally, even though she was itching for it to the tips of her toes, how could the woman contain my huge organ? Woe unto me if I should rupture the noble lady and get thrown to the beasts to provide part of my owner's gladiatorial show. Meantime she kept repeating tender words and constant kisses and sweet moans with eyes that bit into me. Finally she said, "I am holding you, I am holding you, my little dove, my sparrow." And as she spoke she demonstrated that my calculations had been vain and my fear pointless, because she clasped me very tightly and took in absolutely all of me—yes, all of me. In fact every time I tried to spare her and pull back my buttocks, she would push closer with a mad thrust, grab my spine, and cling in an even closer embrace, until, by Hercules, I believed that I did not even have enough to fulfil her desire, and that the Minotaur's mother might have had reason to take her pleasure with her mooing paramour. After we had passed a busy and sleepless night the woman departed, avoiding the complicity of daylight, after agreeing to the same price for another night.

My trainer was not unhappy to dispense these joys at her command, because he was not only taking in a very large profit but also rehearsing a new show for his master, to whom he unhesitatingly disclosed our entire sexual performance. The master rewarded his freedman generously, and decided that I should take part in his public spectacle. Since that excellent wife of mine could not be considered because of her social position, and absolutely no one else could be found even for a high price, a depraved woman was procured, one already sentenced by the governor's order to be thrown to the beasts, to appear with me in a packed theatre and exhibit the loss of her virtue.[7]

. . . .

I awaited the day of the show in a state of terrible suspense and great torment, frequently wishing to kill myself rather than be polluted by the infection of that depraved woman or shamed by the disgrace of a public spectacle. But, lacking a human hand and fingers, I had no way to unsheath a sword with my round, misshapen hoof. In this uttermost catastrophe I consoled myself with just one slender hope: spring in her moment of birth was now painting everything with her flowery jewels and clothing the meadows with crimson brilliance; and recently the roses had burst their thorny covers and sparkled forth, exhaling their spicy fragrance—roses that could restore me to the Lucius I used to be.[8]

And now the day appointed for the show had come. I was led to the outside wall of the theatre, escorted by crowds in an enthusiastic parade. The opening of the show was given over to actors' mimic dances; meanwhile I enjoyed myself standing in front of the gate, browsing on the lush, rich grass which grew right in the entrance-way, and occasionally refreshing my inquisitive eyes with a delightful glimpse of the show through the open gate.

There were boys and girls in the bloom of verdant youth, outstanding in beauty, resplendent in costume, and graceful in movement, all ready to dance the Greek Pyrrhic. They went through beautiful dance-cycles with carefully arranged patterns, now turning into a rounded circle, now linked into a slanting chain, then wedged into a hollow square, then split into separate sections. But when the horn's concluding note had unravelled the knotted complexities of their alternating movements, the curtain was raised, the screens folded back, and the stage was set.

There stood a wooden mountain, constructed with lofty craftsmanship to resemble the famous mountain of which the bard Homer sang, Mount Ida. It was planted with bushes and live trees, and at its very peak, from a flowing fountain made by the designer's hand, it poured river-water. A few goats were browsing among the low grasses, and a young man, beautifully attired like the Phrygian shepherd Paris, with exotic robes flowing over his shoulders and a golden tiara covering his head, was feigning mastery of the flock. Then a radiantly beautiful boy appeared, naked except for an ephebic cape covering his left shoulder. He attracted all eyes with his blond curls, and from his hair projected little golden wings symmetrically attached; a caduceus and wand identified him as Mercury.[9] He danced forward, carrying in his right hand an apple gilded with gold leaf, which he held out to the person who was acting Paris. Then, after indicating Jupiter's instructions with a nod, he quickly and elegantly retraced his steps and disappeared.

---

7. Lucius now recounts the woman's criminal history, omitted here.

8. Lucius can only return to human form by eating roses.

9. Messenger of the gods.

[Indecent Proposal and Judgment of Paris]

[Paris is commanded to judge who is the most beautiful goddess: Juno, queen of the gods; Minerva, goddess of wisdom; or Venus, goddess of love. He awards the prize to Venus after she promises him her human daughter Helen — over whom the Trojan War will subsequently be fought. Lucius comments on his verdict.]

Why are you so surprised, you cheap ciphers—or should I say sheep of the courts, or better still vultures in togas—if nowadays all jurors hawk their verdicts for a price, since at the world's beginning an adjudication between gods and men was corrupted by beauty's influence, and a country shepherd, chosen judge on the advice of great Jupiter, sold the first verdict for a profit of pleasure, resulting in the destruction of himself and his entire race? And it was the same, by Hercules, with a second and yet another celebrated case among the far-famed princes of the Achaeans, when Palamedes, a man of superior learning and wisdom, was condemned for treason because of false accusations, or mediocre Ulysses was preferred to great Ajax, who was supreme in martial valour.[10] And what kind of a trial was that one held by the Athenians, those skilful legislators and teachers of all knowledge? Is it not true that that divinely wise old man,[11] whom the Delphic god pronounced superior to all other mortals in intelligence, was attacked by the lies and malice of an utterly worthless faction, accused of being a corruptor of the young—whom he was in fact keeping in rein—and murdered with the poisonous juice of a baleful herb? He bequeathed to his fellow-citizens the stain of eternal disgrace, because even to this day the best philosophers choose his holy school and in their jealous pursuit of happiness swear by his very name.

But I am afraid one of you may reproach me for this attack of indignation and think to himself, "So, now are we going to have to stand an ass lecturing us on philosophy?" So I shall return to the story at the point where I left it.

After the judgement of Paris was completed, Juno and Minerva went off stage, gloomy and acting angry, proclaiming with gestures their wrath at being defeated. Venus, on the other hand, joyfully and gaily proclaimed her happiness by dancing with her entire chorus. Then, from a hidden pipe at the very peak of the mountain, saffron dissolved in wine came spurting up into the air and rained down in a fragrant shower, sprinkling the goats that were grazing all round, until, dyed to a greater beauty, they exchanged their natural whiteness for a yellow hue. Finally, when the theatre was filled with the delightful fragrance, a chasm in the earth opened and swallowed up the wooden mountain.

And now a soldier came hurrying across the theatre floor in answer to the audience's demands, to fetch the woman from the public prison, the one who I told you had been condemned to the beasts for her manifold crimes and engaged to make an illustrious match with me. And now a bed, evidently meant to serve as our honeymoon couch, was being elaborately made up, shining with Indian tortoise-shell, piled high with a feathered mattress, and spread with a flowery silk coverlet.

---

10. Two famous mythical examples of unjust verdicts.

11. Socrates, condemned to death by drinking hemlock.

But as for me, besides my shame at indulging in sexual intercourse in public, besides the contagion of this damnable polluted woman, I was greatly tormented by the fear of death; for I thought to myself that, when we were in fact fastened together in Venus' embrace, any wild animal that might be let in to slaughter the woman could not possibly turn out to be so intelligently clever or so skilfully educated or so temperately moderate as to mangle the woman lying attached to my loins while sparing me on the grounds that I was unconvicted and innocent. So now I was afraid not for my honour, but for my very life. While my trainer gave his full attention to the proper fitting of our couch, and all the slaves were busy, some occupied with preparations for the hunting-spectacle, the others spellbound by the sensual pleasure of the show, I was allowed free rein for my own devices. Besides, no one thought that such a tame ass needed to be watched very carefully. So I slowly moved forward without being observed until I reached the nearest gate, and then hurled myself forward with the utmost rapidity. I covered six whole miles at full speed and arrived at the town of Cenchreae, which is well-known as part of the illustrious territory of the Corinthians, and is washed by the Aegean Sea and the Saronic Gulf. The port there is a safe harbour for ships and has a large population. I avoided the crowds, therefore, and chose a hidden stretch of shore. There, right next to the spray from the breakers, I stretched out in a soft hollow of sand to refresh my weary body, for the Sun's chariot had raced round the last turning-post of the day. As I surrendered myself to the evening's quiet, sweet sleep overwhelmed me.

About the first watch of the night I awoke in sudden fright and saw, just emerging from the waves of the sea, the full circle of the moon glistening with extraordinary brilliance. Surrounded by the silent mysteries of dark night, I realised that the supreme goddess now exercised the fullness of her power; that human affairs were wholly governed by her providence; that not only flocks and wild beasts but even lifeless things were quickened by the divine favour of her light and might; and that individual bodies on land, in the sky, and in the sea grew at one period in consequence of her waxing and diminished at another in obedience to her waning. Since fate, it seemed, was now satiated with the number and intensity of my sufferings, and was offering me the hope, albeit late, of deliverance, I decided to pray to the august image of the goddess present before me. Quickly I shook off my sluggish sleep and arose happily and eagerly. Desiring to purify myself I went at once to bathe in the sea, plunging my head under the waves seven times, because the divine Pythagoras[12] had declared that number to be especially appropriate to religious rituals. Then, my face covered with tears, I prayed to the mighty goddess.

"O queen of heaven—whether you are bountiful Ceres, the primal mother of crops, who in joy at the recovery of your daughter took away from men their primeval animal fodder of acorns and showed them gentler nourishment, and now dwell in the land of Eleusis; or heavenly Venus, who at the first foundation

---

12. Greek mathematician and philosopher, sixth century B.C.E., who taught of the transmigration of souls.

of the universe united the diversity of the sexes by creating Love and propagated the human race through ever-recurring progeny, and now are worshipped in the island sanctuary of Paphos; or Phoebus' sister,[13] who brought forth populous multitudes by relieving the delivery of offspring with your soothing remedies, and now are venerated at the illustrious shrine of Ephesus; or dreaded Proserpina[14] of the nocturnal howls, who in triple form repress the attacks of ghosts and keep the gates to earth closed fast, roam through widely scattered groves and are propitiated by diverse rites—you who illumine every city with your womanly light, nourish the joyous seeds with your moist fires, and dispense beams of fluctuating radiance according to the convolutions of the Sun—by whatever name, with whatever rite, in whatever image it is meet to invoke you: defend me now in the uttermost extremes of tribulation, strengthen my fallen fortune, grant me rest and peace from the cruel mischances I have endured. Let this be enough toil, enough danger. Rid me of this dreadful four-footed form, restore me to the sight of my own people, restore me to the Lucius I was. But if some divine power that I have offended is harassing me with inexorable savagery, at least let me die, if I may not live."

[Venus appears to Lucius.]

"Behold, Lucius, moved by your prayers I have come, I the mother of the universe, mistress of all the elements, and first offspring of the ages, mightiest of deities, queen of the dead, and foremost of heavenly beings; my one person manifests the aspect of all gods and goddesses. With my nod I rule the starry heights of heaven, the health-giving breezes of the sea, and the plaintive silences of the underworld. My divinity is one, worshipped by all the world under different forms, with various rites, and by manifold names. In one place the Phrygians, first-born of men, call me Pessinuntine Mother of the Gods, in another the autochthonous people of Attica call me Cecropian Minerva, in another the sea-washed Cyprians call me Paphian Venus; to the arrow-bearing Cretans I am Dictynna Diana, to the trilingual Sicilians Ortygian Proserpina, to the ancient people of Eleusis Attic Ceres; some call me Juno, some Bellona, others Hecate, and still others Rhamnusia; the people of the two Ethiopias, who are lighted by the first rays of the Sun-God as he rises every day, and the Egyptians, who are strong in ancient lore, worship me with the rites that are truly mine and call me by my real name, which is Queen Isis. I have come in pity at your misfortunes; I have come in sympathy and good will. Now stop your tears and cease your lamentation; banish your grief. Now by my providence your day of salvation is dawning. So, therefore, pay careful attention to these commands of mine. The day which will be the day born from this night has been proclaimed mine by everlasting religious observance: on that day, when the winter's tempests are lulled and the ocean's storm-blown waves are calmed, my priests dedicate an untried keel to the now navigable sea and consecrate it as the first fruits of voyaging. You must await this

---

13. Diana, patroness of childbirth, was worshipped at Ephesus as an Asiatic fertility
goddess.

14. Queen of the underworld.

rite with an attitude both calm and reverent. At my command, my priest, as part of his equipment for the procession, will carry in his right hand a garland of roses attached to the sistrum.[15] So do not hesitate, but eagerly push through the crowd and join the procession, relying on my good will; go right up to the priest and gently, as if you were going to kiss his hand, pluck the roses and cast off at once the hide of that wretched beast which I have long detested. And do not shrink from any of my instructions because it seems difficult: for at this very moment when I come to you I am present there too and am instructing my priest in his sleep about what he must do next. At my command the tight-packed crowd of people will give way before you, and no one in the midst of the joyous rites and festive revelries will shrink from the unsightly aspect that you present. Nor will anyone misinterpret your sudden transformation and prefer charges against you out of spite.

"You will clearly remember and keep forever sealed deep in your heart the fact that the rest of your life's course is pledged to me until the very limit of your last breath. Nor is it unjust that you should owe all the time you have to live to her by whose benefit you return to the world of men. Moreover you will live in happiness, you will live in glory, under my guardianship. And when you have completed your life's span and travel down to the dead, there too, even in the hemisphere under the earth, you will find me, whom you see now, shining among the shades of Acheron and holding court in the deep recesses of the Styx, and while you dwell in the Elysian fields I will favour you and you will constantly worship me.[16] But if by assiduous obedience, worshipful service, and determined celibacy you win the favour of my godhead, you will know that I—and I alone—can even prolong your life beyond the limits determined by your fate."

This was the end of the holy revelation, and the invincible divinity now withdrew into herself. At once I was quickly released from sleep, and I rose in a confusion of fear and joy, and covered with sweat.

[Lucius Recovers His Human Form]

[Lucius recovers his human form, then undergoes a series of initiations into the worship of Isis and her divine husband Osiris. He moves to Rome and becomes a devotee at the temple of Isis, shaving his head and selling his clothes to do so; he earns his living as a lawyer. The book ends with a final vision.]

Finally, after just a few days, he that is mightiest of the great gods, the highest of the mightiest, the loftiest of the highest, and the sovereign of the loftiest, Osiris, appeared to me in a dream. He had not transformed himself into a semblance other than his own, but deigned to welcome me face to face with his own venerable utterance, bidding me unhesitatingly to continue as now to win fame in the courts as an advocate and not fear the slanders of detractors which my

---

15. A musical instrument, used in rituals of Isis.

16. Acheron and Styx are underworld rivers; the Elysian fields are the dwelling place of blessed souls.

industrious pursuit of legal studies had aroused in Rome. Furthermore, to avoid my serving his mysteries as an undistinguished member of the faithful, he elected me to the college of his *pastophori*,[17] and even made me a member of the quinquennial board of directors. Then, once more shaving my head completely, neither covering up nor hiding my baldness, but displaying it wherever I went, I joyfully carried out the duties of that ancient priesthood, founded in the days of Sulla.[18]

---

17. "Shrine-bearers." 18. Some 250 years earlier.

Lady writing a love letter. Temple
sculpture of the eleventh century C.E.
from Khajuraho in central India.

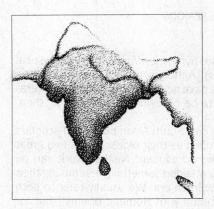

SECTION II
South Asia: Early and Middle Periods

As a physical landscape South Asia, comprising present-day Pakistan, India, Nepal, Bangladesh, and Sri Lanka, is vast and varied. As a literary landscape, it comprises dozens of languages with a complex and fascinating record of literary activity stretching back more than three thousand years. In the "early period" (to the end of the first millennium C.E.) literature in South Asia finds expression above all in Sanskrit and Tamil, languages radically different not only in respect to their linguistic identity but also in respect to their ethnic and regional identities; the next half-millennium or so, the "middle period," is marked by the emergence of new literary languages and new forms of subjectivity and of political, social, and religious consciousness.

Sanskrit belongs to the Indo-European family of languages; its presence in the northwest of the subcontinent is attested to as early as the first millennium B.C.E. During the next thousand years Sanskrit spread throughout South Asia to become the first of several pan-Indian literary languages (the others being Persian in the later middle period and English in the modern period).

The name Sanskrit means, among other things, "refined" or "ritually purified." (It is one of the very few language names that does not commemorate an ethnic identity.) Initially, Sanskrit seems to have been employed principally for religious purposes. Writings related to this religion include the hymns of the Veda ("[sacred] knowledge," from the same Indo-European root, *weid*, that gave us our English words *wit* and *wisdom*), prose commentaries on the hymns (*brahmanas*), and mystical and philosophical speculations (*upanishads*). Although these texts include the most ancient Sanskrit writings, South Asians have never considered them "literature" in as much as they were considered to be of divine origins. Where, then, does the Sanskrit literary tradition begin?

Since at least the fifth or sixth centuries C.E., South Asian poets and scholars reflecting on their literary history have identified as their oldest works two great Sanskrit "epics": the *Mahabharata* and the *Ramayana*. Neither work can be dated with any specificity, but both probably attained something resembling their current form around the beginning of the common era. We usually refer to both works as epics (they share features in common with Homeric poems), but for South Asians they are often thought to represent different genres. The *Ramayana* is regarded as a poem (*kavya*), indeed it is thought to be the first poem, while the *Mahabharata* is classified as history (*itihasa*). Despite this distinction, the two works are similar in form as well as in content.

The concerns of these texts are above all social, political, and male in perspective: What does it mean to live in a world of power, to live with our "own," to deal with "others"? What is a king? What is the nature of war? What is the "right thing to do" (*dharma*)? What is the proper relationship between men and women? The responses the two epics provide to these questions are markedly different. Between them they provide a kind of spectrum of responses to the most pressing questions of the human condition.

The influence that the *Mahabharata* and the *Ramayana* have exerted on the literary history of South Asia has been fundamental. Even Sanskrit literature of a much later period is devoted to rethinking and rewriting their stories. This is especially true of Sanskrit drama (whose relationship to these epics is strikingly close to the relationship that existed between Greek drama and the Homeric epics). The history of virtually every regional literature, too, is marked—in some cases even initiated—by adaptations of the epics. Today their influence continues to be strong, as witnessed by large-scale television versions of both epics in India in the 1980s. The religious associations of Sanskrit were such that apart from the two "epics" we have no "literature" in Sanskrit before the common era.

The literary imagination was to find expression in other languages, probably in the Prakrits—regional dialects related to Sanskrit that are the ancestors of modern languages of northern India. Little of this literature has survived, however, and with few exceptions later Prakrit works are derivative of Sanskrit literature.

Religious movements such as Buddhism and Jainism arose in opposition to Vedic practice during the fifth century B.C.E. and explicitly rejected Sanskrit, at least initially, for their own doctrinal writings. In part, this rejection was a practical decision: The new sects hoped to attract converts by using a common language. However, the decision was also ideological, for the sects defined themselves in opposition to vedic culture and its Sanskrit idiom. Languages espoused by these new sects provided literary opportunities; thus some of the oldest texts that exhibit features of what the later Indian tradition thinks of as literature are in Pali, an early Buddhist language. These texts also include some of the first works ascribed to women, for the Buddhist monastic community included women as members.

Within three or four hundred years of the founding of these religious movements, however, many of their adherents in the north had switched to Sanskrit for their writings. The reasons were undoubtedly as complex as the process is unclear, yet the effect was to "liberate" Sanskrit and make it available for general intellectual use. Among the great innovators in this cultural convergence were Buddhist poets of the first centuries of the common era, who worked in a new environment created by — if not actually at the courts of — central Asians newly immigrant into the subcontinent. The most celebrated of these poets is Ashvaghosha, who turned vernacular tales about the Buddha into a form of Sanskrit poetry that quickly came to be regarded as a "classical" standard.

Freed by the examples of the epics and the efforts of the Buddhists from its exclusively Vedic domain, Sanskrit became the chosen instrument for expressing a vast range of intellectual and artistic concerns. The Sanskrit literature that evolved over the next 1500 years (100–1600 or so) includes every conceivable genre of imaginative and expository writing and constitutes perhaps the largest and richest single body of literature in all premodernity. A truly representative sampling — that would include something from the large number of Sanskrit dramas or from the immensely influential story literature — is impossible within the confines of this book. But the flavor of Sanskrit literature can be suggested by the selections of lyric poetry included here. A decidedly nonreligious species of writing in what is often and quite erroneously represented as a uniquely religion-obsessed culture, lyric poetry is one of the great achievements of Sanskrit art. The lyric was also the single genre to offer women a literary voice in early India, though unfortunately even this was rather rare. (It is only toward the end of the middle period, in the fifteenth to seventeenth centuries, that we find in southern India a few larger-scale compositions in Sanskrit by women.)

Despite the everyday concerns of Sanskrit literature, there is evidence that the language was never widely used for everyday purposes. Instead, Sanskrit was studied as a "father" tongue, and it existed in a state of some tension with the "mother" tongues — the various regional languages. (The situation can be compared with the relationship of Latin to the emerging regional languages of medieval Europe.) Only one regional language, Tamil, the language of the southernmost region of India, succeeded in creating its own distinct literary tradition during the early period (up to about 1000 C.E.)

Tamil belongs to the Dravidian family of languages — a family exclusive to South Asia — and its literary history stretches back to at least a century or two before the common era. The earliest Tamil poetry — called *sangam,* or "literary academic" poetry — shares a highly systematized and detailed repertoire of literary conventions, indicating how acutely aware its poets were that they inhabited a linguistically and culturally distinct region. Central to Tamil poetry is the genre distinction between the "interior" and "exterior" worlds — the inner world of the emotional life of lovers, the outer world of the public lives of warriors and kings. More than just a literary convention, these worlds provided a way of envisioning the human condition in terms of two complementary spheres of experience.

The influence of Tamil poetry spread early into the world of Sanskrit poetry. But the lines of influence were also reversed, as Sanskrit literature exercised a powerful influence on later Tamil poetry. This was far from a passive reception of dominant cultural forms, however, as the adaptation of the *Ramayana* by Kampan, Tamil's greatest poet (twelfth century), makes clear: Kampan did not merely translate the earlier Sanskrit work; he rethought it and reworked some of its key scenes and themes.

A powerful component in the development of South Asian writing, however, is indeed a growing self-conscious differentiation between Sanskrit and the mother tongues. The "Middle Period" of South Asian literary history (roughly 1000–1800) may in fact be taken as constituted by the emergence of new literary languages to express new forms of subjectivity, new worlds of political experience, new kinds of religious consciousness. For example, Kannada, the language of the southern region of India called Karnataka, had been a vehicle for literary work from at least the ninth century C.E. Its earliest writers, however, had largely emulated Sanskrit models. A truly distinctive form of Kannadan literature came into existence in the tenth century, with the rise of new religious movements broadly known as "devotionalism," which expressed a more direct, less socially constrained relationship with the divine. Similarly in the north, regional languages such as Avadhi and Braj (ancestors of modern Hindi) became the vehicles for expressing an altogether new kind of subjectivity, as in the strikingly innovative autobiography from the beginning of the seventeenth century, the *Ardhakathanaka* of Banarasi, and a new kind of religious politics, as in the songs of the low-caste weaver poet Kabir, which contest and seek to transcend the divisions in the social and religious communities of the fifteenth century.

Historical and Cultural Background

An early form of Sanskrit and the Vedic religious practices were brought to South Asia by peoples who are thought to have entered the region from the northwest probably a little before 1000 B.C.E. In successive waves of migration they gradually fanned out over the northern plains and along the Ganges River. Before their arrival the northwest had been home to what is known as the Harappan civilization, in the Indus River valley (largely in present-day Pakistan), which flourished for perhaps five hundred years (about 1500 B.C.E.). Archaeological evidence makes it clear that Harappan civilization was extremely advanced; writing was known, though it has yet to be deciphered. It is probable, though as yet unproven, that something of its culture also survived in the new civilizations that would take shape over the next millennium.

These civilizations began to take on distinctive traits after 1000 B.C.E. with the growth of cities and settled kingdoms, especially in the northeast. The Sanskrit texts often refer to four social orders: Vedic priests (*brahmans*), warriors (*kshatriyas*), merchants (*vaishyas*), and servants (*shudras*). Eventually, numerous "subcastes" would appear. It was especially in the religious world of the Brahman priests and the fire cult they maintained and the sacred texts associated with this cult (the *vedas*) that these social orders were represented as an ideological model. Whatever the everyday reality of this hierarchy, it and the religious worldview in which it was embedded were the objects of frequent contention from about the middle of the first millennium B.C.E. onward. New social-religious communities, such as the Buddhists and the Jains, came into existence then which presented themselves as alternatives to Vedic society. Brahmanic developments in the wake of these movements and interaction with local religious practices initiated the gradual metamorphosis of Vedic practice into the diverse collection of local religions we group together under the umbrella term *Hinduism*.

Political regional autonomy was the rule in South Asia, with numerous dynastic kingdoms fostering great cultural diversity. Regional kingdoms were occasionally, however, brought into loose imperial formations. Among the most important of these were the Maurya Empire (third to fourth centuries B.C.E.), the last of whose kings, Ashoka, patronized the Buddhists; the central Asian Kushan Empire in the north and northwest (first century C.E.), which also adopted Buddhism; and the Gupta Empire (fourth to sixth centuries C.E.), which made its presence felt throughout much of the northern half of the subcontinent. Crippled by repeated invasions of Hun tribes (part of the same wave of invasions that brought down the Roman Empire in the west), the Gupta Empire gradually disintegrated, and autonomous regional kingdoms reasserted themselves. New incursions from central Asia had lasting effects.

Starting in the eleventh century, Turkic peoples from central Asia and Afghanistan began a series of invasions that eventually led to the establishment of the Delhi Sultanate in 1206. The Sultanate lasted for almost two centuries, bringing much of the subcontinent under Turkic rule. A second major period of Islamic influence occurred from the sixteenth to the eighteenth centuries with the Mughal Empire.

Too often painted in stark terms of conquest and mutual animosity, the interactions of the Islamic immigrants with the very heterogeneous peoples of the subcontinent were actually quite complex, creating particularly Indian types of Islamic culture. Sometimes the results were the creation of altogether new forms of religious and cultural identity. From a cultural standpoint, a major consequence was the introduction of Persian, yet another trans-regional language in the South Asian cultural landscape.

NB Alternate spellings (Siva, Shiva, etc.) have been allowed to stand.

Further Readings

Biardeau, Madeleine. *Hinduism: The Anthropology of a Civilization*. Delhi: Oxford University Press, 1989.

Chatterji, Suniti Kumar, ed. ''Part III: Major Languages and Literature of Modern India.'' *The Cultural Heritage of India*. Vol. 5. Calcutta: Ramakrishna Mission Institute of Culture, 1978.

Das, Sisir Kumar. *A History of Indian Literature*. Vol. 8. New Delhi: Sahitya Akademi, 1991.

Davies, C. Collin. *An Historical Atlas of the Indian Peninsula*. Oxford: Oxford University Press, 1959.

Dimock, Edward C. et al. *The Literatures of India: An Introduction*. Chicago: University of Chicago Press, 1974.

Gonda, Jan, ed. *A History of Indian Literature*. 10 vols. Wiesbaden, Germany: Otto Harrossowitz, 1973.

Hardy, Peter. ''Islam in South Asia.'' *Encyclopedia of Religions*. Vol. 7. Ed. Mircea Eliade. New York: Macmillan. 390–404.

Kosambi, D. D. *The Culture and Civilisation of Ancient India in Historical Outline* London: Routledge & Kegan Paul, 1965.

Kulke, Hermann, and Dieter Rothermund. *A History of India*. Totowa, N.J.: Barnes and Noble, 1986.

O'Flaherty, Wendy Doniger. *Hindu Myths: A Sourcebook*. Harmondsworth, England: Penguin, 1975.

Robinson, Richard. *Buddhism: A Historical Introduction*. 3rd ed. Belmont, CA: Dickenson, 1982.

Winternitz, Maurice. *History of Indian Literature*. 3 vols. Delhi: Motilal Banarsidass. 1959–67.

KRISHNA DVAIPAIYANA VYASA

(FOURTH CENTURY B.C.E.)

India

The *Mahabharata,* or the Great Tale of the Bharata War, started as an oral epic. It was composed (that is, recited, modified, and transmitted) over the course of many centuries, beginning in the middle of the first millennium B.C.E. The written text of some 100,000 verses probably dates from early in the common era. It is traditionally attributed to Krishna Dvaipaiyana Vyasa, about whom we know nothing except what emerges from the poem itself.

The story concerns the dispute between two sets of claimants to the throne of Hastinapura, a city the text locates near modern Delhi. Though often referred to in the poem as brothers, they are actually first cousins—the sons of the brothers Pandu and Dhritarashtra. After years of struggle, the kingdom is provisionally partitioned between them. But Duryodhana, the eldest son of Dhritarashtra, decides to seize the share of the Pandavas (the sons of Pandu). He settles on the ruse of a dice game with Yudhishthira, the eldest son of Pandu.

The first selection presents this dramatic gambling match. Yudhishthira, a weak and confused person, is nevertheless an embodiment of "law" (*dharma*) itself as a duly consecrated King. The tricky Duryodhana is playing through a proxy, his uncle Shakuni. The focal point of the selection is the humiliation of Draupadi, the wife of the Pandavas. (They have married her conjointly.) Her humiliation is the key moment of the epic, releasing energies on both sides that cannot be contained. Inexorably, the story builds to the terrible slaughter that will destroy the sons of Dhritarastra, leaving the sons of Pandu victors who, as they realize near the end of the poem, are really dead in life, for they have destroyed everything they fought for.

Just before the great battle begins in the epic from the *Mahabharata* is the celebrated *Bhagavad Gita,* or "Song of the Blessed One." In our second selection, the action begins with a description of "the field of Kuru," "the field of sacred duty (*dharma*)," where the question posed is what actually is "duty" in the context of this war. Krishna, a close companion of Arjuna, one of the Pandavas, discourses on the nature of the war and convinces Arjuna that it is right for him to do battle.

from *The Mahabharata*

The Friendly Dice Game

2.52

VAISHAMPAYANA
Then Vidura[1] set forth with noble steeds
swift and strong, well broken to the car.

Translated by Daniel H. H. Ingalls.

---

1. The half-caste son of Vyasa, and therefore
   half-brother to King Dhritarashtra.

Compelled by order of King Dhritarashtra
he journeyed to the five wise Pandavas.

He flew along the road; he reached the royal city.   5
The wise counselor entered and was honored by the priests.

He came to the king's citadel as bright as Kubera's palace,[2]
and approached the son of Law, the Law itself, Yudhishthira.

Yudhishthira the king, invincible,
ever firm in truth and great of soul,   10
then greeted Vidura with all respect
and asked of Dhritarashtra and his sons.

YUDHISHTHIRA
I see your heart, O half-caste, is unhappy.
And yet, the news you bring is good, I trust?
His sons, I trust, obey the ancient king;   15
the Kuru tribesmen follow his command?

VIDURA
The ancient king is well, as are his children:
He sits among his godlike family
happy with virtuous and obedient sons,
knowing no sorrow, self-reliant, strong.   20

But this is the message given me by the king,
bidding me first ask your health and welfare:
"Your cousins have built a court as fair as yours
that I would gladly have you see, my son.

"Come to it, Pandava, with your four brothers   25
and enjoy yourself at a friendly game of dice.
We will rejoice to see you, as will also
the Kuru lords whom we have brought together."

You will see the stocks of dice provided there
by Dhritarashtra the magnificent,   30
and all the players that he has assembled.
Such was I bid to ask you. Pray accept.

YUDHISHTHIRA
If we should gamble, I fear there will be quarrels.
What man, aware of what it leads to, gambles?
But I ask you what you think the proper course,   35
for all of us take counsel by your word.

---

2. Kubera was the god of riches and treasure
   and presiding deity of the northern quarter
   of space.

VIDURA

I know that gambling is the source of evil
and I made great efforts to prevent it;
in spite of which the king has sent me.
Hear and choose with wisdom what is best.   40

YUDHISHTHIRA

What other gamblers will attend the game
in addition to the sons of Dhritarashtra?
I ask you, Vidura; tell me who they are,
those others brought together by the king.

VIDURA

The king of Gandhara, Shakuni, O king,   45
that gambler swift of hand who knows his dice;
Prince Vivimshati and Citrasena,
Purumitra, true to his word, and Jaya.

YUDHISHTHIRA

Fearful gamblers have been brought together,
experts in the art, who use deceit.   50
But the world, they say, is in the power of fate;
I will not fail to gamble with the experts.

For how can I not wish to come
when Dhritarashtra sends his bidding?
—a son must wish what his father bids—   55
So I accept the invitation.

But with Shakuni I have no wish to gamble
and will not do so unless he challenges.
Only if challenged I will not refuse,
for so I have sworn as my eternal vow.   60

VAISHAMPAYANA

So spoke the King of Law to Vidura
and bid with haste make ready for the journey.
Next morning he departed with his men,
and with his ladies led by Draupadi.

"Fate takes along our wits as a bright light takes our vision, 65
and we are in the power of fate as if bound to it by cords."

So spoke Yudhishthira in setting forth with the half-caste;
the invitation did not please the enemy-taming king.

The slayer of foes mounted the car that Bahlika had given;
surrounded by his brothers the son of Law drove forth,   70

drove shining with royal glory and accompanied by brahmans,[3]
summoned by Dhritarashtra and by the hour of fate.

He drove to Hastinapura to Dhritarashtra's palace
and there the lawful Pandava met the ancient king.

He met the teacher Drona, and Bhishma, Karna, Kripa,   75
greeting each in his degree and greeting Drona's son.

And there the great-armed king met also Somadatta
together with Duryodhana, Shakuni, and Shalya.

He met Jayadratha and Kuru lords by hundreds,
and all the other kings that had assembled there.   80

Then the great-armed king accompanied by his brothers
entered the inner chamber of learned Dhritarashtra.

He saw Queen Gandhari with daughters-in-law beside her,
bright as the star Rohini among its lesser stars.

He greeted Queen Gandhari and in return was greeted.   85
He saw the king his uncle blind except in wit.

The old king kissed his head and the heads of the kneeling princes,
the younger sons of Pandu, Bhima and the rest.

There was joy among the Kurus at the coming of their cousins
to see these handsome Pandavas, these tigers among men.   90

They took their leave and were shown to chambers decked with jewels,
where all their ladies met them, led by Draupadi.

But not so glad of heart were the Dhartarashtra ladies
when they saw how Draupadi fairly blazed with gems.   95

The heroes left their wives with promise to meet later;
they engaged in manly exercise and had their bodies oiled
and rubbed with sandal paste; and so in peaceful spirit
they heard the priestly blessing and said their evening prayers.

After a rich repast they returned to the jeweled chambers,   100
and as their ladies sang to them, the Pandavas lay down.

They passed the happy night in amorous engagement
and awoke refreshed next morning to praises of their bards.

The happy night had passed. They said their morning prayers
and entered the fair court where the gamblers stood in wait.   105

---

3. Priests and scholars.

2.53

SHAKUNI

The carpet is laid, Yudhishthira; all wait upon your coming.
The dice are put in place; let us set the rules of play.

YUDHISHTHIRA

Dicing is deception. It needs no warrior's courage;
it needs no ruler's judgment. Why praise dicing, king?

For men accord no honor to the deceptions of a gambler.   5
Do not beat us, Shakuni, by such dishonest means.

SHAKUNI

He alone can long endure at gambling
who can reckon numbers and recognize deceit,
who never tires in moving of the dice,
who has the wit to understand the play.   10

It is the way you draw the dice that wins
and only that, when you will call it fate.
Let us gamble, king, and no more hesitate;
set stakes and make no more delay.

YUDHISHTHIRA

I would rather heed the words of Devala the holy,   15
who ever visits our battles, those gates to heaven's world.

"That sort of play is evil where gamblers use deception.
To win by rightful war is the proper sort of play.

"Nobles do not act like slaves; they do not use deception.
An honest and straightforward fight is the way of real men."   20

We seek to use our wealth in aid of worthy brahmans;
whether one win or lose, it is wrong to gamble with such wealth.

I like not wealth or pleasure when purchased by deception;
even when the gambler is honest, I do not praise the game.

SHAKUNI

The learned fights the ignorant: by deceit, Yudhishthira?   25
the wise against the foolish: who calls out deceit?

Just so you fight me here. But if you find deception,
or if you are afraid, of course you may withdraw.

YUDHISHTHIRA

Challenged, I will not refuse, for I have made that promise;
and fate is strong, O Shakuni; I stand at its command.   30

So say in this assembly with whom am I to gamble?
Who can set stakes against me? Let the play begin.

DURYODHANA

O lord of tribes, it is I will stake my gold and jewels;
but for my sake my uncle, Shakuni, will dice.

YUDHISHTHIRA

It is wrong that one should gamble on another's wager;   35
you know as well as I. But take him if you wish.

VAISHAMPAYANA

As the game was about to begin, many kings and nobles
followed Dhritarashtra into the fair court.

Bhisma, Drona, Kripa, and wise Vidura
came with the others, but they were not so glad of heart.   40

Singly and in couples the lion-necked heroes
seated themselves about on the many brilliant thrones.

The court was then resplendent with these assembled nobles,
as heaven is resplendent with its assembled gods,

for all of them were brilliant, Veda—knowing[4] heroes.   45
Then straightaway began the friendly game of dice.

YUDHISHTHIRA

I have a pearl necklace born of the deep ocean,
costly and fair, Duryodhana, and the pearls are set in gold.

This is my wager, king. What have you that is equal?
If not, I have won first turn to draw from the stock of dice.   50

DURYODHANA

Indeed I too have pearls and many kinds of treasure.
I am no miser with my wealth. See, I have won the draw.

VAISHAMPAYANA

Then Shakuni drew the dice, who knew the art of dicing.
"I have won," said Shakuni to King Yudhishthira.

SHAKUNI

You have lost much wealth: horses, elephants, and brothers.   55
Tell me, son of Kunti, does any wealth remain?

YUDHISHTHIRA

I am the chief of all and well loved of my brothers;
If beaten I will work for you myself in servitude.

VAISHAMPAYANA

The gambler heard the words; etc. . . . .

---

4. Sacred text.

SHAKUNI

This was most ill done to lose yourself at wager;   60
when wealth remains, O king, it is ill to lose oneself.

VAISHAMPAYANA

He spoke and with proud glance herded his captives singly,
drawing to him the heroes that had stood at stake.

SHAKUNI

There still is left your dear queen, a single unwon wager.
Set Draupadi at stake; by her win back yourself.   65

YUDHISHTHIRA

The mean of tall and short; the mean of black and gold,
whose eyes are lit by passion: with her I wager you.

Whose eyes are autumn lotuses, whose breath is the autumn lotus,
whose beauty is that of Sri[5] who lives in the autumn lotus;

a woman of such kindliness and of such perfect beauty,   70
of such consummate virtue, as ever man could wish;

whose careful management extends to my meanest shepherd,
ever the first to wake, ever the last to sleep;

the sweat upon whose face smells of jasmine flowers;
long-haired, narrow-waisted, smooth-skinned, loving-eyed: 75

with this fair-waisted queen, the daughter of Pancala,
with dear-limbed Draupadi: come, I wager you.

VAISHAMPAYANA

So spoke the King of Law and at his words there mounted
a cry of horror from the elders of the court.

All began to speak; the court was in an uproar.   80
Bhisma, Drona, Kripa, were overwhelmed with grief.

Vidura held his head as if fainting from a blow;
he sat with lowered face, breath hissing like a snake.

But Dhritarashtra was glad. He asked over and over
"Has he won, Has my son won?" unable to hide his joy.   85

Karna was passing glad and Duhshasana exulted;
but others at the court could not hold back their tears.

Shakuni was sure of himself. As though without reflection
he approached the dice once more, and said simply "I have won."

---

5. The goddess of royalty and wealth.

2.59

DURYODHANA

Come, half-caste! Bring Draupadi to court:
the dear consort of the Pandavas.
We'll put her straight to work. It will be a pleasure
to watch her clean the floor with servant girls.

VIDURA

Fool! you put a noose around your neck   5
and yet are unaware of what you do:
a simpleton that teeters on a cliff,
a boy that would show off by teasing tigers.

The snakes are on your head, their fangs filled with poison;
stir them not up, you fool, or you will soon be dead.   10

Queen Draupadi I think has not become your servant;
the king was not her master when he made the bet.

This young king is like the bamboo tree
that comes in fruit only in time to perish.
For gambling brings on deadly enmity: 15
he knows it not but he is ripe for death.

Be not spiteful. Turn not the knife in the wound,
nor summon payment from a helpless man.
Speak not that word by which, although
another trembles, you go yourself to hell.   20

We call it "overspeaking" when a word
so falls upon another's tenderness
that day and night he suffers from the pain.
A wise man guards himself from overspeech.

You know of the goat—the thieves had lost the knife   25
until the goat by digging with his hoof
revealed the means of cutting his own throat.
So you: don't dig at hatred that may kill you.

Some men are silent, saying not a word
of village dweller or of forester;   30
but when a holy man appears in town,
perfect in wisdom, they bark at him like dogs.

You do not realize, Duryodhana,
that at this dice game you have opened up
a gateway sloping down to hell, through which   35
how many Kuru lords must follow you!

Gourds may sink and stones may float,
ships may lose themselves on water,
but this stupid son of Dhritarashtra
will never heed my good advice.   40

The end is near. Destruction of the Kurus,
cruel and all-devouring, will ensue
from this one prince who spurns the words of Kavya,[6]
the advice of friends, and only grows in greed.

2.60

VAISHAMPAYANA
Duryodhana cried out, "I spurn your words,"
and turned away from the half-caste with contempt.
His eyes sought out the usher of the court,
to whom among those noble lords he spoke.

"You, usher, bring us Draupadi.   5
You are not frightened of the Pandavas.
The half-caste here opposes me from fear
and from his never having wished me well."

He spoke. The bard who served the court as usher
left quickly in obedience to the king.   10
As a dog might steal into a pride of lions
he made his way to the Pandavas' chief queen.

THE USHER
Yudhishthira, mad with dicing,
has lost you to Duryodhana.
So come to Dhritarashtra's chamber;   15
I am to lead you to your work.

DRAUPADI
O usher, how can such a thing be true?
What son of kings would put his wife at wager?
Was the king out of his mind with dicing,
or was it that no other wealth remained?   20

THE USHER
It was when no other wealth remained
that King Yudhishthira put up the wager;
for first the king had wagered his four brothers
and next himself; last of all were you.

---

6. Also called Shukra, a mythological authority on politics.

DRAUPADI

Go now, bard's son, to the court and ask my lord this question: 25
whether he first lost himself or whether first lost me.
Find out the answer and come back; then lead me as you say.

VAISHAMPAYANA

He went straight to the court and told Yudhishthira her question:
"Draupadi asks of whom you were master when you lost,
'whether you first lost yourself, or whether first lost me.'"   30

As though he were in a swoon Yudhishthira sat silent.
He said no word to the bard's son, whether of good or ill.

DURYODHANA

Let Krsna Draupadi come here and ask her question,
here in the court where all may hear both her words and his.

VAISHAMPAYANA

Again at the king's command he went to the royal harem   35
and said to Draupadi, trembling as he spoke:

THE USHER

The courtiers, lady, order you to come
and I fear destruction for the Kauravas.
The worthless king will not keep fortune long
if my lady Draupadi goes down to court.   40

DRAUPADI

The ordainer surely has ordained it thus,
for both the wise and foolish feel his hand.
But he has given us one highest law
and he will give me peace if I obey it.

· · ·

VAISHAMPAYANA

In single garment, with knot turned down, weeping and in her courses,[7]   45
the daughter of Panchala kings knelt before her uncle.

From where he stood Duryodhana observed
the expression of their faces. To the bard's son
he spoke exultant: "Bring her here, right here,
where the lords may speak to her directly.   50

The bard was subject to Duryodhana
but feared the anger of the highborn queen.
He faltered in obedience and asked,
"What shall I say to the lady Draupadi?"

---

7. Traditionally Indian women are secluded
   during their menstrual periods and dress in
   a single garment.

DURYODHANA

Duhshasana! My foolish usher   55
trembles with fear of Wolfbelly Bhima.
Go bring us Draupadi yourself.
What can her helpless husbands do?

VAISHAMPAYANA

The younger prince heard his brother's words
and rose with anger-reddened eyes.   60
He strode up to the audience chamber
and thus addressed Queen Draupadi.

"Come, Pancali, come! You have been won.
Look without shame on King Duryodhana.
Your love belongs to the Kurus; the lovely prize   65
is fairly won. Come down with me to the court."

Mindless what to do, the queen arose
and passed a hand across her bloodless face,
then ran in desperation toward the chambers
of the royal ladies of the Kauravas.   70

With speed Duhshasana ran after,
cursing at her in his wrath.
By her hair he seized the fleeing queen,
by her long and wavy, jet-black hair.

That hair that had been bathed in holy water   75
at ending of a royal consecration
the sons of Pandu now could not protect
from insult at a Dhartarastra's hand.

Duhshasana seized and pulled her toward the court
as the wind pulls at the thrashing plantain tree,   80
Pancala's daughter of the jet black hair,
a married queen, like a woman without a man.

With slender body bending at his force
she whispered, "No! I wear a single garment;
I am unclean! You cannot be so vile   85
as to bring me in this state before the court."

To which he answered, seizing with rough hand
the soft black tresses of the trembling queen,
"Call on what gods you wish: not Krishna, Jisnu,
Hari, Nara, shall stop my taking you.   90

"Be you unclean, it makes no difference;
or in a single garment or stark naked.
You have been won at dice and are our slave
and masters do with slave girls as they wish."

Her hair fell disheveled, her garment slipped   95
as she was shaken by Duhshasana.
In deep shame and burning indignation
the beautiful queen spoke with lowered voice.

DRAUPADI
Here present in the court are learned men,
men like Indra,[8] who perform the rites,   100
my elders and lords the equals of my elders;
they must not see me in my present state.

This is an outrage! You are being shameful!
Stop stripping me¡ Stop pulling me about!
These sons of kings will not permit such wrong   105
even if all the gods should give you aid.

The royal son of Law[9] stands in the law,
and law is subtle: only the wise can grasp it.
But even at my lord's command I will not
give up honor and commit a sin.   110

This is a villainy to drag me so
among the Kurus when I am unclean.
But does no one cry out shame upon you?
Surely it cannot be that they approve?

Shame! Shame! The law of Bharatas,   115
the warrior code of honor is destroyed
when all the Kurus gathered here at court
see how the law of Kurus is transgressed.

Drona and Bhisma must have lost their strength
together with the great-souled Vidura.   120
Do not the elders of the Kauravas
perceive the unlawful conduct of their king?

VAISHAMPAYANA
The queen spoke these pitiable words
and cast a glance upon her hero husbands,
raising the anger of the Pandava hearts   125
to blazing fire by her sidelong glance.

Not their lost kingdom, not the wealth,
not all the lost gems of highest price,
gave Pandu's sons such pain as Draupadi
gave by that one anguished sidelong glance.   130

---

8. King of the gods.   9. Yudhishthira, who is viewed as the
                                                 embodiment of Dharma.

Duhshasana, observing how the queen
had looked upon her helpless hero lords,
shook her roughly until she almost swooned,
with cruel laughter calling her his slave.

Karna was passing glad to her that word;   135
he gave honor to the prince and laughed aloud.
The King of Gandhara, son of Subala,
also gave Duhshasana applause.

But others who were present at the court,
except those two and King Duryodhana,   140
felt bitter anguish as they saw the queen,
dark Draupadi, so pulled about the court.

BHISMA
My good lady, the law is a subtle thing;
I cannot answer rightly what you ask.
A gambler cannot bet what is not his: 145
true; but a wife lies in her husband's power.

Again, I know that King Yudhishthira
would forsake the world before forsaking truth,
and Yudhishthira admits that he has lost;
I cannot answer rightly what you ask.   150

There is no equal to Shakuni in dicing,
but he gave to King Yudhishthira his choice;
the king does not accuse him of deceit;
I cannot answer rightly what you ask.

DRAUPADI
No. The king was challenged by these gamblers,   155
villainous, wicked men who use deceit;
of his own free will he never sought to gamble.
How can you tell me that he had his choice?

An honest man, the noblest of you all,
he never recognized the treachery.   160
As he was beaten out of all his wealth
and only then agreed upon the wager—

answer me, Kurus who attend this court,
you nobles who have daughters of your own
and daughters-in-law to spur your rightful judgment,   165
answer me the question I have put!

VAISHAMPAYANA
She spoke these pitiable words and wept,
casting her eyes once more upon her husbands,

the while Duhshasana kept up his cry
of bitter words and cruel epithets.   170

Then Bhima, seeing the defenseless queen
in such condition in a single garment
so treated, looked at King Yudhishthira
and in ungovernable fury spoke.

2.61

BHIMA
A gambler often keeps a wench but never bets her;
even to such a creature he shows some decency.

What stirs my wrath is not that the tribute of Benares
and other tribute given at your assumption of the realm,

not that the chariots and gold, the armor and the weapons,   5
the kingdom, and ourselves, and you, have all been lost:

these things stir not my wrath—for were you not sole master?
but this I say was wrongly done to wager Draupadi;

for she who came to us a blameless maid is by your doing
now tortured by these Kurus, these double-dealing brutes.   10

On her account my wrath is stirred and I bring it down on you.
I will brand your arms. Sahadeva, bring me fire!

ARJUNA
Never have you spoken words like this, Bhima.
Our enemies have broken your respect for law.

Give them no such satisfaction. Hold to what is lawful.   15
The rightful and the eldest brother must not be defied.

Challenged by his foe, he minds the code of warriors
and gambles at the other's wish. Hereby he wins us fame.

BHIMA
If I knew him to have acted so like an egoist
I would hold his two arms in the fire until they burned to ash.   20

VAISHAMPAYANA
Then seeing the sons of Pandu pained and Draupadi mistreated,
a younger son of the Kuru king, Vikarna, rose and spoke.

VIKARNA
Answer the question, nobles, that Draupadi has set us.
If we decide unjustly, we shall pay for it in hell.

Bhisma and Dhritarashtra, the oldest of the Kurus,   25
withhold their word of judgment, as does Vidura the wise.

Kripa too, and Drona, the teacher of us all,
our two foremost brahmans, have answered not a word.

So let the other nobles who are here assembled
put by their love and hatred and answer as they think.   30

Consider well the question that Draupadi has set us
and speak up, every nobleman, what side of it you choose.

VAISHAMPAYANA
He spoke. He spoke to them again, to all those there assembled,
but the nobles answered not a word, either of good or ill.

Then after asking many times those noblemen, Vikarna,   35
wringing his hands in anguish and breathing deeply, spoke.

VIKARNA
So be it, noblemen; speak or speak not your judgment;
I think it proper here in either case to give my own.

Four vices, as they say, are often found in princes:
hunting, drinking, dice, and the vice of fornication.   40

A man attached to one of these lets go his hold on virtue,
and what he does unbridled the world does not approve.

It is true we find here Pandu's son too much attached to dicing,
for on a gambler's challenge he wagered Draupadi.

But not only does the queen belong to all the Pandavas;   45
she was wagered by one Pandava when he had lost himself.

Furthermore, Shakuni sought the wager, naming the queen outright.
Considering these facts, I find she is not won.

VAISHAMPAYANA
When the lords had heard him out, a mighty roar resounded
of nobles favoring Vikarna and blaming Shakuni.   50

At length the sound subsided and Karna, filled with anger,
stretched forth his jeweled arm in challenge and replied.

KARNA
I see in this Vikarna a fatal twist of temper,
a rod to kindle fire that burns the rod itself.

The others have said nothing though urged to give their judgment;   55
I infer their judgment to be that Draupadi is won.

But you, young son of Dhritarashtra, will perish by your nonsense,
a child who rises as an elder to give judgment in the hall.

You do not know the law, young brother of Duryodhana,
if you would call the queen unwon when she is surely won.   60

How think you Draupadi can be unwon, Vikarna,
when the eldest of the Pandavas pledged everything he owned

and Draupadi, as lying within that everything, most surely
and lawfully is won. The conclusion is not to be denied.

Yes, Draupadi was named; but the Pandava consented.   65
What reason can you give by which she becomes unwon?

Perhaps you think it wrong that in a single garment
she was brought to the hall. On that too hear my word.

To one wife, O Kuru prince, the gods allot one husband;
this woman with her many husbands stands ajudged a whore.   70

Bringing her to the hall was nothing strange I think
whether in single garment or in her naked skin.

Whatever property existed in Pandava possession,
their woman and they themselves, all has been rightly won.

This boy Vikarna is a fool who tries to speak with wisdom.   75
Duhshasana! Strip off the clothes of the servants we have won!

VAISHAMPAYANA
The sons of Pandu heard his words. Without delay the brothers
took off their upper robes and sat bare-breasted in the court.

Then Prince Duhshasana in the midst of that assembly
began to strip the single garment by force from Draupadi.   80

But ever as he drew away her robe, another garment
identical in form assumed its very place.

At this there rose a murmur, swelling to an uproar,
from all the courtiers as they saw this wonder of the age;

above which Bhima's voice was heard from lips that shook with anger.   85
Pressing one hand on the other, he shouted out this oath.

BHIMA
Hear my words, O nobles who have come from all countries,
words that no man has spoken and none will speak again;

words that having said, if I should fail to do them,
may I never join my ancestors in the world of joy to come: 90

I will take one day in battle this wicked, lowborn outcaste
and I swear that day I will rip out his breast and drink his living blood.

VAISHAMPAYANA

The nobles heard his oath and shivered as they heard it;
they gave him their applause and blamed Duhshasana.

Only when the garments grew to a heap upon the carpet   95
did the prince, ashamed and weary, give over his attempt.

But a chilling cry of shame arose from every witness,
whether men or gods. Then, seeing there the Pandavas

and that the Kauravas answered not the question,
the common folk cried out, reviling the old king.   100

The Song of the Blessed One [Bhagavad Gita]

THE FIRST TEACHING: ARJUNA'S DEJECTION

DHRITARASHTRA

Sanjaya, tell me what my sons
and the sons of Pandu did when they met,
wanting to battle on the field of Kuru,
on the field of sacred duty?

SANJAYA[1]

Your son Duryodhana, the king,   5
seeing the Pandava forces arrayed,
approached his teacher Drona
and spoke in command.

"My teacher, see
the great Pandava army arrayed   10
by Drupada's son,
your pupil, intent on revenge.

Here are heroes, mighty archers
equal to Bhima[2] and Arjuna[3] in warfare,
Yuyudhana, Virata, and Drupada,   15
your sworn foe on his great chariot.

Here too are Dhrishtaketu, Cekitana,
and the brave king of Benares;

Translated by Barbara Stoler Miller.

---

1. The charioteer and messenger of King Dhritarashtra.

2. The second son of Pandu.
3. The third son of Pandu.

Purujit, Kuntibhoja,
and the manly king of the Shibis.

Yudhamanyu is bold,
and Uttamaujas is brave;
the sons of Subhadra and Draupadi
all command great chariots.

Now, honored priest, mark
the superb men on our side
as I tell you the names
of my army's leaders.

They are you and Bhishma,[4]
Karna and Kripa, a victor in battles,
your own son Ashvatthama,
Vikarna, and the son of Somadatta.

Many other heroes also risk
their lives for my sake,
bearing varied weapons
and skilled in the ways of war.

Guarded by Bhishma, the strength
of our army is without limit;
but the strength of their army,
guarded by Bhima, is limited.

In all the movements of battle,
you and your men,
stationed according to plan,
must guard Bhishma well!"

Bhishma, fiery elder of the Kurus,
roared his lion's roar
and blew his conch horn,
exciting Duryodhana's delight.

Conches and kettledrums,
cymbals, tabors, and trumpets
were sounded at once
and the din of tumult arose.

Standing on their great chariot
yoked with white stallions,
Krishna and Arjuna, Pandu's son,
sounded their divine conches.

4. The grand-uncle of the Pandavas.

Krishna blew Pancajanya,[5] won from a demon;
Arjuna blew Devadatta,[6] a gift of the gods;
fierce wolf-bellied Bhima blew Paundra,[7]
his great conch of the east.   60

Yudhishthira, Kunti's son, the king,
blew Anantavijaya,[8] conch of boundless victory;
his twin brothers Nakula and Sahadeva
blew conches resonant and jewel toned.

The king of Benares, a superb archer,   65
and Shikhandin on his great chariot,
Drishtadyumna, Virata, and indomitable Satyaki,
all blew their conches.

Drupada, with his five grandsons,
and Subhadra's strong-armed son,
each in his turn blew   70
their conches, O King.

The noise tore the hearts
of Dhritarashtra's sons,
and tumult echoed   75
through heaven and earth.

Arjuna, his war flag a rampant monkey,
saw Dhritarashtra's sons assembled
as weapons were ready to clash,
and he lifted his bow.   80

He told his charioteer:
   "Krishna,
   halt my chariot
   between the armies!
   Far enough for me to see   85
   these men who lust for war,
   ready to fight with me
   in the strain of battle.

   I see men gathered here,
   eager to fight,   90
   bent on serving the folly
   of Dhritarashtra's son."

When Arjuna had spoken,
Krishna halted
their splendid chariot   95
between the armies.

---

5. The name of Krishna's conch shell.   7. The name of Bhisma's conch shell.
6. The name of Arjuna's conch shell.   8. The name of Yudhishthira's conch shell.

Facing Bhishma and Drona
and all the great kings,
he said, "Arjuna, see
the Kuru men assembled here!"

Arjuna saw them standing there:
fathers, grandfathers, teachers,
uncles, brothers, sons,
grandsons, and friends.

He surveyed his elders
and companions in both armies,   105
all his kinsmen
assembled together.

Dejected, filled with strange pity,
he said this: 110
    "Krishna, I see my kinsmen
gathered here, wanting war.

My limbs sink,
my mouth is parched,
my body trembles,   115
the hair bristles on my flesh.

The magic bow slips
from my hand, my skin burns,
I cannot stand still,
my mind reels.   120

I see omens of chaos,
Krishna; I see no good
in killing my kinsmen
in battle.

Krishna, I seek no victory,   125
or kingship or pleasures.
What use to us are kingship,
delights, or life itself?

We sought kingship, delights,
and pleasures for the sake of those   130
assembled to abandon their lives
and fortunes in battle.

They are teachers, fathers, sons,
and grandfathers, uncles, grandsons,
fathers and brothers of wives,   135
and other men of our family.

I do not want to kill them
even if I am killed, Krishna;

not for kingship of all three worlds,
much less for the earth!   140

What joy is there for us, Krishna,
in killing Dhritarashtra's sons?
Evil will haunt us if we kill them,
though their bows are drawn to kill.

Honor forbids us to kill
our cousins, Dhritarashtra's sons;   145
how can we know happiness
if we kill our own kinsmen?

The greed that distorts their reason
blinds them to the sin they commit   150
in ruining the family, blinds them
to the crime of betraying friends.

How can we ignore the wisdom
of turning from this evil
when we see the sin   155
of family destruction, Krishna?

When the family is ruined,
the timeless laws of family duty
perish; and when duty is lost,
chaos overwhelms the family.   160

In overwhelming chaos, Krishna,
women of the family are corrupted;
and when women are corrupted,
disorder is born in society.

This discord drags the violators   165
and the family itself to hell;
for ancestors fall when rites
of offering rice and water lapse.

The sins of men who violate
the family create disorder in society   170
that undermines the constant laws
of caste and family duty.

Krishna, we have heard
that a place in hell
is reserved for men   175
who undermine family duties.

I lament the great sin
we commit when our greed

for kingship and pleasures
drives us to kill our kinsmen.

If Dhritarashtra's armed sons
kill me in battle when I am unarmed
and offer no resistance,
it will be my reward." 180

Saying this in the time of war,
Arjuna slumped into the chariot
and laid down his bow and arrows,
his mind tormented by grief. 185

THE SECOND TEACHING:
PHILOSOPHY AND SPIRITUAL DISCIPLINE

SANJAYA
Arjuna sat dejected,
filled with pity,
his sad eyes blurred by tears.
Krishna gave him counsel.

LORD KRISHNA
Why this cowardice
in time of crisis, Arjuna? 5
The coward is ignoble, shameful,
foreign to the ways of heaven.

Don't yield to impotence!
It is unnatural in you!
Banish this petty weakness from your heart. 10
Rise to the fight, Arjuna!

ARJUNA
Krishna, how can I fight
against Bhishma and Drona[9]
with arrows 15
when they deserve my worship?

It is better in this world
to beg for scraps of food
than to eat meals
smeared with the blood 20
of elders I killed

---

9. The former is the grand-uncle of the Pandavas; the latter is their teacher. Both are
allied, albeit reluctantly, with Duryodhana.

at the height of their power
while their goals
were still desires.

We don't know which weight
is worse to bear—
our conquering them   25
or their conquering us.
We will not want to live
if we kill   30
the sons of Dhritarashtra
assembled before us.

The flaw of pity
blights my very being;
conflicting sacred duties   35
confound my reason.
I ask you to tell me
decisively—Which is better?
I am your pupil.
Teach me what I seek!   40

I see nothing
that could drive away
the grief
that withers my senses;
even if I won kingdoms   45
of unrivaled wealth
on earth
and sovereignty over gods.

SANJAYA
Arjuna told this
to Krishna—then saying,   50
"I shall not fight,"
he fell silent.
Mocking him gently,
Krishna gave this counsel
as Arjuna sat dejected,   55
between the two armies.

LORD KRISHNA
You grieve for those beyond grief,
and you speak words of insight;
but learned men do not grieve
for the dead or the living.   60

Never have I not existed,
nor you, nor these kings;
and never in the future
shall we cease to exist.

Just as the embodied self
enters childhood, youth, and old age,
so does it enter another body;
this does not confound a steadfast man.

Contacts with matter make us feel
heat and cold, pleasure and pain.
Arjuna, you must learn to endure
fleeting things—they come and go!

When these cannot torment a man,
when suffering and joy are equal
for him and he has courage,
he is fit for immortality.

Nothing of nonbeing comes to be,
nor does being cease to exist;
the boundary between these two
is seen by men who see reality.

Indestructible is the presence
that pervades all this;
no one can destroy
this unchanging reality.

Our bodies are known to end,
but the embodied self is enduring,
indestructible, and immeasurable;
therefore, Arjuna, fight the battle!

He who thinks this self a killer
and he who thinks it killed,
both fail to understand;
it does not kill, nor is it killed.

It is not born,
it does not die;
having been,
it will never not be;
unborn, enduring,
constant, and primordial,
it is not killed
when the body is killed.

Arjuna, when a man knows the self
to be indestructible, enduring, unborn,
unchanging, how does he kill
or cause anyone to kill?

As a man discards
worn-out clothes
to put on new
and different ones,   105
so the embodied self
discards
its worn-out bodies
to take on other new ones.

Weapons do not cut it,
fire does not burn it,
waters do not wet it,   115
wind does not wither it.

It cannot be cut or burned;
it cannot be wet or withered;
it is enduring, all-pervasive,
fixed, immovable, and timeless.   120

It is called unmanifest,
inconceivable, and immutable;
since you know that to be so,
you should not grieve!

If you think of its birth   125
and death as ever-recurring,
then too, Great Warrior,
you have no cause to grieve!

Death is certain for anyone born,
and birth is certain for the dead;   130
since the cycle is inevitable,
you have no cause to grieve!

Creatures are unmanifest in origin,
manifest in the midst of life,
and unmanifest again in the end.   135
Since this is so, why do you lament?

Rarely someone
sees it,
rarely another
speaks it,   140
rarely anyone

hears it—
even hearing it,
no one really knows it.

The self embodied in the body
of every being is indestructible;   145
you have no cause to grieve
for all these creatures, Arjuna!

Look to your own duty;
do not tremble before it;   150
nothing is better for a warrior
than a battle of sacred duty.

The doors of heaven open
for warriors who rejoice
to have a battle like this   155
thrust on them by chance.

If you fail to wage this war
of sacred duty,
you will abandon your own duty
and fame only to gain evil.   160

People will tell
of your undying shame,
and for a man of honor
shame is worse than death.

The great chariot warriors will think   165
you deserted in fear of battle;
you will be despised
by those who held you in esteem.

Your enemies will slander you,
scorning your skill   170
in so many unspeakable ways—
could any suffering be worse?

If you are killed, you win heaven;
if you triumph, you enjoy the earth;
therefore, Arjuna, stand up   175
and resolve to fight the battle!

Impartial to joy and suffering,
gain and loss, victory and defeat,
arm yourself for the battle,
lest you fall into evil.   180

VALMIKI (SECOND CENTURY B.C.E.)
North India

The *Ramayana* ("adventures of Rama") is not only considerably shorter than the *Mahabharata* (about a quarter of its length), it is also more recent. It began its life as an oral epic well after the *Mahabharata*, although it reached its present form somewhat earlier—perhaps a little before the first century of the common era. The traditional attribution of the poem is to Valmiki. As with Vyasa, the creator of the older epic, we know little about Valmiki other than what the poem itself tells us.

    The *Ramayana* looks back to the *Mahabharata* as it attempts to offer different solutions to the problems raised there. Again, the action centers initially around a dispute over the succession to the throne of a major state—this time Ayodhya, capital of the eastern province of Kosala (in the present-day state of Bihar). The aged king, Dasharatha, wishes to appoint his eldest son, Rama, as his successor. However, one of the king's younger wives, Kaikeyi, demands the appointment of her own son, Bharata. The king once made certain promises to Kaikeyi, and the first selection, from Book 2, focuses on the critical moment when he is forced to keep them by denying the kingship to Rama and instead sending him into exile. Again, the moral fulcrum of the narrative lies in the problem of *dharma,* "what is right." Rama believes that any promise his father made must be kept, no matter what the cost. He adheres to a higher, almost spiritualized vision of kingship by accepting exile rather than launching a struggle for the throne.

    The main action of the epic begins in Book 3, our second selection, which takes place during Rama's banishment in the wilderness. The demon king Ravana abducts the hero's wife, in part as revenge for Rama's attack on Shurpanakha, Ravana's sister. As in the *Mahabharata,* the narrative focuses on violence perpetrated against a woman, and again war ensues. This time the antagonists are not brothers, however, but a demon race dwelling far from the world of Ayodhya.

from THE RAMAYANA

Book 2

SARGA 7 [Now, Kaikeyi's family servant]

1. Now, Kaikeyi's family servant, who had lived with her from the time of her birth, had happened to ascend to the rooftop terrace that shone like the moon.

2–3. From the terrace Manthara could see all Ayodhya—the king's way—newly sprinkled, the lotuses and waterlilies strewn about, the costly ornamental

Translated by Sheldon I. Pollock.

pennants and banners, the sprinkling of sandalwood water, and the crowds of freshly bathed people.

4–5. Seeing a nursemaid standing nearby, Manthara asked, "Why is Rama's mother so delighted and giving away money to people, when she has always been so miserly? Tell me, why are the people displaying such boundless delight? Has something happened to delight the lord of earth? What is he planning to do?"

6. Bursting with delight and out of sheer gladness the nursemaid told the hunchback Manthara about the greater majesty in store for Raghava:

7. "Tomorrow on Pusya day[1] King Dasharatha is going to consecrate Rama Raghava as prince regent, the blameless prince who has mastered his anger."

8. When she heard what the nursemaid said, the hunchback was furious and descended straightway from the terrace that was like the peak of Mount Kailasa.[2]

9. Consumed with rage, the malevolent Manthara approached Kaikeyi as she lay upon her couch, and she said:

10. "Get up, you foolish woman! How can you lie there when danger is threatening you? Don't you realize that a flood of misery is about to overwhelm you?

11. "Your beautiful face has lost its charm. You boast of the power of your beauty, but it has proved to be as fleeting as a river's current in the hot season."

12. So she spoke, and Kaikeyi was deeply distraught at the bitter words of the angry, malevolent hunchback.

13. "Manthara," she replied, "is something wrong? I can tell by the distress in your face how sorely troubled you are."

14. Hearing Kaikeyi's gentle words the wrathful Manthara spoke—and a very clever speaker she was.

15. The hunchback grew even more distraught, and with Kaikeyi's best interests at heart, spoke out, trying to sharpen her distress and turn her against Raghava:

16. "Something is very seriously wrong, my lady, something that threatens to ruin you. For King Dasharatha is going to consecrate Rama as prince regent.

17. "I felt myself sinking down into unfathomable danger, stricken with grief and sorrow, burning as if on fire. And so I have come here, with your best interests at heart.

---

1. An auspicious day in the lunar calendar.   2. Holy mountain in the far north of India; dwelling place of the god Shiva

18. "When you are sorrowful, Kaikeyi, I am too, and even more, and, when you prosper, so do I. There is not the slightest doubt of this.

19. "You were born into a family of kings, you are a queen of the lord of earth. My lady, how can you fail to know that the ways of kings are ruthless?

20. "Your husband talks of righteousness, but he is deceiving you; his words are gentle but he is cruel. You are too innocent to understand, and so he has utterly defrauded you like this.

21. "When expedient, your husband reassures you, but it is all worthless. Now that there is something of real worth he is ready to bestow it upon Kausalya.

22. "Having got Bharata out of the way by sending him off to your family, the wicked man shall tomorrow establish Rama in unchallenged kingship.

23. "He is an enemy pretending to be your husband. He is like a viper, child, whom you have taken to your bosom and lovingly mothered.

24. For what an enemy or a snake would do if one ignored them, King Dasharatha is now doing to you and your son.

25. "The man is evil, his assurances false, and, by establishing Rama in the kingship, dear child who has always known comfort, he will bring ruin upon you and your family.

26. "Kaikeyi, the time has come to act, and you must act swiftly, for your own good. You must save your son, yourself, and me, my enchanting beauty."

27. After listening to Manthara's speech, the lovely woman rose from the couch and presented the hunchback with a lovely piece of jewelry.

28. And, when she had given the hunchback the jewelry, Kaikeyi, most beautiful of women, said in delight to Manthara,

29. "What you have reported to me is the most wonderful news. How else may I reward you, Manthara, for reporting such good news to me?

30. "I draw no distinction between Rama and Bharata, and so I am perfectly content that the king should consecrate Rama as king.

31. "You could not possibly tell me better news than this, or speak more welcome words, my well-deserving woman. For what you have told me I will give you yet another boon, something you might like more—just choose it!"

The end of the seventh *sarga* of the *Ayodhyakanda* of the *Sri Ramayana*.

SARGA 8 [But Manthara was beside herself with rage and sorrow]

1. But Manthara was beside herself with rage and sorrow. She threw the jewelry away and said spitefully:

2. "You foolish woman, how can you be delighted at such a moment? Are you not aware that you stand in the midst of a sea of grief?

3. "It is Kausalya who is fortunate; it is her son the eminent brahmans will consecrate as the powerful prince regent tomorrow, on Pusya day.

4. "Once Kausalya secures this great object of joy, she will cheerfully eliminate her enemies. And you will have to wait on her with hands cupped in reverence, like a serving woman.

5. "Delight is truly in store for Rama's exalted women, and all that is in store for your daughters-in-law is misery, at Bharata's downfall."

6. Seeing how deeply distressed Manthara was as she spoke, Queen Kaikeyi began to extol Rama's virtues:

7. "Rama knows what is right, his gurus have taught him self-restraint. He is grateful, truthful, and honest, and as the king's eldest son, he deserves to be prince regent.

8. "He will protect his brothers and his dependents like a father; and long may he live! How can you be upset, hunchback, at learning of Rama's consecration?

9. "Surely Bharata as well, the bull among men, will obtain the kingship of his fathers and forefathers after Rama's one hundred years.

10. "Why should you be upset, Manthara, when we have prospered in the past, and prosper now, and shall have good fortune in the future? For he obeys me even more scrupulously than he does Kausalya."

11. When she heard what Kaikeyi said, Manthara was still more sorely troubled. She heaved a long and hot sigh and then replied:

12. "You are too simple-minded to see what is good for you and what is not. You are not aware that you are sinking in an ocean of sorrow fraught with disaster and grief.

13. "Raghava will be king, Kaikeyi, and then the son of Raghava, while Bharata will be debarred from the royal succession altogether.

14. "For not all the sons of a king stand in line for the kingship, my lovely. Were all of them to be so placed, grave misfortune would ensue.

15. "That is why kings place the powers of kingship in the hands of the eldest, faultless Kaikeyi, however worthy the others.

16. "Like a helpless boy that son of yours, the object of all your motherly love, will be totally excluded from the royal succession and from its pleasures as well.

17. "Here I am, come on your behalf, but you pay me no heed. Instead, you want to reward me in token of your rival's good luck!

18. "Surely once Rama secures unchallenged kingship he will have Bharata sent off to some other country—if not to the other world!

19. And you had to send Bharata, a mere boy, off to your brother's, though knowing full well that proximity breeds affection, even in insentient things.

20. "Now, Raghava will protect Lakshmana, just as Saumitri will protect Rama, for their brotherly love is as celebrated as that of the Asvins.[3]

21. "And so Rama will do no harm to Lakshmana, but he will to Bharata without question.

22. "So let your son go straight from Rajagriha[4] to the forest. That is the course I favor, and it is very much in your own best interests.

23. "For in this way good fortune may still befall your side of the family—if, that is, Bharata secures, as by rights he should, the kingship of his forefathers.

24. "Your child has known only comfort, and, at the same time, he is Rama's natural enemy. How could the one, with his fortunes lost, live under the sway of the other, whose fortunes are thriving?

25. "Like the leader of an elephant herd attacked by a lion in the forest, your son is about to be set upon by Rama, and you must save him.

26. "Then, too, because of your beauty's power you used to spurn your co-wife, Rama's mother, so proudly. How could she fail to repay that enmity?

27. "When Rama secures control of the land, Bharata will be lost for certain. You must therefore devise some way of making your son the king and banishing his enemy this very day."

The end of the eighth *sarga* of the *Ayodhyakanda* of the *Sri Ramayana*.

SARGA 9 [So Manthara spoke]

1. So Manthara spoke, and Kaikeyi, her face glowing with rage, heaved a long and burning sigh and said to her:

2. "Today, at once, I will have Rama banished to the forest, and at once have Bharata consecrated as prince regent.

3. "But now, Manthara, think: In what way can Bharata, and not Rama, secure the kingship?"

4. So Queen Kaikeyi spoke, and the malevolent Manthara answered her, to the ruin of Rama's fortunes:

5. "Well then, I shall tell you, Kaikeyi—and pay close attention—how your son Bharata may secure sovereign kingship."

---

3. Twin deities, typically represented as beings of great beauty.

4. Bharata is currently visiting his mother's family in the northwest city of Rajagriha.

6. Hearing Manthara's words, Kaikeyi half rose from her sumptuous couch and exclaimed:

7. "Tell me the way, Manthara! How can Bharata, and not Rama, secure the kingship?"

8. So the queen spoke, and the malevolent hunchback answered her, to the ruin of Rama's fortunes:

9–11. "When the gods and *asuras*[5] were at war, your husband went with the royal seers to lend assistance to the king of the gods, and he took you along. He set off toward the south, Kaikeyi, to the Dandakas and the city called Vaijayanta. It was there that Timidhvaja ruled, the same who is called Shambara, a great *asura* of a hundred magic powers. He had given battle to Shakra, and the host of gods could not conquer him.

12–13. "In the great battle that followed, King Dasharatha was struck unconscious, and you, my lady, conveyed him out of battle. But there, too, your husband was wounded by weapons, and once again you saved him, my lovely. And so in his gratitude he granted you two boons.

14. "Then, my lady, you said to your husband, 'I shall choose my two boons when I want them,' and the great king consented. I myself was unaware of this, my lady, until you yourself told me, long ago.

15. "You must now demand these two boons of your husband: the consecration of Bharata and the banishment of Rama for fourteen years.

16. "Now go into your private chamber, daughter of Asvapati, as if in a fit of rage. Put on a dirty garment, lie down on the bare ground, and don't speak to him, don't even look at him.

17. "Your husband has always adored you, I haven't any doubt of it. For your sake the great king would even go through fire.

18. "The king could not bring himself to anger you, nor even bear to look at you when you are angry. He would give up his own life to please you.

19. "The lord of the land is powerless to refuse your demand. Dull-witted girl, recognize the power of your beauty.

20. "King Dasharatha will offer gems, pearls, gold, a whole array of precious gifts—but pay no mind to them.

21. "Just keep reminding Dasharatha of those two boons he granted at the battle of the gods and *asuras*. Illustrious lady, you must not let this opportunity pass you by.

22–23. "When the great king Raghava helps you up himself and offers you a boon, then you must ask him for this one, first making sure he swears to it: 'Banish

---

5. Antigods.

Rama to the forest for nine years and five, and make Bharata king of the land, the bull among kings.'

24. "In this way Rama will be banished and cease to be 'the pleasing prince,' and your Bharata, his rival eliminated, will be king.

25. "And by the time Rama returns from the forest, your steadfast son and his supporters will have struck deep roots and won over the populace.

26. "I think it high time you overcame your timidity. You must forcibly prevent the king from carrying out Rama's consecration."

27. And so Manthara induced her to accept such evil by disguising it as good, and Kaikeyi, now cheered and delighted, replied:

28. "Hunchback, I never recognized your excellence, nor how excellent your advice. Of all the hunchbacks in the land there is none better at devising plans.

29. "You are the only one who has always sought my advantage and had my interests at heart. I might never have known, hunchback, what the king intended to do.

30. "There are hunchbacks who are misshapen, crooked and hideously ugly—but not you, you are lovely, you are bent no more than a lotus in the breeze.

31. "Your chest is arched, raised as high as your shoulders, and down below your waist, with its lovely navel, seems as if it had grown thin in envy of it.

32. "Your girdle-belt beautifies your hips and sets them jingling. Your legs are set strong under you, while your feet are long.

33. "With your wide buttocks, Manthara, and your garment of white linen, you are as resplendent as a wild goose when you go before me.

34. "And this huge hump of yours, wide as the hub of a chariot wheel—your clever ideas must be stored in it, your political wisdom and magic powers.

35. "And there, hunchback, is where I will drape you with a garland made of gold, once Bharata is consecrated and Raghava has gone to the forest.

36. "When I have accomplished my purpose, my lovely, when I am satisfied, I will anoint your hump with precious liquid gold.

37. "And for your face I will have them fashion an elaborate and beautiful forehead mark of gold and exquisite jewelry for you, hunchback.

38. "Dressed in a pair of lovely garments you shall go about like a goddess; with that face of yours that challenges the moon, peerless in visage; and you shall strut holding your head high before the people who hate me.

39. "You too shall have hunchbacks, adorned with every sort of ornament, to humbly serve you, hunchback, just as you always serve me."

40. Being flattered in this fashion, she replied to Kaikeyi, who still lay on her luxurious couch like a flame of fire on an altar:

41. "One does not build a dike, my precious, after the water is gone. Get up, apprise the king, and see to your own welfare!"

42. Thus incited, the large-eyed queen went with Manthara to her private chamber, puffed up with the intoxicating power of her beauty.

43. There the lovely lady removed her pearl necklace, worth many hundred thousands, and her other costly and beautiful jewelry.

44. And then, under the spell of the hunchback Manthara's words, the golden Kaikeyi got down upon the floor and said to her:

45. "Hunchback, go inform the king that I will surely die right here unless Bharata receives as his portion the land and Raghava, as his, the forest."

46. And uttering these ruthless words, the lady put all her jewelry aside and lay down upon the ground bare of any spread, like a fallen *kimnara* woman.[6]

47. Her face enveloped in the darkness of her swollen rage, her fine garlands and ornaments stripped off, the wife of the lord of men grew distraught and took on the appearance of a darkened sky, when all the stars have set.

The end of the ninth *sarga* of the *Ayodhyakanda* of the *Sri Ramayana*.

SARGA 10 [*Now, when the great king had given orders*]

1. Now, when the great king had given orders for Raghava's consecration, he gladly entered the inner chamber to tell his beloved wife the good news.

2. But when the lord of the world saw her fallen on the ground and lying there in a posture so ill-befitting her, he was consumed with sorrow.

3. The guileless old man saw her on the floor, that guileful young wife of his, who meant more to him than life itself.

4. He began to caress her affectionately, as a great bull elephant in the wilderness might caress his cow wounded by the poisoned arrow of a hunter lurking in the forest.

5. And, as he caressed his lotus-eyed wife with his hands, sick with worry and desire, he said to her:

6–7. "I do not understand, my lady, why you should be angry. Has someone offended you, or shown you disrespect, that you should lie here in the dust, my precious, and cause me such sorrow? What reason have you to lie upon

---

6. A semidivine creature of great beauty.

the floor as if possessed by a spirit, driving me to distraction, when you are so precious to me?

8. "I have skilled physicians, who have been gratified in every way. They will make you well again. Tell me what hurts you, my lovely.

9. "Is there someone to whom you would have favor shown, or has someone aroused your disfavor? The one shall find favor at once, the other incur my lasting disfavor.

10. "Is there some guilty man who should be freed, or some innocent man I should execute? What poor man should I enrich, what rich man impoverish?

11–12. "I and my people, we all bow to your will. I could not bring myself to thwart any wish of yours, not if it cost me my life. Tell me what your heart desires, for all the earth belongs to me, as far as the wheel of my power reaches."

13. So he spoke, and now encouraged, she resolved to tell her hateful plan. She then commenced to cause her husband still greater pain.

14. "No one has mistreated me, my lord, or shown me disrespect. But there is one wish I have that I should like you to fulfill.

15. "You must first give me your promise that you are willing to do it. Then I shall reveal what it is I desire."

16. So his beloved Kaikeyi spoke, and the mighty king, hopelessly under the woman's power, said to her with some surprise:

17. "Do you not yet know, proud lady, that except for Rama, tiger among men, there is not a single person I love as much as you?

18. "Take hold of my heart, rip it out, and examine it closely, my lovely Kaikeyi; then tell me if you do not find it true.

19. "Seeing that I have the power, you ought not to doubt me. I will do what will make you happy, I swear to you by all my acquired merit."

20. His words filled her with delight, and she made ready to reveal her dreadful wish, which was like a visitation of death:

21. "Let the three and thirty gods, with Indra at their head, hear how you in due order swear an oath and grant me a boon.

22–23. "Let the sun and moon, the sky, the planets, night and day, the quarters of space, heaven and earth, let all the *gandharvas*[7] and *raksasas*,[8] the spirits that stalk the night, the household gods in every house, and all the other spirits take heed of what you have said.

24. "This mighty king, who is true to his word and knows the ways of

---

7. Heavenly musicians.   8. Demons.

righteousness, in full awareness grants me a boon—let the deities give ear to this for me."

25. Thus the queen ensnared the great archer and called upon witnesses. She then addressed the king, who in his mad passion had granted her a boon.

26. "I will now claim the two boons you once granted me, my lord. Hear my words, your Majesty.

27. "Let my son Bharata be consecrated with the very rite of consecration you have prepared for Raghava.

28. "Let Rama withdraw to Dandaka wilderness and for nine years and five live the life of an ascetic, wearing hides and barkcloth garments and matted hair.

29. "Let Bharata today become the uncontested prince regent, and let me see Raghava depart this very day for the forest."

30. When the great king heard Kaikeyi's ruthless demands, he was shaken and unnerved, like a stag at the sight of a tigress.

31. The lord of men gasped as he sank down upon the bare floor. "Oh damn you!" he cried in uncontrollable fury before he fell into a stupor, his heart crushed by grief.

32. Gradually the king regained his senses and then, in bitter sorrow and anger, he spoke to Kaikeyi, with fire in his eyes:

33. "Malicious, wicked woman, bent on destroying this House! Evil woman, what evil did Rama or I ever do to you?

34. "Raghava has always treated you just like his own mother. What reason can you have for trying to wreck his fortunes, of all people?

35. "It was sheer suicide to bring you into my home. I did it unwittingly, thinking you a princess—and not a deadly poisonous viper.

36. "When praise for Rama's virtues is on the lips of every living soul, what crime could I adduce as pretext for renouncing my favorite son?

37. "I would sooner renounce Kausalya, or Sumitra, or sovereignty, or life itself, than Rama, who so cherishes his father.

38. "The greatest joy I know is seeing my first-born son. If I cannot see Rama, I shall lose my mind.

39. "The world might endure without the sun, or crops without water, but without Rama life could not endure within my body.

40. "Enough then, give up this scheme, you evil-scheming woman. I beg you! Must I get down and bow my head to your feet?"

41. His heart in the grip of a woman who knew no bounds, the guardian of the

earth began helplessly to cry, and as the queen extended her feet he tried in vain to touch them, and collapsed like a man on the point of death.

The end of the tenth *sarga* of the *Ayodhyakanda* of the *Sri Ramayana.*

SARGA 11 [The king lay there, in so unaccustomed a posture]

1–2. The king lay there, in so unaccustomed a posture, so ill-befitting his dignity, like Yayati[9] himself, his merit exhausted, fallen from the world of the gods. But the woman was unafraid, for all the fear she awoke. She was misfortune incarnate and had yet to secure her fortunes. Once more she tried to force him to fulfill the boon.

3. "You are vaunted, great king, as a man true to his word and firm in his vows. How then can you be prepared to withhold my boon?"

4. So Kaikeyi spoke, and King Dasharatha, faltering for a moment, angrily replied:

5. "Vile woman, mortal enemy! Will you not be happy, will you not be satisfied until you see me dead, and Rama, the bull among men, gone to the forest?

6. "To satisfy Kaikeyi Rama must be banished to the forest, but if I keep my word in this, then I must be guilty of another lie. My infamy will be unequaled in the eyes of the people and my disgrace inevitable."

7. While he was lamenting like this, his mind in a whirl, the sun set and evening came on.

8. To the anguished king lost in lamentation, the night, adorned with the circlet of the moon, no longer seemed to last a mere three watches.

9. Heaving burning sighs, aged King Dasharatha sorrowfully lamented in his anguish, his eyes fixed upon the sky.

10. "I do not want you to bring the dawn—here, I cup my hands in supplication. But no, pass as quickly as you can, so that I no longer have to see this heartless, malicious Kaikeyi, the cause of this great calamity."

11. But with this, the king cupped his hands before Kaikeyi and once more, begging her mercy, he spoke:

12. "Please, I am an old man, my life is nearly over. I am desolate, I place myself in your hands. Dear lady, have mercy on me for, after all, I am king.

13. "Truly it was thoughtless of me, my fair-hipped lady, to have said those things just now. Have mercy on me, please, my child. I know you have a heart."

14. So the pure-hearted king lamented, frantically and piteously, his eyes

---

9. A legendary king, who went to heaven for his good deeds, but there committed a sin, and so was exiled.

reddened and dimmed by tears, but the malicious, black-hearted woman only listened and made no reply.

15. And as the king stared at the woman he loved but could not appease, whose demand was so perverse—for the exile of his own son—he once again was taken faint, overcome with grief, and dropped unconscious to the floor.

The end of the eleventh *sarga* of the *Ayodhyakanda* of the *Sri Ramayana*.

SARGA 16 [*Rama saw his father, with a wretched look and his mouth all parched*]

1. Rama saw his father, with a wretched look and his mouth all parched, slumped upon his lovely couch, Kaikeyi at his side.

2. First he made an obeisance with all deference at his father's feet and then did homage most scrupulously at the feet of Kaikeyi.

3. "Rama!" cried the wretched king, his eyes brimming with tears, but he was unable to say anything more or to look at him.

4. As if his foot had grazed a snake, Rama was seized with terror to see the expression on the king's face, one more terrifying than he had ever seen before.

5. For the great king lay heaving sighs, racked with grief and remorse, all his senses numb with anguish, his mind stunned and confused.

6. It was as if the imperturbable, wave-wreathed ocean had suddenly been shaken with perturbation, as if the sun had been eclipsed, or a seer had told a lie.

7. His father's grief was incomprehensible to him, and the more he pondered it, the more his agitation grew, like that of the ocean under a full moon.

8. With his father's welfare at heart, Rama struggled to comprehend, "Why does the king not greet me, today of all days?

9. "On other occasions, when Father might be angry, the sight of me would calm him. Why then, when he looked at me just now, did he instead become so troubled?

10. "He seems desolate and grief-stricken, and his face has lost its glow." Doing obeisance to Kaikeyi, Rama spoke these words:

11. "I have not unknowingly committed some offense, have I, to anger my father? Tell me, and make him forgive me.

12. "His face is drained of color, he is desolate and does not speak to me. It cannot be, can it, that some physical illness or mental distress afflicts him? But it is true, well-being is not something one can always keep.

13. "Some misfortune has not befallen the handsome prince Bharata, has it, or courageous Satrughna,[10] or one of my mothers?

14. "I should not wish to live an instant if his Majesty, the great king, my father, were angered by my failure to satisfy him or do his bidding.

15. "How could a man not treat him as a deity incarnate, in whom he must recognize the very source of his existence in this world?

16. "Can it be that in anger you presumed to use harsh words with my father, and so threw his mind into such turmoil?

17. "Answer my questions truthfully, my lady: What has happened to cause this unprecedented change in the lord of men?

18. "At the bidding of the king, if enjoined by him, my guru, father, king, and benefactor, I would hurl myself into fire, drink deadly poison, or drown myself in the sea.

19. "Tell me then, my lady, what the king would have me do. I will do it, I promise. Rama need not say so twice."

20. The ignoble Kaikeyi then addressed these ruthless words to Rama, the upright and truthful prince:

21. "Long ago, Raghava, in the war of the gods and *asuras*, your father bestowed two boons on me, for protecting him when he was wounded in a great battle.

22. "By means of these I have demanded of the king that Bharata be consecrated and that you, Raghava, be sent at once to Dandaka wilderness.

23. "If you wish to ensure that your father be true to his word, and you to your own, best of men, then listen to what I have to say.

24. "Abide by your father's guarantee, exactly as he promised it, and enter the forest for nine years and five.

25. "Forgo the consecration and withdraw to Dandaka wilderness, live there seven years and seven, wearing matted hair and barkcloth garments.

26. "Let Bharata rule this land from the city of the Kosalans, with all the treasures it contains, all its horses, chariots, elephants."

27. When Rama, slayer of enemies, heard Kaikeyi's hateful words, like death itself, he was not the least disconcerted, but only replied,

28. "So be it. I shall go away to live in the forest, wearing matted hair and barkcloth garments, to safeguard the promise of the king.

---

10. The fourth son of Dasharatha and close companion of Bharata.

29. "But I want to know why the lord of earth, the invincible tamer of foes, does not greet me as he used to?

30. "You need not worry, my lady. I say it to your face: I shall go to the forest—rest assured—wearing barkcloth and matted hair.

31. "Enjoined by my father, my benefactor, guru, and king, a man who knows what is right to do, what would I hesitate to do in order to please him?

32. "But there is still one thing troubling my mind and eating away at my heart: that the king does not tell me himself that Bharata is to be consecrated.

33. "For my wealth, the kingship, Sita, and my own dear life I would gladly give up to my brother Bharata on my own, without any urging.

34. "How much more readily if urged by my father himself, the lord of men, in order to fulfill your fond desire and safeguard his promise?

35. "So you must reassure him. Why should the lord of earth keep his eyes fixed upon the ground and fitfully shed these tears?

36. "This very day let messengers depart on swift horses by order of the king to fetch Bharata from his uncle's house.

37. "As for me, I shall leave here in all haste for Dandaka wilderness, without questioning my father's word, to live there fourteen years."

38. Kaikeyi was delighted to hear these words of Rama's, and trusting them implicitly, she pressed Raghava to set out at once.

39. "So be it. Men shall go as messengers on swift horses to bring home Bharata from his uncle's house.

40. "But since you are now so eager, Rama, I do not think it wise to linger. You should therefore proceed directly from here to the forest.

41. "That the king is ashamed and does not address you himself, that is nothing, best of men, you needn't worry about that.

42. "But so long as you have not hastened from the city and gone to the forest, Rama, your father shall neither bathe nor eat."

43. "Oh curse you!" the king gasped, overwhelmed with grief, and upon the gilt couch he fell back in a faint.

44. Rama raised up the king, pressed though he was by Kaikeyi—like a horse whipped with a crop—to make haste and depart for the forest.

45. Listening to the ignoble Kaikeyi's hateful words, so dreadful in their consequences, Rama remained unperturbed and only said to her,

46. "My lady, it is not in the hopes of gain that I suffer living in this world. You should know that, like the seers, I have but one concern and that is righteousness.

47. "Whatever I can do to please this honored man I will do at any cost, even if it means giving up my life.

48. "For there is no greater act of righteousness than this: obedience to one's father and doing as he bids.

49. "Even unbidden by this honored man, at your bidding alone I shall live for fourteen years in the desolate forest.

50. "Indeed, Kaikeyi, you must ascribe no virtue to me at all if you had to appeal to the king, when you yourself are so venerable in my eyes.

51. "Let me only take leave of my mother, and settle matters with Sita. Then I shall go, this very day, to the vast forest of the Dandakas.

52. "You must see to it that Bharata obeys Father and guards the kingdom, for that is the eternal way of righteousness."

53. When his father heard Rama's words, he was stricken with such deep sorrow that he could not hold back his sobs in his grief and broke out in loud weeping.

54. Splendid Rama did homage at the feet of his unconscious father and at the feet of that ignoble woman, Kaikeyi, then he turned to leave.

55. Reverently, Rama circled his father and Kaikeyi, and withdrawing from the inner chamber, he saw his group of friends.

56. Laksmana, the delight of Sumitra, fell in behind him, his eyes brimming with tears, in a towering rage.

57. Reverently circling the equipment for the consecration, but careful not to gaze at it, Rama slowly went away.

58. The loss of the kingship diminished his great majesty as little as night diminishes the loveliness of the cool-rayed moon, beloved of the world.

59. Though he was on the point of leaving his native land and going to the forest, he was no more discomposed than one who has passed beyond all things of this world.

60. Holding back his sorrow within his mind, keeping his every sense in check, and fully self-possessed he made his way to his mother's residence to tell her the sad news.

61. As Rama entered her residence, where joy still reigned supreme, as he reflected on the sudden wreck of all his fortunes, even then he showed no sign of discomposure, for fear it might endanger the lives of those he loved.

The end of the sixteenth *sarga* of the *Ayodhyakanda* of the *Sri Ramayana*.

Book 3

SARGA 16 [After their bath, Rama, Sita, and Laksmana left the bank of the Godavari for their ashram]

1. After their bath Rama, Sita, and Laksmana left the bank of the Godavari for their ashram.[11]

2. Returning to the ashram, Raghava and Laksmana performed the morning rites and then returned to the leaf hut.

3. Great-armed Rama sat with Sita before the leaf hut, shining like the moon beside the sparkling star Citra, and began to converse with his brother Laksmana about one thing and another.

4. As Rama was sitting there engrossed in conversation, a certain *rakshasa*[12] woman chanced to come that way.

5. She was the sister of Ravana, the ten-necked *rakshasa*, and her name was Shurpanakha. Coming upon Rama, she stared at him as if he were one of the thirty gods.

6–7. Rama had long arms, the chest of a lion, eyes like lotus petals. Though delicate, he was very strong and bore all the signs of royalty. He was swarthy as the blue lotus, radiant as the love-god Kandarpa, the very image of Indra—and when the *rakshasa* woman saw him, she grew wild with desire.

8–10. Rama was handsome, the *rakshasa* woman was ugly, he was shapely and slim of waist, she misshapen and potbellied; his eyes were large, hers were beady, his hair was jet black, and hers the color of copper; he always said just the right thing and in a sweet voice, her words were sinister and her voice struck terror; he was young, attractive, and well mannered, she ill mannered, repellent, an old hag. And yet, the god of love, who comes to life in our bodies, had taken possession of her, and so she addressed Rama:

11. "Your hair is matted in the manner of ascetics, yet you have a wife with you and bear bow and arrows. How is it you have come into this region, the haunt of *rakshasas*?"

12. Questioned in this fashion by the *rakshasa* woman Shurpanakha, the slayer of enemies in his open manner proceeded to tell her everything.

13. "There was a king named Dasharatha, courageous as one of the thirty gods. I am his eldest son, named Rama, known to people far and wide.

14. "This is Laksmana, my devoted younger brother, and this my wife, the princess of Videha, known as Sita.

---

11. Dwelling place of ascetics.   12. A sort of antihuman; demon.

15. "I was compelled to come to live in the forest by command of my mother and my father, the lord of men, and I wanted to do what is right, for doing right has always been my chief concern.

16. "But I should like to know about you. Tell me, who are you? To whom do you belong? For what purpose have you come here? Tell me truthfully."

17. Hearing his words and consumed with passion, the *rakshasa* woman replied, "Listen, then, Rama, I shall tell you, and my words will be truthful.

18. "My name is Shurpanakha. I am a *rakshasa* woman, who can take on any form at will, and I roam this wilderness all alone, striking terror into every living thing.

19. "The *rakshasa* named Ravana, the lord of all *rakshasas,* is my brother, so too the powerful Kumbhakarna, who lies ever fast asleep.

20. "So is Vibhisana, but he is righteous and does not behave like a *rakshasa*. My other brothers are Khara and Dusana, famed for their might in battle.

21. "But I am prepared to defy them all, Rama, for I have never seen anyone like you. I approach you as I would a husband, with true love, best of men. Be my husband forevermore; what do you want with Sita?

22. "She is ugly and misshapen and unworthy of you. I alone am suited to you; look upon me as your wife.

23. "I will devour this misshapen slut, this hideous human female with her pinched waist, along with this brother of yours.

24. "And then, my beloved, you shall roam Dandaka with me, viewing all the different mountain peaks and forests."

25. Thus addressed by the wild-eyed creature, Kakutstha[13] burst out laughing but then went on to reply with customary eloquence.

The end of the sixteenth *sarga* of the *Aranyakanda* of the *Sri Ramayana.*

SARGA 17

1. As Shurpanakha stood there bound tight in the bonds of desire, Rama smiled and, humoring her, replied in jest:

2. "I am already married, my lady, and I love my wife. And for women such as you, to have a rival wife is a source of bitter sorrow.

3. "But my younger brother here is of good character, handsome, powerful, majestic, and still unmarried. His name is Laksmana.

---

13. Another name for Rama.

4. "He has never had a woman before and is in need of a wife. He is young and handsome and will make a good husband, one suited to such beauty as yours.

5. "Accept my brother as your husband, large-eyed, shapely lady. With no rival wife the two of you will be inseparable as sunlight and Mount Meru."

6. When the *rakshasa* woman, wild with desire, heard Rama address her in this way, she promptly forsook him and said to Laksmana:

7. "I shall make you a lovely wife, one befitting your beauty. And together we shall roam so pleasantly all through Dandaka."

8. Lakshman smiled at the words of the *rakshasa* woman Shurpanakha and with customary eloquence made this fitting reply:

9. "Why would you want to be my wife, lotuslike beauty? I am completely subject to the will of my noble brother; I am a slave, and she who is my wife must be a slave as well.

10. "Become instead the junior wife of my noble brother, large-eyed lady of unblemished beauty. He is prosperous, and with him your fortunes, too, will prosper and you will be happy.

11. "Soon enough he will turn away from this misshapen slut, this hideous old wife with her pinched waist, and give his love to you alone.

12. "What man with any sense would reject this singular beauty of yours, my fair and shapely lady, and bestow his affections on a human female?"

13. So Laksmana spoke, and the potbellied, hideous creature, unused to teasing, thought he was in earnest.

14. Then as Rama, the invincible slayer of enemies, sat with Sita before the leaf hut, the *rakshasa* woman addressed him once more, wild with desire.

15. "It is on account of this misshapen slut, this hideous old wife with her pinched waist, that you care so little for me.

16. "I am going to devour this human female at once, before your very eyes; then, free of any rival, I shall live happily with you."

17. And with this, she flew into a rage, and with eyes flashing like firebrands she shot toward the fawn-eyed princess, like a giant meteor toward the star Rohini.

18. But as she was about to fall upon Sita, like the very noose of Death, mighty Rama angrily restrained her and said to Laksmana:

19. "Never tease savage, ignoble creatures, Saumitri. Look at Vaidehi, dear brother; she is frightened half to death.

20. "Now, tiger among men, mutilate this misshapen slut, this potbellied, lustful *rakshasa* woman."

21. So Rama spoke, and powerful Lakshmana, in full view of his brother, drew his sword and in a rage cut off the creature's ears and nose.

22. The dreadful Shurpanakha, her ears and nose hacked off, gave out an earsplitting roar as she fled back into the forest the way she had come.

23. Mutilated, spattered with blood, and all the more dreadful now, the *rakshasa* woman roared incessantly, like a storm cloud when the rains come.

24. Gushing blood all over, a terror to behold, she disappeared into the deep forest, howling, her arms outstretched.

25. She made her way then to her brother, the awesome Khara, who was in Janasthana together with a troop of *rakshasas*. Mutilated, she fell before him to the ground, like a bolt of lightning from the sky.

26. Spattered with blood, wild with fear and confusion, Khara's sister told him the whole story—how Rama had come into the forest with his wife and Lakshmana, and how she herself had been mutilated.

The end of the seventeenth *sarga* of the *Aranyakanda* of the *Sri Ramayana*.

KAMPAN (TWELFTH CENTURY C.E.)
India

Kampan was a Tamil poet who most likely lived in the twelfth century C.E. His *Ramayana* is regarded as one of the literary masterpieces of the Tamil language. The story Kampan narrates is essentially the same as that presented by Valmiki, but the manner in which the story is presented is very different. In the present selection, for instance, the Tamil poet focuses on the woman in a different way, exploring her emotional response in far greater depth. Among the sources Kampan drew on for his narrative are motifs and conventions associated with *sangam* (literary academic) poetry and the folklore of southern India. Perhaps the most distinctive feature of Kampan's text is that it explicitly presents Rama as an incarnation of the god Vishnu, one of the three supreme gods of classical Hinduism (the divinity of Rama in Valmiki's poem is a more complicated matter). In this it follows the tradition established by the poetry of the Tamil saints of the sixth to ninth centuries C.E.

from **The Ramayana**

[Patalam Five: Shurpunakha]

1. 2829

And the heroes saw the river Godavari
   which was like the poems of the great poets,
a sublime ornament for the earth
   with fields of profound wealth
and its episodes that are watering places
   for rescue from the heat, with its flow
through the five landscapes of poetry,[1]
   clear and lovely and sweetly running.

2. 2830

With her bright face glittering, gracious
   as a lotus where the bees gather
and the glowing eyes of her water lilies
   that absorb and hold sweet fragrance
while her hands, the clear waves,
   one after another, were picking up and scattering
beautiful flowers, the holy river shone
   as if bowing at the noble sight of them.

3. 2831

And O the river seemed to cry out,
   cry out and grieve and grieve
with risen love, as if the moving water
   were shedding cool drops of tears
spreading from her lovely eyes
   of newly open water lilies that had to see
this sadness, those young men[2] who were honest
   and faultless living in the forest.

4. 2832

The bowman of the long bow saw
   the cakravaka birds[3] peacefully

Translated by George L. Hart and Hank Heifitz.

---

1. The five different types of Tamil poetry, associated with five stages of love.
2. Rama and Laksmana.

3. Love birds condemned to spend their
nights apart.

closing their eyes on their beds
    of lotuses and looked at the breasts
of his woman, while she whose ornaments
    were lovely looked at the hills
glittering with their jewels and her mind
    turned to her great lord's arms.

5. 2833

And that highest being when he saw
    the swaying walk of a wild goose
smiled a little and looked
    at Sita walking near him
and she saw how a male elephant
    coming back from drinking at the water
moved and a sudden smile
    showed across her face.

. . .

20. 2848

"Has the sun who is lord of light not seen this radiance,
this glow of a being whose smile is like glistening moonlight,
that he goes on his way without shame in his heart, spreading
his lesser light on high through all the distances?

21. 2849

"This man with his huge shoulders like towering mountains
has a lower lip for which no comparison possible
on this earth is adequate. What could I ever find
to say that marks a redness even greater than coral?

22. 2850

"For the happiness of encircling this lovely waist that dispels
the darkness, I think that not even a golden robe
could have done the tapas of that bark garment[4]
for this noble being who shines as brightly as the moon.

23. 2851

"Ah! if instead of matted hair, he was wearing
the black tuft[5] of a young man with its curls

---

4. Religious penance consisting of wearing
   rough garments.

5. The signs, respectively, of an ascetic and
   a warrior.

all through it like long clouds hanging down,
surely he would put an end to every woman's life.

24. 2852

"If the best of ornaments, radiating light, were to embrace
this body, could they make its loveliness grow any more?
Does the beauty of the faultless ruby, king of gems,
shine any brighter by the presence of some other jewel?

25. 2853

"When Brahma[6] created this body, collecting and displaying
every virtue possible, keeping nothing back, then blame
came to him since Indra, ruler of all the worlds, though he beg
for more, in beauty is not worth the dust on those feet!"

. . .

80. 2908

Whenever a dark cloud appeared or she happened to look at a column
of blue sapphires, she would join her palms in praise, with her body
so on fire that even a giant moonstone that is moistened
by the moon's touch would catch fire from her and burn.

81. 2909

So that the huge lovely moon would never find her
nor the cool north wind nor the God of Love, she almost went
to the safety of a deep mountain cave where there lives
an angry snake, with sharp, terrifying fangs.

82. 2910

Then, as the flame grew higher and higher, not knowing
what to do next, with her breasts burning and pouring out
three times more fire than before, she began to roll
around on a bed of long, fresh, golden shoots.

83. 2911

The form of the hero took shape before her burning eyes
and thinking she was seeing him, huge and dark as a monsoon cloud,[7]
she was pained and ashamed and stunned as that body
vanished away and she fell to the ground, in great suffering.

---

6. The creator god.

7. Rama is represented as dark in complexion.

84. 2912

As a black cloud passed, she tried to press it to her breasts,
imagining it was her lord and when she saw those clouds
warming up and dissolving, she would weep! Was there
any end at all to that unholy woman's delusion?

85. 2913

Though it seemed as if she were caught in the blazing fire that consumes
a universe, that mindless woman did not lose her life
saved by the drug of her desire to have that man
with his body the color of the dark ocean and then to live!

99. 2927

She tried to press her nose back on.
    She breathed like fire in a forge.
She hammered her hands on the ground and grasping
    her two large breasts,
she looked at them and her body broke out
    sweating. She went running
on her great strong legs everywhere
    and she weakened as the blood flowed.

100. 2928

She wandered in a flooding swamp of her own blood
    that came streaming down like a waterfall
swollen full by many springs and, through calling out
    all those names of her family
that can frighten even Death, made
    the gods run away in terror.
Unable to bear the pain, she stood there and summoned them,
    speaking in a torrent of words.

101. 2929

"You! with your power on this wide earth, are you not offended by these
holy men wandering carrying bows who have made me not able
any more to raise my head before the gods! O incomparable mountain
who lifted Siva's[8] own mountain! Won't you come look at these things?

---

8. The destroyer god, who dwells on Mt.
Kailasa.

102. 2930

"The world encircled by the roaring ocean believes that no one
takes a tiger's cub even when the mother is gone. Is this
a lie? O you who are stronger than Asuras and gods and the three[9]
who are highest! Won't you come to see the pain I feel?

103. 2931

"You saw the back of Indra when you fought him as he was riding
the king of elephants who trumpeted in battle and, fighting for him,
there was a dense army of gods! You defeated him in war. He broke out sweating
and barely escaped with his life! Won't you come to see the shame I feel?

104. 2932

"You who are served by wind, fire, and water and Death
who is cruel time, and the sky and the planets! Have you lost
your strength? Do you retreat before two men, you who seized
the sword you carry out of the mighty hand of great Siva!

105. 2933

"Though in form they resemble the God of Love, why do you not show
your anger at these men not worth the dust under the soles of your sandals,
O strength! who, lifting your arms, broke Kailasa and the tusks of the Elephants
of Space[10] who flow with musth, whose feet make the dust sparkle!

106. 2934

"Has his strength abandoned Ravana who has the power even to destroy
the gods who wear fragrant garlands that are filled with nectar?
Has strength left his younger brothers? Has it gone to stay
with men, the meat of whose bodies is meant to be food for our race?

107. 2935

"Did this happen because of the power of two holy men who are hiding
in the great forest thick with trees or because Raksasas good at killing
have given up? You! whose hands are so strong your enemies can only
be Siva or Brahma or Visnu! Will you look at the pain I feel?

---

9. Brahma, Visnu, Siva.

10. Mythic beasts said to guard the cardinal points of space.

108. 2936

"Where Indra and Brahma on his flower and the other gods ask for your orders
and the women of heaven sing to wish you long life and the seven worlds
praise you, sitting in the midst of your court under your umbrella unrivaled
like the moon, can I who am your servant, with no shame, show you my face?

109. 2937

"Am I to remain here crying out my pain while that man admires
his arms after he kicked and rolled me across the ground so that my strength
broke and faded and then he cut off my nose? Should I have to endure this
in Khara's forest? O brother who moved Siva's mountain! O my brother!

110. 2938

"Isn't your good name sullied by this stain, because I acted
without a sense of shame and due to my lust, I have lost my nose?
You whose arms have the great fame of having fought and tired
out the Elephants of Space! You broke their tusks! Ravana! Ravana!

111. 2939

"And you my nephew![11] My nephew! You who made the gods serve you,
who put Indra himself in chains and wiped out clans of Asuras!
Am I to die here, because of this disgrace, I who sinned and had
my nose and my ears cut off by those two in the middle of the forest!

112. 2940

"Once the seven worlds grew angry and came against you and you,
strong in your rage, broke them with a single bow and scattered them
in all the directions. Then, chaining Indra's legs, you put him
in a great prison! My nephew! Won't you come face the strength of men?

113. 2941

"You whose murderous force can split rocks with the weapons in your giant
hands! Khara! Dusana![12] You others born as Rakshasas and ornamented
with jewels that flash apart the darkness! Do you sleep on the earth
like Kumbhakarna[13] with his sharply honed weapons? Can't you hear me calling?"

---

11. Indrajit, son of Ravana and "conqueror of
    Indra."

12. Brother of Shurpanakha and Khara's
    general, respectively.
13. Brother of Ravana.

114. 2942

As the Raksasi, she who was the enemy, went on shouting out these things,
wailing and lamenting as she rolled on the beautiful earth, he came,
who by that river had finished the full morning rites of his tapas, a mountain
of emerald, whose long arms with their strong sturdy hands held a bow.

115. 2943

Looking at his face as he came, she beat her belly and her raining
tears and the torrents of her blood turned the rich soil to mud.
"By the sin of love risen in me for the beauty of your body, ah
my lord! See what I have suffered!" and she fell on the ground before him.

116. 2944

Within the beauty of his heart that has no equal, he knew something evil
had been done by this woman whose hair was spreading loose and he realized
it must have been his younger brother that same day who had cut off
her long ears and her nose. He said to her, "Woman! Who are you?"

117. 2945

Hearing these words, the strong Raksasi said, "Don't you know me?
My brother is Ravana whose rage silenced even a single word
raised against him in any of the worlds, he who holds heaven
and all other worlds by his cruel spear with its leaflike blade."

118. 2946

"Why have you left those Raksasas with all their power and come here
so far away, to where we live and carry on our tapas?" he said,
and she answered him, "O best cure for the cruel sickness of desire
burning me like hot charcoal! Don't you remember my coming yesterday?"

119. 2947

"Was it you walking here yesterday, like the goddess Sri on her lotus
full of honey, with your long dark eyes like lovely fishes?"
"When a woman has lost her nipples, her ears with their earrings, her nose
like a vine, O king with handsome eyes! isn't her beauty destroyed?"

120. 2948

The king, looking into the face of his strong younger brother and smiling
just a little said to him, "Hero! What evil thing did she intend
to do that you at once cut off her long ears and her nose like a vine?"
and the great hero, bowing to his brother's feet, gave him this answer.

121. 2949

"Whether she meant to use her sharp teeth and consume what she had tracked
or whether a crowd of malevolent Raksasas somewhere behind her
was urging her on, she came running, evil, with her eyes spitting fire
at your noble woman. She was in a towering rage beyond belief."

122. 2950

Before Laksmana with his curving, well-strung bow had finished, the Raksasi,
their enemy, said, "You are from a rich land bright with rivers where by a stream
a pregnant frog, furious at the sight of her husband hovering near a conch,
troubles the water! Doesn't a woman's heart burn when she sees her rival?"

123. 2951

That being who is past the reach of words said to her, "We came here
searching for the great clan of Raksasas to destroy them all who fight
in their strength against the weak. Run now far from this forest where truth
is sought, or else you will be killed as you give us these vicious answers."

124. 2952

"Since Brahma whose hair never turns white nor does his skin wrinkle
and all the other gods are subjects and pay tribute to Ravana,
it would be wrong of you to hurry me away. I have something else,
something different to tell you, if you have any sense of what's best for you!

125. 2953

"Ravana will tear out the tongue of the man who tells him his sister
has had her nose cut off, lost to her forever. He is not
a cultured gentleman. By cutting off my nose, you ended your clan
without escape! You have poured all your beauty out on barren ground.

126. 2954

"The gods in heaven and the kings on the earth and those who rule
where the great Nagas live will stay where they are now protecting
their own heads! Who is there to protect you? Care for me and I
will protect you, but if you will not, then be aware that Ravana exists!

127. 2955

"Though women who are firmly modest should not boast of their own might,
yet I speak out to you because of my love, great with desire.
Won't you tell your younger brother that I am stronger than anyone
in this world, and the honored sister of him who is stronger than the gods?

128. 2956

"In your mighty battles, I will stand by you and protect you. I can
pick you up and carry you away on the air! I can give you endless fruit
as delicious as meat! Why reject your protector? I will give you anything
you wish for! Tell me what you gain from this one who is delicate as a flower!

129. 2957

"Among women who wear their lovely ornaments here on the earth
or in the sky, who are young and beautiful and accomplished, the finest
in their clans, who can summon for themselves whatever they may want,
will you tell me if there is a single one fit to be compared with me?

130. 2958

"So what if you made me lose my nose, now that it's gone, if you can't bear it,
instantly I will create it again! I will be beautiful again! Am I
any less a woman if in this way I gain the fortune of your grace?
Isn't a long nose rising on a woman's face only a frill?

131. 2959

"If I want someone and he doesn't want me, mustn't he be impotent?
Isn't my life yours, because of the love that has risen in me?
Beauty that others may look at and desire, isn't that a poison?
Shouldn't you welcome a body that only a husband will caress?

132. 2960

"You! as if Siva and Brahma who on his flower faces the directions[14]
and Visnu and Indra with his devastating thunderbolt had joined in one
to stand here! Is Kama whose flower arrows take life away from the worlds
your younger brother too? He is as merciless as this one has been.

133. 2961

"Is there any reason for you to have cut off my nose and made a hole
    show, you with your war anklets
beautifully fashioned of gold! unless you had the thought in your mind,
    'She will stay here with us, she will
not go, she who has this form that is delight.' So that no stranger
    might ever look at me, you cut it,
didn't you? Did you harm me? Because I understood your wish, don't I know
    that my love is twice as strong?

---

14. Brahma has four faces, one looking in each
    direction.

134. 2962

"If the Raksasas with their spears and their great anger like unquenchable fire
    should come to know what has happened
and see it in their rage, all the worlds would be destroyed because of you
    who have wronged me. Born in a lineage
so high, with Righteousness always in your minds, you would not cause the
        worlds
    to be destroyed! Consider carefully
and stay here with me, in happiness, clear of blame, saving all life,"
    she said and, standing up, bowed down to him.

135. 2963

"I still have the arrow that ended the life of Tadaka, the mother
    of your mother who was a Raksasi guilty
of causing pain such as living beings here had never known
    and now I have taken on as my tapas
to live in the forest where I exist to destroy the enemy race
    of Raksasas who around their shoulders
wear garlands of thick, lovely flowers. Strong Raksasi!" said the Lord,
    "Stop behaving in a way so low!

136. 2964

"We are the sons of Dasaratha, the wheel of whose law ruled the world
    unrivaled! Obeying our mother's command,
we entered the forest where fragrance is everywhere. Brahmins and great sadhus
    have asked us to destroy the race
of Raksasas whose army is an ocean with no shore to be seen.
    Only then will we reenter our city
where the mansions of the families rise like ancient mountains. Take these things
    to heart. Understand them clearly,

137. 2965

"You should not be thinking that these are just any two men,
    even though the great gods themselves
were defeated, unable to stand against the Raksasas who do not
    travel the path of virtues.
Bring, if you can, everyone you think is powerful, all of them,
    the Raksasas with their sharp spears
smelling of flesh and all the Yaksas[15] who always win their victories!
    Then right in front of you we will kill them."

---

15. Semidivine beings, whose king is Kubera,
    brother of Shurpanakha.

138. 2966

"Yes, you can kill them," she said, "you can be told what strategies
  they will try, you can win
and end their string of victories, you can overcome every one
  of their tricks if only you see me
not as a woman with a gaping mouth, with all of my teeth showing
  because my upper lip has been cut away!
Listen to me! You who come from a land where water nourishes
  all grains and offers them to the people!

139. 2967

"Even if you don't give her up, she whose arms are as graceful as bamboo,
  would I be nothing at all to you?
If you are determined to go into battle against the Raksasas who are outlaws,
  who are ignorant and murderous, then
since I understand the various magic powers of their intricate weapons,
  won't I be able to repel them?
Don't you know what the proverb says, that a snake is the one
  to search out the lair of a snake?

140. 2968

"If you feel that you must keep this woman in your heart, still you should
  realize that if you intend to fight
and prevail on the battlefield against the Raksasas, we three here together
  could make that field a pool
of blood! Should that give you pain? And if then you will marry me
  to this young prince who does not realize
what there is to gain, I would never weaken even before him
  who has imprisoned[16] the sun and the moon.

141. 2969

"On the day you return to your city, when it will be filled with great joy,
  I will skillfully take on whatever form
you wish for, and if your younger brother should say, 'How can I live
  with a woman who has had her nose
cut off completely?' even though it was he who became enraged and cut at me
  in his anger that could not be satisfied,
won't you tell him he has been living for a very long time
  with a woman who has no waist at all?"

---

16. Ravana.

142. 2970

The younger brother glanced at his spear with its bright blade like a leaf,
   thinking to pierce her as she spoke
and he said, "If we don't free ourselves by killing her right now,
   she will trouble us for a long time.
O king, what is your will?" The Lord said, "That would be the right thing
   to do, if she doesn't leave us alone!"
and the Raksasi thought, "These men will show me no compassion.
   I will lose my life if I stay."

143. 2971

She said to them, "Could I ever bear to live with you after I have
   lost my nose as lovely
as a long vine and my two ears and the nipples of both my breasts?
   What I said was meant to find out
all about you. Now I will bring him who is swifter than the wind,
   him who is crueler than fire,
Khara, who will be your Death!" and she set out, feeling herself
   full of hatred that had no calming.

ASHVAGHOSHA (c. 100 C.E.)
India

The *Life of the Buddha* [*Buddhacarita*] is one of two long poems, three plays, and assorted hymns and discourses written by Ashvaghosha, the first of the great Buddhist poets in Sanskrit. Tradition associates Ashvaghosha with the court of King Kanishka I, who ruled sometime between the middle and the end of the first century C.E. in the northern part of present-day India.

   The passage presented here is known as the episode of the "four signs." It relates a crucial moment in the life of Shakyamuni, a young prince, when a series of events convinces him to undertake the quest for spiritual awakening that will result in his transformation into Buddha (which means "awakened" in Sanskrit). It had been foretold at Shakyamuni's birth that he was destined to become either a great king or a master of *dharma* (here the word takes on a special Buddhist meaning of spiritual teaching). Hoping for a king rather than a holy man, his father, King Shuddhodana, raises Shakyamuni in perfect comfort, shielding him from anything that might provoke a distaste for worldly pleasures. One day, however, the prince accidentally encounters four men: an old man, a sick man, a dead man, and a man who has renounced the world. He thereby realizes the nature of mortality and the possible responses to its inevitable course, and he decides to seek his spiritual enlightenment.

The Enlightenment of the Buddha.
Sandstone sculpture of the first
century C.E. from Sanchi in
central India.

from **The Life of Buddha [Buddhacarita]**

The Four Signs

LIFE IN THE PALACE

The prince passed through infancy and in course of time duly underwent the ceremony of initiation. And it took him but a few days to learn the sciences suitable to his race, the mastery of which ordinarily requires many years.

But, as the king of the Sakyas had heard from the great seer, Asita, that the prince's future goal would be the supreme beatitude, he feared lest he should go to the forests and therefore he turned him to sensual pleasures.

Then from a family possessed of long-standing good conduct he summoned for him the goddess of Fortune in the shape of a maiden, Yasodhara by name, of widespread renown, virtuous and endowed with beauty, modesty and gentle bearing.

The prince, radiant with wondrous beauty like Sanatkumara,[1] took his delight with the Sakya king's daughter-in-law, as the Thousand-eyed with Saci.[2]

The monarch, reflecting that the prince must see nothing untoward that might agitate his mind, assigned him a dwelling in the upper storeys of the palace and did not allow him access to the ground.

Translated by E. H. Johnston.

---

1. "Eternal Youth," one of the four sons of the god Brahmā.

2. The god Indra (who is said to have one thousand eyes) with his wife.

Then in the pavilions, white as the clouds of autumn, with apartments suited to each season and resembling heavenly mansions come down to earth, he passed the time with the noble music of singing-women.

For the palace was glorious as Kailasa,[3] with tambourines whose frames were bound with gold and which sounded softly beneath the strokes of women's fingers, and with dances that rivalled those of the beautiful Apsarases.[4]

There the women delighted him with their soft voices, charming blandishments, playful intoxications, sweet laughter, curvings of eyebrows and sidelong glances.

Then, a captive to the women, who were skilled in the accessories of love and indefatigable in sexual pleasure, he did not descend from the palace to the ground, just as one who has won Paradise by his merit does not descend to earth from the heavenly mansion.

THE PRINCE'S PERTURBATION

Then upon a time he listened to songs celebrating the forests, with their soft grass, with their trees resounding with koïls' calls, and with their adornment of lotusponds.

Then hearing of the entrancing character of the city groves, beloved of the womenfolk, he set his heart on an expedition outside, like an elephant confined inside a house.

Then the king learnt of the state of mind of that heart's desire, styled his son, and directed a pleasure excursion to be prepared worthy of his love and majesty and of his son's youth.

And, reflecting that the prince's tender mind might be perturbed thereby, he forbade the appearance of afflicted common folk on the royal road.

Then with the greatest gentleness they cleared away on all sides those whose limbs were maimed or senses defective, the aged, sick and the like, and the wretched, and made the royal highway supremely magnificent.

Then, when the road had been made beautiful, the prince, after receiving permission, descended at the proper time in full splendour with well-trained attendants from the top of the palace, and approached the king.

Thereon the ruler of men, with tears in his eyes, gazed long at his son and kissed him on the head; and with his voice he bade him set forth, but out of affection he did not let him go in his mind.

Then the prince mounted a golden chariot, to which were harnessed four well-broken horses with golden gear, and with a driver who was manly, skilful and reliable.

Then, like the moon with the constellations mounting to the sky, he proceeded with a suitable retinue towards the road which was bestrewn with

---

3. Mountain in the Himalayas, where the god Siva resides.

4. Divine females, often represented as the dancing girls of the gods.

heaps of brilliant flowers and made gay with hanging wreaths and fluttering banners.

And very slowly he entered the royal highway, which was carpeted with the halves of blue lotuses in the shape of eyes open to their widest in excitement, as all around the citizens gazed at him.

Some praised him for his gracious bearing, others worshipped him for his glorious appearance, but for his benignity others wished him sovereignty and length of days.

From the great houses humpbacks and swarms of dwarfs and Kiratas[5] poured forth, and from the meaner houses women; and all bowed down as to the flag in the procession of the god.

Hearing the news from their servants, "the prince, they say, is going out," the women obtained leave from their elders and went out on to the balconies in their desire to see him.

They gathered together in uncontrollable excitement, obstructed by the slipping of their girdle-strings, as they put their ornaments on at the report, and with their eyes still dazed by sudden awakening from sleep.

They frightened the flocks of birds on the houses with the jingling of belts, the tinkling of anklets and the clatter of their steps on the stairs, and reproached each other for jostling.

But some of these magnificent women, though longing made them try to rush, were delayed in their movements by the weight of their hips and full breasts.

But another, though well able to move with speed, checked her steps and went slowly, modestly shrinking as she covered up the ornaments worn in intimacy.

Unquiet reigned in the windows then, as the women were crowded together in the mutual press, with their earrings ever agitated by collisions and their ornaments jingling.

But the lotus-faces of the women, emerging from the windows and mutually setting their earrings in perpetual commotion, seemed like lotuses stuck on to the pavilions.

Then with its palaces full to bursting with young women, who threw the lattices open in their excitement, the city appeared as magnificent on all sides as Paradise with its heavenly mansions full of Apsarases.

From the narrowness of the windows the faces of these glorious women, with their earrings resting on each other's cheeks, seemed like bunches of lotus-flowers tied to the windows.

The women, looking down at the prince in the street, seemed as if wishing to descend to earth, while the men, gazing up at him with upraised faces, seemed as if wishing to rise to heaven.

Beholding the king's son in the full glory of his beauty and majesty, the

---

5. Usually forest-dwelling hunters: here presumably harem guards.

women murmured low, "Blessed is his wife," with pure minds and from no baser motive;

For they held him in reverent awe, reflecting that he with the long stout arms, in form like the visible presence of the god whose symbols are flowers,[6] would, it was said, resign his royal pomp and follow the religious law.

Thus the first time that the prince saw the royal highway, it was thronged with respectful citizens, clad in cleanly sober guise; and he rejoiced and felt in some degree as if he were being re-created.

But when the Suddhadhivasa gods[7] saw that city as joyful as Paradise itself, they created the illusion of an old man in order to incite the king's son to leave his home.

Then the prince saw him overcome with senility and different in form to other men. His interest was excited and, with gaze steadily directed on the man, he asked the charioteer:—

"Good charioteer, who is this man with white hair, supporting himself on the staff in his hand, with his eyes veiled by the brows, and limbs relaxed and bent? Is this some transformation in him, or his original state, or mere chance?"

When the chariot-driver was thus spoken to, those very same gods confounded his understanding, so that, without seeing his error, he told the prince the matter he should have withheld:—

"Old age it is called, that which has broken him down,—the murderer of beauty, the ruin of vigour, the birthplace of sorrow, the grave of pleasure, the destroyer of memory, the enemy of the senses.

For he too sucked milk in his infancy, and later in course of time he crawled on the ground; in the natural order he became a handsome youth and in the same natural order he has now reached old age."

At these words the king's son started a little and addressed the charioteer thus, "Will this evil come upon me also?" Then the charioteer said to him:—

"Inevitably by force of time my long-lived lord will know this length of his days. Men are aware that old age thus destroys beauty and yet they seek it."

Then, since his mind was purified by his intentions in the past and his good merit had been accumulated through countless epochs, he was perturbed in his lofty soul at hearing of old age, like a bull on hearing the crash of a thunderbolt near by.

Fixing his eyes on the old man, he sighed deeply and shook his head; and looking on the festive multitude he uttered these words in his perturbation:—

"Thus old age strikes down indiscriminately memory and beauty and valour, and yet with such a sight before its eyes the world is not perturbed.

This being so, turn back the horses, charioteer; go quickly home again. For how can I take my pleasure in the garden, when the fear of old age rules in my mind?"

So at the bidding of his master's son the driver turned back the chariot. Then the prince returned to the same palace, but so lost in anxiety that it seemed to him empty.

---

6. The god of love, who (like Cupid) has a bow, made of flowers with a black bow-string of bees.

7. "Dwelling in a pure abode," one of numerous categories of gods in the Buddhist cosmology, who typically announce the birth of the Buddha.

But even there he found no relief, as he ever dwelt on the subject of old age; therefore once more with the permission of the king he went out, all being ordered as before.

Thereupon the same gods created a man with body afflicted by disease, and the son of Śuddhodana saw him, and, keeping his gaze fixed on him, he said to the charioteer:—

"Who is this man with swollen belly and body that heaves with his panting? His shoulders and arms are fallen in, his limbs emaciated and pale. He calls out piteously, "mother," as he leans on another for support."

Then the charioteer replied to him, "Good Sir, it is the mighty misfortune called disease, developed in full force from the disorder of the humours, that has made this man, once so competent, no longer master of himself."

Thereupon the king's son looked at the man compassionately and spoke, "Is this evil peculiar to him, or is the danger of disease common to all men?"

Then the chariot-driver said, "Prince, this evil is shared by all. For men feast and yet they are thus oppressed by disease and racked by pain".

Hearing this truth, he was perturbed in mind and trembled like the reflection of the moon on rippling water; and in his pity he uttered these words in a somewhat low tone:—

"This is the calamity of disease for mankind and yet the world sees it and feels no alarm. Vast, alas, is the ignorance of men, who sport under the very shadow of disease.

Turn back the chariot, charioteer, from going outside; let it go straight to the palace of the chief of men. And on hearing of the danger of disease, my mind is repelled from pleasures and shrinks, as it were, into itself."

Then he turned back with all feeling of joy gone and entered the palace, given over to brooding; and seeing him thus returned a second time, the lord of the earth made enquiry.

But when he learnt the reason for his return, he felt himself already abandoned by him. And he merely reprimanded the officer in charge of clearing the road, and angry though he was, imposed no severe punishment on him.

And he further arranged for his son the application of sensual attractions in the highest degree, hoping, "Perhaps he will be held by the restlessness of the senses and not desert us".

But when in the women's apartments his son took no pleasure in the objects of sense, sounds and the rest, then he directed another excursion outside with the thought that it might cause a change of mood.

And as out of his affection he understood his son's state of mind and took no account of the dangers of passion, he ordered suitable courtesans to be present there, as skilled in the arts.

Then the royal highway was decorated and guarded with especial care; and the king changed the charioteer and chariot and sent the prince off outside.

Then as the king's son was going along, those same gods fashioned a lifeless man, so that only the charioteer and the prince, and none other, saw the corpse being borne along.

Thereon the king's son asked the charioteer, "Who is being carried along yonder by four men and followed by a dejected company? He is dressed out gorgeously and yet they bewail him".

Then the driver's mind was overcome by the pure-natured Suddhadhivasa gods and, though it should not have been told, he explained this matter to the lord of mankind:—

"This is someone or other, lying bereft of intellect, senses, breath and qualities, unconscious and become like a mere log or bundle of grass. He was brought up and cherished most lovingly with every care and now he is being abandoned."

Hearing the driver's reply, he was slightly startled and said, "Is this law of being peculiar to this man, or is such the end of all creatures?"

Then the driver said to him, "This is the last act for all creatures. Destruction is inevitable for all in the world, be he of low or middle or high degree".

Then, steadfast-minded though he was, the king's son suddenly became faint on hearing of death, and, leaning with his shoulder against the top of the chariot rail, he said in a melodious voice:—

"This is the end appointed for all creatures, and yet the world throws off fear and takes no heed. Hardened, I ween, are men's hearts; for they are in good cheer, as they fare along the road.

Therefore, charioteer, let our chariot be turned back; for it is not the time or place for pleasure-resorts. For how could a man of intelligence be heedless here in the hour of calamity, when once he knows of destruction?"

Though the king's son spoke to him thus, he not merely did not turn back but in accordance with the king's command went on to the Padmasanda grove,[8] which had been provided with special attractions.

There the prince saw that lovely grove like the grove of Nandana,[9] with young trees in full bloom, with intoxicated koïls[10] flitting joyously about, and with pavilions and tanks beautiful with lotuses.

THE WOMEN REJECTED

Then the women went forth from the city garden, their eyes dancing with excitement, to meet the king's son, as if he were a bridegroom arriving.

And, as they approached him, their eyes opened wide in wonder and they welcomed him respectfully with hands folded like lotus-buds.

And they stood around him, their minds absorbed in love, and seemed to drink him in with eyes that were moveless and blossomed wide in ecstasy.

For the glory of the brilliant signs on his person,[11] as of ornaments born on him, made the women deem him to be the god of love in bodily form.

---

8. A place where day-lotuses grow.
9. The heavenly garden of Indra.
10. Indian cuckoos.

11. Physical marks—often very specific signs such as the "wheel" on the foot in the case of an emperor—indicate a person's character and destiny.

Some opined from his benignity and gravity that the moon had come down to earth in person with his rays veiled.

Enthralled by his beauty, they writhed suppressedly, and, smiting each other with their glances, softly sighed.

But despite such allurements the prince firmly guarded his senses, and in his perturbation over the inevitability of death, was neither rejoiced nor distressed.

He, the supreme man, saw that they had no firm footing in the real truth, and with mind that was at the same time both perturbed and steadfast he thus meditated:—

"Do these women then not understand the transitoriness of youth, that they are so inebriated with their own beauty, which old age will destroy?

Surely they do not perceive anyone overwhelmed by illness, that they are so full of mirth, so void of fear in a world in which disease is a law of nature.

And quite clearly they sport and laugh so much at ease and unperturbed, because they are ignorant of death who carries all away.

For what rational being would stand or sit or lie at ease, still less laugh, when he knows of old age, disease and death?

But he is just like a being without reason, who, on seeing another aged or ill or even dead, remains indifferent and unmoved.

For when one tree is shorn both of its flowers and its fruit and falls or is cut down, another tree is not distressed thereby."

Then their garlands and ornaments worn in vain, their excellent arts and endearments all fruitless, the women suppressed the god of love in his birthplace, their hearts, and returned to the city with their hopes frustrated.

Then the son of earth's guardian saw the glory of the women in the city garden withdrawn again in the evening and, meditating on the transitoriness of everything, he entered his dwelling.

But when the king heard that his son was averse from the objects of sense, then like an elephant with a dart in its heart, he did not lie down that night. Thereon wearing himself out with all kinds of counsels with his ministers, he found no means, other than the passions, for restraining his son's purpose.

FLIGHT

Though the son of the Sakya king was thus tempted by priceless objects of sense, he felt no contentment, he obtained no relief, like a lion pierced deeply in the heart by a poisoned arrow.

Then longing for spiritual peace, he set forth outside with the king's permission in order to see the forest, and for companions he had a retinue of ministers' sons, chosen for their reliability and skill in converse.

He went out, mounted on the good horse Kanthaka, the bells of whose bit were of fresh gold and whose golden trappings were beautified with waving chowries, and so he resembled a *karṇikāra*[12] emblem mounted on a flagpole.

Desire for the forest as well as the excellence of the land led him on to the more distant jungle-land, and he saw the soil being ploughed, with its surface broken with the tracks of the furrows like waves of water.

When he saw the ground in this state, with the young grass torn up and scattered by the ploughs and littered with dead worms, insects and other creatures, he mourned deeply as at the slaughter of his own kindred.

And as he observed the ploughmen with their bodies discoloured by wind, dust and the sun's rays, and the oxen in distress with the labour of drawing, the most noble one felt extreme compassion.

Then alighting from his horse, he walked slowly over the ground, overcome with grief. And as he considered the coming into being and the passing away of creation, he cried in his affliction, "How wretched this is."

And desiring to reach perfect clearness with his mind, he stopped his friends who were following him, and proceeded himself to a solitary spot at the root of a *jambu*-tree,[13] whose beautiful leaves were waving in all directions.

And there he sat down on the clean ground, with grass bright like beryl; and reflecting on the origin and destruction of creation he took the path of mental stillness.

And his mind at once came to a stand and at the same time he was freed from mental troubles such as desire for the objects of sense. And he entered into the first trance of calmness which is accompanied by gross and subtle cogitation and which is supermundane in quality.

Then he obtained possession of concentration of mind, which springs from discernment and yields extreme ecstasy and bliss, and thereafter, rightly perceiving in his mind the course of the world, he meditated on this same matter.

"A wretched thing it is indeed that man, who is himself helpless and subject to the law of old age, disease and destruction, should in his ignorance and the blindness of his conceit, pay no heed to another who is the victim of old age, disease or death.

For if I, who am myself such, should pay no heed to another whose nature is equally such, it would not be right or fitting in me, who have knowledge of this, the ultimate law."

As he thus gained correct insight into the evils of disease, old age and death, the mental intoxication relating to the self, which arises from belief in one's strength, youth and life, left him in a moment.

He did not rejoice nor yet was he downcast; doubt came not over him, nor sloth, nor drowsiness. And he felt no longing for sensual pleasures, no hatred or contempt for others.

---

12. A type of tree.   13. Rose-apple tree.

The Offering of the Four Bowls. Gandharan, 2nd to 5th century
A.D. Stone (schist); Baltimore Museum of Art

While this pure passionless state of mind grew within his lofty soul, there came up to him a man in mendicant's clothes, unseen of other men.

The king's son asked him, "Tell me, who are you?" On this he explained to him, "O bull among men, I am a *sramana*,[14] who in fear of birth and death have left the home life for the sake of salvation.

Since the world is subject to destruction, I desire salvation and seek the blessed incorruptible stage. I look with equal mind on kinsman and stranger, and longing for and hatred of the objects of sense have passed from me.

I dwell wherever I happen to be, at the root of a tree or in a deserted temple, on a hill or in the forest, and I wander without ties or expectations in search of the highest good, accepting any alms I may receive."

After saying this, he flew up to the sky before the prince's very eyes; for he was a heavenly being who in that form had seen other Buddhas and had encountered him to rouse his attention.

When that being went like a bird to heaven, the best of men was thrilled and amazed. And then he gained awareness of *dharma*[15] and set his mind on the way to leave his home.

---

14. Wandering mendicant, especially Buddhist or Jain.

15. Doctrine of the Buddha.

ANONYMOUS (500–1500 C.E.)
India

Sanskrit epic poetry was written in quatrains—syntactically self-contained four-line stanzas expressing a complete thought and able to stand alone. The quatrain became the basic building block of classical Sanskrit poetry. Poets also explored the possibilities of using the quatrain as a complete poem in its own right (the translations that follow often abandon this rigid form). These four-line works, called *muktaka,* or "separated" poems, were apparently gathered into collections by the poets themselves. From about 1000 C.E., anthologies containing *muktakas* from many poets replaced these earlier collections, and the names of the poets were often lost in the process. It is from these later anthologies that the anonymous poems in this selection derive.

The thousands of *muktaka* thus preserved for us are as manifold and complex as life itself. A typical anthology will begin with invocations of the gods, proceed through all the various stages and domains of human existence, and end with poems dealing with renunciation of the world.

The lyrics illustrate not only the emotional universe of Sanskrit, however, but also its aesthetic project, the ways in which Indian poets sought to produce a complete literary experience in four lines of verse, and to do so by generating as pure a representation of emotion as they could. The anonymity of this poetry, the fact that it is never anchored in a given time or place or historical personality—you will find almost nothing comparable to "Easter 1916." "Westminster Bridge," "miser Catulle"—is a *decision* on the part of the poets rather than a lack. The thousands of poems found in inscriptions, typically praise-poems to kings, show that sensitivity to time and place could be profound when it was felt to be appropriate. But in this genre there operates a literary sensibility that believed the highest forms of poetry were able to express human emotion in a way permitting a sensitive reader to relive that emotion as a pure distillate of aesthetic pleasure; any local specificity would only diminish this potential for universalization.

from Love Poems from the Sanskrit

[Deep in night]

Deep in night
a lonely wanderer listens to heavy
moving clouds crashing
all over sullen heaven
the longing overcomes him
tears fill his eyes   5

Translated by W. S. Merwin and J. Moussaieff Masson.

he sings
the agony of his loneliness
then the villagers know that travelling
away from someone we love   10
is like dying
they will not speak of it
suddenly even their pride
is far behind them

[How have you come to be/ so thin]

How have you come to be
so thin
why are you trembling
why are you so
pale oh   5
simple girl
and she answered the lord of her life
all these things
just happen for no reason
sighing as she said it   10
and turning away to let
tears fall

[She let him in]

She let him in
she did not turn away from him
there was no anger in her words
she simply looked straight at him
as though there had never been   5
anything between them

[Lush clouds]

Lush clouds in
dark sky of tears she saw *my love*
if you leave me now she
said and could not say more
twisting my shirt   5
toe gripping dust
after that what she
did all words

are helpless to repeat and
they know it and give up   10

[Middle of night]

Middle of night
season of rains season
for love
heavy clouds rolling
thunder
small village asleep in soft rain
lonely traveller sings in tears
girl whose lover is far away
hears the singing
shuts her eyes over what she sees
longing longing
still weeping
later and later in the dark

[Conquering the whole earth]

Conquering the whole earth
as I have done
the essence of it is one
city
in that city one house
in that house only one
room
and even there one bed
in that bed the woman above all others
the essence of the kingdom's happiness
shining like a jewel

[I know]

I know
I shook like a vine
he kissed me
touched my two breasts as he pleased
pushed the necklace aside
I remember that much
but what next
the letting go

the body turning to water
but after that
I keep trying to remember
and I cannot

[To go if you have really decided]

To go
if you have really decided
then you will go
why hurry
two or three oh little while stay
while I look at
your face
living we are water running from
a bucket
who knows
whether I will see you
and you will see
me again

[Daughter of the mountain]

Daughter of
the mountain
look at the full moon
you can see a man
who loves a dark woman
night
she is that black shape
lying on top of him
wrapped around him
he exhausted after loving
she dripping nectar onto him[1]

[Lakshman little brother]

Lakshman
little brother
the mouth of the murderous sun

---

1. The black spot of the moon is imagined to
   be a black woman on top of her white lover.

Convention has it that the moon oozes
nectar.

opens on the horizon
let us hide in the shade here   5
of the green tree

> Rama
> beloved brother
> it is night now   10
> we are in the dark
> there is no sun
> what you see is the moon

Gentle Lakshman
how do you know

> I see the face   15
> of a deer
> on the moon

oh god
oh my love where are you
my Sita my wife   20
with the moon your face
and the face of the deer on it[2]

[Some in this world insist]

Some in this world insist
that a certain whatever-it-is
that has no taste of
joy or sorrow
no qualities   5
is Release
they are fools

to my mind her
body unfurling

---

2. The situation is this: Rama is wandering in the forest with his younger brother Laksh-man. Lakshman is no doubt attempting to distract him from brooding over the loss of Sita. He is, the verse suggests, on the verge of madness for he can no longer distinguish night from day. The poetic convention is that for a man burning with the fever of love, even moonbeams, generally regarded as soothing, burn him. But this conven-tional figure is completely forgotten in the next lines. The words "deer" (where we see a face, Indians see a deer or a hare in the moon) and "moon," common epithets for a beautiful woman (referring to her eyes and face respectively) remind Rama of Sita and the depth of his loss. The imaginative experience involves the pathos of lovers separated by forces beyond their control.

with joy of being young
flowering out of love
her eyes floating as with wine and
words wandering with love
then the undoing of the knot
of her sari
that
is Release

[I like sleeping with somebody different]

I like sleeping with somebody
   different

   often

It's nicest when my husband is
   in a foreign country

   and there's rain in the streets at night
   and wind

   and nobody

[He who stole my virginity]

He who stole my virginity
is the same man
I am married to
and these are the same
spring nights and
this is the same moment of
the jasmine's opening
with winds just coming of age carrying
the scent of its flowers mingled.
with pollen from Kadamba trees
to wake desire
in its nakedness
I am no different yet I
long with my heart
for the delicate
love-making back there under
the dense cane-trees
by the bank of the river
Narmada in
the Vindhya mountains

[Hiding in the cucumber garden]

Hiding in the
cucumber garden
simple country girl shivers
with desire
her lover on a low cot   5
lies tired with love
she melts into his body
with joy
his neck tight in her arms
one of her feet   10
flicking a necklace of
sea shells hanging
on a vine
on the fence
rattles them to scare off   15
foxes there in the dark

[Sky dark]

Sky dark
black smudge-fire clouds
earth dark
thick blanket of young grass yes
now is the time for making love   5
those whose lovers are not with them
call softly to death

VARIOUS AUTHORS (100 B.C.E.–250 C.E.)
India

Among the finest literary creations in the Tamil language is a corpus of
approximately 2400 poems collected in eight *sangam* (literary academic poetry)
anthologies. The poems selected here are drawn from the five anthologies
classified as *akam* poems, poems of the interior world. Each *akam* poem depicts
a moment in the story of two lovers. The moment is described by one of the
lovers or by someone who knows of them, such as the girl's close friend or her
mother, or another lover of the man's. An especially striking feature of many
akam poems is the way in which the poet uses landscape as a mirror of the
emotional lives of the characters. The author and the anthology in which it is
found are listed at the end of each selection.

from **Love Poems from the Tamil**

On Mothers

Mothers

That dignified old woman,

with white hair
that has given up
all fragrant things,

and withered breasts
with nipples like eyes
crinkled as the ironwood seed,

she has a much-loved son who, all alone,

    like a drop of curd
    flicked by a childish milkmaid's
    fingernail
    curdling a whole pitcher of milk,

brought grief
to an army of enemies.

                Maturaipputan Ilanakanar
                Purananuru 276

5

10

Mothers

The old woman's hair
was white, feather
of the fisher heron.

Her delight

    when she heard
    that her son fell in battle
    felling an elephant,

was greater
than at his birth,

and her tears
were more than the scatter of drops
hanging from all the great swaying bamboos

5

10

All poems in this selection are translated by A. K. Ramanujan.

after the rains
on the Bamboo Mountains.

Punkanuttiraiyar
Purananuru 277

Mothers

There, in the very middle
of battle-camps
   that heaved like the seas,

pointing at the enemy
   the tongues of lances,
new-forged and whetted,

urging soldiers forward
   with himself at the head
in a skirmish of arrow and spear,

cleaving through
   an oncoming wave of foes,
forcing a clearing,

he had fallen
in that space
   between armies,
his body hacked to pieces:

   when she saw him there
   in all his greatness,
   mother's milk flowed again
   in the withered breasts
   of this mother
   for her warrior son
   who had no thought of retreat.

Auvaiyar
Purananuru 295

A Leaf in Love and War

The chaste trees,[1] dark-clustered,
blend with the land
that knows no dryness;

---

1. "Its dark leaves were used by women in love as leaf-skirts, and as emblematic wreaths by warriors during a siege. The poem points to the irony of this double-edged image" (Ramanujan).

the colors on the leaves
mob the eyes.

    We've seen those leaves
    on jeweled women,
    on their mounds
    of love.

Now the chaste wreath lies slashed
on the ground, so changed, so mixed
with blood, the vulture snatches it
with its beak,
thinking it raw meat.

    We see this too
    just because a young man
    in love with war
    wore it for glory.

Veripatiya Kamakkanniyar
Purananuru 271

Peace Poem

Waist thin as the purslane creeper,
gait heavy as with grief,

the young Brahman came at night
and entered the fortress quickly.

The words he spoke
were few,

and the ladders, the wooden bolts,
came down,

and the war bells
were loosened

from the flanks
of the veteran elephants.

Maturai Velacan
Purananuru 305

What She Said

"O your hair," he said,
"it's like rainclouds
moving between
branches of lightning.

It parts five ways
between gold ornaments,
braided with a length of flowers
and the fragrant screwpine.

"O your smiles, your glistening teeth,
words sheer honey,
mouth red as coral,
O fair brow,
I want to tell you
something,
listen, stop and listen,"

he said, and stopped me.

Came close,
to look closer
at my brow, my hands, my eyes,
my walk, my speech,
and said, searching
for metaphors:

> "Amazed, it grows small, but it isn't the crescent.
> Unspotted, it isn't the moon.
> Like bamboo, yet it isn't on a hill.
> Lotuses, yet there's no pool.
> Walk mincing, yet no peacock.
> The words languish, yet you're not a parrot,"

and so on.[2]

On and on he praised my parts
with words gentle and sly,
looked for my weakening
like a man with a net
stalking an animal,

watched me
as my heart melted,
stared at me
like a butcher at his prey,

O he saluted me, saluted me,
touched me O he touched me,
a senseless lusting elephant
no goad could hold back.

---

2. The flattery used by the suitor is rife with
   clichés.

Salute and touch,
and touch again he did,

but believe me, friend,
I still think he is not really

a fool by nature.

Kapilar
Kalittokai 55

What She Said: to Her Girl Friend

O you, you wear flowers of gold,
their colors made in fire,
complete with pollen,
while the flowers on creeper and branch
are parched, waterless.
Your lovely forearm stacked
with jeweled bracelets,
shoulders soft as a bed of down,

is it right not to let me
live at your feet?

            he said.

And didn't let go at that,
but stayed on to grab
all my hair
scented with lemon grass,
my hair-knot held together
by the gold shark's-mouth,
and with a finger
he twisted tight
the garland in my hair
and smelled it too.

Not only that, he took
my fingers
    (unfolding now
    like crocus buds,
    I suppose)

to cover his bloodshot eyes
and fetched a huge sigh,
blowing hot like a blacksmith
into his bellows.

And,

>   like a deluded bull-elephant
>   fondling with his trunk
>   his beloved female,

he fondled my young painted breasts
till the paint rubbed off
on his rough hands.
Then he stroked me all over,
just about everywhere.

Yet friend,
with that act of his
I was rid
of all my troubles.

And I tell you this
only so that you can go
and persuade Mother:

May the sweet smells
of my marriage in our house
cling to no man
but him,
and that will be good.

It will guarantee a lasting place for us
in this world that doesn't last.

Kapilar
Kalittokai 54

What She Said: to Her Girl Friend, and What Her Girl Friend Said in Reply

"Friend,
like someone who gets drunk secretly
on hard liquor
till his body begins to ooze with it,
and goes on to brag shamelessly
till listeners shiver,
and then gets caught
with the stolen liquor in his hand,

I too got caught
with my secret in my hands:

my goatherd lover's
string of jasmine
that I'd twined in my hair

fell before my foster-mother[3]
as she loosened my hair
to smear it with butter,[4]

and embarrassed her
before Father, Mother,
and others in the house.

And she
didn't ask a thing about it,
or get angry,
but like someone
shaking off a live coal
she shook it off
and moved into the backyard.

Then I
dried my hair perfumed with sandal,
knotted it,
and picking up the end
of my blue flower-border dress
    that comes down to the floor
I tiptoed in fear
and hid
in the thick of the forest."

"O you got scared because of that?
No fears. Even as you wore
your young man's garlands,
they too have conspired
to give you to him.

They'll pour soft sand
in the wide yard,
put curtains all around,
and make a wedding there
very soon.
            Not only all day today,
but all night yesterday,
we've been scheming
to do just that."

Uruttiran
Kalittokai 115

---

3. Either her personal maid or her father's
second wife.

4. Hair is typically oiled in South Asia.

The Girl Friend Describes the Bull Fight

With the first rains

white clusters of the wild jasmine
backed by fresh thorn
are budding
on nodes once dry
in the cool rain lands.

The bud of the glory lily
looks like a ladle first,
then becomes a fire
when the red petals open
gathering the embers,
and it sways like a drunk.

The bilberry, flowering,
gives nothing but blue gems.

Weaving such blossom
in their wreaths,
cowherds vie with all they have,
enter the stalls
to let loose the bulls,
horns whittled sharp
as the Lord's own pickaxes.

There, in the middle ground,
where the brides wait,
men gather
again and again
ready to master the bulls,
sounding like rumbling and thunder,
raising dust clouds, and smoke,
offer the right things
to the gods
in watering places,
under the banyan tree
and the ancient mango.

There, they leap into the field.

Look, the bull,
raised horns and skin tawny
as certain silkmoths,
he skewers to death
the cowherd who sprang
heedless of the look in the animal's eyes,

5

10

15

20

25

30

35

40

carries the carcass high and shakes it
on his horns,

> like the warrior Bhima[5]
> making good his oath
> sworn among enemies,
> cleaving the heart
> of the man
> who dared put a hand
> to the tresses
> of his lovely wife.

Look at that black bull,
a moon-mark on his brow,[6]
carry and shake the cowherd,
skewered and gutted
(the wreaths on his head
were flowers once on the caverned hills):

> like the raging androgynous god,
> whose one half is His woman,
> who dances at the end of time
>   when lives wear all their sorrows,
> cleaves the heart of the Death-god,
> that rider of buffaloes,
> and feeds Death's own guts
> to His famished barbaric minions.

Look at that other bull
with spotted ears,
smooth reds
on his white body.
Teased by the fighters,
he throws that daredevil, that herdsman,
with the points of his horns,

> like Ashvatthama[7] in grief and rage
> not mindful of the darkness
> whirling
> on his shoulders

45

50

55

60

65

70

75

---

5. Second son of Pandu and a hero of the
Mahābhārata. Bhima ripped open the chest
of Duhśāsana, and drank his blood, to fulfil
the vow he took when Duhśasana assaulted
Draupadi during "The Friendly Dice
Game."

6. The bull is being compared to Siva, who
wears a crescent moon in his headdress.
7. Another Mahabharata figure, son of Drona.
He sought to avenge his father's death by a
nighttime raid on the camp of the
Pandavas.

that eunuch
who slew his father.

But now the herdsmen
play flutes,
good omens   80
for you and your man
wearing blue-gem bilberry flowers.

[Saying this, the girl friend went to the man and said:]

That bull is wilder
than an elephant
gone wild: 85
do not loosen
your hand's grip
on him,
and the shoulders of our girl
will bring you victory flags.   90

Only to that man
who takes on that murderous bull,
carries a staff on his shoulder,
plays melancholy notes on his flute,
we will give our girl   95
with dark flowing hair.

Among men who take on a bull,
no one is equal to me, says he,
standing among the cows,
bragging of his power.   100

Surely, one day, not too far,
he will take us too:
for, looking at him,
my left eye throbs,
which is a good omen.   105

There, the bulls are faint,
and the men have wounds all over.
The cowherd girls
with dark fragrant hair,
taking hints   110
from their herdsman-lovers,
move into the cool groves
of jasmine.

Uruttirann
Kalittokai 101

What She Said: to Her Girl Friend, After a Tryst at Night (which Turned Out to Be a Fiasco)

My well-dressed friend,
listen to what happened.
It has set the whole village laughing.

It's the dead of night, very dark,
no sign of life,
and I'm waiting
all dressed up, lovely shawl,
best jewels,
for our soft broad-chested man,

when that old cripple, that Brahman[8]   10
turns up,
the one you're always asking me to respect,
bald head, rough blanket,
hands and legs shortened by leprosy,
the fellow who never leaves our street.   15

He bends low
to take a good look at me
and says,
        "Standing here
at this unearthly hour?
Who are you?"   20

He won't leave my side
like an old bull
who has sighted hay;
he opens his satchel, saying,
"Lady, come, have some betel,[9] won't you?"   25

I stand there, say nothing.
"Listen, girl," he says,
    stepping back a little.

"I've caught you.
I'm a demon too, but not your kind.   30
Be good to me. If you trouble me,
I'll grab all the offerings of this village,
and you'll get nothing."

And he jabbers on.
I can see by now the old fellow is a bit scared,   35
maybe thinking I'm some demon woman,

---

8. Priest, highest of the four social orders.
9. Chewing the tender leaf of betel, containing areca nut, spices, and often tobacco, is a common custom.

so I pick up a fistful of sand and throw it
in his face, and he howls and howls.

It was as if a trap laid by hunters
for a tiger, a fearless, striped, cruel-eyed tiger,
had caught instead a puny jackal.

What a sight for someone
waiting to see a lover!
The whole village is laughing
at this old Brahman whose life
is a daily farce.

Kapilar
Kalittokai 65

The Hunchback and the Dwarf: A Dialogue

Hunchback woman,
the way you move is gentle
and crooked as a reflection
in the water,
                   what good deeds
did you do that I should want you so?

   O mother! (she swore to herself) Some
   auspicious moment made you dwarf,
   so tiny you're almost invisible,
   you whelp born to a man-faced owl,
   how dare you stop us to say
   you want us? Would such midgets
   ever get to touch such as us!

Lovely one,
     curvaceous,
         convex
as the blade of a plough,
you strike me with a love
I cannot bear.
     I can live
only by your grace.

   (Look at this creature!)
   You dwarf, standing piece of timber,
   you've yet to learn the right approach
   to girls. At high noon
   you come to hold
   our hand and ask us to your place.
   Have you had any women?

Good woman,
            your waist is higher
than your head, your face a stork,
plucked and skinned,
with a dagger for a beak,
                        listen to me.
If I take you in the front, your hump
juts into my chest; if from the back
it'll tickle me in odd places.
                    So I'll not
even try it. But come close anyway and let's touch
side to side.

    Chi,[10] you're wicked. Get lost! You half-man!
    As creepers hang on only to the crook of a tree
    there are men who'd love to hold this hunch
    of a body close, though nothing fits. Yet, you lecher,
    you ask for us sideways. What's so wrong
    with us, you ball, you bush of a man.
    Is a gentle hunchback type far worse than a cake
    of black beans?

But I've fallen for you
(he said, and went after her).
O look, my heart,
at the dallying of this hunchback!

    Man, you stand
    like a creepy turtle stood up by somebody,
    hands flailing in your armpits.
    We've told you we're not for you. Yet you hang around.
    Look, he walks now like Kama.[11]

Yes, the love-god with arrows, brother to Cama.
Look at this love-god!
                    Come now, let's find joy.
you in me, me in you; come, let's ask and tell
which parts we touch.

I swear by the feet of my king.
All right, O gentle-breasted one. I too will give up
mockery.
            But I don't want this crowd in the palace
laughing at us, screaming when we do it,

---

10. An exclamation.   11. God of love.

"Hey, hey! Look at them mounting,
leaping like demon on demon!"
                                    O shape   60
of unbeaten gold, let's get away from the palace
to the wild jasmine bush. Come,
let's touch close, hug hard,
and finish the unfinished:
then we'll be   65
like a gob of wax on a parchment
made out in a court full of wise men,
and stamped
to a seal.
            Let's go.

                                    Marutanilanakanar
                                    Kalittokai 94

BASAVANNA (C. 900–1100 C.E.)
DEVARA DASIMAYYA (C. 900–1100 C.E.)
MAHADEVIYAKKA (C. 900–1100 C.E.)
India

The poems selected here—written in Kannada, after Tamil the oldest literary
language of southern India—belong to a genre termed *vachanas* (sayings,
utterances). They were composed between the tenth and twelfth centuries in the
religious community of the Lingayats or Virashaivas. This community arose in
part as a devotionalist movement opposed to the caste system of Hinduism. Thus
many of the *vachana* poets were members of the lowest caste and illiterate. The
poems typically end with a direct address to a local embodiment of the god Shiva,
one of the three major deities of Hinduism. The third poet represented here,
Mahadeviyakka, is one of a number of women who composed *vachanas*.

from **The Kannada**

BASAVANNA

[Like a monkey on a tree]

Like a monkey on a tree
it leaps from branch to branch:

Translated by A. K. Ramanujan.

how can I believe or trust
this burning thing, this heart?[1]
It will not let me go
to my Father,
my lord of the meeting rivers.

[Shiva, you have no mercy]

Shiva, you have no mercy.
Shiva, you have no heart.

Why why did you bring me to birth,
   wretch in this world,
   exile from the other?

Tell me, lord,
don't you have one more
little tree or plant
made just for me?

[You can make them talk]

You can make them talk
if the serpent
has stung
them.

You can make them talk
if they're struck
by an evil planet.[2]

But you can't make them talk
if they're struck dumb
by riches.

   Yet when Poverty the magician
   enters, they'll speak
   at once,

      O lord of the meeting rivers.

---

1. The heart as a monkey is a traditional image
   for the restless distracted heart (*manas*). In
   Kannada, the word *mana* or *manas* could
   mean either heart and mind. In this poem,
   the Lord is the Father: a favorite stance of
   bhakti or personal devotion. Other stances
   are Lover/Beloved and Master/Servant.

2. Struck by misfortune, the action of malefic
   planets. The rich unregenerate worldling is
   a familiar target in the vacanas. The Vi-
   rashaiva movement was a movement of the
   poor, the underdog.

[The crookedness of the serpent]

The crookedness of the serpent
is straight enough for the snake-hole.

The crookedness of the river
is straight enough for the sea.

And the crookedness of our Lord's men
is straight enough for our Lord!

[Before/ the grey reaches the cheek]

Before
    the grey reaches the cheek,
    the wrinkle the rounded chin
    and the body becomes a cage of bones:

before
    with fallen teeth
    and bent back
    you are someone else's ward:

before
    you drop your hand to the knee
    and clutch a staff:

before
    age corrodes
    your form:

before
    death touches you:

        worship
        our lord
        of the meeting rivers!

[Feet will dance]

Feet will dance,
eyes will see,
tongue will sing,
and not find content.
What else, what else
shall I do?

I worship with my hands,
the heart is not content.
What else shall I do?

Shiva as Lord of the Dance. Bronze sculpture from c. 1000 C.E. Tiruppulam, south India.

Listen, my lord,
it isn't enough.
I have it in me
to cleave thy belly
and enter thee

O lord of the meeting rivers!   15

[I don't know anything like time-beats and metre]

I don't know anything like time-beats and metre
nor the arithmetic of strings and drums;
I don't know the count of iamb and dactyl.[3]

My lord of the meeting rivers,
as nothing will hurt you
I'll sing as I love.

[In the mother's womb]

In the mother's womb
the child does not know
his mother's face

---

3. The familiar vacana opposition of *measure*
v. *spontaneity.* Iamb and dactyl are here
used as loose English equivalents for two metric units in Kannada.

nor can *she* ever know
his face.   5

The man in the world's illusion
does not know the Lord

nor the Lord him,

Ramanatha.

DEVARA DASIMAYYA

[A fire in every act and look and word]

A fire
in every act and look and word.
Between man and wife
a fire.
In the plate of food   5
eaten after much waiting
a fire.
In the loss of gain
a fire.
And in the infatuation   10
of coupling
a fire.

You have given us
five fires
and poured dirt in our mouths   15

O Ramanatha.[4]

[For what shall I handle a dagger]

For what
shall I handle a dagger
O lord?

What can I pull it out of,
or stab it in,   5

when You are all the world,

O Ramanatha?

---

4. Name of the devotee's god.

[The earth is your gift]

The earth is your gift,
the growing grain your gift,
the blowing wind your gift.

What shall I call these curs
who eat out of your hand
and praise everyone else?

[I'm the one who has the body]

I'm the one who has the body,
you're the one who holds the breath.

You know the secret of my body,
I know the secret of your breath.

That's why your body
is in mine.

You know
and I know, Ramanatha,

the miracle

of your breath
in my body.

[Fire can burn]

Fire can burn
but cannot move.

Wind can move
but cannot burn.

Till fire joins wind
it cannot take a step.

Do men know
it's like that
with knowing and doing?

[Monkey on a monkeyman's stick]

Monkey on a monkeyman's stick
puppet at the end of a string

I've played as you've played
I've spoken as you've told me
I've been as you've let me be

    O engineer of the world
    lord white as jasmine

    I've run
    till you cried halt.

MAHADEVIYAKKA

[O mother I burned]

O mother[5] I burned
in a flameless fire

O mother I suffered
a bloodless would

mother I tossed
without a pleasure:

loving my lord white as jasmine
I wandered through unlikely worlds.

[Would a circling surface vulture]

Would a circling surface vulture
    know such depths of sky
    as the moon would know?

would a weed on the riverbank
    know such depths of water
    as the lotus would know?

would a fly darting nearby
    know the smell of flowers
    as the bee would know?

O lord white as jasmine
    only you would know
    the way of your devotees:
    how would these,

these
    mosquitoes
    on the buffalo's hide?

---

5. Exclamation of intense feeling.

[Other men are thorn under the smooth leaf]

Other men are thorn
under the smooth leaf.
I cannot touch them,
go near them, nor trust them,
nor speak to them confidences.   5

Mother,
because they all have thorns
in their chests,
                    I cannot take
any man in my arms but my lord

        white as jasmine.   10

[Who cares]

Who cares
    who strips a tree of leaf
    once the fruit is plucked?

Who cares
    who lies with the woman
    you have left?   5

Who cares
    who ploughs the land
    you have abandoned?

After this body has known my lord
    who cares if it feeds   10
    a dog
    or soaks up water?

[Like an elephant lost from his herd]

Like an elephant
lost from his herd
suddenly captured,

remembering his mountains,
his Vindhyas,[6]   5
        I remember.

___
6. Mountain range in central India.

A parrot
came into a cage
remembering his mate,
    I remember.

O lord white as jasmine
show me
your ways.
    Call me: Child, come here,
      come this way.

10

[Better than meeting and mating all the time]

Better than meeting
and mating all the time
is the pleasure of mating once
after being far apart.

When he's away
I cannot wait
to get a glimpse of him.

5

Friend, when will I have it
both ways,
be with Him
yet not with Him,
my lord white as jasmine?

10

KABIR (C. 1450 C.E.)
North India

These songs were composed by Kabir, a fifteenth-century weaver from northern India, in the vernacular of his region. They express with great poignancy the social and religious vision of a man striving to transcend the conflicts facing him in his world—the choice between high caste and low caste, between Hinduism and Islam. The unmistakable candor, sincerity, and power of these songs have kept them an integral part of popular culture in northern India, where to this day one often hears the phrase "As Kabir says . . . ."

from *The Bijak*

[Saints, I see the world is mad]

Saints, I see the world is mad.
If I tell the truth they rush to beat me,
if I lie they trust me.
I've seen the pious Hindus, rule-followers,
early morning bath-takers—   5
killing souls, they worship rocks.
They know nothing.
I've seen plenty of Muslim teachers, holy men
reading their holy books
and teaching their pupils techniques.   10
They know just as much.
And posturing yogis, hypocrites,
hearts crammed with pride,
praying to brass, to stones, reeling
with pride in their pilgrimage,   15
fixing their caps and their prayer-beads,
painting their brow-marks and arm-marks,
braying their hymns and their couplets,
reeling. They never heard of soul.
The Hindu says Ram is the Beloved,   20
the Turk says Rahim.
Then they kill each other.
No one knows the secret.
They buzz their mantras from house to house,
puffed with pride.   25
The pupils drown along with their gurus.
In the end they're sorry.
Kabir says, listen saints:
they're all deluded!
Whatever I say, nobody gets it.   30
It's too simple.

[Brother, where did your two gods come from]

Brother, where did your two gods come from?
Tell me, who made you mad?
Ram, Allah, Keshav, Karim, Hari, Hazrat—

    so many names.
    So many ornaments, all one gold,   5

All poems in this section are translated by Linda Hess and Shukdev Singh.

it has no double nature.
For conversation we make two—
this *namaz,* that *puja,*
this Mahadev, that Muhammed,
this Brahma, that Adam,   10
this a Hindu, that a Turk,
but all belong to earth.
Vedas, Korans, all those books,
those Mullas and those Brahmins—
so many names, so many names,   15
but the pots are all one clay.
Kabir says, nobody can find Ram,
both sides are lost in schisms.
One slaughters goats, one slaughters cows,
they squander their birth in isms.   20

[Pandit, look in your heart for knowledge]

Pandit, look in your heart for knowledge.
Tell me where untouchability
came from, since you believe in it.
Mix red juice, white juice and air—
a body bakes in a body.[1]   5
As soon as the eight lotuses
are ready, it comes
into the world. Then what's
untouchable?
Eighty-four hundred thousand vessels   10
decay into dust, while the potter
keeps slapping clay
on the wheel, and with a touch
cuts each one off.
We eat by touching, we wash   15
by touching, from a touch
the world was born.
So who's untouched? asks Kabir.
Only he
who has no taint of Maya.   20

---

1. *Ghat,* with the conventional double meaning
of body and clay pot, initiates the metaphor
of pot and potter which is worked out in this
poem in detail. The potter is considered
untouchable in North India, and clay vessels
are unclean, the cheap unbaked ones being
thrown away after a single use. The body is
commonly referred to as a pot—one whose
clay, as the poet points out here, surrounds
the eight lotuses or chakras, channels of
spiritual energy. The vessels of line 10 (*ba-
san*) have the obvious secondary meaning of
passions (*basana);* one finds the word printed
both ways. The potter's wheel has been in-
ferred from *pat,* defined as a washerman's
stone slab or a millstone, but basically meaning any level surface. The pots are cut off the
wheel with a string or wire.

[When you die, what do you do with your body]

When you die, what do you do with your body?
Once the breath stops
you have to put it away.
There are several ways to deal
with spoiled flesh.   5
Some burn it, some bury it
in the ground.
Hindus prefer cremation,
Turks burial.
But in the end, one way or another,   10
both have to leave home.
Death spreads the karmic net
like a fisherman snaring fish.
What is a man without Ram?
A dung beetle in the road.   15
Kabir says, you'll be sorry later
when you go from this house
to that one.

[It's a heavy confusion]

It's a heavy confusion.
Veda, Koran, holiness, hell, woman, man,
a clay pot shot with air and sperm . . .
When the pot falls apart, what do you call it?
Numskull! You've missed the point.   5
It's all one skin and bone, one piss and shit,
one blood, one meat.
From one drop, a universe.
Who's Brahman? Who's Shudra?
Brahma *rajas*, Shiva *tamas*, Vishnu *sattva* . . .   10
Kabir says, plunge into Ram!
There: No Hindu. No Turk.

[So much pain, a mine of pain]

So much pain, a mine of pain.
You'll save yourself when you know Ram.
The Ram-knowing trick is the only trick
that doesn't land you in a trap.
The world sticks to its own tricks,   5
it certainly doesn't listen to me.
Gold, silk, horses, women,
a lot of wealth
last a little time.

From a little money
a man goes crazy.
He doesn't hear news
of the King of Death.
When the terror comes,
his face shrivels.
Cheated, he learns
his nectar was poison.
I make, I kill, I burn,
I eat, I fill
the land and water.
Spotless is my name.[2]

[No one knows the secret of the weaver]

No one knows the secret of the weaver
who spread his warp through the universe.
He dug two ditches, sky and earth,[3]
made two spools, sun and moon,[4]
filled his shuttle with a thousand threads,
and weaves till today: a difficult length!
Kabir says, they're joined by actions.
Good threads and bad,
that fellow weaves both.

[The road the pandits took]

The road the pandits took,
crowds took.

Ram's pass is a high one.
Kabir keeps climbing.

[Man in his stupid acts]

Man in his stupid acts—
iron mail from head to toe.
Why bother to raise your bow?
No arrow can pierce that.

---

2. Originally a name for God, Niranjan (without spot/stain) through sectarian mythology came to be associated with *kal* or Death.
3. Indian looms are set in dug-out places in the ground. In tantric symbolism the earth is the lowest chakra (*muladhara*) and sky the highest (*sahasrara*).

4. The *nari* (*nali/nari*, "tube") is a small spool that is inserted in the shuttle; it has a hollow center through which the thread is drawn out. The two *nadi* (channels) on either side of the spine in tantric physiology are often called sun and moon.

BANARASI (SEVENTEENTH CENTURY C.E.)
India

Written in 1641, the heyday of Mughal rule, *Half a Tale [Ardhakathanaka]* is the most striking example of autobiography in premodern India; in fact, it is virtually unique. *Ardhakathanaka* tells the story of a self-aware and articulate merchant-scholar, a member of the Jain community. (The Jains had both monastic and lay orders; members of the latter were typically merchants.) It concerns in part a search for religious meaning, although the tone is far removed from the fervent devotionalism of the preceding selections. Written in the vernacular, in this case a mixed dialect of Braj and eastern Hindi, *Ardhakathanaka* is a rare example of literary expression outside the patronage of any court. Long ignored, it is increasingly held to be an important document for our understanding of the cultural, intellectual, and social history of Mughal India, especially in revealing the new sense of self-awareness that emerged during that period.

Half a Tale [Ardhakathanaka]

My name is Banarasi, a name which carries the stamp of the city that gave birth to two Tirthankaras.[1] I will now relate to you the story of my life because it occurred to me that I should make my history public.

I will speak of my life from my early childhood to the present, describing what I saw and experienced; and to this narrative I will also sometimes add things I have heard from others. In this manner, I will relate the events of my past in broad outlines, but the future I do not know; only the All-knowing can know that.

I will narrate my story in the common language of middle India (madhyadesa), freely revealing all that lies concealed. And though I will speak to you of my virtues, I will also disclose my sins and follies.

Listen attentively friends as I unveil my past.

I am a Jain[2] belonging to the clan of Srimals, who were once princely Rajputs[3] living in Biholi, a village near the town of Rohtak in the region known as Madhyadesa of our good land of Bharat. These Rajputs were converted to Jainism under the influence of a great teacher, and, giving up their earlier life of violence, they took to the practice of wearing a mala, a garland, inscribed with the true mantra; hence they came to be called Srimals. My ancestors bore the gotra-name[4] Biholia, for they had once been defenders of Biholi.

I was now fourteen and began to develop a keen desire to pursue further studies, and so I went to Pandit Devadutt, who was a knowledgeable scholar. I studied with him a number of standard works on a wide variety of subjects. My

Translated by Mukund Lath.

1. Jain deities.
2. Religious sect.
3. Members of a high caste in North India.
4. Lineage name.

studies included two lexical texts, the *Namamala* and the *Anekarthakosa*.[5] I also took lessons in jyotisa (astronomy cum astrology), alankara (poetics), and erotics, in which latter subject I read a work called *Laghukoka*[6] by Pandit Koka. In addition, I also studied the *Khandasphuta*[7] which is a work in four hundred verses. I spent the whole of Vikram[8] 1657 intent upon studying and reflecting deeply on whatever I had learnt.

But I had also another, equally strong, passion. For I was in love and I gave myself up to this consuming passion with the whole-hearted yearning and devotion of a sufi fakir.[9] Single-mindedly I meditated upon the object of my desire. My beloved occupied my entire vision. Forever I thought of her, paying no heed to propriety or family honour. I even stooped to stealing money and jewels from my father so that I could buy her costly presents and offer her the choicest sweets. Following the right etiquette in such matters, I called myself the 'slave' of my beloved, always referring to myself as the 'poor one'.

After four months of summer had passed, the weather turned cool. During this pleasant season, two Jain sadhus[10] named Bhanchand and Ramchand came to sojourn in Jaunpur. Both were disciples of a great teacher called Abhaydharma, who was a Svetambara monk of the Kharataragaccha sect[11] of Jainism, a religion which reveals the path of fearlessness. Bhanchand was the more intelligent and knowledgeable of the two. Ramchand was yet a young boy; he still wore the attire of householders, such as novice sadhus do. Devotees of the sect to which they belonged often came piously to visit these two. I, too, followed the custom of my community and went to see them at the upasraya, a religious building where Jain sadhus stay. I became friendly with Bhanchand and my attachment to him grew so much that I spent all my days in his company, often returning home quite late at night. With him I began earnestly to study the sacred texts of Jainism. I studied a large number of works including hymns to various Tirthankaras,[12] hundreds of well-known verses on different religious topics and a treatise on the proper ritual for bathing a Jina image. I also studied texts dealing with samayika meditation and penances for sin. Besides Jain texts I also studied lexicons and works on prosody. An important work I studied was the famous *Srutabodha*. Another was the *Chandakosa*.[13] I was a diligent student and spent much time memorising texts and reciting them with the right enunciation. I had become quite religious and did my best to acquire the eight merits of a good Jain.

I also began to write and commenced work on a book called *Pancasandhi* dealing with an important aspect of Sanskrit grammar. But I was still leading a dual life. Though I was fully devoted to the task of acquiring knowledge, yet I did not give up my amorous pursuits. I composed a book of poems containing a thousand verses with love as the central theme, though, ostensibly, the book was

---

5. Dictionaries.
6. A treatise on erotics.
7. An unidentified text; its name suggests a work on astronomy.
8. Calendrical reckoning (approx. C.E. minus 57 years).
9. Muslim ascetic.
10. Ascetics.
11. A monk who goes "clothed in white" (as opposed to the naked Jain monks) and belongs to a sect especially devoted to scholarship.
12. Jain saints.
13. Treatises on metrics.

about all the major human sentiments, which have been classified as the nine rasas.[14] Reflecting back, I realize that I had become a false poet, an author of words and sentiments expressing falsehood.

Devoted thus entirely to my two consuming passions, I was doing nothing to earn money. I was so lost in the labours of love and learning that often I even forgot to eat my meals. Where then was the time for thinking of paltry things like money?

I spent two whole years in this state of abandon, despite severe admonitions from my parents. By Vikram 1659, however, I was satiated with books and amour. I now set out to fetch my bride from her father's home. I put on all my finery, and attended by a livery of servants, travelled happily in a palanquin to Khairabad, the home of my father-in-law.

I was now fifteen years and ten months old. After a month in Khairabad, I suddenly fell sick with a disgusting disease caused by a morbid condition of the windy humour (vata). The skin all over my body became like that of a leper. My very bones ached and my hair began to fall. Innumerable eruptions appeared all over my arms and legs and soon I was so unsightly that people shunned my company. My father-in-law and my brother-in-law refused to sit with me at meals. I was so repellant that none wanted even to come near me. My sins were bearing fruit once again.

In Vikram 1662 (A.D. 1605), during the month of Kartik, after the monsoon was over, the great emperor Akbar breathed his last in Agra. The alarming news of his death spread fast and soon reached Jaunpur. People felt suddenly orphaned and insecure without their sire. Terror raged everywhere; the hearts of men trembled with dire apprehension; their faces became drained of colour.

I was sitting upon a flight of stairs in my house when I heard the dreadful news, which came as a sharp and sudden blow. It made me shake with violent, uncontrollable agitation. I reeled, and losing my balance, fell down the stairs in a faint. My head hit the stone floor and began to bleed profusely, turning the courtyard red. Everyone present rushed to my help. My dear parents were in utter agony. My mother put my head in her lap and applied a piece of burnt cloth to my wound in order to stop the flow of blood. I was then quickly put to bed with my sobbing mother at my side.

The whole town was in a tremor. Everyone closed the doors of his house in panic; shop-keepers shut down their shops. Feverishly, the rich hid their jewels and costly attire underground; many of them quickly dumped their wealth and their ready capital on carriages and rushed to safe, secluded places. Every householder began stocking his home with weapons and arms. Rich men took to wearing thick, rough clothes such as are worn by the poor, in order to conceal their status, and walked the streets covered in harsh woolen blankets or coarse cotton wrappers. Women shunned finery, dressing in shabby, lustreless clothes. None could tell the status of a man from his dress and it became impossible to distinguish the rich from the poor. There were manifest signs of panic everywhere

---

14. Aesthetic moods.

although there was no reason for it since there were really no thieves or robbers about.

The commotion subsided after ten days, when a letter arrived from Agra bearing news that all was well in the capital. The situation returned to normal. Let me give you the gist of the news the letter carried. Akbar had died in the month of Kartik, in the year 1662 Vikram, after a reign of fifty-two years; now Akbar's eldest son, Prince Salim, had been enthroned as king to rule from Agra, like his father. Salim had assumed the title of Sultan Nuruddin Jahangir; his power reigned supreme and unchallenged throughout the land.

This news came as a great relief and people heartily hailed the new king.

To the joy of my parents, I, too, soon regained my health. We celebrated the end of the days of gloom with much festivity, distributing alms to the poor and gifts to friends and relations.

Soon after these events I went alone one day to my room at the roof-top and sat down to think and reflect. I began seriously to question the state of my faith and belief.

"I have been an ardent devotee of Siva," I said to myself, "but when I fell down the stairs and was severely hurt, Siva did not come to my aid." This thought nagged me constantly and made me neglect my daily ritual to Siva. My heart was no longer in it, and one day I simply put the Siva-conch[15] away.

Indeed, a strange mood had come over me. For that conch was not the only thing I put away. One day, in the company of a few close friends, I strolled down to the bridge over the Gomti, taking with me the manuscript of my book of poems on love, and began reciting verses from it to my friends. But as I read, a sudden thought violently perturbed me: "A man who utters a single lie," I reflected, "suffers in hell; yet here I am with a whole book full of nothing but falsehood—how can I ever be redeemed?" I looked down at the flowing waters, and on the spur of the moment, flung away the manuscript into the river, as though it was so much waste paper. My friends rushed to stop me from this impulsive act, but the deed was done. The folios of my poems were lying scattered over waters running deep and fearful. The book was now beyond retrieval. My friends were greatly distressed, but all they could do was to lament over the quirks of destiny.

My father was glad to hear the news. "Perhaps this is a sign that my son is undergoing a real change for the better," he happily remarked, "there is yet hope for the future of my family."

. . .

I had made two good friends, both very close and dear to me. One was Narottamdas, the grandson of Benidas of the Khobra gotra. The other was Thanmal Badaliya. The three of us were greatly attached to each other. We made a merry trio, spending all our time in each other's company.

One day, taking a carriage we went together to offer worship at a Jain shrine. After performing the usual rites of propitiation, the three of us approached the deity with folded palms and, in unison, made the following supplication: "O Lord,

---

15. Refers to an earlier episode of Banarasi's
    religious development.

grant us wealth, for then we shall have occasion to come and offer worship at your shrine again."

After that day the three of us became still more attached to each other, one in body and soul. We began to spend every hour of the day together in sweet conversation.

Then, during that year, in the spring month of Phalgun, a rich friend of ours named Tarachand Mothiya, who was a son of Nema, invited me to join him in a marriage party which was soon to proceed out of town. Balchand was the groom. Narottamdas was travelling with it and I, too, was prevailed upon to go. I began to look for some money to take with me, and sold a few pearls which I had put aside for bad times. They fetched me thirty-two rupees, which sum I took with me on my journey.

When I returned I had no money left. I hastened to sell my stock of cloth for whatever I could get and had to be satisfied with four rupees less than my cost price. I used this money to pay off some interest that had fallen due. I was free of debt but a pauper once again.

I went to see Narottam at his house. He welcomed me warmly and forced me to share his meal. I told him I was bankrupt, with nothing left and nowhere to go. He implored me to come and live with him. He assured me that I was like a brother to him and that whatever was his was also mine. His house, he added, was always open to those whom he loved. I was hesitant and protested that others in his family, especially his wife, may not like my being there. But he silenced me with these words: "Can you think of anyone in my family who will say anything to hurt you?"

He insisted that I could not refuse. He now made it a habit to address me as 'brother'; he also treated me like one, and we were always inseparable.

One day, when Narottamdas was with Tarachand Mothiya, Tarachand offered him some work. He asked Narottam to travel as his agent to Patna, taking me with him. He gave us money and we began making preparations for our departure. Then, on an auspicious day, we performed the propitiatory rites customary for people setting out on a long journey and crossed the Yamuna with tilak-marks[16] on our foreheads.

We were three of us, Narottam, I, and his father-in-law: all young, able Srimal men. We hired a carriage for our journey but took no serving men.

We had hired our carriage at Firozabad and we were to travel on it up to Shahzadpur, about half way on the road to Patna. When we reached Shahzadpur we paid our fare and decided to cover the rest of the journey on foot, hiring a porter to carry our luggage.

We decided to leave Shahzadpur as early in the morning as possible. That night, about five hours after sunset, the moonlight suddenly became very bright and we were deceived into thinking that day was about to dawn. So we immediately set out on our way. But as the light was yet dim, we could not properly make out our path. We strayed towards the south and soon entered a

---

16. Dots or stripes drawn on the forehead, here for good luck.

thick forest. It was not long before we realized that we were completely lost in the middle of a desolate jungle. Our porter suddenly lost his wits and began to scream and howl in panic. He threw down the luggage he was carrying and ran away into the wilderness. We had no choice but to carry the load ourselves. We divided it into three bundles, one for each of us. But the journey now became an ordeal. We tried to ease our burden by constantly shifting the weight from head to shoulders, but this was hardly of any help. Soon it was midnight and yet we were still far away from anywhere. We were miserable and almost demented with fatigue, singing and crying in the same breath like men who have suddenly gone mad.

After a little while, we entered a part of the forest where robbers lived in little hamlets of their own. A man espied us and shouted: "Who goes there?" We were seized with terror. Our lips were parched and suddenly glued together. We could not bring ourselves to utter a single word and began fervently to pray to God.

The man we had encountered was the chief of the robbers himself. Seeing him, I had a timely inspiration. I pronounced a benediction upon the man, chanting a sacred verse in Sanskrit in the manner of a pious Brahman. My trick worked. The robber chief took us for learned Brahmans, and approaching us, humbly bowed at our feet with deep respect. He also offered to give us shelter for the night.

"Consider me your humble servant, O venerable ones," he said. "Come with me and I will take you to my village where you can spend the night in the chaupal.[17] Do not be afraid of me, for as God is my witness, I mean you no harm."

We quietly followed the robber chief to his village, and, true to his word, he gave us a place for the night.

But we were still trembling violently with fear, our hearts pounding and our faces drained of all colour. As soon as we were alone, we hurriedly hunted for some loose yarn and quickly spun it into four sacred threads (*janeu*) such as every Brahman must wear. We then hung three of the sacred threads across our shoulders, and kept the fourth conspicuously out for all to see. Then, fetching some mud and a little water from a nearby pond, we smeared our foreheads with holy tilak-marks[18] befitting pious Brahmans. Our disguise now complete, we waited quietly for the morning to come. But we were still seized with fear and remained huddled together in a crouching position till about six hours later when light dawned and the rising sun turned the clouds red.

The robber chief approached us on a horse with a retinue of twenty men. When he came near us, he folded his palms and deeply bowed his head in veneration. I blessed him, again loudly intoning a sacred benedictory verse.

"Come venerable Brahmans, let me lead you out of the forest and show you the road," the chief said.

Obediently, we followed him with our bundles on our head. The man meant well and took us along a path that led out of the forest. After we had walked for about three kos,[19] we reached the road to Fatehpur.

---

17. Assembly hall in a village used also for shelter for travelers.
18. Here the "tilak-marks" are caste signs.

19. Literally "cry," a measure of distance (how far one can hear a human cry; calculated at a little over two miles).

"This road will take you to your destination," the robber chief assured us. Pointing to a clump of trees in the distance, he added: "There, across those trees, lies Fatehpur."

He then begged leave of us and we blessed him heartily, chanting "May you live long," and began to walk towards Fatehpur.

In Vikram 1699, my third son, the only surviving child I had, also died. His death rent my heart with agony. I was wretched and miserable with sorrow. Worldly attachments are powerful bonds, for they bind both the ignorant and the knowing. Two years have now passed since my son's death, and I still feel desolate. I find myself unable to overcome my sorrow and my attachment to his memory remains an unbearable pain.

My story is now complete. I am fifty-five years of age, and I live in Agra with my wife in reasonably comfortable circumstances. I married thrice, and had two daughters and seven sons. But all my children died. And now my wife and I are alone like winter trees that have shed all their greenery, standing bare and denuded. Looking at it in the light of the absolute vision, you may declare that as a man takes unto himself, so he sheds. But can any man rooted in this world ever see things in such a light? A man feels enriched when he takes something unto himself and utterly lost when he is deprived of even a trifle.

I will now end. But before I do so, I would like to speak to you of my present good and bad attributes.

First, then, my good points. As a poet I am matchless in composing verses on spiritual themes, which I recite with great art and impact. I know Prakrit and Sanskrit and can intone these languages with faultless pronunciation. I also know many vernacular languages. In my use of language I am ever alive to nuances of words and meanings.

My temper is naturally forgiving. I am easily content, and not readily moved by worldly cares. I am sweet of tongue and good at mixing with people for I have great forbearance and shun harsh language. My intentions are unsullied; so the counsel I give usually proves helpful to others. I have no foul or vicious habits, and I do not run after other men's wives. I have a true, unwavering faith in Jainism, and a steadfast mind which remains unshaken in its determination. I am pure in heart and always strive for equanimity.

These are my various virtues, both small and big. None of them really touch supreme heights and none are quite without shortcomings.

Now for my bad points. I said I have little of anger, pride or cunning, yet my greed for money is great. A little gain makes me inordinately happy and a little loss plunges me into the depths of despair. I am indolent by nature and slow in my work, hardly ever wanting to stir out of my house.

I do not perform sacred religious rituals; I never utter the holy mantras, never sit for meditations (tapa) and never exercise self-restraint. Neither do I perform puja[20] nor practise charity.

I am overfond of laughter, and love to poke fun at everything. I delight in

---

20. Worship.

playing the clown and acting the buffoon, indulging in these capers with great relish and gusto. I often utter things that should not be said without any sense of shame, revelling in narrating unutterable stories and escapades with much glee. I love to relate fictitious stories, often quite scandalous, and try to pass them off as true especially when I am in the midst of a large gathering. When I am in the mood for fun, nothing can restrain me from telling fanciful lies or untruths.

I sometimes break into a dance when I am alone. Yet I am also prone to sudden, irrational feelings of sheer dread.

Such is my temper. The good in my character alternates with the bad.

I have now done with all that I had to say about myself. Yet what I have said pertains mostly to my visible conduct and actions: things that could be seen or discovered by all. But in a man's life there is much that is too subtle to be so palpable. Of this, however, only God can know.

Also, I must confess that I spoke mostly of things I could best recollect. I have also deliberately remained silent about certain of my deeds which were perversities of such gross proportions that I cannot speak of them to anyone. Yet you must grant that I have not entirely shied away from speaking of my faults and follies. This at least is something quite unusual since people are careful to conceal even their smallest misdoings although they be petty things of common occurrence. A man who confesses to his faults is a Kevalin,[21] a realized soul.

But none can report all that happens, not even the all-knowing Kevalin. Even in the tiny span of a day, a man passes through myriad states of consciousness. The all-knowing Kevalin can perceive them, but even he cannot describe them in their fulness. And who can know more than the Kevalin? The wisest, most occult of sages can know only a part of what the Kevalin knows. Compared to them I am nothing but a primitive earthworm with no more than the haziest of awareness. How could I have revealed all? A man's life has much that is subtly secret and profoundly beyond grasp. What I have reported is certainly the grossest of the gross part of my life. For as I said, I have spoken mainly of my outward conduct and behaviour.

I have narrated to you the story of fifty-five years of my life. The full span of a man's life is a hundred and ten years. I have lived only half of this span. I do not know what is to come in the future. God alone can know that.

All men at all times can be divided into three categories; the truly praiseworthy, the utterly despicable, and those who fall between these two.

The truly praiseworthy men are those who, in speaking of others, speak only of their merits, deliberately drawing a veil over their faults. When such men speak of themselves, they speak only of faults and never of their merits.

The utterly despicable have just the contrary traits. They only speak of faults in others while boasting of their own merits. Never do they utter a word about their own blemishes.

I am one who falls in between. I speak unreservedly of both faults and merits in others as well as myself.

---

21. In Jain theology, one liberated from the
    cycle of rebirth.

Today, as I complete my tale, it is Monday, the fifth of the bright half of the month Agrahayana, Vikram 1698 (A.D. 1641). I now live in Agra and I am, let me repeat, a Jain of the Srimal clan, Banarasi Biholia by name and an Adhyatmi by conviction. It occurred to me that I should make the story of my life public, and so I have narrated the events that have happened during these last fifty-five years. The future I do not know; I shall face it as it comes.

The story of the last fifty-five years of my life covers half the number of days allotted to man. I have, therefore, named my story 'Half a Tale'.

Wicked men will mock at my tale. But friends will surely give it a glad and attentive ear and recite it to each other.

Before I finish I would like to extend my good wishes to all who may read my story or listen to it or recite it to others.

"SAGE IN MEDITATION." KANG HUI-AN,
1419–65. Early Yi dynasty. National
Museum of Korea.

SECTION III

East Asia: Early and Middle Periods

China
Japan
Korea

CHINA

The German philosopher Friedrich Nietzsche once suggested that the value of a nation resided in its ability to give to ordinary, daily experience the "stamp of the eternal." One can imagine the writers in this section agreeing with his criterion, for not only does it perfectly capture the effect of so much of Chinese literature, it also touches on the deepest assumptions underlying Chinese culture itself. In China, what one marvels at is the commonplace, what one celebrates is the mundane. Even as they occasionally note the strange and extraordinary, China's writers never tire of the everyday. If one had to settle on a single characteristic that most clearly distinguishes the literature of China from that of the West, it would be this resolute emphasis on the actual moment, this clear-eyed focus on the here and now.

Readers new to Chinese literature are often struck by its immense time span and essential unity of thought. China is, in fact, the oldest continuous civilization in the world, the keeper of an unbroken literary tradition stretching back some 2500 years. The earliest works of this tradition, a collection of texts known as the Confucian classics, were enshrined at the center of the educational system during the Han Dynasty (206 B.C.E. to 220 C.E.) and remained there until the early years of our own century. Studied and memorized by each succeeding generation of scholars, the histories, anecdotes, poetry, and philosophy of the classics provide an intellectual bond, a common currency of allusion and reference that links China's present effortlessly to its past for 2000 years.

On a deeper level, continuity and unity flow from the Chinese writing system itself, a system unlike those of the West in concept and implication. Unlike Indo-European languages, Chinese is not written phonetically by means of an alphabet. Rather, each word has its own unique sign—a visual emblem of the entire word-idea called a *character* or *calligraph*. Many basic characters originated as *pictographs,* drawings that visually represent what they signify. For example, the character for "sun" (日) originated as a simple line drawing of the sun (⊙). Yet even in the earliest examples of Chinese script that have been discovered—inscriptions on bone from the second millennium B.C.E.,—pictographs were being combined to form *ideographs,* representations of abstract ideas. Thus sun and moon next to each other signify "brightness" (明); the sun showing through a tree (木) signifies "east" (東).

Because they embody the meaning of a word instead of merely recording its sound, Chinese characters overcome the difficulties that arise with phonetic scripts as spoken language changes over the centuries and from region to region. Today, Mandarin and Cantonese, to name only the two most widely spoken Chinese dialects, are farther apart in sound than French and Italian. In Mandarin, the word for "shoe," for example, is pronounced *xie*; the Cantonese word is *hai*. Clearly, if they relied on a phonetic script, the two dialects could no longer communicate. As it is, the gulf between them disappears in writing, for *xie* and *hai* are written with the same character (鞋).

Writing not only links colloquial dialects to each other, it also connects them to a third entity known as classical Chinese (*wen-yen,* or "literary language"). Arising in the late fourth century B.C.E. and formalized during the Han Dynasty, classical Chinese presumably reflected the spoken language of the time. However, it survived as a purely written language, the preferred vehicle for literary expression, until the early twentieth century, even as the spoken language continued to change. Classical Chinese differs from colloquial Chinese (*pai-hua,* or "plain speech") mainly in syntax; the two overlap in vocabulary and use the same characters. Although many characters have shifted in meaning as the spoken language diverged from the classical, many key words have survived the centuries completely intact. Certain words at the heart of the culture—for example, 仁, meaning a sense of human relatedness; or 恕, meaning sympathy, forgiveness; or 孝, meaning devotion to family and respect for one's elders—are a part of today's vernacular but also occurred with virtually the same senses in ancient texts.

These fundamental facts about the Chinese language are certainly important in understanding the "conservative," seemingly immutable nature of Chinese culture. Traditional Chinese literature is still, at least partially, accessible to contemporary readers in a way that ancient literatures of other cultures are not. A student of modern English could not read the works of Chaucer without special training, whereas a student of modern Chinese could make some sense of *The Analects* (*Lun-yü),* purportedly an account of a series of discourses between Confucius and his disciples. Less than 600 years separate us from Chaucer; almost twenty-five centuries separate us from Confucius.

For Western readers approaching Chinese literature in translation, the first challenge is not so much what is said, but what is *not* said. One of the finest Western interpreters of Chinese was misled into believing that, because the word "love" does not often occur in the literature of China, there is no tradition of love poems in Chinese. If he was thinking of effusions of passion, he was right; but if he was thinking of expressions of devotion between two human beings, he could not be more wrong. Chinese writers considered emotions too intense for words. Chinese love poems are indirect—passion is conveyed subtly and with understatement. A neutral and modest reference to "feeling" will touch a Chinese reader deeply, eliciting emotions far more intense than the most lavish verbal display.

Another adjustment that Western readers must make is in their expectations of originality, which does not have the exalted place on the scale of values in China that it does in the modern West. Many images, thoughts, and attitudes encountered in Chinese writing will undoubtedly seem novel and even exotic to Western readers. But more often than not such effects are due to the disparity between Western and Chinese cultures. To Chinese readers, the same passages would probably seem reassuringly familiar, neither exceptional nor exceptionable.

What, then, do the Chinese value in their literature? One clue is a quotation from Confucius's *Analects*: "I merely transmit, I do not create; I love and revere the ancients." Chinese writers took their cue from Confucius even when they had something original to say. The virtue of their writing lay in its affirmation of age-old truths, not in the discovery of new ones. Except for a brief period called the Six Dynasties (roughly from the third century C.E. to the end of the sixth century C.E.), Chinese writers strove toward an elegance that was spare rather than contrived. Modesty of character, a major tenet of Chinese philosophy, was reflected in modesty of means, and readers admired the seeming artlessness and inevitability of the compositions. This seeming effortlessness is, of course, the product of much effort, for there is art of a very high order in Chinese writing. Chinese poets, for example, strove for their limpid style while at the same time fulfilling the demands of intricate poetic forms.

The literature of China is vast, and the selections here can give only a sample of its great variety. In addition to the obvious proportion of poetry, readers will find many snippets and extracts that are more difficult to classify—selections of philosophical discourse and aphorisms; literary anecdotes and criticism; official and legendary history. Chinese forms and genres do not find exact Western counterparts, nor, in fact, does the Chinese concept of literature. The closest Chinese term, *wenxue* (pinyin) includes both our "literature" and "literary studies." Writing commentary on the classics was a scholarly tradition from the Han Dynasty onward. In the West, we would classify such commentary as "secondary" works—derivatives rather than the genuine article. In China, however, commentary on the past is part of the ongoing literary enterprise.

Wen means not only "script" or "text," but refers to any kind of marks that reveal inner essence. The most famous instances of *wen* in this sense are the stripes of the tiger manifesting tigerness and the spots of a leopard manifesting leopardness. (Just so are Chinese characters marks that indicate essence.) *Wen* also refers to culture: the outward manifestation of an inner sense of civility that reflects virtue. *Hsüeh* means "learning," but it can also designate a "school," as in *xuexcao*. "Written learning" is an inadequate translation for *wenxue*, but it conveys something of a sense of what literature is to the Chinese. Official documents, transcribed folksongs, memorial inscriptions, philosophy, history, commentary, poetry, anecdote, fact approached through fiction, fiction grounded in fact—all are *wenxue*.

The problem with many Western presentations of Chinese literature—which includes not only popular translations but scholarly exegeses—is that too often the texts are considered as codes to be broken rather than as worlds to be inhabited. Western students have been misled to look for counterparts to their own genres and literary forms, just as Western linguists have vainly searched in Chinese for exact counterparts to their own grammar. The result has been a distortion of the value of Chinese literature on the basis of its likeness or unlikeness to Western literature. What has fascinated students of early Chinese literature in the West is not always what the Chinese value in their own tradition. To put it perhaps oversimplistically, Chinese literature does not so much embody a constant search for truth as it exemplifies a continuing reaffirmation of traditional verities.

The best of Chinese literature is astonishing by any aesthetic standards, whether Western or Eastern. The Japanese admired the Chinese canon when their own culture was being shaped. Indeed, there is a large body of original poems written in classical Chinese by Japanese scholars. The intellectuals of eighteenth-century France took a special interest in the fugitive translations of Chinese literature that were beginning to appear. Chinese literature influenced the early founders of modernism, especially Ezra Pound and the poets of the imagist group. Just as, in the 1960s, this literature became the favorite reading of many young hippie Americans, it will doubtless continue to enlighten and charm readers for centuries to come.

Historical and Cultural Background

The civilization of China arose in the fertile basin of the Yellow River not long after the first civilizations began in Mesopotamia, Egypt, and the Indus Valley; there is some evidence that Chinese civilization is even older—dating from the fifth millennium B.C.E. Ancient Chinese historical annals date the founding of China to 2852 B.C.E. and describe the eras of the Three Sovereigns, the Five Kings, and the Hsia and Shang dynasties. Modern historians long regarded all of these eras as legendary. However, archaeological finds of the early twentieth century not only validated the existence of the Shang but found that the succession of Shang kings coincided almost exactly with the list given in Chinese literary sources, leading some scholars to speculate that accounts of the Hsia Dynasty may be accurate as well. Excavations of Shang sites also yielded the earliest examples of Chinese writing.

The subsequent history of China has traditionally been told within the framework supplied by the rise and fall of dynasties, which serve as reference points for discussions of culture. We speak, for example, of a Sung Dynasty painting or a T'ang Dynasty porcelain.

In 1027 B.C.E., the Shang were overthrown by the Chou, a Chinese people to the northwest who adopted the more advanced Shang culture and established feudal rule over the Chinese city-states. In 771 B.C.E., the Chou capital fell to invaders from the west. Chou kings reestablished an eastern capital, but they never fully recovered their authority, and the Eastern Chou period was a troubled one. During the first portion, a time known as the Spring and Autumn period (770–476 B.C.E.), subordinate states grew in power and independence. The situation worsened during the treacherous political maneuvering and increasingly ruthless warfare of the Warring States period (403–221 B.C.E.). It was during these chaotic times that China's greatest philosophers were to emerge. Historians speak of "100 schools of philosophy," each offering solutions to the problems of how to govern, social organization, and individual conduct. While none of the philosophers seems to have had an effect on the rulers of his day, the three whose works are included in this section—Confucius, Lao-tzu, and Chuang-tzu— ultimately exerted a profound and lasting influence on Chinese culture.

In 256 B.C.E. the state of Ch'in overthrew the Chou Dynasty and within twenty-five years subjugated the remaining states, unifying China for the first time. As a sign of superiority over the Chou kings, the first Ch'in ruler gave himself the exalted title we translate as emperor. The Ch'in established the mechanism of central bureaucracy that would serve later dynasties well, dividing the empire into administrative units and standardizing weights and measures, currency, the width of cart axles, and the characters of the writing system. China's borders were extended in all directions, and various battlements on the northern frontier were joined to form the Great Wall. Ch'in laws, however, were cruel and severe, the products of a philosophy called Legalism. In 213 B.C.E., all books except for practical manuals on such subjects as agriculture were ordered burned, and scholars were persecuted. Classical texts survived only by being carefully hidden or committed to memory.

A rebellion brought the downfall of the Ch'in in 206 B.C.E. The leader of the victorious forces, a commoner, founded the Han Dynasty and ruled as its first emperor. The Han, divided by historians into Former or Western Han (206 B.C.E.–9 C.E.) and Later or Eastern Han (23–220 C.E.), gave Chinese culture its definitive form and served as a model for subsequent dynasties. Han emperors relaxed the stringent laws of the Ch'in, instituted Confucianism as the state philosophy, recruited scholars to staff the bureaucracy, and set up an imperial academy to train civil servants by teaching the Confucian classics. The empire expanded still farther, and Chinese control over great stretches of the Central Asian steppe resulted in the fabled Silk Road, a trade route that linked China by land to the Kushan Empire and ultimately to the Hellenistic world of Greece and Rome. Over this road, Chinese emissaries traveled to India and Persia. It was also over this road that Buddhism first began to filter back into China, where its influence would ultimately prove more lasting than in its native India.

After the first century C.E., the Han entered into a long decline, and civil unrest, palace intrigues, and rebellious generals finally brought the dynasty to a close. China now began the long era of political disunity called by historians the Six Dynasties (220–589). The history of the period is complex, but a brief summary provides the reference points needed for the literature here. China split first into three kingdoms for more than a generation. The Chin Dynasty united the two northern kingdoms in 265, and in 280 succeeded in briefly reuniting all of China. Constant invasions from the north and west, however, forced the Chin to move their capital south to Nanking, after which the dynasty is known as Eastern Chin (318–420), the first of the six dynasties centered in Nanking, for which the period is named. The north, meanwhile, experienced the rise and fall of successive kingdoms—sixteen in all—established by various invaders from the steppe. Over the course of two centuries, these peoples were gradually assimilated, and the resulting multiethnic society added great vibrancy to Chinese culture.

The Sui Dynasty, the last of the six southern dynasties, succeeded in reuniting all of China in 589, but overextended itself and was quickly succeeded by the T'ang Dynasty (618–907). Under the T'ang emperors, China once again reached out to the world. At its height, T'ang China was a vast, prosperous, cosmopolitan empire with close cultural ties to Persia, Japan, Korea (then known as Silla), and India. Caravan trade along the Silk Road was reestablished. The arts flourished, especially poetry. To search out the most brilliant minds for its bureaucracy, the T'ang emperors introduced a more highly structured version of the civil service examinations of the Han. The most prestigious degree was the *chin-shih,* a literature degree that demanded not only complete mastery of the Confucian classics but also the ability to compose poetry. The examinations established a gentry class of literati in China that served as the backbone of its government until the early twentieth century. From the T'ang on, most men of letters served for a time as government officials, and most high officials were also accomplished in the arts of poetry, calligraphy, and painting.

We use the locution "men of letters" intentionally, for Confucian philosophy relegated women to distinctly second-class citizenship. The imperial examinations were closed to them, and it was generally only in a family setting—and this rarely—that women were encouraged in scholarly or literary pursuits. Thus it was, for example, that one of China's finest historians was a woman, Pan Chao; her brother, Pan Ku, who had learned the family "trade" of writing, died, and she took over. Nevertheless, there were women writers in every dynasty. During the T'ang Dynasty, the *Ch'uan T'ang Shih,* a collection of poetry in the *shih* form included 190 women among its 2200 anthologized poets. Literacy was officially restricted to Buddhist nuns, Taoist priestesses, concubines, and courtesans, though these women were often very well educated indeed. (The situation was to eventually change somewhat: during the Ch'ing Dynasty in the eighteenth and nineteenth centuries, a period outside our present survey, a woman's ability to write poetry was considered part of her dowry.) Possibly the only class of women to keep up a steady stream of literary production were courtesans, who wrote copiously in the folk song genre and who stood by definition outside the realm of Confucian codes.

In the middle of the eighth century, T'ang power began to wane. The armies guarding the distant frontiers gathered power, weakening central bureaucratic control. The event that signaled the beginning of the end was the rebellion led by An Lu-shan, a general from the northeastern frontier who swept across China with his armies, capturing the capital and forcing the emperor to flee to the mountains. The rebellion is particularly notable because it touched the lives of the two greatest T'ang poets, Tu Fu and Li Po, and because the story of the dynasty's fleeing emperor and his concubine forms the subject of Po Chü-yi's masterpiece, "A Song of Unending Sorrow," which is included here.

After the T'ang Dynasty, China experienced fifty years of civil war, during which time the north and south again developed separately. The country was reunited in 960 under the Sung Dynasty. The Sung was another era of great cultural brilliance, especially in painting. Some of the most familiar modern technologies were invented or developed during the Sung—including gunpowder, paper currency, printing (centuries before Gutenberg), and the compass used in navigation. Wealth, luxury, and taste prevailed; trade and commerce flourished, resulting in the growth of great cities. The capital, Kaifeng, held over 260,000 households—a population estimated at more than one million people. By comparison, London at the time had a population of only 18,000.

Invading Chin Tartars forced the Sung to abandon their capital in 1126 and flee south, and for the rest of the period under consideration here China was again divided. The Southern Sung Dynasty (1127–1279) held the south; the powerful Chin Dynasty (1126–1234) ruled the north.

A Note on Transliteration

There are two systems generally used for romanizing or transliterating Chinese words in the English-speaking world. The older of the two, the Wade-Giles system, has today been largely supplanted by the *pinyin* system introduced by the People's Republic of China in the 1950s. However, because so many important scholarly works on China predate *pinyin,* a sensible practice has been established, which we follow here: Wade-Giles is used for discussions of pre-1950 or prerevolutionary China and *pinyin* is used for topics in contemporary China. At the start of each headnote, however, we include the *pinyin* version of the author's name in brackets next to the Wade-Giles version. For example, Chuang-tzu [Zhuangzi]. In some instances, such as "Shanghai" and "Wang Wei," there are no differences in the two systems.

Further Readings

Birch, Cyril, ed. *Anthology of Chinese Literature*. 2 vols. New York: Grove Press, 1972.

Chan, Wing-tsit. *A Source Book in Chinese Philosophy*. Princeton: Princeton University Press, 1963.

Liu, James J.Y. *The Art of Chinese Poetry*. Chicago: University of Chicago Press, 1962.

Liu, Wu-chi, and Irving Lo, eds. *Sunflower Splendor: Three Thousand Years of Chinese Poetry*. Bloomington: Indiana University Press, 1990.

Nienhauser, William. *Indiana Companion to Traditional Chinese Literature*. Bloomington: Indiana University Press, 1986.

CONFUCIUS (551–479 B.C.E.)
China

The man whose honorific name K'ung-fu-tzu (Master K'ung) has been Latinized since the sixteenth century as Confucius was known in his own day as K'ung Ch'iu; the name he chose for himself or his "style"-name was Chung-ni.* Born into a declining aristocratic family in the state of Lu (roughly, present-day Shantung province), Confucius was reduced to relative poverty when young and had to make a living in a number of menial occupations. He served briefly as an official during his middle years but soon returned to private life, lecturing and traveling with his disciples.

Confucius lived during an era of drastic social upheavals known as the Spring and Autumn period, when the disastrous consequences of warfare among China's numerous feudal states bred uncertainties about the meaning of life in the minds of the rulers and ruled alike. During this troubled time, Confucius emerged as a great educator, discussing many issues and addressing numerous problems in life, society, and politics. His doctrines have come to be known as Confucianism.

Lun-yü, familiar in English as the Analects, was not written by Confucius himself but was compiled by his disciples or their followers. Its twenty books or chapters contain brief, concise notes of conversations between Confucius and his disciples. (The English title is actually somewhat misleading. Lun-yü can be literally translated as "discussion talk," but it properly means "conversation" or "discourse.") The notes can be bewilderingly fragmentary, and since much of their original context has undoubtedly been lost, the meaning of certain passages is irretrievable.

During the Han Dynasty, the Analects, along with the rest of the Confucian texts, became the official "core curriculum" for scholars, a position they held until the early years of the twentieth century. As such, they helped shape Chinese thinking for more than two millennia. Probably the only work in Western civilization that can be placed on a par with the Analects, both in terms of generic form and subsequent influence, would be Plato's Republic.

Selected Analects [Lun-yü]

Someone asked Confucius how to elevate virtue, purge evil, and clarify confusion. Confucius said, "Good question! Put service first and gain after; is this not elevating virtue? Attack your own evils, not those of others; is this not purging evil? And suppose you forget yourself and affect your relatives because of a temporary fit of anger; is that not confusion?" (12:21)

Translated by Thomas Cleary.

*A Chinese author is identified not only by his given name (ming), but also by his style or courtesy name (tzu), as well as by his pen name or literary name (hao). Woman authors, however, do not always enjoy the full panoply of nominals.

A pupil asked about friendship. Confucius said, "Speak truthfully and guide them in good ways. If they do not agree, then stop and do not disgrace yourself for them." (12:23)

Confucius said to a student, "Be an exemplary man of learning, not a trivial pedant." (6:13)

Confucius said, "Not cultivating virtue, not learning, not being able to take to justice on hearing it, and not being able to change what is not good: these are my worries." (7:3)

Confucius said, "Be dutiful at home, brotherly in public; be discreet and trustworthy, love all people, and draw near to humanity. If you have extra energy as you do that, then study literature." (1:7)

Confucius said, "At the age of fifteen I set my heart on learning. At thirty I was established. At forty I was unwavering. At fifty I knew the order of Heaven. At sixty I listened receptively. At seventy I followed my heart's desire without going too far." (2:4)

One of the disciples was studying for employment.

Confucius said, "Learn a lot, eliminate the doubtful, and speak discreetly about the rest; then there will be little blame. See a lot, eliminate the perilous, act prudently on the rest; then there will be little regret. When your words are seldom blamed and your actions seldom regretted, employment will be there." (2:18)

Confucius said, "It is after the coldest weather that you know the pine and the cedar outlast the withering." (9:29)

Confucius said of his foremost disciple, "He is wise indeed! He subsists on bare essentials and lives in a poor neighborhood; for other people this would mean intolerable anxiety, but he is consistently happy. Wise indeed is he!" (6:11)

Confucius said, "Don't worry about the recognition of others; worry about your own lack of ability." (14:32)

Confucius said, "Don't worry that other people don't know you; worry that you don't know other people." (1:16)

Confucius said to a disciple, "Shall I teach you how to know something? Realize you know it when you know it, and realize you don't know it when you don't." (2:17)

Confucius said, "Uncle Tai can be said to have been perfect in virtue. He conceded kingship three times, yet the people never found out or appreciated it." (8:1)

Confucius said, "A person can spread the Way, but the Way is not to aggrandize a person." (15:29)

Confucius said, "If you associate with those who are not centered in their actions, you will become either too uninhibited or too inhibited. Those who are too uninhibited are too aggressive, while those who are too inhibited are too passive." (13:21)

Confucius said, "Cultivated people are easy to work for but hard to please. If you try to please them in the wrong way, they are not pleased. When they employ people, they consider their capacities.

"Petty people are hard to work for but easy to please. Even if you please them by something that is wrong, they are still pleased. When they employ people, they expect everything." (13:25)

Confucius said, "Cultivated people are serene but not haughty. Petty people are haughty but not serene." (13:26)

Confucius said, "Clever talkers who put imperious expressions on their faces have little humaneness indeed." (1:3)

Confucius said, "I will have nothing to do with those who are free but not honest, childlike but not sincere, straightforward but not trustworthy." (8:16)

A disciple asked Confucius, "How is it when everyone in your hometown likes you?"
Confucius said, "Not good enough."
The disciple asked, "How about if everyone in your hometown dislikes you?"
Confucius said, "Not good enough. It is better when the good among the people like you and the bad dislike you." (13:24)

Confucius said, "A knight who is concerned about a dwelling place is not worthy of being considered a knight." (14:3)

Confucius said, "When I am with a group of people all day and the conversation never touches on matters of justice but inclines to the exercise of petty wit, I have a hard time." (15:17)

Confucius said of his foremost disciple, "I can talk to him all day, and he doesn't contradict me, as if he were ignorant. From what I observe of his private life after he has gone home, however, I find he has the ability to apply what he's learned. He is no ignoramus." (2:9)

Confucius said, "See what they do, observe the how and why, and examine their basic premises. How can people hide? How can people hide?" (2:10)

Confucius said, "I do not teach the uninspired or enlighten the complacent. When I bring out one corner to show people, if they do not come back with the other three, I do not repeat." (7:8)

Confucius said, "It is all right to talk of higher things to those who are at least middling, but not to those who are less than middling." (6:21)

Confucius said, "Enliven the ancient and also know what is new; then you can be a teacher." (2:11)

Confucius said, "If you don't talk with those worth talking to, you lose people. If you talk with those not worth talking to, you lose words. Knowers do not lose people, and they do not lose words either." (15:8)

Confucius said to a pupil, "Do you think I have come to know many things by studying them?"
The pupil said, "Yes. Isn't it so?"
Confucius said, "No. I penetrate them by their underlying unity." (15:3)

Confucius said, "Study without thinking, and you are blind; think without studying, and you are in danger." (2:16)

A pupil asked Confucius, "If one is poor but does not curry favor, or is rich but not haughty, how would that be?"
Confucius said, "Fine, but not as good as one who is poor but takes pleasure in the Way, or one who is rich but still courteous." (1:15)

Confucius said, "Exemplary people understand matters of justice; small people understand matters of profit." (1:16)

Confucius said, "The knowing enjoy water, the humane enjoy mountains. The knowing are diligent; the humane are quiet. The knowing are happy, the humane are long-lived." (6:23)

When at ease, Confucius was relaxed and genial. (7:4)

Confucius said, "Even if my fare is plain and my lifestyle austere, I still find pleasure in them. Riches and status unjustly attained are to me like floating clouds." (7:15)

An official of the state of Chu asked one of Confucius' disciples about the teacher, but the disciple didn't answer. Confucius remarked, "Why didn't you say, 'His character is such that he gets so enthusiastic that he forgets to eat, and is so happy that he forgets worries; he is not conscious of impending death'?" (7:18)

A certain student was sleeping in the daytime.
Confucius said, "Rotten wood cannot be sculpted, a manure wall cannot be plastered. What admonition is there for me to give?" (5:10)

Confucius also said, "At first the way I dealt with people was to listen to their words and trust they would act on them. Now I listen to their words and observe whether they act on them. It was within my power to change this." (5:10)

Confucius said, "Good people should be slow to speak but quick to act." (4:24)

One of the disciples always used to say, "Neither harming nor importuning— how can this not be good?"
Confucius said, "How can this way be enough to be considered good?" (9:28)

Someone asked Confucius how to serve ghosts and spirits.
Confucius said, "As long as you are unable to serve people, how can you serve ghosts?"
The inquirer also asked about death.
Confucius said, "As long as you do not know life, how can you know death?" (11:12)

Confucius said, "To eat your fill but not apply your mind to anything all day is a problem. Are there no games to play? Even that would be smarter than doing nothing." (17:22)

A disciple asked Confucius, "Do cultivated people value courage?"
Confucius said, "Cultivated people consider justice foremost. When cultivated people have courage without justice, they become rebellious. When petty people have courage without justice, they become brigands." (17:23)

LAO-TZU [LAOZI] (SIXTH CENTURY B.C.E.)
China

Little can be said definitively about the life of the sage who is honorifically called Lao-tzu. According to Ssu-ma Ch'ien, a historian who lived four centuries later, Lao-tzu was named Li Erh and was from the south, possibly the state of Ch'u (roughly the region covering the present-day provinces of Hunan and Hupei). The scarcity of biographical data has fostered a supernaturalized Lao-tzu in popular literature and has led some modern scholars to question whether he actually existed at all.

Like his contemporary Confucius, Lao-tzu (assuming that he existed) rose as a profound philosopher at a time when philosophy was most needed as a remedy for social chaos. The two masters, however, stood for different, if not diametrically opposite, ideals and precepts. While Confucius considered himself a transmitter of ancient tradition, Lao-tzu questioned established values and the status quo. One of his key notions is that of Tao, or the Way things in the universe come into existence as they do. Both individuals and governments must conform to the Tao by practicing *wu wei*, or nondoing. Difficult to translate succinctly, *wu wei* does not imply passivity or inaction, but rather it serves as an injunction against "being or acting as that which you are not." Perhaps the closest we can come in current Western terms would be to say that to practice *wu wei* is to live in a state of constant epiphany before the ordinary, and to let that state guide our relations with all things in the world.

Tao Te Ching, the only work attributed to Lao-tzu, was actually not written by the sage himself. Like the *Analects* of Confucius, it is a compilation by disciples of what they had noted down or remembered of their master's sayings. Apart from its philosophical wisdom, it is marked by its artless simplicity, vivid imagery, and piquant wit.

from *Tao-Te Ching*

[Existence is beyond the power of words]

Existence is beyond the power of words
To define:
Terms may be used
But are none of them absolute.
In the beginning of heaven and earth there were no words,   5
Words came out of the womb of matter;
And whether a man dispassionately
Sees to the core of life
Or passionately
Sees the surface,   10
The core and the surface
Are essentially the same,
Words making them seem different
Only to express appearance.
If name be needed, wonder names them both: 15
From wonder into wonder
Existence opens.

[Thirty spokes are made one]

Thirty spokes are made one by holes in a hub
By vacancies joining them for a wheel's use

Translated by Witter Bynner.

The use of clay in moulding pitchers
Comes from the hollow of its absence;
Doors, windows, in a house,
Are used for their emptiness:
Thus we are helped by what is not
To use what is.

[Rid of formalized wisdom and learning]

19

Rid of formalized wisdom and learning
People would be a hundredfold happier,
Rid of conventionalized duty and honor
People would find their families dear.
Rid of legalized profiteering
People would have no thieves to fear.
These methods of life have failed, all three,
Here is the way, it seems to me:
Set people free,
As deep in their hearts they would like to be,
From private greeds
And wanton needs.

[Existence is infinite, not to be defined]

32

Existence is infinite, not to be defined;
And, though it seem but a bit of wood in your hand, to carve as you please,
It is not to be lightly played with and laid down.
When rulers adhered to the way of life,
They were upheld by natural loyalty:
Heaven and earth were joined and made fertile,
Life was a freshness of rain,
Subject to none,
Free to all.
But men of culture came, with their grades and their distinctions;
And as soon as such differences had been devised
No one knew where to end them,
Though the one who does know the end of all such differences
Is the sound man:
Existence
Might be likened to the course
Of many rivers reaching the one sea.

[There is no need to run outside]

47

There is no need to run outside
For better seeing,
Nor to peer from a window. Rather abide
At the center of your being;
For the more you leave it, the less you learn.   5
Search your heart and see
If he is wise who takes each turn:
The way to do is to be.

[Real words are not vain]

81

Real words are not vain,
Vain words not real;
And since those who argue prove nothing
A sensible man does not argue.
A sensible man is wiser than he knows,   5
While a fool knows more than is wise.
Therefore a sensible man does not devise resources:
The greater his use to others
The greater their use to him,
The more he yields to others   10
The more they yield to him.
The way of life cleaves without cutting:
Which, without need to say,
Should be man's way.

ANONYMOUS (NINTH–FIFTH CENTURY B.C.E.)

The fountainhead of Chinese poetry is the *Book of Songs* [*Shih-ching*], a compilation of 305 songs representing a variety of musical forms. Few of the songs can be accurately dated, but the bulk of them came into being approximately between 1000 and 700 B.C.E., during the Chou Dynasty. More than half are folk songs (*feng*) from various regions; the rest are categorized as courtly songs (*ya*) or ritual songs (*sung*). The bulk of the songs had been passed down orally, constantly

modified in form and language, until they were transcribed and gathered into the
Book of Songs during Confucius's time.

Credit for compiling the songs was in fact traditionally given to Confucius.
When Confucianism established its position as orthodoxy during the Han
Dynasty, the *Book of Songs* was enshrined as one of the Confucian classics—the
central texts of a scholarly education. The diction and imagery of its songs thus
influenced generations of scholars and writers.

Two of the four songs included here, "In the south is a tree with drooping
boughs" and "Where the scrub elm skirts the wood" are *feng.* The first is a song
of benediction; the second describes a hunter's seduction of a lovesick girl. The
other two songs are *ya.* "Pick a fern, pick a fern, ferns are high" is a soldier's
lament and may have been sung by soldiers in unison to keep time as they
marched. "Don't escort the big chariot" is a homily on the travails of life.

from Book of Songs [Shih-ching]

[In the south is a tree with drooping boughs]*

4

In the south is a tree with drooping boughs;
The cloth-creeper binds it.
Oh, happy is our lord;
Blessings and boons secure him!

In the south is a tree with drooping boughs;
The cloth-creeper covers it.
Oh, happy is our lord;
Blessings and boons protect him!

In the south is a tree with drooping boughs;
The cloth-creeper encircles it.
Oh, happy is our lord;
Blessings and boons surround him!

[Where the scrub elm skirts the wood]†

23

Lies a dead deer on yonder plain
whom white grass covers,
A melancholy maid in spring
                    is luck
                        for
                        lovers.

*Translated by Arthur Waley.
†Translated by Ezra Pound.

Where the scrub elm skirts the wood,
be it not in white mat bound,
as a jewel flawless found,
       dead as doe is maidenhood.

Hark!
Unhand my girdle-knot,
      stay, stay, stay
      or the dog
      may
      bark.

[Pick a fern, pick a fern, ferns are high]†

167

Pick a fern, pick a fern, ferns are high,
"Home," I'll say: home, the year's gone by,
no house, no roof, these huns on the hoof.
Work, work, work, that's how it runs,
We are here because of these huns.   5

Pick a fern, pick a fern, soft as they come,
I'll say "Home."
Hungry all of us, thirsty here,
no home news for nearly a year.

Pick a fern, pick a fern, if they scratch,   10
I'll say "Home," what's the catch?
I'll say, "Go home," now October's come.
King wants us to give it all,
no rest, spring, summer, winter, fall,
Sorrow to us, sorrow to you.   15
We won't get out of here till we're through.

When it's cherry-time with you,
we'll see the captain's car go thru,
four big horses to pull that load.
That's what comes along our road,   20
What do you call three fights a month,
and won 'em all?

Four car-horses strong and tall
and the boss who can drive 'em all
as we slog along beside his car,   25
ivory bow-tips and shagreen case

†*Translated by Ezra Pound.*

to say nothing of what we face
sloggin' along in the Hien-yün war.

Willows were green when we set out,
it's blowin' an' snowin' as we go   30
down this road, muddy and slow,
hungry and thirsty and blue as doubt
(no one feels half of what we know).

[Don't escort the big chariot]*

206

Don't escort the big chariot;
You will only make yourself dusty.
Don't think about the sorrows of the world;
You will only make yourself wretched.

Don't escort the big chariot;   5
You won't be able to see for dust.
Don't think about the sorrows of the world;
Or you will never escape from your despair.

Don't escort the big chariot;
You'll be stifled with dust.   10
Don't think about the sorrows of the world;
You will only load yourself with care.

CHUANG-TZU [ZHUANGZI]

(369–286 B.C.E.)

China

Chuang Chou, known by his honorific name of Chuang-tzu, was a native of the
state of Sung, today's Honan province. Born into an aristocratic family, Chuang-
tzu grew up in a rich tradition of learning and refinement. Nevertheless, except
for a short stint as a clerk in the local government, he declined all offers of official
positions. Chuang-tzu's noninvolvement in public affairs was in keeping with his
adherence to the Taoist principle of nondoing, which he learned from his master
Lao-tzu. As a philosopher, Chuang-tzu's major contribution was his exploration
of relativism—the idea that there are no absolute qualities, only individual

*Translated by Arthur Waley.

viewpoints. His concerns are a natural extension of the Taoist insistence on reverence for the uniqueness of all creation.

Chuang-tzu lived during the Warring States period, a time that saw the numerous small states of China consolidated into seven major kingdoms. It was in the wake of this step toward unification of the nation that the formation of the writing style known today as Classical Chinese began. The sophistication of the new style enabled Chuang-tzu to include descriptive amplifications in his narrative, in contrast to the sketchiness of the *Analects* and the *Tao-te Ching*.

In his writings, Chuang-tzu characteristically uses fictions—stories and parables—to illustrate truths. "Wandering About at Large" focuses on the theme that the world of each of us is necessarily provincial, because each person's perspective is limited. We are tempted—both as individuals and as a species—to see our world as the "real" one, but our experience determines what we know and what we can imagine. "The Identity of Things" attacks hierarchical notions of reality (that one thing is more important than another, for example, or that one being is superior to another). It also explores the flaws in our tendency to bipolar logic—the world of either/or choices: this/that, right/wrong, light/dark. All interpretation is an imposition, according to Chuang-tzu, and it has the pitfall of reducing phenomena to abstract meaning—seeing "treeness," for example, rather than the tree itself. Taoism suggests that such abstractions can cause us to lose contact with reality.

"In the World of Men" teaches us that utility is a subjective concept, not an inherent quality in things or ideas. The proper question is not, Is *x* useful? but rather, For whom is *x* useful, and when? To be useless to others, it turns out, may be quite useful to one's self, and wisdom may even reside in being useless to as many others as possible. In "Autumn Waters," the final selection, Chuang-tzu ridicules a famous ancient logician who thought he understood everything because he could reduce everything to analytical abstractions. Chuang-tzu attacks this form of knowledge as narrow and provincial. Persuasive as analytical understanding appears to be, its mode of investigation is to "take apart," whereas true knowledge, Taoists maintain, is direct and unanalytical. True understanding transcends analysis: as Lao-tzu would say, "The truth cannot be told."

Wandering About at Large

In the vast reaches of the north there is a fish named K'un: its size cannot be gauged but it is at least several thousand leagues (*li*). When transformed into a bird, its name is P'eng. P'eng's span is beyond measuring: at least several thousand leagues. When it rages, its wings are like a cloud hung from heaven. This bird, when the sea moves, migrates toward the southern reaches, called the Pool of Heaven. In the Book of Wonders many strange things are recorded: it says there that when the P'eng migrates to the southern reaches, the waters are stirred for three thousand leagues; when it beats its wings, a typhoon results, and when it rises ninety thousand leagues, it leaves behind a gale that lasts for six months. Horses in the wild, bits of dust, living things are all blown about. The blue-azure of the sky, its true color, is distorted; its remoteness and limitless horizon is distorted; from its vantage point from above, it would be as it was.

Translated by Eugene Eoyang.

Moreover, if the depths of the water are not great, then there is not buoyancy enough to float a large boat. Pour out a cup of water into a hollow in the ground, and a mustard seed will float on it; put the *cup* in the water, and it will become stuck: the water is shallow and the vessel large. If a wind lacks force, it will lack the strength to keep great wings airborne. To rise ninety thousand leagues therefore requires this kind of wind from below: only then can it be mounted. With the blue sky at its back, and nothing to stop him and nothing in his way, he heads south.

The cicada and the dove laughed and said: "We take off and dart from elm to elm: there are times when we don't make it and fall to the ground. How can anything travel south flying at ninety thousand leagues? Three meals on an outing to the country and one returns, with the belly still full; for a trip of a hundred miles, grain must be pounded the night before; and for a trip of a thousand miles, three months' provisions must be stored." What do these worms know? A little knowledge does not amount to great wisdom; a few years of life is not the same as many years of experience. How does one know? The morning-glory [literally "the morning mushroom"] knows nothing of moonrise and moonset: one season's cicada knows nothing of spring and autumn. They live only a short term. South of Ch'u, there is a tree called Ming-ling, which counts five hundred years as one spring and five hundred years as one autumn. In very ancient times, there was a great tree for which eight thousand years was one spring, and eight thousand years one autumn. Even down to the present, Peng-tsu is well-known for his longevity. If everyone were to compare themselves to him, wouldn't they feel sorry for themselves?

The questions T'ang asked of Chi say the same thing: "In the sparse wastes of the north there is a vast ocean, the Pool of Heaven, with a fish several thousand leagues wide and who knows how long, named K'un. There is also a bird named P'eng, with a back like T'ai Mountain, wings like clouds hanging down from the sky. Flapping up a whirlwind winding around like goat-horns, it rises ninety thousand leagues, breaking through the clouds, and with only the blue sky at its back, it heads toward the south, and the southern deep. The marsh quail laughed at this and said: "So what? I take off and go up for some distance before I glide down amidst weeds and brambles. This is also the ultimate in flying. So what?" Which shows the difference between the little and the great. So it is that those who know how to govern a district, to administer a region, and who have the virtues of a ruler that qualify them for leading a nation, they all regard themselves in this way. Yet, Sung Jung-tzu would have laughed at them, for though the entire world censures him, he would not have been crushed. He firmly distinguished between what he thought of himself and what the world thought of him and he clearly marked off the limits of honor and of shame. But this is as far as he went. Toward the world, he was in no way unsettled. He had not yet grounded himself firmly.

Lieh-tzu rode on the wind, and took to its airy ways, but he returned in a fortnight. In matters of his own welfare, he had no worries. Still, while this enabled him to avoid moving about on his own, he had, nevertheless, to depend on something else. Whether one depends on the processes of heaven and earth or seizes upon the shifts in the six elements, one will wander ceaselessly, and this is the evil of being dependent. Therefore, it is said that the supreme man is without self; the holy man is without merit; *the exalted man is anonymous.*

Yao wished to yield his throne to Hsü-yu and said: "When the sun and moon come out in the midst of torch fires that burn steadily, wouldn't it be difficult to see them in the glare? When seasonal rains fall, wouldn't irrigating the marshland be too much effort? Then you should take over the reins of government, for if I continue to administer the country, all I would see would be my own shortcomings. Please take over." Hsü-yu answered: "With you in charge, the country is under control; if I were to stand in your place, it would only be for vanity. But vanity is only the shadow of reality, and I would be but a shadow. The wren may build its nest in a thick forest but he uses only one branch; the tapir may drink from the stream, but only to quench his thirst. Go back, my lord, I would be of no use in government. Even if a cook is not attending to the kitchen, the master of ceremonies does not skip over the sacrificial vessels to take his place."

Chien-wu said to Lien-shu: "I have heard Chieh-yü talk. His words are big but not to the point; they wander all over the place but never hit home. I am overwhelmed by his words: they are like the stars of the Milky Way, and as numberless. But they are beside the point and have nothing to do with the world of men."

"What kind of talk?" Lien-shu asked.

"He said: 'Far away in the mountain of Ku-she, there lived a holy man. His flesh was like ice and snow, and he was as tender as a young maiden. He didn't eat five grains but inhaled the wind and imbibed the dew. He rode the cloud-drifts and mounted a flying dragon, and wandered beyond even the four seas. His intense powers spared creatures from disease and caused the crops to flourish every year.' To my mind, these words were mad, so I didn't believe them."

Lien-shu said: "Of course. A blind man cannot appreciate the sight of an elegant figure, nor a deaf man the sound of a bell and drum. Yet who's to say only the body may be afflicted with blindness and deafness? It can happen to the mind as well—as your words demonstrate! This man has the virtues of responsiveness: to comprehend a thousand things as one. Though the world calls out of its chaos, who would manage its affairs? This man cannot be harmed by things: though the floodwaters reach heaven, he would not drown. In a great drought, when metal and stone melt and the hills and mountains are scorched, he will not be hot. From his earthly remains one could fashion a Yao or a Shun, so why would he be willing to manage such things? A man of Sung, who sold ceremonial caps, went to Yüeh, but the people of Yüeh cut their hair short, and decorated their bodies, so had no use for them. Yao ruled over the people in the world, and controlled the governments within the seas, yet after, when he went to see the Four Masters in far-away Ku-she Mountain, south of the Fen River, he mourned deeply for his kingdom.

Hui-tzu said to Chuang-tzu: "The King of Wei left me a melon seed. I planted it and it grew to a size that could contain fully five gallons. With liquid in it, it was too heavy to lift. Cut in two for ladles, there was nothing that it wasn't too big for. Therefore, because it was useless, I broke it up."

Chuang-tzu said: "You are obtuse in matters concerning the importance of usefulness. There was a man of Sung who excelled at concocting an ointment for chapped hands. For generations, his family was in the business of treating silk. A stranger heard of this, and offered to buy the method for a hundred pieces of gold. Whereupon the family was convened, and they all agreed: 'For generations we have treated silk and never earned more than a few pieces of gold. Now one morning we can sell it for a hundred pieces. Give it to him.' The stranger took it and went to advise the King of Wu, who was having difficulties with Yüeh. The King of Wu sent him to command his forces. It was winter. There was a naval battle with Yüeh, and Yüeh suffered a great defeat. The conquered territories were parceled out, and he received a fiefdom. Now, the properties of the ointment were the same—whether to prevent chapped hands (which may be used to gain a fiefdom), or to treat silk. The difference lies in how you use it. Now, you have a gourd that holds five gallons: why not make a large vessel out of it, to float down the river with? Instead, you worry that it is too big. It appears you still have cobwebs in your head."

Hui-tzu said to Chuang-tzu: "I have a big tree which people call 'the tree of heaven.' Its large roots are so dense and swollen as to be beyond measuring; its small branches are so twisted that they can't be lined up with a straightedge. If it were standing in the road, a carpenter wouldn't even take notice. Now your words are equally large and useless. Which is why the multitudes pay no attention."

Chuang-tzu said: "You alone do not notice the wildcat, how it crouches low to lie in ambush for the unwary. It leaps everywhere, nothing is too high or too low until it falls into a trap and perishes in the net. Then, there is the yak—as big as a cloud dropped from heaven, really huge! But it cannot catch mice. Now, your big tree bothers you because it is useless. Why not plant it in Never-never land, in the great barren wastes, where you can stroll to and fro beside it and can lie down free and easy beneath it? It will not be axed, and it will be free from harm. What possible distress could uselessness cause?"

The Oneness of Things

Tzu-ch'i of the Southern Suburb sat at his place, leaning against a table, looking up at the sky, and sighed. Distracted, he looked as if he had lost touch. Yen-ch'eng tzu-yu was standing by, in front of him, and said, "What's this? Your body could be a withered tree, and your mind is like dead ashes. Surely the person leaning at this table today is not the same person who was leaning at this table before?"

Tzu-ch'i said, "Yen, don't you start asking. Just now, I was outside myself. Do you understand? You hear the sounds of humans, but know nothing of the sounds of the earth. Or if you have heard the sounds of the earth, you haven't heard the sounds of heaven."

Tzu-yu said: "Would you please explain that?"

Tzu-ch'i replied: "The Great Earth exhales, and it is called 'wind.' There are times when it doesn't blow. But when it does, a thousand caves will bellow. Are you the only one who has never heard the rushing of the wind? The awesome

Translated by Eugene Eoyang.

heights of the mountain forests, the hollows of huge trees—a hundred span around—are like noses, mouths, ears, goblets, bowls, puddles, pools. And the wind whistles, exclaims, sighs, howls, wails, moans, first high notes, then low notes. A light wind produces minor chords, a gale brings forth major chords. When the fierce wind blows over, all the stops are empty. Have you not noticed this in the swaying and bending of trees in the wind?"

Tzu-yu said: "The music of the earth is made through countless hollows; the music of humans is made on the pipes; may I ask about the music of the spheres?"

Tzu-ch'i said: "These melodies are all different, but every one of them is self-generated, all of them self-realized. Who is there that would initiate these sounds? Great understanding opens up; small knowledge closes in. Great discourse is limpid and clear; small discourse is petty and wordy. Asleep, the soul wanders; awake, the body is set free. Associations mean involvement, and every day one mind contends with another. There are hesitations, inhibitions, and qualms. Small fears are annoying; large fears disturbing. Some set out like a mechanical contrivance with the function of making out what is from what is not; others maintain themselves with alliance pacts, taking charge to keep up their superiority. Some decay and die as in autumn and winter, while their words daily diminish: others sink so far that they cannot come back again. Some are repressed, as if all bound up; their words outdated, like a dried-up moat, their hearts edging toward death, incapable of regeneration.

Joy and outrage, sorrow and happiness, anxiety and relief, flexibility and firmness, sedateness and agitation—these express our moods. Music derives from the void, and moisture produces mushrooms. Day and night alternate with each other and no one knows from whence they sprout. Oh, my! Dawn and dusk bear this out: if we ask their origin. Without them, there is no I; and without an I, there is nothing to experience them. This is very near to the truth, but we do not know what makes it so. If this is the reality of things, it would be difficult to solve their mysteries. I believe this reality to be possible, but I cannot see its manifestations. It exists, but without form. The hundred joints, the nine apertures (eyes, ears, nose, mouth, nostrils, etc.), the six organs (heart, liver, spleen, lungs, kidneys, etc.) all coexist together. Which one am I most attached to? Which would you say? Their existence is an internal matter: as if all were functionaries. These functionaries are not up to governing themselves, and take turns as governor and governed, and thus retain true governance. Whether you find the reality or do not find it, it does not matter, for reality itself is unaffected. Once the parts are in place, they operate without interruption to the very end. Whether on edge with each other, or working smoothly together, the process exhausts itself like a runaway horse that cannot be stopped. Isn't this a shame? To sweat and strain all one's life, with no sign of accomplishment; blithely working oneself to death and not know to what end one is working toward, is this not pitiful? One may say: 'there is no death' but to what purpose? When the body wears out, the spirit goes with it. How can this not be called sad? Is the life of man so thoughtless? Or am I alone so blithe when everyone else is not?

Men are influenced by what they think: Who alone is not so influenced? And not only those who know the ups and downs and who think for themselves: fools also have such thoughts and influences. To not have such thoughts about what is and what is not, is like going to Yüeh today and arriving there yesterday. It would be like making something that isn't, is. To make something that isn't—though one had the powers of the sage Yü—would be impossible to know. How could I know it, then?

Words are not mere wind: words have something to say; what they say, however, is not absolute. So, do words exist? Or don't they? There are those who distinguish words from the chirping of birds. Some see a difference there and some see no difference at all.

How can the Tao be both obscure to the perceptions and distinguishable as true and false? How can words be obscure and real or unreal? How can the Tao be past and yet not present? How can words be present and not possible? The Tao is obscured by small-mindedness. Words are obscured by vain-gloriousness. Thus, the "right" and "wrong" of the Confucians and the Mohists.[1] What one calls "right" the other considers "wrong": and what one calls "wrong," the other considers "right." If one wishes to make "right" the other's "wrong," and to make "wrong" the other's "right," there is nothing better than insight.

There is nothing that is not object (a "that"), and nothing that is not subject (a "this"). The self does not see itself as the "other"; the self, however, knows the "other." Which is why it is said: " 'That' derives from 'this'; and 'this' also proceeds from 'that.' " Which is saying that "this" and "that" arise from each other. Where there is life there is death; where there is death, there is life. Where there is possibility, there is also impossibility, and where there is impossibility, there is possibility. Because reality exists, so too unreality; and if unreality exists, so does reality. Existence in the eyes of the sage is not seen this way, but in the light of eternity, the truth is determined. For "this" is also "that," and "that" is also "this." According to "that" there is a true and false; according to "this" there is a true and false. Thus, there is a "that" and a "this": or is there no "that" and no "this"? To resist opposing "that" and "this" is the very point of the Tao. This point is the center of a sphere of innumerable mutual influences. The "trues" are as number-less as the "untrues." Which is why it is better to use insight. To point to something that is to illustrate something that is not is not as good as to point to something which is not to illustrate what is not. To use a horse to illustrate what isn't a horse, isn't as good as using what isn't a horse to illustrate that a horse is not something else. All creation is an index; everything is a horse.

The possible is possible; the impossible impossible. The Tao follows this course to achieve its purpose. Things are merely labeled to be so. But do they exist? That which exists, exists. Or do they not exist? That which is nonexistent does not exist. Things which are, therefore, exist; things which are, therefore, are possible. Nonexistent things do not exist; nonexistent things are not possible. Which is why a rafter and a pillar, ugliness and the beauty Hsi Shih, greatness,

---

1. The Mohists formed a school that followed the precepts of Mo-tzu, a contemporary of Confucius who preached a doctrine of universal love, and who based his teachings on the concept of righteousness (i)—whereas Confucius based his ethics on the concept of relatedness (jen). From the fifth century to the third century B.C.E., the Mohists constituted the bitterest rivals of the Confucian school.

cunning, craftiness, strangeness, in the scheme of the Tao, are all one. Individual-ities comprise the whole; but the whole diminishes them. All things—incomplete or diminished—can yet be regarded as one. Only those with transcendent wisdom can see through to things as one. Reality is not used but seen from the multiplicity of things. This multiplicity has its "uses"; these "uses" are effective; this "effective-ness" is successful. When success is achieved, the ultimate is reached. When the ultimate is reached, and one doesn't know what it is, we call it the Tao.

To work the spirit and the mind as one, and not know they are identical, is like "three in the morning." What is "three in the morning"? A keeper of monkeys, distributing acorns, said: "Only three acorns and four at night." The monkeys were incensed. "Well, then," he said, "You'll have four in the morning and three at night." At this, the monkeys were well pleased. What one calls reality has no consequences on the reality, but does affect the response, whether of anger or satisfaction. The cause for this is subjectivity.

The sage accommodates himself to reality and nonreality, abides by the scales of Heaven. This is called the two-fold path.

The knowledge of the ancients was ultimate. How? They were not yet aware that things existed. That was ultimate and exhaustive, and could not be improved upon. Then they recognized the existence of things, but had yet to make distinctions between them. Finally, they began to make distinctions, but had yet to distinguish between reality and unreality. When reality and nonreality appear, the Tao is undermined. As the Tao fails, so the affections succeed. Now, is this success and this failure real? Or are they unreal? If this success and failure are real, then Chao-wen plays the lute; and if they aren't, he doesn't play. Chao-wen's lute, Shih-kuang's baton, Hui-tzu's rhetoric: their knowledge—all three—was incom-parable, and each excelled in an art which he practiced to the end of his life. Because they loved their art, they were different from others. And because they loved their art, they wanted to make it clear to others. But they were not enlightened as a result of their efforts. Which is why one ends up with obscure abstractions as hardness (in a stone) and whiteness (in a horse). His son played with Chao-wen's instruments all his life, and all his life never realized anything. If this can be called realization, than I am also realized; but if this cannot be called realization, then everything, including me, remains unrealized. Therefore the glimmerings out of chaos are valued by the Sage. He doesn't use reality but derives what is called insight from within the multitude of things.

Now, there are words, like these. I don't know if they are of the same order as that which is real. Perhaps they are not of the same order. Of, and not of, the same order. They may be of the same order, but they may be different from the other nonentities. Never mind. Let's try these words: There was a beginning; there was a time before the beginning began; there was a time before the beginning of a beginning of a time before the beginning. There is existence; there is nonexis-tence. There is a time before existence and nonexistence; there was a time before the time before there was nonexistence. When, all of a sudden, nonexistence came into being, no one knew whether the roots of nonexistence lay in existence or nonexistence. Now, though I have just said something, I do not know whether what I have said really said something, or whether it said nothing. In all the world, nothing is as big as the tip of a wisp in autumn, and Mount T'ai is small. There's no one older than a child who is short-lived and Peng-tsu is young. The universe and I were both created at the same time, and the multitude of things and I are one. But, if they are one, what about words? If you consider those things as one, they are not words. The one with words would make two. Two and one would make three. And so it goes. If skilled mathematicians are not up to this, how about ordinary people? Thus, from nonexistence proceeding to existence, one reaches three, what would happen if one proceeded from existence to existence? Let's not proceed. Let's stop here.

The Tao existed before there were distinctions, and words existed before posterity. To cope with reality, demarcations were set up. And words indicated those demarcations. There is a "left" and there is a "right"; there are "discussions" and there are "deliberations"; there are "distinctions" and there are "discriminations"; there are "contentions" and there are "rivalries." These are the so-called "eight propositions." Things outside the universe, the sage allows but does not discuss. Things within the universe, the sage discusses but does not decide. In the *Ch'un Ch'iu,* which documents history and the annals of ancient kings, the sages discussed but did not dispute. True, there are distinguishable things, but there are also things not distinguishable, as there are things that can't be discriminated.

"How is that?"

"The sage comprehends the thing itself, while the common man contrasts things with each other. Which is why it is said that the one who makes distinctions does not see. Thus, the great Tao is inexpressible; the great distinctions are beyond words; great virtue is in not being virtuous. Great modesty is not humble; great courage is not bold. The Tao on display is not the Tao; words that split hairs do not see to the heart of the matter. Constant benevolence fails. Flagrant modesty will not be believed. Presumptuous courage will not succeed. These five attributes seem to be round, but tend toward being square. Therefore, wisdom that stops at what it does not know is the highest wisdom."

Who knows the distinction that cannot be expressed, the Way that cannot be expressed, the Way that cannot be followed? If there is such a one who possesses this knowledge, then he holds what is called the "storehouse of the heavens"—which may be replenished but is never full, drained but never empty, the source for which is unknown. This is called "the light within."

Long ago, Yao asked Shun: "I wish to attack Tsung, Kuei, and Hsü-ao in the south, but I can't figure out why? Can you tell me?"

Shun said: "Those are three backwater countries. It's no wonder you can't explain it. Long ago, ten suns emerged among the multitude of things, and shone on everything. By how much does the radiance of virtue exceed these suns?"

Yeh-Chüeh asked Wang I: "Do you know in what way things are identical?"

"How should I know?"

"Do you know those things which you don't know?"

"How should I know?"

"Then, how about the ignorance of things?"

"How should I know?" came the reply once again, "but let me try this: How do I know that what I think I know isn't something I don't know? How do I know that what I think I don't know isn't really something I really do know? Now, let me ask you this: people who sleep in the damp end up half-dead, with an ache in their back—but what about the mudfish? To live in the trees is perilous and precarious,—but what about a monkey? Now, of these three, who has the right idea of a place to live? Men feed on the flesh of herbivores; deer feed on autumn grass; centipedes find locusts tasty; owls relish mice. Of the four, who knows how to eat? Monkeys cohabit with monkeys; buck with doe; mudfish sport with other fish. Men find Mao Ch'iang, or "the beautiful concubine," attractive: but fish would dive for the deep at the sight of her, birds would head for the skies, and deer would dart away for dear life. Of these four, who knows what beauty is? The way I see it, the principles of righteousness and benevolence, the path of right and wrong, is a morass of confusion—how can I possibly know the difference?"

Yeh-Chüeh said: "If you do not know what is good or bad, then must it be that the perfect man also does not know?"

Wang I said: "The Perfect Man is superhuman: when the great marshes are scorched, he is not burned; when the great waterways freeze over, he feels no cold; when the mountains are split asunder by bolts of lightning, and the seas tremble in the typhoon, he is not frightened. Such a man rides the clouds, mounts the sun and the moon, and wanders beyond the four seas. Death and life have no effect on him, so how can notions of good and bad?"

Chü-chüeh-tzu asked Ch'ang-wu-tzu: "I have heard the Masters say, 'The exalted man does not concern himself with the affairs of the world, he does not achieve rewards, nor avoid penalties; he is not curious to find out; nor does he explain the ineffable. He has no utterance for what can be expressed, but he can communicate the inexpressible.' Thus, he roams beyond the reach of the dirt and dust of this world. The Master considered this idle talk, but I consider it the workings of the mysterious Tao. I ask you, what do you think?"

Ch'ang-wu-tzu said: "The Yellow Emperor himself would hear these words with skepticism, so how could you expect Confucius to understand them? Besides, you jump to conclusions: you see an egg and look for a cock to crow; you see a cross-bow and envision a duck roasting on a spit. Let me try out a few conjectures on you, which I want you to consider as conjecture. How does one stand by the sun and moon and hold the universe in one's hands? The one who does, relates one thing to another, puts aside chaos and confusion, and treats menials on a par. The ordinary man shifts about, while the sage is ingenuous. Ten thousand years are as one, pure and simple; ten thousand things pursue their course, and exist together. How do I know that love of life is not an illusion? How do I know that fearing death isn't like the lost soul weeping because he cannot find the way home? "Beautiful concubine" was the daughter of Ai, the border guard. When she was captured by Chin, tears flowed onto her dress but when she arrived at the palace, and shared the royal couch, and ate the most sumptuous food, she then wondered why she had wept at all. How do I know that the dead do not regret their first quest for life? Those who dream of getting drunk may end up by morning in tears; those who dream of crying and sobbing may find themselves hunting in the fields when day breaks. In a dream, one is not aware one is dreaming; indeed, one can even interpret a dream in the midst of the dream. Only when awake does one know one has been dreaming. Maybe there will be one day a great awakening at which we will realize that this life has been one great dream. Fools think they are awake, and know it with insistence, whether prince or pauper. Confucius and you are both part of a dream; when I say you are part of a dream, I am also dreaming. These assertions are paradoxical: thousands of generations from now, a great sage will appear and explain them in a day.

Suppose you and I argue; you win out instead of me; is your argument right, mine wrong? Or, suppose I win out instead of you, is my argument right and yours wrong? Must one be right and the other wrong? Or can both be right, or both wrong? You and I cannot reach any agreement, so meanwhile people are left in the dark. Who should I get to set things right? If I choose someone who agrees with you as the arbiter, then he will agree with you in his judgment, so how can he be fair? And if I choose one who agrees with me as arbiter, then he will agree with me, so how can he be fair? And, if I choose someone who disagrees with both you and me, then he will differ from both of us, so how can he be fair in judging between us? And, if I choose someone who agrees with both you and me, then he will agree with both of us, so how can he judge between us in all fairness? As a result, you, I, everyone cannot come to understand each other, and wait for someone else. What is the so-called "harmony with the workings of heaven"? Let us consider: "We have 'is' and 'is not,' 'right' and 'not right'; but if 'is' exists, then the opposite of 'is' must be 'is not' and there is no distinction. If there is a 'right' then the opposite of 'right' must be 'not right,' and there would be no distinction. The mutual dependency of changing sounds, if they do not depend on each other, is said to "harmonize with the workings of heaven." Because of this, one can live out the years in boundless fulfillment. Forget the years, forget notions of right and wrong, and you will establish yourself in the realm of the infinite."

Shade asked shadow: "Before, you moved about, now you stay still; before, you sat down, now you get up. Why are you so shiftless and lacking in purpose?"

Shadow replied: "My existence depends on the existence of something else; that on which my existence depends itself depends on something else. My dependence is like the skin shed by a snake, or the wings of a cicada. How do I know what will happen? How do I know when something will not happen?"

Once Chuang Chou dreamed he was a butterfly, fluttering happily about like a butterfly. It did not know it was Chuang Chou. Suddenly it awoke and realized it was Chou. Now, we don't know whether it was Chou dreaming he was a butterfly in his dream, or a butterfly now dreaming it was Chou. There must be a difference between Chou and the butterfly: this is the so-called "transformation of things."

from *In the World of Men*

[The Usefulness of Trees]

A carpenter named Shih went to the kingdom of Chi: when he reached Ch'ü-yüan he saw an oak tree used as an altar: its girth was wide enough to hide oxen; it

Translated by Eugene Eoyang.

spanned a hundred cubits, its height approached the mountains; at eighty feet, the branches spread out, a score or more, each the size of a small boat. Crowds milled around it, but the master carpenter didn't give it any notice, and went on without stopping. His apprentice stared his fill and, catching up to Carpenter Shih, said: "Since I picked up the axe and followed in your service, I have never seen a piece of wood to match this tree. Why does the Master walk right by without glancing at it even for a moment?"

"That's enough. Don't waste your breath. That's a worthless piece of wood. If you made a boat out of it, it would sink; if you made a coffin, it would rot in no time; if you made furniture out of it, it would collapse on the spot; if you made a door, the sap would seep through; if you made a pillar, it would be worm-eaten. It's a completely worthless piece of wood, and because it is so useless, it has lived so long."

Later, when Carpenter Shih had returned home, the oak tree appeared to him in a dream: "Why do you make comparisons with me? Are you comparing me with 'usable' trees? Like the pear, the orange, the grapefruit, and all species of fruit-bearing plants? When the fruit ripens, they are stripped and treated ignominiously: first, the big branches are cut, and the little branches are pulled off. Thus the value of the trees embitters their life, they are not allowed to live out their heaven-ordained years, are cut off midway in their life span. They bring upon themselves the mutilation and abuse of the mob. There is nothing that this does not apply to. So I cultivated uselessness for a long time. Near death now, I have reached this state, and that is of great use to me. Let us suppose I were useful, do you think I would have attained such a size as this? Besides, you and I are both things. By what right does one thing judge another? And what does a worthless mortal fellow like you know about a worthless tree like me?"

When Carpenter Shih woke up, he tried to interpret the dream. His disciple said: "If the tree were so set on being useless, then why is it a sacred tree?"

"If secrets have no words, that also must have just happened, since the tree did not know itself as being free from harm and injury. If it were not an altar, would it not have been cut down? Thus its manner of survival was different from that of others, and to compare its disposition with those would be wide of the mark."

Tzu-ch'i of Nan-po was travelling in the mountains of Shang, when he saw a big tree of extraordinary size. A thousand chariot teams could be sheltered in its shade. Tzu-ch'i said: "What kind of tree is this? It must yield an extraordinary amount of wood. Then he looked up and saw the smaller branches all gnarled and twisted, totally unfit for rafters or beams. Looking down, he saw the great roots of the tree, too pliant and supple to make good wood for coffins. He licked the leaves, and his mouth burned and hurt. He sniffed at it, and it made one drunk for fully three days. Tzu-ch'i said: "This tree is not so useful, after all. And because of this, it has attained to such size. Ah! the wise man is useless in the same way."

In the state of Sung, there is a region called Ching-shih, where the catalpa, the cedar, and the mulberry flourish. But those that grow above a few spans are used for monkey posts; they are cut; those of three or four yards are cut down to make roofbeams; those of seven or eight yards, are cut down to make sideboards for the coffins of the aristocrats. As a result they never live out their alloted life-span, and are axed in their prime. This is the calamity of being useful. Thus in the book of Chieh, cows with white faces, pigs with upturned snouts, men with piles were all taboo, and could not be used as offerings to the river. This was known to the shamans, so they considered these things ill-fated. But to the sage, on the other hand, these things were blessed.

There was a deformed man without limbs named Shu, whose chin hung over his navel, whose shoulders were higher than his head, whose top-knot pointed skyward; his viscera were in the upper half of his body, and his thigh-bones were his ribs. By sharpening needles, and by washing clothes, he eked out a living. By winnowing grains of rice, he was able to support ten or more people. When soldiers were conscripted, this misshapen man bared his arms along with the others; when there was great effort required, because he was subject to so many maladies, the burden of the work was never placed on him. But when provisions were distributed, he would receive three bushels of grain and ten bundles of firewood. With his deformity, Shu was still able to take care of his body, and live out his years: how much more than if he were crippled in mind!

Confucius went to Ch'u. There was a madman named Chieh-yü who passed by his door, saying: "Oh phoenix, oh phoenix, that virtue has fallen on such hard times! The world of tomorrow is beyond waiting for, and the world of yesterday cannot be dismissed. When the Tao prevails, the sage achieves his purpose; when the Tao fails, the sage merely survives. Nowadays, he barely escapes punishment. The joys of life are as light as a feather, but no one knows how to keep them going; the calamities of life are as heavy as earth, yet no one knows how to avert them. Enough of this! Approaching men with notions of virtue, watch out, watch out! to mark out the way and rush on ahead. False light, false light, do not mislead me in my journey. My path is erratic; do not injure my steps. Mountain trees undermine themselves; grease-fires consume themselves; the cassia is edible, and for that is cut down; the lacquer tree is useful, so it is scarred with a knife. Everybody knows the use of the useful, but no one knows the use of the useless."

from *Autumn Waters*

[The Boundaries of Knowing and Not Knowing]

Kung-sun Lung asked Wei-mou: "When I was young I learned the wisdom of former kings; when I was older, I could understand the workings of selflessness and right-mindedness, relate similarity to dissimilarity, distinguish between "hardness" and "whiteness," what is and what is not, possibility and impossibility; I struggled through the teachings of the hundred schools, and exhausted the subtleties of innumerable points of view. I thought I had reached the ultimate. Now, I hear Chuang-tzu's words and I am lost and bewildered. I don't know if my arguments are inadequate, or my understanding is awry, but it seems I have nothing to say. Would you explain this?"

Translated by Eugene Eoyang.

Prince Mou leaned on his bench, heaved a sigh, looked up toward heaven, and laughed. He said: "Have you never heard of the frog who lived in a shallow well. Talking to the turtle of the Eastern Sea, he said: "How happy I am! I hop out onto the railing of the well, then go in for a rest whenever I want into the crevices where a brick is missing; when I go in the water, it comes up to my haunches and holds up my chin; when I slip into the mud, my feet are covered and my ankles disappear. When I look at small crabs and tadpoles, they can't do what I can, for I have the waters of this ditch all to myself, and can enjoy the pleasures of the well. This is the greatest! Why don't you come and look for yourself?"

The turtle of the Eastern Sea had hardly put his left foot in when his right knee got caught. Whereupon, he drew back and began telling about the sea: "A thousand leagues wouldn't be enough to measure its vastness; a thousand yards wouldn't be enough to plumb its depths. In the days of Yü, when it flooded nine years out of ten, its water level did not rise; in the days of T'ang, when there was drought seven years out of eight, its shoreline did not recede. No pushing or shifting, for a moment or for long, no matter how much the tide advances and recedes—this is the great joy of the Eastern Sea. When the frog heard this, he was suddenly stupefied, and found himself at a loss. How you are at the boundaries of knowing and not-knowing, right and wrong, and still you look askance at Chuang-tzu's words. This is like making a gnat shoulder a mountain, or a millipede race the river. That won't do!"

"The detailed and subtle discussions on knowing and not-knowing will provide an advantage for a time—but isn't it like the frog in the broken-down well? Whereas the other [Chuang-tzu] is just now walking about in the Yellow Springs [the underworld] or ascending into heaven. For him, there is no south, no north, he is free in every direction: he is awash in the bottomless depths; with no east, no west, he starts out with dark mysteries, and ends up with great insight. You come blithely along and analyze him for petty points! Isn't this like looking at the sky through a straw or pointing to the earth with an awl? Those things are too small! Off with you! Or, haven't you heard of the youngest children of Shou-ling, who were learning to walk in Han-tan: but before they went home, they had lost the knack, so they had to crawl back on their hands and knees. Now, if you don't go, you may forget what you knew before, and lose your means of livelihood."

Kung-sun Lung's mouth was wide open and would not close, his tongue was stuck and would not come loose. There and then, he withdrew and walked away.

ANONYMOUS (THIRD CENTURY B.C.E.)
China

Consisting of thirty-three books, each on an individual state, *Intrigues of the Warring States [Chan-kuo Ts'e]* records, or rather recreates, the major events during the Warring States period (403–221 B.C.E.). The stories were first recorded during the third century B.C.E., although the text that has come down to us is the product of later editing during the Western Han and Northern Sung periods.

With several states waging deadly wars and treacherous diplomacy against each other, the Warring States period saw the decline of feudal patriotism—the system of loyalties that had provided political stability during the preceding Chou Dynasty. Scholars no longer dutifully served their own state, wandering instead from one state to the next, offering their expertise in statecraft to the highest bidder. The eloquent Su Ch'in, in the selection from the *Book of Yen,* was such a figure. With other scholars, however, feudal patriotism died hard. Among these was Ching K'o, whose abortive attempt to assassinate the King of Ch'in, the archenemy of his native state, has remained for centuries the model for heroic self-sacrifice.

A hallmark of this historic work is its extensive use of dialogues, such as the one between Su-Ch'in and the King of Yen. Also characteristic is a penchant for parables, many of which, frequently alluded to by later writers, have furnished expressions and aphorisms still current in everyday Chinese conversation. In a literary tradition where the demarcation between history and fiction was never clear-cut, *Intrigues of the Warring States* exerted a strong influence on later narratives.

from *Intrigues of the Warring States [Chan-kuo Ts'e]*

THE BOOK OF CH'I

[Lord Meng-ch'ang Is Persuaded to Keep His Retainer]

Lord Meng-ch'ang had a retainer he was not too happy with and he wanted to get rid of him. But Lu (Chung-)lien said to Lord Meng-ch'ang: "If apes and monkeys left the woods and took to the water, they would not be the equals of fish and turtles; for passing through rugged terrain and for climbing cliffs, thousand-league horses are not as good as the fox. When Ts'ao Mei flashed his three-foot sword, an army couldn't subdue him; but take the three-foot sword away, put a hoe in his hands, let him live with farmers in the field, and he wouldn't be even as good as a farmer. If strengths are abandoned in favor of shortcomings, then Yao himself would be found inadequate. Now if we force someone to do something he can't and call him incompetent; if we teach someone who cannot understand and call him dense; and because of their stupidity get rid of them, and because of their incompetence, abandon them, we will have removed any means of communicating with the rejected and the abandoned, and they will come back seeking revenge. This, surely, wouldn't be the example you would want to set for the world, would it?"

Lord Meng-ch'ang said: "All right, then," and he did not send the man away.

Translated by Eugene Eoyang.

[Feng Hsuan Provides Loyalty for Lord Meng-ch'ang]

There was a man of Ch'i named Feng Hsuan who was so poor he couldn't support himself, so he sent word to Lord Meng-ch'ang that he wished to serve as his attendant. Lord Meng-ch'ang said: "What ambitions does he have?"

"No ambitions," came the reply.

"What abilities?"

"No abilities," he was told. Lord Meng-ch'ang then laughed, and received him, saying: "Alright."

The staff assumed that their lord did not think much of the newcomer, so they fed him the humblest fare. He stayed for a while, then, leaning on a post, stroking his longsword, he sang a song with these words: "Longsword! Let's go home! Not even a fish in our meals." The staff reported this to Lord Meng-ch'ang, who said: "Feed him as a guest of the court." He stayed for a while, and then once again he stroked his sword, and sang this song: "Longsword! Let's go home! We don't even have a chariot to ride out in!" The retainers all laughed and reported this to Lord Meng-ch'ang, who said: "Give him a chariot, like those of the others!" Thereupon, he mounted his chariot, raised his sword, and passing among his friends, he would say: "Lord Meng-ch'ang treats me like a guest!" But, after a while, once again he stroked his sword and sang: "Longsword! Let's go home! I'm not treated as one of them!" The staff began to hate him, for they thought him grasping and insatiable. Lord Meng-ch'ang asked: "Does he have a family?"

"A mother," came the reply.

Lord Meng-ch'ang sent someone to her with provisions, so that she would never go hungry. And after that, Feng Hsuan never sang his song again.

Some time later, Lord Meng-ch'ang issued a proclamation, asking if there were any among his retainers with experience handling accounts who could collect revenues in the region of Hsieh. Feng Hsuan replied that he could. Lord Meng-ch'ang marveled at this: "Who is this?" he asked.

"He is the one who sang to his sword that they should go home," said the retainers.

Lord Meng-ch'ang laughed: "So he can do something after all! I have been remiss and haven't taken much notice of him." He then asked Feng Hsuan to step forward and addressed him, apologetically: "I have been much occupied, vexed by worries, and have become abstracted and inattentive: I am swamped by affairs of state, and therefore have treated you most reprehensibly. Yet, you are not offended, and are even willing to collect revenues for me in the region of Hsieh?"

Feng Hsuan replied: "Yes, I am."

So he prepared his cart and arranged his baggage, taking along the tax records. As he left, he said: "When I have finished collecting the tax revenue, is there anything you would like me to bring back for you?"

Lord Meng-ch'ang said: "Take a look around, and see if I need anything."

Feng Hsuan hurried to Hsieh, sent out messengers calling everyone to straighten out their accounts. When the accounts had all been settled, he announced a mythical edict which returned all the revenue back to the people, and burned the records. At this, the people all cheered.

Feng hurried back to Ch'i, and asked for an audience early in the morning. Lord Meng-ch'ang wondered at his quickness, put on his ceremonial robes, and gave him an audience:

"Did you collect the revenues? How comes it that you've returned so quickly?"

"The revenues have been collected," came the reply.

"And what have you brought back for me?"

Feng Hsuan said: "You asked me to bring back whatever I thought you seem to need. I concluded that in your palace, since there was an abundance of wealth, stables teeming with horses and dogs, beautiful women of every rank, that what you lacked was loyalty. I therefore took it upon myself to secure loyalty for you."

Lord Meng-ch'ang said: "And where is this loyalty?"

"Now, you have the territory of Hsieh, but you do not much care for its people, which is why you exploit them. I proclaimed a mythical edict from you, which released the people from their tax obligation, and burned the records. The populace all cheered. This is how I secured loyalty for you."

Lord Meng-ch'ang was not happy about this, but he said: "Alright. You may go."

A full year later, the King of Ch'i called Lord Meng-ch'ang and told him: "I cannot afford to continue in my service a minister of my predecessor." So Lord Meng-ch'ang left the country for Hsieh: he had not gone one hundred leagues before the people, holding their old folk up, and with their children in tow, all turned out to welcome him as he came down the road. At the end of the day, Lord Meng-ch'ang looked up Feng Hsuan: "Sir, the loyalty which you secured for me I saw for myself today."

Feng Hsuan said: "The crafty hare has three burrows, to avoid being killed. Now, we have but one burrow. It isn't time yet to sit down and relax. Let me dig out a second burrow."

Lord Meng-ch'ang conferred upon him fifty chariots, five hundred catties[1] of gold, and with it, he journeyed west to Liang. There, he said to King Hui: "The kingdom of Ch'i has just released its great minister Lord Meng-ch'ang, and he is now free to serve someone else. Whoever secures his services will be prosperous and mighty in arms."

Immediately, the King of Liang vacated a high post by making his minister a general, and sent an envoy with a thousand vessels of gold and a hundred carts to offer to Lord Meng-ch'ang. But Feng Hsuan rushed there first to forewarn Lord Meng-ch'ang. "A thousand vessels of gold is quite a treasure; a hundred carts is no small caravan. Ch'i should hear of this."

The Liang emissary approached Lord Meng-ch'ang three times, but each time Lord Meng-ch'ang adamantly refused their offer to go back with them. The King of Ch'i heard of it, and both he and his ministers were nervous and apprehensive. They sent the Assistant Grand Tutor with an offer of a thousand catties of gold, two beautifully tooled chariots, a formal ceremonial sword, and a letter, in which he apologized to Lord Meng-ch'ang in these words: "I am terribly unfortunate, bedeviled by evil spirits haunting my ancestral temples and surrounded by toadies

---

1. A Chinese pound.

for ministers. We have committed offenses against you, which I cannot allow. Would you consider looking after the ancestral temples of the former kings? Would you come back now and govern the people?"

Feng Hsuan advised Lord Meng-ch'ang: "Ask him to place the sacred vessels of the former kings in ancestral temples set up in Hsieh."

When the temples were completed, Feng Hsuan reported to Lord Meng-ch'ang: "The three burrows are now finished, sir. You may now relax and enjoy yourself."

That Lord Meng-ch'ang was able to serve as minister for several decades without the slightest mishap befalling him was due largely to the foresight of Feng Hsuan.

[King Hsuan Learns About Fear]

King Hsuan of Ching (Ch'u) asked his assembled ministers: "I hear that the people in the North fear Chao Hsi-hsu. Is that true?" The assembled ministers kept silent, all except Chiang Yi, who said: "The tiger hunts all the animals for food, but when he caught a fox, the fox said: 'You dare not eat me. The almighty has made me leader of all the animals. If you eat me now, you will be violating the will of Heaven. Now if you don't believe, come with me and we'll see, with me in front and you behind. You will see that when all the animals see us, no one will dare to face us; they will run away.' "

The tiger wondered about this, so he followed him. When the animals saw them, indeed, they all ran away. The tiger did not know that the animals feared him: he thought it was the fox. Now, your majesty's territory spans some five thousand leagues, and you have a million soldiers who bear arms for you, which you have delegated to Chao Hsi-hsu. This is why the northern regions fear Hsi-hsu. What they really fear is your majesty's army, in the same way that the animals were all actually afraid of the tiger."

THE BOOK OF CH'U

[A Rogue Becomes a Lord]

Chuang Hsin said to King Hsiang of Ch'u: "Your majesty has Marquis Chou on his left, and Marquis Hsia on his right; in your entourage are Lord Yen-ling and Lord Shou-ling. Since all they do is to indulge in wanton pleasures, and no one looks after how well the country is governed, Ying (the capital of Ch'u) is in peril."

King Hsiang said: "You are a contrary old rogue! Do you want to wish misfortune on Ch'u?"

Chuang Hsin said: "I merely report honestly the way things really are: I wouldn't dare wish ill-fortune on this country. But if your majesty indulges these four men without let-up, then the state of Ch'u is doomed. I request permission to repair to Chao, where I can wait and watch."

He stayed there five months. In that time, Ch'in moved against the territories of Yen, the city of Ying (the capital of Ch'u), the regions of Wu, Shang Tsai, and

Ch'en. King Hsiang took cover in Ch'eng-yang, whereupon he sent messengers to seek out Chuang Hsin in Chao. Chuang Hsin agreed to come. When he arrived, King Hsiang said: "I was not able to follow your advice, so that now, things have come to this. What shall I do?"

Chuang Hsin replied: "I have heard folk say, 'When the hare is spotted, it's still not too late to send the hound; when sheep have strayed off, it's not too late to repair the pen.' I have heard that in times past, T'ang and Wu flourished with a hundred leagues, while Chieh and Chou came to nought even with everything under the sun. Now, although Ch'u is small, if you take the long and short of it, it still extends several thousand leagues. And what's wrong with even a hundred?

Haven't you seen the dragonfly, with his six legs, four wings, darting and hovering between heaven and earth, diving down to peck on mosquitoes for food, soaring upward for sweet dew to drink? He thinks himself free from calamity, and has no conflict with man. He does not know that a boy, scarce four feet tall, is dabbing honey on some sticky string, and will bring him down from twenty feet and above to become food for ants. But, after all, what's a small thing like a dragonfly?

The yellow sparrow, for example, dips down to peck at grain, perches upon a branch of a luxuriant tree, flaps his wings and flies off. He thinks himself free from calamity, and has no conflict with man. He does not know that a young prince, with bird-shot in his left hand and pellets in his right, will bring him down from a height of nearly sixty feet, and does not know that decoys will lure him to his death. Flying among the trees in the morning, in no time he will end up a tasty dish at night, when he falls into the hands of a young prince. But, after all, what's a small thing like a sparrow?

Consider the yellow crane, who roams the rivers and oceans, and dwells in a great swamp, diving down for eel and carp, and reaching up for chestnuts and tasty shoots. He flaps his six pinions and glides on thin air, banking here and there, soaring high on the wind. He thinks himself free from calamity, and has no conflict with man. He doesn't know that an archer is sharpening his shaft, arranging his black bow, and adjusting his retrieving line, all designed to bring him down from more than five hundred feet, where, struck by the arrow, and pulled by the line, he is brought down from thin air. Roaming the rivers and streams in the morning, he falls into a boiling pot by night. But, after all, what's a small thing like a yellow crane?

So let us take the case of the Marquis Tsai-ling: he traveled in the south around the high range, climbed Mount Wu in the north, drank from the streams of Ju-ch'i, and tasted the fish of the Hsiang river. Here he embraces young girls, there he sports with old favorites, gallivanting about in the middle of Kao-ts'ai, with no concern for affairs of state. Little does he know that Tzu-fa has received orders from King Hsuan to bring him to court, bound with the vermilion cord. But, after all, what's a small thing like the troubles of Marquis Ling?

Your majesty's affair, for example, involves Marquis Chou on the one side and Marquis Hsia on the other, and Prince Yen-ling and Prince Shou-ling in attendance: they feed off the grain collected from the fiefs, carry away gold tribute from all directions, and go off gallivanting in Yun-meng [a district in Hupei province]. They do not attend to affairs of state. Little do they know that Marquis Jang has already received an order from the King of Ch'in to cut off the Min pass, to strand the King of Ch'u outside."

King Hsiang, when he heard this, turned pale and trembled with fear. Whereupon he then and there grasped his sceptre and enfeoffed Chuang Hsin with the title, Lord of Yang-ling, and gave him the region of Huai-pei.

[Loyalty Is Sometimes Punished]

There was a man who hated Su Ch'in and said to the King of Yen: "Lord Wu-an (i.e., Su Ch'in), is the most faithless man in the empire. Your majesty has equipped him with ten thousand chariots, honored him at court, as if to proclaim to all the world that you prefer the company of small people."

When Lord Wu-an came back from Ch'i, the King of Yen would not give him hospitality. He addressed the King of Yen: "I was a mere rustic from Eastern Chou (Tung Chou) when I first met you, without a thing to commend me, yet you welcomed me from the outside, and singled me out within your palace. Now that I have served you, Sir, as minister, annexed ten cities, shored up a faltering state, you won't even listen to me. It must be because someone has spoken to you against me behind my back, claiming that I am disloyal. If what I do is disloyal, it is unfortunate for you, for ministers as loyal as Wei-sheng, as upright as Po Yi, as devoted as Tseng Shen, three of the noblest models, could hardly serve you, could they?"

"And why not?"

"If I were that kind of minister, I'd hardly serve you," Su Ch'in said, "for as devoted as Tseng Shen was, he would never leave his parents for even one night abroad, so how could I have gone to Ch'i? If I were as upright as Po Yi, I couldn't accept the fruits of indolence, and would consider even fealty to King Wu demeaning: I would not serve him but leave the lord of Ku-chu and starve to death alone in the mountains of Shou-yang. Would anyone so upright have been willing, as I was, to travel a thousand leagues to serve a weak ruler of Yen in trouble? Or say I were as faithful as Wei-sheng, who waited for his loved one even when she did not come, holding onto the pilings of the pier until he drowned to death. Were I that faithful would I have been willing to further the interest of Yen and Ch'in in Ch'i and still receive great distinction doing it? For those who are faithful are faithful for themselves, and not for others. Pretenses at self-abnegation, do not achieve results. The Three Kings stayed in power, the Five Rulers maintained their preeminence, not by abnegating themselves, so why should your majesty? Otherwise, Ch'i would not have exploited Ying-ch'iu, and you, Sir, would not have crossed the borders of Ch'u or be eyeing the regions outside your territories. When I left my aged mother in Chou to serve you, I had to abandon the arts of self-denial, and plot out ways of advancing and making progress. My bent evidently does not coincide with yours: you want a self-denying minister, whereas

I am ambitious and eager to move ahead. This is why I say that loyalty and piety would be punished by your majesty."

The King of Yen said: "How can loyalty and faithfulness be punished?"

"Your majesty does not know about a neighbor of mine who was sent far from home on a mission. His wife had a lover and when the husband came back, the lover became apprehensive, but the wife reassured him: 'My lord, don't worry, I have already poisoned the wine that my husband will be served when he returns.' When the husband arrived after two days, the wife sent the concubine to bring in the jug of wine. The concubine knew the wine was poisoned, and that if she brought it in, her master would die, and that if she betrayed her mistress, then she would be dispatched, so she fell flat out, and spilled the wine. The husband was furious and gave her a sound thrashing. But, because the concubine fell down and spilled the wine, the husband was saved and the wife spared. Loyalty as devoted as this, however, didn't spare her a thrashing. This is the kind of loyalty that is punished."

"Now my conduct of affairs is ill-fated, and I am like the concubine who spilled the wine. For though I serve you, Sir, in honor and for the benefit of the state, I am being punished today. I fear that those who will serve you in the future will not dare to act on their own. Where I have won the confidence of Ch'i for you, and have never misled her, those who will be sent to negotiate with Ch'i will not have my say, and though they have the intelligence of a Yao or Shun, they will not dare to exercise their own initiative."

THE BOOK OF YEN

[Sword Play in Ch'in's Territories]

Prince Tan of Yen, the heir to the throne, after being hostage at Ch'in, returned to see Ch'in destroy the Six States, and poise its armies on the Yi River. Fearing the worst, the Prince addressed his tutor Chu Wu with apprehension: "Yen and Ch'in cannot both stand. Would the Grand Tutor devise a well-conceived scheme?" Wu replied: "Ch'in's territories are all over the place. If they can intimidate Han, Wei, and Chao, then the region north of the Yi River will not be secure. Of what use is your grievance if it will only goad the dragon?" The Prince said: "Alright, then, what do I do?" The Grand Tutor said: "Let me think of something."

Meanwhile, a certain General Fan ran away from Ch'in and arrived in Yen: the Prince offered him sanctuary. The Grand Tutor Chu Wu remonstrated with him: "You can't do that! The savagery of Ch'in and his growing hostilities toward Yen are enough to make the heart shudder; what will happen when he hears that General Fan is here? It would be like leaving meat in the path of a hungry tiger. Nothing can save us from catastrophe now! Even if you had the wise Kuan-tzu or the clever Yen-tzu, they couldn't come up with a way out. You must quickly abandon him to the Hsiung-nu to dispose of, then negotiate treaties in the west with the three Tsin [Han, Chao, and Wei], conclude an alliance in the south with Ch'i and Ch'u, and make a parley in the north with the Ch'an-yu [the chieftain of the Huns]. Only then can you figure out what to do next!"

Prince Tan said: "The Grand Tutor's plan wastes time and would take forever.

It's completely confused and couldn't be done in a little while. And that's not the only consideration. General Fan has gone through many obstacles in order to get here, and we will not, in the end, be pressured by the might of Ch'in to abandon all principles of mercy by leaving him to the Hsiung-nu. My mind is made up, and my fate is sealed. Think of something else!"

Chu Wu said: "In Yen, there is a Master T'ien Kuang, who is profoundly wise and deeply courageous. Perhaps he can help."

The Prince said: "You have to but command!" He went to see T'ien Kuang and told him that the Prince wanted to discuss affairs of state with him. T'ien Kuang said, "I shall obey, with all due respect," and went with him. The Prince welcomed him on his knees, led him to his place, and asked him to sit down. When he was seated, and they were alone, the Prince left his seat and said: "Yen and Ch'in cannot both stand. Would you, Sir, give this matter your attention?"

T'ien Kuang said: "I have heard when the fabulous Ch'i-ch'i horse was hale and hearty, it could cover a thousand leagues in one day, but when it was in its last days, even an old nag could outrun it. Now, the Prince has heard of me as I was in my prime, and you are not aware that my powers have long ago deserted me. Although I cannot presume to settle momentous affairs of state myself, I can recommend Ching K'o as someone who might help."

The Prince said: "Would you, Sir, be good enough to introduce us to Ching K'o?"

"Most assuredly!" T'ien Kuang said, and got up to go.

The Prince saw him to the gate, and said: "I am indebted to you for your good counsel, but as these are important affairs of state, I would wish that you wouldn't let word of this get out."

T'ien Kuang bowed with a smile: "Of course." And with this he took his leave and went to see Ching K'o.

"You and I have been good friends," he said to Ching K'o, "as everyone in Yen knows. Now, the Prince has heard of me in my prime, and not knowing that I am not what I used to be, he said to me, 'Yen and Ch'in cannot both stand, please give this matter your attention.' I could not overlook you, so I spoke of you to the Prince, and now he wants you to go see him in the palace."

Ching K'o said: "You have but to command."

T'ien Kuang said: "I have heard that honorable men conduct themselves in such a way as to leave no cause for anyone to doubt them. But just now the Prince said to me, 'The things we've just discussed are important matters of state, please don't let any word of this get out.' Which means that the Prince has doubts about me. And anyone whose conduct is not above suspicion is not a true man of integrity." And since he wanted his suicide to be a spur to Ching K'o, he said: "Please hurry on to the Prince, and tell him that I am already dead, and am silenced forever." With that, he cut his own throat and died.

When K'o saw the Prince, he told him that T'ien Kuang had died, silenced by his own hand forever. The Prince bowed again and again, knelt down and wept, and said, after a while: "When I asked Master T'ien to keep close counsel, I was thinking only of the success of any plans we may make. Now, Master T'ien has died to protect our confidence. How could I imagine that he would do such a thing?"

Ching K'o sat down. The Prince got up, bowed toward him, and said: "Master T'ien did not know that I was not worthy of him. Yet he sent you to me, and you seem willing to give me counsel, so Heaven has taken pity on Yen, and has not abandoned us. At the moment, Ch'in has a voracious appetite, and her wants cannot be satisfied. Not until she has all the territories under the sun, or the fealty of all the kings within the oceans, will she have enough. As of now, Ch'in has already seized the King of Han, and absorbed her territories, also has raised an army south against Ch'u, north toward Chao, and Wang Chien with troops in the tens of thousands, is heading for Chang Yeh, and Li Hsin is coming out right into Tai-yuan and Yun-chung. Chao cannot hold out against Ch'in, and will be subjugated, and when that happens, it will be a catastrophe for Yen, for Yen is too small and weak to survive several military engagements. Now we figure the country is not up to facing Ch'in, even if the whole population were mobilized. All the various clans now swear fealty to Ch'in: they would not dare support any attempt to oppose her. But I have a secret plan. I'm foolish enough to think that if we found the bravest man there is, sent him to Ch'in to look around and gave him lots of wealth, the king would be so greedy for his goods that he would be able to have his way. Truly to steal back and return to everyone the territories invaded by the King of Ch'in—just like Ts'ao Mei with the Duke Huan of Ch'i—would be a marvelous thing. But if that isn't possible, he will be assassinated. Then, the generals would seize control of the army on the outside, and there would be great confusion within; lord and minister would suspect each other, and the various clans would band together and force restitutions that would break Ch'in's hold. This is my fondest wish, but I do not know who to send, if my minister Ching won't consider it."

After some time, Ching K'o said: "This is a very important affair of state: I doubt whether I am up to the task." The Prince implored him, kept insisting and wouldn't take no for an answer, until finally he agreed. Thereupon he was promoted to the highest rank, lodged in the best apartments, consulted daily by the Prince, and was given the best of everything—chariots, women, whatever he wanted was duly granted Ching K'o.

A considerable period of time passed, and Ching K'o still had not shown any signs of proceeding with the plan. Meantime, Ch'in, through General Wang Chien, invaded Chao, capturing the King of Chao, taking all her lands, advancing the army to the northern reaches, all the way to the southern border of Yen. Prince Tan was fearful, and asked Ching K'o: "The Ch'in army is about to cross the Yi River any day or night now, and though I would like to indulge you indefinitely, I can't afford to any longer."

Ching K'o said: "If my prince hadn't mentioned it, I would have broached the subject myself. But to proceed now would be pointless: I have nothing yet with which to gain Ch'in's confidence. But now there's General Fan, for whom the King of Ch'in has offered a reward of a thousand catties of gold and a fiefdom of ten thousand families. If only one could get one's hands on General Fan's head, that along with the map of the Tu-k'ang region of Yen would surely secure an audience with the Ch'in king, and then I would be able to avenge my prince."

The Prince said: "General Fan has undergone many hardships to seek refuge here. I will not tolerate any breach of propriety while he is in my custody. Please, Sir, consider another alternative!"

Ching K'o knew that the Prince would not permit it, so he went to see Fan Yu-ch'i in secret: "Ch'in's offense against you is grave. Your father and mother and the rest of your family have all been massacred. And now I hear there is a price on the General's head of a thousand catties of gold and a fiefdom of ten thousand families! What do you make of this?"

General Fan raised his head toward heaven, sighed aloud, and with tears in his eyes, he said: "My every thought pierces me to the marrow. But I don't know what I should do!"

K'o replied: "What would you say if I had an idea that could save the state of Yen from calamity, and also repay the General's enemy?"

Fan Yu-ch'i leaned forward and asked: "What is it?"

Ching K'o: "Let me deliver your head to Ch'in, and the Ch'in king will be delighted to grant me an audience. Then, with my left hand holding his sleeve, my right will strike at his heart. Thus the General will be avenged on his enemy, and the state of Yen will be rid of the shame of grave insult. What does the General say to this?"

Fan Yu-ch'i bared his throat, grasped his wrist, and said: "Day and night, I have gnashed my teeth and afflicted my heart, but now I have heard what I want!" With this he cut his throat and died.

When the Prince heard this, he hurried to the prostrate corpse in tears, moaning in lamentation: but since there was nothing that could be done about it, he took Fan Yu-ch'i's head, and put it in a sealed box. Then he looked high and low for the best dagger in all the land, and found the dagger of a certain Hsu of Chao, which he bought for a hundred gold pieces, and had workman temper in poison. He also tested it on people: when so much as a trickle of blood was drawn, not one survived. It was wrapped up and sent along to Ching K'o. Now, in the state of Yen, there was someone named Ch'in Wu-yang, who had killed a man when he was in his thirteenth year, whom no one dared cross, and he was assigned to accompany Ching K'o on his mission. Ching K'o was waiting for someone else whom he wanted along with him, but lived very far away and had not yet arrived. Still, Ching K'o waited for him and did not set out. The Prince bore with him, but he was anxious lest Ching K'o change his mind, so he asked again: "Time is running out. Why isn't the minister Ching carrying out our plan? Perhaps I had better send Ch'in Wu-yang on ahead."

Ching K'o was indignant, and he yelled at the Prince: "Since I am the poor fool who is going and will not return, and since I am the one to go straight into the invulnerable and invincible Ch'in army with only a dagger, I naturally delayed a bit, waiting for my friend whom I wanted along as a companion. But since the Prince is so impatient, I'll be on my way right now!" And with that, he set out at last.

The Prince and those who knew of the mission all donned their white robes and caps to see him off. When they reached the waters of the Yi, they invoked the gods and asked for a blessing on the mission. Kao Chien-li struck up a mournful melody on his lute, and Ching K'o sang along, harmonizing in a minor key. The men all had tears running down their cheeks, as Ching K'o stepped forward and sang:

> The wind blows and blows,
> The Yi waters are cold!
> Stout fellows once gone,
> Oh, will never come back!

Then he sang of The Magnanimous Knight, and the other officers glared at him, their hair bristling under their caps. Ching K'o mounted his chariot and went, without so much as a glance back. When he arrived in Ch'in, he made gifts of a thousand pieces of gold to the Tutor Meng Chia, who was a key member of the King's privy council. Chia spoke on his behalf to the King of Ch'in: "The King of Yen is truly awed by the might of your majesty, and does not dare to organize troops to raise a hand against you; he wishes to offer his fealty to you, to serve you as one of your vassals, and to make tributes as a protectorate if he is allowed to retain his ancestral temples. And since he was fearful and did not want to come in person, he sent the decapitated head of Fan Yu-ch'i, along with the maps of the Tu-k'ang region of Yen, all under seal. The King of Yen has sent an envoy to pay his respects, and to attend to your majesty's wishes!"

When the King of Ch'in heard this, he was very pleased. He instructed the entire court to turn out to receive the envoy from Yen in the Hsien-yang palace. Ching K'o offered up the box with Fan Yu-ch'i's head, and Ch'in Wu-yang presented the portfolio with the map. When they approached the throne, however, Ch'in Wu-yang grew pale with fear, and the assembly wondered at this. Ching K'o noticed this and laughed. Stepping forward, he apologized to the throne: "He's a rube who comes from among the northern barbarians, and since he has never seen real royalty, naturally, he is a bit terrified. If your majesty would make allowances for him and let him stay out here until the audience is over."

Ching K'o took the map and presented it, unrolling the map until the dagger wrapped up in it was exposed, whereupon he seized the sleeve of the King with his left hand and with his right, he struck out at him. But, before he could get to him, the King of Ch'in jumped, drew back, got up, tearing his sleeve, and reached for his sword. As the sword was long, it wouldn't come out of its scabbard, for in his panic, the King left the scabbard upright, which is why it was hard to draw out. Ching K'o chased the King, who circled around a pillar and darted away. The assembled court was aghast, and all collapsed into chaos, without any notion of what to do. According to the rules of the Ch'in court, courtiers who approached the throne were not allowed to carry arms, so the assembled guards were all some distance from the royal dais, and could not approach. Further, at this critical point, there was no time to call the guards, which is why Ching K'o could—unchecked—pursue the King of Ch'in. The King, in his disarray, had nothing with which to strike back at K'o, so he resorted to using his fists. Just then, the physician Hsia Wu-ch'ieh threw his medicine pouch at K'o, which enabled the Ch'in king to go behind a pillar, but being still confused, he was at a loss as to what to do next. Everyone around then yelled: "Your majesty, pull out your sword!" And the King managed to draw it, and with it struck out at K'o, cutting his left thigh. Ching K'o withdrew, and threw his dagger at the Ch'in king, but he missed, hitting the pillar. The King of Ch'in then struck K'o repeatedly, inflicting eight wounds. K'o realized at this point that he had failed, and spreading his legs against a pillar, he laughed derisively and cursed out: "The mission has failed! And all because I tried to strip him alive, and force him to return the lands that he had invaded, thus avenging my Prince." At this the attendants all surrounded him and stabbed him to death, while the King fell into a dead faint. When it came time later to mete out rewards for meritorious action, everyone at court was found undeserving, except for Hsia Wu-ch'ieh who was awarded two thousand taels of gold with these words: "Wu-ch'ieh is devoted to me, for he threw his medicine pouch at K'o." From then on, Ch'in was furious at Yen: she sent additional troops to besiege Chao and called upon General Wang Chien to attack Yen. In ten months, the town of Chi in Yen fell. King Hsi, and Prince Tan, together with the remnants of their army, fled east to Liao-tung for safety. But the Ch'in general Li Hsin tracked them down and attacked the Yen king, who in his panic, took the suggestion of King Chia of Tai, and had Prince Tan executed, and with his head sued for peace. But Ch'in pressed on, and after five years, destroyed Yen completely, capturing Hsi, the King. Ch'in then proceeded to consolidate all her territories. Afterward, Ching K'o's old companion Kao Chien-li, playing on his lute, caught sight of the Ch'in emperor, and tried to beat him over the head with his lute to avenge the state of Yen, but he too failed and was killed.

CH'Ü YÜAN [QU YUAN] (378?–340 B.C.E.)
China

Ch'ü Yüan, China's first known poet, was born into an aristocratic family in the southern state of Ch'u, one of the seven major powers during the Warring States period. After finishing his schooling, he was appointed to a prominent official position. Political rivals succeeded in turning the King of Ch'u against him, however, and he was dismissed from court in disgrace. Ch'ü Yüan was bitterly sorrowful over the future of the state and of its people, as well as his own personal fate. According to legend, he eventually drowned himself in the Milo River.

Paradoxically, what was unfortunate for Ch'ü Yüan turned out to be most fortunate for literature, for he gave form to his profound sorrow in one of China's greatest lyric poems, "On Encountering Sorrow" ["Li-sao"]. The first part of the poem presents a biographical account of the poet's ancestry, his efforts at self-cultivation, and his ideal of an enlightened government. The second part is devoted to the poet's imaginary travels to a heavenly world, travels that represent his frustrated quest for his ideals. In the last part, the poet continues his travels in search of an understanding goddess but ends up in despair. Finally, he decides to join P'eng Hsien, a legendary courtier who drowned himself after his counsel was ignored by his king.

The style of the poetry of the state of Ch'ü, represented by the exuberant imagery and magnificent diction of "On Encountering Sorrow," greatly influenced later poets, especially those of the Han Dynasty.

On Encountering Sorrow [Li Sao]

UNLIKE *the other Chu-tzu poems, for whose authorship the second-century commentator Wang I is often our only authority, this poem was from a fairly early date associated with the name of Ch'ü Yüan, and there seems little reason for quarrelling with the traditional attribution. It may, however, be of interest to consider to what extent the personality which confronts us in Li Sao corresponds to the Ch'ü Yüan of Ssŭ-ma Ch'ien's biography.*

Like him, the author of Li Sao is a Ch'u nobleman. (All noblemen in ancient China were descended from the gods, and Li Sao opens with a declaration of the poet's divine ancestry from Kao Yang.) Like him, he is a victim of slanderous misrepresentation and royal folly. Like him, his conception of honor and purity sets him at odds with a society fallen into evil ways.

Beyond that the resemblances end. The Li Sao poet is a magician who journeys in an airborne chariot to the fairyland of the West, compelling gods and spirits to wait upon him. Somehow the magic is not quite strong enough, however, and the dispirited poet ends in complete despair, disillusioned alike with the world of men and with the supernatural world through which he has been travelling.

The way in which we interpret Li Sao rests ultimately on whether or not we believe the last two lines of the poem to be authentic. If they are, it looks as though the poet's celestial journey in quest of fair women is an allegory of the rejected courtier's unsuccessful search for a wise prince. The 'place where P'eng Hsien dwells' used to be taken as a reference to the waters of the river, and the poet's final resolution to go there as an announcement of his intention to drown himself. This is by no means certain, and I am inclined to believe that 'following P'eng Hsien' meant devoting oneself to occult training.

In a sense the interpretation makes little difference to our picture of the poet. Allegory or no allegory, the fact remains that Ch'ü Yüan took a rather specialized kind of magic-making as the central theme of his poem, thereby demonstrating that he was familiar with such matters and perhaps expert in them.

The escape from human miseries by means of a journey into the supernatural world, in which the poet, like a lord of the universe, seizes the stars in his grasp and commands the gods as his lackeys, later became a stock-in-trade of the Chinese poet. But it was Ch'ü Yüan who first used this theme and who wrote the earliest long narrative poem to survive. It seems not unreasonable to suppose that he may have got the idea for his theme and also for the form of his poem from hearing recitals by Ch'u shamans in which they gave an account of their journeys through the spirit-lands. Recitals of this kind are extremely common among shamans in other parts of the world and references to 'spirit-journeys' are by no means uncommon in early Chinese literature.

—DAVID HAWKES

Scion of the High Lord Kao Yang,[1]
Po Yung was my father's name.
When She T'i[2] pointed to the first month of the year,
On the day *keng yin*,[3] I passed from the womb.
My father, seeing the aspect of my nativity,   5

Translated by David Hawkes.

---

1. Divine ancestor of both the Ch'u and Ch'in royal houses.
2. A constellation.

3. Name of the twenty-seventh day in the sexagenary cycle.

Took omens to give me an auspicious name.
The name he gave me was True Exemplar;
The title he gave me was Divine Balance[4]

Having from birth this inward beauty,
I added to it fair outward adornment;   10
I dressed in selinea and shady angelica,
And twined autumn orchids to make a garland.
Swiftly I sped, as in fearful pursuit,
Afraid Time would race on and leave me behind.
In the morning I gathered the angelica on the mountains;   15
In the evening I plucked the sedges of the islets.

The days and months hurried on, never delaying;
Springs and autumns sped by in endless alternation:
And I thought how the trees and flowers were fading and falling,
And feared that my Fairest's beauty would fade too.   20
'Gather the flower of youth and cast out the impure!
'Why will you not change the error of your ways?
'I have harnessed brave coursers for you to gallop forth with:
'Come, let me go before and show you the way!

'The three kings[5] of old were most pure and perfect: 25
'Then indeed fragrant flowers had their proper place.
'They brought together pepper and cinnamon;
'All the most-prized blossoms were woven in their garlands.
'Glorious and great were those two, Yao and Shun,[6]
'Because they had kept their feet on the right path.   30
'And how great was the folly of Chieh and Chou,[7]
'Who hastened by crooked paths, and so came to grief.

'The fools enjoy their careless pleasure,
'But their way is dark and leads to danger.
'I have no fear for the peril of my own person,   35
'But only lest the chariot of my lord should be dashed.
'I hurried about your chariot in attendance,
'Leading you in the tracks of the kings of old.'
But the Fragrant One refused to examine my true feelings:
He lent ear, instead, to slander, and raged against me.   40

How well I know that loyalty brings disaster;
Yet I will endure: I cannot give it up.
I called on the ninefold heaven to be my witness,

---

4. "True Exemplar" and "Divine Balance" are
pseudonyms. They could be word-plays on
"P'ing" and "Yüan".
5. Yü, T'ang, and Wu, founders of the Hsia,
Shang, and Chou dynasties.

6. Legendary Sage-kings.
7. Last kings of the Hsia and Shang dynasties,
traditionally described as monsters of iniquity.

And all for the sake of the Fair One, and no other.
                                        [Interpolation]   45
There once was a time when he spoke with me in frankness;
But then he repented and was of another mind.
I do not care, on my own count, about this divorcement,
But it grieves me to find the Fair One so inconstant.

I had tended many an acre of orchids,   50
And planted a hundred rods of melilotus;
I had raised sweet lichens and the cart-halting flower,
And asarums mingled with fragrant angelica,
And hoped that when leaf and stem were in fullest bloom,
When the time had come, I could reap a fine harvest.   55
Though famine should pinch me, it is small matter;
But I grieve that all my blossoms should waste in rank weeds.

All others press forward in greed and gluttony,
No surfeit satiating their demands:
Forgiving themselves, but harshly judging others;   60
Each fretting his heart away in envy and malice.
Madly they rush in the covetous chase,
But not after that which *my* heart sets store by.
For old age comes creeping and soon will be upon me,
And I fear I shall not leave behind an enduring name.   65

In the mornings I drank the dew that fell from the magnolia;
At evening ate the petals that dropped from chrysanthemums.
If only my mind can be truly beautiful,
It matters nothing that I often faint for famine.
I pulled up roots to bind the valerian   70
And thread the castor plant's fallen clusters with;
I trimmed sprays of cassia for plaiting melilotus,
And knotted the lithe, light trails of ivy.

I take my fashion from the good men of old:
A garb unlike that which the rude world cares for: 75
Though it may not accord with present-day manners,
I will follow the pattern that P'eng Hsien[8] has left.
Heaving a long sigh, I brush away my tears,
Grieving for man's life, so beset with hardships.
I have always loved pretty things to bind myself about with,   80
And so mornings I plaited and evenings I twined.

When I had finished twining my girdle of orchids,
I plucked some angelicas to add to its beauty.

---

8. A shaman ancestor, i.e. a long-dead shaman   late tradition says that he lived in the Shang
   who has become a guide to the initiate. A   Dynasty and that he drowned himself.

It is this that my heart takes most delight in,
And though I died nine times, I should not regret it.   85
What I do resent is the Fair One's waywardness:
Because he will never look to see what is in men's hearts.
All your ladies were jealous of my delicate beauty;
They chattered spitefully, saying I loved wantonness.

Truly, this generation are cunning artificers!   90
From square and compass they turn their eyes and change the true measurement,
They disregard the ruled line to follow their crooked fancies:
To emulate in flattery is their only rule.
But I am sick and sad at heart and stand irresolute:
I alone am at a loss in this generation.   95
But I would rather quickly die and meet dissolution
Before I ever would consent to ape *their* behaviour.

Eagles do not flock like birds of lesser species;
So it has ever been since the olden time.
How can the round and square ever fit together?   100
How can different ways of life ever be reconciled?
Yet humbling one's spirit and curbing one's pride,
Bearing blame humbly and enduring insults,
But keeping pure and spotless and dying in righteousness:
Such conduct was greatly prized by the wise men of old.   105

Repenting, therefore, that I had not conned the way more closely,
I halted, intending to turn back again—
To turn about my chariot and retrace my road
Before I had advanced too far along the path of folly.
I walked my horses through the marsh's orchid-covered margin;   110
I galloped to the hill of pepper-trees and rested there.
I could not go in to him for fear of meeting trouble,
And so, retired, I would once more fashion my former raiment.

I made a coat of lotus and water-chestnut leaves,
And gathered lotus petals to make myself a skirt.   115
I will no longer care that no one understands me,
As long as I can keep the sweet fragrance of my mind.
High towered the lofty hat on my head;
The longest of girdles dangled from my waist.
Fragrance and richness mingled in sweet confusion.   120
The brightness of their lustre has remained undimmed.

· · ·

Pepper is all wagging tongue and lives only for slander;
And even stinking Dogwood seeks to fill a perfume bag.
Since they only seek advancement and labour for position,
What fragrance have they deserving our respect?   125

Since, then, the world's way is to drift the way the tide runs,
Who can stay the same and not change with all the rest?
Seeing the behaviour of Orchid and Pepper flower,
What can be expected from cart-halt and selinea?
They have cast off their beauty and come to this: 130
Only my garland is left to treasure.
Its penetrating perfume does not easily desert it,
And even to this day its fragrance has not faded.

I will follow my natural bent and please myself;
I will go off wandering to look for a lady.   135
While my adornment is in its pristine beauty
I will travel all around looking both high and low.
Since Ling Fen had given me a favourable oracle,
I reckoned a lucky day to start my journey on.
I broke a branch of jasper to take for my meat,   140
And ground fine jasper meal for my journey's provisions.

'Harness winged dragons to be my coursers;
'Let my chariot be of fine work of jade and ivory!
'How can I live with men whose hearts are strangers to me?
'I am going a far journey to be away from them.'   145
I took the way that led towards the K'un-lun mountain:
A long, long road with many a turning in it.
The cloud-embroidered banner flapped its great shade above us;
And the jingling jade yoke-bells tinkled merrily.

I set off at morning from the Ford of Heaven;   150
At evening I came to the world's western end.
Phoenixes followed me, bearing up my pennants,
Soaring high aloft with majestic wing-beats.
'See, I have come to the desert of Moving Sands!'
Warily I drove along the banks of the Red Water;[9]   155
Then, beckoning the water-dragons to make a bridge for me,
I summoned the God of the West to take me over.

Long was the road that lay ahead and full of difficulties;
I sent word to my other chariots to take a short route and wait.
The road wound leftwards round the Pu Chou Mountain:[10]   160
I marked out the Western Sea as our meeting-place.
There I marshalled my thousand chariots,
And jade hub to jade hub we galloped on abreast.

---

9. The Moving Sands of mythological geography no doubt derive from travelers' tales of the Gobi Desert. The Red Water is one of the colored rivers that flow from K'un-lun.

10. The northwest pillar of heaven against which Kung Kung butted his head in the theomachia which tilted the earth downward in the southeast. It is also the gate of the underworld.

My eight dragon-steeds flew on with writhing undulations;
My cloud-embroidered banners flapped on the wind.   165

I tried to curb my mounting will and slacken the swift pace;
But the spirits soared high up, far into the distance.
We played the Nine Songs and danced the Nine Shao dances:[11]
I wanted to snatch some time for pleasure and amusement.
But when I had ascended the splendour of the heavens,   170
I suddenly caught a glimpse below of my old home.
The groom's heart was heavy and the horses for longing
Arched their heads back and refused to go on.

ENVOI

Enough! There are no true men in the state: no one to understand me.
Why should I cleave to the city of my birth?   175
Since none is worthy to work with in making good government,
I will go and join P'eng Hsien in the place where he abides.

FU HSÜAN [FU XUAN]

(THIRD CENTURY C.E.)

China

Fu Hsüan was a poet of the early Chin Dynasty. During his time, the period of the Three Kingdoms (220 C.E.–262 or 280 C.E.), which had seen the tripartition of China, was ended, and the nation was once again unified. Peace and relative social stability brought about a period in which both literature and art prospered.

From the time of the Han Dynasty, when a taste for elaborate court poetry was established, Chinese poetry had primarily moved in an elitist direction, cultivating intricate forms, ornate rhetorical devices, and inbred allusions. Alongside this learned tradition, however, existed a breath of fresh air: a genre called *yüeh-fu,* which had its roots in folk song. *Yüeh-fu* refers literally to a division of the bureaucracy, the Bureau of Music. Scholars employed in this bureau were charged with collecting folk songs as a means of gauging the national mood: "Find out what the people are singing about and report back to me," was the essence of their edicts. The poetic virtues of the songs did not go unnoticed, and a tradition began of writing in their simple, down-to-earth style.

Fu Hsüan wrote in the *yüeh-fu* tradition. In plain language, his poems depict

---

11. Not the Nine Songs of *Ch'u Tz'ü,* but those of Ch'i. The Nine Shao were danced to these songs.

with sympathy the poor and the unfortunate, especially women who were downtrodden and suppressed by male-dictated ethical codes.

Woman*

How sad it is to be a woman!
Nothing on earth is held so cheap.
Boys standing leaning at the door
Like Gods fallen out of Heaven.
Their hearts brave the Four Oceans,   5
The wind and dust of a thousand miles.
No one is glad when a girl is born;
By her the family sets no store.
When she grows up, she hides in her room
Afraid to look a man in the face.   10
No one cries when she leaves her home—
Sudden as clouds when the rain stops.
She bows her head and composes her face,
Her teeth are pressed on her red lips:
She bows and kneels countless times.   15
She must humble herself even to the servants.
His love is distant as the stars in Heaven,
Yet the sunflower bends toward the sun.
Their hearts more sundered than water and fire—
A hundred evils are heaped upon her.   20
Her face will follow the years' changes;
Her lord will find new pleasures.
They that were once like substances and shadow
Are now as far as Hu from Ch'in.[1]
Yet Hu and Ch'in shall sooner meet   25
Than they whose parting is like Ts'an and Ch'en.[2]

T'AO CH'IEN [TAO QIAN] (365–427 C.E.)
China

A native of Hsinyang in present-day Kiangsi province, T'ao Ch'ien (also known as T'ao Yüan-ming), was the literary giant of the late Chin period and arguably

Translated by Arthur Waley.

---

1. Two lands.   2. Two stars.

China's greatest pastoral poet. Despite the fact that he was the scion of a bureaucratic family, T'ao Ch'ien was reduced to poverty because he did not want a job in the bureaucracy, and had occasionally even to resort to begging in order to support his aging mother and himself. At thirty-two, he was made a magistrate, but he resigned this post after only one year, and after ten years in public service, returned to his rustic life.

The late Chin period was marked by turbulent disorder. In the face of repeated barbarian invasions from the north, the imperial court had moved southward to Nanjing in 318 C.E. Subsequently, the Chin house (today referred to as Eastern or Later Chin by historians) was plagued by the factional strife and political corruption that would eventually cause its downfall. T'ao Ch'ien's withdrawal into a rural life was his way of distancing himself from corrupt bureaucratic politics.

However, T'ao Ch'ien was not merely an escapist. During his time, the influence of Confucianism had significantly waned, yielding ground to Taoism and to a newcomer, Buddhism. T'ao Ch'ien's philosophy has often been said to be a harmonious combination of elements from these three sources, but in his love of nature and adherence to a natural way of living, involving no extraneous efforts, he was clearly closer to Taoism than anything else.

The Seasons Come and Go, Four Poems*

The seasons come and go: late spring is upon us. The spring garments are ready and, as the scenery is inviting, I stroll out by myself, with feelings of joy mixed with sadness.

1

By and by, the seasons come and go,
My, my! What a fine morning!
I put on my spring cloak
And set out east for the outskirts.
Mountains are cleansed by lingering clouds;   5
Sky is veiled by fine mist.
A wind comes up from the south,
Winging over the new sprouts.

2

Bank to bank, the stream is wide;
I rinse, then douse myself.
Scene by scene, the distant landscape;
I am happy as I look out.
People have a saying: 5
"A heart at peace is easy to please."
So I brandish this cup,
Happy to be by myself.

*Translated by Eugene Eoyang.

3

Peering into the depths of the stream,[1]
I remember the pure waters of the Yi,
There students and scholars worked together,
And, carefree, went home singing.
I love their inner peace,   5
Awake or asleep, I'd change places,
But, alas, those times are gone—
We can no longer bring them back.

4

In the morning and at night
I rest in my house.
Flowers and herbs are all in place;
Trees and bamboos cast their shadows.
A clear-sounding lute lies on my bed,   5
And there's half a jug of coarse wine.
Huang and T'ang[2] are gone forever:
Sad and alone, here I am.

On Returning to My Garden and Field, Two Selections[†]

1

When I was young, I did not fit into the common mold,
By instinct, I love mountains and hills.
By error, I fell into this dusty net
And was gone from home for thirteen years.
A caged bird yearns for its native woods;   5
The fish in a pond recalls old mountain pool.
Now I shall clear the land at the edge of the southern wild,
And, clinging to simplicity, return to garden and field.
My house and land on a two-acre lot,
My thatched hut of eight or nine rooms—   10
Elms and willows shade the eaves back of the house,
Peach and plum trees stand in a row before the hall.
Lost in a haze is the distant village,
Where smoke hovers above the homes.
Dogs bark somewhere in deep lanes,   15
Cocks crow atop the mulberry trees.
My home is free from dust and care,

[†]Translated by Wu-chi Liu.

---

1. Alluding to the ancient lustration rites held
   in the spring, on the bank of the Yi River.

2. The legendary emperors Huang-ti and Yao.

In a bare room there is leisure to spare.
Long a prisoner in a cage,
I am now able to come back to nature.   20

2

I plant beans at the foot of the southern hill;
The grass is thick and bean sprouts are sparse.
At dawn, I rise and go out to weed the field;
Shouldering the hoe, I walk home with the moon.
The path is narrow, grass and shrubs are tall,   5
And evening dew dampens my clothes.
Wet clothes are no cause for regret
So long as nothing goes contrary to my desire.

Miscellaneous Poems, Six Selections*

1

A man has no roots.
Blown about—like dust on the road,
In all directions, he tumbles with the wind:
Our lives are brief enough.
We come into this world as brothers and sisters: 5
But why must we be tied to flesh and blood?
Let's enjoy our happiness:
Here's a jug of wine, call in the neighbors.
The best times don't come often:
Each day dawns only once.   10
The seasons urge us on—
Time waits for no man.

2

Bright sun lights out over the western bank,
Pale moon comes out from behind the eastern ridge.
Far-reaching, this million-mile brilliance;
Transcendent, this scene in space.
A breeze comes through the window in my room.   5
At night the mat and pillow are cold.
The weather shifts: I sense the seasons change;
Unable to sleep, I know how long the night is.
I'd like to say something, but no one's around,
So I raise my cup, and toast my own shadow.   10
Days and months pass by—

*Translated by Eugene Eoyang

One cannot keep pace with ambition.
Thinking these thoughts, I am depressed;
Right through till dawn, I find rest impossible.

3

Bright blossoms seldom last long;
Life's ups-and-downs can't be charted.
What was a lotus flower in spring,
Is now the seed-husk of autumn.
Severe frost freezes the wild grass:
Decay has yet to finish it off.
Sun and moon come back once more,
But where I go, no sun will shine.
I look back longingly on times gone by—
Remembering the past wounds my soul.   10

4

A noble ambition spans the four seas;
Mine is simpler: not to grow old.
I'd like my family all in one place,
My sons and grandsons all caring for each other.
I want a goblet and a lute to greet each day,   5
And my wine casks never to run dry.
Belt loosened, I drink pleasure to the dregs:
I rise late, and retire early.
How can today be compared to yesterday?
My heart harbored both ice and coal.   10
In time, ashes return to ashes, dust to dust—
And vain is the way of fame and glory.

5

When I was young and in my prime,
If times were sad, I was happy on my own.
With brave plans that went beyond the sea,
I spread my wings, and dreamt of great flights.
But the course of time has run me down,   5
And my zest for life has begun to wane.
Enjoyment no longer makes me happy,
Each and every thing means more worry.
My strength is beginning to peter out,
I sense the change: one day's not like the last.   10
The hurrying barge can't wait for a moment:
It pulls me along and gives no rest.
The road ahead: how much farther?

Ch'en Hung-shou (1598–1652). Handscroll illustrating an ode of T'ao Ch'ien.

I don't know where I will come to rest.
The ancients begrudged a shadow's inch-of-time: 15
When I think of this, it makes me shudder.

6

Years ago, when I heard the words of my elders,
I'd cover my ears, not liking what they said.
Now that I am fifty years old,
These things suddenly matter.
To recapture the joys of my youth—   5
Does not appeal to me in the slightest.
Going, going, it's very quickly gone.
Who ever lives this life twice?
Let's use the household money for entertainment,
Before the years catch up with us.   10
I have children, but no money left:
No use leaving post-mortem trusts.

In Praise of Poor Scholars*

All creatures, each has a home:
The solitary cloud alone has none.
Here and there, into thin air, it vanishes:

*Translated by Eugene Eoyang

When do you ever see its traces?
Morning glow breaks through night's mist;   5
Flocks of birds fly off together—
One by one, winging out of the woods,
Not to return again until nightfall.
Know your strengths, keep to trodden ways.
Who hasn't known cold and hunger?   10
Those who know me: if they are no longer here—
That's it then. Why complain?

LIU I-CH'ING [LIU YIQING]

(403–444 C.E.)

China

Liu I-ch'ing was a prince of the royal family of the Sung Dynasty. Although known as a generous patron of literary talent, he was reportedly not a particularly gifted writer himself, and his *New Talk of the Town,* [*Shih-shuo hsin-yu*] therefore, may actually have been compiled by many hands.

Although fictional elements are by no means rare in China's early historical narratives, prose fiction as a genre arose relatively late. During the fifth century, Buddhism, with its emphasis on the other world, inspired a number of prose works telling stories of the supernatural and the miraculous. During this same period, Taoism (which considers other-worldly speculation pointless) inspired a vogue among the intelligentsia for *ch'ing-t'an*, or pure discourse unsullied by worldly (i.e., everyday, practical) concerns. Both genres had a significant impact on the evolution of Chinese fictional narrative.

New Talk of the Town, a collection of anecdotes and sayings of literati past and present, is an example of *ch'ing-t'an*. Written in a pithy style approaching oral presentation, these short pieces aim at entertainment rather than edification, but they do reflect the spirit of the age.

from **New Talk of the Town [Shih-shuo hsin-yu]**

Repartee [The Presence of the Two Sons of an Official Is Requested by the Twelve-Year-Old Emperor, to the Official's Trepidation]

[The ceremonial respect for authority in Chinese history was not mere ritual, for rulers were often terrifying in their absolute power. A minister was admired not only for loyalty, bordering on servility, but for his wit and tact. The following exchange involves the two sons

Translated by Eugene Eoyang.

of Chūng Yú (died 230 C.E.), both of whom were successful officials; it records a disarming instance of the awe in which the two held the Emperor.]*

Chūng Yú and Chūng Húi were much praised when they were small. At around the age of twelve, the Emperor of Wèn of Wéi heard about them, and said to their father Chūng Yú: "You may bring your two sons to court." They were thus commanded to appear. At the audience, Chung Yu's face broke out in beads of sweat. The Emperor asked: "Why are you perspiring?" To this, Chūng Yü replied:

> "Overcome with fear and trepidation,
> I cannot control my perspiration."

Then, turning to Chung Hui, the Emperor asked:
"And why do you *not* sweat?" To which, Hui replied:

> "Here I'm trembling and shivering yet,
> How could I possibly dare to sweat!"

[Learning: Pettiness and Envy Among Brilliant Minds]

[The following story concerns pettiness and envy among brilliant minds. Ma Jung (79–166 C.E.) was perhaps the most famous scholar of his generation, whose commentaries on the classics won him a great reputation and attracted a considerable following. Cheng Hsüan (127–200 C.E.) one of his most brilliant students, eventually surpassed his master, as this anecdote indicates.]

Cheng Hsüan was a disciple of Ma Jung, and had not been able to meet with the master for three years. Ma Jung's chief assistant would relay what the master said, and that was it. One day, the calculations on the astrolabe did not come out correctly and no one among the students could work it out. Someone said that Cheng Hsüan might be able to figure it out, so Ma Jung sent for him. With one turn, Cheng Hsüan was able to solve the problem, to the astonishment of all.

Later, Cheng Hsüan, upon completing his studies, took his leave and went home (east to Shantung). At that point, Ma Jung was sorry that his secrets on the Classic of Music and the Classic of Rites would go east with Hsüan. Afraid that Hsüan would now make a name for himself, Ma Jung became jealous. Hsüan, for his part, was on the alert, for he suspected an ambush. So he sat under a bridge, on top of the water, in wooden overshoes. Jung consequently turned his divining wheel to locate him, and then announced to those around him, "Hsüan is under the ground, above the water, and resting on wood. This must mean he is dead." And with that, he called off the search. Hsüan was thus able to escape in the end.

[Noble Ladies: The Story of Wang Chao-chün]

[The story of Wang Chao-chün is one of the most celebrated in all of Chinese literature: recounted in the official histories as well as in other chronicles; memorialized in verse (Li Po, for one, has two poems on the theme); recorded on a scroll found at Tun-huang; alluded to

---

*Through an accident of transliteration, Chung Yü and Chung Yu look very similar; in the Chinese, the names and the way they are pronounced are, of course, very different.

in many *tz'u* during the Sung period; the subject of dramas during the Yuan period; the variants differ in technique and in their details, but the essential story is the same. In the Han palace there were so many concubines that the emperor gave away his most beautiful woman by mistake to a Hsiung-nu chieftain. The ill-starred concubine, going out of loyalty to her country into what was considered an unspeakable exile among barbarians, became the central figure in a drama of pathos and self-sacrifice.]

In the palace of the Han emperor Yüan (who reigned 48 B.C.E. to 32 B.C.E.), there were so many ladies that he had portraits painted of each of them for reference. Instead of calling for them in person, they were summoned right away by means of the portraits. Now, among the ladies, there was a long-standing practice of offering bribes to the court painter.

Wang Chao-chün was exceptionally beautiful, but her disposition was such that she would not stoop to a bribe. The painter, as a result, spitefully distorted her portrait.

Later, when the Hsiung-nu came to the Han court to conclude an alliance, he sought a beautiful lady from the Han emperor. The emperor thought Wang Chao-chün dispensable and decided to give her up, but when he summoned her and saw her in person, he regretted his decision. But, since he had affixed his seal to the pact, there was no turning back on his word, and so he had to let her go.

[Outlandish Figures: The Drunkard]

[The total abandon of the drunkard has about it something of the aura of innocence. Vulnerable, totally without inhibitions, the drunkard seems to undercut the hypocrisy of social conventions, as the following episode shows.]

Liu Ling was constantly under the influence and totally abandoned in his behavior. Once he took off all his clothes and stood stark naked in the room. The people all made fun of him, but Ling said: "Heaven and earth are my abode; these rooms, this house are my trousers. What are you doing in my trousers?"

ANONYMOUS (FIRST CENTURY? C.E.)
China

Circulated in the second century C.E., this *yüeh-ju* is attributed to Lady Pan, a concubine of the Han emperor Ch'ung, who reigned from 32 to 37 C.E.

Song of Regret

To begin I cut fine silk of Ch'i,
white and pure as frost or snow,

Translated by Burton Watson.

shape it to make a paired-joy fan,
round, round as the luminous moon,
to go in and out of my lord's breast;   5
when lifted, to stir him a gentle breeze.
But always I dread the coming of autumn,
cold winds that scatter the burning heat,
when it will be laid away in the hamper,
love and favor cut off midway.   10

WANG WEI (701–761 C.E.)
China

Wang Wei was born in Hotung (present-day Jungchi in Shanhsi province). From
early childhood, he was recognized as a prodigy and began to compose poems at
the age of nine. After earning the *chin-shih* degree at twenty-one, he was
appointed to various official positions. In addition to his fame as one of the
leading poets of the T'ang Dynasty, a period regarded by the Chinese as their
golden age of poetry, Wang Wei was also a great innovator in calligraphy and
landscape painting.

A spiritual heir to T'ao Ch'ien, Wang Wei was a great admirer of natural
beauty and idyllic country life. His poems, like his paintings, never delineate the
details of nature, but rely instead on a few suggestive strokes to convey an effect
of pure elegance. In his later years, Wang Wei became increasingly absorbed in
the beauty of nature and thus detached himself from society: "I love only the
stillness, / The world's affairs no longer trouble my heart."

Seeing Someone Off*

Dismounting, I offer you wine
And ask, "Where are you bound?"
You say, "I've found no fame or favors;
"I must return to rest in the South Mountain."
You leave, and I ask no more—   5
White clouds drift on and on.

To Subprefect Chang*

In late years, I love only the stillness,
The world's affairs no longer trouble my heart.

*Translated by Irving Y. Lo.

Looking at myself: no far-reaching plans;
All I know: to return to familiar woods—
The pine winds blow and loosen my sash;   5
The mountain moon shines upon me playing the lute.
You ask for reasons for failure or success—
Fisherman's song enters the riverbanks deep.

Birdsong Brook*

Mind at peace, cassia flowers fall,
Night still, spring mountain empty.
Moon rising startles mountain birds
Now and again sing from spring brook.

Suffering from Heat†

The red sun fills the sky and the earth,
And fiery clouds are packed into hills and mountains.
Grasses and trees are all parched and shriveled;
Rivers and swamps, all utterly dried.
In light white silks I feel that my clothes are heavy;   5
Under dense trees I grieve that the shade is thin.
My mat of rushes cannot be approached;
My clothes of linen are washed again and again.

I long to escape beyond space and time;
In vast emptiness, dwell alone and apart.   10
Then long winds from a myriad miles would come;
Rivers and seas would cleanse me of trouble and dirt.
Then would I find that my body causes suffering;
Then would I know that my mind is still unawake.
I would suddenly enter the Gate of Pleasant Dew   15
And be at ease in the clear, cool joy.

†*Translated by Hugh M. Stimson.*

LI PO [LI BAI] (701?–762? C.E.)
China

Li Po's ancestral home was probably in Ch'engchi (near present-day T'ienshi, in Kansu province). Early in the seventh century, however, his ancestors were banished to Central Asia, where they lived for almost a century before Li Po's father brought the family back to China proper, settling in Ssuchuan [Sichuan] when Li Po was about six years old.

Li Po spent most of his life joining various reclusive groups or traveling around the country visiting friends and scenic spots. When he was forty-two, he was introduced by a friend to the imperial court, where his poetic talent so impressed the emperor that he was immediately appointed to an official position. But Li Po was too unconventional to confine himself to the rigors of court life, and three years later he found himself roaming again. Toward the end of his life, Li Po was exiled for his involvement in the famous An Lu-shan rebellion; he died shortly after the punishment was lifted.

More than any other T'ang poet, Li Po is "romantic" in the full sense of the word. In his poems we hear him deriding various forms of social vanity that suppress spontaneous individuality ("Bringing in the Wine"); we feel the pulse of

Su Han-ch'en (active 1124–1162 C.E.), *A Lady on a Garden Terrace.*

human psyche and emotions ("The River-Merchant's Wife: A Letter" and "Written in Behalf of My Wife"). Above all we see the poet's true self—forthright, unconstrained, and somewhat hedonistic.

Fully exploring the possibilities of folk songs, Li Po was versatile stylistically. His poems are known for their grandeur and forcefulness, but they do not lack subtlety. Deservedly, Li Po keeps a supreme place in the history of Chinese poetry, where he is known as "The Transcendent Exile from Heaven."

The River-Merchant's Wife: A Letter*

While my hair was still cut straight across my forehead
I played about the front gate, pulling flowers.
You came by on bamboo stilts, playing horse,
You walked about my seat, playing with blue plums.
And we went on living in the village of Chokan: 5
Two small people, without dislike or suspicion.

At fourteen I married My Lord you.
I never laughed, being bashful.
Lowering my head, I looked at the wall.
Called to, a thousand times, I never looked back.   10

At fifteen I stopped scowling,
I desired my dust to be mingled with yours
For ever and for ever and for ever.
Why should I climb the look out?

At sixteen you departed,   15
You went into far Ku-to-yen, by the river of swirling eddies,
And you have been gone five months.
The monkeys make sorrowful noise overhead.

You dragged your feet when you went out.
By the gate now, the moss is grown, the different mosses,   20
Too deep to clear them away!
The leaves fall early this autumn, in wind.
The paired butterflies are already yellow with August
Over the grass in the West garden:
They hurt me. I grow older.   25

If you are coming down through the narrows of the river Kiang
Please let me know beforehand.
And I will come out to meet you
            As far as Cho-fu-Sa.

*Translated by Ezra Pound.

Written in Behalf of My Wife[†]

To cleave a running stream with a sword,
The water will never be severed.
My thoughts that follow you in your wanderings
Are as interminable as the stream.
Since we parted, the grass before our gate   5
In the autumn lane has turned green in spring.
I sweep it away but it grows back,
Densely it covers your footprints.
The singing phoenixes were happy together;
Startled, the male and the female each flies away.   10
On which mountaintop have the drifting clouds stayed?
Once gone, they never are seen to return.
From a merchant traveling to Ta-lou,
I learn you are there at Autumn Cove.
In the Liang Garden[1] I sleep in an empty embroidered bed;   15
On the Yang Terrace you dream of the drifting rain.[2]
Three times my family has produced a prime minister;
Then moved to west Ch'in since our decline.
We still have our old flutes and songs,
Their sad notes heard everywhere by neighbors.   20
When the music rises to the purple clouds,
I cry for the absence of my beloved.
I am like a peach tree at the bottom of a well,
For whom will the blossoms smile?
You are like the moon high in the sky,   25
Unwilling to cast your light on me.
I cannot recognize myself when I look in the mirror,
I must have grown thin since you left home.
If only I could own the fabled parrot
To tell you of the feelings in my heart!   30

Bringing in the Wine[‡]

[written to music]

See how the Yellow River's waters move out of heaven.
Entering the ocean, never to return.
See how lovely locks in bright mirrors in high chambers,

[†]*Translated by Joseph J. Lee.*
[‡]*Translated by Witter Bynner.*

---

1. A region in southeastern Honan.
2. Yang Terrace refers to the general area on the Yangtze. The line alludes not only to Li

Po's whereabouts, but also to Sung Yü's "Shen-nü Fu."

Though silken-black at morning, have changed by night to snow.
. . . Oh, let a man of spirit venture where he pleases   5
And never tip his golden cup empty toward the moon!
Since heaven gave the talent, let it be employed!
Spin a thousand pieces of silver, all of them come back!
Cook a sheep, kill a cow, whet the appetite,
And make me, of three hundred bowls, one long drink!   10
. . . To the old master, Ts'ên,
And the young scholar, Tan-ch'iu,

Bring in the wine!
Let your cups never rest!
Let me sing you a song!   15
Let your ears attend!
What are bell and drum, rare dishes and treasure?
Let me be forever drunk and never come to reason!
Sober men of olden days and sages are forgotten,
And only the great drinkers are famous for all time.   20
. . . Prince Ch'ên paid at a banquet in the Palace of Perfection
Ten thousand coins for a cask of wine, with many a laugh and quip.
Why say, my host, that your money is gone?
Go and buy wine and we'll drink it together!
My flower-dappled horse,   25
My furs worth a thousand,
Hand them to the boy to exchange for good wine,
And we'll drown away the woes of ten thousand generations!

Farewell to Meng Hao-jan[§]

I took leave of you, old friend, at the
Yellow Crane Pavilion;
In the mist and bloom of March, you went
down to Yang-chou:
A lonely sail, distant shades, extinguished   5
by blue—
There, at the horizon, where river meets sky.

Drinking Alone in the Moonlight[‡]

From a pot of wine among the flowers
I drank alone. There was no one with me—
Till, raising the cup, I asked the bright moon
To bring me my shadow and make us three.

[§]Translated by Eugene Eoyang.
[‡]Translated by Witter Bynner

Alas, the moon was unable to drink   5
And my shadow tagged me vacantly;
But still for a while I had these friends
To cheer me through the end of spring. . . .
I sang, the moon encouraged me.
I danced. My shadow tumbled after.   10

As long as I knew, we were boon companions.
And then I was drunk, and we lost one another.
. . . Shall goodwill ever be secure?
I watch the long road of the River of Stars.

TU FU [DU FU] (712–772 C.E.)
China

Tu Fu was a native of Hsiangyang, located in present-day Honan province. When he was twenty, he began traveling around the country, meeting scholars and poets, including Li Po. The two poets became lifelong friends, and their friendship found sincere expression in poems such as "Dreaming of Li Po." Tu Fu sat for the civil service examination several times but never passed it, and he was in his forties before he was finally appointed to a minor official position. In his later years Tu Fu lived mostly in Ch'engtu. In 772, he died on his way to visit friends.

Tu Fu's life was marked by poverty, instability, anxiety, and frustration. He was especially affected by the devastation and human suffering he witnessed in the aftermath of the An Lu-shan rebellion, and in his poems he voiced his concern for his family, for the people of China, and for the state. In the history of Chinese literature, Tu Fu's name is most often mentioned in the same breath with that of Li Po, the two forming twin peaks in the land of poetry. Although Li Po's poetry largely transcends social realities, Tu Fu was in fact a realist—"a poet-historian," as he is often called—and he used his gifts to call attention to the urgent social conditions of his time.

Meandering River, Two Poems*

1

A single petal swirling diminishes the spring.
Ten thousand dots adrift in the wind, they sadden me.
Shouldn't I then gaze at flowers about to fall before my eyes?

*Translated by Irving Y. Lo.

Never disdain the hurtful wine that passes through my lips.
In a small pavilion by the river nest the kingfisher birds;   5
Close by a high tomb in the royal park lie stone unicorns.
This, a simple law of nature: seek pleasure while there's time.
Who needs drifting fame to entangle this body?

2

Returning from court day after day, I pawn my spring clothes;
Every time I come home drunk from the riverbank.
A debt of wine is a paltry, everyday affair;
To live till seventy is rare since Time began.
Deep among the flowers, butterflies press their way;   5
The slow-winged dragonflies dot the water.
I'd whisper to the wind and light: "Together let's tarry;
We shall enjoy the moment, and never contrary be."

Dreaming of Li Po, Two Poems[†]

1

Parted by death, we swallow remorse;
Apart in life, we always suffer.
South of the river, miasmal place,
From the banished exile, not a word!
Old friend, you appeared in a dream,   5
It shows you have long been in my thoughts.
Perhaps it wasn't your living soul[1]
The way's too far, it couldn't be done.
Your spirit came: and the maples were green:
Your spirit left: the mountain pass darkened.   10
Friend, now that you're ensnared down there,[2]
How did you manage to wing away?
Moonlight shines full on the rafters,
Yet I wonder if it isn't your reflection.
The waters are deep, the waves expansive: 15
They won't let the water-dragon prevail!

[†]Translated by Eugene Eoyang.

"Dreaming of Li Po, Two Poems"

1. The popular conception distinguished between the soul of a living being and the soul
of a dead being. The soul of a living being
was more circumscribed in its movements,
but the soul of the deceased could roam at
will across great distances.
2. The image of the net plays an important

role in both this and the next poem. Here
reference is made to the net of the law. The
injustice of this net moves Tu Fu to write in
"Twenty Rhymes to Li Po": "When they
applied the old laws to your case,/Was
there no one to point this out?" It is against
this net of the law, which has kept Li Po in
exile away from the capital, that Tu Fu rails.

2

Drifting clouds pass by all day long;
The wanderer is long in getting here.
Three nights now you've entered my dreams—
Which shows how good a friend you are.
But your leave-takings are hurried,   5
Bitterly you say, it's not easy to come;
The river's waters are wind-blown and choppy,
And you're afraid to lose your oars.
Outside the door, you scratch your white head,
As if a lifetime's ambition were forfeit.   10
Officials teem in the capital city,[3]
Yet you alone are wretched.
Who says the net is wide,[4]
When it tangles such a man in his old age?
An imperishable fame of a thousand years   15
Is but a paltry, after-life affair.

*Random Pleasures: Nine Quatrains**

1

See a traveler in sorrow: deeper is his grief
As wanton spring steals into the river pavilion—
True, the flowers will rush to open,
Yet how the orioles will keep up their songs.

2

Those peach and plum trees planted by hand are not without a master:
The rude wall is low; still it's my home.
But 'tis just like the spring wind, that master bully:
Last night it blew so many blossomed branches down.

---

*Translated by Irving Y. Lo

---

3. Cf. "For Li Po," "Two years I've been in the
   Eastern Capital,/And had my fill of cunning
   and conniving."
4. Here, the net is the net of Heaven (cf. Ch.
   78 of the *Tao Te Ching*: "Heaven's net is
   wide; Coarse are the meshes, yet nothing
   slips through"—Waley translation).
   Hawkes (*A Little Primer of Tu Fu*, Oxford
   University Press, 1967, p. 97) contrasts the
   net here with that in the first poem: "The

net here is not the net of the law . . . but the
net with which the Emperor, as a fisher of
men, gathers up men of talent to put in
positions of responsibility. Li Po, one of the
biggest fish of all, has managed to elude the
imperial fisherman." This contrast, between
the "net of the law" and "the net of
Heaven," is critical to an understanding of
both poems.

3

How well they know my study's low and small—
The swallows from the riverside find reason to visit me often:
Carrying mud to spot and spoil my lute and books,
And trailing a flight of gnats that strike my face.

4

March is gone, and April's come:
Old fellow, how many more chances to welcome the spring?
Don't think of the endless affairs beyond the hereafter;
Just drain your lifetime's few allotted cups.

5

Heartbroken—there springtime river trickles to its end:
Cane in hand, I slowly pace and stand on fragrant bank.
How impertinent the willow catkins to run off with the wind;
So fickle, the peach blossoms to drift with the stream!

6

I've grown so indolent I never leave the village;
At dusk I shout to the boy to shut the rustic gate.
Green moss, raw wine, calm in the grove;
Blue water, spring breeze, dusk on the land.

7

Path-strewn catkins spread out a white carpet;
Stream-dotting lotus leaves mound up green coins.
By the bamboo roots, a young pheasant unseen;
On the sandbank, ducklings by their mother, asleep.

8

West of my house, young mulberry leaves are ready for picking;
Along the river, new wheat, so tender and soft.
How much more is left of life when spring has turned to summer?
Don't pass up good wine, sweeter than honey.

9

The willows by the gate are slender and graceful
Like the waist of a girl at fifteen.
Morning came, and who could fail to see
Mad wind had snapped the longest branch.

Two Quatrains†

1

I lounge on the jetty in the fragrance of catalpa
The fresh young buds all seem too young to fly
I'll stay drunk until the wind's through blowing
Could I bear, if I were sober, the rains come smash, and scatter?

2

Beyond the gate the cormorant had gone and not returned
Now on the sandbank, suddenly, he greets my waiting eye
From this moment he must know my mind
And every day return a hundred times.

Night§

Over sheer banks a menacing wind moves,
In a cold room the candle shadow dims,
The mountain ape sleeps out in the frost,
And the river bird flies deep into night.
Sitting alone I befriend a manly sword,
With a mournful song, sigh at my short gown.
Smoke and dust encircle the palace gate;
White head pays no heed to a stout heart.

Jade Flower Palace**

The stream swirls. The wind moans in
The pines. Grey rats scurry over
Broken tiles. What prince, long ago,
Built this palace, standing in

†*Translated by Jerome P. Seaton.*
§*Translated by Jan W. Walls.*
****Translated by Kenneth Rexroth.*

Ruins beside the cliffs? There are   5
Green ghost fires in the black rooms.
The shattered pavements are all
Washed away. Ten thousand organ
Pipes whistle and roar. The storm
Scatters the red autumn leaves.   10
His dancing girls are yellow dust.
Their painted cheeks have crumbled
Away. His gold chariots
And courtiers are gone. Only
A stone horse is left of his   15
Glory. I sit on the grass and
Start a poem, but the pathos of
It overcomes me. The future
Slips imperceptibly away.
Who can say what the years will bring?   20

Restless Night††

The cool of bamboo invades my room;
moonlight from the fields fills the corners of the court;
dew gathers till it falls in drops;
a scattering of stars, now there, now gone.
A firefly threading the darkness makes his own light;   5
birds at rest on the water call to each other;
all these lie within the shadow of the sword—
Powerless I grieve as the clear night passes.

PO CHÜ-YI [BAI JUYI] (772–846 C.E.)
China

Po Chü-yi is generally regarded as the third greatest poet of the T'ang period, surpassed only by Li Po and Tu Fu. A native of the province of Shensi, Po Chü-yi was born into a scholar official's family. After earning the *chin-shih* degree at twenty-nine, Po Chü-yi was appointed to a succession of official posts in various parts of the empire. His long life and broad experience enabled him to be the most prolific poet of the T'ang period, leaving us a corpus of over three thousand poems.

Despite his successful official career, Po Chü-yi was an advocate of the impoverished and underprivileged. With Yüan Chen, another poet, Po Chü-yi formed a literary comradeship, one purpose of which was to promote the socially

††*Translated by Burton Watson.*

utilitarian functions of poetry. In many of his poems, such as "Bitter Cold, Living in the Village," "The Old Man of Hsin-feng with the Broken Arm" and "An Old Charcoal Seller," Po Chü-yi expresses his boundless sympathy for unfortunate people and protests social inequities. In the famous "A Song of Unending Sorrow," however, Po Chü-yi was more ambivalent; he castigates the rulers for their sumptuous way of living, but he obviously savors the love between the emperor and his beautiful consort.

Stylistically, Po Chü-yi endeavored to revitalize the *yüeh-fu*, a poetic genre that came into being during the Han period and was rooted in folk song. Indeed, many of Po Chü-yi's poems were written in such a colloquial diction that some critics have called them "pseudo–folk songs."

Bitter Cold, Living in the Village*

In the twelfth month of the Eighth Year,
On the fifth day, a heavy snow fell.
Bamboos and cypress all perished from the freeze.
How much worse for people without warm clothes!

As I looked around the village,   5
Of ten families, eight or nine were in need.
The north wind was sharper than the sword,
And homespun cloth could hardly cover one's body.
Only brambles were burnt for firewood,
And sadly people sat at night to wait for dawn.   10

From this I know that when winter is harsh,
The farmers suffer most.
Looking at myself, during these days—
How I'd shut tight the gate of my thatched hall,
Cover myself with fur, wool, and silk,   15
Sitting or lying down, I had ample warmth.
I was lucky to be spared cold or hunger,
Neither did I have to labor in the field.

Thinking of that, how can I not feel ashamed?
I ask myself what kind of man am I.   20

The Old Man of Hsin-feng with the Broken Arm†1

An old man from Hsin-feng, eighty-eight years old,
Hair on his temples and his eyebrows white as snow.

*Translated by Irving Y. Lo.
†Translated by Eugene Eoyang.

---

1. Author's subtitle "To Warn Against Militarism: New Music Bureau Ballads" (*Hsin Yüeh-fu*), No. 9. Each poem in Po Chü-yi's "New Music Bureau Ballads" carries a similar subtitle, which states the moral implied.

Leaning on his great-great-grandson, he walks to the front of the inn,
His left arm on the boy's shoulder, his right arm broken.
I ask the old man how long has his arm been broken,
And how it came about, how it happened.   5
The old man said he grew up in the Hsin-feng district.
He was born during blessed times, without war or strife.
And he used to listen to the singing and dancing in the Pear Garden,
Knew nothing of banner and spear, or bow and arrow.   10
Then, during the T'ien-pao period, a big army was recruited:
From each family, one was taken out of every three,
And of those chosen, where were they sent?
Five months, ten thousand miles away, to Yunnan,
Where, it is said, the Lu River runs,   15
Where, when flowers fall from pepper trees, noxious fumes rise;
Where, when a great army fords the river, with its seething eddies,
Two or three out of ten never reach the other side.

The village, north and south, was full of the sound of wailing,
Sons leaving father and mother, husbands leaving wives.   20
They all said, of those who went out to fight the barbarians,
Not one out of a thousand lived to come back.
At the time, this old man was twenty-four,
And the army had his name on their roster.

"Then, late one night, not daring to let anyone know,   25
By stealth, I broke my arm, smashed it with a big stone.
Now I was unfit to draw the bow or carry the flag,
And I would be spared the fighting in Yunnan.
Bone shattered, muscles ached, it wasn't unpainful,
But I could count on being rejected and sent home.   30

"This arm has been broken now for over sixty years:
I've lost one limb, but the body's intact.
Even now, in cold nights, when the wind and rain blow,
Right up to daybreak, I hurt so much I cannot sleep,
But I have never had any regrets.   35
At least, now I alone have survived.
Or else, years ago at the River Lu,
I would have died, my spirit fled, and my bones left to rot:
I would have wandered, a ghost in Yunnan looking for home,
Mourning over the graves of ten thousands."   40

So the old man spoke: I ask you to listen.
Have you not heard of the Prime Minister of the K'ai-yüan period,
    Sung K'ai-fu?
How he wouldn't reward frontier campaigns, not wanting to glorify war?
And, have you not heard of Yang Kuo-chung, the Prime Minister of the T'ien-pao
    period?

Wishing to seek favor, he achieved military deeds at the frontier,   45
But, before he could pacify the frontier, the people became disgruntled:
Ask the old man of Hsin-feng with the broken arm!

An Old Charcoal Seller†

An old charcoal seller
Cuts firewood, burns coal by the southern mountain.
His face, all covered with dust and ash, the color of smoke,
The hair at his temples is gray, his ten fingers black.
The money he makes selling coal, what is it for?   5
To put clothes on his back and food in his mouth.
The rags on his poor body are thin and threadbare;
Distressed at the low price of coal, he hopes for colder weather.
Night comes, an inch of snow has fallen on the city,
In the morning, he rides his cart along the icy ruts,   10
His ox weary, he hungry, and the sun already high.
In the mud by the south gate, outside the market, he stops to rest.
All of a sudden, two dashing riders appear;
An imperial envoy, garbed in yellow (his attendant in white),
Holding an official dispatch, he reads a proclamation.   15
Then turns the cart around, curses the ox, and leads it north.
One cartload of coal—a thousand or more vessels!
No use appealing to the official spiriting the cart away:
Half a length of red lace, a slip of damask
Dropped on the ox—is payment in full!   20

To My Brothers and Sisters Adrift in Troubled Times
This Poem of the Moon‡

[Since the disorders in Ho-nan and the famine in Kuan-nêi, my brothers and sisters have
been scattered. Looking at the moon, I express my thoughts in this poem, which I send to my
eldest brother at Fou-liang, my seventh brother at Yü-ch'ien, my fifteenth brother at
Wu-chiang and my younger brothers and sisters at Fu-li and Hsia-kuêi.]

My heritage lost through disorder and famine,
My brothers and sisters flung eastward and westward,
My fields and gardens wrecked by the war,
My own flesh and blood become scum of the street,
I moan to my shadow like a lone-wandering wildgoose,   5
I am torn from my root like a water-plant in autumn:
I gaze at the moon, and my tears run down
For hearts, in five places, all sick with one wish.

†Translated by Eugene Eoyang.
‡Translated by Witter Bynner.

A Song of Unending Sorrow[†]

China's Emperor, craving beauty that might shake an empire,
Was on the throne for many years, searching, never finding,
Till a little child of the Yang clan, hardly even grown,
Bred in an inner chamber, with no one knowing her,
But with graces granted by heaven and not to be concealed,   5
At last one day was chosen for the imperial household.
If she but turned her head and smiled, there were cast a hundred spells,
And the powder and paint of the Six Palaces faded into nothing.
. . . It was early spring. They bathed her in the Flower-Pure Pool,
Which warmed and smoothed the creamy-tinted crystal of her skin,   10
And, because of her languor, a maid was lifting her
When first the Emperor noticed her and chose her for his bride.
The cloud of her hair, petal of her cheek, gold ripples of her crown when she
    moved,
Were sheltered on spring evenings by warm hibiscus-curtains;
But nights of spring were short and the sun arose too soon,   15
And the Emperor, from that time forth, forsook his early hearings
And lavished all his time on her with feasts and revelry,
His mistress of the spring, his despot of the night.
There were other ladies in his court, three thousand of rare beauty,
But his favours to three thousand were concentered in one body.   20
By the time she was dressed in her Golden Chamber, it would be almost evening;
And when tables were cleared in the Tower of Jade, she would loiter, slow with
    wine.
Her sisters and her brothers all were given titles;
And, because she so illumined and glorified her clan,
She brought to every father, every mother through the empire,   25
Happiness when a girl was born rather than a boy.
. . . High rose Li Palace, entering blue clouds,
And far and wide the breezes carried magical notes
Of soft song and slow dance, of string and bamboo music.
The Emperor's eyes could never gaze on her enough—   30
Till war-drums, booming from Yü-yang, shocked the whole earth
And broke the tunes of *The Rainbow Skirt and the Feathered Coat*.
The Forbidden City, the nine-tiered palace, loomed in the dust
From thousands of horses and chariots headed southwest.
The imperial flag opened the way, now moving and now pausing—   35
But thirty miles from the capital, beyond the western gate,
The men of the army stopped, not one of them would stir
Till under their horses' hoofs they might trample those moth-eyebrows . . .
Flowery hairpins fell to the ground, no one picked them up,
And a green and white jade hair-tassel and a yellow-gold hairbird.   40
The Emperor could not save her, he could only cover his face.
And later when he turned to look, the place of blood and tears

Was hidden in a yellow dust blown by a cold wind.
. . . At the cleft of the Dagger-Tower Trail they criss-crossed through a cloud-line
Under O-mêi Mountain. The last few came.   45
Flags and banners lost their colour in the fading sunlight . . .
But as waters of Shu are always green and its mountains always blue,
So changeless was His Majesty's love and deeper than the days.
He stared at the desolate moon from his temporary palace.
He heard bell-notes in the evening rain, cutting at his breast.   50
And when heaven and earth resumed their round and the dragon-car faced home,
The Emperor clung to the spot and would not turn away
From the soil along the Ma-wêi Slope, under which was buried
That memory, that anguish. Where was her jade-white face?
Ruler and lords, when eyes would meet, wept upon their coats   55
As they rode, with loose rein, slowly eastward, back to the capital.
. . . The pools, the gardens, the palace, all were just as before,
The Lake T'ai-yi hibiscus, the Wêi-yang Palace willows;
But a petal was like her face and a willow-leaf her eyebrow—
And what could he do but cry whenever he looked at them?   60
. . . Peach-trees and plum-trees blossomed, in the winds of spring;
Lakka-foliage fell to the ground, after autumn rains;
The Western and Southern Palaces were littered with late grasses,
And the steps were mounded with red leaves that no one swept away.
Her Pear-Garden Players became white-haired   65
And the eunuchs thin-eyebrowed in her Court of Pepper-Trees;
Over the throne flew fire-flies, while he brooded in the twilight.
He would lengthen the lamp-wick to its end and still could never sleep.
Bell and drum would slowly toll the dragging night-hours
And the River of Stars grow sharp in the sky, just before dawn,   70
And the porcelain mandarin-ducks on the roof grow thick with morning frost
And his covers of kingfisher-blue feel lonelier and colder
With the distance between life and death year after year;
And yet no beloved spirit ever visited his dreams.
. . . At Lin-ch'iung lived a Taoist priest who was a guest of heaven,   75
Able to summon spirits by his concentrated mind.
And people were so moved by the Emperor's constant brooding
That they besought the Taoist priest to see if he could find her.
He opened his way in space and clove the ether like lightning,
Up to heaven, under the earth, looking everywhere.   80
Above, he searched the Green Void, below, the Yellow Spring;
But he failed, in either place, to find the one he looked for.
And then he heard accounts of an enchanted isle at sea,
A part of the intangible and incorporeal world,
With pavilions and fine towers in the five-coloured air,   85
And of exquisite immortals moving to and fro,
And of one among them—whom they called The Ever True—
With a face of snow and flowers resembling hers he sought.

So he went to the West Hall's gate of gold and knocked at the jasper door
And asked a girl, called Morsel-of-Jade, to tell The Doubly-Perfect.   90
And the lady, at news of an envoy from the Emperor of China,
Was startled out of dreams in her nine-flowered canopy.
She pushed aside her pillow, dressed, shook away sleep,
And opened the pearly shade and then the silver screen.
Her cloudy hair-dress hung on one side because of her great haste,   95
And her flower-cap was loose when she came along the terrace,
While a light wind filled her cloak and fluttered with her motion
As though she danced *The Rainbow Skirt and the Feathered Coat*.
And the tear-drops drifting down her sad white face
Were like a rain in spring on the blossom of the pear.   100
But love glowed deep within her eyes when she bade him thank her liege,
Whose form and voice had been strange to her ever since their parting—
Since happiness had ended at the Court of the Bright Sun,
And moons and dawns had become long in Fairy-Mountain Palace.
But when she turned her face and looked down toward the earth   105
And tried to see the capital, there were only fog and dust.
So she took out, with emotion, the pledges he had given
And, through his envoy, sent him back a shell box and gold hairpin,
But kept one branch of the hairpin and one side of the box,
Breaking the gold of the hairpin, breaking the shell of the box;   110
"Our souls belong together," she said, "like this gold and this shell—
Somewhere, sometime, on earth or in heaven, we shall surely meet."
And she sent him, by his messenger, a sentence reminding him
Of vows which had been known only to their two hearts:
"On the seventh day of the Seventh-month, in the Palace of Long Life,   115
We told each other secretly in the quiet midnight world
That we wished to fly in heaven, two birds with the wings of one,
And to grow together on the earth, two branches of one tree."
. . . Earth endures, heaven endures; some time both shall end,
While this unending sorrow goes on and on for ever.   120

LI CH'ING-CHAO [LI QINGZHAO]

(1084?–c.1151 C.E.)

China

Indisputably China's most noted woman poet, Li Ch'ing-chao lived during a
period straddling the Northern and the Southern Sung dynasties. The daughter
of a distinguished man of letters from Tsi-nan, Shantung, she married a scholar

named Chao Ming-ch'eng. At the time of the invasion of the Chin Tartars (the event that caused the Sung to move their capital south, ushering in the Southern Sung period), the couple hastily made their escape southward, but the husband died after they reached Chienk'ang (present-day Nanjing). Lonely and wretched, the poet spent the rest of her life in Hangchou and Chinhua.

In addition to inheriting an extremely rich tradition of poetry from the T'ang, the Sung Dynasty saw the flourishing of a newly popular form called *tz'u*. Originating in popular song, *tz'u* were written to fit certain specified tunes. Like many other Sung poets, Li Ch'ing-chao wrote mostly in the *tz'u* tradition.

In Li Ch'ing-chao's poems, of which only some fifty are extant, we hear the many voices of the poet, the facets of a distinctly feminine sensibility. To her, the blissful matrimonial life was only to be recaptured in poetry ("Tune: 'Magnolia Blossoms, Abbreviated' " and "Tune: 'Song of Picking Mulberry' "). Except for a few bright moments of delight ("Tune: 'Manifold Little Hills' "), most of her poems convey the sorrow and melancholy of widowhood. She was incomparable in depicting personal feelings with vigor and honesty and in transcending the subjective and the merely anecdotal.

Tune: *Spring at Wu-ling*

The wind subsides—a fragrance
    of petals freshly fallen;
it's late in the day—I'm too tired
    to comb my hair.
Things remain but he is gone
    and with him everything.
On the verge of words: tears flow.

I hear at Twin Creek spring it's still lovely;
how I long to float there on a small boat—
But I fear at Twin Creek my frail "grasshopper" boat
could not carry this load of grief.

Tune: *A Southern Song*

In the sky the Milky Way turns;
here on earth a curtain drops.
A chill collects on the pillow-mat, wet with tears.
I get up to untie my silk gown,
    wondering what hour of night it is.

The blue-tinted lotus pod is small
the gold-spotted lotus leaves are sparse.
Old-time weather, old-time clothes

Translated by Eugene Eoyang.

only bring back memories
  but nothing like real old times.   10

Tune: Tipsy in the Flower's Shade

Thin mists—thick clouds—sad all day long.
The gold animal spurts incense from its head.
Once more it's the Festival of Double Nine[1]:
On the jade pillow—through mesh bed curtains—
the chill of midnight starts seeping through.   5

At the eastern hedge[2] I drink a cup after dusk;
furtive fragrances fill my sleeve.
Don't say one can't be overwhelmed:
when the west wind furls up the curtain,
I'm more fragile than the yellow chrysanthemum.   10

Tune: Manifold Little Hills

Spring has come to the gate—spring's grasses green;
some red blossoms on the plum tree burst open,
others have yet to bloom.
Azure clouds gather, grind out jade into dust.
Let's keep this morning's dream: 5
break open a jug of spring!

Flower's shadows press at the gate;
translucent curtains thin out pale moonlight.
It's a lovely evening!
Over two years—three times—you've missed the spring.   10
Come back!
Let's enjoy this one to the full!

Tune: Magnolia Blossoms, Abbreviated

From the pole of the flower vendor
I bought a sprig of spring about to bloom,

---

1. The Double Nine refers to the ninth day of
   the ninth month by the lunar calendar
   (which corresponds to early October),
   which the Chinese call *Ch'ung Yang*. On this
   day, the custom is to climb to high ground,
   take some wine in which chrysanthemum
   petals have been dropped, and compose
   poetry. The festival was especially important to Li Ch'ing-chao, because it was asso-

   ciated with T'ao Ch'ien, the poet whom she
   and her husband preferred to all others and
   who was known for his poems on the
   chrysanthemum.
2. Referring to T'ao Ch'ien's famous lines:
   "Picking chrysanthemums by the eastern
   hedge / I catch sight of the distant southern
   hills."

tear-speckled, lightly sprinkled,
still touched by a rose mist and dawn's early dew.

Should my beloved chance to ask,   5
if my face weren't fair as a flower's,
I'd put one aslant in my hair,
then ask him to look and compare.

Tune: The Charm of Nien-nu

Lonely courtyard,
once more slanting wind, misty rain,
the double-hinged door must be shut.
Graceful willow, delicate blossoms,
    Cold Food Day approaches,   5
and with it every kind of unsettling weather.
    I work out a few ingenious rhymes,
    clear my head of weak wine,
    exceptional, the taste of idleness.
Migrating wild geese wing out of sight   10
but they cannot convey my teeming thoughts.

In my pavilion, cold for days with spring chill,
    the curtains are drawn on all sides.
I am too weary to lean over the balustrade.
The incense sputters, the quilt feels cold,   15
    I am just awake from a dream.
No dallying in bed for one who grieves,
    when clear dew descends with the dawn,
    and the *wu-t'ung* tree is about to bud.
There are so many diversions in spring.   20
The sun is rising: the fog withdraws;
see: it will be a fine day after all.

Tune: As in a Dream: A Song (Two Lyrics)

1

How many evenings in the arbor by the river,
when flushed with wine we'd lose our way back.
The mood passed away, returning late by boat
we'd stray off into a spot thick with lotus,
    and thrashing through   5
            and thrashing through
startle a shoreful of herons by the lake.

2

Last night, a bit of rain, gusty wind,
a deep sleep did not dispel the last of the wine.
I ask the maid rolling up the blinds—
but she replies: "The crab apple is just as it was."
   Doesn't she know?
          doesn't she know?
The leaves should be lush and the petals frail.

Tune: *Sand of Silk-washing Stream* (Two Lyrics)

1

Mild and peaceful spring glow, Cold Food Day.
From a jade censer, incense curls out in wisps of smoke.
My dream returns me to the hills of my pillow, hiding my hairpins.
The sea swallows have not yet come,
   idly we duel with blades of grass.
By the river the plum trees have bloomed,
   catkins sprout from the willow,
and at dusk scattered showers
   sprinkle the garden swing.

2

In the little courtyard, by the side window,
   spring's colors deepen,
with the double blinds unfurled
   the gloom thickens.
Upstairs, wordless,
   the strumming of a jasper lute.

Far-off hills, jutting peaks,
   hasten the thinning of dusk,
Gentle wind blowing rain
   plays with light shade.
Pear blossoms are about to fall
   but there's no helping that.

Tune: *Song of Picking Mulberry*[1]

In the evening gusts of wind and rain
   washed away embers of daylight.

---

1. This lyric has also been attributed to anonymous authorship and appeared under the
tune-title *Ch'ou nu-erh*.

I stop playing on the pipe
and touch up my face in front of my mirror.

Through the thin red silk my cool flesh glistens 5
    lustrous as snow fresh with fragrance.
    With a smile I say to my beloved:
"Tonight, inside the mesh curtains, the pillow and mat are cool."

Tune: Telling of Innermost Feelings

Night found me so flushed with wine;
    I was slow to undo my hair.
The plum petals still stuck onto a dying branch.
Waking up, the scent of wine stirred me from spring sleep;
    my dream once broken, there was no going back. 5

    Now it's quiet,
    the moon hovers above,
    the kingfisher blinds are drawn.
Still: I feel the fallen petals;
still: I touch their lingering scent; 10
still: I hold onto a moment of time.

JAPAN

Premodern or classical Japanese literature extends from earliest times to the Meiji
Restoration of 1868, a change in government that ended a long period of
isolationism and opened Japan to the West. The date is a convenience, of course,
for literary practice did not change overnight. Nevertheless, the Japanese themselves find it a useful reference point for separating the world of "then" from the
world of "now." In its classical period, Japanese literature defined itself largely
against the influence and example of China; in the modern period, it has
responded in various ways to the literature of the West. This section treats
Japanese literature up to 1600, the beginning of the Edo period (a change in
government that moved the capital to Edo, present-day Tokyo).

Like almost all literatures except those of the West, Japanese literature was
founded on the lyric. That is, it holds the lyric poem to be the highest form of
artistic expression, and the lyric sensibility infuses its other literary genres, such
as drama and prose narrative. So close is the Japanese identification with the lyric
that its most characteristic poetic form, the *tanka,* or "short poem," is alternatively called *waka,* which means simply "Japanese poem." Exceedingly brief by

Western norms, the *tanka* consists of 31 syllables divided into five lines. (The pattern is 5-7-5-7-7.) For centuries, Japanese poets cultivated this small plot, and from it entire worlds of human experience blossomed.

The poetics (a treatise on poetic theory) for a lyric-based literature was supplied early on, though not, interestingly, at the very dawn of the tradition. The earliest extant Japanese works are three compilations of the eighth century C.E., *Kojiki* ("Records of Ancient Matters"), *Nihon Shoki* ("Records of Japan"), and *Man'yōshū* ("Collection for Ten Thousand Generations" or "of Ten Thousand Leaves"). *Kojiki* and *Nihon Shoki* were considered historical accounts of the Age of the Gods through the early sovereigns of Japan. Today, we would say they combine myth, legend, anecdote, and history. Both are prose narratives, though they also include poems and songs, and both anthologize traditional, orally transmitted material as well as earlier written sources, now lost. As such, they served as valuable sourcebooks for later writers, and they remain essential for understanding early Japan.

The *Man'yōshū* is the first extant collection of poetry and the glory of early Japanese literature. It would be impossible to overstate the esteem in which the collection is held in Japan. Compiled in the latter portion of the eighth century, in part from no longer extant earlier collections, it contains well over four thousand poems, ranging from anonymous works transmitted orally from early times through contemporary poems by the anthology's compilers. In view of later developments, the variety of its forms is most remarkable. *Tanka* are certainly well represented, but there are also many long poems, *chōka,* and these often contain narrative elements and a decidedly public voice, addressing issues of concern to society such as war, historical events, and affairs of state.

The earliest writings of Japan, then, offered many possible directions for development. Yet, for whatever reason, no critical intelligence of sufficient power or influence arose in response to these works to formulate a literary theory based on prose, on narrative, or on poetry of the public realm. After the *Man'yōshū,* Japan's poets grew more subjective, and it is this intimate, personal, yet social lyricism that came to distinguish most Japanese poetry.

In the early part of the tenth century, the poet Ki no Tsurayuki and others compiled the *Kokinshū,* the first of twenty-one royally comissioned *waka* collections. The collection came to be considered a standard, so much so that to refer to something as the *Kokinshū* of its kind was a formula of high praise. Tsurayuki's preface to the collection is the first major work of Japanese literary criticism in Japan, and it formulated the poetics that set the essential project of Japanese literature for centuries. In the opening of the preface, often referred to by later writers, Tsurayuki set out to differentiate Japanese poetry:

> The poetry of Japan has its roots in the human heart [or, mind] and flourishes in the countless leaves of words. Because human beings possess interests of so many kinds, it is in poetry that they give expression [to what they think and experience]. Hearing the warbler sing among the blossoms and the frog that lives in the waters—is there any living being not given to song? It is poetry which, without exertion, moves heaven and earth, stirs the feelings of gods and spirits invisible to the eye, softens relations between men and women, calms the hearts of fierce warriors.

The human heart (or, mind), Tsurayuki says, is the seed or cause of words. Japanese poetry is thus *expressionist,* that is, it concerns itself with giving form to an inner, emotional response to the outer world of experience. (In lieu of a title, collections like the *Kokinshū* precede each poem with a brief statement of the circumstances or subject the poem responds to.) Japanese poetry is also *affective,* that is, its goal is to produce in the reader the response that moved the poet. The expressive-affective ideal of poetry is that of a "transfer" from heart to heart of what is most moving.

The third sentence is also important. Tsurayuki asks rhetorically whether poetry is not the natural expression of *all* living things. That emphasis shows how we Western readers ought not to suppose that Japanese poetry—for all its valuing of cultivated lyricism—is inherently elitist. It is true that the majority of poems that have come down to us were written by a small elite largely centered around the court, and that in this rarified milieu the crafting of verse became a subtle and exquisite affair. But the assumption underlying the Japanese view of poetry is something quite different: Poetry is a natural form of expression, something everyone is presumed capable of creating. An experience of sufficient emotional intensity was as likely to prompt a *tanka* from a peasant as from a courtier. The royal anthologies, the most famous repositories of classical poetry, underscored this point by including poetry by illiterates, by a beggar or a prostitute, for example. Even *renga* linked verse, a particularly intricate and demanding form, was mastered by illiterate peasants, who composed orally and recited their efforts.

Orality in general retained a strong presence in Japanese literature. Correspondence commonly included poetry, and the recipient of a letter was expected to read any poems it contained aloud in a sort of heightened speech-song called cantillation. Even lengthy prose works were written to be recited rather than read. Versions of this practice still survive. Tsurayuki's invocation of warbler- and frog-song thus strikes deeper than the casual reader first realizes: literature in Japan was human song and to be voiced.

In another work, Tsurayuki has his narrator write in her diary, "Surely both in China and Japan art is that which is created when we are unable to suppress our feeling." Japanese ideas about literature were founded to no little extent by knowledge of the "classical" model of China, whose civilization was already highly advanced when Japan's was newly forming. There is a consistent lag of about 350 years between Chinese practice and Japanese adaptation. The insular nation guarded itself from its huge continental neighbor by the time lag to adapt to native tastes, by periodic rejection of the foreign, as well as by an almost religious veneration of the unique properties, real and supposed, of Japanese language and society.

As is often pointed out, classical Chinese served much the same purpose in East and Southeast Asia as Latin did in medieval Europe. It was the language of scholarship, of education and cultivation. (There is a sizeable body of poetry by both Korean and Japanese poets in classical Chinese.) The Japanese initially borrowed Chinese characters to write their own language. While the gift of writing was, of course, a great step for Japan, the system was extremely cumbersome, for the Japanese language is much different from Chinese. During the ninth century, the Japanese developed two syllabaries based on simplified Chinese characters. (A syllabary is a writing system in which each symbol stands for a syllable.) However, links with Chinese, both spoken and written, remained in the language to varying degrees. (Today, Japanese is written with a mixture of Chinese characters and Japanese syllabic symbols.)

Classical Chinese remained the preferred medium for most philosophical and legal texts, histories, essays and religious writings in Japan until the nineteenth century. But classical Japanese poetry, the foundation of Japanese literature, shunned Sinified pronunciations (words pronounced in the Chinese manner) and Chinese loanwords, emphasizing instead pure Japanese, which could be written entirely with the syllabaries, avoiding Chinese characters altogether. A syllabary, like an alphabet, is inherently democratic: Anyone can learn to write "by ear," connecting the limited repertoire of signs with sounds. Perhaps the happiest consequence was the opening of the literary enterprise to women. Women did not normally receive a formal education in classical Chinese, but because literature emphasized pure Japanese, women could write—and not as marginal voices but straight to the heart of the tradition. Women were authors in Japan from earliest mythic times, and Japanese is the sole literature for which it is agreed that the greatest writer is a woman: Murasaki Shikibu, author of *The Tale of Genji*.

Japanese poetics is distinguished from other lyric-based aesthetics in its early acceptance of fictionality. To simplify complex matters, we can say that literature is assumed to be factual in the absence of evidence to the contrary. That is, we assume that the poet actually had the experience that prompted the poem. Fictionality is accommodated to factuality when a poet responds to an imagined experience as though it were real. A poem attributed to an animal, for example, is clearly fictional. (Poems were attributed to animals in the spirit of the *Kokinshū* preface.) A more pervasive practice was the poetry match, in which poets composed on set topics. By the eleventh century, most poetry was created in response to the topics set for competitions. Fictional poetry is now judged by how intensely it affects a reader, not how faithfully it reports an actual experience.

A second distinguishing mark of Japanese literature is the early acceptance of prose narrative and drama as critically esteemed genres. By 1010, less than a century after the *Kokinshū* preface, Murasaki Shikibu had, in her *Tale of Genji*, produced in prose the greatest work in the whole literature, justifying it (in the "Fireflies" chapter) by analogy both to histories and to Buddhist practice: Fiction gives what is lacking, most moving, and religiously suggestive to cold fact.

The Tale of Genji is studded with lyrics—the characters often communicate in verse. In this we discover another distinctive feature of Japanese literature, the compatibility of narrative and lyric: poems are typically embedded like gemstones in longer prose works, where they serve to embody moments of particular emotional intensity. The selections from the *Tales of Ise* included here show this trait in its ideal form.

This tendency to use brief poetic units as building blocks of larger artistic wholes is evident in its purest form in the royal *waka* anthologies themselves. These did not order their contents chronologically or by author, but by subject matter (the seasons, love, and so on). Organization grew increasingly subtle, reaching perfection with the eighth anthology, the *Shinkokinshū* of the early thirteenth century, which can actually be read as a single, extended work of nearly 2,000 poems (10,000 lines).

With *nō* plays and their comic interludes, *kyōgen*, drama obtained admired status. *Nō* developed gradually from a variety of popular entertainment forms. Its sudden flowering and achievement of literary prestige was largely the work of two men, the actor and playwright Kan'ami (1333–1384) and his even greater son, the actor, playwright, and critic Zeami (?1364–?1443). Zeami's critical writings in particular were instrumental in positioning *nō* within the framework of Japan's lyric poetics (as amplified to include narratives). In the manner of narrative works, *nō* texts combine prose and poetry. But the essence of *nō* theatre is, of course, performance, and the text must be understood as only one element of what in contemporary terms we might call total theatre. *Nō* performance includes masks, music, mime, dance, chant, and a stylized form of acting. In its method of performance and its central use of narrative and lyric, it is unique in the theatres of the world.

The selections here illustrate the progression of the lyric-based literature in pure Japanese that has been the subject of this introduction. Thus, the usual "narrow" definition of Japanese literature has been used, excluding Japanese writings in Chinese, as well as writings in Ainu (the language of an earlier people in the Japanese islands), or in the Ryukyuan dialect-language. By modern western convention, we ignore many histories included in the broader Japanese concept of literature. Space constraints account for omission of many kinds of poetry and song, of performance, and of narrative.

Historical Background

The early Stone Age culture of Japan seems to have given way around 300 B.C.E. to communities based on agriculture and metal-working—developments that paved the way there as elsewhere for the beginning of civilization. The technologies had probably been brought by a new wave of arrivals from the nearby Korean peninsula. After a period of warfare (a Chinese chronicle of the Han Dynasty speaks of Japan as comprising "more than one hundred countries" at war), a more or less stable configuration of regional states seems to have emerged—tribal confederations, more accurately—ruled by a dominant aristocratic warrior class headed by royalty.

By around 300 C.E., a warrior clan on the Yamato plain, near present day Osaka, had accrued enough power to style themselves as "great kings" over the regional aristocracy. From here on, the political history of Japan is customarily divided into periods according to the seat of the government, and literary history follows suit. (It also uses designations such as medieval, modern, etc.)

During the Yamato era, which lasted roughly four centuries, close relations with Korea continued, and Chinese culture, which the Korean ruling class had adopted, passed increasingly into Japan. During the sixth century, Buddhism, Confucianism, administrative systems, and writing all entered Japan mostly through Korea. Beginning in the seventh century, Japan began to send students and ambassadors directly to China, a practice that continued for some 200 years.

Though it persisted, the philosophy of Confucius did not find especially fertile ground in Japan. Buddhism, however, proved a lasting and powerful influence. The Japanese took especially to the religious aspects of Buddhism (the Chinese, in contrast, had focused on the philosophical side). Buddhism had the advantage of meshing easily with the ancient state religion, Shintō. Shintō is a shamanistic religion, shamans being mediums between humankind and divinities. When not protective deities or spirits of the dead, the divinities of Shintō are largely natural divinities—mountains, rivers, thunder, and so on. The chief divinity is female, the sun goddess. Shamans, too, are almost all female (the chief exception being the monarch, who ruled as the leading shaman). Shintō is a religion of communion with, invocation of, and appeasement of spirits, including the recent dead. Its strong feminine component is another cultural factor supporting the uncontested acceptance of women as writers and the relatively high position of women in society generally: women monarchs were common in early times.

Toward the end of the seventh century centralized power increased, and administrative systems adapted from Chinese models were instituted. While Western histories have generally referred to the rulers of Japan as emperors from this point on, the concept of empire had no place in classical Japan. "Sovereign" or "monarch" remain more accurate titles.

In 710, the capital was moved to Nara. With the Nara period, we enter true historical time, though our knowledge is far from complete. This was the period of Japanese literature's three founding works, *Kojiki, Nihon Shoki,* and *Man'yōshū.* In 794, the capital moved again, this time to Heian (present-day Kyoto), where it remained for over one thousand years. The Heian era was one of courtly refinement and great artistic brilliance. Literary development was rapid, as was development in other social and cultural spheres. The capital grew to perhaps the most populous city in the world, and decade upon decade passed in peace.

The Heian also witnessed the rise of the *samurai* — regional warriors nominally in the service of the government but capable of stirring up trouble. Regional military forces emerged, increasing in strength and sapping the power of the nobility of the ruling Fujiwara houses. That vast family grew to preeminence in the ninth century and retained its grip on power for 200 years. They monopolized all key government posts and, by marrying their daughters to the sovereign, controlled the court as well: after the birth of an heir, the Fujiwara would force the sovereign into retirement and rule as regents for the child. Things began to change when a series of "retired" sovereigns reasserted control from 1072 to 1156. But struggles over royal succession brought in rival military forces with their taste for conflict. At first the Taira family (who had supplanted the Fujiwara in power) triumphed over the armies of the Minamoto family. Their control was brief—they were overthrown by the Minamoto in 1185. The long rivalry and bloody warfare between the Taira and Minamoto clans furnished a rich subject for later literature.

The ensuing period, dated from either 1156 or 1186 and extending to 1603, is often referred to as medieval or feudal Japan, though it is more specifically divided into four periods, Kamakura, Nambokuchō, Muromachi, and Azuchi-Momoyama. The victorious Minamoto generals moved the administrative center east to Kamakura, away from the distractions of the Heian court. Their control lasted until 1339, when the country was plunged into disastrous civil war over two rival lines of sovereigns (the Nambokuchō period). Peace was forged in 1399 with the formation of a military and increasingly "feudal" society. Powerful regional lords ruled under the central control (now waxing, now waning) of a *bakufu* (government by military aristocracy) run by the *shogun,* the commander-in-chief to the figurehead sovereign. Regional warfare was common. In this newly militaristic society, the status of women declined. Buddhism offered a consolation to many in these chaotic times, especially the Pure Lands and Zen sects, which ascended over the Tendai and Shingon sects that had dominated the Heian period. In literature, this was the time of the flowering *nō* drama and *renga* linked verse.

A Note on Japanese Names and Pronunciation

Names are given here in contemporary style and according to representations of contemporary Japanese pronunciation. Surnames precede given names, as in

Ariwara (surname) Narihira (given name). Beyond this point, the matter of names in Japan is more complicated. Modern abbreviations simplify more ancient practice and have been used here: thus, Kakinomoto Hitomaro instead of Kakinomoto no Asomi no Hitomaro. By convention, some writers are known by their pen name versions of given names, while others are known by their (sometimes pseudo-) surnames. There is no single rule or style to be followed. One simply adopts some version of current Japanese practice.

A rough approximation of modern Japanese pronunciation is possible with vowels sounded as in Spanish (or Italian, Latin) and consonants as in English except for *r*, which is pronounced with the slightest touch of *the tip* of the tongue behind the area touched for English *l*, so giving it features of English *l*, *r*, and *d*. The stress accent on Japanese syllables is lighter than in English. There is also a light accent. Following the usual practice, Old Japanese has here been standardized into modern. Two diacritical marks are used: an apostrophe to indicate the end of a syllable and a macron to indicate lengthening of *o* or *u*. Thus, *Man'yōshū* is pronounced divided as *man-yō-shū* rather than *ma-nyō-shū*, and with the second and third vowels longer in duration than the first. Long *a*, *e*, and *i* are represented doubled as *aa*, *ee*, and *ii*.

Further Reading

Keene, Donald. *World Within Walls*. New York: Holt Rinehart Winston, 1976. (premodern, ca. 1600–1868)

———. *Dawn to the West*. 2 vols. New York: Holt Rinehart Winston, 1984.

Konishi, Jin'ichi. *A History of Japanese Literature*. 5 vols., Princeton: Princeton University Press. Volume 1: *The Archaic and Ancient Ages*, 1984; Volume 2: *The Early Middle Ages*, 1986; Volume 3: *The High Middle Ages*, 1991.

Miner, Earl, Hiroko Odagiri, and Robert E. Morrell. *The Princeton Companion to Classical Japanese Literature*. Princeton: Princeton University Press, 1985.

Note: At present the most authoritative version in English consists of Konishi's three volumes followed by Keene's two in the 1984 work, but both authors assume certain kinds of knowledge. In Miner et al. there is a concise literary history (Part 1); there are also chronologies (Part 2) and other information. But all is premodern.

KAKINOMOTO HITOMARO

(fl. 680–700; d. 708–715 C.E.)

YAMANO(U)E OKURA (660–c. 733 C.E.)

Japan

Kakinomoto Hitomaro and Yamano(u)e Okura are generally regarded as the foremost poets of the *Man'yōshū* (c. 760), the first great anthology of Japanese poetry, containing about 4,500 poems.

Kakinomoto Hitomaro has long been revered as a virtual deity within the world of poetry. For centuries after his death, the supposed date of his birth was a closely guarded secret, known only to a few. He perfected the chōka (long poem), which dealt with both official and personal subjects.

In Hitomaro's poetry, the simple and the complex are impossible to distinguish. The first poem selected here, ("at Cape Kara . . .") which concerns a man who is parting from his wife, reflects enormously complicated Japanese marriage customs. Family property was passed down matrilineally—that is, from mother to daughter. Thus a husband moved in with (or visited) his wife. If he was then assigned duty to another part of the county, as is assumed to be the case in this poem, separation or divorce was the result. Over a lifetime, both sexes might have a series of spouses, official or unofficial.

In the second poem, ("The Quick Gallop"), a man mourns the death of his wife. In the Shinto religion, efforts were made to remember the newly dead, both to comfort mourners and to pacify the possibly angry spirit of the deceased. In the third poem ("The land of Sanuki . . .") the poet describes his shipwreck during a typhoon. He encounters a lifeless body and addresses it—or its spirit—in order to pacify it. Hitomaro seeks to pacify and console himself as well. He speaks in gentle ironies: We meet disaster, yet the world is divine; if your wife were here . . . ; what a rough place to sleep. In Japanese the poem can be read so that the complete text is an incomplete sentence stressing its last word, wife; the same word begins the first envoy—or short concluding stanza—which finally brings the sentence to a close.

Yamano(u)e Okura studied for a while in China, and in the dialogue presented here he writes Chinese-style social criticism. The criticism is implicit; no names are provided. But the poet makes the point that the country is not well ruled—hence the apologetic prose at the end to soften the criticism. The poem consists of a double chōka, something very rare. In the first chōka (lines 1–29), a poor man speaks, emphasizing the cold as an image of his bad fortune. In the second chōka (lines 30–70), a man wholly destitute replies. Traces of new (Chinese) learning appear in references to Buddhist and Confucian tenets. Thus to be born human (line 38) is a blessing, since it is a requisite for Buddhist enlightenment. The greater care of parents than of wife and children (lines 50–53) is Confucian. (We could not guess from this poem that property in Japan was inherited matrilineally.)

The translator follows the usual interpretation wherein the poet himself speaks the envoy. The original, however, has no noun or pronoun as a subject.

It is conceivable that the destitute man continues talking, or that a voice speaks on behalf of the human race.

The morality based on rational grounds, the striking imagery appealing to all our senses, and the uneven, jerky, hard-hitting style are typical of Okura's poetry. By the end, we feel Okura's concern: we know that poverty and hunger continue in "this world."

from **Man'Yōshū**

KAKINOMOTO HITOMARO

On Parting from His Wife as He Set Out from Iwami for the Capital

At Cape Kara
on the Sea of Iwami,
where the vines
   crawl on the rocks,
rockweed of the deep   5
grows on the reefs
and sleek seaweed
grows on the desolate shore.
As deeply do I
think of my wife   10
who swayed toward me in sleep
   like the lithe seaweed.
Yet few were the nights
we had slept together
before we were parted   15
like crawling vines uncurled.
And so I look back,
still thinking of her
with painful heart,
this clench of inner flesh,   20
but in the storm
of fallen scarlet leaves
on Mount Watari,
crossed as on
   a great ship,   25
I cannot make out the sleeves
she waves in farewell.
For she, alas,
is slowly hidden
like the moon   30
   in its crossing

Translated by Ian Hideo Levy.

between the clouds
over Yagami Mountain
just as the evening sun
coursing through the heavens
has begun to glow,   35
          and even I
who thought I was a brave man
find the sleeves
of my well-woven robe   40
drenched with tears.

Envoys

The quick gallop
of my dapple-blue steed
races me to the clouds,
passing far away   45
from where my wife dwells.

O scarlet leaves
falling on the autumn mountainside:
stop, for a while, the storm
your strewing makes, that I might glimpse   50
the place where my wife dwells.

On the Death of His Wife

She was my wife,
to whom my thoughts gathered
thick as the spring leaves,
like the myriad branches budding
on the zelkova tree
on the embankment (a short step
from her gate),
that we would bring
and look at together
while she was of this world.   10
She was my wife,
on whom I depended,
but now, unable to break
the course of this world,
she shrouds herself from me
in heavenly white raiments   15
on a withered, sun-simmered plain,
and rises away in the morning
like a bird,

and conceals herself
like the setting sun.
Each time our infant,   20
the memento she left,
cries out in hunger,
I, though a man,
having nothing to give it,   25
hug it to my breast.
Inside the wedding house
where the pillows we slept on
lie pushed together,
I live through the days   30
desolate and lonely
and sigh through the nights.
Lament as I may,
I know nothing I can do.
Long for her as I may,   35
I have no way to meet her.
And so when someone said,
"The wife you long for
dwells on Hagai Mountain,
    of the great bird,"   40
I struggled up here,
kicking the rocks apart,
but it did no good:
my wife, whom I thought   45
was of this world,
is ash.[1]

Envoys

The autumn moon crosses the heavens
as it did when I watched last year,
but my wife, who watched with me—   50
the drift of the year has taken her.

Leaving my wife on Hikide Mountain
by the Fusuma Road,
I think of the path she has taken,
and I am hardly alive.   55

I come home
and gaze inside:
facing outward

---

1. "Is ash": the line alludes to the Buddhist
   practice of cremation, then new to Japan.

Since there is so little Buddhism elsewhere
in Hitomaro, it may be an addition.

on the haunted floor,
my wife's boxwood pillow.   60

[Upon seeing a dead man lying among the rocks on the island of Samine in Sanuki]

The land of Sanuki,
   fine in sleek seaweed:
is it for the beauty of the land
that we do not tire
   to gaze upon it?   5
Is it for its divinity
that we deem it most noble?
Eternally flourishing,
   with the heavens
     and the earth,
   with the sun   10
     and the moon,
the very face of a god—
so it has come down
   through the ages.   15

Casting off
from Naka harbor,
we came rowing.
Then tide winds
blew through the clouds;   20
on the offing
we saw the rustled waves,
on the strand
we saw the roaring crests.
Fearing the whale-hunted seas,   25
our ship plunged through—
we bent those oars!
Many were the islands
near and far,
but we beached on Samine—   30
   beautiful its name—
and built a shelter
   on the rugged shore.
Looking around,
     we saw you   35
lying there
on a jagged bed of stones,
the beach
   for your finely woven pillow,

by the breakers' roar.
    If I knew your home,
I would go and tell them.
If your wife knew,
she would come and seek you out.
But she does not even know the road,
    straight as a jade spear.
Does she not wait for you,
    worrying and longing,
your beloved wife?

Envoys

If your wife were here,
she would gather and feed you
the starwort that grows
on the Sami hillsides,
but is its season not past?

Making a finely woven pillow
of the rocky shore
    where waves from the offing
        draw near,
you, who sleep there!

YAMANO(U)E OKURA

A Dialogue of the Poor with the Destitute

"On nights when rain falls,
    mixed with wind,
on nights when snow falls,
    mixed with rain,
I am cold.
And the cold
    leaves me helpless:
I lick black lumps of salt
and suck up melted dregs of *sake*.
Coughing and sniffling,
I smooth my uncertain wisps
    of beard.
I am proud—
    I know no man
        is better than me.
But I am cold.
I pull up my hempen nightclothes

and throw on every scrap
of cloth shirt that I own.
But the night is cold.
And I wonder how a man like you,
 even poorer than myself,
with his father and mother
starving and freezing,
with his wife and children
begging and begging
  through their tears,
can get through the world alive
 at times like this."
"Wide, they say,
  are heaven and earth—
but have they shrunk for me?
Bright, they say,
  are the sun and moon—
but do they refuse to shine for me?
Is it thus for all men,
 or for me alone?
Above all, I was born human,
I too toil for my keep—
as much as the next man—
yet on my shoulders hangs
a cloth shirt
not even lined with cotton,
these tattered rags
thin as strips of seaweed.
In my groveling hut,
 my tilting hut,
sleeping on straw
cut and spread right on the ground,
with my father and mother
  huddled at my pillow
and my wife and children
  huddled at my feet,
I grieve and lament.
Not a spark rises in the stove,
and in the pot
a spider has drawn its web.
I have forgotten
what it is to cook rice!
As I lie here,
a thin cry tearing from my throat—
  a tiger thrush's moan—
then, as they say,

to slice the ends
of a thing already too short,
to our rough bed
comes the scream of the village headman
    with his tax collecting whip.
Is it so helpless and desperate,
the way of life in this world?"

Envoy

I find this world
a hard and shameful place.
But I cannot fly away—
I am not a bird.

ONO NO KOMACHI (fl. 835–857 C.E.)
ARIWARA NARIHIRA (825–880 C.E.)
KI NO TSURAYUKI (c. 872?–945? C.E.)
IZUMI SHIKIBU (b. 976? C.E.)
Japan

The four poets presented here are among the most admired of the *Kokinshū* (910 C.E.), the first and most prestigious of twenty-one royal anthologies. The *Kokinshū* is ordered topically (poems about the seasons, poems about love, and so on) rather than by author. The result is less an anthology than a complete artistic whole in which each individual poem takes its place. Ono no Komachi and Ariwara Narihira are numbered among the Six Poetic Sages, a title that comes from their having been singled out in the *Kokinshū* preface. Komachi focused attention on the poetic figure of the passionate woman. Indeed, the legends that have evolved about Komachi's life as a woman of passion have been so enduring that her historical reality remains veiled for us today. Narihira was also famous as a lover, though he was less intense, and more reflective and difficult in his style. Ki no Tsurayuki was the complete poet and critic, and his was presumably the genius behind the *Kokinshū*. Izumi Shikibu, the greatest poet of her time, was, with Murasaki Shikibu, one of the many brilliant writers at the salon of Joto Mon'in, a royal consort. Quickwitted, amorous, religious, maternal and a prolific poet, she is often difficult to interpret.

These poets mark the dawn of a continuous poetic tradition in Japan. They are confident even in their questions, certain even of their bewilderment. Their world is one in which things can be named, collected, and confidently arranged.

It is no accident that this was the age that articulated a systematic poetics (in Ki no Tsurayuki's preface to the *Kokinshū*) that has outlasted the centuries. There were great works before, but the unbroken tradition of Japanese literature in all its guises begins here.

from The Early Royal Anthologies [Kokinshū]

ONO NO KOMACHI

[The cherry blossoms]

The cherry blossoms
Have passed with loss of color,
    While to no avail
Age takes my beauty as it falls
In the long rain of my regret.

[For waking daylight]

For waking daylight,
Then it can be understood!
    But even in dreams!
To avoid me there in fear of gossip—
That is too much misery to be borne.

[Although my feet / never rest in running to you]

Although my feet
Never rest in running to you
    On the path of dreams,
Such nights of spectral love
Match no moment face-to-face.

[No hue of passion / marks that thing which fades away]

No hue of passion
Marks that thing which fades away:
    In the world of love
Find that in the male heart
Pretending to be abloom with love!

All poems in this selection translated by Earl Miner.

[Longing for your loving]

Longing for your loving,
Without a moon to light my way,
Waking in passion's fire
My breast swift conflagration,
My yearning heart reduced to char.

ARIWARA NARIHIRA

[Though the blackness]

Through the blackness
Of the darkness of desiring heart
Wandering bewildered—
Is this called reality or dream?
You who know the world of love, decide!

[Full sleep does not come]

Full sleep does not come.
Full waking still eludes me,
And night breaks with dawn:
So far am I a listless spring thing
Imbued with reverie's long rain.

[This is not that moon]

This is not that moon.
It cannot be this is the spring
Known as spring before.
I myself am that alone
Remaining as it ever was . . .

[At last we find ourselves / upon the road that all must travel]

"At last we find ourselves
Upon the road that all must travel"—
So had I heard, too,
But never had it occurred to me
The time is then and now.

KI NO TSURAYUKI

[Composed when I visited a mountain temple]

"Composed when I visited a mountain temple."
   I found my dwelling;
It was on hillslopes of spring
   That I slept the night,
And even throughout my dreams
The cherry blossoms kept up their fall.

[On hearing the hototogisu sing]

"On hearing the hototogisu sing."[1]
   During June's long rains
The sky itself fills with music,
   And, hototogisu,
What anguish is that you feel
To give the whole night to song?

[Composed at royal command]

"Composed at royal command."
   Is it Kasuga,
The fields where they go for greens,
   Those young women
With sleeves of whitened linen
Beckoning the one who sees?

[As urged by desire]

   As urged by desire
I go in hunt of my beloved,
   On the winter night
The river wind blows up so cold
That I hear the plovers cry.

[On the death of his cousin, Ki no Tomonori]

On the death of his cousin, Ki no Tomonori.
   Tomorrow is unknown,
So much of myself have I been sure,

---

1. A sort of cuckoo, rather like a nightingale.

But all has turned to dark:
Today it is him I think of
That casts me into all this grief!

[A mother returning to the capital from Tosa]

A mother returning to the capital from Tosa thinks
of her daughter who died in that province.
    Thinking her alive,
I keep forgetting she is not,
    Asking of one now dead,
"Where has that girl slipped off to?"
And the shock renews the grief.

IZUMI SHIKIBU

Love

    Whether my long dark hair
Be tangled is more than I can care:
    As I lie beside you,
You, darling, are so loving
As to start by stroking it aside.

The same

The same
    My darling will believe
He dwells in lapis lazuli,
    Because our bedding
Sparkles with string after string
Of drops of our bejewelled tears.

[Composed after my lover had abandoned me]

Composed after my lover had abandoned me. On a
pilgrimage to Kibune Shrine I saw fireflies by
the sacred river.
    Heavy at heart,
I take the fireflies from the marsh
    To be my very soul
Departed somehow from my body
And flickering in the gloom.

[Written to someone when I was ill]

Written to someone when I was ill.
  Soon to be no more!
As a keepsake of this world
  Taken to the next,
I long to have you come for loving
If just once more but make it now.

[Sent to her lover]

Sent to her lover "on seeing the extraordinary
whiteness of the frost."
  Marking everything
The frost also lies on the sleeve
  Of the pillowing arm,
And in morning light it looks
Like "whitened hemp" of olden times.
          (Izumi Shikibu Diary)

[Sent to His Eminence Shōku]

Sent to His Eminence Shōku.
  Out of darkness
To travel yet a darker path
  I must set forth:
Illuminate the great distance,
Blest moon arising on the hills!

ANONYMOUS (c. 950 C.E.)
Japan

An evocative, romantic mystery, the *Tales of Ise* consists of some 125 brief episodes centering on 209 poems. No satisfactory explanation exists for its title (though episode 69, included here, does indeed take place in Ise). The date is also uncertain: the earliest estimate is c. 875; the latest and more likely is c. 950 C.E. The episodes usually begin with a recurring phrase: "Once there was a certain man . . ." This man is generally presumed to be modeled on Ariwara Narihira, one of the foremost poets of the *Kokinshū*, the first royal anthology (910 C.E.). Episodes often seem to be taken verbatim, or with slight modifications, from *Kokinshū*, although some scholars believe the influence flowed the other way. In the first episode, the man appears newly dressed in adult clothing; he will be an "old man" before the tales are over. Quick-witted and amorous, he is the model for numerous courtly males in later literature. A certain air of doom also hangs over him: the Ariwaras were losers in the political struggles at court.

Together with *The Tale of Genji*, the *Tales of Ise* came to define the essence of court romance for later centuries. Both works, but especially the *Tales,* illustrate the compatibility of prose and verse in Japanese literature. The *Tales* also shows the distinctive Japanese tendency to consolidate ever briefer artistic units into new, larger wholes. Few things looking so simple are so complex. A first reading reveals little of the Shinto and esoteric Buddhist depths of these brief accounts. And few works, when fully understood, are so revealing about the possibilities of literature.

from **The Tales of Ise [Ise Monogatari]**

[Glimpsing Two Sisters]

Once a man who had lately come of age went hunting on his estate at Kasuga village, near the Nara capital. In the village there lived two beautiful young sisters. The man caught a glimpse of the sisters through a gap in their hedge. It was startling and incongruous indeed that such ladies should dwell at the ruined capital, and he wished to meet them. He tore a strip from the skirt of his hunting costume, dashed off a poem, and sent it in. The fabric of the robe was imprinted with a moss-fern design.

> Like the random pattern of this robe,
> Dyed with the young purple
> From Kasuga Plain—
> Even thus is the wild disorder
> Of my yearning heart.

No doubt it had occurred to him that this was an interesting opportunity for an adaptation of the poem that runs,

> My thoughts have grown disordered
> As random patterns dyed on cloth
> Reminiscent of Shinobu in Michinoku—
> And who is to blame?
> Surely not I.

People were remarkably elegant in those days.

[Plum Blossoms and the Past][1]

Once when the ex-empress was living in the eastern Fifth Ward, a certain lady occupied the western wing of her house. Quite without intending it, a man fell

---

Translated by Helen Craig McCullough; the translation of the first poem "Like the random pattern" and the preceding three sentences ("It was startling . . . moss-fern design") by Earl Miner.

1. This episode features Narihira's greatest
   and, for the translator, most difficult poem.

deeply in love with the lady and began to visit her; but around the Tenth of the First Month she moved away without a word, and though he learned where she had gone, it was not a place where ordinary people could come and go. He could do nothing but brood over the wretchedness of life. When the plum blossoms were at their height in the next First Month, poignant memories of the year before drew him back to her old apartments. He stared at the flowers from every conceivable standing and sitting position, but it was quite hopeless to try to recapture the past. Bursting into tears, he flung himself onto the floor of the bare room and lay there until the moon sank low in the sky. As he thought of the year before, he composed this poem:

> Is not the moon the same?
> The spring
> The spring of old?
> Only this body of mine
> Is the same body . . .

He went home at dawn, still weeping.

[Weeping Over Poems]

Once a certain man decided that it was useless for him to remain in the capital. With one or two old friends, he set out toward the east in search of a province in which to settle. Since none of the party knew the way, they blundered ahead as best they could, until in time they arrived at a place called Yatsuhashi in Mikawa Province. (It was a spot where the waters of a river branched into eight channels, each with a bridge, and thus it had come to be called Yatsuhashi—"Eight Bridges.") Dismounting to sit under a tree near this marshy area, they ate a meal of parched rice. Someone glanced at the clumps of sweet flags blooming luxuriantly in the marsh. "Compose a poem on the topic, 'A Traveler's Emotions,' beginning each line with a letter from 'flags,' " he said. The man recited,

> From far Cathay,
> Long has the robe been a comfort
> As is the wife I miss,
> Gone from sight into the distance,
> Sorrows being what travel brings.

They all wept onto their dried rice until it swelled with the moisture.

On they journeyed to the province of Suruga. At Mount Utsu the road they were to follow was dark, narrow, and overgrown with ivy vines and maples. As they contemplated it with dismal forebodings, a wandering ascetic appeared and asked, "What are you doing on a road like this?" The man, recognizing him as someone he had once known by sight, gave him a message for a lady in the capital:

> Beside Mount Utsu
> In Suruga
> I can see you
> Neither waking
> Nor, alas, even in my dreams.

At Mount Fuji a pure white snow had fallen, even though it was the end of the Fifth Month.

> Fuji is a mountain
> That knows no seasons.
> What time does it take this for,
> That it should be dappled
> With fallen snow?

To speak in terms of the mountains hereabout, Mount Fuji is as tall as twenty Mount Hiei's piled on top of one another. In shape it resembles a salt-cone.

Continuing on their way, they came to a mighty river flowing between the provinces of Musashi and Shimōsa. It was called the Sumidagawa. The travelers drew together on the bank, thinking involuntarily of home. "How very far we have come!" The ferryman interrupted their laments: "Come aboard quickly; it's getting late." They got into the boat and prepared to cross, all in wretched spirits, for there was not one among them who had not left someone dear to him in the capital.

A bird about the size of a snipe—white, with a red bill and red legs—happened to be frolicking on the water as it ate a fish. Since it was of a species unknown in the capital, none of them could identify it. They consulted the ferryman, who replied with an air of surprise, "It is a capital-bird, of course." Then one of the travelers recited this poem:

> If you are what your name implies,
> Let me ask you,
> Capital-bird,
> Does all go well
> With my beloved?

Everyone in the boat burst into tears.

[A Poem Gets Completed] [2]

Once a man went to the province of Ise as an Imperial Huntsman. The Ise [Shrine Priestess's] mother had sent word that he was to be treated better than the ordinary run of imperial representatives, and the [Priestess] accordingly looked after his needs with great solicitude, seeing him off to hunt in the morning and allowing him to come to her own residence when he returned in the evening.

On the night of the second day of this hospitable treatment, the man suggested that they might become better acquainted. The [Priestess] was not unwilling, but with so many people about it was impossible to arrange a meeting in private. However, since the man was in charge of the hunting party, he had not

---

2. This episode is thought by some to explain the title. The Shrine Priestess seems so dazzled that she cannot wait for the man to send his *aubade* (next-morning poem, or poem of dawn, when the lovers separate, from *alba*, literally "white").

been relegated to some distant quarter, but had been lodged rather close to the [Priestess's] own sleeping chamber, and so the [Priestess] went to his room around eleven o'clock that night, after the household had quieted down. He was lying on his bed wide awake, staring out into the night. When he saw her by the faint light of the moon, standing with a little girl in front of her, he led her joyfully into the bedchamber; but though she stayed from eleven o'clock until two-thirty, she took her leave without exchanging vows with him.

The man, bitterly disappointed, spent a sleepless night. The next morning, despite his impatience, he could not very well send a message, and was obliged to wait anxiously for word from the [Priestess]. Soon after dawn she sent this poem without an accompanying letter:

> Did you, I wonder, come here,
> Or might I have gone there?
> I scarcely know . . .
> Was it dream or reality—
> Did I sleep or wake?

Shedding tears of distress, he sent her this:

> I too have groped
> In utter darkness.
> Can you not determine tonight
> Which it might have been—
> Whether dream or reality?

Then he went off on a hunting excursion. As he galloped over the plain his thoughts strayed to the coming night. Might he not hope to meet [her] as soon as the others had gone to bed? But word of his presence had reached the governor of the province, who was also in charge of the [Priestess's] affairs, and that official proceeded to entertain him at a drinking party that lasted all night. It was impossible to see [her], and since he was to leave at dawn for Owari Province there could be no further opportunity, even though he was quite frantic with longing, as indeed was [she].

As dawn approached, [she] sent him a farewell cup of wine with a poem inscribed on the saucer. He picked up the vessel and examined it.

> Since ours was a relationship no deeper
> Than a creek too shallow
> To wet a foot-traveler's garb . . .

The last two lines were missing. He took a bit of charcoal from a pine torch and supplied them:

> I shall surely again cross
> Osaka Barrier.

At daybreak he set out toward the province of Owari.

The [Priestess] was the one who served during the reign of Emperor Seiwa; she was a daughter of Emperor Montoku and a sister of Prince Koretaka.

SEI SHŌNAGON (c. 966?–1017? C.E.)
Japan

Sei (shorthand for "Kiyowara family") Shōnagon was a star in the literary circle of the royal consort Teishi. Her masterpiece, *The Pillow Book (Makura no Soshi)*, consists of numerous prose sections—jottings, we are to presume, made in a bedside notebook—and sixteen poems. The sections are conventionally viewed as falling into two broad categories: diary-like entries and the now-famous lists of things or enumerations of such modern appeal ("Things That Make One's Heart Beat Faster," "Rare Things"). Yet the very first section, given here, shows this distinction to be inadequate. Two features in particular deserve special attention. One is the almost total and unparalleled absence of verse with the courtly prose. The other is the author's exquisite sense of her own subjectivity: it will be five centuries before a European author, the French essayist Montaigne, writes with such an awareness.

Sei Shōnagon knew her way around a royal court and all its intrigues. Her chief demand was that the court—and the world, for that matter—be observable. She knew how to make it memorable. Her education included Chinese, and while she may not have known as much of that language as she liked to pretend, the point is that she knew it at all. Had the occasion arisen, she could easily have invented a list called "Things Concealed from Others in Order to Understand Ourselves."

from *The Pillow Book [Makura no Soshi]*

In Spring It Is the Dawn[1]

In spring it is the dawn that is most beautiful. As the light creeps over the hills, their outlines are dyed a faint red and wisps of purplish cloud trail over them.

In summer the nights. Not only when the moon shines, but on dark nights too, as the fireflies flit to and fro, and even when it rains, how beautiful it is!

In autumn the evenings, when the glittering sun sinks close to the edge of the hills and the crows fly back to their nests in threes and fours and twos; more charming still is a file of wild geese, like specks in the distant sky. When the sun has set, one's heart is moved by the sound of the wind and the hum of the insects.

In winter the early mornings. It is beautiful indeed when snow has fallen during the night, but splendid too when the ground is white with frost; or even when there is no snow or frost, but it is simply very cold and the attendants hurry from room to room stirring up the fires and bringing charcoal, how well this fits

Translated by Ivan Morris.

---

1. These associations between hours and seasons become essential to understanding Japanese literature.

the season's mood! But as noon approaches and the cold wears off, no one bothers to keep the braziers alight, and soon nothing remains but piles of white ashes.

Things That Make One's Heart Beat Faster

Sparrows feeding their young. To pass a place where babies are playing. To sleep in a room where some fine incense has been burnt. To notice that one's elegant Chinese mirror has become a little cloudy. To see a gentleman stop his carriage before one's gate and instruct his attendants to announce his arrival. To wash one's hair, make one's toilet, and put on scented robes; even if not a soul sees one, these preparations still produce an inner pleasure.

It is night and one is expecting a visitor. Suddenly one is startled by the sound of rain-drops, which the wind blows against the shutters.

Once I Saw Yukinari[2]

Once I saw Yukinari, the Controller First Secretary, engaged in a long conversation with a lady near the garden fence by the western side of the Empress's Office. When at last they had finished, I came out and asked, "Who was she?" "Ben no Naishi," he replied. "And what on earth did you find to discuss with her for such a long time? If the Major Controller had seen you, she would have left you quickly enough." "And who can have told you about that business?" asked Yukinari, laughing. "As a matter of fact, that is precisely what I was discussing with her. I was trying to persuade her not to leave me even if the Major Controller did see us."

Yukinari is a most delightful man. To be sure, he does not make any particular effort to display his good points and simply lets people take him as he appears, so that in general he is less appreciated than he might be. But I, who have seen the deeper side of his nature, know what an unusual person he really is. I said this one day to the Empress, who was well aware of it herself. In the course of our conversations he often says, "A woman yields to one who has taken pleasure in her; a knight dies for one who has shown him friendship." We used to say that our feelings for each other were like the willows on Tōtōmi Beach.

Yet the young women at Court heartily detest Yukinari and openly repeat the most disagreeable things about him. "What an ugly man he is!" they say. "Why can't he recite sutras and poems like other people? He really is most unpleasant." Yukinari, for his part, never speaks to any of them.

"I could love a woman," he said one day, "even if her eyes were turned up, her eyebrows spread all over her forehead, and her nose crooked. But she must have a prettily shaped mouth and a good chin and neck, and I couldn't stand an unattractive voice. Of course I would prefer her not to have any bad feature. There's really something sad about a woman with an ugly face." As a result, all the Court ladies with pointed chins or other unattractive features have become Yukinari's bitter enemies, and some of them have even spoken badly of him to the Empress.

---

2. This study of Yukinari is really a self-study.

I was the first person he employed to take messages to the Empress, and he always called on me when he wanted to communicate with her. If I was in my room, he would send for me to the main part of the Palace, or else he would come directly into the women's quarters to give me his message. Even if I was at home, he would write to me or come himself, saying, "In case you are not returning to Court at once, would you please send someone to Her Majesty informing her that I have such-and-such a message." "Surely you could tell a messenger yourself directly," I said; but he would have none of it.

On one such occasion I suggested to Yukinari that one should "take things as they are" and not always stick to the same habits. "But such is my nature," he replied, "and that is something one cannot change."

"Well then," I said in a surprised tone, "what is the meaning of 'Do not be afraid'?"

Yukinari laughed and said, "There has no doubt been a lot of talk lately about our being so friendly. But what of it? Even if we were as intimate as people think, that would be nothing to be ashamed of. Really you could let me see your face."

"O no," I replied, "I cannot possibly do that. I am extremely ugly, and you said you could never love an ugly woman."

"Are you really?" he said. "In that case you had better not let me see you."

Often thereafter, when it would have been easy for Yukinari to look at me in the normal course of things, he covered his face with a fan or turned aside. In fact he never once saw me. To think that he took what I said about my ugliness quite seriously!

Towards the end of the Third Month it becomes too warm for winter cloaks, and often Chamberlains who are on night watch in the Senior Courtiers' Chamber wear only the over-robes of their Court costumes, leaving off their trouser-skirts and trains. Early one morning in that month, when Lady Shikibu and I had been sleeping in the outer part of a room in the Empress's Office, the sliding-door was pushed open and the Emperor and Empress entered. We were thrown into utter confusion and did not know what to do with ourselves, which greatly amused Their Majesties. Hastily we threw on our Chinese jackets, tucking our hair inside, and then we heaped the bed-clothes and everything else in a great pile. Their Majesties walked across the room and, standing behind this pile, watched the men going between the Palace and the guard house. Several courtiers approached our room and spoke to us, without suspecting who was inside the room. "Do not let them see we are here," His Majesty said with a chuckle.

Before long Their Majesties left. "Come along, both of you," said the Empress. I replied that we would come as soon as we had made up our faces, and we stayed where we were.

Lady Shikibu and I were still discussing how splendid Their Majesties had looked when, through a small opening in the blinds (where the frame of our curtain of state was pressed against the sliding-door in the back of the room), we noticed the dark silhouette of a man. At first we thought that it must be Noritaka and continued to talk without paying any particular attention. Presently a beaming face appeared through the opening in the blinds. We still took it to be Noritaka, but after a quick look we were amused to find that we were mistaken.

Laughing heartily, we rearranged our curtain of state so that we were properly hidden. Too late, though. The man turned out to be none other than Yukinari; and he had seen me full-face. After all my past efforts this was extremely vexing. Lady Shikibu, on the other hand, had been looking safely in the other direction.

"Well," said Yukinari, stepping forward, "now I have really managed to see you completely."

"We thought it was Noritaka," I explained, "and so we didn't bother to hide properly. But why, may I ask, did you examine me so carefully when in the past you said that you would never look at me?"

"I have been told," said he, "that a woman's face is particularly attractive when she rises in the morning. So I came here hoping for a chance to peep into one of the ladies' rooms and see something interesting. I was already watching you when Their Majesties were here, but you suspected nothing."

Then, as I recall, he walked straight into the room.

Unsettling Things

The feeling of a mother whose son is a priest and has gone into the mountains for a twelve-year retreat.

One arrives after nightfall in an unfamiliar place. For fear of being too conspicuous, one refrains from lighting a lamp; but one prefers to sit near the other people in the room, even though they are hidden by the dark.

A servant is newly employed and his character unfamiliar; yet one has entrusted a valuable object to him. He is supposed to deliver it to someone's house and now he is late in returning.

A baby who is still unable to talk falls over backwards. Someone picks him up, but he starts crying.

Eating strawberries in the dark.

A festival where one does not recognize any of the participants.

Rare Things

A son-in-law who is praised by his adoptive father; a young bride who is loved by her mother-in-law.

A silver tweezer that is good at plucking out the hair.

A servant who does not speak badly about his master.

A person who is in no way eccentric or imperfect, who is superior in both mind and body, and who remains flawless all his life.

People who live together and still manage to behave with reserve towards each other. However much these people may try to hide their weaknesses, they usually fail.

To avoid getting ink stains on the notebook into which one is copying stories, poems, or the like. If it is a very fine notebook, one takes the greatest care not to make a blot; yet somehow one never seems to succeed.

When people, whether they be men or women or priests, have promised each other eternal friendship, it is rare for them to stay on good terms until the end.

A servant who is pleasant to his master.

One has given some silk to the fuller and, when he sends it back, it is so beautiful that one cries out in admiration.

Adorable Things

The face of a child drawn on a melon.

A baby sparrow that comes hopping up when one imitates the squeak of a mouse; or again, when one has tied it with a thread round its leg and its parents bring insects or worms and pop them in its mouth—delightful!

A baby of two or so is crawling rapidly along the ground. With his sharp eyes he catches sight of a tiny object and, picking it up with his pretty little fingers, takes it to show to a grown-up person.

A child, whose hair has been cut like a nun's, is examining something; the hair falls over his eyes, but instead of brushing it away he holds his head to the side. The pretty white cords of his trouser-skirt are tied round his shoulders, and this too is most adorable.

A young Palace page, who is still quite small, walks by in ceremonial costume.

One picks up a pretty baby and holds him for a while in one's arms; while one is fondling him, he clings to one's neck and then falls asleep.

The objects used during the Display of Dolls.[3]

One picks up a tiny lotus leaf that is floating on a pond and examines it. Not only lotus leaves, but little hollyhock flowers, and indeed all small things, are most adorable.

An extremely plump baby, who is about a year old and has a lovely white skin, comes crawling towards one, dressed in a long gauze robe of violet with the sleeves tucked up.

A little boy of about eight who reads aloud from a book in his childish voice.

Pretty, white chicks who are still not fully fledged and look as if their clothes are too short for them; cheeping loudly, they follow one on their long legs, or walk close to the mother hen.

Duck eggs.

An urn containing the relics of some holy person.

Wild pinks.

One Day, When Her Majesty Was Surrounded by Several Ladies[4]

One day, when Her Majesty was surrounded by several ladies, I remarked in connexion with something that she had said, "There are times when the world so

---

3. The Display of Dolls fell on the third day of the third Month.

4. This describes the way in which *The Pillow Book* was begun. For all its bows to royalty, this shows the author's self-analysis.

exasperates me that I feel I cannot go on living in it for another moment and I want to disappear for good. But then, if I happen to obtain some nice white paper, Michinoku paper, or white decorated paper, I decide that I can put up with things as they are a little longer. Or, if I can spread out a finely woven, green straw mat and examine the white bordering with its vivid black patterns, I somehow feel that I cannot turn my back on this world, and life actually seems precious to me."

"It really doesn't take much to console you," said the Empress, laughing. "I wonder what sort of a person it was who gazed at the moon on Mount Obasute."

The ladies who were in attendance also teased me. "You've certainly found a cheap prayer for warding off evil," they said.

Some time later, when I was staying at home and absorbed in various petty worries, a messenger brought me twenty rolls of magnificent paper from Her Majesty. "Come back quickly," she wrote, adding, "I am sending you this because of what you told me the other day. It seems to be of poor quality, however, and I am afraid you will not be able to use it for copying the Sutra of Longevity." It delighted me that Her Majesty should have remembered something that I myself had completely forgotten. Even if an ordinary person had sent me the present, I should have been overjoyed. How much more pleasing when it came from the Empress herself! I was so excited that I could not frame a proper reply, but simply sent Her Majesty this poem:

> Thanks to the paper that the Goddess gave,
> My years will now be plenteous as the crane's.

"Make sure that the Empress is asked the following," I told the messenger. "Am I expecting too many years?" My reward for the messenger, a general maid from the Table Room, was an unlined green costume.

Then I immediately used the paper I had received to write my collection of notes. I felt a glow of delight and all my worries began to disappear.

A couple of days later a messenger dressed in red arrived with a straw mat. "Here you are," he said. "And who may you be?" said my maid severely. "Such impudence!" However, the man simply put down the mat and left. I told the maid to ask him where he came from, but he had already disappeared. She brought me the mat, which was an unusually beautiful one with a splendid white border, of the type used by high dignitaries. I felt it must be the Empress who had sent it, but as I was not quite sure I told someone to look for the messenger. Everyone was greatly puzzled, but I did not think the matter was worth discussing since the messenger was nowhere to be found. It occurred to me that, if he had delivered the mat to the wrong place, he would be sure to come back and say so. I should have liked to send someone to Her Majesty's palace to discover the truth of the affair. Then I decided that the mystery must be deliberate and that the mat could only have come from the Empress. This thought filled me with joy. Having heard nothing further after two days, I knew there could be no doubt about the matter, and I sent a message to Lady Sakyō telling her what had happened. "Has any of this come to your ears?" I asked. "Please inform me secretly of what you have heard. In any case do not let anyone know that I have asked you."

"Her Majesty did it all in great secret," was Lady Sakyō's reply. "On no account tell anyone now or later that I informed you."

Delighted that everything I had suspected was now clear, I wrote a letter, telling the messenger to lay it on the balustrade in Her Majesty's palace when no one was looking. In his nervousness, however, he placed it in such a way that it fell off the side and landed under the stairs.

MURASAKI SHIKIBU (978?–1014? C.E.)
Japan

"Evening Faces" ("Yūgao") is the fourth chapter of *The Tale of Genji*, the greatest work of Japanese literature. Genji, the hero of the book, was born fifteen years before we meet him here. He is the son of a low-ranking but favorite royal concubine and the emperor. To spare him from palace intrigues, his father made him a commoner, assigning him to the Marimoto clan, or Genji. Hence his name, which gave no hint of his royal lineage. Because of his magical aura or charisma, he was given the name Radiant Genji [Hikaru Genji]. (No character in the book has a name in the standard sense of an inherited family name and a given name.)

The book begins by focusing on Genji's relations with women throughout the first three chapters. The rainy-night discussion of women in the second chapter is one of the most self-contained of the work's fifty-four chapters, but a few connections and conventions need to be explained. Rokujō, who is mentioned in the opening paragraph, is identified later: it is the place where Genji has an affair with a high-born, somewhat older woman. It is perhaps her jealous spirit that kills Yūgao, the chapter's heroine. The ties that children formed with a wetnurse were considered close ones; Genji's visit to his is aided by her son, Koremitsu. He is Genji's faithful attendant, as Yūgao's is Ukon.

4   Yūgao ("Evening Faces") takes her name, as do so many characters in the story, from a poem mentioning a flower having the same name. When she hands the flower to Genji, she is permitting him to woo her. (Today the eroticism may be missed, but in the time of *Genji* the gesture was highly charged.) Yūgao's poem is more important than her appearance; as is clear from Chapter 51 of the *Pillow Book,* women even preferred not to be seen. Genji also hides his appearance from Yūgao. The courtly romance here involves youth, glimpses of the couple making love, essential communications by means of poems, the shock of a malevolent spirit bringing darkness and death, and the revelation that the precious beauty and anguish of life are mutually dependent.

Other characters appear late in the chapter. Tō no Chūjō is Genji's closest friend and an often comic foil. He preceded Genji as Yūgao's lover. (In fact, he has unknowingly had a daughter by her, as Ukon will discover many chapters later.) The "lady of the locust shell," Utsusemi, had been pursued in vain earlier by Genji; their attachment remains unconsummated.

The chapter concludes with the longest example of the author's intervention in the story. The Japanese suppose a number of court ladies as the narrators of

Frontispiece to a sutra scroll. Japanese, Heian period, 12th century C.E. Itsukushi-ma Jinja Homotsukan, Hiroshima

Genji's story, but imagine that the author herself may intrude at moments such as this.

The clear and appealing translation obscures the complex style of the original, which usually omits mention of persons and flows on unceasingly as if each chapter were a single sentence. Older manuscripts include no punctuation at all and use indentation solely to set off poems. A more beautiful, more complex, and yet more natural style cannot be imagined. Seven or eight centuries before the English novel was born, a Japanese lady serving in the salon of a royal consort created one of the greatest literary works in the world.

from The Tale of Genji

Evening Faces

On his way from court to pay one of his calls at Rokujō, Genji stopped to inquire after his old nurse, Koremitsu's mother, at her house in Gojō. Gravely ill, she had become a nun. The carriage entrance was closed. He sent for Koremitsu and while he was waiting looked up and down the dirty, cluttered street. Beside the nurse's house was a new fence of plaited cypress. The four or five narrow shutters above had been raised, and new blinds, white and clean, hung in the apertures. He caught outlines of pretty foreheads beyond. He would have judged, as they moved about, that they belonged to rather tall women. What sort of women might they

Translated by Edward G. Seidensticker.

be? His carriage was simple and unadorned and he had no outrunners. Quite certain that he would not be recognized, he leaned out for a closer look. The hanging gate, of something like trelliswork, was propped on a pole, and he could see that the house was tiny and flimsy. He felt a little sorry for the occupants of such a place—and then asked himself who in this world had more than a temporary shelter.[1] A hut, a jeweled pavilion, they were the same. A pleasantly green vine was climbing a board wall. The white flowers, he thought, had a rather self-satisfied look about them.

" 'I needs must ask the lady far off yonder,' "[2] he said, as if to himself.

An attendant came up, bowing deeply. "The white flowers far off yonder are known as 'evening faces,' "[3] he said. "A very human sort of name—and what a shabby place they have picked to bloom in."

It was as the man said. The neighborhood was a poor one, chiefly of small houses. Some were leaning precariously, and there were "evening faces" at the sagging eaves.

"A hapless sort of flower. Pick one off for me, would you?"

The man went inside the raised gate and broke off a flower. A pretty little girl in long, unlined yellow trousers of raw silk came out through a sliding door that seemed too good for the surroundings. Beckoning to the man, she handed him a heavily scented white fan.

"Put it on this. It isn't much of a fan, but then it isn't much of a flower either."

Koremitsu, coming out of the gate, passed it on to Genji.

"They lost the key, and I have had to keep you waiting. You aren't likely to be recognized in such a neighborhood, but it's not a very nice neighborhood to keep you waiting in."

Genji's carriage was pulled in and he dismounted. Besides Koremitsu, a son and a daughter, the former an eminent cleric, and the daughter's husband, the governor of Mikawa, were in attendance upon the old woman. They thanked him profusely for his visit.

The old woman got up to receive him. "I did not at all mind leaving the world, except for the thought that I would no longer be able to see you as I am seeing you now. My vows seem to have given me a new lease on life, and this visit makes me certain that I shall receive the radiance of Lord Amitābha with a serene and tranquil heart." And she collapsed in tears.

Genji was near tears himself. "It has worried me enormously that you should be taking so long to recover, and I was very sad to learn that you have withdrawn from the world. You must live a long life and see the career I make for myself. I am sure that if you do you will be reborn upon the highest summits of the Pure Land. I am told that it is important to rid oneself of the smallest regret for this world."

Fond of the child she has reared, a nurse tends to look upon him as a paragon even if he is a half-wit. How much prouder was the old woman, who somehow

---

1. Compare Anonymous, *Kokinshū* 987:
   Where in all this world shall I call home?
   A temporary shelter is my home.
2. Compare: Anonymous, *Kokinshū* 1007:
   I needs must ask the lady far off yonder

What flower it is off there that blooms so white.
3. The *Yūgao, Lagenaria siceraria*, is a kind of gourd.

gained stature, who thought of herself as eminent in her own right for having been permitted to serve him. The tears flowed on.

Her children were ashamed for her. They exchanged glances. It would not do to have these contortions taken as signs of a lingering affection for the world.

Genji was deeply touched. "The people who were fond of me left me when I was very young. Others have come along, it is true, to take care of me, but you are the only one I am really attached to. In recent years there have been restrictions upon my movements, and I have not been able to look in upon you morning and evening as I would have wished, or indeed to have a good visit with you. Yet I become very depressed when the days go by and I do not see you. 'Would that there were on this earth no final partings.' "[4] He spoke with great solemnity, and the scent of his sleeve, as he brushed away a tear, quite flooded the room.

Yes, thought the children, who had been silently reproaching their mother for her want of control, the fates had been kind to her. They too were now in tears.

Genji left orders that prayers and services be resumed. As he went out he asked for a torch, and in its light examined the fan on which the "evening face" had rested. It was permeated with a lady's perfume, elegant and alluring. On it was a poem in a disguised cursive hand that suggested breeding and taste. He was interested.

"I think I need not ask whose face it is,
So bright, this evening face, in the shining dew."

"Who is living in the house to the west?" he asked Koremitsu. "Have you perhaps had occasion to inquire?"

At it again, thought Koremitsu. He spoke somewhat tartly. "I must confess that these last few days I have been too busy with my mother to think about her neighbors."

"You are annoyed with me. But this fan has the appearance of something it might be interesting to look into. Make inquiries, if you will, please, of someone who knows the neighborhood."

Koremitsu went in to ask his mother's steward, and emerged with the information that the house belonged to a certain honorary vice-governor.[5] "The husband is away in the country, and the wife seems to be a young woman of taste. Her sisters are out in service here and there. They often come visiting. I suspect the fellow is too poorly placed to know the details."

His poetess would be one of the sisters, thought Genji. A rather practiced and forward young person, and, were he to meet her, perhaps vulgar as well—but the easy familiarity of the poem had not been at all unpleasant, not something to be pushed away in disdain. His amative propensities, it will be seen, were having their way once more.

---

4. Compare Ariwara Narihira, *Kokinshū* 901 and *Tales of Ise* 84:
    Would that my mother might live a thousand years.
    Would there were on this earth no final partings.

5. The word in original text is *Yōmei no suke.* Once thought among the undecipherables in the *Genji,* it is now thought to refer to someone who has the title but not the perquisites of vice-governor.

Carefully disguising his hand, he jotted down a reply on a piece of notepaper and sent it in by the attendant who had earlier been of service.

"Come a bit nearer, please. Then might you know
Whose was the evening face so dim in the twilight."

Thinking it a familiar profile, the lady had not lost the opportunity to surprise him with a letter, and when time passed and there was no answer she was left feeling somewhat embarrassed and disconsolate. Now came a poem by special messenger. Her women became quite giddy as they turned their minds to the problem of replying. Rather bored with it all, the messenger returned empty-handed. Genji made a quiet departure, lighted by very few torches. The shutters next door had been lowered. There was something sad about the light, dimmer than fireflies, that came through the cracks.

At the Rokujō house, the trees and the plantings had a quiet dignity. The lady herself was strangely cold and withdrawn. Thoughts of the "evening faces" quite left him. He overslept, and the sun was rising when he took his leave. He presented such a fine figure in the morning light that the women of the place understood well enough why he should be so universally admired. On his way he again passed those shutters, as he had no doubt done many times before. Because of that small incident he now looked at the house carefully, wondering who might be within.

"My mother is not doing at all well, and I have been with her," said Koremitsu some days later. And, coming nearer: "Because you seemed so interested, I called someone who knows about the house next door and had him questioned. His story was not completely clear. He said that in the Fifth Month or so someone came very quietly to live in the house, but that not even the domestics had been told who she might be. I have looked through the fence from time to time myself and had glimpses through blinds of several young women. Something about their dress suggests that they are in the service of someone of higher rank.[6] Yesterday, when the evening light was coming directly through, I saw the lady herself writing a letter. She is very beautiful. She seemed lost in thought, and the women around her were weeping."

Genji had suspected something of the sort. He must find out more.

Koremitsu's view was that while Genji was undeniably someone the whole world took seriously, his youth and the fact that women found him attractive meant that to refrain from these little affairs would be less than human. It was not realistic to hold that certain people were beyond temptation.

"Looking for a chance to do a bit of exploring, I found a small pretext for writing to her. She answered immediately, in a good, practiced hand. Some of her women do not seem at all beneath contempt."

"Explore very thoroughly, if you will. I will not be satisfied until you do."

The house was what the guardsman would have described as the lowest of the low, but Genji was interested. What hidden charms might he not come upon!

---

6. They wear *shibira*, apparently a sort of
   apron or jacket indicating a small degree of
   formality.

Suzumushi ("The Bell Cricket") painting from The Tale of Genji Scroll. Attributed to Takayoshi. Japanese, Heian period, 12th century C.E. In the Gotoh Museum, Tokyo

He had thought the coldness of the governor's wife, the lady of "the locust shell," quite unique. Yet if she had proved amenable to his persuasions the affair would no doubt have been dropped as a sad mistake after that one encounter. As matters were, the resentment and the distinct possibility of final defeat never left his mind. The discussion that rainy night would seem to have made him curious about the several ranks. There had been a time when such a lady would not have been worth his notice. Yes, it had been broadening, that discussion! He had not found the willing and available one, the governor of Iyo's daughter, entirely uninteresting, but the thought that the stepmother must have been listening coolly to the interview was excruciating. He must await some sign of her real intentions.

The governor of Iyo returned to the city. He came immediately to Genji's mansion. Somewhat sunburned, his travel robes rumpled from the sea voyage, he was a rather heavy and displeasing sort of person. He was of good lineage, however, and, though aging, he still had good manners. As they spoke of his province, Genji wanted to ask the full count of those hot springs, but he was somewhat confused to find memories chasing one another through his head. How foolish that he should be so uncomfortable before the honest old man! He remembered the guardsman's warning that such affairs are unwise,[7] and he felt sorry for the governor. Though he resented the wife's coldness, he could see that from the husband's point of view it was admirable. He was upset to learn that the governor meant to find a suitable husband for his daughter and take his wife to the provinces. He consulted the lady's young brother upon the possibility of another meeting. It would have been difficult even with the lady's cooperation, however, and she was of the view that to receive a gentleman so far above her would be extremely unwise.

---

7. This is curious, since the guardsman's warning was not against women of the lower classes but against fickle women. There have been theories that some part of his discourse has been lost.

Yet she did not want him to forget her entirely. Her answers to his notes on this and that occasion were pleasant enough, and contained casual little touches that made him pause in admiration. He resented her chilliness, but she interested him. As for the stepdaughter, he was certain that she would receive him hospitably enough however formidable a husband she might acquire. Reports upon her arrangements disturbed him not at all.

Autumn came. He was kept busy and unhappy by affairs of his own making, and he visited Sanjō infrequently. There was resentment.

As for the affair at Rokujō, he had overcome the lady's resistance and had his way, and, alas, he had cooled toward her. People thought it worthy of comment that his passions should seem so much more governable than before he had made her his. She was subject to fits of despondency, more intense on sleepless nights when she awaited him in vain. She feared that if rumors were to spread the gossips would make much of the difference in their ages.

On a morning of heavy mists, insistently roused by the lady, who was determined that he be on his way, Genji emerged yawning and sighing and looking very sleepy. Chūjō, one of her women, raised a shutter and pulled a curtain aside as if urging her lady to come forward and see him off. The lady lifted her head from her pillow. He was an incomparably handsome figure as he paused to admire the profusion of flowers below the veranda. Chūjō followed him down a gallery. In an aster robe that matched the season pleasantly and a gossamer train worn with clean elegance, she was a pretty, graceful woman. Glancing back, he asked her to sit with him for a time at the corner railing. The ceremonious precision of the seated figure and the hair flowing over her robes were very fine.

He took her hand.

"Though loath to be taxed with seeking fresher blooms,
I feel impelled to pluck this morning glory."

"Why should it be?"
She answered with practiced alacrity, making it seem that she was speaking not for herself but for her lady:

"In haste to plunge into the morning mists,
You seem to have no heart for the blossoms here."

A pretty little page boy, especially decked out for the occasion, it would seem, walked out among the flowers. His trousers wet with dew, he broke off a morning glory for Genji. He made a picture that called out to be painted.

Even persons to whom Genji was nothing were drawn to him. No doubt even rough mountain men wanted to pause for a time in the shade of the flowering tree,[8] and those who had basked even briefly in his radiance had thoughts, each in accordance with his rank, of a daughter who might be taken into his service, a

---

8. In the preface to the *Kokinshū* one of the "poetic immortals" is likened to a woodcutter resting under a cherry tree in full bloom.

not ill-formed sister who might perform some humble service for him. One need not be surprised, then, that people with a measure of sensibility among those who had on some occasion received a little poem from him or been treated to some little kindness found him much on their minds. No doubt it distressed them not to be always with him.

I had forgotten: Koremitsu gave a good account of the fence peeping to which he had been assigned. "I am unable to identify her. She seems determined to hide herself from the world. In their boredom her women and girls go out to the long gallery at the street, the one with the shutters, and watch for carriages. Sometimes the lady who seems to be their mistress comes quietly out to join them. I've not had a good look at her, but she seems very pretty indeed. One day a carriage with outrunners went by. The little girls shouted to a person named Ukon that she must come in a hurry. The captain[9] was going by, they said. An older woman came out and motioned to them to be quiet. How did they know? she asked, coming out toward the gallery. The passage from the main house is by a sort of makeshift bridge. She was hurrying and her skirt caught on something, and she stumbled and almost fell off. 'The sort of thing the god of Katsuragi might do,'[10] she said, and seems to have lost interest in sightseeing. They told her that the man in the carriage was wearing casual court dress and that he had a retinue. They mentioned several names, and all of them were undeniably Lord Tō no Chūjō's guards and pages."

"I wish you had made positive identification." Might she be the lady of whom Tō no Chūjō had spoken so regretfully that rainy night?

Koremitsu went on, smiling at this open curiosity. "I have as a matter of fact made the proper overtures and learned all about the place. I come and go as if I did not know that they are not all equals. They think they are hiding the truth and try to insist that there is no one there but themselves when one of the little girls makes a slip."

"Let me have a peep for myself when I call on your mother."

Even if she was only in temporary lodgings, the woman would seem to be of the lower class for which his friend had indicated such contempt that rainy evening. Yet something might come of it all. Determined not to go against his master's wishes in the smallest detail and himself driven by very considerable excitement, Koremitsu searched diligently for a chance to let Genji into the house. But the details are tiresome, and I shall not go into them.

Genji did not know who the lady was and he did not want her to know who he was. In very shabby disguise, he set out to visit her on foot. He must be taking her very seriously, thought Koremitsu, who offered his horse and himself went on foot.

"Though I do not think that our gentleman will look very good with tramps for servants."

To make quite certain that the expedition remained secret, Genji took with him only the man who had been his intermediary in the matter of the "evening

---

9. Tō no Chūjō.
10. Tradition held that the god of Katsuragi,   south of Nara, was very ugly and built a
     bridge which he used only at night.

faces" and a page whom no one was likely to recognize. Lest he be found out even so, he did not stop to see his nurse.

The lady had his messengers followed to see how he made his way home and tried by every means to learn where he lived; but her efforts came to nothing. For all his secretiveness, Genji had grown fond of her and felt that he must go on seeing her. They were of such different ranks, he tried to tell himself, and it was altogether too frivolous. Yet his visits were frequent. In affairs of this sort, which can muddle the senses of the most serious and honest of men, he had always kept himself under tight control and avoided any occasion for censure. Now, to a most astonishing degree, he would be asking himself as he returned in the morning from a visit how he could wait through the day for the next. And then he would rebuke himself. It was madness, it was not an affair he should let disturb him. She was of an extraordinarily gentle and quiet nature. Though there was a certain vagueness about her, and indeed an almost childlike quality, it was clear that she knew something about men. She did not appear to be of very good family. What was there about her, he asked himself over and over again, that so drew him to her? *mysteriousness*

He took great pains to hide his rank and always wore travel dress, and he did not allow her to see his face. He came late at night when everyone was asleep. She was frightened, as if he were an apparition from an old story. She did not need to see his face to know that he was a fine gentleman. But who might he be? Her suspicions turned to Koremitsu. It was that young gallant, surely, who had brought the strange visitor. But Koremitsu pursued his own little affairs unremittingly, careful to feign indifference to and ignorance of this other affair. What could it all mean? The lady was lost in unfamiliar speculations.

Genji had his own worries. If, having lowered his guard with an appearance of complete unreserve, she were to slip away and hide, where would he seek her? This seemed to be but a temporary residence, and he could not be sure when she would choose to change it, and for what other. He hoped that he might reconcile himself to what must be and forget the affair as just another dalliance; but he was not confident.

On days when, to avoid attracting notice, he refrained from visiting her, his fretfulness came near anguish. Suppose he were to move her in secret to Nijō. If troublesome rumors were to arise, well, he could say that they had been fated from the start. He wondered what bond in a former life might have produced an infatuation such as he had not known before.

"Let's have a good talk," he said to her, "where we can be quite at our ease."

"It's all so strange. What you say is reasonable enough, but what you do is so strange. And rather frightening."

Yes, she might well be frightened. Something childlike in her fright brought a smile to his lips. "Which of us is the mischievous fox spirit? I wonder. Just be quiet and give yourself up to its persuasions."

Won over by his gentle warmth, she was indeed inclined to let him have his way. She seemed such a pliant little creature, likely to submit absolutely to the most outrageous demands. He thought again of Tō no Chūjō's "wild carnation," of the equable nature his friend had described that rainy night. Fearing that it would be useless, he did not try very hard to question her. She did not seem likely to indulge in dramatics and suddenly run off and hide herself, and so the fault must have been Tō no Chūjō's. Genji himself would not be guilty of such negligence—though it did occur to him that a bit of infidelity[11] might make her more interesting.

The bright full moon of the Eighth Month came flooding in through chinks in the roof. It was not the sort of dwelling he was used to, and he was fascinated. Toward dawn he was awakened by plebeian voices in the shabby houses down the street.

"Freezing, that's what it is, freezing. There's not much business this year, and when you can't get out into the country you feel like giving up. Do you hear me, neighbor?"

He could make out every word. It embarrassed the woman that, so near at hand, there should be this clamor of preparation as people set forth on their sad little enterprises. Had she been one of the stylish ladies of the world, she would have wanted to shrivel up and disappear. She was a placid sort, however, and she seemed to take nothing, painful or embarrassing or unpleasant, too seriously. Her manner elegant and yet girlish, she did not seem to know what the rather awful clamor up and down the street might mean. He much preferred this easygoing bewilderment to a show of consternation, a face scarlet with embarrassment. As if at his very pillow, there came the booming of a foot pestle,[12] more fearsome than the stamping of the thunder god, genuinely earsplitting. He did not know what device the sound came from, but he did know that it was enough to awaken the dead. From this direction and that there came the faint thump of fulling hammers against coarse cloth; and mingled with it—these were sounds to call forth the deepest emotions—were the calls of geese flying overhead. He slid a door open and they looked out. They had been lying near the veranda. There were tasteful clumps of black bamboo just outside and the dew shone as in more familiar places. Autumn insects sang busily, as if only inches from an ear used to wall crickets at considerable distances. It was all very clamorous, and also rather wonderful. Countless details could be overlooked in the singleness of his affection for the girl. She was pretty and fragile in a soft, modest cloak of lavender and a lined white robe. She had no single feature that struck him as especially beautiful, and yet, slender and fragile, she seemed so delicately beautiful that he was almost afraid to hear her voice. He might have wished her to be a little more assertive, but he wanted only to be near her, and yet nearer.

"Let's go off somewhere and enjoy the rest of the night. This is too much."

"But how is that possible?" She spoke very quietly. "You keep taking me by surprise."

There was a newly confiding response to his offer of his services as guardian in this world and the next. She was a strange little thing. He found it hard to believe that she had had much experience of men. He no longer cared what people might think. He asked Ukon to summon his man, who got the carriage ready. The

---

11. On whose part, his or the girl's? The passage is obscure.

12. *Karausu.* The mortar was sunk in the floor and the pestle was raised by foot and allowed to fall.

women of the house, though uneasy, sensed the depth of his feelings and were inclined to put their trust in him.

Dawn approached. No cocks were crowing. There was only the voice of an old man making deep obeisance to a Buddha, in preparation, it would seem, for a pilgrimage to Mitake.[13] He seemed to be prostrating himself repeatedly and with much difficulty. All very sad. In a life itself like the morning dew, what could he desire so earnestly?

"Praise to the Messiah to come," intoned the voice.

"Listen," said Genji, "He is thinking of another world.

"This pious one shall lead us on our way
As we plight our troth for all the lives to come."

The vow exchanged by the Chinese emperor and Yang Kuei-fei seemed to bode ill, and so he preferred to invoke Lord Maitreya, the Buddha of the Future; but such promises are rash.

"So heavy the burden I bring with me from the past,
I doubt that I should make these vows for the future."

It was a reply that suggested doubts about his "lives to come."

The moon was low over the western hills. She was reluctant to go with him. As he sought to persuade her, the moon suddenly disappeared behind clouds in a lovely dawn sky. Always in a hurry to be off before daylight exposed him, he lifted her easily into his carriage and took her to a nearby villa. Ukon was with them. Waiting for the caretaker to be summoned, Genji looked up at the rotting gate and the ferns that trailed thickly down over it. The groves beyond were still dark, and the mist and the dews were heavy. Genji's sleeve was soaking, for he had raised the blinds of the carriage.

"This is a novel adventure, and I must say that it seems like a lot of trouble.

"And did it confuse them too, the men of old,
This road through the dawn, for me so new and strange?

"How does it seem to you?"
She turned shyly away.

"And is the moon, unsure of the hills it approaches,
Foredoomed to lose its way in the empty skies?

"I am afraid."
She did seem frightened, and bewildered. She was so used to all those swarms of people, he thought with a smile.

The carriage was brought in and its traces propped against the veranda while a room was made ready in the west wing. Much excited, Ukon was thinking about earlier adventures. The furious energy with which the caretaker saw to preparations made her suspect who Genji was. It was almost daylight when they alighted

---

13. In the Yoshino Mountains, south of Nara.

from the carriage. The room was clean and pleasant, for all the haste with which it had been readied.

"There are unfortunately no women here to wait upon His Lordship." The man, who addressed him through Ukon, was a lesser steward who had served in the Sanjō mansion of Genji's father-in-law. "Shall I send for someone?"

"The last thing I want. I came here because I wanted to be in complete solitude, away from all possible visitors. You are not to tell a soul."

The man put together a hurried breakfast, but he was, as he had said, without serving women to help him.

Genji told the girl that he meant to show her a love as dependable as "the patient river of the loons."[14] He could do little else in these strange lodgings.

The sun was high when he arose. He opened the shutters. All through the badly neglected grounds not a person was to be seen. The groves were rank and overgrown. The flowers and grasses in the foreground were a drab monotone, an autumn moor. The pond was choked with weeds, and all in all it was a forbidding place. An outbuilding seemed to be fitted with rooms for the caretaker, but it was some distance away.

"It is a forbidding place,"[15] said Genji. "But I am sure that whatever devils emerge will pass me by."

He was still in disguise. She thought it unkind of him to be so secretive, and he had to agree that their relationship had gone beyond such furtiveness.

"Because of one chance meeting by the wayside
The flower now opens in the evening dew.

"And how does it look to you?"

"The face seemed quite to shine in the evening dew.
But I was dazzled by the evening light."

Her eyes turned away. She spoke in a whisper.
To him it may have seemed an interesting poem.

As a matter of fact, she found him handsomer than her poem suggested, indeed frighteningly handsome, given the setting.

"I hid my name from you because I thought it altogether too unkind of you to be keeping your name from me. Do please tell me now. This silence makes me feel that something awful might be coming."

"Call me the fisherman's daughter."[16] Still hiding her name, she was like a little child.

"I see. I brought it all on myself? A case of *warekara*?"[17]

---

14. Compare: Umanofuhito Kunihito, *Man-yōshū* 4458:
   The patient river of the patient loons
   Will not run dry. My love will still
   outlast it.

15. The repetition in almost identical language suggests a miscopying.

16. Compare: Anonymous, *Shinkokinshū* 1701, and "Courtesan's Song," *Wakan Rōeishū* 722:

A fisherman's daughter, I spend my life by the waves,
The waves that tell us nothing. I have no home.

17. Compare: Fujiwara Naoiko, *Kokinshū* 807:
   The grass the fishermen take, the *warekara*:
   "I did it myself." I shall weep but I shall not hate you.

And so, sometimes affectionately, sometimes reproachfully, they talked the hours away.

Koremitsu had found them out and brought provisions. Feeling a little guilty about the way he had treated Ukon, he did not come near. He thought it amusing that Genji should thus be wandering the streets, and concluded that the girl must provide sufficient cause. And he could have had her himself, had he not been so generous.

Genji and the girl looked out at an evening sky of the utmost calm. Because she found the darkness in the recesses of the house frightening, he raised the blinds at the veranda and they lay side by side. As they gazed at each other in the gathering dusk, it all seemed very strange to her, unbelievably strange. Memories of past wrongs quite left her. She was more at ease with him now, and he thought her charming. Beside him all through the day, starting up in fright at each little noise, she seemed delightfully childlike. He lowered the shutters early and had lights brought.

"You seem comfortable enough with me, and yet you raise difficulties."

At court everyone would be frantic. Where would the search be directed? He thought what a strange love it was, and he thought of the turmoil the Rokujō lady was certain to be in.[18] She had every right to be resentful, and yet her jealous ways were not pleasant. It was that sad lady to whom his thoughts first turned. Here was the girl beside him, so simple and undemanding; and the other was so impossibly forceful in her demands. How he wished he might in some measure have his freedom.

It was past midnight. He had been asleep for a time when an exceedingly beautiful woman appeared by his pillow. _In a dream_.

"You do not even think of visiting me, when you are so much on my mind. Instead you go running off with someone who has nothing to recommend her, and raise a great stir over her. It is cruel, intolerable." She seemed about to shake the girl from her sleep. He awoke, feeling as if he were in the power of some malign being. The light had gone out. In great alarm, he pulled his sword to his pillow and awakened Ukon. She too seemed frightened.

"Go out to the gallery and wake the guard. Have him bring a light."

"It's much too dark."

He forced a smile. "You're behaving like a child."

He clapped his hands and a hollow echo answered. No one seemed to hear. The girl was trembling violently. She was bathed in sweat and as if in a trance, quite bereft of her senses.

"She is such a timid little thing," said Ukon, "frightened when there is nothing at all to be frightened of. This must be dreadful for her."

Yes, poor thing, thought Genji. She did seem so fragile, and she had spent the whole day gazing up at the sky.

"I'll go get someone. What a frightful echo. You stay here with her." He pulled Ukon to the girl's side.

---

18. We do not learn much about "the Rokujō lady" until Chapter 9. There is a theory that "Evening Faces" was written consid- erably later than the present succession of chapters has it.

The lights in the west gallery had gone out. There was a gentle wind. He had few people with him, and they were asleep. They were three in number: a young man who was one of his intimates and who was the son of the steward here, a court page, and the man who had been his intermediary in the matter of the "evening faces." He called out. Someone answered and came up to him.

"Bring a light. Wake the other, and shout and twang your bowstrings. What do you mean, going to sleep in a deserted house? I believe Lord Koremitsu was here."

"He was. But he said he had no orders and would come again at dawn."

An elite guardsman, the man was very adept at bow twanging. He went off with a shouting as of a fire watch. At court, thought Genji, the courtiers on night duty would have announced themselves, and the guard would be changing. It was not so very late.

He felt his way back inside. The girl was as before, and Ukon lay face down at her side.

"What is this? You're a fool to let yourself be so frightened. Are you worried about the fox spirits that come out and play tricks in deserted houses? But you needn't worry. They won't come near me." He pulled her to her knees.

"I'm not feeling at all well. That's why I was lying down. My poor lady must be terrified."

"She is indeed. And I can't think why."

He reached for the girl. She was not breathing. He lifted her and she was limp in his arms. There was no sign of life. She had seemed as defenseless as a child, and no doubt some evil power had taken possession of her. He could think of nothing to do. A man came with a torch. Ukon was not prepared to move, and Genji himself pulled up curtain frames to hide the girl.

"Bring the light closer."

It was a most unusual order. Not ordinarily permitted at Genji's side, the man hesitated to cross the threshold.

"Come, come, bring it here! There is a time and place for ceremony."

In the torchlight he had a fleeting glimpse of a figure by the girl's pillow. It was the woman in his dream. It faded away like an apparition in an old romance. In all the fright and horror, his confused thoughts centered upon the girl. There was no room for thoughts of himself. *The jealous woman occurred her.*

He knelt over her and called out to her, but she was cold and had stopped breathing. It was too horrible. He had no confidant to whom he could turn for advice. It was the clergy one thought of first on such occasions. He had been so brave and confident, but he was young, and this was too much for him. He clung to the lifeless body.

"Come back, my dear, my dear. Don't do this awful thing to me." But she was cold and no longer seemed human.

The first paralyzing terror had left Ukon. Now she was writhing and wailing. Genji remembered a devil a certain minister had encountered in the Grand Hall.[19]

---

19. The *Okagami* tells how Fujiwara Tadahira met a devil in the Shishinden. It withdrew when informed that he was on the emperor's business.

"She can't possibly be dead." He found the strength to speak sharply. "All this noise in the middle of the night—you must try to be a little quieter." But it had been too sudden.

He turned again to the torchbearer. "There is someone here who seems to have had a very strange seizure. Tell your friend to find out where Lord Koremitsu is spending the night and have him come immediately. If the holy man is still at his mother's house, give him word, very quietly, that he is to come too. His mother and the people with her are not to hear. She does not approve of this sort of adventure."

He spoke calmly enough, but his mind was in a turmoil. Added to grief at the loss of the girl was horror, quite beyond describing, at this desolate place. It would be past midnight. The wind was higher and whistled more dolefully in the pines. There came a strange, hollow call of a bird. Might it be an owl? All was silence, terrifying solitude. He should not have chosen such a place—but it was too late now. Trembling violently, Ukon clung to him. He held her in his arms, wondering if she might be about to follow her lady. He was the only rational one present, and he could think of nothing to do. The flickering light wandered here and there. The upper parts of the screens behind them were in darkness, the lower parts fitfully in the light. There was a persistent creaking, as of someone coming up behind them. If only Koremitsu would come. But Koremitsu was a nocturnal wanderer without a fixed abode, and the man had to search for him in numerous places. The wait for dawn was like the passage of a thousand nights. Finally he heard a distant crowing. What legacy from a former life could have brought him to this mortal peril? He was being punished for a guilty love, his fault and no one else's, and his story would be remembered in infamy through all the ages to come. There were no secrets, strive though one might to have them. Soon everyone would know, from his royal father down, and the lowest court pages would be talking; and he would gain immortality as the model of the complete fool.

Finally Lord Koremitsu came. He was the perfect servant who did not go against his master's wishes in anything at any time; and Genji was angry that on this night of all nights he should have been away, and slow in answering the summons. Calling him inside even so, he could not immediately find the strength to say what must be said. Ukon burst into tears, the full horror of it all coming back to her at the sight of Koremitsu. Genji too lost control of himself. The only sane and rational one present, he had held Ukon in his arms, but now he gave himself up to his grief.

"Something very strange has happened," he said after a time. "Strange—'unbelievable' would not be too strong a word. I wanted a priest—one does when these things happen—and asked your reverend brother to come."

"He went back up the mountain yesterday. Yes, it is very strange indeed. Had there been anything wrong with her?"

"Nothing."

He was so handsome in his grief that Koremitsu wanted to weep. An older man who has had everything happen to him and knows what to expect can be depended upon in a crisis; but they were both young, and neither had anything to suggest.

Koremitsu finally spoke. "We must not let the caretaker know. He may be dependable enough himself, but he is sure to have relatives who will talk. We must get away from this place."

"You aren't suggesting that we could find a place where we would be less likely to be seen?"

"No, I suppose not. And the women at her house will scream and wail when they hear about it, and they live in a crowded neighborhood, and all the mob around will hear, and that will be that. But mountain temples are used to this sort of thing. There would not be much danger of attracting attention." He reflected on the problem for a time. "There is a woman I used to know. She has gone into a nunnery up in the eastern hills. She is very old, my father's nurse, as a matter of fact. The district seems to be rather heavily populated, but the nunnery is off by itself."

It was not yet full daylight. Koremitsu had the carriage brought up. Since Genji seemed incapable of the task, he wrapped the body in a covering and lifted it into the carriage. It was very tiny and very pretty, and not at all repellent. The wrapping was loose and the hair streamed forth, as if to darken the world before Genji's eyes.

He wanted to see the last rites through to the end, but Koremitsu would not hear of it. "Take my horse and go back to Nijō, now while the streets are still quiet."

He helped Ukon into the carriage and himself proceeded on foot, the skirts of his robe hitched up. It was a strange bedraggled sort of funeral procession, he thought, but in the face of such anguish he was prepared to risk his life. Barely conscious, Genji made his way back to Nijō.

"Where have you been?" asked the women. "You are not looking at all well."

He did not answer. Alone in his room, he pressed a hand to his heart. Why had he not gone with the others? What would she think if she were to come back to life? She would think that he had abandoned her. Self-reproach filled his heart to breaking. He had a headache and feared he had a fever. Might he too be dying? The sun was high and still he did not emerge. Thinking it all very strange, the women pressed breakfast upon him. He could not eat. A messenger reported that the emperor had been troubled by his failure to appear the day before.

His brothers-in-law came calling.

"Come in, please, just for a moment." He received only Tō no Chūjō and kept a blind between them. "My old nurse fell seriously ill and took her vows in the Fifth Month or so. Perhaps because of them, she seemed to recover. But recently she had a relapse. Someone came to ask if I would not call on her at least once more. I thought I really must go and see an old and dear servant who was on her deathbed, and so I went. One of her servants was ailing, and quite suddenly, before he had time to leave, he died. Out of deference to me they waited until night to take the body away. All this I learned later. It would be very improper of me to go to court with all these festivities coming up,[20] I thought, and so I stayed

---

20. There were many Shinto rites during the Ninth Month.

away. I have had a headache since early this morning—perhaps I have caught cold. I must apologize."

"I see. I shall so inform your father. He sent out a search party during the concert last night, and really seemed very upset." Tō no Chūjō turned to go, and abruptly turned back. "Come now. What sort of brush did you really have? I don't believe a word of it."

Genji was startled, but managed a show of nonchalance. "You needn't go into the details. Just say that I suffered an unexpected defilement. Very unexpected, really."

Despite his cool manner, he was not up to facing people. He asked a younger brother-in-law to explain in detail his reasons for not going to court. He got off a note to Sanjō with a similar explanation.

Koremitsu came in the evening. Having announced that he had suffered a defilement, Genji had callers remain outside, and there were few people in the house. He received Koremitsu immediately.

"Are you sure she is dead.?" He pressed a sleeve to his eyes.

Koremitsu too was in tears. "Yes, I fear she is most certainly dead. I could not stay shut up in a temple indefinitely, and so I have made arrangements with a venerable priest whom I happen to know rather well. Tomorrow is a good day for funerals."

"And the other woman?"

"She has seemed on the point of death herself. She does not want to be left behind by her lady. I was afraid this morning that she might throw herself over a cliff. She wanted to tell the people at Gojō, but I persuaded her to let us have a little more time."

"I am feeling rather awful myself and almost fear the worst."

"Come, now. There is nothing to be done and no point in torturing yourself. You must tell yourself that what must be must be. I shall let absolutely no one know, and I am personally taking care of everything."

"Yes, to be sure. Everything is fated. So I tell myself. But it is terrible to think that I have sent a lady to her death. You are not to tell your sister, and you must be very sure that your mother does not hear. I would not survive the scolding I would get from her."

"And the priests too: I have told them a plausible story." Koremitsu exuded confidence.

The women had caught a hint of what was going on and were more puzzled than ever. He had said that he had suffered a defilement, and he was staying away from court; but why these muffled lamentations?

Genji gave instructions for the funeral. "You must make sure that nothing goes wrong."

"Of course. No great ceremony seems called for."

Koremitsu turned to leave.

"I know you won't approve, said Genji, a fresh wave of grief sweeping over him, "but I will regret it forever if I don't see her again. I'll go on horseback."

"Very well, if you must." In fact Koremitsu thought the proposal very ill advised. "Go immediately and be back while it is still early."

Genji set out in the travel robes he had kept ready for his recent amorous excursions. He was in the bleakest despair. He was on a strange mission and the terrors of the night before made him consider turning back. Grief urged him on. If he did not see her once more, when, in another world, might he hope to see her as she had been? He had with him only Koremitsu and the attendant of that first encounter. The road seemed a long one.

The moon came out, two nights past full. They reached the river. In the dim torchlight, the darkness off towards Mount Toribe was ominous and forbidding; but Genji was too dazed with grief to be frightened. And so they reached the temple.

It was a harsh, unfriendly region at best. The board hut and chapel where the nun pursued her austerities were lonely beyond description. The light at the altar came dimly through cracks. Inside the hut a woman was weeping. In the outer chamber two or three priests were conversing and invoking the holy name in low voices. Vespers seemed to have ended in several temples nearby. Everything was quiet. There were lights and there seemed to be clusters of people in the direction of Kiyomizu. The grand tones in which the worthy monk, the son of the nun, was reading a sutra brought on what Genji thought must be the full flood tide of his tears.

He went inside. The light was turned away from the corpse. Ukon lay behind a screen. It must be very terrible for her, thought Genji. The girl's face was unchanged and very pretty.

"Won't you let me hear your voice again?" He took her hand. "What was it that made me give you all my love, for so short a time, and then made you leave me to this misery?" He was weeping uncontrollably.

The priests did not know who he was. They sensed something remarkable, however, and felt their eyes mist over.

"Come with me to Nijō," he said to Ukon.

"We have been together since I was very young. I never left her side, not for a single moment. Where am I to go now? I will have to tell the others what has happened. As if this weren't enough, I will have to put up with their accusations." She was sobbing. "I want to go with her."

"That is only natural. But it is the way of the world. Parting is always sad. Our lives must end, early or late. Try to put your trust in me." He comforted her with the usual homilies, but presently his real feelings came out. "Put your trust in me—when I fear I have not long to live myself." He did not after all seem likely to be much help.

"It will soon be light," said Koremitsu. "We must be on our way."

Looking back and looking back again, his heart near breaking, Genji went out. The way was heavy with dew and the morning mists were thick. He scarcely knew where he was. The girl was exactly as she had been that night. They had exchanged robes and she had on a red singlet of his. What might it have been in other lives that had brought them together? He managed only with great difficulty to stay in his saddle. Koremitsu was at the reins. As they came to the river Genji fell from his horse and was unable to remount.

"So I am to die by the wayside? I doubt that I can go on."

Koremitsu was in a panic. He should not have permitted this expedition, however strong Genji's wishes. Dipping his hands in the river, he turned and made supplication to Kiyomizu. Genji somehow pulled himself together. Silently invoking the holy name, he was seen back to Nijō.

The women were much upset by these untimely wanderings. "Very bad, very bad. He has been so restless lately. And why should he have gone out again when he was not feeling well?"

Now genuinely ill, he took to his bed. Two or three days passed and he was visibly thinner. The emperor heard of the illness and was much alarmed. Continuous prayers were ordered in this shrine and that temple. The varied rites, Shinto and Confucian and Buddhist, were beyond counting. Genji's good looks had been such as to arouse forebodings. All through the court it was feared that he would not live much longer. Despite his illness, he summoned Ukon to Nijō and assigned her rooms near his own. Koremitsu composed himself sufficiently to be of service to her, for he could see that she had no one else to turn to. Choosing times when he was feeling better, Genji would summon her for a talk, and she soon was accustomed to life at Nijō. Dressed in deep mourning, she was a somewhat stern and forbidding young woman, but not without her good points.

"It lasted such a very little while. I fear that I will be taken too. It must be dreadful for you, losing your only support. I had thought that as long as I lived I would see to all your needs, and it seems sad and ironical that I should be on the point of following her." He spoke softly and there were tears in his eyes. For Ukon the old grief had been hard enough to bear, and now she feared that a new grief might be added to it.

All through the Nijō mansion there was a sense of helplessness. Emissaries from court were thicker than raindrops. Not wanting to worry his father, Genji fought to control himself. His father-in-law was extremely solicitous and came to Nijō every day. Perhaps because of all the prayers and rites the crisis passed—it had lasted some twenty days—and left no ill effects. Genji's full recovery coincided with the final cleansing of the defilement. With the unhappiness he had caused his father much on his mind, he set off for his apartments at court. For a time he felt out of things, as if he had come back to a strange new world.

By the end of the Ninth Month he was his old self once more. He had lost weight, but emaciation only made him handsomer. He spent a great deal of time gazing into space, and sometimes he would weep aloud. He must be in the clutches of some malign spirit, thought the women. It was all most peculiar.

He would summon Ukon on quiet evenings. "I don't understand it at all. Why did she so insist on keeping her name from me? Even if she *was* a fisherman's daughter it was cruel of her to be so uncommunicative. It was as if she did not know how much I loved her."

"There was no reason for keeping it secret. But why should she tell you about her insignificant self? Your attitude seemed so strange from the beginning. She used to say that she hardly knew whether she was waking or dreaming. Your refusal to identify yourself, you know, helped her guess who you were. It hurt her that you should belittle her by keeping your name from her."

"An unfortunate contest of wills. I did not want anything to stand between us; but I must always be worrying about what people will say. I must refrain from things my father and all the rest of them might take me to task for. I am not permitted the smallest indiscretion. Everything is exaggerated so. The little incident of the 'evening faces' affected me strangely and I went to very great trouble to see her. There must have been a bond between us. A love doomed from the start to be fleeting—why should it have taken such complete possession of me and made me find her so precious? You must tell me everything. What point is there in keeping secrets now? I mean to make offerings every week, and I want to know in whose name I am making them."

"Yes, of course—why have secrets now? It is only that I do not want to slight what she made so much of. Her parents are dead. Her father was a guards captain. She was his special pet, but his career did not go well and his life came to an early and disappointing end. She somehow got to know Lord Tō no Chūjō—it was when he was still a lieutenant. He was very attentive for three years or so, and then about last autumn there was a rather awful threat from his father-in-law's house. She was ridiculously timid and it frightened her beyond all reason. She ran off and hid herself at her nurse's in the western part of the city. It was a wretched little hovel of a place. She wanted to go off into the hills, but the direction she had in mind has been taboo since New Year's. So she moved to the odd place where she was so upset to have you find her. She was more reserved and withdrawn than most people, and I fear that her unwillingness to show her emotions may have seemed cold."

So it was true. Affection and pity welled up yet more strongly.

"He once told me of a lost child. Was there such a one?"

"Yes, a very pretty little girl, born two years ago last spring."

"Where is she? Bring her to me without letting anyone know. It would be such a comfort. I should tell my friend Tō no Chūjō, I suppose, but why invite criticism? I doubt that anyone could reprove me for taking in the child. You must think up a way to get around the nurse."

"It would make me very happy if you were to take the child. I would hate to have her left where she is. She is there because we had no competent nurses in the house where you found us."

The evening sky was serenely beautiful. The flowers below the veranda were withered, the songs of the insects were dying too, and autumn tints were coming over the maples. Looking out upon the scene, which might have been a painting, Ukon thought what a lovely asylum she had found herself. She wanted to avert her eyes at the thought of the house of the "evening faces." A pigeon called, somewhat discordantly, from a bamboo thicket. Remembering how the same call had frightened the girl in that deserted villa, Genji could see the little figure as if an apparition were there before him.

"How old was she? She seemed so delicate, because she was not long for this world, I suppose."

"Nineteen, perhaps? My mother, who was her nurse, died and left me behind. Her father took a fancy to me, and so we grew up together, and I never once left her side. I wonder how I can go on without her. I am almost sorry that we were so close.[21] She seemed so weak, but I can see now that she was a source of strength."

"The weak ones do have a power over us. The clear, forceful ones I can do without. I am weak and indecisive by nature myself, and a woman who is quiet and withdrawn and follows the wishes of a man even to the point of letting herself be used has much the greater appeal. A man can shape and mold her as he wishes, and becomes fonder of her all the while."

"She was exactly what you would have wished, sir." Ukon was in tears. "That thought makes the loss seem greater."

The sky had clouded over and a chilly wind had come up. Gazing off into the distance, Genji said softly:

"One sees the clouds as smoke that rose from the pyre,
And suddenly the evening sky seems nearer."

Ukon was unable to answer. If only her lady were here! For Genji even the memory of those fulling blocks was sweet.

"In the Eighth Month, the Ninth Month, the nights are long,"[22] he whispered, and lay down.

The young page, brother of the lady of the locust shell, came to Nijō from time to time, but Genji no longer sent messages for his sister. She was sorry that he seemed angry with her and sorry to hear of his illness. The prospect of accompanying her husband to his distant province was a dreary one. She sent off a note to see whether Genji had forgotten her.

"They tell me you have not been well.

"Time goes by, you ask not why I ask not.
Think if you will how lonely a life is mine.

"I might make reference to Masuda Pond."[23]

This was a surprise; and indeed he had not forgotten her. The uncertain hand in which he set down his reply had its own beauty.

"Who, I wonder, lives the more aimless life.

"Hollow though it was, the shell of the locust
Gave me strength to face a gloomy world.

"But only precariously."

So he still remembered "the shell of the locust." She was sad and at the same time amused. It was good that they could correspond without rancor. She wished no further intimacy, and she did not want him to despise her.

As for the other, her stepdaughter, Genji heard that she had married a guards lieutenant. He thought it a strange marriage and he felt a certain pity for the

---

21. This would seem to be a poetic allusion, but none has been satisfactorily identified.

22. Po Chü-i, Collected Works, XIX, "The Fulling Blocks at Night."

23. Compare: Anonymous, *Shūishū* 804:
Long the roots of the Masuda water shield,
Longer still the aimless, sleepless nights.

lieutenant. Curious to know something of her feelings, he sent a note by his young messenger.

"Did you know that thoughts of you had brought me to the point of expiring?

"I bound them loosely, the reeds beneath the eaves,[24]
And reprove them now for having come undone."

He attached it to a long reed.

The boy was to deliver it in secret, he said. But he thought that the lieutenant would be forgiving if he were to see it, for he would guess who the sender was. One may detect here a note of self-satisfaction.

Her husband was away. She was confused, but delighted that he should have remembered her. She sent off in reply a poem the only excuse for which was the alacrity with which it was composed:

"The wind brings words, all softly, to the reed,
And the under leaves are nipped again by the frost."

It might have been cleverer and in better taste not to have disguised the clumsy handwriting. He thought of the face he had seen by lamplight. He could forget neither of them, the governor's wife, seated so primly before him, or the younger woman, chattering on so contentedly, without the smallest suggestion of reserve. The stirrings of a susceptible heart suggested that he still had important lessons to learn.

Quietly, forty-ninth-day services were held for the dead lady in the Lotus Hall on Mount Hiei. There was careful attention to all the details, the priestly robes and the scrolls and the altar decorations. Koremitsu's older brother was a priest of considerable renown, and his conduct of the services was beyond reproach. Genji summoned a doctor of letters with whom he was friendly and who was his tutor in Chinese poetry and asked him to prepare a final version of the memorial petition. Genji had prepared a draft. In moving language he committed the one he had loved and lost, though he did not mention her name, to the mercy of Amitābha.

"It is perfect, just as it is. Not a word needs to be changed." Noting the tears that refused to be held back, the doctor wondered who might be the subject of these prayers. That Genji should not reveal the name, and that he should be in such open grief—someone, no doubt, who had brought a very large bounty of grace from earlier lives.

Genji attached a poem to a pair of lady's trousers which were among his secret offerings:

"I weep and weep as today I tie this cord.
It will be untied in an unknown world to come."

He invoked the holy name with great feeling. Her spirit had wandered

---

24. The girl is traditionally called Nokiba-no-ogi, "the reeds beneath the eaves."

uncertainly these last weeks. Today it would set off down one of the ways of the future.

His heart raced each time he saw Tō no Chūjō. He longed to tell his friend that "the wild carnation" was alive and well; but there was no point in calling forth reproaches.

In the house of the "evening faces," the women were at a loss to know what had happened to their lady. They had no way of inquiring. And Ukon too had disappeared. They whispered among themselves that they had been right about that gentleman, and they hinted at their suspicions to Koremitsu. He feigned complete ignorance, however, and continued to pursue his little affairs. For the poor women it was all like a nightmare. Perhaps the wanton son of some governor, fearing Tō no Chūjō, had spirited her off to the country? The owner of the house was her nurse's daughter. She was one of three children and related to Ukon. She could only long for her lady and lament that Ukon had not chosen to enlighten them. Ukon for her part was loath to raise a stir, and Genji did not want gossip at this late date. Ukon could not even inquire after the child. And so the days went by bringing no light on the terrible mystery.

Genji longed for a glimpse of the dead girl, if only in a dream. On the day after the services he did have a fleeting dream of the woman who had appeared that fatal night. He concluded, and the thought filled him with horror, that he had attracted the attention of an evil spirit haunting the neglected villa.

Early in the Tenth Month the governor of Iyo left for his post, taking the lady of the locust shell with him. Genji chose his farewell presents with great care. For the lady there were numerous fans,[25] and combs of beautiful workmanship, and pieces of cloth (she could see that he had had them dyed specially) for the wayside gods. He also returned her robe, "the shell of the locust."

"A keepsake till we meet again, I had hoped,
And see, my tears have rotted the sleeves away."

There were other things too, but it would be tedious to describe them. His messenger returned empty-handed. It was through her brother that she answered his poem.

"Autumn comes, the wings of the locust are shed.
A summer robe returns, and I weep aloud."

She had remarkable singleness of purpose, whatever else she might have. It was the first day of winter. There were chilly showers, as if to mark the occasion, and the skies were dark. He spent the day lost in thought.

"The one has gone, to the other I say farewell.
They go their unknown ways. The end of autumn."

He knew how painful a secret love can be.

---

25. Because the sound of the word *ōgi*, "fan,"
bodes well for a reunion, fans were often
given as farewell presents.

I had hoped, out of deference to him, to conceal these difficult matters; but I have been accused of romancing, of pretending that because he was the son of an emperor he had no faults. Now, perhaps, I shall be accused of having revealed too much.

MONK SAIGYŌ (1118–1190 C.E.)
FUJIWARA SHUNZEI (c. 1175?–?1250 C.E.)
FUJIWARA TEIKA (1162–1241 C.E.)
PRINCESS SHOKUSHI (d. 1201 C.E.)
FUJIWARA SHUNZEI'S DAUGHTER
(c. 1175?–?1250 C.E.)
Japan

These poets are five of the brightest lights of the *Shinkokinshū* ("New Kokinshū"), the eighth and, by general consent, finest of the twenty-one royal poetry anthologies. The Japanese regard the poets of the *Shinkokinshū* period (1183–1235) as their most profound, admiring in particular their subtle allusions to earlier poetry, their meditations on Tendai Buddhism, their descriptions of nature, and the depth they bring to the conventional poetic figure of the passionate woman.

Poetry by now had become largely fictional—imagined responses to artificially posed situations. Such poetry required intense depth and a supremely magical quality in order to appeal to readers—or even to poets, who looked on poetry as both a contest for fame and a religious vocation. The compilers of the *Shinkokinshū* brought to perfection the practice, which had begun with the *Kinkoshū,* of creating a new artistic continuum from sequences of brief poems. The collection is organized in sequences of 100 poems each and can actually be read as a single, extended work of almost 10,000 lines.

As for the poets, the monk Saigyō is counted as one of the three most beloved poets in Japan. Fujiwara Shunzei defined the poetic ideals of the age in terms of affecting deprivation (*sabi,* the beauty and desolation of loneliness or solitude), ethereal beauty (*yōen*) and, especially, mystery and depth (*yūgen*). His son, Fujiwara Teika, is increasingly being considered one of the three or four greatest Japanese poets. Too difficult a person to sentimentalize, he was his own harshest critic. To him we also owe a number of the best manuscript transcriptions of earlier great works, including *The Tale of Genji.* He also distinguished himself in a rare way: his gifted imitators were also to achieve greatness. Among them was the poet known simply as Fujiwara Shunzei's Daughter. Her talent was so great that Fujiwara Teika, who was her uncle, adopted her. Another gifted woman writer, Princess Shokushi, shows that the beauty sought was truly refined and proud.

from **The Eighth Royal Anthology [Shinkokinshū]**

MONK SAIGYŌ

[While denying his heart]

While denying his heart,
Even a monk cannot but know
    The bleak beauty.
From the marsh a single snipe
Flies off into autumn dusk.

[I hope no longer]

I hope no longer
That any friend will come to visit
    This village in the hills,
Where if not for loneliness
Living would be a wretched thing.

[The crickets cry]

The crickets cry—
With the quelling cold of night
    Autumn takes its way,
As they gradually seem to falter,
Those cries that fade afar.

[In Tsu province]

In Tsu province
Naniwa knew spring glories
    Now no more than dream!
Over the frost-withered reed leaves
The cold winds cross to farther ends.

[We realized our love]

We realized our love.
And from those nights of vanished dreams

All poems in this selection translated by Earl Miner.

Would I never wake,
In spite of everlasting sleep
In the darkness of vain desire.[1]

FUJIWARA SHUNZEI

[As evening falls]

As evening falls,
Along the fields the autumn wind
    Pierces to the bone,
And quails raise their anguished cries
Among Fukakusa's deep grass.[2]

[Longing for the past]

Longing for the past,
The hermit's grass-thatched hut
    In a shower at night:
Do not call a freshening of tears,
Hototogisu singing here at last.[3]

[Will some other poet]

Will some other poet,
When once again the orange trees bloom
    Recall with longing
Something of me when I as well
Will have become a person of the past?

[Upon Fushimi Hill]

Upon Fushimi Hill,
From this dark shelter of the pines
    I gaze off beyond,
Where with daybreak on the fields
The ripples of the breeze pass by.

---

1. The dream of love is held in balance with the reality of religion.
2. Recalling Ariwara Narihira's exchange of poems with a woman in Fukakusa, a place that had disappeared.
3. The hototogisu is a variety of cuckoo, similar to the western nightingale.

[Shining with raindrops]

Shining with raindrops
Across the blooms of orange trees
    The breeze makes way,
And at last the hototogisu
Sings from somewhere in low clouds.

[Worldly attachments]

Worldly attachments
Join together numerous desires,
    And while I ponder this,
In the emptiness of the sky[4]
A white cloud melts away from view.

[The imagined image]

The imagined image
Of the form of cherry blossoms
    I hold as ideal view,
And how many ridges have I crossed
For what were white clouds on those peaks?[5]

FUJIWARA TEIKA

[Looking far beyond]

Looking far beyond
Neither blossoms nor colored leaves[6]
    Need be wished for:
Wretched thatched huts along the cove
In the thickening autumn dusk.

[A woman on love at dawn parting]

My image of you—
It too alters with your departure
    At dawn's temple bell

---

4. The character for "sky" designates literal "emptiness" and also the Buddhist doctrine of lack of real existence.

5. The clouds imagined as flowers are more attractive than actual flowers.

6. A dispute exists as to whether or not these are autumnal leaves.

When it is always sad to find
The sky streaked with first light.[7]

[Across the heavens]

Across the heavens
In the fragrance of plum blossoms[8]
   The haze increases;
The smoke-like pallor does not exempt
The moon on the brief spring night.

[On the brief spring night]

On the brief spring night
The floating bridge of dreams
   Breaks all apart,
And from the peak a bank of clouds
Takes leave into the empty sky.[9]

[Blossoms of the plum]

Blossoms of the plum
Transfer from the tree their fragrance
   To rest upon the sleeve,
Where moonbeams vie in glistening
As they filter through the eaves.

[Crimson it is]

Crimson it is,
The dew catching and reflecting
   The morning sunlight
And the whole region all aglow
With wild carnation flowers.

[A single traveler]

A single traveler,
His sleeves blow back and forth

---

7. A woman on her lover's rare and too brief
   visit.
8. Plum and haze are spring emblems in section 1 of *The Pillow Book*.

9. The imagery of lines 1–3 conveys waking
   up; the personification of lines 4–5 describes the scene. Line 2 is the title of the
   last chapter of *The Tale of Genji*. "Sky" is
   discussed in note 4.

In the autumn wind
When the evening sun turns desolate[10]
The hanging bridge between the peaks.

[One of three love poems presented at the palace in the Third Month of 1213]

Our reflections—
Where the two Streams of Longing met,
    Let them at least join!
What matter if, like drifting foam,
We soon vanish in the current.

[I leave the capital]

I leave the capital
As morning rises on the mountain,
    Where upon the crest
The tearful dew of parting
Scatters with gusts of autumn wind.

[For straw-mat bedding / in the waiting night]

For straw-mat bedding—
In the waiting night the autumn
    Wind grows very late,
And she spreads out the moonlight—
The Lady of the Uji Bridge.[11]

["Like whitened hemp"]

The sleeves that mark our parting
    Accumulate the dew,
And with its flesh-piercing color
The chill wind of autumn blows.[12]

---

10. "Desolate" modifies both "sun" and "bridge."

11. This poem echoes a questioning earlier poem. "The Bridge Lady" is the title of one of the Uji chapters of *The Tale of Genji*; it may also indicate a goddess.

12. Parting in tears and in the dew, (with additional erotic suggestions) the lovers don garments used as bedclothes. The man leaves the woman's house in a white wind, contrary to an earlier poem, which depicts wind without any color.

PRINCESS SHOKUSHI

[The dawn arrives]

The dawn arrives
Announced by the crowing cocks
    That call some hope
To a pillow fraught with longing
In the long dream of vain desire.

[Hidden Love]

O cord of life,
If you must break, then break now!
    If I must live on,
The fearful strain of holding out
Will be too much for me to bear.

[Guide me on my way]

Guide me on my way—
Across waves that leave no trace
    My boat rows on
And its destination uncertain—
O salt wind gusting from all sides!

[The cherry petals gone]

The cherry petals gone,
No special color makes its claim;
    Gazing in reverie,
From somewhere in the vacant sky[13]
The spring rain gently falls.

FUJIWARA SHUNZEI'S DAUGHTER

[On the topic "Love and Clouds"]

"On the topic 'Love and Clouds' "
    Its flames suppressed,
Desire's great fire will consume me.
    Its very smoke

---

13. Sky and emptiness are discussed in note 4.

Vanishing without trace in clouds
Whose only end is desolation.[14]

[On the topic "Love in Spring"]

An image of you
Forms in the hazed over moon
　　That has found lodging:
In a spring not that of old
On sleeves glistening with tears.[15]

[The orange flowers]

The orange flowers
Glow all about the region
　　Of some brief sleep,
And in a dream of times bygone
His scented sleeves return to mind.[16]

[Haze by the river]

The Lady of the Bridge—[17]
The morning frost upon her sleeves
　　Chills them further,
And the spring haze drifts along
In the Uji River's wind.

[To my house]

To my house his path
Has along its wayside grasses
　　Withered, withered,
And rarer still his footprints
In the frost that makes all pale.

[A gentle breeze]

A gentle breeze
Comes to a sleeve that dozes

---

14. The imagery suggests cremation.
15. See Narihira's poem, *Tales of Ise,* episode 4.
16. Alluding to an anonymous *Kokinshū*

poem in which the blossoms recall a lover who used them to scent sleeves.
17. See note 11.

Scenting with blossoms
A pillow rich in the fragrance
Of dream on a brief spring night.

A SEQUENCE OF SEVEN POEMS BY VARIOUS POETS FROM THE SHINKOKINSHŪ

These poems are taken from Book 6 of the twenty divisions of the *Shinkokinshū*. Among the winter poems, the seven presented here belong to a group of twenty-eight poems having snow as their central image, as well as to a briefer subsequence of thirteen poems emphasizing human concerns. The first four poems are by older and, on the whole, lesser poets; the more recent poems are by more impressive poets. (This controlled fluctuation in poetic quality was part of the aesthetic strategy of the anthology's compilers. Lesser poems provided a mental respite, in preparation for the more challenging greater poems.)

In the poems presented below, the customary headnote (a statement describing the occasion the poem is responding to) has been omitted. Following each translation is the poet's name and a review of motifs. By paying close attention to the motifs, we see how the techniques used by these poets were able to integrate poems written on widely varied subjects into a kind of continuous narrative or sequence. Beyond their intrinsic interest, sequences of this kind foretell the genius of *renga* or linked poetry (like the selections from *One Hundred Stanzas* by *Three Poets at Ginase* included later in this section), which was at this period only a pastime from the rigors of composing serious poems such as the ones presented here.

[As they sound]

As they sound—
The bamboo wattlings of the fence
Crack beneath the piling snow.

[Fujiwara Norikane. Indoors, bamboo fence, snow. Sleeper awaking. Predawn. Surprise.]

[The crowing cock]

The crowing cock
Announces arrival of the dawn—
But it is the snow
That radiates the peak of Otowa,
"Mountain of Feathered Sound."

[Fujiwara Takakura. Bird(s), light, mountains, snow. Observer of daybreak sounds and sights. Dawn. Pleasure in beauty. Hearing from, and looking at, the outside of the house.]

All poems in this selection translated by Earl Miner and Robert H. Brower.

[In the mountains]

In the mountains
Even the single path must lie
　Buried from the sight,
For in the capital snow has fallen
Together with the colored leaves.

[Fujiwara Ietsune. Distant mountains, trees, snow. Capital dweller thinking of life in the mountains (and someone dear?). Day. Pensive tone. Only outdoors conceived; speaker's position unclear.]

[Was it not enough / to know loneliness]

Was it not enough
To know loneliness without this?
　Along the hillslopes
The oaks drop their withered leaves
And silently the snow still falls.

[Fujiwara Kunifusa. Hills, trees, snow. Observer out of doors (hills). Daytime. Loneliness.]

[There is no shelter]

There is no shelter
Where I can rest my weary horse
　And brush my laden sleeves:
Sano ford and adjoining fields
Spread with a twilight in the snow.

[Fujiwara Teika. Horse, river and neighborhood, snow. Rider during heavy snowfall. Out of doors. Bleak scene as light is failing.]

[The path of him I long for]

The path of him I long for
Across foothills to where I wait
　Must be all hidden:
The snow weighs unbearably
In the cedars beyond my eaves.

[Teika. Hills (and mountains), narrow road, trees, snow. Evening (when a lover visits). Lonely scene imagined by a waiting woman.]

[Beneath the piling snow]

Beneath the piling snow
The bamboos at Fushimi village

Crack loudly in the dark:
Even the path to love in dreams
Snaps to waking underneath the snow.

[Fujiwara Ariie. Village south of the capital, bamboos, snow. Night. Dream of visiting her lover broken by sound of bamboos cracking under heavy snowfall. Pathos of romance.]

ANONYMOUS (1300–1330 C.E.)

Japan

The Tale of the Heike describes the defeat of the Heike (or Taira) family by the Genji (or Minamoto) family. The story is as familiar in Japan as is the Bible or the Arthurian legend in the West. Covering the bloody period between c. 1131 and 1191, the *Tale* existed in numerous versions, the best known of which were those of the *biwa hōshi* or "lute priests"—itinerant blind minstrels who recited to their own lute accompaniment. The extracts here are taken from the most respected of these oral versions, the one associated with the reciter Kakuichi (c. 1300–1371). It consists of twelve parts subdivided into numbered, titled episodes, and a sequel.

In its imaginative role, majesty, and sweep, this is the Japanese epic, a miscellaneous grouping in the manner of the Western romance epic (there is no agreement on the "structure" of its parts); in many ways, it is epic-by-collection. The *Tale* also differs from most Western epics in the prominence given to women and children. The collective viewpoint is that of the people of Kyoto. They had trembled before the mighty Heike family, who are now reported dead or humiliatingly led captive through the streets of the capital. Yet the Heike receive admiration and sympathy in defeat, for they had taken up the refined ways of the court. Among the iron-willed, militaristic Genji, on the other hand, only the doomed Yoshitsune seems to receive full approval.

The selections here begin with the famous opening words and thereafter come from later books: the death of the impetuous Yoshinaka (9:4); the death of the young Atsumori (9:16); and the separation of Yokubue from her beloved (10:8). The first of these episodes displays the ethos of the warrior, including women warriors. The second is a favorite that has inspired dramatic versions in both nō and kabuki. The third, one of the most popular, shows both how Japanese concepts of love involve yearning for the unattainable and how Buddhism offered consolation for human misery. The elegiac emphasis heard here increases as the work progresses, a quality which brings the *Tale* closer to epics outside the Graeco-Roman tradition.

The *Tale* is a typically Japanese work in three respects. First, it combines prose narrative with verse lyrics. Second, the assembly of diverse matter is more important than the plot. Third, the boundaries of fact and fiction are the harder to draw because they so often cross. The *Tale* is a fitting counterpart, in a later age, to *The Tale of Genji*, showing the heartrending beauty of human suffering in war.

Buddhism, with its stress on evanescence, underlies the opening passage, in which the first sentence alludes to the death of Shakamuni (depicted by his entry into Nirvana as a Buddha) at the Jetavana Temple (Gion Shoja in Japanese, providing the title for the opening chapter). Shakamuni's passing causes the great teak trees to shed their leaves and animals to weep tears. As this rich tapestry unfolds, Buddhism is only one of the many designs included.

from *The Tale of the Heike [Heike Monogatari]*

[Opening]*

At the Jetavana Temple / the bell sounds out / the impermanence of all things / as it tolls its knell. / That the color of the flowers / on the great teak trees / foretells the fall of the proud / is wholly suitable. / Those who utter large claims / will not long continue— / their times like a spring night / when dreams quickly break. / Those who display bravery / fall down in the end: / as victims of the tempest / are blown off like the dust.

[The Death of Kiso]†

Kiso no Yoshinaka had brought with him from Shinano two female attendants, Tomoe and Yamabuki. Yamabuki had fallen ill and stayed in the capital. Of the two, Tomoe was especially beautiful, with white skin, long hair, and charming features. She was also a remarkably strong archer, and as a swordswoman she was a warrior worth a thousand, ready to confront a demon or god, mounted or on foot. She handled unbroken horses with superb skill; she rode unscathed down perilous descents. Whenever a battle was imminent, Yoshinaka sent her out as his first captain, equipped with strong armor, an oversized sword, and a mighty bow; and she performed more deeds of valor than any of his other warriors. Thus she was now one of the seven who remained after all the others had fled or perished.

There were rumors that Yoshinaka was making for the Tanba Road by way of Nagasaka, and also that he was heading north through the Ryūge Pass. In actuality, he was fleeing toward Seta in the hope of finding Imai no Shirō Kanehira. Kanehira himself had started back toward the capital with furled banner, worried about his master, after having lost all but fifty of his eight hundred defenders at Seta. The two arrived simultaneously at Uchide-no-hama in the vicinity of Ōtsu, recognized one another from about three hundred and fifty feet away, and galloped together.

Lord Kiso took Kanehira by the hand, "I meant to die at the Rokujō riverbed, but I broke through a swarm of enemies and came away here because I wanted to find you."

"Your words do me great honor," Kanehira said. "I meant to die at Seta, but I have come this far because I was worried about you."

*Translated by Earl Miner.

†Translated by Helen McCullough.

"I see that our karma tie is still intact. My warriors scattered into the mountains and woods after the enemy broke our formations; some of them must still be nearby. Have that furled banner of yours raised!"

More than three hundred riders responded to the unfurling of Imai's banner—men who had fled from the capital or Seta, or who had come from some other place. Yoshinaka was overjoyed. "Why can't we fight one last battle, now that we have a force of this size? Whose is the band I see massed over there?"

"They say the commander is Ichijō no Jirō Tadayori from Kai."

"What is his strength?"

"He is supposed to have six thousand riders."

"Then we are well matched! If we must meet death, let it be by galloping against a worthy foe and falling outnumbered." Yoshinaka rode forward in the lead.

That day, Lord Kiso was attired in a red brocade *hitatare,* a suit of armor laced with thick Chinese damask, and a horned helmet. At his side, he wore a magnificent oversized sword; high on his back, there rode a quiver containing the few arrows left from his earlier encounters, all fledged with eagle tail feathers. He grasped a rattan-wrapped bow and sat in a gold-edged saddle astride his famous horse Oniashige [Roan Demon], a very stout and brawny animal. Standing in his stirrups, he announced his name in a mighty voice. "You must have heard of Kiso no Kanja in the past; now you see him! I am the Morning Sun Commander Minamoto no Yoshinaka, Director of the Imperial Stables of the Left and Governor of Iyo Province. They tell me you are Ichijō no Jirō from Kai. We are well matched! Cut off my head and show it to Yoritomo!" He galloped forward, shouting.

"The warrior who has just announced his name is their Commander-in-Chief," Ichijō no Jirō said. "Wipe out the whole force, men! Get them all, young retainers! Kill them!"

The easterners moved to surround Yoshinaka with their superior numbers, each hoping to be the one to take his head. Yoshinaka's three hundred riders galloped lengthwise, sidewise, zigzag, and crosswise in the midst of the six thousand foes and finally burst through to the rear, only fifty strong.

As the fifty went on their way after having broken free, they came to a defensive position manned by two thousand riders under the command of Toi no Jirō Sanehira. Again, they broke through and went on. Again, they galloped through enemy bands—here four or five hundred, there two or three hundred, or a hundred and forty or fifty, or a hundred—until only five of them were left. Even then, Tomoe remained alive.

"Quickly, now," Lord Kiso said to Tomoe. "You are a woman, so be off with you; go wherever you please. I intend to die in battle, or to kill myself if I am wounded. It would be unseemly to let people say, 'Lord Kiso kept a woman with him during his last battle.' "

Reluctant to flee, Tomoe rode with the others until she could resist no longer. Then she pulled up. "Ah! If only I could find a worthy foe! I would fight a last battle for His Lordship to watch," she thought.

As she sat there, thirty riders came into view, led by Onda no Hachirō Moroshige, a man renowned in Musashi Province for his great strength. Tomoe galloped into their midst, rode up alongside Moroshige, seized him in a powerful grip, pulled him down against the pommel of her saddle, held him motionless, twisted off his head, and threw it away. Afterward, she discarded armor and helmet and fled toward the eastern provinces.

Tezuka no Tarō Mitsumori died in battle; Tezuka no Bettō fled. Only two horsemen remained, Imai no Shirō Kanehira and Lord Kiso.

"I have never noticed it before, but my armor seems heavy today," Lord Kiso said.

"You are not tired yet, and your horse is still strong. Why should you find a suit of armor heavy? You are discouraged because there is nobody left to fight on our side. But you should think of me as a man worth a thousand ordinary warriors. I will hold off the enemy awhile with my last seven or eight arrows. That place over there is the Awazu Pine Woods: kill yourself among the trees."

As the two rode, whipping their horses, a new band of fifty warriors appeared. "Get into the pine woods. I will hold these enemies at bay," Kanehira said.

"I ought to have perished in the capital. My only reason for fleeing here was that I wanted to die with you. Let's not be killed in different places; let's go down together." Lord Kiso brought his mount alongside Kanehira's, ready to gallop forward.

Kanehira leaped down and took his master's horse by the mouth. "No matter how glorious a warrior's earlier reputation may have been, an ignoble death means eternal disgrace. You are tired; there are no forces following you. If you are isolated by the enemy and dragged down to your death by some fellow's insignificant retainer, people will say, 'So-and-So's retainer killed the famous Lord Kiso, the man known throughout Japan.' I would hate to see that happen. Please, please, go into the pine woods."

"Well, then . . ." Lord Kiso galloped toward the Awazu Pine Woods.

Kanehira dashed into the fifty riders alone, stood in his stirrups, and announced his name in a mighty voice. "You must have heard of me long ago; see me now with your own eyes! I am Imai no Shirō Kanehira, aged thirty-three, foster brother to Lord Kiso. The Kamakura Lord Yoritomo himself must know that such a person exists. Kill me and show him my head!" He fired off his remaining eight arrows in a fast and furious barrage that felled eight men on the spot. (It is impossible to say whether or not they were killed.) Then he drew his sword and galloped slashing from place to place, without meeting a man willing to face him. Many were the trophies he amassed! The easterners surrounded him and let fly a hail of arrows, hoping to shoot him down, but none of their shafts found a chink in his armor or penetrated its stout plates, and he remained uninjured.

Lord Kiso galloped toward the Awazu Pine Woods, a lone rider. The shadows were gathering on the Twenty-First of the First Month, and a thin film of ice had formed. Unaware that a deep paddy field lay in front of him, he sent his horse plunging into the mire. The animal sank below its head and stayed there, motionless, despite furious flogging with stirrups and whip. Lord Kiso glanced backward, worried about Kanehira, and Ishida no Jirō Tamehisa, who was hard on his heels, drew his bow to the full and sent an arrow thudding into his face. Mortally wounded, he sagged forward with the bowl of his helmet against the horse's neck.

Two of Tamehisa's retainers went up and took Lord Kiso's head. Tamehisa impaled it on the tip of his sword, raised it aloft, and announced in a mighty voice,

"Miura no Ishida no Jirō Tamehisa has killed Lord Kiso, the man known throughout Japan!"

Kanehira heard the shout as he battled. "I don't need to fight to protect anyone now. Take a look, easterners! This is how the bravest man in Japan commits suicide!" He put the tip of his sword in his mouth, jumped headlong from his horse, and perished, run through. Thus, it turned out that there was no combat worthy of the name at Awazu.

[The Death of Atsumori]

Kumagae no Jirō Naozane walked his horse toward the beach after the defeat of the Heike. "The Taira nobles will be fleeing to the water's edge in the hope of boarding rescue vessels," he thought. "Ah, how I would like to grapple with a high-ranking Commander-in-Chief!" Just then, he saw a lone rider splash into the sea, headed toward a vessel in the offing. The other was attired in a crane-embroidered *nerinuki* silk *hitatare,* a suit of armor with shaded green lacing, and a horned helmet. At his waist, he wore a sword with gilt bronze fittings; on his back, there rode a quiver containing arrows fledged with black-banded white eagle feathers. He grasped a rattan-wrapped bow and bestrode a white-dappled reddish horse with a gold-edged saddle. When his mount had swum out about a hundred and fifty or two hundred feet, Naozane beckoned him with his fan.

"I see that you are a Commander-in-Chief. It is dishonorable to show your back to an enemy. Return!"

The warrior came back. As he was leaving the water, Naozane rode up alongside him, gripped him with all his strength, crashed with him to the ground, held him motionless, and pushed aside his helmet to cut off his head. He was sixteen or seventeen years old, with a lightly powdered face and blackened teeth—a boy just the age of Naozane's own son Kojirō Naoie, and so handsome that Naozane could not find a place to strike.

"Who are you? Announce your name. I will spare you," Naozane said.

"Who are you?" the youth asked.

"Nobody of any importance: Kumagae no Jirō Naozane, a resident of Musashi Province."

"Then it is unnecessary to give you my name. I am a desirable opponent for you. Ask about me after you take my head. Someone will recognize me, even if I don't tell you."

"Indeed, he must be a Commander-in-Chief," Naozane thought. "Killing this one person will not change defeat into victory, nor will sparing him change victory into defeat. When I think of how I grieved when Kojirō suffered a minor wound, it is easy to imagine the sorrow of this young lord's father if he were to hear that the boy had been slain. Ah, I would like to spare him!" Casting a swift glance to the rear, he discovered Sanehira and Kagetoki coming along behind him with fifty riders.

"I would like to spare you," he said, restraining his tears, "but there are Genji warriors everywhere. You cannot possibly escape. It will be better if I kill you than if someone else does it, because I will offer prayers on your behalf."

"Just take my head and be quick about it."

Overwhelmed by compassion, Naozane could not find a place to strike. His senses reeled, his wits forsook him, and he was scarcely conscious of his surroundings. But matters could not go on like that forever: in tears, he took the head.

"Alas! No lot is as hard as a warrior's. I would never have suffered such a dreadful experience if I had not been born into a military house. How cruel I was to kill him!" He pressed his sleeve to his face and shed floods of tears.

Presently, since matters could not go on like that forever, he started to remove the youth's armor *hitatare* so that he might wrap it around the head. A brocade bag containing a flute was tucked in at the waist. "Ah, how pitiful! He must have been one of the people I heard making music inside the stronghold just before dawn. There are tens of thousands of riders in our eastern armies, but I am sure none of them has brought a flute to the battlefield. Those court nobles are refined men!"

When Naozane's trophies were presented for Yoshitsune's inspection, they drew tears from the eyes of all the beholders. It was learned later that the slain youth was Tayū Atsumori, aged seventeen, a son of Tsunemori, the Master of the Palace Repairs Office.

After that, Naozane thought increasingly of becoming a monk.

The flute in question is said to have been given by Retired Emperor Toba to Atsumori's grandfather Tadamori, who was a skilled musician. I believe I have heard that Tsunemori, who inherited it, turned it over to Atsumori because of his son's proficiency as a flautist. Saeda [Little Branch] was its name. It is deeply moving that music, a profane entertainment, should have led a warrior to the religious life.

Yokobue

Although the corporeal being of the Komatsu Middle Captain Koremori remained at Yashima, his spirit strayed ceaselessly to the capital. The figures of his wife and children at home were always by his side, never forgotten for an instant. It was meaningless to live on with matters thus, he told himself. Shortly before dawn on the Fifteenth of the Third Month in the first year of Genryaku, he stole away from his Yashima quarters with three attendants—Yosōbyōe Shigekage, a page called Ishidōmaru, and a groom known as Takesato, whom he took because he was said to understand boats. Setting out from Yūki-no-ura in Awa Province aboard a small craft, he rowed across the Naruto Straits toward Kii Province, passed Waka, Fukiage, the Tamatsushima Shrine (where Sotoorihime had once appeared as a divinity), and the shrines at Nichizen and Kokuken, and so arrived at Kii Harbor.

"I would like to follow the mountains from here to the city, to see and be seen by my beloved family one last time," he thought. "But it is bad enough that Shigehira has already been captured, paraded through the avenues, and humiliated in the capital and Kamakura. What a terrible disgrace for my dead father if I should be taken too!" Time after time, he was seized by the urge to go, but he always fought it down, and in the end he went to Mount Kōya instead.

On Mount Kōya, there dwelt a holy man who was an old acquaintance of Koremori's, Saitō Takiguchi Tokiyori (a son of Saitō Saemondaifu Mochiyori of Sanjō), who had been one of Shigemori's samurai. As a thirteen-year-old boy, Tokiyori had taken up a post in the Palace Guards, where he had proceeded to fall in love with one of Kenreimon'in's lesser attendants, a girl called Yokobue. His father gave him a severe scolding when he heard about it. "I had intended to marry you into an influential family so you could rise in the world. Now I find you have got yourself involved with a nobody."

"There was once a Queen Mother of the West," the youth said to himself, "but she no longer exists; we hear of Dongfang Shuo, but we cannot see him. In a world where the young may die before the old, human existence is like a spark from a flint. Even what we call a long life does not last more than seventy or eighty years, and the prime of that span is a mere two decades or thereabouts. What is to be gained by spending even a brief time with an uncongenial wife in this dreamlike, evanescent existence? Yet I will seem disobedient to my father if I marry the one I love. The situation is a friend to me: it shows that I ought to renounce the harsh world for the path of truth." He cut off his hair and went to perform pious exercises at the Ōjōin in Saga, aged nineteen.

"I could have accepted it if he had broken with me," Yokobue thought when she heard the news, "but it was unkind to go to such lengths. Why couldn't he have told me if he was planning to become a monk? Even though he may not want to see me, I will find him and tell him how I feel." One day toward dusk, she left the capital and wandered off in the direction of Saga. As was to have been expected of the season, which was past the Tenth of the Second Month, the spring breeze from Umezu carried the nostalgic scent of plum blossoms, and haze veiled the moonlight on the Ōi River. She must have considered it entirely Tokiyori's fault that she was suffering such unhappiness.

Yokobue had been told that the Takiguchi Novice was at the Ōjōin, but she did not know which cloister was his, and she began a pathetic search, pausing here and stopping there. At length, she heard a voice intoning sacred words inside a ruined monks' dwelling. Thinking that it sounded like his, she sent in a message by the maid who had accompanied her. "I have come all this way looking for you. Please let me see you just once as a monk."

The Takiguchi Novice peeped through a crack in the sliding partition, his heart racing. Even the most resolute pursuer of enlightenment would have wavered at such a moment, moved to pity by her exhausted appearance. But he turned her away without a meeting. "The person you want is not here," he sent someone out to say. "You must have come to the wrong place." Although Yokobue's heart swelled with indignation at his coldness, she had to restrain her tears and go home.

"This is a quiet place where a man can recite the sacred name without interference," the Takiguchi Novice said to a cloister mate. "But I parted from a girl I still loved, and now she has found me here. Even though I hardened my heart the first time, I don't think I can do it if she comes again. I must bid you farewell." He left Saga for Mount Kōya and took up residence at the Shōjōshin'in.

Word reached the Takiguchi Novice that Yokobue had also entered the religious life. He sent her a poem:

> Although you harbored
> such feelings of resentment
> that you shaved your head,
> what happiness to know
> you have entered the true Way!

Yokobue answered with this:

> That I shaved my head
> was not because I harbored
> resentment toward you.
> Yours is a heart praiseworthy
> for steadfast devotion.

Perhaps because Yokobue was borne down by the heavy burden of her sorrows, she soon breathed her last at the Hokkeji in Nara, where she had gone to live. Upon hearing the news, the Takiguchi Novice redoubled his pious exertions, displaying a zeal so intense that his father recognized him as his son again. Everyone close to him revered him and called him "the holy man at Mount Kōya."

Middle Captain Koremori went to visit the Novice. In the old days at the capital, this samurai had been an elegant gentleman in an unfigured hunting robe and high cap, his garments stylishly draped and his side hair smoothed. Now, when the Middle Captain saw him for the first time since his renunciation of the world, it must have cost him a pang of envy to recognize a true seeker after enlightenment—a man who resembled an emaciated old monk (though he was not yet thirty), dressed in a deep black robe and a black surplice. It seemed that the Seven Sages of the Bamboo Groves in Jin or the Four Graybeards of Mount Shang in Han could have been no more impressive to behold.

ZEAMI (KANZE MOTOKIYO)

(1364–1443 C.E.)

Japan

Nō plays are traditionally divided into five categories by the kind of character represented by the principal or *shite* role: plays of gods, of warriors, of women, of mad ones, and of devils. *Kagekiyo,* a play of anonymous authorship, belongs to the fourth and most numerous category—plays in which the *shite* is a mad person (male or female) or a person from "modern" times. The plays are also placed in two additional categories, depending on whether the *shite* represents a spirit or a living person. A play featuring a spirit is a dream play (*mugen*); one whose chief character is alive is called a "present" play (*genzaimono*). Finally, some *nō* plays consist of a single act (*tanshiki*) and some of two acts (*fukushiki*). The form the Japanese consider the most beautiful—that is, the most fully expressive of the essence of nō—is the two-act dream play (*fukushiki mugen nō*) with the spirit of a woman in the *shite* role. In such plays, the secondary or *waki* role is commonly that of a visiting monk. There are various accompanying characters (*tsure*) and other refinements as well.

   Kagekiyo is a one-act "present" play. Its four characters include the title character (the *shite* role), his daughter Hitomaru (*tsure* or *shitezure*), an attendant (*tomo, shitezure no tomo*), and a village headman (the *waki* role). Having supported the Heike cause (see headnote to *The Tale of the Heike*), Kagekiyo is banished by the victorious Genji to what is now southeastern Kyushu. Although near death, he remains hot-tempered. The drama turns on deep motives that are sometimes contradictory and not always resolved. Kagekiyo is self-centered and proud of his military feats, but he is also shamed by his present status as a beggar. He speaks contemptuously about his daughter, but when he meets her after a long separation their bond is fully established. Hitomaru has searched for him out of filial devotion and shares his strong spirit. The other characters handle the events of the plot.

   The seeming simplicity of the plot is belied by various formal features, the most typical of which is the ending in two phases. The first phase involves Kagekiyo's deeds at the crucial Battle of Yashima, which begins with high bravery and concludes in comedy. The second phase contains the final speech, in which the chorus speaks for Kagekiyo for nine lines, for Hitomaru for one line, and finally for a narrator who speaks the last three lines, which may be more literally rendered: "Their final words mingle as one voice, / this the sole relic of parent and child, / this the sole relic of parent and child." The comedy at the end of the first phase and the abrupt conclusion of the second phase with its switches from mind to mind are very Japanese and typical of nō drama.

Kagekiyo, A Nō Drama

Persons

HITOMARU, *Daughter of Kagekiyo*	*Tsure*
ATTENDANT	*Tomo*
AKUSHICHIBYŌE KAGEKIYO,	
(Kagekiyo the Hot-tempered)	*Shite*
VILLAGE HEADMAN	*Waki*

Place

Miyazaki, Hyūga Province (in southeastern Kyushu)

Season

Indefinite

Stage-attendants bring in a framework straw-thatched hut hung all round with a curtain and place it before the Orchestra.

Translated by Gakujutsu Shinkōkai

1

      HITOMARU, *wearing a tsure mask, wig, brocade outer-kimono, and painted gold-patterned under-kimono and her* ATTENDANT, *wearing a suō robe, trailing divided skirt, plain kimono and carrying a short sword at his side, appear, cross the Bridgeway and enter the stage.*

HITOMARU and ATTENDANT: A zephyr whispered he was living still,
shidai   A zephyr whispered he was living still,
        But what has become of his life of dew?
CHORUS: A zephyr whispered he was living still,
jidori   But what has become of his life of dew?   5
HITOMARU: I am Hitomaru, a girl living
sashi   At Kamegae-ga-yatsu in Kamakura.
        My father, Kagekiyo the Hot-tempered,
        sided with the Heike clan,
        And incurred the hatred of the Genji.   10
        They banished him to Miyazaki,
        A village, in Hyūga Province,
        And there in exile he has lived for many years.
        Though unused to journeying far,
        I am armed against all perils,   15
        Encouraged by the thought
        Of seeing my dear father.
HITOMARU and ATTENDANT: Yearning after him, on the pillow
sage-uta I lay my head and weep
        And wet my sleeves already moist   20
        With the evening dew of the wayside grass.
age-uta Sagami lies behind us,
        Sagami lies behind us,
        Whom shall we ask for guidance
        On our distant journey?   25
        Through Tōtōmi Province we pass,
        Crossing the lake[1] by ferry-boat,
        And on to Mikawa with the Eight Bridges.
        Inured to wind and road,
        Oh! how long before we see Miyako!
        Oh! how long before we see Miyako!   30
ATTENDANT: Travelling in haste, we have already reached Miyazaki in Hyūga.
        Here it would be well to ask where your father lives.

    [HITOMARU *stands by the Waki seat, and the* ATTENDANT *stands beside her.*]

2

    KAGEKIYO *is sitting in the hut, wearing a "Kagekiyo" mask, pointed hood, broad-sleeved robe and plain kimono.*

---

1. I.e. Lake Hamana.

KAGEKIYO: *[Speaks from within the hut.]* Behind the gate the pine-trees shadow
          I live alone year in, year out.
          Blind to the serene light of sun and moon,
          I hardly feel the passing of the hours.
          In the deep, unending darkness of my hut   5
          I only wake and sleep.
          Owning not a change of robe
          To shield me from the sun and snow,
          My bones are bent, my flesh decayed.
CHORUS: If to leave the world it be one's fate,
age-uta If to leave the world it be one's fate,
          Better far to wear the holy robes of black.
          A different way I chose, and now I find
          My plight repulsive even to myself.
          None pities me nor comes to solace me,
          None pities me nor comes to solace me.

          [The curtain is removed from the hut.]

          [HITOMARU and the ATTENDANT turn toward the hut.]

HITOMARU: How strange that from within this hut of thatch,
          Desolate beyond a habitation,
          A human voice is heard.
          Is it a beggar dwelling there?
          Better that we stand beyond
          The shadow of its eaves.
KAGEKIYO: Our eyes know not when autumn first comes in, yet we know it from
          the murmur of the wind; so do I feel a visitor from some unknown place.
HITOMARU: Alas! Not knowing where to seek my father,
          There is no house in which to rest.
KAGEKIYO: In truth, the Three Worlds do not exist in space, and can to
          nothingness diminish.
          Whom then should you ask for in this void?
            How could we reply
            Where the sought one lives?
ATTENDANT: O master of the hut! I have something to ask you.
KAGEKIYO: Who are you?
ATTENDANT: Do you know where lives the exile?
KAGEKIYO: The exile? Whom do you mean? What is his name?
ATTENDANT: It is Kagekiyo the Hot-tempered, a Heike warrior.
KAGEKIYO: I have heard of him, indeed, but being blind never have I seen him.
            A wretched life, they say, he lives
            And my pity stirs for him.
            Go elsewhere
            And others ask for information.

ATTENDANT: He is not to be found here. We must go farther and enquire again.

[HITOMARU *and the* ATTENDANT *retire to the stage-attendants' seat.*]

4

KAGEKIYO: How strange! For who should be the visitor but the daughter of this blind man? Long ago I fell in love with a courtesan of Atsuta in Owari Province, and in course of time a child was born to me. She was a girl, and therefore being not important, I left her in the charge of the mistress of a pleasure-house at Kamegae-ga-yatsu in Kamakura.

> Desolate at the years of parting,
> From afar she comes to speak to me.

CHORUS: Her speech I heard,

age-uta Her face I could not see.
> Oh! the pity of my sightless eyes!
> I let her pass without my name revealing,
> Out of my dear love for her,
> Out of my dear love for her.

[KAGEKIYO *lowers his face.*]

5

[HITOMARU *and the* ATTENDANT *go along the bridgeway as far as the first pine and the* ATTENDANT *turns toward the curtain.*]

ATTENDANT: Is there anyone about?

The VILLAGE HEADMAN, *wearing a striped kimono and* suō *robe and trailing skirt and carrying a short sword at his side, appears on the bridgeway.*

HEADMAN: You ask for some one. What do you want?

ATTENDANT: Do you know the house of the exile?

HEADMAN: There are several, which one are you seeking?

ATTENDANT: We are seeking a Heike warrior by the name of Kagekiyo the Hot-tempered.

HEADMAN: *[Turns toward the* Metsuke *Pillar.]* On your way you must have passed a thatched hut beneath the hill. Was there no one inside?

ATTENDANT: Yes, there was a blind beggar.

HEADMAN: That blind beggar is the man you seek. How strange! [HITOMARU *starts weeping.*] When I spoke about Kagekiyo, the lady wept bitter tears of sorrow. What, I wonder, ails her?

ATTENDANT: You have reason to wonder. I shall tell you. This lady is the daughter of Kagekiyo, and longing to see her father once again before he dies, has travelled from afar to find him. If I presume not too much on your kindness, please persuade him to receive his daughter.

HEADMAN: How strange! Is this lady Kagekiyo's daughter? Pray calm yourself and hear me speak. Your father has become blind. In distress he has shaved his head and taken the name of Kōtō of Hyūga to live on the charity of travellers and villagers like myself. Perhaps, he was too ashamed to reveal himself to you. I will accompany you once more to his hut, and call him by his real name. If he answers, then you may present yourself and together you can talk of all things past and present. Please come this way.

[HITOMARU *and the* ATTENDANT *enter the stage and go to the* Waki *seat. The* HEADMAN *stands near the* shite *pillar, facing the hut.*]

6

HEADMAN: Kagekiyo! Are you in? [*Approaches the hut and taps the pillar twice. Then he steps away and stands near the* Metsuke *pillar. Stops his ears with his hands. Lowers his hands.*]

KAGEKIYO: Quiet, Fellow! Quiet! My mind is troubled enough without your noisy shouting. Only a little while ago some one came from my distant home, but ashamed of my poverty and my state, I could not reveal my name and turned her from my door.
A thousand streams of tears drench my sleeves![2]
    I have now awakened to the thought that all is a dream and I myself but a dream shadow. If you call a beggar dead to the world 'Kagekiyo the Hot-tempered,' how will he answer?

CHORUS: In Hyūga, the sun-facing land,
In Hyūga, the sun-facing land,
I find a name becoming me.
Call me by the old name
I myself cast off
When my bow was laid aside
And I, whose passion now lies dead,
Will burn with bitter wrath.

KAGEKIYO: [KAGEKIYO *strikes his knee with his right hand.*] Here must I live,

CHORUS: Here must I live;
A blind man losing his staff
Could I be likened to,
If I the hatred bring upon my head
Of those, whose charity I seek.

[KAGEKIYO *fumbles for the staff.*]

Deformity brings ill reason
As with me now.
Forgive my bitter tongue.

[2]Line from a Chinese poem by Sugawara-no-Michizane:
  More than three years have passed since I left home;
  Tears fall in a thousand lines.
  All, all is like a dream;
  From time to time I look up at the sky.
The poem was composed when he was in exile in Dazaifu.

KAGEKIYO: [KAGEKIYO *turns toward the* HEADMAN *and joins his hands.*] My eyes are
      darkened,
CHORUS: My eyes are darkened,
      Yet I can tell the thoughts of man
      By a single uttered word.

      [KAGEKIYO *looks upward to the left.*]

      If there is a breeze in the hill-top pines,
      I know what it will scatter blooms like snow.
      From dreams like these to wake,
      Wherein alone a blind man sees
      The cherries blooming,
      Oh! how bitter, how bitter!

      [KAGEKIYO *lowers his face.*]

      And on the rocky beach
      I hear the noise of falling waves,
      And know the evening tide is flowing.

      [KAGEKIYO *makes a gesture of listening.*]

      I am a former warrior of the Heike;
      And I will entertain you with the tales of battle.

      [KAGEKIYO *comes out of the hut, taking the staff in his hand, and sits down in
      the center.*]

7

KAGEKIYO: I said harsh things to you just now. My mind was over-wrought. Pray
      forgive me.
HEADMAN: Never mind. We understand and do not take it seriously. Were there
      not some people here before me?
KAGEKIYO: No, no one came to see me save yourself.
HEADMAN: You are not telling the truth. You know a young lady came here,
      who called herself Kagekiyo's daughter. Why do you conceal it? Hearing
      her tale, so deeply was my heart moved that I have brought her back
      again.
         Come here at once, and speak with your father.

      [*Speaks to* HITOMARU.]

HITOMARU: Father! It is I, Hitomaru, who have come.

      [*Sits down by* KAGEKIYO's *side and takes hold of his sleeve with her hand.*]

      Where lies your pity
      To receive me thus, after my long journey,
      Through rain and wind, dew and frost?

[Weeps.]

> Is your father's love the less
> Because his child's a girl?
> O cruel, cruel!

[Weeps again.]

KAGEKIYO: I thought to have disguised myself,
But all in vain; I know not what to do
With my shameful, wretched self.

[Lowers his face.]

> If you in all your youthful grace
> Should own this wretch your father,
> All the world would talk.
> Oh! Think me not heartless
> For deceiving you.

[Puts his hand on her shoulder.]

CHORUS: I, whose house was ever warm
sage-uta   To greet the passing stranger,
             Was angry if he did not call,
             Now close my door to hide myself
             From my own child.
             Oh! how wretched I am!

[KAGEKIYO lets go of HITOMARU and weeps.]

age-uta   On the warships of the Heike,
             On the warships of the Heike,
             Warriors were crowded,
             Shoulder to shoulder, knee to knee,
             Leaving no space between.
             Among them all,
             Kagekiyo shone like the moon.
             My advice was sought
             By war commanders
             Of the Imperial ship.
             The clan of Heike boasted many
             Brave in battle and in counsel wise,
             But none to equal Kagekiyo.
             I, envied by all
             When called to live
             With my princely masters,
             An now a broken horse
             Outstripped by every jade.

[KAGEKIYO sinks to the floor, lowering his face.]

8

HEADMAN: O pathetic speech! Dear child, be seated here. Kagekiyo, your daughter has a favour to ask of you.

[*Speaks to* HITOMARU. *She resumes her seat, while the* HEADMAN *sits down next the* ATTENDANT.]

KAGEKIYO: What is it?

HEADMAN: She says that she would like to hear your exploits at the battle of Yashima. Please tell her the tale.

KAGEKIYO: Such a desire is not quite becoming in a girl, but out of compassion for her filial love in coming here from such a distance, I will comply with her request. When the tale is finished, you must persuade her to return home at once.

HEADMAN: Yes, I will persuade her, as soon as your tale is over.

KAGEKIYO: It was towards the end of the third month of the third year of Juei. We
katari of the Heike in ships and the Genji on land were arrayed along the coast
    for the impending decisive battle.

      Then said Noritsune, Lord of Noto,
      "All last year,
      Neither at Muroyama of Harima,
      Nor Mizushima of Bitchū,
      Nor again at Hiyodorigoe,
      Did our warriors a single victory gain,
      Because of Yoshitsune's battle strategy.
      O for some strategic plan
      To destroy this Yoshitsune!"
    I thought to myself, "After all the Hōgan is not above an ordinary mortal; it would be easy to destroy him, if I am prepared to give my life for it." Telling Noritsune what was in my heart I bade him a long farewell. The moment I set foot on land,
      The Genji troops rush towards me,
      Crying "Death to the enemy."

[KAGEKIYO *dances while the following lines are being chanted.*]

CHORUS: At sight of this, I, Kagekiyo,
age-uta At sight of this, I, Kagekiyo,
    Say to myself, "What noise!"
    And brandishing my halberd in the setting sun,
    I cut and slash to right and left;
    The flinching foemen take to flight
    In disarray in all directions.
    Pressing hard upon them,

KAGEKIYO: "Fie on you, you cowards!

CHORUS: "Fie on you, you cowards!" I shout;
    "Be ashamed before the watching eyes
    Of both the Genji and the Heike!"

Confident in victory in single combat,
I cry and cry again, with my halberd by my side,
"I am Kagekiyo of the Heike clan!"
And pursue them fiercely,
Trying to stop and capture one.
I grasp the neck-piece
Of Mionoya's helmet,
But alas! I fail to hold it.
Two, three times he flees from me;
I pursue him still;
He is a foe too worthy to let slip.
At last I leap upon him, seize his helmet,
And pull and tug at it with violent shouts.
Suddenly it breaks, leaving the neck-piece in my hand,
Giving its owner another chance to flee.
Some distance off he stops to turn and say,
"You have, indeed, a devilish strength of arm."
In reply I say to him,
"You have a neck-bone more powerful still!"
And we parted from each other
With shouts of laughter.

9

CHORUS: Such tales of ancient times I still remember,
But I am old and weak, and to my shame confess
My mind confused is growing.
My life with all its ills is coming to a close.
Go home now, and pray for my departed soul.
Your prayers for me will be
A light in darkest night,
A bridge across the desolate plain.
"Farewell, daughter!" I say.

[KAGEKIYO *takes hold of his staff and stands up.* HITOMARU, *the* ATTENDANT
and the HEADMAN *all stand up with him.* KAGEKIYO *goes toward the* shite
pillar, and as HITOMARU *passes him on her way to the bridgeway, he turns
around and places his hand on her shoulder.*]

"Farewell, father! I go."

[HITOMARU *goes along the Bridgeway, followed by the* ATTENDANT *and the*
HEADMAN, *and all disappear behind the curtain.*]

In the sorrowing minds of child and father
This simple parting forever dwells,
This simple parting forever dwells.

[KAGEKIYO *looks after* HITOMARU *and then, turning to the front, weeps.*]

IIO SŌGI (1421–1502 C.E.)
BOTANKA SHŌHAKU (1443–1527 C.E.)
SAIOKUEN SŌCHŌ (1448–1532 C.E.)

The three poets included here are not represented by their individual works but by extracts from a joint effort, a long poem called *One Hundred Stanzas by Three Poets at Minase* (*Minase Sangin Hyakuin*). The poem is probably the most famous example of *renga*, one of two forms of linked poetry—a fascinating and distinctively Japanese genre. *Renga* began as a diversion, a sort of game for facile poets. It was later accepted as serious literature by modeling its language on that of court poetry (*waka*), establishing elaborate canons and gaining court approval.

The typical *renga* sequence of 100 stanzas was composed by three or four poets writing stanzas in rapid alternation. Decades of poetic practice had made the writers so adept that a stanza might be composed, checked, written down, and repeated aloud in less than three minutes. The most fundamental principle of composition was that each stanza had to form a semantic unit with, and only with, its immediate predecessor. Thus the hundred stanzas emerged linked in an ongoing chain.

Linked poetry was written on the fronts and backs of four folded sheets (eight sides in all). The front of the first sheet was devoted to a dignified introduction of eight stanzas. The first stanza, or *hokku,* was a factual description of the scene at the poets' meeting; subsequent stanzas were predominantly fictional. The back of the last sheet contained an eight-stanza conclusion. In between, with fourteen stanzas per side, was the development, the most varied and agitated part of the sequence. The remaining conventions of *renga* were so elaborate that they defy simple description. The code covered topics and subtopics, imagery, motifs, and even variations in quality and degrees of connectedness between stanzas.

The greatest *renga* sequences are characterized by controlled variation. They honor the *renga* code, manipulate it, and transform it with originality. In successful practice, a single strong poet exercised a role like that of a conductor. Sogi, for example, ensured that the beauty of the total sequence always took precedence over the brilliance of any one part, and other able *renga* poets never composed as well as with him.

For its spirit and principles, linked poetry is indebted to collections of court poetry such as the *Shinkokinshū*, which first explored ways of gathering independent poetic units into a larger artistic whole. Linked poetry bequeathed its three-part structure to the *nō* drama. It is quintessentially Japanese in its asymmetry and poetic associations (see the opening section to Sei Shōnagon's *Pillow Book*). Some critics have been tempted to trace the principles of linked poetry throughout later and even contemporary literature. This goes perhaps too far. Yet its uniqueness and influence is undisputed. Linked poetry is a truly Japanese phenomenon, both in its aesthetic spirit and its lack of counterparts in other literatures.

One Hundred Stanzas by Three Poets at Minase
[Minase Sangin Hyakuin]

SŌGI

[Despite some snow]

   Despite some snow
the base of hills spreads with haze
   the twilight scene

Design. No relation. Spring. Rising Things. Peaks.
In this most famous of renga *hokku,* haze designates spring, a season long thought best for dawn, as autumn was for evening. Gotoba had a royal palace at Minase, where he wrote a tanka Sōgi echoes.

SHŌHAKU

[Despite some snow]

   Despite some snow
the base of hills spreads with haze
   the twilight scene
where the waters flow afar
the village glows with sweet plum flowers

Design. Close. Spring. Waters. Trees. Residences.
The movement suggests temporal progress with the melting of snow in 1. "Yuku mizu" seems to recall a poem in the *Kokinshū* (15: 793) on Minase River. This *waki* (or second stanza) is not a flower stanza, because it uses a named flower, the plum.

SŌCHŌ

[Where the waters flow afar]

Where the waters flow afar
the village glows with sweet plum flowers
   in the river wind
a single stand of willow trees
   shows spring color

Design-Ground. Close. Spring. Waters. Trees.
This *daisan* (third stanza) advances spring a bit more, suggesting that willows are in full leaf but still fresh. When stirred by wind they were thought loveliest.

Translated by Earl Miner.

SŌGI

[In the river wind]

In the river wind
a single stand of willow trees
   shows spring color
the break of day shows distinct
sounds of the punting of a boat

Ground-Design. Distant-Close. Miscellaneous. Waters. Night.
Daybreak is considered nightbreak: hence, Night. So also does Sōgi emphasize what is heard. The connection is that between the boat and the river of 3. "Distinct" governs both "day shows" and "sounds," as "spreads with haze" does "hills" and "scene" in the opening stanza: a form of zeugma or yoking common in linked poetry.

SHŌHAKU

[The break of day]

The break of day shows distinct
sounds of the punting of a boat
   does not the moon
of a fog-enveloped night
   stay yet in the sky

Ground-Design. Close-Distant. Autumn. Radiance. Night. Rising Things.
The language is somewhat prosaic (although it would be poetic in haikai), but the image of the moon ensures that this is not a ground stanza. Shōhaku emphasizes the stillness implied by 5 with night fog. In it a faint glow suggests that the moon has not yet set. The first moon stanza, expected as stanza 8.

SŌCHŌ

[Does not the moon]

   Does not the moon
of a fog-enveloped night
   stay yet in the sky
as wide fields settle with the frost
autumn has approached its end

Ground. Close-Distant. Autumn. Falling Things.
The stanza has commonplace imagery and is syntactically fragmented, but it fits well in the sequence, opposing a falling to a rising thing and suggesting that the end of autumn made the moon more appreciated in 5.

SŌGI

[As wide fields settle with the frost]

As wide fields settle with the frost
autumn has approached its end
   the insects cry out
but without regard for such desires
   the grasses wither

Design. Close-Distant. Autumn. Insects. Plants.
This is fresh in conception and yet central to Japanese thinking about autumn and insects.
Given the essential character (hon'i) of renga imagery, unnamed insects were thought more
comprehensive and moving. This is, therefore, the sole use allowed in a hundred stanzas.

SHŌHAKU

[The insects cry out]

   The insects cry out
but without regard for such desires
   the grasses wither
as I come to the fence in visit
the once covered path is clear

Design-Ground. Close-Distant. Miscellaneous. Residences.
"The once-covered path" is new in renga diction, and it suggests that the person visited is
as much gone as the path is changed. This concludes the front of the first sheet: three poems
on spring and three on autumn, the two most esteemed seasons.

KOREA

In considering Korean literature, we must first make it clear that we mean
literature written in the Korean language, not all literature written by Koreans. The
distinction is important, for the fundamental fact that confronts students of
Korean literature is this: until well into the nineteenth century, literate Koreans
wrote almost exclusively in classical Chinese, which in East Asia enjoyed the same
authority and prestige as did Latin in the medieval West. Of the writings that have
come down to us from before 1850, less than one percent are in Korean. Nor did
a script for Korean exist until the fifteenth century, when scholars devised an

alphabet under the patronage of King Sejong. Prior to this, writers interested in recording Korean borrowed Chinese graphs to transcribe the sound and sense of Korean words.

Linguistic and literary evidence indicates that Koreans learned to use the Chinese script at the earliest stage of their history, from at least the fourth century C.E. on. In the mid-seventh century, a royal academy was established, modeled on the Chinese system of the T'ang Dynasty. As in China, the curriculum was grounded in the Confucian classics, and the goal was to train scholars for civil service examinations. Again as in China, the system produced a privileged social class of *literati,* or lettered men. (Women were excluded from both the academy and the examinations.) It was this class that controlled the canon of classical literature and critical discourse in Korea. The literati adopted as official the Chinese genres and their hierarchy, with their clear distinction between most esteemed genres (poetry and certain prose genres) and lesser genres (literary miscellany, fictional narratives, and drama), and they intended their writings as contributions to Chinese culture.

And how they wrote! Poems were produced on every conceivable occasion; the courtiers must have thought in verse. If a soldier, merchant, female entertainer, or slave is mentioned in history, it is because of his or her unexpected ability to write poetry in Chinese. It was even common practice to write poems on house walls or in public places for passersby to enjoy; this poetry was not considered graffiti. Some literati, and some enterprising women, wrote in Korean, although vernacular poetry and prose enjoyed little esteem. Still, within the native Korean tradition, poetry held pride of place, as it did in China. Other genres in Korean remained low in status and have not been fully appreciated until modern times.

Generalizations about early Korean poetry are difficult to frame, for very little has come down to us. From the unified Silla period (beginning in the mid-seventh century) through the Koryŏ period (935–1392), we know of only forty-one extant poems. Twenty-five of these, dating from the Silla and early Koryŏ, are known as *hyangga,* ''native songs'' (as opposed to poetry in classical Chinese). Eleven *hyangga* are devotional poems written by the Buddhist monk Kyunyŏ; the remaining fourteen were written by members of the elite corps of knights or by Buddhist monks. The other sixteen poems, known simply as Koryŏ songs, are folk songs and poems by commoners.

After the creation of the Korean alphabet, writing in Korean grew more common. The two most enduring poetic forms to develop were the *sijo* and *kasa.* Both were written initially by the literati, then from the eighteenth century on largely by commoners. The selections in this section—a sampling of *hyangga, sijo,* and *kasa,* as well as prose works by women writers—thus represent a spectrum of native sensibility and experience.

Aside from basic similarities in topics, imagery, tropes, allusions, and other devices, Korean poetry is characterized by its musicality, the consistency with which it celebrates cultural values, and its close relationship to the audience. In Korea, all poetry was meant to be sung, and its forms and styles reflect melodic origins. The basis of its prosody is a line of alternating metric segments of three or four syllables, the rhythm that is probably most natural to the Korean language. Extant musical notations indicate that the musical divisions of, for example, a popular song of medieval Korea are different from its poetic (stanzaic) division; a musical division is signaled by an interjection followed by a refrain. Nonsense jingles or onomatopoetic representations of the sound of musical instruments attest to the refrain's musical origin and function.

Considered as a living performance art, poetry becomes a collective enterprise involving the poet, the singer, and the audience. The singer of a poem takes on the role of lyric persona—the disembodied voice of poetry itself. (If the singer is also the poet, he or she has multiple roles of composer and singer, poet and lyric persona.) The audience, for its part, validates the song through its understanding and appreciation, which derive from a shared knowledge of traditional poetic norms and conventions. We can even say that the audience helps shape the song through its expectations. Thus, poet and audience together reaffirm their common culture.

We can see this reaffirmation in the recurrence of certain themes—such as nature, love, friendship, time, and praise—as well as certain topics and images. Taken up again and again, by generation after generation, such themes become cultural touchstones, and the poetry of the past—the poet's own tradition—takes on the character of a resource to be freely drawn on rather than a burden to be thrown off. Like their Chinese and Japanese counterparts, Korean poets knew that a literary text that draws nothing from its predecessors is inconceivable, and that originality does not mean repudiating all that has gone before. Indeed, links to the past were valued, for they endow poems with rich overtones and multiple meanings unavailable through any other means. Far from being overwhelmed by tradition, successful poets found their own unique voice through a skillful use of the poetic techniques at their disposal.

Historical Background

From the time of the emergence of the Three Kingdoms in the early centuries of our era, Korea maintained its independence and cultural identity throughout history. The three kingdoms—Koguryŏ in the north, and Paekche and Silla in the south—consolidated earlier tribal federations and states, which in turn had evolved from the earliest Stone Age cultures of the peninsula. Relations with the more advanced neighboring culture of China were complex. Elements of Chinese culture such as writing, Confucianism, and Buddhism were quickly absorbed, yet China's recurring territorial ambitions were a source of tension. During the first century B.C.E., the Chinese had overthrown an earlier state in northern Korea and colonized the area. During the early- and mid-seventh century C.E., Koguryŏ, which extended north into southern Manchuria, successfully fought off invasions by the Chinese as well as by northeastern nomadic peoples.

Supported by T'ang Dynasty China, Silla conquered the other two kingdoms during the latter part of the seventh century, unifying the peninsula. The northern territories of Koguryŏ (into Manchuria) reformed as the state of Parhae—as seen by many Korean historians—and soon came into direct confrontation with Silla. But Parhae eventually collapsed and was overtaken by nomadic peoples, and the development of Korean society and culture henceforth takes place on the peninsula proper.

During the Silla period, Buddhism flourished and a royal academy was established on the Chinese model. The eighth century saw a gradual weakening of the Silla government and the corresponding growth of numerous regional powers. After the final disintegration of Silla in the ninth century, the ruler of one of these regional powers again unified the peninsula, founding the Koryŏ dynasty, from which we derive our word "Korea." The Koryŏ lasted almost five hundred years surviving even the Mongol invasions and overlordship of the thirteenth and fourteenth centuries.

Following the collapse of the Mongol empire in the fourteenth century, a Korean general named Yi Sŏnggye declared himself king, founding the Chosŏn Dynasty. Chosŏn ruled in a succession of twenty-six monarchs until Japan annexed Korea in 1910. The early Chosŏn was a time of great cultural flowering, with development of movable type for printing, the creation of the Korean alphabet, and the establishment of many centers of learning, including a prestigious royal academy. Buddhism, hitherto the official state religion, was replaced with the ethical system of neo-Confucianism.

A Japanese invasion of 1592 inaugurated a period of disturbances. The Japanese withdrew in defeat in 1598, but trouble came soon after from the north with invasions by the Manchu, who also threatened, and eventually toppled, the Ming dynasty in China.

Beginning in the mid-seventeenth century, significant changes occurred in Korean society. Agricultural advances raised the standard of living for common people. Many scholars set aside the abstract theorizing dear to Confucianists to found the Sirhak, or Practical Learning School, which held that theory should have practical applications for society and the nation. The Sirhak turned their attention to such matters as administrative reform, education, commerce, technology, history, and the Korean language. This language was increasingly used for the lengthy prose works called *sosŏl*, or narrative fiction. The *sosŏl* is not a literary form equivalent to the novel, as many Western scholars mistakenly think. Originally, it was a derogatory term meaning "small talk," and the term was eventually used by writers when they translated the English term "novel," hence the confusion. By the twentieth century, but not before, *sosŏl* came to correspond to the Western novel. But even in our day, the East Asian *sosŏl* is different from the Western novel, as some critics are beginning to point out (e.g., Fujii, *Complicit Fictions*, Berkeley, 1993).

Further Reading

Eckert, Carter J. et al. *Korea Old and New: A History*. Seoul: Ilchokak, 1990.

Lee, Peter H. *Celebration of Continuity: Themes in Classic East Asian Poetry*. Cambridge: Harvard University Press, 1979.

———. *Anthology of Korean Literature from Early Times to the Nineteenth Century*. 2nd ed. Honolulu: University of Hawaii Press, 1990.

Rutt, Richard. *The Bamboo Grove: An Introduction to Sijo*. Berkeley: University of California Press, 1971.

Fujii, *Complicit Fictions*. Berkeley: University of California Press, 1993.

Pronounciation Guide

Chŏng Ch'ŏl (jung chul)
Chosŏn (cho-sun)
Ch'ungdam (choong-dahm)
Hŏ Nansŏrhŏn (huh nan-sol-hun)
Hwang Chini (hwang jin-ee)
hyangga (hyang-gah)
Kwangdŏk (kwang-duhk)

Kyunyŏ (kyun-yuh)
sasŏl sijo (sah-sol si-jo)
Sejong (se-jong)
sijo (si-jo)
Silla (shilla)
Yŏngjae (young-jay)
Yun Sŏndo (yoon son-do)

KWANGDŎK (fl. 661–681 C.E.)
MASTER WŎLMYŎNG (fl. 742–765 C.E.)
MASTER CH'UNGDAM (fl. 742–765 C.E.)
HŬIMYŎNG (fl. 742–765 C.E.)
MONK YŎNGJAE (fl. 785–798 C.E.)
CH'ŎYONG (fl. 875–886 C.E.)
GREAT MASTER KYUNYŎ (923–973 C.E.)
Korea

Vernacular poetry dating from the seventh through the tenth centuries is called *hyangga* [hyang-gah], meaning "native songs" or "Korean songs" as opposed to poetry written in classical Chinese. As in most vernacular poetry in Korea, *hyangga* are songs, emphasizing orality, the vibrant relation between poet and audience, and between poetry and music. On the basis of the surviving examples, we may say that there are three forms: a stanza of four lines; two stanzas of four lines; and two stanzas of four lines plus a stanza of two lines. In the ten-line version, the ninth line usually begins with an interjection, analogous to the English "Ah," which indicates heightened emotions an a change in tempo and pitch and also presages the poem's conclusion. Buddhist poems occupy two-thirds of extant *hyangga*—a reflection of the fact that Buddhism was the dominant religion for almost nine hundred years (527–1392) during the earlier kingdoms of Silla and Koryŏ.[1]

---

1. Silla [shilla] (57 B.C.–A.D. 935), an ancient Korean kingdom, had its capital in Kyŏngju in southeastern Korea. Koryŏ (918–1392), a medieval Korean kingdom, had its capital in Kaesŏng in west-central Korea.

KWANGDŎK

[In the first stanza the speaker asks the moon to undertake a journey to the West where Amitāyus (Infinite Life) resides. The second amplifies the praise of the virtues of Amitāyus. The last stanza presents a rhetorical question in which the speaker affirms that flesh, that stands between the promised land and this world, must be annihilated.]

Prayer to Amitāyus

O Moon,
Go to the West, and
Pray to Amitāyus
And say

That there is one who
Adores the judicial throne, and
Longs for the Pure Land,
Praying before Him with folded hands.

Can the forty-eight vows be met
If this flesh remains unannihilated?

MASTER WŎLMYŎNG

[Written by Master Wŏlmyŏng (Moon Brightness) in memory of his sister, the poem is built on a single theme of separation through death, in the first stanza on the image of a crossroad and in the second on the image of the tree. The branches come from the same source, the trunk: but leaves which grow on the branches, when fallen, are permanently separated from one another. In the final line, the assurance of a meeting after death consoles the speaker, dispelling the uncertainty expressed in the second stanza, and the image echoes that of Homer, who, underscoring the brevity of human life, compared the generation of men to leaves (*Iliad* 6:146–150).]

Requiem

On the hard road of life and death
That is near our land.
You went, afraid,
Without words.

All poems in this selection translated by Peter H. Lee.

We know not where we go,
Leaves blown, scattered,
Though fallen from the same tree,
By the first winds of autumn.

Abide, Sister, perfect your ways,
Until we meet in the Pure Land.

MASTER CH'UNGDAM

[This is a eulogy by Master Ch'ungdam written to praise Knight Kip'a, a member of the *hwarang,* a group of leading knights in the ancient kingdom of Silla. By introducing a correspondence between the knight and the pine, the poet asserts that his moral beauties endure. The knight, through his integrity, not only scorns mutability but imposes a sense of order on the landscape.]

Ode to Knight Kip'a

The moon that pushes her way
Through the thickets of clouds,
Is she not pursuing
The white clouds?

Knight Kip'a once stood by the water,
Reflecting his face in the blue.
Henceforth I shall seek and gather
Among pebbles the depth of his mind.

Knight, you are the towering pine
That scorns frost, ignores snow.

HŬIMYŎNG

[On behalf of her son who has lost his eyesight, Hŭimyŏng implores the Thousand-Armed and Thousand-Eyed "Sound Observer" (Bodhisattva Who Observes the Sounds of the World), painted on the north wall of Punhwang Monastery.]

Hymn to the Thousand-Eyed Sound Observer

Falling on my knees,
Pressing my hands together,
Thousand-Eyed Merciful Goddess,
I implore thee.

Yield me,
Who lacks,
One among your thousand eyes,
By your mystery restore me whole.

If you grant me one of your many eyes,
O the bounty, then, of your charity.

MONK YŎNGJAE

[Intending to spend his last days on South Peak in retirement, the monk Yŏngjae was crossing Taehyŏn Ridge when he met sixty thieves. The bandits drew their swords and threatened him; but he showed no fear and revealed his identity. Since the bandits had heard of his reputation as a poet, they asked him to compose an impromptu poem. The poem is a revelation of the process of attaining enlightenment: the swords that "glitter in the bushes" aid the poet to comprehend the relations between illusion and enlightenment. It is the enlightened poet who in turn enlightens the bandits.]

Meeting with Bandits

My mind that knew not its true self,
The mind that wandered in the dark and deep,
Now is started out for bodhi,
Now is awakened to light.

But on my way to the city of light,
I meet with a band of thieves.
Their swords glitter in the bushes—
Things-as-they-are and things-as-they are not.

Well, bandits and I both meditate on the Truth;
But is that sufficient for tomorrow?

CH'ŎYONG

Ch'ŏyong, one of the seven sons of the Dragon King of the Eastern Sea, married a beautiful woman. Seeing that she was extremely beautiful, a demon of plague transformed himself into a man and attacked her in her room while Ch'ŏyong was away. But Ch'ŏyong returned, and witnessing the scene, he calmly sang the following song, which so moved the demon that he went away. The Ch'ŏyong mask was later used to exorcise evil spirits, usually on New Year's Eve, and his image was pasted on the gates.]

Song of Ch'ŏyong

Having caroused far into the night
In the moonlit capital,
I return home and in my bed,
Behold, four legs.

Two were mine,
Whose are the other two?
Two were mine.
No, no, they are taken.

GREAT MASTER KYUNYŎ

[This is the sixth of eleven poems inspired by "Vows on the Practices of the Bodhi-sattva." The mind is the ignorant soil which suffers from "the blight of affliction." If "sweet dharma rain" falls over the dried and barren soil of the mind, the blight will be dispelled, the grass will grow, and the soil will bear the "golden fruit of knowledge." The autumn field must be illuminated by the moon, a recurring symbol for enlightenment.]

from **Eleven Devotional Poems**

To the Majestic Assembly of Buddhas

To the majestic assembly of Buddhas
In the dharma realm.
I fervently pray
For the sweet rain of truth.

Dispel the blight of affliction
Rooted deep in the soil of ignorance,
And wet the mind's field of the living,
Where good grasses struggle to grow.

Ah, the mind is a moonlit autumn field
Ripe with the golden fruit of knowledge.

HWANG HŬI (1363–1452 C.E.)
KING SŎNGJONG (1457–1494 C.E.)
SONG SUN (1493–1583 C.E.)
YI HWANG (1501–1571 C.E.)
YU HŬI-CH'UN (1513–1577 C.E.)
HWANG CHINI (c. 1506–1544 C.E.)
KWŎN HOMUN (1532–1587 C.E.)
SŎNG HON (1535–1598 C.E.)
CHŎNG CH'ŎL (1537–1594 C.E.)
YI TŎKHYŎNG (1561–1613 C.E.)
YUN SŎNDO (1587–1671 C.E.)
YI MYŎNGHAN (1595–1645 C.E.)

Korea

SIJO

Each line of the *sijo,* the most popular, elastic, and mnemonic of Korean poetic forms, consists of four metric segments, with a minor pause occurring at the end of the second segment and a major one at the end of the fourth. An emphatic syntactic division is usually introduced in the third line in the form of a countertheme, paradox, resolution, judgment, command, or exclamation. The introduction of a deliberate twist in phrasing or meaning is often a test of a poet's originality. The following scheme shows the syllable-count pattern of the *sijo:*

¾	4	¾	4
¾	4	¾	4
3	5	4	¾

The *sijo* was transmitted orally, as a song. It was not until the beginning of the eighteenth century that such poems were written down.

The great number of variants of a given poem reflects the oral nature of the *sijo.* We are not sure which *sijo* are composed spontaneously during performances. In any event, the singer was free to alter phrases or lines whenever his memory failed him or his creativity inspired him. Always, the spoken word was the basis of his artistic creation. The *sijo* has proved to be a form well-suited to express the poet's sense of the world and response to a given situation. Simplicity and sensitive rendering of the poet's own microcosm in relation to the world at large characterize the form.

The last song included in this selection is an example of the *sasŏl sijo*, in which more than two metric segments in each line, except for the first in the third line, are added. Most *sasŏl sijo* are written anonymously, usually not at court. What hastened the rise of this poetic form was the eighteenth-century rupture of a system of beliefs that served to perpetuate existing social formations and power structures. Innovations introduced by the *sasŏl sijo* writers include the introduction of new topics regarding love and other matters as well as a change of scale, voice, diction, and rhetorical patterns. A marked feature is enumeration, or listing of details.

HWANG HŬI

[Spring has come to a country village]*

Spring has come to a country village;
How much there is to be done!
I knit a net and
A servant tills the fields and sows:
But who will pluck the sweet herbs
That grow on the back-hill?

KING SŎNGJONG

[Stay]*

Stay:
Will you go? Must you go?
Is it in weariness you go? From disgust?
Who advised you, who persuaded you?
Say why you are leaving,
You, who are breaking my heart.[1]

SONG SUN

[I have spent ten years]*

I have spent ten years
Building a grass hut;
Now winds occupy half,
The moon fills the rest.

*Translated by Peter H. Lee.

1. Addressed to Yu Hoin (1445–1494), assistant section chief of the Ministry of Works and the king's favorite courtier.

Alas, I cannot let you come in.
But I shall receive you outside.[1]

[I discuss with my heart]*

I discuss with my heart
Whether to retire from court.
My heart scorns the intent:
"How could you leave the king?"
"Heart, stay here and serve him,
My old body must go."

[Do not grieve, little birds]*

Do not grieve, little birds,
Over the falling blossoms:
They're not to blame, it's the wind
Who loosens and scatters the petals.
Spring is leaving us.
Don't hold it against her.

YI HWANG

[The green hills—how can it be]*

The green hills—how can it be
           that they are green eternally?
Flowing streams—how can it be;
           night and day do they never stand still?
We also, we can never stop,
           we shall grow green eternally.

YU HŬICH'UN

[A little bunch of parsley]†

A little bunch of parsley,
           which I dug and rinsed myself.
I did it for no one else,
           but simply to give it to you.

†*Translated by Richard Rutt.*

---

1. Also attributed to Kim Changsaeng (1548–
   1631).

The flavor is not so very pungent;
       taste it, once more taste it, and see.

HWANG CHINI

[I will break the back]†

I will break the back
       of this long, midwinter night,
folding it double,
       cold beneath my spring quilt,
that I may draw out
       the night, should my love return.

KWŎN HOMUN

[Nature makes clear the windy air]*

Nature makes clear the windy air,
And bright the round moon.
In the bamboo garden, on the
Pine fence, not a speck of dust.
How fresh and fervent my life
With a long lute and piled scrolls!

SŎNG HON

[The mountain is silent]*

The mountain is silent,
The water without form.
A clear breeze has no price,
The bright moon no lover.
Here, after their fashion,
I will grow old in peace.

CHŎNG CH'ŎL

[Snow has fallen on the pine-woods]*

Snow has fallen on the pine-woods,
       and every bough has blossomed.
I should like to pluck a branch
       and send it to where my lord is.

---

†*Translated by David R. McCann.*

After he has looked at it,
    what matter if the snow-flowers melt?

[Could my heart but be removed]†

Could my heart but be removed
    and assume the moon's bright shape
To be hung there bright and shining
    in the vast expanse of heaven.
I could go where my dear lord is,
    and pour my light upon him.

YI TŎKHYŎNG

[The moon hangs in the sky, bright, full]*

The moon hangs in the sky, bright, full.
Since the dawn,
It has met wind and frost.
Alas, soon it will sink.
But no, wait, I say,
And shine on the gold cup of my drunken guest.

YUN SŎNDO

Songs of Five Friends*

How many friends have I? Count them:
Water and stone, pine and bamboo—
The rising moon on the east mountain,
Welcome, it too is my friend.
What need is there, I say,
To have more friends than five?

They say clouds are fine: I mean the color.
But, alas, they often darken.
They say winds are clear; I mean the sound.
But, alas, they often cease to blow.
It is only the *water*, then,
That is perpetual and good.

Why do flowers fade so soon
Once they are in their glory?
Why do grasses yellow so soon
Once they have grown tall?
Perhaps it is the *stone*, then,
That is constant and good.

Flowers bloom when it is warm;
Leaves fall when days are cool.
But, O *pine*, how is it
That you scorn frost, ignore snow?
I know now even your roots are,
Straight among the Nine Springs.

You are not a tree, no,
Nor a plant, not even that.
Who let you shoot so straight;
What makes you empty within?
You are green in all seasons,
Welcome, *bamboo*, my friend.

YI MYŎNGHAN

[Do not draw back your sleeves and go]*

Do not draw back your sleeves and go,
My own,
With tears I beg you.
Over the long dike green with grass
Look, the sun goes down.
You will regret it, lighting the lamp
By the tavern window,
Sleepless and alone.

[If my dreams]*

If my dreams
Left their footprints on the road,
The path beneath my love's window
Would be worn down, though it is stone.
Alas, in the country of dream
No roads endure, no traces remain.

ANONYMOUS

from Sasŏl Sijo

[Cricket, cricket]*

Cricket, cricket,
O sad cricket,

you keep vigil till the moon sinks,
with your long and short notes;
each sad note
of your lonely cry
wakes me from a fitful sleep.
Chirp on, tiny insect,
you alone know my misery
in this empty room.

HŎ NANSŎRHON (1563–1589 C.E.)
KIM INGYŎM (1707–?)
Korea

Kasa

The *kasa* originated as song lyrics written to prevailing *kasa* tunes. It is characterized by a lack of stanzaic division, varying length, a tendency toward description and exposition, as well as, at times, lyricism, and by its verbally and syntactically balanced parallel phrases. Emerging as a new genre toward the middle of the fifteenth century, the form was perfected by such masters as Chŏng Ch'ŏl (1537–1594) and Hŏ Nansŏrhon, who was an accomplished poet in Chinese and Korean. Hŏ Nansŏrhon's is a dramatic narrative written by a woman on unrequited love.

As third secretary, Kim Ingyŏm accompanied the Korean diplomatic mission to Japan. The party, consisting of some five hundred members, left Seoul on September 9, 1763 and arrived in Edo (Tokyo) in 1764. They returned to Seoul on August 5, 1764. The work runs to some four thousand lines, and the present selection shows what was expected of a writer in a foreign country such as Japan. The scenes depicted occurred on two days in February 1764.

HŎ NANSŎRHON

A Woman's Sorrow

Yesterday I fancied I was young;
But today, I am aging.
What use is there in recalling
The joyful days of my youth?

Translated by Peter H. Lee.

Now I am old, to recount
My sad story chokes me.
When Father begot me, Mother reared me,
When they took pains to bring me up,
They dreamed, not of a duchess or marchioness,
But at least of a bride fit for a gentleman.
Through the retribution of karma
And the ties chanced by a matchmaker,
I met as if in a dream
A valiant man known as frivolous,
And I served him with care, as if trodding on ice.
When I reached fifteen, counted sixteen,
The inborn beauty in me blossomed,
And with this face and this body
I vowed a union of a hundred years.
The flow of time was sudden;
The gods too were jealous of my beauty,
Spring breezes and autumn water,
They flew like a shuttle.
And my face once young and fair
Has become ugly to look at.
I know my image in the mirror;
So who will love me now?
Blush not, my self, and reproach no one.
Do you say a new customer showed up
At a tavern where men cluster?
When flowers smiled in the setting sun,
He left home for no fixed place
On a white horse with a gold whip.
Where does he stop to enjoy himself?
How far he went I don't know;
I'll hear no word from him.
Our ties are broken,
But I still think of him.
I don't see him at all, but I still yearn for him.
Long is a day, cruel is a month.
The plum trees by my window,
How many times have they fallen?
The winter night is bitter cold,
And snow, or some mixture, descends.
Long, long is a summer's day,
And a dreary rain comes too.
And spring with flowers and willows
Have no feeling for me.
When the autumn moon enters my room

And crickets chirp on the couch,
A long sigh and salty tears
In vain make me recall the past.
It is hard to bring this cruel life to an end.
But when I examine myself, I shouldn't despair so.
Turning the blue lamp around,
I play "A Song of Blue Lotus,"
Holding the green zither aslant,
As my sorrow commands me.
As though the rain on the Hsiao and Hsiang
Beat over the rustling bamboo leaves,
As though the crane returned whooping
After a span of a thousand years,
Fingers may stylishly pluck
The old familiar tune;
But who will listen in the room
Except for the lotus-brocade curtains?
I feel that my entrails are torn to pieces.
I would rather fall asleep
To see him at least in a dream.
But for what enmity
Do the leaves falling in the wind
And the insects piping among the grasses
Wake me from sleep?
The Weaver and Herdboy in the sky[1]
Meet once on the seventh day of the seventh moon—
However hard it is to cross the Milky Way—
And never miss this yearly encounter.
But since he left me alone,
What magic water separates him from me,
And what makes him silent about his comings and goings?
Leaning on the balustrade, I gaze at the path he took—
Dewdrops glitter on the grass,
Evening clouds pass by, birds sing sadly
In the green bamboo grove.
Numberless are the sorrowful;
But can there by anyone as wretched as I?
Love, you caused me this grief;
I don't know whether I shall live or die.

---

1. The Herdboy and Weaver were constellations in Chinese astronomy, on both sides
of the Milky Way. Condemned to a year-
long separation, they meet once on the
night of the seventh day of the seventh
lunar month, when magpies form a bridge
across the river of stars. The motif is as old
as the *Book of Songs*.

KIM INGYŎM

Grand Trip to Japan

On the twenty-third I fell ill,
lying in the official hostel.
Our hosts bring me their poems,
they are heaped like a hill.
Sickness aside, I answer them;
how taxing this chore is!
Regulated verse, broken-off lines,
old style verse, regulated couplets—
some one hundred thirty pieces.
Because I dashed them off on draft paper,
upon revision I've discarded a half.
If I have to work like this every day,
it will be too much to bear. . . .
The rich and noble in the city
bring presents, many in kind and amount.
But I return them all as before.
One scholar, his hand on the brow,
begs me a hundred times to accept,
rubbing hands together sincerely.
Touched with pity,
I accept a piece of ink stick.
When I offer him Korean paper,
brushes and ink sticks,
he too takes only one ink stick. . . .
Before dawn on the twenty-fourth,
they arrive in streams.
How hard to talk by means of writing,
how annoying to cap their verses.
Braving my illness,
and mindful of our mission
to awe them and enhance our prestige,
I exert myself for dear life,
wield my brush like wind and rain,
and harmonize with them.
When they revise their verses,
they put their heads together—
their writings bid fair to inundate me.
I compose for another round;
they respond with another pile.
I am old and infirm,
and the task saps my vigor.

Translated by Peter H. Lee.

I wouldn't mind it if I were young,
but they traveled thousands of miles
with packed food and waited for months
just to get our opinions.
If we deny them our writing,
how disappointed they would be!
We write on and on
for the old and young, the high and low.
We work as a matter of duty
night and day, without rest.

ANONYMOUS (NINETEENTH CENTURY)
Korea

Prose by Women

Women have not been silent in Korean literature. Some secretly taught themselves classical Chinese, much as Lady Wortley Montague taught herself Latin, and some were gifted poets in Chinese forms. Because the Korean alphabet, which was invented between 1443 and 1444, was easier to learn than Chinese, it was thought to be a script for women who used it as the medium for refined literature.

"Lament for a Needle" is a delightful prose piece gracefully written by an anonymous woman. The author of "The Dispute of a Woman's Seven Companions," also anonymous, rebukes those members of her own sex concerned with self-recognition. Her engaging story is told with great simplicity to her friends gathered around a brazier on a winter night. It is interesting to note that she praises the humility of the thimble, portrayed as the loyal servant of the house who has mastered the secret of life.

Lament for a Needle

On a certain day of a certain month in a certain year, a certain widow addresses a needle with a few words. To a woman the needle is an indispensable tool, though commonly people do not cherish it. You are only a small thing, but I mourn you greatly, because so many memories are connected with you. Alas, what a loss, what a pity! It has been twenty-seven years since I first held you in my hand. How could a sensitive human being feel otherwise? How sad! Holding back my tears and calming my heart, I bid my last farewell to you by hastily writing down this account of your deeds and my memories.

Translated by Peter H. Lee.

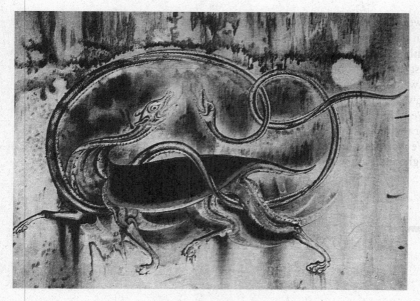

Tortoise-Serpent in the mural painting in a Koguryo tomb (500–650 AD). From *Korea: Tradition and Transformation* by Andrew C. Nahm. Courtesy, Andrew C. Nahm.

Years ago, my uncle-in-law was chosen as the head of the Winter Solstice Felicitation mission to China, and upon his return from Peking he gave me dozens of needles. I sent some to my parents' home, some to my relatives, and divided the rest among my servants. I then chose you, and got to know you, and we have been together ever since. How sad! The ties between us are of an extraordinary nature. Although I have lost or broken many other needles, I have kept you for years. You may be unfeeling, but how could I not love you and be charmed by you! What a loss, what a disappointment!

I was unlucky, I had no children, but I went on living. Moreover, our fortunes began to fail, so I devoted myself to sewing, and you helped me forget my sorrow and manage my household. Today I bid you farewell. Alas, this must have come about through the jealousy of the spirits and the enmity of Heaven.

How regrettable, my needle, how pitiful! You were a special gift of fine quality, a thing out of the ordinary, prominent among ironware. Deft and swift like some knight-errant, straight and true like royal subject, your sharp point seemed to talk, your round eye seemed to see. When I embroidered phoenixes and peacocks on thick or thin silk, your wondrously agile movements seemed the workings of a spirit. No human effort could have matched yours.

Alas! Children may be precious, but they leave when the time comes. Servants may be obedient, but they grumble at times. When I consider your subtle talents, so responsive to my needs, you are far better than children or servants. I made you a silver case enameled in five colors and carried you on the tie-string of my blouse, a lady's trinket. I used to feel you there whenever I ate or slept, and we became friends. Before beaded screens in summer or by lamplight in winter, I used to quilt, broad-stitch, hem, sew, or make finishing stitches with double thread, and your movement was like a phoenix brandishing its tail. When I sewed stitch by stitch, your two ends went together harmoniously to attach seam to seam. Indeed, your creative energy was endless.

I intended to live with you for a hundred years, but, alas, my needle! On the tenth day of the tenth month of this year, at the hour of the Dog (7–9 P.M.), while I was attaching a collar to a court robe in dim lamplight, you broke. You caught me unawares, and I was stunned. Alas, you had broken in two. My spirit was numbed and my soul flew away, as if my heart had been pulverized and my brain smashed. When I recovered from my long faint, I touched you and tried to put you back together, but it was no use. Not even the mystic arts of a renowned physician could prolong your life nor a village artisan patch you up. I felt as if I had lost an arm or a leg. How pitiful, my needle! I felt at my collar, but no trace of you remained.

Alas, it was my fault. I ended your innocent life, so whom else could I loathe or reproach? How can I ever hope to see an adept nature or ingenious talent like yours again? Your exquisite shape haunts my eyes, and your special endowments fill me with yearning. If you have any feeling, we will meet again in the underworld to continue our companionship. I hope we may share happiness and sorrow, and live and die together. Alas, my needle!

The Dispute of a Woman's Seven Companions

The lifelong companions of a woman are seven: a yardstick, a pair of scissors, a needle, blue and pink threads, a thimble, a long-handled iron, and a regular iron. The lady of a household is in charge of them all, and none of them can keep a secret from the others.

A certain lady who often used to work with the help of her seven indispensable companions one day felt sleepy and dozed off.

Brandishing her slender body, the yardstick said, "Friends, listen. I am so perceptive I can measure the long, the short, the narrow and the wide. It's because of me that my lady does not fail in her work. Don't you think my merits far exceed yours?"

Thereupon, the scissors grew angry. Shaking her long mouth, she replied, "Don't praise yourself so. Without my mouth nothing could be shaped or formed. It is only through my services that your measurements become reality. Hence my merits excel yours."

The needle reddened. "Don't argue, my two friends. However well you measure or cut, nothing is accomplished without me. So I am the first in merit," she retorted.

The blue and pink threads roared with laughter. "Don't talk nonsense. The

Translated by Peter H. Lee.

proverb says, 'Three bushels of pearls have to be strung to become a treasure.' What could you accomplish without us?"

Then the old thimble laughed. "Don't quarrel, threads. Let me cut in. I cover tactfully the sore spot in the fingers of the old and young, so that they can finish their work easily. So how can you say I'm without merit? Like a shield on the battlefield, I help to get the work done, no matter how difficult it is."

The long-handled iron, fuming with rage, moved forward in a single stride. "You all want to show off your talents, but listen to me if you don't want to be called fools. My foot can smooth out wrinkles and correct what is crooked and bent. It's my work you're taking the credit for. Without me, you'd be ashamed to face our mistress no matter how hard you tried."

Choking with laughter the iron said, "How true the word of the long-handled iron. Were it not for our services, who could talk about rewards?"

Their wordy warfare woke up the lady, who suddenly rose up in anger. "What merits are you talking about? It is my eyes and hands that make you do what you do. How can you wrangle impudently behind my back and indulge in self-praise?"

The yardstick sighed and mumbled, "How unkind and unfeeling is humankind. How could she measure anything without me? As if this is not enough, she uses me to thrash the maidservants. I've held out this long only because I happen to be strong, and it saddens me that our mistress takes no notice of this."

The scissors joined in tearfully, "How unkind my mistress is. Day after day she forces open my mouth and cuts thick and hard fabrics just as she pleases. But if I am not to her liking, she strikes my two cheeks with an iron hammer, accuses me of having thick lips or blunt edges and whets me. For her to talk like that after all she's done to me."

The needle heaved a long sigh, "I was made from an iron stick belonging to the fairy Ma-ku of Mount Ti'en-t'ai and polished for ten years on a rock: She inserts thick and thin threads through my eye and makes a hole with my leg through all kinds of dress goods. What an odious chore! Overcome with fatigue, sometimes I pierce her under the fingernail and draw blood, but there's no relief."

The blue and pink threads chimed in, "How can we tell all our sorrow? Clothes of men and women, fine quilts, children's colorful dresses—how could one sew a single seam of these without us? When lazy ladies and girls pull us through the needle's eye too hard, or when we cannot pass through it easily, they curse us in unspeakable language. What is our crime, and how can we bear this grief?"

"My resentment is immeasurable," the long-handled iron complained. "For what retribution am I stuck in a brazier day and night throughout the seasons? After children have used me sloppily to iron the clothes for their dolls, they stick me in any old way until some woman picks me up and scolds me for not being warm enough, or for being too light or too heavy. They make me feel there is no place for me in the world."

"Your sorrow is like mine," the iron said, "so there is no point rehearsing it. They put burning charcoal in my mouth; it's like the tyrant Chou's cruel punishments of roasting and branding. Only because my face is tough and hardened can I bear it. And that's not all. Lazy women will put off their work for ten or even fifteen days. Then they blame me for the wrinkles that will not come out."

The old thimble leaped forward and waved her hand, saying, "Listen, girls. I'm half dead from overwork too; stop chattering on and on. If our mistress hears, all your sins will be visited on me."

"What if she does?" all replied. "She cannot manage without us."

The lady finally scolded, "You dared to criticize my behavior while I was asleep," and dismissed them all. They were withdrawing in despair when the old thimble fell prostrate. "The young ones acted thoughtlessly. Please calm your anger and forgive them," she begged the lady.

Thereupon the lady called all of them together. "I forgive you for the sake of the old thimble," she said. She promised the thimble never to be parted from her, and to this day she cherishes her as her most intimate friend.

"The Birth of Tristram." Woodcut from Wynkyn de Worde's *Morte D'Arthur*, 1498. Rylands Library, Manchester, England.

SECTION IV
Medieval Europe

The term *Middle Ages,* (or *medieval*) coined during the Renaissance in Italy, was not intended as a compliment. It looks backward to ancient Rome and forward to a beginning Renaissance, dismissing what happened in between. The most striking aspect of medieval literature in western Europe is variety. Despite the predominance of Christianity, there is influence from ancient Roman and Germanic pagan cultures, and to a lesser extent from Islamic and Jewish cultures as well. Despite the prevalence of Latin as the language of literacy, there are literary traditions of some sophistication in both Germanic vernaculars (German, Anglo-Saxon, Old Norse) and Romance vernaculars (Provençal, French, Italian, Gallego-Portuguese, Spanish). The literature of this period takes many forms—from learned treatises in prose and learned allegories in poetry, religious sermons and saints' lives, to love lyrics, courtly romances, heroic epics, and animal fables. But with all the different influences, languages, and genres, common sources and common themes provide continuity across the many centuries and peoples of medieval Europe. The classics of ancient Rome from the Mediterranean, the Judeo-Christian bible from the Near East, the myths of King Arthur and his knights from the Celtic northwest, and the concept of courtly love from southern France make their way into virtually all medieval literatures.

Medieval literature begins in the last years of the ancient Roman Empire, as that civilization was being attacked spiritually by Christianity and physically by various tribes. The early fathers of the church (e.g., Augustine), like the philosopher Boethius, were Roman-educated and wrote in Latin for Roman audiences, but their works were formative influences on Christian thought and literature throughout the Middle Ages.

Augustine, the major theologian of the early Catholic faith in the West, traces in his *Confessions* his own conversion from pagan to Christian, from self-centered, lustful, and ambitious man of the world to devoted servant of God, in part through episodes that most of his readers can identify with. Boethius, whose writings transmitted classical philosophy, Platonic and Aristotelian, to the early Middle Ages, presents himself in *The Consolation of Philosophy* as an intellectual caught up in self-pity, who must be led by the figure of Philosophy (classical learning and logical thinking) to understand and accept his fate within the larger scheme of good and evil in the world. Most of the issues that concern these early writers and the philosophical and allegorical modes they use to deal with them recur frequently in succeeding centuries, and their works offer powerful models to later writers and messages that have relevance for later readers.

The historical struggle between Christianity and pagan religions is reflected in the stories of early martyrs.[1] Some of the twelfth-century French epics (*chansons de geste* like the *Song of Roland*) also draw on historic conflicts between pagans and Christians, particularly Saracens and Franks in Spain, but these are treated as military rather than intellectual encounters. For the most part, it is the personal struggle that dominates the texts presented in this medieval section, whether in moral terms — individuals struggling against their baser instincts — or in social terms — individual needs in opposition to the claims of society. The settings of these conflicts are vastly different from those we face today, but the human problems, social and moral, are quite similar at times.

Hildegard of Bingen, a renowned abbess of the same period, preached and wrote against the corruption of her world; her contemporaries, even religious and secular leaders, widely sought her advice because of her visions in which the voice of God spoke to her. She does not reveal her motives as openly as the monk Abelard,[2] but her struggles both with herself and with authority are nonetheless revealed in her letters, while her extraordinary powers of imagination are evident in her visions and poems.

Jean de Meun, a learned man of the thirteenth century, continued in a more polemical and didactic vein the open-ended *Romance of the Rose,* a poem that Guillaume de Lorris had written as an allegory of young, self-centered love. Dante (1265–1321), a lyric poet and author of prose treatises in philosophy, language, and political theory, brings together the moral, philosophical, religious, and cultural issues of earlier writers with political concerns of his own time and experience in an all-encompassing narrative poem, *The Divine Comedy*. The

---

1. The dramas of the tenth-century nun, Hrotsvit, offer an interesting example, with a touch of early feminism and sometimes with humor. Her Christian martyrs are mainly women who expose the emptiness of the faith of pagan men by their courageous acceptance of torture and death and also by their learning and eloquence.

2. Abelard, one of the most important philosophers in the early twelfth century, recounts in "The Story of His Misfortunes" the history of his problems with what he sees as a hostile world, though he provokes much of the hostility by his intellectual arrogance and his self-indulgence, particularly the showing up of his teachers and the seduction of his brilliant student Heloise.

Comedy sets the conversion of the individual from sin to grace within the vast context of contrasting worlds, the corrupt world of Hell and the ideal world of Paradise, which together house an impressive array of characters from contemporary life, history, and literature. They tell their own stories of political, moral, or emotional struggles, some in victory, some in defeat, driven by the same kinds of lust and ambition that moved Augustine and that move us still today.

Much later in the fourteenth century, Christine de Pizan (c. 1364–c. 1429) wrote an allegory that also deals with religion, history, philosophy, and the arts, but in a world entirely inhabited and fashioned by women. *The City of Ladies* is her answer to the vast literature of misogyny she had been exposed to. Christine's interest in learning had been encouraged by her father, a physician and astrologer at the court of Charles V of France, and by various powerful friends, including the king and the chancellor of the University of Paris. But it was only when her husband died, leaving her as the sole support for herself, her children, and her mother, that she used that learning to write on a variety of subjects — from warfare and political theory to biography, love, and women. She went on to become a highly successful author, with an international reputation and invitations from English and Italian courts.

The focus of writers mentioned so far is on the morality and behavior of the individual, though some are also concerned with the effects of individual actions on society. Their mode of presentation is mainly prose or allegorical poetry, often entertaining and moving but primarily didactic, unlike the lyrics, heroic epics, and romances, secular genres composed primarily for entertainment; these lighter works, however, can also carry serious messages about personal conduct and social responsibility. The lyrics offer a brief but intense expression of the human condition, the emotions of grief, desire, joy, anger, unsatisfied yearning or frustrated desire for a love that either is never satisfied or can no longer be satisfied, fear of death and decay, or religious devotion. The Provençal lyrics of the twelfth century, such as those of Bernart de Ventadorn, introduce the concept of "courtly love," a love befitting a member of a court, which involves devoted service and striving to be worthy of the person loved, and which contributes to the quality of life at the court. This concept, with its idealization of the beloved, makes its way into other vernacular lyric and romance traditions, and continues to influence their treatment of love, even when they move beyond the original courtly and aristocratic audiences. Indeed, with considerable modification, the influence of such lyrics has persisted to the present.

The narrative genres of heroic epic and romance fulfill a different purpose. Though the plot may hinge on the hero's conflicting motivations or desires, the resolution of such conflict must be in harmony with the needs and values of his society. In the epics the hero's story is part of the history of his people, and his death may well mean their destruction as in *Beowulf*. To serve society, the hero must perform heroic actions, fighting monsters or defeating hostile armies, and these actions can provoke envy and betrayal, even death. Violent deaths in a heroic society demand revenge; the endless cycle of fighting and death ultimately means the end of a people or of a dynasty. The mood of epic is therefore tragic, while courtly romance is comic (in the sense of ending happily). In Arthurian romance the setting is not historic, but ideal; in this world, conflicts can be resolved, and death, when it occurs, is not allowed to determine the action. The values of Arthur's court are ideal social values: justice, defense of the weak and oppressed, condemnation of evil or violence for its own sake. Individuals learn to harmonize their personal needs and desires with the demands of their societies, so they can satisfy the one while serving the other. Love is an inspiration to social service rather than an obstacle to it.

At least, that is true of the genre of medieval romance in its early stages, in most of the works of twelfth and early thirteenth-century French and German poets, whom Chrétien de Troyes and Wolfram von Eschenbach represent here. It is not true of the many versions of the Tristan story, where the adulterous nature of the love puts it into insoluble conflict with society. It is not always true in the *Lais* of Marie de France (late twelfth century), where the social setting, court, family, or marriage can be oppressive and sterile, and the trapped individual can only be rescued by a love that is freely given. Nor is it true of the later Arthurian romances—the thirteenth-century prose romances, particularly the Grail romances, or their last medieval expression in Thomas Malory's *Morte D'Arthur* (c. 1471) where the problems can no longer be resolved because they have struck at the center of the court, the king and queen, and because the Grail quest is now perceived as an individual quest for salvation that takes the best knights away from the secular world, instead of inspiring them in its service.

To some extent, the seeds of trouble were always present in the Arthurian court, even in the earliest romances of Chrétien, where court customs threatened to provoke hostilities, but they were contained there. The problems of envy and jealousy, of lust for undeserved honor and power, are inherent in the human condition. They are treated satirically in the animal stories collected around Renard the Fox beginning in the late twelfth century and in the fables of Marie de France. These and other aspects are satirized by Chaucer (c. 1340–c. 1400), on all levels of society and in a variety of literary genres, in *Canterbury Tales*.

There is satire and much else in the Spanish texts of the late Middle Ages included here. Juan Ruiz's *Book of Good Love* has been described variously as an erotic pseudo-autobiography and an "art of love," and as a sober example of proper Christian behavior and an "art of poetry"; its multicultural perspective reflects the coexistence in medieval Spain of Christians, Jews, and Moors. Equally rich and ambiguous is Fernando de Rojas's *Celestina,* which has been called a tragicomedy, the first European novel, and a "novel in disguise." Janus-like, it looks both backward toward medieval literary and philosophical concerns and forward toward new interrogations of these traditions and the ensuing development of new forms, while presenting individual human lives in a society that it views as chaotically meaningless and godless.

Historical Background

Two momentous decisions of the Roman emperor Constantine (ruled 310–337) helped set the stage for the Middle Ages. In 313, Constantine extended official recognition to Christianity, whose adherents had been growing in both numbers and wealth. In 330, he moved the capital east to the ancient Greek city of Byzantium, renamed Constantinople (which is present-day Istanbul).

By 400, Christianity had become the state religion, and the empire was partitioned for administrative purposes. The Eastern, or Byzantine, empire survived into the fifteenth century. The Western empire, long decaying internally, collapsed over the course of the fifth century, overwhelmed by a massive influx of

Germanic tribes. The last Roman emperor was deposed by a Germanic chieftain named Odoacer in 476.

The ensuing thousand years — to roughly 1500 — are conventionally called the Middle Ages. The early Middle Ages (to 1000) was a time of invasion and instability. Determined to reassert its authority over the West, Constantinople sent the Ostrogoths, a neighboring Germanic tribe, to retake Italy. Their leader, Theodoric, reinstituted Roman law and ruled until 526. Elsewhere, Germanic kingdoms rose and fell — Visigoths in Spain, Franks in France — whose rulers acknowledged the sovereignty of Constantinople and were given Roman titles in return. All in all, the period saw a gradual interpenetration of cultures rather than the total eclipse of one by the other.

After Theodoric's death, Byzantine armies conquered North Africa and Italy. The Eastern empire's presence in Italy was reduced to a mere foothold, however, when the peninsula was overrun from the north by yet another Germanic tribe, the Lombards. North Africa in turn fell to an entirely new regional power, Islam: during the seventh and eighth centuries, Arab armies consolidated an empire that reached from the borders of Byzantium across Africa and up into Spain. Islam retained a strong presence in Spain throughout the Middle Ages, and Arab ships dominated the Mediterranean for several centuries. Ultimately, it was not Constantinople but the Latin Church that reestablished the frontiers of Europe. Having grown up within the empire, the Church had adopted imperial organization, with an administrative hierarchy of clergy in provincial cities and a central authority, the pope, in Rome.

The Church was central to the medieval world: when the kingdoms of the Middle Ages thought of themselves as part of a whole, it was not Europe they called it, but Christendom. From the clergy, schooled in Latin, came most of the literate members of society. Education remained in the hands of the Church. Monasteries were important scholarly as well as spiritual centers, and it was in their libraries that the classical texts known to the early Middle Ages survived. Convents offered education and some realm of authority to women, but only to daughters of the nobility. Male monasteries, too, were largely the province of the well-born and/or well-off, closed to all but the most gifted poor men. In general, the lines of literacy in the early Middle Ages were less male/female then religious/secular. Later, as universities became centers of learning, dominated by the clergy, women were denied entry even to the profession of medicine, which had long been open to them. Certainly women were excluded from the priesthood and therefore from the church hierarchy. But outside the Church women had more access to power than misogynist doctrines would seem to suggest. When there was no male heir, women might inherit land and, in some cases, rule it. In the absence of a husband or the minority of a son, women frequently exercised authority as regents.

The Church also had a hand in secular government. Bishops, abbots, and abbesses (into the twelfth century) were drawn from the nobility and some ruled as lords over extensive estates. These swore fealty as vassals to secular lords and fulfilled a vassal's military obligations: a bishop might even lead troops in battle. Later government bureaucracy relied on the services of clerics because of their training and literacy, and some higher clergy held administrative or advisory positions. The relationship between church and state, however, was rarely untroubled, and the history of the Middle Ages traces an ongoing struggle between popes and kings to define respective spheres of authority.

In the secular sphere, different forces dominated in different periods. The early Middle Ages witnessed the ascendancy of the Franks. Under their leader Clovis, who was converted with the help of his Christian wife Clotilda—not an unusual circumstance—the Franks were the first important conquest of the Church in the sixth century. During the next two centuries, they extended their rule over much of France and into Germany. In 732 Frankish troops turned back Arab armies at Tours, an important battle that ended Islamic attempts to push beyond the Pyrenees.

Under Charlemagne (who ruled from 768 to 814), Frankish dominion reached its height. Charlemagne conquered the Lombards in Italy, extended German holdings, and pushed Frankish power over the Pyrenees into Moorish Spain. In 800, Pope Leo III crowned Charlemagne "Emperor and Augustus," recognizing a new Western empire and sending a signal of independence to Constantinople. Charlemagne ruled from Aachen in present-day Germany, where his court was the center of a brief intellectual and artistic renaissance, but his empire was short-lived. His grandsons divided it into three kingdoms, which were later consolidated into two; these developed separately as France and Germany. Legends of Charlemagne's achievements persisted, however, furnishing a rich subject for later medieval literature.

The ninth and tenth centuries brought new waves of invasions: Norsemen (northmen, also known as Vikings), who raided coastal towns and moved inland up rivers; Magyar horsemen (Hungarians), who swept in from the east; Arab ships that attacked from the Mediterranean. The Vikings in particular had a lasting influence on the new civilization of Europe, especially through their assimilation in Germany and their presence in France, where as the Normans they controlled a large territory. The Norman Conquest in 1066 placed the French-speaking ex-Vikings legitimately on the English throne, affecting the subsequent history not only of England but also of the English language: hitherto purely Germanic, English entered into a new cycle of development that integrated French (Latin) elements.

The Magyar invasions were turned back by Otto I, the German king who emerged as the most powerful ruler since Charlemagne. His kingdom united an expanded Germany with northern Italy, and he was crowned emperor by the pope in 961. For the rest of the Middle Ages and beyond, Germany formed the core of the Holy Roman Empire, the nominal protector of the papacy. German kings had the strongest claim to the imperial throne, though they could only secure it through coronation in Rome. Disagreements between emperors and popes over whose authority was supreme provoked the most explosive of the many medieval confrontations between spiritual and secular authority.

The early Middle Ages also saw the development of feudalism, a hierarchy of loyalties and obligations that structured medieval society. Based on the holding of land by one lord from another, the central relationship of feudalism was the bond between lord and vassal. A vassal pledged fealty (loyalty) to a lord in return for a fief—an estate from the lord's holdings. Peasants worked the land either as serfs, essentially owned by the local lord, or as his tenants. The vassal might in turn have vassals of his own; the lord might be vassal to another lord. The obligations between lord and vassal were many, but the fundamental exchange was that of the lord to protect his vassal and the vassal to serve his lord, especially militarily. In theory, feudalism produced a hierarchy of vassalage that extended from the lowliest knight to the king—a gigantic cavalry in perpetual readiness for mobilization. In reality, feudalism suffered fragmentation and fostered a powerful regional nobility, technically vassals to the king, yet largely autonomous.

Knights, originally mounted soldiers quartered in a lord's household as a private army, came to constitute a lesser nobility, often holding fiefs and earning a large degree of independence. With the increasingly elaborate and ritualized character of knightly warfare and the influence of courtly literature, knighthood became central to the nobility's self-image, and there grew around it a system of ethical ideals known as chivalry (from *chevalier,* the French word for knight). A fusion of Christian and military values, chivalry emphasized honor, bravery, courtesy, piety, and loyalty. During the Crusades—the military expeditions undertaken by the European Christians in the eleventh, twelfth, and thirteenth centuries to recover the Holy Land from the Moslems—chivalry found its ultimate expression in the creation of knightly orders and monastic communities of knights such as the Knights Templar.

The clergy formed its own privileged class, although some were also feudal lords. The upper ranks usually came from the nobility, while the lower clergy—especially parish priests—tended to come from the peasantry and were often little better educated than their flock.

The high Middle Ages (1100–1300) began with a sense of confidence, with the borders of Europe largely secured. The economy, in decline since the late Roman empire, started to revive. A newly rich merchant class evolved and spread throughout Europe. As the economy revived, so did the cities and towns, home not only to merchants but also to artisans and tradespeople. To the three classes of feudal society—the nobles, the church, and the peasants—the towns added a new and disturbing "middle class" virtually outside the feudal system.

The Church's power and prestige reached its apex. In 1095 the pope declared the First Crusade, calling on the sovereigns of Europe to retake the Holy Land from Islam. Although faith certainly played a role in the Crusades, the expeditions—eight in all—increasingly became acts of plunder and conquest, deepening the mutual antagonism between the Latin West and East whether Byzantium or Islam. Viewed from a political or religious standpoint, the Crusades were a failure. In the long run, their contribution lay in stimulating trade.

Intellectually, the high Middle Ages were marked by the dissemination of Roman learning and the recovery of Greek learning from the Moors in Spain. Islamic scholars had preserved the works of Greek thinkers and had themselves made important advances in mathematics and other fields. Latin texts and basic works of Roman law were also newly available. Universities began to form in Bologna in the twelfth century and in Paris in the thirteenth century. A major project of medieval scholars was the reconciliation of Church doctrine with the newly recovered works of Aristotle, a synthesis of faith and reason.

Politically, England and France began a gradual movement toward national monarchies. Lawyers staffed government bureaucracies replacing feudal custom with centralized Roman law. Nobility, clergy, and townspeople organized councils to represent their concerns in the shifting power structure, laying the foundations for parliamentary systems of government. The Holy Roman Empire, in contrast, began a long process of fragmentation that saw Germany splinter into ever smaller, increasingly autonomous principalities. In Italy independent cities made rich by trade annexed surrounding lands to form city-states. Neither Germany nor Italy would unify as a centralized nation-state until the nineteenth century.

The late Middle Ages (1300–1500) were a troubled period of transition.

Crop failures led to recurrent famine; trade routes that had brought wealth now brought disease, and pestilence swept Europe. The most famous plague, the Black Death, struck around 1348 and wiped out as much as two-fifths of the population. The futile Hundred Years' War between France and England (1337–1453), fought entirely on French soil, wreaked terrible suffering on the population. New military technology—gunpowder, artillery, and professional armies—made knights increasingly obsolete and finally destroyed the power base of the feudal structure. Gangs of disbanded mercenary troops roamed the countryside, causing as much terror as the war itself. The disastrous conditions of the time ignited social unrest in three great peasant revolts and many lesser urban riots. France emerged from the war as a centralized state with a strong monarchy, but not before the duchy of Burgundy almost carved out its own empire. England gave up its claims to French soil and turned its attention to becoming a naval power, but not before suffering a lengthy civil war of succession.

Emerging national sentiments lessened the hold of the Church, and the papacy, in disarray and disrepute for most of the late Middle Ages, lost much of its political influence. Intellectually, the Church was increasingly challenged by an emphasis on rational inquiry, and the synthetic systems of the high Middle Ages crumbled. Classical humanism flourished in Italy; independently of the Church-sponsored universities, humanist scholars pursued knowledge for its own sake, reestablishing a tradition of secular education whose greatest weapon would be the newly invented printed book. Even spiritually, the Church was losing ground, and internal dissent and calls for reform would soon culminate in the Protestant Reformation.

Spain, whose small Christian principalities had been slowly pushing back the Moorish frontier, suddenly arrived as a major power when the kingdoms of Castile and Aragon merged through marriage. In 1492 the Spanish recaptured the last Moorish stronghold at Granada, exiling the Jews and attempting to convert the Muslims by force. In the same year Spain sponsored a voyage by an explorer named Christopher Columbus, who failed in his mission to find a sea route to India but accidentally stumbled onto something of even greater potential.

Further Reading

Erich Auerbach, *Mimesis*. Princeton: Princeton University Press, 1953.

Marc Bloch, *The Feudal Society*. Chicago: University of Chicago Press, 1961.

Caroline Walker Bynum, *Jesus as Mother: Studies in the Spirituality of the High Middle Ages*. Berkeley: University of California Press, 1982.

Norman F. Cantor, *The Meaning of the Middle Ages*. Boston: Allyn and Bacon, 1973.

Ernst Curtius, *European Literature and the Decline of the High Middle Ages*. Princeton: Princeton University Press, Bollingen, 1953.

Joan Ferrante, *Woman as Image in Medieval Literature*. New York: Columbia University Press, 1975. (Labyrinth Paperback.)

Penelope Schine Gold, *The Lady and the Virgin*. Chicago: Chicago University Press, 1985.

Frederick Goldin, *The Mirror of Narcissus in the Courtly Love Lyric*. Ithaca: Cornell University Press, 1967.

Robert Hanning, *The Individual in Twelfth Century Romance*. New Haven: Yale University Press, 1977.

Friedrich Heer, *The Medieval World*. New York: Mentor, 1961.

J. Huizinga, *The Waning of the Middle Ages*. New York: Doubleday Anchor, 1973.

W. T. H. Jackson, *The Literature of the Middle Ages*. New York: Columbia University Press, 1960.

SAINT AUGUSTINE
[AURELIUS AUGUSTINUS] (354–430)
Roman North Africa

In the *Confessions,* the first autobiography in Western Christendom, Augustine tells the story of his early life in what is today Algeria and of his conversion to Christianity. After 376, he went to Rome where he taught rhetoric and then to Milan. He was converted in 387, joined a monastic community, and in 395, became the bishop of Hippo, where he died during the siege of the Vandals. Beginning with his childhood, and writing in Latin, he describes his experiences as the son of an educated pagan father and a Christian mother, St. Monica, whose devotion was ultimately an important influence on him, and he dwells on the defects in his character: his impatience with his studies and his delight in bouts of delinquency like the theft of the pears, the incident described in the first selection here; his pursuit of sex and the distractions of the stage when he is sent to school in the city; and his early career, teaching young men to practice law for profit, preferring honesty but clearly not rejecting manipulation of the truth ("the tricks of pleading"), while living with a woman to whom he was not married. In many details Augustine led the life typical of a middle-class suburban youth, with all the advantages of devoted parents, good education, and easy access to a profitable career, aided by native intelligence and abetted by a desire for comfort and pleasure. It is not the way we might expect the life of a major saint and theologian of the Catholic faith to begin, nor is it the way the lives of most saints begin. Augustine's writing holds us with the honesty of its introspection and the liveliness of its description.

from Confessions

Book 2 [Stealing the Pears]

It is certain, O Lord, that theft is punished by your law, the law that is written in men's hearts and cannot be erased however sinful they are. For no thief can bear that another thief should steal from him, even if he is rich and the other is driven to it by want. Yet I was willing to steal, and steal I did, although I was not compelled by any lack, unless it were the lack of a sense of justice or a distaste for what was right and a greedy love of doing wrong. For of what I stole I already had plenty, and much better at that, and I had no wish to enjoy the things I coveted by stealing, but only to enjoy the theft itself and the sin. There was a pear-tree near our vineyard, loaded with fruit that was attractive neither to look at nor to taste. Late one night a band of ruffians, myself included, went off to shake down the fruit and carry it away, for we had continued our games out of doors until well after dark, as was our pernicious habit. We took away an enormous quantity of

Translated by R. S. Pine-Coffin.

pears, not to eat them ourselves, but simply to throw them to the pigs. Perhaps we ate some of them, but our real pleasure consisted in doing something that was forbidden.

Look into my heart, O God, the same heart on which you took pity when it was in the depths of the abyss. Let my heart now tell you what prompted me to do wrong for no purpose, and why it was only my own love of mischief that made me do it. The evil in me was foul, but I loved it. I loved my own perdition and my own faults, not the things for which I committed wrong, but the wrong itself. My soul was vicious and broke away from your safe keeping to seek its own destruction, looking for no profit in disgrace but only for disgrace itself.

Book 3 [Love and Lust]

I went to Carthage, where I found myself in the midst of a hissing cauldron of lust. I had not yet fallen in love, but I was in love with the idea of it, and this feeling that something was missing made me despise myself for not being more anxious to satisfy the need. I began to look around for some object for my love, since I badly wanted to love something. I had no liking for the safe path without pitfalls, for although my real need was for you, my God, who are the food of the soul, I was not aware of this hunger. I felt no need for the food that does not perish, not because I had had my fill of it, but because the more I was starved of it the less palatable it seemed. Because of this my soul fell sick. It broke out in ulcers and looked about desperately for some material, worldly means of relieving the itch which they caused. But material things, which have no soul, could not be true objects for my love. To love and to have my love returned was my heart's desire, and it would be all the sweeter if I could also enjoy the body of the one who loved me.

So I muddied the stream of friendship with the filth of lewdness and clouded its clear waters with hell's black river of lust. And yet, in spite of this rank depravity, I was vain enough to have ambitions of cutting a fine figure in the world. I also fell in love, which was a snare of my own choosing. My God, my God of mercy, how good you were to me, for you mixed much bitterness in that cup of pleasure! My love was returned and finally shackled me in the bonds of its consummation. In the midst of my joy I was caught up in the coils of trouble, for I was lashed with the cruel, fiery rods of jealousy and suspicion, fear, anger, and quarrels.

Book 3 [The Attractions of the Theatre]

I was much attracted by the theatre, because the plays reflected my own unhappy plight and were tinder to my fire. Why is it that men enjoy feeling sad at the sight of tragedy and suffering on the stage, although they would be most unhappy if they had to endure the same fate themselves? Yet they watch the plays because they hope to be made to feel sad, and the feeling of sorrow is what they enjoy. What miserable delirium this is! The more a man is subject to such suffering himself, the more easily he is moved by it in the theatre. Yet when he suffers himself, we call it misery: when he suffers out of sympathy with others, we call it pity. But what sort of pity can we really feel for an imaginary scene on the stage? The audience is not called upon to offer help but only to feel sorrow, and the more they are pained the more they applaud the author. Whether this human agony is based on fact or is simply imaginary, if it is acted so badly that the audience is not moved to sorrow, they leave the theatre in a disgruntled and critical mood; whereas, if they are made to feel pain, they stay to the end watching happily.

This shows that sorrow and tears can be enjoyable. Of course, everyone wants to be happy; but even if no one likes being sad, is there just the one exception that, because we enjoy pitying others, we welcome their misfortunes, without which we could not pity them? If so, it is because friendly feelings well up in us like the waters of a spring. But what course do these waters follow? Where do they flow? Why do they trickle away to join that stream of boiling pitch, the hideous flood of lust? For by their own choice they lose themselves and become absorbed in it. They are diverted from their true course and deprived of their original heavenly calm.

Book 4 [Playing Shepherd to the Wind]

During those years I was a teacher of the art of public speaking.[1] Love of money had gained the better of me and for it I sold to others the means of coming off the better in debate. But you know, Lord, that I preferred to have honest pupils, in so far as honesty has any meaning nowadays, and I had no evil intent when I taught the tricks of pleading, for I never meant them to be used to get the innocent condemned but, if the occasion arose, to save the lives of the guilty. From a distance, my God, you saw me losing my foothold on this treacherous ground, but through clouds of smoke you also saw a spark of good faith in me; for though, as I schooled my pupils, I was merely abetting their futile designs and their schemes of duplicity, nevertheless I did my best to teach them honestly.

In those days I lived with a woman, not my lawful wedded wife but a mistress whom I had chosen for no special reason but that my restless passions had alighted on her. But she was the only one and I was faithful to her. Living with her I found out by my own experience the difference between the restraint of the marriage alliance, contracted for the purpose of having children, and a bargain struck for lust, in which the birth of children is begrudged, though, if they come, we cannot help but love them.

I remember too that once, when I had decided to enter a competition for reciting dramatic verse, a sorcerer sent to ask me how much I would pay him to make certain that I won. I loathed and detested these foul rites and told him that even if the prize were a crown of gold that would last for ever, I would not let even a fly be killed to win it. For he would have slaughtered living animals in his ritual, and by means of these offerings he would have pretended to invoke the aid of his demons in my favour. But, O God of my heart, it was not from a pure love of you that I rejected this wickedness. I had not learnt how to love you, for when I

---

1. The art of public speaking is rhetoric—the art of using language to persuade an audience, here in a court of law.

thought of you I imagined you as some splendid being, but entirely physical. Does not the soul which pines for such fantasies *break its troth with you?* Does it not trust in false hopes and *play shepherd to the wind?* But while I would not let this man offer sacrifice for me to his devils, all the time I was offering myself as a sacrifice to them because of my false beliefs. For if we play shepherd to the wind, we find pasture for the devils, because by straying from the truth we give them food for laughter and fill their cup of pleasure.

BOETHIUS [ANICIUS MANLIUS SEVERINUS] (c. 480–524)
Roman Empire

The Roman philosopher Boethius wrote Latin commentaries and translations of Greek philosophers and treatises on logic and music that were major sources of medieval learning. Accused of treason, he was imprisoned by Theodoric, king of the Ostrogoths. While awaiting execution, he wrote *The Consolation of Philosophy,* which influenced medieval poets as well as philosophers. His personification of Philosophy is a model for Jean de Meun's Reason (in *The Roman de la Rose*) and Dante's Philosophy (in his *Convivio* or *The Banquet*) and his Virgil and Beatrice (in the *Divine Comedy*), to name only the most obvious. A personification of learning and logical thought, she comes to the imprisoned philosopher when he is consumed by self-pity and giving vent to his grief in poetry. She appears as a separate character, though in fact she represents the learning and logic that is already present in his mind but is not functioning. By the end of the work, which is written mainly in prose, with poems interspersed, she has brought him around to see himself not as the victim of an unjust fate but as someone who is finally happier than those fortune seems to favor; in their evil and ignorance, they are unable to achieve the good that is really desired by all, while he, for all his apparent misfortune, has achieved it, and with it a power and a reality they can never attain.

from *The Consolation of Philosophy*

BOOK 1

[Philosophy and the Muses]

While I was quietly thinking these thoughts over to myself and giving vent to my sorrow with the help of my pen, I became aware of a woman standing over me.

Translated by V. E. Watts.

She was of awe-inspiring appearance, her eyes burning and keen beyond the usual power of men. She was so full of years that I could hardly think of her as of my own generation, and yet she possessed a vivid colour and undiminished vigour. It was difficult to be sure of her height, for sometimes she was of average human size, while at other times she seemed to touch the very sky with the top of her head, and when she lifted herself even higher, she pierced it and was lost to human sight. Her clothes were made of imperishable material, of the finest thread woven with the most delicate skill. (Later she told me that she had made them with her own hands.) Their colour, however, was obscured by a kind of film as of long neglect, like statues covered in dust. On the bottom hem could be read the embroidered Greek letter Pi, and on the top hem the Greek letter Theta.[1] Between the two a ladder of steps rose from the lower to the higher letter. Her dress had been torn by the hands of marauders who had each carried off such pieces as he could get. There were some books in her right hand, and in her left hand she held a sceptre.

At the sight of the Muses of Poetry at my bedside dictating words to accompany my tears, she became angry.

"Who," she demanded, her piercing eyes alight with fire, "has allowed these hysterical sluts to approach this sick man's bedside? They have no medicine to ease his pains, only sweetened poisons to make them worse. These are the very women who kill the rich and fruitful harvest of Reason with the barren thorns of Passion. They habituate men to their sickness of mind instead of curing them. If as usual it was only some ordinary man you were carrying off a victim of your blandishments, it would matter little to me—there would be no harm done to my work. But this man has been nourished on the philosophies of Zeno and Plato.[2] Sirens is a better name for you and your deadly enticements: be gone, and leave him for my own Muses to heal and cure."

These rebukes brought blushes of shame into the Muses' cheeks, and with downcast eyes they departed in a dismal company. Tears had partly blinded me, and I could not make out who this woman of such imperious authority was. I could only fix my eyes on the ground overcome with surprise and wait in silence for what she would do next. She came closer and sat down on the edge of my bed. I felt her eyes resting on my face, downcast and lined with grief. Then sadly she began to recite . . .

[The Good and Strong, the Bad, the Weak]

Then I cried out in wonder at the magnitude of her promises. "Not that I don't think you can do it," I said. "Only do not keep me waiting, now that you have whetted my appetite."

"First then," she said, "that the good are always strong and that the wicked always bereft of all power, these are facts you will be able to see, the one being

---

1. In another work, Boethius speaks of two kinds of philosophy, practical (moral philosophy and ethics) and theoretical or speculative (theology, metaphysics and phys-

   ics), represented here by the first letters of their names in Greek, Pi and Theta.
2. The Greek philosopher Zeno is credited with the invention of logic.

proved by the other. For since good and evil are opposites, the weakness of evil is shown by establishing the strength of good, and vice versa. So to strengthen your confidence in my teaching, I will proceed along both ways and prove my assertions doubly.

"Now, there are two things on which all the performance of human activity depends, will and power. If either of them is lacking, there is no activity that can be performed. In the absence of the will, a man is unwilling to do something and therefore does not undertake it; and in the absence of the power to do it, the will is useless. So that if you see someone who wants to get something which he cannot get, you can be sure that what he has been lacking is the power to get what he wanted."

"It is obvious," I said, "and cannot be denied."

"And if you see a man who has done what he wanted, you will hardly doubt that he had the power to do it, will you?"

"No."

"Therefore, men's power or ability is to be judged by what they can do, and their weakness by what they can't do."

"I agree."

"Do you, then, remember how earlier in the argument we reached the conclusion that the instinctive direction of the human will, manifested through a variety of pursuits, was entirely towards happiness?"

"I remember that this was proved as well."

"And you recall that happiness is the good itself and similarly that since they seek happiness, all men desire the good?"

"Not so much recall it, as hold it fixed in my mind."

"So that without any difference of instinct all men, good and bad alike, strive to reach the good."

"Yes, that follows."

"But surely men become good by acquiring goodness?"

"Yes."

"So that good men obtain what they are looking for?"

"It seems so."

"But if the wicked obtained what they want—that is goodness—they could not be wicked?"

"No."

"Since, then, both groups want goodness, and one obtains it and the other doesn't, surely there can be no doubt of the power of the good and the weakness of the bad?"

"Anyone who does doubt it is no judge either of reality or the logic of argument."

"Again," she said, "suppose there were two men who are set the same natural task, and one of them performs and completes it by natural action, while the other cannot manage the natural action, but uses another method contrary to nature, and does not actually complete the task but approximates to someone completing it; which would you say had the more power?"

"I can guess what you mean," I said, "but I would like to have it more clearly put."

"You will not deny that the action of walking is natural and human, will you?"

"No."

"And presumably you have no doubt that it is the natural function of the feet?"

"No, indeed."

"If, then, one man is able to proceed on foot and goes walking, and another lacks the natural function of the feet and tries to walk on his hands, which may properly be considered the more able or powerful?"

"Ask me another! No one could doubt that the man who can do the natural action is more able than the one who can't."

"Well, the supreme good is the goal of good men and bad alike, and the good seek it by means of a natural activity—the exercise of their virtues—while the bad strive to acquire the very same thing by means of their various desires, which isn't a natural method of obtaining the good. Or don't you agree?"

"Yes, for what follows is also obvious; from what I have already admitted it follows that the good are powerful and the bad weak."

"You anticipate correctly. As the doctors like to think, it is a sign of a constitution strong and fighting back. But seeing you are so quick of understanding, I will pile the arguments on. Just think how great the weakness is that we see in wicked men; they can't even reach the goal to which almost by compulsion their natural inclination leads them. What if they were deserted by this great and almost invincible help, and nature ceased to show them the way?

"Think of the extent of the weakness impeding the wicked. It is not as if the prizes they failed to win were mere sports trophies. The quest in which they fail is the quest for the highest and most important of all things, and success is denied these wretched men in the very pursuit they toil at night and day to the exclusion of all else, the same pursuit in which the strength of the good stands out.

"If a man by walking could reach a point beyond which there was nowhere for him to go, you would consider him the champion at walking. In the same way you must judge the man who achieves the goal of all endeavour, beyond which there is nothing, to be supreme in power. The opposite of this is also true; those who do not gain it are obviously lacking in all power.

"For I ask you, what is the cause of this flight from virtue to vice? If you say it is because they do not know what is good, I shall ask what greater weakness is there than the blindness of ignorance. And if you say that they know what they ought to seek for, but pleasure sends them chasing off the wrong way, this way too, they are weak through lack of self control because they cannot resist vice. And if you say they abandon goodness and turn to vice knowingly and willingly, this way they not only cease to be powerful, but cease to be at all. Men who give up the common goal of all things that exist, thereby cease to exist themselves. Some may perhaps think it strange that we say that wicked men, who form the majority of men, do not exist; but that is how it is. I am not trying to deny the wickedness of the wicked; what I do deny is that their existence is absolute and complete existence. Just as you might call a corpse a dead man, but couldn't simply call it a man, so I would agree that the wicked are wicked, but could not agree that they have unqualified existence. A thing exists when it keeps its proper place and preserves its own nature. Anything which departs from this ceases to exist, because its existence depends on the preservation of its nature.

"To the objection that evil men do have power, I would say that this power of theirs comes from weakness rather than strength. For they would not have the power to do the evil they can if they could have retained the power of doing good. This power only makes it more clear that they can do nothing, for if, as we concluded a short time ago, evil is nothing, it is clear that since they can only do evil, the wicked can do nothing."

"Obviously."

"But I want you to understand the exact nature of the power we are talking about. A moment ago we decided that there is nothing with greater power than the supreme good."

"That is so."

"But supreme goodness cannot do evil."

"No."

"Now, no one thinks of human beings as omnipotent, do they?"

"Not unless they are mad."

"But men can do evil?"

"I only wish they couldn't."

"It is obvious, therefore, that since a power that can only do good is omnipotent, while human beings who can also do evil are not, these same human beings who can do evil are less powerful. In addition to this we have shown that all forms of power are to be included among those things worth pursuing, and that all these worthwhile objects of pursuit are related to the good as to a kind of aggregate of their nature. Now, the ability to commit a crime cannot be a form of goodness, and is therefore not worth pursuing. But all forms of power are worth seeking after, so that it is obvious that the ability to do evil is not a form of power.

"From all this the power of good men is obvious and, beyond all doubt, so is the weakness of bad men. And it is clear that what Plato said in the *Gorgias* is true, namely that only the wise can achieve their desire, while the wicked busy themselves with what gives pleasure without being able to achieve their real objective. Their actions depend on the belief that they are going to obtain the good they desire through the things that give them pleasure. But they do not obtain it, because evil things cannot reach happiness."

ANONYMOUS (EIGHTH CENTURY)
England

Dating from the eighth century, "The Seafarer," an Old English elegy of 124 lines in all, is composed in alliterative verse. The first section, given here, deals with the wonders and miseries of life at sea, whereas the second contains moral reflections on the brevity of human existence and the glories of the heavens. It is generally supposed that there are at least two authors of this text, which may be a secular poem with a Christian appendage, or an allegory for human exile upon life's waters. Ezra Pound's rendering of the first part, free and remarkably evocative, conveys, as few texts have, a feeling of and for the sea.

The Seafarer

May I for my own self song's truth reckon,
Journey's jargon, how I in harsh days
Hardship endured oft.
Better breast-cares have I abided,
Known on my keel many a care's hold,   5
And dire sea-surge, and there I oft spent
Narrow nightwatch nigh the ship's head
While she tossed close to cliffs. Coldly afflicted,
My feet were by frost benumbed.
Chill its chains are; chafing sighs   10
Hew my heart round and hunger begot
Mere-weary[1] mood. Lest man know not
That he on dry land loveliest liveth,
List how I, care-wretched, on ice-cold sea,
Weathered the winter, wretched outcast   15
Deprived of my kinsmen;
Hung with hard ice-flakes, where hail-scur[2] flew,
There I heard naught save the harsh sea
And ice-cold wave, at whiles the swan cries,
Did for my games the gannet's clamor,   20
Sea-fowls' loudness was for me laughter,
The mews' singing all my mead-drink.
Storms, on the stone-cliffs beaten, fell on the stern
In icy feathers; full oft the eagle screamed
With spray on his pinion.
              Not any protector   25
May make merry man faring needy.
This he little believes, who aye in winsome life
Abides 'mid burghers some heavy business,
Wealthy and wine-flushed, how I weary oft
Must bide above brine.   30
Neareth nightshade, snoweth from north,
Frost froze the land, hail fell on earth then,
Corn of the coldest. Nathless[3] there knocketh now

Translated by Ezra Pound.

---

1. Sea-weary.   3. Notwithstanding.
2. Hail-storms.

The heart's thought that I on high streams
The salt-wavy tumult traverse alone.   35
Moaneth always my mind's lust
That I fare forth, that I afar hence
Seek out a foreign fastness.
For this there's no moody-lofty man over earth's midst,
Not though he be given his good, but will have in his youth greed;   40
Nor his deed to the daring, nor his king to the faithful
But shall have his sorrow for sea-fare
Whatever his lord will.
He hath not heart for harping, nor in ring-having
Nor winsomeness to wife, nor world's delight   45
Nor any whit else save the wave's slash,
Yet longing comes upon him to fare forth on the water.
Bosque[4] taketh blossom, cometh beauty of berries,
Fields to fairness, land fares brisker,
All this admonisheth man eager of mood,   50
The heart turns to travel so that he then thinks
On flood-ways to be far departing.
Cuckoo calleth with gloomy crying,
He singeth summerward, bodeth sorrow,
The bitter heart's blood. Burgher knows not—   55
He the prosperous man—what some perform
Where wandering them widest draweth.
So that but now my heart burst from my breastlock,
My mood 'mid the mere-flood,
Over the whale's acre, would wander wide.   60
On earth's shelter cometh oft to me,
Eager and ready, the crying lone-flyer,
Whets for the whale-path the heart irresistibly,
O'er tracks of ocean; seeing that anyhow
My lord deems to me this dead life   65
On loan and on land, I believe not
That any earth-weal eternal standeth
Save there be somewhat calamitous
That, ere a man's tide go, turn it to twain.
Disease or oldness or sword-hate   70
Beats out the breath from doom-gripped body.
And for this, every earl whatever, for those speaking after—
Laud of the living, boasteth some last word,
That he will work ere he pass onward,
Frame on the fair earth 'gainst foes his malice,   75

---

4. Grove.

Daring ado,[5] . . .
So that all men shall honor him after
And his laud beyond them remain 'mid the English,
Aye, for ever, a lasting life's-blast,
Delight 'mid the doughty.
                           Days little durable,   80
And all arrogance of earthen riches,
There come now no kings nor Caesars
Nor gold-giving lords like those gone.
Howe'er in mirth most magnified,
Whoe'er lived in life most lordliest,   85
Drear all this excellence, delights undurable!
Waneth the watch, but the world holdeth.
Tomb hideth trouble. The blade is layed low.
Earthly glory ageth and seareth.
No man at all going the earth's gait,   90
But age fares against him, his face paleth,
Gray-haired he groaneth, knows gone companions,
Lordly men, are to earth o'ergiven,
Nor may he then the flesh-cover, whose life ceaseth,
Nor eat the sweet nor feel the sorry,   95
Nor stir hand nor think in mid heart,
And though he strew the grave with gold,
His born brothers, their buried bodies
Be an unlikely treasure hoard.

ANONYMOUS (EIGHTH CENTURY)
England

Anonymously composed, like virtually all the heroic epics of the Middle Ages, *Beowulf* is a poem about a mythic hero of a historic sixth-century tribe, the Geats. It is interspersed with references to historic people and events, and realistic descriptions of the tragic effects of heroic values. Beowulf wins honor in his youth by saving the Danes from the ravages of the monster Grendel (the first excerpt included here) and the monster's mother. Half a century later, when he is king of the Geats, Beowulf defeats but is killed by a dragon who has ravaged his own land. After Beowulf's death, his people do not survive long. There is a self-destructive aspect to the heroic ethos, in which honor can be won only by defeating an enemy, and it can be maintained only if the deaths of relatives are

---

5. Brave deeds.

avenged. The second excerpt describes the hopelessness of attempts to control the destruction with peace-making marriages.

from *Beowulf*

[Beowulf Defeats the Archbeast Grendel]

The fiend wasted no time, but for a start snatched up a sleeping man. He tore him apart in an instant, crunched the body, drank blood from its veins, and gulped it down in great bites until he had wholly swallowed the dead man, even the hands and feet. Then he advanced nearer. Reaching out with his open hand, the fiend was about to take hold of the hero on his bed. But Beowulf at once saw the hostile move and propped himself up on his elbow. The archbeast soon realized that nowhere in the world had he ever met a man with such might in the grip of his hand. Although terror-struck, he could get away none the faster. He had never met anything like this in his life before; his one idea was to slink off to his hiding-place to rejoin the fellowship of devils. But at this point Beowulf remembered the promise which he had made earlier in the evening. He stood upright and gripped Grendel so tightly that the talons cracked to bursting. The monster fought to escape, but Beowulf closed with him. The fiend was trying to break loose and make a bolt for his fen-refuge; yet, as he knew only too well, his talons were fast in an enemy clutch. That was a fatal expedition which the demon made to Heorot.[1] The hall thundered with the hubbub. Every one of the Danes who lived in the stronghold, soldiers and chieftains alike, was seized with extreme panic. The furious contestants for the mastery of the hall raged till the building rang. It was a miracle that the beautiful banqueting hall withstood such combatants without falling flat to the ground; but it was firmly braced inside and out with iron clamps forged by skilled craftsmen. They say that where the two antagonists fought, bench after bench inlaid with gold was uprooted from the floor. Till then the most farsighted among the Danes had never imagined that anybody might wreck their splendid ivory-inlaid hall by ordinary means, or destroy it by dint of cunning (barring fire, which would envelop it in flame). A stupendous din went up. Pure terror laid hold of the Danes, and of everyone outside the hall who heard the howling; the dreadful scream of God's adversary wailing his defeat; the prisoner of hell bellowing over his wound. He was fast in the clutch of the strongest man alive.

[The Uselessness of a Treaty]

Sometimes Hrothgar's[2] daughter carried goblets of ale to the senior chieftains in succession—as she handed the flagon round I heard people call her Freawaru. Young and adorned with gold, she was promised in marriage to Froda's

Translated by David Wright.

---

1. Heorot is the great hall of the Danes, which Grendel invades.

2. Hrothgar is king of the Danes.

good-looking son, Prince Ingeld of the Heathobards.[3] King Hrothgar arranged it, and thinks it a good plan to end the many bitter feuds between the Danes and the Heathobards through this girl. But after the death of a prince it seldom happens that the spear lies idle for long, however beautiful the bride may be.

"For it may gall Prince Ingeld, and every man of his race, when he enters the banqueting hall with his bride, that the treasures of the Heathobards, the arms and armour that their ancestors once wielded, should glitter upon the backs of her Danish retainers now being banqueted.

"But in the battle the Heathobards had led their comrades, as well as their own lives, to destruction. Sooner or later, when drinking has begun, some fierce old spearman who remembers everything, including the massacre of his comrades, will recognize one of the swords. In bitterness of heart he will begin to sound some young fellow and stir up trouble with talk like this: 'My friend, can you recognize that weapon which your own father last carried into battle, when these brave Danes killed him and held the field after the death of Withergyld and the destruction of our men? Now the son of one of his killers is swaggering in his armour in our banqueting hall, bragging of that slaughter and flaunting a sword which by rights should be yours.' In this manner he will egg him on at every turn, and lash him with blistering words, until the day shall come when one of Freawaru's Danish retainers, drenched in blood from a sword-thrust, forfeits his life for what his father did; while the man who killed him escapes because he knows the neighbourhood. Then on both sides the oaths of the chieftains will quickly be broken. Bitter hatred must swell in Ingeld's breast, while, owing to his anguish of mind, his love for his wife must cool. That is why I do not think much of this friendship of the Heathobards, or consider the peace treaty with the Danes to be either real or lasting."

ALCUIN (c. 735–804)
England/France

Alcuin was a distinguished scholar and teacher, born in England and active there for most of his life. In 782 he accepted Charlemagne's invitation to the imperial court in Aachen, where he was a principal force in the revival of classical learning and the establishment of an enduring educational system. This lyric, written like nearly all his verse in classical Latin meter, begins as a personal lament for a lost nightingale; but the grief is forgotten as soon as it is expressed, and the poem concentrates on the message embodied in the sweetly singing bird. Hearing this creature, guided by instinct, singing to its Creator, the listener may sense something of

---

3. The Heathobards are an unidentified tribe. They were apparently seafaring and lived for a while along the Baltic Sea.

the rapture of the angels in their eternal song of praise; for the nightingale was given
by God and Nature to man to wake him to his own true life of praise and devotion.

The Nightingale

Nightingale in the broom, the hand which stole you
from me was envious of my joy.
You filled my heart with sweet-sounding poetry
and my unhappy mind with honeyed song.
May throngs of birds come at once from all sides   5
to lament with me for you in Pierian song. Spurned though you were
for your colour, for your singing you were not spurned;
your swelling voice sounded in your narrow throat,
repeating its sweet tunes in different melodies,
always singing odes to the Creator.   10
On gloomy nights your adorable voice never ceased
your sacred songs, my pride and beauty.
What wonder is it that the cherubim and seraphim praise
the Almighty in eternal song, if your voice has such power?
How happy is he who both day and night   15
with such zeal always has songs for the Lord on his lips!
Neither food and drink were sweeter to you than song,
nor were the bonds of companionship with other birds.
This was the gift of Nature and of Nature's kindly creator
whom you praised with unceasing voice,   20
in order to urge us when sodden with wine and slumber
to shake off the idleness of our minds, clogged with sleep.
What you did, ignorant of reason or understanding,
with natural instinct as your much nobler guide,
everyone with active understanding and powerful reason   25
ought to have done for some time with their speech.
The greatest rewards shall await eternally in the heights of heaven
the man who forever praises the eternal king.

ANONYMOUS (c. 1000)
Germany

The lyric presented here is preserved in a manuscript of the eleventh century that
contains forty-eight other poems of various types—some on religious and historical

subjects, some of themes of secular love—known collectively as the *Cambridge Songs*. This song is written in quatrains of rhymed iambic couplets, which was the most common meter of liturgical hymns. (Secular and religious lyrics adopted each other's meters and expressions throughout the Middle Ages). The strategy of beginning a lyric with a description of the season and then comparing the mood of nature with that of the speaker is a widespread feature of the medieval lyric, in both Latin and the vernacular languages. The contrast between the joyful reawakening of life in spring and the sadness of the speaker became one of the most common themes of the medieval lyric in the centuries that followed.

The Sighs of a Woman in Spring

Softly the west wind blows;
Gaily the warm sun goes;
The earth her bosom sheweth,
And with all sweetness floweth.

Goes forth the scarlet spring,   5
Clad with all blossoming,
Sprinkles the fields with flowers,
Leaves on the forest.

Dens for four-footed things,
Sweet nests for all with wings.   10
On every blossomed bough
Joy ringeth now.

I see it with my eyes,
I hear it with my ears,
But in my heart are sighs,   15
And I am full of tears.

Alone with thought I sit,
And blench, remembering it;
Sometimes I lift my head,
I neither hear nor see.   20

Do thou, O Spring most fair,
Squander thy care
On flower and leaf and grain.
—Leave me alone with pain![1]

Translated by Helen Waddell.

---

1. The translation of this last line trivializes the original: *Nam mea lanquet anima,* ("For my soul languishes.")

Hildegard of Bingen, a Vision from *Scivias*. Otto Müller Verlag, Salzburg, 1954.

HILDEGARD OF BINGEN (1098–1179)
Germany

This German Benedictine nun had many talents: her opinions on theology, prophecies, attacks on corruption, and advice on professional, personal, and medical problems were widely valued. She was an able administrator of a convent, who could hold her own with the bishops of her district. She was a gifted poet and composer of music, a student of female physiology, and a prolific correspondent (hundreds of letters to and from her survive—she corresponded with four popes, two emperors, and St. Bernard of Clairvaux). She had had, from her childhood, divine visions in which the voice of God interpreted the extraordinary things she saw or decried the corruption of the world and the Church, or gave her answers to questions that people put to her, in her extensive travels around Germany, about the conduct of their lives. She described these visions in three books, written in Latin, of which one, the *Scivias*, has survived in a manuscript with illustrations done probably under her guidance. The passages cited here give only a limited sense of the scope of her imagination and the power of her expression.

from Scivias

Book 1: Vision Three, The Universe and Its Symbolism

After this I saw a vast instrument, round and shadowed, in the shape of an egg, small at the top, large in the middle and narrowed at the bottom; outside it, surrounding its circumference, there was bright fire with, as it were, a shadowy zone under it. And in that fire there was a globe of sparkling flame so great that the whole instrument was illuminated by it, over which three little torches were arranged in such a way that by their fire they held up the globe lest it fall. And that globe at times raised itself up, so that much fire flew to it and thereby its flames lasted longer; and sometimes sank downward and great cold came to it, so that its flames were more quickly subdued. But from the fire that surrounded the instrument issued a blast with whirlwinds, and from the zone beneath it rushed forth another blast with its own whirlwinds, which diffused themselves hither and thither throughout the instrument. In that zone, too, there was a dark fire of such great horror that I could not look at it, whose force shook the whole zone, full of thunder, tempest and exceedingly sharp stones both large and small. And while it made its thunders heard, the bright fire and the winds and the air were in commotion, so that lightning preceded those thunders; for the fire felt within itself the turbulence of the thunder.

But beneath that zone was purest ether, with no zone beneath it, and in it I saw a globe of white fire and great magnitude over which two little torches were placed, holding that globe so that it would not exceed the measure of its course. And in that ether were scattered many bright spheres, into which the white globe from time to time poured itself out and emitted its brightness, and then moved back under the globe of red fire and renewed its flames from it, and then again sent them out into those spheres. And from that ether too a blast came forth with its whirlwinds, which spread itself everywhere throughout the instrument.

And beneath that ether I saw watery air with a white zone beneath it, which diffused itself here and there and imparted moisture to the whole instrument. And when it suddenly contracted it sent forth sudden rain with great noise, and when it gently spread out it gave a pleasant and softly falling rain. But from it too came a blast with its whirlwinds, which spread itself throughout the aforementioned instrument.

And in the midst of these elements was a sandy globe of great magnitude, which these elements had so surrounded that it could not waver in any direction. But as these elements and these blasts contended with each other, by their strength they made it move a little.

And I saw between the North and the East a great mountain, which to the North had great darkness and to the East had great light, but in such a way that the light could not reach the darkness, nor the darkness the light.

And again I heard the voice from Heaven, saying to me:

1.   The visible and temporal is a manifestation of the invisible and eternal   God, Who made all things by His will, created them so that His Name would be known and glorified, showing in them not just the things that are visible and temporal, but also the things that are invisible and eternal. Which is demonstrated by this vision you are perceiving.

2.   The firmament in the likeness of an egg and what it signifies   For this *vast instrument, round and shadowy, in the shape of an egg, small at the top, large in the middle and narrowed at the bottom,* faithfully shows Omnipotent God,

Translated by Mother Columba Hart and Jane Bishop.

incomprehensible in His Majesty and inestimable in His mysteries and the hope of all the faithful; for humanity at first was rude and rough and simple in its actions, but later was enlarged through the Old and New Testaments, and finally at the end of the world is destined to be beset with many tribulations.

3. On the bright fire and the shadowy zone   *Outside it, surrounding its circumference, there is bright fire with, as it were, a shadowy zone under it.* This shows that God consumes by the fire of His vengeance all those who are outside the true faith, and those who remain within the Catholic faith He purifies by the fire of His consolation; thus He throws down the darkness of devilish perversity, as He did also when the Devil wanted to oppose himself to God though God had created him, and so fell defeated into perdition.

4. On the placement of the sun and the three stars   *And in that fire there is a globe of sparkling flame, so great that the whole instrument is illuminated by it,* which in the splendour of its brightness shows that within God the Father is His ineffable Only-Begotten, the sun of justice with the brilliance of burning charity, of such great glory that every creature is illumined by the brightness of His light; *over which three little torches are arranged in such a way that by their fire they hold up the globe lest it fall;* that is, [the Trinity] shows how by its arrangement the Son of God, leaving the angels in the heavenly places, descended to earth and showed humans, who exist in soul and body, heavenly things, so that, glorifying Him by serving Him, they reject all harmful error, and magnify Him as the true Son of God incarnate through the true Virgin, when the angel foretold Him and when humans, living in soul and body, with faithful joy received Him.

. . .

6. On the descent of the sun and what it signifies   So, indeed, *sometimes it sinks downwards and great cold comes to it, so that its flames are more quickly subdued.* This shows that the Only-Begotten of God, born of a virgin and hence inclined to be merciful to human poverty, incurred many miseries and sustained great physical anguish; but after He had shown Himself to the world in a bodily shape, He passed from the world and returned to the Father, while His disciples stood by, as it is written:

. . .

9. On the second wind and its whirlwinds   *But from the zone beneath it rushes forth another blast with its own whirlwinds* because the rage of the Devil, knowing God and fearing Him, sends out the worst dishonor and the most evil utterances, *which diffuse themselves hither and thither throughout the instrument,* since in the world useful and useless rumors spread themselves abroad in many ways among the peoples.

10. On the dark fire and the thunder and the sharp stones   *In this zone also there is a dark fire of such horror that you cannot look at it.* This means that the ancient betrayer's most evil and most vile snares vomit forth blackest murder with such great passion that the human intellect cannot fathom its insanity; *whose force shakes the whole zone,* because murder includes in its horror all diabolical malignities. In the first man born hatred boiled up out of anger and led to fratricide, *full of thunder, tempest and exceedingly sharp stones large and small,* for murder is full of avarice, and drunkenness and extreme hardness of heart, which run riot relentlessly both in great murders and in minor vices. *While it makes its thunders heard, the bright fire and the winds and the air are all in commotion,* because when murder cries out in its eagerness to shed blood, it arouses the justice of Heaven and an outburst of flying rumors and an increased disposition to vengeance on the part of right judgment; *so that lightning precedes those thunders, for the fire feels in itself the turbulence of the thunder,* for the manifestation of divine scrutiny exceeds and suppresses evil, since the Divine Majesty, before the sound of that insanity manifests itself in public, forsees it with that watchful eye to which all things are naked.

ANONYMOUS (c. 1100?)
France

The term "chanson de geste" can mean song of great deeds or song of the race or family. It denotes medieval epic French poems whose plots arise from an historical setting, very often the court of Charlemagne or his son; the first and greatest of these is *La Chanson de Roland*. There are historic elements in *The Song of Roland*—the French invasion of Spain under Charlemagne in 778 and the destruction of their rearguard—but it was Christian Basques, not Saracens, who ambushed them, and it was a disaster, not a glorious victory. Among the slain was Hruodlandus, Prefect of Brittany. *The Chanson de Roland* transforms this kernel into a combat between Christians and pagans or good and evil. The embarrassing defeat was slowly transformed in oral tradition into the victory described in the second part of this *chanson de geste,* where Charlemagne takes revenge for the deaths of his nephew Roland and the other heroes of the rearguard. Roland contributes to the tragedy by publicly offending his stepfather, Ganelon, who is already envious of Roland's glory. Ganelon plots with the Saracen enemy to ambush and kill Roland and coincidentally the entire rearguard, the flower of Charlemagne's army. In the first excerpt, Roland and his friend Oliver have just realized that the Saracens are approaching in overwhelming numbers. Oliver wants Roland to sound his horn and alert Charlemagne to their danger so he will return with the rest of the army, but Roland considers it shameful to ask for help and refuses, preferring to die rather than to lose his honor. Once they have been defeated and know they are dying, Roland is ready to sound the horn, so Charlemagne can come back and take revenge, but Oliver objects, throwing Roland's words back at him. The dying Oliver strikes Roland, whom he does not recognize, asks his forgiveness, and dies reconciled with him. Roland's consistent opposition to the pagans and his absolute acceptance of what he regarded as his duty are ultimately rewarded when he alone is escorted to heaven by angels. The gap in the lines of this translation is intended to suggest the rhythm of the original; it does not occur in the text.

from Song of Roland

[Roland Refuses to Blow His Horn]

84

"Roland, my friend,   let the Oliphant[1] sound!
King Charles will hear it,   his host will all turn back,
His valiant barons   will help us in this fight."
Roland replies,   "Almighty God forbid
That I bring shame   upon my family,   5
And cause sweet France   to fall into disgrace!
I'll strike that horde   with my good Durendal;[2]
My sword is ready,   girded here at my side,
And soon you'll see   its keen blade dripping blood.
The Saracens   will curse the evil day   10
They challenged us,   for we will make them pay."

85

"Roland, my friend,   I pray you, sound your horn!
King Charlemagne,   crossing the mountain pass,
Won't fail, I swear it,   to bring back all his Franks."
"May God forbid!"   Count Roland answers then.   15
"No man on earth   shall have the right to say
That I for pagans   sounded the Oliphant!
I will not bring   my family to shame.
I'll fight this battle;   my Durendal shall strike
A thousand blows   and seven hundred more;   20
You'll see bright blood   flow from the blade's keen steel.
We have good men;   their prowess will prevail,
And not one Spaniard   shall live to tell the tale."

86

Oliver says,   "Never would you be blamed;
I've seen the pagans,   the Saracens of Spain.   25
They fill the valleys,   cover the mountain peaks;
On every hill,   and every wide-spread plain,
Vast hosts assemble   from that alien race;
Our company   numbers but very few."
Roland replies,   "The better, then, we'll fight!   30
The saints and angels,   almighty God forbid
That I betray   the glory of sweet France!

Translated by Patricia Terry.

1. The oliphant is Roland's ivory horn.   2. Durendal is Roland's sword.

Better to die   than learn to live with shame—
Charles loves us more   as our keen swords win fame."

87

Roland's a hero,   and Oliver is wise;   35
Both are so brave   men marvel at their deeds.
When they mount chargers,   take up their swords and shields,
Not death itself   could drive them from the field.
They are good men;   their words are fierce and proud.
With wrathful speed   the pagans ride to war.   40
Oliver says,   "Roland, you see them now.
They're very close,   the King too far away.
You were too proud   to sound the Oliphant:
If Charles were with us,   we would not come to grief.
Just look up there!   Close to the Aspre Pass,   45
The rearguard stands,   grieving for what must come.
To fight this battle   means not to fight again."
Roland replies,   "Don't speak so foolishly!"
Cursed be the heart   that cowers in the breast!
We'll hold our ground;   if they will meet us here,   50
Our foes will find us   ready with sword and spear."

88

When Roland sees   the fight will soon begin,
Lions and leopards   are not so fierce as he.
Calling the Franks,   he says to Oliver:
"Noble companion,   my friend, don't talk that way!   55
The Emperor Charles,   who left us in command
Of twenty thousand   he chose to guard the pass,
Made very sure   no coward's in their ranks.
In his lord's service   a man must suffer pain,
Bitterest cold   and burning heat endure;   60
He must be willing   to lose his flesh and blood.
Strike with your lance,   and I'll wield Durendal—
The king himself   presented it to me—
And if I die,   whoever takes my sword
Can say its master   has nobly served his lord."   65

[Oliver and Roland Before the Battle]
91

At Roncevaux   Count Roland passes by,
Riding his charger,   swift-running Veillantif.
He's armed for battle,   splendid in shining mail.

As he parades,   he brandishes his lance,
Turning the point   straight up against the sky,   5
And from the spearhead   a banner flies, pure white,
With long gold fringes   that beat against his hands.
Radiant, fair to see,   he laughs for joy.
Now close behind him   comes Oliver, his friend,
With all the Frenchmen   cheering their mighty lord.   10
Fiercely his eyes   confront the Saracens;
Respectfully, fondly   he gazes at the Franks,
Speaking these gallant words   to cheer their hearts:
"Barons, my lords,   softly now, keep the pace!
Here come the pagans   looking for martyrdom.   15
We'll have such plunder   before the day is out,
As no French king   has ever won before!"
And at this moment   the armies join in war.

92

Oliver says,   "I have no heart for words.
You were too proud   to sound the Oliphant: 20
No help at all   you'll have from Charlemagne.
It's not his fault—   he doesn't know our plight,
Nor will the men   here with us be to blame.
But now, ride on,   to fight as you know how.
Barons, my lords,   in battle hold your ground!   25
And in God's name,   I charge you, be resolved
To strike great blows   for those you have to take.
Let's not forget   the war-cry of King Charles!"
He says these words,   and all the Franks cry out;
No one who heard   that mighty shout, "Montjoie!"   30
Would soon forget   the valor of these men.
And then, how fiercely,   God! they begin to ride,
Spurring their horses   to give their utmost speed,
They race to strike—   what else is there to do?
The Saracens stand firm;   they won't retreat.   35
Pagans and Christians,   behold! in battle meet.

[Angels Take Roland's Soul to Paradise]
128

Count Roland sees   the slaughter of the Franks.
He says these words   to Oliver his friend:
"Noble companion,   how does it look to you?
So many Franks   lie dead upon the field—
Well could we weep   for that fair land, sweet France,
Which will not see   these valiant lords again.   5

Oh! Charles, my friend,   if only you were here!
Oliver, brother,   how can we call him back?
Is there no way   for us to send him word?"
Oliver answers,   "No, I do not know how.   10
Better to die   than lose our honor now."

129

Then Roland says,   "I'll sound the Oliphant.
King Charles will hear it   on the high mountain pass;
I promise you,   the Franks will all turn back."
Oliver answers,   "Then you would bring disgrace   15
And such dishonor   on your whole family
The shame of it   would last them all their lives.
Three times I asked,   and you would not agree;
You still can do it,   but not with my consent.
To sound the horn   denies your valor now.   20
And both your arms   are red with blood of foes!"
The Count replies,   "I've struck some pretty blows."

[Roland and Oliver in Battle]

147

Oliver knows   he has a fatal wound.
He longs for vengeance—   he'll never have enough.
In the melee   he fights on valiantly,
He cuts through spears,   the pagans' studded shields,
And feet and fists   and saddle-trees and spines.
Whoever watched him   cut pagans limb from limb,   5
Bodies piled up   around him on the ground,
Would know that once   he'd seen a noble lord.
The Count remembers   the war-cry of King Charles,
And loud and clear   his voice rings out, "Montjoie!"
He calls to Roland,   summons his friend and peer,   10
"My lord, companion,   come fight beside me now!
We'll part in sorrow   before the sun goes down."

148

Roland is there;   he sees Oliver's face,
The skin is ashen,   so pallid it looks grey,   15
And from his wounds   bright blood is spurting out;
Its heavy drops   flow down him to the ground.
"O God!" says Roland,   "I don't know what to do

Was such great valor   destined to be cut down!
My noble friend,   you'll have no peer on earth.   20
Alas, sweet France!   Now you have fallen low,
Bereft of vassals,   so many valiant men;
The Emperor Charles   will sorely feel the lack."
With these words Roland   faints on his horse's back.

149

Here is Count Roland   unconscious on his horse;   25
Oliver, wounded   and very close to death,
Has bled so much   that both his eyes are dimmed:
Now far or near   he can't see well enough
To give a name   to any man alive.
When he encounters   Count Roland in the field,   30
Oliver strikes him,   cleaving his golden helm
Brilliant with jewels—   the nose-piece cracks in two—
And yet the blade   does not touch face or head.
Roland's eyes open,   and looking at his friend,
Softly and gently   he asks him only this: 35
"My lord, companion,   it's Roland—did you know?
I've always loved you;   did you intend that blow?
You gave no challenge   before you charged at me."
Oliver says,   "I recognize your voice,
But I can't see you—   God keep you in His sight!   40
I struck at you!   I pray you, pardon me."
Roland replies,   "I am not hurt at all;
I do forgive you,   here and in front of God."
When he had spoken,   each leaned down toward his friend.
So, with great love,   they parted in the end.   45

[Death of Count Roland]
169

High are the hills   and very high the trees,
The four great blocks   of polished marble shine;
On the green grass   the Count is lying still.
A Saracen   watches with steady eyes:
This man feigned death,   hiding among the slain;   5
His face and body   he had besmeared with blood.
Now he stands up   and dashes forward fast—
He's handsome, strong   and very valiant too,
But he won't live   to profit from his pride;
He falls on Roland,   seizing him and his arms,   10

And says these words: "Charles' nephew lost the fight!
When I go home,   his sword shall be my prize."
But as he pulls it,   Roland comes back to life.

170

Count Roland feels   the pagan take his sword,
And opening his eyes,   he says just this: 15
"You look to me   like no one on our side!"
Raising the horn   he'd wanted to keep safe,
He strikes the helmet   shining with gold and jewels,
Shatters the steel,   smashes the skull and bones;
He puts both eyes   out of the pagan's head,   20
And sends his body   crashing against the ground.
And then he asks him,   "How did you get so brave,
Dog, to attack me   with or without just cause?
Whoever heard this   would say you were insane!
But I have cracked   the Oliphant's broad bell;   25
Its gold and crystals   were shattered as it fell."

171

Now Roland feels   that he is going blind.
The Count stands upright,   using what strength remains;
All of the color   has vanished from his face.
In front of him   there is a dark grey stone.   30
He strikes ten blows   in bitterness and grief;
The steel blade grates   but will not break or dent.
Then Roland cries: "O Holy Mary, help!
O Durendal,   alas for your fair fame!
My life is over,   you won't be in my care.   35
We've won such battles   together in the field,
So many lands   we've conquered, you and I,
For Charles to rule   whose beard is silver-grey.
No man must have you   who fights and runs away!
You have been long   in a good vassal's hands;   40
You'll have no equal   in all of holy France."

172

Count Roland strikes   the hard sardonyx stone;
The steel blade grates   but will not chip or break.
When Roland sees   he can't destroy his sword,
Then, to himself,   grieving, he speaks its praise: 45
"O Durendal,   how fair you are, and bright!
Against the sunlight   your keen steel gleams and flames!

Charles was that time   in Moriane's Vales
When by God's will   an angel from the sky
Said to bestow you   upon a chieftain Count:
The noble King   girded you at my side.   50
With you I won him   Anjou and Brittany,
Conquered Poitou   and after that all Maine,
With you I won him   that free land, Normandy,
Conquered Provence,   and then all Aquitaine,   55
And Lombardy,   Romagna after that.
With you I won him   Bavaria, Flanders,
Bulgaria,   and all of Poland too.
Constantinople   paid homage to King Charles,
In Saxony   he does as he desires.   60
With you I conquered   the Irish and the Scots,
And England too   the King holds as his own.
So many countries   we've won him, many lands
Ruled by King Charles   whose flowing beard is white.
For your sake now   I suffer grief and pain—   65
Better to die   than leave you here in Spain.
Almighty Father,   keep sweet France from that shame!"

173

Count Roland strikes   against a dark grey stone;
More of it falls   than I can make you see.
The steel blade grates   but will not crack or break;   70
Against the sky   it springs back up again.
Count Roland knows   he can't destroy his sword.
Then, to himself,   he quietly laments:
"O Durendal,   holy you are, and fair!
You have great relics   within your hilt of gold: 75
Saint Peter's tooth,   drops of Saint Basil's blood,
Hairs from the head   of my lord Saint Denis,
Part of a garment   that Holy Mary wore—
For any pagan   to hold you would be wrong;
Only by Christians   can you be rightly served.   80
May you not fall   into a coward's hands!
Many wide lands   we've conquered, you and I,
For Charles to rule   whose flowing beard is white;
They have increased   his majesty and might."

174

Count Roland feels   the very grip of death   85
Which from his head   is reaching for his heart.
He hurries then   to go beneath a pine;

In the green grass   he lies down on his face,
Placing beneath him   the sword and Oliphant;
He turns his head   to look toward pagan Spain.   90
He does these things   in order to be sure
King Charles will say,   and with him all the Franks,
The noble Count   conquered until he died.
He makes confession,   for all his sins laments,
Offers his glove   in God in penitence.   95

175

Now Roland feels   his time has all run out.
He looks toward Spain   from high on a steep hill,
And with one hand   beating his breast, he says:
"God, I have sinned   against Thy holy name.
Forgive the sins,   the great ones and the less,   100
That I committed   from my first hour of life
To this last day   when I have been struck down."
And now toward God   he raises his right glove;
A flight of angels   comes from the skies above.

176

And now Count Roland,   lying beneath a pine,   105
Has turned his face   to look toward pagan Spain;
And he begins   remembering these things:
The many lands   his valor won the King,
Sweet France, his home,   the men of his own line,
And Charlemagne   who raised him in his house—   110
The memories   make him shed tears and sigh.
But not forgetting   how close he is to death,
He prays that God   forgive him all his sins:
"O my true Father,   O Thou who never lied,
Thou who delivered   Lazarus from the grave,   115
Who rescued Daniel   out of the lions' den,
Keep now my soul   from every peril safe,
Forgive the sins   that I have done in life."
Roland's right glove   he offers now to God.
Saint Gabriel comes   and takes it from his hand.   120
His head sinks down   to rest upon his arm;
Hands clasped in prayer,   Roland has met his end.
God sends from heaven   the angel Cherubin,
Holy Saint Michael   who saves us from the sea,
And with these two   the angel Gabriel flies.   125
Count Roland's soul   they bring to Paradise.

MARCABRU (fl. 1129–1150)
France

Marcabru was one of the earliest troubadours, the poet-musicians of Provence in the eleventh, twelfth, and thirteenth centuries, and one of the most inventive in language, form, and imagery. He wrote in Provençal, the language of medieval southern France. Though he did not compose love songs, he attacked the circumstances that fostered the deterioration of the ideals represented in such songs. He denounces the immorality of the courtly class, the lost sense of its mission, the false, seductive, language of its entertainments. In his prophetic stance he used rough words and striking images whose vernacular immediacy and rich allusiveness often make them hard to understand today. But there is considerable variety in his work, and other songs of his assume the voice of a degenerate high-born character—the kind he elsewhere excoriates—who unwittingly condemns himself. In still other songs, such as "By the Fountain in the Orchard," Marcabru sets a dialogue going that draws its significance from the situation of the two speakers: both characters are outside the walls of the court; the woman is alone in the open, the man sees a sexual conquest, both are free of the policing presence of society. This situation tests the class quality and the ethical integrity of the two characters, and, as is usual in Marcabru, the woman emerges with the dignity appropriate to her station, while the man is exposed and defeated. This song dramatizes the conception of passionate love fostered by the troubadours and adopted in lyrics and romances in succeeding generations in European literature: human love is true and sanctionable when it accords with social order and Providential design; otherwise it is false, bitter, lustful, and destructive. This is a dialogue between the voices of true and false love. The differences in the language of the two speakers, their misunderstandings, their mutually incomprehensible desires reveal the ethical status of each one. Observing how they talk past each other, we can make out the courtly ideals promoted by the early vernacular lyric. We can sense, too, in the young woman's situation and in her lament and longing, the spirit of the time during the Crusades.

By the Fountain in the Orchard

I

By the fountain in the orchard,
where the grass is green along the sandy banks,
under the shade of a planted tree,
beset among white flowers
and the ancient song of the new season,   5
I found her alone, without companion,
this girl who wants no pleasure with me.

Translated by Frederick Goldin.

II

She was a young girl, the body on her beautiful,
the daughter of a castle lord.
And just as I ventured the thought that the birds   10
must be filling her with joy, and all the green,
and this sweet new season, this spring,
and she would gladly hear my patter—
just then the look and manner of her changed.

III

Her eyes welled up with tears beside the fountain,   15
she sighed from the depths of her heart.
"Jesus," she said, "King of the world,
because of You my great grief increases,
the shame done unto You now brings me down,
for the best of all this world   20
are going off to serve You, such is Your pleasure.

IV

"Away with You goes my beloved,
my handsome, gentle, valiant, noble friend;
no part of him stays here with me but the great distress,
the constant desire, and the tears.   25
Ai! cursed be King Louis,[1]
who gave the orders and preached the sermons
that brought on grief invading my heart."

V

When I heard how the spirit in her was gone,
I came up to her along the clear stream.   30
"O beautiful," I said, "with too much weeping
the face grows pale, the color fades.
You have no reason to despair, now,
for He Who makes the woods burst into leaf
can give you all the joy you need."   35

VI

"Lord," she said, "I do believe
that God may pity me

---

1. Louis VII, king of France, was a leader of
   the Second Crusade in 1147.

in the world to come, time without end,
like many another sinner.
But in this world He wrests from me the only one   40
who made my joy grow great; who cares but little for me,
for he has gone so far away."

BERNART DE VENTADORN

(fl. 1150–1180)

France

This is one of the most famous and most widely praised lyrics of the troubadours, the poet-musicians of southern France, in part because of the entrancing image in the first strophe. All we know of its author is that he was a commoner. This song is a *canso*, a song of several strophes (usually five to seven), often concluding (as here) with an envoi or *tornada*. The *canso* was devoted exclusively to the theme of *fin' amors*, or "courtly love." Such love was befitting a person of the court, and it distinguished that individual from those lacking the refinement and self-discipline of the courtly class. The object of this love never appears in the *canso*; she is present only in the lover's praise and complaints. In his praise he depicts her as ideally beautiful, a radiant figure in whom the distinguishing virtues of courtliness are fully realized; in his complaints he curses the obstacles that keep him at a distance, and reproaches her for her imperiousness and lack of concern. For at the heart of courtly love is a strange erotic paradox: this long-enduring love reveals and perfects the lover's courtly quality *as long as distance separates him from the beloved;* she may respond to his courtship and his song but always across an ineradicable distance and always leaving his longing and uncertainty intact. Though courtly love was strictly a literary theme, a fiction in which the noble audience could behold its high-minded image and justify its privileged position, the troubadours depicted the lover's joy and suffering as actual experiences. They analyzed the consequences of the courtly love relation—the enhanced refinement, the tested loyalty, the celebration of courtly worth, the perpetual tension, the moral uncertainty, the dangers of disillusionment—through a series of subsidiary themes, many of which are powerfully realized in this song.

When I See the Lark Moving

I

When I see the lark moving
its wings in joy against the light,

Translated by Frederick Goldin.

rising up into forgetfulness, letting go, and falling
for the sweetness that comes to its heart,
ai! such envy then comes over me   5
of everyone I see rejoicing,
it makes me wonder that my heart
at once does not melt with desire.

II

I, weary, how much I thought I knew
about love, and how little I know,   10
because I cannot keep myself from loving
her from whom I shall get no favor.
She has it all: she bore off my heart, and me,
and herself, and the whole world.
And when she took herself away from me, she left me nothing   15
but desire and a heart still wanting.

III

I have no longer had the power of myself,
I have not been my own man, from that moment
when she let me look into her eyes,
into a mirror that gives me pleasure, even now.   20
Mirror, since I beheld myself in you,
the sighs from my depths have slain me,
and I am lost to myself, as he was lost—
the fair Narcissus in the fountain.

IV

I give up all hope in fair ladies,
I shall not put my faith in them again.   25
As much as I used to exalt them,
now I shall abandon them.
For I do not see a single one who stands by me
against her who destroys me and brings me down.
I shall fear and distrust them all,   30
for they are all alike, I know it well.

V

This is how she shows herself a woman indeed,
my lady, and I reproach her for it:
she does not want what one ought to want,
and that which one forbids her to do, she does.   35

I have fallen in evil grace,
I have acted like the madman on the bridge,
and why this happens to me I do not know,
except that I climbed too high on the mountain.   40

VI

Kindness, in truth, is lost,
and I never knew it till now;
for she who ought to have it most
has none, and where shall I seek it?
Ah, to look at her it does not seem   45
that she would let this man, miserable with desire,
who can know no health without her,
die, and never come to his aid.

VII

Since these things do not avail me with my lady:
prayer, pity, the rights I have;   50
and since it brings her no pleasure
that I love her, I shall not tell her again.
Thus I part from her, I renounce my service and song.
She has given me death, and I will answer her with death,
and I go away, since she does not retain me,   55
a broken man, in exile, I know not where.

VIII

Tristan, you shall have nothing more from me,
for I go away, a broken man, I know not where.
I forsake all song, I renounce it,
and far from joy and love shall hide myself away.   60

MARIE DE FRANCE (fl. 1160–1190)
France

We do not know the exact identity of the French medieval poet, Marie de France,
although some have suggested she was a half-sister of Henry II of England. She
probably wrote for the French-speaking English court. Besides her *Lais*, she
wrote a collection of beast fables, based on Aesop (*Isopet* or *Little Aesop*.)
    The *lai* is a short verse narrative poem related to the romance in setting and

theme and composed for the same sort of audience. In the prologue to the *Lais,* Marie de France begins with a standard remark about the duty to share the knowledge one has, but then she suggests a deeper meaning in her work. She might have translated some of her material from Latin to French, as many of her contemporaries did, thereby establishing her scholarly credentials; but, she chose to put these tales into verse. In her twelve *lais,* Marie deals with love in a variety of forms and human relations: love between husband and wife, between adulterous lovers, between young lovers, between a possessive father and his daughter; self-indulgent love and self-sacrificing love; sterile love and fertile love; enduring devotion and brief flirtation.

In "Yonec" she describes a love that is willed by the imagination of a young woman trapped in marriage with an old and jealous husband who imprisons her in a tower. A knight comes to her as a bird and visits her whenever she wants him, until the husband, alerted by the joy she cannot conceal, sets a trap that fatally wounds the lover. The woman is empowered by this treachery to leap from the tower and follow her lover to his land, where he gives her a ring to make her husband forget what has happened and a sword for the son she will have, who will eventually avenge his father when he visits his tomb with his mother and his stepfather.

In the *Fables* Marie tells old and new stories and derives morals from them, frequently using them to make a point about social responsibility, which seems to take direct aim at members of her audience, as we see in "The Wolf and the Lamb."

from Lais

Prologue

Whoever has received knowledge
and eloquence in speech from God
should not be silent or secretive
but demonstrate it willingly.
When a great good is widely heard of,   5
then, and only then, does it bloom,
and when that good is praised by many,
it has spread its blossoms.
The custom among the ancients—
as Priscian testifies—   10
was to speak quite obscurely
in the books they wrote,
so that those who were to come after
and study them
might gloss the letter   15
and supply its significance from their own wisdom.
Philosophers knew this,
they understood among themselves

Translated by Robert Hanning and Joan Ferrante.

that the more time they spent,
the more subtle their minds would become   20
and the better they would know how to keep themselves
from whatever was to be avoided.
He who would guard himself from vice
should study and understand
and begin a weighty work   25
by which he might keep vice at a distance,
and free himself from great sorrow.
That's why I began to think
about composing some good stories
and translating from Latin to Romance;   30
but that was not to bring me fame:
too many others have done it.
Then I thought of the *lais* I'd heard.
I did not doubt, indeed I knew well,
that those who first began them   35
and sent them forth
composed them in order to preserve
adventures they had heard.
I have heard many told;
and I don't want to neglect or forget them.   40
To put them into word and rhyme
I've often stayed awake.

Yonec

The lady lived in great sorrow,
with tears and sighs and weeping;
she lost her beauty,
as one does who cares nothing for it.
She would have preferred   5
death to take her quickly.

It was the beginning of April
when the birds begin their songs.
The lord arose in the morning
and made ready to go to the woods.   10
He had the old woman get up
and close the door behind him—
she followed his command.
The lord went off with his men.
The old woman carried a psalter   15
from which she intended to read the psalms.
The lady, awake and in tears,
saw the light of the sun.

She noticed that the old woman
had left the chamber.
She grieved and sighed   20
and wept and raged:
"I should never have been born!
My fate is very harsh.
I'm imprisoned in this tower
and I'll never leave it unless I die.   25
What is this jealous old man afraid of
that he keeps me so imprisoned?
He's mad, out of his senses;
always afraid of being deceived   30
I can't even go to church
or hear God's service.
If I could speak to people
and enjoy myself with them
I'd be very gracious to my lord   35
even if I didn't want to be.
A curse on my family,
and on all the others
who gave me to this jealous man,
who married me to his body.   40
It's a rough rope that I pull and draw.
He'll never die—
when he should have been baptized
he was plunged instead in the river of hell;
his sinews are hard, his veins are hard,   45
filled with living blood.
I've often heard
that one could once find
adventures in this land
that brought relief to the unhappy.   50
Knights might find young girls
to their desire, noble and lovely;
and ladies find lovers
so handsome, courtly, brave, and valiant
that they could not be blamed,   55
and no one else would see them.
If that might be or ever was,
if that has ever happened to anyone,
God, who has power over everything,
grant me my wish in this."   60
When she'd finished her lament,
she saw, through a narrow window,
the shadow of a great bird.
She didn't know what it was.

It flew into the chamber;
its feet were banded; it looked like a hawk
of five or six moultings.
It alighted before the lady.
When it had been there awhile
and she'd stared hard at it,
it became a handsome and noble knight.
The lady was astonished;
her blood went cold, she trembled,
she was frightened—she covered her head.
The knight was very courteous,
he spoke first:
"Lady," he said, "don't be afraid.
The hawk is a noble bird,
although its secrets are unknown to you.
Be reassured
and accept me as your love.
That," he said, "is why I came here.
I have loved you for a long time,
I've desired you in my heart.
Never have I loved any woman but you
nor shall I ever love another,
yet I couldn't have come to you
or left my own land
had you not asked for me.
But now I can be your love."
The lady was reassured;
she uncovered her head and spoke.
She answered the knight,
saying she would take him as her lover
if he believed in God,
and if their love was really possible.
For he was of great beauty.
Never in her life
had she seen so handsome a knight—
nor would she ever.
"My lady," he said, "you are right.
I wouldn't want you to feel
guilt because of me,
or doubt or suspicion.
I do believe in the creator
who freed us from the grief
that Adam, our father, led us into
when he bit into the bitter apple.
He is, will be, and always was
the life and light of sinners.

65

70

80

85

90

95

100

105

110

With that the knight departed,
leaving his love in great joy.
In the morning she rose restored;
she was happy all week.
Her body had now become precious to her,   115
she completely recovered her beauty.
Now she would rather remain here
than look for pleasure elsewhere.
She wanted to see her love all the time
and enjoy herself with him.   120
As soon as her lord departed,
night or day, early or late,
she had him all to her pleasure.
God, let their joy endure!
Because of the great joy she felt,   125
because she could see her love so often,
her whole appearance changed.
But her lord was clever.
In his heart he sensed
that she was not what she had been.   130
He suspected his sister.
He questioned her one day,
saying he was astonished
that the lady now dressed with care.
He asked her what it meant.   135
The old woman said she didn't know—
no one could have spoken to her,
she had no lover or friend—
it was only that she was now more willing
to be alone than before.   140
His sister, too, had noticed the change.
Her lord answered:
"By my faith," he said, "I think that's so.
But you must do something for me.
In the morning, when I've gotten up   145
and you have shut the doors,
pretend you are going out
and leave her lying there alone.
Then hide yourself in a safe place,
watch her and find out   150
what it is, and where it comes from,
that gives her such great joy."
With that plan they separated.
Alas, how hard it is to protect yourself

Handwritten annotations: Her lover revitalized her self-esteem + began to think good thoughts again. Carried his child within her. Saw each other often. Plan of deceit toward his wife by her sister.

from someone who wants to trap you,
to betray and deceive you!

He left in great sorrow.
She followed him with loud cries.
She leapt out a window—
it's a wonder that she wasn't killed,
for it was at least twenty feet high
where she made her leap,
naked beneath her gown.
She followed the traces of blood
that flowed from the knight
onto the road.
She followed that road and kept to it
until she came to a hill.
In the hill there was an opening,
red with his blood.
She couldn't see anything beyond it
but she was sure
that her love had gone in there.
She entered quickly.
She found no light
but she kept to the right road
until it emerged from the hill
into a beautiful meadow.
When she found the grass there wet with blood,
she was frightened.
She followed the traces through the meadow
and saw a city not far away.
The city was completely surrounded by walls.
There was no house, no hall or tower,
that didn't seem entirely of silver.
The buildings were very rich.
Going toward the town there were marshes,
forests, and enclosed fields.
On the other side, toward the castle,
a steam flowed all around,
where ships arrived—
there were more than three hundred sails.
The lower gate was open;
the lady entered the city,
still following the fresh blood
through the town to the castle.
No one spoke to her,
she met neither man nor woman.

When she came to the palace courtyard,
she found it covered with blood.
She entered a lovely chamber   200
where she found a knight sleeping.
She did not know him, so she went on
into another larger chamber.
There she found nothing but a bed   205
with a knight sleeping on it;
she kept going.
She entered the third chamber
and on that bed she found her love.

     . . .

On their way, they passed the chapter house,   210
where they found a huge tomb
covered with a cloth of embroidered silk,
a band of precious gold running from one side to the other.
At the head, the feet, and at the sides
burned twenty candles.   215
The chandeliers were pure gold,
the censers amethyst,
which through the day perfumed
that tomb, to its great honor.
They asked and inquired   220
of people from that land
whose tomb it was,
what man lay there.
The people began to weep
and, weeping, to recount   225
that it was the best knight
the strongest, the most fierce,
the most handsome and the best loved,
that had ever lived.
"He was king of this land;   230
no one was ever so courtly.
At Caerwent he was discovered
and killed for the love of a lady.
Since then we have had no lord,
but have waited many days,   235
just as he told and commanded us,
for the son the lady bore him."
When the lady heard that news,
she called aloud to her son.
"Fair son," she said, "you hear   240
how God has led us to this spot.
Your father, whom this old man murdered,
lies here in this tomb.

Now I give and commend his sword to you.
I have kept it a long time for you."   245
Then she revealed, for all to hear,
that the man in the tomb was the father and this was his son,
and how he used to come to her,
how her lord had betrayed him—
she told the truth.   250
Then she fainted over the tomb
and, in her faint, she died.
She never spoke again.
When her son saw that she had died,
he cut off his stepfather's head.   255
Thus with his father's sword
he avenged his mother's sorrow.
When all this had happened,
when it became known through the city,
they took the lady with great honor   260
and placed her in the coffin.
Before they departed
they made Yonec their lord.

Long after, those who heard this adventure
composed a lay about it,   265
about the pain and the grief
that they suffered for love.

from *The Fables*

The Wolf and the Lamb

This tells of wolf and lamb who drank
Together once along a bank.
The wolf right at the spring was staying
While lambkin down the stream was straying.
The wolf then spoke up nastily,   5
For argumentative was he,
Saying to lamb, with great disdain,
"You give me such a royal pain!"
The lamb made this reply to him,
"Pray sir, what's wrong?"—"Are your eyes dim!   10
You've so stirred up the water here,
I cannot drink my fill, I fear,
I do believe I should be first,
Because I've come here dying of thirst."

Translated by Harriet Spiegel.

The little lamb then said to him,   15
"But sir, 'twas you who drank upstream.
My water comes from you, you see."
"What!" snapped the wolf. "You dare curse me?"
"Sir, I had no intention to!"
The wolf replied, "I know what's true.   20
Your father treated me just so
Here at this spring some time ago—
It's now six months since we were here."
"So why blame me for that affair?
I wasn't even born, I guess."   25
"So what?" the wolf responded next;
"You really are perverse today—
You're not supposed to act this way."
The wolf then grabbed the lamb so small,
Chomped through his neck, extinguished all.   30
   And this is what our great lords do,
The viscounts and the judges too,
With all the people whom they rule:
False charge they make from greed so cruel.
To cause confusion they consort   35
And often summon folk to court.
They strip them clean of flesh and skin,
As the wolf did to the lambkin.

CHRÉTIEN DE TROYES (fl. 1170–1190)
France

Chrétien de Troyes, a French poet who spent some time at the court of Marie de
Champagne and Phillip of Flanders, was the author of some of the earliest
Arthurian romances. Although fighting is still a main element of the plot in his
romances, new values of public service have replaced the old ones of honor and
revenge. Knights are expected to fight for justice and to defend the weak and
oppressed, not simply to increase their own glory. The most successful knights
in this world are inspired by their love for a woman, but that love is supposed to
inspire them to serve society, not to interfere with their service. In *The Knight with
the Lion,* however, the hero, Yvain, is so obsessed with winning honor by fighting
that he leaves his wife and his responsibilities to defend her land and goes off on
unspecified adventures with Gawain. When he does not return within the
allotted time, she sends a messenger to denounce and reject him. He goes mad
and must work his way back to sanity and to his wife by a series of battles in
defense of women who are endangered or exploited or abused. The most striking

is presented in "The Weaving Maidens," which describes women working in a silk factory, a medieval sweatshop, with conditions that may have parallels with those of the cloth manufacturers of northern France. Certainly Chrétien seems to be making a comment on the indifference of his audience to the women's plight, when he shows the noble family who live in the same castle. They presumably benefit from the work done there but seem oblivious to the workers' suffering as they sit in a garden listening to their daughter read a romance.

Yvain's companion in his adventures is not a fellow knight—indeed, Gawain is not available even for those adventures that should have been his responsibility—but a lion, whom the knight had rescued. In "The Devotion of a Lion," the animal shows extraordinary gratitude and devotion, to the point of attempting suicide when he thinks Yvain is dead.

from **The Knight with the Lion**

[The Devotion of a Lion]

When he reached a clearing, he saw a lion and a serpent, which was holding the lion by the tail and scorching his haunches with burning fire. Sir Yvain spent little time looking at this strange sight. When he considered which of the two he would help, he decided to go to aid the lion, because a serpent with its venom and treachery deserved nothing but harm. The serpent was venomous, and fire was darting from its mouth, so full of evil was the creature.

Intending first to kill the serpent, Sir Yvain drew his sword and advanced. He held his shield before his face as a protection against the flames gushing from the serpent's throat, which was more gaping than a pot. If the lion attacked him later, there would be a fight; yet whatever happened after, he still wished to aid the lion. Pity urged him and pleaded that he help and support the noble and honorable beast.

With his keen-cutting sword he attacked the evil serpent, pinning it to the ground and slicing it in two. He then struck it again and again until he had cut and hacked it to pieces. But he had to sever a piece of the lion's tail because the head of the wretched serpent still gripped the tail. He cut off as little as necessary; in fact, he could not have removed less. When he had freed the lion, he expected that the lion would spring at him and he would have to fight, but to the lion such an idea never occurred. Hear what the lion did. In a manner befitting the worthy and nobly born, he began to show that he was surrendering. He stood on his hind legs, stretched out his forepaws together to the knight, and bowed his head to the ground. Then he knelt down, his whole face wet with tears of humility. For certain Sir Yvain realized that the lion was thanking him and humbling himself before him, since he had delivered him from death by killing the serpent. This adventure delighted Yvain. He cleaned the serpent's venomous filth from his sword, which he then placed back in its scabbard. Then he resumed his journey. The lion

Translated by David Staines.

walked close beside him, never to leave him, but to accompany him always to serve and to protect him.

The lion went ahead on the road. Because he was in front, he caught in the wind the scent of wild beasts grazing. Hunger and his natural instinct urged him to go hunting prey for his own food. This was the way Nature intended him to act. He set out on the trail a little until he had shown his master that he had sniffed out and taken up the scent of a wild animal. He then stopped and looked at him, for he sought to please him and had no intention of acting against his will. By such behavior, Yvain realized that the lion was showing him that he awaited his direction. He understood and knew that if he held back, the lion would hold back, and if he followed him, the lion would catch the game he had scented.

. . .

Alas, Sir Yvain almost lost sense when this time he neared the spring and the stone and the chapel.[1] A thousand times he called himself wretched and miserable. He was so distraught that he fell in a faint; his sharp sword dropped from its scabbard and the point pierced through the meshes of his hauberk close to the neck below the cheek. There is no mail that does not break open, and the sword cut the skin of the neck beneath the gleaming mail and made his blood spill. The sight convinced the lion that his master and companion was dead. Greater than ever before was the anger he experienced, as the display of his grief commenced. Never have I heard told or described such grief. He threw himself about, clawing himself and screaming. He wanted to kill himself with the sword he thought had killed his good master. With his teeth he grabbed the sword from him, laid it on a fallen tree, and steadied it on a trunk behind, fearing it might slip when he hurled his breast against it. He had almost accomplished his desire when Yvain recovered from his swoon. The lion had been rushing at death like a wild boar, careless of where he impaled himself. Now, however, he took restraint.

[The Weaving Maidens]

Pressured and provoked into coming up by the porter's rude insolence, Sir Yvain went straight past him without saying a word and came upon a great high hall that was recently built. In front of it was a courtyard enclosed by large, round, pointed stakes, between which he saw as many as three hundred maidens inside, engaged in different kinds of embroidery, sewing threads of gold and silk as best they could. They were so poor that many had nothing on their heads and no belts around their waists. Their jackets were torn at the breasts and elbows; the shifts on their backs were soiled. From hunger and pain their faces were

---

1. The spring, the stone, and the chapel are the setting of Yvain's first adventure, in which he fatally wounded the knight defending the spring. Pursuing the knight to his castle, Yvain was trapped there, fell in love with his widow, and married her, thereby accepting responsibility to defend the spring. When he sees it again, he is reminded of his wife, his neglect of her, and her rejection of him.

pale, their necks thin. They all noticed him looking at them, and bowed their heads and wept. For a long time they remained there without the will to do anything. Wretched as they were, they were unable to raise their eyes from the ground.

When Sir Yvain had watched them a while, he turned and rode back to the gate. The porter barred the way. "It is no use, dear master, you will not go away now," he yelled at him. "You will want to be outside now, but wanting that, I swear, avails you not. Before you leave, you will have suffered so much shame that you will be unable to bear more. It was unwise of you to enter here, for there is no escape."

"Dear brother, I have no wish to escape," he replied. "But tell me, on your father's soul, the young ladies I have seen in this castle weaving cloths of silk and gold embroidery, whence have they come? I am delighted by their work. But I am disturbed by their thin bodies and the sad expressions on their pale faces. I believe they would be beautiful and charming if they had what pleased them."

"I shall say nothing to you," he replied. "Find someone else to tell you."

"So I will, since there's nothing more to do."

Yvain searched until he found the entrance to the courtyard where the young ladies were working. He stood before them all and greeted them together. He saw the teardrops running from their eyes and falling as they wept. "May it be God's pleasure to take this sorrow from your hearts and turn it to joy," he said to them. "I do not know the cause of your sorrow."

"God hear your call!" one answered. "You shall know who we are and from what land. I suppose that is what you wish to ask."

"Yes, that is why I came here," he said.

"Sir, a long time ago it happened that the King of the Isle of Maidens was traveling through many courts and countries in search of news. He continued traveling, like a born fool, until he fell into this peril. It was an evil hour when he arrived here. We prisoners undeservedly suffer the misery and disgrace of it. You can be certain such awful shame will be yours too unless they agree to accept ransom for you.

"In any case, it happened that our lord came to this castle, which is the home of two sons of the devil. Do not think this an idle tale, for they are the offspring of a woman and a demon. They were to fight the king, who was exceedingly alarmed. He was not yet eighteen years old, and they would have cut him in half as though he were a gentle lamb. The king was terrified, and escaped as best he could, swearing to send here every year, as long as he lived, thirty maidens from his kingdom. This tribute brought about his release. And it was settled by oath that the tribute should last as long as the two demons were alive. On the day they were overcome and defeated in combat, he would be released from this duty, and we, who are subjected to painful lives of misery and disgrace, would be set free. We shall never have anything to please us. Now I chatter like a child in referring to being set free. We shall never leave here.

"Always we shall weave cloths of silk. Never shall we be better dressed. Always we shall be poor and naked, and always suffer hunger and thirst. Never shall we be able to earn enough to have better food. We have hardly any bread, a little in the morning and less in the evening. Never, for her handiwork, will any maiden earn more than four deniers[2] from the pound to live on, and that cannot give us enough clothing and food. Those who earn twenty sous[3] a week are still not without burden. The truth, be certain, is that every one of us does at least twenty sous' worth of work or more. That amount would make a duke wealthy. We are destitute, and our employer becomes rich from our earnings. We lie awake most of the night, and work all day to earn our living, for he threatens us with bodily harm when we rest. So we dare not rest. But why talk more? We have so much misery and disgrace that I cannot tell you the fifth of it. Still we are often furious and enraged at the sight of young and worthy knights dying in combat against the two demons; they pay much for their accommodation, as you will tomorrow. Whether you wish to or not, tomorrow you will have to fight entirely on your own and lose your reputation against two devils incarnate."

"May God, the true King of Heaven, protect me and give you honor and joy, if it be His will," Sir Yvain answered, "Now I must go and see the people inside and learn how they will receive me."

"Go now, sir. The Giver of All Goodness save you."

He then went away and entered the hall, where he found no one, good or evil, who would speak to them of anything.

Sir Yvain, the maiden, and the lion passed through the house and went out into a garden. They did not discuss or even mention stabling their horses, but it did not matter; those who expected to have the horses had done the stabling. I do not know if they were wise in their expectations, for in the end the knight will have a horse that is all rested. The horses had oats and hay and straw up to their bellies.

Sir Yvain entered the garden with his party following him. He saw a noble man reclining on his side on a silk rug. In front of him a maiden was reading from a romance—I do not know about whom. A lady had come to recline there and hear the romance. She was the maiden's mother, and the lord was her father. They enjoyed watching and listening to her very much, for they had no other children. Not more than sixteen, she was so beautiful and charming that the god of Love, had he seen her, would have become her servant and caused her never to love anyone but him. To be her servant, he would have set aside his divinity and taken on human form. He would have struck his own body with the arrow whose wound never heals unless an untrue physician tends it. It is wrong for anyone to recover unless treachery is discovered there, and anyone healed another way is not a true lover. If the story pleased you, I could go on telling you of these wounds until I reached some ending. But soon there would be someone who would say I was telling you of a dream. People today do not fall in love or love as they used to. They do not even have the desire to hear talk of love.

---

2. The *denier* is a penny, a twelfth of a *sou.*
3. The *sou* is the equivalent of an English shilling,

a twentieth of a pound, a little more than a dime.

WALTHER VON DER VOGELWEIDE

(c. 1170–1230)

Germany

Walther von der Vogelweide created a greater variety of lyrical forms, and treated a greater range of poetic themes, than any other *Minnesinger*. During the Civil War in Germany, he supported first one side, then the other, and finally turned to Frederick II, the grandson of Barbarossa, who gave him a house with the fireside he had always longed for. His love songs differ from others in their emphasis on reciprocity: he depicts *Minne*—courtly love—as a bond between equals and in some lyrics challenges traditional representations of love by imagining a simpler, more direct relation. He composed the first sustained and specifically pointed political songs of the German Middle Ages. He represents the singer—that is, himself—as the creator and guarantor of the renown of those he serves: of his lady in the (fictional) love songs, of his noble patron in the political and didactic songs. The inventiveness and boldness of his thought, the continual assertion of his performer's pride, the brilliant structure of his strophes, the immediacy of his needy presence (he continually proclaims both his unsurpassed merit and his undeserved indigence), the beauty and directness of his language— the combination of all these traits is unique, and he is generally considered the greatest German lyric poet of the Middle Ages.

    The lyric presented here has come to be known as Walther's "elegy," largely because of the painful awakening depicted in the first two strophes. But these bitter complaints, which sound so personal, are meant to exemplify the inability of human beings to save themselves, and of any society to endure on its own strength without corruption. The song then brings forth its triumphant theme, the Crusade. The horrified awakening can be the beginning of a new life, of redemption in service of God; the knight's profession can be the way to his salvation, sanctified forever in the voyage across the sea.

Alas, Where Have They Vanished

I

Alas, where have they vanished, all my years!
Have I dreamed my life, or is it real?
That which I thought was something, *was* it something?
Then I have long been sleeping and do not know it.
Now I have awakened, and everything seems strange   5
that used to be familiar as this hand of mine.
The people and the land where from a child I was raised—

Translated by Frederick Goldin.

have all turned strange to me, as though it were all lies.
The children that I played with now are old and slow.
The field is cultivated, all the woods cut down.   10
If the water did not flow still as it used to flow,
in truth I would consider my misfortune great.
Many are slow to greet me who knew me once quite well.
The world is everywhere full of the loss of grace.
When I think back on many and many a glorious day   15
all fallen from me like a blow struck on the water, then
evermore, alas.

II

Alas, how poorly these young people present themselves today,
whose spirits soared rejoicing, once, in times gone by.
They know only worries, ach, how can they live that way?   20
Wherever in this world I turn, no one is content,
dancing, laughing, singing pass on into care.
No Christian man has ever seen a year so wretched.
Look at the ladies, how they dress their hair,
and our knights, so splendid, clothed in peasant dress.   25
Now here are these cruel letters come to us from Rome:[1]
we are authorized to suffer, we are despoiled of joy.
It offends me deeply—we used to live well in this land—
that I must trade away my laughter, that I must choose to weep.
The birds in the wild forests are cast down by our lament: 30
then what wonder is it if I come to despair?
Ach, fool, what am I saying in my worthless rage?
Who chases after pleasures *here* has lost them *there,*
evermore, alas.

III

Alas, how we are poisoned with things that taste so sweet.   35
I see amidst the honey the bitter gall afloat.
Outside the world is fair—white, green, and red,
and inside black, black the darkness of death.
Let him whom the world has misled now look upon his hope:
he is, with such soft penance, set free from mighty sin.   40
You who are knights, reflect on this, it is for you.

---

1. The excommunication of Frederick II, the
   Holy Roman Emperor, by Pope Gregory IX,
   in 1227.

You bear the brilliant helms, the meshes of hard rings,
the strong shields, the consecrated swords.
Would God that I were worthy of that victory!
Then I, a needy man, would win great wages, 45
but I do not mean vast acres or the gold of kings.
Salvation's crown of ages I myself would wear,
that a soldier fighting for pay could win with his spear.[2]
Could I make that beloved voyage across the sea,
then I would sing rejoicing, and nevermore "alas," 50
nevermore "alas."

GACE BRULÉ (fl. 1180–1212)
France

The *trouvères* of northern France also took up the themes and ideas of the troubadours. Among the most celebrated of the singers of France was Gace Brulé, a knight of Champagne, who knew the songs of the troubadours well and was especially influenced by Bernart de Ventadorn, to whose lyrics he alludes explicitly. The lyric presented here is a skillfully wrought fabric of courtly themes. The songs of the birds heard in Brittany remind him of his native land, Champagne, where he first heard them; the mood of remembrance and contemplation evokes the image of his beloved. The succeeding strophes continue this intricate and unending alternation of distant memory and live experience: the central event of the past, the kiss, continues to take place in the lonely present: his lips still feel it; the lingering feeling of the kiss is the cause of his torment, which recalls the joy of its first occurrence. The inaccessibility of the beloved, the crazed look of the lover, the competition of the false lovers who win the favor denied to the true one—these too are traditional themes; here their expressive power is renewed through the pattern of the song.

The Little Birds of My Homeland

I

The little birds of my homeland
I have heard here in Brittany.
By their song I realize

Translated by Frederick Goldin.

---

2. A possible reference to Longinus, a Roman soldier who, according to legend, was con-verted at the foot of the Cross at the Crucifixion.

I heard them, once,
in sweet Champagne,   5
if I am not mistaken.
They've put me into such a pleasant study,
I have started out on this new song,
so that I may attain
what Love has now for so long promised me.   10

II

By long waiting I am discomfited,
and speak not one word of complaint.
That takes away my joy in song, my laughter,
for no one whom Love rules and torments
can think of anything else.   15
My body and my face
I find so many times beset,
that I have taken on a madman's look:
whatever others may transgress in love,
I never did her any other wrong.   20

III

On a kiss my sweet gentle lady
stole away my heart.
How mad of my heart to quit me
for her who torments me.
Alas! I never felt it   25
when it went from me.
She ravished it away so gently,
drew it to her on a sigh.
She fills my mad heart with desire,
but will never feel pity for me.   30

IV

That kiss I remember well,
so well that in my mind
not an hour passes but on my lips
I feel what has betrayed me.
When she allowed,   35
Lord God! what I am telling of,
why did she not warn me of my death!
She is aware that I am dying

of the pain of this long waiting,
wherefor my face loses color, has grown pale.   40

V

Thus she bears away my laughter and play
and causes me to die of longing.
Love makes me pay dearly again
and again for her company.
Alas, I dare not go to her: 45
the false lovers get me condemned there
for the madman's look on me.
Seeing them ply their words with her, I am undone,
for not one of them can find
the smallest treachery in her.   50

GOTTFRIED VON STRASSBURG

(fl. 1210)

Germany

This great German Romantic poet was probably well read in Latin and in French.
He had a gift for language and an affinity for classical poetry, mythology, and
music. Basing his German version of the popular story of the doomed lovers
Tristan and Isolde on the Anglo-Norman text by the poet Thomas, with its echoes
of Abelard and Heloise (the gifted pair of intellectuals who fell in love over their
studies) Gottfried raises the love to an almost mystic level. He uses religious
language to describe it in the prologue, calling their story a kind of eucharist
("bread") to all noble hearts, treating the love potion as a symbol of the bond
between them that makes one being of the two, and describing the cave in which
they spend their exile as an allegorical shrine of ideal love, where they need no
food or company but subsist on love, on mutual desire and on the literature and
music they share. Unfortunately, they also have to exist in the real world, in
which Isolde is married to Tristan's uncle, King Mark. Eventually Mark's jealousy
of Isolde, despite his love for Tristan, forces Tristan to leave court.

In other versions the lovers meet again before they die, but we do not know
if Gottfried would have included those episodes, had he finished the poem, or
whether he deliberately left their fate suspended because he was uncomfortable
with Thomas's ending. Either way, his audience would have known that the
lovers could not be truly united except in death.

from **Tristan**

Doomed love.

from the *Prologue* [*The Sorrow and Joy of Love*]

He that never had sorrow of love never had joy of it either! In love, joy and sorrow ever went hand in hand! With them we must win praise and honour or come to nothing without them! If the two of whom this love-story tells had not endured sorrow for the sake of joy, love's pain for its ecstasy within one heart, their name and history would never have brought such rapture to so many noble spirits! Today we still love to hear of their tender devotion, sweet and ever fresh, their joy, their sorrow, their anguish, and their ecstasy. And although they are long dead, their sweet name lives on and their death will endure for ever to the profit of well-bred people, giving loyalty to those who seek loyalty, honour to those who seek honour. For us who are alive their death must live on and be for ever new. For wherever still today one hears the recital of their devotion, their perfect loyalty, their hearts' joy, their hearts' sorrow—

This is bread to all noble hearts. With this their death lives on. We read their life, we read their death, and to us it is sweet as bread.

Their life, their death are our bread. Thus lives their life, thus lives their death. Thus they live still and yet are dead, and their death is the bread of the living.

And whoever now desires to be told of their life, their death, their joy, their sorrow, let him lend me his heart and ears—he shall find all that he desires!

Fell in love from love potion.

[*Enduring Sorrow for the Sake of Joy*]

Denial

Now when the maid and the man, Isolde and Tristan, had drunk the draught, in an instant that arch-disturber of tranquility was there, Love, waylayer of all hearts, and she had stolen in! Before they were aware of it she had planted her victorious standard there and bowed them beneath her yoke. They who were two and divided now became one and united. No longer were they at variance. Isolde's hatred was gone. Love, the reconciler, had purged their hearts of enmity, and so joined them in affection that each was to the other as limpid as a mirror. They shared a single heart. Her anguish was his pain: his pain her anguish. The two were one both in joy and in sorrow, yet they hid their feelings from each other. This was from doubt and shame. She was ashamed, as he was. She went in doubt of him, as he of her. However blindly the craving in their hearts was centered on one desire, their anxiety was how to begin. This masked their desire from each other.

When Tristan felt the stirrings of love he at once remembered loyalty and honour, and strove to turn away. 'No, leave it, Tristan,' he was continually thinking to himself, 'pull yourself together, do not take any notice of it.' But his heart was impelled towards her. He was striving against his own wishes, desiring against his desire. He was drawn now in one direction, now in another. Captive that he was, he tried all that he knew in the snare, over and over again, and long maintained his efforts.

Translated by A. T. Hatto.

Relationship evolves . . .

[The Blind Sweetness of Love]

The loyal man was afflicted by a double pain: when he looked at her face and sweet Love began to wound his heart and soul with her, he bethought himself of Honour, and it retrieved him. But this in turn was the sign for Love, his liege lady, whom his father had served before him, to assail him anew, and once more he had to submit. Honour and Loyalty harassed him powerfully, but Love harassed him more. Love tormented him to an extreme, she made him suffer more than did Honour and Loyalty combined. His heart smiled upon Isolde, but he turned his eyes away: yet his greatest grief was when he failed to see her. As is the way of captives, he fixed his mind on escape and how he might elude her, and returned many times to this thought: 'Turn one way, or another! Change this desire! Love and like elsewhere!' But the noose was always there. He took his heart and soul and searched them for some change: but there was nothing there but Love—and Isolde.

And so it fared with her. Finding this life unbearable, she, too, made ceaseless efforts. When she recognized the lime that bewitching Love had spread and saw that she was deep in it, she endeavoured to reach dry ground, she strove to be out and away. But the lime kept clinging to her and drew her back and down. The lovely woman fought back with might and main, but stuck fast at every step. She was succumbing against her will. She made desperate attempts on many sides, she twisted and turned with hands and feet and immersed them ever deeper in the blind sweetness of Love, and of the man. Her limed senses failed to discover any path, bridge, or track that would advance them half a step, half a foot, without Love being there too. Whatever Isolde thought, whatever came uppermost in her mind, there was nothing there, of one sort or another, but Love, and Tristan.

This was all below the surface, for her heart and her eyes were at variance— Modesty chased her eyes away, Love drew her heart towards him. That warring company, a Maid and a Man, Love and Modesty, brought her into great confusion; for the Maid wanted the Man, yet she turned her eyes away: Modesty wanted Love, but told no one of her wishes. But what was the good of that? A Maid and her Modesty are by common consent so fleeting a thing, so short-lived a blossoming, they do not long resist. Thus Isolde gave up her struggle and accepted her situation. Without further delay the vanquished girl resigned herself body and soul to Love and to the man.

Isolde glanced at him now and again and watched him covertly, her bright eyes and her heart were now in full accord. Secretly and lovingly her heart and eyes darted at the man rapaciously, while the man gave back her looks with tender passion. Since Love would not release him, he too began to give ground. Whenever there was a suitable occasion the man and the maid came together to feast each other's eyes. These lovers seemed to each other fairer than before—such is Love's law, such is the way with affection. It is so this year, it was so last year and it will remain so among all lovers as long as Love endures, that while their affection is growing and bringing forth blossom and increase of all loveable things, they please each other more than ever they did when it first began to burgeon. Love that bears increase makes lovers fairer than at first. This is the seed of Love, from which it never dies.

Love seems fairer than before and so Love's rule endures. Were Love to seem the same as before, Love's rule would soon wither away.

Give in to such feelings.

[The Nourishment of Love]

Some people are smitten with curiosity and astonishment, and plague themselves with the question how these companions, Tristan and Isolde, nourished themselves in this wasteland? I will tell them and assuage their curiosity. They looked at one another and nourished themselves with that! Their sustenance was the eye's increase. They fed in their grotto on nothing but love and desire. The two lovers who formed its court had small concern for their provender. Hidden away in their hearts they carried the best nutriment to be had anywhere in the world, which offered itself unasked ever fresh and new. I mean pure devotion, love made sweet as balm that consoles body and sense so tenderly, and sustains the heart and spirit—this was their best nourishment. Truly, they never considered any food but that from which the heart drew desire, the eyes delight, and which the body, too, found agreeable. With this they had enough. Love drove her ancient plough for them, keeping pace all the time, and gave them an abundant store of all those things that go to make heaven on earth.

Nor were they greatly troubled that they should be alone in the wilds without company. Tell me, whom did they need in there with them, and why should anyone join them? They made an even number: there were simply one and one. Had they included a third in the even pair which they made, there would have been an uneven number, and they would have been much encumbered and embarrassed by the odd one. Their company of two was so ample a crowd for this pair that good King Arthur never held a feast in any of his palaces that gave keener pleasure or delight. In no land could you have found enjoyment for which these two would have given a brass farthing to have with them in their grotto. Whatever one could imagine or conceive elsewhere in other countries to make a paradise, they had with them there. They would not have given a button for a better life, save only in respect of their honour. What more should they need? They had their court, they were amply supplied with all that goes to make for happiness. Their loyal sevitors were the green lime, the sunshine and the shade, the brook and its banks, flowers, grass, blossoms, and leaves, so soothing to the eye. The service they received was the song of the birds, of the lovely, slender nightingale, the thrush and blackbird, and other birds of the forest. Siskin and calander-lark vied in eager rivalry to see who could give the best service. These followers served their ears and sense unendingly. Their high feast was Love, who gilded all their joys; she brought them King Arthur's Round Table as homage and all its company a thousand times a day! What better food could they have for body or soul? Man was there with Woman, Woman there with Man. What else should they be needing? They had what they were meant to have, they had reached the goal of their desire.

Now some people are so tactless as to declare (though I do not accept it myself) that other food is needed for this pastime. I am not so sure that it is. There is enough here in my opinion. But if anyone has discovered better nourishment in this world let him speak in the light of his experience. There was a time when I, too, led such a life, and I thought it quite sufficient.

. . .

Those faithful denizens, Tristan and his mistress, had arranged their leisure and exertions very pleasantly in the woods and glades of their wilderness. They were always at each other's side. In the mornings they would stroll to the meadow through the dew, where it had cooled the grass and the flowers. The cool field was their recreation. They talked as they walked to and fro, and they listened as they went to the sweet singing of the birds. Then they would turn aside to where the cool spring murmured, and would hearken to its music as it slid down on its path. Where it entered the glade they used to sit and rest and listen to its purling and watch the water flow, a joy they never tired of.

But when the bright sun began to climb and the heat to descend, they withdrew to their lime-tree in quest of its gentle breezes. This afforded them pleasure within and without their breasts—the tree rejoiced both their hearts and their eyes. With its leaves the fragrant lime refreshed both air and shade for them; from its shade the breezes were gentle, fragrant, cool. The bench beneath the lime was flowers and grass, the best-painted lawn that ever lime-tree had. Our constant lovers sat there together and told love-tales of those whom love had ruined in days gone by. *Much like a Wisteria bush in Texas.*

When they tired of stories they slipped into their refuge and resumed their well-tried pleasure of sounding their harp, and singing sadly and sweetly. They busied their hands and their tongues in turn. They performed amorous lays and their accompaniments, varying their delight as it suited them: for if one took the harp it was for the other to sing the tune with wistful tenderness. And indeed the strains of both harp and tongue, merging their sound in each other, echoed in that cave so sweetly that it was dedicated to sweet Love for her retreat most fittingly as 'La fossiure a la gent amant'.[1]

[Tristan and Isolde Shall Forever Remain One] *(in death)*

If Isolde was ever united with Tristan in one heart and bond, it will always remain fresh, it will endure for ever! But I will ask one thing: to whichever corners of the earth you go, take care of yourself, my life! For when I am orphaned of you, then I, your life, will have perished. I will guard myself, your life, with jealous care, not for my sake but yours, knowing that our two lives are one. We are one life and flesh. Keep your thoughts on me, your very life, your Isolde. Let me see my life again, in you, as soon as ever possible; and may you see yours in me! The life we share is in your keeping. Now come here and kiss me. You and I, Tristan and Isolde, shall for ever remain one and undivided! Let this kiss be a seal upon it that I am yours, that you are mine, steadfast till death, but one Tristan and Isolde!

Denial — evolve — give into feelings —

---

1. "The cave of lovers," which gives its title to the chapter.

divided in love — nourish the love — not truly united except in death.

WOLFRAM VON ESCHENBACH

(fl. 1200–1210)
Germany

Little is known about the author, except that he must have begun *Parzival* around 1197 or 1198. We assume, from the text, that he must have been a knight, proud though poor. He spent some time at the court of Landgrave Hermann, and may have competed in the singing contest there, the subject of the second act of Wagner's*Tannhauser*. Also working with a French source, Chrétien's *Perceval* or *The Story of the Grail,* though he denies it, Wolfram resolves the problems of loyalty and love, and their occasional clash, which had troubled Chrétien in the Arthurian world, by moving his hero into a higher world, the realm of the Grail, where he can serve God and man and his lady all at the same time. And by not making the Grail world very different from the Arthurian, except in the religious symbolism of its central ritual, seen in the last selection presented here, Wolfram manages to keep chivalric adventure as the main plot device. Chrétien had condemned fighting and violence in the beginning of his story, and then had no action for his hero to engage in, but Wolfram, who was a knight himself and approved of fighting, allows his hero to fight, because his Grail knights are a military order, like the Knights Templar.

Parzival is brought up in the woods, ignorant of the chivalry that killed his father because his mother wants to protect him from his father's fate. She has taught him little about religion except that God is brilliant, so when he first sees knights in bright armor, he mistakes them for gods, as is described in the first selection presented here. Subsequently, he learns what Knights are, and he decides he wants to be one and goes to Arthur's court to be made a knight without any sense of what it involves. He learns quickly and is able to rescue the woman whom he will marry from a devastating siege, whose effects on the population are described with realistic touches (that contrast with the splendor of the Grail procession).

from *Parzival*

[Parzival Mistakes the Knights for Gods]

One day he went out hunting along a mountain slope. He broke off a branch from a tree for the whistle the leaf would make. Right near him ran a path, and there he heard the sound of horses' hooves. He began to brandish his javelot and said, "What is this I hear? O, if only the Devil would just come along now in his furious rage! I would stand up to him for sure. My mother says he is a terror, but I think her bravery is a little daunted." And thus he stood eager for battle, when look!

Translated by Helen M. Mustard and Charles E. Passage.

there came three knights galloping along, as fair as anyone could wish and armed from the feet upward. The lad thought for sure that each one was a god, and so he stood there no longer but fell to his knees on the path. Loud cried the lad then, "Help, God! You surely have help to give!"

The rider in front flew into a rage to see the lad laying there in the path: "This stupid Waleis[1] is holding up our swift journey."—A thing we Bavarians get praise for I have to say about Waleis people too: they are stupider than Bavarian folks, and yet, like them, of manly stout-heartedness. Anyone born in these two countries grows up a marvel of cleverness.

Just then there came along at a gallop a splendidly adorned knight who was in a great hurry. He was riding in pursuit of those who had got a head start on him, two knights, namely, who had abducted a lady in his land. He considered this a disgrace and grieved at the plight of the maiden, who had ridden on before him in a deplorable state. These three knights here were his own vassals. He was riding a fine Castilian horse; there was very little of his shield that was whole; and his name was Karnahkarnanz, *le comte* Ulterlec. "Who is blocking our way?" said he, and rode over to the lad, to whom he seemed to have the form of a god, for never had he seen anything so bright. His surcoat swept the dew, his stirrups, adjusted to either foot to just the right length, rang with little golden bells, and his right arm chimed with bells whenever he raised it in greeting or to strike. It was meant to ring loud at his sword strokes, for this hero was eager for renown. Thus rode the rich prince, woundrously adorned.

Then of him who was a garland of all the flowers of manly beauty Karnahkarnanz asked, "Young Sir, have you seen two knights ride past who could not keep the knightly code? They are perpetrating rape and are lacking in honor. They are abducting a maiden."

But say what he might, the lad still thought he was God, just as Lady Herzeloyde[2] the Queen had told him when she explained His bright shining. And so he cried out in all seriousness, "Help me now, God of help!" And *le fils du roi* Gahmuret fell down in an attitude of prayer.

The prince said, "I am not God, though I gladly do His commandment. What you see here are four knights, if you would only look aright."

The lad asked further, "You speak of *knights*: what is that? If you do not have God's kind of power, then tell me: who bestows knighthood?"

"That King Arthur does. Young Sir, if you come to his house, he will give you the name of knight so that you will never need to be ashamed of it. You may well be of knightly race."—And by the warriors he was scrutinized, and God's handiwork was manifest in him.—I have this from the adventure, which with truth was told me so. Never had man's beauty been more nobly realized since Adam's time, and hence his praise was wide among women.

---

1. A Welshman.

2. Parzival's mother, whose name means "heart's grief" in German.

But then the lad spoke again, and laughter arose at it, "Ay, Knight God, what may you be? You have so many rings tied around your body, up there, and down here."[3] And therewith the lad's hand laid hold of iron wherever he could find it on the prince, and he began to inspect the armor. "My mother's ladies wear their rings on strands and they don't fit so close together as these." The lad spoke further to the prince, just as the thoughts came to him, "What is this good for, that fits you so well? I can't pick it off."

Then the prince showed him his sword. "You see, anyone seeking battle with me I ward off with blows, and to protect myself against his, I have to put this on, and both for shot and for stab I have to wear armor like this."

But the lad quickly replied, "If stags wore pelts like that, my javelot would not wound a single one. And a good many fall dead before me."

The knights were chafing at his delay with the lad who was so simple. "God shield you," said the prince. "Would that your beauty were mine! God would have conferred upon you the uttermost that could be wished for, if only you had intelligence. May God's power keep you from harm."

[Parzival Is About to Be a Knight]

The lad said, "God keep you! as my mother told me to say before I left her house. I see many Arthurs here: which one will make me a knight?"

Iwanet[4] burst out laughing and said, "The right one you do not see, but it won't be long before you do." He led him inside the great hall where the worthy company was.

In spite of the din he was able to say, "God keep you gentlemen all, and especially the King and his wife. My mother charged me on my life to greet *them* in particular. And those that have a place at the Round Table because of their deserved renown, she bade me greet them too. But one piece of knowledge I lack: I don't know which one of you is the host. To *him* a knight has sent a message—I saw him and he was red all over[5] . . . and he says he will wait for him outside there. I think he wants to fight. Also, he is sorry that he spilled wine on the Queen. O, if only I had received those clothes of his from the King's hand! I would be very pleased: they look so knightly!"

The free-spoken lad was much elbowed about, hustled this way and that. They noticed his beauty. Their own eyes saw that never was more lovely form lorded or ladied, for God was in a good humor when He created Parzival. And thus he who feared terror but little was brought before Arthur. No one could be hostile to him in whom God invented perfection. The Queen too gazed at him before she left the great hall where she had had the wine spilled on her.

---

3. Parzival has never seen armor or chain mail.
4. Iwanet is a squire in Arthur's court.
5. The knight in red armor is Ither, who came to Arthur's court to claim land, and seized the goblet as a symbolic gesture, but spilled the wine on the queen.

Then Arthur looked at the lad, and to the simple youth he said, "Young Sir, may God repay your greeting. I will gladly serve you with my life and my possessions. I am indeed of a mind to do so."

"God grant that that is really so! The time seems to me a year since I was supposed to become a knight, and that is more bad than good. Now do not make me wait any longer, grant me the honor of knighthood!"

"That I will and gladly," said his host, "if my dignity suffices. You are so pleasing that my gift to you shall be of precious worth. Indeed I will not fail to do it, but you must wait until tomorrow morning and I will fit you out properly."

The high-born lad halted there awkward as a crane, and said "I will not beg for anything here. A knight came riding toward me. If I can't get his armor I don't care who talks about kingly gifts. Those my mother can give me, for after all she is a queen."

Then Arthur said to the lad, "That armor is worn by such a man that I would not dare give to you. I have had to live with worry as it is, and through no fault of mine, ever since I lost his homage. He is Ither of Gaheviez, who rammed sorrow through my joy."

"A generous king *you* would be, if a gift like that were too great for you!" said Keie[6] then. "Let him have it, and let him go out there and face him on the meadow! As long as someone has to bring us the goblet, here is the string and there is the top: let the boy do the spinning. He will be praised for it among the women. He will often have to risk quarrels and take such chances, and I don't care about either of their lives. You have to lose a dog or two to get a boar's head."

"I hate to deny him," said Arthur in good faith, "only I fear he may be killed just when I am about to help him to knighthood."

. . .

On both sides of the street stood a great crowd of people. Slingers and foot soldiers, a long line of them, came bearing arms, and a large number of dart throwers. At the same time he saw many brave foot soldiers, the best in the country, with long stout lances, sharp and whole. Also, as I heard the story, many merchants stood there too with axes and javelots, as their guild masters had ordered. They all had skins slack from hunger. The queen's marshal led him with difficulty through their midst as far as the courtyard. There defenses had been prepared. There were towers over the living quarters, mural towers, tower keeps, and half turrets, certainly more of them than he had ever seen before. From all sides knights came forth to greet him, some on horseback, some on foot, and this sorry crowd was also the color of ashes or sickly clay.—My master, the Count of Wertheim,[7] would not have liked to be a soldier there: he couldn't have survived on their allowance.—Want had reduced them to starvation. They had neither cheese, nor meat, nor bread; they had no use for toothpicks, and no grease from

---

6. Keie (or Kay) is Arthur's seneschal, who is normally insulting or mocking, as he is here.

7. Wolfram was apparently a vassal of the Count of Wertheim, and a poor one at that.

their lips soiled the wine they drank. Their bellies had caved in, their hips were protruding and lean, and their skin was shriveled right to their ribs like Hungarian leather. Hunger had driven their flesh away, and from privation they could do nothing but endure it. There was mighty little to drip into their fires.

But if I were to twit them about it, I would show very poor sense, for where I have often dismounted and where I am addressed as Sir, at home in my own house, it is uncommon for a mouse to find delight. Mice have to steal their food, but I, from whom nobody has to hide it, can't even find it openly. And it happens all too often to me, Wolfram of Eschenbach, that I put up with such comfort!

[The Procession of the Grail]

There where sat many a valorous knight, Sorrow itself was borne into their presence. In through the door dashed a squire, bearing a lance in his hand. This rite sharpened their sorrow. Blood gushed from the point and ran down the shaft to the hand that bore it and on into the sleeve. And now there was weeping and wailing throughout the whole wide hall. The people of thirty lands could not have wept so many tears. The squire bore the lance in his hands all around the four walls until he reached the door again and ran out. Stilled then was the people's mourning, called forth by the sorrow of which they had been reminded by this lance borne in the hand of the squire.

If it will not weary you, I shall tell you now with what courtesy service was offered here. At the end of the great hall a door of steel was opened and in came two maidens of noble birth—now note how they are attired—so fair that they could have given love's reward if any knight there had earned it with his service. Each wore a wreath of flowers on her loose-flowing hair and bore in her hand a golden candlestick in which was a burning candle. Their hair was wavy, long, and fair—but we must not forget to tell how they were dressed. The Countess of Tenabroc and her companion wore gowns of brown wool, each drawn tight with a girdle about the waist. Following them came a duchess and her companion, their lips aglow like the red of the fire, carrying two little ivory stools. They bowed, all four, and the two set the stools in front of the host. This service was performed to perfection. Then they stood in a group together, all four dressed alike and fair to see.

But look how quickly they have been joined by more ladies, four times two, who had a duty to perform. Four carried tall candles, the other four were not displeased to be the bearers of a precious stone so clear that in the day the sun shone through. It was a garnet hyacinth, long and wide, and he who measured it for a table top had cut it thin that it might be light to carry. At this sumptuous table the host ate. All eight maidens went straight to the host and bowed their heads before him. Four laid the table top on the snow-white ivory of the stools placed there before, and stepped back decorously to stand with the first four.

Two princesses were seen approaching now, most beautifully dressed. They carried two knives as sharp as fishbones, displaying them, since they were so rare, on two cloths, each one separately. They were of silver hard and white and wrought with cunning skill, so keenly sharpened they could very likely have cut even steel. Preceding the silver knives came other ladies needed for service here, four maids of a purity free from reproach, carrying candles that cast a gleam upon the silver.

After them came the queen.[8] So radiant was her countenance that everyone thought the dawn was breaking. She was clothed in a dress of Arabian silk. Upon a deep green achmardi she bore the perfection of Paradise, both root and branch. That was a thing called the Grail,[9] which surpasses all earthly perfection. Repanse de Schoye was the name of her whom the Grail permitted to be its bearer. Such was the nature of the Grail that she who watched over it had to preserve her purity and renounce all falsity.

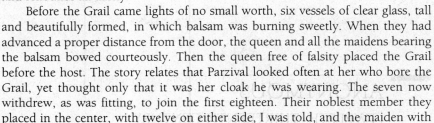

Before the Grail came lights of no small worth, six vessels of clear glass, tall and beautifully formed, in which balsam was burning sweetly. When they had advanced a proper distance from the door, the queen and all the maidens bearing the balsam bowed courteously. Then the queen free of falsity placed the Grail before the host. The story relates that Parzival looked often at her who bore the Grail, yet thought only that it was her cloak he was wearing. The seven now withdrew, as was fitting, to join the first eighteen. Their noblest member they placed in the center, with twelve on either side, I was told, and the maiden with the crown stood there in all her beauty.

For the knights assembled in the great hall stewards were assigned, one for each group of four, all bearing heavy gold basins and followed by comely pages carrying white towels. Splendor enough was there to be seen. A hundred tables—there must have been that many—were now brought into the hall, each was placed before four of the noble knights, and white cloths were spread carefully upon them. The host then took water for washing his hands—he had long since lost his joyful spirits—and Parzival too washed in the same water and, like his host, dried his hands on a bright-colored silk towel which a count's son on bended knee was quick to offer them. In the spaces between, where . . . no tables were, four squires were stationed to serve those who sat at each table. Two of them knelt and carved; the other two brought food and drink and attended them zealously.

---

8. The "queen," Repanse de Schoye, is the sister of the Grail king. Her name, apparently French, may mean "thought of joy," though it could also be "refuge" or "regret of joy." Wolfram frequently played with French names.

9. The Grail is a vessel—supposedly containing the blood of Christ—with power from God to sustain those who serve it, and the

Grail quest adds a religious motivation to the secular culture of chivalry. In Wolfram it draws the finest knight away from Arthur's service—Parzival becomes the Grail king—without disrupting Arthur's court, but in the Morte D'Arthur by Malory, the quest contributes to the disintegration of the Arthurian world.

Listen now as I tell you more of this splendor. Four carts brought costly vessels of gold to every knight who was there. Around the four walls they were drawn, and four knights with their own hands placed the vessels on the tables, each one followed by a clerk whose duty it was to collect and count them later after the meal was over.

Now listen and you shall hear more. A hundred squires, so ordered, reverently took bread in white napkins from before the Grail, stepped back in a group and, separating, passed the bread to all the tables. I was told, and I tell you too, but on *your* oath, not mine—hence if I deceive you, we are liars all of us—that whatsoever one reached out his hand for, he found it ready, in front of the Grail, food warm or food cold, dishes new or old, meat tame or game. "There never was anything like that," many will say. But they will be wrong in their angry protest, for the Grail was the fruit of blessedness, such abundance of the sweetness of the world that its delights were very like what we are told of the kingdom of heaven.

ANONYMOUS
(TWELFTH–THIRTEENTH CENTURY)
France

Renard the Fox is the greatest of the beast epics—a sociopolitical satire in which predatory animals and their natural prey represent the various inhabitants of a monarchy. The authors of these tales attack with gusto and an implied idealism the government of their country, its legal system and Church, the formalities of feudalism, the hollow protection offered the underprivileged, and the unredeemed brutality of peasants.

When Renard the Fox, a great lord in the court of King Noble the Lion, is tried and condemned for murdering a chicken, the effect is richly comic, but the underlying message is that the predations of a human *seigneur* would similarly be part of his nature. The Renard stories spread throughout European vernacular literatures, leaving their mark on Chaucer's "Nun's Priest's Tale" and Goethe's famous adaptation, *Reineke Fuchs*.

In the passage that follows, the badger, Grinbert, kinsman to Renard, goes to visit the fox at Maupertuis, described as a fortress but also clearly a den. Grinbert has been preceded as ambassador by Tibert the cat and Bruin the bear, both of whom were grievously mistreated by Renard. Grinbert persuades Renard to confess his sins, which gives the fox a chance to rejoice in past successes. Then they must leave for the court of King Noble, where Renard is to be tried for committing adultery with the wolf's wife, Hersent. Renard bids farewell to his family and says a moving prayer, but he is soon shown to be unreformed.

King Noble the Lion furious with Renard the Fox - manuscript illumination.
Bibliothèque Nationale, Paris.

from **Renard the Fox**

[Renard's Confession]

Then Grinbert,[1] with the king's permission,
Started out to perform his mission.
Through meadow and wood he went; no lack
Of sweat was pouring off his back,
And still he had far to go before   5
He would be close to Renard's front door.
At vespers he came upon a lane,
And at nightfall found Renard's domain.
The walls rose high above his head;
There were narrow passageways that led   10
To where he found a low-vaulted door
Into a courtyard. Then, still more*
Afraid of what Renard would do
If he should hear him coming through,
He hugged the walls and waited to see—   15
That was Grinbert at Maupertuis.[2]
As soon as his visitor had stepped
Onto the turning bridge* and crept

Translated by Patricia Terry.

*The translation conforms to the octosyllabic couplets of the original.

---

1. Grinbert (Gran BER): the king's ambassador, a badger.

2. Maupertuis (Mow pair TWEE): Renard's
   home.

Along the passageways—even then,
Before Grinbert came into his den,   20
Hindquarters first and head to the rear,
Renard knew who was coming near.
He welcomed Grinbert with warm delight,
Wrapped both arms around him tight,
And two soft pillows behind him pressed,   25
Because his cousin was his guest.
I think Grinbert was very wise
To keep his message for a surprise
Until he'd had enough to eat,
But after dinner, feeling replete,   30
"My lord," he said, "everyone knows
The way you lie and cheat—it shows.
I'm here to tell you the king demands,
No, not demands—the king commands
That at his palace you submit   35
To whatever sentence he deems fit.
Why wage a war you cannot win?
What did you want of Ysengrin?[3]
Why harm Tibert? Why hurt Bruin?
You have betrayed them to your ruin.   40
I'd like to offer you some cheer,
But I think your time to die is near,
And all your children will share your fate.
Break this seal and you'll get it straight.
Just read the words that are written here."   45
Renard listens, and shakes with fear.
He trembles, as he breaks the seal,
For what that gesture may reveal.
He reads the first few words and sighs,
Well understanding what meets his eyes.   50
   "Noble the lion, whose majesty
Prevails throughout these lands where he
Over all the beasts is king and lord,
Promises Renard he cannot afford
To ignore this summons: he'll pay dear   55
If tomorrow he does not appear
To make amends for his misdeeds.
Not silver and not gold he needs,
And let no champion give him hope;
He'll pay his debt with a hangman's rope."   60
   A terrible message for Renard!
Inside his chest his heart beat hard,

---

3. Ysengrin the wolf.

His face took on a somber hue.
"For God's sake, Grinbert, what shall I do?
Pity a poor defenseless captive!
Alas that I have this hour to live,
If I must hang until I'm dead
Tomorrow. I wish I'd been instead
A monk at Cluny or Citeaux!
But many of them are false, and so
I'd soon have wanted to depart;
In that case better not to start."
"You've other things to worry about!"
Said Grinbert. "And while you're here without
People around you, I suggest
That it would be well if you confessed.
Confess your sins to me at least—
Since I don't see any closer priest."
"My lord Grinbert," Renard replies,
I think your counsel very wise;
I'm close to death for my transgression,
And if you hear my true confession
I've nothing at all to lose thereby,
And I am saved if I have to die
    Listen! I heartily repent
For what I did with Dame Hersent[4]
Who is the wife of Ysengrin.
She tried to cover up that sin
But no one believed her—that was shrewd
For she was well and truly screwed.
May God preserve my soul from Hell,
So many time I rang her bell—
Mea culpa!—if I have to face
Ysengrin, I'll lose the case.
How to deny that he's been cheated,
Three times imprisoned and defeated!
Now I will tell you all about it.
I made him fall into the pit
Just as he carried off a sheep.
Lucky for him he got to keep
Any skin at all, for it was shed
In a hundred blows before he fled.
When I had trapped him as I planned,
There were three shepherds close at hand
Who beat him like a balky ass."
Another time I helped him pass

65

70

75

80

85

90

95

100

105

---

4. Hersent the wolf's wife.

Through an entrance to a rich man's larder,
But getting out was a great deal harder,
For his belly swelled still more with each
Of three hams he found within his reach.   110
I set him to fishing through the ice;
His tail was caught as in a vise.
I made him fish in a pool one night
When the full moon was very bright,
And its reflection, white and round,   115
Looked like a lovely cheese he'd found.
So once again I had my wish—
He ended up on a load of fish.
A hundred times I took him in
With the guileful schemes my wits can spin.   120
Thanks to me he had a tonsured head.
Then he saw how well the canons fed
And thought their life wouldn't be so hard;
Those fools gave him their sheep to guard!
I could talk all day and not be done   125
Telling you how I had my fun.
There's not one beast in Noble's court
Who wouldn't give me a bad report.
When I led Tibert into the net
He thought that it was rats he'd get.   130
In all Pinte's[5] family there lives
One aunt; her other relatives,
Cocks and hens alike, were able
To fill a place at my dinner table.
When a cow and ox and the mighty boar   135
With other beasts stood at my door
Well armed, Ysengrin, in the lead,
Was sure that he had all he'd need
To win. There were on his side as well,
With the watchdog, Loudmouth Roenel,   140
Seven times twenty dogs and bitches
All of whom soon needed stitches,
Having most foully been betrayed—
I'd gotten to everyone they paid.
I certainly have no cause to boast   145
Of how I routed that great host—
Only by guile were they defeated.
I watched as long as they retreated

---

5. Pinte the hen who came to King Noble's
   court to accuse Renard of murdering her
   relatives.

And in salute stuck out my tongue.
God! What I did when I was young!
But now, *mea culpa!* true remorse
Turns my life from its sinful course."
"Renard, Renard," Grinbert begins,
"I've heard the confession of your sins
And all the evil you have done.
Your trial, By God's will, may yet be won.
Take care from now on to do no wrong."
"May God not let me live so long,"
Renard replied, "that all my ways
Are not deserving of His praise."
He shows a pious resolution,
Kneels, and Grinbert gives absolution
In French and in the tongue of Rome.
Next morning, before Renard left home,
He kissed his children and his wife,
All of them fearing for his life.
When the time of separation came,
"My sons," he said, "defend our name!
However this misadventure goes,
Protect my castles against our foes.
Against a count, against a king,
For months you won't need to fear a thing—
No count or baron, no lord would dare
Rob your head of a single hair.
You'll never be so much as grazed,
If you keep every drawbridge raised
And are well provisioned—for seven years
You'll stand them off and have no fears.
What more is there for me to say?
I commend you now to God, and pray
That He will bring me back once more."
With that he knelt down on the floor;
Because he would have to leave his lair,
Renard began to say a prayer.
    "God, King, in your omnipotence,
Let my craft and my common sense
Not be lost to me out of fear
When before the king I must appear
To answer Ysengrin in court.
Whatever he chooses to report
Let me make it harmless to admit,
Or find some way of denying it;
And let me come back to Maupertuis
Alive and well, so that I may be

150

155

160

165

170

175

180

185

190

Avenged on those who seek my disgrace."   195
Renard fell down upon his face,
Then, beating his breast for what he'd done,
Made the sign against the evil one.
    And now the noble lords will go
To court; on their way swift rivers flow;   200
There are narrow trails to follow past
High mountain ridges until at last
They ride across a level plain.
Renard is really feeling the strain;
That's why, in the woods, they go astray   205
And find no footpath, road or way
Until, where farmland had been cleared,
A barn that belonged to nuns appeared.
Surely one would find inside
The best of what the world can provide: 210
Cheese and milk and lambs they keep,
Geese and oxen, cows and sheep,
And young ones they fatten up to eat.
"Come on!" said Renard. "Don't drag your feet!
Now I can see where we went wrong.   215
There's underbrush to follow along
To the henyard, then it's straight ahead."
"Renard, Renard," the badger said,
"Does God not know what you say that for?
Foul unbelieving son of a whore,   220
Stinking glutton—I thought you craved,
Pleading for mercy, to be saved!
I heard your confession, did I not?"
Replied Renard, "I quite forgot.
I'm ready now. Let's go on like friends."   225
"Renard, Renard, it never ends!
God himself you will try to trick!
On you repentance can never stick.
How you came to be so mad, God knows!
Your life may be coming to a close,   230
And scarcely have you confessed before
You turn around and sin once more.
Evil has marked you out as prey.
Let's go now. A curse upon the day
When you were severed from your mother!"   235
"You do very well to say so, brother!
But now let's go our way in peace."
To make his cousin's scolding cease
Renard was keeping very quiet
As to the farm—he dared not try it,   240

But he craned his neck a little when
He caught a sight of a lovely hen,
Sadly thinking he'd rather have fed
And paid the price, though it were his head!

NA CASTELLOZA
(EARLY THIRTEENTH CENTURY)
France

Castelloza is an unusual name, perhaps a pseudonym. It appears attached to three Provençal poems in the found texts, but we know nothing about her. In the scant information that is provided in the prose poems, the poet speaks of a husband and a lover, and she also addresses another woman poet, but none of this has helped to identify her. In the text presented here she asserts her love and the pleasure she takes in pleading her case, even though it is not considered proper for a lady to do so. Elsewhere she explains her unusual forthrightness: "I shall have set a very bad example for other women in love, because it's the man who usually sends a message . . . yet . . . this was right for me." And: "the more a lady happens to love, [the more] she should court a knight, if she sees prowess and heroism in him."

Friend, If I Found You Charming

I. Friend, if I found you charming, humble, open, and compassionate, I would love you indeed—since now I realize that I find you wicked, despicable, and haughty toward me, yet I make songs to make your good name heard; which is why I cannot keep from making everyone praise you when most you cause me harm and anger.

II. Never shall I consider you worthy, nor shall I love you from the heart or with trust; in truth I'll see if ever it would do me any good to show you a cruel and hateful heart.—I will never do it, for I don't want you to be able to say that I ever had the heart to be negligent toward you; you would have some defense, if I had committed negligence toward you.

III. I know well that it pleases me, even though everyone says that it's very improper for a lady to plead her own cause with a knight, and make him so long a sermon all the time. But whoever says that doesn't know how to discern well at

Translated by William Paden.

all. I want to pray before I let myself die, since in prayer I find much sweet healing when I pray to the one from whom I get great care.

IV. He is quite a fool who reproaches me for loving you, since it is so very pleasing to me; and he who says it doesn't know how it is with me, nor has he seen you with the eyes I saw you with when you told me not to worry, for at any time it could happen that I would again have joy. From your mere word I have a rejoicing heart.

V. All other love I consider nothing—so know well that joy no longer sustains me, but for yours which delights me and heals me when most pain and distress come to me. By my lamentation and lays I always hope to enjoy you, friend, because I cannot convert; I have no joy, nor do I expect help, except only as much as I'll get while sleeping.

VI. From now on I don't know why I present myself to you, for I've tested with evil and with good your hard heart—which my own doesn't renounce. And I don't send you this, for I say it to you myself: I shall die if you don't want to make me rejoice with whatever joy; and if you let me die you will commit a sin, and you'll be in torment for it, and I'll be more sought after at Judgment.

HEINRICH VON MORUNGEN

(fl. 1200; d. 1222)

Germany

The form and the defining themes of the troubadour *canso* were adopted in other areas and languages. In German-speaking lands the influence of the troubadours of southern France and the *trouvères* of northern France combined with a native lyric tradition to produce a distinctive body of lyrics, known collectively as the *Minnesang,* that is, songs about *Minne* or courtly love. (The word *Minne* is etymologically related to English "mind" and designates that elevated passion—sexual desire complicated and enhanced by thought, and channeled into courtly forms of behavior—which the troubadours called *fin' amors.*)

The songs of Heinrich von Morungen—a nobleman, who died in a cloister—are characterized by the variety of their forms, their immediacy to the audience, and their arresting imagery. The lyric presented here is one of the most famous and most variously interpreted of the entire *Minnesang*. It depicts the deepest traits of the courtly love relation: the tense and unending—and unendable—oscillation of the lover between adoration and disillusionment, soaring joy and painful doubt; the tantalizing unreadability of the beloved (reflected in the instability of her image); and the intensification of self-consciousness in the "I." From another point of view one can detect the awareness of the performer before his audience—notice the dramatic strategy in the second strophe ("Behold!"), and the allusions to elements of their common

culture, to Narcissus in the third strophe, for example, and to the Virgin in the
fourth: ("The very heaven . . . she is the good one").

It Fared with Me as with a Child

I

It fared with me as with a child
that caught sight of its glowing image in a mirror
and reached in toward its own reflection
so long, till it broke the mirror to pieces;
then all its pleasure turned to pain and discontent.   5
So I, once, thought I'd live in joy forever
when I beheld my lady, beautiful, dearly loved,
through whom, beside the pleasure, it has fared painfully with me.

II

Minne, who increases the joy of the world,
behold! she brought me my lady in the way of a dream   10
where my body was turned toward sleep,
lost in the vision of its great delight.
Then I beheld her excellence, her noble radiance,
beautiful, exalted among women,
only there was some little wound upon   15
her small red mouth, the source of every joy.

III

I felt great dread therefore,
that her sweet mouth should pale, that was so red.
And so I now raised up new laments,
since my heart offered itself to such tribulation,   20
that my eyes made me look on such distress—
like a certain child, unthinking, inexperienced,
who caught sight of his shadow in a spring
and now must love it till he dies.

IV

Women more exalted in character and spirit   25
the very heaven can nowhere embrace—
she is the good one.[1] To my loss, and fearing loss,

Translated by Frederick Goldin.

---

1. The virtue of the beloved, compared to that
   of the Virgin.

I must keep my distance and cleave to her forever.
Ach, the pain of it! I imagined I had reached the goal:
her noble and rejoicing love.   30
Now here I stand, barely at the beginning.
Therefore my joy is gone, and my soaring dream.

GIACOMO DA LENTINO (fl. 1200–1250)
Italy

Giacomo da Lentino was a notary in the imperial court of Frederick II in Sicily, a
setting that favored the continuation of the themes and poetic practices of the
troubadours. He was among the first to write lyrics in Italian in this courtly manner,
even adopting many of the key terms of his poetic ancestors. He is generally
regarded as the inventor of the sonnet. In the example that follows, he uses the
sonnet form in exemplary fashion. The second quatrain, celebrating the physical
beauty of his lady and the joy that she gives, seems to undo the impression of piety
conveyed by the first, which speaks only of devotion to God and the joys of
Paradise; the last six lines, or sestet, resolve this conflict, revealing that the two
devotions coincide, that the beloved, as the magnet of his gaze, draws him to his
salvation. The role played by the lady in this sonnet is a development of one of the
fundamental themes of the courtly love lyric, that of the ameliorating effect of the
beloved image. The extension of this effect to the gates of Paradise is an innovation
that continues through all the "schools" of Italian lyric poetry in the Middle Ages.
Until Dante, it is used simply as an elaborate literary compliment. In Dante this
figurative theme illustrates a literal belief with narrative details.

I Have Set My Heart to Serving God

I have set my heart to serving God
so that I may go to Paradise,
the holy place, where, as I have heard,
there is no end of converse, laughter, joys.

Without my lady I would not want to go there—   5
she of the blonde hair and radiant face—
for lacking her I can rejoice nowhere,
parted from my lady in that place.

But I do not mean by this pronouncement
that I would want to sin in Heaven—I forswear;   10
but only to behold her beautiful deportment,

Translated by Frederick Goldin.

that gentle, loving look, that face so fair;
for I would dwell forever in contentment
to see my lady standing in glory there.

ANONYMOUS (THIRTEENTH CENTURY)
Norway/Iceland

"The Grief of Gudrun" comes from the pre-Christian oral tradition of Norway
and Iceland. Its written form, dating from the tenth century, was preserved in a
thirteenth-century collection called *The Elder Edda,* a collection of poems
primarily lyric rather than narrative. It comes from the legends of the Volsungs,
King Sigmond and his descendants, familiar in modern times from Wagner's
operas. The tradition reflects ancient conflicts between the Burgundians and the
Huns. Brynhild, originally one of Odin's valkyries—the shield-maidens who
guide the dead to Valhalla—is portrayed here as the sister of Atli (Attila the Hun).

In all versions of the Gudrun/Sigurd/Brynhild triangle, Gudrun is the
innocent victim of her brother's (Gunnar's) treachery. Gunnar, desiring the gold
that Sigurd acquired when he killed the dragon Fafnir, deceived Sigurd with a
magical drink that caused him to forget his commitment to Brynhild and marry
Gudrun instead. Brynhild then conspired in Sigurd's murder and killed herself.

The gap in the lines exists in the original text.

from *The Elder Edda*

The Grief of Gudrun

Close to death   in her despair,
Gudrun sat grieving   over Sigurd.
She did not wail   or wring her hands,
nor did she weep   like other women.

Noblemen came   to give her comfort,   5
spoke wise words   to soothe her heart.
Yet Gudrun could not   give way to tears;
burdened by grief,   her heart would break.

Great ladies   decked in gold
sat with Gudrun;   each one spoke.   10
telling the sorrows   she had suffered,
the bitterest   each one had borne.

Translated by Patricia Terry.

Gjuki's sister,   Gjaflaug said:
"I think no woman   in the world
hapless as I am—   five husbands,   15
three daughters,   three sisters,
eight brothers lost;   and I live on."

Yet Gudrun could not   give way to tears;
hating those   who had killed her husband,
she sat with Sigurd,   her heart like stone.   20

Then said Herborg,   queen of the Huns:
"I have greater   griefs to tell.
At war in the south,   my seven sons,
and then my husband—   all have been slain;
my father and mother,   my four brothers,   25
all, when the wind   whipped the waves,
were struck down   in their ship at sea.

"I alone laid them out,   I alone buried them,
I alone gave them   an honored grave.
All this I suffered   in just one season,   30
and no one came   to comfort me.

"Then I was caught   and held a captive
in that same season;   I was a slave.
Every day   I had to dress
my lord's lady,   and lace her shoes.   35

"Her jealous spite   spared me no threats,
and she would beat me   hard blows.
No house could boast   a better master,
not have I met   a mistress worse."

Yet Gudrun could not   give way to tears;   40
hating those   who had killed her husband,
she sat with Sigurd,   her heart like stone.

Gjuki's daughter,   Gullrond, spoke:
"Foster-mother,   your wisdom fails you—
how shall a young wife   listen to words?"   45
She told them not to keep   the dead prince concealed.

She swept off the sheet   that covered Sigurd,
and placed a pillow   at Gudrun's knees:
"Look at your beloved!   Lay your lips on his,
the way you kissed   when the king was alive."   50

Gudrun looked   once at her lord;
she saw his hair   streaming with blood,

the keen eyes dead   in the king's face,
the great sword wound   in Sigurd's breast.

She sank to the ground   against the pillow,   55
her hair fell loose,   her cheeks flushed red;
drops as of rain   ran down to her knees.

Then Gjuki's daughter,   Gudrun, wept
so that the tears   streamed through her hair;
geese in the yard   began to shriek,   60
the famous birds   that belonged to Gudrun.

Gjuki's daughter,   Gullrond, said:
"No man and woman   in all the world
were ever given   so great a love.
Sister, I know   you never felt at peace   65
anywhere   away from Sigurd."

Gudrun said:
"My Sigurd was   to Gjuki's sons
as garlic stands   taller than grass,
or like a bright stone   on a string of beads,   70
a priceless jewel   among the princes.

"My lord's warriors   honored me once
more than any   of Odin's maids:
now I am so little,   like a winter leaf
clinging to a willow,   since the king is dead.   75

"I miss in the hall,   I miss in bed,
my companion   killed by Gjuki's sons,
Gjuki's sons   who gave me to grief,
who made their sister's   bitter sorrow.

"May all who live here   leave your lands   80
as you cast aside   the oaths you swore!
Gunnar, you'll get   no joy from the gold—
the rings will drive you   to your death,
because you swore   an oath with Sigurd.

"There was greater happiness   in this house   85
before my Sigurd   saddled Grani,
and they left   on a luckless day
to woo Brynhild,   the worst of women,"

Then said Brynhild,   Budli's daughter:
"May she mourn   her man and children,   90
who taught you, Gudrun,   to shed tears,
and gave you this day   the gift of speech."

Gjuki's daughter,   Gullrond, said:
"Accursed woman,   don't speak such words!
Ever have you proved   the bane of princes,   95
all the world   wishes you ill;
seven kings   you've brought to sorrow,
widows you've made   of many wives."

Then said Brynhild,   Budli's daughter:
"Atli bears the guilt   of all this grief,   100
Atli, my brother,   Budli's son.

"Around a hero   in the Hunnish hall
flickered the light   of Fafnir's lair,
and I paid   for the prince's journey,
for that sight   I still can see."   105

She stood by a pillar,   summoning her strength;
fire burned   in Brynhild's eyes,
baneful venom   flew from her lips,
when she saw the wounds,   how Sigurd died.

GUILLAUME DE LORRIS (fl. 1230–1235)
JEAN DE MEUN [JEAN CHOPINEL]
(c. 1240–1305)

France

Guillaume de Lorris began *The Romance of the Rose,* a poem written in French
about a young lover who in a dream enters an idyllic garden of Love in the spring,
joins in the dance of Love's companions (Idleness, Diversion, Courtesy, Joy, and
others), sees himself in the mirror of Narcissus, is shot by the arrows of Love, and
falls in love with a rosebud. The rosebud seems to represent a woman, the Rose
for whom Guillaume claims to write the poem, though the Narcissism of this
kind of love is also obvious. The poet describes the pursuit of the rosebud and her
reactions up to the kiss and the imprisonment of the rosebud in a tower, with a
sympathetic if ironic view of the lover's folly. Whether Guillaume died before he
could finish, as Jean de Meun says, or intentionally left the story suspended, as
some have argued, we do not know.

　　In any case, Jean de Meun went on with it in a rather different tone, putting
extensive polemical or didactic discourses in the mouths of various personifications
and human characters, who speak on a variety of subjects from justice to optics,
with emphasis on clerical corruption and misogyny, though Jean also developed

Translated by Charles Dahlberg.

the struggle between the forces or attributes of the lover and those of the lady into a full-scale psychoneurosis. Though there is a good deal of antifeminism in the text, and the poem ends with what can only be called a rape of the rosebud, there is also the curiously affecting speech of an old woman who laments the loss of her beauty and the gifts and attention it brought her, and who wants the young woman to profit from her mistakes, not by avoiding a life of pleasure, but by making it work for her. Though the old woman is morally offensive in her deceptiveness and greed and in her desire for revenge, she also makes a case for the mistreatment of women by men and the natural desire of women to be free—a subject that influenced Chaucer in his treatment of the wife of Bath in the *Canterbury Tales* and that has understandably attracted the attention of modern feminists.

from *The Romance of the Rose*

[The Dream of Narcissus and the Fountain]

Many men say that there is nothing in dreams but fables and lies, but one may have dreams which are not deceitful, whose import becomes quite clear afterward. We may take as witness an author named Macrobius, who did not take dreams as trifles, for he wrote of the vision which came to King Scipio.[1] Whoever thinks or says that to believe in a dream's coming true is folly and stupidity may, if he wishes, think me a fool; but, for my part, I am convinced that a dream signifies the good and evil that come to men, for most men at night dream many things in a hidden way which may afterward be seen openly.

In the twentieth year of my life, at the time when Love exacts his tribute from young people, I lay down one night, as usual, and slept very soundly. During my sleep I saw a very beautiful and pleasing dream; but in this dream was nothing which did not happen almost as the dream told it. Now I wish to tell this dream in rhyme, the more to make your hearts rejoice, since Love both begs and commands me to do so. And if anyone asks what I wish the romance to be called, which I begin here, it is the Romance of the Rose, in which the whole art of love is contained. Its matter is good and new; and God grant that she for whom I have undertaken it may receive it with grace. It is she who is so precious and so worthy to be loved that she should be called Rose.

I became aware that it was May, five years or more ago; I dreamed that I was filled with joy in May, the amorous month, when everything rejoices, when one sees no bush or hedge that does not wish to adorn itself with new leaves.

. . .

When I heard the birds singing, I began to go out of my mind wondering by what art or what device I could enter the garden. But I could never discover any place where I could get in; you see, I didn't know whether there were opening, path, or place by which one might enter. There was not even any one there who might show me one, for I was alone. I was very distressed and anguished until at

---

1. The commentary of the Latin writer and philosopher Macrobius (fl. 400) on the dream of Scipio in Cicero's *Republic*, dis- cusses the various kinds of dreams, their divine, demonic, or physiological causes, and their prophetic meanings.

last I remembered that it had never in any way happened that such a beautiful garden had no door or ladder or opening of some sort. Then I set out rapidly, tracing the outline of the enclosure and extent of the square walled area until I found a little door that was very narrow and tight. No man entered there by any other place. Since I didn't know how to look for any other entrance, I began to knock on the door. I knocked and rapped a great deal and listened many times to see whether I might hear anyone coming. Finally a very sweet and lovely girl opened the wicket, which was made of hornbeam. She had hair as blond as a copper basin, flesh more tender than that of a baby chick, a gleaming forehead, and arched eyebrows. The space between her eyes was not small but very wide in measure. She had a straight, well-made nose, and her eyes, which were gray-blue like those of a falcon, caused envy in the harebrained. Her breath was sweet and savory, her face white and colored, her mouth small and a little full; she had a dimple in her chin. Her neck was of good proportion, thick enough and reasonably long, without pimples or sores. From here to Jerusalem no woman has a more beautiful neck; it was smooth and soft to the touch. She had a bosom as white as the snow upon a branch, when it has just fallen. Her body was well made and svelte; you would not have had to seek anywhere on earth to find a woman with a more beautiful body. She had a pretty chaplet of gold embroidery. There was never a girl more elegant or better arrayed; nor would I have described her right. Above the chaplet of gold embroidery was one of fresh roses, and in her hand she held a mirror. Her hair was arranged very richly with a fine lace. Both sleeves were well sewn into a beautifully snug fit, and she had white gloves to keep her white hands from turning brown. She wore a coat of rich green from Ghent, cord-stiched all around. It certainly seemed from her array that she was hardly busy. By the time that she had combed her hair carefully and prepared and adorned herself well, she had finished her day's work. She led a good and happy life, for she had no care nor trouble except only to turn herself out nobly.

When the girl with gracious heart had opened the door to me, I thanked her nicely and asked her name and who she was. She was not haughty toward me, nor did she disdain to reply.

"I am called Idleness,"[2] she said, "by people who know me. I am a rich and powerful lady, and I have a very good time, for I have no other purpose than to enjoy myself and make myself comfortable, to comb and braid my hair. I am the intimate acquaintance of Diversion, the elegant charmer who owns this garden and who had the trees imported from Saracen land and planted throughout the garden.

. . .

When the inscription had made clear to me that this was indeed the true fountain of the fair Narcissus,[3] I drew back a little, since I dared not look within. When I remembered Narcissus and his evil misfortune, I began to be afraid. But

---

2. Idleness is the gatekeeper of the garden of Love because courtly love is a game that can be played only by the rich and the leisured.

3. Narcissus scorned the love of a young woman, Echo, who cursed him to a similar

fate of unrequited love. When he saw his own reflection in water, he fell in love with its beauty, and when he finally recognized that his love could never be satisfied, he died.

then I thought that I might be able to venture safely to the fountain, without fear of misfortune, and that I was foolish to be frightened of it. I approached the fountain, and when I was near I lowered myself to the ground to see the running water and the gravel at the bottom, clearer than fine silver. It is the fountain of fountains; there is none so beautiful in all the world. The water is always fresh and new; night and day it issues in great waves from two deep, cavernous conduits. All around, the short grass springs up thick and close because of the water. In winter it cannot die, nor can the water stop flowing.

At the bottom of the fountain were two crystal stones upon which I gazed with great attention. There is one thing I want to tell you which, I think, you will consider a marvel when you hear it: when the sun, that sees all, throws its rays into the fountain and when its light descends to the bottom, then more than a hundred colors appear in the crystals which, on account of the sun, become yellow, blue, and red. The crystals are so wonderful and have such power that the entire place—trees, flowers, and whatever adorns the garden—appears there all in order. To help you understand, I will give you an example. Just as the mirror shows things that are in front of it, without cover, in their true colors and shapes, just so, I tell you truly, do the crystals reveal the whole condition of the garden, without deception, to those who gaze into the water, for always, wherever they are, they see one half of the garden, and if they turn, then they may see the rest. There is nothing so small, however hidden or shut up, that is not shown there in the crystal as if it were painted in detail.

It is the perilous mirror in which proud Narcissus gazed at his face and his gray eyes; on account of this mirror he afterward lay dead, flat on his back. Whoever admires himself in this mirror can have no protection, no physician, since anything that he sees with his eyes puts him on the road of love. This mirror has put many a valiant man to death, for the wisest, most intelligent and carefully instructed are all surprised and captured here. Out of this mirror a new madness comes upon men. Here hearts are changed; intelligence and moderation have no business here, where there is only the simple will to love, where no one can be counseled. For it is here that Cupid, son of Venus, sowed the seed of love that has dyed the whole fountain, here that he stretched his nets and placed his snares to trap young men and women; for Love wants no other birds. Because of the seed that was sown this fountain has been rightly called the Fountain of Love, about which several have spoken in many places in books and in romances; but, when I have revealed the mystery, you will never hear the truth of the matter better described.

I wanted to remain there forever, gazing at the fountain and the crystals, which showed me the hundred thousand things that appeared there; but it was a painful hour when I admired myself there. Alas! How I have sighed since then because of that deceiving mirror. If I had known its powers and qualities, I would never have approached it, for now I have fallen into the snare that has captured and betrayed many a man.

Among a thousand things in the mirror, I saw rosebushes loaded with roses; they were off to one side, surrounded closely by a hedge. I was seized by so great a desire for them that not for Pavia or Paris would I have left off going there where I saw this splendid thicket. When this madness, by which many other men have been seized, had captured me, I straightway drew near to the rosebushes. Mark well; when I was near, the delicious odor of the roses penetrated right into my entrails. Indeed, if I had been embalmed, the perfume would have been nothing in comparison with that of the roses. Had I not feared to be attacked or roughly treated, I would have cut at least one that I might hold it in my hand to smell the perfume; but I was afraid that I might repent such an action which might easily provoke the wrath of the lord of the garden. There were great heaps of roses; none under heaven were as beautiful. There were small, tight buds, some a little larger, and some of another size that were approaching their season and were ready to open. The little ones are not to be despised; the broad, open ones are gone in a day, but the buds remain quite fresh at least two or three days. These buds pleased me greatly. I did not believe that there were such beautiful ones anywhere. Whoever might grasp one should hold it a precious thing. If I could have a chaplet of them, I would love no possession as much.

Among these buds I singled out one that was so very beautiful that, after I had examined it carefully, I thought that none of the others was worth anything beside it; it glowed with a color as red and as pure as the best that Nature can produce, and she had placed around it four pairs of leaves, with great skill, one after the other. The stem was straight as a sapling, and the bud sat on the top, neither bent nor inclined. Its odor spread all around; the sweet perfume that rose from it filled the entire area. And when I smelled its exhalation, I had no power to withdraw, but would have approached to take it if I had dared stretch out my hand to it. But the sharp and piercing thorns that grew from it kept me at a distance. Cutting, sharp spikes, nettles, and barbed thorns allowed me no way to advance, for I was afraid of hurting myself.

[Women Maintain Their Freedom as Best They Can]

"Certainly, dear son, my tender young one, if my youth were present, as yours is now, the vengeance that I would take on them could not rightly be written. Everywhere I came I would work such wonders with those scoundrels, who valued me so lightly and who vilified and despised me when they so basely passed by near me, that one would never have heard the like. They and others would pay for their pride and spite; I would have no pity on them. For with the intelligence that God has given me—just as I have preached to you—do you know what condition I would put them in? I would so pluck them and seize their possessions, even wrongly and perversely, that I would make them dine on worms and lie naked on dunghills, especially and first of all those who loved me with more loyal heart and who more willingly took trouble to serve and honor me. If I could, I wouldn't leave them anything worth one bud of garlic until I had everything in my purse and had put them all into poverty; I would make them stamp their feet in living rage behind me. But to regret it is worth nothing; what has gone cannot come. I would never be able to hold any man, for my face is so wrinkled that they don't even protect themselves against my threat. A long time ago the scoundrels who despised me told me so, and from that time on I took to weeping. O God. But it still pleases me when I think back on it. I rejoice in my thought and my limbs become lively again. Remembering all that happened gives me all the blessings of the world, so that however they may have deceived me, at least I have had my fun.

A young lady is not idle when she leads a gay life, especially she who thinks about acquiring enough to take care of her expenses.

. . .

"Moreover, women are born free. The law, which takes away the freedom in which Nature placed them, has put them under conditions. Nature is not so stupid that she has Marotte born only for Robichon, if we put our wits to work, nor Robichon only for Marietta or Agnes or Perette. Instead, fair son, never doubt that she has made all us women for all men and all men for all women, each woman common to every man and every man common to each woman. Thus, when they are engaged, captured by law, and married, in order to prevent quarreling, contention, and murder and to help in the rearing of children, who are their joint responsibility, they still exert themselves in every way, these ladies and girls, ugly or beautiful, to return to their freedoms. They maintain their freedom as best they can; as a result, many evils will come, do come, and have come many times in the past. In fact, I would count over ten of them straightway, but I pass on, since I would be worn out and you overburdened with listening before I had numbered them.

"But pay good attention to Nature, for in order that you may see more clearly what wondrous power she has I can give you many examples which will show this power in detail. When the bird from the green wood is captured and put in a cage, very attentively and delicately cared for there within, you think that he sings with a gay heart as long as he lives; but he longs for the branching woods that he loved naturally, and he would want to be on the trees, no matter how well one could feed him. He always plans and studies how to regain his free life. He tramples his food under his feet with the ardor that his heart fills him with, and he goes trailing around his cage, searching in great anguish for a way to find a window or hole through which he might fly away to the woods. In the same way, you know, all women of every condition, whether girls or ladies, have a natural inclination to seek out voluntarily the roads and paths by which they might come to freedom, for they always want to gain it.

"It is the same, I tell you, with the man who goes into a religious order and comes to repent of it afterward. He needs only a little more grief to hang himself. He complains and goes frantic until he is completely tormented by the great desires that come to him. He wants to find out how he can regain the freedom that he has lost. The will is not moved on account of any habit that one may take, no matter what place one goes to give oneself up to religion.

DANTE ALIGHIERI (1265–1321)
Italy

Born in Florence, Dante was a lyric poet and political figure exiled because of his politics in 1302. He spent the rest of his life in exile, living in different cities and

courts of Northern Italy. During this time, he wrote his *Divine Comedy*, perhaps
as a political message to his countrymen.

from **The Divine Comedy**

HELL

Canto 5 [From that initial circle I went down]

*The first active sinners Dante meets in Hell are the lustful, those who indulged their sexual desires
with no thought to their social responsibilities. It is the obsessive aspect of their passion and their
willful self-deception that Dante condemns, not sexual love, witness the former lovers Dante puts
in Paradise in Canto 9. Most of the souls Dante sees here are reigning queens, who satisfied their
personal appetites at great cost to their lands. The bestial aspect of such obsession is shown in King
Minos, the infernal guardian at the beginning of the section who now communicates his judgments
by coiling his tail; the surrender to uncontrolled passion is represented by the "hurricane," and the
self-deceptive aspect of the sin is seen in the story Francesca tells about her affair, casting it in the
romantic frame of the tale of Lancelot and Guinevere, blaming the legendary lovers for inspiring
her affair. But she rewrites their story, making Lancelot the active partner in the first kiss instead
of Guinevere, as she presumably revises her own story, to whitewash her role, and to disguise the
physical aspect under the clichés of courtly love ("Love, that can quickly seize the gentle heart,"
"Love, that releases no beloved from loving").*

From that initial circle I went down
descending to the second, which contains,
enclosing as it does a lesser space,
a harsher pain to sting them till they shriek.
There horrifying Minos[1] stands and snarls   5
upon the threshold, scrutinising sins:
he judges and despatches with his coils,
by which I mean that when the hapless soul
appears before him, it confesses all,
and this great connoisseur of sinfulness   10
decides on its allotted place in hell;
the times he twines his tail determining
how many levels down the soul must fall.
Before him always stands a crowd, and each
comes forward for the verdict in his turn.   15
They speak, they hear and then are hurled below.
'Oh you who come to pain's own residence,'
said Minos when he saw me, and left off
performance of his high official rites,
'be careful how you enter; whom you trust;   20

Translated by Tom Phillips.

Hell, Canto 5

1. According to Greek myth, Minos, king of
Crete, was the son of Europa and Zeus in
the guise of a bull. He is judge of the
underworld in Vergil's *Aeneid*. Dante adds
the tail.

and don't be fooled by this wide entranceway.'
And then my guide to him, 'Why shout like that?
Do not obstruct his destined way ahead,
for this is willed where will and power are one;
all further questions are superfluous.'   25
From now I start to hear the tones of grief,
and come where frequent wailing strikes my ears.
I came into a place where light was dumb,
which bellowed like the tempest-beaten sea
when warring winds assault it from all sides.   30
The hellish hurricane unresting sweeps
the swirling souls in its rapacious wake
and thrashes and torments them as they whirl.
With devastation now they're face to face,
a scene of weeping, howling and lament   35
where they revile divine omnipotence.
It dawned on me that those who undergo
such torture must be carnal sinners, who
submit all reason to their appetite.
And just as starlings when cold weather comes   40
are lofted by their wings in huge dense flocks,
so back and forth and up and down are swept
the wicked spirits in that blast of wind;
nor are they comforted at all by hope
of any rest, much less relief from pain.   45
And just as cranes strung out in stretching lines
chant dirges as they travel through the air,
I watched the moaning shades go passing by
suspended in the maelstrom I described;
which made me ask, 'Oh master, who are they,   50
the beings whom the black air scourges so?'
And straight away he said, 'The first of them
whose history you'd want me to relate
was Empress over many different tongues
and so abandoned to luxurious vice   55
she legalised her own licentiousness
and thus forestalled the censure she deserved.
She is Semiramis,[2] who as we read
was wife to Ninos and succeeded him:
she held the land where now the Sultan rules.   60
Next, faithless to Sichaeus' ashes,[3] comes

---

2. Semiramis was supposed to have succeeded
   her husband as ruler of Assyria, to have
   founded the city of Babylon, and to have
   had an affair with her son, which she
   justified by making incest legal.

3. The widow of Sychaeus was Dido, who had
   an affair with Aeneas, which kept him
   temporarily from pursuing his destiny to
   found Trojan civilization in Italy, ultimately
   in Rome.

the one who killed herself possessed by love.
Luxurious Cleopatra follows her:
see Helen now, round whom revolved an age
of tragedy: see great Achilles too   65
who fought his final battle against love.
See Paris, Tristan[4] . . . and a thousand shades
or more he singled out to show and name
whom love had severed from this life of ours.
Then, having heard my mentor name these Knights   70
and Ladies of times past, my pity grew,
and I was lost in my bewilderment.
'Oh poet,' I began, 'I'd like to speak
with those that fly together as a pair
and seem to be so weightless on the wind.'   75
And he, 'You'll see, when they draw nearer us,
if you request them by that love of theirs,
the force that drives them on, that they will come.'
The wind steered them towards us, and at once
I raised my voice. 'Oh wearied souls, unless   80
Another One forbids it, come and speak.'
Like doves with wings held high and motionless
that drift on air supported by their will
when drawn by longing for their pleasant nest,
these separated now from Dido's flock   85
and came towards us through the sickly air,
such was the tender force of my appeal.
'Oh living creatures, gracious and benign
that brave the purple darkness of the air
to visit us who stained the world blood red;   90
were He our friend, the Universal King,
we'd pray to Him to grant you peace, since you
have pity on our sad calamity.
Whatever you would like to speak about
or hear, we'll hear and speak about with you   95
within the present respite of the wind.
My birthplace hugs that shore, where, making peace
with its attendant streams, the Po descends.
Love that so quickly fires the gentle heart
ensnared this man through that fair body's form   100
I now am stripped of (it still grieves me how).
Love that releases none, if loved, from love
ensnared me with such strong delight in him
it still won't let me go, as you can see.

---

4. Achilles, Paris, and Tristan shared, in medieval legend, the role of royal princes who
became involved in illicit affairs to their
own and their countries' harm.

Love led us on towards a single death.
Caïna's depth greets him who quenched our lives.'
Such were the words that floated down from them.
And when I'd listened to these injured souls
I bowed my head and held it low so long
the Poet asked at last, 'What's on your mind?'
And then I answered him and said, 'Alas
how many sweet reflections and desires
have led them on to this distressing state.'
Then turning back to speak to them, I said,
'Francesca,[5] how your torment makes me weep
for sadness and for sympathy; but say,
by what, in your delightful time of sighs,
and how, did love announce itself, and bring
the stirrings of those dubious desires?'
And she to me, 'There is no greater grief
than when in wretchedness one calls to mind
one's happy times: your mentor knows this too.
But if you've such a keen desire to know
the story of our love, how it took root,
I'll talk of it as one who speaks and weeps.
One day for our amusement we began
to read the tale of Lancelot,[6] how love
had made him prisoner. We were alone,
without the least suspicion in our minds:
but more and more our eyes were forced to meet,
our faces to turn pale by what we read.
One passage in particular became
the source of our defeat: when we read how
the infatuated lover saw the smile
he'd longed to see and kissed it, this man here
who never shall be parted from my side,
all trembling as he did it, kissed my mouth.
The book was Gallehault, a go-between
and he who wrote it played that role for us.
That day we read no further word of it.'
As this first spirit spoke the other wept.

105

110

115

120

125

130

135

140

---

5. Francesca da Rimini, according to early accounts, had an affair with her husband's younger brother, Paolo, who was himself married but had served as proxy at their betrothal. As she tells it, the husband surprised them in the first flush of love and killed them both, but in reality the deaths took place at least a decade after the marriage, and long after the birth of children to both. Dante's Francesca expects her husband to go to the section reserved for fratricides (Caina) in the lowest circle of Hell (for traitors).

6. The story of Lancelot and Guinevere is told in a thirteenth-century French prose romance; Gallehault is the friend who arranged for the lovers to meet.

For pity like a dying man, I swooned
and fell as bodies fall that fall down dead.

Canto 10 [Onwards through a hidden alleyway]

*Just inside the inner city of Hell, Dante finds a vast cemetery of open tombs. This is the circle of
heretics, specifically of those who did not believe in an afterlife, so they are condemned to tombs
representing the death they expected, but the lids are open, revealing the life they did not expect.
They are grouped with their followers because leading others into error is part of their sin, and the
souls will involve Dante temporarily in error. Dante has strong ties to the two souls he meets
here— political in one case, personal in the other—but he distresses both of them; the souls are
also connected with each other, by the marriage of their children, but they ignore each others'
feelings throughout.*

*The first soul, Farinata, recognizes Dante as a fellow Tuscan and Florentine. Farinata had
been the leader of the Ghibelline faction, the party that supported the emperor, while Dante's
family is Guelph, the party that supported the pope and the republic; in fact, Dante is actually a
White Guelph, a member of the pro-empire faction, which had evolved after Farinata's time, so
their political positions are not opposed. But Farinata does not know that and does not wait to find
out. He attacks Dante as an enemy, and Dante responds in kind; they exchange taunts of exile,
Dante announcing that Farinata's party was never allowed to return to the city, and Farinata that
Dante would soon know what exile was like. (Dante was in exile by the time he wrote the poem,
but the poem is set in the year 1300, two years before his exile began, so the Dante in the poem
is disturbed by the news.) They attack each other even though they are on the same side, a good
example of the way political factionalism works mindlessly against peace.*

*Their argument is interrupted by the other soul, Cavalcanti, the father of one of Dante's
closest friends and fellow poets, Guido Cavalcanti, who asks why his son is not there. He and
Dante confuse each other because, like heretics, both are working from limited knowledge. Dante
does not know that Cavalcanti is unaware of the present (a particular punishment of these heretics
who were concerned only with the present), and Cavalcanti does not know that Dante does not
know. All three are left worse off for the encounter, Farinata because of the fate of his people,
Cavalcanti because he thinks his son is dead, and Dante because he learns he will be exiled.*

Now onwards through a hidden alleyway
between these tortures and the city walls
my master went and I came close behind.
'Oh paragon of moral strength,' I said,
'who lead me down according to your will   5
along the spirals of iniquity,
speak, satisfy my anxious need to know;
these people, lying in the sepulchres,
is one allowed to see them? All the lids
are open wide and nobody stands guard.'   10
And he to me, 'They'll all be well locked up

Translated by Tom Phillips.

when they come back here from Jehosophat[1]
and bring their bodies which they left above.
This cemetery is the ground reserved
for Epicurus[2] and his followers   15
who state that soul and body die one death.
And as for that you questioned me about
it shall be answered soon, and in this place,
as shall that other wish you've kept from me.'
'Kind guide, it's not that I conceal my heart,'   20
I said, 'but only keep my speeches short
as often you've encouraged me to do.'
'Tuscan! who make your way, a living man
across the fiery city, and who speak
with such refinement, please stay here awhile.   25
Your dialect reveals that you were born
a native of that noble fatherland
of which my treatment was perhaps too harsh.'
This sound it was that suddenly burst out
of one such grave and made me in my fear   30
draw even closer to my master's side,
who said to me, 'Turn round! Why act like that?
Look now, at Farinata, risen there;
waist upwards he's entirely visible.'
But I was staring at his face by then.   35
He'd now stretched upright, chest and brow thrown back
as though he had a high contempt for hell.
At once my guide with prompt decisive hands
urged me towards him through the sepulchres,
and as he did so told me, 'Watch your words.'   40
When I had reached the limits of his tomb
he eyed me half-contemptuously awhile
then asked me, 'You, who were your ancestors?'
And I who was most willing to comply
left nothing out but openly told all.   45
He raised his eyebrows somewhat as I spoke,
and said, 'Their bitter animosity towards
myself, my forbears, and my party too
obliged me twice to scatter them abroad.'
I answered him, 'Though they were driven out,   50
they still came back, both times, from every point,

Hell, Canto 10.

1. Jehosophat is the valley in which the Last
   Judgment is supposed to have taken place
   (Joel 3:2, 3:12).

2. Epicurus was an ancient Greek philosopher
   whose followers taught that pleasure or the
   lack of pain is the highest good; they were
   thought also to deny an afterlife of the soul.

an art your faction hasn't mastered yet.'
Alongside him another shade reared up,
with face and chin emerging into view;
he must have heaved himself on to his knees.
He looked each side of me, as though impelled   55
to check if someone else was with me there
but when this expectation had proved vain
he said, through tears, 'If your high genius
allows you passage through this purblind gaol   60
then where's my son? Why isn't he with you?'
'I do not come here on my own,' I said,
'for he that waits there guides me through, to her[3]
your Guido held perhaps in low esteem.'
The words he spoke, his mode of punishment   65
had by this time spelled out his name for me;
that's why I'd given such a full reply.
Then all at once he sprang up straight and cried,
'What? You said, "held". Is he not still alive?
Is gentle light not visiting his eyes?'   70
When he became aware that I had made
some kind of pause before I answered him
he just fell backwards and was seen no more.
That first imposing soul at whose request
I'd halted did not move meanwhile   75
a muscle on his face, nor turn his neck
nor shift his body's attitude at all
but carried on from where he had left off,
'To think they're not yet masters of that art;
why, that torments me more than does this bed.   80
The face of her that rules this lower realm
shall not become rekindled fifty times
before you'll know what price that art exacts.
So tell me, by your wish to reach again
the lovely world, why with their every law   85
these people treat my clan so brutally?'
'The havoc and the heavy massacre,'
I said, 'that dyed the Arbia[4] red, make this
the issue upon which our temple dwells.'
He sighed and shook his head and then replied,   90

---

3. The translator takes the Italian pronoun *cui*
   to refer to Beatrice, who will be mentioned
   at the end of the canto as the one who will
   tell Dante about his destiny. It might also
   refer to Vergil, Dante's guide.
4. The Arbia is a river at the site of the battle of
   Monataperti at which Ghibelline forces

killed many Florentine Guelphs in 1260.
The Guelphs never forgave them for that
slaughter, but they seem to have forgotten
that Farinata was the one who alone kept
his party from destroying the city after the
defeat, as he reminds Dante.

'I was not on my own when that was done
nor surely would have joined in without cause:
yet I was on my own when all the rest
resolved to stamp out Florence. It was I
that spoke out openly in her defense.'   95
'And now,' I begged him, 'to ensure your seed
eventually might come to find repose
untie this knot that's tangled up my wits.
It seems, if I hear right, that you can see
events which time has yet to bring about   100
while no such process makes the present clear.'
'Like those who have defective sight,' he said,
'we see what lies a long way off, for such
is what the high Lord's light still shines upon.
When things approach or actually take place   105
our intellects are wholly at a loss;
and so, unless some other brings us word
we have no knowledge of your human state.
From this you'll understand, that instantly
the doors of future time have been shut fast   110
our own awareness will die utterly.'
Whereat, regretting my offence, I said,
'Would you inform the one who just fell back
his son is still in living company,
and let him know that if I earlier   115
was silent in response to what he said
it's just that my ideas were still confused
by that misapprehension you've resolved.'
But now my master called for my return
and so I pressed the soul more urgently   120
to speak of those who shared that place with him.
'A thousand shades or more,' he said, 'lie here;
the second Frederick[5] and the cardinal
are both within, but I'll not mention more.'
With that he disappeared, and I walked back   125
towards the poet of antiquity
turning that message over in my mind
which seemed to carry threats against myself.
He started off, and as we went along
enquired, 'What's this that's made you so perplexed?'   130
I answered him as fully as I could.

---

5. Frederick II was emperor from 1215 to
1250; Dante respected him as a political
leader but places him in this circle because
of his reputed refusal to believe in the life of
the soul. The cardinal is Ottaviano degli

Ubaldini (born sometime after 1273), who
was reported to have said, "If there is a soul,
I have lost it a thousand times for the
Ghibellines."

'Keep fresh within your mind the things you've heard
against yourself,' the sage advised, 'and note,'
and here his finger pointed up above
'when you shall face the gentle radiance   135
of her whose lovely eyes see everything,
you'll understand from her your quest in life.'
This said he turned his feet towards the left
and, veering from the wall, we made our way
towards the centre following a path   140
that struck across a valley whose foul stench
was nauseating high up as we were.

PURGATORY

Canto 4 [When any of our faculties retains/ a strong impression]

*Along the lower edge of the mountain of Purgatory, outside the gate where purgation really begins,
Dante meets a series of souls who are literally "doing time," waiting for a period that corresponds
to the time they neglected their religious duties, before they can begin to climb the mountain and
purify themselves in order to enter paradise. Among these souls Dante meets an old friend, Belacqua, who is still as lazy and cynical as he was on earth. He makes fun of Vergil's lecture on
astronomy and of Dante's desire to climb. In comparison to Belacqua, who sits like a rock, scarcely
moving his head and speaking in very short sentences, Dante seems all energy and action, even
though he has been exhausted by his earlier climb. In contrast to other mountains, the mountain
of Purgatory is steepest at the bottom: the climb to purge oneself of sinful impulses is hard to begin,
but increasingly easier to finish.*

When any of our faculties retains
a strong impression of delight or pain,
the soul will wholly concentrate on that,
    neglecting any other power it has[1]
(and this refutes the error that maintains   5
that—one above the other—several souls
    can flame in us); and thus, when something seen
or heard secures the soul in stringent grip,
time moves and yet we do not notice it.
    The power that perceives the course of time   10
is not the power that captures all the mind;
the former has no force—the latter binds.
    And I confirmed this by experience,

Translated by Allen Mandelbaum.

Purgatory, Canto 4

1. The soul has different powers, including
   the senses and reason, but it is one soul, not
   several, as some believe.

hearing that spirit in my wonderment;
for though the sun had fully climbed fifty   15
 degrees, I had not noticed it, when he
came to the point at which in unison
those souls cried out to us: "Here's what you want."
 The farmer, when the grape is darkening,
will often stuff a wider opening   20
with just a little forkful of his thorns,
 than was the gap through which my guide and I,
who followed after, climbed, we two alone,
after that company of souls had gone.
 San Leo can be climbed, one can descend   25
to Noli and ascend Cacume and
Bismantova[2] with feet alone, but here
 I had to fly: I mean with rapid wings
and pinions of immense desire, behind
the guide who gave me hope and was my light.   30
 We made our upward way through rifted rock;
along each side the edges pressed on us;
the ground beneath required feet and hands.
 When we had reached the upper rim of that
steep bank, emerging on the open slope,   35
I said: "My master, what way shall we take?"
 And he to me: "Don't squander any steps;
keep climbing up the mountain after me
until we find some expert company."
 The summit was so high, my sight fell short;   40
the slope was far more steep than the line drawn
from middle-quadrant to the center point.
 I was exhausted when I made this plea:
"O gentle father, turn around and see—
I will be left alone unless you halt."   45
 "My son," he said, "draw yourself up to there,"
while pointing to a somewhat higher terrace,
which circles all the slope along that side.
 His words incited me; my body tried;
on hands and knees I scrambled after him   50
until the terrace lay beneath my feet.
 There we sat down together, facing east,
in the direction from which we had come:
what joy—to look back at a path we've climbed!
 My eyes were first set on the shores below,   55

---

2. San Leo in Urbino and Bismantova in
 Emilia refer to very steep ascents, and Noli
 in Liguria, to a steep descent.

and then I raised them toward the sun; I was
amazed to find it fall upon our left.

And when the poet saw that I was struck
with wonder as I watched the chariot
of light passing between the north and us,[3]

he said to me: "Suppose Castor and Pollux
were in conjunction with that mirror there,
which takes the light and guides it north and south,

then you would see the reddish zodiac
still closer to the Bears as it revolves—
unless it has abandoned its old track.

If you would realize how that should be,
then concentrate, imagining this mountain
so placed upon this earth that both Mount Zion

and it, although in different hemispheres,
share one horizon; therefore, you can see,
putting your mind to it attentively,

how that same path which Phaethon drove so poorly
must pass this mountain on the north, whereas
it skirts Mount Zion on the southern side."

I said: "My master, surely I have never—
since my intelligence seemed lacking—seen
as clearly as I now can comprehend,

that the mid-circle of the heavens' motion
(one of the sciences calls it Equator),
which always lies between the sun and winter,

as you explained, lies as far north of here
as it lies southward of the site from which
the Hebrews, looking toward the tropics, saw it.

But if it please you, I should willingly
learn just how far it is we still must journey:
the slope climbs higher than my eyes can follow."

And he to me: "This mountain's of such sort
that climbing it is hardest at the start;
but as we rise, the slope grows less unkind.

Therefore, when this slope seems to you so gentle
that climbing farther up will be as restful
as traveling downstream by boat, you will

be where this pathway ends, and there you can

60

65

70

75

80

85

90

---

3. Dante is amazed to see the sun in the
northeast rather than the southeast, and
Vergil has to explain why with a combination of astronomic and mythological terms.

The main point is that Purgatory is at the
center of the southern hemisphere on the
opposite side of the earth from Jerusalem,
the center of the northern hemisphere.

expect to put your weariness to rest.
I say no more, and this I know as truth."

And when his words were done, another voice
nearby was heard to say: "Perhaps you will
have need to sit before you reach that point!"

Hearing that voice, both of us turned around,
and to the left we saw a massive boulder,
which neither he nor I—before—had noticed.

We made our way toward it and toward the people
who lounged behind that boulder in the shade,
as men beset by listlessness will rest.

And one of them, who seemed to me exhausted,
was sitting with his arms around his knees;
between his knees, he kept his head bent down.

"O my sweet lord," I said, "look carefully
at one who shows himself more languid than
he would have been were laziness his sister!"

Then that shade turned toward us attentively,
lifting his face, but just along his thigh,
and said: "Climb, then, if you're so vigorous!"

Then I knew who he was, and the distress
that still was quickening my breath somewhat
did not prevent my going to him; and

when I had reached him, scarcely lifting up
his head, he said: "And have you fathomed how
the sun can drive his chariot on your left?"

The slowness of his movements, his brief words
had stirred my lips a little toward a smile;
then I began: "From this time on, Belacqua,

I need not grieve for you; but tell me, why
do you sit here? Do you expect a guide?
Or have you fallen into your old ways?"

And he: "O brother, what's the use of climbing?
God's angel, he who guards the gate, would not
let me pass through to meet my punishment.

Outside that gate the skies must circle round
as many times as they did when I lived—
since I delayed good sighs until the end—

unless, before then, I am helped by prayer
that rises from a heart that lives in grace;
what use are other prayers—ignored by Heaven?"

And now the poet climbed ahead, before me,
and said: "It's time; see the meridian
touched by the sun; elsewhere, along the Ocean,
night now has set its food upon Morocco."

95

100

105

110

115

120

125

130

135

PARADISE

Canto 9 [Fair Clemence, after I had been enlightened]

The souls Dante meets in the heaven of Venus, those who succumbed to the influence of passionate love in their lives, are very different from the self-centered souls of the two previous selections, the hostile souls of the heretics or the lazy Belacqua. These souls are moved by the love of God to share their joy with others and to share the joy of others with Dante. They do not need to hear Dante's desire to satisfy it, reading his thoughts reflected in God as in a mirror, and they are eager to pass him on to other souls in the same section who can satisfy his desire further. The first to speak to him in Canto 9 is Cunizza, a woman famous for her love affairs and many marriages, who is now able to say "this planet's radiance conquered me." She shows no trace of sinful lust, though she is still passionate about the corruption in her land. She introduces Dante to the love-poet Folco, who later became a monk and bishop. Folco compares himself without shame to the most passionate classical lovers, and then introduces Dante to the most surprising soul of all, Rahab, the prostitute in the book of Joshua, the first in this group of souls, Folco tells us, to be led out of Hell by Christ, when he rescued the souls of the Jews in the Old Testament. Rahab the prostitute, who was interpreted by medieval Christians as a figure for the Church because she had helped Joshua, a Christ figure, to enter Jericho, is contrasted with the pope and cardinals of the contemporary Church, who are committing adultery with Christ's bride (the Church) and who neglect Christ's teachings in their concern with worldly matters.

Fair Clemence,[1] after I had been enlightened
by your dear Charles, he told me how his seed
would be defrauded, but he said: "Be silent
    and let the years revolve." All I can say
is this: lament for vengeance well-deserved   5
will follow on the wrongs you are to suffer.
    And now the life-soul of that holy light
turned to the Sun that fills it even as
the Goodness that suffices for all things.
    Ah, souls seduced and creatures without reverence,   10
who twist your hearts away from such a Good,
who let your brows be bent on emptiness!
    And here another of those splendors moved
toward me; and by its brightening without,
it showed its wish to please me. Beatrice,   15
    whose eyes were fixed on me, as they had been
before, gave me the precious certainty
that she consented to my need to speak.
    "Pray, blessed spirit, may you remedy—
quickly—my wish to know," I said. "Give me   20
proof that you can reflect the thoughts I think."

Translated by Allen Mandelbaum.

Paradise, Canto 9

1. Clemence is either the wife or the daughter of Charles Martel (1271–1295), the King of Hungary, whom Dante met in the previous canto.

Botticelli, illustration to Dante's *Paradiso*, Canto XX. Kupferstichka-binett, Staatliche Museen, Berlin.

At which that light, one still unknown to me,
out of the depth from which it sang before,
continued as if it rejoiced in kindness:
    "In that part of indecent Italy   25
that lies between Rialto and the springs
from which the Brenta and the Piave stream,
    rises a hill—of no great height—from which
a firebrand[2] descended, and it brought
much injury to all the land about.   30
    Both he and I were born of one same root:
Cunizza was my name, and I shine here
because this planet's radiance conquered me.
    But in myself I pardon happily
the reason for my fate; I do not grieve—   35
and vulgar minds may find this hard to see.
    Of the resplendent, precious jewel that stands
most close to me within our heaven, much
fame still remains and will not die away
    before this hundredth year returns five times: 40
see then if man should not seek excellence—
that his first life bequeath another life.

. . .

---

2. The firebrand is Cunizza's brother, Ezzelino
   III da Romano, a tyrant whom Dante saw in
   Canto 12 of Hell.

Feltre[3] shall yet lament the treachery
of her indecent shepherd—act so filthy
that for the like none ever entered prison.   45
   The vat to hold the blood of the Ferrarese
would be too large indeed, and weary he
who weighs it ounce by ounce—the vat that he,
   generous priest, will offer up to show
fidelity to his Guelph party; and   50
such gifts will suit the customs of that land.
   Above are mirrors—Thrones[4] is what you call them—
and from them God in judgment shines on us;
and thus we think it right to say such things."
   Here she was silent and appeared to me   55
to turn toward other things, reentering
the wheeling dance where she had been before.
   The other joy, already known to me
as precious, then appeared before my eyes
like a pure ruby struck by the sun's rays.   60
   On high, joy is made manifest by brightness.
as, here on earth, by smiles; but down below,
the shade grows darker when the mind feels sorrow.
   "God can see all," I said, "and, blessed spirit,
your vision is contained in Him, so that   65
no wish can ever hide itself from you.
   Your voice has always made the heavens glad.
as has the singing of the pious fires
that make themselves a cowl of their six wings:
   why then do you not satisfy my longings?   70
I would not have to wait for your request
if I could enter you as you do me."[5]
   "The widest valley into which the waters
spread from the sea that girds the world," his words
began, "between discrepant shores, extends   75
   eastward so far against the sun, that when
those waters end at the meridian,
that point—when they began—was the horizon.
   I lived along the shoreline of that valley
between the Ebro and the Magra, whose   80

---

3. The bishop of Feltre surrendered political
   refugees who had put themselves under his
   protection to their enemies and they were
   all killed.
4. Thrones are one of the orders of angels,
   called "mirrors" because they reflect God's
   will to the souls. The Seraphim, referred to

in ll 68–69 as the "fires" with six wings, are
a higher order of angels.
5. The line reads literally, "if I could *inyou*
   myself as you *inme* yourself." The verbs
   created out of pronouns emphasize the
   intense union of the souls.

brief course divides the Genoese and Tuscans.[6]

Beneath the same sunset, the same sunrise,
lie both Bougie and my own city, which
once warmed its harbor with its very blood.

Those men to whom my name was known, called me   85
Folco; and even as this sphere receives
my imprint, so was I impressed with its;

for even Belus' daughter, wronging both
Sychaeus and Creusa, did not burn
more than I did, as long as I was young;[7]   90

nor did the Rhodopean woman whom
Demophoön deceived, nor did Alcides
when he enclosed Iole in his heart.

Yet one does not repent here; here one smiles—
not for the fault, which we do not recall,   95
but for the Power that fashioned and foresaw.

For here we contemplate the art adorned
by such great love, and we discern the good
through which the world above forms that below.

But so that all your longings born within   100
this sphere may be completely satisfied
when you bear them away, I must continue.

You wish to know what spirit is within
the light that here beside me sparkles so,
as would a ray of sun in limpid water.   105

Know then that Rahab lives serenely in
that light, and since her presence joins our order.
she seals that order in the highest rank.

This heaven, where the shadow cast by earth
comes to a point, had Rahab as the first   110
soul to be taken up when Christ triumphed.

And it was right to leave her in this heaven
as trophy of the lofty victory
that Christ won, palm on palm, upon the cross,

for she had favored the initial glory   115
of Joshua within the Holy Land—
which seldom touches the Pope's memory.

Your city, which was planted by that one
who was the first to turn against his Maker,[8]

---

6. Folco identifies his city Marseilles by its
position along the Mediterranean coast between Italy and Spain, and directly across
from the North African city of Bougie.

7. Belus's daughter is Dido, who wronged
both her dead husband Sychaeus and
Aeneas's wife Creusa by her affair with

Aeneas and then killed herself when he
deserted her. The Rhodopean woman is
Phyllis, who hanged herself when she
thought her lover, Demophoön, had left
her. Alcides is Hercules, who was killed
because of his wife's jealousy of his new
love, Iole.

the one whose envy cost us many tears—   120
    produces and distributes the damned flower
that turns both sheep and lambs from the true course,
for of the shepherd it has made a wolf.
    For this the Gospel and the great Church Fathers
are set aside and only the Decretals[9]   125
are studied—as their margins clearly show.
    On these the Pope and cardinals are intent.
Their thoughts are never bent on Nazareth,
where Gabriel's open wings were reverent.
    And yet the hill of Vatican as well   130
as other noble parts of Rome that were
the cemetery for Peter's soldiery
    will soon be freed from priests' adultery."

GUIDO CAVALCANTI (c. 1259–1300)
Italy

Guido Cavalcanti was the most important of a group of Florentine poets who
produced a body of lyrics that has come to be known as the Dolce Stil
Nuovo—the "sweet new style," a phrase drawn from a critical passage in Dante's
Purgatorio (XXIV, 52ff). Both the physical setting of the court and the social
tenets of courtly love have disappeared in the lyrics of the stilnovists. Love
remains the chief subject, however, and they speculate about its origin, its nature,
and its effect. The phenomenon of love takes place now in a more complex
setting, which includes the mental and physical organization of the lover, the
urban space across which the beloved lady's inspiring image is borne to him, and
the cosmic order, which is connected to the love relation through influence and
analogy. The primary agents of this communication are the "spirits"—highly
refined and specialized material substances produced in the body, which
maintain the network of human faculties and make human beings sentient in the
world. Visual spirits, for example, bear the image of the thing seen to the eyes and
then to the brain, which abstracts the essence of the thing from its "accidents" or
inessential properties; spirits then carry the commands of the mind back to the

---

8. Florence is Dante's city, planted by the
devil, "the first to turn against his maker"; it
distributes the florin, "the damned flower,"
one of the strongest currencies in contemporary Europe, and turns the shepherd, the

pope, and other clerics, into a wolf, a
symbol of greed in the *Comedy*.
9. Decretals are papal decrees, usually comments on or modifications in ecclesiastical
law.

senses and sinews. Sighs, too, are spirits that go out into the world—and even to the border of this world and the next—bearing and receiving images. The stilnovisti drew their imagery and many of their ideas from the fields of medicine, natural philosophy, and theology; in so doing, they were able to work out in detail the universal context of inner experience, setting humans in a world that extended from the streets of the city to the highest heaven. By excluding everything in the poetic tradition that was no longer expressive, and by broadening the sources of poetry, they gave new life and new possibilities to the lyric. Through their innovations, the lyric was able to express the concerns and experiences of a world far removed from that of the court—a city world under the stress of dynamic forces, rather than a court world ordered by stable, endlessly circling patterns.

In the following lyric, one can observe many of the distinctive traits of the stilnovist lyric. The action of the spirits, the processes of desire and intellection, the longing to decode the metaphysical message of beauty, and the ambition of the stilnovisti to compose lyrics that only a spiritually privileged elite could understand—these are all brilliantly conveyed in the proliferating image of the lady and the star.

[I see in the eyes of my lady]

I see in the eyes of my lady
a light full of spirits of love,
bearing to my heart a sweetness never known,
so that a joyous life awakens there.

Something happens to me in her presence,   5
which I cannot describe to the intellect:
it seems to me as I gaze that a lady issues forth
from her lips—one so beautiful that the mind
cannot grasp it, because at once
another is born of her, of a beauty never seen,   10
from whom it seems a star arises
and proclaims: "Your blessedness is come forth."

There, where this beautiful lady appears,
a voice is heard preceding her; and seems,
moved by goodness and humility, to sing her name   15
so sweetly, that if I try to recount it,
I feel that her greatness makes me tremble;
and sighs in my soul bestir themselves,
which say: "Behold, if you gaze upon this one,
you will see her goodness and power ascended into heaven." 20

Translated by Frederick Goldin.

JUAN RUIZ (1283–1350)
Spain

All that we know about the creator of this intriguing text (composed in 1330 and revised by him in 1343) is his identity, summed up in a single laconic phrase: "I, Juan Ruiz, archpriest of Hita." Not only is this a small amount of information, but the name "Juan Ruiz" is most probably a pseudonym, akin to the English "John Doe." The author may have chosen to disguise his true identity because the irreverent nature of this book may have jeopardized his position as archpriest. Despite the lack of specific biographical data, however, the author offers us a very well developed profile of himself and his ethical and literary values by means of his self-presentation as the protagonist and author of his text.

While acknowledging—indeed celebrating—racial and religious diversity in his text, Juan Ruiz is most concerned with the perennial problem of human interpretation on its broadest level. This interest is illustrated by his presentation of many perspectives on the same issue or event. "Debate between the Greeks and Romans" offers us a prime example of the archpriest's exploration of interpretation per se, offering, in essence, a parable of interpretation (and its inevitable ambiguities) whereby each of the two disputants is convinced by the definitive truth of his own view. Both nonetheless are mistaken.

So that we do not miss the point of the archpriest's treatment of interpretation (simultaneously comical but very serious) and its challenges for the reader or listener, he follows the sign-language debate between the Greek scholar and the Roman ruffian with an episode detailing five mutually contradictory astrological predictions regarding the untimely death of King Alcáraz's son. Much to our astonishment, they all prove to be true.

This profound interrogation of interpretation is thematized by the archpriest in his text, where the term "Good Love" has various meanings: it serves as the book's title and it also refers to the go-between who helps him to meet women as well as (very daringly) both to the carnal love between the sexes and to the spiritual love of God.

from *The Book of Good Love*

Debate Between the Greeks and Romans

Here it tells how every man in the midst of his cares should be merry; and of the debate that the Greeks and the Romans had with one another.

It is the saying of a wise man, and Cato said it, that among the cares man has in his heart he should intersperse pleasures and merry words, for much sadness brings much sin.

Translated by Raymond S. Willis.

And since a person cannot laugh at sensible things, I will insert a few jokes here; whenever you hear them pay attention only to the way they are put into song and verse.

Understand my words correctly and ponder their meaning; don't let it happen to you as it happened to the wise man from Greece with the Roman hoodlum of very little knowledge, when Rome petitioned Greece for learning.

Once upon a time the Romans had no laws, and they went to ask for them from the Greeks who did have them; the Greeks answered that the Romans did not deserve them, nor would they be able to understand them because they had so little knowledge;

although, if the Romans did want laws in order to conduct themselves by them, it was first of all necessary for them to hold a debate with the wise men of Greece in order to determine whether the Romans could understand laws and deserved to have them: this was the gracious answer they gave in order to get out of it.

The Romans answered that this suited them [and they would do it] gladly; they drew up a signed agreement for the debate; but since they would not be able to understand the language which they themselves did not speak, they asked to debate by means of gestures and the sign-language used by learned men.

Both parties agreed on a specified day for the contest; the Romans were in distress; they did not know what to do because they were not educated and would not be able to understand the Greek doctors nor their great wisdom.

While they were in this difficulty, a certain citizen told them to select a hoodlum, a Roman roughneck, and [tell him that] whatever gestures God might inspire him to make with his hand, these he should make; and it was good advice for them.

They approached a hoodlum, who was very big and pugnacious; they told him: "We have an appointment with the Greeks to debate by gestures; ask for anything you want and we will give it to you: only spare us from this contest."

They put on him rich robes of great price, as though he were a doctor of philosophy; he climbed up onto the lecture seat and said boastfully: "Now let those Greeks come, challenge and all."

A Greek stepped forth, a very polished doctor, selected from among the Greeks and highly renowned among all; he mounted the other high seat, with all the people assembled; they began their gestures, as had been agreed upon.

The Greek rose, calmly, slowly, and held out one finger, the one next to the thumb; then he sat down in his place. The hoodlum rose, savage and in a bad temper;

he held out three fingers towards the Greek, the thumb and the two fingers next to it, like a trident, with the last two fingers folded in; quickly he sat down, gazing at his robes.

The Greek stood up and held out his open palm, and then he sat down, he with his fine mind; the hoodlum got up, he with his vacuous fancies, and stuck out his clenched fist: he wanted to get into a brawl.

The Greek sage said to all the Greeks: "The Romans deserve laws, I will not deny them to them." All the people arose in peace and with calm; Rome gained great honor through a worthless tramp.

They asked the Greek what he had said to the Roman by his gestures, and what he had answered him. He said: "I said that there is one God; the Roman said He was One in Three Persons, and made a sign to that effect.

Next I said that all was by the will of God; he answered that God held everything in his power, and he spoke truly. When I saw that they understood and believed in the Trinity, I understood that they deserved assurance of [receiving] laws."

They asked the hoodlum what his notion was; he replied: "He said that with his finger he would smash my eye; I was mighty unhappy about this and I got mighty angry, and I answered him with rage, with anger, and with fury,

that, right in front of everybody, I would smash his eyes with my two fingers and his teeth with my thumb; right after that he told me to watch him because he would give me a big slap on my ears [that would leave them] ringing.

I answered him that I would give him such a punch that in all his life he would never get even for it. As soon as he saw that he had the quarrel in bad shape, he quit making threats in a spot where they thought nothing of him."

This is why the proverb of the shrewd old woman says: "No word is bad if you don't take it badly." You will see that my word is well said if it is well understood: understand my book well and you will have a lovely lady.

Whatever joke you may hear, don't despise it; the nature of the book must be understood by you as subtle, an art [knowledge] of praising and vilifying, cryptic and graceful; you won't find here just one of a thousand troubadours.

You will find many herons, you won't find a single egg; not every new tailor can do a good job of mending; don't imagine that I am impelled to compose poems as a fool does: what good love says, I will prove to you with good reasoning.

The text speaks to everyone in general; people of good sense will discern its wisdom; as for frivolous young people, let them refrain from folly: let him who is fortunate select the better side.

The utterances of good love are veiled: strive to find their true meanings; if you understand the meaning of what is said or hit upon the sense, you will not speak ill of the book which you now censure.

Where you think it is telling lies, it is speaking the greatest truth; in the bright-colored stanzas is where great ugliness lies; judge a statement to be complimentary or derogatory, point by point [with hairsplitting reasoning]; praise or condemn the stanzas for their points [musical notes].

I, this book, am akin to all instruments of music: according as you point [play music] well or badly, so, most assuredly, will I speak; in whatever way you choose to speak, make a point [stop] there and hold fast; if you know how to point me [pluck my strings], you will always hold me in mind.

Here it says how by nature men and the other beasts desire to couple with females.

As Aristotle says, and a true thing it is, the whole world exerts itself for two things: the first is to find sustenance, the other thing is to couple with a pleasant female.

GIOVANNI BOCCACCIO (1313–1375)
Italy

After spending part of his youth at Naples (1327–1341), Boccaccio lived mostly in Florence. He is considered, with Petrarch, one of the first writers of the Italian Renaissance; his scholarly works in Latin were written toward the end of his life, when a spiritual crisis caused him to reject vernacular writing as sinful. Framed within a story of ten young Florentines fleeing the plague in the city and amusing themselves in the country, partly by storytelling, Boccaccio presents 100 short stories, ten each day—which explains the word "decameron," ten days in Greek. The stories come in a variety of moods—comic, tragic, romantic—and in a variety of settings—ancient and contemporary, exotic and familiar. Boccaccio values love (of body and of soul), justice, generosity, and cleverness, (learning from one's experiences, coping with life and other people, often by a clever use of words). A storyteller who uses his ongoing or "frame" characters, to tell the stories of other characters themselves using stories or witty remarks to get what they want or to get out of trouble. Boccaccio is fascinated by the power of words and the power of laughter. The tale of Chichibio is a good example.

from *Decameron*

Sixth Day, Fourth Tale

Chichibio, cook to Currado Gianfigliazzi, changes Currado's anger to laughter, and so escapes the punishment with which Currado had threatened him.

Lauretta was silent, and they all praised Nonna; whereupon the queen ordered Neifile to follow next. And she said:

Amorous ladies, although quick wits often provide speakers with useful and witty words, yet Fortune, which sometimes aids the timid, often puts words into their mouths which they would never have thought of in a calm moment. This I intend to show you by my tale.

As everyone of you must have heard and seen, Currado Gianfigliazzi was always a noble citizen of our city, liberal and magnificent, leading a gentleman's life, continually delighting in dogs and hawks, and allowing his more serious affairs to slide. One day near Peretola his falcon brought down a crane, and finding it to be plump and young he sent it to his excellent cook, a Venetian named Chichibio, telling him to roast it for supper and see that it was well done.

Chichibio, who was a bit of a fool, prepared the crane, set it before the fire, and began to cook it carefully. When it was nearly done and giving off a most savoury odour, there came into the kitchen a young peasant woman, named Brunetta, with

Translated by Richard Aldington.

whom Chichibio was very much in love. Smelling the odour of the bird and seeing it, she begged Chichibio to give her a leg of it. But he replied with a snatch of song:

"You won't get it from me, Donna Brunetta, you won't get it from me."

This made Donna Brunetta angry, and she said:

"God's faith, if you don't give it me, you'll never get anything you want from me."

In short, they had high words together. In the end Chichibio, not wanting to anger his lady-love, took off one of the crane's legs, and gave it to her. A little later the one-legged crane was served before Currado and his guests. Currado was astonished at the sight, sent for Chichibio, and asked him what had happened to the other leg of the crane. The lying Venetian replied:

"Sir, cranes only have one leg and one foot."

"What the devil d'you mean," said Currado angrily, "by saying they have only one leg and foot? Did I never see a crane before?"

"It's as I say, Sir," Chichibio persisted, "and I'll show it you in living birds whenever you wish."

Currado would not bandy further words from respect to his guests, but said:

"Since you promise to show me in living birds something I never saw or heard of, I shall be glad to see it tomorrow morning. But, by the body of Christ, if it turns out otherwise I'll have you tanned in such a way that you'll remember my name as long as you live."

When day appeared next morning, Currado, who had not been able to sleep for rage all night, got up still furious, and ordered his horses to be brought. He made Chichibio mount a pad, and took him in the direction of a river where cranes could always be seen at that time of day, saying:

"We'll soon see whether you were lying or not last night."

Chichibio, seeing that Currado was still angry and that he must try to prove his lie, which he had not the least idea how to do, rode alongside Currado in a state of consternation, and would willingly have fled if he had known how. But as he couldn't do that, he kept gazing round him and thought everything he saw was a crane with two legs. But when they came to the river, he happened to be the first to see a dozen cranes on the bank, all standing on one leg as they do when they are asleep. He quickly pointed them out to Currado, saying:

"Messer, you can see that what I said last evening is true, that cranes have only one leg and one foot; you have only to look at them over there."

"Wait," said Currado, "I'll show you they have two."

And going up closer to them, he shouted: "Ho! Ho!" And at this the cranes put down their other legs and, after running a few steps, took to flight. Currado then turned to Chichibio, saying:

"Now, you glutton, what of it? D'you think they have two?"

In his dismay Chichibio, not knowing how the words came to him, replied:

"Yes, messer, but you didn't shout 'ho! ho!' to the bird last night. If you had shouted, it would have put out the other leg and foot, as those did."

Currado was so pleased with this answer that all his anger was converted into merriment and laughter, and he said:

"Chichibio, you're right; I ought to have done so."

So with this quick and amusing answer Chichibio escaped punishment, and made his peace with his master.

GEOFFREY CHAUCER (1340–1400)
England

The most important writer of Middle English, the poet Geoffrey Chaucer, joined the English army's invasion of France in 1359, was captured, and was ransomed by King Edward III in 1360; after 1367, when he was given a life pension by the King, he remained in the royal service. After periods of French and Italian influence, he began *The Canterbury Tales* in 1387. Chaucer created a vivid social satire in his *Canterbury Tales*. In the prologue he describes a group of people of different ranks and professions setting off together on a pilgrimage. He focuses on each of them, detailing their physical characteristics, their clothes, and something of their lives and habits. He rarely criticizes his characters directly, but uses clothes or actions that are not appropriate to their position to satirize them. The characters also reveal themselves, for good or bad, in their conversations, in the prologues to the individual tales, and in the tales themselves, which range from courtly to coarse, from saint's life to dirty tricks, from tragic to farcical. The prologue for the Wife of Bath describes her various marriages, the domination of some of her husbands, and her rebellion against the misogyny of others. The tale she tells, set in the world of Arthurian knights, questions stereotypical notions of sexual hierarchy, of class, even of age. Beginning with a snide attack on friars who abuse their positions of trust to seduce women, it focuses on a knight who commits a rape but is saved from execution by the queen (Guinevere) if he can discover what it is that all women want. The trick, however, is that to discover the answer he has to act it out—that is, he has to give himself and his body into the power of his wife, who thereby avenges the rape. And, it is implied, if he wants to continue to have a beautiful and faithful wife, he must leave the relationship in her control.

from *The Canterbury Tales*

The Wife of Bath's Tale

In the old days when King Arthur ruled the nation,
Whom Welshmen speak of with such veneration,
This realm we live in was a fairy land.
The fairy queen danced with her jolly band
On the green meadows where they held dominion.   5

Translated by Theodore Morrison.

This was, as I have read, the old opinion;
I speak of many hundred years ago.
But no one sees an elf now, as you know,
For in our time the charity and prayers
And all the begging of these holy friars   10
Who swarm through every nook and every stream
Thicker than motes of dust in a sunbeam,
Blessing our chambers, kitchens, halls, and bowers,
Our cities, towns, and castles, our high towers,
Our villages, our stables, barns, and dairies,   15
They keep us all from seeing any fairies,
For where you might have come upon an elf
There now you find the holy friar himself
Working his district on industrious legs
And saying his devotions while he begs.   20
Women are safe now under every tree.
No incubus is there unless it's he,
And all they have to fear from him is shame.

   It chanced that Arthur had a knight who came
Lustily riding home one day from hawking,   25
And in his path he saw a maiden walking
Before him, stark alone, right in his course.
This young knight took her maidenhead by force,
A crime at which the outcry was so keen
It would have cost his neck, but that the queen,   30
With other ladies, begged the king so long
That Arthur spared his life, for right or wrong,
And gave him to the queen, at her own will,
According to her choice, to save or kill.

   She thanked the king, and later told this knight,   35
Choosing her time, "You are still in such a plight
Your very life has no security.
I grant your life, if you can answer me
This question: what is the thing that most of all
Women desire? Think, or your neck will fall   40
Under the ax! If you cannot let me know
Immediately, I give you leave to go
A twelvemonth and a day, no more, in quest
Of such an answer as will meet the test.
But you must pledge your honor to return   45
And yield your body, whatever you may learn."

   The knight sighed; he was rueful beyond measure.
But what! He could not follow his own pleasure.
He chose at last upon his way to ride
And with such answer as God might provide   50
To come back when the year was at the close.

Geoffrey Chaucer, from an illuminated manuscript, now in the National Portrait Gallery, London.

He seeks out every house and every place
Where he has any hope, by luck or grace,
Of learning what thing women covet most.   55
But he could never light on any coast
Where on this point two people would agree,
For some said wealth and some said jollity,
Some said position, some said sport in bed
And often to be widowed, often wed.   60
Some said that to a woman's heart what mattered
Above all else was to be pleased and flattered.
That shaft, to tell the truth, was a close hit.
Men win us best by flattery, I admit,
And by attention. Some say our greatest ease   65
Is to be free and do just as we please,
And not to have our faults thrown in our eyes,
But always to be praised for being wise.
And true enough, there's not one of us all
Who will not kick if you rub us on a gall.   70
Whatever vices we may have within,
We won't be taxed with any fault or sin.
     Some say that women are delighted well
If it is thought that they will never tell
A secret they are trusted with, or scandal.   75
But that tale isn't worth an old rake handle!

We women, for a fact, can never hold
A secret. Will you hear a story told?
Then witness Midas! For it can be read
In Ovid that he had upon his head   80
Two ass's ears that he kept out of sight
Beneath his long hair with such skill and sleight
That no one else besides his wife could guess.
He loved her well, and trusted her no less.
He begged her not to make his blemish known,   85
But keep her knowledge to herself alone.
She swore that never, though to save her skin,
Would she be guilty of so mean a sin,
And yet it seemed to her she nearly died
Keeping a secret locked so long inside.   90
It swelled about her heart so hard and deep
She was afraid some word was bound to leap
Out of her mouth, and since there was no man
She dared to tell, down to a swamp she ran—
Her heart, until she got there, all agog—   95
And like a bittern booming in the bog
She put her mouth close to the watery ground:
"Water, do not betray me with your sound!
I speak to you, and you alone," she said.
"Two ass's ears grow on my husband's head!   100
And now my heart is whole, now it is out.
I'd burst if I held it longer, past all doubt."
Safely, you see, awhile you may confide
In us, but it will out; we cannot hide
A secret. Look in Ovid if you care   105
To learn what followed; the whole tale is there.

   This knight, when he perceived he could not find
What women covet most, was low in mind;
But the day came when homeward he must ride,
And as he crossed a wooded countryside   110
Some four and twenty ladies there by chance
He saw, all circling in a woodland dance,
And toward this dance he eagerly drew near
In hope of any counsel he might hear.
But the truth was, he had not reached the place   115
When dance and all, they vanished into space.
No living soul remained there to be seen
Save an old woman sitting on the green,
As ugly a witch as fancy could devise.
As he approached her she began to rise   120
And said, "Sir knight, here runs no thoroughfare.
What are you seeking with such anxious air?

Tell me! The better may your fortune be.
We old folk know a lot of things," said she.
    "Good mother," said the knight, "my life's to pay,   125
That's all too certain, if I cannot say
What women covet most. If you could tell
That secret to me, I'd requite you well."
    "Give me your hand," she answered. "Swear me true
That whatsoever I next ask of you,   130
You'll do it if it lies within your might
And I'll enlighten you before the night."
    "Granted, upon my honor," he replied.
    "Then I dare boast, and with no empty pride,
Your life is safe," she told him. "Let me die   135
If she, the queen, won't say the same as I.
Let's learn if the haughtiest of all who wear
A net or coverchief upon their hair
Will be so forward as to answer 'no'
To what I'll teach you. No more; let us go."   140
With that she whispered something in his ear,
And told him to be glad and have no fear.
    When they had reached the court, the knight declared
That he had kept his day, and was prepared
To give his answer, standing for his life.   145
Many the wise widow, many the wife,
Many the maid who rallied to the scene,
And at the head as justice sat the queen.
Then silence was enjoined; the knight was told
In open court to say what women hold   150
Precious above all else. He did not stand
Dumb like a beast, but spoke up at command
And plainly offered them his answering word
In manly voice, so that the whole court heard.
    "My liege and lady, most of all," said he,   155
"Women desire to have the sovereignty
And sit in rule and government above
Their husbands, and to have their way in love.
This is what most you want. Spare me or kill
As you may like; I stand here by your will."   160
    No widow, wife, or maid gave any token
Of contradicting what the knight had spoken.
He should not die; he should be spared instead;
He well deserved his life, the whole court said.
    The old woman whom the knight met on the green   165
Sprang up at this. "My sovereign lady queen,
Before your court has risen, do me right!
I taught, myself, this answer to the knight,

For which he pledged his honor in my hand,
Solemnly, that the first thing I demand,   170
He'd do it, if it lay within his might.
Before the court I ask you, then, sir knight,
To take me," said the woman, "as your wife,
For well you know that I have saved your life.
Deny me, on your honor, if you can."   175
    "Alas," replied this miserable man,
"That was my promise, it must be confessed.
For the love of God, though, choose a new request!
Take all my wealth, and let my body be."
    "If that's your tune, then curse both you and me,"   180
She said. "Though I am ugly, old, and poor,
I'll have, for all the metal and the ore
That under earth is hidden or lies above,
Nothing, except to be your wife and love."
    "My love? No, my damnation, if you can!   185
Alas," he said, "that any of my clan
Should be so miserably misallied!"
    All to no good; force overruled his pride,
And in the end he is constrained to wed,
And marries his old wife and goes to bed.   190
    Now some will charge me with an oversight
In failing to describe the day's delight,
The merriment, the food, the dress at least.
But I reply, there was no joy nor feast;
Nothing but sorrow and sharp misery.   195
He married her in private, secretly,
And all day after, such was his distress,
Hid like an owl from his wife's ugliness.
    Great was the woe this knight had in his head
When in due time they both were brought to bed.   200
He shuddered, tossed, and turned, and all the while
His old wife lay and waited with a smile.
"Is every knight so backward with a spouse?
Is it," she said, "a law in Arthur's house?
I am your love, your own, your wedded wife.   205
I am the woman who has saved your life.
I've never done you anything but right.
Why do you treat me this way the first night?
You must be mad, the way that you behave!
Tell me my fault, and as God's love can save,   210
I will amend it, truly, if I can."
    "Amend it?" answered this unhappy man.
"It never can be amended, truth to tell.
You are so loathsome and so old as well,

And your low birth besides is such a cross 215
It is no wonder that I turn and toss.
God take my woeful spirit from my breast!"
   "Is this," she said, "the cause of your unrest?"
   "No wonder!" said the knight. "It truly is."
   "Now sir, she said, "I could amend all this 220
Within three days, if it should please me to,
And if you deal with me as you should do.
   "But since you speak of that nobility
That comes from ancient wealth and pedigree,
As if *that* constituted gentlemen, 225
I hold such arrogance not worth a hen!
The man whose virtue is pre-eminent,
In public and alone, always intent
On doing every generous act he can,
Take him—he is the greatest gentleman! 230
Christ wills that we should claim nobility
From him, not from old wealth or family.
Our elders left us all that they were worth
And through their wealth and blood we claim high birth,
But never, since it was beyond their giving, 235
Could they bequeath to us their virtuous living;
Although it first conferred on them the name
Of gentlemen, they could not leave that claim!
   "Dante the Florentine on this was wise:
'Frail is the branch on which man's virtues rise'— 240
Thus runs his rhyme—'God's goodness wills that we
Should claim from him alone nobility.'
Thus from our elders we can only claim
Such temporal things as men may hurt and maim.
   "It's plain enough that true nobility 245
Is not bequeathed along with property,
For many a lord's son does a deed of shame
And yet, God knows, enjoys his noble name.
But he, though scion of a noble house
And elders who were wise and virtuous, 250
Who will not follow his elders, who are dead,
But leads, himself, a shameful life instead,
He is not noble, be he duke or earl.
It is the churlish deed that makes the churl.
And therefore, my dear husband, I conclude 255
That though my ancestors were rough and rude,
Yet may Almighty God confer on me
The grace to live, as I hope, virtuously.
Call me of noble blood when I begin
To live in virtue and to cast out sin. 260

"As for my poverty, at which you grieve,
Almighty God in whom we all believe
In willful poverty chose to lead his life,
And surely every man and maid and wife
Can understand that Jesus, heaven's king,   265
Would never choose a low or vicious thing.
A poor and cheerful life is nobly led;
So Seneca and others have well said.
The man so poor he doesn't have a stitch
Who thinks himself repaid, I count as rich.   270
He that is covetous, he is the poor man,
Pining to have the things he never can.
It is of cheerful mind, true poverty.
Juvenal says about it happily:
'The poor man as he goes along his way   275
And passes thieves is free to sing and play.'
Poverty is a good we loathe, a great
Reliever of our busy worldly state,
A great amender also of our minds
As he that patiently will bear it finds.   280
And poverty, for all it seems distressed,
Is a possession no one will contest.
Poverty, too, by bringing a man low,
Helps him the better God and self to know.
Poverty is a glass where we can see   285
Which are our true friends, as it seems to me.
So, sir, I do not wrong you on this score;
Reproach me with my poverty no more.

"Now, sir, you tax me with my age; but, sir,
You gentlemen of breeding all aver   290
That men should not despise old age, but rather
Grant an old man respect, and call him 'father.'
"If I am old and ugly, as you have said,
You have less fear of being cuckolded,
For ugliness and age, as all agree,   295
Are notable guardians of chastity.
But since I know in what you take delight,
I'll gratify your worldly appetite.

"Choose now, which of two courses you will try:
To have me old and ugly till I die   300
But evermore your true and humble wife,
Never displeasing you in all my life,
Or will you have me rather young and fair
And take your chances on who may repair
Either to your house on account of me   305
Or to some other place, it well may be.

Now make your choice, whichever you prefer."
   The knight took thought, and sighed, and said to her
At last, "My love and lady, my dear wife,
In your wise government I put my life. 310
Choose for yourself which course will best agree
With pleasure and honor, both for you and me.
I do not care, choose either of the two;
I am content, whatever pleases you."
   "Then have I won from you the sovereignty, 315
Since I may choose and rule at will?" said she.
   He answered, "That is best, I think, dear wife."
   "Kiss me," she said. "Now we are done with strife,
For on my word, I will be both to you,
That is to say, fair, yes, and faithful too. 320
May I die mad unless I am as true
As ever wife was since the world was new.
Unless I am as lovely to be seen
By morning as an empress or a queen
Or any lady between east and west, 325
Do with my life or death as you think best.
Lift up the curtain, see what you may see."
   And when the knight saw what had come to be
And knew her as she was, so young, so fair,
His joy was such that it was past compare. 330
He took her in his arms and gave her kisses
A thousand times on end; he bathed in blisses.
And she obeyed him also in full measure
In everything that tended to his pleasure.
   And so they lived in full joy to the end. 335
And now to all us women may Christ send
Submissive husbands, full of youth in bed,
And grace to outlive all the men we wed.
And I pray Jesus to cut short the lives
Of those who won't be governed by their wives; 340
And old, ill-tempered niggards who hate expense,
God promptly bring them down with pestilence!

CHRISTINE DE PIZAN (c. 1364–1429)
France

In the *Mutation of Fortune,* a narrative poem written in 1403, the French author
Christine de Pizan describes how Fortune appears to her when she is in deep

depression over the death of her husband—Etienne de Castel—whom she married in 1379, and who was to become secretary to Charles VI—and turns her into a man so she can face the demands of her new life, support her three children, fight with the government bureaucracy over her husband's claims, and succeed as a professional writer. She is not comfortable with her new role, but she accepts it as a necessity for herself and her family.

Christine's interest in learning had been encouraged by her father, a physician and astrologer at the court of Charles V of France, and by various powerful friends, including the king and the chancellor of the University of Paris. In the beginning of the *The Book of the City of Ladies,* a French prose work of 1405, she is again in a moment of depression, this time brought on by reading the latest in a series of misogynous texts that make women out to be hopelessly sinful creatures. Though the descriptions of women in these books contrast with Christine's own experience of women of every class, she is unsettled by them and begins to feel that God has mistreated her by making her a woman, until three personifications appear to her (reflecting the influence of Boethius's *The Consolation of Philosophy*) and console her. They are Reason, Rectitude, and Justice, and they tell her of all the contributions women have made to civilization. It is from this knowledge that she builds her city of ladies.

from The Mutation of Fortune

[Fortune Changes Christine into a Man]

I was in this state [of grief for her husband] for a long time, refusing all pleasures, without hope of joy or solace. Our troubled ship was carried now here, now there, all winds harmful to it, for there was no one who knew enough to pilot it. I thought that I could never guide it back, but would remain on that sea that divides grief from joy all my life, on the wrong side of happiness which had fled from me, and that alarmed me. But it did not continue; I was later to take many steps on land. To be brief, my sorrow and my weeping were such that even Fortune had pity on my distress and wanted to befriend and help me, as a good mistress. But her help was wondrous—perhaps it was even more dangerous.

Exhausted by long weeping, I remained as if dead. Then I fell asleep and my mistress, who has offered joy to many, came towards me and touched me all over my body. Each part, I remember well, she held in her hands and massaged. Then she left and I remained. When our ship, carried by the waves of the sea, broke against a rock with a great crash, I awoke and immediately, without any doubt, felt myself completely transformed. I felt my body to be much stronger, the weeping I had been engaged in abated. Then I touched myself and was amazed. Fortune did not hate me if she so transformed me, for quite suddenly she changed the fear and doubt in which I had been floundering. I felt myself much relieved, my flesh changed and strengthened, my voice deepened, and my body harder and swifter. But the ring that Hymen [marriage] had given me, fell from my finger which troubled me, with good reason, for I loved it dearly.

Translated by Joan M. Ferrante.

I got up easily. I did not remain in the indolence of weeping which had increased my distress. I found a strong and bold heart in me, which astonished me, but then I recognized that I had become a true man. I was amazed by the adventure. I raised my eyes, by chance, saw the sail and mast all broken, for the bad weather had torn the ropes. Our ship was badly shattered and cracked and the water was pouring in. It was already so filled that if the rocks on which we struck had not interfered, it would have sunk to the bottom. When I saw it thus in danger, I began to fix it myself. With nails and mortar, I rejoined and hammered the planks and gathered moss on the rocks and fixed it in the cracks in great bunches to make it watertight. I had the water bailed. In short, I knew what to do to handle the ship. What I did not know myself about guiding it, I learned, so I became a good pilot, as I had to be to help myself and my people, if I didn't want us to die there.

Now I was a true man—this is no fable—capable of piloting a ship. Fortune taught me that craft, and so took hold of me. As you hear this, I am still a man, and have been so already for more than thirteen years, though it would please me three times as much to be a woman still, as I was when I spoke with Hymen. But since Fortune has estranged me from that life, so that I shall never be lodged there again, I shall remain a man and keep myself with my lady [Fortune] however much I find a harshness in her service that destroys me. But I have to live there until I die—God deliver me to salvation. So I drew myself away from those rocks, I steered my ship and brought it to the place from which I had departed.

from *The Book of the City of Ladies*

[Here Begins the Book of the City of Ladies]

1. *Here begins* The Book of the City of Ladies, *whose first chapter tells why and for what purpose this book was written.*

One day as I was sitting alone in my study surrounded by books on all kinds of subjects, devoting myself to literary studies, my usual habit, my mind dwelt at length on the weighty opinions of various authors whom I had studied for a long time. I looked up from my book, having decided to leave such subtle questions in peace and to relax by reading some light poetry. With this in mind, I searched for some small book. By chance a strange volume came into my hands, not one of my own, but one which had been given to me along with some others. When I held it open and saw from its title page that it was by Mathéolus,[1] I smiled, for though I had never seen it before, I had often heard that like other books it discussed respect for women. I thought I would browse through it to amuse myself. I had not been reading for very long when my good mother called me to refresh myself with some supper, for it was

Translated by Earl Jeffrey Richards.

1. Mathéolus wrote a *Book of Lamentations* in Latin in about 1300, expressing misogyny in Ovidian verse. It was translated into French in the late fourteenth century.

evening. Intending to look at it the next day, I put it down. The next morning, again seated in my study as was my habit, I remembered wanting to examine this book by Mathéolus. I started to read it and went on for a little while. Because the subject seemed to me not very pleasant for people who do not enjoy lies, and of no use in developing virtue or manners, given its lack of integrity in diction and theme, and after browsing here and there and reading the end, I put it down in order to turn my attention to more elevated and useful study. But just the sight of this book, even though it was of no authority, made me wonder how it happened that so many different men—and learned men among them—have been and are so inclined to express both in speaking and in their treatises and writings so many wicked insults about women and their behavior. Not only one or two and not even just this Mathéolus (for this book had a bad name anyway and was intended as a satire) but, more generally, judging from the treatises of all philosophers and poets and all the orators—it would take too long to mention their names—it seems that they all speak from one and the same mouth. They all concur in one conclusion: that the behavior of women is inclined to and full of every vice. Thinking deeply about these matters, I began to examine my character and conduct as a natural woman and, similarly, I considered other women whose company I frequently kept, princesses, great ladies, women of the middle and lower classes, who had graciously told me of their most private and intimate thoughts, hoping that I could judge impartially and in good conscience whether the testimony of so many notable men could be true. To the best of my knowledge, no matter how long I confronted or dissected the problem, I could not see or realize how their claims could be true when compared to the natural behavior and character of women. Yet I still argued vehemently against women, saying that it would be impossible that so many famous men—such solemn scholars, possessed of such deep and great understanding, so clear-sighted in all things, as it seemed—could have spoken falsely on so many occasions that I could hardly find a book on morals where, even before I had read it in its entirety, I did not find several chapters or certain sections attacking women, no matter who the author was. This reason alone, in short, made me conclude that, although my intellect did not perceive my own great faults and, likewise, those of other women because of its simpleness and ignorance, it was however truly fitting that such was the case. And so I relied more on the judgment of others than on what I myself felt and knew. I was so transfixed in this line of thinking for such a long time that it seemed as if I were in a stupor. Like a gushing fountain, a series of authorities, whom I recalled one after another, came to mind, along with their opinions on this topic. And I finally decided that God formed a vile creature when He made woman, and I wondered how such a worthy artisan could have deigned to make such an abominable work which, from what they say, is the vessel as well as the refuge and abode of every evil and vice. As I was thinking this, a great unhappiness and sadness welled up in my heart, for I detested myself and the entire feminine sex, as though we were monstrosities in nature. And in my lament I spoke these words:

"Oh, God, how can this be? For unless I stray from my faith, I must never doubt that Your infinite wisdom and most perfect goodness ever created anything which was not good. Did You yourself not create woman in a very special way and since that time did You not give her all those inclinations which it pleased You for her to have? And how could it be that You could go wrong in anything? Yet look at all these accusations which have been judged, decided, and concluded against women. I do not know how to understand this repugnance. If it is so, fair Lord God, that in fact so many abominations abound in the female sex, for You Yourself say that the testimony of two or three witnesses lends credence, why shall I not doubt that this is true? Alas, God, why did You not let me be born in the world as a man, so that all my inclinations would be to serve You better, and so that I would not stray in anything and would be as perfect as a man is said to be? But since Your kindness has not been extended to me, then forgive my negligence in Your service, most fair Lord God, and may it not displease You, for the servant who receives fewer gifts from his lord is less obliged in his service." I spoke these words to God in my lament and a great deal more for a very long time in sad reflection, and in my folly I considered myself most unfortunate because God had made me inhabit a female body in this world.

[Here Christine Describes How Three Ladies Appeared to Her]

2. Here Christine describes how three ladies appeared to her and how the one who was in front spoke first and comforted her in her pain.

So occupied with these painful thoughts, my head bowed in shame, my eyes filled with tears, leaning on the pommel of my chair's armrest, I suddenly saw a ray of light fall on my lap, as though it were the sun. I shuddered then, as if wakened from sleep, for I was sitting in a shadow where the sun could not have shone at that hour. And as I lifted my head to see where this light was coming from, I saw three crowned ladies standing before me, and the splendor of their bright faces shone on me and throughout the entire room. Now no one would ask whether I was surprised, for my doors were shut and they had still entered. Fearing that some phantom had come to tempt me and filled with great fright, I made the Sign of the Cross on my forehead.

Then she who was the first of the three smiled and began to speak, "Dear daughter, do not be afraid, for we have not come here to harm or trouble you but to console you, for we have taken pity on your distress, and we have come to bring you out of the ignorance which so blinds your own intellect that you shun what you know for a certainty and believe what you do not know or see or recognize except by virtue of many strange opinions. You resemble the fool in the prank who was dressed in women's clothes while he slept; because those who were making fun of him repeatedly told him he was a woman, he believed their false testimony more readily than the certainty of his own identity. Fair daughter, have you lost all sense? Have you forgotten that when fine gold is tested in the furnace, it does not change or vary in strength but becomes purer the more it is hammered and handled in different ways? Do you not know that the best things are the most debated and the most discussed? If you wish to consider the question of the highest form of reality, which consists in ideas or celestial substances, consider whether the greatest philosophers who have lived and whom you support against your own sex have ever resolved whether ideas are false and contrary to the truth. Notice how these same philosophers contradict and criticize one another, just as you have seen in the *Metaphysics* where Aristotle takes their opinions to task and speaks similarly of Plato and other philosophers. And note, moreover, how even Saint Augustine and the Doctors of the Church have criticized Aristotle in certain passages, although he is known as the prince of philosophers in whom both natural and moral philosophy attained their highest level. It also seems that you think that all the words of the philosophers are articles of faith, that they could never be wrong. As far as the poets of whom you speak are concerned, do you not know that they spoke on many subjects in a fictional way and that often they mean the contrary of what their words openly say? One can interpret them according to the grammatical figure of *antiphrasis,* which means, as you know, that if you call something bad, in fact, it is good, and also vice versa. Thus I advise you to profit from their works and to interpret them in the manner in which they are intended in those passages where they attack women. Perhaps this man, who called himself Mathéolus in his own book, intended it in such a way, for there are many things which, if taken literally, would be pure heresy. As for the attack against the estate of marriage—which is a holy estate, worthy and ordained by God—made not only by Mathéolus but also by others and even by the *Romance of the Rose* where greater credibility is averred because of the authority of its author, it is evident and proven by experience that the contrary of the evil which they posit and claim to be found in this estate through the obligation and fault of women is true. For where has the husband ever been found who would allow his wife to have authority to abuse and insult him as a matter of course, as these authorities maintain? I believe that, regardless of what you might have read, you will never see such a husband with your own eyes, so badly colored are these lies. Thus, in conclusion, I tell you, dear friend, that simplemindedness has prompted you to hold such an opinion. Come back to yourself, recover your senses, and do not trouble yourself anymore over such absurdities. For you know that any evil spoken of women so generally only hurts those who say it, not women themselves."

FRANÇOIS VILLON [FRANÇOIS DE MONTCORBIER, OR FRANÇOIS DE LOGES] (1431–1463?)
France

François de Montcorbier adopted the last name of his patron, the chaplain of a university church who adopted him in about 1438. Villon received a Master of Arts degree from the Sorbonne before he was twenty-one, and spent his life repeatedly under arrest, or wandering to escape it, for brawls, robberies, and other escapades. His *Petit Testament* parodies the style of a legal testament; his *Grand Testament,* of

2000 lines, is more melancholy, without losing its humor. In 1462, he was sentenced to be hanged, after a street fight, but the sentence was commuted in 1463 to ten years of banishment. He then disappeared, and remains popular as a colorful outlaw. Villon's lyrics are deeply rooted in tradition and in the facts of life of their time; drawing on these two sources, he gives a vivid and permanent form to the ephemeral moment. As a university student, a criminal, a jailbird, and a wanderer, Villon had a broad schooling in the varieties of human life and language. He was no less broadly acquainted with the poetic movements of his time. He organized most of his lyrics into two cycles, in each of which the speaker—an outlaw and a fugitive, possessing nothing—bequeaths a "legacy" to various persons who shared his times. There are many figures represented and voices heard—those of pimps and prostitutes as well as those of prominent personages—and many kinds of language—from street slang and obscenities to learned and refined speech. The speaker's body is given a voice as well, for it is the object of his continual awareness and concern, a principal source of his moods and of his self-recognition as a mortal, as a participant in the mortality of all God's creatures. For human beings, however much they differ in fortune and circumstance, are all human through their bodies, and all bodies come to the same end.

Most of these elements in Villon's poetry—the arrangement of lyrics into cycles that follow the movements of the speaker's inner life; the immediate presence of historical and personal reality, as well as gloom and the awareness of disaster and decay; the inclusion of different voices and points of view, and of various metrical forms in which to express them—are characteristic of lyric poetry in France in the fourteenth and fifteenth centuries. It is partly through the immense increase in the subjects of poetic representation, and the inclusion of many kinds of popular language not previously recognized as poetic, that Villon surpasses other poets of his time and tradition. With his outlaw's point of view, his mortal and physical consciousness, and his urban attitude—he is the poet of the city, of Paris. Villon was to enlarge the domain of poetry so that there remained no subject unworthy of poetic language, and no language unworthy of poetic form.

Hanged Men

Brother humans who live on after us
Don't let your hearts harden against us
For if you have pity on wretches like us
More likely God will show mercy to you
You see us five, six, hanging here   5
As for the flesh we loved too well
A while ago it was eaten and has rotted away
And we the bones turn to ashes and dust
Let no one make us the butt of jokes
But pray God that he absolve us all.   10

Don't be insulted that we call you
Brothers, even if it was by Justice
We were put to death, for you understand

Translated by Galway Kinnell.

Not every person has the same good sense
Speak up for us, since we can't ourselves   15
Before the son of the virgin Mary
That his mercy toward us shall keep flowing
Which is what keeps us from hellfire
We are dead, may no one taunt us
But pray God that he absolve us all.   20

The rain has rinsed and washed us
The sun dried us and turned us black
Magpies and ravens have pecked out our eyes
And plucked our beards and eyebrows
Never ever can we stand still   25
Now here, now there, as the wind shifts
At its whim it keeps swinging us
Pocked by birds worse than a sewing thimble

Therefore don't join in our brotherhood
But pray God that he absolve us all.   30

Prince Jesus, master over all
Don't let us fall into hell's dominion
We've nothing to do or settle down there
Men, there's nothing here to laugh at
But pray God that he absolve us all.   35

Our Lady[1]

Lady of heaven, regent of earth
Empress over the swamps of hell
Receive me your humble Christian
Let me be counted among your elect
Even though I'm without any worth   5
My lady and mistress your merits
Are greater by far than my sinfulness
And without them no soul could deserve
Or enter heaven, I'm not acting
In this faith I want to live and die.   10

Tell your son I belong to him
May he wash away my sins
And forgive me as he did the Egyptian woman[2]

---

1. In his poetic *Testament* or Will, Villon be-
   queathes this ballade to his "poor mother,"
   to help her pray to the Virgin.
2. Saint Mary the Egyptian was a prostitute in
   Alexandria who joined a pilgrimage out of
   mere curiosity, paying for her passage, ac-

cording to legend, by plying her trade—a
Villonesque touch; she was converted in
Jerusalem through the influence of the Virgin's image and thereafter lived a reclusive
life of penance in the wilderness.

Or Theophilus[3] the priest
Who with your help was acquitted and absolved   15
Though he'd made a pact with the devil
Keep me from ever doing that
Virgin who bore with unbroken hymen
The sacrament we celebrate at Mass
In this faith I want to live and die.   20

I'm just a poor old woman
Who knows nothing and can't read
On the walls of my parish church I see
A paradise painted with harps and lutes
And a hell where they boil the damned   25
One gives me a fright, one great bliss and joy
Let me have the good place, mother of God
To whom sinners all must turn
Filled with faith, sincere and eager
In this faith I want to live and die.   30

Virgin so worthy, princess, you bore
Iesus who reigns without end or limit
Lord Almighty who took on our weakness
Left heaven and came down to save us
Offering his precious youth to death   35
Now such is our Lord, such I acknowledge him
In this faith I want to live and die.[4]

THOMAS MALORY (c. 1471)
England

Sir Thomas Malory, who belonged to an old Warwickshire family, was, at various times, a soldier—a loyalist, then a rebel—a member of Parliament, and five or six years later, a fugitive from justice. Imprisoned eight times, he made two dramatic escapes; it was during his last imprisonment that he wrote his Arthurian romance: *Le Morte D'Arthur,* testifying to England's heroic past. Drawing on the vast compendia of Arthurian, Tristan, and Grail stories in the French vulgate cycles of the thirteenth century, Malory set the Tristan-Isolde affair at the center of *Le Morte D'Arthur,* his long prose romance.

---

3. The story of Theophilus, saved from his pact with the Devil through the intervention of the Virgin, was popular all through the Middle Ages.

4. In this concluding stanza, or envoi, the first letters of the first six lines, read downward, form an acrostic of the poet's name.

The Launcelot-Guinevere affair, with certain important similarities, is told on either side of the Tristan story. It brings the problem of adultery with the king's wife to the heart of the Arthurian court, which it will help to destroy. Malory makes Launcelot an exemplum of the courtly paradox—the knight who has achieved the highest level of chivalry through his service to his lady, Guinevere, but who fails in the highest quest of all, for the Grail, precisely because of that love. Though he remains the finest knight within the Arthurian circle, Launcelot is unable to give up chivalric values, like helping the weaker side in a tournament even if it is the sinners' side (the black knights in the second selection). He is therefore unable to achieve the Grail quest, while the knights who do, Galahad and Perceval, do not continue to serve in the world but die shortly after their quests are accomplished.

from *Le Morte D'Arthur*

[How Sir Launcelot Found the Old Chapel and Saw the Altar]

Then Sir Launcelot looked by him, and saw an old chapel, and there he weened to have found people; and Sir Launcelot tied his horse till a tree, and there he did off his shield and hung it upon a tree. And then he went to the chapel door, and found it waste and broken. And within he found a fair altar, full richly arrayed with cloth of clean silk, and there stood a fair clean candlestick, which bare six great candles, and the candlestick was of silver. And when Sir Launcelot saw this light he had great will for to enter into the chapel, but he could find no place where he might enter; then was he passing heavy and dismayed. Then he returned and came to his horse and did off his saddle and bridle, and let him pasture, and unlaced his helm, and ungirt his sword, and laid him down to sleep upon his shield tofore the cross.

How Sir Launcelot, half sleeping and half waking, saw a sick man borne in a litter, and how he was healed by the Sangrail

And so he fell asleep; and half waking and sleeping he saw come by him two palfreys all fair and white, the which bare a litter, therein lying a sick knight. And when he was nigh the cross he there abode still. All this Sir Launcelot saw and beheld, for he slept not verily; and he heard him say,

"O sweet Lord, when shall this sorrow leave me? And when shall the holy vessel come by me, wherethrough I shall be blessed? For I have endured thus long, for little trespass."

A full great while complained the knight thus, and always Sir Launcelot heard it.

With that Sir Launcelot saw the candlestick with the six tapers come before the cross, and he saw nobody that brought it. Also there came a table of silver, and

Edited by Janet Cowen.

the holy vessel of the Sangrail,[1] which Launcelot had seen aforetime in King Petchere's house.[2]

And therewith the sick knight sat up, and held up both his hands, and said, "Fair sweet Lord, which is here within this holy vessel, take heed unto me that I may be whole of this malady."

And therewith on his hands and on his knees he went so nigh that he touched the holy vessel and kissed it, and anon he was whole; and then he said, "Lord God, I thank Thee, for I am healed of this sickness."

So when the holy vessel had been there a great while it went unto the chapel with the chandelier and the light, so that Launcelot wist not where it was become; for he was overtaken with sin that he had no power to rise against[3] the holy vessel; wherefore after that many men said of him shame, but he took repentance after that.

Then the sick knight dressed him up and kissed the cross; anon his squire brought him his arms, and asked his lord how he did.

"Certes," said he, "I thank God right well, through the holy vessel I am healed. But I have marvel of this sleeping knight that had no power to awake when this holy vessel was brought hither."

"I dare right well say," said the squire, "that he dwelleth in some deadly sin whereof he was never confessed."

"By my faith," said the knight, "whatsomever he be he is unhappy, for as I deem he is of the fellowship of the Round Table, the which is entered into the quest of the Sangrail."

"Sir," said the squire, "here I have brought you all your arms save your helm and your sword, and therefore by mine assent now may ye take this knight's helm and his sword;" and so he did.

And when he was clean armed he took Sir Launcelot's horse, for he was better than his; and so departed they from the cross.

[How Sir Launcelot Heard a Voice and Called Himself Wretched, Unhappy, and Ashamed]

Then anon Sir Launcelot waked, and sat him up, and bethought him what he had seen there, and whether it were dreams or not.

Right so heard he a voice that said, "Sir Launcelot, more harder than is the stone, and more bitter than is the wood, and more naked and barer than is the leaf of the fig tree;[4] therefore go thou from hence, and withdraw thee from this holy place."

And when Sir Launcelot heard this he was passing heavy and wist not what

---

1. The Sangrail is the Holy Grail. In Malory, God's blood is in the vessel, giving it the power to cure the sick knight when he kisses it.

2. King Petchere or Pescheors is the Fisher King, the Grail king who appears in Chrétien and in Wolfram. It is a play on the French word *pescheor,* "sinner," which in Middle French also means "fisherman." Since Saint Peter was a "fisher of men," and a fish is an ancient symbol of Christians, the pun is particularly suitable.

3. In the presence of the holy vessel.

4. A fig tree becomes barren in the gospel when Christ curses it (Matthew 21:19).

to do, and so departed sore weeping, and cursed the time that he was born. For then he deemed never to have had worship more. For those words went to his heart, till that he knew wherefore he was called so.

Then Sir Launcelot went to the cross and found his helm, his sword, and his horse taken away. And then he called himself a very wretch, and most unhappy of all knights; and there he said,

"My sin and my wickedness have brought me unto great dishonour. For when I sought worldly adventures for worldly desires, I ever achieved them and had the better in every place, and never was I discomfit in no quarrel, were it right or wrong. And now I take upon me the adventures of holy things, and now I see and understand that mine old sin hindereth me and shameth me, so that I had no power to stir nor speak when the holy blood appeared afore me."

[Sir Launcelot and the Black Knights]

How Sir Launcelot jousted with many knights, and he was taken

And then mounted upon his horse, and rode into a forest, and held no highway. And as he looked afore him he saw a fair plain, and beside that a fair castle, and afore the castle were many pavilions of silk and of diverse hue. And him seemed that he saw there five hundred knights riding on horseback; and there were two parties; they that were of the castle were all on black horses and their trappers black, and they that were without were all on white horses and trappers, and every each hurtled to other that it marvelled Sir Launcelot. And at the last him thought they of the castle were put to the worse.

Then thought Sir Launcelot for to help there the weaker party in increasing of his chivalry. And so Sir Launcelot thrust in among the party of the castle, and smote down a knight, horse and man, to the earth. And then he rushed here and there, and did marvellous deeds of arms and then he drew out his sword, and struck many knights to the earth, so that all those that saw him marvelled that ever one knight might do so great deeds of arms.

But always the white knights held them nigh about Sir Launcelot, for to tire him and wind him. But at the last, as a man may not ever endure, Sir Launcelot waxed so faint of fighting and travailing, and was so weary of his great deeds, but he might not lift up his arms for to give one stroke, so that he weened never to have borne arms; and then they all took and led him away into a forest, and there made him to alight and to rest him.

And then all the fellowship of the castle were overcome for the default of him.

Then they said all unto Sir Launcelot, "Blessed be God that ye be now of our fellowship, for we shall hold you in our prison;" and so they left him with few words.

And then Sir Launcelot made great sorrow, "For never or now was I never at tournament nor jousts but I had the best, and now I am shamed." And then he said, "Now I am sure that I am more sinfuller than ever I was."

Thus he rode sorrowing, and half a day he was out of despair, till that he came into a deep valley. And when Sir Launcelot saw he might not ride up into the mountain, he there alit under an apple tree, and there he left his helm and his shield, and put his horse unto pasture. And then he laid him down to sleep.

And then him thought there came an old man afore him, the which said, "Ah, Launcelot of evil faith and poor belief, wherefore is thy will turned so lightly toward thy deadly sin?" And when he had said thus he vanished away, and Launcelot wist not where he was become.

Then he took his horse, and armed him; and as he rode by the way he saw a chapel where was a recluse, which had a window that she might see up to the altar. And all aloud she called Launcelot, for that he seemed a knight errant. And then he came, and she asked him what he was, and of what place, and where about he went to seek.

[How Sir Launcelot Recounted His Vision, and Had It Interpreted for Him]

And then he told her all together word by word, and the truth how it befell him at the tournament. And after told her his advision that he had had that night in his sleep, and prayed her to tell him what it might mean, for he was not well content with it.

"Ah, Launcelot," said she, "as long as ye were knight of earthly knighthood ye were the most marvellous man of the world, and most adventurous. Now," said the lady, "sithen ye be set among the knights of heavenly adventures, if adventure fell thee contrary at that tournament have thou no marvel, for that tournament yesterday was but a tokening of Our Lord. And notforthan there was none enchantment, for they at the tournament were earthly knights.

. . .

"The day of Pentecost, when King Arthur held his court, it befell that earthly kings and knights took a tournament together, that is to say the quest of the Sangrail. The earthly knights were they the which were clothed all in black, and the covering betokeneth the sins whereof they be not confessed. And they with the covering of white betokeneth virginity, and they that chose chastity. And thus was the quest begun in them. Then thou beheld the sinners and the good men, and when thou sawest the sinners overcome, thou inclinest to that party for bobaunce and pride of the world, and all that must be left in that quest, for in this quest thou shalt have many fellows and thy betters. For thou are so feeble of evil trust and good belief, this made it when thou were there where they took thee and led thee into the forest.

"And anon there appeared the Sangrail unto the white knights, but thou was so feeble of good belief and faith that thou mightest not abide it for all the teaching of the good man, but anon thou turnest to the sinners, and that caused thy misadventure that thou shouldst know good from evil and vain glory of the world, the which is not worth a pear. And for great pride thou madest great sorrow that thou haddest not overcome all the white knights with the covering of white by whom was betokened virginity and chastity; and therefore God was wroth with you, for God loveth no such deeds in this quest. And this advision signifieth that thou were of evil faith and of poor belief, the which will make thee to fall into the deep pit of hell if thou keep thee not.

"Now have I warned thee of thy vain glory and of thy pride, that thou hast many times erred against thy Maker. Beware of everlasting pain, for of all earthly knights I have most pity of thee, for I know well thou hast not thy peer of any earthly sinful man."

FERNANDO DE ROJAS (c. 1465–1541)
Spain

Fernando de Rojas was a *converso*—a Jew who converted to Christianity in order to avoid permanent expulsion from his homeland as a result of a royal decree of 1492. Few other biographical facts are known about him and the circumstances under which he wrote *La Celestina*. However, he does offer some information in an acrostic poem that precedes the text proper. If we combine the first letters of each stanza, we learn the following: "The Bachelor [i.e., lawyer] Fernando de Rojas finished the comedy of Calisto and Melibea and was born in Puebla de Montalbán." Some further indirectly communicated information is supplied by a letter from "the author to a friend," which also precedes the narrative. In the letter he explains that he found the first act he reproduces in his text in Salamanca with no indication as to its author. Rojas goes on to say that during a two-week vacation he added the subsequent acts (offering a total of sixteen acts in the 1499 version and twenty-one acts in the expanded 1502 edition). Also new in the later edition is a prologue that officially changed the title of the work from the *Comedy of Calixto and Melibea* to the *Tragicomedy of Calixto and Melibea*.

In spite of this significant renaming of his text (intended to emphasize its more somber aspects), it has since the sixteenth century been referred to as *La Celestina* because of the powerful portrayal of the bawd who effects the liaison between the two young lovers, Melibea and Calixto. Celestina is characterized very vividly in her various vocations as peddler, procuress, and witch, and Rojas defies literary norms by combining a story about upper-class lovers with a striking fascination for the world of the underclass in all its seaminess. The clash of values extends to the upper class as well, however, for we see that even Calixto and Melibea are driven by a very uncourtly lust and a craving for domination.

The passages included here are among the most famous speeches in all of Spanish literature, for they testify with great eloquence to the power of human subjectivity and its defiance of social strictures. Melibea confesses her illicit affair to her father, killing herself thereafter, since life without Calixto would be meaningless. Even more surprisingly, her father, Pleberio, who has functioned not only as an exemplary and loving father but as a spokesman for Stoic *ataraxia* (restraint), is utterly devastated by Melibea's untimely death. It is important to note that Pleberio does not condemn his daughter's behavior as a revengeful father of Spanish Golden Age *comedia* (or traditional drama) would do—as a horrible stain on the family's honor. He is too deeply destroyed on a personal level to care about social sanctions. In these passages, as throughout this text, Rojas brilliantly explodes the convention of character decorum, whereby individuals are made to function as expressions of class, gender, or other sociocultural typecasting.

from **The Celestina**

[Melibea Confesses Her Affair and Kills Herself]

MELIBEA: Everyone has left me, and I've now contrived a way of dying. It gives me
some consolation to know that soon we shall be together, I and my dear
lover Calisto. I will shut the door, so that no one may come up to prevent
my death. They shan't prevent my going. No one shall stop the way by
which very soon I shall be able to visit him today who visited me last
night. Everything has conformed to my plan, and I shall have time to tell
my lord Pleberio the cause of my premature end. I am greatly wronging
his grey hairs, bringing much grief to his old age. Many sorrows will fall
on him because of my sin. I leave him in great desolation. But even if my
death should shorten my parents' days, others have certainly been
crueller to theirs. Prusias, king of Bithynia killed his father, for no reason,
having no grievance against him; Ptolemy king of Egypt killed his father,
his mother, his brothers, and his wife in order to enjoy a mistress; and
Orestes murdered his mother Clytemnestra; the cruel Emperor Nero had
his mother Agrippina killed just for the joy he took in murder. They are
wicked, they are the true parricides, but I am not. If I give pain by my
death, at least I am expiating the crime of causing them grief. Others have
been far more cruel, and killed sons and brothers. Beside their crimes
mine will appear slight. Philip, king of Macedon; Herod, king of Judah;
Constantine, emperor of Rome; Laodice, queen of Cappadocia, and the
witch Medea: all of them killed their dear children and lovers for no
reason and preserved their own lives. Finally I remember the great
cruelty of Phrates, king of the Parthians, who killed his old father
Orodos, his only son, and thirty brothers and sisters in order to leave no
heir. These crimes were wicked indeed, for they killed their elders,
descendants, and brothers, while remaining safe themselves. It is true
that even so we should not imitate their evil-doing. But it is now out of
my hands. You, Lord, who have been witness to what I've said, you see
how little is my strength, how my liberty is lost, how my feelings have
been captured by love for that gentleman who is dead, a love so powerful
that it destroys the love I have for my living parents.

PLEBERIO: What are you doing up there, Melibea? Why are you alone? What do
you want to say to me? Would you like me to come up?

MELIBEA: Don't attempt to come up here, Father, or you'll interrupt what I want to
say to you. Soon you'll be weeping for the death of your only daughter. I
have come to my end. I am drawing near to my rest and you to your sorrow, I to my comfort and you to your grief. Now is the time when I shall
have company and you will be alone. There'll be no need of instruments to
soothe my sorrow, only of bells for the burial of my body. If you can listen
without weeping you'll hear the desperate cause of my forced but happy

Translated by J. M. Cohen.

departure. Do not interrupt me with words or tears, or you'll suffer more by not knowing why I have died than by seeing me dead. Ask me no questions, and do not demand to know more than I wish to tell you. For when the heart is heavy with grief, the ears are closed to counsel, and at such times good advice rather inflames than allays the passions. Listen, dear Father, to my last words, and if you receive them as I hope, you will not blame my fault. You can see and hear the mourning that afflicts the whole city. You can hear the tolling of bells, the shouting of the people, the barking of dogs and the clash of arms. I was the cause of all this. I have today clothed in sackcloth and mourning the majority of the city's gentlemen, I have left many servants masterless, I have robbed many poor and destitute people of alms and relief, I have been the occasion for sending the most accomplished man ever endowed with graces to keep company with the dead. I have sent out of the land of the living the pattern of nobility and gallantry, of charm and adornment, of speech, carriage, courtesy, and virtue. Thanks to me earth enjoys before her time the noblest body and freshest youth ever born into the world in our days. Though it will astonish you to hear of my strange sin, I will tell you more fully what happened.

Many days ago, Father, a knight named Calisto, whom you knew well, was grieving for love of me. You knew his parents also, and his noble descent; he was famous for his virtues and his courtesy to everyone. He was so tortured by his love and had so little opportunity of speaking to me that he disclosed his passion to a wise and cunning old woman called Celestina, whom he sent to visit me and who dragged the secret of my love from my heart. I told her what I had concealed from my beloved mother. She found a way of winning me to her will, and brought his desires and mine to fruition. He loved me greatly and he was not disappointed. She contrived the sweet and ill-fated consummation of his desires. Subdued by love for him I let him into your house. He scaled the walls of your garden with a ladder, and overcame my resistance. I lost my virginity, and we enjoyed the sinful pleasures of our love for almost a month. Last night he came in the usual way, and just as he was about to return home, Fortune, in her mutability, disposing of all things in her disorderly way, put an end to our joy. The walls were high, the night was dark, the ladder was weak, and the servants he brought with him unused to this kind of service. He was descending in a hurry, having heard a noise in the road where his servants were waiting, and in his confusion failed to see the rungs, put a foot out into the void and fell. Alas, he fell on his head and scattered his brains over the stones and the wall. The Fates cut short his life. They cut him off unconfessed and with him all my hopes, my joy and delight in his company. How cruel it would be, Father, after his death from that fall, that I should live on in grief! His death calls for mine. It invites me, it compels me to be swift and allows no delay. It summons me to fall also, so that I may follow him in everything. It shall not be said of me that dead and gone is soon forgotten. I shall content him in my death, since I had not time to do so in my life. O my loved lord Calisto! Wait for me, I am coming. Wait if you expect me, and don't blame me for staying to give this last account to my father, for I owe him this and much more. Beloved father, I beg you if you loved me in my painful life that is now over, that we may be buried together and our funerals be celebrated together also. Before my welcome release I would say some words of consolation to you that I have chosen and gathered from those ancient books that you made me read for the improvement of my mind. But alas, my memory is confused by the tumult of my grief, and by the sight of your ill-restrained tears trickling down your wrinkled cheeks, and so I have forgotten them. Carry my farewell to my dear mother, and tell her carefully the sad reasons for my death. I am glad not to see her here. Accept, dear father, the penalties of old age; for in a long life sorrows must be endured. Receive this tribute to your years, and receive your beloved daughter in your arms. I grieve for myself, I grieve for you, and much more for my old mother. God be with you and her. To him I offer my soul, and to you for burial my body, that is now coming down to you.

[Pleberio Bewails His Misery and Curses Celestina]

Pleberio returns to his room weeping bitterly, and Alisa asks him the cause of his sudden grief. He tells her of their daughter's death, and shows her Melibea's shattered body. The work concludes with his lamentation.

ALISA: What's the matter, Pleberio? Why are you weeping and crying? I have been lying here senseless since I fainted on hearing that our daughter was in pain. But now your shouts and groans have roused me. Your tears and grief and unaccustomed lamentations have struck me to the heart, revived my numbed senses, and dispelled my previous sorrow. One grief, one passion has driven out the other. Tell me what you are bewailing. Why are you cursing your honourable old age? Why are you tearing your white hair? Why do you call on death? Why are you scratching your venerable face? Has something terrible happened to Melibea? In God's name tell me, for if she is suffering I no longer want to live.

PLEBERIO: Oh, oh, noble wife! Our joy is drowned, and all our happiness gone. Our life is worth nothing now. There is no pain like that of sudden grief, one unexpected blow following on another. It will drive you quickly to the tomb. But I cannot weep alone for the sad loss that has struck us both. Here is the daughter you bore and I engendered. Gaze on her shattered body. She told me the cause, but I learnt it more fully from her sorrowful maid. Join me in weeping our latter years that have now come upon us, all of you who come to share my grief. Help me, my friends, to bewail my misery. My daughter who was my sole treasure! It would be cruelty in me to outlive you. My seventy years were riper for the grave than your twenty. The due order of death was reversed by the grief that overwhelmed you. My hair has grown white only from sorrow, and earth should receive it more gladly than the fair locks that lie here. The rest of my days will be too many. I will complain against death for being so slow and leaving me here alone, now that you have gone. What have I left in life now that I have lost your delightful company? Get up from where she lies, Alisa, and if any life is left in you join me in bewailing her, pour it out in groans and sighs and lamentations. But if your spirit has joined hers, if you have already left this life of grief, why have you wished me to suffer everything alone? You women have the advantage over us that a great grief can painlessly remove you from the world, or at least make you swoon and thus give you some ease. What a hard heart has a father, that it does not break with grief at the loss of its one beloved child! For whom did I build towers? For whom did I acquire honours? For whom did I plant trees? For whom construct ships? O hard earth, how can you still support my steps? Where will my disconsolate old age find shelter? O Fortune, you are indeed minister and steward of temporal wealth, how mutable you are! Why did you not turn your cruel wrath on me? Why did you not overwhelm with your changing tides me who am truly your subject? Why did you not destroy my wealth? Why did you not burn my house? Why did you not reduce my great inheritance to dust? You might have left me that flourishing plant, over which you should have had no power. O fickle Fortune, if you had given me an unhappy youth and a glad old age, you would not have perverted nature. I could have borne the cruelty of your deceptions better in my strong and vigorous youth than in my weak and declining age.

O life full of griefs and miseries! O world, world! Many men have said many things of you, many have inveighed against you for your deceits. they have said many things of you by hearsay, but I will speak from the sad experience of one whose sales and purchases at your deceptive fair have not gone well, of one who has long concealed your double-dealing for fear of arousing your wrath by my hatred, and so that you should not prematurely wither this flower that has today fallen into your grasp. But now I am not afraid, for I have nothing more to lose. Now I am weary of your company. I am like a poor traveller who sings loudly on his way since he has nothing to fear from the cruel highwaymen. I believed in my youth that you and your deeds were governed by some order. But now that I have seen the pro and contra of your dealings, I find in you only a maze of error, a frightful desert, a den of wild beasts, a game in which men go round in circles, a lake full of mud, a country choked with thorns, a high mountain, a stony meadow, a field swarming with snakes, an orchard all blossom and no fruit, a fountain of cares, a river of tears, a sea of miseries, labour without profit, sweet poison, vain hope, false joy, and real sorrow. Feed us, false world, with the food of your delights, and in the tastiest morsel we find the hook. We cannot escape it for it has ensnared our wills. You promise much but perform nothing. You throw us from you so that we shall not beg you to keep your empty promises. Carelessly and thoughtlessly we run in the meadows of your rank vices, and you show us the trap when we have no chance of turning back. Many have forsaken you for fear you might suddenly forsake them, and they will count themselves lucky when they see the reward you have given this poor old man in payment for his long services. You put out our eyes and then anoint our brows to comfort us. So that no sad man shall find himself alone in adversity, you hurt everyone. You tell us that it consoles miserable men like myself to have companions in sorrow. But I am alone in my grief, disconsolate and old.

No man's misfortune is like mine. Though I search my weary memory of the present and the past I can find no one who has suffered a similar grief. If I recall the stoical patience of Paulus Emilius, whose two sons were killed within a week yet who bore his loss with such courage that the Roman people took more comfort from him than he from them, I am not consoled, for he had two sons left to him, whom he had adopted. What sort of companion in my grief should I find in the Athenian captain Pericles, or in the valiant Xenophon, since their sons died in foreign lands? It could not have cost Pericles much not to change countenance but to keep a calm expression, or for Xenophon to tell the messenger who brought him the sad news of his son's death that he would receive no penalty because he himself felt no sorrow. There is no resemblance here to my misfortune.

Even less could you say, O world full of evils, that Anaxagoras and I were alike in our grief and loss, and that I could repeat of my beloved daughter what he said of his only son: 'Being mortal, I knew that whatever I engendered must die.' For my Melibea killed herself before my eyes, of her own free will, driven to it by the cruel love that tortured her, whereas his son was killed in righteous battle. There is no loss like mine. A stricken old man, I seek comfort but find nothing to comfort me. The royal prophet David, who wept when his son was sick, refused to weep for him dead since he said it was almost madness to weep for what could not be remedied, and he had many children left to comfort him in his loss. But I am not weeping for her sad death, but for the terrible manner of it. O my unhappy daughter, with you I lose the fears and apprehensions that alarmed me every day. Your death alone has had the power to free me from anxieties.

What shall I do when I go to your room and find it empty? What shall I do when you do not answer my knock? Who could fill the void that you leave in me? No one has lost what I have lost today, not the valiant Lambas of Auria, Duke of Athens, who with his own hands threw his wounded son overboard into the sea. All these were deaths suffered in the cause of honour. But what forced my daughter to slay herself was the mighty power of love. False world, what comfort can you give me in my tired old age? How can you expect me to remain alive, now that I know the tricks and snares, the chains and nets, in which you capture our weak wills? Where have you taken my daughter? Who will be my companion in my companionless home? Who will look after me in my failing years? O love, love, I did not think you had the strength and power to kill your victims. You wounded me in my youth, but I survived your fires. Why did you let me go, only to pay me out for my escape in my old age? I thought myself free from your snares when I came to the age of forty and was happy in my wife's company and in the fruit of our union that you have plucked today. I did not think you would visit your spite against the fathers upon the children, or know that you could wound with the sword and burn with fire. You leave the clothes untouched but wound the heart. You make men love the ugly and think it beautiful. Who gave you such power? Who gave you so unsuitable a name? If you were love indeed, you would love your servants. If they lived happily they would not kill themselves, as my beloved daughter has done.

What is the fate of your servants and ministers? The false pander Celestina died at the hands of the most faithful servants she had ever recruited in your poisonous cause. They were beheaded, Calisto fell from the wall, and my beloved daughter chose to die the same death in order to follow him. You were the cause of all this. They have given you a sweet name, but you perform bitter deeds, and you do not give equal rewards. The law is wicked that is not fair to all. We rejoice at the sound of your name, but our dealings with you make us sad. Happy are those whom you have never known or never noticed. Some, induced by an error of the senses, have called you a god. But it is a strange god that kills its own children, as you kill your followers. In defiance of all reason, you give the richest gifts to those who serve you least, so that in the end you may draw them into your painful dance. You are an enemy to your friends, a friend to your enemies. Why do you act without rhyme or reason? They paint you as a poor blind boy, and put a bow in your hand with which you shoot at random; but it is your ministers that are blind, for they never feel or see how harsh is the reward you give to those who serve you. Your fire is a burning flash that leaves no mark where it strikes. Its flames are fed with the souls and lives of human beings, so numberless that if I tried to count them I do not know where I should begin. Not only of Christians, but of pagans and Jews; and all in requital for their worship of you. What would you say of Macias, who in our day died of love, and of whose sad end you were the cause? What did Paris do for you? And Helen? And Hypermnestra? And Aegisthus? Everyone knows the answer. What payment did you give to Sappho, Ariadne, and Leander? You would not leave even David and Solomon unharmed. And did not Samson pay the penalty for trusting her in whom you forced him to put his faith? There are many more whom I leave unmentioned, for my own evils are a sufficient theme.

I complain of the world because it created me in its bosom; because if it had not given me life I should not have fathered Melibea. If she had not been born I should not have loved her; if I had not loved I would cease to complain and my old age would not be desolate. O my daughter, my dear companion, dashed to pieces on the ground, why would you not let me prevent your death? Why did you not take pity on your darling mother, whom you loved? Why did you behave so cruelly to your old father? Why did you leave me in torment? Why did you leave me sad and alone in this vale of tears?

ANONYMOUS (FIFTEENTH CENTURY)
England

In this poem we see some of the defining features of the Middle English lyric at its best. The meaning and effect are conveyed by vivid images that are both simple and rich in allusiveness (the dew, for example, is a symbol of multiple significance, including the Holy Spirit and divine grace in its range of meaning; its initiating text is the story of Gideon's fleece, Judges 6:37–40). The language is simple and close to popular usage, but it can convey complex ideas and feelings. The word *makeles,* for example, in the second line, means "matchless," signifying not only the Virgin's uniqueness as the mother of God, but also her exemption from the ordinary "match," since the Middle English word *make* also means "mate"; consider also the different meanings of *stille.* The message is simple and directly stated, but its enterprise is tremendous: it seeks to translate mystery into experience—the greatest mystery of all, the miracle of the Virgin Birth, the beginning of human redemption, and also the most interior experience, that of the sentient imagination. The tone of wonder and admiration is strengthened by a powerful irony: the maiden, a simple girl, chooses as her son the King of Kings.

I Sing of a Maiden

I sing of a maiden
that is makeles,[1]
Kings of alle kinges
to[2] here sone she ches.[3]

He cam also[4] stille   5
ther[5] his moder was
as dew in Aprille
that falleth on the gras.

He cam also stille
to his moderes bowr   10
as dew is Aprille
that falleth on the flowr.

He cam also stille
ther his moder lay
as dew in Aprille   15
that falleth on the spray.[6]

Moder and maiden
was never none but she:
well may swich[7] a lady
Godes moder be.   20

---

1. Matchless/mateless.
2. For, as.
3. Chose.
4. As.

5. Where.
6. Small branches and foliage.
7. Such.

Dervishes dancing to music, from a Persian manuscript, c. 1485 C.E. Dublin, Chester Beatty Library (mms. 163).

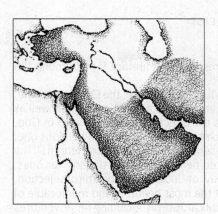

SECTION V
Early and Classical Middle East

The development of Arabic, Persian, and Turkish literatures was closely bound up with the emergence of the Islamic religion in seventh-century Arabia, the Arab conquests that followed, and the classical Islamic civilization that resulted in most of what we today call the Middle East.

When the Qur'an (Arabic *qur'ān*, recitation; also familiar as the Koran) the holy book of Islam, was revealed to the Arabian Prophet Muhammad during the seventh century C.E., it heralded the advent not only of a new religious civilization but of a sophisticated literary culture as well. The first literature of the Islamic world was in Arabic, the language of the Arabs and of the Qur'an. For a few centuries, Arabic remained the sole literary language. But later, literatures developed in Persian, Turkish, and other languages. These literary cultures drew from their progenitor; their writers were usually schooled in Arabic letters as well as their own.

Arabic literature began before Islam in a period called the Jāhiliyya. This literature of a partly Bedouin society was dominated by poetry, the poet often acting as the oracle of his tribe. Poems such as "Arabian Ode in 'L,' " written by the sixth-century poet Shanfarā, are still considered by modern Arabs to be among the finest examples of their art. Alongside the dominant male poetic voice was a female one, generally specialized in elegiac verse, like that of al-Khansā', whose elegies for her brother have ensured her literary immortality. Indeed, poetry has remained to the present time the most prestigious of literary forms among the Arabs.

With its powerful imagery and its often incantatory style, the Qur'an became, along with the pre-Islamic poetic corpus, a literary and aesthetic model as well as a religious one. For Muslims, the Qur'an is the direct, unmediated word of God, and as such it is as perfect from a literary point of view as it is from a religious one. The Qur'an is divided into 114 chapters or *suras* in Arabic of varying length. "The Forenoon" and "The Darkening," presented here, are among the shorter ones, dealing with the call to Islam and the Day of Judgment. The third selection, "Joseph," is generally agreed to be one of the most beautiful and memorable of the longer *suras,* relating the story of the biblical Joseph, including his adventures with his brothers and his period in Egypt. Joseph is represented as the paragon of beauty in Islam; this confrontation with the Egyptian ruler's wife becomes one of the most haunting incidents recurring in later literary and mystical texts, where the wife is known as Zulaykhā.

The Arab-Islamic conquests of the seventh and eighth centuries created a multinational empire from Spain to Afghanistan. This cosmopolitan society drew virtually without prejudice from the cultures of the region, spawning a sophisticated literature far greater in richness and quantity than the literatures of either the classical Mediterranean world or medieval Europe. Paper had recently been invented in China and its dissemination throughout the Islamic world had much to do with this literary florescence, but so too did the opening of cultural channels and the circulation of ideas across an unprecedented geographical expanse. Scholars and writers could begin their careers in what is today Portugal and end them on the banks of the Red Sea or on the borders of the Hindu Kush.

The works that have come down to us from the classical period of this highly sophisticated culture are numerous.[1] One of the literary genres dominating the prose corpus is *adab,* an anecdotal genre designed at once to be edifying and entertaining. To characterize it strictly as prose can be, however, misleading. In its various forms, *adab* can include Qur'anic verses, poetry, and traditions of the Prophet. These traditions, called *hadīth,* are collections of sayings and descriptions of the actions of the Prophet, designed to serve as guides for the daily life of the Muslim. The ninth-century Arab writer, al-Jāhiz is generally recognized as the greatest master of Arabic *adab.*

The heterogeneous nature of the Islamic empire led eventually to linguistic diversity, and even al-Jāhiz used some Persian in his Arabic works. Given the diversity of the culture, it should come as no surprise that literary genres once conceived as typically Arabic should surface in other languages of the Islamic empire, such as Persian. It is here that a connection can be seen with the works of the thirteenth-century writer, Saᶜdī and the fourteenth-century writer ᶜUbayd-i Zākānī. That they are, in fact, literary cousins of the Arabic *adab* can be seen from their similar discourse, with its mixture of prose, verse, and interwoven religious text.

The characters who populated medieval Arabic anecdotal works ranged from rulers and judges to misers and party crashers. This anecdotal literature was a generic cousin to an indigenous Arabic form invented by the tenth-century writer

---

1. The classical period of Islamic civilization coincided with the European Middle Ages. "Classical" and "medieval" are thus loosely interchangeable in general discussions of Islamic culture.

Badīᶜ al-Zamān al-Hamadhānī. His *Maqāmāt* (loosely translated as "seances") were a literary tour de force executed in rhymed prose *sajᶜ* and featuring a sort of picaresque hero whose existence centered around his eloquence on the one hand and his ability to outwit his listeners and gain from them on the other.

Literature flourished in the Islamic West as it did in the Islamic East. The eleventh-century Andalusian author Ibn Hazm, shows us another dimension of anecdotal prose literature in *The Dove's Neckring,* his treatise on the psychology of love. The emergence of courtly love themes in Hispano-Arabic literature has often been linked to the popularity of the troubadours in neighboring Provence.

From quite early on in the development of Islamic orthodoxy, rumblings of asceticism and mysticism could be heard. Islamic mysticism spawned its own literature in Arabic, and especially, in Persian. Farīd al-Dīn ᶜAttār, Rūmī, and Jāmī are but a few of the names. One of the most beloved of stories in Islam, that of Joseph and the Egyptian ruler's wife was redefined and recast in a mystical setting. Generally, asceticism and mysticism attracted individuals dissatisfied with what they perceived to be the loss of the personal dimension in the religious experience, buried under legalistic discussions and ritualized practice. These competing trends, the mystical and the legal, were harmonized by the great thinker al-Ghazālī, whose autobiography focuses on this dilemma.

Al-Ghazālī's autobiography, like that of Saint Augustine, recounts a religious quest. The autobiographical writing of the great twelfth-century Syrian warrior-writer, Usāma ibn Munqidh is different. His saga takes place during the Crusades and some of his observations of the Western combatants are by now classic, their insights into cultural differences as illuminating today as they were seven centuries ago.

The Islamization of regions such as Iran and Turkey did not mean a homogenization of culture. Distinctive genres flourished; distinctive discourses developed. The Persian epic, for example, finds no parallel in Arabic letters. The Persian poet Firdawsī's famous epic, *Shāh Nāma,* dramatically recounts the adventures of the heroes of pre-Islamic Iran. As such, it has remained a monument to Iranian (as opposed to Islamic) cultural identification. Its influence in the twentieth century is still felt: one of the first cultural acts of the Khomeini regime was to ban this work.

Fortunately, literature seems to be able to transcend politics and political borders. Names may change, but genres, like the *ghazal*—a lyric form cultivated by Arab, Persian, and Turkish poets alike—remind us that the Islamic world, despite its linguistic diversity, had a unified and rich culture.

Historical Background

Muhammad (570?–632 C.E.), the Prophet of Islam, was born in Mecca, a thriving commercial center in Arabia. When he was about forty, he felt himself selected to be the prophet of God, the same unique God that had spoken through such prophets as Abraham, Moses, and Jesus. Against the idolatry, materialism, and social injustice he perceived around him, Muhammad preached an uncompromising monotheism. *Islām*, "submission" or "surrender," to God's will was the paramount principle of faith; by acknowledging God's transcendence, one became *muslim*, "submissive."

In 622 Muhammad left an increasingly hostile Mecca for Yathrib, an agricultural town to the north. His voyage subsequently became known as the Hegira (*hijra,* "emigration"), the town as Medina (*al-Madina,* "the City [of the Prophet]"), and the year as the first of the new Islamic calendar. (The era before 622 is known simply as the Jāhiliyya, or "pagan" era.) In Medina, Muhammad consolidated his political and spiritual authority, and the basic practices of the Islamic community, or *umma,* evolved. By 630 the entire Arabian peninsula had been brought under Muhammad's leadership, and traditionally divisive tribal and blood loyalities were subsumed—at least theoretically—in the unifying idea of *umma.*

After Muhammad's death, leadership passed to a series of four caliphs (from *khalīfa,* successor) distinguished by their close ties to the Prophet. Arab armies began to expand Islamic domination, winning Syria, Egypt, and northern Libya from the Byzantine empire, and conquering the Sassanian Persian empire to the east. From these territories, the heritage of eastern Hellenism—especially its philosophic and scientific writings—passed into Islamic culture, laying the foundation for a brilliant scholarly tradition that produced important advances in astronomy, medicine, natural sciences, and mathematics. From Iran, long open to Indian as well as Mediterranean influence, materials of Hindu civilization passed into the Islamic intellectual storehouse.

A civil war of succession followed, and power passed to the founder of the Umayyad Dynasty (661–750), the first dynastic caliphate. Expansion continued: in the West newly converted Berber tribes helped extend Muslim rule across North Africa and into the Iberian Peninsula; in the east the frontier was pushed to the Indus River. Everywhere, Arabic followed as the language of religion and administration. The importance of preserving the meaning of the Qur'an encouraged the crystalization of a "classical" Arabic language, which remained the literary standard even as spoken dialects continued to evolve.

A rebellion in 750 brought the Abbasid Dynasty (750–1258) to power. Within a few years, however, a new Umayyad Dynasty (756–1031) established itself in Spain, ending forever the political unity of Islam. Henceforth, the empire comprised a shifting mosaic of major powers, these often further fragmented into semiautonomous kingdoms and principalities.

The Abbasid Dynasty, with its capital in Baghdad, witnessed the rise of a strong Persian presence in Islam as the Arabic warrior elite that had prevailed during the Umayyad Dynasty gave way to a bureaucracy staffed largely by Persian gentry.

By the time of the Islamic conquest, the Persian civilization was already an ancient one. The first Persian empire, founded in the sixth century B.C.E., fell to Alexander the Great in 331 B.C.E., ushering in a period of Hellenistic influence under the Seleucids. Parthian rule followed, succeeded in turn by the Sassanian empire (224–642). These changes had been accompanied by a linguistic evolution from Old Iranian to Pahlavi, or Middle Iranian. Little literature survives from these early eras, although an important epic tradition had clearly been established.

For the first 200 years of Abbasid rule, Arabic remained the sole literary language, and, fueled in no small part by Arabic-speaking Persians, the period marks a high point in Arabic letters and scholarship. Jews and Christians, protected as always under Islamic law, added still more facets to the intellectual community. At the same time, the Persian language was undergoing a further metamorphosis, absorbing Arabic vocabulary and borrowing the Arabic script.

This newly formulated "classical" Persian began an independent literary life in the tenth century, inspired both by the vigorous Arabic-Islamic literary culture and Persia's own heroic past.

Turkish tribes, meanwhile, had become an important new ethnic presence. Initially brought from the central Asian steppe to serve as slave troops, Turks gradually assumed virtually all political power, with the rule of the Seljuk Turks in Iran beginning in the eleventh century serving as a decisive moment. The most lasting Turkish formation, however, was the Ottoman empire, which began to consolidate its power in Anatolia (Asia Minor) during the fourteenth century, lasting another six centuries until World War I. During the course of the fifteenth century, the Ottoman Turks finished off the Byzantine empire, and made inroads into Eastern Europe. During the following century, they extended their rule over virtually the entire Arabic-speaking world.

Writings in various Turkic dialects exist from the onset of the Turkish presence in the Islamic world. As the Ottomans came to prominence, however, so did their dialect. Culturally oriented toward Persia, Ottoman Turkish absorbed Persian and Arabic elements and adopted the Arabic script. During the latter part of the fifteenth century, the language of the Ottoman capital at Istanbul (formerly Constantinople) became the literary standard, and the stability and wealth of the new empire contributed to the flowering of the third major Islamic literature.

A Note on Transliteration

There is no single, universally accepted system for transliterating from the Arabic alphabet. The differences between systems, however, are minimal, and generations of readers have learned to take minor variations in spellings and diacritical marks (symbols added to a letter to modify its pronounciation) in stride. Here, readers will notice occasional discrepancies between our text and the translations.

One fact that accounts for many spelling variations is that written Arabic does not usually indicate short vowels, and thus vowel sounds are open to some interpretation. The Persian poet here spelled Firdawsī, for example, may be found in other works listed as Ferdousī or Firdausī. Long vowels may be marked with an accent (á), a circumflex (â), or a macron (ā). The macron is currently the most widely accepted symbol; some of the translations, however, use the accent or the circumflex. Full scholarly transliteration also demands the use of subscript dots to distinguish "emphatic" consonants (ḥ, ṣ, ṭ, and so on), for which the Arabic alphabet has separate letters. Again, a few of the translations here employ them, others do not. Necessary for specialists, they can safely be ignored by the general reader.

Finally, readers will notice two diacritical marks that are especially prevalent in Arabic, the hamza (ʾ) and the ʿayn (ʿ). The hamza indicates a glottal stop, the ʿayn a sort of gargling sound deep in the throat. While special characters are sometimes used for these, common substitutes are a turned comma for the hamza (') and an apostrophe for ʿayn (').

N. B. In this section, headings to the notes offer the language of the original text instead of the writer's country or region.

Further Readings

Grunebaum, G. E. von. *Medieval Islam: A Study in Cultural Orientation*. 2d ed. Chicago: University of Chicago Press, 1971.

Nicholson, R. A. *A Literary History of the Arabs*. 1907. Reprint. Cambridge: Cambridge University Press, 1969.

Rahman, Fazlur. *Islam*. Anchor Books Edition. Garden City, N.Y.: Doubleday, 1968.

Rypka, Jan. *History of Iranian Literature*. Translated from the German by P. van Popta-Hope, and edited and revised by the authors. Dordrecht: D. Reidel Publishing Co., 1968.

Schimmel, Annemarie. *Mystical Dimensions of Islam*. Chapel Hill: University of North Carolina Press, 1975.

Yarshater, Ehsan, ed. *Persian Literature*. Albany, N.Y.: Bibliotheca Persica, 1988.

SHANFARĀ (SIXTH CENTURY)

Arabic

"Arabian Ode in 'L' " [*Lāmīyat al-'Arab*], attributed to the poet Shanfarā, is one of the most famous pre-Islamic odes. The ode (*qasīda*) was a favored classical Arabic poetic form. Technically, it challenged a poet to sustain not only the same meter but also the same rhyme throughout. The title of this example comes from the fact that the rhyme that repeats at the end of each line of the original Arabic employs the letter "L." As in the case for other pre-Islamic poets, Shanfara's name and works lived for generations in the mouths of professional reciters (*rāwīs*) before being transcribed and collected by early Islamic scholars. Tradition classifies him as one of the brigand or outlaw poets. Proud exiles from the tribal communities, their poetry often celebrates the fierce independence of their existence.

Arabian Ode in "L"

Get up the chests of your camels
    and leave, sons
of my mother, I lean to a tribe
    other than you.

    What must be is at hand.   5
The moon is full,
    mounts and saddle frames secured
for distant crossings.

In this land is a refuge for a man
    from wrongs,   10
for one fearing scalding hatred,
    a place to withdraw.

    By your life! It crowds on no man
who travels by night,
    in fear or in desire,   15
and keeps his wits about him.

I have in place of you other kin:
    the wolf, unwearying runner,
the darting sand leopard,
    the bristle-necked hyena.   20

    These are my clan. They don't reveal
a secret given in trust,

Translated by Michael A. Sells.

and they don't abandon a man
for his crimes.

They are the scornful ones,
      the fierce, though I
at first sight of the prey
      am fiercer.

      As recompense for losing those
who don't repay a favor,
      in whose nearness
I cannot feel ease,

I have three friends: a brave
      heart, a bare
blade, and a long
      bow of yellow wood,

      Smooth and taut,
sonorous,
      bedecked with jeweled tokens,
secured with a crossbelt.

And when it lets the arrow slip
      it twangs,
like a child-bereft mother,
      grief-struck, who moans and wails.

——————

      I'm no quick-to-thirst,
herd ill-pastured at dusk,
      calves ill-fed
though their mother's udders are untied,

No foul-breathed cringer,
      wife-clinging,
asking her in every affair
      what to do,

      No ostrich,
gangly, stupefied,
      as if a sparrow were beating up and down
in his heart,

No malingerer, stay-at-home,
      woman-chaser,
evening and morning coated with kohl
      and perfume,

      No tick,
worthless, indolent,

25

30

35

40

45

50

55

60

leaping up, when startled,
unarmed,

Nor bewildered by the dark
    when the towering emptiness
turns astray the traveler, lagging,
    frantic, losing his way.

    When my sole pads
meet the gravel flint
    it flies up sparking,
shattered.

I push hunger on
    until it dies,
drive attention from it,
    forget.

    I'd sooner slurp the dust,
a dry mouthful,
    than take some man's
condescending favors.

Where I not shunning blame
    I would lack
no food, no drink,
    no ease of life,

    But this hard soul
gives me no rest
    when wronged
until I move on,

Wrapping my insides
    around an empty stomach pit,
like a weaver's threads
    spun and twisted.

    ————————

    I part at dawn on meager fare
like a wolf
    led on, desert into desert,
scrawny, grey.

He sets out at dawn, hungry,
    quick into the wind,
slicing down where the ravine ends
    and veering.

    He moves on in pursuit of food.
It eludes him.

He howls. His mates respond,
hunger-worn,

Thin as the new moon,   105
    ashen-faced, like arrow shafts
rattling around
    in the hand of a gambler,

    Like a queen bee,
swarm roused   110
    by the two poles of a cliff-dangling
honey-gatherer,

Wide-jawed, gape-mouthed,
    as if their jaws
were the sides of a split stick,   115
    grinning, grim.

    He howls in the empty spaces,
they howl,
    as if they and he were bereaved women
on the high ridge, wailing.   120

His eyelids sag. He grows silent.
    They follow his lead.
They, he, forlorn,
    take heart from one another.

    He turns back. They turn back,   125
surging, hard pressed,
    keeping composure
over what they hide.

The sand grouse drink what I leave behind.
    They approach the water hole   130
after a night journey,
    their sides rumbling.

    I resolved. They did.
We raced. Their wings fell limp
    while I stood in front at ease   135
with my robe tucked up.

I turned away.
    They tumbled to the rim,
crops and gullets
    squeezing and pulsing,   140

    As if their clatter
on both sides of the water hole

were groups of men from caravans,
letting themselves down,

Congregating from all sides
   and taken in
like droves of camels
   at a wayside pool.   145

   They gulped swiftly and passed on
at dawn
   like panic-stricken riders
from Uháza.   150

———————

I know the earth's face well.
   There I stretch out,
restless,
   dried out vertebrae and a crooked back,   155

   An arm for a pillow,
worn to the bone,
   joints standing up like bone cubes
strewn by a gambler.   160

And if the mother of dust
   grieves for Shánfara now,
long did she find satisfaction in him
   before!

   His crimes track him down,   165
They cast lots
   for the choicest piece
of his hamstrung flesh.

When he sleeps
   they spend the night,   170
eyes open, quick to his ruin,
   working their way in.

   Shánfara, friend of cares!
Time after time they return
   like quartan fever   175
or worse.

When they come down
   I drive them out.
They turn back from all sides
   upon me.   180

   Though you might see me
sun-beaten as a sand daughter,

ragged, shoeless,
with worn feet,

Still am I the master of patience,   185
    wearing its armor
over the heart of a sand cat,
    shod with resolution.

    Sometimes I have nothing,
sometimes all I need.   190
    Only one who gives himself,
far-seeing, will prosper.

I don't lose nerve in adversity,
    exposing weakness,
nor do I prance, self-satisfied,   195
    in my riches.

    The hot-neck fool will not provoke
my self-command, and I am not seen
    begging at the heels of conversations
and slandering.   200

———————

On how many a night of ill luck
    when the hunter burns his bow
for fuel.
    and his arrow wood.

    Have I trodden through darkness and drizzle,   205
on fire with hunger,
    grinding inside, shivering,
filled with dread.

Then have I widowed women
    and orphaned children,   210
returning as I began,
    the night a blacker black.

    When next morning in Ghumaysá[1]
two groups met,
    one asking about me,   215
the other being asked:

"Last night our dogs were whining."
    "A wolf prowling, or a hyena?"
"Just a faint sound, then silence."
    "Perhaps a startled grouse, or a hawk?" 220

———————————————————

1. An obscure place name.

"If a jinni,[2]
   what an ill-boding night visitor!
and a man, no,
   men don't act like that."

To how many a day of the dog star,   225
when the sun drools heat
   and snakes writhe
on the burning ground,

Have I turned my face,
   no veil to protect it   230
but the tattered shreds
   of an Athami cloak.[3]

With hair down my back,
flying up
   when the wind takes it   235
in uncombed clumps,

Unoiled, unloused,
   encrusted,
a full turn of seasons
   without a rinse of mallow.   240

How many a desert plain, wind-swept,
like the surface of a shield,
   empty, impenetrable,
have I cut through on foot,

Joining the near end to the far,   245
   then looking out from a summit,
crouching sometimes,
   then standing,

While mountain goats, flint-yellow,
graze around me,   250
   meandering like maidens
draped in flowing shawls.

They become still in the setting sun,
   around me, as if I were a white-foot,
bound for the high mountain meadow,   255
   tall-horned.

---

2. A spirit capable of assuming human or
animal form to exercise supernatural powers over people. *Jinn* were part of pre-
Islamic beliefs.

3. A cloak from Atham, an obscure place
name.

AL-KHANSĀ' (SEVENTH CENTURY)
Arabic

Al-Khansā' was a pre-Islamic poet famous for her elegies mourning the death of her brother, Sakhr, who was killed in battle (c. 615 C.E.). The genre in which she wrote, the *rithā'*, or poetic elegy, became associated more with the female voice than with the male voice. Most often, the *rithā'*, was written to mourn the death of a father or a brother.

[Oh, would that my mother]

Oh, would that my mother had never borne me sound and straight,
   and that I had been dust in the hands of the midwives,
And that heaven had fallen on the earth and covered it over,
   and that everyone, barefoot and shod, had died,
On the morning that the announcer of Sakhr's death came   5
   and frightened me, and bequeathed to me grief full of anxieties.
I said to him, "What are you saying?" And he replied, "Ibn
   ᶜAmr is dead." May his mother be bereft of him!
After you I will never enjoy any favor, and I will never weep
   at the request of a woman bereft.   10
Let death work its will with my relatives after him; let them
   get a second draught of it after the first.

[It is as if Sakhr]

It is as if Sakhr had never made a morning raid with
   his horsemen, and had never urged on the thin noble she-camels,
And had never requited his true friends, nor clad himself in the
   gray dust of battle raised by the horses' hooves,
Had never made in the noonday heat for his men a canopy of his   5
   beautiful cloak.
So weep for Sakhr ibn ᶜAmr, for he was an easy man to deal with
   whenever fate was harsh to the people,
Generous and sweet when his aid was requested, but bitter and
   sour when he wished to be.   10
And Khansā' weeps sadly in the dark and calls to her brother,
   but he, dust-covered, makes no reply.

Translated by James Bellamy.

THE QUR'AN (THE KORAN)

(SEVENTH CENTURY)

Arabic

As the sacred book of Islam, the Qur'an (Arabic *qur'ān,* meaning "recitation" or "text to be recited") is considered by Muslim believers to be the direct word of God revealed to the Prophet Muhammad through the intervention of the angel Gabriel. Preserved both orally and in written form during the Prophet's lifetime, the revelations were collected under the caliph 'Uthmān some twenty years after the Prophet's death and an authorized text was prepared. The Qur'an is organized by chapters (*sūras*), not in chronological order of revelation but according to the length of the *sūra.* After the brief opening *sūra* known as *al-fātiha,* the chapters are arranged from the longest to the shortest. The *sūras* are also classified by their locus of revelation, the Meccan having been revealed in Mecca, the Medinan in Medina. The Meccan chapters, shorter and more dynamic, are often exhortations and calls to religion with appropriate interjections about events such as the Day of Judgment. The typical Medinan chapters (which occur later than the Meccan chapters) tend to be more legally oriented, directed to the organization of the Muslim community (*umma*). The *sūra* of Joseph (*sūra* 12) is universally considered by Muslims and non-Muslims alike to be a narrative masterpiece. Because of the Qur'an's religious nature as the revealed word of the deity, Muslim scholars speak of its inimitability (*iᶜjâz al-Qur'ān*). This doctrine signifies both literary and aesthetic as well as doctrinal and moral perfection on the part of the Holy Book.

from **The Qur'an [Koran]**

SÛRA 81

The Darkening

In the Name of God, the Merciful, the Compassionate

When the sun shall be darkened,
when the stars shall be thrown down,
when the mountains shall be set moving,
when the pregnant camels shall be neglected,
when the savage beasts shall be mustered,
when the seas shall be set boiling,
when the souls shall be coupled,

5

Translated by Arthur J. Arberry.

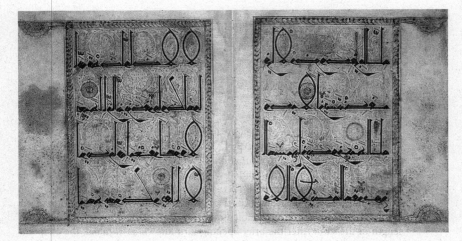

A page from the Qur'an, from a manuscript produced in Iraq or Iran, eleventh century C.E.

when the buried infant shall be asked for what sin she was slain,
when the scrolls shall be unrolled,
when heaven shall be stripped off,   10
when Hell shall be set blazing,
when Paradise shall be brought nigh,
then shall be a soul know what it has produced.

No! I swear by the slinkers,
the runners, the sinkers,   15
by the night swarming,
by the dawn sighing,
truly this is the word of a noble Messenger
having power, with the Lord of the Throne secure,
obeyed, moreover trusty.   20

Your companion is not possessed;
he truly saw him on the clear horizon;
he is not niggardly of the Unseen.

And it is not the word of an accursed Satan;
where then are you going?   25

It is naught but a Reminder
unto all beings,
for whosoever of you who would go straight;
but will you shall not, unless God wills,
the Lord of all Being.   30

SÛRA 93

The Forenoon

In the Name of God, the Merciful, the Compassionate

By the white forenoon
and the brooding night!
Thy Lord has neither forsaken thee nor hates thee
and the Last shall be better for thee than the First.
Thy Lord shall give thee, and thou shalt be satisfied.   5

Did He not find thee an orphan, and shelter thee?
Did He not find thee erring, and guide thee?
Did He not find thee needy, and suffice thee?

As for the orphan, do not oppress him,
and as for the beggar, scold him not;   10
and as for thy Lord's blessing, declare it.

SÛRA 12

Joseph

In the Name of God, the Merciful, the Compassionate

Alif Lam Ra[1]
Those are the signs of the Manifest Book.
We have sent it down as an Arabic Koran;
    haply you will understand.

We will relate to thee the fairest of stories
in that We have revealed to thee this Koran,
though before it thou wast one of the heedless.   5

When Joseph said to his father, "Father, I saw
eleven stars, and the sun and the moon; I saw them
    bowing down before me."
He said, "O my son, relate not thy vision
to thy brothers, lest they devise against thee   10
some guile. Surely Satan is to man
    a manifest enemy.
So will thy Lord choose thee, and teach thee
the interpretation of tales, and perfect His   15

---

1. Three Arabic letters. Groups of two to five
   letters appear at the beginning of 29 *sūras*.
   Known as the "isolated letters" (*al-harūf
   al-muqatta^Cāt*), their meaning, while the

   subject of much speculation, remains a
   mystery. A certain mystical significance has
   become attached to them.

blessing upon thee and upon the House of Jacob,
as He perfected it formerly on thy fathers
Abraham and Isaac; surely thy Lord is
   All-knowing, All-wise."
(In Joseph and his brethren were signs for those   20
   who ask questions.)
When they said, "Surely Joseph and his brother
are dearer to our father than we, though
we are a band. Surely our father is
   in manifest error.   25
Kill you Joseph, or cast him forth into
some land, that your father's face may be
free for you, and therefore you may be
   a righteous people."
One of them said, "No, kill not Joseph,   30
but cast him into the bottom of the pit
and some traveller will pick him out,
   if you do aught."
They said, "Father, what ails thee, that thou
trustest us not with Joseph? Surely we are his   35
   sincere well-wishers.
Send him forth with us tomorrow, to
frolic and play; surely we shall be
   watching over him."
He said, "It grieves me that you should go with him,   40
and I fear the wolf may eat him, while you
   are heedless of him."
They said, "If the wolf eats him, and we a band,
   then are we losers!"
So when they went with him, and agreed to put him   45
in the bottom of the well, and We revealed to him,
"Thou shalt tell them of this their doing
   when they are unaware,"
And they came to their father in the evening,
   and they were weeping.   50
They said, "Father, we went running races, and
left Joseph behind with our things; so the wolf
ate him. But thou wouldst never believe us,
   though we spoke truly."
And they brought his shirt with false blood on it.   55
He said, "No; but your spirits tempted you
to do somewhat. But come, sweet patience!
And God's succour is ever there to seek against
   that you describe."
Then came travellers, and they sent one of them,   60
a water-drawer, who let down his bucket.

"Good news!" he said. "Here is a young man."
So they hid him as merchandise; but God knew
   what they were doing.
Then they sold him for a paltry price, a   65
handful of counted dirhams; for they set
   small store by him.
He that bought him, being of Egypt,
said to his wife, "Give him goodly lodging,
and it may be that he will profit us,   70
or we may take him for our own son."
So We established Joseph in the land, and
that We might teach him the interpretation
of tales. God prevails in His purpose, but
   most men know not.   75
And when he was fully grown, We gave him
judgment and knowledge. Even so We recompense
   the good-doers.

Now the woman in whose house he was
solicited him, and closed the doors on them.   80
"Come," she said, "take me!" "God be my refuge,"
he said, "Surely my lord has given me
a goodly lodging. Surely the evildoers
   do not prosper."
For she desired him; and he would have taken her,   85
but that he saw the proof of his Lord.
So was it, that We might turn away from him
evil and abomination; he was one of
   Our devoted servants.
They raced to the door; and she tore his shirt   90
from behind. They encountered her master
by the door. She said, "What is the recompense
of him who purposes evil against thy folk,
but that he should be imprisoned, or
   a painful chastisement?"   95
Said he, "It was she that solicited me";
and a witness of her folk bore witness,
"If his shirt has been torn from before
then she has spoken truly, and he is
   one of the liars;   100
but if it be that his shirt has been torn
from behind, then she has lied, and he is
   one of the truthful."
When he saw his shirt was torn from behind
he said, "This is of your women's guile; surely   105
   your guile is great.

Joseph, turn away from this; and thou, woman,
ask forgiveness of thy crime; surely thou art
   one of the sinners."
Certain women that were in the city said,   110
"The Governor's wife has been soliciting her
page; he smote her heart with love; we see her
   in manifest error."
When she heard their sly whispers, she sent
to them, and made ready for them a repast,   115
then she gave to each one of them a knife.
"Come forth, attend to them," she said.
And when they saw him, they so admired him
that they cut their hands, saying, "God save us!
This is no mortal; he is no other   120
   but a noble angel."
"So now you see," she said. "This is he you
blamed me for. Yes, I solicited him, but
he abstained. Yet if he will not do what I
command him, he shall be imprisoned, and be   125
   one of the humbled."
He said, "My Lord, prison is dearer to me
than that they call me to; yet if Thou
turnest not from me their guile, then I
shall yearn towards them, and so become   130
   one of the ignorant."
So his Lord answered him, and He turned
away from him their guile; surely He is
   the All-hearing, the All-knowing.
Then it seemed good to them, after they had   135
seen the signs, that they should imprison
   him for a while.
And there entered the prison with him
two youths. Said one of them. "I dreamed
that I was pressing grapes." Said the other,   140
"I dreamed that I was carrying on my head
bread, that birds were eating of. Tell us
its interpretation; we see that thou art
   of the good-doers."
He said, "No food shall come to you   145
for your sustenance, but ere it comes to you
I shall tell you its interpretation.
That I shall tell you is of what God
has taught me. I have forsaken the creed
of a people who believe not in God   150
and who moreover are unbelievers in
   the world to come.

And I have followed the creed of my fathers,
Abraham, Isaac and Jacob. Not ours is it
to associate aught with God. That is of God's 155
bounty to us, and to men; but most men
   are not thankful.
Say, which is better, my fellow-prisoners—
many gods at variance, or God the One,
   the Omnipotent? 160
That which you serve, apart from Him, is
nothing but names yourselves have named,
you and your fathers; God has sent down
no authority touching them. Judgment
belongs only to God; He has commanded 165
that you shall not serve any but Him.
That is the right religion; but
   most men know not.
Fellow-prisoners, as for one of you, he shall
pour wine for his lord; as for the other, 170
he shall be crucified, and birds will eat
of his head. The matter is decided
   whereon you enquire."
Then he said to the one he deemed
should be saved of the two, "Mention me 175
in thy lord's presence." But Satan caused him
to forget to mention him to his master,
so that he continued in the prison
   for certain years.

And the king said, "I saw in a dream 180
seven fat kine,[2] and seven lean ones
devouring them; likewise seven green ears
of corn, and seven withered. My counsellors,
pronounce to me upon my dream, if you are
   expounders of dreams." 185
"A hotchpotch of nightmares!" they said.
"We know nothing of the interpretation
   of nightmares."
Then said the one who had been delivered,
remembering after a time, "I will 190
myself tell you its interpretation;
   so send me forth."

"Joseph, thou true man, pronounce to us
regarding seven fat kine, that seven lean ones

---

2. Cattle.

were devouring, seven green ears of corn, and
seven withered; haply I shall return to the men,
     haply they will know."
He said, "You shall sow seven years
after your wont; what you have harvested
leave in the ear, excepting a little
     whereof you eat.
Then thereafter there shall come upon you
seven hard years, that shall devour what
you have laid up for them, all but a little
     you keep in store.
Then thereafter there shall come a year
wherein the people will be succoured
     and press in season."

The king said, "Bring him to me!" And
when the messenger came to him, he
said, "Return unto thy lord, and ask
of him, 'What of the women who cut
their hands?' Surely my Lord has knowledge
     of their guile."
"What was your business, women," he said,
"when you solicited Joseph?" "God save us!"
they said, "We know no evil against him."
The Governor's wife said, "Now the truth
is at last discovered; I solicited him; he
     is a truthful man."
"That, so that he may know I betrayed him not
secretly, and that God guides not the guile
     of the treacherous.
Yet I claim not that my soul was innocent—
surely the soul of man incites to evil—
except inasmuch as my Lord had mercy;
truly my Lord is All-forgiving,
     All-compassionate."
The king said, "Bring him to me! I would
attach him to my person." Then, when he
had spoken with him, he said, "Today
thou art established firmly in our favour
     and in our trust."
He said, "Set me over the land's storehouses; I
     am a knowing guardian."
So We established Joseph in the land, to
make his dwelling there wherever he would.
We visit with Our mercy whomsoever We
will, and We leave not to waste the wage

195

200

205

210

215

220

225

230

235

of the good-doers.   240
Yet is the wage of the world to come better
for those who believe, and are godfearing.

And the brethren of Joseph came, and
entered unto him, and he knew them, but
    they knew him not.   245
When he had equipped them with their equipment
he said, "Bring me a certain brother of yours
from your father. Do you not see
that I fill up the measure, and am
    the best of hosts?   250
But if you bring him not to me, there shall
be no measure for you with me, neither shall
    you come nigh me."
They said, "We will solicit him of our father;
    that we will do."   255
He said to his pages, "Put their merchandise
in their saddlebags; haply they will recognize it
when they have turned to their people; haply
    they will return."
So, when they had returned to their father,   260
they said, "Father, the measure was denied
to us; so send with us our brother, that we
may obtain the measure; surely we shall be
    watching over him."
He said, "And shall I entrust him to you   265
otherwise than as I entrusted before
his brother to you? Why, God is the best
guardian, and He is the most merciful
    of the merciful."
And when they opened their things, they found   270
their merchandise, restored to them. "Father,"
they said, "what more should we desire?
See, our merchandise here is restored to us.
We shall get provision for our family,
and we shall be watching over our brother;   275
we shall obtain an extra camel's load—that
    is an easy measure."
He said, "Never will I send him with you
until you bring me a solemn pledge by God
that you will surely bring him back to me   280
unless it be that you are encompassed."
When they had brought him their solemn pledge
he said, "God shall be Guardian
    over what we say."

He also said, "O my sons, enter not   285
by one door; enter by separate doors.
Yet I cannot avail you anything
against God; judgment belongs not to any
but God. In Him I have put my trust;
and in Him let all put their trust   290
    who put their trust."

And when they entered after the manner
their father commanded them, it availed them
nothing against God; but it was a need
in Jacob's soul that he so satisfied.   295
Verily he was possessed of a knowledge
for that We had taught him; but
    most men know not.
And when they entered unto Joseph, he said,
taking his brother into his arms,   300
"I am thy brother; so do not despair of
    that they have done."
Then, when he had equipped them with
their equipment, he put his drinking-cup
into the saddlebag of his brother.   305
Then a herald proclaimed, "Ho, cameleers,
    you are robbers!"
They said, turning to them, "What is it that
    you are missing?"
They said, "We are missing the king's goblet.   310
Whoever brings it shall receive a camel's load;
    that I guarantee."
"By God," they said, "you know well that we
came not to work corruption in the land.
    We are not robbers."   315
They said, "And what shall be its recompense
    if you are liars?"
They said, "This shall be its recompense—
in whoever's saddlebag the goblet is found,
he shall be its recompense. So we recompense   320
    the evildoers."
So he made beginning with their sacks, before
his brother's sack, then he pulled it out
of his brother's sack. So We contrived
for Joseph's sake; he could not have taken his   325
brother, according to the king's doom, except
that God willed. Whomsoever We will, We
raise in rank; over every man of knowledge
    is One who knows.

They said, "If he is a thief, a brother of his
was a thief before." But Joseph secreted it
in his soul and disclosed it not to them, saying,
"You are in a worse case; God knows very well
   what you are describing."
They said, "Mighty prince, he has a father,
aged and great with years; so take one of us
in his place; we see that thou art one
   of the good-doers."
He said, "God forbid that we should take
any other but him in whose possession
we found the goods; for if we did so, we
   would be evildoers."
When they despaired of moving him, they
conferred privily apart. Said the eldest of
them, "Do you not know how your father has taken
a solemn pledge from you by God, and aforetime
you failed regarding Joseph? Never will I
quit this land, until my father gives me
leave, or God judges in my favour; He is
   the best of judges.
Return you all to your father, and say,
'Father, thy son stole; we do not testify
except that we know; we were no guardians
   of the Unseen.
Enquire of the city wherein we were, and the
caravan in which we approached; surely
   we are truthful men.' "

"No!" he said. "But your spirits tempted you
to do somewhat. But come, sweet patience!
Haply God will bring them all to me; He is
   the All-knowing, the All-wise."
And he turned away from them, and said,
"Ah, woe is me for Joseph!" And his eyes
turned white because of the sorrow that
   he choked within him.
"By God," they said, "thou wilt never cease
mentioning Joseph till thou art consumed, or
   among the perishing."
He said, "I make complaint of my anguish
and my sorrow unto God; I know from God
   that you know not.
Depart, my sons, and search out tidings
of Joseph and his brother. Do not despair
of God's comfort; of God's comfort

330

335

340

345

350

355

360

365

370

no man's despairs, excepting the people   375
   of the unbelievers.''

So, when they entered unto him, they said,
''O mighty prince, affliction has visited us
and our people. We come with merchandise
of scant worth. Fill up to us the measure,   380
and be charitable to us; surely God recompenses
   the charitable.''
He said, ''Are you aware of what you did
with Joseph and his brother, when you
   were ignorant?''   385
They said, ''Why, art thou indeed Joseph?''
''I am Joseph,'' he said. ''This is my brother.
God has indeed been gracious unto us.
Whosoever fears God, and is patient—
surely God leaves not to waste the wage   390
   of the good-doers.''
''By God,'' they said, ''God has indeed
preferred thee above us, and certainly
   we have been sinful.''
He said, ''No reproach this day shall be on you;   395
God will forgive you; He is the most merciful
   of the merciful.
Go, take this shirt, and do you cast it
on my father's face, and he shall recover
his sight; then bring me your family   400
   all together.''

So, when the caravan set forth, their father
said, ''Surely I perceive Joseph's scent, unless
   you think me doting.''
The said, ''By God, thou art certainly in   405
   thy ancient error.''
But when the bearer of good tidings came
to him, and laid it on his face, forthwith
   he saw once again.
He said, ''Did I not tell you I know from God   410
   that you know not?''
They said, ''Our father, ask forgiveness
of our crimes for us; for certainly
   we have been sinful.''
He said, ''Assuredly I will ask my Lord   415
to forgive you; He is the All-forgiving,
   the All-compassionate.''

So, when they entered unto Joseph,
he took his father and mother into his arms

saying, "Enter you into Egypt, if God will,   420
   in security."
And he lifted his father and mother
upon the throne; and the others fell down
prostrate before him: "See, father," he said,
"this is the interpretation of my vision   425
of long ago; my Lord has made it true.
He was good to me when He brought me forth
from the prison, and again when He
brought you out of the desert, after that
Satan set at variance me and my brethren.   430
My Lord is gentle to what He will; He is
   the All-knowing, the All-wise.
O my Lord, Thou has given me to rule,
and Thou hast taught me the interpretation
of tales. O Thou, the Originator of the   435
heavens and earth, Thou art my Protector
in this world and the next. O receive me
to Thee in true submission, and join me
   with the righteous."

That is of the tidings of the Unseen that   440
We reveal to thee; thou wast not with them
when they agreed upon their plan, devising.
Yet, be thou ever so eager, the most part of
   men believe not.
Thou askest of them no wage for it;   445
it is nothing but a reminder
   unto all beings.
How many a sign there is in the heavens
and in the earth that they pass by, turning
   away from it!   450
And the most part of them believe not in God,
   but they associate
other gods with Him. Do they feel secure
that there shall come upon them no enveloping
of the chastisement of God, or that the   455
Hour shall not come upon them suddenly
   when they are unaware?

   Say: "This is my way.
I call to God with sure knowledge,
I and whoever follows after me.
To God be glory! And I am not   460
   among the idolaters."

We sent not forth any before thee, but
men We revealed to of the people living
in the cities. Have they not journeyed   465
in the land? Have they not beheld
how was the end of those before them? Surely
the abode of the world to come is better
for those that are godfearing. What,
　　do you not understand?   470
Till, when the Messengers despaired, deeming
they were counted liars, Our help came to them
and whosoever We willed was delivered. Our
might will never be turned back from the people
　　of the sinners.   475
In their stories is surely a lesson to
men possessed of minds; it is not a tale
forged, but a confirmation of what is before
it, and a distinguishing of every thing,
and a guidance, and a mercy to a people   480
　　who believe.

DHŪ AL-RUMMA (696?–735?)
Arabic

Dhū al-Rumma was the nickname of Ghaylān ibn ᶜUkba, a famous Arab poet of the
early Islamic period. He hailed from a family of poets and was himself an authority
on poetry. His extensive use of rare terms earned him great visibility among the
later lexicographers, who quoted profusely from his verses. He earned the title of
"seal (i.e., the last) of the classical poets," because of the close links of his poetry to
the Bedouin ode, or *qasīda*—a form widely cultivated by the pre-Islamic Arab
poets. *Qasīdas* would continue to be written for some time—the form, in fact,
would later be taken up by Persian poets—but the distinctive voice of the early
desert poets sounds for the last time in the work of Dhū al-Rumma.

To the Encampments of Máyya

To the encampments of Máyya,[1]
　　both of you,

Translated by Michael A. Sells.

---

1. A woman's name. Al-Rumma's love for
　Máyya was constant; he is said to have
　courted her for twenty years.

a well-meant word
   and distant greeting:

   May the rain-star Arcturus
be over you still . . .
   and the rains of the Pleiades,
pouring down and spreading,

Though it was you
   who stirred a lover's
disheartened desire,
   until the eye shed

   Tears, yes, that nearly,
on knowing a campsite as Máyya's,
   if not released,
would have killed,

Though I was already nearing thirty
   and my friends had learned better
and good sense had begun
   to weigh down folly.

   When distance turns other lovers,
the first premonition
   of loving Máyya
will still be with me.

Nearness of her
   cannot impoverish desire,
nor distance, wherever she might be,
   run it dry.

   The inner whisper
of memory,
   reminiscence of Máyya,
is enough to bruise your heart.

Desires have their way,
   circulate freely,
but I can't see your share of my heart
   given away.

   Though in parting some love
is effaced and disappears,
   yours in me is made over
and compounded.

You came to mind
   when a doe ariel passed us,

right flank turned to the camel mounts,
   neck lowered,

   A doe of the sands, earth-hued,   45
with a white blaze on the forehead
   and the forenoon sun
clear upon her back.

She leaves her fawn
   on a dune, a grassy dune   50
in Múshrif, the glance of her eye
   gleaming around him,

   Gazing at us as if we intended harm
where we would meet him,
   approaching us,   55
then backing away.

She is her like, in shoulder,
   neck and eye,
but Máyya is more radiant than she, still—
   more beautiful.   60

   After sleep she is languor.
The house exudes her fragrance.
   She adorns it
when she appears in the morning,

As if her anklets and ivory   65
   were entwined around a calotrope
stopping the water's flow
   in the bed of a wadi,

   With buttocks like a soft dune
over which a rain shower falls   70
   matting the sand
as it sprinkles down,

Her hair-fall
   over the lower curve of her back,
soft as the moringa's gossamer flowers,   75
   curled with pins and combed,

   With long cheek hollows
where tears flow,
   and a lengthened curve at the breast sash
where it crosses and falls.   80

You see her ear pendant
   along the exposed ridge of her neck,

swaying out,
    dangling over the abyss.

    With a red thornberry tooth-twig,
fragrant as musk and Indian ambergris
    brought in in the morning,
she reveals

Petals of a camomile
    cooled by the night
to which the dew has risen at evening
    from Ráma oasis,

    Wafting in on all sides
with the earth scent of the garden,
    redolent as a musk pod
falling open.

The white gleam of her teeth,
    her immoderate laugh,
almost, to the unhearing
    speak secrets.

    She is the cure, she the disease,
memory of her, misgiving,
    desire dead
were it not for the affliction of distance.

———————

Far-flung!
    her tribe cut off
behind biting winds
    that scour the hard ground.

    How many a crow,
cawing separation,
    like a highborn Nubian woman
wailing the dead.

Has confirmed my foreboding,
    Máyya changing direction,
striking fire
    with the staff of parting.

    Let the spouse of Máyya weep
that purebred camels kneel
    worn out at the end of night
before the house of Mai.

Die miserably
    husband of Mai!

85

90

95

100

105

110

115

120

Hearts belonging to Máyya
  are free to blemish, pure.

  Had they left her a choice,   125
she would have chosen well.
  One like Máyya does not belong
with the likes of you.

As if I sleep on a bed of awls
  while her spouse sleeps,   130
stretched out,
  on a sandy hillock.

  When I say Máyya is near
the desert stretches out,
  dust-hued,   135
as far as the eye can see.

Mai has packed up and gone.
  Right there is her abode!
Left to the limping crow
  and ring-necked dove.   140

  When I complained to Máyya of love
that she might reward me
  for my affections, she said:
You're not being serious!

Keeping me off,   145
  leading me on,
when she saw that the spector of love
  had almost made off with my body.

  ———————

  How many a noonday heat,
far from Mai,   150
  the pace of my thick-humped mare unbroken,
the black-white locusts twitching

In pathless wastelands
  whose stillness
in the mirage of forenoon and midday   155
  almost blots out the gaze,

  As if the flat hill summits
were entwined in pure silk
  parting at times to reveal them,
then sewed back,   160

When the chameleon
  struck by the heat

begins to twist his head
   and reel—

How many a rider   165
drunk on sleeplessness
   as if swaying from the two ropes
on a concave well

Have I shaken from his stupor
   as he nodded his head   170
like a staggering drinker
   after his last drop of wine.

   When he expires in the saddle
I bring him back to life
   with your memory. The fleet roans   175
lean to their gallop.

When the end of the whip frays
   and the bodies of the camels
are worn to sickles
   then Sáydah besets them.   180

  —————

   She has stubby ears
and a long upper nape,
   a cheek polished
like the mirror of a foreign lady,

The eyes of a black-horn,   185
   solitary,
lips like Yemeni leather
   that flap loosely when she paces,

   A leg like the shadow of a wolf,
stride met   190
   by the lower foreleg
twisted out wide by the shinbone,

At full gallop
   when the black of night
is parted from the riders   195
   by the pale horizon of dawn.

   When I call out "aaj!"
or intone the camel driver's song
   she lifts a tail like under-wing feathers
as if pregnant or false-pregnant.   200

You see her
   when I have imposed upon her

every hardship, before the trail camels,
  their forelegs pulling in air,

  Her legs surging,
body lunging,
  wary of threats,
head raised,

Tawny, towering,
  as if a bite-scarred rough-flank
bore me in the saddle
  through the empty regions.

———————

  He turns the herd,
driving and urging, their flanks
  like boulder-strewn ground
in a field of brush grass.

They grazed dry pastures
  until they became as thin
as well-straightened spear shafts
  from Khatt.

  Until there came a day
when in their sand hollows
  ostrich eggs
nearly split in the blaze.

He continued to beguile them,
  as they stood, thirst-parched,
as if on the crowns of their heads
  were a flock of birds,

  One a promontory
at the dust hour
  when locusts expire
from the force of heat.

———————

You see the wind play
  where she travels at nightfall
between her and what she will find
  where she arrives at dawn.

  As if the camels
through the far-flung, trackless barrens
  were boats floating
in the desert of the Tigris.

My heart refused everything
    but memory of Máyya.
She-with-many-guises, playful and serious,
    troubled it.

AL-JĀHIZ (776?–868?)
Arabic

Al-Jāhiz, the master stylist of classical Arabic prose, is most notably associated
with *adab,* a medieval Arabic genre that combined anecdotal prose, poetry,
sacred text, proverb, and story. Al-Jāhiz (whose name means "the goggle-eyed")
was born and died in Basra (in present-day Iraq), one of the major centers of
medieval Islamic scholarship. He had an astounding literary and scholarly range,
extending from philosophy and religion to works oriented to the general reader.
His works on rhetoric and poetic composition are as renowned as his works on
varied character types, such as misers. Al-Jāhiz was a master at observing his
fellow human beings, and all his works demonstrate a lively wit. His *Book of
Misers* [*Kitāb al-Bukhalā'*] is a classic; some of its anecdotes appear even today in
children's magazines all over the Arab world.

from *Book of Misers*

The Glass Lamp

One day Abū 'Abd Allāh al-Marwazī paid a visit to a *shaikh** from Khurāsān, and
the latter had just lit one of those green pottery lamps. "Upon my soul," exclaimed
Abū 'Abd Allāh, "you do nothing right. I grumbled at you for using stone lamps,
and you think to please me [by replacing them] with pottery. Do you not know
that stone and earthenware literally drink oil?" "Excuse me," replied the *shaikh,* "I
gave this lamp to a friend of mine who is an oil merchant, and he put it in his filter
for a month, so that it is super-saturated and will never absorb any more." "That
is not my point. That may be a good way you have discovered of dealing with that
problem. But do you not know that the flame continually burning at the end of the
wick dries out the part of the lamp it is in contact with? When this place is
saturated the flame soaks up the oil from it and burns it. If you were to compare
the amount of oil absorbed from this place with the amount drawn up into the
wick, you would find that the former is greater."

   "Moreover the part of the lamp that is in contact with the wick is always
running with oil. I am told that if a lighted lamp is placed inside a empty one, after

Translated by Charles Pellat.
**A religious official or leader of an Arab village.*

one night or two at the outside the underneath one is full of oil. You can observe it also if you look at the salt and bran placed underneath a lamp to level it: they are absolutely soaked in oil. All this represents loss and waste such as can be condoned only by spendthrifts. Such people are continually providing others with food and drink, but at least they occasionally reap some benefit from it, trifling though it may be; whereas all you are doing is giving food and drink to the flame. And on the Day of Resurrection God will feed the flames with those that have fed them during their lifetime!"

"Then what should one do, pray?" asked the *shaikh*.

"Get a glass lamp. Glass is better than any other material: it is non-porous and non-absorbent, and does not collect dust. As a rule the only way to remove dust is either to rub the lamp hard or else to set light to it, and either way the effect is to dry the lamp out still further. Glass, on the other hand, withstands water and wine better than pure gold; and moreover it is manufactured, whereas gold is in its natural state. If gold is to be preferred for its hardness, glass is superior by virtue of its cleanness. Finally, glass is transparent, while gold is opaque. Furthermore, since the wick in a glass lamp is situated at the centre, the edges do not get heated by the flame as they do in an ordinary lamp. When a ray of light strikes the glass, the flame and the lamp together become a single source of light, reflecting each other's rays. This effect can be observed when a ray of light strikes a mirror, the surface of water or a piece of glass: its brightness is doubled, and if it shines in someone's eye it dazzles and may even blind him. It is said in the Koran: 'God is the light of the heavens and of the earth. This light is like a niche in which is a torch set in a glass like a glittering star; the torch is lit with oil from a sacred tree, an olive neither of the East nor of the West, whose oil glows even when no fire touches it. It is light upon light. God guides to His light whom He pleases.' Oil in a glass lamp is 'light upon light,' brightness upon twofold brightness. In addition to this advantage there is the point that a glass lamp is handsomer than a stone or pottery one."

A Tale About Tammām b. Ja'far

Tammām b. Ja'far was mean about food with an excessive meanness. He would heap reproaches on people who had eaten his bread and pursue them with his spite, sometimes even going as far as to claim that it was lawful for him to put them to death.

If a guest of his should say: "There is no one on earth better than me at walking and running," he would reply: "What else do you expect, seeing that you eat enough for ten? It is not the belly that gives strength to the legs? May God not reward him that praises you."

But if the same guest said: "No, by God, I cannot walk, for I am too weak, and get out of breath after thirty paces," he would reply: "And how do you expect to be able to walk, seeing that you have put twenty porters' loads into your belly? Do you not know that to be spry one must eat lightly? How can anyone move freely when sated? A man who is overburdened with food cannot kneel down and prostrate himself, let alone go for a long walk."

Suppose the guest complained of a bad tooth, explaining that he did not sleep a wink the previous night because of the shooting pain. He would retort: "I am surprised that you complain of one tooth and not of all of them, and that you still have one left in your head! What molar could stand up to such crushing and grinding? By God, the mills of Syria would soon grow weary and the stoutest pestle be worn out by such a task! Indeed, your toothache seems to me to have come very late. Spare yourself, for moderation is a blessing; and do not maltreat yourself, for abuse is a calamity!"

But if he said: "I have never suffered from toothache; not one tooth of mine has ever shifted in my life," Tammām would reply: "Idiot! Chewing hardens the gum tissue, strengthens the teeth, tans the skin and consolidates the roots, whereas disuse weakens the teeth. The mouth is a part of the human body, and the same is true of the jaw as of the whole organism: work and exercise strengthen it, whereas prolonged inactivity makes it weak and soft. But go gently: overwork will weaken the strongest, for there is a limit and a compass to everything. [And have a care:] if you have not got toothache, have you not got a bellyache?"

If the same guest said: "By God, I drink a lot of water: I doubt whether there is anyone in the world who drinks more than I," he would reply: "Earth and clay need water to moisten and soak them: is not the amount needed proportional to the amount of soil to be moistened? It would not surprise me if you drank all the water of the Euphrates, seeing the quantity of food you eat and the size of your mouthfuls! Do you know what you do? You take your pleasure and do not see yourself. Ask someone who will speak straightforwardly to you, and you will see that all the water of the Tigris would not suffice [to wet] the contents of your stomach!"

But if he said: "I have not drunk a drop of water all day, and yesterday I did not take so much as half a pint: no one on earth drinks less than I do," Tammām would reply: "Obviously you leave no room for water: you put away such a hoard in your belly that there would be no space for it. Indeed, it is surprising that you have not got indigestion. For the man who does not drink with meals does not realize how much he is eating, and if he overdoes it he runs the risk of getting indigestion."

If he said: "I cannot sleep a wink all night, and insomnia is killing me," Tammām would reply: "How on earth do you expect to sleep, with your stomach swollen and rumbling? Thirst alone would prevent you sleeping and keep you awake all night? If a man drinks a lot it makes him piss, and how can he get to sleep if he spends all night drinking and pissing?"

But if he said: "I go off to sleep the moment I lay my head [on the pillow], and sleep like a log till morning," he would reply: "Good heavens! Food intoxicates, numbs and clouds the mind; it saturates the brain and arteries, and makes the whole body sodden. I would expect you to sleep day and night!"

If he said: "I do not feel like anything to eat this morning," Tammām would reply: "Beware of eating very lightly, for to eat little when you are not hungry is worse for you than eating a lot when you are. Indeed, the very table says, 'Alas for the man who never feels like anything to eat!' Besides, how could you possibly have an appetite today, seeing that yesterday you ate enough for ten?"

A Fine Line of Patter

An old vagrant met a young one new to the profession, and asked him how he was. "God's curses on vagrancy," he cried, "and on them that follow such a miserable, unprofitable calling! It lines the face all unbeknownst, and drags a man down. Have you ever come across a successful vagrant?" The old vagrant turned angrily to his young colleague and said: "Just you talk a little less, for you exaggerate. A man such as you cannot succeed because you are not predestined to, and anyway you are not grown-up yet. Vagrancy demands men. Why do you say such things?" Then he turned [to the crowd] and said: "Pray listen to me. Do you not know that vagrancy is a noble, enjoyable, pleasing calling? Vagrants enjoy boundless happiness; their task it is to rove the world by stages, and to pace out the earth; they are the successors of Alexander the Great, who reached the East and the West. No matter where they stop, they need fear no harm. They go wherever they wish, getting the best there is to be had in every town . . . They are serene and content with their lot, and have no worries about families, possessions, houses or property: wherever they stop they find their pittance. I myself once went just as I am to a town in Media and stopped in the great mosque, with a towel round [my body], a palmetto cord round my head and an oleander stick in my hand. Quite a crowd collected around me, as though I were al-Hajjāj b. Yūsuf[1] in his pulpit. I said to them: 'Good people, I come from Syria, to be precise from a town called al-Maṣṣīṣa,[2] and I am descended from conquerors and monks [who walked] in the way of God, from the gallopers and the protectors of Islam. I have taken part with my father in fourteen expeditions, seven by sea and seven on land; I have fought with the Armenian (say "God's blessing on Abū al-Ḥasan"), with 'Amr b. 'Ubaid Allāh[3] (say "God's blessing on Abū Ḥafs"), with al-Baṭṭāl b. al-Husain[4] and many more. I have been to Constantinople and prayed in the mosque of Maslama b. 'Abd al-Malik.[5] If you have heard my name, so much the better; if not, let me introduce myself: I am Ibn al-Ghuzayyil b. al-Rakkān al-Maṣṣīṣī, known and celebrated on all the borders, he who smites with sword and lance. I am one of the bulwarks of Islam, and I challenged the king of Byzantium under the walls of Tarsus . . . I fled with a party of merchants, but we were cut off by brigands. I call on God and on you for protection. If you see fit to restore one of the pillars of Islam to his home and country, [I rely on you].' By God, before I had finished my speech the *dirhams*[6] were raining on me from all sides: I went away with more than a hundred pieces of silver."

Then the young man fell on him and kissed his head, crying: "You are the master of goodness. May God reward you on behalf of your brothers!"

---

1. A famous governor, known for his cruelty, who died in 714 C.E.
2. A town in Asia Minor.
3. Emir of Melitene, who died in 863 C.E.

4. A warrior from the Umayyad period who becomes a legendary hero.
5. Son of the caliph ᶜAbd al-Malik, who fought the Byzantines.
6. Silver coin.

A Late Supper

Maḥfūz an-Naqqāsh accompanied me one night from the Friday Mosque.[7] When I got near his house, and his house was closer to the Friday Mosque than mine, he asked me to spend the night at his home saying: "Where will you go in this rain and cold, given that my house is your house, and you are in darkness and you have no lantern? I have some colostrum[8] the like of which no one has seen and some excellent dates which can only be eaten with the colostrum." So I went along with him. He delayed a while, then brought me a cup of colostrum and a platter of dates. But when I stretched out [my arm], he said: "Abū 'Uthmān, this is colostrum with its thickness, and it is nighttime with its sluggishness. Besides, it is a rainy and damp night and you are a man already advanced in age and you still complain of hemiplegia. You get extremely thirsty and, in principle, you do not eat dinner. If you eat the colostrum and do not overdo it, you will be neither an eater nor an abstainer, you will irritate your nature and then will stop eating, no matter how appetizing it might be for you. If, however, you overdo it, we will spend a bad night worrying about your state, and we will not prepare any wine or honey for you. I have only said this to you lest you say tomorrow: it was such and such. By God, I am on the horns of a dilemma: because if I did not bring it to you after having mentioned it to you, you would say: he has been miserly with it and has changed his mind about it. But if I brought it to you and did not warn you nor mention all that would happen to you with it, you would say: he had no pity on me and did not advise me. However, I am cleared from both sides: if you wish, it is eating and dying and if you wish, then some suffering but sleeping in health."

I have never laughed the way I laughed that night. I ate it all and it was only the laughter, liveliness, and delight which digested it, as far as I know. If there had been someone with me who understood the flavor of what he said, the laughter would have destroyed me or killed me. But the laughter of he who is alone is not the same as that shared with friends.

AL-KHATĪB AL-BAGHDĀDĪ (d. 1071)
Arabic

Al-Khatīb al-Baghdādī, whose name means the Baghdadi preacher, was, like al-Jāhiz, an author with an immense literary range. Al-Khatīb's broader fame is linked to his abilities as a *muhaddith*, a specialist in the transmission of *hadīth*, the traditions of the Prophet Muhammad. But as an author, al-Khatīb has to his name works of history, such as *The History of Baghdad* [*Ta'rīkh Baghdād*], a text that is

---

7. The mosque where obligatory Friday prayers are held.

8. Milk secreted shortly before and after parturition.

still widely used as a source for that city's history, as well as works more theological and literary in orientation. His *Book of Misers* [*Kitāb al-Bukhalā'*] is less concrete but no less sophisticated than that of his predecessor al-Jāhiz.

from *Book of Misers*

A Delicate Sensibility

A certain important man wished to have people come to his table and eat his food, except that he could not bear to see a mouth chewing anything. So he complained about that to a friend of his with whom he was on intimate terms. His friend said to him: "What if you were to take some food which they would eat without chewing?" He said: "Is that possible?" "Yes," he said, "prepare for them a *siriṭrāṭa*, and it is a *fālūdhaja* [sweetmeat composed of starch, water, and honey], which would not be well cooked over fire and would therefore not thicken. They will swallow it and will not need to chew it." So the man said to his friend: "You have comforted me. This is the easiest thing for me, nothing is difficult for me except the noise of the chewing only." So he ordered the stew, and it was made and placed in a large bowl and he brought those whom he wished to invite. People then sat in the courtyard of the house while the man sat in a room overlooking them so that he could watch how they ate. After a while, his friend with whom he was on intimate terms went up to see him and found him unconscious. So he waited until he regained his consciousness and then said to him: "How are you, Sir, and what hit you?" He said, "My friend, swallowing, by God, is harder on me than chewing!"

FIRDAWSĪ (941?–1020?)
Persian

The *Shāh Nāma* is the Iranian national epic. Replete with adventure and romance, it chronicles the majestic history of pre-Islamic Iran from the first mythological ruler to the last Sassanian king, defeated in the seventh century by the Muslim Arab forces. About its author, Firdawsī, we know little other than that he was born near Tus, in eastern Iran, into a landed though not particularly wealthy family. As befits the man regarded as the immortal national poet of Iran, however, his life is surrounded with legends. Relying on at least one written source that we know of, and most likely on other sources both written and oral as well, he worked on his epic for about thirty years, finally completing it around 1000 C.E. Structurally, the *Shāh Nāma* consists of some fifty thousand lines divided into an introduction and fifty chapters, each of which chronicles the reign of a king.

Translated by Fedwa-Malti Douglas.

Integrated into the first half of this historical framework is a traditional cycle of
Iranian stories known as the Seistan cycle, which relate the adventures of the
great hero Rostam and his descendents. As with other heroes of world literature,
Rostam is of extraordinary descent (from a long line of Seistan kings—hence the
name of the cycle) and birth (by caesarean section). His strength and endurance
are superhuman, yet he is human in his feelings and failings. His long life—he
lives for three hundred years—uncoils relentlessly according to a pre-ordained
fate, and after heroic deeds in the service of king after king, he dies a ignoble and
unheroic death. Rostam spends only one night with a woman, but from that night
issues a son, Sohrāb. Here, the two meet in deadly battle, each unaware of the
other's identity. The story of Sohrāb and Rostam has had great appeal for English
readers, and translations appeared as early as the mid-nineteenth century.

from *The Shâh Nâma*

The Tragedy of Sohráb and Rostám

The Death of Sohráb

Again they firmly hitched their steeds, as ill—
Intentioned fate revolved above their heads.
Once more they grappled hand to hand. Each seized
The other's belt and sought to throw him down.
Whenever evil fortune shows its wrath,   5
It makes a block of granite soft as wax.
Sohráb had mighty arms, and yet it seemed
The skies above had bound them fast. He paused
In fear; Rostám stretched out his hands and seized
That warlike leopard by his chest and arms.   10
He bent that strong and youthful back, and with
A lion's speed, he threw him to the ground.
Sohráb had not the strength; his time had come.
Rostám knew well he'd not stay down for long.
He swiftly drew a dagger from his belt   15
And tore the breast of that stout-hearted youth.
He writhed upon the ground; groaned once aloud,
Then thought no more of good and ill. He told
Rostám, "This was the fate allotted me.
The heavens gave my key into your hand.   20
It's not your fault. It was this hunchback fate,
Who raised me up then quickly cast me down.
While boys my age still spent their time in games,
My neck and shoulders stretched up to the clouds.
My mother told me who my father was.   25
My love for him has ended in my death.

Translated by Jerome W. Clinton.

Whenever you should thirst for someone's blood,
And stain your silver dagger with his gore,
Then Fate may thirst for yours as well, and make
Each hair upon your trunk a sharpened blade.   30
Now should you, fishlike, plunge into the sea,
Or cloak yourself in darkness like the night,
Or like a star take refuge in the sky,
And sever from the earth your shining light,
Still when he learns that earth's my pillow now,   35
My father will avenge my death on you.
A hero from among this noble band
Will take this seal and show it to Rostám.
'Sohráb's been slain, and humbled to the earth,'
He'll say, 'This happened while he searched for you.' "   40
    When he heard this, Rostám was near to faint.
The world around grew dark before his eyes.
And when Rostám regained his wits once more,
He asked Sohráb with sighs of grief and pain,
"What sign have you from him—Rostám? Oh, may   45
His name be lost to proud and noble men!"
"If you're Rostám," he said, "you slew me while
Some evil humor had confused your mind.
I tried in every way to draw you forth,
But not an atom of your love was stirred.   50
When first they beat the war drums at my door,
My mother came to me with bloody cheeks.
Her soul was racked by grief to see me go.
She bound a seal upon my arm, and said,
'This is your father's gift, preserve it well.   55
A day will come when it will be of use.'
Alas, its day has come when mine has passed.
The son's abased before his father's eyes.
My mother with great wisdom thought to send
With me a worthy pahlaván[1] as guide.   60
The noble warrior's name was Zhende Razm,
A man both wise in action and in speech.
He was to point my father out to me,
And ask for him among all groups of men.
But Zhende Razm, that worthy man, was slain.   65
And at his death my star declined as well.
Now loose the binding of my coat of mail,
And look upon my naked, shining flesh."

---

1. A hero; becomes *paladin* in English.

When he unloosed his armor's ties and saw
That seal, he tore his clothes and wept.   70
"Oh, brave and noble youth, and praised among
All men, whom I have slain with my own hand!"
He wept a bloody stream and tore his hair;
His brow was dark with dust, tears filled his eyes.
Sohráb then said, "But this is even worse.   75
You must not fill your eyes with tears. For now
It does no good to slay yourself with grief.
What's happened here is what was meant to be."
     When the radiant sun had left the sky,
And Tahamtán had not returned to camp,   80
Some twenty cavaliers rode off to see
How matters stood upon the field of war.
They saw two horses standing on the plain,
Both caked with dirt. Rostám was somewhere else.
Because they did not see his massive form   85
Upon the battlefield and mounted on
His steed, the heroes thought that he'd been slain.
The nobles all grew fearful and perplexed.
They sent a message swiftly to the shah,[2]
"The throne of majesty has lost Rostám."   90
From end to end the army cried aloud,
And suddenly confusion filled the air.
Kavús commanded that the horns and drums
Be sounded, and his marshal, Tus, approached.
Then Kavús spoke, "Be quick, and send a scout   95
From here to view the battlefield
And see how matters stand with bold Sohráb.
Must we lament the passing of Irán?
If by his hand the brave Rostám's been slain,
Who from Irán will dare approach this foe?   100
We now must strike a wide and general blow;
We dare not tarry long upon this field."
     And while a tumult rose within their camp,
Sohráb was speaking thus with Tahamtán,
"The situation of the Turks has changed   105
In every way, now that my days are done.
Be kind to them, and do not let the shah
Pursue this war or urge his army on.
It was for me the Turkish troops rose up,
And mounted this campaign against Irán.   110

---

2. Iranian ruler.

I it was who promised victory, and I
Who strove in every way to give them hope.
They should not suffer now as they retreat.
Be generous with them, and let them go."
　　Rostám then mounted Rakhsh, as swift as dust.　　115
His eyes bled tears, his lips were chilled with sighs.
He wept as he approached the army's camp,
His heart was filled with pain at what he'd done.
When they first spied his face, the army of Irán
Fell prostrate to the earth in gratitude,　　120
And loudly praised the Maker of the World,
That he'd returned alive and well from war.
But when they saw him thus, his chest and clothes
All torn, his body heavy and his face
Begrimed by dust, they asked him all at once,　　125
"What does this mean? Why are you sad at heart?"
He told them of his strange and baffling deed,
Of how he'd slain the one he held most dear.
They all began to weep and mourn with him,
And filled the earth and sky with loud lament.　　130
At last he told the nobles gathered there,
"It seems my heart is gone, my body too.
Do not pursue this battle with the Turks.
The evil I have done is quite enough."
And when he left that place, the pahlaván　　135
Returned with weary heart to where he lay.
The noble lords accompanied their chief,
Men like Gudárz and Tus and Gostahám.
The army all together loosed their tongues,
And gave advice and counsel to Rostám,　　140
"Yazdán alone can remedy this wound;
He yet may ease this burden's weight for you."
He grasped a dagger in his hand, and made
To cut his worthless head from his own trunk.
The nobles hung upon his arm and hand, and tears　　145
Of blood poured from the lashes of their eyes.
Gudárz said to Rostám, "What gain is there
If by your death you set the world in flames?
Were you to give yourself a hundred wounds,
How would that ease the pain of brave Sohráb?　　150
If some time yet remains for him on earth,
He'll live, and you'll remain with him, at peace.
But if this youth is destined to depart,
Look on the world, who's there that does not die?
The head that wears a helmet and the head　　155
That wears a crown, to death we all are prey."

Rostám Asks Kay Kavús for the Nushdarú

Rostám called wise Gudárz and said to him,
"Depart from here upon your swiftest steed,
And take a message to Kavús the shah.
Tell him what has befallen me. With my   160
Own dagger I have torn the breast of my
Brave son—oh, may Rostám not live for long!
If you've some recollection of my deeds,
Then share with me a portion of my grief,
And from your store send me the *nushdarú*,   165
That medicine which heals whatever wound.
It would be well if you sent it to me
With no delay, and in a cup of wine.
By your good grace, my son may yet be cured,
And like his father stand before your throne."   170
The *sepahbód*[3] Gudárz rode like the wind,
And gave Kavús the message from Rostám.
    Kavús replied, "If such an elephant
Should stay alive and join our royal court,
He'll make his father yet more powerful.   175
Rostám will slay me then, I have no doubt.
When I may suffer evil at his hands,
What gift but evil should I make him now?
You heard him, how he said, 'Who is Kavús?'
If he's the shah, then who is Tus?' And with   180
That chest and neck, that mighty arm and fist,
In this wide world, who's there to equal him?
Will he stand humbly by my royal seat,
Or march beneath my banner's eagle wings?"
    Gudárz heard his reply, then turned and rode   185
Back to Rostám as swift as wind-borne smoke.
"The evil nature of the shah is like
The tree of war, perpetually in fruit.
You must depart at once and go to him.
Perhaps you can enlighten his dark soul."   190

Rostám Mourns Sohráb

Rostám commanded that a servant bring
A robe and spread it by the river's bank.
He gently laid Sohráb upon the robe,
Then mounted Rakhsh and rode toward the shah.

---

3. A title that means general; can be used for
   shahs and heroes as well.

But as he rode, his face toward the court,   195
They overtook him swiftly with the news,
"Sohráb has passed from this wide world; he'll need
A coffin from you now, and not a crown.
'Father!' he cried, then sighed an icy wind,
Then wept aloud and closed his eyes at last."   200
   Rostám dismounted from his steed at once.
Dark dust replaced the helmet on his head.
He wept and cried aloud, "Oh, noble youth,
And proud, courageous seed of pahlaváns!
The sun and moon won't see your like again,   205
No more will shield or mail, nor throne or crown.
Who else has been afflicted as I've been?
That I should slay a youth in my old age
Who is the grandson of world-conquering Sam,
Whose mother's seed's from famous men as well.   210
It would be right to sever these two hands.
No seat be mine henceforth save darkest earth.
What father's ever done a deed like this?
I now deserve abuse and icy scorn.
Who else in all this world has slain his son,   215
His wise, courageous, youthful son?
How Zal the golden will rebuke me now,
He and the virtuous Rudabé as well.
What can I offer them as my excuse?
What plea of mine will satisfy their hearts?   220
What will the heroes and the warriors say
When word of this is carried to their ears?
And when his mother learns, what shall I say?
How can I send a messenger to her?
What can I say? Why did I slay him when   225
He'd done no crime? Why blacken all his days?
How will her sire, that worthy pahlaván,
Report this to his pure and youthful child?
He'll call this seed of Sam[4] a godless wretch,
And heap his curses on my ancient head.   230
Alas, who could have known this precious child
Would quickly grow to cypress height, or that
He'd raise this host and think of arms and war,
Or that he'd turn my shining day to night."
   Rostám commanded that the body of   235
His son be covered with a royal robe.

---

4. Rostám's grandfather.

He'd longed to sit upon the throne and rule;
His portion was a coffin's narrow walls.
The coffin of Sohráb was carried from
The field. Rostám returned to his own tent.   240
They set aflame Sohráb's pavilion while
His army cast dark dust upon their heads.
They threw his tents of many colored silk,
His precious throne and leopard saddle cloth
Into the flames, and tumult filled the air.   245
    He cried aloud, "Oh, youthful conqueror!
Alas, that stature and that noble face!
Alas, that wisdom and that manliness!
Alas, what sorrow and heart-rending loss—
No mother near, heart pierced by father's blade!"   250
His eyes wept bloody tears, he tore the earth,
And rent the kingly garments on his back.
    Then all the pahlaváns and Shah Kavús
Sat with him in the dust beside the road.
They spoke to him with counsel and advice—   255
In grief Rostám was like one driven mad—
"This is the way of fortune's wheel. It holds
A lasso in this hand, a crown in that.
As one sits happily upon his throne,
A loop of rope will snatch him from his place.   260
Why is it we should hold the world so dear?
We and our fellows must depart this road.
The longer we have thought about our wealth,
The sooner we must face that earthy door.
If heaven's wheel knows anything of this,   265
Or if its mind is empty of our fate,
The turning of the wheel it cannot know,
Nor can it understand the reason why.
One must lament that he should leave this world,
Yet what this means at last, I do not know."   270
    Then Kay Kavús spoke to Rostám at length,
"From Mount Alborz to the frailest reed,
The turning heavens carry all away.
You must not fix your heart upon this world.
One sets off quickly on the road, and one   275
Will take more time, but all pass on to death.
Content your heart with his departure and
Give careful heed to what I tell you now.
If you should bring the heavens down to earth,
Or set the world aflame from end to end,   280
You won't recall from death the one who's gone.

His soul's grown ancient in that other manse.
Once from afar I saw his arms and neck,
His lofty stature and his massive chest.
The times impelled him and his martial host   285
To come here now and perish by your hand.
What can you do? What remedy is there
For death? How long can you bewail his loss?"
    Rostám replied, "Though he himself is gone,
Humán still sits upon this ample plain,   290
His Turkish and his Chinese chiefs as well.
Retain no hint of enmity toward them,
But strengthened by Yazdán and your command,
Let Zavaré guide all their army home."
    "Oh, famous pahlaván," said Shah Kavús,   295
"This war has caused you suffering and loss.
Though they have done me many grievous wrongs,
And though Turán has set Irán aflame,
Because my heart can feel your heavy pain,
I'll think no more of them and let them go,"   300

BADĪᶜ AL-ZAMĀN AL-HAMADHĀNĪ

(969?–1008)

Arabic

The *maqāma* (plural, *maqāmāt*) is an indigenous Arabic literary form, a tale crafted in rhymed prose (*sajᶜ*) with occasional portions in verse. Usually translated as "seance" or "assembly," it is closely related to the anecdotal *adab*. Al-Hamadhānī is credited by most literary historians with having invented the *maqāma*. Born, as his name reveals, in Hamadān, he seems to have spent his life traveling from one court to another. He died in Herāt, in present-day Afghanistan. According to a delighted account by a contemporary, al-Hamadhānī's verbal virtuosity was dazzling; his nickname, Badīᶜ al-Zaman, means "wonder of the age." The hero of the *maqāma* is likewise a verbal virtuoso—a clever rogue whose exploits are related by a narrator whose path continually crosses the hero's. The two even share adventures. Eloquence and a ready wit are among the chief tools of the rogue hero's trade. This and other literary qualities have led some scholars to link the classical Arabic maqāma to the Spanish picaresque novel, a genre named for *its* rogue hero, or *picaro*. Certain is that al-Hamadhānī's invention, including its stock hero and narrator, spread throughout the Islamic world, and the ensuing centuries saw *Maqāmāt* written in Persian, Turkish, and even Hebrew.

from *The Maqāmāt*

Portrait of a Parvenu

THE MADĪRA[1] (LATE TENTH CENTURY)

'Isā ibn Hishām told us the following: I was in Basra with Abu'l-Fatḥ al-Iskandarī, a master of language—when he summoned elegance, it responded; when he commanded eloquence, it obeyed. I was present with him at a reception given by some merchant, and we were served a *madīra,* one that commended the civilization of cities. It quivered in the dish and gave promise of bliss and testified that Muꜥāwiya,[2] God have mercy on him, was Imam.[3] It was in a bowl such that looks glided off it and brilliance rippled in it. When it took its place on the table and its home in our hearts, Abu'l-Fatḥ al-Iskandarī started to curse it and him who offered it, to abuse it and him who ate it, to revile it and him who cooked it. We thought that he was jesting, but the fact was the reverse, for his jest was earnest, indeed. He withdrew from the table and left the company of brothers. We had the *madīra* removed, and our hearts were removed with it, our eyes followed behind it, our mouths watered after it, our lips smacked, and our livers were kindled. Nevertheless, we joined with him in parting with it and inquired of him concerning it, and he said, "My story about the *madīra* is longer than the pain of my being deprived of it, and if I tell you about it, I am in danger of arousing aversion and wasting time."

We said, "Come on!" and he continued.

"When I was in Baghdad a certain merchant invited me to a *madīra* and stuck to me like a creditor and like the dog to the companions of al-Raqīm.[4] So I accepted his invitation, and we set out for his house. All the way he praised his wife, for whom, he said, he would give his life's blood. He described her skill in preparing the *madīra* and her refinement in cooking it, and he said, 'O my master, if you could see her, with the apron round her middle, moving about the house, from the oven to the pots and from the pots to the oven, blowing on the fire with her mouth and pounding the spices with her hand; if you could see the smoke blacken that beautiful face and leave its marks on that smooth cheek, then you would see a sight which would dazzle the eyes! I love her because she loves me. It is bliss for a man to be vouchsafed the help of his wife and to be aided by his helpmate, especially if she is of his kin. She is my cousin on my father's side, her

Translated by Bernard Lewis.

1. A stew of spiced meat.
2. Caliph, founder of the Umayyad Dynasty.
3. leader of the community, a reference to the disputed legitimacy of this ruler.
4. A reference to the story of the People of the Cave which appears in Sûra 18 of the Qur'an. The People of the Cave are often associated with the Seven Sleepers of Eph-

esus, in the Christian tradition a group of young men who escaped persecution under the Emperor Decius by hiding in a cave and sleeping there for many years. Al-Raqīm may be the dog or the village closest to the cave. Others understand this reference to allude to a separate incident altogether.

flesh is my flesh, her town is my town, her uncles are my uncles, her root is my root. She is however better natured and better looking that I.'

"So he wearied me with his wife's qualities until we reached the quarter where he lived, and then he said, 'O my master, look at this quarter! It is the noblest quarter of Baghdad. The worthy vie to settle here, and the great compete to dwell here. None but merchants live here, for a man can be judged by his neighbor. My house is the jewel in the middle of a necklace of houses, the center of their circle. How much, O my master, would you say was spent on each house? Make a rough guess, if you don't know exactly.'

"I answered, 'A lot.'

"He said, 'Glory be to God, how great is your error! You just say "a lot." ' Then he sighed deeply and said, 'Glory to Him who knows all things.'

"Then we came to the door of his house, and he said, 'This is my house. How much, O my master, would you say I spent on this doorway? By God, I spent more than I could afford and enough to reduce me to poverty. What do you think of its workmanship and shape? By God, have you seen its like? Look at the fine points of craftsmanship in it, and observe the beauty of its lattice-work; it is as if it had been drawn with a compass. Look at the skill of the carpenter in making this door. From how many pieces did he make it? You may well say, "How should I know?" It is made of a single piece of teak, free from worm or rot. If it is moved, it moans, and if it is struck, it hums. Who made it, sir? Abū Isḥāq ibn Muḥammad al-Baṣrī made it, and he is, by God, of good repute, skillful in the craft of doors, dextrous with his hands in his work. God, what a capable man he is! By my life, I would never call on anyone but him for such a task.'

" 'And this door ring which you see, I bought it in the curio market from 'Imrān the curio dealer, for three Mu'izzī dinars. And how much yellow copper does it contain, sir? It contains six *raṭls!* It turns on a screw in the door. Turn it, by God! Then strike it and watch. By my life, one should not buy a door ring from anyone but " 'Imrān, who sells nothing but treasures.' "

"Then he rapped on the door, and we entered the hall, and he said, 'May God preserve you, O house! May God not destroy you, O walls! How strong are your buttresses, how sound your construction, how firm your foundation! By God, observe the steps and scrutinize the inside and the outside of the house, and ask me, "How did you obtain it, and by what devices did you acquire and gain possession of it?" I had a neighbor called Abū Sulaymān, who lived in this quarter. He had more wealth than he could store and more valuables than he could weigh. He died, may God have mercy on him, leaving an heir who squandered his inheritance on wine and song and dissipated it between backgammon and gambling. I feared lest the guide of necessity lead him to sell the house and he sell it in a moment of desperation or leave it exposed to ruination. Then I would see my chance of buying it slip away, and my grief would continue to the day of my death.'

" 'So I got some clothes of a kind difficult to sell and brought them and offered them to him and chaffered with him until he agreed to buy them on credit. The luckless regard credit as a gift, and the unsuccessful reckon it as a present. I asked him for a document for the amount, and he drew one up in my favor. Then

I neglected to claim what was due until he was in the direst straits. And then I came and demanded what he owed. He asked for a delay, to which I agreed; he asked me for more clothes, which I brought him; and I asked him to give me his house as security and as a pledge in my hand. He did so, and then I induced him in successive negotiation to sell it to me so that it became mine by rising fortune, lucky chance, and a strong arm. Many a man works unwittingly for others, but I, praise be to God, am lucky and successful in matters such as these. Just think, O my master, that a few nights ago when I was sleeping in the house together with my household, there was a knock at the door. I asked, "Who is this untimely caller?" and there was a woman with a necklace of pearls, as clear as water and as delicate as a mirage, offering it for sale. I took it from her as if by theft, so low was the price for which I bought it. It will be of obvious value and abundant profit, with the help and favor of God. I have only told you this story so that you may know how lucky I am in business, for good luck can make water flow from stones. God is great! Nobody will inform you more truthfully than you yourself, and no day is nearer than yesterday. I bought this mat at an auction. It was brought out of the houses of the Ibn al-Furāt family when their assets were confiscated and seized. I had been looking for something like this for a long time and had not found it. "Fate is a pregnant woman;" no one knows what it will bear. It chanced that I was at Bāb al-Ṭāq, and this mat was displayed in the market. I weighed out so many dinars[5] for it. By God, look at its fineness, its softness, its workmanship, its color, for it is of immense value. Its like occurs only rarely. If you have heard of Abū ʿImrān the mat maker, it is he who made it. He has a son who has now succeeded him in his shop, and only with him can the finest mats be found. By my life, never buy mats from any shop but his, for a true believer gives good advice to his brothers, especially those admitted to the sanctity of his table. But let us return to the *madīra,* for the hour of noon has come. Slave! Basin and water!'

"God is great, I thought, release draws nearer and escape becomes easier.

"The slave stepped forward, and the merchant said, 'Do you see this slave? He is of Greek origin and brought up in Iraq. Come here, slave! Uncover your head! Raise your leg! Bare your arm! Show your teeth! Walk up and down!'

"The slave did as he said, and the merchant said, 'By God, who bought him? By God, Abu'l-Abbās bought him from the slave-dealer. Put down the basin and bring the jug!'

"The slave put it down and the merchant picked it up, turned it around, and looked it over; then he struck it and said, 'Look at this yellow copper—like a glowing coal or a piece of gold! It is Syrian copper, worked in Iraq. This is not one of those wornout valuables, though it has known the houses of kings and has circulated in them. Look at its beauty and ask me, "When did you buy it?" By God, I bought it in the year of the famine, and I put it aside for this moment. Slave! The jug!'

"He brought it, and the merchant took it and turned it around and said, 'Its spout is part of it, all one piece. This jug goes only with this basin, this basin goes

---

5. Gold coins.

only with this seat of honor, this seat of honor fits only in this house, and this house is beautiful only with this guest! Pour the water, slave, for it is time to eat! By God, do you see this water? How pure it is, as blue as a cat's eye, as clear as a crystal rod! It was drawn from the Euphrates and served after being kept overnight so that it comes as bright as the tongue of flame from a candle and clear as a tear. What counts is not the liquid, but the receptacle. Nothing will show you the cleanliness of the receptacles more clearly than the cleanliness of what you drink. And this kerchief! Ask me about its story! It was woven in Jurjān and worked in Arrajān. I came across it and I bought it. My wife made part of it into a pair of drawers and part of it into a kerchief. Twenty ells went into her drawers, and I snatched this amount away from her hand. I gave it to an embroiderer who worked it and embroidered it as you see. Then I brought it home from the market and stored it in a casket and reserved it for the most refined of my guests. No Arab of the common people defiled it with his hands, nor any woman with the corners of her eyes. Every precious thing has its proper time, and every tool its proper user. Slave! Set the table, for it is growing late! Bring the dish, for the argument has been long! Serve the food, for the talk has been much!'

"The slave brought the table, and the merchant turned it in its place and struck it with his fingertips and tested it with his teeth and said, 'May God give prosperity to Baghdad! How excellent are its products, how refined its craftsmen! By God, observe this table, and look at the breadth of its surface, the slightness of its weight, the hardness of its wood, and the beauty of its shape.'

"I said, 'This is all fine, but when do we eat?'

"'Now,' he said. 'Slave! Bring the food quickly. But please observe that the legs and the table are all of one piece.'"

Abu'l-Fatḥ said, "I was fuming, and I said to myself, 'There is still the baking and its utensils, the bread and its qualities, and where the wheat was originally bought, and how an animal was hired to transport it, in what mill it was ground, in what tub it was kneaded, in what oven it was baked, and what baker was hired to bake it. Then there is still the firewood, when it was cut, when it was brought, and how it was set out to dry; and then the baker and his description, the apprentice and his character, the flour and its praises, the yeast and its commentary, the salt and its saltiness. And then there are the plates, who got them, how he acquired them, who used them, and who made them; and the vinegar, how its grapes were selected or its fresh dates were bought, how the press was limed, how the juice was extracted, how the jars were tarred, and how much each cask was worth. And then there were the vegetables, by what devices they were picked, in what grocery they were packed, with what care they were cleaned. And then there is the *madīra*, how the meat was bought, the fat was paid for, the pot set up, the fire kindled, the spices pounded so that the cooking might excell and the gravy be thick. This is an affair that overflows and a business that has no end.'

"So I rose, and he asked, 'What do you want?'

"I said, 'A need that I must satisfy.'

"He said, 'O my master! You are going to a privy which shames the spring residence of the amir and the autumn residence of the vizier! Its upper part is plastered and its lower part is whitewashed; its roof is terraced and its floor is paved with marble. Ants slip off its walls and cannot grip; flies walk on its floor and slither along. It has a door with panels of teak and ivory combined in the most perfect way. A guest could wish to eat there.'

" 'Eat there yourself,' I said. 'The privy is not part of the bargain.'

"Then I made for the door and hurried as I went. I began to run, and he followed me, shouting, 'O Abu'l-Fath, the *maḍīra!* The youngsters thought that *al-maḍīra* was my byname, and they began to shout it. I threw a stone at one of them, so angry was I, but the stone hit a man on his turban and pierced his head. I was seized and beaten with shoes, both old and new, and showered with blows, both worthy and vicious, and thrown into prison. I remained for two years in this misfortune, and I swore that I would never eat a *maḍīra* as long as I lived. Have I done wrong in this, O people of Hamadān?"

'Isā ibn Hishām said, "We accepted his excuse and joined in his vow, saying 'The *maḍīra* has brought misfortune on the noble and has exalted the unworthy over the worthy.' "

IBN HAZM (d. 1064)
Arabic

The Dove's Neckring (*Twaq al-Hamāma*), written by the Andalusian scholar and legist Ibn Hazm, is a work of great universal appeal. It was supposedly written in answer to a request by a friend who wished Ibn Hazm to describe love and its various manifestations. Part of the appeal of the work lies in its autobiographical elements. It also provides readers with a personal view of Andalusian society during the eleventh century.

from *The Dove's Neckring*

[Of Various Loves]

Because betrayal is so common a characteristic of the beloved, fidelity on her part has come to be regarded as extraordinary; therefore its rare occurrence in persons loved is thought to counterbalance its frequency among lovers. I have a little poem on this subject.

> Small faithfulness in the beloved
> Is most exceedingly approved,
> While lovers' great fidelity
> Is taken unremarkably.

Translated by A. J. Arberry.

> So cowards, rarely brave in war,
> Are more applauded when they are
> Than heroes, who sustain all day
> The heat and fury of the fray.

A particularly base type of betrayal is when the lover sends an emissary to the beloved, entrusting all his secrets to his keeping, and then the messenger strives and contrives to convert the beloved's interest to himself, and captures her affection to the exclusion of his principal. I put this situation in rhyme as follows.

> I sent an envoy unto thee,
>   Intending so my hopes to gain;
> I trusted him too foolishly;
>   Now he has come between us twain.
>
> He loosed the cords of my true love,
>   Then neatly tied his own instead;
> He drove me out of all whereof
>   I might have well been tenanted.
>
> I, who had called him to the stand,
>   Am now a witness to his case:
> I fed him at my table, and
>   Now hang myself upon his grace.

Finally there is the separation which is caused by death, that final parting from which there is no hope of a return. This is indeed a shattering and back-breaking blow, a fateful catastrophe; it is a lamentable woe, overshadowing the blackness of night itself; it cuts off every hope, erases all ambition, and causes the most sanguine to despair of further meeting. Here all tongues are baffled; the cord of every remedy is severed; no other course remains open but patient fortitude, willing or perforce. It is the greatest affliction that can assail true lovers; and he who is struck down by it has nothing left but to lament and weep, until either he perishes himself or wearies of his lamentations. It is the wound which cannot heal, the anguish which never passes, the sorrow which is constantly renewed, as ever his poor body crumbles that thou hast committed to the dust. On this matter I have the following to say.

> What things soe'er
> May come to pass,
> Cry not alas
> While hope is there.
>
> Haste not thy heart
> To gloom to yield:
> All is not sealed
> Till life depart.
>
> But when the veil
> Of death descends
> Then all hope ends,
> All comforts fail.

I have seen this happen to many people, and can relate to you a personal experience of the same order; for I am also one who has been afflicted by this calamity and surprised by this misfortune. I was deeply in love with, and passionately enamoured of, a certain slave-girl once in my possession, whose name was Nu'm. She was a dream of desire, a paragon of physical and moral beauty, and we were in perfect harmony. She had known no other man before me, and our love for each other was mutual and perfectly satisfying. Then the fates ravished her from me, and the nights and passing days carried her away; she became one with the dust and stones. At the time of her death I was not yet twenty, and she younger than I. For seven months thereafter I never once put off my garments; my tears ceased not to flow, though I am a man not given to weeping, nor discovering relief in lamentation. And by Allah, I have not found consolation for her loss even to this day. If ransoms could have been of avail, I would have ransomed her with everything of which I stand possessed, my inheritance and all my earnings, aye, and with the most precious limb of my body, swiftly and willingly. Since her death life has never seemed sweet to me; I have never forgotten her memory, nor been intimate with any other woman. My love for her blotted out all that went before, and made anathema to me all that came after it.

I can tell you with regard to myself, that in my youth I enjoyed the loving friendship of a certain slave-girl who grew up in our house, and who at the time of my story was sixteen years old. She had an extremely pretty face, and was moreover intelligent, chaste, pure, shy, and of the sweetest disposition. She was not given to jesting, and was most sparing of her favours; she had a wonderful complexion, which she always kept closely veiled. Innocent of every vice, and of very few words, she kept her eyes modestly cast down. Moreover she was extremely cautious, and guiltless of all faults, ever maintaining a serious mien; charming in her withdrawal, she was naturally reserved, and most graceful in repelling unwelcome advances. She seated herself with becoming dignity, and was most sedate in her behaviour; the way she fled from masculine attentions like a startled bird was delightful to behold. No hopes of easy conquest were to be entertained so far as she was concerned; none could look to succeed in his ambitions if these were aimed in her direction; eager expectation found no resting-place in her. Her lovely face attracted all hearts, but her manner kept at arm's length all who came seeking her; she was far more glamorous in her refusals and rejections than those other girls, who rely upon easy compliance and the ready lavishing of their favours to make them interesting to men. In short, she was dedicated to earnestness in all matters, and had no desire for amusement of any kind; for all that she played the lute most beautifully. I found myself irresistibly drawn towards her, and loved her with all the violent passion of my youthful heart. For two years or thereabouts I laboured to the utmost of my powers to win one syllable of response from her, to hear from her lips a single word, other than the usual kind of banalities that may be heard by everyone; but all my efforts proved in vain.

Now I remember a party that was held in our residence, on one of those occasions that are commonly made the excuse for such festivities in the houses of persons of rank. The ladies of our household and of my brother's also, God have mercy on his soul, were assembled together, as well as the womenfolk of our retainers and faithful servants, all thoroughly nice and jolly folk. The ladies remained in the house for the earlier part of the day, and then betook themselves to a belvedere that was attached to our mansion, overlooking the garden and giving a magnificent view of the whole of Cordova; the bays were constructed with large open windows. They passed their time enjoying the panorama through the lattice openings, myself being among them.

I recall that I was endeavouring to reach the bay where she was standing, to enjoy her proximity and to sidle up close to her. But no sooner did she observe me in the offing than she left that bay and sought another, moving with consummate grace. I endeavoured to come to the bay to which she had departed, and she repeated her performance and passed on to another. She was well aware of my infatuation, while the other ladies were entirely unconscious of what was passing between us; for there was a large company of them, and they were all the time moving from one alcove to another to enjoy the variety of prospects, each bay affording a different view from the rest.

You must realize, my friend, that women have keener eyes to detect admiration in a man's heart, than any benighted traveller has to discover a track in the desert. Well, at last the ladies went down into the garden; and the dowagers and duchesses among them entreated the mistress of the girl to let them hear her sing. She commanded her to do so; and she thereupon took up her lute and tuned it with a pretty shyness and modesty, the like of which I had never seen; though it is true of course that things are doubly beautiful in the eyes of their admirers. Then she began to sing those famous verses of al-'Abbās ibn al-Ahnaf.

> My heart leapt up, when I espied
> A sun sink slowly in the west,
> Its beauty in that bower to hide
> Where lovely ladies lie at rest:
>
> A sun embodied in the guise
> Of a sweet maiden of delight,
> The ripple of her rounded thighs
> A scroll of parchment, soft and white.
>
> No creature she of human kind,
> Though human fair and beautiful,
> And neither sprite, although designed
> In faery grace ineffable.
>
> Her body was a jasmine rare,
> Her perfume sweet as amber scent,
> Her face a pearl beyond compare,
> Her all, pure light's embodiment.
>
> All shrouded in her pettigown
> I watched her delicately pass,

> Stepping as light as thistledown
> That dances on a crystal glass.

And by my life, it was as though her plectrum was plucking at the strings of my heart. I have never forgotten that day, nor shall forget it until the time comes for me to leave this transient world. That was the most I was ever given to see her, or to hear her voice.

Then my father, the vizier, God rest his soul, moved from our new mansion in Rabad al-Zāhira on the eastern side of Cordova to our old residence on the western side, in the quarter of Balat Mughith; this was on the third day of the accession of Muhammad al-Mahdī, to the Caliphate.[1] I followed him in February 1009; but the girl did not come with us, for reasons that obliged her to remain behind. Thereafter, when Hishām al-Mu'aiyad[2] succeeded to the throne, we were sufficiently preoccupied with the misfortunes which came upon us, thanks to the hostility of his ministers; we were sorely tried by imprisonment, surveillance and crushing fines, and were finally obliged to go into hiding. Civil war raged far and wide; all classes suffered from its dire effects, and ourselves in particular. At last my father the vizier died, God have mercy on his soul, our situation being still as I have described, on the afternoon of Saturday, June 22, 1012.

Things remained unchanged with us thereafter, until presently the day came when we again had a funeral in the house, one of our relatives having deceased. I saw her standing there amid the clamour of mourning, all among the weeping and wailing women. She revived that passion long buried in my heart, and stirred my now still ardour, reminding me of an ancient troth, an old love, an epoch gone by, a vanished time, departed months, faded memories, periods perished, days forever past, obliterated traces. She renewed my griefs and reawakened my sorrows; and though upon that day I was afflicted and cast down for many reasons, yet I had indeed not forgotten her; only my anguish was intensified, the fire smouldering in my heart blazed into flame, my unhappiness was exacerbated, my despair was multiplied. Passion drew forth from my breast all that lay hidden within it; my soul answered the call, and I broke out into plaintive rhyme.

> They weep for one now dead,
> High honoured in his tomb;
> Those tears were better shed
> For him who lives in gloom.
>
> O wonder, that they sigh
> For him who is at rest
> Yet mourn not me, who die
> Most cruelly oppressed.

Then destiny struck its heaviest blows, and we were banished from our loved abodes; the armies of the Berbers triumphed over us. I set forth from Cordova[3] on July 13, 1013, and after that one glimpse of her she vanished from my sight for six

---

1. Muhammad al-Mahdī reigned from 1009 to 1010.

2. Hisham al-Mu'aiyad reigned from 976 to 1009 and from 1010 to 1013.

3. A city in Spain.

long years and more. Then I came again into Cordova in February 1019, and lodged with one of our womenfolk; and there I saw her. I could scarcely recognize her, until someone said to me, 'This is So-and-so'; her charms were so greatly changed. Gone was her radiant beauty, vanished her wondrous loveliness; faded now was that lustrous complexion which once gleamed like a polished sword or an Indian mirror; withered was the bloom on which the eye once gazed transfixed seeking avidly to feast upon its dazzling splendour only to turn away bewildered. Only a fragment of the whole remained, to tell the tale and testify to what the complete picture had been. All this had come to pass because she took too little care of herself, and had lacked the guardian hand which had nourished her during the days of our prosperity, when our shadow was long in the land; as also because she had been obliged to besmirch herself in those inevitable excursions to which her circumstances had driven her, and from which she had formerly been sheltered and exempted.

For women are as aromatic herbs, which if not well tended soon lose their fragrance; they are as edifices which, if not constantly cared for, quickly fall into ruin. Therefore it has been said that manly beauty is the truer, the more solidly established, and of higher excellence, since it can endure, and that without shelter, onslaughts the merest fraction of which would transform the loveliness of a woman's face beyond recognition: such enemies as the burning heat of the noonday, the scorching wind of the desert, every air of heaven, and all the changing moods of the seasons.

If I had enjoyed the least degree of intimacy with her, if she had been only a little kind to me, I would have been beside myself with happiness; I verily believe that I would have died for joy. But it was her unremitting aloofness which schooled me in patience, and taught me to find consolation. This then was one of those cases in which both parties may excusably forget, and not be blamed for doing so: there has been no firm engagement that should require their loyalty, no covenant has been entered into obliging them to keep faith, no ancient compact exists, no solemn plighting of troths, the breaking and forgetting of which should expose them to justified reproach.

Here is a story which I have often heard told concerning a certain Berber king. An Andalusian gentleman, finding himself in financial difficulties, had sold a female slave whom he loved passionately; she was bought by a man of the Berber country. The poor fellow who sold her never imagined that his heart would follow her in the way it did. When she reached her purchaser's home, her former owner almost expired. So he searched out the man to whom he had sold her and offered him all his possessions, and himself to boot, if he would restore her to him; but the Berber refused.

The Andalusian then besought the inhabitants of the town to prevail upon him; but not one of them came to his assistance. Almost out of his mind, he bethought himself of appealing to the king; he therefore stood without the palace, and uttered a loud cry. The king, who was seated in a lofty chamber overlooking the courtyard, heard his shout and ordered him to be admitted. The Andalusian entered the royal presence, and standing before his Berber majesty he told his story, and implored and supplicated him to have compassion.

The king, much touched by his plight, commanded that the man who had bought the girl should be summoned to court. He duly came; and the king said, "This poor fellow is a stranger; you can see what a state he is in. I intercede with you personally on his behalf." But the purchaser refused, saying, "I am more deeply in love with her than he is, and I fear that if you return her to him I myself shall be standing here tomorrow imploring your aid, and in an even worse case." The king and all his courtiers offered him of their own riches to let her go; but he persisted in his refusal, pleading as his excuse the affection he bore her.

The audience having by now dragged on a long time, and there being no sign whatsoever that the purchaser would give way and consent, the king said to the Andalusian, "My good sir, I can do nothing more for you than this. I have striven to the utmost of my powers on your behalf; and you see how he excuses himself on the grounds that he loves her more than you do, and fears he may come to even greater evil than yourself. You had best endure patiently what Allah has decreed for you."

The Andalusian thereupon exclaimed, "Have you no means at all then of helping me?"

"Can I do anything more for you than entreat him, and offer him money?" the king answered.

The Andalusian, being in despair, bent himself double, and with his hands clutching his feet he threw himself down from the topmost height of the audience-chamber to the earth. The king cried out in alarm, and his slaves below ran to where the man was lying. It was his fate not to be greatly injured by the fall, and he was brought up to the king again.

"What did you intend by doing that?" the king said to him.

"O king," the man replied, "I cannot live any longer, now that I have lost her."

Then he would have thrown himself down a second time, but he was prevented.

"Allah is great!" the king thereupon exclaimed. "I have hit upon the just arbitrament of this problem." Turning to the purchaser he said, "Good sir, do you claim that your love for the girl is greater than his, and do you state that you fear to come to the same pass as he is in?"

"Yes," replied the Berber.

"Very well," went on the king. "Your friend here has given us a clear indication of his love; he hurled himself down, and would have died, but that Almighty God preserved him. Now do you stand up and prove your love is true; cast yourself down from the topmost point of this pavilion, as your friend did. If you die, it will mean that your appointed time has come; if you live, you will have the better right to the girl, seeing that she is at present your property; and your companion in distress shall then go away. But if you refuse to jump, I will take the girl from you, whether you like it or not, and will hand her over to him."

At first the Berber held back, but then he said, "I will cast myself down." But when he came near the opening, and looked into the yawning void below him, he drew himself back again.

"By Allah," cried the king, "it shall be as I have said."

The man tried again, but shrunk away once more.

When he would not take the plunge, the king shouted to him, "Do not make sport of us! Ho, slaves, seize his hands and pitch him to the ground!"

The Berber, seeing the king thus resolved, exclaimed, "O king, I am content: let him have the girl."

The king replied, "Allah give thee a good recompense!"

So saying, he bought the girl from him and gave her over to her former owner; and the two departed.

AL-GHAZĀLĪ (1058?–1111)
Arabic

A brilliant legist, philosopher-theologian, and professor, al-Ghazālī has entered the annals of world literature through his spiritual autobiography. Al-Ghazālī began his career as a professor of religious sciences in Baghdad, where he produced important works on philosophy and Islamic orthodoxy. Dissatisfied with the intellectual life he was leading, however, he left his teaching post, abandoned his family, and for ten years explored the mystical side of Islam. *The Rescuer from Error [al-Munqidh min al-Dalā]* is his autobiographical account of this intellectual and spiritual saga. Al-Ghazālī was more than simply someone who solved his own personal crisis, however. In a later work, *Revitalization of Religious Sciences [Ihyā' ʿ-Ulūm ad-Dīn]*, he turned his personal experience to use in unifying two divergent strands in medieval Islamic society: religious orthodoxy and mysticism.

from *The Rescuer from Error*

The Ways of Mysticism

When I had finished with these sciences, I next turned with set purpose to the method of mysticism (or Sufism). I knew that the complete mystic "way" includes both intellectual belief and practical activity; the latter consists in getting rid of the obstacles in the self and in stripping off its base characteristics and vicious morals, so that the heart may attain to freedom from what is not God and to constant recollection of Him.

The intellectual belief was easier to me than the practical activity. I began to acquaint myself with their belief by reading their book, such as *The Food of the Hearts* by Abū Ṭālib al-Makkī (God have mercy upon him), the works of al-Ḥārith al-Muḥāsibī, the various anecdotes about al-Junayd, ash-Shiblī and Abū Yazīd al-Bistāmī (may God sanctify their spirits),[1] and other discourses of their leading

Translated by W. Montgomery Watt.

men. I thus comprehended their fundamental teachings on the intellectual side, and progressed, as far as is possible by study and oral instruction, in the knowledge of mysticism. It became clear to me, however, that what is most distinctive of mysticism is something which cannot be apprehended by study, but only by immediate experience (*ahawq*—literally "tasting"), by ecstasy and by a moral change. What a difference there is between *knowing* the definition of health and satiety, together with their causes and presuppositions, and *being,* healthy and satisfied! What a difference between being acquainted with the definition of drunkenness—namely, that it designates a state arising from the domination of the seat of the intellect by vapours arising from the stomach—and being drunk! Indeed, the drunken man while in that condition does not know the definition of drunkenness nor the scientific account of it; he has not the very least scientific knowledge of it. The sober man, on the other hand, knows the definition of drunkenness and its basis, yet he is not drunk in the very least. Again the doctor, when he is himself ill, knows the definition and causes of health and the remedies which restore it, and yet is lacking in health. Similarly there is a difference between knowing the true nature and causes and conditions of the ascetic life and actually leading such a life and forsaking the world.

I apprehended clearly that the mystics were men who had real experiences, not men of words, and that I had already progressed as far as was possible by way of intellectual apprehension. What remained for me was not to be attained by oral instruction and study but only by immediate experience and by walking in the mystic way.

Now from the sciences I had laboured at and the paths I had traversed in my investigation of the revelational and rational sciences (that is, presumably, theology and philosophy), there had come to me a sure faith in God most high, in prophet-hood (or revelation), and in the Last Day. These three credal principles were firmly rooted in my being, not through any carefully argued proof, but by reason of various causes, coincidences and experiences which are not capable of being stated in detail.

It had already become clear to me that I had no hope of the bliss of the world to come save through a God-fearing life and the withdrawal of myself from vain desire. It was clear to me too that the key to all this was to sever the attachment of the heart to worldly things by leaving the mansion of deception and returning to that of eternity, and to advance towards God most high with all earnestness. It was also clear that this was only to be achieved by turning away from wealth and position and fleeing from all time-consuming entanglements.

Next I considered the circumstances of my life, and realized that I was caught in a veritable thicket of attachments. I also considered my activities, of which the best was my teaching and lecturing, and realized that in them I was dealing with sciences that were unimportant and contributed nothing to the attainment of eternal life.

After that I examined my motive in my work of teaching, and realized that it

---

1. Al-Makkī, al-Muhāsibī, al-Junayd, ash-Shiblī, and al-Bistāmī are all well-known mystics.

was not a pure desire for the things of God, but that the impulse moving me was the desire for an influential position and public recognition. I saw for certain that I was on the brink of a crumbling bank of sand in imminent danger of hell-fire unless I set about to mend my ways.

I reflected on this continuously for a time, while the choice still remained open to me. One day I would form the resolution to quit Baghdad and get rid of these adverse circumstances; the next day I would abandon my resolution. I put one foot forward and drew the other back. If in the morning I had a genuine longing to seek eternal life, by the evening the attack of a whole host of desires had reduced it to impotence. Worldly desires were striving to keep me by their chains just where I was, while the voice of faith was calling, "To the road! to the road! What is left of life is but little and the journey before you is long. All that keeps you busy, both intellectually and practically, is but hypocrisy and delusion. If you do not prepare *now* for eternal life, when will you prepare? If you do not now sever these attachments, when will you sever them?" On hearing that the impulse would be stirred and the resolution made to take to flight.

Soon, however, Satan would return. "This is a passing mood," he would say; "do not yield to it, for it will quickly disappear; if you comply with it and leave this influential position, these comfortable and dignified circumstances where you are free from troubles and disturbances, this state of safety and security where you are untouched by the contentions of your adversaries, then you will probably come to yourself again and will not find it easy to return to all this."

For nearly six months beginning with Rajab 488 A.H.[2] I was continuously tossed about between the attractions of worldly desires and the impulses towards eternal life. In that month the matter ceased to be one of choice and become one of compulsion. God caused my tongue to dry up so that I was prevented from lecturing. One particular day I would make an effort to lecture in order to gratify the hearts of my following, but my tongue would not utter a single word nor could I accomplish anything at all.

This impediment in my speech produced grief in my heart, and at the same time my power to digest and assimilate food and drink was impaired; I could hardly swallow or digest a single mouthful of food. My powers became so weakened that the doctors gave up all hope of successful treatment. "This trouble arises from the heart; they said, "and from there it has spread through the constitution; the only method of treatment is that the anxiety which has come over the heart should be allayed."

Thereupon, perceiving my impotence and having altogether lost my power of choice, I sought refuge with God most high as one who is driven to Him, because he is without further resources of his own. He answered me, He who 'answers him who is driven (to Him by affliction) when he calls upon Him'.[3] He made it easy for my heart to turn away from position and wealth, from children and friends. I openly professed that I had resolved to set out for Mecca, while privately I made arrangements to travel to Syria. I took this precaution in case the Caliph and all my friends should oppose my resolve to make my residence in Syria. This stratagem

---

2. July 1095 C.E.   3. Qur'an 27, 63.

for my departure from Baghdad I gracefully executed, and had it in my mind never to return there. There was much talk about me among all the religious leaders of 'Iraq, since none of them would allow that withdrawal from such a state of life as I was in could have a religious cause, for they looked upon that as the culmination of a religious career; that was the sum of their knowledge.

Much confusion now came into people's minds as they tried to account for my conduct. Those at a distance from 'Iraq supposed that it was due to some apprehension I had of action by the government. On the other hand those who were close to the governing circles and had witnessed how eagerly and assiduously they sought me and how I withdrew from them and showed no great regard for what they said, would say, "This is a supernatural affair; it must be an evil influence which has befallen the people of Islam and especially the circle of the learned."

I left Baghdad, then, I distributed what wealth I had, retaining only as much as would suffice myself and provide sustenance for my children. This I could easily manage, as the wealth of 'Iraq was available for good works, since it constitutes a trust fund for the benefit of the Muslims. Nowhere in the world have I seen better financial arrangements to assist a scholar to provide for his children.

In due course I entered Damascus, and there I remained for nearly two years with no other occupation then the cultivation of retirement and solitude, together with religious and ascetic exercises, as I busied myself purifying my soul, improving my character and cleansing my heart for the constant recollection of God most high, as I had learnt from my study of mysticism. I used to go into retreat for a period in the mosque of Damascus, going up the minaret of the mosque for the whole day and shutting myself in so as to be alone.

At length I made my way from Damascus to the Holy House (that is, Jerusalem). There I used to enter into the precinct of the Rock every day and shut myself in.

Next there arose in me a prompting to fulfill the duty of the Pilgrimage, gain the blessings of Mecca and Medina, and perform the visitation of the Messenger of God most high (peace be upon him), after first performing the visitation of al-Khalīl, the Friend of God (God bless him).[4] I therefore made the journey to the Hijaz.[5] Before long, however, various concerns, together with the entreaties of my children, drew me back to my home (country); and so I came to it again, though one time no one had seemed less likely than myself to return to it. Here, too, I sought retirement, still longing for solitude and the purification of the heart for the recollection (of God). The events of the interval, the anxieties about my family, and the necessities of my livelihood altered the aspect of my purpose and impaired the quality of my solitude, for I experienced pure ecstasy only occasionally, although I did not cease to hope for that; obstacles would hold me back, yet I always returned to it.

I continued at this stage for the space of ten years, and during these periods of solitude there were revealed to me things innumerable and unfathomable. This much I shall say about that in order that others may be helped: I learnt with certainty

---

4. That is, Abraham, who is buried in the cave of Machpelah under the mosque at Hebron, which is called 'al-Khalīl' in Arabic; similarly the visitation of the Messenger is the formal visit to his tomb at Medina.

5. A district of western Arabia that includes the holy cities of Mecca and Medina.

that it is above all the mystics who walk on the road of God; their life is the best life, their method the soundest method, their character the purest character; indeed, were the intellect of the intellectuals and the learning of the learned and the scholarship of the scholars, who are versed in the profundities of revealed truth, brought together in the attempt to improve the life and character of the mystics, they would find no way of doing so; for to the mystics all movement and all rest, whether external or internal, brings illumination from the light of the lamp of prophetic revelation; and behind the light of prophetic revelation there is no other light on the face of the earth from which illumination may be received.

In general, then, how is a mystic "way" (tarīqah) described? The purity which is the first condition of it (as bodily purity is the prior condition of formal Worship for Muslims) is the purification of the heart completely from what is other than God most high; the key to it, which corresponds to the opening act of at adoration in prayer,[6] is the sinking of the heart completely in the recollection of God; and the end of it is complete absorption (fanā) in God. At least this is its end relatively to those first steps which almost come within the sphere of choice and personal responsibility; but in reality in the actual mystic "way" it is the first step, what comes before it being, as it were, the antechamber for those who are journeying towards it.

With this first stage of the "way" there begin the revelations and visions. The mystics in their waking state now behold angels and the spirits of the prophets; they hear their speaking to them and are instructed by them. Later, a higher state is reached; instead of beholding forms and figures, they come to stages in the "way" which it is hard to describe in language; if a man attempts to express these, his words inevitably contain what is clearly erroneous.

In general what they manage to achieve is nearness to God; some, however, would conceive of this as "inherence" (hulūl) some as "union" (ittihād), and some as "connection" (wuṣūl) All that is erroneous. In my book, The Noblest Aim, I have explained the nature of the error here. Yet he who has attained the mystic "state" need do no more than say:

> Of the things I do not remember, what was, was;
> Think it good; do not ask an account of it.
>   (Ibn al-Mu'tazz).

In general the man to whom He has granted no immediate experience at all, apprehends no more of what prophetic revelation really is than the name. The miraculous graces given to the saints are in truth the beginnings of the prophets; and that was the first "state" of the Messenger of God (peace be upon him) when he went out to Mount Ḥirā,[7] and was given up entirely to his Lord, and worshipped, so that the bedouin said, "Muhammad loves his Lord passionately."

Now this is a mystical "state" which is realized in immediate experience by

---

6. Literally, the "prohibition," tahrīm; the opening words of the rites of the Muslim Worship, "God is great," are known as takbīrat at-tahrīm, the prohibitory adora-tion, "because it forbids to the worshipper what was previously allowable."

7. The place where the Prophet Muhammad received the first revelations.

those who walk in the way leading to it. Those to whom it is not granted to have immediate experience can become assured of it by trial (contact with mystics or observation of them) and by hearsay, if they have sufficiently numerous opportunities of associating with mystics to understand that (ecstasy) with certainty means of what accompanies the "states." Whoever sits in their company derives from them this faith; and none who sits in their company is pained.

Those to whom it is not even granted to have contacts with mystics may know with certainty the possibility of ecstasy by the evidence of demonstration, as I have remarked in the section entitled *The Wonders of the Heart* of my *Revival of the Religious Sciences.*

Certainly reached by demonstration is *knowledge* (*'ilm*); actual acquaintance with that "state" is *immediate experience* (*dhawq*); the acceptance of it as probable from hearsay and trial (or observation) is *faith* (*īmān*). These are three degrees. "God will raise those of you who have faith and those who have been given knowledge in degrees (of honour)."[8]

Behind the mystics, however, there is a crowd of ignorant people. They deny this fundamentally, they are astonished at this line of thought, they listen and mock. "Amazing," they say, "What nonsense they talk!" About such people God most high has said: "Some of them listen to you, until, upon going out from you, they say to those to whom knowledge has been given, 'What did he say just now?' These are the people on whose hearts God sets a seal and they follow their passions."[9] He makes them deaf, and blinds their sight.

Among the things that necessarily became clear to me from my practice of the mystic "way" was the true nature and special characteristics of prophetic revelation. The basis of that must undoubtedly be indicated in view of the urgent need for it.

YEHUDA HALEVY (1085?–1141?)
Hebrew

Although classified in this section with Arabic writers and poets, Yehuda Halevy was one of the most brilliant of the Hebrew poets who modeled themselves after Arabic literature in medieval Spain, Provençe, and the Near East. He was born in Muslim Toledo on the borders of Christian Spain, and then traveled to various centers of Jewish scholarship. In Andalusia, he formed a lasting friendship with the famous poet and philosopher Moses Ibn Ezra. He later settled in Toledo, where he practiced medicine; after concerted attacks there on Jews by Christians, he returned to the Muslim area of Cordoba.

Halevy was also known as a philosopher. In his *Book of the Kuzari* he

---

8. Qur'an 58, 12.
9. Qur'an 47, 18.

developed a philosophy of history, as a dialogue between intuitive religious truths and speculative logical or rational truths, giving preference to the former. He left on a pilgrimage to Palestine around 1140, staying in Alexandria on the way. The place of his death has never been determined.

[Soaring Wind]*

Soaring wind, when the day's
heat begins to wane, bear

greetings to my companion:
All I ask is remembrance

of that parting day,
love's first pact

under the leaves
of an apple tree.

[Life's Source]*

Toward life's true source I run,
fleeing senseless barren days, to
see my King's visage my sole intent:
only before Him do I tremble, I
exalt no other—if I but beheld
Him in a dream I would sleep an
endless sleep and never rise—
having gazed at His face within
my heart's core, my eyes would
no longer seek vision without.

USĀMA IBN MUNQIDH (1095–1188)
Arabic

The Crusades began in 1095, the same year that Usāma ibn Munqidh was born in Syria. Usāma was a nobleman and a warrior, and his family's castle can still be visited in the mountains of western Syria. In his classic work, *The Book of Reflections* (*Kitāb al-Iᶜtibār*), East meets West, but also, autobiography meets anecdote. Usāma is an interesting narrator: he describes life with his family and

*Translated by Ammiel Alcalay.

life with the Crusaders. These delightful and candid evaluations are unparalleled in medieval Arabic literature. At the same time, they show what Arabs of the period felt about the Western invaders.

from *The Book of Reflections*

USAMAH: *A Muslim View of the Crusaders*

Mysterious are the works of the Creator, the author of all things! When one comes to recount cases regarding the Franks, he cannot but glorify Allah (exalted is he!) and sanctify him, for he sees them as animals possessing the virtues of courage and fighting, but nothing else, just as animals have only the virtues of strength and carrying loads. I shall now give some instances of their doings and their curious mentality.

In the army of King Fulk, son of Fulk, was a Frankish reverend knight who had just arrived from their land in order to make the holy pilgrimage and then return home. He was of my intimate fellowship and kept such constant company with me that he began to call me "my brother." Between us were mutual bonds of amity and friendship. When he resolved to return by sea to his homeland, he said to me:

"My brother, I am leaving for my country and I want thee to send with me thy son (my son, who was then fourteen years old, was at that time in my company) to our country, where he can see the knights and learn wisdom and chivalry. When he returns, he will be like a wise man."

Thus there fell upon my ears words which would never come out of the head of a sensible man; for even if my son were to be taken captive, his captivity could not bring him a worse misfortune than carrying him into the lands of the Franks. However, I said to the man:

"By thy life, this has been exactly my idea. But the only thing that prevented me from carrying it out was the fact that his grandmother, my mother, is so fond of him that she did not this time let him come out with me until she exacted an oath from me to the effect that I would return him to her."

Thereupon he asked, "Is thy mother still alive?" "Yes," I replied. "Well," said he, "disobey her not."

A case illustrating their curious medicine is the following:

The lord of al-Munaytirah[1] wrote to my uncle asking him to dispatch a physician to treat certain sick persons among his people. My uncle sent him a Christian physician named Thābit. Thābit was absent but ten days when he returned. So we said to him, "How quickly hast thou healed thy patients!" He said:

Translated by Philip K. Hitt.

1. In Lebanon near Afqah, the source of Nahr-Ibrāhīm, i.e., ancient Adonis.

They brought before me a knight in whose leg an abscess had grown, and a woman afflicted with imbecility.[2] To the knight I applied a small poultice until the abscess opened and became well; and the woman I put on diet and made her humor wet. Then a Frankish physician came to them and said, "This man knows nothing about treating them." He then said to the knight, "Which wouldst thou prefer, living with one leg or dying with two?" The latter replied, "Living with one leg." The physician said, "Bring me a strong knight and a sharp ax." A knight came with the ax. And I was standing by. Then the physician laid the leg of the patient on a block of wood and bade the knight strike his leg with the ax and chop it off at one blow. Accordingly he struck it—while I was looking on—one blow, but the leg was not severed. He dealt another blow, upon which the marrow of the leg flowed out and the patient died on the spot. He then examined the woman and said, "This is a woman in whose head there is a devil which has possessed her. Shave off her hair." Accordingly they shaved it off and the woman began once more to eat their ordinary diet—garlic and mustard. Her imbecility took a turn for the worse. The physician then said, "The devil has penetrated through her head." He therefore took a razor, made a deep cruciform incision on it, peeled off the skin at the middle of the incision until the bone of the skull was exposed, and rubbed it with salt. The woman also expired instantly. Thereupon I asked them whether my services were needed any longer, and when they replied in the negative I returned home, having learned of their medicine what I knew not before.

I have, however, witnessed a case of their medicine which was quite different from that.

The king of the Franks[3] had for treasurer a knight named Bernard, who (may Allah's curse be upon him!) was one of the most accursed and wicked among the Franks. A horse kicked him in the leg, which was subsequently infected and which opened in fourteen different places. Every time one of these cuts would close in one place, another would open in another place. All this happened while I was praying for his perdition. Then came to him a Frankish physician and removed from the leg all the ointments which were on it and began to wash it with very strong vinegar. By this treatment all the cuts were healed and the man became well again. He was up again like a devil.

Another case illustrating their curious medicine is the following:

In Shayzar we had an artisan named abu-al-Fatḥ, who had a boy whose neck was afflicted with scrofula. Every time a part of it would close, another part would open. This man happened to go to Antioch on business of his, accompanied by his son. A Frank noticed the boy and asked his father about him. Abu-al-Fatḥ replied, "This is my son." The Frank said to him, "Wilt thou swear by thy religion that if I prescribe to thee a medicine which will cure thy boy, thou wilt charge nobody fees for prescribing it thyself? In that case, I shall prescribe to thee a medicine which will cure the boy." The man took the oath and the Frank said:

---

2. Arabic *nashāf*, "dryness," is not used as a name of a disease. I take the word therefore to be Persian *nishāf*—"imbecility."

3. Fulk of Anjou, king of Jerusalem (1131–1142).

"Take uncrushed leaves of glasswort, burn them, then soak the ashes in olive oil and sharp vinegar. Treat the scrofula[4] with them until the spot on which it is growing is eaten up. Then take burnt lead, soak it in ghee butter[5] and treat him with it. That will cure him."

The father treated the boy accordingly, and the boy was cured. The sores closed, and the boy returned to his normal condition of health.

I have myself treated with this medicine many who were afflicted with such disease, and the treatment was successful in removing the cause of the complaint.

Everyone who is a fresh emigrant from the Frankish lands is ruder in character than those who have become acclimatized and have held long association with the Moslems. Here is an illustration of their rude character.

Whenever I visited Jerusalem I always entered the Aqsa Mosque,[6] beside which stood a small mosque which the Franks had converted into a church. When I used to enter the Aqsa Mosque, which was occupied by the Templars[7] who were my friends, the Templars would evacuate the little adjoining mosque so that I might pray in it. One day[8] I entered this mosque, repeated the first formula, "Allah is great," and stood up in the act of praying, upon which one of the Franks rushed on me, got hold of me and turned my face eastward, saying, "This is the way thou shouldst pray!" A group of Templars hastened to him, seized him and repelled him from me. I resumed my prayer. The same man, while the others were otherwise busy, rushed once more on me and turned my face eastward, saying, "This is the way thou shouldst pray!" The Templars again came in to him and expelled him. They apologized to me, saying, "This is a stranger who has only recently arrived from the land of the Franks and he has never before seen anyone praying except eastward." Thereupon I said to myself, "I have had enough prayer." So I went out, and have ever been surprised at the conduct of this devil of a man, at the change in the color of his face, his trembling, and his sentiment at the sight of one praying towards the *qiblah*.[9]

I saw one of the Franks come to al-Amīr Muᶜīn-al-Dīn (may Allah's mercy rest upon his soul!) when he was in the Dome of the Rock,[10] and say to him, "Dost thou want to see God as a child?" Muᶜīn-al-Dīn said, "Yes." The Frank walked ahead of us until he showed us the picture of Mary with Christ (may peace be upon him!) as an infant in her lap. He then said, "This is God as a child." But Allah is exalted far above what the infidels say about him!

The Franks are void of all zeal and jealousy. One of them may be walking along with his wife. He meets another man who takes the wife by the hand and steps aside to converse with her while the husband is standing on one side waiting

---

4. A skin disease.
5. Clarified butter.
6. A holy mosque in Jerusalem.
7. Knights of the Temple, a crusading order.
8. About 1140.

9. The direction of the Kaᶜbah in the holy city, Mecca.
10. *al-ṣakhrah*, the mosque, standing near al-Aqsa in Jerusalem.

for his wife to conclude the conversation. If she lingers too long for him, he leaves her alone with the conversant and goes away.

Here is an illustration which I myself witnessed:

When I used to visit Nāblus,[11] I always took lodging with a man named Muᶜizz, whose home was a lodging house for the Moslems. The house had windows which opened to the road, and there stood opposite to it on the other side of the road a house belonging to a Frank who sold wine for the merchants. He would take some wine in a bottle and go around announcing it by shouting, "So and so, the merchant, has just opened a cask full of this wine. He who wants to buy some of it will find it in such and such a place." The Frank's pay for the announcement made would be the wine in that bottle. One day this Frank went home and found a man with his wife in the same bed. He asked him, "What could have made thee enter into my wife's room?" The man replied, "I was tired, so I went in to rest." "But how," asked he, "didst thou get into my bed?" The other replied, "I found a bed that was spread, so I slept in it." "But," said he, "my wife was sleeping together with thee!" The other replied, "Well, the bed is hers. How could I therefore have prevented her from using her own bed?" "By the truth of my religion," said the husband, "if thou shouldst do it again, thou and I would have a quarrel." Such was for the Frank the entire expression of his disapproval and the limit of his jealousy.

Another illustration:

We had with us a bath-keeper named Sālim, originally an inhabitant of al-Maᶜarrah,[12] who had charge of the bath of my father (may Allah's mercy rest upon his soul!). This man related the following story:

"I once opened a bath in al-Maᶜarrah in order to earn my living. To this bath there came a Frankish knight. The Franks disapprove of girding a cover around one's waist while in the bath. So this Frank stretched out his arm and pulled off my cover from my waist and threw it away. He looked and saw that I had recently shaved off my pubes. So he shouted, "Sālim!" As I drew near him he stretched his hand over my pubes and said, "Sālim, good! By the truth of my religion, do the same for me." Saying this, he lay on his back and I found that in that place the hair was like his beard. So I shaved it off. Then he passed his hand over the place and, finding it smooth, he said, "Sālim, by the truth of my religion, do the same to madame [al-dāma]" (al-dāma in their language means the lady), referring to his wife. He then said to a servant of his, "Tell madame to come here." Accordingly the servant went and brought her and made her enter the bath. She also lay on her back. The knight repeated, "Do what thou hast done to me." So I shaved all that hair while her husband was sitting looking at me. At last he thanked me and handed me the pay for my service."

Consider now this great contradiction! They have neither jealousy nor zeal, but they have great courage, although courage is nothing but the product of zeal and of ambition to be above ill repute.

Here is a story analogous to the one related above:

---

11. Neapolis, ancient Shechem.

12. Maᶜarrat-al-Nuᶜmān, between Hamāh and Aleppo.

I entered the public bath in Ṣūr [Tyre] and took my place in a secluded part. One of my servants thereupon said to me, "There is with us in the bath a woman." When I went out, I sat on one of the stone benches and behold! the woman who was in the bath had come out all dressed and was standing with her father just opposite me. But I could not be sure that she was a woman. So I said to one of my companions, "By Allah, see if this is a woman," by which I meant that he should ask about her. But he went, as I was looking at him, lifted the end of her robe and looked carefully at her. Thereupon her father turned toward me and said, "This is my daughter. Her mother is dead and she has nobody to wash her hair. So I took her in with me to the bath and washed her head." I replied, "Thou hast well done! This is something for which thou shalt be rewarded [by Allah]!"

A curious case relating to their medicine is the following, which was related to me by William of Bures, the lord of Ṭabarayyah [Tiberias], who was one of the principal chiefs among the Franks. It happened that William had accompanied al-Amīr Muᶜīn-al-Dīn (may Allah's mercy rest upon his soul!) from ᶜAkka to Ṭabarayyah when I was in his company too. On the way William related to us the following story in these words:

"We had in our country a highly esteemed knight who was taken ill and was on the point of death. We thereupon came to one of our great priests and said to him, 'Come with us and examine so and so, the knight.' 'I will,' he replied, and walked along with us, while were were assured in ourselves that if he would only lay his hand on him the patient would recover. When the priest saw the patient, he said, 'Bring me some wax.' We fetched him a little wax, which he softened and shaped like the knuckles of fingers, and he stuck one in each nostril. The knight died on the spot. We said to him, 'He is dead.' 'Yes,' he replied, 'he was suffering great pain, so I closed up his nose that he might die and get relief.'

Let this go and let us resume the discussion regarding Harim.[13]

We shall now leave the discussion of their treatment of the orifices of the body to something else.

I found myself in Ṭabarayyah at the time the Franks were celebrating one of their feasts. The cavaliers went out to exercise with lances. With them went out two decrepit, aged women whom they stationed at one end of the race course. At the other end of the field they left a pig which they had scalded and laid on a rock. They then made the two aged women run a race while each one of them was accompanied by a detachment of horsemen urging her on. At every step they took, the women would fall down and rise again, while the spectators would laugh. Finally one of them got ahead of the other and won that pig for a prize.

I attended one day a duel in Nāblus between two Franks. The reason for this was that certain Moslem thieves took by surprise one of the villages of Nāblus. One of the peasants of that village was charged with having acted as guide for the

---

13. A hemistich quoted from the pre-Islamic poet Zuhayr ibn-abi-Sulma al-Muzani.

thieves when they fell upon the village. So he fled away. The king[14] sent and arrested his children. The peasant thereupon came back to the king and said, "Let justice be done in my case. I challenge to a duel the man who claimed that I guided the thieves to the village." The king then said to the tenant who held the village in fief, "Bring forth someone to fight the duel with him." The tenant went to his village, where a blacksmith lived, took hold of him and ordered him to fight the duel. The tenant became thus sure of the safety of his own peasants, none of whom would be killed and his estate ruined.

I saw this blacksmith. He was a physically strong young man, but his heart failed him. He would walk a few steps and then sit down and ask for a drink. The one who had made the challenge was an old man, but he was strong in spirit and he would rub the nail of his thumb against that of the forefinger in defiance, as if he was not worrying over the duel. Then came the viscount, the seignior of the town, and gave each one of the two contestants a cudgel and a shield and arranged the people in a circle around them.

The two met. The old man would press the blacksmith backward until he would get him as far as the circle, then he would come back to the middle of the arena. They went on exchanging blows until they looked like pillars smeared with blood. The contest was prolonged and the viscount began to urge them to hurry, saying, "Hurry on." The fact that the smith was given to the use of the hammer proved now of great advantage to him. The old man was worn out and the smith gave him a blow which made him fall. His cudgel fell under his back. The smith knelt down over him and tried to stick his fingers into the eyes of his adversary, but could not do it because of the great quantity of blood flowing out. Then he rose up and hit his head with the cudgel until he killed him. They then fastened a rope around the neck of the dead person, dragged him away and hanged him. The lord who brought the smith now came, gave the smith his own mantle, made him mount the horse behind him, and rode off with him. This case illustrates the kind of jurisprudence and legal decisions the Franks have—may Allah's curse be upon them!

I once went in the company of al-Amīr Muʿīn-al-Dīn (may Allah's mercy rest upon his soul!) to Jerusalem. We stopped at Nāblus. There a blind man, a Moslem, who was still young and was well dressed, presented himself before al-Amīr carrying fruits for him and asked permission to be admitted into his service in Damascus. The Amīr consented. I inquired about this man and was informed that his mother had been married to a Frank whom she had killed. Her son used to practice ruses against the Frankish pilgrims and co-operate with his mother in assassinating them. They finally brought charges against him and tried his case according to the Frankish way of procedure.

They installed a huge cask and filled it with water. Across it they set a board of wood. They then bound the arms of the man charged with the act, tied a rope around his shoulders, and dropped him into the cask, their idea being that in case he was innocent, he would sink in the water and they would then lift him up with

---

14. Fulk of Anjou, king of Jerusalem again.

the rope so that he might not die in the water; and in case he was guilty, he would not sink in the water. This man did his best to sink when they dropped him into the water, but he could not do it. So he had to submit to their sentence against him—may Allah's curse be upon them! They pierced his eyeballs with red-hot awls.

Later this same man arrived in Damascus. Al-Amīr Muʿīn-al-Dīn (may Allah's mercy rest upon his soul!) assigned him a stipend large enough to meet all his needs and said to a slave of his, "Conduct him to Burhān-al-Dīn al-Balkhi (may Allah's mercy rest upon his soul!) and ask him on my behalf to order somebody to teach this man the Koran and something of Moslem jurisprudence." Hearing that, the blind man remarked, "May triumph and victory be thine! But this was never my thought." "What didst thou think I was going to do for thee?" asked Muʿīn-al-Dīn. The blind man replied, "I thought thou wouldst give me a horse, a mule and a suit of armor and make me a knight." Muʿīn-al-Dīn then said, "I never thought that a blind man could become a knight."

Among the Franks are those who have become acclimatized and have associated long with the Moslems. These are much better than the recent comers from the Frankish lands. But they constitute the exception and cannot be treated as a rule.

Here is an illustration. I dispatched one of my men to Antioch on business. There was in Antioch at that time al-Ra'īs Theodoros Sophianos, to whom I was bound by mutual ties of amity. His influence in Antioch was supreme. One day he said to my man, "I am invited by a friend of mine who is a Frank. Thou shouldst come with me so that thou mayest see their fashions." My man related the story in the following words:

"I went along with him and we came to the home of a knight who belonged to the old category of knights who came with the early expeditions of the Franks. He had been by that time stricken off the register and exempted from service, and possessed in Antioch an estate on the income of which he lived. The knight presented an excellent table, with food extraordinarily clean and delicious. Seeing me abstaining from food, he said, "Eat, be of good cheer! I never eat Frankish dishes, but I have Egyptian women cooks and never eat except their cooking. Besides, pork never enters my home." I ate, but guardedly, and after that we departed.

As I was passing in the market place, a Frankish woman all of a sudden hung to my clothes and began to mutter words in their language, and I could not understand what she was saying. This made me immediately the center of a big crowd of Franks. I was convinced that death was at hand. But all of a sudden that same knight approached. On seeing me, he came and said to that woman, "What is the matter between thee and this Moslem?" She replied, "This is he who has killed my brother Hurso." This Hurso was a knight in Afāmiyah who was killed by someone of the army of Hamāh. The Christian knight shouted at her, saying, "This is a bourgeois (i.e., a merchant) who neither fights nor attends a fight." He also yelled at the people who had assembled, and they all dispersed. Then he took me by the hand and went away. Thus the effect of that meal was my deliverance from certain death."

FARĪD AL-DĪN ᶜATTĀR (1142?–1230?)
Persian

A poet and mystic, Farīd al-Dīn ᶜAttār lived in Nishapur, an important center of mysticism, where he practiced as a pharmacist (hence "attar"). He produced mystical literature in poetry and prose, as well as an influential collection of biographies of mystic saints. His epic poem *The Conference of the Birds* [*Mantiq al-Tayr*], given here in a prose translation, is his most enduringly popular work. This poetic adventure tells of the search on the part of all the birds for the mythical bird known as the Sīmurgh, whom they regard as their king. Of the thousands of birds that gather, only thirty birds (*sī murgh* in Persian) finally embark on the journey. A mystical allegory of the pilgrim soul's search for union with God, the poem ends when the thirty, *sī murgh,* understand that they themselves are the being they so ardently seek.

from *The Conference of the Birds*

The Bird Parliament

All of the birds of the world, known and unknown, were assembled together. They said: "No country in the world is without a king. How comes it, then, that the kingdom of the birds is without a ruler? This state of things cannot last. We must make effort together and search for one; for no country can have a good administration and a good organization without a king."

So they began to consider how to set out on their quest. The Hoopoe,[1] excited and full of hope, came forward and placed herself in the middle of the assembled birds. On her breast was the ornament which symbolized that she had entered the way of spiritual knowledge; the crest on her head was as the crown of truth, and she had knowledge of both good and evil.

"Dear Birds," she began, "I am one who is engaged in divine warfare, and I am a messenger of the world invisible. I have knowledge of God and of the secrets of creation. When one carries on his beak, as I do, the name of God, Bismillah, it follows that one must have knowledge of many hidden things. Yet my days pass restlessly and I am concerned with no person, for I am wholly occupied by love for the King. I can find water by instinct, and I know many other secrets. I talk with Solomon and am the foremost of his followers. It is astonishing that he neither asked nor sought for those who were absent from his kingdom, yet when I was away from him for a day he sent his messengers everywhere, and, since he could not be without me for a moment, my worth is established forever. I carried his letters, and I was his confidential companion. The bird who is sought after by

Translated by S. C. Nott.

1. A bird.

means "30 birds"

the prophet Solomon merits a crown for his head. The bird who is well spoken of by God, how can he trail his feathers in the dust? For years I have travelled by sea and land, over mountains and valleys. I covered an immense space in the time of the deluge; I accompanied Solomon on his journeys, and I have measured the bounds of the world.

"I know well my King, but alone I cannot set out to find him. Abandon your timidity, your self-conceit and your unbelief, for he who makes light of his own life is delivered from himself; he is delivered from good and evil in the way of his beloved. Be generous with your life. Set your feet upon the earth and step out joyfully for the court of the King. We have a true King, he lives behind the mountains called Kāf. His name is Simurgh and he is the King of birds. He is close to us, but we are far from him. The place where he dwells is inaccessible, and no tongue is able to utter his name. Before him hang a hundred thousand veils of light and darkness, and in the two worlds no one has power to dispute his kingdom. He is the sovereign lord and is bathed in the perfection of his majesty. He does not manifest himself completely even in the place of his dwelling, and to this no knowledge or intelligence can attain. The way is unknown, and no one has the steadfastness to seek it, though thousands of creatures spend their lives in longing. Even the purest soul cannot describe him, neither can the reason comprehend: these two eyes are blind. The wise cannot discover his perfection nor can the man of understanding perceive his beauty. All creatures have wished to attain to this perfection and beauty by imagination. But how can you tread that path with thought? How measure the moon from the fish? So thousands of heads go here and there, like the ball in polo, and only lamentations and sighs of longing are heard. Many lands and seas are on the way. Do not imagine that the journey is short; and one must have the heart of a lion to follow this unusual road, for it is very long and the sea is deep. One plods along in a state of amazement, sometimes smiling, sometimes weeping. As for me, I shall be happy to discover even a trace of him. That would indeed be something, but to live without him would be a reproach. A man must not keep his soul from the beloved, but must be in a fitting state to lead his soul to the court of the King. Wash your hands of this life if you would be called a man of action. For your beloved, renounce this dear life of yours, as worthy men. If you submit with grace, the beloved will give his life for you.

"An astonishing thing! The first manifestation of the Simurgh took place in China in the middle of the night. One of his feathers fell on China and his reputation filled the world. Everyone made a picture of this feather, and from it formed his own system of ideas, and so fell into a turmoil. This feather is still in the picture-gallery of that country; hence the saying, 'Seek knowledge, even in China!'

"But for his manifestation there would not have been so much noise in the world concerning this mysterious Being. This sign of his existence is a token of his glory. All souls carry an impression of the image of his feather. Since the description of it has neither head nor tail, beginning nor end, it is not necessary to say more about it. Now, any of you who are for this road, prepare yourselves, and put your feet on the Way."

When the Hoopoe had finished, the birds began excitedly to discuss the glory of this King, and seized with longing to have him for their own sovereign, they were all impatient to be off. They resolved to go together; each became a friend to the other and an enemy to himself. But when they began to realize how long and painful their journey was to be, they hesitated, and in spite of their apparent good will began to excuse themselves, each according to his type.

One bird said to the Hoopoe: "O you who know the road of which you have told us and on which you wish us to accompany you, to me the way is dark, and in the gloom it appears to be very difficult, and many parasangs in length."

The Hoopoe replied: "We have seven valleys to cross, and only after we have crossed them shall we discover the Simurgh. No one has ever come back into the world who has made this journey, and it is impossible to say how many parasangs there are in front of us. Be patient, O fearful one, since all those who went by this road were in your state.

"The first valley is the Valley of the Quest, the second the Valley of Love, the third is the Valley of Understanding, the fourth is the Valley of Independence and Detachment, the fifth of Pure Unity, the sixth is the Valley of Astonishment, and the seventh is the Valley of Poverty and Nothingness, beyond which one can go no farther."

When the birds had listened to this discourse of the Hoopoe their heads dropped down, and sorrow pierced their hearts. Now they understood how difficult it would be for a handful of dust like themselves to bend such a bow. So great was their agitation that numbers of them died then and there. But others, in spite of their distress, decided to set out on the long road. For years they travelled over mountains and valleys, and a great part of their life flowed past on this journey. But how is it possible to relate all that happened to them? It would be necessary to go with them and see their difficulties for oneself, and to follow the wanderings of this long road. Only then could one realize what the birds suffered.

In the end, only a small number of all this great company arrived at that sublime place to which the Hoopoe had led them. Of the thousands of birds, almost all had disappeared. Many had been lost in the ocean; others had perished on the summits of the high mountains, tortured by thirst; others had had their wings burnt and their hearts dried up by the fire of the sun; others were devoured by tigers and panthers; others died of fatigue in the deserts and in the wilderness, their lips parched and their bodies overcome by the heat. Some went mad and killed each other for a grain of barley; others, enfeebled by suffering and weariness, dropped on the road, unable to go farther; others, bewildered by the things they saw, stopped where they were, stupefied; and many who had started out from curiosity or pleasure, perished without an idea of what they had set out to find.

So then out of all those thousands of birds, only thirty reached the end of the journey. And even these were bewildered, weary and dejected, with neither feathers nor wings. But now they were at the door of this Majesty that cannot be described, whose essence is incomprehensible—that Being who is beyond human reason and knowledge. Then flashed the lightning of fulfilment, and a hundred worlds were consumed in a moment. They saw thousands of suns, each more resplendent than the other, thousands of moons and stars all equally beautiful, and seeing all this they were amazed and agitated like a dancing atom of dust, and they cried out: "O Thou who art more radiant than the sun! Thou who hast reduced the sun to an atom, how can we appear before Thee? Ah, why have we so uselessly endured all this suffering on the Way? Having renounced ourselves and all things, we now cannot obtain that for which we have striven. Here it little matters whether we exist or not."

Then the birds, who were so disheartened that they resembled a cock half-killed, sank into despair. A long time passed. When, at a propitious moment, the door suddenly opened, there stepped out a noble Chamberlain, one of the courtiers of the Supreme Majesty. He looked them over and saw that out of thousands, only these thirty birds were left.

He said: "Now then, O Birds, where have you come from, and what are you doing here? What is your name? O you who are destitute of everything, where is your home? What do they call you in the world? What can be done with a feeble handful of dust like you?"

"We have come," they said, "to acknowledge the Simurgh as our King. Through love and desire for him we have lost our reason and our peace of mind. Very long ago, when we started on this journey, we were thousands, and now only thirty of us have arrived at this sublime court. We cannot believe that the King will scorn us after all the sufferings we have gone through. Ah, no! He cannot but look on us with the eye of benevolence!"

The Chamberlain replied: "O you whose minds and hearts are troubled, whether you exist or do not exist in the universe, the King has his being always and eternally. Thousands of worlds of creatures are no more than an ant at his gate. You bring nothing but moans and lamentations. Return then to whence you came, O vile handful of earth!"

At this the birds were petrified with astonishment. Nevertheless, when they came to themselves a little, they said: "Will this great King reject us so ignominiously? And if he really has this attitude to us, may he not change it to one of honour? Remember Majnūn, who said: 'If all the people who dwell on earth wished to sing my praises, I would not accept them; I would rather have the insults of Laila.[2] One of her insults is more to me than a hundred compliments from another woman!'"

"The lightning of his glory manifests itself," said the Chamberlain, "and it lifts up the reason of all souls. What benefit is there if the soul be consumed by a hundred sorrows? What benefit is there at this moment in either greatness or littleness?"

The birds, on fire with love, said: "How can the moth save itself from the flame when it wishes to be one with the flame? The friend we seek will content us by allowing us to be united to him. If now we are refused, what is there left for us

---

2. The classic Arabic star-crossed lovers.

to do? We are like the moth who wished for union with the flame of the candle. They begged him not to sacrifice himself so foolishly and for such an impossible aim, but he thanked them for their advice and told them that since his heart was given to the flame forever, nothing else mattered."

Then the Chamberlain, having tested them, opened the door; and as he drew aside a hundred curtains, one after the other, a new world beyond the veil was revealed. Now was the light of lights manifested, and all of them sat down on the masnad, the seat of the Majesty and Glory. They were given a writing which they were told to read through; and reading this, and pondering, they were able to understand their state. When they were completely at peace and detached from all things, they became aware that the Simurgh was there with them, and a new life began for them in the Simurgh. All that they had done previously was washed away. The sun of Majesty sent forth his rays, and in the reflection of each other's faces these thirty birds (si-murgh) of the outer world contemplated the face of the Simurgh of the inner world. This so astonished them that they did not know if they were still themselves or if they had become the Simurgh. At last, in a state of contemplation, they realized that they were the Simurgh and that the Simurgh was the thirty birds. When they gazed at the Simurgh they saw that it was truly the Simurgh who was there, and when they turned their eyes toward themselves they saw that they themselves were the Simurgh. And perceiving both at once, themselves and Him, they realized that they and the Simurgh were one and the same being. No one in the world has ever heard of anything to equal it.

Then they gave themselves up to meditation, and after a little they asked the Simurgh, without the use of tongues, to reveal to them the secret of the mystery of the unity and plurality of beings. The Simurgh, also without speaking, made this reply: "The sun of my majesty is a mirror. He who sees himself therein sees his soul and his body, and sees them completely. Since you have come as thirty birds, si-murgh, you will see thirty birds in this mirror. If forty or fifty were to come, it would be the same. Although you are now completely changed, you see yourselves as you were before.

"Can the sight of an ant reach to the far-off Pleiades? And can this insect lift an anvil? Have you ever seen a gnat seize an elephant in its teeth? All that you have known, all that you have seen, all that you have said or heard—all this is no longer that. When you crossed the valleys of the Spiritual Way and when you performed good tasks, you did all this by my action; and you were able to see the valleys of my essence and my perfections. You, who are only thirty birds, did well to be astonished, impatient and wondering. But I am more than thirty birds. I am the very essence of the true Simurgh. Annihilate then yourselves gloriously and joyfully in me, and in me you shall find yourselves."

Thereupon the birds at last lost themselves forever in the Simurgh—the shadow was lost in the sun, and that is all.

All that you have heard or seen or known is not even the beginning of what you must know, and since the ruined habitation of this world is not your place you must renounce it. Seek the trunk of the tree, and do not worry about whether the branches do or do not exist.

When a hundred thousand generations had passed, the mortal birds surrendered themselves spontaneously to total annihilation. No man, neither young nor old, can speak fittingly of death or immortality. Even as these things are far from us, so the description of them is beyond all explanation or definition. If my readers wish for an allegorical explanation of the immortality that follows annihilation, it will be necessary for me to write another book. So long as you are identified with the things of the world you will not set out on the Path, but when the world no longer binds you, you enter as in a dream, and knowing the end, you see the benefit. A germ is nourished among a hundred cares and loves so that it may become an intelligent and acting being. It is instructed and given the necessary knowledge. Then death comes and everything is effaced, its dignity is thrown down. This that was a being has become the dust of the street. It has several times been annihilated; but in the meanwhile it has been able to learn a hundred secrets of which previously it had not been aware, and in the end it receives immortality, and is given honour in place of dishonour. Do you know what you possess? Enter into yourself and reflect on this. So long as you do not realize your nothingness and so long as you do not renounce your self-pride, your vanity and your self-love, you will never reach the heights of immortality. On the Way you are cast down in dishonour and raised in honour.

And now my story is finished; I have nothing more to say.

IBN AL-ʿARABĪ (d. 1240)
Arabic

Known as al-Shaykh al-Akbar (The Greatest Shaykh), Ibn al-ʿArabī is possibly one of the greatest mystics of Islam. He was born in Andalusia, and lived in Spain and North Africa. An inveterate traveler, he journeyed East to perform the pilgrimage to Mecca and expand his intellectual and geographical horizons to include the Eastern lands of the Islamic world. Ibn al-ʿArabī was the most prolific of the mystic writers, with *The Meccan Revelations [al-Futūhāt al-Makkiyya]* being his most famous work. His influence extended beyond his own century and continues today. The poem here, "Gentle Now, Doves of the Thornberry and Moringa Thicket" (*alā yā hammāmāti l-arākati wa l-bāni*) typically mingles the thought and vocabulary of sacred and profane love.

Gentle Now, Doves of the Thornberry and Moringa Thicket

Gentle now,
doves of the thornberry and moringa thicket,
don't add to my heart-ache
your sighs.

Translated by Michael A. Sells.

Gentle now,
or your sad cooing
will reveal the love I hide
the sorrow I hide away.

I echo back, in the evening,
in the morning, echo,
the longing of a love-sick lover,
the moaning of the lost.

In a grove of tamarisks
spirits wrestled,
bending the limbs down over me,
passing me away.

They brought yearning,
breaking of the heart,
and other new twists of pain,
putting me through it.

Who is there for me in Jám^c,
and the Stoning-Place at Mína,
who for me at Tamarisk Grove,
or at the way-station of Na^{c}mān?

Hour by hour
they circle my heart
in rapture, in love-ache,
and touch my pillars with a kiss.

As the best of creation
circled the Ka^{c}ba,
which reason with its proofs
called unworthy,

And kissed the stones there—
and he was the Natiq!
And what is the house of stone
compared to a man or a woman?

They swore, and how often!
they'd never change—piling up vows.
She who dyes herself red with henna
is faithless.

A white-blazed gazelle
is an amazing sight,
red-dye signalling,
eyelids hinting,

5

10

15

20

25

30

35

40

Pasture between breastbones   45
and innards.
Marvel,
a garden among the flames!

My heart can take on
any form: 50
a meadow for gazelles,
a cloister for monks,

For the idols, sacred ground,
Kaᶜba for the circling pilgrim,
the tables of the Torah,   55
the scrolls of the Qurʾán.

I profess the religion of love;
wherever its caravan turns long the way,
that is the belief,
the faith I keep.   60

Like Bishr,
Hind and her sister,
love-mad Qays and his lost Láyla,
Máyya and her lover Ghaylán.

JALĀL AL-DĪN RŪMĪ (1207?–1273)
Persian

A theologian and a mystic, Jalāl al-Dīn Rūmī was born in Balkh. As a child, he
fled with his family from his native city and after years of traveling through the
central Islamic lands, the group finally made Konya, the Seljug capital, their
home. There, Rūmī's infatuation with another mystic, Shams al-Dīn, known as
Shams-i Tabrīzī (*shams* means sun), altered his life: the poem here speaks of their
reunion in the language of mystical love. Generally considered the most brilliant
of the Persian mystic poets, Rūmī founded the Mawlawi order, one of the
fraternal mystical orders that began to form during the thirteenth century.

[Blessed Moment]

Blessed moment. Here we sit in this palace of love, you and I.
We have two shapes, two bodies, but a single soul, you and I.

Translated by Talat Sait Halman.

The colors of the gardens and the songs of the birds
Among the flower-beds will make us immortal, you and I.

The stars of heaven will come out to gaze at us—
We shall show the stars the moon herself, you and I.

United in ecstasy, we shall no longer be you or I.
Rescued from foolish babble, we shall rejoice, you and I.

All the bright-plumed birds of paradise will plunge into grief
When they hear us laughing merrily, you and I.

SAᶜDÎ (1200?–1292)
Persian

Born in Shiraz, Saᶜdî studied in Baghdad, made more than one pilgrimage to
Mecca, and travelled widely. He is best known for *The Rose Garden [Gulistan]*, a
marvelous example of Persian *adab* literature. Like its Arabic cousin, the Persian
adab runs the gamut from prose to poetry. *The Rose Garden* covers topics ranging
from rulers to mystics to erotic exploits. (On the cover of an English translation,
for example, it is billed as "the Persian counterpart to the Kama Sutra.") This is
certainly quite a claim, but it does testify to the appeal of the work, which was one
of the first oriental texts translated into a European language, and this as early as
the seventeenth century. As a compendium of worldly wisdom, it is unsurpassed.

from *The Rose Garden [Gulistan]*

[The Thorn Without the Rose]

The beautiful wife of a man died but her mother, a decrepit old hag, remained in
the house on account of the dowry. The man saw no means of escaping from
contact with her until a company of friends paid him a visit of condolence and one
of them asked him how he bore the loss of his beloved. He replied: "It is not as
painful not to see my wife as to see the mother of my wife."

> The rose has been destroyed and the thorn remained.
> The treasure has been taken and the serpent left[1]
> It is better that one's eye be fixed on a spear-head
> Than that it should behold the face of an enemy.

Translated by Edward Rehatsek.

---

1. Generally in Eastern legend, the serpent
   guarding a treasure is killed before the
   treasure is removed; here, the opposite
   takes place.

It is incumbent to sever connection with a thousand friends
Rather than to behold a single foe.

[A Beauty Brings a Beverage]

I remember having in the days of my youth passed through a street, intending to see a moon-faced beauty. It was in Temuz[2] whose heat dried up the saliva in the mouth and whose simum[3] boiled the marrow in my bones. My weak human nature being unable to endure the scorching sun, I took refuge in the shadow of a wall, wishing someone might relieve me from the summer heat and quench my fire with some water; and lo, all of a sudden, from the darkness of the porch of a house a light shone forth, namely a beauty, the grace of which the tongue of eloquence is unable to describe. She came out like the rising dawn after an obscure night or the water of immortality gushing from a dark cavern, carrying in her hand a bowl of snow-water, into which sugar had been poured and essence of roses mixed. I knew not whether she had perfumed it with rose-water or whether a few drops from her rosy face had fallen into it. In short, I took the beverage from her beautiful hands, drank it and began to live again.

> The thirst of my heart cannot be quenched
> By sipping limpid water even if I drink oceans of it.

Blessed is the man of happy destiny whose eye
Alights every morning on such a countenance.
One drunk of wine awakens at midnight,
One drunk of the cupbearer on the morn of resurrection.

[A Leave-Taking]

In the year when Muhammad Khovarezm Shah concluded peace with the king of Khata to suit his own purpose, I entered the cathedral mosque of Kashgar and saw an extremely handsome, graceful boy as described in the simile:

Thy master has taught thee to coquet and to ravish hearts,
Instructed thee to oppose, to dally, to blame and to be severe.
A person of such figure, temper, stature and gait
I have not seen; perhaps he learnt these tricks from a fairy.

He was holding in his hand the introduction of Zamak-sharni's Arabic syntax and reciting: *Zaid struck Amru and was the injurer of Amru*. I said: "Boy! Khovarezm and Khata have concluded peace, and the quarrel between Zaid and Amru still subsists!" He smiled and asked for my birthplace. I replied: "The soil of Shiraz." He continued: "What rememberest thou of the compositions of Sa'di?" I recited:

---

2. The month of July.

3. The name of a fearfully hot wind blowing in the African deserts.

"I am tired by a nahvi⁴ who makes a furious attack
Upon me, like Zaid in his opposition to Amru.
When Zaid submits he does not raise his head
And how can elevation subsist when submission is the regent."⁵

He considered awhile and then said: "Most of his poetry current in this
country is in the Persian language. If thou wilt recite some, it will be more easily
understood." Then I said:

"When thy nature has enticed thee with syntax
It blotted out the form of intellect from our heart.
Alas, the hearts of lovers are captive in thy snare.
We are occupied with thee but thou with Amru and Zaid."

The next morning, when I was about to depart, some people told him that I
was Sa'di, whereon he came running to me and politely expressed his regret that
I had not revealed my identity before so that he might have girded his loins to
serve me in token of the gratitude due to the presence of a great man.

In spite of thy presence no voice came to say: I am he.

He also said: "What would it be if thou wert to spend in this country some
days in repose that we might derive advantage by serving thee?" I replied: "I
cannot on account of the following adventure which occurred to me:

I beheld an illustrious man in a mountain region
Who had contentedly retired from the world into a cave.
Why, said I, comest thou not into the city
For once to relax the bonds of thy heart?
He replied: "Fairy-faced maidens are there.
When clay is plentiful, elephants will stumble."

This I said. Then we kissed each other's heads and faces and took leave of
each other.

What profits it to kiss a friend's face
And at the same time to take leave of him?
Thou wouldst say that he who parts from friends is an apple.
One half of his face is red and the other yellow.

If I die not of grief on the day of separation
Reckon me not faithful in friendship.

[A Dervish Utters Wise Words]

A man in patched garments⁶ accompanied us in a caravan to the Hejaz and one of
the Arab amirs presented him with a hundred dinars to spend upon his family but

---

4. A student of syntax.
5. The play on words is on two grammatical
terms, the nominative *refa'*, which also

means raising, elevating, and the genitive
jarr, which also means pulling, submitting.
6. A dervish.

robbers of the Kufatcha tribe suddenly fell upon the caravan and robbed it clean of everything. The merchants began to wail and to cry, uttering vain shouts and lamentations.

> Whether thou implorest or complainest
> The robber will not return the gold again.

The dervish[7] alone had not lost his equanimity and showed no change. I asked: "Perhaps they have not taken thy money?" He replied: "Yes, they have but I was not so much accustomed to that money that separation therefrom could grieve my heart":

> The heart must not be tied to any thing or person
> Because to take off the heart is a difficult affair.

I replied: "What thou hast said resembles my case because, when I was young, my intimacy with a young man and my friendship for him were such that his beauty was the Qiblah[8] of my eye and the chief joy of my life union with him":

> Perhaps an angel in heaven but no mortal
> Can be on earth equal in beauty of form to him.
> I swear by the amity, after which companionship is illicit,
> No human sperm will ever become a man like him.

All of a sudden the foot of his life sank into the mire of non-existence. The smoke[9] of separation arose from his family. I kept him company on his grave for many days and one of my compositions on his loss is as follows:

> Would that on the day when the thorn of fate entered thy foot
> The hand of heaven had struck a sword on my head;
> So that this day my eye could not see the world without thee.
> Here I am on thy grave, would that it were over my head.

> He who could take neither rest nor sleep
> Before he had first scattered roses and narcissi.
> The turns of heaven have strewn the roses of his face.[10]
> Thorns and brambles are growing on his tomb.

After separation from him I resolved and firmly determined to fold up the carpet of pleasure during the rest of my life and to retire from mixing in society:

> Last night I strutted about like a peacock in the garden of union
> But today, through separation from my friend, I twist my head like a snake.
> The profit of the sea would be good if there were no fear of waves.
> The company of the rose would be sweet if there were no pain from thorns.

---

7. A Muslim mystic.
8. The direction toward Mecca in which all Moslems are bound to turn when they say their orisons; in Bombay they turn to the west and do not err much in doing so.

9. Grief.
10. More freely translated this would be "have blanched the roses of his cheeks."

[Looking from a Lover's Eye]

A king of the Arabs, having been informed of the relations subsisting between Laila and Mejnun, with an account of the latter's insanity, to the effect that he had in spite of his great accomplishments and eloquence, chosen to roam about in the desert and to let go the reins of self-control from his hands; he ordered him to be brought to his presence, and this having been done, he began to reprove him and to ask him what defect he had discovered in the nobility of the human soul that he adopted the habits of beasts and abandoned the society of mankind. Mejnun replied:

> *"Many friends have blamed me for loving her.*
> *Will they not see her one day and understand my excuse?"*

> Would that those who are reproving me
> Could see thy face, O ravisher of hearts,
> That instead of a lemon in thy presence
> They might heedlessly cut their hands.[11]

That the truth may bear witness to the assertion: *This is he for whose sake ye blamed me.*[12]

The king expressed a wish to see the beauty of Laila in order to ascertain the cause of so much distress. Accordingly he ordered her to be searched for. The encampments of various Arab families having been visited, she was found, conveyed to the king and led into the courtyard of the palace. The king looked at her outward form for some time and she appeared despicable in his sight because the meanest handmaids of his harem excelled her in beauty and attractions. Mejnun, who shrewdly understood the thoughts of the king, said: "It would have been necessary to look from the window of Mejnun's eye at the beauty of Laila when the mystery of her aspect would have been revealed to thee."

> *If the record of the glade which entered my ears*
> *Had been heard by the leaves of the glade they would have lamented with me.*
> *O company of friends, say to him who is unconcerned*
> *"Would that thou knewest what is in a pining heart!"*

> Who are healthy have no pain from wounds.
> I shall tell my grief to no one but a sympathizer.
> It is useless to speak of bees to one
> Who never in his life felt their sting.
> As long as thy state is not like mine
> My state will be but an idle tale to thee.

---

11. Zuleikha, the wife of Potiphar, knowing that her female friends would be extremely surprised at the wonderful beauty of Joseph, of whom they previously thought ill, used a stratagem to change their mind, as appears from the Qur'an, Ch. XII. v. 31, which gave rise to the allusion in the above verses; 'and when she had heard of their subtle behaviour, she sent unto them and prepared a banquet for them and she gave to each of them a knife; and then said to Joseph come forth to them. And when they saw him they praised him greatly and they cut their own hands and said: "O Allah, this is not a mortal, he is no other than an angel, deserving the highest respect." '

12. Qur'an, Ch. XII, part of v. 32.

[A Qazi Is Saved by His Wit]

It is related that the qazi[13] of Hamdan, having conceived affection towards a farrier-boy and the horseshoe of his heart being on fire, he sought for some time to meet him, roaming about and seeking for opportunities, according to the saying of chroniclers:

> That straight tall cypress my eyes beheld
> It robbed me of my heart and threw me down.
> Those wanton eyes have taken my heart with a lasso.
> If thou desirest to preserve thy heart shut thy eyes.

I was informed that the boy, who had heard something of the qazi's passion, happening to meet him in a thoroughfare, manifested immense wrath, assailed the qazi with disrespectful and insulting words, snatched up a stone and left no injury untried. The qazi said to an ullemma[14] of repute who happened to be of the same opinion with him:

> "Look at that sweetheart and his getting angry,
> And that bitter knot of his sweet eyebrow."

The Arab says: "*A slap from a lover is a raisin.*"[15]

> A blow from the hand on the mouth
> Is sweeter than eating bread with one's own hand.

In the same way the boy's impudence might be indicating kindness as padshahs utter hard words whilst they secretly wish for peace:

> Grapes yet unripe are sour.
> Wait two or three days, they will become sweet.

After saying these words he returned to his court of justice, where some respectable men connected with him kissed the ground of service and said: "With thy permission we shall, doing obeisance, speak some words to thee although they may be contrary to politeness because illustrious men have said:

> It is not permissible to argue on every topic.
> To find fault with great men is wrong.

"But as in consequence of favours conferred by thy lordship in former times upon thy servants it would be a kind of treachery to withhold the opinion they entertain, they inform thee that the proper way is not to yield to thy inclinations concerning this boy but to fold up the carpet of lascivious desires because thy dignity as qazi is high and must not be polluted by a base crime. The companion thou hast seen is this, and our words thou hast heard are these:

> One who has done many disreputable things
> Cares nothing for the reputation of anyone.

---

13. Or qadi, a Muslim judge.
14. In Arabic, ʿulamâ', plural of ʿâlim, meaning a class of learned men in Islam.

15. 'Sweet like a raisin.'

> Many a good name of fifty years
> Was trodden under foot by one bad name."[16]

The qazi approved of the unanimous advice of his friends and appreciated their good opinion as well as their steadfast fidelity, saying that the view taken by his beloved friends on the arrangement of his case was perfectly right and their arguments admitting of no contradiction. Nevertheless:

> *Although love ceases in consequence of reproval*
> *I heard that just men sometimes concoct falsehoods.*

> Blame me as much as thou listest
> Because blackness cannot be washed off from a negro.

> Nothing can blot out my remembrance of thee.
> I am a snake with broken head and cannot turn.

These words he said and sent some persons to make inquiries about him,[17] spending boundless money because it is said that whoever has gold in his hand possesses strength of arm and he who has no worldly goods has no friends in the whole world:

> Whoever has seen gold droops his head,
> Although he may be hard to bend like iron-backed scales.[18]

In short, one night he obtained privacy but during that night the police obtained information that the qazi is spending the whole of it with wine in his hand and a sweetheart on him bosom, enjoying himself, not sleeping, and singing:

> Has this cock perhaps not crowed at the proper time this night
> And have the lovers not had their fill of embrace, and kiss
> Whilst alas for only a moment the eye of confusion is asleep?
> Remain awake that life may not elapse in vain
> Till thou hearest the morning call from the Friday-mosque
> Or the noise of kettle-drums on Atabek's palace-gate.
> Lips against lips like the cock's eye[19]
> Are not to part at the crowing of a silly cock.

Whilst the qazi was in this state one of his dependants entered and said: "Arise and run as far as thy feet will carry thee because the envious have not only obtained a handle for vexation but have spoken the truth. We may, whilst the fire of confusion is yet burning low, perchance extinguish it with the water of stratagem but when it blazes up high it may destroy a world." The qazi, however, replied:

> "When the lion has his claws on the game
> What boots it if a jackal makes his appearance?

---

16. Or "by one imprudent act deserving a bad name."

17. That is to say, about the above-mentioned farrier boy.

18. Because when the scales are very heavily filled, even the iron rod from which they are suspended must bend.

19. The cock's eye designates a certain brilliant red flower to which beautiful lips are also sometimes compared.

Keep thy face on the face of the friend and leave
The foe to chew the back of his own hand in rage."

The same night information was also brought to the king that in his realm such a wickedness had been perpetrated and he was asked what he thought of it. He replied: "I know that he is one of the most learned men, and I account him to be the paragon of our age. As it is possible that enemies have devised a plot against him, I give no credit to this accusation unless I obtain ocular evidence because philosophers have said:

He who grasps the sword in haste
Will repenting carry the back of his hand to his teeth and bite it."

I heard that at dawn the king with some of his courtiers arrived at the pillow of the qazi, saw a lamp standing, the sweetheart sitting, the wine spilled, the goblet broken and the qazi plunged in the sleep of drunkenness, unaware of the realm of existence. The king awakened him gently and said: "Get up for the sun has risen." The qazi, who perceived the state of affairs, asked: "From what direction?" The sultan was astonished and replied: "From the east as usual." The qazi exclaimed: "Praise be to Allah! The door of repentance is yet open because according to tradition *the gate of repentance will not be locked against worshippers till the sun rises in its setting place.*"[20]

These two things impelled me to sin:
My ill-luck and my imperfect understanding.
If thou givest me punishment I deserve it
And if thou forgivest pardon is better than revenge.

The king replied: "As thou knowest that thou must suffer capital punishment, it is of no use to repent. *But their faith availed them not after they had beholden our vengeance.*[21]

"What is the use to promise to forego thieving
When a lasso cannot be thrown up to the palace?
Say to the tall man: 'Do not pluck the fruit,'
For he who is short cannot reach the branch.

"For thee, who hast committed such wickedness, there is no way of escape." After the king had uttered these words, the men appointed for the execution took hold of him, whereon he said: "I have one word more to speak in the service of the sultan." The king, who heard him, asked: "What is it?" And he recited:

"Thou who shakest the sleeve of displeasure upon me
Expect not that I shall withdraw my hand from thy skirt.
If escape be impossible from this crime which I committed
I trust to the clemency which thou possessest."

---

20. It is well known that the rising of the sun in the west instead of the east will be one of the signs of the resurrection and Day of Judgment.

21. Qur'an, Ch. XL, last verse, i.e., 85.

The king replied: "Thou hast adduced this wonderful sally and hast enounced a strange maxim but it is impossible according to reason and contrary to usage that thy accomplishments and eloquence should this day save thee from the punishment which I have decreed; and I consider it proper to throw thee headlong from the castle that others may take an example." He continued: "O lord of the world, I have been nourished by the bounty of this dynasty, and this crime was not committed only by me in the world. Throw another man headlong that I may take the example." The king burst out laughing, pardoned his crime and said to his dependents who desired the qazi to be slain:

> "Everyone of you who are bearers of your own faults
> Ought not to blame others for their defects."

[Falling into the Sea]

A virtuous and beauteous youth
Was pledged to a chaste maiden.
I read that in the great sea
They fell into a vortex together.
When a sailor came to take his hand,
Lest he might die in that condition,
He said in anguish from the waves:
"Leave me. Take the hand of my love."
Whilst saying this, he despaired of life.
In his agony he was heard to exclaim:
"Learn not the tale of love from the wretch
Who forgets his beloved in distress."
Thus the lives of the lovers terminated.
Learn from what has occurred that thou mayest know
Because Sa'di is of the ways and means of love affairs
Well aware in the Arabian city of Baghdad.
Tie thy heart to the heart-charmer thou possessest
And shut thy eye to all the rest of the world.
If Mejnun and Laila were to come to life again
They might indite a tale of love on this occurrence.

ᶜUBAYD-I ZĀKĀNĪ (d. 1371)
Persian

Zākānī can justifiably be considered the master satirist of medieval Persian literature. Born in Qazvīn, he studied in Baghdad before settling in Shiraz, where he was a contemporary of the poet Hāfiz. Much of the wit in his satirical works derives from a juxtaposition of the sacred and profane, sometimes tending to the obscene. Zākānī's satire is not for everyone: his works, as one Western critic puts it, "were, and continue to be, condemned as self-serving vulgarity."

[A Sequence of Satiric Anecdotes]

Sultan Maḥmūd[1] was attending a sermon in the Mosque. Talhak went there after him. When he arrived, the preacher stood up and said that if anyone had committed pederasty, then on the Day of Judgment the youth whom he had abused would be placed on his neck, and he would have to carry him over the Bridge of Doom. Sultan Maḥmūd wept. Talhak said, "O Sultan, do not weep but be of good cheer. On that day you won't have to go on foot either."

The Caliph al-Mahdī once got separated from his party during a hunt. In the night he came to a Bedouin's house. The Bedouin was sitting at a meal and had a jug of wine in front of him. When they had drunk a glass, al-Mahdī said, "I am one of al-Mahdī's courtiers." They drank another glass, and al-Mahdī said, "I am one of al-Mahdī's amirs." When they had drunk a third glass, he said, "I am al-Mahdī." The Bedouin took the jug away and said, "You drank the first glass and claimed to be a courtier. With the second glass you claimed to be an amir, and with the third, to be Caliph. If you drink another glass, you will surely claim to be God Almighty." The next day when the Caliph's party arrived, the Bedouin fled in fear. Al-Mahdī commanded that he should be found and brought before him, whereupon he gave him some gold pieces. The Bedouin said, "I bear witness that you speak truth, even if you make the fourth claim."

A man announced that he was God. He was brought before the Caliph who said to him. "Last year there was someone here who claimed to be a prophet. He was executed." "That was well done," said the man, "for I had not sent him."

A Qazvīnī[2] went to war against the heretics with a huge shield. From the fortress they threw a stone which hit him on the head and wounded him. The Qazvīnī was furious and said, "Are you blind, man? Can't you see a shield as big as this that you have to throw a stone straight on to my head?"

A number of Qazvīnīs went to war against the heretics. When they came back from the battle, each of them was carrying the head of a heretic on a pole. One of them had a foot on his pole. They asked him, "Who killed this one?" He answered, "I did." They asked him, "Why didn't you bring his head?" He answered, "They took his head away before I got there."

Translated by Bernard Lewis.

1. Sultan Maḥmūd of Ghazna, who reigned from 998 to 1030.
2. Qazvin, where ʿUbayd-i Zākānī was born, was the main base for campaigns against the Ismāʿīlī stronghold at Alamūt.

Someone asked Mawlānā 'Aḍud al-Dīn, "How is it that in the time of the Caliphs many men claimed to be God or Prophet, and now they do not?" He replied, "The men of our time are so beset by oppression and hunger that they reck nothing of God or Prophet."

A Rāzī, Gīlānī, and a Qazvīnī went together on pilgrimage. The Qazvīnī was bankrupt, the Rāzī and the Gīlānī were rich. When the Rāzī put his hand on the curtain ring of the Ka'ba, he said, "O God, in thanksgiving to Thee for bringing me here safely I set free my slaves Balban and Banafsha." When the Gīlānī grasped the curtain ring, he said, "In thanksgiving for this I set free my slaves Mubārak and Sunqur." When the Qazvīnī grasped the curtain ring he said, "O God, Thou knowest I have neither Balban nor Sunqur, neither Banafsha nor Mubārak. In thanksgiving for this, therefore, I set free my old Fāṭima with a triple divorce."

In the time of the Caliph Wāthiq a woman laid claim to prophethood. The Caliph asked her, "Was Muḥammad a Prophet?" "Certainly," she replied. "Then," said the Caliph, "since Muḥammad said, 'There will be no Prophet after me,' your claim is false." The woman replied, "He said, 'There will be no Prophet after me,' He did not say, 'There will be no Prophetess after me.'"

One day when Sultan Maḥmūd was hungry, they brought him a dish of eggplant. He liked it very much and said, "Eggplant is an excellent food." A courtier began to praise the eggplant with great eloquence. When the sultan grew tired of the dish he said, "Eggplant is a very harmful thing," whereupon the courtier began to speak in hyperbole of the harmful qualities of the eggplant. "Man alive," said the sultan, "have you not just now uttered the praises of the eggplant?" "Yes," said the courtier, "but I am your courtier and not the eggplant's courtier. I have to say what pleases you, not what pleases the eggplant."

A tumbler scolded his son and said, "You do no work and you waste your life in idleness. How often must I tell you to practice somersaults and to learn how to dance on a rope and to make a dog jump through a hoop so that you can achieve something with your life. If you don't listen to me, I swear by God I shall abandon you to the *madrasa* to learn their dead and useless science and to become a scholar so as to live in contempt and misery and adversity and never be able to earn a penny wherever you go."

Shaykh Sharaf al-Dīn Darguzīnī asked Mawlānā 'Aḍud al-Dīn, "Where in the Qur'ān has God spoken of shaykhs?" He answered, "At the side of the learned in this verse, 'Shall the learned and the ignorant be treated in the same manner?'"

Mawlānā Sharaf al-Dīn Dāmghānī was passing by the door of a mosque just as the mosque servant got hold of a dog and beat him inside the mosque. The dog howled. Mawlānā opened the mosque door, and the dog fled. The mosque servant abused Mawlānā. "My friend," said Mawlānā, "excuse the dog. He has no understanding; that is why he went into the mosque. We others, who have understanding, you will never see us in the mosque."

A Khurāsānī went to a physician and said, "My wife is ill. What should I do?" The physician said, "Bring me a specimen in a bottle tomorrow. Then I will look and tell you." By chance the Khurāsānī himself felt ill later that day. Next day he came to the physician with a bottle with a piece of string tied round the middle. The physician asked, "Why did you tie on this string?" The man said, "I also felt sick. The upper half is my water and the lower half is my wife's." Next day the physician repeated this story to everybody. A Qazvīnī was present and said, "Master, please excuse him, for the Khurāsānī has no sense. Was the string tied inside or outside the bottle?"

They asked a wise man, "Why do the nomads never need a physician?" He answered, "As the wild ass needs no vet."

Shams-i Muzaffar said one day to his disciples, "One should learn when one is young. What one learns in youth one never forgets in age. It is now fifty years since I learned the first verse of the Qur'ān and I can still remember it, though I never read it since."

A man said, "I have pain in my eyes and as a cure I use Qur'ān verses and prayers." Talhak said to him, "But you should use a little eye-salve too."

The devil was asked, "Which group of people do you love best?" He replied, "The market brokers [dallāl]." They asked him why. He answered, "Not only do they speak falsehood, which in itself delights me, but they swear to it as well."

A king had three wives, one Persian, one Arab, and one Coptic. One night he lay beside the Persian woman and asked her, "What time is it?" She answered, "It is the hour of dawn." He asked her, "How do you know?" She answered, "Because the scent of the roses and basil is rising and the birds are beginning to sing." The next night he lay with the Arab woman and asked her the same question. She answered, "It is the hour of dawn. I know it because the pearls of my necklace feel cold against my breast." On the third night he lay with the Coptic woman and he asked her the same question and she answered, "It is the hour of dawn. I know because I have to go to stool."[3]

In the month of Ramadān someone said to a dealer, "In this month there is no business." He answered "God give long life to the Jews and the Christians."

A man met another man who was riding on a wretched donkey. "Where are you going?" he asked. "I am going to the Friday prayer," answered the other. "Woe

---

3. The first two answers contain well-known literary themes used in dawn poetry.

betide you, it's only Tuesday," said the first. "Yes," said the rider, "but I shall be lucky if this donkey can bring me to the mosque by Saturday."

Abū Dulaf became a Shi'ite and used to say that whoever did not declare himself a Shi'ite was a child of fornication. His son said to him, "I am not of your sect." Abū Dulaf answered, "Yes, indeed, by God. I bedded your mother before I bought her."

A man said to a woman, "I would like to taste you, to know which has a better flavor, you or my wife." She answered, "Ask my husband, he has tasted us both."

Abū Nuwās saw a drunken man and looked at him in wonderment. He was asked, "Why do you find this funny? You yourself are in the same state every day." Abū Nuwās replied, "I have never seen a drunken man before." "How is that?" they asked him. "Because," he replied, "I am always the first to get drunk and the last to recover so I don't know what happens to those who get drunk after I do."

One day Abū Nuwās was seen with a glass of wine in his hand, a bunch of grapes on his right, and a dish of raisins on his left, and every time he drank from the glass he took a grape and a raisin. "What does this mean?" they asked him, and he replied, "This is the Father, the Son, and the Holy Ghost."

A Bedouin was eating with all five fingers. He was asked, "Why do you behave like this?" "If I were to eat with only three," he replied, "the other fingers would be angry." They said to another Bedouin, "You are eating with five fingers." "Yes," he said, "what can I do? I have no more."

Abu'l-Hārith was asked, "Can a man of eighty have a child?" He answered them, "Yes, if he has a neighbor of twenty."

A man with bad breath came to a physician and complained of a toothache. When the physician opened his mouth, a terrible smell came out. The physician said, "This is not my job. Go to the sweepers."

A bore visited a sick man and stayed with him too long. The sick man said, "I am plagued with too many visitors." The bore said, "I will go and shut the door." "Yes," said the sick man, "but from the outside."

A man who claimed to be a prophet was brought before the Caliph al-Mu'taṣim. Al-Mu'taṣim said, "I bear witness that you are a stupid prophet." The man replied, "I have only come to people like you."

A man said to Ḥajjāj, "I saw you yesterday in a dream, and it seemed that you were in Paradise!" Ḥajjāj replied, "If your dream is true, then the injustice in the hereafter is even greater than in this world."

They said to a Ṣūfī, "Sell your cloak." He replied, "If a fisherman sells his net, with what shall he fish?"

A Bedouin went on pilgrimage and reached Mecca ahead of the others. He grasped the curtains of the Kaʿba and said, "O God, forgive me before the crowd gets to You."

A man married a woman, and on the fifth day after the wedding she bore a child. The man went to the market and bought tablets and ink. They asked him, "What is this?" He answered, "A child that can come into the world after five days can go to school after another three."

The mark of the fool is that he comes at the wrong time and stays too long.

HĀFIZ (1300?–1388?)
Persian

Hāfiz is the master of the *ghazal,* a short lyrical poem. His name means "he who has memorized the *Qur'an.*" Little is certain of his life other than that he lived in Shiraz and was apparently attached to a mystical order. It is perhaps not coincidental, then, that much of his lyrical and often apparently erotic poetry can be understood in mystical terms.

I Cease Not from Desire*

I cease not from desire till my desire
Is satisfied; or let my mouth attain
My love's red mouth, or let my soul expire,
Sighed from those lips that sought her lips in vain.
Others may find another love as fair;   5
Upon her threshold I have laid my head,
The dust shall cover me, still lying there,
When from my body life and love have fled.

My soul is on my lips ready to fly,
But grief beats in my heart and will not cease,   10
Because not once, not once before I die,
Will her sweet lips give all my longing peace.
My breath is narrowed down to one long sigh

*Translated by Gertrude Bell.

For a red mouth that burns my thoughts like fire;
When will that mouth draw near and make reply   15
To one whose life is straitened with desire?
When I am dead, open my grave and see
The cloud of smoke that rises round thy feet:
In my dead heart the fire still burns for thee;
Yea, the smoke rises from my winding-sheet!   20
Ah, come, Beloved! for the meadows wait
Thy coming, and the thorn bears flowers instead
Of thorns, the cypress fruit, and desolate
Bare winter from before thy steps has fled.
Hoping within some garden ground to find   25
A red rose soft and sweet as thy soft cheek,
Through every meadow blows the western wind,
Through every garden he is fain to seek.
Reveal thy face! that the whole world may be
Bewildered by thy radiant loveliness;   30
The cry of man and woman comes to thee,
Open thy lips and comfort their distress!
Each curling lock of thy luxuriant hair
Breaks into barbèd hooks to catch my heart,
My broken heart is wounded everywhere   35
With countless wounds from which the red drops start.
Yet when sad lovers meet and tell their sighs,
Not without praise shall Hafiz' name be said,
Not without tears, in those pale companies
Where joy has been forgot and hope has fled.   40

Light in Darkness[†]

High-nesting in the stately fir,
The enduring nightingale again
Unto the rose in passionate strain
Singeth: "All ill be far from her!

"In gratitude for this, O rose,   5
That thou the Queen of Beauty art,
Pity nightingales' mad heart,
Be not contemptuous of those."

I do not rail against my fate
When thou dost hide thy face from me;   10
Joy wells not of propinquity
Save in the heart once desolate.

[†]*Translated by Arthur S. Arberry.*

If other men are gay and glad
That life is joy and festival,
I do exult and glory all
Because her beauty makes me sad.

And if for maids of Paradise
And heavenly halls the monk aspires,
The Friend fulfils my heart's desires,
The Tavern will for heaven suffice.

Drink wine, and let the lute vibrate;
Grieve not; if any tell to thee,
"Wine is a great iniquity",
Say, "Allah is compassionate!"

Why, Hafiz, art thou sorrowing,
Why is thy heart in absence rent?
Union may come of banishment,
And in the darkness light doth spring.

15

20

25

O Ask Not[†]

O love, how have I felt thy pain!
  Ask me not how—
O absence, how I drank thy bane!
  Ask me not how—

In quest, throughout the world I err'd,
And whom, at last, have I preferr'd?
  O ask not whom—

In hope her threshold's dust to spy,
How streamed down my longing eye!
  O ask not how—

Why bite my friends their lips, displeas'd?
Know they what ruby lip I seiz'd?
  O ask not when—

But yester-night, this very ear
Such language from her mouth did hear—
  O ask not what—

Like Hafiz, in love's mazy round,
My feet, at length, their goal have found,
  O ask not where.

5

10

15

[†]*Translated by H. H.*

[If I follow in her tracks she stirs up trouble]

If I follow in her tracks she stirs up trouble,
and if I rest from the search she rises up in anger.

And if on the road for a moment, out of loyalty,
I fall on her tracks like dust, like the wind she flees.

And if I seek half a kiss, a hundred taunts, like sugar,   5
spill down from the jewel-box of her mouth.

That deceit which I see in your eyes
mixes many a good name with the dust of the road.

The rise and fall of Love's desert is the snare of affliction.
Where is the lionhearted who is unafraid of affliction?   10

Seek life and patience, for the great wheel, with its sleight-of-hand,
plays a thousand tricks more strange than these.

Hafiz, place your head on the threshold of submission,
for if you argue, time will argue back.

[Don't ask how many complaints I have about her black curls]

Don't ask how many complaints I have about her black curls.
I am so undone because of her that it's beyond telling.

Let no one abandon heart and faith in hope of fidelity.
I did. Do not ask me how sorry I am.

With one gulp of wine which troubles no one
I drew such fire from the ignorant that it's beyond telling.

Ascetic, leave us in peace. And this ruby wine,
do not ask how it steals my heart and faith.

Seclusion and peace were my desire but
the glance I caught from that narcissus is beyond telling.

On this road there are conversations which melt the soul.
Each man has such a quarrel that it's beyond telling.

I asked the great sphere of Heaven about his condition.
He said, "Don't ask how much pain I feel from the mallet's blow."

Translated by H. H.

I said to her, "With whose blood did you color your hair?"
She said, "Hafiz, by the Koran, this story is so long it's beyond telling."

JÂMÎ (1414–1492)
Persian

Regarded as one of the greatest authors of the medieval Persian romance, Jâmî was a member of a mystical order and spent most of his life at the Timurid court at Herāt. Prolific and versatile, he excelled in all literary genres and also produced works on such subjects as theory, poetics, rhetoric and grammar. Among his finest creations are seven epic poems, known collectively as *The Seven Thrones* (*Haft Ourang,* the Persian name for the constellation Ursa Major). Three of these poems are romances. For his topics, Jâmî drew from both Islamic and Greco-Islamic materials, ranging from the beloved Joseph and Zulaykhā story to the legend of the star-crossed lovers, Laylā and Majnūn. His frequent use of allegory links his romantic plots with the world of mysticism.

The Women of Memphis
[from Yūsuf u Zulaikhā, *Joseph and Zulaikha]*

Love is ill suited with peace and rest:
Scorn and reproaches become him best.
Rebuke gives strength to his tongue, and blame
Wakes the dull spark to a brighter flame.
Blame is the censor of Love's bazaar: 5
It suffers no rust the pure splendour to mar.
Blame is the whip whose impending blow
Speeds the willing lover and wakes the slow;
And the weary steed who can hardly crawl
Is swift of foot when reproaches fall.   10
When the rose of the secret had opened and blown,
The voice of reproach was a bulbul in tone.[1]

The women of Memphis, who heard the tale first,
The whispered slander received and nursed.

Translated by Ralph T. H. Griffith.

---

1. An allusion to the bulbul's love of the rose,
   whose beauty, according to Persian legend,
   he sings.

Then, attacking Zulaikha for right and wrong,   15
Their uttered reproaches were loud and long:
"Heedless of honour and name she gave
The love of her heart to the Hebrew slave,
Who lies so deep in her soul enshrined
That to sense and religion her eyes are blind.   20
She loves her servant. 'Tis strange to think
That erring folly so low can sink;
But stranger still that the slave she woos
Should scorn her suit and her love refuse.
His cold eye to hers he never will raise;   25
He never will walk in the path where she strays.
He stops if before him her form he sees;
If she lingers a moment he turns and flees.
When her lifted veil leaves her cheek exposed,
With the stud of his eyelash his eye is closed.   30
If she weeps in her sorrow he laughs at her pain,
And closes each door that she opens in vain.
It may be that her form is not fair in his eyes,
And his cold heart refuses the proffered prize.
If once her beloved one sat with us   35
He would sit with us ever, not treat us thus.
Our sweet society ne'er would he leave,
But joy unending would give and receive.
But not all have this gift in their hands: to enthral   40
The heart they would win is not given to all.
There is many a woman, fair, good, and kind,
To whom never the heart of a man inclined;
And many a Laila with soft black eye.
The tears of whose heart-blood are never dry."

Zulaikha heard, and resentment woke   45
To punish the dames for the words they spoke.
She summoned them all from the city to share
A sumptuous feast which she bade prepare.
A delicate banquet meet for kings
Was spread with the choicest of dainty things.   50
Cups filled with sherbet of every hue
Shone as rifts in a cloud when the sun gleams through.
There were goblets of purest crystal filled
With wine and sweet odours with art distilled.
The golden cloth blazed like the sunlight; a whole   55
Cluster of stars was each silver bowl.
From goblet and charger rare odours came;
There was strength for the spirit and food for the frame.

All daintiest fare that your lip would taste,
From fish to fowl, on the cloth was placed.   60
It seemed that the fairest their teeth had lent
For almonds, their lips for the sugar sent.
A mimic palace rose fair to view
Of a thousand sweets of each varied hue,
Where instead of a carpet the floor was made   65
With bricks of candy and marmalade.
Fruit in profusion, of sorts most rare,
Piled in baskets, bloomed fresh and fair.
Those who looked on their soft transparency felt
That the delicate pulp would dissolve and melt.   70
Bands of boys and young maidens, fine
As mincing peacocks, were ranged in line;
And the fair dames of Memphis, like Peris eyed,
In a ring on their couches sat side by side.
They tasted of all that they fancied, and each   75
Was courteous in manner and gentle in speech.

    The feast was ended; the cloth was raised,
And Zulaikha sweetly each lady praised.
Then she set, as she planned in her wily breast,
A knife and an orange beside each guest: 80
An orange, to purge the dark thoughts within
Each jaundiced heart with its golden skin.
One hand, as she bade them, the orange clasped,
The knife in the other was firmly grasped.
Thus she addressed them: "Dames fair and sweet,   85
Most lovely of all when the fairest meet,
Why should my pleasure your hearts annoy?
Why blame me for loving my Hebrew boy?
If your eyes with the light of his eyes were filled,
Each tongue that blames me were hushed and stilled.   90
I will bid him forth, if you all agree,
And bring him near for your eyes to see."
"This, even this," cried each eager dame,
"Is the dearest wish that our hearts can frame.
Bid him come; let us look on the lovely face   95
That shall stir our hearts with its youthful grace.
Already charmed, though our eyes never fell
On the youth we long for, we love him well.
These oranges still in our hands we hold,
To sweeten the spleen with their skins of gold.   100
But they please us not, for he is not here:
Let not one be cut till the boy appear."

She sent the nurse to address him thus:
"Come, free-waving cypress, come forth to us.
Let us worship the ground which thy dear feet press,   105
And bow down at the sight of thy loveliness.
Let our love-stricken hearts be thy chosen retreat,
And our eyes a soft carpet beneath thy feet."

But he came not forth, like a lingering rose
Which the spell of the charmer has failed to unclose.   110
Then Zulaikha flew to the house where he dwelt,
And in fond entreaty before him knelt:
"My darling, the light of these longing eyes,
Hope of my heart," thus she spoke with sighs,
"I fed on the hope which thy words had given;   115
But that hope from my breast by despair is driven.
For thee have I forfeited all: my name
Through thee has been made a reproach and shame.
I have found no favour: thou wouldst not fling
One pitying look on so mean a thing.   120
Yet let not the women of Memphis see
That I am so hated and scorned by thee.
Come, sprinkle the salt of thy lip to cure
The wounds of my heart and the pain I endure.
Let the salt be sacred: repay the debt   125
Of the faithful love thou shouldst never forget."

The heart of Yusuf grew soft at the spell
Of her gentle words, for she charmed so well.
Swift as the wind from her knees she rose,
And decked him gay with the garb she chose.   130
Over his shoulders she drew with care,
The scented locks of his curling hair,
Like serpents of jet-black lustre seen
With their twisted coils where the grass is green.
A girdle gleaming with gold, round the waist   135
That itself was fine as a hair, she braced.
I marvel so dainty a waist could bear
The weight of the jewels that glittered there.
She girt his brow with bright gems; each stone
Of wondrous beauty enhanced his own.   140
On his shoes were rubies and many a gem,
And pearls on the latchets that fastened them.
A scarf, on whose every thread was strung
A loving heart, on his arm was hung.
A golden ewer she gave him to hold,   145
And a maid brow-bound with a fillet of gold
In her hand a basin of silver bore,

And shadow-like moved as he walked before.
If a damsel had looked, she at once had resigned
All joy of her life, all the peace of her mind.   150
Too weak were my tongue if it tried to express
The charm of his wonderful loveliness.

    Like a bed of roses in perfect bloom
The secret treasure appeared in the room.
The women of Memphis beheld him, and took   155
From that garden of glory the rose of a look.
One glance at his beauty o'erpowered each soul
And drew from their fingers the reins of control.
Each lady would cut through the orange she held,
As she gazed on that beauty unparalleled.   160
But she wounded her finger, so moved in her heart,
That she knew not her hand and the orange apart.
One made a pen of her finger, to write
On her soul his name who had ravished her sight—
A reed which, struck with the point of the knife,   165
Poured out a red flood from each joint in the strife.
One scored a calendar's lines in red
On the silver sheet of her palm outspread,
And each column, marked with the blood-drops, showed
Like a brook when the stream o'er the bank has flowed.   170

    When they saw that youth in his beauty's pride:
"No mortal is he," in amaze they cried.
"No clay and water composed his frame,
But, a holy angel, from heaven he came."
" 'Tis my peerless boy," cried Zulaikha, "long   175
For him have I suffered reproach and wrong.
I told him my love for him, called him the whole
Aim and desire of my heart and soul.
He looked on me coldly; I bent not his will
To give me his love and my hope fulfill.   180
He still rebelled: I was forced to send
To prison the boy whom I could not bend.
In trouble and toil, under lock and chain,
He passed long days in affliction and pain.
But his spirit was tamed by the woe he felt,   185
And the heart that was hardened began to melt.
Keep your wild bird in a cage and see
How soon he forgets that he once was free."

    Of those who wounded their hands, a part
Lost reason and patience, and mind and heart.   190
To weak the sharp sword of his love to stay,

They gave up their souls ere they moved away.
The reason of others grew dark and dim,
And madness possessed them for love of him.
Bare-headed, bare-footed, they fled amain,   195
And the light that had vanished ne'er kindled again.
To some their senses at length returned,
But their hearts were wounded, their bosoms burned.
They were drunk with the cup which was full to the brim,
And the birds of their hearts were ensnared by him.   200
Nay, Yusuf's love was a mighty bowl
With varied power to move the soul.
One drank the wine till her senses reeled;
To another, life had no joy to yield;
One offered her soul his least wish to fulfil;   205
One dreamed of him ever, but mute and still.
But only the woman to whom no share
Of the wine was vouchsafed could be pitied there.

ANONYMOUS
Arabic

An established classic in both Eastern and Western literature, *The Thousand and One Nights* (*Alf Layla wa-Layla,* also known in English as *The Arabian Nights*) enjoyed little success among the medieval Arab intelligentsia, who favored the stylistically more ambitious *adab* works. But the *Nights* did have strong links to *adab* literature, in much the same way that the *maqâma* did. Narratively, the *Nights* is composed of enframed stories. The frame story itself is the tale of Shahrasād (long familiar in English as Sheherazade), the new bride of King Shahryār. Once betrayed, the king has come to fear infidelity so much that he kills each wife after but one night with her. To forestall her own death, Shahrasād tells the king each night a story, stopping always at its climax: to learn the ending, he must let her live for one more day. After one thousand and one nights, his heart is finally melted. Into this frame are set stories gathered from various parts of the Islamic world and India. *The Nights* was not composed all at once, but evolved over many centuries. The frame story has been traced to India, and it was possibly as a collection of Hindu and Buddhist tales that *The Nights* first made its way into Persian. During the ninth century, a Persian version was translated into Arabic. *The Nights* continued to evolve in Arabic, with new stories in all probability replacing old ones. The collection was especially popular in Egypt during the period of Mamlūk rule (1250–1517), and it was then that the *Nights* probably took its final form, though the word "final" is somewhat misleading:

there is no single canonical text, and some versions include stories not found in other versions.

from *The Thousand and One Nights*

[The Tale of King Yunan and the Sage Duban]

There was once a king call Yunan, who reigned in one of the cities of Persia, in the province of Zuman.[1] This king was afflicted with leprosy, which had defied the physicians and the sages, who, for all the medicines they gave him to drink and all the ointments they applied, were unable to cure him. One day there came to the city of King Yunan a sage called Duban. This sage had read all sorts of books, Greek, Persian, Turkish, Arabic, Byzantine, Syriac, and Hebrew, had studied the sciences, and had learned their groundwork, as well as their principles and basic benefits. Thus he was versed in all the sciences, from philosophy to the lore of plants and herbs, the harmful as well as the beneficial. A few days after he arrived in the city of King Yunan, the sage heard about the king and his leprosy and the fact that the physicians and the sages were unable to cure him. On the following day, when God's morning dawned and His sun rose, the sage Duban put on his best clothes, went to King Yunan and, introducing himself, said, "Your Majesty, I have heard of that which has afflicted your body and heard that many physicians have treated you without finding a way to cure you. Your Majesty, I can treat you without giving you any medicine to drink or ointment to apply." When the king heard this, he said, "If you succeed, I will bestow on you riches that would be enough for you and your grandchildren. I will bestow favors on you, and I will make you my companion and friend." The king bestowed robes of honor on the sage, treated him kindly, and then asked him, "Can you really cure me from my leprosy without any medicine to drink or ointment to apply?" The sage replied, "Yes, I will cure you externally." The king was astonished, and he began to feel respect as well as great affection for the sage. He said, "Now, sage, do what you have promised." The sage replied, "I hear and obey. I will do it tomorrow morning, the Almighty God willing." Then the sage went to the city, rented a house, and there he distilled and extracted medicines and drugs. Then with his great knowledge and skill, he fashioned a mallet with a curved end, hollowed the mallet, as well as the handle, and filled the handle with his medicines and drugs. He likewise made a ball. When he had perfected and prepared everything, he went on the following day to King Yunan and kissed the ground before him.

But morning overtook Shahrazad, and she lapsed into silence. Then her sister Dinarzad said, "What a lovely story!" Shahrazad replied, "You have heard nothing yet."

Translated by Husain Haddawy.

---

1. Modern Armenia.

Tomorrow night I shall tell you something stranger and more amazing if the king spares me and lets me live!"

THE TWELFTH NIGHT

The following night Dinarzad said to her sister Shahrazad, "Please, sister, finish the rest of the story of the fisherman and the demon." Shahrazad replied, "With the greatest pleasure":

I heard, O King, that the fisherman said to the demon:

The sage Duban came to King Yunan and asked him to ride to the playground to play with the ball and mallet. The king rode out, attended by his chamberlains, princes, viziers,[2] and lords and eminent men of the realm. When the king was seated, the sage Duban entered, offered him the mallet, and said, "O happy King, take this mallet, hold it in your hand, and as you race on the playground, hold the grip tightly in your fist, and hit the ball. Race until your perspire, and the medicine will ooze from the grip into your perspiring hand, spread to your wrist, and circulate through your entire body. After you perspire and the medicine spreads in your body, return to your royal palace, take a bath, and go to sleep. You will wake up cured, and that is all there is to it." King Yunan took the mallet from the sage Duban and mounted his horse. The attendants threw the ball before the king, who, holding the grip tightly in his fist, followed it and struggled excitedly to catch up with it and hit it. He kept galloping after the ball and hitting it until his palm and the rest of his body began to perspire, and the medicine began to ooze from the handle and flow through his entire body. When the sage Duban was certain that the medicine had oozed and spread through the king's body, he advised him to return to his palace and go immediately to the bath. The king went to the bath and washed himself thoroughly. Then he put on his clothes, left the bath, and returned to his palace.

As for the sage Duban, he spent the night at home, and early in the morning, he went to the palace and asked for permission to see the king. When he was allowed in, he entered and kissed the ground before the king; then, pointing toward him with his hand, he began to recite the following verses:

> The virtues you fostered are great;
> For who but you could sire them?
> Yours is the face whose radiant light
> Effaces the night dark and grim.
> Forever beams your radiant face;
> That of the world is still in gloom.

---

2. Ministers.

You rained on us with ample grace,
As the clouds rain on thirsty hills,
Expending your munificence,
Attaining your magnificence.

When the sage Duban finished reciting these verses, the king stood up and embraced him. Then he seated the sage beside him, and with attentiveness and smiles, engaged him in conversation. Then the king bestowed on the sage robes of honor, gave him gifts and endowments, and granted his wishes. For when the king had looked at himself the morning after the bath, he found that his body was clear of leprosy, as clear and pure as silver. He therefore felt exceedingly happy and in a very generous mood. Thus when he went in the morning to the reception hall and sat on his throne, attended by the Mamluks[3] and chamberlains, in the company of the viziers and the lords of the realm, and the sage Duban presented himself, as we have mentioned, the king stood up, embraced him, and seated him beside him. He treated him attentively and drank and ate with him.

But morning overtook Shahrazad, and she lapsed into silence. Then her sister Dinarzad said, "Sister, what a lovely story!" Shahrazad replied, "The rest of the story is stranger and more amazing. If the king spares me and I am alive tomorrow night, I shall tell you something even more entertaining."

THE THIRTEENTH NIGHT

The following night Dinarzad said to her sister Shahrazad, "Sister, if you are not sleepy, tell us one of your lovely little tales to while away the night." Shahrazad replied, "With the greatest pleasure":

I heard, O happy King who is praiseworthy by the Grace of God, that King Yunan bestowed favors on the sage, gave him robes of honor, and granted his wishes. At the end of the day he gave the sage a thousand dinars and sent him home. The king, who was amazed at the skill of the sage Duban, said to himself, "This man has treated me externally, without giving me any draught to drink or ointment to apply. His is indeed a great wisdom for which he deserves to be honored and rewarded. He shall become my companion, confidant, and close friend." Then the king spent the night, happy at his recovery from his illness, at his good health, and at the soundness of his body. When morning came and it was light, the king went to the royal reception hall and sat on the throne, attended by his chief officers, while the princes, viziers, and lords of the realm sat to his right and left. Then the king called for the sage, and when the sage entered and kissed

---

3. Literally "slaves," members of a military force, originally of Caucasian slaves, who made themselves masters of Egypt in 1254 C.E. until their massacre in 1811.

the ground before him, the king stood up to salute him, seated him beside him, and invited him to eat with him. The king treated him intimately, showed him favors, and bestowed on him robes of honor and many other gifts. Then he spent the whole day conversing with him, and at the end of the day he ordered that he be given a thousand dinars. The sage went home and spent the night with his wife, feeling happy and thankful to God the Arbiter.

In the morning, the king went to the royal reception hall, and the princes and viziers came to stand in attendance. It happened that King Yunan had a vizier who was sinister, greedy, envious, and fretful, and when he saw that the sage had found favor with the king, who bestowed on him much money and many robes of honor, he feared that the king would dismiss him and appoint the sage in his place; therefore, he envied the sage and harbored ill will against him, for 'nobody is free from envy.' The envious vizier approached the king and, kissing the ground before him, said, "O excellent King and glorious Lord, it was by your kindness and with your blessing that I rose to prominence; therefore, if I fail to advise you on a grave matter, I am not my father's son. If the great King and noble Lord commands, I shall disclose the matter to him." The king was upset and asked, "Damn you, what advice have you got?" The vizier replied, "Your Majesty, 'He who considers not the end, fortune is not his friend.' I have seen your Majesty make a mistake, for you have bestowed favors on your enemy who has come to destroy your power and steal your wealth. Indeed, you have pampered him and shown him many favors, but I fear that he will do you harm." The king asked, "Whom do you accuse, whom do you have in mind, and at whom do you point the finger?" The vizier replied, "If you are asleep, wake up, for I point the finger at the sage Duban, who has come from Byzantium." The king replied, "Damn you, is he my enemy? To me he is the most faithful, the dearest, and the most favored of people, for this sage has treated me simply by making me hold something in my hand and has cured me from the disease that had defied the physicians and the sages and rendered them helpless. In all the world, east and west, near and far, there is no one like him, yet you accuse him of such a thing. From this day onward, I will give him every month a thousand dinars, in addition to his rations and regular salary. Even if I were to share my wealth and my kingdom with him, it would be less than he deserves. I think that you have said what you said because you envy him. This is very much like the situation in the story told by the vizier of King Sindbad[4] when the king wanted to kill his own son.

But morning overtook Shahrazad, and she lapsed into silence. Then her sister Dinarzad said, "Sister, what a lovely story!" Shahrazad replied, "What is this compared with what I shall tell you tomorrow night! It will be stranger and more amazing."

---

4. Not to be confused with Sindbad the Sailor.

THE FOURTEENTH NIGHT

The following night, when the king got into bed and Shahrazad got in with him, her sister Dinarzad said, "Please, sister, if you are not sleepy, tell us one of your lovely little tales to while away the night." Shahrazad replied, "Very well":

I heard, O happy King, that King Yunan's vizier asked, "King of the age, I beg your pardon, but what did King Sindbad's vizier tell the king when he wished to kill his own son?" King Yunan said to the vizier, "When King Sindbad, provoked by an envious man, wanted to kill his own son, his vizier said to him, 'Don't do what you will regret afterward.'"

[The Tale of the Husband and the Parrot]

I have heard it told that there was once a very jealous man who had a wife so splendidly beautiful that she was perfection itself. The wife always refused to let her husband travel and leave her behind, until one day when he found it absolutely necessary to go on a journey. He went to the bird market, bought a parrot, and brought it home. The parrot was intelligent, knowledgeable, smart, and retentive. Then he went away on his journey, and when he finished his business and came back, he brought the parrot and inquired about his wife during his absence. The parrot gave him a day-by-day account of what his wife had done with her lover and how the two carried on in his absence. When the husband heard the account, he felt very angry, went to his wife, and gave her a sound beating. Thinking that one of her maids had informed her husband about what she did with her lover in her husband's absence, the wife interrogated her maids one by one, and they all swore that they had heard the parrot inform the husband.

When the wife heard that it was the parrot who had informed the husband, she ordered one of her maids to take the grinding stone and grind under the cage, ordered a second maid to sprinkle water over the cage, and ordered a third to carry a steel mirror and walk back and forth all night long. That night her husband stayed out, and when he came home in the morning, he brought the parrot, spoke with it, and asked about what had transpired in his absence that night. The parrot replied, "Master, forgive me, for last night, all night long, I was unable to hear or see very well because of the intense darkness, the rain, and the thunder and lightning." Seeing that it was summertime, during the month of July, the husband replied, "Woe unto you, this is no season for rain." The parrot said, "Yes, by God, all night long, I saw what I told you." The husband, concluding that the parrot had lied about his wife and had accused her falsely, got angry, and he grabbed the parrot and, taking it out of the cage, smote it on the ground and killed it. But after the parrot's death, the husband heard from his neighbors that the parrot had told the truth about his wife, and he was full of regret that he had been tricked by his wife to kill the parrot.

King Yunan concluded, "Vizier, the same will happen to me."

not to kill the sage because of vizier's envy + insecurity

But morning overtook Shahrazad, and she lapsed into silence. Then her sister Dinarzad said, "What a strange and lovely story!" Shahrazad replied, "What is this compared with what I shall tell you tomorrow night! If the king spares me and lets me live, I shall tell you something more amazing." The king thought to himself, "By God, this is indeed an amazing story."

THE FIFTEENTH NIGHT

The following night Dinarzad said to her sister Shahrazad, "Please, sister, if you are not sleepy, tell us one of your lovely little tales, for they entertain and help everyone to forget his cares and banish sorrow from the heart." Shahrazad replied, "With the greatest pleasure." King Shahrayar added, "Let it be the remainder of the story of King Yunan, his vizier, and the sage Duban, and of the fisherman, the demon, and the jar." Shahrazad replied, "With the greatest pleasure":

I heard, O happy King, that King Yunan said to his envious vizier, "After the husband killed the parrot and heard from his neighbors that the parrot had told him the truth, he was filled with remorse. You too, my vizier, being envious of this wise man, would like me to kill him and regret it afterward, as did the husband after he killed the parrot." When the vizier heard what King Yunan said, he replied, "O great king, what harm has this sage done to me? Why, he has not harmed me in any way. I am telling you all this out of love and fear for you. If you don't discover my veracity, let me perish like the vizier who deceived the son of the king." King Yunan asked his vizier, "How so?" The vizier replied:

[The Tale of the King's Son and the She-Ghoul]

It is said, O happy King, that there was once a king who had a son who was fond of hunting and trapping. The prince had with him a vizier appointed by his father the king to follow him wherever he went. One day the prince went with his men into the wilderness, and when he chanced to see a wild beast, the vizier urged him to go after it. The prince pursued the beast and continued to press in pursuit until he lost its track and found himself alone in the wilderness, not knowing which way to turn or where to go, when he came upon a girl, standing on the road, in tears. When the young prince asked her, "Where do you come from?" she replied, "I am the daughter of an Indian king. I was riding in the wilderness when I dozed off and in my sleep fell of my horse and found myself alone and helpless." When the young prince heard what she said, he felt sorry for her, and he placed her behind him on his horse and rode on. As they passed by some ruins, she said, "O my lord, I wish to relieve myself here." He let her down and she went into the ruins. Then he went in after her, ignorant of what she was, and discovered that she was a she-ghoul, who was saying to her children, "I brought you a good, fat boy."

They replied, "Mother, bring him to us, so that we may feed on his innards." When the young prince heard what they said, he shook with terror, and fearing for his life, ran outside. The she-ghoul followed him and asked, "Why are you afraid?" and he told her about his situation and his predicament, concluding, "I have been unfairly treated." She replied, "If you have been unfairly treated, ask the Almighty God for help, and he will protect you from harm." The young prince raised his eyes to Heaven . . .

Kill the sage, now. For he may go behind back to hole King done in

But morning *overtook Shahrazad, and she lapsed into silence. Then her sister Dinarzad said, "What a strange and lovely story!" Shahrazad replied, "What is this compared with what I shall tell you tomorrow night! It will be even stranger and more amazing."*

THE SIXTEENTH NIGHT

The following night Dinarzad said, "Please, sister if you are not sleepy, tell us one of your lovely little tales." Shahrazad replied, "I shall with pleasure":

I heard, O King, that the vizier said to King Yunan:

When the young prince said to the she-ghoul, "I have been unfairly treated," she replied, "Ask God for help, and He will protect you from harm." The young prince raised his eyes to Heaven and said, "O Lord, help me to prevail upon my enemy, for 'everything is within your power,'" When the she-ghoul heard his invocation, she gave up and departed, and he returned safely to his father and told him about the vizier and how it was he who had urged him to pursue the beast and drove him to his encounter with the she-ghoul. The king summoned the vizier and had him put to death.

The vizier added, "You too, your Majesty, if you trust, befriend, and bestow favors on this sage, he will plot to destroy you and cause your death. Your Majesty should realize that I know for certain that he is a foreign agent who has come to destroy you. Haven't you seen that he cured you externally, simply with something you held in your hand?" King Yunan, who was beginning to feel angry, replied, "You are right, vizier. The sage may well be what you say and may have come to destroy me. He who has cured me with something to hold can kill me with something to smell." Then the king asked the vizier, "My vizier and good counselor, how should I deal with him?" The vizier replied, "Send for him now and have him brought before you, and when he arrives, strike off his head. In this way, you will attain your aim and fulfill your wish." The king said, "This is good and sound advice." Then he sent for the sage Duban, who came immediately, still feeling happy at the favors, the money, and the robes the king had bestowed on him. When he entered, he pointed with his hand toward the king and began to recite the following verses:

If I have been remiss in thanking you,
For whom then have I made my verse and prose?
You granted me your gifts before I asked,
Without deferment and without excuse.
How can I fail to praise your noble deeds,
Inspired in private and in public by my muse?
I thank you for your deeds and for your gifts,
Which, though they bend my back, my care reduce.

The king asked, "Sage, do you know why I have had you brought before me?" The sage replied, "No, your Majesty." The king said "I brought you here to have you killed and to destroy the breath of life within you." In astonishment Duban asked, "Why does your Majesty wish to have me put to death, and for what crime?" The king replied, "I have been told that you are a spy and that you have come to kill me. Today I will have you killed before you kill me. I will have you for lunch before you have me for dinner." Then the king called for the executioner and ordered him, saying, "Strike off the head of this sage and rid me of him! Strike!"

When the sage heard what the king said, he knew that because he had been favored by the king, someone had envied him, plotted against him, and lied to the king, in order to have him killed and get rid of him. The sage realized then that the king had little wisdom, judgment, or good sense, and he was filled with regret, when it was useless to regret. He said to himself, "There is no power and no strength, save in God the Almighty, the Magnificent. I did a good deed but was rewarded with an evil one." In the meantime, the king was shouting at the executioner, "Strike off his head." The sage implored, "Spare me, your Majesty, and God will spare you; destroy me, and God will destroy you." He repeated the statement, just as I did, O demon, but you too refused, insisting on killing me. King Yunan said to the sage, "Sage, you must die, for you have cured me with a mere handle, and I fear that you can kill me with anything." The sage replied, "This is my reward from your Majesty. You reward good with evil." The king said, "Don't stall; you must die today without delay." When the sage Duban became convinced that he was going to die, he was filled with grief and sorrow, and his eyes overflowed with tears. He blamed himself for doing a favor for one who does not deserve it and for sowing seeds in a barren soil and recited the following verses:

Maimuna was a foolish girl,
Though from a sage descended,
And many with pretense to skill
Are e'en on dry land upended.

The executioner approached the sage, bandaged his eyes, bound his hands, and raised the sword, while the sage cried, expressed regret, and implored, "For God's sake, your Majesty, spare me, and God will spare you; destroy me, and God will destroy you." Then he tearfully began to recite the following verses:

> They who deceive enjoy success,
> While I with my true counsel fail
> And am rewarded with disgrace.
> If I live, I'll nothing unveil;
> If I die, then curse all the men,
> The men who counsel and prevail.

Then the sage added, "Is this my reward from your Majesty? It is like the reward of the crocodile." The king asked, "What is the story of the crocodile?" The sage replied, "I am in no condition to tell you a story. For God's sake, spare me, and God will spare you. Destroy me, and God will destroy you," and he wept bitterly.

Then several noblemen approached the king and said, "We beg your Majesty to forgive him for our sake, for in our view, he has done nothing to deserve this." The king replied, "You do not know the reason why I wish to have him killed. I tell you that if I spare him, I will surely perish, for I fear that he who has cured me externally from my affliction, which had defied the Greek sages, simply by having me hold a handle, can kill me with anything I touch. I must kill him, in order to protect myself from him." The sage Duban implored again, "For God's sake, your Majesty, spare me, and God will spare you. Destroy me, and God will destroy you." The king insisted, "I must kill you."

Demon, when the sage realized that he was surely going to die, he said, "I beg your Majesty to postpone my execution until I return home, leave instructions for my burial, discharge my obligations, distribute alms, and donate my scientific and medical books to one who deserves them. I have in particular a book entitled *The Secret of Secrets,* which I should like to give you for safekeeping in your library." The king asked, "What is the secret of this book?" The sage replied, "It contains countless secrets, but the chief one is that if your Majesty has my head struck off, opens the book on the sixth leaf, reads three lines from the left page, and speaks to me, my head will speak and answer whatever you ask."

The king was greatly amazed and said, "Is it possible that if I cut off your head and, as you say, open the book, read the third line, and speak to your head, it will speak to me? This is the wonder of wonders." Then the king allowed the sage to go and sent him home under guard. The sage settled his affairs and on the following day returned to the royal palace and found assembled there the princes, viziers, chamberlains, lords of the realm, and military officers, as well as the king's retinue, servants, and many of his citizens. The sage Duban entered, carrying an old book and a kohl[5] jar containing powder. He sat down, ordered a platter, and poured out the powder and smoothed it on the platter. Then he said to the king, "Take this book, your Majesty, and don't open it until after my execution. When my head is cut off, let it be placed on the platter and order that it be pressed on

---

5. Cosmetic, used by Eastern, especially Muslim, women to darken the eyelids.

the powder. Then open the book and begin to ask my head a question, for it will then answer you. There is no power and no strength save in God, the Almighty, the Magnificent. For God's sake, spare me, and God will spare you; destroy me, and God will destroy you." The king replied, "I must kill you, especially to see how your head will speak to me." Then the king took the book and ordered the executioner to strike off the sage's head. The executioner drew his sword and, with one stroke, dropped the head in the middle of the platter, and when he pressed the head on the powder, the bleeding stopped. Then the sage Duban opened his eyes and said, "Now, your Majesty, open the book." When the king opened the book, he found the pages stuck. So he put his finger in his mouth, wetted it with his saliva, and opened the first page, and he kept opening the pages with difficulty until he turned seven leaves. But when he looked in the book, he found nothing written inside, and he exclaimed, "Sage, I see nothing written in this book." The sage replied, "Open more pages." The king opened some more pages but still found nothing, and while he was doing this, the drug spread through his body—for the book had been poisoned—and he began to heave, sway, and twitch.

But morning overtook Shahrazad, and she lapsed into silence. Then her sister Dinarzad said, "Sister, what an amazing and entertaining story!" Shahrazad replied, "What is this compared with what I shall tell you tomorrow night if the king spares me and lets me live!"

THE SEVENTEENTH NIGHT

The following night Dinarzad said to her sister Shahrazad, "Please, sister, if you are not sleepy, tell us one of your lovely little tales to while away the night." The king added, "Let it be the rest of the story of the sage and the king and of the fisherman and the demon." Shahrazad replied, "Very well, with the greatest pleasure":

I heard, O King, that when the sage Duban saw that the drug had spread through the king's body and that the king was heaving and swaying, he began to recite the following verses:

> For long they ruled us arbitrarily,
> But suddenly vanished their powerful rule.
> Had they been just, they would have happily
> Lived, but they oppressed, and punishing fate
> Afflicted them with ruin deservedly,
> And on the morrow the world taunted them,
> " 'Tis tit for tat; blame not just destiny."

As the sage's head finished reciting the verses, the king fell dead, and at that very moment the head too succumbed to death. Demon, consider this story.

But morning overtook Shahrazad, and she lapsed into silence. Then her sister Dinarzad said, "Sister, what an entertaining story!" Shahrazad replied, "What is this compared with what I shall tell you tomorrow night if I live!"

FUZŪLĪ (1480?–1556?)
Turkish

Muhammad ibn Sulaymān, whose pen name was Fuzūlī, is considered one of the most illustrious figures in classical Turkish literature. Fuzūlī came from an educated family and was an accomplished author in all three classical Islamic languages: Arabic, Persian, and Turkish. It is, however, his literary output in Turkish, in the Azerbaijan dialect, that has placed Fuzūlī's name in the limelight. His popularity has not waned over the centuries among Turkish speakers. The poem here, a *ghazal,* is from his collection of lyrics in Turkish.

[My love has tired me of my life]

My love has tired me of my life—will she not tire of cruelty?
My sigh has set the spheres on fire—will not the candle of my passion burn?

On those who faint and fail for her, my love bestows a healing drug
Why does she give none to me; does she not think that I am sick?

I hid my pain from her. They said tell it to your love.
And if I tell that faithless one—I do not know, will she believe, or will she not?

In the night of separation, my soul burns, my eye weeps blood
My cries awaken; does my black fate never wake?

Against the rose of your cheek red tears stream from my eye
Dear love, this is the time of roses, will not these flowing waters cloud?

It was not I who turned to you but you who drove my sense away
When the fool who blames me sees you, will he not be put to shame?

Fuzuli is a crazy lover and a byword among folk
Ask then what kind of love is this—of such a love does he not tire?

Translated by Bernard Lewis.

Bronze Benin head (sixteenth century).
The Metropolitan Museum of Art.

SECTION VI
Africa: The Epic Tradition

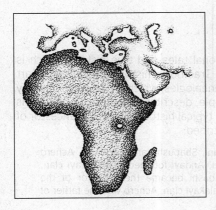

The epic in Africa is born again and again; it combines several oral genres: songs, incantations, proverbs, praise poetry, narrative, and sometimes genealogy. Oral praise poetry, which is equivalent to a panegyric, is produced throughout Africa to celebrate a hero or heroine, or a respected animal, or sometimes both at the same time as in S. K. Lekgothoane's "Praises of Animals in Northern Section":

It is the yellow leopard with the spots
The yellow leopard of the cliffs
It is the leopard of the broad cheeks
Yellow leopard of the broad face, I-do-not-fear

The real subjects in this excerpt are the chiefs of the Tlokwa of Lesotho. An equally well-known genre in Africa is the traditional narrative of an important historical figure such as Chaka the Zulu, Liongo Fumo of East Africa, Muhammed Toure of Songhay, or Idris Alooma of Kanem-Bornu. Dedan Kimathi, the Kenyan freedom fighter, is made legendary through the eyes of a Gikuyu schoolboy in *Weep Not Child,* a novel by Ngugi wa Thiong'o:

Dedan can change himself into anything—a white man, a bird, or a tree. He can also turn himself into an aeroplane. He learnt all this in the Big War.

The accounts of such figures, presented as fact, often contain elements difficult for the outsider to believe, but it is this legendary quality that enforces belief and a sense of affiliation. An essential distinction is always maintained between invented, fictional tales and true history, which is often the province only of elders or priests. Traditional history is an integral part of the life of many African peoples, as are genealogies, which are performed orally and function as a charter for a group of people, describing their present relations in terms of their lineages from the past. In a typical historical text, the ancestor of the Abasamia clan in western Kenya is described:

> [He] had five sons: Achero, Andaayi, Aswani, Shabushi, and Andakayi. Achero became the ancestor of the Abachero clan; Andayi founded the Abatayi clan; Aswani founded the Abayonga clan; Shabushi became the ancestor of the Abakambuli; and Andakayi founded the Abalakayi clan. Achero was the father of Luyo, father of Mwamba, father of Miya.

The recitation is in fact a poetic exercise in name-dropping, since every name alludes to some person or group the hearer is expected to recognize.

When we combine praise with narrative, we get epic. Today researchers keep uncovering so much new epic and heroic poetry that the form cannot be thought of as confined to any one of Africa's four language groups: Click (macro-khoisan), Afro-Asiatic, Savanna-Sahara, and Niger-Congo. Heroic epics are as common in Africa as anywhere else, for the same reasons. Just as the Greek Oedipus and Theseus, the Hebrew Moses, the German Siegfried, and the Irish Cu Chulainn—heroes of the ancient Mediterranean and Europe—are historically related because the peoples are contiguous, so the lives of African heroes often include similar incidents: unusual birth, precocious growth, enormous physical strength and bravery in slaying monsters or enemies, and eventual leadership or fathering of a people. Anthropologist Clyde Kluckhohn found the theme of slaying monsters in thirty-seven of the fifty world-wide cultures he studied for their myth themes. He interpreted it psychologically in his *Myth and Mythmaking*:

> Not infrequently, the elaboration of the theme has a faintly Oedipal flavor. Thus in Bantu Africa (and beyond) a hero is born to a woman who survives after a monster has eaten her spouse (and everyone else). The son immediately turns into a man, slays a monster or monsters, restores his people—but not his father—and becomes chief.

In African forms of this hero legend, the Oedipal theme is often disguised by making it seem that the son is avenging his father. The components of this epic also include a favorite African motif, the all-devouring monster who swallows whole towns of people and buildings. The final incident will then be the rescuing of the victims from the monster's belly.

The epic selections presented here refer to events that happened as early as the eighth or tenth century. All were recorded in modern times. Face-to-face oral transmission was for many centuries, and still is, a perfectly adequate channel for the production and enjoyment of this kind of art. Although writing, recording, broadcasting, or printing an epic alters its status as living entertainment, it does not diminish it. In an age of increased African literacy, print affords recognition to an ancient art, especially when the many nights required for a full performance do not seem to be available any more. Printed texts and translations can manage sometimes to reflect the active intervention of audiences, commenting on the action, applauding the narrator, and even helping out the person running the tape recorder. Historical reconstruction enables us to imagine where and when an epic would have been performed, and what audience would have especially appreciated it. All these texts, then, should be read as libretti for performance, like Sophocles' *Antigone* or Racine's *Phaedra*.

Historical Background

The epics in this section are drawn from West Africa, Egypt, and the island of Madagascar. The borders of the region known as West Africa are the Sahara to the north, the Atlantic Ocean to the west and south, and the basin of Lake Chad to the east. Its northern portion forms the greater part of the Sudan, a broad belt of sahel (semidesert) modulating to savanna (flat grasslands) that stretches across Africa south of the Sahara. Below the Sudan is a forested coastal region called Guinea.

The West African epics included in this section come from three Sudanese empires: Ghana, Mali, and Songhay. They flourished successively from the eighth through the sixteenth centuries, and each in its time controlled lucrative trade between West Africa and the Mediterranean. The trans-Sahara trade routes were ancient — probably as old as the desert itself (which emerged by around 2000 B.C.E.). Mediterranean civilizations offered horses, luxury goods, and — above all — salt. West Africa offered ivory, slaves, and gold from the valleys of the Senegal and Niger rivers. During the sixth century B.C.E., the Phoenician colony of Carthage (near present-day Tunis) tried to establish direct contact with West Africa by sea. But the attempt failed, and the desert routes remained the monopoly of mediating Saharan peoples.

The first written mention of Ghana appears in an Arab chronicle of the late eighth century. Arabs united under Islam had by this time amassed an empire that stretched from Spain across North Africa and east as far as Afghanistan. In the process they came into possession of the northern ends of the trans-Sahara trade routes. Over the ensuing centuries, Islam spread gradually into West Africa, largely through trading contacts, and Muslim geographers and chroniclers left descriptions of the kingdoms they encountered.

Ghana arose in the Sahel between the Senegal and Niger rivers (far north of the present-day coastal nation of Ghana, to which it is unrelated). By the time the Arabs encountered it, the kingdom—if not the empire—was probably several centuries old. Excavations have confirmed Arabic records that tell of stone cities and surrounding farmlands. The court was wealthy and powerful, and the king commanded the allegiance of numerous lesser rulers. Muslims found welcome not only as traders but also as administrators and legal advisers to the king.

In the mid-eleventh century, Ghana was attacked and occupied for a time by the Almoravids, a group of North African nomadic peoples united under a militant version of Islam. The occupation—possibly combined with a series of droughts—undermined the empire, and its satellite kingdoms grew increasingly independent.

During the early thirteenth century, the Keita kings of Mali, a gold-rich region of the uppermost Niger valley, emerged as the new regional power. Under King Son-Jara (or Sundiata, r. 1230–1255), Mali extended its dominion along the length of the upper Niger, around the Niger Bend, and west to the Atlantic coast, subsuming the former empire of Ghana in a much larger formation. Mali controlled the Sahara trade far more effectively than Ghana had. The West African commercial centers of Gao, Walata, and Jenne were firmly under Malian control, and the capital, Niani, grew into a major city.

The Keita kings were Muslim. Several even made the pilgrimage to Mecca, among them Mansa Musa, who ruled in the early fourteenth century. Musa's pilgrimage earned him lasting fame when, during his stay in Egypt, so much gold flowed from his purse that a decade-long inflation ensued. He returned to Mali with a retinue of scholars, scientists, artists, and architects, transforming Timbuktu into the most important intellectual center of Islam south of the Sahara.

Mali went into a decline in the fifteenth century, and, as with Ghana, its subject kingdoms began to splinter away. The next power to arise were the Songhay, whose kings ruled from the city of Gao on the Niger Bend. The Songhay were brought into the Mali empire by Mansa Musa but succeeded in throwing off Malian control in 1375. In the fifteenth century, they reached out to form their own empire, which extended in a broad arc along the Niger River and north to the Sahara. Songhay dominance lasted until 1591, when the empire was conquered by the Saʿdi Dynasty of Morocco.

Madagascar lies off the southeastern coast of Africa. Its people, the Malagasy, are of Indonesian and Afro-Arab ancestry; the Malagasy language is Malayo-Polynesian with some Bantu and Arabic vocabulary. This multicultural mixture is typical of the East African coastal territories, which from ancient times were visited by ships trading along the coast of South Asia. In all likelihood, Indonesian migrations to Africa and Madagascar began before the birth of Christ or what we now call the common era. Muslim traders arrived from East Africa between the ninth and fourteenth centuries. Europeans discovered Madagascar in 1500, and in the seventeenth century the French established settlements.

The Malagasy epic excerpted here is from the Merina people, who inhabit the central plateau of the island. Their kingdom, Imerina, was founded by a forceful visionary ruler Andrianampoinimerina (r. 1782–1810), known as the "Prince in the Heart of Imerina." His son, Radama I, who ruled from 1810 to 1828, opened the island to British influence; Christian missionaries put the Malagasy language into writing and started schools. After his death, his xenophobic widow Ranavalona I (r. 1828–1861) expelled all Europeans and reinstated traditional beliefs and customs. Then in another reversal, Ranavalona's successors again welcomed Europeans. Despite much resistance, Madagascar eventually succumbed to the French and underwent sixty-two years of colonial rule. Independence was won in 1958.

Further Readings

Davidson, Basil. *African Civilization Revisited from Antiquity to Modern Times*. Trenton N.J.: Africa World Press, 1991.

Finnegan, Ruth. *Oral Literature in Africa*. Oxford: Clarendon Press, 1970.

Okpewho, Isidore. *African Oral Tradition*. Bloomington: Indiana University Press, 1992.

Scheub, Harold. *African Oral Narratives, Proverbs, Riddles, Poetry and Song*. Boston: G. K. Hall, 1977.

———. "A Review of African Oral Traditions and Literature." *African Studies Review* June–September 1985: 1–72.

Zell, Hans M., et al. *A New Reader's Guide to African Literature*. New York: Africana, 1983.

MERINA PEOPLE
Madagascar

The Merina (pronounced *Mairn'*, the "Elevated People") are the largest and most influential (1,200,000) of Madagascar's eighteen dialect groups. From the seventeenth century until 1896, when France invaded and colonized the island, the Merina state ("Imerina") expanded through military conquest and forced labor. The colossus of Merina history is Andrianampoinimerina ("Prince in the heart of Imerina"), whose imposing presence was the incarnation of kingly authority. Ibonia's heroic deeds in the epic seem to allude to this divine king. The Merina have produced eloquent oratory, innumerable proverbs, and a remarkable kind of oral poetry, *hainteny* (pron. *hine-tenny*), in which men and women court each other. Famous for blending this poetry with European literary forms is the poet Jean-Joseph Rabearivelo (1901–1937).

The epic from which this episode comes narrates the typical biography of a legendary hero of royal parentage: unusual birth, precocious strength, a quest for his betrothed, tests and combats, supernatural aid, a struggle with the abductor of the beloved, final victory, and marriage. The epic was probably recited in and for the royal court of nineteenth-century Imerina, a rigidly stratified society having a female sovereign. This early episode depicts the testing of Beautiful-Rich, the hero's mother, who proves to be nearly as heroic as her son will be. By featuring the mother early in this recitation, the Merina bard combines praise poetry, flattering his audience, with narration.

At the beginning of this excerpt, Skyfather expresses dismay that his favorite son, Prince of the Center, has no heir. The prince sends Beautiful-Rich, his barren wife, to the diviner, Great-Echo, who in turn sends her to a certain rock to capture a locust that will enable her to conceive. Beautiful-Rich displays perfect determination in seeking out the diviner and "masculine" courage in her quest for a magical object that will fulfill her destiny. She returns home pregnant with the hero.

from *Ibonia*

[Beautiful-Rich Goes to Seek the Locust]

Skyfather then went out and mounted his golden throne.
He made a speech:
"Now I have completed the welcome meal for the four men,
    but not the one for Prince of the Center.
We will arrange two groups facing each other.
    That means a hundred bulls, a hundred oxen and the rest.
I have had the guns and cannons fired with a single charge,

Collected by L. Dahle, a Norwegian missionary; translated by Lee Haring from the published version.

and the discharge was lost in the earth,
        because there is no child to cry.[1]
Beautiful-Rich is barren.   10
The Prince of the Center has fathered no child.
What I have to say to you then,
    Beautiful-Rich and Prince of the Center, is this:
        All now is well,
            your greatness up to now is all very well—   15
        but there is no child to cry."

Now when Beautiful-Rich heard that,
    she was perturbed. She wept, she cried out,
        she covered her husband with tears up to the neck,
    Prince of the Center. Then she said,   20
"Prince, men are assembled here;
    much wealth is here.
    Only a single calabash[2] is denied to us,
        and swine and curs must inherit this kingdom and land."
"I will not take another wife," said Prince of the Center.   25
"Go you to get help from Great-Echo [the diviner].
Get a childbearing charm from him."

So Beautiful-Rich set out to get help from Great-Echo.
    With her she took ten women
        and a hundred men carrying guns, spears, and muskets.   30

When they reached Great-Echo's place, Great-Echo said,
"The 'line for two' is not made by my foot,
The 'line for four' is not made by my hand.[3]
What will happen next year I see this year,
    what will happen tomorrow I see today.   35
So I know even before you open your mouth
    what brings you here grieving. It is your need for a child.
How many men accompany you, how many women accompany you?"

Beautiful-Rich said, "A hundred men,
carrying a hundred guns, a hundred spears, and a hundred muskets,   40
    and ten women carrying ten round stones."

"Eehh, woman!" said Great-Echo.
    "He will be a hard man on earth.
        A thousand years in your womb,
            a hundred men inside you,   45

---

1. Crying means that the child is alive but also
that there will be no child to weep for
Skyfather himself when he dies.
2. A bowl-shaped container made from a large
gourd.

3. Refers to arrangements of stones used in
sikidy, or divination. The divine says he is
the channel, not the creator, of the divination signs.

and ten years will you carry him, O Beautiful-Rich.
If you consent, then that is what I will give you.
But if you do not consent, you will have no other child.
Then go home—
    for he is a trouble child. Trouble, that one,   50
      and a calamity child.
He is a thunderbolt, he is lightning.
    On earth he will kill his father,
                in the womb he will kill his mother."

Then Beautiful-rich said, "Oh yes, sir,   55
    for it is bad to have nothing, even trouble,
      and the child is the heir to the father."

              Great-Echo said, "So be it.
If you agree, then go you to Male-Rock-of-Thousand-Corners.
    Lightning will also be there.   60
      Animals will be there.
        Deadly things will be there too.
But when you go there,
    have each of your women carry two cannonballs
      and you carry three.   65
A locust you will get there, as your childbearing charm.
A thousand strong men will meet you there,
        but those thousand strong men will flee,
    for the male locust will madden the ox
      and will pass over the Male-Rock-of-Thousand-Corners."   70

        Then she set out.
When she arrived near the stone,
    waterspouts, winds, thunderbolts, hail fell upon her.
    So did all deadly things.
Seven times did the ten women fall,   75
    but Beautiful-Rich was the only one who did not fall.
As she approached Male-Rock-of-Thousand-Corners,
    there were more deadly things.
When she came to the north of the rock,
            there was the locust, on top of it.   80
Male-Rock-of-Thousand-Corners sank down
    level with the ground.
Then again her ten servant women fell, crushing their hands,
    but Beautiful-Rich was the only one who did not fall.
The locust was bombarded with bullets   85
    so that Beautiful-Rich could catch him,
but that locust did not die.
    He seemed ever more alive, to look at him.
Then Beautiful-Rich bound up her loins like a man

to catch the locust.   90
       and she caught the locust.
It carried them up, flying.
  Beautiful-Rich almost reached the sky—
    but she would not fall:
      she was sitting atop the stone.   95
Then it came down to earth,
  but did not enlarge its hole;
  it fell into the same place as before.
Beautiful-Rich slid into the stone[4]
    and took the locust to make a childbearing charm.   100

Then each of the oldest trees in the world began to speak:
  "I am the childbearing charm."
  "I am the childbearing charm."
When Beautiful-Rich had arrived
  among the childbearing charms—   105
  among Does-Not-Wither-When-Transplanted,
    and Does-Not-Dry-When-Planted,
      Thousand-Goat-Horns,
      Hundred-in-the-Womb—
she went into the forest to get Single-Trunk.[5]   110
But when she reached the top of Single-Trunk,
      it was the locust who seized the charm.
Then came back Beautiful-Rich, traversing on spiderwebs,
  not touching the sky,
  not touching the blossoms on the trees as she passed,   115
    not walking on the ground.

SONINKÉ PEOPLE
West Africa

These excerpts come from two versions of poetic narratives about the Ghana empire and were recounted by Soninké *griots*—a regional term of uncertain origin for professional wordsmiths found throughout the Sahel. Known in Soninké as *geseré, griots* serve as historians, genealogists, praise-singers, compos-

---

4. Victory over the stone and the locust establish her supremacy over the mineral and animal realms. By the time she enters the male rock, she is carrying the seed.

5. A second charm will give force to the first one.

ers, musicians, spokesmen, arbiters, tutors, and ambassadors. Their female counterparts, *griottes,* perform many of the same functions.

Ghana, once called Wagadu, was described by eighth-century Arab writers as the "land of gold." With its capital at Kumbi Saleh in southeastern Mauritania, Ghana controlled trade in gold, ivory, salt, and slaves between North Africa and the forest region to the south. After reaching its peak in the eleventh century, Ghana declined and many of its Soninké-speaking peoples scattered across West Africa, carrying with them the story of the Bida snake and its role in the empire's fall.

The first text was recorded from a Soninké *griot* named Diara Sylla, transcribed and translated by Mamadou Soumare, and annotated by Germaine Dieterlen and Youssouf Cissé for publication in French in 1977. The second text was recorded from Jiri Silla in 1965 at Yerere, Mali, by Malamine Cissé and translated by Abdoulaye Bathily for publication in French in 1977.

from The Oral Epic of the Ghana Empire

[A Message Left for a Vulture to Convey]

[Diara Sylla first tells his listeners about Dinga Khoré, ancestor of the descendants of the Ghana empire. In this version, they came from India via Yemen and Israel to an unidentified place in Africa approximately a thousand miles east of present-day Mauritania. Toward the end of his life, Dinga left a message for a vulture to convey to his descendants.]

. . . I have a message I would like to entrust to you.

The vulture replied, "We are at your service."

Dinga spoke again: "After my death, when all the sacrifices have been made, you
　　will tell my descendants to go toward the West.

There is a place there called Kumbi, there is a well at that place, and there is
　　something in the well. People talk with that creature, for it is not an ordinary
　　creature. My descendants will only settle down there after they have reached
　　an understanding with the creature in question."

[The vulture transmitted the message to one of Dinga's sons, Djabé Cissé.]

Djabé Cissé asked, "How can one find this place?"

The vulture replied, "You will kill forty fillies for us, one a day."

The lungs and the liver are for me, the vulture, and the remainder of the meat you
　　will give to the hyena."

[After the sacrifices were made, the vulture explained what the descendants of Dinga would find at Kumbi.]

. . . . after their arrival at Kumbi, they will find there a well and inside the well a
　　monster.

They will be called upon to make a contract with this creature.

[Djabé Cissé and his people set off with the hyena and the vulture for Kumbi.]

Told by Diara Sylla and Jiri Silla; translated and summarized by Thomas A. Hale.

They walked for forty days before reaching Kumbi. At their arrival the hyena
  stopped at the edge of a well and the vulture perched at the top of a tree near
  the well.
The vulture said then to the children of Dinga, "Here is Kumbi, here is the well."
Then a loud noise arose from the well.
The voice asked who was there, and the vulture replied that they were the children
  of Dinga, and that they had come to settle there.
At these words, an enormous snake rose out of the well. He was very black, he had
  a crest on his head like that of a rooster, and the crest was very red.
He said, "No one will settle here."
Djabé replied, "We will settle here, for our father at the end of his life ordered us
  to come to Kumbi. And this is certainly Kumbi: here is the well! We shall
  settle here."
"Agreed!" said the snake called Bida. "But there are conditions for that."
Djabé declared then, "We are ready to listen to these conditions."
"Fine!" replied Bida.
"Each year," he said, "in the seventh month, on the seventh day of the seventh
  month, you will offer me 100 heifers, 100 fillies, and 100 girls."
"Agreed," said Djabé, "but each year, the loss of 100 heifers, 100 fillies, and 100
  girls will amount to the ruin of the country."
They bargained and finally agreed on one filly and one girl—but the filly will be the
  best in the entire country and the girl the most beautiful in the entire country.

[Djabé won the title of King of Wagadu as the result of a competition to lift four heavy drums.
The snake then gave him conditional power to rule.]

When Djabé was installed as ruler, Bida declared to him that he will be supplied
  with people and goods as long as he honors the contract that links them
  together.

[A Time for Sacrifice]

[When the time for the sacrifice came next year, the people prepared themselves.]

At the end of the rainy season, in the seventh month and on the seventh day, all
  the people gathered and the sacrifice was carried out.
The morning of the sacrifice, the morning of the solemn day, everyone turned up
  before the door of the ruler, drummers as well as citizens, all gathered in this
  spot.
As for the girl, she was already dressed, dressed in such an extraordinary way that
  you had to see it to appreciate it.
The filly was so fat that it was beyond commentary.
When they arrived near the well, the cortege divided in two.
The *griots* were always in front of the ruler, competing with each other in turn
  until they arrived at the edge of the well.
Before the *griots* could return to the ruler with their songs, Bida the snake
  suddenly surged out of the well and made a terrifying loud noise.

[After coming out and going back into the well twice, the snake appeared again for a final time.]

He wrapped himself around the girl and the filly. He carried them in his lair.
The ruler and his people returned to the town.

[The snake kept his promise. Gold rained down on the country and the people prospered. But during the annual sacrifice to Bida another year, after the third appearance of the snake from the well, a man attacked it.]

Mahamadu the Taciturn cut off his head with his sabre.
At the very moment his head fell away, the serpent cried out: "Seven stars, seven
    luminous stars,"
"Seven famines, seven great famines,"
"Seven rainy seasons, seven entire rainy seasons."
"No rain will fall in the country of Wagadu."
"And even less gold."
"People will say that Mahamadu the Taciturn ruined Wagadu!"

[The Flight of Wagadu]

[After the flight of the Wagadu people from the land, some people went home to see what was left.]

They found that everyone was dead.
Wagadu emigrated.
It divided into three groups.
One went along the banks of the river.
One group headed toward the Sahel.
And the third left by the middle way.
The one that left by the middle maintained the use of the Soninké language.

[Today, all that remains at Kumbi are some ruins. But the Soninké people live on in many parts of the Sahel from Senegal to Niger. An archaic form of their language has become the occult tongue of Songhay sorcerors and *griots*.]

SONGHAY PEOPLE
West Africa

Mali began to lose control of its territory by the mid-fifteenth century. The Songhay empire, based in Gao on the Niger River in southeastern Mali, expanded to absorb a large part of Mali and other areas. From 1463 to 1492, Sonni Ali Ber laid the foundation for Askia Mohammed, a ruler of Soninké origin who built a vast empire from 1493 to 1528.

Tomb of
the Askia
Dynasty
near Gao,
Mali.

Our knowledge of Songhay history comes both from the Timbuktu
chronicles, written in Arabic by Moslem scribes close to the ruling elite, and from
griots, known in Songhay as *jeseré,* derived from the Soninké *geseré.* Songhay oral
narratives were originally chanted in Soninké.

Askia Mohammed spread Islam to new areas of West Africa, and for this
reason the religion has a much higher profile here than in the other epics in this
section. But traditional Songhay beliefs and magic play equally significant roles.
Like Son-Jara and other epic heroes, Askia Mohammed was born under
extraordinary circumstances and had to overcome great obstacles. Called Mamar
Kassaye (Mohammed, son of Kassaye), he appears as the killer of Sonni Ali Ber,
referred to here as his uncle Si.

from *The Oral Epic of Askia Mohammed*

[By Subterfuge, Kassaye Saves Her Son]

Kassaye is the woman.
It is Si who is the man, it is he who is on the throne, it is he who is the chief.
Kassaye is his sister, she is in his compound.
Any husband who marries Kassaye, and if she gives birth,
The seers have said "Listen"—they told Si it is Kassaye who   5
    will give birth to a child who will kill him and take over the
    throne of Gao.
It is Kassaye who will give birth to a child.
That child will kill Si and will take the position of ruler.

*Excerpted from a 1602-line version chanted in Songhay by Nouhou Malio in Saga, Niger, on December 30,
1980, and January 26, 1981. Recorded, translated, annotated, and published by Thomas A. Hale; this is the
first English version of the epic.*

Si also heard about this.
All the children that Kassaye gave birth to,
As soon as Kassaye delivered it, Si killed it.   10
Every child that Kassaye delivered, as soon as it was born, Si killed it.
Until she had given birth to seven children,
Which her brother Si killed.
Kassaye had enough, she said she would no longer take a husband.   15
She stayed like that.
Si is on his throne,
While Kassaye remained like that.
Until, until, until, until one day, much later, in the middle of the night,
A man came who was wearing beautiful clothes.   20
He was a real man, he was tall, someone who looked good in
white clothes, his clothes were really beautiful.
One could smell perfume everywhere.
He came in to sit down next to Kassaye.
They chatted with each other, they chatted, they chatted.   25
He said to her, "It is really true.
"Kassaye, I would like to make love with you.
"Once we make love together,
"You will give birth to a boy,
"Whom Si will not be able to kill,   30
"It is he who will kill Si and will become the ruler."
Kassaye said to him, "What?"
He said, "By Allah."
She said, "Good, in the name of Allah."
Each night the man came.   35
It is during the late hours that he came.
Each time during the coolness of the late evening.
Until Kassaye became pregnant by him.
Kassaye carried her pregnancy.
Kassaye had a Bargantché captive.   40
It is the Bargantché woman who is her captive, she lives in her house, and she too
    is pregnant.
They remained like that.
Kassaye kneeled down to give birth.
The captive kneeled down to give birth.
So Kassaye, Kassaye gave birth to a boy.   45
The captive gave birth to a girl.
Then Kassaye took the daughter of the captive, she took her home with her.
She took her son and gave it to the captive.
So the people left for the palace.
They said to Si: 50
"The Bargantché captive has given birth."
He said, "What did she get?"
They said, "A boy."

He said, "May Allah be praised, may our Lord give him a long life and may he be
    useful."
Then they were thoughtful for a moment.   55
They got up and informed him that Kassaye had given birth.
They asked, "What did she get?"
They answered, "A girl."
He said, "Have them bring it to me."
They brought it to him, he killed it.   60
It is the boy who remained with the captive and Kassaye.

[By this subterfuge, Kassaye saves her son, who becomes a servant working for his uncle. Of
noble origin, he must nevertheless pass as a slave.]

[Mamar Kassaye Sees His Father]

He became a young man tall and very strong, a tall young man.
The children in the compound,
They are the ones who insult him by saying that they don't know his father.
Also, they call him the little slave of Si.
"The little slave of Si, the little slave of Si."   5
They called him "little slave of Si," and said, "We don't know your father, you
    don't have a father.
"Who is your father?"
Then he came home to his mother's house and told her that the children in the
    compound were really bothering him.
They say to him, "Who is your father?"
She told him, "Go sit down, you'll see your father."   10
She said to him, "Look, take this ring in your hand.
"But don't put it on your finger,
"Until you get to the river.
"Then you put it on your finger.
"At that moment, you will see your father."   15
Mamar took the ring to the river.
Then he put the ring on his middle finger.
The water opened up.
Under the water there are so many cities, so many cities, so many cities, so many
    villages, and so many people.
It is his father too who is the chief.   20
They too get themselves ready, they go out to go to the prayer ground.
He said, "That's the way it is."
His father greets him with an embrace.
There is his son, there is his son.
Yes, the prince whom he fathered while away,   25
The chief's son whom he fathered while away has come.
He said to him, "Now go return to your home, you do not stay here.

"Go return home."
His father gave him a white stallion, really white, really, really, really, really, really,
    really, really white like, like percale.[1]
He gave him all the things necessary.
He gave him two lances.
He gave him a saber, which he wore.
He gave him a shield.
He bid him good-bye.

[Armed by his real father from the underwater spirit world, Mamar Kassaye sets out to take power from his evil uncle. He chooses to do so on a Moslem holy day. Pretending to demonstrate his loyalty to Si, he races his horse up to the ruler three times in succession, stopping each time just before the ruler.]

[Mamar Kassaye Kills His Uncle]

He and his people go out, they went to the prayer ground.
They are at the prayer ground.
Then Mamar went around them and headed directly for them.
They were about to start the prayer.
They said, "Stop, just stop, a prince from another place is coming to pray with us.   5
"A prince from another place is coming to pray with us."
The horse gallops swiftly, swiftly, swiftly, swiftly, swiftly, swiftly he is
    approaching.
He comes into view suddenly, leaning forward on his mount.
Until, until, until, until, until, until, until he touches the prayer skin of his uncle,
    then he reins his horse there.
Those who know him say that he is like the little captive of Si.   10
Actually, he does resemble the little captive of Si, he has the same look as the little
    captive of Si.
Did you see him! When I saw him I thought that it was the little captive of Si.
He retraced his path only to return again.
Until be brought the horse to the same place, where he reined it again.
Now he made it gallop again.   15
As he approaches the prayer skin of his uncle,
He reins his horse.
He unslung his lance, and pierced his uncle with it until the lance touched the
    prayer skin.
Until the spear went all the way to the prayer skin.

[Mamar Kassaye decides to atone for the killing of his uncle by making a pilgrimage to Mecca, an event that actually took place between 1497 and 1498. On his way, he forces Islam on many peoples.]

---

1. A type of finely woven cotton cloth.

[Mamar Kassaye Imposes Islam on Many Villages]

In each village where he stopped during the day, for example, this place,
If he arrives in mid-afternoon, he stops there and spends the night.
Early in the morning, they pillage and they go on to the next village, for example,
     Liboré.
The cavalier who goes there,
He traces on the ground for the people the plan for the mosque.   5
Once the plan for the foundation is traced,
The people build the mosque.
It is at that time,
Mamar Kassaye comes to dismount from his horse.

             . . .

They teach them prayers from the Koran.   10
Any villages that refuse, he destroys the village, burns it, and moves on.

[After his return from Mecca, Mamar Kassaye continues to impose Islam on the territories he conquers. But he does not always succeed. He cannot escape the fact that, when
he was an infant, he was nursed during the day by a woman from another ethnic group,
the Bargantché of northern Benin. This milk tie is as strong as the tie of blood that
links people together in families and clans. For this reason, when Mamar Kassaye sets
out to conquer the Bargantché, he encounters difficulty and must call upon his mother for
help.]

[Mamar Kassaye Asks His Mother For Help and Escapes]

His mother, Kassaye, had told him, "Long ago,
"I told him not to fight against the Bargantché.
"He cannot beat them, for he has in his stomach the milk of a Bargantché."

Now, she took some cotton seeds in her hand and said, "Take."
She took an egg, a chicken egg, and she said to him, "Take."   5
She took a stone, a river stone, she told him, "Take."
"If you go," if he goes to the Bargantché,
If the Bargantché chase him,
He should put all his horses before him and he should be the only one behind.
He should scatter the cotton seeds behind him.   10
They will become a dense bushy barrier between him and them.
If they chop it down,
This dense bush will not prevent anything.
They will clear the bush in order to find him.
If the bush does not help at all,   15
This time, if they are still hunting him,
He should put all his cavalry in front of him.
He should throw the stone behind him.
It will become a big mountain that will be a barrier between them.

If the big mountain does not help them,
And when they chase him again,
He should put all his cavalry in front of him again,
Leaving himself in the rear.
He should throw the egg behind him.
The egg will become a river to separate them.

He escaped from the Bargantché, the Bargantché who live along the river.
He never again fought against them.
Now, he just passed through their country, to go and start again his reign.

[Nouhou Malio does not tell us what happened to Mamar Kassaye. But we know from the chronicles that he was overthrown by one of his sons, Askia Moussa, in 1528, and exiled to an island in the Niger River. He died ten years later. The empire then experienced a series of rulers descended from Askia Mohammed—some good, some bad—for the remainder of the century. On April 12, 1591, an army sent by the Sultan of Morocco across the Sahara defeated the Songhay, an event that not only destroyed their empire, but marked the final chapter in the rise of a great Sahelian civilization whose stories still echo across the region in the tales of modern *griots*.]

BEDOUIN PEOPLE
Egypt

The action of *Sirat Bani Hilal,* an epic that recounts the migration of the Hilali, a group of Bedouin Arabs, from Arabia to Tunis, takes place in the eighth or ninth century. The excerpt presented here was recorded on March 10, 1983, by one of the many Egyptian poet-reciters who keep this ancient tradition alive. "The Story of Amir Khafaji" recounts the rescue of Dawaba, daughter of King Amir Khafaji of Iraq, by the hero Abu Zayd (who, however, does not marry her, as he would in a European folktale). Enjoying the king's hospitality as they travel westward, Abu Zayd and his three nephews are assumed to be slaves because they say they are wandering poets and praise-singers. Abu Zayd entertains the court. Dawaba, Amir's daughter, violates custom to descend among the Arabs because she hopes that Abu Zayd's nephew, the handsome Yunis, will perform. To save the situation, Abu Zayd, who really is a poet, recites until dawn. Then when a black slave arrives bearing a letter, Abu Zayd asks to see it; the slave, incredulous at his literacy, accompanies him into Amir's *diwan,* or men's council. The king weeps on discovering that the rival king al-Tash al-Khorasani is extorting tribute, including Dawaba, from him and that he threatens the destruction of Iraq if it is not delivered. During the recitation, the audience comments upon the behavior of the characters.

from *Sirat Bani Hilal*

The Story of Amir Khafaji

Dawaba descended in full regalia [*adalha*[1]]
(Audience: Really.)

from atop the lofty fortress,
kohl[2]-darkened eyes beautifying her form, as was her custom
at her father's, and she went to the dwelling.
The maiden entered the *diwans*,   5
she is eloquent with wisdom for all,
she meets the Arabs in session,
Arabs honored with chairs.[3]
"Dawaba," he said, "O handsome of stature,
O maiden, perform now your duties,   10
I hope you know the proper art.
Why do you come among the Arabs?
Why do you come inside the *diwans*?
O woman wearing earrings, coquettish,
a scandal, a lack of conduct: 15
you are a dishonor among the tribes.
Is this a council for women?
I swear by the path of trust,
a scandal, a lack of conduct,
O maiden, be wary of censure!"   20
Dawaba says to him, "O my father,
yield me the sanctuary of your trust."
"Dawaba, your words speak to me,
may you be welcome among the Arabs."
"O my father, if the slave's like this,   25
then how are his masters in poetry?
Then how are his masters in poetry?
O dark one, why not be silent,
let the handsome one bring forth an ode."
(Audience: Really she wants to get Yunis[4] to speak any way she can)
Yunis said, said the Emir Yunis: 30
"What's to be done about unjust times?
We are neither poets nor praise-singers,
have not even a verse inside a poem,
we shut fast a window on those troubles

Told by Awadallah Abd aj-Jalil Ali; translated by Susan Slyomovic.

---

1. Makeup, earrings.
2. Black eye makeup used by women.

3. Chairs are a sign of government and authority according to the bard.
4. Nephew of the hero, Abu Zayd.

and Abu Zayd flings wide paths and doors." 35
Abu Zayd said to him, "O my nephew,"
in the language of Najd, a strange language,
"O my son, cease your words,
O Yunis, your words are childish words.
I am your uncle the hero Abu Zayd, 40
the lion does not eat my portion,
neither in our *wadis*[5] nor our homeland.
I myself am the warrior Abu Zayd,
I have sworn not to pass by the wretched.
O son, cease your speaking, 45
when am I ever confused how to reject a request?"
Abu Zayd said to him, "O Amir,
hear my words, O Sultan:
the day we set forth from our country
we spread forth our hands praying for the inhabitants, 50
each made poetry for thirty,
every last one, thirty days.
They were standing in rows,
by God, this night we spend with you, O Sultan,
if you bid me to stop I shall stop, 55
as my gift, I refuse no fee."
He said to him, "O poet, divert us,
your night will be the happiest of times."
He said, "O night," to invoke the Beautiful One,[6]
an invocation to the Prophet, sheltered by clouds. 60
He drew on the bowstring, sang of the Beloved
until dawn's rays widened into light.

Abu Zayd stared with his eyes,
yet performed the obligatory prayer to the Merciful One.
He observes the slave coming forward, 65
with a firman[7] stuck in his head,
with a letter stuck in his head.
See the slave, purchased with money!
Abu Zayd went towards him,
he said to him, "Good morning, O lad of Mirgan, 70
good morning, O my cousin.
(*Audience: Really*)
My mother and your mother were sisters,
as for you, your mother is Masuda
and I, my mother was named Zayd al-Mal,
but where are you going and from where do you come? 75

---

5. Oases.
6. The Prophet.

7. Royal order in writing.

The news of yourself, give me a sign."
The slave said to him, "I come from al-Khorasani,
from al-Tash al-Khorasani."
Abu Zayd said to him, "Good, show me the letter,
I would see the writing of the title."   80
He said to Abu Zayd, "Enough, O vile black slave
ill-mannered, you show no respect.
How can Mameluke[8] writing
be read by slaves from Sunnar?"
Abu Zayd nagged at him   85
until he caused him to enter the diwan,
(*Audience: he is politicking*)
when he caused him to enter the diwans
he found the assembly abustle.
(*Audience: he fell into the trap*)

The slave said to Amir, "Behold, O father of Dawaba,
a letter from al-Tash al-Khorasani."
When Amir saw the letter,   90
his tears fell first, wetting his caftan
(*Audience: his color changed*)
Amir wept, tears of his eyes,
his tears upon the cheek, descending,
fate and parting tormented him,   95
all present were astonished by him.
Amir wept, tears of his eyes,
when no one fulfills one's needs
when no one asks after one's sadness, why?
His tears fell first, wetting his cheeks,   100
he wept, drenching his clothes.
Salama the hero had said to him:
"Why tears descending, what happened to you?
O stalwart camel, you spit in rage,
O Amir, why weep, what happened to you?   105
You weep, O Shaykh, and what to do?
I swear by the path of trust!"
Amir said to Abu Zayd, "Then forbear your words,
an evil day brought you among us,
(*Audience: O Protector*)
so you O little slave are ill-omened,   110
they turn you loose in the wadis,[9]
The night you passed in my home
you brought it, like the close walls, down upon me."
Abu Zayd said to him, "Show me the letter,

---

8. The Mamelukes were the dominant class in
   Egypt.

9. River valleys.

I shall explain what the address contains."   115
Amir said to him, "Then you know how to read?"
Abu Zayd said to him, "I am schooled in the Koran.
(*Audience: ya salam*)[10]
First, this old man[11] is a healer,
I heal all the sick,
secondly, this old man is a preacher,   120
I read the a's and d's,
thirdly, this old man is a poet,
I make art and bring forth poems,
fourthly, this old man is a horseman,
my spirit is young in my spear thrust."   125
Then Amir gave him the letter,
Abu Zayd set forth the firman:
"The letter begins, the Jew says:
O Amir,[12] I want tribute.
Beware refusing the tithe of goods!   130
I want ninety she-camels,
fruitful, long-necked ones,
I want ninety he-camels
of the spitting kind, roaring ones,
I want ninety kohl-black horses,   135
their tail hairs sweeping the sands,
I want ninety portions of flour,
the choice grains that sleep on the sieve
(*Audience: that's the way it is*)
and ninety portions of henna
for the hair of the foreigner's daughters.   140
We want ninety lances,
their spearpoints, two thirds of a gintar.
I want ninety spears,
whose teeth wound men
and besides all these,   145
hear my words, O son of Durgham,
from you, I want Dawaba
in the temple, she will bring forth poems.
I want, I want ninety fair maidens,
the choicest of the daughters of Islam.   150
If you bring all these
we shall meet as friends meet,
and if you do not bring all these
I proclaim destruction for your homeland!"

---

10. An exclamation.
11. Conversing with Amir, Abu Zayd refers to himself as "your uncle" in the sense of "this old man in front of you."
12. Prince.

MANINKA PEOPLE
Mali

"Son-Jara" is an epic of the Mandé, whose languages include Mandinka, Maninka, Khasonke, Bamana, Jula, and Wangara. The indigenous term for the old empire of Mali, which flourished in the thirteenth and fourteenth centuries, is *Manden,* sometimes spelled *Mandin* or *Manding.* A person from the Manden heartland is a *Maninka,* sometimes spelled Malinké.

    In the wake of the regional instability left by the decline of Ghana, Mali rose in the thirteenth century because of the efforts of Son-Jara (or Sundiata) Keita. Mali reached a peak in the mid-fourteenth century, when Mansa Musa made an extraordinary pilgrimage to Mecca. Today the cultural heritage of the Mali empire is preserved by *griots* who are called *jeli* or *jali* in the many Mandé languages of Mali, eastern Senegal, The Gambia, Guinea-Bissau, upper Guinea, northern Liberia, and northwestern Côte d'Ivoire*. The peoples of the ancient Manden region—the Maninka, the Bambana, the Jula, and the Mandinka, among others—recognize Son-Jara and his accomplishments every seven years by sending representatives to reroof a sacred house in Kangaba, a town in southwestern Mali that is the center of the Manden. From Ghana to Mali we see an evolution in the form of the West African epic. The 3083-line source of these excerpts is more detailed and more focused on the rise and exploits of a single hero, and it contains references to the new religion in the region, Islam.

from *The Oral Epic of Son-Jara*

[A Family Rivalry]

[Fa-Digi Sisòkò explains how two hunters managed to kill a buffalo that had been devastating the farmers of Du. They received as a reward a woman named Sugulun Kòndè, who rejected them. They then traded her to the King of the Manden,[1] Fata Magan, in exchange for his sister, Nakana Tiliba, and a token that the King had received from his ancestor Bilal, a man of African origin who was the first *muezzin* or prayer-caller for Muhammad, founder of Islam.]

"You must give me your ugly maid.   (Mmm)
"My forefather Bilal,   (Indeed)
"When he departed from the Messenger of God,   (True)
"He designed a certain token,   (Mmm)
"Saying that his ninth descendant,   (Indeed)   5

Told by Fa-Digi Sisòkò in the Maninka language on March 9, 1968, in Kita, Mali; recorded by Charles S. Bird and translated, annotated, and published by John W. Johnson in 1986. This is the first linear, or verse, version in English from the Mandé heartland of what has become the most widely read epic from West Africa.

*Previously known in English as the Ivory Coast.

---

1. The homeland of the Mandé-speaking peoples.

"Having taken his first wife,   (True)
"When he takes his second wife,   (Indeed)
"Must add that token to that marriage.   (Mmm)
"I am adding that token
"Together with Nakana Tiliba,   (Mmm)   10
"And giving them to you,
"You must give me your ugly little maid."
That token was added to Nakana Tiliba,
Exchanging her for Sugulun Kòndè.   (Indeed)
It is said that Fata Magan, the Handsome   15
Took the Kòndè maiden to bed.   (Mmm)
His Berete wife became pregnant.   (Indeed)
His Kòndè wife became pregnant.   (Indeed)

[Birth of Son-Jara]

[The birth of children both to the new wife and the King's first wife set the stage for family
rivalry known in the Manden as *fadenya,* or father-centeredness. It is marked by competition between sons of the same father but different mothers. In the short run the outcome of
the rivalry between Son-Jara and his half-brother determined who would rule the Manden.
In the excerpts that follow, Wizard, Biribiriba, and Magan Konate are praise names for
Son-Jara based on his talents, actions, and paternal lineage. Couscous is a dish of North
African origin composed of a meat-and-vegetables stew on a bed of steamed semolina.]

One day as dawn was breaking,   (Indeed)
The Berete woman gave birth to a son.   (Indeed)
She cried out, "Ha! Old Women!   (Indeed)
"That which causes co-wife conflict
"Is nothing but the co-wife's child.   (True)   5
"Go forth and tell my husband   (Indeed)
"His first wife has borne him a son."   (Indeed)

The Berete woman,
She summoned to her a holy-man,
Charging him to pray to God,   (Indeed)   10
So Son-Jara would not walk.   (Indeed)
And summoned to her an Omen Master,   (Indeed)
For him to read the signs in sand,   (Indeed)
So Son-Jara would not walk.   (Indeed)

For nine years, Son-Jara crawled upon the ground.   (Indeed)   15
Magan Kònatè could not rise.   (Indeed)

                                . . .

On the tenth day of Dòmba,   (Indeed)
The Wizard's mother cooked some couscous,   (Indeed)
Sacrificial couscous for Son-Jara.
Whatever woman's door she went to,   (Indeed)   20
The Wizard's mother would cry: (Indeed)

"Give me some sauce of baobab[2] leaf."
The woman would retort,
"I have some sauce of baobab leaf,
"But it is not to give to you.
"Go tell that cripple child of yours

"That he should harvest some for you.   (Mmm)
"'Twas my son harvested these for me."   (True)

[Baobab Tree]

[The scene of the baobab tree marks the beginning of Son-Jara's rise to power. *Griots*, realizing the significance of what is happening, begin to compose praises to celebrate him. He shows his hunting prowess early and gives other signs of his future greatness. The audience constantly replies to and reinforces the bard. His mother is the first to praise him.]

   "O Kapok Tree and Flame Tree!"   (Fa-Digi, that's true)
"My mother,   (Mmm)
"That baobab there in Manden country,
"That baobab from which the best sauce comes,   (Indeed)
"Where is that baobab, my mother?"   (Indeed)   5
"Ah, my lame one,   (Indeed)
"You have yet to walk,"   (Indeed)

The Wizard took his right foot,
And put it before his left.
His mother followed behind him,   (Indeed)
And sang these songs for him: (Indeed)   10
   "Tunyu Tanya!   (Indeed)
   "Brave men fit well among warriors!   (Indeed)
   "Tunyu tanya!   (Indeed)
   "Brave men fit well among warriors!   (Indeed)
   "Ma'an Kònatè, you have risen!"   (Indeed)   15

   "Muddy water,   (Indeed)
   "Do not compare yourself to water among the stones.   (Indeed)
   "That among the stones is pure, wasili!   (Indeed)
   "   (Indeed)   20
   . . .
   "   (Indeed)
   . . .
   "And a good reputation.   (Indeed)
   "Khalif Magan Kònatè has risen.   (True)

   "Great snake, O great snake,   (Indeed)
   "I will tolerate you.   (Indeed)   25
   "Should you confront me, toleration.   (Indeed)

---

2. A very large and distinctive tree that serves
as a rich source of sustenance for both
humans and animals throughout the Sahel.

"O great snake upon the path, (Indeed)
"Whatever confronts me, I will tolerate." (Indeed)

"Arrow-shaft of happiness. (Indeed)
"It is in one hundred. (Indeed) 30
"The one hundred dead,
"All but Son-Jara.
"The higher stones get crushed! (True)
"Who can mistake the Destroyer-of-Origins! (Indeed)
"And this by the hand of Nare Magan Kònatè!" 35

Hey! Biribiriba came forward.
He shook the baobab tree. (Indeed)
A young boy fell out. (Indeed)
His leg was broken.
The bards thus sing, "Leg-Crushing-Ruler! 40
"Magan Kònatè has risen!" (Indeed)
He shook the baobab again. (Indeed)
Another young boy fell out.
His arm was broken
The bards thus sing, "Arm-Breaking-Ruler! (Indeed)
"Magan Kònatè has risen!" 45
He shook the baobab again. (Indeed)
Another young boy fell out. (Indeed)
His neck was broken. (Indeed)
And thus the bards sing, "Neck-Breaking-Ruler! 50
"Magan Kònatè has risen!" (Indeed)
The Wizard uprooted the baobab tree,
And laid it across his shoulder. (Mmm)
Nare Magan Kònatè rose up. (Indeed)

A crowd of women surged out: yrrrrrrr. (Indeed) 55
"Why have you come today? (Indeed)
"What a spectacle! (Indeed)
"Have they no reason to be here? (Indeed)
"What a spectacle! (Indeed)

"O witch-wives! (Indeed) 60
"O witch-wives of the Manden!
"You go find the answer. (Indeed)
"Today's cannot be found by searching." (Indeed)

"The Master of men, O power, power, power. (Indeed)
"One without people, the wind, the wind. 65
"The woman put the child in a web,
"A web of sorcery!" (Mmm)

They fixed their eyes on Magan Son-Jara standing there:
"Come, let us go!

"Nare Magan Kònatè has risen!   70

    "*Living alone, I know it.*   (Indeed)
    "*After coming to understand that,*   (Indeed)
    "*Bearer of good children, have no shame.*   (Indeed)
    "*Whenever there's a crowd, have no shame.*"

    "*Having power,*   (Indeed) 75
    "*If you prepare yourself for the powerful,*
    "*They will respect you.*"   (Indeed)

    "*The pocket sees only today,*
    "*Its eye is not on tomorrow.*   (Indeed)
    "*The pocket sees only today,*   (Indeed) 80
    "*Its eye is not on tomorrow.*
    "*A fortunate man's happiness occurs while he lives.*   (Indeed)
    "*The unfortunate man's happiness occurs after he dies.*
    "*O misery!*   (Indeed)
    "*But one should not kill himself for misery.*   85
    "*No one knows where misery leads.*   (True)
    "*Khalif Magan Kònatè!*

    "*The one for those behind is Kapok.*
    "*Tunyu tanya!*   (Indeed)
    "*Ours is the Flame Tree,*   90
    "*The golden Flame Tree!*   (Mmm)
    "*Khalif Magan Kònatè has risen!*"

Biribiriba came forward.   (Mmm)
He planted the baobab behind his mother's house:
"In and about the Manden,   (Mmm) 95
"From my mother they must seek these leaves!"   (Mmm)
To which his mother said, "I do not think I heard."   (Mmm)
"Ah, my mother,   (Indeed)
"Now all the Manden baobabs are yours."
"I do not think I heard."   100
"Ah, my mother,   (Indeed)
"All those women who refused you leaves,
"They all must seek those leaves from you."   (Indeed)
His mother fell upon her knees, gejebu![3]
On both her knees,   105
And laid her head aside the baobab.   (Indeed)

    "*For years and years,*
    "*My ear was deaf.*   (Indeed)

---

3. An ideophone—a descriptive word that creates an emotion—for the sound of Son-Jara's mother kneeling on the ground; later ideophones are found on lines 184, 187, and 235: "fèsè," "dèndèlen," and "bilika." (See footnote 6.)

"Only this year
"Has my ear heard news.   110
"Khalif Magan Kònatè has risen!"   (That's true)
Biribiriba!   (Indeed)
Since he began to walk,   (Indeed)
Whenever he went into the bush,   (Mmm)
Were he to kill some game,   (Indeed) 115
He would give his elder the tail,
And think no more of it.

Took up the bow!   (Indeed)
Simbon, Master-of-the-Bush!
Took up the bow!   120
Took up the bow!   (Indeed)
Ruler of bards and smiths
Took up the bow!
Took up the bow!
The Kòndè woman's child,   125
Answerer-of-Needs,
He took up the bow.
Sugulun's Ma'an took up the bow!

The Wizard has risen!
King of Nyani, Nare Magan Kònatè!   130
The Wizard has risen!
Ah! Bèmba!   (Indeed)
Whenever he went to the bush,   (Indeed)
Were he to kill some game,   (Indeed)
He would give to his elder the tail,   135
And think no more of it.

As Biribiriba walked forth one day,   (That's true)
A jinn[4] came upon him,
And laid his hand on Son-Jara's shoulder:
"O Son-Jara!   (Mmm)   140
"In the Manden, there's a plot against you.   (Mmm)
"That spotted dog you see before you,   (Indeed)
"Is an offering made against you,   (Indeed) 145
"So that you not rule the bards,   (Indeed)
"So that you not rule the smiths,
"So, the three and thirty warrior clans,
"That you rule over none of them.
"When you go forth today,   (Mmm)
"Make an offering of a safo-dog,   (Mmm)   150
                                                                          (Indeed)

---

4. A spirit.

"Should God will it,
"The Manden will be yours!"   (Indeed)

Ah! Bèmba!
On that, Biribiriba went forth, my father,   155
And made an offering of a safo-dog,[5]
And hung a weight around its neck,
And fastened an iron chain about it.   (Indeed)
Even tomorrow morning,
The Europeans will imitate him.   160
Whenever the Europeans leave a dog,   (Mmm)
Its neck weight,
They fasten that dog with an iron chain, Manden!   (Indeed)

O! Bèmba!
He hung a weight around the dog's neck,   165
And fastened it with a chain.
That done, whatever home he passed before,   (Mmm)
The people stood gaping at him: (Indeed)
"Causer-of-Loss!   (Indeed)
"A cow with its neckweight,   170
"But a dog with a neckweight?"
To which the Wizard did retort: (Indeed)
"Leave me be!   (True)
"Cast your eyes on the dog of the prince.
"There's not a tooth in that dog's mouth!   175
"But there are teeth in my dog's mouth,
"My commoner's dog. Leave me be!   (Indeed)
"My dog's name is Tomorrow's Affair."

Son-Jara's sacrificial dog,
That dog was called Tomorrow's Affair.   180

From his neckweight he broke loose,
And also from his chain,   (Indeed)
And charged the dog of Dankaran Tuman,   (Indeed)
And ripped him into shreds, fèsè fèsè fèsè!   (Indeed)
And stacked one piece atop the other.   (Indeed)   185
The mother of Dankaran Tuman, she wrung her hands atop her head,
And gave a piercing cry: "dèndèlen!   (Indeed)
"That a dog would bite a dog,   (Indeed)
"A natural thing in the Manden.   (Indeed)
"That a dog would kill a dog,   190

---

5. A favorite sacrifice, but its exact nature is
   obscure. The dog is considered an animal
   possessed of extraordinary occult power.

"A natural thing in the Manden.
"That a dog shred another like an old cloth,
"My mother, there must be something with his master!"
Dankaran Tuman replied, "Ah! my mother,   (Mmm)
"I called my dog Younger-Leave-Me-Be.   (Mmm) 195
"Ah! My mother, do not sever the bonds of family.   (True)
"My mother!   (Indeed)
"That is the dog that stalked the bush
"To go and kill some game,
"Bringing it back to me, my mother.   (True) 200
"Do not sever the bonds of family, my mother!"   (True)

The mother of Dankaran Tuman had no answer: (Indeed)
"One afternoon, the time will come for Son-Jara to depart.   (Mmm)
"Indeed what the wise men have said,   (Mmm)
"His time is for the morrow.   (Mmm) 205
"The one that I have borne,   (Mmm)
"He is being left behind without explanation.   (Mmm)
"Son-Jara,   (Mmm)
"The Kòndè woman's offspring,   (Mmm)
"He will take the Manden tribute,   (Mmm) 210
"And he will rule the bards,   (Mmm)
"And he will rule the smiths,   (Indeed)
"And rule the funès and the cordwainers.   (Indeed)
"The Manden will be his.
"That time will yet arrive,   (Indeed) 215
"And that by the hand of Nare Magan Kònatè.
"Nothing leaves its time behind."
    O Biribiriba!
    Kirikisa, Spear-of-Access, Spear-of-Service!
    People of Kaya, Son-Jara entered Kaya. 220
    All this by the hand of Nare Magan Kònatè.
    Gaining power is not easy!   (Indeed)
Ah! Bèmba!   (Indeed)
The mother of King Dankaran Tuman,   (Indeed)
When the Wizard had left the bush,   (Indeed) 225
And offered his flesh-and-blood-brother the tail,   (Indeed)
And when he said, "Here take the tail,"
She retorted: "Your mother, Sugulun Kòndè, will take the tail!"   (Indeed)
"And your younger sister, Sugulun Kulukan,   (Indeed)
"And your younger brother, Manden Bukari.   (Indeed) 230
"Go and seek a place to die,   (Indeed)
"If not, I will chop through your necks,
"Cutting a handspan down into the ground.
"Be it so; you'll never return to the Manden again."   (Indeed)

Son-Jara bitterly wept, bilika[6] bilika!	(Indeed) 235
And went to tell his mother.	(Indeed)
His mother said,	(Indeed)
"Ah! My child,	(Indeed)
"Be calm. Salute your brother.	(Indeed) 240
"Had he banished you as a cripple,	
"Where would you have gone?	
"Let us at least agree on that.	
"Let us depart.	
"What sitting will not solve,	245
"Travel will resolve."	(That's true)

[Son-Jara's Sister Is of Help]

[Son-Jara grows up, becomes a great hunter, and relinquishes his claim to the throne after the death of his father. His half-brother, Dankaran Tuman, forces Son-Jara into exile at the insistence of his mother, the powerful and jealous first wife. Son-Jara returns later to a homeland conquered by the sorcerer king Sumamuru. Unable to defeat the enemy at first because of Sumamuru's far greater occult power, Son-Jara retreats. But his sister offers to help.]

Son-Jara's flesh-and-blood-sister, Sugulun Kulunkan,	(Indeed)
She said, "O Magan Son-Jara,	(Indeed)
"One person cannot fight this war.	(Indeed)
"Let me go seek Sumamuru.	(Indeed)
"Were I then to reach him,	5
"To you I will deliver him,	(Indeed)
"So that the folk of the Manden be yours,	(Indeed)
"And all the Mandenland your shield."	(Indeed)
Sugulun Kulunkan arose,	(Indeed)
And went up to the gates of Sumamuru's fortress:	(Indeed) 10
"*Brave child of the Warrior,*	
"*And Deliverer-of-the-Benign.*	(Indeed)
"*Sumamuru came amongst us*	
"*With pants of human skin.*	(Indeed)
"*Sumamuru came amongst us*	15
"*With shirt of human skin.*	(Indeed)
"*Sumamuru came amongst us*	
"*With helm of human skin.*	(Indeed)
"Come open the gates, Susu Mountain Sumamuru!	(Indeed) 20
"Come make me your bed companion!"	(Indeed)
Sumamuru came to the gates:	(Indeed)

---

6. An ideophone for the sound of falling tears. An *ideophone* is a descriptive word that creates an emotion. "It creates a picture; it is sensual, enabling the listener to identify a feeling, a sound, color, texture, expression, movement, or silence through his own senses. The ideophone is poetic; it is in the purest sense imagery" (Philip A. Noss, "Description in Gbaya Literary Art," in *African Folklore*, ed. Richard M. Dorson. Garden City: Doubleday, 1972, p. 75).

"What manner of person are you?"   (Indeed)
"It is I Sugulun Kulunkan!"   (Indeed)
"Well, now, Sugulun Kulunkan,   (Indeed)   25
"If you have come to trap me,   (Indeed)
"To turn me over to some person,   (Indeed)
"Know that none can ever vanquish me.   (Indeed)
"I have found the Manden secret,   (Indeed)

He lay Sugulun Kulunkan down on the bed.   (Indeed)   30
After one week had gone by,
Sugulun Kulunkan spoke up: (Indeed)
"Ah, my husband,   (Indeed)
"Will you not let me go to the Manden,   (Indeed)
"That I may get my bowls and spoons,   35
"For me to build my household here?"   (Indeed)

Sugulun returned to reveal those secrets
To her flesh-and-blood-brother, Son-Jara.   (Indeed)
The sacrifices did Son-Jara thus discover.   (Indeed)

[Son-Jara Defeats Sumamuru]

[Armed with the information needed to defeat Sumamuru, Son-Jara sets off with his army to attack the enemy. After a series of battles, he and his lieutenants close in on Sumamuru. Their victory sets the stage for the rise of the Mali empire. In the final lines, Sumamuru disappears into a mountain at the village of Kulu-Kòrò, thirty miles northeast of Bamako, capital of present-day Mali.]

Fa-Koli with his darts charged up:
  "O Colossus,   (Indeed)
  "We have taken you!   (That's the truth)
  "We have taken you, Colossus!
  "We have taken you, Colossus!   5
  "We have taken you!"   (Indeed)
Tura Magan held him at bladepoint.   (Indeed)
Sura, the Jawara patriarch held him at bladepoint.   (Indeed)
Fa-Koli came up and held him at bladepoint.
Son-Jara held him at bladepoint: (Indeed)   10
  "We have taken you, Colossus!   (That's the truth)
  "We have taken you!"   (Indeed)
Sumamuru dried up on the spot: nyònyòwu!   (Indeed)
He has become the sacred fetish of Kulu-Kòrò   (Indeed)
The Bambara[7] worship that now, my father.   15
Susu Mountain Sumamuru,
He became that sacred fetish.   (That's the truth, indeed, father, yes, yes, yes, yes)

---

7. A Mandè people living in Mali. They have remained most strongly attached to their own belief system and most resistant to Islam.

Gianlorenzo Bernini, *The Ecstasy of St. Teresa,* 1645–52. Marble, lifesize. Cornaro Chapel, S. Maria della Vittoria, Rome.

SECTION VII
Early Modern Europe

The early modern period in European literature extends from the late fourteenth century to about 1750, from the Renaissance to the Baroque period, and finally to neoclassicism. The Renaissance is most clearly distinguished from the medieval period by a distinctly different attitude toward the culture of ancient Greece and Rome. Although there was an awareness during the Middle Ages of the many remains, physical and literary, of ancient culture, such things were not at the center of medieval concerns. The Renaissance had begun in Italy in the fourteenth century and from there spread to the other parts of Europe. Ancient culture was viewed as a kind of model, a way to understand human experience. It was a time of cultural rebirth, "rebirth" being the meaning of the French word "renaissance," which was later applied to the period. Renaissance scholars eagerly cultivated the artifacts of ancient culture. In literature this meant locating, editing, and publishing ancient manuscripts, often hidden away and preserved in monastery libraries. Understanding these texts involved mastering the intricacies of the classical languages, especially Latin. This led to the birth of the science of philology, the technical study of the language found in these texts.

Complicating this enterprise was the fact that ancient Greek and Roman culture had been pagan while European culture was now Christian. The Catholic Church was the only organized religious body—aside from small Jewish communities—at the beginning of the Early Modern period. The new methods of studying and editing ancient literary texts could be applied to Christian texts as well, to the Bible and to the early Christian writings of the fathers of the Church. These techniques, combined with nationalist stirrings in many countries and what were perceived as abuses within the Catholic Church, resulted in a period of religious upheaval that swept through the sixteenth century. The result was that the sixteenth century was racked by religious wars, which finally ended in a permanent division of Europe: the Protestant North and the Catholic South.

A basic preoccupation of Renaissance scholars was the search for self-knowledge. It was here that the classical models seemed especially useful: if you could understand your own experience in terms of the experiences described in classical literature, your own experience became more meaningful. This secular movement was known as humanism, for its concentration on human values and possibilities. Renaissance literature thus often had an introspective quality that was lacking during the Middle Ages. It was a period that developed a new interest in autobiographical writing, as we will see in Montaigne's "Of Cannibals," presented in this section.

Technological developments also generated a reshaping of European society at the beginning of the late medieval period. Contemporary observers were ambivalent. The invention of the printing press was a benefit while the newly discovered gunpowder was an evil. The fact that a common soldier could lay low a nobleman with a simple firearm, or that artillery made armor increasingly useless except for show, transformed military chivalry into mere display, although display itself was significant for this culture. Nevertheless, the development of the printed book was to be the distinctive hallmark of the period. Texts, ancient and modern, could be disseminated in a standardized form more quickly and more inexpensively than handwritten manuscripts, thus making the knowledge of the period accessible to a far greater number of readers.

A single event was to decisively reshape the view of the world in this period: the discovery of the New World by Columbus in 1492. It was an era of exploration, of colonization and economic expansion, which rarely was for the good of native populations but inspired the European imagination. Such discoveries had few precedents in classical literature and previous European experience. The chief European contact with an alien civilization had been a long and complex interaction with the Muslim countries around the Mediterranean. The discovery of America encouraged other voyages that led to a bewildering variety of cultural otherness and brought Europe into more intimate contact with the cultures of Asia and Africa. This confrontation with non-European otherness resulted in two conflicting tendencies. On the one hand, there was the kind of self-questioning we see in Montaigne's essay on the cannibals. On the other, there was the conviction that the Christian culture of Europe was superior to other cultures, an attempted denial of the other that was to result in the seventeenth century in the rise of racism and colonialism. But the disquieting presence of the other remained impossible to ignore.

Renaissance culture, like the periods that immediately followed it, was obsessed by form. A renewed interest in the rules of art and writing of the ancient classics focused attention on the careful creation of form, on what we would call technique. Form itself became a kind of meaning, and some literary forms became very closely associated with certain kinds of subject matter. In poetry, the sonnet is a clear example of this, perfected according to Renaissance standards, by

Petrarch in the fourteenth century. The sonnet was associated with frustrated love, both physical and spiritual. Merely glancing at a poem and seeing that it was a sonnet raised expectations in a reader that skillful poets could shape through the way they made use of the sonnet form. In prose, the concern for form resulted in a renewed interest in the principles of classical rhetoric, the art of arranging language so as to make it more persuasive. The Roman orator Cicero was a model in this area, a model that writers could imitate or—as often in the seventeenth century—react against.

The baroque period responded to Renaissance form by distorting it, by twisting its shapes to express a vision of a world of extremes, such as that of God and man, very difficult to reconcile. Neoclassicism was to emerge in the seventeenth century as a reaction to this. Obsessed with symmetry and balance, it dominated Europe through the eighteenth century. The neoclassicists sought to express attitudes and ideas that were seen as having universal value, and Renaissance practice was codified into neoclassical law, which allowed no exceptions. The center of neoclassical culture in Europe by the middle of the seventeenth century was in France, where it had become the official artistic policy of the French court, and from there it spread to the rest of Europe where it was eagerly, and more or less effectively, imitated.

The works in this section exemplify these movements and impulses. The central figure in the early northern Renaissance was Erasmus, who dominated the European intellectual culture of his time. His editions of the New Testament and of the church fathers, his voluminous writings on social and religious questions, his many letters, and his varied humorous works offered a stature few have had since. But in the sixteenth century Europe was splitting into Protestant and Catholic camps and his attempts to mediate between the two had little lasting effect, and his vision of a harmonious society organized around a Christianity that was understood primarily as perfect charity was not a forecast of what would follow.

At the same time in Italy Machiavelli was working out ideas about the control of political power, a view that he believed much more realistic. Italy was still the center of European culture in the early sixteenth century. A key figure, because of the brilliance of his work as a sculptor, painter, and architect, and because of his long life, was Michelangelo, who has since also come to be recognized as one of the most accomplished poets of his time. His exchange of sonnets with Vittoria Colonna emphasized spiritual love and demonstrated one set of possibilities for the form. The contrast between Michelangelo's muscular energy and agitation and Colonna's serenity is a striking one for two people who were so close. A different kind of longing is expressed in the sonnets of Gaspara Stampa, in which physical desire is central and overpowering. But in all these poems, the energy is controlled by the tight and precise form that focuses the energy all the more sharply.

In Spain religious and mystical impulses were given striking expression in the prose writings of Saint Teresa of Avila, whose accounts of her own religious experience bear classical and definitive witness to human consciousness overwhelmed by a sense of God's presence.

The literary culture of France in the mid-sixteenth century was especially brilliant, as Italian and classical forms and impulses were being adopted by an already vigorous native tradition. Here too the contribution of women writers is significant. The sonnet was effectively transposed into French and Lyons became an important poetic center. Among the several women active there, Louise Labé was especially successful in using this cultivated form for the elegant expression of her own longings. Marguerite d' Angoulême, sister of Francis I and later to become Queen of Navarre, made herself the center of a literary circle in which her own writing stands out most sharply. Her chief work is the *Heptameron,* which follows the tradition of story collections begun by Boccaccio in his *Decameron* but relies heavily on experiences she herself was familiar with.

Two prose writers, supreme and idiosyncratic, dominate French Renaissance literature: Rabelais and Montaigne. François Rabelais created a unique synthesis of many branches of learning and of popular culture in the five volumes of his *Gargantua and Pantagruel.* This enormous text, outsized as are its giant heroes, satirizes Renaissance ideas about balance and order at the same time that it expresses and embodies Renaissance ideas about education and about social and political concerns. At the end of the sixteenth century, the measured, reflective voice of Michel de Montaigne expresses, in his *Essays,* an equally individual reaction to the ideas and events of his time. He questions, without quite rejecting, the accepted values of style and education, using his own experience as a constant test of the value of what his culture has passed on to him.

England became another vibrant center for later Renaissance literature toward the end of the sixteenth century, with Shakespeare as its undisputed master. His plays have become central to world theater, and his sonnets reveal his supreme skills of formal control, combining passion and precision in their expression. Equally accomplished in his own way was John Donne. With restless virtuosity he shifted from the erotic to the spiritual. The culmination of English Renaissance literature, with neoclassicism now the dominant form is found in the works of John Milton. In *Paradise Lost,* the last great Renaissance epic, Milton carefully worked out a powerful synthesis of classical and Christian themes.

In Spain, Miguel Cervantes partakes of both the Renaissance and the baroque; *Don Quixote,* a comic masterpiece, is a complex novel that has provided the world with an archetype of the man engaged in a mad attempt to enact his fantasies in a world finding no use for them.

The center of European neoclassical culture was France. Especially important are the writers encouraged by Louis XIV, the Sun King, as he liked to be called, and some of the most brilliant of these writers were dramatists. The supreme achievement of neoclassical tragedy is found in the work of Racine, whose dark and stately dramas achieve a synthesis of elegance and intensity that was the ideal of neoclassical culture.

We can thus see that the early modern period was a time both like and unlike our own. Although obsession with religious matters and the belief in the supreme importance of form may seem somewhat strange to us, the questions raised about the status of the individual, about the exercise of political power, and about the presence of cultural otherness are questions we are still wrestling with. The vitality of the literature of this period comes from just these questions.

Historical Background

What we now think of as modern Europe actually had its beginnings in the sixteenth century when the feudalism of the Middle Ages began to yield to a more dynamic structure of society. The decisive turning point was the Renaissance, which by 1600 had reached its final flourishing. During this latter period there arose a number of features we recognize as distinctively modern, including the revival of both urban life and a fertile urban culture, growth of business enterprises stoked by private capital, dedication to classical scholarship and observation of the world, rising literacy, a surge of works written not in Latin but in the vernacular, an expanding bureaucracy, and establishment of increasingly independent, powerful and often warring city-states. As towns expanded into the surrounding countryside and consolidated themselves into corporate and more highly organized states, conflict between—and within—city states proliferated. In *The Prince,* Machiavelli pragmatically counseled would-be rulers how to acquire power, found a state, and keep it—in a very real and unidealized world marked by human weakness and desire.

When Machiavelli proclaimed that he loved his country (Florence) more than his soul, he aligned himself with civil rather than Christian virtues. In this, he signals a crucial shift away from Christian ethics and toward humanist and republican values. Besides Martin Luther, no other figure exerted a greater impact on western culture in the first half of the sixteenth century. In the north, the humanist movement brought the study of the classics within the compass of a larger Christian framework, and a Christian humanist such as Erasmus was able to make sophisticated fun of human foibles even as he championed down-to-earth Christian values. Similarly, Rabelais lampooned the Church's excesses, even as he argued the essential goodness of human nature. Linked with humanism was an increase in literacy and rise of national feeling expressed in vernacular works.

All of these wide-ranging social and political developments were linked to dramatic changes in the economic structure of early modern Europe, a period marked by an ever more rapid revolution. During that time, Europe saw tremendous economic expansion, the explosion of sea and land trade, the replacement of serfdom with a system of capitalist rent, and the general advance and maturation of western capitalism. After two centuries of stagnation, famine, and plagues throughout Europe, populations began to increase after 1500. This, along with technological advances, fueled Europe's transformation into a world economic system. New commodities were transported from new lands, particularly spices and luxury goods from the East. During the sixteenth century, Venice reached prominence as a commercial and shipping center. A century later, the Atlantic coast had begun to replace the Mediterranean as the center of commerce. The Dutch, with the help of a new and cheaper cargo ship, dominated much Baltic trade. Merchants, traders, entrepreneurs, and bankers amassed capital in unprecedented quantities. Not surprisingly, the sixteenth century is known as "the bourgeois century."

In the first half of the sixteenth century, the most important political development was the emergence of the modern sovereign state. In the era of the Tudor sovereigns in England, the monarchial system grew stronger, more centralized, and more organized. In addition to larger bureaucracies and mounting national debts, states now marshalled large and professional armies, sent out diplomats, and supported a princely court—where music, painting, and poetry were pursued in a refined and exclusionary manner. The Renaissance paragon was the perfect gentleman, reinforcing the point that education and statecraft were directed at young men. The efforts to regulate the economy in order to reinforce state power—what is known as mercantilism—had its beginnings but did not fully emerge until after 1650, when more systematic economic plans were drawn up. From roughly 1494 to 1564, Europe's internationally regulated political arena was dominated by France and Spain under the Valois kings and Charles I, respectively. Both countries regularly sent armies into weaker states while England remained aloof from continental matters. By the last forty years of the century, most wishes for a united Europe and Christendom were erased by increasing national consciousness as well as by Charles V's abdication in 1555 of the largest empire the world has ever known: the Holy Roman Empire.

Yet it was not only nation-states, monarchies, and trade patterns that changed. Social patterns altered as well. What demographers label the modern marriage pattern emerged. Unlike the Middle Ages when wives were usually younger than their husbands, brides in late sixteenth century were generally mature and usually the same age as their grooms. The consolidation of state power brought a number of problems having to do with race and ethnicity. As the state power increased, so, too, did an ideal of unquestioning allegiance to the state, conformity to the prevailing culture, and intolerance for those different. Witches were fervidly hunted. The status of Jews progressively worsened, not only in England and France but also in Spain, where in 1492 they were offered the choice of expulsion or conversion. Elsewhere, however, in Holland as well as Italian states, exiled Jews were admitted, though often forced to live in segregated communities or ghettos (the word originates in Venice).

At about the same time that Italy had its High Renaissance, Germany became the center of the Protestant Reformation, a spiritual watershed that thwarted forever any hopes for the religious unity of the West. The crusade began in 1517 with Martin Luther's *Ninety-five Theses,* a protest against the profligacy and materialism of the Church, in particular the generation of papal revenue by selling indulgences or pardons for sins. Luther's act led to excommunication in 1520 but he retained protection from German princes. Within four years, Luther had a sizable following for his theology, known as Lutheranism; he advocated a return to an earlier and simpler Christianity, grounded not in the popes, bishops, or councils, not in rituals and relics, but in the Bible. Such religious reforms succeeded in fragmenting Western Christianity into a number of camps, including Lutheranism, a more militant Protestantism known as Calvinism, and Anabaptism, as well as Anglicanism, which took form under Henry VIII as the Church of England. To this general movement may be added the reforms staged by the Catholic Church upon itself—particularly at the Council of Trent in Italy (1545–1563)—a movement known as the Counter-Reformation that by 1600 had begun to win back adherents. Nonetheless, the religious problem was ultimately settled in Germany, France, and the Netherlands by the Religious Wars, a series of conflicts that did not end until 1609.

With the seventeenth century came the dawning of the baroque era, a name that itself suggests the age's opulence, grandeur, nonclassical dynamism, and sweeping gestures as well as a search for supreme order and stability. The idea of Europe was fully in place, though it was no longer centered in Rome, stretching instead across the entire continent. The period from 1648 to 1789, the Age of Monarchy, was characterized by a new breed of ruler who aspired to absolute power in both name and deed. Among the new rulers was Louis XIV, the self-proclaimed Sun King who immortalized his name with a palace at Versailles, and a court life that established France as an artistic and literary center. Similarly in England, under Elizabeth I as well as the first two Stuarts, James I and Charles I, a system of court patronage and court literature flourished. Yet the Stuart Accession that begins with James I in 1603 also charts a gradual course away from monarchy and court life to a republic in 1649, and finally in 1660, after twenty years of civil war and revolution, to a restored but limited monarchy wherein the crown had to acknowledge a citizen's rights as well as Parliament's power in financial matters. After 1688, private businesses as well as Parliament offered a formidable rival to the power and prestige of court, and this too exerted a profound pressure on the period's literature and art. Despite the Thirty Years' War, the last continent-wide conflict between the Protestants and the Roman Catholics, the idea of Europe continued to be fortified; by 1715, a tenuous but workable balance of power existed between five principal military states—England, Austria, France, Prussia, and Russia.

It has been argued that the Scientific Revolution did more to prepare the world for modernity than the Renaissance and Reformation combined. The crisis of conscience that Europe underwent from 1685 to 1715 was largely prompted by the Scientific Revolution, when age-old beliefs about the universe—as well as the place of humanity in it—were displaced by discoveries in physics and astronomy. The telescope and the microscope, both invented around 1600, enabled scientists to see what had never before been seen. In such a climate, the ground was prepared for reason to replace faith, skepticism to meet dogma, and natural law to contest Scripture; human nature was seen as potentially good and people were thought to be capable of self-government. Such beliefs would find their fullest flowering in the later period known alternatively as the Enlightenment and the Age of Reason.

Further Reading

Burckhardt, Jakob. *The Civilization of the Renaissance in Italy*. New York: Mentor Classic, New American Library, (1960).

Bush, Douglas. *The Renaissance and English Humanism*. Toronto: University of Toronto Press (1968).

Ferguson, Wallace K. *The Renaissance*. New York: Holt, Rinehart and Winston (1940).

Ferguson, Wallace K., Robert S. Lopez, George Sarton, Roland H. Bainton, Leicester Bradner, and Erwin Panofsky. *The Renaissance: Six Essays*. New York: Harper Paperback Editions (1962).

Kristeller, Paul Oskar. *Renaissance Thought and Its Sources*. New York: Columbia University Press (1979).

Rabil, Albert, Jr., ed. *Renaissance Humanism: Foundations, Forms and Legacy*. Philadelphia: University of Pennsylvania Press, (1988).

FRANCESCO PETRARCH (1304–1374)
Italy

Francesco Petrarca, known in English as Petrarch, was born in Arezzo, Italy, but spent much of the first part of his life in Avignon in southern France. Here he met the woman he called Laura: his feelings for her are the subject of his love poems. She died of the plague in 1348, and her death is a crucial event in the *Rime sparse* (*Scattered Rhymes or Lyrics*), as they are called, including sonnets, songs, sestinas, ballads, and madrigals.

Petrarch was famous in his lifetime for his extensive writings in Latin, but his love poetry in Italian started a tradition that spread throughout Europe and was the basic model for European love poetry for centuries to come. Though Petrarch is a contemporary of Chaucer, he is a figure who dissociates himself from the Middle Ages. Even in his return to the classical, he is seen to mark an opening to the modern.

[O Heavenly Father: after wasted days]*

O Heavenly Father: after wasted days,
And all these hungry nights when my desire
Ran in my veins with new replenished fire
At recollection of her lovely ways;
O Heavenly Father, lend the hand to raise   5
Me to the good life whereto I aspire,
Rescue my feet from the encompassing mire
And from the traps my adversary lays.
Father, today the eleventh year is turning
Since that unhappy day of desolation   10
When the yoke first upon my shoulders lay.
Have mercy, Lord, on my long shameful yearning,
Lead thou my thoughts to a better destination,
Remind them, thou wast crucified today.

[She used to let her golden hair fly free]*

She used to let her golden hair fly free
For the wind to toy and tangle and molest;
Her eyes were brighter than the radiant west.
(Seldom they shine so now.) I used to see

*Translated by Morris Bishop.

Pity look out of those deep eyes on me.   5
('It was false pity,' you would now protest.)
I had love's tinder heaped within my breast;
What wonder that the flame burned furiously?
She did not walk in any mortal way,
But with angelic progress; when she spoke,   10
Unearthly voices sang in unison.
She seemed divine among the dreary folk
Of earth. You say she is not so today?
Well, though the bow's unbent, the wound bleeds on.

[Charged with oblivion my ship careers / through stormy combers][†]

Charged with oblivion my ship careers
Through stormy combers in the depth of night;
Left lies Charybdis, Scylla[1] to the right;
My master—nay, my foe sits aft and steers.
Wild fancies ply the oars, mad mutineers,   5
Reckless of journey's end or tempest's might;
The canvas splits 'gainst the relentless spite
Of blasts of hopes and sighs and anxious fears.
A rain of tears, a blinding mist of wrath
Drench and undo the cordage, long since worn   10
And fouled in knots of ignorance and error;
The two sweet lights[2] are lost that showed my path,
Reason and art lie 'neath the waves forlorn:
What hope of harbor now? I cry in terror.

[Life hurries on, a frantic refugee][*]

Life hurries on, a frantic refugee,
And Death, with great forced marches, follows fast;
And all the present leagues with all the past
And all the future to make war on me.
Anticipation joins to memory   5
To search my soul with daggers; and at last,
Did not damnation set me so aghast,
I'd put an end to thinking, and be free.

[†]*Translated by Thomas G. Bergin.*

---

1. Charybdis and Scylla were legendary monsters who threatened sailors in the strait between Italy and Sicily.

2. The two lights in this and the following sonnet are Laura's eyes.

The few glad moments that my heart has known
Return to me; then I foresee in dread   10
The winds upgathering against my ways,
Storm in the harbor, and the pilot prone,
The mast and rigging down; and dark and dead
The lovely lights whereon I used to gaze.

[The ardour and the odour and dark wonder]‡

The ardour and the odour and dark wonder
Of my sweet laurel and her golden glamour
That offered quiet from the dusty clamour,
Death the Despoiler tramples down in thunder.
As when the moon presses the proud sun under,   5
So now my lights go out, my voices stammer;
On Death I cry to halt Death's heavy hammer—
With such black thoughts Love tears my heart asunder.
O lovely lady, brief the sleep you slumbered:
An instant only, then amid the numbered   10
You woke to gaze with them on God's deep glory:
And if my verse its cunning still recovers,
Among the noble minds, the noble lovers
It shall record your name, your deathless story.

DESIDERIUS ERASMUS (1466–1536)
Netherlands / Switzerland

Desiderius Erasmus was born in Rotterdam in the Netherlands around 1466.
Trained in schools that emphasized religious practice as opposed to theological
dogma, he was himself ordained a priest in 1492. Through his writings, all of
which were in Latin, he became the central European intellectual figure of his
time. He died in Basel, Switzerland, in 1536. *The Praise of Folly,* his best known
work, was published in 1511. It is a satiric work in which the female figure of
Folly, the goddess of foolishness, speaks in the first person.

‡*Translated by Joseph Auslander.*

Fool sees himself in mirror from
Erasmus, *The Praise of Folly*.

from *The Praise of Folly*

[Sweetening the Sourness of the Masculine Mind with Female Folly]

But because it was necessary to add just a pinch more of reason to the male, who
is naturally destined for the administration of affairs, Jupiter took me into his
counsel on this occasion (as on others) so that he might provide for this extra bit
of reason as well as he could; and I very quickly gave him advice worthy of myself,
namely, that he join woman to man (for women are foolish and silly creatures, but
nevertheless amusing and pleasant) so that by living with him she can season and
sweeten the sourness of the masculine mind with her folly. For where Plato is
uncertain whether to place women among rational or irrational creatures, he
intended no more than to point out the extraordinary folly of that sex. And if by
chance a woman should wish to be considered wise, she simply shows that she is
twice foolish, since she is attempting something 'completely against the grain,' as
they say, like someone bringing 'a bull to a chinashop.' For a fault is redoubled if
someone tries to gloss it over with unnatural disguises and to work against the

Translated by Clarence Miller.

inborn bias of the mind. The Greek proverb says "An ape is still an ape, even if it is dressed up in royal purple"; just so, a woman is still a woman—that is, a fool—no matter what role she may try to play.

Still, I don't think women are so foolish as to be angry at me because I, who am both a woman and Folly herself, attribute folly to them. For if they see the matter in the right light, they will recognize that they owe it to folly that they are better off than men in so many ways. First, because of their beauty, which they quite rightly value above everything else and which protects them so well that they can tyrannize even over tyrants. Where do men get their rough features, coarse skin, bushy beards—all of them clearly signs of old age? Where but from the vice of prudence? Women, on the other hand, have soft cheeks, a high voice, a delicate and smooth complexion, so that they seem to preserve forever unchanged the marks of adolescence. Then again, what do women want more than anything else in the world? Isn't it to be most attractive to men? Isn't that the reason for so many toiletries, cosmetics, baths, coiffures, lotions, perfumes, so many clever ways of highlighting, painting, disguising their faces, eyes, and skin? Now, is there anything which makes them more attractive to men than folly? What is there that men will not grant to women? But what recompense do men expect but pleasure? Now, women have no way of giving pleasure except through folly. No one will deny this if he takes the trouble to consider how childishly men talk, how frivolously they act when they have decided to indulge in the pleasure to be found in women. There you have it: the source from which springs the first and foremost pleasure in life.

But there are some people—especially old men—who are boozers rather than woman-chasers and who find the greatest pleasure in drinking bouts. Whether there can be a really fine party with no women present is a question I leave to others. But this much is certain: without the spice of folly there is no such thing as an enjoyable party. So much so that if there is no one who can make people laugh, either by genuine or simulated folly, they get some *comedian*—and pay him a good fee too—or find some ridiculous hanger-on to dispel the silence and boredom of the party with his laughable (that is, foolish) quips. What good would it do to stuff the belly with so many hors d'oeuvres, so many tidbits and delicacies, unless the eyes and ears too, indeed, unless the whole mind be replenished with laughter, jokes, and witticisms? But I am the one and only deviser of such delicacies. Of course, those customary amusements at parties—such as choosing a master of the revels, playing dice, drinking each other's health, *passing the bottle around the table,* having everybody (one after the other) sing a song, dancing around and cutting up—all these pastimes were hardly invented by the seven sages of Greece but rather were thought up by us for the well-being of the human race. But the nature of all such amusements is that the more foolish they are, the more they contribute to the life of mortals. Indeed, a sad life can hardly be called life at all. But sad it must be unless you employ such entertainments to dispel the inherent tedium of living.

But perhaps there will be some who do not care for this kind of pleasure either, who find their satisfaction in the mutual affection and companionship of friends. Friendship, they keep insisting, takes precedence over everything else. It is just as essential as air or fire or water, so pleasurable that we can no more do without it than we can do without the sun, and (finally) so honorable (as if that had anything to do with it) that philosophers have not hesitated to place it among the chief goods of life. But what if I can show that I constitute this great blessing 'from stem to stern'? I will not demonstrate it through the crocodile's dilemma, or the argument of the growing heap, or the argument of the horns,[1] or any other dialectical subtlety of that sort. Rather I will use simple evidence to make it 'as plain as the nose on your face,' as they say. Tell me now, to wink at a friend's faults, to be deceived, to be blind to his vices, to imagine them away, even to love and admire certain notorious vices as if they were virtues—surely this is not far from folly? What about the man who kisses the mole on his mistress or the one who is delighted with his sweetheart's polyp, or the doting father who insists his cross-eyed boy merely has a slight squint—what is all this, I say, but sheer folly? They can call it as foolish as they like—they can say it over and over again—but it is this very same foolishness that brings friends together and keeps them together. I am talking about mortal men, none of whom is born without faults (indeed, he is best who is afflicted with the fewest); as for these gods of wisdom, either they never strike up any friendship at all, or they occasionally fall into a gloomy and unpleasant sort of friendship, and even that with very few men (I hesitate to say with none at all) because most men are foolish—indeed, there is no one who does not have many foolish delusions—and, of course, friendship cannot spring up except between those who are alike. But if it should happen that some of these severe wisemen should become friendly with each other, their friendship is hardly stable or long-lasting, because they are so sour and sharp-sighted that they detect their friends' faults with an eagle eye and 'a bloodhound's nostril,' so to speak. Nevertheless, they are completely blind to their own faults and utterly ignore the wallet hanging on their own backs.[2] Therefore, since man's nature is such that no personality can be discovered which is not subject to many faults, and when you add to this the great variety of temperaments and interests, the many mistakes and errors and accidents to which the lives of mortals are subject, how could the joy of friendship possibly last even for a single hour among these 'critics who ferret out every fault' if it were not for that quality which the Greeks designate by the remarkable word υη, which may be translated either "folly" or "an easy-going temperament"? And what about this: isn't Cupid, the author and father of all friendship, completely blind? Just as *things not beautiful seem beautiful to him,* so too he is responsible for a similar phenomenon among you: to each his own seems fair, 'Punch dotes on Judy, Jack must have his Jill.' Such things happen everywhere and are laughed at everywhere, but still it is just such laughable absurdities that fit and join together the whole frame-work of society and make the wheels of life run smoothly.

Now, what has been said about friendship is even more applicable to marriage, which is, after all, no more than an inseparable joining of two lives into one. Good lord! how many divorces (or things worse than divorces) would be

---

1. The names of certain technical kinds of dialectical argumentation.

2. A wallet in Erasmus's time was a large sack.

happening everywhere if it were not that the everyday life of married couples is supported and sustained by flattery, laughing things off, taking it easy, being deceived, pretending things are not as they are—all of which belong to my retinue. Good grief! how few marriages would take place if the bridegroom prudently investigated the pranks played long before the wedding by that refined and (to all appearances) modest maiden. And then, of the marriages actually entered into, how very few would last if many of the wife's carryings on did not remain secret from her husband, either through his negligence or his stupidity. Such blindness is quite rightly attributed to folly, but it is this same folly which makes it possible for the wife to remain in her husband's good graces and he in hers, for the home to remain peaceful and their relatives to remain on good terms. The deceived husband is a standing joke. People call him cuckold. They make fun of his horns and whatnot when he kisses away the tears of his whorish wife. But how much happier it is to be thus deceived than to eat out your own heart with jealous suspicion and to turn everything into a tragic uproar!

In short, without me no companionship among friends, no blending of lives in marriage can be either pleasant or stable. The people would no longer tolerate their prince, nor the master his servant, nor the maidservant her mistress, nor the teacher his pupil, nor one friend another, nor the wife her husband, nor the landlord his tenant, nor a soldier his barracks-buddy, nor one messmate another, if in their relations with one another they did not sometimes err, sometimes flatter, sometimes wisely overlook things, sometimes soothe themselves with the sweet salve of folly.

* * *

Even so, I can imagine the philosophers' objections: "But to be caught in the toils of such folly, to err, to be deceived, to be ignorant—such an existence is itself miserable." One thing is sure: such it is to be a man. But I don't see why they should call him miserable, since this is the way you are born, this is the way you are formed and fashioned, this is the common lot of everyone. But nothing is miserable merely because it follows its own nature, unless perhaps someone thinks man's lot is deplorable because he cannot fly like the birds, or run on all fours like other animals, and is not armed with horns like a bull. But by the same token, he should argue that even a fine, thoroughbred horse is unhappy because he has never learned grammar and doesn't eat pancakes, or that a bull is miserable because he cannot work out in the gym. Therefore, just as a horse who is ignorant of grammar is not miserable, so too, a man who is a fool is not unhappy, because these things are inherent in their natures.

But these word-jugglers are back at it again: "The knowledge of various branches of learning," they say, "was especially added to human nature so that with their help he could use his mental skill to compensate for what Nature left out." As if it were the least bit likely that Nature, who was so alert in providing for gnats (and even for tiny flowers and blades of grass), should have nodded only in equipping mankind, so that there should be a need for the different branches of learning—which were actually thought up by Theutus, a spirit quite hostile to mankind, as instruments of man's utter ruination. So little do they contribute to man's happiness, that they defeat the very purpose for which they were supposedly invented—as that most wise king in Plato clever-ly argues concerning the invention of writing. Thus, the branches of learning crept in along with the other plagues of man's life, and from the very same source from which all shameful crimes arise, namely, the demons—who also derive their name from this fact, since "demon" comes from δαημονες ("scientes," knowing ones). Now the simple people of the golden age, who were not armed with any formal learning, lived their lives completely under the guidance of natural impulses. What need was there for grammar when everyone spoke the same language and when speech served no other purpose than to let one person understand another? What use was there for dialectic, when there was no disagreement among conflicting opinions? What room was there for rhetoric when there were no litigious troublemakers? What demand was there for legal learning when there was no such thing as bad morals—for good laws undoubtedly sprang from bad conduct. Then too, they had more reverence than to pry into the secrets of Nature with irreligious curiosity—to measure the stars, their motions and effects, to seek the causes of mysterious phenomena—for they considered it unlawful for mortals to seek knowledge beyond the limits of their lot. As for what is beyond the range of the furthest stars, the madness of exploring such things never even entered their minds. But when the purity of the golden age had gradually declined, then evil spirits, as I said, first began to invent the learned disciplines, but only a few at first and even those taken up only by a few. Afterwards, the superstition of the Chaldeans and the idle frivolity of the Greeks added hundreds more, all of them nothing but forms of mental torture, so painful that the grammar of even one language is more than enough to make life a perpetual agony.

Still, even among these disciplines, the ones held in highest esteem are those which come closest to the ordinary understanding—that is, the folly—of man-kind. Theologians starve, physicists freeze, astronomers are ridiculed, logicians are ignored. *"One physician alone is worth whole hosts of other men."* And even among physicians, the more ignorant, bold, and thoughtless one of them is, the more he is valued by these high and mighty princes. Besides, medicine ⟨(certainly as it is now practiced by most doctors)⟩ is nothing but a subdivision of flattery, just like rhetoric. The next rank beneath the doctors belongs to pettifogging lawyers; in fact, I wonder if they don't hold the highest rank of all, since their profession—not to speak of it myself—is universally ridiculed as asinine by the philosophers. Still, all business transactions, from the smallest to the greatest, are absolutely controlled by these asses. They acquire large estates, while a theologian who has carefully read through whole bookcases of divinity nibbles on dried peas, waging continual warfare with bedbugs and lice.

Moreover, just as those disciplines which are most closely related to Folly contribute most to happiness, so too, those men who have nothing whatever to do with any branch of learning and follow Nature as their only guide are by far the happiest of all. For she is completely adequate in every way, unless perhaps someone wants to leap over the bounds of human destiny. Nature hates disguises, and whatever has not been spoiled by artifice always produces the happiest results.

* * *

Do not all these witnesses cry out with one voice that all mortals are fools, even the pious? And that even Christ, though he was the wisdom of the Father, became somehow foolish in order to relieve the folly of mortals when he took on human nature and appeared in the form of a man? Just as he became sin in order to heal sins. Nor did he choose any other way to heal them but through the folly of the cross, through ignorant and doltish apostles. For them, too, he carefully prescribed folly, warning them against wisdom, when he set before them the example of children, lilies, mustard seed, and sparrows—stupid creatures lacking all intelligence, leading their lives according to the dictates of nature, artless and carefree—and also when he forbad them to be concerned about how they should speak before magistrates, and when he enjoined them not to examine dates and times, so as to keep them from relying on their own wisdom and make them depend on him heart and soul. To the same effect is the prohibition of God, the architect of the world, that they should not eat any fruit from the tree of knowledge, as if knowledge would poison their happiness. For that matter, Paul openly condemns knowledge as dangerous because it puffs men up. St. Bernard, I imagine, was following Paul when he interpreted the mountain on which Lucifer established his throne as the mountain of knowledge.

* * *

And now, to stop running through endless examples and to put it in a nutshell, it seems to me that the Christian religion taken all together has a certain affinity with some sort of folly and has little or nothing to do with wisdom. If you want some proof of this, notice first of all that children, old people, women, and retarded persons are more delighted than others with holy and religious matters and hence are always nearest to the altar, simply out of a natural inclination. Moreover, you see how those first founders of religion were remarkably devoted to simplicity and bitterly hostile to literature. Finally, no fools seem more senseless than those people who have been completely taken up, once and for all, with a burning devotion to Christian piety: they throw away their possessions, ignore injuries, allow themselves to be deceived, make no distinction between friend and foe, shudder at the thought of pleasure, find satisfaction in fasts, vigils, tears, and labors, shrink from life, desire death above all else—in short, they seem completely devoid of normal human responses, just as if their minds were living somewhere else, not in their bodies. Can such a condition be called anything but insanity? In this light, it is not at all surprising that the apostles seemed to be intoxicated with new wine and that Paul seemed mad to the judge Festus.

NICCOLÒ MACHIAVELLI (1469–1527)
Italy

Niccolò Machiavelli was born in Florence in 1469. He became actively involved in the administration of the Florentine republic, as an envoy, and was closely acquainted with figures like Caesar Borgia, but when the government was overthrown in 1512, when the Medicis returned, he was forced to retreat from the city. It was during this semiexile that he wrote the twenty-six chapters of *The Prince* in 1513, a work that has been a source of controversy since its publication in 1532. Since *The Prince* seems to advise the ruler to adopt a course that is expedient rather than moral, Machiavelli's name, rightly or wrongly, has become associated with political practices whose goal is success by any means. His other best-known works are the *Discorsi* (*Discourses,* (1513-17) and the comedy *La Mondragola* (*The Mandrake,* c. 1518).

from *The Prince*

[On Things for Which Men, and Particularly Princes, Are Praised or Blamed]

We now have left to consider what should be the manners and attitudes of a prince toward his subjects and his friends. As I know that many have written on this subject I feel that I may be held presumptuous in what I have to say, if in my comments I do not follow the lines laid down by others. Since, however, it has been my intention to write something which may be of use to the understanding reader, it has seemed wiser to me to follow the real truth of the matter rather than what we imagine it to be. For imagination has created many principalities and republics that have never been seen or known to have any real existence, for how we live is so different from how we ought to live that he who studies what ought to be done rather than what is done will learn the way to his downfall rather than to his preservation. A man striving in every way to be good will meet his ruin among the great number who are not good. Hence it is necessary for a prince, if he wishes to remain in power, to learn how not to be good and to use his knowledge or refrain from using it as he may need.

Putting aside then the things imagined as pertaining to a prince and considering those that really do, I will say that all men, and particularly princes because of their prominence, when comment is made of them, are noted as having some characteristics deserving either praise or blame. One is accounted liberal, another stingy, to use a Tuscan term—for in our speech avaricious (*avaro*) is

Translated by Thomas G. Bergin.

applied to such as are desirous of acquiring by rapine whereas stingy (*misero*) is the term used for those who are reluctant to part with their own—one is considered bountiful, another rapacious; one cruel, another tender-hearted; one false to his word, another trustworthy; one effeminate and pusillanimous, another wild and spirited; one humane, another haughty; one lascivious, another chaste; one a man of integrity and another sly; one tough and another pliant; one serious and another frivolous; one religious and another skeptical, and so on. Everyone will agree, I know, that it would be a most praiseworthy thing if all the qualities accounted as good in the above enumeration were found in a Prince. But since they cannot be so possessed nor observed because of human conditions which do not allow of it, what is necessary for the prince is to be prudent enough to escape the infamy of such vices as would result in the loss of his state; as for the others which would not have that effect, he must guard himself from them as far as possible but if he cannot, he may overlook them as being of less importance. Further, he should have no concern about incurring the infamy of such vices without which the preservation of his state would be difficult. For, if the matter be well considered, it will be seen that some habits which appear virtuous, if adopted would signify ruin, and others that seem vices lead to security and the well-being of the prince.

[Cruelty and Clemency and Whether It Is Better to Be Loved or Feared]

Now to continue with the list of characteristics. It should be the desire of every prince to be considered merciful and not cruel, yet he should take care not to make poor use of his clemency. Cesare Borgia[1] was regarded as cruel, yet his cruelty reorganized Romagna and united it in peace and loyalty. Indeed, if we reflect, we shall see that this man was more merciful than the Florentines who, to avoid the charge of cruelty, allowed Pistoia to be destroyed. A prince should care nothing for the accusation of cruelty so long as he keeps his subjects united and loyal; by making a very few examples he can be more truly merciful than those who through too much tender-heartedness allow disorders to arise whence come killings and rapine. For these offend an entire community, while the few executions ordered by the prince affect only a few individuals. For a new prince above all it is impossible not to earn a reputation for cruelty since new states are full of dangers. Virgil indeed has Dido[2] apologize for the inhumanity of her rule because it is new, in the words:

> Res dura et regni novitas me talia cogunt
> Moliri et late fines custode tueri.[3]

---

1. Cesare Borgia, the illegitimate son of Pope Alexander VI, had conquered the Northern Italian region of Romagna on behalf of his father, who made him Duke of Romagna. Famous for his violence and treachery, he became a noted example of the unscrupulous Renaissance warlord.

2. In Virgil's *Aeneid*, Dido is the queen of the newly established settlement of Carthage on the hostile North African coast.

3. Harsh conditions and the newness of my kingdom force me to undertake such things and to watch my boundaries far and wide with guards.

Machiavelli, oil painting by Santi di Tito (1536 –1603). In the Palazzo Vecchio, Florence.

Nevertheless a prince should not be too ready to listen to talebearers nor to act on suspicion, nor should he allow himself to be easily frightened. He should proceed with a mixture of prudence and humanity in such a way as not to be made incautious by overconfidence nor yet intolerable by excessive mistrust.

Here the question arises; whether it is better to be loved than feared or feared than loved. The answer is that it would be desirable to be both but, since that is difficult, it is much safer to be feared than to be loved, if one must choose. For of men in general this observation may be made: they are ungrateful, fickle, and deceitful, eager to avoid dangers, and avid for gain, and while you are useful to them they are all with you, offering you their blood, their property, their lives, and their sons so long as danger is remote, as we noted above, but when it approaches they turn on you. Any prince, trusting only in their words and having no other preparations made, will fall to his ruin, for friendships that are bought at a price and not by greatness and nobility of soul are paid for indeed, but they are not owned and cannot be called upon in time of need. Men have less hesitation in offending a man who is loved than one who is feared, for love is held by a bond of obligation which, as men are wicked, is broken whenever personal advantage suggests it, but fear is accompanied by the dread of punishment which never relaxes.

Yet a prince should make himself feared in such a way that, if he does not thereby merit love, at least he may escape odium, for being feared and not hated may well go together. And indeed the prince may attain this end if he but respect the property and the women of his subjects and citizens. And if it should become necessary to seek the death of someone, he should find a proper justification and a public cause, and above all he should keep his hands off another's property, for men forget more readily the death of their father than the loss of their patrimony. Besides, pretexts for seizing property are never lacking, and when a prince begins to live by means of rapine he will always find some excuse for plundering others, and conversely pretexts for execution are rarer and are more quickly exhausted.

A prince at the head of his armies and with a vast number of soldiers under his command should give not the slightest heed if he is esteemed cruel, for without such a reputation he will not be able to keep his army united and ready for action. Among the marvelous things told of Hannibal is that, having a vast army under his command made up of all kinds and races of men and waging war far from his own country, he never allowed any dissension to arise either as between the troops and their leaders or among the troops themselves, and this both in times of good fortune and bad. This could only have come about through his most inhuman cruelty which, taken in conjunction with his great valor, kept him always an object of respect and terror in the eyes of his soldiers. And without the cruelty his other characteristics would not have achieved this effect. Thoughtless writers have admired his actions and at the same time deplored the cruelty which was the basis of them. As evidence of the truth of our statement that his other virtues would have been insufficient let us examine the case of Scipio,[4] an extraordinary leader not only in his own day but for all recorded history. His army in Spain revolted and for no other reason than because of his kind-heartedness, which had allowed more license to his soldiery than military discipline properly permits. His policy was attacked in the Senate by Fabius Maximus, who called him a corrupter of the Roman arms. When the Locrians had been mishandled by one of his lieutenants, his easy-going nature prevented him from avenging them or disciplining his officer, and it was à propos of this incident that one of the senators remarked, wishing to find an excuse for him, that there were many men who knew better how to avoid error themselves than to correct it in others. This characteristic of Scipio would have clouded his fame and glory had he continued in authority, but as he lived under the government of the Senate, its harmful aspect was hidden and it reflected credit on him.

Hence, on the subject of being loved or feared I will conclude that since love depends on the subjects, but the prince has it in his own hands to create fear, a wise prince will rely on what is his own, remembering at the same time that he must avoid arousing hatred, as we have said.

[In What Manner Princes Should Keep Their Word]

How laudable it is for a prince to keep his word and govern his actions by integrity rather than trickery will be understood by all. Nonetheless we have in our times seen great things accomplished by many princes who have thought little of keeping their promises and have known the art of mystifying the minds of men. Such princes have won out over those whose actions were based on fidelity to their word.

---

4. Publius Cornelius Scipio, called "Africanus," was a Roman general who conquered   Spain and defeated Carthage in the Second Punic War.

It must be understood that there are two ways of fighting, one with laws and the other with arms. The first is the way of men, the second is the style of beasts, but since very often the first does not suffice it is necessary to turn to the second. Therefore a prince must know how to play the beast as well as the man. This lesson was taught allegorically by the ancient writers who related that Achilles and many other princes were brought up by Chiron the Centaur, who took them under his discipline. The clear significance of this half-man and half-beast preceptorship is that a prince must know how to use either of these two natures and that one without the other has no enduring strength. Now since the prince must make use of the characteristics of beasts he should choose those of the fox and the lion, though the lion cannot defend himself against snares and the fox is helpless against wolves. One must be a fox in avoiding traps and a lion in frightening wolves. Such as choose simply the rôle of a lion do not rightly understand the matter. Hence a wise leader cannot and should not keep his word when keeping it is not to his advantage or when the reasons that made him give it are no longer valid. If men were good, this would not be a good precept, but since they are wicked and will not keep faith with you, you are not bound to keep faith with them.

A prince has never lacked legitimate reasons to justify his breach of faith. We could give countless recent examples and show how any number of peace treaties or promises have been broken and rendered meaningless by the faithlessness of princes, and how success has fallen to the one who best knows how to counterfeit the fox. But it is necessary to know how to disguise this nature well and how to pretend and dissemble. Men are so simple and so ready to follow the needs of the moment that the deceiver will always find some one to deceive. Of recent examples I shall mention one. Alexander VI[5] did nothing but deceive and never thought of anything else and always found some occasion for it. Never was there a man more convincing in his asseverations nor more willing to offer the most solemn oaths nor less likely to observe them. Yet his deceptions were always successful for he was an expert in this field.

So a prince need not have all the aforementioned good qualities, but it is most essential that he appear to have them. Indeed, I should go so far as to say that having them and always practising them is harmful, while seeming to have them is useful. It is good to appear clement, trustworthy, humane, religious, and honest, and also to be so, but always with the mind so disposed that, when the occasion arises not to be so, you can become the opposite. It must be understood that a prince and particularly a new prince cannot practise all the virtues for which men are accounted good, for the necessity of preserving the state often compels him to take actions which are opposed to loyalty, charity, humanity, and religion. Hence he must have a spirit ready to adapt itself as the varying winds of fortune command him. As I have said, so far as he is able, a prince should stick to the path of good but, if the necessity arises, he should know how to follow evil.

---

5. Pope Alexander VI, Rodrigo Borgia, who
   ruled from 1492 to 1503, was notorious for
   his corruption and his worldliness.

A prince must take great care that no word ever passes his lips that is not full of the above mentioned five good qualities, and he must seem to all who see and hear him a model of piety, loyalty, integrity, humanity, and religion. Nothing is more necessary than to seem to possess this last quality, for men in general judge more by the eye than the hand, as all can see but few can feel. Everyone sees what you seem to be, few experience what you really are and these few do not dare to set themselves up against the opinion of the majority supported by the majesty of the state. In the actions of all men and especially princes, where there is no court of appeal, the end is all that counts. Let a prince then concern himself with the acquisition or the maintenance of a state; the means employed will always be considered honorable and praised by all, for the mass of mankind is always swayed by appearances and by the outcome of an enterprise. And in the world there is only the mass, for the few find their place only when the majority has no base of support. A certain prince of our own times, whom it would not be well to name, preaches nothing but peace and faith and yet is the enemy of both, and if he had observed either he would already on numerous occasions have lost both his state and his renown.

[The Influence of Fortune on Human Affairs and How It May Be Countered]

I am not ignorant of the fact that many have held and hold the opinion that the things of this world are so ordered by fortune and God that the prudence of mankind may effect little change in them, indeed is of no avail at all. On this basis it could be argued that there is no point in making any effort, but we should rather abandon ourselves to destiny. This opinion has been the more widely held in our day on account of the great variations in things that we have seen and are still witnessing and which are entirely beyond human conjecture. Sometimes indeed, thinking on such matters, I am minded to share that opinion myself. Nevertheless I believe, if we are to keep our free will, that it may be true that fortune controls half of our actions indeed but allows us the direction of the other half, or almost half. I would compare fortune to a river in flood, which when it breaks its bonds, deluges the surrounding plains, tears up trees and dwellings, here washing away the land and there building up new deposits. All flee before it, everyone must bow before the fury of the flood, for there is no checking it. Yet though this be so it does not signify that in quiet times men cannot make some provision against it, building levees and dikes so that when the river rises it may follow a channel prepared for it or at least have its first onrush rendered less impetuous and harmful. In like fashion fortune displays her greatest effect where there is no organized ability to resist and hence she directs her bolts where there have been no defenses or bulwarks prepared against her. And if you will consider Italy, the scene of the variations we have mentioned above and the motivating center thereof, you will find it an open field without dikes and without any kind of protection. Had it been protected by proper valor and ability, as were Germany, France, and Spain, it would not have suffered such great changes from the flood, which indeed might never have come. This I think should suffice as an argument against fortune in general.

Coming now to particular cases, I will note how we see such a prince reign happily today and meet his downfall tomorrow without any visible change in his nature and character. This is a result of causes we have already discussed, and a prince who depends entirely on fortune will not prosper when fortune changes. I further believe that a prince is fortunate when his conduct is in accord with the times and unsuccessful if his behavior is not so in tune. For we observe of men as they follow out the course of action necessary to the ends they seek, whether glory or riches, that one works cautiously, another impetuously, or one uses violence and another astuteness, or one is patient and another the contrary, yet success may attend any of these methods. And we may see that of two of the cautious type one attains his ends where the other fails, and similarly we may see two succeed though using different methods, one deliberate and the other impetuous, and this all depends on the temper of the times and whether or not it be in accord with the method of procedure. Hence it comes about, as I have said, that two using different methods may come to the same end, and of two following the same method one may succeed and the other fail. Herein lies the variation in prosperity, for if one prince conducts himself with patience and caution and the times are right for such conduct he will prosper, but if times and circumstances change and he does not alter his behavior he will fall. Nor is there any man so wise as to be able to adapt himself to such changes, both because we cannot be other than as nature inclines us and because one who has prospered by following one kind of policy will not be persuaded to abandon it. Hence the cautious man, when the time comes for bold action, is incapable of it and so falls, for if nature could be changed with the variation of times and circumstances fortune would not change.

My conclusion is, then, that, as fortune is variable and men fixed in their ways, men will prosper so long as they are in tune with the times and will fail when they are not. However, I will say that in my opinion it is better to be bold than cautious, for fortune is a woman and whoever wishes to win her must importune and beat her, and we may observe that she is more frequently won by this sort than by those who proceed more deliberately. Like a woman, too, she is well disposed to young men, for they are less circumspect and more violent and more bold to command her.

BALDESSARE CASTIGLIONE

(1478–1529)

Italy

Baldesar Castiglione was born in Mantua; he served in various official capacities at the courts of northern Italy, especially at the court of the Duke of Urbino. It was there that he set his chief work, *The Book of the Courtier,* in which a group of

Portrait of Baldassare
Castiglione by Raphael, 1516.
In the Louvre, Paris.

nobles hold a series of conversations in which they attempt to describe the ideal
courtier. Published in 1528, this work defined the standards of the ideal courtier
for the rest of Renaissance Europe. Castiglione, himself regarded as a model
courtier, died in 1529 in Spain where he had been sent as papal envoy.

from *The Book of the Courtier*

[Should the Courtier Be Deprived of Love]

Then signor Gasparo[1] said: "I remember that last evening, in discussing the
accomplishments of the Courtier, these gentlemen wished him to be in love; and
since, in summarizing what has been said so far, we might conclude that a Courtier
who has to lead his prince to virtue by his worth and authority will almost have to
be old (because knowledge very rarely comes before a certain age, and especially
knowledge in those things that are learned through experience)—I do not know
how it can be fitting for him, if he is advanced in age, to be in love. For, as has been
said this evening, love is not a good thing in old men, and those things which in
young men are the delights, courtesies, and elegances so pleasing to women, in old
men amount to madness and ridiculous ineptitude, and whoever indulges in them
will cause some women to despise him and others to deride him. So if this Aristotle
of yours, as an old Courtier, were in love and did the things that young lovers do

Translated by Charles Singleton.

---

1. Gasparo Pallavicino, a friend of Castiglione's.

(like some whom we have seen in our time), I fear he would forget to instruct his prince, and children would perhaps mock him behind his back, and women would scarcely have any pleasure from him except to poke fun at him."

Then signor Ottaviano[2] said: "As all the other accomplishments assigned to the Courtier suit him, even though he be old, I do not think that we ought at all to deprive him of this happiness of loving."

"Nay," said signor Gasparo, "to deprive him of love is to give him a further perfection and to make him live happily, free of misery and calamity."

* * *

Then the Duchess[3] said: "I am glad, messer Pietro,[4] that you have had little to do in our discussion this evening, for now we shall the more confidently give you the burden of speaking, and of teaching the Courtier a love so happy that it brings with it neither blame nor displeasure; for it could well be one of the most important and useful conditions that have yet been attributed to him. Therefore, by your faith, tell us all that you know about it."

* * *

Whereupon messer Pietro, having first remained silent for a while, made ready as if to speak of something important, then said: "Gentlemen, in order to show that old men can love not only without blame but sometimes more happily than young men, I am obliged to enter upon a little discourse to explain what love is, and wherein lies the happiness that lovers can have. So I beg you to follow me attentively, for I hope to bring you to see that there is no man here to whom it is unbecoming to be in love. . . .

"I say, then, that, according to the definition of ancient sages, love is nothing but a certain desire to enjoy beauty; and, as our desire is only for things that are known, knowledge must always precede desire, which by its nature turns to the good but in itself is blind and does not know the good. Therefore nature has ordained that to every cognitive power there shall be joined an appetitive power; and as in our soul there are three modes of cognition, namely, by sense, by reason, and by intellect: so, from sense comes appetite, which we have in common with animals; from reason comes choice, which is proper to man; from intellect, whereby man can communicate with the angels, comes will. Thus, even as sense knows only those things which the senses perceive, appetite desires these and no other; and even as intellect is turned solely to the contemplation of intelligible things, the will feeds only upon spiritual good. Being by nature rational and placed as in the middle between these two extremes, man can choose (by descending to sense or rising to intellect) to turn his desires now in one direction and now in the other. In these two ways, therefore, men can desire beauty, which name is universally applied to all things, whether natural or artificial, that are made in the good proportion and due measure that befit their nature.

"But to speak of the beauty we have in mind, namely, that only which is seen in the human person and especially in the face, and which prompts the ardent

---

2. Ottaviano Fregoso, a nobleman of Genoa.
3. Elisabetta Gonzaga, the Duchess of Urbino, who presides over the gathering.
4. Pietro Bembo, a Venetian nobleman, famous as a poet and as an authority on the Neoplatonic theory of love.

desire we call love, we will say that it is an effluence of the divine goodness, which (although it is shed, like the sun's light, upon all created things), when it finds a face well proportioned and composed of a certain radiant harmony of various colors set off by light and shadow and by measured distance and limited outline, infuses itself therein and shines forth most beautifully and adorns and illumines with grace and a wondrous splendor the object wherein it shines, like a sunbeam striking upon a beautiful vase of polished gold set with precious gems. Thus, it agreeably attracts the eyes of men to itself, and, entering through them, impresses itself upon the soul, and moves and delights it throughout with a new sweetness; and, by kindling it, inspires it with a desire of itself."

MICHELANGELO BUONARROTI

(1475–1564)

Italy

Michelangelo Buonarroti, the greatest sculptor of the Renaissance, wrote poetry on and off throughout his long life. He was born in 1475 in a rural area near Florence, where he was trained as an artist. He eventually settled in Rome, working for Pope Julius II and gaining great fame as a sculptor and also as the painter (although a reluctant one) of the frescoes of the Sistine Chapel in the Vatican. He died in Rome in 1564. A tormented man, Michelangelo expressed many of the tensions in his life in his vigorous poetry, which was not published until 1623.

To Giovanni, the One from Pistoia, on Painting the Vault of the Sistine Chapel (1508–1512)[1]

I've already grown a goiter from this toil
as water swells the cats in Lombardy
or any other country they might be,
forcing my belly to hang under my chin,
My beard to heaven, and my memory   5
I feel above its coffer. My chest a harp.
And ever above my face, the brush dripping,
making a rich pavement out of me.
My loins have been shoved into my guts,

Translated by Sidney Alexander.

---

1. This poem, addressed to the humanist Giovanni di Benedetto da Pistoia, is the artist's
   description of himself painting the ceiling
   of the Sistine Chapel.

My arse serves to counterweigh my rump,
Eyelessly I walk in the void.   10
   Ahead of me my skin lies outstretched,
and to bend, I must knot my shoulders taut,
holding myself like a Syrian bow.
   Therefore, fallacious, strange   15
the judgment carried in the mind must fly,
for from a twisted gun one shoots awry.
   My dead picture defend
now, Giovanni, and also my honor,
for I'm in no good place, nor I a painter.   20

For Vittoria Colonna

High-born soul whose limbs and features fair
Mirror within your chaste and mollient members dear
How nature and heaven can draw near
And shape for us beauty beyond compare.

Resplendent spirit in whom one hopes and believes that there   5
Inwardly, as on your outward face appear,
Love, pity, mercy are—states so rare
Never so intimately bound with beauty were.

Love seizes me, locks me in beauty's prison
Pity and mercy with gentle glances beckoning   10
Seem to ring my heart with hopes to the horizon.

What usage, what governance, what reckoning
Denies this world? What cruelty? What ultimate negation
That soon or late death spares not so lovely a creation?[2]

[What marvel is it, if close to the fire]

What marvel is it, if close to the fire
I melted and burned; and now that it is spent
from without, from within I am afflicted and rent
and bit by bit reduced to ashes of a perished pyre?

Burning I used to see the source of my desire,   5
the lucent place whence depended my torment.
That sight alone lent me content
And death and dole to me were festivals and gyre.

---

2. The sonnet was written on the death of
   Michelangelo's friend, the poet Vittoria Colonna.

But when the splendor of that incendiary food
that burnt me and nurtured me flew off to heaven   10
One coal though covered, yet remained glowing.

And if love heap not up other wood
to see me aflame, not a single spark even
will remain of me, all to cinders and ashes going.

VITTORIA COLONNA (1490–1547)
Italy

Vittoria Colonna, born in 1490 into a noble family in Rome, was married to the
Marquis of Pescara. Although he was absent on military campaigns during most
of the marriage, his death in 1525 had a decisive effect on her. For the rest of her
life she lived in convents and became intensely interested in religion. In 1534 she
met Michelangelo, who became a close friend. In 1538 she published a collection
of sonnets, very spiritual in tone, on the death of her husband. Michelangelo was
present when she died in 1547, and he wrote several of his most notable sonnets
on her death.

[I live on this depraved and lonely cliff]*

I live on this depraved and lonely cliff
like a sad bird abhorring a green tree
or plashing water; I move forcefully
away from those I love, and I am stiff
even before myself, so that my thoughts   5
may rise and fly to him: sun I adore
and worship. Though their wings could hurry more,
they race only to him; the forest rots
until the instant when they reach that place.
Then deep in ecstasy, though brief, they feel   10
a joy beyond all earthly joy. I reel,
and yet if they could recreate his face
as my mind, craving and consuming, would,
then here perhaps I'd own the perfect good.

*Translated by Willis Barnstone.

[As when some hungry fledgling hears and sees]*

As when some hungry fledgling hears and sees
   His mother's wings beating around him, when
   She brings him nourishment, from which loving
   Both meal and her, he cheers up and rejoices,
   And deep within the nest, chafes and worries   5
      With desire to follow her, even flying,
      And offers thanks with such a caroling
      His tongue seems loosed beyond its usual power;
   So I, at times, when warm and living rays
      Come from the heavenly sun by which my heart   10
      Is fed, shine forth with such a lightening,
   And I find my pen moves, urged on always
      By an inner love, as if it had no part
      In what I say: it is his praise I sing.

MARGUERITE DE NAVARRE (MARGUERITE DE VALOIS) (1492–1549)
France

Marguerite was born in Angoulême in 1492. Her younger brother would become King Francis I of France. She had a literary education and was married in 1527 to the king of Navarre (of whose court she made a refuge for humanists). Often at the French court, she was much involved in the political events of her time and was associated with attempts to reform the Catholic Church from within. The *Heptameron* was apparently left incomplete at her death in 1549. In this first collection of French tales, which continues the tradition of Boccaccio's *Decameron*, a group of ten men and women, caught in the mountains by flooded streams, amuse themselves by telling each other stories.

from *Heptameron*

[Passion and Vengeance in the Naples Court]†

In the town of Amboise there was a certain mule-driver in the service of the Queen of Navarre, the sister of King Francis I, and it all happened while the Queen was

---

*Translated by Barbara Howes.
†Translated by P. A. Chilton; revised by Marcel Tetel.

staying at Blois, around the time when she gave birth to a son.[1] The mule-driver had gone over to collect his quarterly pay, while his wife stayed behind in their house on the other side of the bridges in Amboise. Now the husband had a servant, and this man had been desperately in love with the wife for quite a while. One day, unable to stand it any longer, he had come out with his declaration. But being a very virtuous woman, she had given him a very sharp reply, and threatened to get her husband to give him a beating and throw him out of the house. After that the man had never dared open his mouth to her in this fashion again, or in any other way indicate his feelings. However, the flames of passion smoldered secretly away, until the fateful day when the husband went off to Blois. The lady of the house had gone to vespers in the church of Saint-Florentin, in the castle, and a long way from the house. Left to himself in the house, the servant got it into his head that he would take by force what he had failed to obtain by supplication and service. He broke an opening in the partition that separated the room where he slept from that of his mistress. The hole could not be seen, because it was covered by the curtain of his master's bed on one side, and by the curtain round the servant's bed on the other. So his foul intentions were not suspected, until the good lady had actually got into bed, accompanied by a little lass of eleven or twelve years of age. The poor woman had just fallen asleep, when the servant jumped through the hole and into bed with her, wearing nothing but his shirt, and clutching his bare sword in his hand. The moment she felt him by her side, she jumped up, and told him what she thought of him, like the virtuous woman she was. His love was no more than animal lust, and he would have understood the language his mules spoke better than he understood the virtuous appeals to reason that she now made. Indeed, what he did next proved him even more bestial than the animals with whom he had spent so much of his life. She ran too fast round the table for him to catch her, and was in any case so strong that she had already twice managed to struggle free from his clutches. He despaired of taking her alive, and stabbed her violently in the small of the back, thinking no doubt that the pain would make her surrender, where terror and manhandling had failed. However, the very opposite happened. Just as a good soldier will fight back all the more fiercely if he sees his own blood flowing, so the chaste heart of this lady was only strengthened in its resolve to run, and escape falling into the hands of this desperate man. As she struggled to get away, she reasoned with him as well as she was able, thinking she might somehow bring him to recognize the wrongness of his acts. But by now he was worked up into a frenzy, and was in no state to be moved by words of wisdom. He went on lunging at her with his sword, while she ran as fast as she could to get away. When at last she had lost so much blood that she felt death approaching, she raised her eyes to heaven and, joining her hands in prayer, gave thanks to her God.

"Thou art my strength, my virtue, my suffering and my chastity," she prayed, humbly beseeching that He would receive the blood, which, according to His commandment, was shed in veneration of the blood of His son. For she truly

---

1. The Queen is Marguerite herself. The teller of this story is Cisille, who is usually identified with Louise of Savoy, the mother of Marguerite and King Francis.

believed that through Him were all her sins cleansed and washed from the memory of His wrath. And as she sank with her face to the floor, she sighed, "Into thy hands I commend my spirit, my spirit that was redeemed by thy great goodness."

Then the vicious brute stabbed her several times again, and, once she could no longer speak, and all her physical resistance was gone, he took the poor defenseless creature by force. When he had satisfied his lusts he made a speedy getaway, and in spite of all subsequent attempts to track him down, it had proved impossible to find him. The young girl who had been sleeping with the poor woman had been terrified, and had hidden under the bed. Once the man had disappeared she came out and went to her mistress. Finding that she was unable to speak and just lay there motionless, she ran to the window and called out for help from the neighbors. There were plenty of people in the town who were fond of her and thought highly of her, and they now rallied round immediately and fetched doctors to tend her. When they examined her they found twenty-five fatal wounds. They did what they could to help her, but to no avail. She lingered on for another hour, unable to speak, but indicating by movements of her eyes, and gestures of the hands, that her mind was still clear. A man of the church came and questioned her about the faith in which she died, and about her hope for salvation through Christ alone. Although she could only reply by signs, no words could have conveyed her meaning more clearly. And so, with joy on her face, and her eyes turned heavenward, her soul left this chaste body to return to its Creator. No sooner had the corpse been lifted from where it lay, prepared for burial and placed before the door of the house to await the burial party, than the poor husband arrived. There, completely unforewarned, he was confronted with the spectacle of his wife lying dead in front of his own house. When he heard how she had died, his grief was doubled. Indeed, so deep was his sorrow that he too came near to death. His wife, this martyr of chastity, was then laid to rest in the church of Saint-Florentin. All the virtuous women of the town were present, as was their duty, to do all possible honor to her name. For them it was a great blessing to have lived in the same town as one so virtuous. For women of more wanton ways the sight of such respect being paid to her body made them resolve to amend their lives.

FRANÇOIS RABELAIS (c. 1494–1553)
France

François Rabelais was born around 1494 in the French province of Touraine. Although ordained a priest and having entered first the Franciscan and then the Benedictine order, Rabelais left the monastery to work as a doctor. In 1532 he published his *Pantagruel,* and two years later, *Gargantua.* These works made him famous, but because they were frequently condemned by the authorities, he often moved from one place to another, while revising and expanding them, until his death in Paris in 1553. The story of the adventures of the giant Gargantua and his son Pantagruel is an exuberant mixture of popular culture and great learning that has always fascinated and perplexed readers.

from *Gargantua*

Chapter 7: How a Monk of Seuilly Saved the Abbey-Close from Being Sacked by the Enemy

So they went on, wasting, pillaging, and stealing till they arrived at Seuilly, where they robbed men and women alike and took everything they could; nothing was too hot or too heavy for them.[1] Although there was plague in almost every house, they broke into all of them and plundered everything inside; and none of them caught any infection, which is a most wonderful thing. For the priests, curates, preachers, physicians, surgeons, and apothecaries who went to visit, dress, heal, preach to, and admonish the sick had all died of the infection. Yet these robbing and murdering devils never took any harm. What is the reason for that, gentlemen? Consider the problem, I beg of you.

When the town was thus pillaged they went to the abbey in a horrible tumult, but they found it well bolted and barred. So the main body of their army marched on towards the ford of Vède, except for seven companies of foot and two hundred knights with their retainers, who remained there and broke down the walls of the close in order to ravage the vineyard. The poor devils of monks did not know which of their saints to turn to. Whatever the risk, they had the bell tolled for a meeting of the chapter, at which it was decided to march in a stately procession, rendered more effective by grand chants and litanies *contra hostium insidias,* and fine responses *pro pace.*[2]

There was in the abbey at that time a cloister monk, named Friar John of the Hashes, a young, gallant, sprightly, jovial, resourceful, bold, adventurous, resolute, tall, and thin fellow with a great gaping mouth and a fine outstanding nose. He was grand mumbler of matins, dispatcher of masses, and polisher off of vigils, and, to put it briefly, a true monk if ever there has been one since the monking world monked its first monkery; and moreover in the matter of his breviary he was a clerk to his very teeth.

Now when this monk heard the noise that the enemy were making in the close of their vineyard, he came out to see what they were doing; and finding them to be picking the grapes of their close, on which their provision for the whole year depended, he returned to the choir of the church, where the rest of the monks,

Translated by J. M. Cohen.

---

1. Gargantua's kingdom has been attacked by the disorganized army of King Picrochole.

2. "Against the treachery of the enemy"; "for peace."

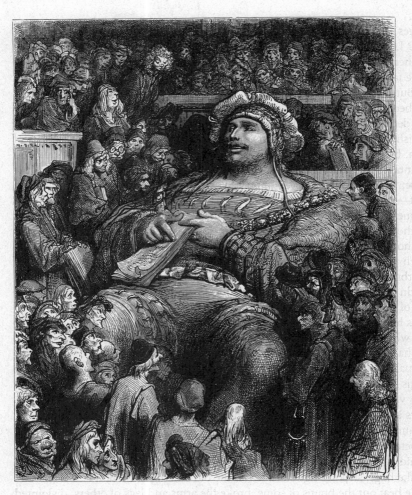

Pantagruel tests his wits against the Parisian scholars (II.10). Illustration by Gustave Doré from *OEuvres de Rabelais* published by Garnier Freres, Paris, n. d. (1873 or shortly thereafter).

gaping like so many stuffed pigs, were singing: *Ini nim, pe, ne, ne, ne, ne, ne, ne, mum, num, ini, i, mi, i, mi, co, o, ne, no, ne, no no, no, rum, ne, num, num.*[3]

"That's shitten well sung!" he cried when he saw them. "But, for God's sake, why don't you sing: 'Baskets farewell; the harvest's done'? The devil take me if they aren't in our close, and so thoroughly cutting both vines and grapes that, God's body, there'll be nothing but gleanings there for the next four years. Tell me, by

---

3. The trembling monks garble the Latin words *impetum inimicorum*, "the attack of our enemies," which they are praying to be delivered from.

St James's belly, what shall we drink in all that time? What'll there be for us poor devils? Lord God, *da mihi potum*."[4]

Then said the Prior of the convent: "What does this drunkard want here? Let him be taken to the punishment cell for disturbing the divine service!"

"But," said the monk, "what about the wine service? Let's see that isn't disturbed. For you yourself, my lord Prior, like to drink of the best, and so does every decent fellow. Indeed, no man of honour hates a good wine; which is a monkish saying. But these responses you're singing here are very much out of season, by God. Now tell me, why are our services short at the harvest-tide and the vintage, and during Advent too, and all the winter? The late Friar Mace Pelosse, of blessed memory, a true zealot for our faith—devil take me if he wasn't—told me the reason, as I remember. It was that we might press and make the wine properly at the vintage, and in winter drink it down. So listen to me, all you who love wine; and follow me too, in God's name. For I tell you boldly, may St Anthony's fire burn me if anyone tastes the grape who hasn't fought for the vine. Church property it is, by God, and hands off it! Devil take it, St Thomas of Canterbury was willing to die for the Church's goods, and if I were to die for them, shouldn't I be a Saint as well? But I shan't die, for all that. It's I that will be the death of others."

As he said this he threw off his heavy monk's cloak and seized the staff of his cross, which was made of the heart of a sorb-apple tree. It was as long as a lance, a full hand's grip round, and decorated in places with lily flowers, which were almost all rubbed away. Thus he went out in a fine cassock, with his frock slung over his shoulder, and rushed so lustily on the enemy, who were gathering grapes in the vineyard without order or ensign, trumpet or drum. For the standard-bearers and ensigns had put down their standards and ensigns beside the walls, the drummers had knocked in one side of their drums to fill them with grapes, the trumpeters were loaded with the fruit, and everyone was in disorder. He rushed, as I said, so fiercely on them, without a word of warning, that he bowled them over like hogs, striking right and left in the old fencing fashion.

He beat out the brains of some, broke the arms and legs of others, disjointed the neck-bones, demolished the kidneys, slit the noses, blackened the eyes, smashed the jaws, knocked the teeth down the throats, shattered the shoulder-blades, crushed the shins, dislocated the thigh-bones, and cracked the fore-arms of yet others. If one of them tried to hide among the thickest vines, he bruised the whole ridge of his back and broke the base of his spine like a dog's. If one of them tried to save himself by flight, he knocked his head into pieces along the lambdoidal suture. If one of them climbed into a tree, thinking he would be safe there, Friar John impaled him up the arse with his staff. If any one of his old acquaintance cried out: "Ha, Friar John, my friend, Friar John, I surrender!" he replied: "You can't help it. But you'll surrender your soul to all the devils as well." And he gave the fellow a sudden thumping.

---

4. "Give me a drink."

If any man was seized with such a spirit of rashness as to try to face up to him, then he showed his muscular strength by running him through the chest by way of the mediastine to the heart. In the case of others, thrusting under the hollow of their short ribs, he turned their stomachs over, so that they died immediately. Others he smote so fiercely through the navel that he made their bowels gush out. Others he struck on the ballocks and pierced their bum-gut. It was, believe me, the most hideous spectacle that ever was seen.

Some invoked St Barbara, others St George, other St Hands-off, others Our Lady of Cunault, of Loretto, of Good Tidings, of Lenou, of Rivière. Some called on St James, others on the Holy Shroud of Chambéry—but it was burnt three months later so completely that they could not save a single thread—others on the Shroud of Cadouin, others on St John of Angély, others on St Eutropius of Saintes, St Maximus of Chinon, St Martin of Candes, St Cloud of Cinais, the relics of Javarzay, and a thousand other pleasant little saints.

Some died without a word, others spoke without dying; some died as they spoke, others spoke as they died, and others cried aloud: "Confession! Confession! *Confiteor! Miserere! In manus!*"[5]

Such was the shouting of the wounded that the Prior of the abbey came out with all his monks; and when they saw these poor creatures tumbled there among the vines and mortally wounded, they confessed some of them. But whilst the priests amused themselves by taking confessions, the little monklings ran to the place where Friar John stood, and asked him how they could help him.

His reply was that they should slit the throats of those lying on the ground. So, leaving their great cloaks on the nearest fence, they began to cut the throats of those whom he had already battered, and to dispatch them. Can you guess with what instruments? With fine *whittles,* which are the little jack-knives with which the small children of our country shell walnuts.

Meanwhile, still wielding the staff of his cross, Friar John reached the breach which the enemy had made, while some of the little monks carried off the ensigns and standards to their cells, to cut them into garters. But when those who had made their confession tried to get out through this breach, the monk rained blows upon them, crying: "These men are shriven and repentant, and have earned their pardons. They'll go right to paradise, as straight as a sickle or the road to Faye."

Thus, by his prowess, all that part of the army that had got into the close was discomfited, to the number of thirteen thousand, six hundred and twenty-two, not counting the women and small children—as is always understood. For never did Maugis the Hermit—of whom it is written in the Deeds of the Four Sons of Aymon—wield his pilgrim's staff so valiantly against the Saracens as this monk swung the staff of his cross in his encounter with the enemy.

---

5. "I confess! Have mercy! Into your hands (I commit myself)!"

from *Pantagruel*

Chapter 2: Of the Nativity of the Most Redoubted Pantagruel

Gargantua at the age of four hundred, four score, and forty-four years begat his son Pantagruel upon his wife Badebec, daughter of the king of the Amaurots in Utopia, who died in childbirth; for he was so amazingly large and so heavy that he could not come into the world without suffocating his mother.

But in order fully to understand the cause and reason of the name which was given to him at baptism, you will note that in that year there was so great a drought throughout all the land of Africa, that thirty-six months, three weeks, four days, thirteen hours, and somewhat more passed without rain, and with the sun's heat so torrid that the whole earth was parched by it. Indeed the heat was no more violent in the days of Elijah than it was then. For there was not a tree in the land that had either leaf or flower. The grass lost its green; the rivers drained away; the springs ran dry; the poor fish, abandoned by their own element, strayed and cried on the ground most horribly; the birds fell from the air through lack of dew; the wolves, foxes, stags, boars, deer, hares, rabbits, weasels, martens, badgers, and other animals were to be found dead in the fields, with their throats gaping. As for men, their case was most piteous. You would have seen them lolling out their tongues like greyhounds that have run for six hours; many threw themselves into wells; others crept into a cow's belly, to be in the shade, and these Homer calls *Alibantes*. The whole country was at a standstill. It was pitiable to see the pains that mortals took to save themselves from this dreadful plight. It was hard work to keep the holy water in the churches from being exhausted. But they so organized it, by the advice of My Lords the Cardinals and the Holy Father, that no one dared to take more than one dip. Yet when anyone entered the church you might have seen scores of poor thirsty souls coming up behind him, and him distributing it to anyone who had his mouth wide open to catch a drop of it, like the wicked rich man, in order that nothing should be lost. Oh, how fortunate in that year was the man who had a cool and well furnished cellar!

The Philosopher relates, in debating the question why the waters of the sea are salt, that at the time when Phoebus handed over the driving of his light-giving chariot to his son Phaeton, the said Phaeton, unskilled in the art and not knowing how to follow the ecliptic line between the two tropics of the sun's orbit, strayed from his track and approached so near to the earth that he dried up all the lands beneath him, scorching a large portion of the sky which the philosophers call *Via lactea*[6] and simpletons call St James's Path, although the more highfalutin' poets say that it is the region where Juno's milk fell when she suckled Hercules. That was the time when the earth was so heated that it burst into a great sweat, which caused it to sweat out the whole sea, which for that reason is salt, for all sweat is salt; which you will admit to be true if you taste your own, or that of pox-patients when they make them sweat. It is all one to me.

An almost similar case occurred in that year. For one Friday, when everyone

---

6. The Milky Way.

was at devotions, and they were making a fine procession with all manner of litanies and grand sermons, calling on God Almighty to deign with his eye of mercy to look down on them in their great distress, great drops of water were plainly seen to break out of the earth, as when someone bursts into a copious sweat. And the poor people began to rejoice, as if this had been something to their profit. For some said that there was not a drop of moisture in the air from which they could expect rain, and that the earth was making up for this lack. Other learned people said that it was rain from the Antipodes, about which Seneca tells in the fourth book of his *Questiones naturales,* in speaking of the origin and source of the River Nile. But they were mistaken. For after the procession, when each one wanted to gather up some of this dew and drink it by the bowlful, they found that it was only brine, saltier and far nastier than sea-water.

And because Pantagruel was born on that very day, his father gave him the name he did: for *Panta* in Greek is equivalent to *all,* and *Gruel,* in the Hagarene language, is as much as to say *thirsty;* by this meaning to infer that at the hour of the child's nativity the world was all thirsty, and also seeing, in a spirit of prophecy, that one day his son would be ruler over the thirsty, as was demonstrated to him at that very hour by another sign even more convincing. For when the child's mother Badebec was being delivered of him and the midwives were waiting to receive him, there came first out of her womb sixty-eight muleteers, each pulling by the collar a mule heavily laden with salt; after which came out nine dromedaries loaded with hams and smoked ox-tongues, seven camels loaded with salted eels; and then twenty-four cartloads of leeks, garlics, and onions: all of which greatly alarmed the said midwives.

But some of them said: "Here is fine fare. We were only drinking slackly, not like Saxons. This is bound to be a good sign. These are spurs to wine." And whilst they were gossiping amongst themselves about such little matters, out came Pantagruel, as shaggy as a bear. Whereupon one of them said in a spirit of prophecy: "He is born with all his hair. He will perform wonders; and if he lives he'll reach a ripe age."

Chapter 8: How Pantagruel, When at Paris, Received a Letter from his Father Gargantua, Together with a Copy of the Same

As you may well suppose, Pantagruel studied very hard. For he had a double-sized intelligence and a memory equal in capacity to the measure of twelve skins and twelve casks of oil. But while he was staying in Paris, he one day received a letter from his father which read as follows:

Most dear Son,

Among the gifts, graces, and prerogatives with which the Sovereign Creator, God Almighty, endowed and embellished human nature in the beginning, one seems to me to stand alone, and to excel all others; that is the one by which we can, in this mortal state, acquire a kind of immortality and, in the course of this transitory life, perpetuate our name and seed; which we do by lineage sprung from us in lawful marriage. By this means there is in some sort restored to us what was taken from us by the sin of our first parents, who were told that, because they had not been obedient to the commandment of God the Creator, they would die, and that by death would be brought to nothing that magnificent form in which man has been created.

But by this method of seminal propagation, there remains in the children what has perished in the parents, and in the grandchildren what has perished in the children, and so on in succession till the hour of the Last Judgement, when Jesus Christ shall peacefully have rendered up to God His Kingdom, released from all danger and contamination of sin. Then all generations and corruptions shall cease, and the elements shall be free from their continuous transformations, since peace, so long desired, will then be perfect and complete, and all things will be brought to their end and period.

Not without just and equitable cause, therefore, do I offer thanks to God, my Preserver, for permitting me to see my grey-haired age blossom afresh in your youth. When, at the will of Him who rules and governs all things, my soul shall leave this mortal habitation, I shall not now account myself to be absolutely dying, but to be passing from one place to another, since in you, and by you, I shall remain in visible form here in this world, visiting and conversing with men of honour and my friends as I used to do. Which conversation of mine has been, thanks to God's aid and grace, although not free from sin, I confess—for we all sin, and continually pray to God to wipe out our sins—at least without evil intention.

If the qualities of my soul did not abide in you as does my visible form, men would not consider you the guardian and treasure-house of the immortality of our name; in which case my pleasure would be small, considering that the lesser part of me, which is my body, would persist, and the better part, which is the soul, and by which our name continues to be blessed among men, would be bastardized and degenerate. This I say not out of any distrust of your virtue, which I have already tried and approved, but in order to encourage you more strongly to proceed from good to better. For what I write to you at present is not so much in order that you may live in this virtuous manner as that you may rejoice in so living and in so having lived, and may strengthen yourself in the like resolution for the future, for the furtherance and perfection of these ends I have, as you will easily remember, spared no expense. Indeed, I have helped you towards them as if I treasured nothing else in this world but to see you, in my lifetime, a perfect model of virtue, honour, and valour, and a paragon of liberal and high-minded learning. I might seem to have desired nothing but to leave you, after my death, as a mirror representing the person of me your father, and if not as excellent and in every way as I wish you, at least desirous of being so.

But although my late father Grandgousier, of blessed memory, devoted all his endeavours to my advancement in all perfection and political knowledge, and although my labour and study were proportionate to—no, even surpassed—his desire; still, as you may well understand, the times were not as fit and favorable for learning as they are to-day, and I had no supply of tutors such as you have. Indeed the times were still dark, and mankind was perpetually reminded of the miseries and disasters wrought by those Goths who had destroyed all sound scholarship. But, thanks be to God, learning has been restored in my age to its former dignity and enlightenment. Indeed I see such improvements that nowadays I should have difficulty in getting a place among little schoolboys, in the lowest class, I who in my youth was reputed, with some justification, to be the most learned man of the century. Which I do not say out of vain boastfulness, although I might commendably do so in writing to you,—for which you have the authority of Marcus Tullius in his work on Old Age, and Plutarch's statement in his book entitled: *How a Man may praise himself without Reproach*—but in order to inspire you to aim still higher.

Now every method of teaching has been restored, and the study of languages has been revived: of Greek, without which it is disgraceful for a man to call himself a scholar, and of Hebrew, Chaldean, and Latin. The elegant and accurate art of printing, which is now in use, was invented in my time, by divine inspiration; as, by contrast, artillery was inspired by diabolical suggestion. The whole world is full of learned men, of very erudite tutors, and of most extensive libraries, and it is my opinion that neither in the time of Plato, of Cicero, nor of Papinian were there such facilities for study as one finds today. No one, in future, will risk appearing in public or in any company, who is not well polished in Minerva's workshop. I find robbers, hangmen, free-booters, and grooms nowadays more learned than the doctors and preachers were in my time.

Why, the very women and girls aspire to the glory and reach out for the celestial manna of sound learning. So much so that at my present age I have been compelled to learn Greek, which I had not despised like Cato, but which I had not the leisure to learn in my youth. Indeed I find great delight in reading the *Morals* of Plutarch, Plato's magnificent *Dialogues,* the *Monuments* of Pausanias, and the *Antiquities* of Athenaeus, while I wait for the hour when it will please God, my Creator, to call me and bid me leave this earth.

Therefore, my son, I beg you to devote your youth to the firm pursuit of your studies and to the attainment of virtue. You are in Paris. There you will find many praiseworthy examples to follow. You have Epistemon for your tutor, and he can give you living instruction by word of mouth. It is my earnest wish that you shall become a perfect master of languages. First of Greek, as Quintilian advises; secondly, of Latin; and then of Hebrew, on account of the Holy Scriptures; also of Chaldean and Arabic, for the same reason; and I would have you model your Greek style on Plato's and your Latin on that of Cicero. Keep your memory well stocked with every tale from history, and here you will find help in the Cosmographes of the historians. Of the liberal arts, geometry, arithmetic, and music, I gave you some smattering when you were still small, at the age of five or six. Go on and learn the rest, also the rules of astronomy. But leave divinatory astrology and Lully's art alone, I beg of you, for they are frauds and vanities. Of Civil Law I would have you learn the best texts by heart, and relate them to the art of philosophy. And as for the knowledge of Nature's works, I should like you to give careful attention to that too; so that there may be no sea, river, or spring of which you do not know the fish. All the birds of the air, all the trees, shrubs, and bushes of the forest, all the herbs of the field, all the metals deep in the bowels of the earth, the precious stones of the whole East and the South—let none of them be unknown to you.

Then scrupulously peruse, the books of the Greek, Arabian, and Latin doctors once more, not omitting the Talmudists and Cabalists, and by frequent dissertations gain a perfect knowledge of that other world which is man. At some hours of the day also, begin to examine the Holy Scriptures. First the New Testament and the Epistles of the Apostles in Greek; and then the Old Testament, in Hebrew. In short, let me find you a veritable abyss of knowledge. For, later, when you have grown into a man, you will have to leave this quiet and repose of study, to learn chivalry and warfare, to defend my house, and to help our friends in every emergency against the attacks of evil-doers.

Furthermore, I wish you shortly to show how much you have profited by your studies, which you cannot do better than by publicly defending a thesis in every art against all persons whatsoever, and by keeping the company of learned men, who are as common in Paris as elsewhere.

But because, according to the wise Solomon, Wisdom enters not into the malicious heart, and knowledge without conscience is but the ruin of the soul, it befits you to serve, love, and fear God, to put all your thoughts and hopes in Him, and by faith grounded in charity to be so conjoined with Him that you may never be severed from Him by sin. Be suspicious of the world's deceits and set not your heart on vanity; for this life is transitory, but the word of God remains eternal. Be helpful to all your neighbours, and love them as yourself. Respect your tutors, avoid the company of those whom you would not care to resemble, and do not omit to make use of those graces which God has bestowed on you. Then, when you see that you have acquired all the knowledge to be gained in those parts, return to me, so that I may see you and give you my blessing before I die.

My son, the peace and grace of Our Lord be with you. Amen.

From Utopia, this seventeenth day of the month of March,

Your father, Gargantua

After receiving and reading this letter, Pantagruel took fresh courage and was inspired to make greater advances than ever. Indeed, if you had seen him studying and measured the progress he made, you would have said that his spirit among the books was like fire among the heather, so indefatigable and ardent was it.

SAINT TERESA OF AVILA (1515–1582)
Spain

Teresa de Cepeda y Ahumada, generally known as Saint Teresa of Avila, was born there to a noble family in 1515. After a devout childhood—she ran away at the age of seven to seek martyrdom among the Moors—she became a Carmelite nun and mystic, as Teresa de Jesus, leading a life of intense personal religious experience, and she also led a movement to reform the Carmelite community, (the Discalced or Barefoot Carmelites). With St. John of the Cross, she founded seventeen new convents of friars and traveled widely. Her mystical writings focus on prayer as the essential expression of the love of God and are based on her own experience, which she describes vividly and effectively: the piercing of her heart (described in her *Vida* [Life, 1552–1565]), is thought to have taken place in 1559. She died in 1582 and was canonized in 1622. In 1970 she was the first woman to be proclaimed doctor of the Catholic Church.

from *The Life of Saint Teresa*

[The Pain and Bliss of Saint Teresa]

The infant soul should be soothed by the caresses of love, which shall draw forth its love in a gentle way, and not, as they say, by force of blows. This love should be inwardly under control, and not as a cauldron, fiercely boiling because too much fuel has been applied to it, and out of which everything is lost. The source of the fire must be kept under control, and the flame must be quenched in sweet tears, and not with those painful tears which come out of these emotions, and which do so much harm.

In the beginning, I had tears of this kind. They left me with a disordered head and a wearied spirit, and for a day or two afterwards unable to resume my prayer. Great discretion, therefore, is necessary at first, in order that everything may proceed gently, and that the operations of the spirit may be within; all outward manifestations should be carefully avoided.

These other impetuosities are very different. It is not we who apply the fuel; the fire is already kindled, and we are thrown into it in a moment to be consumed. It is

Translated by David Lewis.

by no efforts of the soul that it sorrows over the wound which the absence of our Lord has inflicted on it; it is far otherwise; for an arrow is driven into the entrails to the very quick, and into the heart at times, so that the soul knows not what is the matter with it, nor what it wishes for. It understands clearly enough that it wishes for God, and that the arrow seems tempered with some herb which makes the soul hate itself for the love of our Lord, and willingly lose its life for Him. It is impossible to describe or explain the way in which God wounds the soul, nor the very grievous pain inflicted, which deprives it of all self-consciousness; yet this pain is so sweet, that there is no joy in the world which gives greater delight. As I have just said, the soul would wish to be always dying of this wound.

This pain and bliss together carried me out of myself, and I never could understand how it was. Oh, what a sight a wounded soul is!—a soul, I mean, so conscious of it, as to be able to say of itself that it is wounded for so good a cause; and seeing distinctly that it never did anything whereby this love should come to it, and that it does come from that exceeding love which our Lord bears it. A spark seems to have fallen suddenly upon it, that has set it all on fire. Oh, how often do I remember, when in this state, those words of David: "Quemadmodum desiderat cervus ad fontes aquarum"![1] They seem to me to be literally true of myself.

When these impetuosities are not very violent, they seem to admit of a little mitigation—at least, the soul seeks some relief, because it knows not what to do—through certain penances; the painfulness of which, and even the shedding of its blood, are no more felt than if the body were dead. The soul seeks for ways and means to do something that may be felt, for the love of God; but the first pain is so great, that no bodily torture I know of can take it away. As relief is not to be had here, these medicines are too mean for so high a disease. Some slight mitigation may be had, and the pain may pass away a little, by praying God to relieve its sufferings: but the soul sees no relief except in death, by which it thinks to attain completely to the fruition of its good. At other times, these impetuosities are so violent, that the soul can do neither this nor anything else; the whole body is contracted, and neither hand nor foot can be moved: if the body be upright at the time, it falls down, as a thing that has no control over itself. It cannot even breathe; all it does is to moan—not loudly, because it cannot: its moaning, however, comes from a keen sense of pain.

Our Lord was pleased that I should have at times a vision of this kind: I saw an angel close by me, on my left side, in bodily form. This I am not accustomed to see, unless very rarely. Though I have visions of angels frequently, yet I see them only by an intellectual vision, such as I have spoken of before. It was our Lord's will that in this vision I should see the angel in this wise. He was not large, but small of stature, and most beautiful—his face burning, as if he were one of the highest angels, who seem to be all of fire: they must be those whom we call cherubim. Their names they never tell me; but I see very well that there is in heaven so great a difference between one angel and another, and between these and the others, that I cannot explain it.

---

1. Psalm 51: "As the longing of the hart for the fountains of waters, so is the longing of my soul for Thee, O my God."

I saw in his hand a long spear of gold, and at the iron's point there seemed to be a little fire. He appeared to me to be thrusting it at times into my heart, and to pierce my very entrails; when he drew it out, he seemed to draw them out also, and to leave me all on fire with a great love of God. The pain was so great, that it made me moan; and yet so surpassing was the sweetness of this excessive pain, that I could not wish to be rid of it. The soul is satisfied now with nothing less than God. The pain is not bodily, but spiritual; though the body has its share in it, even a large one. It is a caressing of love so sweet which now takes place between the soul and God, that I pray God of His goodness to make him experience it who may think that I am lying.

During the days that this lasted, I went about as if beside myself. I wished to see, or speak with, no one, but only to cherish my pain, which was to me a greater bliss than all created things could give me.

I was in this state from time to time, whenever it was our Lord's pleasure to throw me into those deep trances, which I could not prevent even when I was in the company of others, and which, to my deep vexation, came to be publicly known. Since then, I do not feel that pain so much, but only that which I spoke of before—I do not remember the chapter—which is in many ways very different from it, and of greater worth. On the other hand, when this pain, of which I am now speaking, begins, our Lord seems to lay hold of the soul, and to throw it into a trance so that there is no time for me to have any sense of pain or suffering, because fruition ensues at once. May He be blessed for ever, who hath bestowed such great graces on one who has responded so ill to blessings so great!

LOUISE LABÉ (c. 1520–1565)
France

Little is known about the details of Louise Labé's life, although there has been much speculation. She was born in Lyons, France, about 1520 and was married to a prosperous ropemaker: thus her nickname, "La Belle Cordière" or the beautiful ropemaker. She was a prominent figure in the literary life of Lyons at a time when it was an important cultural center. In 1555 her *Works* were published, including twenty-three sonnets admired for their striking combination of high literary polish, expression of classical learning, and intense emotion. The poems describe the feelings of a woman involved in an absorbing love affair, and they are forthright and carefully crafted.

[I'm living and dying]*

I'm living and dying, as I burn and drown.
I scorch even as I freeze:

Translated by Patricia Terry and Mary Ann Caws.

My life is too sweet and yet too harsh.
Together mingle there great pain and joy:
   I laugh and tears come sudden to my eyes,
Grief torments me even in my pleasure:
I am verdant even as I wither.
My happiness departs; it will not stay.
   So does love inconstant lead me on:
And when I think I cannot bear the pain,
I am surprised to find that it has gone.
   Then when I believe my joy is sure,
That I am close to what I most desire,
Love restores me to my grief again.

[O handsome chestnut eyes]†

O handsome chestnut eyes, evasive gaze,
O fiery sighs and falling tears, O night
obscurely black through which I wait for light
for nothing, O clear dawn of futile days!
O lamentations, O obstinate desires,
O wasted time, O grief scattered about,
O thousand deaths, O thousand nets throughout
my life among the worst insidious fires,
O laughing lips, brow, hair, arms, hands, and fingers,
O funereal lute, viol, bow, and voice!
A woman's heart always has a burned mark.
I sob because of you. Your fire lingers
in every place my seared heart would rejoice,
except in you who keep no single spark.

[Although I cry]†

Although I cry and though my eyes still shed
tears for the seasons I once spent with you,
and while my voice—suppressing sobs, subduing sighs—still rings out vaguely spirited,
while my hand can still pluck the supple string
of the exquisite Lute to sing your grace
and while my arms care only to embrace
your lovely body and to share your being,
while this is true I have no wish to die.
But when I feel my eyes begin to spin,
my voice is broken and my fingers lack
all power, then waiting in my mortal skin

†*Translated by Willis Barnstone.*

my spirit has no lover's glow, and I
pray death to make my brightest day turn black.

[Don't blame me, ladies, if I've loved]†

Don't blame me, ladies, if I've loved. No sneers
if I have felt a thousand torches burn,
a thousand wounds, a thousand daggers turn
in me, if I have burnt my life with tears.
Especially, leave my good name alone.
If I have failed, my hurt is very plain.
Don't sharpen razors to increase my pain,
but know that love, whom none of you have known,
needing no Vulcan to excuse your flame,
nor beautiful Adonis for your shame,
can make you fall in love and anywhere.
You will have fewer chances for relief,
your passion will be stronger and more rare,
and so beware of a more shattering grief.

ANONYMOUS CATALAN BALLAD

(SIXTEENTH CENTURY)

Spain

This sixteenth-century ballad is written in Catalan, the language of Barcelona and the surrounding province, which resembles Provençal. The sentiment of this "romance" is expressed with a typical directness and an autobiographical feeling. As with many anonymous writings, this one is ascribed to a woman. "Anon" is a woman, said Virginia Woolf.

Two Gifts

When I was a girl
I had many lovers.
Now that I'm big,
I only have two:
one a fancy tailor,
the other a weaver.
What can I do?
Both want my love.

†*Translated by Willis Barnstone.*

Spring is coming
with many flowers,
carnations, roses,
violets of all colors.
I'll go to my father's
garden, pick a few,
give the tailor flowers
and the weaver my love.
If they don't want them,
God rid me of both.

GASPARA STAMPA (c. 1523–1554)
Italy

Gaspara Stampa was born in Padua around 1523 but lived most of her life in Venice. There her literary and musical talent made her the object of considerable attention in the society of the cultured nobility in which she moved. Her poetry was published shortly after her death in 1554 as *Rhymes*. The most intense of her sonnets are the result of her passionate affair with Count Collaltino di Collalto. It is his name, derived from the Italian word *colle* (hill), that she often plays on in her poetry. She is much admired for the force and directness of the feelings expressed in her work.

from *Rhymes*

Night of Love

O night to me more splendid and more blessèd
Than the most blessèd and most splendid days;
Night worthy of the most exalted praise,
Not just of mine, unworthy and distressèd;

You alone have been the faithful giver
Of all my joys; you've made the bitter taste
Of this life sweet and dear, for you've replaced
Within my arms the one who's bound me ever.

I just regret that I did not become
Lucky Alemena[1] then, for whom the dawn

Translated by Frank Warnke.

---

1. Alemena was the mother of Hercules by the
   god Zeus. Engendering the hero was a
   project that lasted three nights.

Postponed, against all custom, its returning;
But I can never say such good has come
From you, clear night, for even now my song
Cannot subdue the matter of its yearning.

Send Back My Heart to Me, Relentless One

Send back my heart to me, relentless one,
Who, tyrant-like, do hold and tear it so,
And do to it, and me, just what is done
By tigers and lions to the hapless doe.

Eight days have passed, at least a year to me;
No messages, no letters, do I get,
Despite the vows with which you were so free:
Fountain of valor, Count, and of deceit!

Am I Hercules or Samson, do you suppose,
To bear such sorrow now that we're apart?
I'm young, a woman, half out of my mind,
And, most of all, I'm here without my heart,
You being gone, in whom I used to find
Defense, who were for me strength and repose.

Love, Having Elevated Her to Him, Inspires Her Verses

If, being a woman so abject and vile,
I nonetheless can bear so high a flame,
Why should I not give to the world the same,
At least in part, in proper wealth and style?

If Love, with a new, unprecedented spark,
Could raise me to a place I could not reach,
Why cannot pain and pen combine to teach
Such arts as, never known, shall find their mark?

And if this does not lie in Nature's art,
Then let it be by miracle, whose power

Can conquer, transcend, and every limit break.
How this may be I cannot say for sure,
But well I know the fortune I partake,
And through it a new style engraves my heart.

By Now This Waiting So Has Wearied Me

By now this waiting so has wearied me,
So vanquished am I by desire and grief
For him who, absent, grants me no relief,
So faithless, so forgetful, still is he,

That I turn and beg that she will give me ease,
Who with her sickle makes the world turn white
And gives to all the final blow; my plight
Such sorrow wrings from me, such anguished pleas.

But she is deaf to this my wretched crying,
And scorns my scattered thoughts disturbed and vain,
Like him who, deaf to me, grants no replying.
Thus with lament that from my eyes distills
I wake the pity of these waves, this main,
While he, lighthearted, lives among his hills.

MICHEL DE MONTAIGNE (1533–1592)
France

Michel de Montaigne was born in 1533 on his family's estate in southwestern France. After an excellent humanist education, he studied law but then withdrew from public life and retired into a tower on his estate to devote himself to his reading. There in 1572 he began to write his essays, a form that he is credited with inventing and naming. His *Essays,* first published in 1580, would occupy him until his death in 1592. With their reflective and skeptical tone, they earned him long-lasting fame as an author within his own lifetime and beyond.

from *Essays*

Of Cannibals

When King Pyrrhus passed over into Italy, after he had reconnoitered the formation of the army that the Romans were sending to meet him, he said: "I do not know what barbarians these are" (for so the Greeks called all foreign nations), "but the formation of this army that I see is not at all barbarous." The Greeks said as much of the army that Flamininus brought into their country, and so did Philip, seeing from a knoll the order and distribution of the Roman camp, in his kingdom, under Publius Sulpicius Galba. Thus we should beware of clinging to vulgar opinions, and judge things by reason's way, not by popular say.

I had with me for a long time a man who had lived for ten or twelve years in that other world which has been discovered in our century, in the place where Villegaignon landed, and which he called Antarctic France.[1] This discovery of a boundless country seems worthy of consideration. I don't know if I can guarantee

Translated by Donald M. Frame.

---

1. The region that is now Brazil.

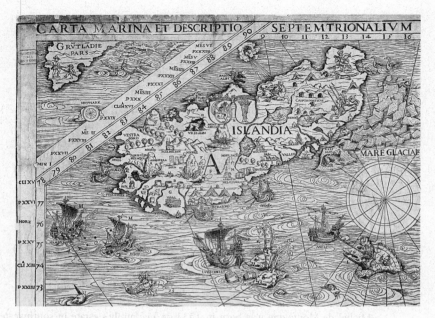

Piglike Sea Monster near Iceland north of Faroe Islands. From Olaus Magnus, *Carta Marina*. Bayerische Staatsbibliothek, Munich.

that some other such discovery will not be made in the future, so many personages greater than ourselves having been mistaken about this one. I am afraid we have eyes bigger than our stomachs, and more curiosity than capacity. We embrace everything, but we clasp only wind.

Plato brings in Solon, telling how he had learned from the priests of the city of Saïs in Egypt that in days of old, before the Flood, there was a great island named Atlantis, right at the mouth of the Strait of Gibraltar, which contained more land than Africa and Asia put together, and that the kings of that country, who not only possessed that island but had stretched out so far on the mainland that they held the breadth of Africa as far as Egypt, and the length of Europe as far as Tuscany, undertook to step over into Asia and subjugate all the nations that border on the Mediterranean, as far as the Black Sea; and for this purpose crossed the Spains, Gaul, Italy, as far as Greece, where the Athenians checked them; but that some time after, both the Athenians and themselves and their island were swallowed up by the Flood.

It is quite likely that that extreme devastation of waters made amazing changes in the habitations of the earth, as people maintain that the sea cut off Sicily from Italy—

'Tis said an earthquake once asunder tore
These lands with dreadful havoc, which before
Formed but one land, one coast

—VIRGIL

Cyprus from Syria, the island of Euboea from the mainland of Boeotia; and elsewhere joined lands that were divided, filling the channels between them with sand and mud:

> A sterile marsh, long fit for rowing, now
> Feeds neighbor towns, and feels the heavy plow.
> —HORACE

But there is no great likelihood that that island was the new world which we have just discovered; for it almost touched Spain, and it would be an incredible result of a flood to have forced it away as far as it is, more than twelve hundred leagues; besides, the travels of the moderns have already almost revealed that it is not an island, but a mainland connected with the East Indies on one side, and elsewhere with the lands under the two poles; or, if it is separated from them, it is by so narrow a strait and interval that it does not deserve to be called an island on that account.

It seems that there are movements, some natural, others feverish, in these great bodies, just as in our own. When I consider the inroads that my river, the Dordogne, is making in my lifetime into the right bank in its descent, and that in twenty years it has gained so much ground and stolen away the foundations of several buildings, I clearly see that this is an extraordinary disturbance; for if it had always gone at this rate, or was to do so in the future, the face of the world would be turned topsy-turvy. But rivers are subject to changes: now they overflow in one direction, now in another, now they keep to their course. I am not speaking of the sudden inundations whose causes are manifest. In Médoc, along the seashore, my brother, the sieur d'Arsac, can see an estate of his buried under the sands that the sea spews forth; the tops of some buildings are still visible; his farms and domains have changed into very thin pasturage. The inhabitants say that for some time the sea has been pushing toward them so hard that they have lost four leagues of land. These sands are its harbingers; and we see great dunes of moving sand that march half a league ahead of it and keep conquering land.

The other testimony of antiquity with which some would connect this discovery is in Aristotle, at least if that little book *Of Unheard-of Wonders* is by him. He there relates that certain Carthaginians, after setting out upon the Atlantic Ocean from the Strait of Gibraltar and sailing a long time, at last discovered a great fertile island, all clothed in woods and watered by great deep rivers, far remote from any mainland; and that they, and others since, attracted by the goodness and fertility of the soil, went there with their wives and children, and began to settle there. The lords of Carthage, seeing that their country was gradually becoming depopulated, expressly forbade anyone to go there any more, on pain of death, and drove out these new inhabitants, fearing, it is said, that in course of time they might come to multiply so greatly as to supplant their former masters and ruin their state. This story of Aristotle does not fit our new lands any better than the other.

This man I had was a simple, crude fellow—a character fit to bear true witness; for clever people observe more things and more curiously, but they interpret them; and to lend weight and conviction to their interpretation, they cannot help altering history a little. They never show you things as they are, but bend and disguise them according to the way they have seen them; and to give credence to their judgment and attract you to it, they are prone to add something to their matter, to stretch it out and amplify it. We need a man either very honest, or so simple that he has not the stuff to build up false inventions and give them plausibility; and wedded to no theory. Such was my man; and besides this, he at various times brought sailors and merchants, whom he had known on that trip, to see me. So I content myself with his information, without inquiring what the cosmographers say about it.

We ought to have topographers who would give us an exact account of the places where they have been. But because they have over us the advantage of having seen Palestine, they want to enjoy the privilege of telling us news about all the rest of the world. I would like everyone to write what he knows, and as much as he knows, not only in this, but in all other subjects; for a man may have some special knowledge and experience of the nature of a river or a fountain, who in other matters knows only what everybody knows. However, to circulate this little scrap of knowledge, he will undertake to write the whole of physics. From this vice spring many great abuses.

Now, to return to my subject, I think there is nothing barbarous and savage in that nation, from what I have been told, except that each man calls barbarism whatever is not his own practice; for indeed it seems we have no other test of truth and reason than the example and pattern of the opinions and customs of the country we live in. *There* is always the perfect religion, the perfect government, the perfect and accomplished manners in all things. Those people are wild, just as we call wild the fruits that Nature has produced by herself and in her normal course; whereas really it is those that we have changed artificially and led astray from the common order, that we should rather call wild. The former retain alive and vigorous their genuine, their most useful and natural, virtues and properties, which we have debased in the latter in adapting them to gratify our corrupted taste. And yet for all that, the savor and delicacy of some uncultivated fruits of those countries is quite as excellent, even to our taste, as that of our own. It is not reasonable that art should win the place of honor over our great and powerful mother Nature. We have so overloaded the beauty and richness of her works by our inventions that we have quite smothered her. Yet wherever her purity shines forth, she wonderfully puts to shame our vain and frivolous attempts:

> Ivy comes readier without our care;
> In lonely caves the arbutus grows more fair;
> No art with artless bird song can compare.
> —PROPERTIUS

All our efforts cannot even succeed in reproducing the nest of the tiniest little bird, its contexture, its beauty and convenience; or even the web of the puny spider. All things, says Plato, are produced by nature, by fortune, or by art; the greatest and most beautiful by one or the other of the first two, the least and most imperfect by the last.

These nations, then, seem to me barbarous in this sense, that they have been fashioned very little by the human mind, and are still very close to their original naturalness. The laws of nature still rule them, very little corrupted by ours; and they are in such a state of purity that I am sometimes vexed that they were unknown earlier, in the days when there were men able to judge them better than we. I am sorry that Lycurgus and Plato did not know of them; for it seems to me that what we actually see in these nations surpasses not only all the pictures in which poets have idealized the golden age and all their inventions in imagining a happy state of man, but also the conceptions and the very desire of philosophy. They could not imagine a naturalness so pure and simple as we see by experience; nor could they believe that our society could be maintained with so little artifice and human solder. This is a nation, I should say to Plato, in which there is no sort of traffic, no knowledge of letters, no science of numbers, no name for a magistrate or for political superiority, no custom of servitude, no riches or poverty, no contracts, no successions, no partitions, no occupations but leisure ones, no care for any but common kinship, no clothes, no agriculture, no metal, no use of wine or wheat. The very words that signify lying, treachery, dissimulation, avarice, envy, belittling, pardon—are unheard of. How far from this perfection would he find the republic that he imagined: *Men fresh sprung from the gods* [Seneca].

> These manners nature first ordained.
> —VIRGIL

For the rest, they live in a country with a very pleasant and temperate climate, so that according to my witnesses it is rare to see a sick man there; and they have assured me that they never saw one palsied, bleary-eyed, toothless, or bent with age. They are settled along the sea and shut in on the land side by great high mountains, with a stretch about a hundred leagues wide in between. They have a great abundance of fish and flesh which bear no resemblance to ours, and they eat them with no other artifice than cooking. The first man who rode a horse there, though he had had dealings with them on several other trips, so horrified them in this posture that they shot him dead with arrows before they could recognize him.

Their buildings are very long, with a capacity of two or three hundred souls; they are covered with the bark of great trees, the strips reaching to the ground at one end and supporting and leaning on one another at the top, in the manner of some of our barns, whose covering hangs down to the ground and acts as a side. They have wood so hard that they cut with it and make of it their swords and grills to cook their food. Their beds are of a cotton weave, hung from the roof like those in our ships, each man having his own; for the wives sleep apart from their husbands.

They get up with the sun, and eat immediately upon rising, to last them through the day; for they take no other meal than that one. Like some other Eastern peoples, of whom Suidas tells us, who drank apart from meals, they do not drink then; but they drink several times a day, and to capacity. Their drink is made of some root, and is of the color of our claret wines. They drink it only lukewarm. This beverage keeps only two or three days; it has a slightly sharp taste, is not at all heady, is good for the stomach, and has a laxative effect upon those who are not used to it; it is a very pleasant drink for anyone who is accustomed to it. In place of bread they use a certain white substance like preserved coriander. I have tried it; it tastes sweet and a little flat.

The whole day is spent in dancing. The younger men go to hunt animals with bows. Some of the women busy themselves meanwhile with warming their drink, which is their chief duty. Some one of the old men, in the morning before they begin to eat, preaches to the whole barnful in common, walking from one end to the other, and repeating one single sentence several times until he has completed the circuit (for the buildings are fully a hundred paces long). He recommends to them only two things: valor against the enemy and love for their wives. And they never fail to point out this obligation, as their refrain, that it is their wives who keep their drink warm and seasoned.

There may be seen in several places, including my own house, specimens of their beds, of their ropes, of their wooden swords and the bracelets with which they cover their wrists in combats, and of the big canes, open at one end, by whose sound they keep time in their dances. They are close shaven all over, and shave themselves much more cleanly than we, with nothing but a wooden or stone razor. They believe that souls are immortal, and that those who have deserved well of the gods are lodged in that part of heaven where the sun rises, and the damned in the west.

They have some sort of priests and prophets, but they rarely appear before the people, having their home in the mountains. On their arrival there is a great feast and solemn assembly of several villages—each barn, as I have described it, makes up a village, and they are about one French league from each other. The prophet speaks to them in public, exhorting them to virtue and their duty; but their whole ethical science contains only these two articles: resoluteness in war and affection for their wives. He prophesies to them things to come and the results they are to expect from their undertakings, and urges them to war or holds them back from it; but this is on the condition that when he fails to prophesy correctly, and if things turn out otherwise than he has predicted, he is cut into a thousand pieces if they catch him, and condemned as a false prophet. For this reason, the prophet who has once been mistaken is never seen again.

Divination is a gift of God; that is why its abuse should be punished as imposture. Among the Scythians, when the soothsayers failed to hit the mark, they were laid, chained hand and foot, on carts full of heather and drawn by oxen, on which they were burned. Those who handle matters subject to the control of human capacity are excusable if they do the best they can. But these others, who come and trick us with assurances of an extraordinary faculty that is beyond our ken, should they not be punished for not making good their promise, and for the temerity of their imposture?

They have their wars with the nations beyond the mountains, further inland, to which they go quite naked, with no other arms than bows or wooden swords ending in a sharp point, in the manner of the tongues of our boar spears. It is astonishing what firmness they show in their combats, which never end but in slaughter and bloodshed; for as to routs and terror, they know nothing of either.

Each man brings back as his trophy the head of the enemy he has killed, and sets it up at the entrance to his dwelling. After they have treated their prisoners well for a long time with all the hospitality they can think of, each man who has a prisoner calls a great assembly of his acquaintances. He ties a rope to one of the prisoner's arms, by the end of which he holds him, a few steps away, for fear of being hurt, and gives his dearest friend the other arm to hold in the same way; and these two, in the presence of the whole assembly, kill him with their swords. This done, they roast him and eat him in common and send some pieces to their absent friends. This is not, as people think, for nourishment, as of old the Scythians used to do; it is to betoken an extreme revenge. And the proof of this came when they saw the Portuguese, who had joined forces with their adversaries, inflict a different kind of death on them when they took them prisoner, which was to bury them up to the waist, shoot the rest of their body full of arrows, and afterward hang them. They thought that these people from the other world, being men who had sown the knowledge of many vices among their neighbors and were much greater masters than themselves in every sort of wickedness, did not adopt this sort of vengeance without some reason, and that it must be more painful than their own; so they began to give up their old method and to follow this one.

I am not sorry that we notice the barbarous horror of such acts, but I am heartily sorry that, judging their faults rightly, we should be so blind to our own. I think there is more barbarity in eating a man alive than in eating him dead; and in tearing by tortures and the rack a body still full of feeling, in roasting a man bit by bit, in having him bitten and mangled by dogs and swine (as we have not only read but seen within fresh memory, not among ancient enemies, but among neighbors and fellow citizens, and what is worse, on the pretext of piety and religion), than in roasting and eating him after he is dead.

Indeed, Chrysippus and Zeno, heads of the Stoic sect, thought there was nothing wrong in using our carcasses for any purpose in case of need, and getting nourishment from them; just as our ancestors, when besieged by Caesar in the city of Alésia, resolved to relieve their famine by eating old men, women, and other people useless for fighting.

> The Gascons once, 'tis said, their life renewed
> By eating of such food.
> —JUVENAL

And physicians do not fear to use human flesh in all sorts of ways for our health, applying it either inwardly or outwardly. But there never was any opinion so disordered as to excuse treachery, disloyalty, tyranny, and cruelty, which are our ordinary vices.

So we may well call these people barbarians, in respect to the rules of reason, but not in respect to ourselves, who surpass them in every kind of barbarity.

Their warfare is wholly noble and generous, and as excusable and beautiful as this human disease can be; its only basis among them is their rivalry in valor. They are not fighting for the conquest of new lands, for they still enjoy that natural abundance that provides them without toil and trouble with all necessary things in such profusion that they have no wish to enlarge their boundaries. They are still in that happy state of desiring only as much as their natural needs demand; anything beyond that is superfluous to them.

They generally call those of the same age, brothers; those who are younger, children; and the old men are fathers to all the others. These leave to their heirs in common the full possession of their property, without division or any other title at all than just the one that Nature gives to her creatures in bringing them into the world.

If their neighbors cross the mountains to attack them and win a victory, the gain of the victor is glory, and the advantage of having proved the master in valor and virtue; for apart from this they have no use for the goods of the vanquished, and they return to their own country, where they lack neither anything necessary nor that great thing, the knowledge of how to enjoy their condition happily and be content with it. These men of ours do the same in their turn. They demand of their prisoners no other ransom than that they confess and acknowledge their defeat. But there is not one in a whole century who does not choose to die rather than to relax a single bit, by word or look, from the grandeur of an invincible courage; not one who would not rather be killed and eaten than so much as ask not to be. They treat them very freely, so that life may be all the dearer to them, and usually entertain them with threats of their coming death, of the torments they will have to suffer, the preparations that are being made for that purpose, the cutting up of their limbs, and the feast that will be made at their expense. All this is done for the sole purpose of extorting from their lips some weak or base word, or making them want to flee, so as to gain the advantage of having terrified them and broken down their firmness. For indeed, if you take it the right way, it is in this point alone that true victory lies:

It is no victory
Unless the vanquished foe admits your mastery.
—CLAUDIAN

The Hungarians, very bellicose fighters, did not in olden times pursue their advantage beyond putting the enemy at their mercy. For having wrung a confession from him to this effect, they let him go unharmed and unransomed, except, at most, for exacting his promise never again to take up arms against them.

We win enough advantages over our enemies that are borrowed advantages, not really our own. It is the quality of a porter, not of valor, to have sturdier arms and legs; agility is a dead and corporeal quality; it is a stroke of luck to make our enemy stumble, or dazzle his eyes by the sunlight; it is a trick of art and technique, which may be found in a worthless coward, to be an able fencer. The worth and value of a man is in his heart and his will; there lies his real honor. Valor is the strength, not of legs and arms, but of heart and soul; it consists not in the worth of our horse or our weapons, but in our own. He who falls obstinate in his courage, *if he has fallen, he fights on his knees* [Seneca]. He who relaxes none of his assurance, no matter how great the danger of imminent death; who, giving up his soul, still looks firmly and scornfully at his enemy—he is beaten not by us, but by fortune; he is killed, not conquered.

The most valiant are sometimes the most unfortunate. Thus there are triumphant defeats that rival victories. Nor did those four sister victories, the fairest that the sun ever set eyes on—Salamis, Plataea, Mycale, and Sicily—ever dare match all their combined glory against the glory of the annihilation of King Leonidas[2] and his men at the pass of Thermopylae.

Who ever hastened with more glorious and ambitious desire to win a battle

2. During the invasion of Greece by the Persians in 480 B.C., King Leonidas of Sparta and a small army held off a vastly superior Persian force for two days at Thermopylae before being wiped out.

than Captain Ischolas to lose one? Who ever secured his safety more ingeniously and painstakingly than he did his destruction? He was charged to defend a certain pass in the Peloponnesus against the Arcadians. Finding himself wholly incapable of doing this, in view of the nature of the place and the inequality of the forces, he made up his mind that all who confronted the enemy would necessarily have to remain on the field. On the other hand, deeming it unworthy both of his own virtue and magnanimity and of the Lacedaemonian name to fail in his charge, he took a middle course between these two extremes, in this way. The youngest and fittest of his band he preserved for the defense and service of their country, and sent them home; and with those whose loss was less important, he determined to hold this pass, and by their death to make the enemy buy their entry as dearly as he could. And so it turned out. For he was presently surrounded on all sides by the Arcadians, and after slaughtering a large number of them, he and his men were all put to the sword. Is there a trophy dedicated to victors that would not be more due to these vanquished? The role of true victory is in fighting, not in coming off safely; and the honor of valor consists in combating, not in beating.

To return to our story. These prisoners are so far from giving in, in spite of all that is done to them, that on the contrary, during the two or three months that they are kept, they wear a gay expression; they urge their captors to hurry and put them to the test; they defy them, insult them, reproach them with their cowardice and the number of battles they have lost to the prisoners' own people.

I have a song composed by a prisoner which contains this challenge, that they should all come boldly and gather to dine off him, for they will be eating at the same time their own fathers and grandfathers, who have served to feed and nourish his body. "These muscles," he says, "this flesh and these veins are your own, poor fools that you are. You do not recognize that the substance of your ancestors' limbs is still contained in them. Savor them well; you will find in them the taste of your own flesh." An idea that certainly does not smack of barbarity. Those that paint these people dying, and who show the execution, portray the prisoner spitting in the face of his slayers and scowling at them. Indeed, to the last gasp they never stop braving and defying their enemies by word and look. Truly here are real savages by our standards; for either they must be thoroughly so, or we must be; there is an amazing distance between their character and ours.

The men there have several wives, and the higher their reputation for valor the more wives they have. It is a remarkably beautiful thing about their marriages that the same jealousy our wives have to keep us from the affection and kindness of other women, theirs have to win this for them. Being more concerned for their husbands' honor than for anything else, they strive and scheme to have as many companions as they can, since that is a sign of their husbands' valor.

Our wives will cry "Miracle!" but it is no miracle. It is a properly matrimonial virtue, but one of the highest order. In the Bible, Leah, Rachel, Sarah, and Jacob's wives gave their beautiful handmaids to their husbands; and Livia seconded the appetites of Augustus, to her own disadvantage; and Stratonice, the wife of King Deiotarus, not only lent her husband for his use a very beautiful young chambermaid in her service, but carefully brought up her children, and backed them up to succeed to their father's estates.

And lest it be thought that all this is done through a simple and servile bondage to usage and through the pressure of the authority of their ancient customs, without reasoning or judgment, and because their minds are so stupid that they cannot take any other course, I must cite some examples of their capacity. Besides the warlike song I have just quoted, I have another, a love song, which begins in this vein: "Adder, stay; stay, adder, that from the pattern of your coloring my sister may draw the fashion and the workmanship of a rich girdle that I may give to my love; so may your beauty and your pattern be forever preferred to all other serpents." This first couplet is the refrain of the song. Now I am familiar enough with poetry to be a judge of this: not only is there nothing barbarous in this fancy, but it is altogether Anacreontic. Their language, moreover, is a soft language, with an agreeable sound, somewhat like Greek in its endings.

Three of these men, ignorant of the price they will pay some day, in loss of repose and happiness, for gaining knowledge of the corruptions of this side of the ocean; ignorant also of the fact that of this intercourse will come their ruin (which I suppose is already well advanced: poor wretches, to let themselves be tricked by the desire for new things and to have left the serenity of their own sky to come and see ours!)—three of these men were at Rouen, at the time the late King Charles IX was there.[3] The king talked to them for a long time; they were shown our ways, our splendor, the aspect of a fine city. After that, someone asked their opinion, and wanted to know what they had found most amazing. They mentioned three things, of which I have forgotten the third, and I am very sorry for it; but I still remember two of them. They said that in the first place they thought it very strange that so many grown men, bearded, strong, and armed, who were around the king (it is likely that they were talking about the Swiss of his guard) should submit to obey a child, and that one of them was not chosen to command instead. Second (they have a way in their language of speaking of men as halves of one another), they had noticed that there were among us men full and gorged with all sorts of good things, and that their other halves were beggars at their doors, emaciated with hunger and poverty; and they thought it strange that these needy halves could endure such an injustice, and did not take the others by the throat, or set fire to their houses.

I had a very long talk with one of them; but I had an interpreter who followed my meaning so badly, and who was so hindered by his stupidity in taking in my ideas, that I could get hardly any satisfaction from the man. When I asked him what profit he gained from his superior position among his people (for he was a captain, and our sailors called him king), he told me that it was to march foremost in war. How many men followed him? He pointed to a piece of ground, to signify as many as such a space could hold; it might have been four or five thousand men. Did all his authority expire with the war? He said that this much remained, that when he visited the villages dependent on him, they made paths for him through the underbrush by which he might pass quite comfortably.

All this is not too bad—but what's the use? They don't wear breeches.

---

3. Charles IX became king of France in 1560 at the age of ten; he died in 1574.

MIGUEL DE CERVANTES SAAVEDRA
(1547–1616)

Spain

Miguel de Cervantes Saavedra, the greatest figure in Spanish literature, was born in Alcalá de Henares in 1547. He had an eventful military career, in Italy, fighting in the battle of *Lepanto* (1571), in which he lost his left hand; returning to Spain with his brother, he was captured by Barbary pirates. Both brothers were taken to Algiers as slaves. When his ransom was paid by the Trinitarian friars, he returned to Spain. He wrote in a variety of forms including the twelve short stories of the *Novelas ejemplares* (*Exemplary Stories*), the pastoral romance *La Galatea* (1585), many plays after 1585, as well as verse and verse romance. His masterpiece is *Don Quixote*: the first part was published in 1605 and the second in 1615, a year before the author's death. A satire on the romances of chivalry, this tale of the adventures of a mad and impoverished nobleman who becomes a wandering knight, a role which in his own time existed only in literature, is one of the world's most influential novels and—as is now recognized—one of the most complex.

from *Don Quixote*

[The Quality and Way of Life of the Famous Knight Don Quixote]

In a certain village in La Mancha, which I do not wish to name, there lived not long ago a gentleman—one of those who have always a lance in the rack, an ancient shield, a lean hack and a greyhound for coursing. His habitual diet consisted of a stew, more beef than mutton, of hash most nights, boiled bones on Saturdays, lentils on Friday, and a young pigeon as a Sunday treat; and on this he spent three-quarters of his income. The rest of it went on a fine cloth doublet, velvet breeches and slippers for holidays, and a homespun suit of the best in which he decked himself on weekdays. His household consisted of a housekeeper of rather more than forty, a niece not yet twenty, and a lad for the field and market, who saddled his horse and wielded the pruning-hook.

Our gentleman was verging on fifty, of tough constitution, lean-bodied, thin-faced, a great early riser and a lover of hunting. They say that his surname was Quixada or Quesada—for there is some difference of opinion amongst authors on this point. However, by very reasonable conjecture we may take it that he was called Quexana. But this does not much concern our story; enough that we do not depart by so much as an inch from the truth in the telling of it.

The reader must know, then, that this gentleman, in the times when he had nothing to do—as was the case for most of the year—gave himself up to the reading of books of knight errantry; which he loved and enjoyed so much that he almost entirely forgot his hunting, and even the care of his estate. So odd and foolish, indeed, did he grow on this subject that he sold many acres of cornland to buy these books of chivalry to read, and in this way brought home every one he could get. And of them all he considered none so good as the works of the famous Feliciano de Silva. For his brilliant style and those complicated sentences seemed to him very pearls, especially when he came upon those love-passages and challenges frequently written in the manner of: 'The reason for the unreason with which you treat my reason, so weakens my reason that with reason I complain of your beauty'; and also when he read: 'The high heavens that with their stars divinely fortify you in your divinity and make you deserving of the desert that your greatness deserves.'

These writings drove the poor knight out of his wits; and he passed sleepless nights trying to understand them and disentangle their meaning, though Aristotle himself would never have unravelled or understood them, even if he had been resurrected for that sole purpose. He did not much like the wounds that Sir Belianis gave and received, for he imagined that his face and his whole body must have been covered with scars and marks, however skillful the surgeons who tended him. But, for all that, he admired the author for ending his book with the promise to continue with that interminable adventure, and often the desire seized him to take up the pen himself, and write the promised sequel for him. No doubt he would have done so, and perhaps successfully, if other greater and more persistent preoccupations had not prevented him.

Often he had arguments with the priest of his village, who was a scholar and a graduate of Siguenza, as to which was the better knight—Palmerin of England or Amadis of Gaul.[1] But Master Nicholas, the barber of that village, said that no one could compare with the Knight of the Sun. Though if anyone could, it was Sir Galaor, brother of Amadis of Gaul. For he had a very accommodating nature, and was not so affected nor such a sniveller as his brother, though he was not a bit behind him in the matter of bravery.

In short, he so buried himself in his books that he spent the nights reading from twilight till daybreak and the days from dawn till dark; and so from little sleep and much reading, his brain dried up and he lost his wits. He filled his mind with all that he read in them, with enchantments, quarrels, battles, challenges, wounds, wooings, loves, torments and other impossible nonsense; and so deeply did he steep his imagination in the belief that all the fanciful stuff he read was true, that to his mind no history in the world was more authentic. He used to say that the Cid Ruy Diaz must have been a very good knight, but that he could not be compared to the Knight of the Burning Sword, who with a single backstroke had cleft a pair of fierce and monstrous giants in two. And he had an even better opinion of Bernardo del Carpio for slaying the enchanted Roland at Roncesvalles,[2] by making use of Hercules' trick when he throttled the Titan Antaeus in his arms.

---

1. Heroes of narrative works about knights-errant. The many volumes of the adventures of Amadis, written in several western European languages, were especially popular.

2. There are many stories about Roland, the heroic nephew of Charlemagne, who supposedly died in battle against the Moors at Roncesvalles in the Pyrenees.

He spoke very well of the giant Morgante; for, though one of that giant brood who are all proud and insolent, he alone was affable and well-mannered. But he admired most of all Reynald of Montalban, particularly when he saw him sally forth from his castle and rob everyone he met, and when in heathen lands overseas he stole that idol of Mahomet, which history says was of pure gold. But he would have given his housekeeper and his niece into the bargain, to deal the traitor Galaon a good kicking.

In fact, now that he had utterly wrecked his reason he fell into the strangest fancy that ever a madman had in the whole world. He though it fit and proper, both in order to increase his renown and to serve the state, to turn knight errant and travel through the world with horse and armour in search of adventures, following in every way the practice of the knights errant he had read of, redressing all manner of wrongs, and exposing himself to chances and dangers, by the overcoming of which he might win eternal honour and renown. Already the poor man fancied himself crowned by the valour of his arm, at least with the empire of Trebizond; and so, carried away by the strange pleasure he derived from these agreeable thoughts, he hastened to translate his desires into action.

The first thing that he did was to clean some armour which had belonged to his ancestors, and had lain for ages forgotten in a corner, eaten with rust and covered with mould. But when he had cleaned and repaired it as best he could, he found that there was one great defect: the helmet was a simple head-piece without a visor. So he ingeniously made good this deficiency by fashioning out of pieces of pasteboard a kind of half-visor which, fitted to the helmet, gave the appearance of a complete head-piece. However, to see if it was strong enough to stand up to the risk of a sword-cut, he took out his sword and gave it two strokes, the first of which demolished in a moment what had taken him a week to make. He was not too pleased at the ease with which he had destroyed it, and to safeguard himself against this danger, reconstructed the visor, putting some strips of iron inside, in such a way as to satisfy himself of his protection; and, not caring to make another trial of it, he accepted it as a fine jointed headpiece and put it into commission.

Next he went to inspect his hack, but though, through leanness, he had more quarters than there are pence in a groat, and more blemishes than Gonella's horse,[3] which was nothing but skin and bone, he appeared to our knight more than the equal of Alexander's Bucephalus[4] and the Cid's Babieca.[5] He spent four days pondering what name to give him; for, he reflected, it would be wrong for the horse of so famous a knight, a horse so good in himself, to be without a famous name. Therefore he tried to fit him with one that would signify what he had been before his master turned knight errant, and what he now was; for it was only right that as his master changed his profession, the horse should change his name for a sublime and high-sounding one, befitting the new order and the new calling he

---

3. Gonella was the court jester of the Duke of Ferrara and became a legendary personality in his own right. There were jokes about his incredibly skinny horse.
4. Alexander the Great, ruler of Macedon and conqueror of much of the known world, had a famous horse named Bucephalus.
5. The horse of Rodrigo Díaz de Bivar, called "The Cid" and hero of the twelfth-century Spanish poem of the same name.

professed. So, after many names invented, struck out and rejected, amended, cancelled and remade in his fanciful mind, he finally decided to call him Rocinante, a name which seemed to him grand and sonorous, and to express the common horse he had been before arriving at his present state: the first and foremost of all hacks in the world.

Having found so pleasing a name for his horse, he next decided to do the same for himself, and spent another eight days thinking about it. Finally he resolved to call himself Don Quixote. And that is no doubt why the authors of this true history, as we have said, assumed that his name must have been Quixada and not Quesada, as other authorities would have it. Yet he remembered that the valorous Amadis had not been content with his bare name, but had added the name of his kingdom and native country in order to make it famous, and styled himself Amadis of Gaul. So, like a good knight, he decided to add the name of his country to his own and call himself Don Quixote de la Mancha. Thus, he thought, he very clearly proclaimed his parentage and native land and honoured it by taking his surname from it.

Now that his armour was clean, his helmet made into a complete head-piece, a name found for his horse, and he confirmed in his new title, it struck him that there was only one more thing to do: to find a lady to be enamoured of. For a knight errant without a lady is like a tree without leaves or fruit and a body without a soul. He said to himself again and again: 'If I for my sins or by good luck were to meet with some giant hereabouts, as generally happens to knights errant, and if I were to overthrow him in the encounter, or cut him down the middle or, in short, conquer him and make him surrender, would it not be well to have someone to whom I could send him as a present, so that he could enter and kneel down before my sweet lady and say in tones of humble submission: "Lady, I am the giant Caraculiambro, lord of the island of Malindrania, whom the never-sufficiently-to-be-praised knight, Don Quixote de la Mancha, conquered in single combat and ordered to appear before your Grace, so that your Highness might dispose of me according to your will"?' Oh, how pleased our knight was when he had made up this speech, and even gladder when he found someone whom he could call his lady. It happened, it is believed, in this way: in a village near his there was a very good-looking farm girl, whom he had been taken with at one time, although she is supposed not to have known it or had proof of it. Her name was Aldonza Lorenzo, and she it was he thought fit to call the lady of his fancies; and, casting around for a name which should not be too far away from her own, yet suggest and imply a princess and great lady, he resolved to call her Dulcinea del Toboso—for she was a native of El Toboso—,a name which seemed to him as musical, strange and significant as those others that he had devised for himself and his possessions.

[Don Quixote's Success in the Dreadful and Never Before Imagined Adventure of the Windmills]

At that moment they caught sight of some thirty or forty windmills, which stand on that plain, and as soon as Don Quixote saw them he said to his squire: "Fortune is guiding our affairs better than we could have wished. Look over there, friend Sancho Panza, where more than thirty monstrous giants appear. I intend to do battle with them and take all their lives. With their spoils we will begin to get rich, for this is a fair war, and it is a great service to God to wipe out such a wicked brood from the face of the earth."

"What giants?" asked Sancho Panza.

"Those you see there," replied his master, "with their long arms. Some giants have them about six miles long."

"Take care, your worship," said Sancho; "those things over there are not giants but windmills, and what seem to be their arms are the sails, which are whirled round in the wind and make the millstone turn."

"It is quite clear," replied Don Quixote, "that you are not experienced in this matter of adventures. They are giants, and if you are afraid, go away and say your prayers, whilst I advance and engage them in fierce and unequal battle."

As he spoke, he dug his spurs into his steed Rocinante, paying no attention to his squire's shouted warning that beyond all doubt they were windmills and no giants he was advancing to attack. But he went on, so positive that they were giants that he neither listened to Sancho's cries nor noticed what they were, even when he got near them. Instead he went on shouting in a loud voice: "Do not fly, cowards, vile creatures, for it is one knight alone who assails you."

At that moment a slight wind arose, and the great sails began to move. At the sight of which Don Quixote shouted: "Though you wield more arms than the giant Briareus, you shall pay for it!" Saying this, he commended himself with all his soul to his Lady Dulcinea, beseeching her aid in his great peril. Then, covering himself with his shield and putting his lance in the rest, he urged Rocinante forward at a full gallop and attacked the nearest windmill, thrusting his lance into the sail. But the wind turned it with such violence that it shivered his weapon to pieces, dragging the horse and his rider with it, and sent the knight rolling badly injured across the plain. Sancho Panza rushed to his assistance as fast as his ass could trot, but when he came up he found that the knight could not stir. Such a shock had Rocinante given him in their fall.

"Oh my goodness!" cried Sancho. "Didn't I tell your worship to look what you were doing, for they were only windmills? Nobody could mistake them, unless he had windmills on the brain."

"Silence, friend Sancho," replied Don Quixote. "Matters of war are more subject than most to continual change. What is more, I think—and that is the truth—that the same sage Friston who robbed me of my room and my books has turned those giants into windmills, to cheat me of the glory of conquering them. Such is the enmity he bears me; but in the very end his black arts shall avail him little against the goodness of my sword."

"God send it as He will," replied Sancho Panza, helping the knight to get up and remount Rocinante, whose shoulders were half dislocated.

WILLIAM SHAKESPEARE (1564–1616)
England

William Shakespeare was born in Stratford-upon-Avon in 1564, and worked as an actor and as a playwright in London. His history plays, tragedies, comedies, and romances have made him the world's most famous and most frequently performed playwright. He later retired from the stage and withdrew to Stratford, dying there in 1616. His 154 sonnets, written in the mid 1590s, were published in 1609. They are concerned with a tangle of relationships between the first person speaker and a handsome young man, a dark complexioned older woman, and a rival poet. They have generated an enormous amount of criticism and commentary of every conceivable kind. The late romance, *The Tempest* (1611), one of Shakespeare's last plays, is often seen as the culmination of his dramatic art.

Shall I Compare Thee to a Summer's Day

Shall I compare thee to a summer's day?
Thou art more lovely and more temperate.
Rough winds do shake the darling buds of May,
And summer's lease hath all too short a date.
Sometimes too hot the eye of heaven shines,   5
And often is his gold complexion dimmed;
And every fair from fair sometime declines,
By chance, or nature's changing course, untrimmed;
But thy eternal summer shall not fade,
Nor lose possession of that fair thou ow'st,   10
Nor shall Death brag thou wand'rest in his shade,
When in eternal lines to time thou grow'st.
  So long as men can breathe or eyes can see,
  So long lives this, and this gives life to thee.

When, in Disgrace with Fortune and Men's Eyes

When, in disgrace with Fortune and men's eyes,
I all alone beweep my outcast state,
And trouble deaf heaven with my bootless cries,
And look upon myself and curse my fate,
Wishing me like to one more rich in hope,
Featured like him, like him with friends possessed,
Desiring this man's art, and that man's scope,
With what I most enjoy contented least;
Yet in these thoughts myself almost despising,

Haply I think on thee, and then my state,
Like to the lark at break of day arising
From sullen earth, sings hymns at heaven's gate;
　　For thy sweet love rememb'red such wealth brings,
　　That then I scorn to change my state with kings.

My Mistress' Eyes Are Nothing Like the Sun

My mistress' eyes are nothing like the sun;
Coral is far more red than her lips' red;
If snow be white, why then her breasts are dun;
If hairs be wires, black wires grow on her head.
I have seen roses damasked, red and white,
But no such roses see I in her cheeks,
And in some perfumes is there more delight
Than in the breath that from my mistress reeks.
I love to hear her speak, yet well I know
That music hath a far more pleasing sound.
I grant I never saw a goddess go;
My mistress when she walks treads on the ground.
　　And yet, by heaven, I think my love as rare
　　As any she belied with false compare.

on film

The Tempest   1611

Names of the Actors

ALONSO, *King of Naples*
SEBASTIAN, *his brother*
PROSPERO, *the right Duke of Milan* — Greedy, demeaning, demanding
ANTONIO, *his brother, the usurping*
Duke of Milan
FERDINAND, *son to the King of Naples*
GONZALO, *an honest old councillor*
ADRIAN *and*
FRANCISCO, ⎬ *lords*
CALIBAN, *a savage and deformed slave*
TRINCULO, *a jester*
STEPHANO, *a drunken butler*
MASTER *of a ship*

BOATSWAIN
MARINERS
MIRANDA, *daughter to Prospero*

ARIEL, *an airy spirit*
IRIS
CERES,
JUNO, ⎬ *[presented by] spirits*
NYMPHS
REAPERS,

[Other Spirits attending on Prospero]

Scene
An uninhabited island

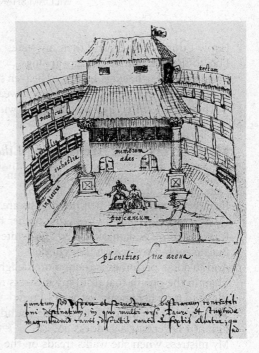

Sketch of the Swan made in 1596 by Aernout van Buchell. Drawing by Johannes de Witt. Bibliotheek der Rijksuniversiteit Utrecht.

Act I

on Board Ship . . .

Scene 1[1]

> [*A tempestuous noise of thunder and lighting heard. Enter a Shipmaster and a Boatswain.*]

MASTER: Boatswain!

BOATSWAIN: Here, Master. What cheer?

MASTER: Good,[2] *My good fellow* speak to the mariners. Fall to 't yarely,[3] *Nimbly* or we run ourselves aground. Bestir, bestir! [*Exit.*]

> [*Enter Mariners.*]

BOATSWAIN: Heigh, my hearts! Cheerly, cheerly, my hearts! Yare, yare! Take in the   5
topsail. Tend[4] to the Master's whistle.—Blow[5] till thou burst thy wind, if room enough![6] *as long as there is enough sea. To the wind . . .*

> [*Enter Alonso, Sebastian, Antonio, Ferdinand, Gonzalo, and others.*]

Act I, Scene 1

1. Location: on board ship, off the island's coast.
2. I.e., it's good you've come, or, my good fellow.
3. Nimbly.
4. Attend.
5. Addressed to the wind.
6. As long as we have sea room enough.

King of Naples
ALONSO: Good Boatswain, have care. Where's the Master? Play the men.[7]
BOATSWAIN: I pray now, keep below.
Brother of Duke
ANTONIO: Where is the Master, Boatswain?   10
BOATSWAIN: Do you not hear him? You mar our labor. Keep[8] your cabins! You do
    assist the storm.
Old Councillor
GONZALO: Nay, good,[9] be patient.
BOATSWAIN: When the sea is. Hence! What cares these roarers[10] for the name of
    king? To cabin! Silence! Trouble us not.   15
GONZALO: Good, yet remember whom thou hast aboard.
BOATSWAIN: None that I more love than myself. You are a councillor; if you can
    command these elements to silence and work the peace of the present,[11]
    we will not hand[12] a rope more. Use your authority. If you cannot, give
    thanks you have lived so long and make yourself ready in your cabin for   20
    the mischance of the hour, if it so hap.[13]—Cheerly, good hearts!—Out
    of our way, I say. [Exit.]
GONZALO: I have great comfort from this fellow. Methinks he hath no drowning
    mark upon him; his complexion is perfect gallows.[14] Stand fast, good
    Fate, to his hanging! Make the rope of his destiny our cable, for our own   25
    doth little advantage.[15] If he be not born to be hanged, our case is
    miserable.[16] [Exeunt (courtiers).]

    [Enter Boatswain.]

BOATSWAIN: Down with the topmast! Yare! Lower, lower! Bring her try wi' the
    main course.[17] (A cry within.) A plague upon this howling! They are
    louder than the weather or our office.[18]   30

    [Enter Sebastian, Antonio, and Gonzalo.]

    Yet again? What do you here? Shall we give o'er[19] and drown? Have you
    a mind to sink?
Bro: of King
SEBASTIAN: A pox o' your throat, you bawling, blasphemous, incharitable dog!
BOATSWAIN: Work you, then.
ANTONIO: Hang, cur! Hang, you whoreson, insolent noisemaker! We are less   35
    afraid to be drowned than thou art.

---

7. Act like men (?) ply, urge the men to exert
   themselves (?).
8. Remain in.
9. Good fellow.
10. Waves or winds, or both: spoken to as
    though they were "bullies" or blusterers.
11. Bring calm to our present circumstances.
12. Handle.
13. Happen.

14. Appearance shows he was born to be
    hanged (and therefore, according to the
    proverb, in no danger of drowning).
15. Our own cable is of little benefit.
16. Circumstances are desperate.
17. Sail her close to the wind by means of the
    mainsail.
18. I.e., the noise we make at our work.
19. Give up.

GONZALO: I'll warrant him for drowning,[20] though the ship were no stronger than a nutshell and as <u>leaky</u> as an unstanched[21] wench. *(on the rag)*

BOATSWAIN: Lay her ahold, ahold![22] Set her two courses.[23] Off to sea again! Lay her off! *Close to the wind*

[*Enter Mariners, wet.*]

MARINERS: All lost! To prayers, to prayers! All lost!   40

[*The Mariners run about in confusion, exiting at random.*]

BOATSWAIN: What, must our mouths be cold?[24] *Can't we have a drink (alcohol) Whiskey*

GONZALO:
The King and Prince at prayers! Let's assist them,
For our case is as theirs.

SEBASTIAN: I am out of patience.

ANTONIO:
We are merely[25] cheated of our lives by drunkards.   45
This wide-chapped[26] rascal! Would thou mightst lie drowning
The washing of ten tides![27]

GONZALO: He'll be hanged yet,
Though every drop of water swear against it
And gape at wid'st[28] to glut[29] him.   50
swallow

[*A confused noise within.*] "Mercy on us!"—
"We split,[30] we split!"—"Farewell my wife and children!"—
Break apart
"Farewell, brother!"—"We split, we split, we split!"

[*Exit Boatswain.*]
Ship destroyed by storm + sink torn apart

ANTONIO: Let's all sink wi' the King.
Bro Duke / Bro King

SEBASTIAN: Let's take leave of him.

[*Exit (with Antonio).*]

GONZALO: Now would I give a thousand furlongs of sea for an acre of barren   55
ground: long heath,[31] brown furze,[32] anything. The wills above be done!
But I would fain[33] die a dry death. *Desperate*
Old Councillor   *Die =*   *to the land*

[*Exit.*]
Don't want to drown — saying prayers.

---

20. Guarantee that he will never be drowned.
21. Insatiable, loose, unrestrained (suggesting also "incontinent" and "menstrual").
22. Ahull, close to the wind.
23. Sails, i.e., foresail as well as mainsail, set in an attempt to get the ship back out into open water.
24. I.e., must we drown in the cold sea, or, let us heat up our mouths with liquor.
25. Utterly.
26. With mouth wide open.
27. Pirates were hanged on the shore and left until three tides had come in.
28. Wide open.
29. Swallow.
30. Break apart.
31. Heather.
32. Furze gorse, a weed growing on waste-land.
33. Rather.

[Handwritten top margin: They are on the island wondering about the ship on the high seas & those on board...]

[Handwritten left margin: ON AN ISLAND]

Scene 2[1]

[Enter Prospero (in his magic cloak) and Miranda.]

[Handwritten: Antonio — Duke Brother; Miranda — daughter to Prospero, niece to Antonio; Prospero/Antonio — brothers]

MIRANDA:
[Handwritten: Antonio/Miranda — Uncle/niece]
[Handwritten left margin: Daughter to Prospero]

If by your art,[2] my dearest father, you have
Put the wild waters in this roar, allay[3] them. *[Handwritten: Pacify]*
The sky, it seems, would pour down stinking pitch,
But that the sea, mounting to th' welkin's cheek,[4] *[Handwritten: sky face, high seas]*
Dashes the fire out. O, I have suffered
With those that I saw suffer! A brave[5] vessel, *[Handwritten: gallant]*
Who had, no doubt, some noble creature in her,
Dashed all to pieces. O, the cry did knock
Against my very heart! Poor souls, they perished.
Had I been any god of power, I would
Have sunk the sea within the earth or ere[6] *[Handwritten: Before]*
It should the good ship so have swallowed and
The freighting[7] souls within her.

[Handwritten left margin: Still Stormy ...]
[Handwritten right margin: Speaking of the sunken ship]

PROSPERO: Be collected.[8] *[Handwritten: Calm]*
No more amazement.[9] Tell your piteous[10] heart
There's no harm done. *[Handwritten: Consternation / pitying]*

MIRANDA: O, woe the day!

PROSPERO: No harm.
I have done nothing but[11] in care of thee,
Of thee, my dear one, thee, my daughter, who
Art ignorant of what thou art, naught knowing
Of whence I am, nor that I am more better[12] *[Handwritten: of higher rank]*
Than Prospero, master of a full[13] poor cell, *[Handwritten: Very]*
And thy no greater father.

[Handwritten: grammatically incorrect]

MIRANDA: More to know
Did never meddle[14] with my thoughts. *[Handwritten: mingle]*

PROSPERO: 'Tis time
I should inform thee farther. Lend thy hand
And pluck my magic garment from me. So,

[Laying down his magic cloak and staff.]

Act I, Scene 2

1. Location: the island, near Prospero's cell.
   On the Elizabethan stage, this cell is implicitly at hand throughout the play, although
   in some scenes the convention of flexible
   distance allows us to imagine characters in
   other parts of the island.
2. Magic.
3. Pacify.
4. Sky's face.
5. Gallant, splendid.
6. Before.
7. Forming the cargo.
8. Calm, composed.
9. Consternation.
10. Pitying.
11. Except.
12. Of higher rank.
13. Very.
14. Mingle.

Lie there, my art.—Wipe thou thine eyes. Have comfort.   25
The direful spectacle of the wreck,[15] which touched
The very virtue[16] of compassion in thee,
I have with such provision[17] in mine art
So safely ordered that there is no soul—
No, not so much perdition[18] as an hair   30
Betid[19] to any creature in the vessel
Which[20] thou heard'st cry, which thou saw'st sink. Sit down,
For thou must now know farther.

MIRANDA [*sitting*]:   You have often
     Begun to tell me what I am, but stopped
     And left me to a bootless inquisition,[21]   35
     Concluding, "Stay, not yet."

PROSPERO: The hour's now come;
     The very minute bids thee ope thine ear.
     Obey, and be attentive. Canst thou remember
     A time before we came unto this cell?
     I do not think thou canst, for then thou wast not   40
     Out[22] three years old.

MIRANDA: Certainly, sir, I can.

PROSPERO:
     By what? By any other house or person?
     Of anything the image, tell me, that
     Hath kept with thy remembrance.

MIRANDA: 'Tis far off,
     And rather like a dream than an assurance   45
     That my remembrance warrants.[23] Had I not
     Four or five women once that tended me?

PROSPERO:
     Thou hadst, and more, Miranda. But how is it
     That this lives in thy mind? What seest thou else
     In the dark backward and abysm of time?[24]   50
     If thou rememberest aught[25] ere thou cam'st here,
     How thou cam'st here thou mayst.

MIRANDA: But that I do not.

PROSPERO:
     Twelve year since, Miranda, twelve year since,
     Thy father was the Duke of Milan and
     A prince of power.   55

MIRANDA: Sir, are not you my father?

---

15. Shipwreck.   21. Profitless inquiry.
16. Essence.   22. Fully.
17. Foresight.   23. Certainty that my memory guarantees.
18. Loss.   24. Abyss of the past.
19. Happened.   25. Anything.
20. Whom.

PROSPERO:
    Thy mother was a piece[26] of virtue, and
    She said thou wast my daughter; and thy father
    Was Duke of Milan, and his only heir
    And princess no worse issued.[27]

MIRANDA:
               O the heavens!
    What foul play had we, that we came from thence?   60
    Or blessed was 't we did?

PROSPERO:
             Both, both, my girl.
    By foul play, as thou sayst, were we heaved thence,
    But blessedly holp[28] hither.

MIRANDA:
            O, my heart bleeds
    To think o' the teen[29] that I have turned you to,
    Which is from[30] my remembrance! Please you, farther.   65

PROSPERO:
    My brother and thy uncle, called Antonio—
    I pray thee mark me—that a brother should
    Be so perfidious!—he whom next[31] thyself
    Of all the world I loved, and to him put
    The manage[32] of my state, as at that time   70
    Through all the seigniories[33] it was the first,
    And Prospero the prime[34] duke, being so reputed
    In dignity, and for the liberal arts
    Without a parallel; those being all my study,
    The government I cast upon my brother   75
    And to my state grew stranger,[35] being transported[36]
    And rapt in secret studies. Thy false uncle—
    Dost thou attend me?

MIRANDA:
            Sir, most heedfully.

PROSPERO:
    Being once perfected[37] how to grant suits,
    How to deny them, who t' advance and who
    To trash[38] for overtopping,[39] new created
    The creatures[40] that were mine, I say, or changed 'em,   80
    Or else new formed 'em;[41] having both the key[42]

---

26. Masterpiece, exemplar.
27. No less nobly born, descended.
28. Helped.
29. To trouble I've caused you to remember or put you to.
30. Out of.
31. Next to.
32. Management, administration.
33. I.e., city-states of northern Italy.
34. First in rank and importance.
35. I.e., withdrew from my responsibilities as duke.
36. Carried away.
37. Grown skillful.
38. Check a hound by tying a cord or weight to its neck.
39. Running too far ahead of the pack; surmounting, exceeding one's authority.
40. Dependents.
41. I.e., either changed their loyalties and duties or else created new ones.
42. (1) key for unlocking (2) tool for tuning stringed instruments.

Of officer and office, set all hearts i' the state
To what tune pleased his ear, that[43] now he was 85
The ivy which had hid my princely trunk
And sucked my verdure out on 't.[44] Thou attend'st not.

MIRANDA:
O, good sir, I do.

PROSPERO: I pray thee, mark me.
I, thus neglecting worldly ends, all dedicated
To closeness[45] and the bettering of my mind 90
With that which, but by being so retired,
O'erprized all popular rate,[46] in my false brother
Awaked an evil nature; and my trust,
Like a good parent,[47] did beget of[48] him
A falsehood in its contrary as great 95
As my trust was, which had indeed no limit,
A confidence sans[49] bound. He being thus lorded[50]
Not only with what my revenue yielded
But what my power might else[51] exact, like one
Who,[52] having into[53] truth by telling of it, 100
Made such a sinner of his memory
To[54] credit his own lie, he did believe
He was indeed the Duke, out o'[55] the substitution
And executing th' outward face of royalty[56]
With all prerogative. Hence his ambition growing— 105
Dost thou hear?

MIRANDA: Your tale, sir, would cure deafness.

PROSPERO:
To have no screen between this part he played
And him he played it for,[57] he needs will be[58]
Absolute Milan.[59] Me, poor man, my library
Was dukedom large enough. Of temporal[60] royalties 110

---

43. So that.
44. Vitality. Out of it.
45. Retirement, seclusion.
46. I.e., were it not that its private nature caused me to neglect my public responsibilities, had a value far beyond what public opinion could appreciate, or, simply because it was done in such seclusion, had a value not appreciated by popular opinion.
47. (Alludes to the proverb that good parents often bear bad children.)
48. In.
49. Without.
50. Raised to lordship, with power and wealth.
51. Otherwise, additionally.

52. I.e., who, by repeatedly telling the lie (that he was indeed Duke of Milan,) made his memory such a confirmed sinner against truth that he began to believe his own lie.
53. Unto, against.
54. So as to.
55. As a result of.
56. And (as a result of) his carrying out all the visible functions of royalty.
57. To have no separation or barrier between his role and himself. (Antonio wanted to act in his own person, not as substitute.)
58. Insisted on becoming.
59. Unconditional Duke of Milan.
60. Practical prerogatives and responsibilities of a sovereign.

He thinks me now incapable; confederates[61]— *conspire*

thirsty So dry[62] he was for sway[63] *power* wi' the King of Naples

To give him[64] annual tribute, do him homage,

Subject his[65] coronet to his[66] crown, and bend[67] *bow down*

The dukedom yet[68] unbowed—alas, poor Milan!— 115

To most ignoble stooping.

MIRANDA: O the heavens!

PROSPERO:

Mark his condition[69] *Pact* and th' event,[70] then tell me

If this might be a brother.

MIRANDA: *other than* I should sin

To think but[71] nobly of my grandmother. 120

Good wombs have borne bad sons. 120

PROSPERO: Now the condition.

This King of Naples, being an enemy

To me inveterate, hearkens[72] *listens to* my brother's suit,

Which was that he,[73] in lieu o' the premises[74] *In lieu of stipulation*

Of homage and I know not how much tribute,

Should presently *removed at once* extirpate[75] me and mine 125

Out of the dukedom and confer fair Milan,

With all the honors, on my brother. Whereon,

A treacherous army levied, one midnight

Fated to th' purpose did Antonio open

The gates of Milan, and, i' the dead of darkness, 130

The ministers for the purpose[76] hurried thence[77]

Me and thy crying self.

MIRANDA: Alack, for pity!

I, not remembering how I cried out then,

Will cry it o'er again. It is a hint[78] *occassion* 135

That wrings[79] mine eyes to 't. *Constrans*

PROSPERO: Hear a little further,

And then I'll bring thee to the present business

Which now's upon 's, without the which this story

Were most impertinent.[80] *irrelevant*

MIRANDA: *Why* Wherefore[81] did they not

That hour destroy us?

---

61. Conspires, allies himself.
62. Thirsty.
63. Power.
64. I.e., the King of Naples.
65. Antonio's.
66. The King of Naples.
67. Make bow down.
68. Hitherto.
69. Pact.
70. Outcome.
71. Other than.

72. Listens to.
73. The King of Naples.
74. In return for the stipulation.
75. At once remove.
76. Agents employed to do this.
77. From there.
78. Occasion.
79. (1) constrains (2)wrings fears from.
80. Irrelevant.
81. Why.

PROSPERO: Well demanded,[82] wench.[83]   *(asked   endearment)*   140
My tale provokes that question. Dear, they durst not,
So dear the love my people bore me, nor set
A mark so bloody[84] on the business, but
With colors fairer[85] painted their foul ends.
In few,[86] they hurried us aboard a bark,[87] *(ship)*
Bore us some leagues to sea, where they prepared   145
A rotten carcass of a butt,[88] not rigged, *(tub)*
Nor tackle,[89] sail, nor mast; the very rats   *(neither rigging)*
Instinctively have quit[90] it. There they hoist us,   *(abandoned)*
To cry to th' sea that roared to us, to sigh
To th' winds whose pity, sighing back again,   150
Did us but loving wrong.[91]

MIRANDA: Alack, what trouble
Was I then to you!

PROSPERO: O, a cherubin
Thou wast that did preserve me. Thou didst smile,
Infused with a fortitude from heaven,   155
When I have decked[92] the sea with drops full salt,   *(covered)*
Under my burden groaned, which[93] raised in me
An undergoing stomach,[94] to bear up *(courage to go on)*
Against what should ensue.

MIRANDA: How came we ashore?

PROSPERO: By Providence divine.   160
Some food we had, and some fresh water, that
A noble Neapolitan, Gonzalo,
Out of his charity, who being then appointed
Master of this design, did give us, with
Rich garments, linens, stuffs,[95] and necessaries,   165
Which since have steaded much.[96] So, of[97] his gentleness,
Knowing I loved my books, he furnished me
From mine own library with volumes that
I prize above my dukedom.

MIRANDA: *(I wish)* Would[98] I might
But ever[99] see that man!   *(someday)*   170

---

82. Asked.
83. (Here a term of endearment.)
84. I.e., make obvious their murderous intent.
    (From the practice of marking with the
    blood of the prey those who have partici-
    pated in a successful hunt.)
85. Apparently more attractive.
86. Few words.
87. Ship.
88. Cask, tub.
89. Neither rigging.
90. Abandoned.

91. I.e., the winds pitied Prospero and Mi-
    randa, though of necessity they blew them
    from shore.)
92. Covered (with salt tears); adorned.
93. I.e., the smile.
94. Courage to go on.
95. Supplies.
96. Been of much use.
97. Similarly, out of.
98. I wish.
99. I.e., someday.

PROSPERO: Now I arise.

[*He puts on his magic cloak.*]

Sit still, and hear the last of our sea sorrow.[100]
Here in this island we arrived; and here
Have I, thy schoolmaster, made thee more profit[101]
Than other princess'[102] can, that have more time
For vainer[103] hours and tutors not so careful.   175

MIRANDA:
Heavens thank you for 't! And now, I pray you, sir—
For still 'tis beating in my mind—your reason
For raising this sea storm?

PROSPERO: Know thus far forth:
By accident most strange, bountiful Fortune,
Now my dear lady,[104] hath mine enemies   180
Brought to this shore; and by my prescience
I find my zenith[105] doth depend upon
A most auspicious star, whose influence[106]
If now I court not, but omit,[107] my fortunes
Will ever after droop. Here cease more questions.   185
Thou art inclined to sleep. 'Tis a good dullness,[108]
And give it way.[109] I know thou canst not choose.

[*Miranda sleeps.*]

Come away,[110] servant, come! I am ready now.
Approach, my Ariel, come.

[*Enter Ariel.*]

ARIEL: 190
All hail, great master, grave sir, hail! I come
To answer thy best pleasure; be 't to fly,
To swim, to dive into the fire, to ride
On the curled clouds, to thy strong bidding task[111]
Ariel and all his quality.[112]

PROSPERO: Hast thou, spirit,
Performed to point[113] the tempest that I bade thee?   195

---

100. Sorrowful adventure at sea.
101. Profit more.
102. Princesses. (Or the word may be *princes,* referring to royal children both male and female.)
103. More foolishly spent.
104. Refers to Fortune, not Miranda.
105. Height of fortune. (Astrological term.)
106. Astrological power.
107. Ignore.
108. Drowsiness.
109. Let it happen (i.e., don't fight it).
110. Come away.
111. Make demands upon.
112. (1) Fellow spirits; (2) abilities.
113. To the smallest detail.

ARIEL: To every article.
 I boarded the King's ship. Now on the beak,[114] *Prow*
 Now in the waist,[115] the deck,[116] in every cabin, *midships*
 I flamed amazement.[117] Sometimes I'd divide
 And burn in many places; on the topmast,   200
 The yards, and bowsprit would I flame distinctly,[118]
 Then meet and join. Jove's lightning, the precursors
 O' the dreadful thunderclaps, more momentary
 And sight-outrunning[119] were not.[120] The fire and cracks
 Of sulfurous roaring the most mighty Neptune[121] *(Roman god of sea)* 205
 Seem to besiege and make his bold waves tremble,
 Yea, his dread trident shake.
PROSPERO: My brave spirit!
 Who was so firm, so constant, that this coil[122] *tumult*
 Would not infect his reason?
ARIEL: Not a soul
 But felt a fever of the mad[123] and played   210
 Some tricks of desperation. All but mariners
 Plunged in the foaming brine and quit the vessel,
 Then all afire with me. The King's son, Ferdinand,
 With hair up-staring[124]—then like reeds, not hair—
 Was the first man that leapt; cried, "Hell is empty, 215
 And all the devils are here!"
PROSPERO: Why, that's my spirit!
 But was not this nigh shore?
ARIEL: Close by, my master.
PROSPERO:
 But are they, Ariel, safe?
ARIEL: Not a hair perished.
 On their sustaining garments[125] not a blemish, *garments kept them afloat*
 But fresher than before; and, as thou bad'st[126] me, *Ordered* 220
 In troops[127] I have dispersed them 'bout the isle. *Groups*
 The King's son have I landed by himself,
 Whom I left cooling[128] of the air with sighs
 In an odd angle[129] of the isle, and sitting, *corner*
 His arms in this sad knot.[130] *(folded)*   [*He folds his arms.*] 225

---

114. Prow.
115. Midships.
116. Poop deck at the stern.
117. Struck terror in the guise of fire, i.e, Saint Elmo's fire.
118. In different places.
119. Swifter than sight.
120. Could not have been.
121. Roman god of the sea.
122. Tumult.

123. I.e., such as madmen feel.
124. Standing on end.
125. Garments that buoyed them up in the sea.
126. Ordered.
127. Groups.
128. Cooling.
129. Corner.
130. (Folded arms are indicative of melancholy.)

PROSPERO: Of the King's ship,
The mariners, say how thou hast disposed,
And all the rest o' the fleet.

ARIEL: Safely in harbor
Is the King's ship; in the deep nook,[131] where once
Thou called'st me up at midnight to fetch dew[132] *(See line 324)*
From the still-vexed Bermudas,[133] there she's hid;   230
The mariners all under hatches stowed,
Who, with a charm joined to their suffered labor,[134]
I have left asleep. And for the rest o' the fleet,
Which I dispersed, they all have met again
And are upon the Mediterranean float[135] *Sea*   235
Bound sadly home for Naples,
Supposing that they saw the King's ship wrecked
And his great person perish.

PROSPERO: Ariel, thy charge
Exactly is performed. But there's more work.
What is the time o' the day?   240

ARIEL: Past the mid season.[136] *Noon*

PROSPERO:
At least two glasses.[137] The time twixt six and now
Must by us both be spent most preciously.

ARIEL:
Is there more toil? Since thou dost give me pains,[138] *labors/work*
Let me remember[139] thee what thou hast promised,
Which is not yet performed me.   245

PROSPERO: How now? Moody?
What is't thou canst demand?

ARIEL: My liberty.

PROSPERO:
Before the time be out? No more!

ARIEL: I prithee,
Remember I have done thee worthy service,
Told thee no lies, made thee no mistakings, served
Without or grudge or grumblings. Thou did promise   250
To bate[140] me a full year.

PROSPERO: Dost thou forget
From what a torment I did free thee?

---

131. Bay.
132. (Collected at midnight for magical purposes; compare with line 324.)
133. Ever stormy Bermudas. (Perhaps refers to the then recent Bermuda shipwreck; see play Introduction. The Folio text reads "Bermoothes.")
134. By means of a spell added to all the labor they have undergone.
135. Sea.
136. Noon.
137. Hourglasses.
138. Labors.
139. Remind.
140. Remit, deduct.

ARIEL: No.

PROSPERO:

Thou dost, and think'st it much to tread the ooze
Of the salt deep,
To run upon the sharp wind of the north,
To do me[141] business in the veins[142] o' the earth   *as in veins of the*   255
When it is baked[143] with frost.   *hardened*   *human body, but of the ground.*

ARIEL: I do not, sir.

PROSPERO:

Thou liest, malignant thing! Hast thou forgot
The foul witch Sycorax, who with age and envy[144]   *malice*
Was grown into a hoop?[145] Hast thou forgot her?   260

ARIEL: No, sir.   *bent w/ age*

PROSPERO:

Thou hast. Where was she born? Speak. Tell me.

ARIEL:

Sir, in Argier.[146]   *Algiers*

PROSPERO: O, was she so? I must

Once in a month recount what thou hast been
Which thou forgett'st. This damned witch Sycorax,   265
For mischiefs manifold and sorceries terrible
To enter human hearing, from Argier,
Thou know'st, was banished. For one thing she did[147]   *pregnant,*
They would not take her life. Is not this true?   *w/ child*

ARIEL: Ay, sir.   270

PROSPERO:

This blue-eyed[148] hag was hither brought with child[149]   *pregnant*
And here was left by the sailors. Thou, my slave,   *once hers, now*
As thou report'st thyself, was then her servant;   *Prospero's*
because
And, for[150] thou wast a spirit too delicate
To act her earthy and abhorred commands,   275
Refusing her grand hests,[151] she did confine thee,   *commands*
By help of her more potent ministers
And in her most unmitigable rage,
Into a cloven pine, within which rift
Imprisoned thou didst painfully remain   280
A dozen years; within which space she died

Kept Ariel captive for 12 yrs. till she (the witch) died.

---

141. Do for me.
142. Veins of minerals, or, underground
      streams, thought to be analogous to the
      veins of the human body.
143. Hardened.
144. Malice.
145. I.e., so bent over with age as to resemble
      a hoop.

146. Algiers.
147. (Perhaps a reference to her pregnancy,
      for which her life would be spared.)
148. With dark circles under the eyes or with
      blue eyelids, implying pregnancy.
149. Pregnant.
150. Because.
151. Commands.

And left thee there, where thou didst vent thy groans
As fast as mill wheels strike.[152] Then was this island—
Save[153] for the son that she did litter[154] here,
A freckled whelp,[155] hag-born[156]—not honored with
A human shape.   285

ARIEL: Yes, Caliban her son.[157]

PROSPERO:
Dull thing, I say so:[158] he, that Caliban
Whom now I keep in service. Thou best know'st
What torment I did find thee in. Thy groans
Did make wolves howl, and penetrate the breasts   290
Of ever-angry bears. It was a torment
To lay upon the damned, which Sycorax
Could not again undo. It was mine art,
When I arrived and heard thee, that made gape[159]   295
The pine and let thee out.

ARIEL: I thank thee, master.

PROSPERO:
If thou more murmur'st, I will rend an oak
And peg thee in his[160] knotty entrails till
Thou hast howled away twelve winters.

ARIEL: Pardon, master.
I will be correspondent[161] to command
And do my spiriting[162] gently.[163]   300

PROSPERO: Do so, and after two days
I will discharge thee.

ARIEL: That's my noble master!
What shall I do? Say what? What shall I do?

PROSPERO:
Go make thyself like a nymph o' the sea. Be subject
To no sight but thine and mine, invisible   305
To every eyeball else. Go take this shape
And hither come in 't. Go, hence with diligence!

[Exit (Ariel).]

Awake, dear heart, awake! Thou hast slept well.
Awake!

---

152. As the blades of a mill wheel strike the
     water.
153. Except.
154. Give birth to.
155. Offspring. (Used of animals.)
156. Born of a female demon.
157. (Ariel is probably concurring with Pro-
     spero's comment about a "freckled

whelp," not contradicting the point
about "A human shape.")
158. I.e., exactly, that's what I said, you dull-
     ard.
159. Open wide.
160. Its.
161. Responsive, submissive.
162. Duties as a spirit.
163. Willingly, ungrudgingly.

MIRANDA: The strangeness of your story put   310
Heaviness[164] in me.
PROSPERO: Shake it off. Come on,
We'll visit Caliban, my slave, who never
Yields us kind answer.
MIRANDA: 'Tis a villain, sir,
I do not love to look on.
PROSPERO: But, as 'tis,
We cannot miss[165] him. He does make our fire,
Fetch in our wood, and serves in offices[166]   315
That profit us.—What ho! Slave! Caliban!
Thou earth, thou! Speak.
CALIBAN(within): There's wood enough within.
PROSPERO:
Come forth, I say! There's other business for thee.
Come, thou tortoise! When?[167]

[Enter Ariel like a water nymph.]

Fine apparition! My quaint[168] Ariel,   320
Hark in thine ear.   [He whispers.]
ARIEL: My lord, it shall be done.   [Exit.]
PROSPERO:
Thou poisonous slave, got[169] by the devil himself
Upon thy wicked dam,[170] come forth!

[Enter Caliban.]

CALIBAN:
As wicked[171] dew as e'er my mother brushed
With raven's feather from unwholesome fen[172]   325
Drop on you both! A southwest[173] blow on ye
And blister you all o'er!
PROSPERO:
For this, be sure, tonight thou shalt have cramps,
Side-stitches that shall pen thy breath up. Urchins[174]
Shall forth at vast[175] of night that they may work   330
All exercise on thee. Thou shalt be pinched

---

164. Drowsiness.
165. Do without.
166. Functions, duties.
167. (An exclamation of impatience.)
168. Ingenious.
169. Begotten, sired.
170. Mother. (Used of animals.)
171. Mischievous, harmful.
172. Marsh, bog.
173. I.e., wind thought to bring disease.
174. Hedgehogs; here, suggesting goblins in the guise of hedgehogs.
175. Lengthy, desolate time. (Malignant spirits were thought to be restricted to the hours of darkness.)

As thick as honeycomb,[176] each pinch more stinging

[handwritten: all over]

Than bees that made 'em.[177]

CALIBAN: I must eat my dinner.
This island's mine, by Sycorax my mother,
Which thou tak'st from me. When thou cam'st first,   335
Thou strok'st me and made much of me, wouldst give me
Water with berries in 't, and teach me how
To name the bigger light, and how the less,[178]   [handwritten: Sun/moon]
That burn by day and night. And then I loved thee   340
And showed thee all the qualities o' th' isle,
The fresh springs, brine pits, barren place and fertile.
Cursed be I that did so! All the charms[179]   [handwritten: Spells]
Of Sycorax, toads, beetles, bats, light on you!
For I am all the subjects that you have,
Which first was mine own king; and here you sty[180] me   [handwritten: confine]   345
In this hard rock, whiles you do keep from me
The rest o' th' island.
PROSPERO: Thou most lying slave,
Whom stripes[181] may move, not kindness! I have used thee,   [handwritten: lashes]
Filth as thou art, with humane[182] care, and lodged thee
In mine own cell, till thou didst seek to violate   350
The honor of my child.

[handwritten margin note: "The island belonged to Caliban first & Prospero wooed him for all the secrets of the island then enslaved him."]

CALIBAN:
Oho, Oho! Would 't had been done!
Thou didst prevent me; I had peopled else[183]   [handwritten: if you'd keep her away from me / populated]
This isle with Calibans.
MIRANDA: Abhorred slave,[184]
Which any print[185] of goodness wilt not take,   355
Being capable of all ill! I pitied thee,
Took pains to make thee speak, taught thee each hour
One thing or other. When thou didst not, savage,
Know thine own meaning, but wouldst gabble like
A thing most brutish, I endowed thy purposes[186]   [handwritten: desires]   360
With words that made them known. But thy vile race,[187]   [handwritten: species]
Though thou didst learn, had that in 't which good natures
Could not abide to be with; therefore wast thou

---

176. I.e., all over, with as many pinches as a
   honeycomb has cells.
177. I.e., the honeycomb.
178. I.e., the sun and the moon. (See Genesis
   1:16: "God then made two great lights:
   the greater light to rule the day, and the
   less light to rule the night.")
179. Spells.
180. Confine as in a sty.

181. Lashes.
182. (Not distinguished as a word from *human*.)
183. Otherwise populated.
184. "Abhorred slave . . . prison (Sometimes
   assigned by editors to Prospero.)
185. Imprint, impression.
186. Meanings, desires.
187. Natural disposition: species, nature.

Deservedly confined into this rock,
Who hadst deserved more than a prison   365

CALIBAN:

You taught me language, and my profit on 't
Is I know how to curse. The red plague[188] rid[189] you
For learning[190] me your language!

PROSPERO: Hagseed,[191] hence!
Fetch us in fuel, and be quick, thou'rt best,[192]
To answer other business.[193] Shrugg'st thou, malice?   370
If thou neglect'st or dost unwillingly
What I command, I'll rack thee with old[194] cramps,
Fill all thy bones with aches,[195] make thee roar
That beasts shall tremble at thy din.

CALIBAN: No, pray thee.
[Aside.] I must obey. His art is of such power   375
It would control my dam's god, Setebos,[196]
And make a vassal of him.

PROSPERO: So, slave, hence!

[Exit Caliban.]

[Enter Ferdinand; and Ariel, invisible,[197] playing and singing. (Ferdinand
does not see Prospero and Miranda)]

[Ariel's Song.]

ARIEL:

Come unto these yellow sands,
    And then take hands;
Curtsied when you have,[198] and kissed   380
    The wild waves whist;[199]
Foot it featly[200] here and there,
    And, sweet sprites,[201] bear
The burden.[202] Hark, hark!

                              [Burden, dispersedly[203] (within).] Bow-wow.   385
    The watchdogs bark.

                              [Burden, dispersedly within.] Bow-wow.

---

188. Plague characterized by red sores and
     evacuation of blood.
189. Destroy.
190. Teaching.
191. Offspring of a female demon.
192. You'd be well advised.
193. Perform other tasks.
194. Such as old people suffer, or, plenty of.
195. (Pronounced "aitches.")
196. (A god of the Patagonians, named in
     Robert Eden's *History of Travel,* 1577.)

197. (Ariel wears a garment that by conven-
     tion indicates he is invisible to the other
     characters.)
198. When you have curtsied.
199. Kissed the waves into silence, or, kissed
     while the waves are being hushed.
200. Dance nimbly.
201. Spirits.
202. Refrain, undersong.
203. I.e., from all directions, not in unison.

Hark, hark! I hear
The strain of strutting chanticleer
   Cry Cock-a-diddle-dow. 390

FERDINAND:

[handwritten: King's son]

Where should this music be? I' th' air or th' earth?
It sounds no more; and sure it waits upon[204] *[handwritten: serves]*
Some god o' th' island. Sitting on a bank,[205] *[handwritten: sandbank]*
Weeping again the King my father's wreck,
This music crept by me upon the waters, 395
Allaying both their fury and my passion[206] *[handwritten: grief]*
With its sweet air. Thence[207] I have followed it,
Or it hath drawn me rather. But 'tis gone.
No, it begins again.

[*Ariel's Song.*]

ARIEL:

Full fathom five thy father lies. *[handwritten: to the bottom of the sea]* 400
   Of his bones are coral made.
Those are pearls that were his eyes.
   Nothing of him that doth fade
But doth suffer a sea change
Into something rich and strange. 405
Sea nymphs hourly ring his knell.[208] *[handwritten: announce death by tolling a bell.]*

                    [*Burden (within).*] Ding dong.

Hark, now I hear them, ding dong bell.

FERDINAND:

The ditty does remember[209] my drowned father.
This is no mortal business, nor no sound 410
That the earth owes.[210] *[handwritten: owns]* I hear it now above me.

PROSPERO [*to Miranda*]:

The fringed curtains of thine eye advance[211] *[handwritten: raise]*
And say what thou seest yond.

MIRANDA: What is 't? A spirit?
Lord, how it looks about! Believe me, sir,
It carries a brave[212] form. But 'tis a spirit. *[handwritten: Excellent]* 415

PROSPERO:

No, wench, it eats and sleeps and hath such senses
As we have, such. This gallant which thou seest

---

204. Serves, attends.
205. Sandbank.
206. Grief.
207. I.e, from the bank on which I sat.
208. Announcement of a death by the tolling of a bell.

209. Commemorate.
210. Owns.
211. Raise.
212. Excellent.

Was in the wreck; and, but[213] he's something stained
With grief, that's beauty's canker,[214] thou mightst call him
A goodly person. He hath lost his fellows
And strays about to find 'em.

MIRANDA: I might call him
A thing divine, for nothing natural
I ever saw so noble.

PROSPERO [aside]:   It goes on,[215] I see,
As my soul prompts it.—Spirit, fine spirit, I'll free thee
Within two days for this.   425

FERDINAND [seeing Miranda]: Most sure, the goddess
On whom these airs[216] attend!—Vouchsafe[217] my prayer
May[218] know if you remain[219] upon this island,
And that you will some good instruction give
How I may bear me[220] here. My prime[221] request,
Which I do last pronounce, is—O you wonder![222]   430
If you be maid or no?[223]

MIRANDA: No wonder, sir,
But certainly a maid.

FERDINAND: My language? Heavens!
I am the best[224] of them that speak this speech,
Were I but where 'tis spoken.

PROSPERO [coming forward]   How? The best?
What wert thou if the King of Naples heard thee?   435

FERDINAND:
A single[225] thing, as I am now, that wonders
To hear thee speak of Naples.[226] He does hear me,[227]
And that he does I weep.[228] Myself am Naples,
Who with mine eyes, never since at ebb,[229] beheld
The King my father wrecked.   440

MIRANDA: Alack, for mercy!

FERDINAND:
Yes, faith, and all his lords, the Duke of Milan
And his brave son[230] being twain.

---

213. Except that.
214. Somewhat disfigured; cankerworm
  (feeding on buds and leaves).
215. I.e., My plan works,
216. Songs.
217. Grant.
218. I.e,.that I may know.
219. Dwell.
220. Conduct myself.
221. Chief.
222. (Miranda's name means "to be wondered
  at.")

223. I.e, a human maiden as opposed to a
  goddess or married woman.
224. I.e., in birth.
225. Solitary, being at once King of Naples
  and myself; (2) feeble.
226. The King of Naples.
227. I.e., the King of Naples does hear my
  words, for I am King of Naples.
228. I.e., and I weep at this reminder that my
  father is seemingly dead, leaving me heir.
229. I.e., dry, not weeping.
230. (The only reference in the play to a son of
  Antonio.)

PROSPERO [aside]: ~~splendid~~ The Duke of Milan ~~refute~~
And his more braver[231] daughter could control[232] thee,
If now 'twere fit to do 't. At the first sight
They have changed eyes.[233]—Delicate Ariel,   445
I'll set thee free for this. [To Ferdinand.] A word, good sir.
I fear you have done yourself some wrong.[234] A word!   *spoken falsely*

MIRANDA [aside]:
Why speaks my father so ungently? This   *be kind, Miranda*
Is the third man that e'er I saw, the first   *shows an interest in*   450
That e'er I sighed for. Pity move my father   *Ferdinand. Don't*
To be inclined my way!   *scare away.*

FERDINAND: O, if a virgin, ← *you love no one else*
And your affection not gone forth, I'll make you *we can marry.*
The Queen of Naples.

PROSPERO: Soft, sir! One word more.
[Aside.] They are both in either's power's; but this[235]   *in each other's*
~~swift business~~
I must uneasy[236] make, lest too light[237] winning   *difficult* *easy*   455
Make the prize light.[238] [to Ferdinand.] One word more: I charge thee   *cheap*
That thou attend[239] me. Thou dost here usurp   *obey*
The name thou ow'st[240] not, and hast put thyself   *Prospero*
Upon this island as a spy, to win it   *accuses*
From me, the lord on 't.[241] *If it*   *Ferdinand of being*   460
                                        a spy to steal from
FERDINAND: | No, as I am a man. | *him* *in jest.*

MIRANDA:
There's nothing ill can dwell in such a temple.
If the ill spirit have so fair a house,
Good things will strive to dwell with 't.[242]

PROSPERO: Follow me.— *to Ferdinand*
Speak not you for him; he's a traitor.—Come,
I'll manacle thy neck and feet together.   465
Seawater shalt thou drink; thy food shall be
The fresh-brook mussels, withered roots, and husks
Wherein the acorn cradled. Follow.

FERDINAND: | No! | *treatment*
I will resist such entertainment[243] till
Mine enemy has more power.   470

[He draws, and is charmed[244] from moving.]
magically prevented

---

231. More splendid.
232. Refute.
233. Exchanged amorous glances.
234. I.e., spoken falsely.
235. Each in the other's.
236. Difficult.
237. Easy.
238. Cheap.
239. Follow, obey.
240. Ownest.
241. Of it.
242. I.e., expel the evil and occupy the *temple,* the body.
243. Treatment.
244. Magically prevented.

MIRANDA: O, dear father,
Make not too rash[245] a trial of him, for
He's gentle,[246] and not fearful.[247]

PROSPERO: What, I say,
My foot[248] my tutor?—Put thy sword up, traitor,
Who mak'st a show but dar'st not strike, thy conscience
Is so possessed with guilt. Come, from thy ward,[249]   475
For I can here disarm thee with this stick
And make thy weapon drop. *[He brandishes his staff.]*

MIRANDA *[trying to hinder him]*: Beseech you, father!

PROSPERO:
Hence! Hang not on my garments.

MIRANDA: Sir, have pity!
I'll be his surety.[250]

PROSPERO: Silence! One word more
Shall make me chide thee, if not hate thee. What,   480
An advocate for an impostor? Hush!
Thou think'st there is no more such shapes as he,
Having seen but him and Caliban. Foolish wench,
To the most of men this is a Caliban,
And they to[251] him are angels.   485

MIRANDA: My affections
Are then most humble; I have no ambition
To see a goodlier man.

PROSPERO *[to Ferdinand]*: Come on, obey.
Thy nerves[252] are in their infancy again
And have no vigor in them.

FERDINAND: So they are.
My spirits,[253] as in a dream, are all bound up.   490
My father's loss, the weakness which I feel,
The wreck of all my friends, nor this man's threats
To whom I am subdued, are but light[254] to me,
Might I but through my prison once a day
Behold this maid. All corners else[255] o' th' earth   495
Let liberty make use of; space enough
Have I in such a prison.

PROSPERO *[aside]*: It works. *[To Ferdinand.]* Come on.—
Thou hast done well, fine Ariel! *[To Ferdinand.]* Follow me.
[To Ariel.] Hark what thou else shalt do me.[256]

---

245. Harsh.
246. Wellborn.
247. Frightening, dangerous, or perhaps, cowardly.
248. Subordinate, (Miranda, the foot, presumes to instruct Prospero, the head.)
249. Defensive posture (in fencing).
250. Guarantee.
251. Compared to.
252. Sinews.
253. Vital powers.
254. Unimportant.
255. Other corners, regions.
256. For me.

MIRANDA *[to Ferdinand]*:   Be of comfort.
 My father's of a better nature, sir,   500
 Than he appears by speech. This is unwonted[257]
 Which now came from him.
PROSPERO *[to Ariel]*:   Thou shalt be as free
 As mountain winds; but then[258] exactly do
 All points of my command.
ARIEL: To th' syllable.
PROSPERO *[to Ferdinand]*:
 Come, follow. *[To Miranda.]* Speak not for him.   505

 [Exeunt.]

Act II

Scene 1[1]

 [Enter Alonso, Sebastian, Antonia, Gonzalo, Adrian, Francisco, and others.]

GONZALO *[to Alonso]*:
 Beseech you, sir, be merry. You have cause,
 So have we all, of joy, for our escape
 Is much beyond our loss. Our hint[2] of woe
 Is common; every day some sailor's wife,
 The masters of some merchant, and the merchant,[3]   5
 Have just our theme of woe. But for the miracle,
 I mean our preservation, few in millions
 Can speak like us. Then wisely, good sir, weigh
 Our sorrow with[4] our comfort.
ALONSO: Prithee, peace.
SEBASTIAN *[aside to Antonio]*: He receives comfort like cold porridge.[5]   10
ANTONIO *[aside to Sebastian]*: The visitor[6] will not give him o'er[7] so
SEBASTIAN: Look, he's winding up the watch of his wit; by and by it will strike.
GONZALO *[to Alonso]*: Sir—
SEBASTIAN *[aside to Antonio]*: One. Tell.[8]
GONZALO: When every grief is entertained[9]   15
 That's offered, comes to th' entertainer—

---

257. Unusual.
258. Until then, or, if that is to be so.

 Act II, Scene 1

1. Location: another part of the island.
2. Occasion.
3. Officers of some merchant vessel and the merchant himself, the owner.
4. Against.
5. (Punningly suggested by *peace,* i.e., "peas" or "pease," a common ingredient of porridge.)
6. One taking nourishment and comfort to the sick, as Gonzalo is doing.
7. Abandon him.
8. Keep count.
9. When every sorrow that presents itself is accepted without resistance, there comes to the recipient.

SEBASTIAN: A dollar.[10]

GONZALO: Dolor comes to him, indeed. You have spoken truer than you purposed.

SEBASTIAN: You have taken it wiselier than I meant you should.

GONZALO: [to Alonso]: Therefore, my lord—   20

ANTONIO: Fie, what a spendthrift is he of his tongue!

ALONSO [to Gonzalo]: I prithee, spare.[11]

GONZALO: Well, I have done. But yet—

SEBASTIAN [aside to Antonio]: He will be talking.

ANTONIO [aside to Sebastian]: Which, of he or Adrian, for a good wager, first begins   25
    to crow?[12]

SEBASTIAN: The old cock.[13]

ANTONIO: The cockerel.[14]

SEBASTIAN: Done, The wager?

ANTONIO: A laughter.[15]   30

SEBASTIAN: A match![16]

ADRIAN: Though this island seem to be desert[17]—

ANTONIO: Ha, ha, ha!

SEBASTIAN: So, you're paid.[18]   35

ADRIAN: Uninhabitable and almost inaccessible—

SEBASTIAN: Yet—

ADRIAN: Yet—

ANTONIO: He could not miss 't.[19]

ADRIAN: It must needs be[20] of subtle, tender, and delicate temperance.[21]   40

ANTONIO: Temperance[22] was a delicate[23] wench.

SEBASTIAN: Ay, and a subtle,[24] as he most learnedly delivered.[25]

ADRIAN: The air breathes upon us here most sweetly.

SEBASTIAN: As if it had lungs, and rotten ones.

ANTONIO: Or as 'twere perfumed by a fen.   45

---

10. Widely circulated coin, the German thaler and the Spanish piece of eight. (Sebastian puns on *entertainer* in the sense of innkeeper; to Gonzalo, *dollar* suggests "dolor," grief.)
11. Forbear, cease.
12. Which of the two, Gonzalo or Adrian, do you bet will speak (crow) first?
13. I.e., Gonzalo.
14. I.e., Adrian.
15. (1) Burst of laughter; (2) sitting of eggs. (When Adrian, the *cockerel*, begins to speak two lines later, Sebastian loses the bet. The Folio speech prefixed in lines 38–39 are here reversed so that Antonio enjoys his laugh as the prize for winning, as in the proverb "He who laughs last laughs best" or "He laughs that wins." The Folio assignment can work in the theater, however, if Sebastian pays for losing with a sardonic laugh of concession.)

16. A bargain; agreed.
17. Uninhabited.
18. I.e., you've had your laugh.
19. (1) Avoid saying "Yet"; (2) miss the island.
20. Has to be.
21. Mildness of climate.
22. A girl's name.
23. (Here it means "given to pleasure, voluptuous"; in line 44, "pleasant." Antonio is evidently suggesting that *tender, and delicate temperance* sounds like a Puritan phrase, which Antonio then mocks by applying the words to a woman rather than an island. He began this bawdy comparison with a double entendre on *inaccessible*, (line 40.)
24. (Here it means "tricky, sexually crafty"; in line 44 "delicate.")
25. Uttered. (Sebastian joins Antonio in baiting the Puritans with his use of the pious cant phrase *learnedly delivered*.)

GONZALO: Here is everything advantageous to life.   50
ANTONIO: True, save[26] means to live.
SEBASTIAN: Of that there's none, or little.
GONZALO: How lush and lusty[27] the grass looks! How green!
ANTONIO: The ground indeed is tawny.[28]
SEBASTIAN: With an eye[29] of green in 't.   55
ANTONIO: He misses not much.
SEBASTIAN: No. He doth but[30] mistake the truth totally.
GONZALO: But the rarity of it is—which is indeed almost beyond credit—
SEBASTIAN: As many vouched[31] rarities are.
GONZALO: That our garments, being, as they were, drenched in the sea, hold   60
        notwithstanding their freshness and glosses, being rather new-dyed than
        stained with salt water.
ANTONIO: If but one of his pockets[32] could speak, would it not say he lies?
SEBASTIAN: Ay, or very falsely pocket[33] up his report.[34]
GONZALO: Methinks our garments are now as fresh as when we put them on first   65
        in Afric, at the marriage of the King's fair daughter Claribel to the King
        of Tunis.
SEBASTIAN: 'Twas a sweet marriage, and we prosper well in our return.
ADRIAN: Tunis was never graced before with such a paragon to[35] their queen.
GONZALO: Not since widow Dido's[36] time.   70
ANTONIO [aside to Sebastian]: Widow? A pox o' that! How came that "widow" in?
        Widow Dido!
SEBASTIAN: What if he had said, "widower Aeneas" too? Good Lord, how you
        take[37] it!
ADRIAN [to Gonzalo]: "Widow Dido" said you? You make me study of[38] that. She 75
        was of Carthage, not of Tunis.
GONZALO: This Tunis, sir, was Carthage.
ADRIAN: Carthage?
GONZALO: I assure you, Carthage.
ANTONIO: His word is more than the miraculous harp.[39]   80

---

26. Except.
27. Healthy.
28. Dull brown, yellowish.
29. Tinge, or spot (perhaps with reference to Gonzalo's eye or judgment).
30. Merely.
31. Allegedly real though strange sights.
32. I.e., because they are muddy.
33. I.e., conceal, suppress; often used in the sense of "receive unprotestingly, fail to respond to a challenge."
34. (Sebastian's jest is that the evidence of Gonzalo's soggy and sea-stained pockets would confute Gonzalo's speech and his reputation for truth telling.)
35. For.

36. Queen of Carthage, deserted by Aeneas. (She was, in fact, a widow when Aeneas, a widower, met her, but Antonio may be amused at Gonzalo's prudish use of the term "widow" to describe a woman deserted by her lover.)
37. Understand, respond to, interpret.
38. Think about.
39. (Alludes to Amphion's harp, with which he raised the walls of Thebes: Gonzalo has exceeded that deed by recreating ancient Carthage—wall and houses—mistakenly on the site of modern-day Tunis. Some Renaissance commentators believed, like Gonzalo, that the two sites were near each other.)

SEBASTIAN: He hath raised the wall, and houses too.

ANTONIO: What impossible matter will he make easy next?

SEBASTIAN: I think he will carry this island home in his pocket and give it his son
for an apple.

ANTONIO: And, sowing the kernels[40] of it in the sea, bring forth more islands. 85

GONZALO: Ay.[41]

ANTONIO: Why, in good time.[42]

GONZALO [to Alonso]: Sir, we were talking[43] that our garments seem now as fresh
as when we were at Tunis at the marriage of your daughter, who is now
queen. 90

ANTONIO: And the rarest[44] that e'er came there.

SEBASTIAN: Bate,[45] I beseech you, widow Dido.

ANTONIO: O, widow Dido? Ay, widow Dido.

GONZALO: Is not, sir, my doubtlet[46] as fresh as the first day I wore it? I mean, in
a sort.[47] 95

ANTONIO: That "sort"[48] was well fished for.

GONZALO: When I wore it at your daughter's marriage.

ALONSO:
You cram these words into mine ears against
The stomach of my sense.[49] Would I had never
Married[50] my daughter there! For, coming thence, 100
My son is lost and, in my rate,[51] she too,
Who is so far from Italy removed
I ne'er again shall see her. O thou mine heir
Of Naples and of Milan, what strange fish
Hath made his meal on thee? 105

FRANCISCO: Sir, he may live.
I saw him beat the surges[52] under him
And ride upon their backs. He trod the water,
Whose enmity he flung aside, and breasted
The surge most swoll'n that met him. His bold head 110
'Bove the contentious waves he kept, and oared
Himself with his good arms in lusty[53] stroke.
To th' shore, that o'er his[54] wave-worn basis bowed,[55]

---

40. Seeds.
41. (Gonzalo may be reasserting his point
about Carthage, or he may be responding
ironically in Antonio, who, in turn, answers sarcastically.)
42. (An expression of ironical acquiescence or
amazement, i.e., "sure, right away.")
43. Saying.
44. Most remarkable, beautiful.
45. Abate, except, leave out. (Sebastian says
sardonically, surely you should allow
widow Dido to be an exception.)
46. Close-fitting jacket.

47. In a way.
48. (Antonio plays on the idea of drawing lots
and on "fishing" for something to say.)
49. My appetite for hearing them.
50. Given in marriage.
51. Estimation, opinion.
52. Waves.
53. Vigorous.
54. Its.
55. I.e., that projected out over the base of the
cliff that had been eroded by the surf, thus
seeming to bend down toward the sea.

As[56] stooping to relieve him. I not doubt   115
He came alive to land.

ALONSO: No, no, he's gone.

SEBASTIAN [to Alonso]:
Sir, you may thank yourself for this great loss,
That[57] would not bless our Europe with your daughter,
But rather[58] loose[59] her to an African,   120
Where she at least is banished from your eye,[60]
Who hath cause to wet the grief on 't.[61]

ALONSO: Prithee, peace.

SEBASTIAN:
You were kneeled to and importuned[62] otherwise
By all of us, and the fair soul herself   125
Weighed between loathness and obedience at
Which end o' the beam should bow.[63] We have lost your son,
I fear, forever. Milan and Naples have
More widows in them of this business' making[64]
Than we bring men to comfort them.   130
The fault's your own.

ALONSO: So is the dear'st[65] o' the loss.

GONZALO: My lord Sebastian.
The truth you speak doth lack some gentleness
And time[66] to speak it in. You rub the sore   135
When you should bring the plaster.[67]

SEBASTIAN: Very well.

ANTONIO: And most chirurgeonly.[68]

GONZALO [to Alonso]:
It is foul weather in us all, good sir,   140
When you are cloudy.

SEBASTIAN [to Antonio]: Fowl[69] weather?

ANTONIO [to Sebastian]:   Very foul.

GONZALO:
Had I plantation[70] of this isle, my lord—

---

56. As if.
57. You who.
58. Would rather.
59. (1) Release, let loose; (2) lose.
60. Is not constantly before your eye to serve as a reproachful reminder of what you have done.
61. I.e., your eye, which has good reason to weep because of this, or, Claribel, who has good reason to weep for it.
62. Urged, implored.
63. Claribel herself was poised uncertainly between unwillingness to marry and obedience to her father as to which end of the scales should sink, which should prevail.

64. On account of this marriage and subsequent shipwreck.
65. Heaviest, most costly.
66. Appropriate time.
67. (A medical application.)
68. Like a skilled surgeon. (Antonio mocks Gonzalo's medical analogy of a plaster applied curatively to a wound.)
69. With a pun on foul, returning to the imagery of lines 30–35.
70. Colonization (with subsequent wordplay on the literal meaning, "planting.")

ANTONIO *[to Sebastian]*:
    He'd sow 't with nettle seed.   145

SEBASTIAN: Or docks, or mallows.[71]

GONZALO:
    And were the king on 't, what would I do?

SEBASTIAN: Scape[72] being drunk for want[73] of wine.

GONZALO:
    I' the commonwealth I would by contraries[74]
    Execute all things; for no kind of traffic[75]   150
    Would I admit; no name of magistrate;
    Letters[76] should not be known; riches, poverty,
    And use of service,[77] none; contract, succession,[78]
    Bourn, bound of land, tilth,[79] vineyard, none;
    No use of metal, corn,[80] or wine, or oil;   155
    No occupation; all men idle, all,
    And women too, but innocent and pure;
    No sovereignty—

SEBASTIAN: Yet he would be king on 't.   160

ANTONIO: The latter end of his commonwealth forgets the beginning.

GONZALO:
    All things in common nature should produce
    Without sweat or endeavor. Treason, felony,
    Sword, pike,[81] knife, gun, or need of any engine[82]
    Would I not have; but nature should bring forth,   165
    Of its own kind, all foison,[83] all abundance,
    To feed my innocent people.

SEBASTIAN: No marrying 'mong his subjects?

ANTONIO: None, man, all idle—whores and knaves.

GONZALO:
    I would with such perfection govern, sir,   170
    T' excel the Golden Age.[84]

SEBASTIAN: 'Save[85] His Majesty!

ANTONIO:
    Long live Gonzalo!

GONZALO: And—do you mark me, sir?

---

71. (Weeds used as antidotes for nettle stings.)
72. Escape.
73. Lack. (Sebastian jokes sarcastically that this hypothetical ruler would be saved from dissipation only by the barrenness of the island.)
74. By what is directly opposite to usual custom.
75. Trade.
76. Learning.
77. Custom of employing servants.

78. Holding of property by right or inheritance.
79. Boundaries, property limits, tillage of soil.
80. Grain.
81. Lance.
82. Instrument of warfare.
83. Plenty.
84. The age, according to Hesiod, when Cronus, or Saturn, ruled the world; an age of innocence and abundance.
85. God save.

ALONSO:
    Prithee, no more. Thou dost talk nothing to me.

GONZALO: I do well believe Your Highness, and did it to minister occasion[86] to   175
    these gentlemen, who are of such sensible[87] and nimble lungs that they
    always use[88] to laugh at nothing.

ANTONIO: 'Twas you we laughed at.

GONZALO: Who in this kind of merry fooling am nothing to you; so you may
    continue, and laugh at nothing still.   180

ANTONIO: What a blow was there given!

SEBASTIAN: An[89] it had not fallen flat-long.[90]

GONZALO: You are gentlemen of brave mettle;[91] you would lift the moon out of
    her sphere[92] if she would continue in it five weeks without changing.

    [Enter Ariel (invisible) playing solemn music.]

SEBASTIAN: We would so, and then go a-batfowling.[93]   185

ANTONIO: Nay, good my lord, be not angry.

GONZALO: No, I warrant you, I will not adventure my discretion so weakly.[94] Will
    you laugh me asleep? For I am very heavy.[95]

ANTONIO: Go sleep, and hear us.[96]

    [All sleep except Alonso, Sebastian, and Antonio.]

ALONSO:
    What, all so soon asleep? I wish mine eyes   190
    Would, with themselves, shut up my thoughts.[97] I find
    They are inclined to do so.

SEBASTIAN: Please you, sir,
    Do not omit[98] the heavy[99] offer of it.
    It seldom visits sorrow; when it doth,   195
    It is a comforter.

ANTONIO: We two, my lord,
    Will guard your person while you take your rest,
    And watch your safety.

ALONSO: Thank you. Wondrous heavy.   200

---

86. Furnish opportunity.
87. Sensitive.
88. Are accustomed.
89. If.
90. With the flat of the sword, i.e., ineffectually. (Compare with "fallen flat.")
91. Temperament, courage. (The sense of *metal*, indistinguishable as a form from *mettle*, continues the metaphor of the sword.)
92. Orbit. (Literally, one of the concentric zones occupied by planets in Ptolemaic astronomy.)
93. Hunting birds at night with lantern and

bat, or "stick"; also, gulling a simpleton. (Gonzalo is the simpleton, or fowl, and Sebastian will use the moon as his lantern.)
94. Risk my reputation for discretion for so trivial a cause (by getting angry at these sarcastic fellows).
95. Sleepy.
96. I.e., get ready for sleep, and we'll do our part by laughing.
97. Would shut off my melancholy brooding when they close themselves in sleep.
98. Neglect.
99. Drowsy.

[Alonso sleeps. Exit Ariel.]

SEBASTIAN:
What a strange drowsiness possesses them!

ANTONIO:
It is the quality o' the climate.

SEBASTIAN: Why
Doth it not then our eyelids sink? I find not
Myself disposed to sleep.   205

ALONSO: Nor I. My spirits are nimble.
They[100] fell together all, as by consent;[101]
They dropped, as by a thunderstroke. What might,
Worthy Sebastian. O, what might—? No more.
And yet methinks I see it in thy face,   210
What thou shouldst be. Th' occasion speaks thee,[102] and
My strong imagination sees a crown
Dropping upon thy head.

SEBASTIAN: What, art thou waking?

ANTONIO:
Do you not hear me speak?   215

SEBASTIAN: I do, and surely
It is a sleepy[103] language, and thou speak'st
Out of thy sleep. What is it thou didst say?
This is a strange repose, to be asleep
With eyes wide open—standing, speaking, moving—   220
And yet so fast asleep.

ANTONIO: Noble Sebastian,
Thou lett'st thy fortune sleep—die, rather; wink'st[104]
Whiles thou art waking.

SEBASTIAN: Thou dost snore distinctly;[105]   225
There's meaning in thy snores.

ANTONIO:
I am more serious than my custom. You
Must be so too if heed[106] me, which to do
Trebles thee o'er.[107]

SEBASTIAN: Well, I am standing water.[108]   230

ANTONIO:
I'll teach you how to flow.

---

100. The sleepers.
101. Common agreement.
102. Opportunity of the moment calls upon
     you, i.e., proclaims you usurper of
     Alonso's crown.
103. Dreamlike, fantastic.

104. (You) shut your eyes.
105. Articulately.
106. If you heed.
107. Makes you three times as great and rich.
108. Water that neither ebbs nor flows, at a
     standstill.

SEBASTIAN: Do so. To ebb[109]
      Hereditary sloth[110] instructs me.

ANTONIO: O,
      If you but knew how you the purpose cherish   235
      Whiles thus you mock it![111] How, in stripping it,[112]
      You more invest[113] it! Ebbing men, indeed,
      Most often do so near the bottom[114] run
      By their own fear or sloth.

SEBASTIAN: Prithee, say on.   240
      The setting[115] of thine eye and cheek proclaim
      A matter[116] from thee, and a birth indeed
      Which throes[117] thee much to yield.[118]

ANTONIO: Thus, sir:
      Although this lord[119] of weak remembrance,[120] this   245
      Who shall be of as little memory
      When he is earthed,[121] hath here almost persuaded—
      For he's a spirit of persuasion, only
      Professes to persuade[122]—the King his son's alive,
      'Tis as impossible that he's undrowned   250
      As he that sleeps here swims.

SEBASTIAN: I have no hope
      That he's undrowned.

ANTONIO: O, out of that "no hope"
      What great hope have you! No hope that way[123] is   255
      Another way so high a hope that even
      Ambition[124] cannot pierce a wink[125] beyond,
      But doubt discovery there. Will you grant with me
      That Ferdinand is drowned?

SEBASTIAN: He's gone.   260

ANTONIO: Then tell me,
      Who's the next heir of Naples?

---

109. Decline.
110. Natural laziness and the position of younger brother, one who cannot inherit.
111. If you only knew how much you really enhance the value of ambition even while your words mock your purpose.
112. I.e., how the more you speak flippantly of ambition, the more you, in effect, affirm it.
113. Clothe. (Antonio's paradox is that, by skeptically stripping away illusions, Sebastian can see the essence of a situation and the opportunity it presents or that, by disclaiming and deriding his purpose, Sebastian shows how valuable it really is.)
114. I.e., on which unadventurous men may go aground and miss the tide of fortune.

115. Set expression (of earnestness).
116. Matter of importance.
117. Causes pain, as in giving birth.
118. Give forth, speak about.
119. I.e., Gonzalo.
120. (1) Power of remembering; (2) being remembered after his death.
121. Buried.
122. Whose whole function (as a privy councillor) is to persuade.
123. I.e., in regard to Ferdinand's being saved.
124. Ambition itself cannot see any further than that hope (of the crown), is unsure of finding anything to achieve beyond it or even there.
125. Glimpse.

SEBASTIAN: Claribel.
ANTONIO:
    She that is Queen of Tunis; she that dwells
    Ten leagues beyond man's life;[126] she that from Naples   265
    Can have no note,[127] unless the sun were post[128]—
    The Man i' the Moon's too slow—till newborn chins
    Be rough and razorable;[129] she that from[130] whom
    We all were sea-swallowed, though some cast[131] again,
    And by that destiny to perform an act   270
    Whereof what's past is prologue, what to come
    In yours and my discharge.[132]

SEBASTIAN: What stuff is this? How say you?
    'Tis true my brother's daughter's Queen of Tunis,
    So is she heir of Naples, twixt which regions   275
    There is some space.

ANTONIO: A space whose every cubit[133]
    Seems to cry out, "How shall that Claribel
    Measure us[134] back to Naples? Keep[135] in Tunis,
    And let Sebastian wake."[136] Say this were death   280
    That now hath seized them, why, they were no worse
    Than now they are. There be[137] that can rule Naples
    As well as he that sleeps, lords that can prate[138]
    As amply and unnecessarily
    As this Gonzalo. I myself could make   285
    A chough of as deep chat.[139] O, that you bore
    The mind that I do! What a sleep were this
    For your advancement! Do you understand me?

SEBASTIAN:
    Methinks I do.

ANTONIO: And how does your content[140]   290
    Tender[141] your own good fortune?

SEBASTIAN: I remember
    You did supplant your brother Prospero.

ANTONIO: True.
    And look how well my garments sit upon me,   295

---

126. I.e., further than the journey of a life-
    time.
127. News, intimation.
128. Messenger.
129. Ready for shaving.
130. On our voyage from.
131. Were disgorged (with a pun on *casting* of
    parts for a play).
132. Performance.
133. Ancient measure of length of about
    twenty inches.

134. I.e., traverse the cubits, find her way.
135. Stay. (Addressed to Claribel.)
136. I.e., to his good fortune.
137. There are those.
138. Speak foolishly.
139. I could teach a jackdaw to talk as wisely,
    or, be such a garrulous talker myself.
140. Desire, inclination.
141. Regard, look after.

Much feater[142] than before. My brother's servants
Were then my fellows. Now they are my men.

SEBASTIAN: But, for your conscience?

ANTONIO:
Ay, sir, where lies that? If 'twere a kibe,[143]
'Twould put me to[144] my slipper; but I feel not   300
This deity in my bosom. Twenty consciences
That stand twixt me and Milan,[145] candied[146] be they[147]
And melt ere they molest![148] Here lies your brother,
No better than the earth he lies upon,
If he were that which now he's like—that's dead,   305
Whom, I, with this obedient steel, three inches of it,
Can lay to bed forever; whiles you, doing thus,[149]
To the perpetual wink[150] for aye[151] might put
This ancient morsel, this Sir Prudence, who
Should not[152] upbraid our course. For all the rest,   310
They'll take suggestion[153] as a cat laps milk;
They'll tell the clock[154] to any business that
We say befits the hour.

SEBASTIAN: Thy case, dear friend,
Shall be my precedent. As thou gott'st Milan,   315
I'll come by Naples. Draw thy sword. One stroke
Shall free thee from the tribute[155] which thou payest,
And I the king shall love thee.

ANTONIO: Draw together;
And when I rear my hand, do you the like   320
To fall it[156] on Gonzalo.   *[They draw.]*

SEBASTIAN: O, but one word.

[They talk apart.]

[Enter Ariel (invisible), with music and song.]

ARIEL: *[to Gonzalo]*
My master through his art foresees the danger
That you, his friend, are in, and sends me forth—
For else his project dies—to keep them living.   325

[Sings in Gonzalo's ear.]

---

142. More becomingly, fittingly.
143. Chilblain, here a sore on the heel.
144. Oblige me to wear.
145. The dukedom of Milan.
146. Frozen, congealed in crystalline form.
147. May they be.
148. Interfere.
149. Similarly. (The actor makes a stabbing gesture.)

150. Sleep, closing of eyes.
151. Ever.
152. Would not then be able to.
153. Respond to prompting.
154. I.e., agree, answer appropriately, chime.
155. (See 1.2.z 113–124.)
156. Let it fall.

> While you here do snoring lie,
> Open-eyed conspiracy
>   His time[157] doth take.
> If of life you keep a care,
> Shake off slumber, and beware.
>   Awake, awake!   330

ANTONIO: Then let us both be sudden.[158]

GONZALO: *[waking]* Now, good angels preserve the King!

[The others wake.]

ALONSO:
> Why, how now, ho, awake? Why are you drawn?
> Wherefore this ghastly looking?   335

GONZALO: What's the matter?

SEBASTIAN:
> Whiles we stood here securing[159] your repose,
> Even now, we heard a hollow burst of bellowing
> Like bulls, or rather lions. Did 't not wake you?
> It struck mine ear most terribly.   340

ALONSO: I heard nothing.

ANTONIO:
> O, 'twas a din to fright a monster's ear,
> To make an earthquake! Sure it was the roar
> Of a whole herd of lions.

ALONSO: Heard you this, Gonzalo?   345

GONZALO:
> Upon mine honor, sir, I heard a humming,
> And that a strange one too, which did awake me.
> I shaked you, sir, and cried.[160] As mine eyes opened,
> I saw their weapons drawn. There was a noise,
> That's verily.[161] 'Tis best we stand upon our guard,   350
> Or that we quit this place. Let's draw our weapons.

ALONSO:
> Lead off this ground, and let's make further search
> For my poor son.

GONZALO: Heavens keep him from these beasts!
> For he is, sure, i' th' island.   355

ALONSO: Lead away.

ARIEL *[aside]*:
> Prospero my lord shall know what I have done.
> So, King, go safely on to seek thy son.

[Exeunt (separately).]

---

157. Opportunity.   160. Called out.
158. Quick.   161. True.
159. Standing guard over.

Scene 2[1]

[Enter Caliban with a burden of wood. A noise of thunder heard.]

CALIBAN:

All the infections that the sun sucks up
From bogs, fens, flats,[2] on Prosper fall, and make him
By inchmeal[3] a disease! His spirits hear me,
And yet I needs must[4] curse. But they'll nor[5] pinch,
Fright me with urchin shows,[6] pitch me i' the mire,   5
Nor lead me, like a firebrand,[7] in the dark
Out of my way, unless he bid 'em. But
For every trifle are they set upon me,
Sometimes like apes, that mow[8] and chatter at me
And after bite me; then like hedgehogs, which   10
Lie tumbling in my barefoot way and mount
Their pricks at my footfall. Sometimes am I
All wound with[9] adders, who with cloven tongues
Do hiss me into madness.

[Enter Trinculo.]

              Lo, now, lo!
Here comes a spirit of his, and to torment me   15
For bringing wood in slowly. I'll fall flat.
Perchance he will not mind[10] me.   *[He lies down.]*

TRINCULO: Here's neither bush nor shrub to bear off[11] any weather at all. And
another storm brewing; I hear it sing i' the wind. Yond same black cloud,
yond huge one, looks like a foul bombard[12] that would shed his[13] liquor.   20
If it should thunder as it did before, I know not where to hide my head.
Yond same cloud cannot choose but fall by pailfuls. *[Seeing Caliban.]*
What have we here, a man or a fish? Dead or alive? A fish, he smells like
a fish; a very ancient and fishlike smell; a kind of not-of-the-newest Poor
John.[14] A strange fish! Were I in England now, as once I was, and had but   25
this fish painted,[15] not a holiday fool there but would give a piece of
silver. There would this monster make a man.[16] Any strange beast there
makes a man. When they will not give a doit[17] to relieve a lame beggar,

---

Act II, Scene 2

1. Location: another part of the island.
2. Swamps.
3. Inch by inch.
4. Have to.
5. Neither.
6. Elvish apparitions shaped like hedgehogs.
7. They in the guise of a will-o'-the-wisp.
8. Make faces.
9. Entwined by.
10. Notice.

11. Keep off.
12. Dirty leather jug.
13. Its.
14. Salted fish, type of poor fare.
15. I.e., painted on a sign set up outside a
    booth or tent at a fair.
16. (1) Make one's fortune; (2) be indistin-
    guishable from an Englishman.
17. Small coin.

they will lay out ten to see a dead Indian. Legged like a man, and his fins like arms! Warm, o' my troth![18] I do now let loose my opinion, hold it[19] no longer: this is no fish, but an islander, that hath lately suffered[20] by a thunderbolt. [Thunder.] Alas, the storm is come again! My best way is to creep under his gaberdine.[21] There is no other shelter hereabout. Misery acquaints a man with strange bedfellows. I will here shroud[22] till the dregs[23] of the storm be past.

[He creeps under Caliban's garment.]

[Enter Stephano, singing, (a bottle in his hand).]

STEPHANO:
        "I shall no more to sea, to sea,
        Here shall I die ashore—"
    This is a very scurvy tune to sing at a man's funeral.
    Well, here's my comfort.   [Drinks.]

    [Sings.]

        "The master, the swabber,[24] the boatswain, and I,
        The gunner and his mate,
        Loved Mall, Meg, and Marian, and Margery,
        But none of us cared for Kate.
        For she had a tongue with a tang,[25]
        Would cry to a sailor, 'Go hang!'
        She loved not the savor of tar nor of pitch,
        Yet a tailor might scratch her where'er she did itch.[26]
        Then to sea, boys, and let her go hang!"
    This is a scurvy tune too. But here's my comfort.

    [Drinks.]

CALIBAN: Do not torment me![27] O!

STEPHANO: What's the matter?[28] Have we devils here? Do you put tricks upon 's[29] with savages and men of Ind,[30] ha? I have not scaped drowning to be afeard now of your four legs. For it has been said, "As proper[31] a man as ever went on four legs[32] cannot make him give ground"; and it shall be said so again while Stephano breathes at[33] nostrils.

---

18. By my faith.
19. Hold it in.
20. I.e., died.
21. Cloak, loose upper garment.
22. Take shelter.
23. I.e., last remains (as in a *bombard* or jug, line 20)
24. Crew member whose job is to wash the decks.
25. Sting.
26. (A dig at tailors for their supposed effeminacy and a bawdy suggestion of satisfying a sexual craving.)

27. (Caliban assumes that one of Prospero's spirits has come to punish him.)
28. What's going on here?
29. Trick us with conjuring shows.
30. India.
31. Handsome.
32. (The conventional phrase would supply *two legs,* but the creature Stephano thinks he sees has four).
33. At the.

CALIBAN: This spirit torments me! O!

STEPHANO: This is some monster of the isle with four legs, who hath got, as I take
it, an ague.[34] Where the devil should he learn[35] our language? I will give
him some relief, if it be but for that.[36] If I can recover[37] him and keep him
tame and get to Naples with him, he's a present for any emperor that ever
trod on neat's leather.[38] 60

CALIBAN: Do not torment me, prithee. I'll bring my wood home faster.

STEPHANO: He's in his fit now and does not talk after the wisest.[39] He shall taste
of my bottle. If he have never drunk wine afore,[40] it will go near to[41]
remove his fit. If I can recover[42] him and keep him tame, I will not take 65
too much[43] for him. He shall pay for him that hath[44] him,[45] and that
soundly.

CALIBAN: Thou dost me yet but little hurt; thou wilt anon,[46] I know it by thy
trembling. Now Prosper works upon thee.

STEPHANO: Come on your ways. Open your mouth. Here is that which will give 70
language to you, cat. Open your mouth.[47] This will shake your shaking.
I can tell you, and that soundly. *[Giving Caliban a drink.]* You cannot tell
who's your friend. Open your chaps[48] again.

TRINCULO: I should know that voice. It should be—but he is drowned, and these
are devils. O, defend me! 75

STEPHANO: Four legs and two voices—a most delicate[49] monster! His forward
voice now is to speak well of his friend; his backward voice[50] is to utter
foul speeches and to detract. If all the wine in my bottle will recover
him,[51] I will help[52] his ague. Come. *[Giving a drink.]* Amen! I will pour
some in thy other mouth. 80

TRINCULO: Stephano!

STEPHANO: Doth thy other mouth call me?[53] Mercy, mercy! This is a devil, and no
monster. I will leave him. I have no long spoon.[54]

TRINCULO: Stephano! If thou beest Stephano, touch me and speak to me, for I am
Trinculo—be not afeard—thy good friend Trinculo. 85

STEPHANO: If thou beest Trinculo, come forth. I'll pull thee by the lesser legs. If

---

34. Fever. (Probably both Caliban and Trinculo are quaking; see lines 56 and 81.)
35. Could he have learned.
36. I.e., for knowing our language.
37. Restore.
38. Cowhide.
39. In the wisest fashion.
40. Before.
41. Be in a fair way to.
42. Restore.
43. I.e., no sum can be too much.
44. Possesses, receives.
45. I.e., anyone who wants him will have to
pay dearly for him.
46. Presently.
47. (Allusion to the proverb "Good liquor will
make a cat speak.")

48. Jaws.
49. Ingenious.
50. (Trinculo and Caliban are facing in opposite directions. Stephano supposes the
monster to have a rear end that can emit
foul speeches or foul-smelling wind at the
monster's *other mouth,* line 95.)
51. Even if it takes all the wine in my bottle to
cure him.
52. Cure.
53. I.e., call me by name, know supernaturally
who I am.
54. (Allusion to the proverb "He that sups
with the devil has need of a long spoon.")

any be Trinculo's legs, these are they. *[Pulling him out.]* Thou art very
Trinculo indeed! How cam'st thou to be the siege[55] of this mooncalf?[56]
Can he vent[57] Trinculos?

TRINCULO: I took him to be killed with a thunderstroke. But art thou not   90
    drowned, Stephano? I hope now thou art not drowned. Is the storm
    overblown?[58] I hid me under the dead mooncalf's gaberdine for fear of
    the storm. And art thou living, Stephano? O Stephano, two Neapolitans
    scaped! *[He capers with Stephano.]*

STEPHANO: Prithee, do not turn me about. My stomach is not constant.[59]   95

CALIBAN:

    These be fine things, an if[60] they be not spirits.
    That's a brave[61] god, and bears[62] celestial liquor.
    I will kneel to him.

STEPHANO: How didst thou scape? How cam'st thou hither? Swear by this bottle
    how thou cam'st hither. I escaped upon a butt of sack[63] which the sailors   100
    heaved o'erboard—by this bottle,[64] which I made of the bark of a tree
    with mine own hands since[65] I was cast ashore.

CALIBAN *[kneeling]:* I'll swear upon that bottle to be thy true subject, for the liquor
    is not earthly.

STEPHANO: Here. Swear then how thou escapedst.   105

TRINCULO: Swum ashore, man, like a duck. I can swim like a duck, I'll be sworn.

STEPHANO: Here, kiss the book.[66] Though thou canst swim like a duck, thou art
    made like a goose.

    [Giving him a drink.]

TRINCULO: O Stephano, hast any more of this?

STEPHANO: The whole butt, man. My cellar is in a rock by the seaside, where my   110
    wine is hid.—How now, mooncalf? How does thine ague?

CALIBAN: Hast thou not dropped from heaven?

STEPHANO: Out o' the moon, I do assure thee. I was the Man i' the Moon when
    time was.[67]

CALIBAN:

    I have seen thee in her, and I do adore thee.
    My mistress showed me thee, and thy dog, and thy bush.[68]   115

STEPHANO: Come, swear to that. Kiss the book. I will furnish it anon with new
    contents. Swear.

---

55. Excrement.
56. Monstrous or misshapen creature (whose deformity is caused by the malignant influence of the moon).
57. Excrete, defecate.
58. Blown over.
59. Unsteady.
60. If.
61. Fine, magnificent.
62. He carries.

63. Barrel of Canary wine.
64. I.e., I swear by this bottle.
65. After.
66. I.e., bottle (but with ironic reference to the practice of kissing the Bible in swearing an oath; see *I'll be sworn* in line 128)
67. Once upon a time.
68. (The Man in the Moon was popularly imagined to have with him a dog and a bush of thorn.)

[Giving him a drink.]

TRINCULO: By this good light,[69] this is a very shallow monster! I afeard of him? A
very weak monster! The Man i' the Moon? A most poor credulous
monster! Well drawn,[70] monster, in good sooth![71]   120

CALIBAN *[to Stephano]*:
I'll show thee every fertile inch o' th' island,
And I will kiss thy foot. I prithee, be my god.

TRINCULO: By this light, a most perfidious and drunken monster! When 's god's
asleep, he'll rob his bottle.[72]

CALIBAN:
I'll kiss thy foot. I'll swear myself thy subject.   125

STEPHANO: Come on then. Down, and swear.

[Caliban kneels.]

TRINCULO: I shall laugh myself to death at this puppy-headed monster. A most
scurvy monster! I could find in my heart to beat him—

STEPHANO: Come, kiss.

TRINCULO: But that the poor monster's in drink.[73] An abominable monster!   130

CALIBAN:
I'll show thee the best springs. I'll pluck thee berries.
I'll fish for thee and get thee wood enough.
A plague upon the tyrant that I serve!
I'll bear him no more sticks, but follow thee,
Thou wondrous man.   135

TRINCULO: A most ridiculous monster, to make a wonder of a poor drunkard!

CALIBAN:
I prithee, let me bring thee where crabs[74] grow,
And I with my long nails will dig thee pignuts,[75]
Show thee a jay's nest, and instruct thee how
To snare the nimble marmoset.[76] I'll bring thee   140
To clustering filberts, and sometimes I'll get thee
Young scamels[77] from the rock. Wilt thou go with me?

STEPHANO: I prithee now, lead the way without any more talking.—Trinculo, the
King and all our company else[78] being drowned, we will inherit[79]

---

69. By God's light, by this good light from
heaven.
70. Well pulled (on the bottle).
71. Truly, indeed.
72. I.e., Caliban wouldn't even stop at robbing
his god of his bottle if he could catch him
asleep.
73. Drunk.
74. Crab apples, or perhaps crabs.
75. Earthnuts, edible tuberous roots.

76. Small monkey.
77. (Possibly *seamews*, mentioned in Stra-
chey's letter, or shellfish, or perhaps from
squamelle "furnished with little scales."
Contemporary French and Italian travel
accounts report that the natives of Patago-
nia in South America ate small fish described as *tort scameux* and *squame*.)
78. In addition, besides ourselves.
79. Take possession.

here.—Here, bear my bottle.—Fellow Trinculo, we'll fill him by and by   145
again.

CALIBAN (*sings drunkenly*):
    Farewell, master, farewell, farewell!

TRINCULO: A howling monster; a drunken monster!

CALIBAN:
    No more dams I'll make for fish,
      Nor fetch in firing[80]   150
      At requiring,
    Nor scrape trenchering,[81] nor wash dish.
      'Ban, 'Ban, Ca–Caliban
      Has a new master. Get a new man![82]
    Freedom, high-day! High-day, freedom! Freedom, high-day,[83]   155
freedom!

STEPHANO: O brave monster! Lead the way.   [*Exeunt.*]

Act III

Scene 1[1]

[*Enter Ferdinand, bearing a log.*]

FERDINAND:
    There be some sports are painful, and their labor
    Delight in them sets off.[2] Some kinds of baseness[3]
    Are nobly undergone,[4] and most poor[5] matters
    Point to rich ends. This my mean[6] task
    Would be as heavy to me as odious, but[7]   5
    This mistress which I serve quickens[8] what's dead
    And makes my labors pleasures. O, she is
    Ten times more gentle than her father's crabbed,
    And he's composed of harshness, I must remove
    Some thousands of these logs and pile them up,   10
    Upon a sore injunction.[9] My sweet mistress
    Weeps when she sees me work and says such baseness

---

80. Firewood.
81. Trenchers, wooden plates.
82. (Addressed to Prospero.)
83. Holiday.

    Act III, Scene 1
1. Location: Before Prospero's cell.
2. Some pastimes are laborious, but the pleasure we get from them compensates for
   the effort. (Pleasure is *set off* by labor as a
   jewel is set off by its foil.)
3. Menial activity.

4. Undertaken.
5. Poorest.
6. Lowly.
7. Were it not that.
8. Gives life to.
9. Severe command.

Had never like executor.[10] I forget;[11]
But these sweet thoughts do even refresh my labors,
Most busy lest when I do it.[12]   15

[Enter Miranda; and Prospero (at a distance, unseen).]

MIRANDA: Alas now, pray you,
Work not so hard, I would the lightning had
Burnt up those logs that you are enjoined[13] to pile!
Pray, set it down and rest you. When this[14] burns,
'Twill weep[15] for having wearied you. My father
Is hard at study. Pray now, rest yourself.   20
He's safe for these[16] three hours.
FERDINAND: O most dear mistress,
The sun will set before I shall discharge[17]
What I must strive to do.
MIRANDA: If you'll sit down,
I'll bear your logs the while. Pray, give me that.   25
I'll carry it to the pile.
FERDINAND: No, precious creature,
I had rather crack my sinews, break my back,
Than you should such dishonor undergo
While I sit lazy by.
MIRANDA: It would become me
As well as it does you; and I should do it
With much more ease, for my good will is to it,   30
And yours it is against.
PROSPERO *[aside]:*   Poor worm, thou art infected!
This visitation[18] shows it.
MIRANDA: You look wearily.
FERDINAND:
No, noble mistress, 'tis fresh morning with me
When you are by[19] at night. I do beseech you—
Chiefly that I might set it in my prayers—   35
What is your name?
MIRANDA: Miranda.—O my father,
I have broke your hest[20] to say so.

---

10. I.e., was never before undertaken by so
    noble a being.
11. I.e., I forget that I'm supposed to be
    working, or, I forget my happiness, op-
    pressed by my labor.
12. I.e., busy at my labor but with my mind on
    other things (?) (The line may be in need
    of emendation.)
13. Commanded.

14. I.e., the log.
15. I.e., exude resin.
16. The next.
17. Complete.
18. (1) Miranda's visit to Ferdinand; (2) visita-
    tion of the plague, i.e., infection of love.
19. Nearby.
20. Command.

FERDINAND: Admired Miranda![21]
Indeed the top of admiration, worth
What's dearest[22] to the world! Full many a lady
I have eyed with best regard,[23] and many a time   40
The harmony of their tongues hath into bondage
Brought my too diligent[24] ear. For several[25] virtues
Have I liked several women, never any
With so full soul but some defect in her
Did quarrel with the noblest grace she owed[26]   45
And put it to the foil.[27] But you, O you,
So perfect and so peerless, are created
Of[28] every creature's best!

MIRANDA: I do not know
One of my sex; no woman's face remember,
Save, from my glass, mine own. Nor have I seen   50
More that I may call men than you, good friend,
And my dear father. How features are abroad[29]
I am skilless[30] of; but, my modesty,
The jewel in my dower, I would not wish
Any companion in the world but you;   55
Nor can imagination form a shape,
Besides yourself, to like of.[32] But I prattle
Something[33] too wildly, and my father's precepts
I therein do forget.

FERDINAND: I am in my condition[34]
A prince, Miranda; I do think, a king—   60
I would,[35] not so!—and would no more endure
This wooden slavery[36] than to suffer
The flesh-fly[37] blow[38] my mouth. Hear my soul speak:
The very instant that I saw you did
My heart fly to your service, there resides   65
To make me slave to it, and for your sake
Am I this patient log-man.

MIRANDA: Do you love me?

---

21. (Her name means "to be admired or wondered at.")
22. Most treasured.
23. Thoughtful and approving attention.
24. Attentive.
25. Various (also in line 43).
26. Owned.
27. (1) overthrew it (as in wrestling) (2)
 served as a *foil,* or "contrast," to set it off.
28. Out of.

29. What people look like in other places.
30. Ignorant.
31. Virginity.
32. Be pleased with, be fond of.
33. Somewhat.
34. Rank.
35. Wish (it were).
36. Being compelled to carry wood.
37. Insect that deposits its eggs in dead flesh.
38. Befoul with fly eggs.

FERDINAND:
> O heaven, O earth, bear witness to this sound,
> And crown what I profess with kind event[39]
> If I speak true! If hollowly,[40] invert[41]
> What best is boded[42] me to mischief?[43] I
> Beyond all limit of what[44] else i' the world
> Do love, prize, honor you.

MIRANDA [weeping]:　　　I am a fool
> To weep at what I am glad of.

PROSPERO [aside]:　　　　　Fair encounter
> Of two most rare affections! Heavens rain grace
> On that which breeds between 'em!

FERDINAND:　　　　　　　Wherefore weep you?

MIRANDA:
> At mine unworthiness, that dare not offer
> What I desire to give, and much less take
> What I shall die[45] to want.[46] But this is trifling,
> And all the more it seeks to hide itself
> The bigger bulk it shows. Hence, bashful cunning,[47]
> And prompt me, plain and holy innocence!
> I am your wife, if you will marry me;
> If not, I'll die your maid.[48] To be your fellow[49]
> You may deny me, but I'll be your servant
> Whether you will[50] or no.

FERDINAND:　　My mistress,[51] dearest,
> And I thus humble ever.

MIRANDA: My husband, then?

FERDINAND: Ay, with a heart as willing[52]
> As bondage e'er of freedom. Here's my hand

MIRANDA [clasping his hand]:
> And mine, with my heart in 't. And now farewell
> Till half an hour hence.

FERDINAND:　A thousand thousand![53]

[Exeunt (Ferdinand and Miranda, separately).]

70

75

80

85

90

---

39. Favorable outcome.
40. Insincerely, falsely.
41. Turn.
42. In store for.
43. Harm.
44. Whatever.
45. (Probably with an unconscious sexual meaning that underlies all of lines 77–81.)
46. Through lacking.

47. Coyness.
48. Handmaiden, servant.
49. Mate, equal.
50. Desire it.
51. I.e., the woman I adore and serve (not an illicit sexual partner).
52. Desirous.
53. I.e., a thousand thousand farewells.

PROSPERO:

> *not as happy as they about this situation*
>
> So glad of this as they I cannot be,
> Who are surprised with all;[54] but my rejoicing
> At nothing can be more. I'll to my book,
> For yet ere suppertime must I perform
> Much business appertaining.[55]   [Exit.]   95

another part of island   Scene 2[1]   *slave   butler   jester   Speaking of Prospero's demise*
                                                                            to kill him
[Enter Caliban, Stephano, and Trinculo.]   *empty*

STEPHANO: Tell not me. When the butt is out,[2] we will drink water, not a drop
before. Therefore bear up and board 'em.[3] Servant monster, drink to me.

TRINCULO: Servant monster? The folly[4] of this island! *stupidity found on*
They say there's but five upon this isle. We are three of them; if th' other
two be brained[5] like us, the state totters.   *intelligent*   5

STEPHANO: Drink, servant monster, when I bid thee.   *drunken stare*
Thy eyes are almost set[6] in thy head. [Giving a drink.]

TRINCULO: Where should they be set[7] else? He were a brave[8] monster indeed if
they were set in his tail.

STEPHANO: My man-monster hath drowned his tongue in sack. For my part, the   10
reach
sea cannot drown me. I swam, ere I could recover[9] the shore, five and
105 miles   *oath*
thirty leagues[10] off and on.[11] By this light,[12] thou shalt be my lieutenant,   *ensign*
monster, or my standard.[13]   *prefer*

1 league = 3 miles + 5 more

TRINCULO: Your lieutenant, if you list;[14] he's no standard.[15]   *not able to stand up*

35 / 3 = 105

STEPHANO: We'll not run,[16] Monsieur Monster.   *urinate*   15

TRINCULO: Nor go[17] neither, but you'll lie[18] like dogs and yet say nothing neither.

STEPHANO: Mooncalf, speak once in thy life, if thou beest a good mooncalf.

CALIBAN:

> How does thy honor? Let me lick thy shoe.
> I'll not serve him. He is not valiant.

---

54. By everything that has happened, or,
    withal, "with it."
55. Related to this.

    Act III, Scene 2

1. Location: another part of the island.
2. Empty.
3. (Stephano uses the terminology of maneuvering at sea and boarding a vessel under
   attack as a way of urging an assault on the
   liquor supply.)
4. I.e., stupidity found on.
5. Are endowed with intelligence.
6. Fixed in a drunken stare, or, sunk, like the
   sun.
7. Placed.

8. Fine, splendid.
9. Gain, reach.
10. Units of distance, each equaling about
    three miles.
11. Intermittently.
12. (An oath: by the light of the sun.)
13. Standard-bearer, ensign (as distinguished
    from *lieutenant,* lines 16–17).
14. Prefer.
15. I.e., not able to stand up.
16. (1) retreat; (2) urinate (taking Trinculo's
    standard, line 17, in the old sense of
    "conduit.")
17. Walk.
18. (1) Tell lies; (2) lie prostrate (3) excrete.

TRINCULO: Thou liest, most ignorant monster, I am in case to jostle a constable.[19] 20
Why, thou debauched[20] fish thou, was there ever man a coward that
hath drunk so much sack[21] as I today? Wilt thou tell a monstrous lie
being but half a fish and half a monster?

CALIBAN:
Lo, how he mocks me! Wilt thou let him, my lord?

TRINCULO: "Lord," quoth he? That a monster should be such a natural![22] 25

CALIBAN:
Lo, lo, again! Bit him to death, I prithee.

STEPHANO: Trinculo, keep a good tongue in your head.
If you prove a mutineer—the next tree![23] The poor monster's my subject,
and he shall not suffer indignity.

CALIBAN:
I thank my noble lord. Wilt thou be pleased
To hearken once again to the suit I made to thee? 30

STEPHANO: Marry,[24] will I. Kneel and repeat it. I will stand, and so shall Trinculo.

[Caliban kneels.]

[Enter Ariel, invisible.][25]

CALIBAN:
As I told thee before, I am subject to a tyrant,
A sorcerer, that by his cunning hath
Cheated me of the island. 35

ARIEL [mimicking Trinculo]:
Thou liest.

CALIBAN: Thou liest, thou jesting monkey, thou!
I would my valiant master would destroy thee.
I do not lie.

STEPHANO: Trinculo, if you trouble him any more in's tale, by this hand, I will 40
supplant[26] some of your teeth.

TRINCULO: Why, I said nothing.

STEPHANO: Mum, then, and no more.—Proceed.

CALIBAN:
I say by sorcery he got this isle;
From me he got it. If thy greatness will 45
Revenge it on him—for I know thou dar'st,
But this thing[27] dare not—

STEPHANO: That's most certain.

---

19. I.e., in fit condition, made valiant by
drink, to taunt or challenge the police.
20. (1) Seduced away from proper service and
allegiance; (2) depraved.
21. Spanish white wine.
22. (1) idiot; (2) natural as opposed to unnatural, monsterlike.

23. I.e., you'll hang.
24. I.e., indeed. (Originally an oath, "by the
Virgin Mary.")
25. I.e., wearing a garment to connote invisi-
bility.
26. Uproot, displace.
27. I.e., Trinculo.

CALIBAN:

Thou shalt be lord of it, and I'll serve thee.

STEPHANO: How now shall this be compassed?[28] Canst thou bring me to the   50
party?

CALIBAN:

Yea, yea, my lord. I'll yield him thee asleep,
Where thou mayst knock a nail into his head.

ARIEL: Thou liest; thou canst not.

CALIBAN:

What a pied ninny's[29] this! Thou scurvy patch![30]   55
I do beseech thy greatness, give him blows
And take his bottle from him. When that's gone
He shall drink naught but brine, for I'll not show him
Where the quick freshes[31] are.

STEPHANO: Trinculo, run into no further danger. Interrupt the monster one word   60
further[32] and, by this hand, I'll turn my mercy out o' doors[33] and make
a stockfish[34] of thee.

TRINCULO: Why, what did I? I did nothing. I'll go farther off.[35]

STEPHANO: Didst thou not say he lied?

ARIEL: Thou liest.   65

STEPHANO: Do I so? Take thou that. [He beats Trinculo.]
As you like this, give me the lie[36] another time.

TRINCULO: I did not give the lie. Out o' your wits and hearing too? A pox o' your
bottle! This can sack and drinking do. A murrain[37] on your monster, and
the devil take your fingers!   70

CALIBAN: Ha, ha, ha!

STEPHANO: Now, forward with your tale. [To Trinculo.]
Prithee, stand further off.

CALIBAN:

Beat him enough. After a little time
I'll beat him too.   75

STEPHANO: Stand farther.—Come, proceed.

CALIBAN:

Why, as I told thee, 'tis a custom with him
I' th' afternoon to sleep. There thou mayst brain him,
Having first seized his books; or with a log
Batter his skull, or paunch[38] him with a stake,   80
Or cut his weasand[39] with thy knife. Remember
First to possess his books, for without them

---

28. Achieved.
29. Fool in motley.
30. Fool.
31. Running springs.
32. I.e., one more time.
33. I.e., forget about being merciful.
34. Dried cod beaten before cooking.
35. Away.
36. Call me a liar to my face.
37. Plague. (Literally, a cattle disease.)
38. Stab in the belly.
39. Windpipe.

He's but a sot,[40] *[fool]* as I am, nor hath not
One spirit to command. They all do hate him
As rootedly as I. Burn but his books.   85
He has brave utensils[41]—*[fine furnishings]* for so he calls them—
Which, when he has a house, he'll deck withal.[42]
And that most deeply to consider is
The beauty of his daughter. He himself
Calls her a nonpareil. I never saw a woman   90
But only Sycorax my dam and she;
But she as far surpasseth Sycorax
As great'st does least.

STEPHANO: Is it so brave[43] a lass? *[Splendid]*

CALIBAN:
  Ay, lord. She will become[44] *[suit satisfy]* thy bed, I warrant,   95
  And bring thee forth brave brood.

STEPHANO: *[Brother]* Monster, I will kill this man. His daughter and I will be king and
  queen—save Our Graces!—and Trinculo and thyself shall be viceroys.
  Dost thou like the plot, Trinculo?

TRINCULO: Excellent.   100

STEPHANO: Give me thy hand. I am sorry I beat thee; but, while thou liv'st, keep
  a good tongue in thy head.

CALIBAN:
  Within this half hour will he be asleep.
  Wilt thou destroy him then?

STEPHANO: Ay, on mine honor.   105

ARIEL [aside]: This will I tell my master.

CALIBAN:
  Thou mak'st me merry; I am full of pleasure.
  Let us be jocund.[45] *[merry]* Will you troll the catch[46] *[sing the round]*
  You taught me but whilere?[47] *[short time ago]*

STEPHANO: At thy request, monster, I will do reason,   110
  any reason.[48]—Come on, Trinculo, let us sing.   [Sings.]
  "Flout[49] 'em and scout[50] 'em
  And scout 'em and flout 'em!
  Thought is free."

CALIBAN: That's not the tune.   115

  [Ariel plays the tune on a tabor[51] *[drum]* and pipe.]

STEPHANO: What is this same?

IDEA! Stephano/Miranda kill Prospero. Trinculo + Caliban to be viceroys

---

40. Fool.   46. Sing the round.
41. Fine furnishings.   47. Only a short time ago.
42. Furnish it with.   48. Anything reasonable.
43. Splendid, attractive.   49. Scoff at.
44. Suit (sexually).   50. Deride.
45. Jovial, merry.   51. Small drum.

TRINCULO: This is the tune of our catch, played by the picture of Nobody.[52]

STEPHANO: If thou beest a man, show thyself in thy likeness. If thou beest a devil, take 't as thou list.[53] *Take my defiance*

TRINCULO: O, forgive me my sins!   120

STEPHANO: He that dies pays all debts.[54] I defy thee. Mercy upon us!

CALIBAN: Art thou afeard?

STEPHANO: No, monster, not I.

CALIBAN:

Be not afeard. The isle is full of noises,   125
Sounds, and sweet airs, that give delight and hurt not.
Sometimes a thousand twangling instruments
Will hum about mine ears, and sometimes voices
That, if I then had waked after long sleep,
Will make me sleep again; and then, in dreaming,   130
The clouds methought would open and show riches
Ready to drop upon me, that when I waked
I cried to dream[55] again.

musical noises to this

STEPHANO: This will prove a brave kingdom to me, where I shall have my music for nothing.   135

CALIBAN: When Prospero is destroyed.

STEPHANO: That shall be by and by.[56] I remember the story. *Very soon*

TRINCULO: The sound is going away. Let's follow it, and after do our work.

STEPHANO: Lead, monster; we'll follow. I would I could see this taborer! He lays it on.[57] *plays drum vigorously*   140

TRINCULO: Wilt come? I'll follow, Stephano.

[Exeunt (following Ariel's music).]

Scene 3[1] *any part of the island*

[Enter Alonso, Sebastian, Antonio, Gonzalo, Adrian, Francisco, etc.]
Naples   brother   usurping Duke of Milan   took from Prospero
kings   councillor lords

GONZALO:

By 'r lakin,[2] I can go no further, sir.   *our Lady*
My old bones aches. Here's a maze trod indeed
Through forthrights and meanders![3] By your patience,   *paths straight & crooked*
I needs must[4] rest me.   *time to rest*

---

52. (Refers to a familiar figure with head, arms, and legs but no trunk.)
53. I.e., take my defiance as you please, as best you can.
54. I.e., if I have to die, at least that will be the end of all my woes and obligations.
55. Desirous of dreaming.
56. Very soon.

57. I.e., plays the drum vigorously.

Act III, Scene 3.

1. Location: another part of the island.
2. By our Ladykin, by our Lady.
3. Paths straight and crooked.
4. Have to.

(Bananepages) ——→

ALONSO: Old lord, I cannot blame thee, *I am also tired*
Who am myself attached[5] with weariness,   5
To th' dulling of my spirits.[6] Sit down and rest.
Even here I will put off my hope, and keep it
No longer for[7] my flatterer. He is drowned
Whom thus we stray to find, and the sea mocks
Our frustrate[8] search on land. Well, let him go.   10

[*Alonso and Gonzalo sit.*]

ANTONIO [*aside to Sebastian*]:
I am right[9] glad that he's so out of hope. *very*
Do not, for[10] one repulse, forgo the purpose
That you resolved t' effect.

SEBASTIAN [*to Antonio*]: The next advantage
Will we take throughly.[11] *thoroughly*

ANTONIO [*to Sebastian*]: Let it be tonight,
For, now[12] they are oppressed with travel,[13] they   15
Will not, nor cannot, use[14] such vigilance *employ*
As when they are fresh.

SEBASTIAN [*to Antonio*]: I say tonight. No more.

[*Solemn and strange music; and Prospero on the top,[15] invisible.*] *up above the stage can't be seen.*

ALONSO:
What harmony is this? My good friends, hark!

GONZALO: Marvelous sweet music!

[*Enter several strange shapes, bringing in a banquet, and dance about it with
gentle actions of salutations; and, inviting the King, etc., to eat, they depart.*]

ALONSO: *guardian angels*
Give us kind keepers,[16] heavens! What were these?   20

SEBASTIAN   *live actors, puppet show*
A living[17] drollery.[18] Now I will believe
That there are unicorns; that in Arabia
There is one tree, the phoenix'[19] throne, one phoenix
At this hour reigning there. *mythical bird*

---

5. Seized.
6. To the point of being dull-spirited.
7. As.
8. Frustrated.
9. Very.
10. Because of.
11. Thoroughly.
12. Now that.
13. (Spelled *trauaile* in the Folio and carrying the sense of labor as well as traveling.)
14. Apply.

15. At some high point of the tiring-house or the theatre, on a third level above the gallery.
16. Guardian angels.
17. With live actors.
18. Comic entertainment, caricature, puppet show.
19. Mythical bird consumed to ashes every five hundred to six hundred years, only to be renewed into another cycle.

ANTONIO: I'll believe both;
                And what does else want credit,[20] come to me   25
                And I'll be sworn 'tis true. Travelers ne'er did lie,
                Though fools at home condemn 'em.
GONZALO: If in Naples
                I should report this now, would they believe me
                If I should say I saw such islanders?
                For, certes,[21] these are people of the island,   30
                Who, though they are of monstrous[22] shape, yet note,
                Their manners are more gentle, kind, than of
                Our human generation you shall find
                Many, nay, almost any.
PROSPERO [aside]:   Honest lord,
                Thou hast said well, for some of you there present   35
                Are worse than devils.
ALONSO: I cannot too much muse[23]
                Such shapes, such gesture, and such sound, expressing—
                Although they want[24] the use of tongue—a kind
                Of excellent dumb discourse.
PROSPERO [aside]:   Praise in departing.[25]
FRANCISCO:
                They vanished strangely.
SEBASTIAN: No matter, since   40
                They have left their viands[26] behind, for we have stomachs.[27]
                Will 't please you taste of what is here?
ALONSO: Not I.
GONZALO:
                Faith, sir, you need not fear. When we were boys,
                Who would believe that there were mountaineers[28]
                Dewlapped[29] like bulls, whose throats had hanging at 'em   45
                Wallets[30] of flesh? Or that there were such men
                Whose heads stood in their breasts?[31] Which now we find
                Each putter-out of five for one[32] will bring us
                Good warrant[33] of.

---

20. Lack credence.
21. Certainly.
22. Unnatural.
23. Wonder at.
24. Lack.
25. I.e., save your praise until the end of the performance. (Proverbial.)
26. Provisions.
27. Appetites.
28. Mountain dwellers.
29. Having a dewlap, or fold of skin hanging from the neck, like cattle.
30. Pendent folds of skin, wattles.
31. (I.e., like the Anthropophagi described in *Othello*, 1.3.146)
32. One who invests money or gambles on the risks of travel on the condition that the traveler who returns safely is to receive five times the amount deposited; hence, any traveler
33. Assurance.

ALONSO: I will stand to[34] and feed,
                 Although my last[35]—no matter, since I feel   50
                 The best[36] is past. Brother, my lord the Duke,
                 Stand to, and do as we.   *[They approach the table.]*

                 [Thunder and lightning. Enter Ariel, like a harpy,[37] claps his wings upon the
                 table, and with a quaint device[38] the banquet vanishes.[39]]

ARIEL:
                 You are three men of sin, whom Destiny—
                 That hath to instrument this lower world
                 And what is in 't—the never-surfeited sea
                 Hath caused to belch up you,[40] and on this island   55
                 Where man doth not inhabit, you 'mongst men
                 Being most unfit to live. I have made you mad;
                 And even with suchlike valor[41] men hang and drown
                 Their proper[42] selves. *[Alonso, Sebastian, and Antonio draw their swords.]*
                      You fools! I and my fellows
                 Are ministers of Fate. The elements
                 Of whom[43] your swords are tempered[44] may as well
                 Wound the loud winds, or with bemocked-at[45] stabs
                 Kill the still-closing waters, as diminish
                 One dowl[46] that's in my plume. My fellow ministers   65
                 Are like[47] invulnerable. If[48] you could hurt,
                 Your swords are now too massy[49] for your strengths
                 And will not be uplifted. But remember—
                 For that's my business to you—that you three
                 From Milan did supplant good Prospero;   70
                 Exposed unto the sea, which hath requit[50] it,
                 Him and his innocent child; for which foul deed
                 The powers, delaying, not forgetting, have
                 Incensed the seas and shores, yea, all the creatures,
                 Against your peace. Thee of thy son, Alonso,   75
                 They have bereft; and do pronounce by me
                 Ling'ring perdition,[51] worse than any death

---

34. Fall to; take the risk.
35. Even if this were to be my last meal.
36. Best part of life.
37. A fabulous monster with a woman's face
    and breasts and a vulture's body, sup-
    posed to be a minister of divine venge-
    ance.
38. Ingenious stage contrivance.
39. I.e., the food vanishes; the table remains
    until line 82.
40. You whom Destiny, controller of the
    sublunary world as its instrument, has
    caused the ever hungry sea to belch up.

41. I.e., the reckless valor derived from mad-
    ness.
42. Own.
43. Which.
44. Composed and hardened.
45. Scorned.
46. Soft, fine feather.
47. Likewise, similarly.
48. Even if.
49. Heavy.
50. Requited, avenged.
51. Ruin, destruction.

Can be at once, shall step by step attend
You and your ways; whose[52] wraths to guard you from—
Which here, in this most desolate isle, else[53] falls   80
Upon your heads—is nothing[54] but heart's sorrow
And a clear[55] life ensuing.

*[He vanishes in thunder; then, to soft music, enter the shapes again, and
dance, with mocks and mows,[56] and carrying out the table.]*

PROSPERO:
Bravely[57] the figure of this harpy hast thou
Performed, my Ariel; a grace it had devouring.[58]
Of my instruction hast thou nothing bated[59]   85
In what thou hadst to say. So,[60] with good life[61]
And observation strange,[62] my meaner[63] ministers
Their several kinds[64] have done. My high charms work,
And these mine enemies are all knit up
In their distractions.[65] They now are in my power;
And in these fits I leave them, while I visit   90
Young Ferdinand, whom they suppose is drowned,
And his and mine loved darling.   *[Exit above.]*

GONZALO:
I' the name of something holy, sir, why[66] stand you
In this strange stare?   95

ALONSO: O, it[67] is monstrous, monstrous!
Methought the billows[68] spoke and told me of it;
The winds did sing it to me, and the thunder,
That deep and dreadful organ pipe, pronounced
The name of Prosper; it did bass my trespass.[69]
Therefor[70] my son i' th' ooze is bedded; and   100
I'll seek him deeper than e'er plummet[71] sounded.[72]
And with him there lie mudded.   *[Exit.]*

---

52. (Refers to the heavenly powers.)
53. Otherwise.
54. There is no way.
55. Unspotted, innocent.
56. Mocking gestures and grimaces.
57. Finely, dashingly.
58. I.e., you gracefully caused the banquet to
    disappear as if you had consumed it (with
    puns on *grace*, meaning "gracefulness"
    and "a blessing on the meal," and on
    devouring, meaning "a literal eating" and
    "an all-consuming or ravishing grace").
59. Abated, omitted.
60. In the same fashion.
61. Faithful reproduction.
62. Exceptional attention to detail.

63. I.e., subordinate to Ariel.
64. Individual parts.
65. Trancelike state.
66. (Gonzalo was not addressed in Ariel's
    speech to the *three men of sin*, line 53, and
    is not, as they are, in a maddened state; see
    lines 105–107.)
67. I.e., my sin (also in line 96)
68. Waves.
69. Proclaim my trespass like a bass note in
    music.
70. In consequence of that.
71. A lead weight attached to a line for testing
    depth.
72. Probed, tested the depth of.

SEBASTIAN: But one fiend at a time,
    I'll fight their legions o'er.[73]
ANTONIO: I'll be thy second.

                           [Exeunt (Sebastian and Antonio).]

GONZALO:
    All three of them are desperate.[74] Their great guilt,   105
    Like poison given to work a great time after,
    Now 'gins to bite the spirits.[75] I do beseech you,
    That are of suppler joints, follow them swiftly
    And hinder them from what this ecstasy[76]
    May now provoke them to.   110
ADRIAN   Follow, I pray you.

                           [Exeunt omnes.]

Act IV

Scene 1[1]

[Enter Prospero, Ferdinand, and Miranda.]

PROSPERO:
    If I have too austerely punished you,
    Your compensation makes amends, for I
    Have given you here a third[2] of mine own life,
    Or that for which I live; who once again
    I tender[3] to thy hand. All thy vexations   5
    Were but my trials of thy love, and thou
    Hast strangely[4] stood the test. Here, afore heaven,
    I ratify this my rich gift. O Ferdinand,
    Do not smile at me that I boast her off,[5]
    For thou shalt find she will outstrip all praise   10
    And make it halt[6] behind her.
FERDINAND: I do believe it
    Against an oracle.[7]

---

73. One after another.
74. Despairing and reckless.
75. Sap their vital powers through anguish.
76. Mad frenzy.

    Act IV, Scene 1

1. Location: before Prospero's cell.
2. I.e., Miranda, into whose education Prospero has put a third of his life (?) or who represents a large part of what he cares about, along with his dukedom and his learned study (?)
3. Offer.

4. Extraordinarily.
5. I.e., praise her so, or, perhaps an error for "boast of her"; the Folio reads "boast her of."
6. Limp.
7. Even if an oracle should declare otherwise.

PROSPERO:

    Then, as my gift and thine own acquisition
    Worthily purchased, take my daughter. But
    If thou dost break her virgin-knot before   15
    All sanctimonious[8] ceremonies may
    With full and holy rite be ministered,
    No sweet aspersion[9] shall the heavens let fall
    To make this contract grow; but barren hate,
    Sour-eyed disdain, and discord shall bestrew   20
    The union of your bed with weeds[10] so loathly
    That you shall hate it both. Therefore take heed,
    As Hymen's lamps shall light you.[11]

FERDINAND: As I hope
    For quiet days, fair issue,[12] and long life,
    With such love as 'tis now, the murkiest den,   25
    The most opportune place, the strong'st suggestion[13]
    Our worser genius[14] can,[15] shall never melt
    Mine honor into lust, to[16] take away
    The edge[17] of that day's celebration
    When I shall think or[18] Phoebus' steeds are foundered[19]   30
    Or Night kept chained below.

PROSPERO: Fairly spoke.
    Sit then and talk with her. She is thine own.

[Ferdinand and Miranda sit and talk together.]

    What,[20] Ariel! My industrious servant, Ariel!

[Enter Ariel.]

ARIEL:

    What would my potent master? Here I am.

PROSPERO:

    Thou and thy meaner fellows[21] your last service   35
    Did worthily perform, and I must use you
    In such another trick.[22] Go bring the rabble,[23]

---

8. Sacred.
9. Dew, shower.
10. (In place of the flowers customarily strewn on the marriage bed.)
11. I.e., as you long for happiness and concord in your marriage. (Hymen was the Greek and Roman god of marriage; his symbolic torches, the wedding torches, were supposed to burn brightly for a happy marriage and smokily for a troubled one.)
12. Offspring.
13. Temptation.
14. Evil genius, or, evil attendant spirit.
15. Is capable of.
16. So as to.
17. Keen enjoyment, sexual ardor.
18. Either.
19. Broken down, made lame. (Ferdinand will wait impatiently for the bridal night.)
20. Now then.
21. Subordinates.
22. Device.
23. Band, i.e., the *meaner fellows* of line 35.

O'er whom I give thee power, here to this place.
Incite them to quick motion, for I must
Bestow upon the eyes of this young couple   40
Some vanity[24] of mine art. It is my promise,
And they expect it from me.

ARIEL: Presently?[25]

PROSPERO: Ay, with a twink.[26]

ARIEL:
Before you can say "Come" and "Go,"
And breathe twice, and cry "So, so,"   45
Each one, tripping on his toe,
Will be here with mop and mow.[27]
Do you love me, master? No?

PROSPERO:
Dearly, my delicate Ariel. Do not approach
Till thou dost hear me call.

ARIEL: Well; I conceive.[28]   [Exit.]   50

PROSPERO:
Look thou be true;[29] do not give dalliance
Too much the rein. The strongest oaths are straw
To the fire i' the blood. Be more abstemious,
Or else good night[30] your vow!

FERDINAND: I warrant[31] you, sir,
The white cold virgin snow upon my heart[32]   55
Abates the ardor of my liver.[33]

PROSPERO: Well.
Now come, my Ariel! Bring a corollary,[34]
Rather than want[35] a spirit. Appear, and pertly![36]—
No tongue![37] All eyes! Be silent.   [Soft music.]

[Enter Iris.][38]

IRIS:
Ceres,[39] most bounteous lady, thy rich leas[40]   60
Of wheat, rye, barley, vetches,[41] oats, and peas;

---

24. (1) illusion; (2) trifle; (3) desire for admiration, conceit.
25. Immediately.
26. In the twinkling of an eye.
27. Gestures and grimaces.
28. Understand.
29. True to your promise.
30. I.e., say good-bye to.
31. Guarantee.
32. I.e., the ideal of chastity and consciousness of Miranda's chaste innocence enshrined in my heart.

33. (As the presumed seat of the passions.)
34. Surplus, extra supply.
35. Lack.
36. Briskly.
37. All the beholders are to be silent (lest the spirits vanish).
38. Goddess of the rainbow and Juno's messenger.
39. Goddess of the generative power of nature.
40. Meadows.
41. Plants for forage, fodder.

Thy turfy mountains, where live nibbling sheep,
And flat meads[42] thatched with stover,[43] them to keep;
Thy banks with pionèd and twillèd[44] brims,
Which spongy[45] April at thy hest[46] betrims   65
To make cold nymphs chaste crowns; and thy broom groves,[47]
Whose shadow the dismissed bachelor[48] loves,
Being lass-lorn; thy poll-clipped[49] vineyard;
And thy sea marge,[50] sterile and rocky hard,
Where thou thyself dost air:[51] the queen o' the sky,[52]   70
Whose watery arch[53] and messenger am I,
Bids thee leave these, and with her sovereign grace,

[Juno descends[54] (slowly in her car).]

Here on this grass plot, in this very place,
To come and sport. Her peacocks[55] fly amain.[56]
Approach, rich Ceres, her to entertain.[57]   75

[Enter Ceres.]

CERES:

Hail, many-colored messenger, that n'er
Dost disobey the wife of Jupiter,
Who with thy saffron[58] wings upon my flowers
Diffusest honeydrops, refreshing showers,
And with each end of thy blue bow[59] dost crown   80
My bosky[60] acres and my unshrubbed down,[61]
Rich scarf[62] to my proud earth. Why hath thy queen
Summoned me hither to this short-grassed green?

IRIS:

A contract of true love to celebrate,
And some donation freely to estate[63]   85
On the blest lovers.

CERES: Tell me, heavenly bow,

---

42. Meadows.
43. Winter fodder for cattle.
44. Undercut by the swift current and protected by roots and branches that tangle to form a barricade.
45. Wet.
46. Command.
47. Clumps of broom, gorse, yellow-flowered shrub.
48. Rejected male lover.
49. Pruned, lopped at the top, or *pole-clipped,* "hedged in with poles"
50. Shore.
51. You take the air, go for walks.
52. I.e., Juno.

53. Rainbow.
54. I.e., starts her descent from the "heavens" above the stage (?)
55. Birds sacred to Juno and used to pull her chariot.
56. With full speed.
57. Receive.
58. Yellow.
59. I.e., rainbow.
60. Wooded.
61. Open upland.
62. (The rainbow is like a colored silk band adorning the earth.)
63. Bestow.

If Venus or her son,[64] as[65] thou dost know,
Do now attend the Queen? Since they did plot
The means that[66] dusky[67] Dis my daughter got,[68]
Her and her[69] blind boy's scandaled[70] company   90
I have forsworn.

IRIS: Of her society[71]
Be not afraid: I met her deity[72]
Cutting the clouds towards Paphos,[73] and her son
Dove-drawn[74] with her. Here thought they to have done[75]
Some wanton[76] charm upon this man and maid,   95
Whose vows are that no bed-right shall be paid
Till Hymen's torch be lighted; but in vain.
Mars's hot minion[77] is returned[78] again;
Her waspish-headed[79] son has broke his arrows,
Swears he will shoot no more, but play with sparrows[80]   100
And be a boy right out.[81]

[Juno alights.]

CERES: Highest Queen of state,[82]
Great Juno, comes; I know her by her gait.[83]

JUNO

How does my bounteous sister?[84] Go with me
To bless this twain, that they may prosperous be,
And honored in their issue.[85]   [They sing.]   105

JUNO:

Honor, riches, marriage blessing,
Long continuance, and increasing,
Hourly joys be still[86] upon you!
Juno sings her blessings on you.

CERES:

Earth's increase, foison plenty,[87]   110
Barns and garners[88] never empty,

---

64. I.e., Cupid.
65. As far as.
66. Whereby.
67. Dark.
68. (Pluto, or *Dis,* god of the infernal regions, carried off Proserpina, daughter of Ceres, to be his bride in Hades.)
69. I.e., Venus'.
70. Scandalous.
71. Company.
72. I.e., Her Highness.
73. Place on the island of Cyprus, sacred to Venus.
74. (Venus' chariot was drawn by doves.)
75. Placed.
76. Lustful spell.
77. I.e., Venus, the beloved of Mars.
78. I.e., returned to Paphos.
79. Hotheaded, peevish.
80. (Supposedly lustful, and sacred to Venus.)
81. Outright.
82. Most majestic Queen.
83. I.e., majestic bearing.
84. I.e., fellow goddess (?)
85. Offspring.
86. Always.
87. Plentiful harvest.
88. Granaries.

Vines with clustering bunches growing,
Plants with goodly burden bowing;

Spring come to you at the farthest
In the very end of harvest![89]   115
Scarcity and want shall shun you;
Ceres' blessing so is on you.

FERDINAND:
This is a most majestic vision, and
Harmonious charmingly.[90] May I be bold
To think these spirits?   120

PROSPERO: Spirits, which by mine art
I have from their confines called to enact
My present fancies.

FERDINAND: Let me live here ever!
So rare a wondered[91] father and a wife
Makes this place Paradise.

[Juno and Ceres whisper, and send Iris on employment.]

PROSPERO: Sweet now, silence!
Juno and Ceres whisper seriously;   125
There's something else to do. Hush and be mute,
Or else our spell is marred.

IRIS *[calling offstage]*:
You nymphs, called naiads,[92] of the windring[93] brooks,
With your sedged[94] crowns and ever-harmless[95] looks,
Leave your crisp[96] channels, and on this green land   130
Answer your summons; Juno does command.
Come, temperate[97] nymphs, and help to celebrate
A contract of true love. Be not too late.

[Enter certain nymphs.]

You sunburned sicklemen,[98] of August weary,[99]
Come hither from the furrow[100] and be merry.   135
Make holiday; your rye-straw hats put on,
And these fresh nymphs encounter[101] every one
In country footing.[102]

---

89. I.e., with no winter in between.
90. Enchantingly.
91. Wonder-performing, wondrous.
92. Nymphs of springs, rivers, or lakes.
93. Wandering, winding (?).
94. Made of reeds.
95. Ever innocent.
96. Curled, rippled.

97. Chaste.
98. Harvesters, field workers who cut down grain and grass.
99. I.e., weary of the hard work of the harvest.
100. I.e., plowed fields.
101. Join.
102. Country dancing.

[Enter certain reapers, properly[103] habited. They join with the nymphs in a graceful dance, towards the end whereof Prospero starts suddenly, and speaks; after which, to a strange, hollow, and confused noise, they heavily[104] vanish.]

PROSPERO *[aside]:*

    I had forgot that foul conspiracy
    Of the beast Caliban and his confederates   140
    Against my life. The minute of their plot
    Is almost come. *[To the Spirits.]* Well done! Avoid;[105] no more!

FERDINAND *[to Miranda]:*

    This is strange. Your father's in some passion
    That works[106] him strongly.

MIRANDA: Never till this day
    Saw I him touched with anger so distempered.   145

PROSPERO:

    You do look, my son, in a moved sort,[107]
    As if you were dismayed. Be cheerful, sir.
    Our revels[108] now are ended. These our actors,
    As I foretold you, were all spirits and
    Are melted into air; into thin air;   150
    And, like the baseless fabric[109] of this vision,
    The cloud-capped towers, the gorgeous palaces,
    The solemn temples, the great globe[110] itself,
    Yea, all which it inherit,[111] shall dissolve,
    And, like this insubstantial pageant faded,
    Leave not a rack[112] behind. We are such stuff   155
    As dreams are made on,[113] and our little life
    Is rounded[114] with a sleep. Sir, I am vexed.
    Bear with my weakness. My old brain is troubled.
    Be not disturbed with[115] my infirmity.   160
    If you be pleased, retire[116] into my cell
    And there repose. A turn or two I'll walk
    To still my beating[117] mind.

FERDINAND, MIRANDA: We wish your peace.

    [Exeunt (Ferdinand and Miranda).]

---

103. Suitably.
104. Slowly, dejectedly.
105. Withdraw.
106. Affects, agitates.
107. Troubled state, condition.
108. Entertainment, pageant.
109. Unsubstantial theatrical edifice or contrivance.
110. (With a glance at the Globe Theatre.)
111. Who subsequently occupy it.
112. Wisp of cloud.
113. Of.
114. Surrounded (before birth and after death), or crowned, rounded off.
115. By.
116. Withdraw, go
117. Agitated.

PROSPERO:

Come with a thought![118] I thank thee, Ariel, Come.

[Enter Ariel.]

ARIEL:

Thy thoughts I cleave[119] to. What's thy pleasure?   165

PROSPERO: Spirit,
We must prepare to meet with Caliban.

ARIEL:

Ay, my commander. When I presented[120] Ceres,
I thought to have told thee of it, but I feared
Lest I might anger thee.

PROSPERO:

Say again, where didst thou leave these varlets?   170

ARIEL:

I told you, sir, they were red-hot with drinking;
So full of valor that they smote the air
For breathing in their faces, beat the ground
For kissing of their feet; yet always bending[121]
Towards their project. Then I beat my tabor,   175
At which, like unbacked[122] colts, they pricked their ears,
Advanced[123] their eyelids, lifted up their noses
As[124] they smelt music. So I charmed their ears
That calflike they my lowing[125] followed through
Toothed briers, sharp furzes, pricking gorse,[126] and thorns,   180
Which entered their frail shins. At last I left them
I' the filthy-mantled[127] pool beyond your cell,
There dancing up to the chins, that the foul lake
O'erstunk[128] their feet.

PROSPERO: This was well done, my bird.
Thy shape invisible retain thou still.   185
The trumpery[129] in my house, go bring it hither,
For stale[130] to catch these thieves.

ARIEL: I go, I go.   *[Exit.]*

---

118. I.e., on the instant, or, summoned by my thought, no sooner thought of than here.
119. Cling, adhere.
120. Acted the part of, or, introduced.
121. Aiming.
122. Unbroken, unridden.
123. Lifted up.
124. As if.
125. Mooing.
126. Prickly shrubs.

127. Covered with a slimy coating.
128. Smelled worse than, or, caused to stink terribly.
129. Goods, the *glistering apparel* mentioned in the following stage direction.
130. (1) Decoy; (2) out-of-fashion garments (with possible further suggestions of "horse piss," as in line 198, and "steal," pronounced like *stale*). *For stale* could also mean "fit for a prostitute."

PROSPERO:
> A devil, a born devil, on whose nature
> Nurture can never stick; on whom my pains,
> Humanely taken, all, all lost, quite lost!
> And as with age his body uglier grows,
> So his mind cankers.[131] I will plague them all,
> Even to roaring.

[Enter Ariel, loaden with glistering apparel, etc.]

> Come, hang them on this line.[132]

[(Ariel hangs up the showy finery; Prospero and Ariel remain,[133] invisible.) Enter Caliban, Stephano, and Trinculo, all wet.]

CALIBAN:
> Pray you, tread softly, that the blind mole may
> Not hear a foot fall. We now are near his cell.

STEPHANO: Monster, your fairy, which you say is a harmless fairy, has done little better than played the jack[134] with us.

TRINCULO: Monster, I do smell all horse piss, at which my nose is in great indignation.

STEPHANO: So is mine. Do you hear, monster? If I should take a displeasure against you, look you—

TRINCULO: Thou wert but a lost monster.

CALIBAN:
> Good my lord, give me thy favor still.
> Be patient, for the prize I'll bring thee to
> Shall hoodwink this mischance.[135] Therefore speak softly.
> All's hushed as midnight yet.

TRINCULO: Ay, but to lose our bottles in the pool—

STEPHANO: There is not only disgrace and dishonor in that monster, but an infinite loss.

TRINCULO: That's more to me than my wetting. Yet this is your harmless fairy, monster!

STEPHANO: I will fetch off my bottle, though I be o'er ears[136] for my labor.

CALIBAN:
> Prithee, my king, be quiet. Seest thou here,
> This is the mouth o' the cell. No noise, and enter.
> Do that good mischief which may make this island
> Thine own forever, and I thy Caliban
> For aye thy footlicker.

---

131. Festers, grows malignant.
132. Lime tree or linden.
133. (The staging is uncertain. They may instead exit here and return with the spirits at line 256.)
134. (1) Knave; (2) will-o'-the-wisp.

135. (Misfortune is to be prevented from doing further harm by being hooded like a hawk and also put out of remembrance.)
136. I.e., totally submerged and perhaps drowned.

STEPHANO: Give me thy hand. I do begin to have bloody thoughts.   220

TRINCULO *[seeing the finery]:* O King Stephano! O peer![137]

    O worthy Stephano! Look what a wardrobe here is for thee!

CALIBAN:

    Let it alone, thou fool, it is but trash.

TRINCULO Oho, monster! We know what belongs to a frippery.[138] O King

    Stephano!   *[He puts on a gown.]*   225

STEPHANO: Put off[139] that gown, Trinculo. By this hand,

    I'll have that gown.

TRINCULO Thy Grace shall have it.

CALIBAN:

    The dropsy[140] drown this fool! What do you mean

    To dote thus on such luggage?[141] Let 't alone   230

    And do the murder first. If he awake,

    From toe to crown[142] he'll fill our skins with pinches,

    Make us strange stuff.

STEPHANO: Be you quiet, monster.—Mistress line,[143] is not this my jerkin?[144] *[He*

    takes it down.] Now is the jerkin under the line.[145] Now, jerkin, you are   235

    like[146] to lose your hair and prove a bald[147] jerkin.

TRINCULO Do, do![148] We steal by line and level,[149] an 't like[150] Your Grace.

STEPHANO: I thank thee for that jest. Here's a garment for 't. *[He gives a garment.]*

    Wit shall not go unrewarded while I am king of this country. "Steal by

    line and level" is an excellent pass of pate.[151] There's another garment   240

    for 't.

TRINCULO Monster, come, put some lime[152] upon your fingers, and away with the

    rest.

CALIBAN:

    I will have none on 't. We shall lose our time,

---

137. (Alludes to the old ballad beginning,
"King Stephen was a worthy peer.")

138. Place where cast-off clothes are sold.

139. Put down, or, take off.

140. Disease characterized by the accumulation of fluid in the connective tissue of the body.

141. Cumbersome trash.

142. Head.

143. (Addressed to the linden or lime tree upon which, at line 193, Ariel hung the *glistering apparel.*)

144. Jacket made of leather.

145. Under the lime tree (with punning sense of being south of the equinoctial line or equator; sailors on long voyages to the southern regions were popularly supposed to lose their hair from scurvy or

other diseases. Stephano also quibbles bawdily on losing hair through syphilis, and in *Mistress* and *jerkin.*)

146. Likely

147. (1) Hairless, napless; (2) meager.

148. I.e., bravo. (Said in response to the jesting or to the taking of the jerkin, or both.)

149. I.e., by means of plumb lime and carpenter's level, methodically (with pun on *line,* "lime tree," line 238, and *steal,* pronounced like *stale,* i.e, prostitute, continuing Stephano's bawdy quibble).

150. If it please.

151. Sally of wit. (The metaphor is from fencing.)

152. Birdlime, sticky substance (to give Caliban sticky fingers).

And all be turned to barnacles,[153] or to apes   245
With foreheads villainous[154] low.
STEPHANO: Monster, lay to[155] your fingers. Help to bear this[156] away where my
hogshead[157] of wine is, or I'll turn you out of my kingdom. Go to,[158]
carry this.
TRINCULO And this.   250
STEPHANO: Ay, and this.

[They load Caliban with more and more garments.]

*[A noise of hunters heard. Enter divers spirits, in shape of dogs and hounds,
hunting them about, Prospero and Ariel setting them on.]*

PROSPERO: Hey, Mountain, hey!
ARIEL: Silver! There it goes, Silver!   255
PROSPERO: Fury, Fury!, There, Tyrant, there! Hark! Hark!

[Caliban, Stephano, and Trinculo are driven out.]

Go, charge my goblins that they grind their joints
With dry[159] convulsions,[160] shorten up their sinews
With aged[161] cramps, and more pinch-spotted make them
Than pard[162] or cat o' mountain.[163]
ARIEL: Hark, they roar!   260
PROSPERO:
Let them be hunted soundly.[164] At this hour
Lies at my mercy all mine enemies.
Shortly shall all my labors end, and thou
Shalt have the air at freedom. For a little[165]
Follow, and do me service.   *[Exeunt.]*   265

Act V

Scene 1[1]

[Enter Prospero in his magic robes, (with his staff) and Ariel.]

PROSPERO:
Now does my project gather to a head.

---

153. Barnacle geese, formerly supposed to be
     hatched from barnacles attached to trees
     or to rotting timber; here, evidently used,
     like *apes,* as types of simpletons.
154. Miserably.
155. Start using.
156. I.e., the *glistering apparel.*
157. Large cask.
158. (An expression of exhortation or remon-
     strance.)
159. Associated with age, arthritic (?).

160. Cramps.
161. Characteristic of old age.
162. Panther or leopard.
163. Wildcat.
164. Thoroughly (and suggesting the sounds
     of the hunt).
165. Little while longer.

Act V, Scene 1
1. Location: before Prospero's cell.

My charms crack[2] not, my spirits obey, and Time
Goes upright with his carriage.[3] How's the day?

ARIEL:
                    On[4] the sixth hour, at which time, my lord,
You said our work should cease.   5

PROSPERO: I did say so,
When first I raised the tempest. Say, my spirit,
How fares the King and 's followers?

ARIEL: Confined together
In the same fashion as you gave in charge,
Just as you left them; all prisoners, sir,
In the line grove[5] which weather-fends[6] your cell.   10
They cannot budge till your release.[7] The King,
His brother, and yours abide all three distracted,[8]
And the remainder mourning over them.
Brim full of sorrow and dismay; but chiefly
Him that you termed, sir, the good old lord, Gonzalo.   15
His tears runs down his beard like winter's drops
From eaves of reeds.[9] Your charm so strongly works 'em
That if you now beheld them your affections[10]
Would become tender.

PROSPERO: Dost thou think so, spirit?

ARIEL:

Mine would, sir, were I human.[11]   20

PROSPERO: And mine shall.
Hast thou, which art but air, a touch,[12] a feeling
Of their afflictions, and shall not myself,
One of their kind, that relish all as sharply
Passion as they,[13] be kindlier[14] moved than thou art?
Though with their high wrongs I am struck to the quick,   25
Yet with my nobler reason 'gainst my fury
Do I take part. The rarer[15] action is
In virtue than in vengeance. They being penitent,
The sole drift of my purpose doth extend
Not a frown further. Go release them, Ariel.   30

---

2. Collapse, fail. (The metaphor is probably alchemical, as in *project* and *gather to a head,* line 1.)
3. Its burden. (Time is no longer heavily burdened and so can go *upright,* "standing straight and unimpeded.")
4. Approaching.
5. Grove of lime trees.
6. Protects from the weather.
7. You release them.
8. Out of their wits.

9. Thatched roofs.
10. Disposition, feelings.
11. (Spelled *humane* in the Folio and encompassing both senses.)
12. Sense, apprehension.
13. Who experience human passions as acutely as they.
14. (1) More sympathetically; (2) more naturally, humanly
15. Nobler.

My charms I'll break, their senses I'll restore,
And they shall be themselves.

ARIEL: I'll fetch them, sir.

[Exit.]

[Prospero traces a charmed circle with his staff.]

PROSPERO:
Ye elves of hills, brooks, standing lakes, and groves,[16]
And ye that on the sands with printless foot
Do chase the ebbing Neptune, and do fly him   35
When he comes back; you demi-puppets[17] that
By moonshine do the green sour ringlets[18] make,
Whereof the ewe not bites; and you whose pastime
Is to make midnight mushrooms,[19] that rejoice
To hear the solemn curfew;[20] by whose aid,   40
Weak masters[21] though ye be, I have bedimmed
The noontide sun, called forth the mutinous winds,
And twixt the green sea and the azured vault[22]
Set roaring war; to the dread rattling thunder
Have I given fire,[23] and rifted[24] Jove's stout oak[25]   45
With his own bolt;[26] the strong-based promontory
Have I made shake, and by the spurs[27] plucked up
The pine and cedar; graves at my command
Have waked their sleepers, oped, and let 'em forth
By my so potent art. But this rough[28] magic   50
I here abjure, and when I have required[29]
Some heavenly music—which even now I do—
To work mine end upon their senses that[30]
This airy charm[31] is for, I'll break my staff,
Bury it certain fathoms in the earth,   55
And deeper than did ever plummet sound
I'll drown my book.   *[Solemn music.]*

*[Here enters Ariel before; then Alonso, with a frantic gesture, attended by
Gonzalo; Sebastian and Antonio in like manner, attended by Adrian and*

---

16. (This famous passage is an embellished paraphrase of Goldring's translation of Ovid's *Metamorphoses,* 7.197–219.)
17. Puppets of half size, i.e., elves and fairies.
18. Fairy rings, circles in grass (actually produced by mushrooms).
19. Mushrooms appearing overnight.
20. Evening bell, usually rung at nine o'clock ushering in the time when spirits are abroad.
21. I.e., subordinate spirits, as in 4.1.35 (?)
22. I.e., the sky.
23. I have discharged the dread rattling thunderbolt.
24. Riven, split.
25. A tree that was sacred to Jove.
26. Lightning bolt.
27. Roots.
28. Violent.
29. Requested.
30. The senses of those whom.
31. I.e., music.

Francisco. They all enter the circle which Prospero had made, and there stand charmed; which Prospero observing, speaks:]

[*To Alonso.*] A solemn air,[32] and[33] the best comforter
To an unsettled fancy,[34] cure thy brains,
Now useless, boiled[35] within thy skull! [*To Sebastian and Antonio.*] There
    stand, 60
For you are spell-stopped.—
Holy Gonzalo, honorable man,
Mine eyes, e'en sociable[36] to the show[37] of thine,
Fall[38] fellowly drops. [*Aside.*] The charm dissolves apace, 65
And as the morning steals upon the night,
Melting the darkness, so their rising senses
Begin to chase the ignorant fumes[39] that mantle[40]
Their clearer[41] reason.—O good Gonzalo,
My true preserver, and a loyal sir 70
To him thou follow'st! I will pay thy graces[42]
Home[43] both in word and deed.—Most cruelly
Didst thou, Alonso, use me and my daughter.
Thy brother was a furtherer[44] in the act.—
Thou art pinched[45] for 't now, Sebastian. [*To Antonio.*] Flesh and blood, 75
You, brother mine, that entertained ambition,
Expelled remorse[46] and nature,[47] whom,[48] with Sebastian,
Whose inward pinches therefore are most strong,
Would here have killed your king, I do forgive thee,
Unnatural though thou art.—Their understanding 80
Begins to swell, and the approaching tide
Will shortly fill the reasonable shore[49]
That now lies foul and muddy. Not one of them
That yet looks on me, or would know me.—Ariel,
Fetch me the hat and rapier in my cell.

[*Ariel goes to the cell and returns immediately.*]

---

32. Song.
33. I.e., which is
34. imagination
35. I.e., extremely agitated.
36. Sympathetic.
37. Appearance.
38. Let fall
39. Fumes that render them incapable of comprehension.
40. Envelop.

41. Growing clearer.
42. Requite your favors and virtues.
43. Fully.
44. Accomplice.
45. Punished, afflicted.
46. Pity.
47. Natural feeling.
48. I.e., who.
49. Shores of reason, i.e., minds. (Their reason returns, like the incoming tide.)

I will discase[50] me and myself present   85
As I was sometime Milan.[51] Quickly, spirit!
Thou shalt ere long be free.

[Ariel sings and helps to attire him.]

ARIEL:

    Where the bee sucks, there suck I.
    In a cowslip's bell I lie;
    There I couch[52] when owls do cry.   90
    On the bat's back I do fly
    After[53] summer merrily.
    Merrily, merrily shall I live now
    Under the blossom that hangs on the bough.

PROSPERO:

    Why, that's my dainty Ariel! I shall miss thee,   95
    But yet thou shalt have freedom. So, so, so.[54]
    To the King's ship, invisible as thou art!
    There shalt thou find the mariners asleep
    Under the hatches. The Master and the Boatswain
    Being awake, enforce them to this place,   100
    And presently,[55] I prithee.

ARIEL:

    I drink the air before me and return
    Or ere[56] your pulse twice beat.   *[Exit.]*

GONZALO:

    All torment, trouble, wonder, and amazement
    Inhabits here. Some heavenly power guide us   105
    Out of this fearful[57] country!

PROSPERO: Behold, sir King,
    The wronged Duke of Milan, Prospero.
    For more assurance that a living prince
    Does now speak to thee, I embrace thy body;
    And to thee and thy company I bid   110
    A hearty welcome.   *[Embracing him.]*

ALONSO: Whe'er thou be'st he or no,
    Or some enchanted trifle[58] to abuse[59] me,
    As late[60] I have been, I not know. Thy pulse

---

50. Disrobe.
51. In my former appearance as Duke of Milan.
52. Lie.
53. I.e., pursuing.
54. (Expresses approval of Ariel's help as valet.)

55. Immediately.
56. Before.
57. Frightening.
58. Trick of magic.
59. Deceive.
60. Lately.

Beats as of flesh and blood; and, since I saw thee,
Th' affliction of my mind amends, with which   115
I fear a madness held me. This must crave[61]—
An if this be at all[62]—a most strange story.[63]
Thy dukedom I resign,[64] and do entreat
Thou pardon me my wrongs.[65] But how should Prospero
Be living, and be here?
PROSPERO *[to Gonzalo]:* First, noble friend,
    Let me embrace thine age,[66] whose honor cannot
    Be measured or continued.   *[Embracing him.]*
GONZALO: Whether this be
    Or be not, I'll not swear.
PROSPERO: You do yet taste
    Some subtleties[67] o' th' isle, that will not let you
    Believe things certain. Welcome, my friends all!   125
    [Aside to Sebastian and Antonio.] But you, my brace[68] of lords, were I so
        minded,
    I here could pluck His Highness' frown upon you
    And justify you[69] traitors. At this time
    I will tell no tales.
SEBASTIAN: The devil speaks in him.
PROSPERO: No.
    [To Antonio.] For you, most wicked sir, whom to call brother   130
    Would even infect my mouth, I do forgive
    Thy rankest fault—all of them; and require
    My dukedom of thee, which perforce[70] I know
    Thou must restore.
ALONSO: If thou be'st Prospero,
    Give us particulars of thy preservation,   135
    How thou hast met us here, whom[71] three hours since
    Were wrecked upon this shore; where I have lost—
    How sharp the point of this remembrance is!—
    My dear son Ferdinand.
PROSPERO: I am woe[72] for 't, sir.
ALONSO:
    Irreparable is the loss, and Patience   140
    Says it is past her cure.

---

61. Require.
62. If this is actually happening.
63. I.e., explanation.
64. (Alonso made arrangement with Antonio
    at the time of Prospero's banishment for
    Milan to pay tribute to Naples; see
    1.2.113–127.)
65. Wrongdoings.

66. Your venerable self.
67. Illusions, magical powers (playing on the
    idea of "pastries, concoctions").
68. Pair.
69. Prove you to be
70. Necessarily.
71. I.e., who.
72. Sorry.

PROSPERO: I rather think
   You have not sought her help, of whose soft grace[73]
   For the like loss I have her sovereign[74] aid
   And rest myself content.
ALONSO: You the like loss?
PROSPERO:
   As great to me as late,[75] and supportable   145
   To make the dear loss, have I[76] means much weaker
   Than you may call to comfort you; for I
   Have lost my daughter.
ALONSO: A daughter?
   O heavens, that they were living both in Naples,   150
   The king and queen there! That[77] they were, I wish
   Myself were mudded[78] in that oozy bed
   Where my son lies. When did you lose your daughter?
PROSPERO:
   In this last tempest. I perceive these lords
   At this encounter do so much admire[79]   155
   That they devour their reason[80] and scarce think
   Their eyes do offices of truth, their words
   Are natural breath.[81] But, howsoever you have
   Been jostled from your senses, know for certain
   That I am Prospero and that very duke   160
   Which was thrust forth of[82] Milan, who most strangely
   Upon this shore, where you were wrecked, was landed
   To be the lord on 't. No more yet of this,
   For 'tis a chronicle of day by day.[83]
   Not a relation for a breakfast nor   165
   Befitting this first meeting. Welcome, sir.
   This cell's my court. Here have I few attendants,
   And subjects none abroad.[84] Pray you, look in.
   My dukedom since you have given me again,
   I will requite[85] you with as good a thing,   170
   At least bring forth a wonder to content ye
   As much as me my dukedom.

[*Here Prospero discovers*[86] *Ferdinand and Miranda, playing at chess.*]

---

73. By whose mercy
74. Efficacious.
75. Recent.
76. To make the deeply felt loss bearable, I have.
77. So that.
78. Buried in the mud.
79. Wonder
80. I.e., are openmouthed, dumbfounded.

81. Scarcely believe that their eyes inform them accurately as to what they see or that their words are naturally spoken.
82. From.
83. Requiring days to tell.
84. Away from here, anywhere else.
85. Repay.
86. I.e., by opening a curtain, presumably rearstage.

MIRANDA: Sweet lord, you play me false.[87] *press your advantage*

FERDINAND: No, my dearest love,
   I would not for the world.   175

MIRANDA:
   Yes, for a score of kingdoms you should wrangle,
   And I would call it fair play.[88]

ALONSO: If this prove
   A vision[89] of the island, one dear son
   Shall I twice lose.

SEBASTIAN: A most high miracle!

FERDINAND *[approaching his father]*:
   Though the seas threaten, they are merciful;   180
   I have cursed them without cause.   *[He kneels.]*

ALONSO: Now all the blessings
   Of a glad father compass[90] thee about!
   Arise, and say how thou cam'st here.

[Ferdinand rises.]

MIRANDA: O, wonder!
   How many goodly creatures are there here!
   How beauteous mankind is! O brave[91] new world   185
   That has such people in 't!

PROSPERO: 'Tis new to thee.

ALONSO:
   What is this maid with whom thou wast at play?
   Your eld'st[92] acquaintance cannot be three hours.
   Is she goddess that hath severed us,
   And brought us thus together?   *Miranda a Goddess?*   190

FERDINAND: Sir, she is mortal;
   But by immortal Providence she's mine.
   I chose her when I could not ask my father
   For his advice, nor thought I had one. She
   Is daughter to this famous Duke of Milan,
   Of whom so often I have heard renown,   195
   But never saw before; of whom I have
   Received a second life; and second father
   This lady makes him to me.

---

87. I.e., press your advantage
88. I.e., yes, even if we were playing for twenty kingdoms, something less than the whole world, you would still press your advantage against me, and I would lovingly let you do it as though it were fair play, or, if you were to play not just for stakes but literally for kingdoms, my complaint would be out of order in that your "wrangling" would be proper
89. Illusion.
90. Encompass, embrace.
91. Splendid, gorgeously appareled, handsome.
92. Longest.

ALONSO: I am hers.
    But O, how oddly will it sound that I
    Must ask my child forgiveness!   200
PROSPERO: There, sir, stop.
    Let us not burden our remembrances with
    A heaviness[93] that's gone.
GONZALO: I have inly[94] wept,
    Or should have spoke ere this. Look down, you gods,
    And on this couple drop a blessed crown!
    For it is you that have chalked forth the way[95]   205
    Which brought us hither.
ALONSO: I say amen, Gonzalo!
GONZALO:
    Was Milan thrust from Milan,[96] that his issue
    Should become kings of Naples? O, rejoice
    Beyond a common joy, and set it down
    With gold on lasting pillars: In one voyage   210
    Did Claribel her husband find at Tunis,
    And Ferdinand, her brother, found a wife
    Where he himself was lost; Prospero his dukedom
    In a poor isle; and all of us ourselves
    When no man was his own.[97]   215
ALONSO: *[to Ferdinand and Miranda]:* Give me your hands.
    Let grief and sorrow still[98] embrace his[99] heart
    That[100] doth not wish you joy!
GONZALO: Be it so! Amen!

[Enter Ariel, with the Master and Boatswain amazedly following.]

    O, look, sir, look, sir! Here is more of us.
    I prophesied, if a gallows were on land,
    This fellow could not drown.—Now, blasphemy,[101] 220
    That swear'st grace o'erboard,[102] not an oath[103] on shore?
    Hast thou no mouth by land? What is the news?
BOATSWAIN:
    The best news is that we have safely found
    Our King and company; the next, our ship—
    Which, but three glasses[104] since, we gave out[105] split— 225

---

93. Sadness.
94. Inwardly.
95. Marked as with a piece of chalk the pathway.
96. Was the Duke of Milan.
97. All of us have found ourselves and our sanity when we all had lost our senses.
98. Always.

99. That person's.
100. Who.
101. I.e., blasphemer.
102. I.e., you who banish heavenly grace from the ship by your blasphemies.
103. Aren't you going to swear an oath
104. I.e., hours.
105. Reported, professed to be.

Is tight and yare[106] and bravely[107] rigged as when
We first put out to sea.

ARIEL: *[aside to Prospero]:* Sir, all this service
Have I done since I went.

PROSPERO: *[aside to Ariel]:* My tricksy[108] spirit!

ALONSO:
These are not natural events; they strengthen[109]
From strange to stranger. Say, how came you hither? 230

BOATSWAIN:
If I did think, sir, I were well awake,
I'd strive to tell you. We were dead of sleep,[110]
And—how we know not—all clapped under hatches,
Where but even now, with strange and several[111] noises
Of roaring, shrieking, howling, jingling chains, 235
And more diversity of sounds, all horrible,
We were awaked; straightway at liberty;
Where we, in all her trim, freshly beheld
Our royal, good, and gallant ship, our Master
Cap'ring to eye her.[112] On a trice,[113] so please you, 240
Even in a dream, were we divided from them[114]
And were brought moping[115] hither.

ARIEL: *[aside to Prospero]:* Was 't well done?

PROSPERO: *[aside to Ariel]:*
Bravely, my diligence. Thou shalt be free. *Still telling (promising) Ariel freedom.*

ALONSO:
This is as strange a maze as e'er men trod,
And there is in this business more than nature 245
Was ever conduct[116] of. Some oracle
Must rectify our knowledge.

PROSPERO: Sir, my liege,
Do not infest[117] your mind with beating on[118]
The strangeness of this business. At picked[119] leisure,
Which shall be shortly, single[120] I'll resolve[121] you, 250
Which to you shall seem probable,[122] of every
These[123] happened accidents;[124] till when, be cheerful
And think of each thing well.[125] *[Aside to Ariel.]* Come hither, spirit.

---

106. Ready.
107. Splendidly.
108. Ingenious, sportive.
109. Increase.
110. Deep in sleep.
111. Diverse.
112. Dancing for joy to see.
113. In an instant.
114. I.e., the other crew members.
115. In a daze.

116. Guide.
117. Harass, disturb.
118. Worrying about.
119. Chosen, convenient.
120. Privately, by my own human powers.
121. Satisfy, explain to.
122. Plausible.
123. About every one of these.
124. Occurrences.
125. Favorably.

Set Caliban and his companions free.
Untie the spell. *[Exit Ariel.]* How fares my gracious sir?   255
There are yet missing of your company
Some few odd[126] lads that you remember not.

[Enter Ariel, driving in Caliban, Stephano, and Trinculo, in their stolen apparel]

STEPHANO: Every man shift[127] for all the rest,[128] and let no man take care for himself; for all is but fortune. Coragio,[129] bully monster,[130] coragio!   260

TRINCULO: If these be true spies[131] which I wear in my head, here's a goodly sight.

CALIBAN:
O Setebos, these be brave[132] spirits indeed!
How fine[133] my master is! I am afraid
He will chastise me.   265

SEBASTIAN: Ha, ha!
What things are these, my lord Antonio?
Will money buy 'em?

ANTONIO: Very like. One of them
Is a plain fish, and no doubt marketable.

PROSPERO:
Mark but the badges[134] of these men, my lords,   270
Then say if they be true.[135] This misshapen knave,
His mother was a witch, and one so strong
That could control the moon, make flows and ebbs,
And deal in her command without her power.[136]
These three have robbed me, and this demidevil—   275
For he's a bastard[137] one—had plotted with them
To take my life. Two of these fellows you
Must know and own.[138] This thing of darkness I
Acknowledge mine.

CALIBAN: I shall be pinched to death.

ALONSO:
Is not this Stephano, my drunken butler?   280

SEBASTIAN: He is drunk now. Where had he wine?

---

126. Unaccounted for.
127. Provide.
128. (Stephano drunkenly gets wrong the saying "Every man for himself.")
129. Courage.
130. Gallant monster. (Ironical.)
131. Accurate observers (i.e., sharp eyes)
132. Handsome.
133. Splendidly attired
134. Emblems of cloth or silver worn by re-

tainers to indicate whom they serve. (Prospero refers here to the stolen clothes as emblems of their villainy.)
135. Honest.
136. Wield the moon's power, either without her authority or beyond her influence, or, even though to do so was beyond Sycorax's own power
137. Counterfeit.
138. Recognize, admit as belonging to you.

ALONSO:
>And Trinculo is reeling ripe.[139] Where should they
>Find this grand liquor that hath gilded[140] 'em?
>[To Trinculo.] How cam'st thou in this pickle?[141]

TRINCULO: I have been in such a pickle since I saw you last that, I fear me, will   285
never out of my bones. I shall not fear flyblowing.[142]

SEBASTIAN: Why, how now, Stephano?

STEPHANO: O, touch me not! I am not Stephano, but a cramp.

PROSPERO: You'd be king o' the isle, sirrah?[143]   290

STEPHANO: I should have been a sore[144] one, then.

ALONSO: [pointing to Caliban]:
>This is a strange thing as e'er I looked on.

PROSPERO:
>He is as disproportioned in his manners
>As in his shape.—Go, sirrah, to my cell.
>Take with you your companions. As you look   295
>To have my pardon, trim[145] it handsomely.

CALIBAN:
>Ay, that I will; and I'll be wise hereafter
>And seek for grace.[146] What a thrice-double ass
>Was I to take this drunkard for a god
>And worship this dull fool!   300

PROSPERO: Go to. Away!

ALONSO:
>Hence, and bestow your luggage where you found it.

SEBASTIAN: Or stole it, rather.

>[Exeunt Caliban, Stephano, and Trinculo.]

PROSPERO:
>Sir, I invite Your Highness and your train
>To my poor cell, where you shall take your rest
>For this one night; which, part of it, I'll waste[147]   305
>With such discourse as, I not doubt, shall make it
>Go quick away: the story of my life,
>And the particular accidents[148] gone by
>Since I came to this isle. And in the morn

---

139. Stumblingly drunk.
140. (1) Flushed, made drunk; (2) covered with gilt (suggesting the horse urine)
141. (1) Fix, predicament (2) pickling brine (in this case, horse urine).
142. I.e., being fouled by fly eggs (from which he is saved by being pickled).
143. (Standard form of address to an inferior, here expressing reprimand.)

144. (1) Tyrannical; (2) sorry, inept; (3) wracked by pain.
145. Prepare, decorate.
146. Pardon, favor.
147. Spend.
148. Occurrences.

I'll bring you to your ship, and so to Naples,   310
Where I have hope to see the nuptial
Of these our dear-beloved solemnized;
And thence retire me[149] to my Milan, where
Every third thought shall be my grave.

ALONSO: I long
To hear the story of your life, which must   315
Take[150] the ear strangely.

PROSPERO: I'll deliver[151] all;
And promise you calm seas, auspicious gales,
And sail so expeditious that shall catch
Your royal fleet far off.[152] *[Aside to Ariel.]* My Ariel, chick,
That is thy charge. Then to the elements   320
Be free, and fare thou well!—Please you, draw near.[153]

[Exeunt omnes (except Prospero).]

Epilogue

[Spoken by PROSPERO.]

Now my charms are all o'erthrown,
And what strength I have 's mine own,
Which is most faint. Now, 'tis true,
I must be here confined by you
Or set to Naples. Let me not,   5
Since I have my dukedom got
And pardoned the deceiver, dwell
In this bare island by your spell,
But release me from my bands[1]   *Bonds*
With the help of your good hands.[2]   *applause*   10
Gentle breath[3] of yours my sails   *breeze from hand clapping*
Must fill, or else my project fails,
Which was to please. Now I want[4]   *Lack*
Spirits to enforce,[5] art to enchant, *control*
And my ending is despair,   15
Unless I be relieved by prayer,[6]   *petition to the audience for approval*

---

149. Return.
150. Take effect upon, enchant.
151. Declare, relate.
152. Enable you to catch up with the main part of your royal fleet, now afar off enroute to Naples (see 1.2.235–236)
153. I.e., enter my cell.

Epilogue

1. Bonds.
2. I.e., applause (the noise of which would break the spell of silence).
3. Favorable breeze (produced by hands clapping or favorable comment).
4. Lack.
5. Control.
6. I.e., Prospero's petition to the audience.

Which pierces so that it assaults[7] *gains attention*
Mercy itself, and frees[8] all faults. *Obtaines forgiveness*
As you from crimes[9] would pardoned be, *sins*
Let your indulgence[10] set me free. *approval*

[Exit.]   20

JOHN DONNE (1572–1631)
England

John Donne was born in London in 1572 to a good family; he was reared as a Roman Catholic, attended Oxford, Cambridge, and Lincoln's Inn, where he was well educated in theology and law. Overcoming his own religious scruples, he was ordained an Anglican priest in 1615. He became dean of Saint Paul's Cathedral in London in 1621, and was famous for the sermons he preached there. Throughout his lifetime, Donne composed poetry, concerned with both love (in the various senses of the word including the erotic) and religion, which was only published after his death in 1631. The main figure of the group known as the metaphysical poets, Donne is now recognized as the greatest lyric poet in English of his time.

Holy Sonnet [Death be not proud]

Death be not proud, though some have called thee
Mighty and dreadfull, for, thou are not soe,
For, those, whom thou think'st, thou dost overthrow,
Die not, poore death, nor yet canst thou kill mee;
From rest and sleepe, which but thy pictures bee,   5
Much pleasure, then from thee, much more must flow,
And soonest our best men with thee doe goe,
Rest of their bones, and soules deliverie.
Thou'art slave to Fate, chance, kings, and desperate men,
And dost with poyson, warre, and sickness dwell,   10
And poppie, 'or charmes can make us sleepe as well,
And better then thy stroke; why swell'st thou then?
One short sleepe past, wee wake eternally,
And death shall be no more, Death thou shalt die.

---

7. Rightfully gains the attention of.
8. Obtains forgiveness for.
9. Sins.

10. (1) humoring, lenient approval; (2) remission of punishment for sin.

Holy Sonnet [*Batter my heart, three person'd God*]

Batter my heart, three person'd God; for, you
As yet but knocke, breathe, shine, and seeke to mend;
That I may rise, and stand, o'erthrow mee, 'and bend
Your force, to breake, blowe, burn and make me new.
I, like an usurpt towne, to'another due,   5
Labour to'admit you, but Oh, to no end,
Reason your viceroy in mee, mee should defend,
But is captiv'd, and proves weake or untrue,
Yet dearely'I love you, and would be lov'd faine,
But am betroth'd unto your enemie,   10
Divorce mee,'untie, or breake that knot againe,
Take mee to you, imprison mee, for I
Except you'enthrall mee, never shall be free,
Nor ever chast, except you ravish mee.

Goodfriday, 1613. Riding Westward.

Let man's Soule be a Spheare, and then, in this,
The'intelligence that moves, devotion is,
And as the other Spheares, by being growne
Subject to forraigne motions, lose their owne,
And being by others hurried every day,   5
Scarce in a yeare their naturall forme obey:
Pleasure or businesse, so, our Soules admit
For their first mover, and are whirld by it.
Hence is't, that I am carryed towards the West
This day, when my Soules forme bends toward the East.   10
There I should see a Sunne, by rising set,
And by that setting endlesse day beget;
But that Christ on this Crosse, did rise and fall,
Sinne had eternally benighted all.
Yet dare I'almost be glad, I do not see   15
That spectacle of too much weight for mee.
Who sees Gods face, that is selfe life, must dye;
What a death were it then to see God dye?
It made his owne Lieutenant Nature shrinke,
It made his footstoole crack, and the Sunne winke.   20
Could I behold those hands which span the Poles,
And turne all spheares at once peirc'd with those holes?
Could I behold that endlesse height which is
Zenith to us, and to'our Antipodes,
Humbled below us? or that blood which is   25
The seat of all our Soules, if not of his,
Make durt of dust, or that flesh which was worne

By God, for his apparell, rag'd, and torne?
If on these things I durst not looke, durst I
Upon his miserable mother cast mine eye,   30
Who was Gods partner here, and furnish'd thus
Halfe of that Sacrifice, which ransom'd us?
Though these things, as I ride, be from mine eye,
They'are present yet unto my memory,
For that looks towards them; and thou look'st towards mee,   35
O Saviour, as thou hang'st upon the tree;
I turne my backe to thee, but to receive
Corrections, till thy mercies bid thee leave.
O thinke mee worth thine anger, punish mee,
Burne off my rusts, and my deformity,   40
Restore thine Image, so much, by thy grace,
That thou may'st know mee, and I'll turne my face.

The Anniversary

All kings, and all their favorites,
    All glory' of honors, beauties, wits,
The sun itself, which makes times, as they pass,
Is elder by a year, now, than it was
When thou and I first one another saw;   5
All other things to their destruction draw,
    Only our love hath no decay;
This, no tomorrow hath, nor yesterday;
Running it never runs from us away,
But truly keeps his first, last, everlasting day,   10

    Two graves must hide thine and my corse;
If one might, death were no divorce:
Alas, as well as other princes, we
(Who prince enough in one another be)
Must leave at last in death, these eyes, and ears,   15
Oft fed with true oaths, and with sweet salt tears;
    But souls where nothing dwells but love
(All other thoughts being inmates) then shall prove
This, or a love increaséd there above,
When bodies to their graves, souls from their graves remove.   20

    And then we shall be throughly blest,
But we no more than all the rest;
Here upon earth, we're kings, and none but we
Can be such kings, nor of such subjects be;

Who is so safe as we, where none can do 25
Treason to us, except one of us two?
   True and false fears let us refrain,
Let us love nobly, 'and live, and add again
Years and years unto years, till we attain
To write threescore, this is the second of our reign. 30

JOHN MILTON (1608–1674)
England

John Milton was born in London in 1608 and was educated at St. Paul's School
and Cambridge University, afterward making a long trip to Italy, on a two-year
European tour, to perfect his learning. He devoted himself to the Puritan cause
and primary school,—then becoming Latin secretary to Cromwell. By 1652, at
the age of 44, he had lost his eyesight from too much intense work; hampered
by political disappointments in later life, he consecrated himself exclusively to
his poetry until his death in 1674. His greatest work is *Paradise Lost,* first
published in 1667. It is an epic poem dealing with God's creation of the universe,
Satan's revolt against God, and especially the fall of Adam and Eve through their
original sin, which has tainted all humankind. The poem, controversial from
Milton's own time on, is regarded as one of the great monuments of English
literature.

from *Paradise Lost*

From Book 1 *[Of Man's First Disobedience]*

Of Man's First Disobedience, and the Fruit
Of that Forbidden Tree, whose mortal taste
Brought Death into the World, and all our woe,
With loss of *Eden,* till one greater Man
Restore us, and regain the blissful Seat, 5
Sing Heav'nly Muse, that on the secret top
Of *Oreb,* or of *Sinai,* didst inspire
That Shepherd, who first taught the chosen Seed,
In the Beginning how the Heav'ns and Earth
Rose out of *Chaos:* Or if *Sion* Hill 10
Delight thee more, and *Siloa's* Brook that flow'd
Fast by the Oracle of God; I thence

Invoke thy aid to my advent'rous Song,
That with no middle flight intends to soar
Above th' *Aonian* Mount,[1] while it pursues   15
Things unattempted yet in Prose or Rhyme.
And chiefly Thou O Spirit, that dost prefer
Before all Temples th' upright heart and pure,
Instruct me, for Thou know'st; Thou from the first
Wast present, and with mighty wings outspread   20
Dove-like satst brooding on the vast Abyss
And mad'st it pregnant: What in me is dark
Illumine, what is low raise and support;
That to the highth of this great Argument
I may assert Eternal Providence,   25
And justify the ways of God to men.
    Say first, the Heav'n hides nothing from thy view
Nor the deep Tract of Hell, say first what cause
Mov'd our Grand Parents in that happy State,
Favor'd of Heav'n so highly, to fall off   30
From thir Creator, and transgress his Will
For one restraint, Lords of the World besides?
Who first seduc'd them to that foul revolt?
Th' infernal Serpent;[2] hee it was, whose guile
Stirr'd up with Envy and Revenge, deceiv'd   35
The Mother of Mankind; what time his Pride
Had cast him out from Heav'n, with all his Host
Of Rebel Angels, by whose aid aspiring
To set himself in Glory above his Peers,
He trusted to have equall'd the most High,   40
If he oppos'd; and with ambitious aim
Against the Throne and Monarchy of God
Rais'd impious War in Heav'n and Battle proud
With vain attempt. Him the Almighty Power
Hurl'd headlong flaming from th' Ethereal Sky   45
With hideous ruin and combustion down
To bottomless perdition, there to dwell
In Adamantine Chains and penal Fire,
Who durst defy th' Omnipotent to Arms.
Nine times the Space that measures Day and Night   50
To mortal men, hee with his horrid crew
Lay vanquisht, rolling in the fiery Gulf
Confounded though immortal: But his doom
Reserv'd him to more wrath; for now the thought

---

1. Mount Helicon, sacred to the Muses, the
   goddesses of classical poetic inspiration.

2. Satan, the archangel whose revolt against
   God has just been defeated.

Both of lost happiness and lasting pain   55
Torments him, round he throws his baleful eyes
That witness'd huge affliction and dismay
Mixt with obdúrate pride and steadfast hate:
At once as far as Angels' ken he views
The dismal Situation waste and wild,   60
A Dungeon horrible, on all sides round
As one great Furnace flam'd, yet from those flames
No light, but rather darkness visible
Serv'd only to discover sights of woe,
Regions of sorrow, doleful shades, where peace   65
And rest can never dwell, hope never comes
That comes to all; but torture without end
Still urges, and a fiery Deluge, fed
With ever-burning Sulphur unconsum'd:
Such place Eternal Justice had prepar'd   70
For those rebellious, here thir Prison ordained
In utter darkness, and thir portion set
As far remov'd from God and light of Heav'n
As from the Center thrice to th' utmost Pole.
O how unlike the place from whence they fell!   75
There the companions of his fall, o'erwhelm'd
With Floods and Whirlwinds of tempestuous fire,
He soon discerns, and welt'ring by his side
One next himself in power, and next in crime,
Long after known in *Palestine,* and nam'd   80
Beëlzebub. To whom th' Arch-Enemy,
And thence in Heav'n call'd Satan, with bold words
Breaking the horrid silence thus began.
    If thou beest hee; But O how fall'n! how chang'd
From him, who in the happy Realms of Light   85
Cloth'd with transcendent brightness didst outshine
Myriads though bright: If he whom mutual league,
United thoughts and counsels, equal hope,
And hazard in the Glorious Enterprise,
Join'd with me once, now misery hath join'd   90
In equal ruin: into what Pit thou seest
From what highth fall'n, so much the stronger prov'd
He with his Thunder: and till then who knew
The force of those dire Arms? yet not for those,
Nor what the Potent Victor in his rage   95
Can else inflict, do I repent or change,
Though chang'd in outward luster; that fixt mind
And high disdain, from sense of injur'd merit,
That with the mightiest rais'd me to contend,

And to the fierce contention brought along 100
Innumerable force of Spirits arm'd
That durst dislike his reign, and mee preferring,
His utmost power with adverse power oppos'd
In dubious Battle on the Plains of Heav'n,
And shook his throne. What though the field be lost? 105
All is not lost; the unconquerable Will,
And study of revenge, immortal hate,
And courage never to submit or yield:
And what is else not to be overcome?
That Glory never shall his wrath or might 110
Extort from me. To bow and sue for grace
With suppliant knee, and deify his power
Who from the terror of this Arm so late
Doubted his Empire, that were low indeed,
That were an ignominy and shame beneath 115
This downfall; since by Fate the strength of Gods
And this Empyreal substance cannot fail,
Since through experience of this great event
In Arms not worse, in foresight much advanc't,
We may with more successful hope resolve 120
To wage by force or guile eternal War
Irreconcilable to our grand Foe,
Who now triúmphs, and in th' excess of joy
Sole reigning holds thy Tyranny of Heav'n.

From Book 4 [Two of far nobler shape erect and tall]

Two of far nobler shape erect and tall,
Godlike erect, with native Honor clad
In naked Majesty seem'd Lords of all,
And worthy seem'd, for in thir looks Divine
The image of thir glorious Maker shone, 5
Truth, Wisdom, Sanctitude severe and pure,
Severe, but in true filial freedom plac't;
Whence true authority in men; though both
Not equal, as thir sex not equal seem'd;
For contemplation hee and valor form'd, 10
For softness shee and sweet attractive Grace,
Hee for God only, shee for God in him:
His fair large Front and Eye sublime declar'd
Absolute rule; and Hyacinthine Locks
Round from his parted forelock manly hung 15
Clust'ring, but not beneath his shoulders broad:

Shee as a veil down to the slender waist
Her unadorned golden tresses wore
Dishevell'd, but in wanton ringlets wav'd
As the Vine curls her tendrils, which impli'd   20
Subjection, but requir'd with gentle sway,
And by her yielded, by him best receiv'd,
Yielded with coy submission, modest pride,
And sweet reluctant amorous delay.
Nor those mysterious parts were then conceal'd,   25
Then was not guilty shame: dishonest shame
Of Nature's works, honor dishonorable,
Sin-bred, how have ye troubl'd all mankind
With shows instead, mere shows of seeming pure,
And banisht from man's life his happiest life,   30
Simplicity and spotless innocence.
So pass'd they naked on, nor shunn'd the sight
Of God or Angel, for they thought no ill:
So hand in hand they pass'd, the loveliest pair
That ever since in love's imbraces met,   35
Adam the goodliest man of men since born
His Sons, the fairest of her Daughters *Eve.*
Under a tuft of shade that on a green
Stood whispering soft, by a fresh Fountain side
They sat them down, and after no more toil   40
To thir sweet Gard'ning labor than suffic'd
To recommend cool *Zephyr,* and made ease
More easy, wholesome thirst and appetite
More grateful, to thir Supper Fruits they fell,
Nectarine Fruits which the compliant boughs   45
Yielded them, side-long as they sat recline
On the soft downy Bank damaskt with flow'rs:
The savory pulp they chew, and in the rind
Still as they thirsted scoop the brimming stream;
Nor gentle purpose, nor endearing smiles   50
Wanted, nor youthful dalliance as beseems
Fair couple, linkt in happy nuptial League,
Alone as they. About them frisking play'd
All Beasts of th' Earth, since wild, and of all chase
In Wood or Wilderness, Forest or Den;   55
Sporting the Lion ramp'd, and in his paw
Dandl'd the Kid; Bears, Tigers, Ounces, Pards
Gamboll'd before them, th' unwieldy Elephant
To make them mirth us'd all his might, and wreath'd
His Lithe Proboscis; close the Serpent sly   60
Insinuating, wove with Gordian twine

His braided train, and of his fatal guile
Gave proof unheeded; others on the grass
Coucht, and now fill'd with pasture gazing sat,
Or Bedward ruminating; for the Sun   65
Declin'd was hasting now with prone career
To th' Ocean Isles, and in th' ascending Scale
Of Heav'n the Stars that usher Evening rose:
When *Satan* still in *gaze*, as first he stood,
Scarce thus at length fail'd speech recover'd sad.   70
     O Hell! what do mine eyes with grief behold,
Into our room of bliss thus high advanc't
Creatures of other mould, earth-born perhaps,
Not Spirits, yet to heav'nly Spirits bright
Little inferior; whom my thoughts pursue   75
With wonder, and could love, so lively shines
In them Divine resemblance, and such grace
The hand that form'd them on thir shape hath pour'd.
Ah gentle pair, yee little think how nigh
Your change approaches, when all these delights   80
Will vanish and deliver ye to woe,
More woe, the more your taste is now of joy;
Happy, but for so happy ill secur'd
Long to continue, and this high seat your Heav'n
Ill fenc't for Heav'n to keep out such a foe   85
As now is enter'd; yet no purpos'd foe
To you whom I could pity thus forlorn
Though I unpitied: League with you I seek,
And mutual amity so strait, so close,
That I with you must dwell, or you with me   90
Henceforth; my dwelling haply may not please
Like this fair Paradise, your sense, yet such
Accept your Maker's work; he gave it me,
Which I as freely give; Hell shall unfold,
To entertain you two, her widest Gates,   95
And send forth all her Kings; there will be room,
Not like these narrow limits, to receive
Your numerous offspring; if no better place,
Thank him who puts me loath to this revenge
On you who wrong me not for him who wrong'd.   100
And should I at your harmless innocence
Melt, as I do, yet public reason just,
Honor and Empire with revenge enlarg'd,
By conquering this new World, compels me now
To do what else though damn'd I should abhor.   105

From Book 9 [Confounded long they sat, as struck'n mute]

Confounded long they sat, as struck'n mute,[3]
Till *Adam,* though not less than *Eve* abasht,
At length gave utterance to these words constrain'd.
    O *Eve,* in evil hour thou didst give ear
To that false Worm, of whomsoever taught   5
To counterfeit Man's voice, true in our Fall,
False in our promis'd Rising; since our Eyes
Op'n'd we find indeed, and find we know
Both Good and Evil, Good lost, and Evil got,
Bad Fruit of Knowledge, if this be to know,   10
Which leaves us naked thus, of Honor void,
Of Innocence, of Faith, of Purity,
Our wonted Ornaments now soil'd and stain'd,
And in our Faces evident the signs
Of foul concupiscence; whence evil store;   15
Even shame, the last of evils; of the first
Be sure then. How shall I behold the face
Henceforth of God or Angel, erst with joy
And rapture so oft beheld? those heav'nly shapes
Will dazzle now this earthly, with thir blaze   20
Insufferably bright. O might I here
In solitude live savage, in some glade
Obscur'd, where highest Woods impenetrable
To Star or Sun-light, spread thir umbrage broad,
And brown as Evening: Cover me ye Pines,   25
Ye Cedars, with innumerable boughs
Hide me, where I may never see them more.
But let us now, as in bad plight, devise
What best may for the present serve to hide
The Parts of each from other, that seem most   30
To shame obnoxious, and unseemliest seen,
Some Tree whose broad smooth Leaves together sew'd,
And girded on our loins, may cover round
Those middle parts, that this new comer, Shame,
There sit not, and reproach us as unclean.   35
    So counsell'd hee, and both together went
Into the thickest Wood, there soon they chose
The Figtree, not that kind for Fruit renown'd,

---

3. At this point Satan in the form of a serpent has persuaded Eve to eat the fruit of the Tree of Knowledge, and she has persuaded Adam to eat it as well.

But such as at this day to *Indians* known
In *Malabar* or *Decan* spreads her Arms   40
Branching so broad and long, that in the ground
The bended Twigs take root, and Daughters grow
About the Mother Tree, a Pillar'd shade
High overarch't, and echoing Walks between;
There oft the *Indian* Herdsman shunning heat   45
Shelters in cool, and tends his pasturing Herds
At Loopholes cut through thickest shade: Those Leaves
They gather'd, broad as *Amazonian* Targe,
And with what skill they had, together sew'd,
To gird thir waist, vain Covering if to hide   50
Thir guilt and dreaded shame; O how unlike
To that first naked Glory. Such of late
Columbus found th' *American* so girt
With feather'd Cincture, naked else and wild
Among the Trees on Isles and woody Shores.   55
Thus fenc't, and as they thought, thir shame in part
Cover'd, but not at rest or ease of Mind,
They sat them down to weep, nor only Tears
Rain'd at thir Eyes, but high Winds worse within
Began to rise, high Passions, Anger, Hate,   60
Mistrust, Suspicion, Discord, and shook sore
Thir inward State of Mind, calm Region once
And full of Peace, now toss't and turbulent:
For Understanding rul'd not, and the Will
Heard not her lore, both in subjection now   65
To sensual Appetite, who from beneath
Usurping over sovran Reason claim'd
Superior sway: From thus distemper'd breast,
Adam, estrang'd in look and alter'd style,
Speech intermitted thus to *Eve* renew'd.   70
     Would thou hadst heark'n'd to my words, and stay'd
With me, as I besought thee, when that strange
Desire of wand'ring this unhappy Morn,
I know not whence possess'd thee; we had then
Remain'd still happy, not as now, despoil'd   75
Of all our good, sham'd, naked, miserable.
Let none henceforth seek needless cause to approve
The Faith they owe; when earnestly they seek
Such proof, conclude, they then begin to fail.
     To whom soon mov'd with touch of blame thus *Eve*.   80
What words have past thy Lips, *Adam* severe,
Imput'st thou that to my default, or will

Of wand'ring, as thou call'st it, which who knows
But might as ill have happ'n'd thou being by,
Or to thyself perhaps: hadst thou been there,   85
Or here th' attempt, thou couldst not have discern'd
Fraud in the Serpent, speaking as he spake;
No ground of enmity between us known,
Why hee should mean me ill, or seek to harm.
Was I to have never parted from thy side?   90
As good have grown there still a lifeless Rib.
Being as I am, why didst not thou the Head
Command me absolutely not to go,
Going into such danger as thou said'st?
Too facile then thou didst not much gainsay,   95
Nay, didst permit, approve, and fair dismiss.
Hadst thou been firm and fixt in thy dissent,
Neither had I transgress'd, nor thou with mee.
     To whom then first incenst *Adam* repli'd.
Is this the Love, is this the recompense   100
Of mine to thee, ingrateful *Eve,* express't
Immutable when thou wert lost, not I,
Who might have liv'd and joy'd immortal bliss,
Yet willingly chose rather Death with thee:
And am I now upbraided, as the cause   105
Of thy transgressing? not enough severe,
It seems, in thy restraint: what could I more?
I warn'd thee, I admonish'd thee, foretold
The danger, and the lurking Enemy
That lay in wait; beyond this had been force,   110
And force upon free Will hath here no place.
But confidence then bore thee on, secure
Either to meet no danger, or to find
Matter of glorious trial; and perhaps
I also err'd in overmuch admiring   115
What seem'd in thee so perfet, that I thought
No evil durst attempt thee, but I rue
That error now, which is become my crime,
And thou th' accuser. Thus it shall befall
Him who to worth in Woman overtrusting   120
Lets her Will rule; restraint she will not brook,
And left to herself, if evil thence ensue,
Shee first his weak indulgence will accuse.
     Thus they in mutual accusation spent
The fruitless hours, but neither self-condemning,   125
And of thir vain contést appear'd no end.

From Book 12 [*To whom thus also th'Angel last repli'd*]

To whom thus also th' Angel last repli'd:[4]
This having learnt, thou hast attain'd the sum
Of wisdom; hope no higher, though all the Stars
Thou knew'st by name, and all th' ethereal Powers,
All secrets of the deep, all Nature's works,   5
Or works of God in Heav'n, Air, Earth, or Sea,
And all the riches of this World enjoy'dst,
And all the rule, one Empire; only add
Deeds to thy knowledge answerable, add Faith,
Add Virtue, Patience, Temperance, add Love,   10
By name to come call'd Charity, the soul
Of all the rest: then wilt thou not be loath
To leave this Paradise, but shalt possess
A paradise within thee, happier far.
Let us descend now therefore from this top   15
Of Speculation; for the hour precise
Exacts our parting hence; and see the Guards,
By mee encampt on yonder Hill, expect
Thir motion, at whose Front a flaming Sword,
In signal of remove, waves fiercely round;   20
We may no longer stay: go, waken *Eve*;
Her also I with gentle Dreams have calm'd
Portending good, and all her spirits compos'd
To meek submission: thou at season fit
Let her with thee partake what thou hast heard,   25
Chiefly what may concern her Faith to know,
The great deliverance by her Seed to come
(For by the Woman's Seed) on all Mankind,
That ye may live, which will be many days,
Both in one Faith unanimous though sad,   30
With cause for evils past, yet much more cheer'd
With meditation on the happy end.
    He ended, and they both descend the Hill;
Descended, *Adam* to the Bow'r where *Eve*
Lay sleeping ran before, but found her wak't;   35
And thus with words not sad she him receiv'd.
    Whence thou return'st, and whither went'st, I know;

---

4. The Archangel Michael has explained to
Adam God's plan for the redemption of
humankind.

For God is also in sleep, and Dreams advise,
Which he hath sent propitious, some great good
Presaging, since with sorrow and heart's distress   40
Wearied I fell asleep: but now lead on;
In mee is no delay; with thee to go,
Is to stay here; without thee here to stay,
Is to go hence unwilling; thou to mee
Art all things under Heav'n, all places thou,   45
Who for my wilful crime art banisht hence.
This further consolation yet secure
I carry hence; though all by mee is lost,
Such favor I unworthy am voutsaf't,
By mee the Promis'd Seed shall all restore.   50
    So spake our Mother *Eve,* and *Adam* heard
Well pleas'd, but answer'd not; for now too nigh
Th' Arch-Angel stood, and from the other Hill
To thir fixt Station, all in bright array
The Cherubim descended; on the ground   55
Gliding meteorous, as Ev'ning Mist
Ris'n from a River o'er the marish glides,
And gathers ground fast at the Laborer's heel
Homeward returning. High in Front advanc't,
The brandisht Sword of God before them blaz'd   60
Fierce as a Comet; which with torrid heat,
And vapor as the *Libyan* Air adust,[5]
Began to parch that temperate Clime; whereat
In either hand the hast'ning Angel caught
Our ling'ring Parents, and to th' Eastern Gate   65
Led them direct, and down the Cliff as fast
To the subjected Plain; then disappear'd.
They looking back, all th' Eastern side beheld
Of Paradise, so late thir happy seat,
Wav'd over by that flaming Brand, the Gate   70
With dreadful Faces throng'd and fiery Arms:
Some natural tears they dropp'd, but wip'd them soon;
The World was all before them, where to choose
Thir place of rest, and Providence thir guide:
They hand in hand with wand'ring steps and slow,   75
Through *Eden* took thir solitary way.

---

5. Burned like the air in the desert of Libya.

ANDREAS GRYPHIUS [ANDREAS GREIF] (1616–1664)
Germany

Andreas Gryphius, poet and playwright, was born and died in Glogau in Silesia, a part of Germany devastated by the Thirty Years' War. After studying in Holland, he returned to his native city to occupy a position as a municipal official. After early work in Latin, he began to publish poetry in German in 1637. In his lifetime he came to be recognized as the foremost German poet of his age and the first great master of the sonnet in the language. The violent contrasts in his poetry and its preoccupation with mortality are characteristic of the German baroque.

Human Misery*

What are we men indeed? Grim torment's habitation,
A toy of fickle luck, wisp in time's wilderness,
A scene of bitter fear and filled with keen distress,
And tapers burned to stubs, snow's quick evaporation.

This life does flee away like jest or conversation;
Those who before us laid aside the body's dress
And in the domesday-book of monster mortalness
Old entry found, have left our mind's and heart's sensation.

Just as an empty dream from notice lightly flees,
And as a stream is lost whose course no might may cease,
So must our honor, fame, our praise and name be ended.

What presently draws breath, must perish with the air,
What after us will come, someday our grave will share.
What do I say? We pass as smoke on strong winds wended.

SOR VIOLANTE DO CÉU (VIOLANTE MONTESINO) (1602?–1693)
Portugal

In 1630 Sor Violante entered the order of Our Lady of the Rosary. She was a playwright (*Saint Eufemia*) as well as a baroque poet, under the influence of the

---

Translated by George C. Schoolfield.

baroque Spanish poet Góngora and given to meditating on life's passing and on divine love. She practices the conceit or *concetto* (the keystone of the movement called *conceptismo*), the idea with a twist toward which the writing leads necessarily, through turnings and deviations.

Voice of a Dissipated Woman Inside a Tomb, Talking to Another Woman Who Presumed to Enter a Church with the Purpose of Being Seen and Praised by Everyone, Who Sat Down Near a Sepulcher Containing This Epitaph, Which Curiously Reads:*

You fool yourself and live a crazy day
or year, dizzy with adventures, and bent
solely on pleasures! Know the argument
of rigid doom and find a wiser way.
Consider that here, buried in the earth,
a dazzling and commended beauty lies,
and all live things are nothing, dust, and worth
less than the nothing of your life and lies.
Consider that when rigid death is come,
it laughs at beauty and discernment, and
what seems entirely certain fades in doubt.
Learn from this tomb what you will soon become,
and live more prudently till that command
is heard: the end which ends with no way out.

CATHERINA REGINA VON GREIFFENBERG (1633–1694)
Germany

Catherina Regina von Greiffenberg was born into a noble Austrian family; because her family was Protestant, she was forced to flee from Catholic Austria and she spent the later years of her life in Nuremberg, Germany, where she died in 1694. Her collected poems, including 250 sonnets, were published in 1662. Her intensely religious poetry, based on her own inner experiences rather than on dogmatic teaching, made a deep impression on her contemporaries. Long

---

*Translated by Willis Barnstone.

neglected, she has in recent years come to be seen as one of the most forceful poets in German of her time.

On the Ineffable Inspiration of the Holy Ghost*

Lightning invisible, you dark bright light
Heart-filling strength, being yet ungrasped!
A godlike thing has come upon the spirit
That moves and rules me; I sense a spare light.

Of itself the soul is not so very light.
It is a wonder-wind, a spirit, a being weaving,
The eternal power of breath become arch-enemy,
Kindling energy in me, this heaven flaming.

You mirror-color-sight, you wonder-tinted shining!
You shimmer in and out, ungraspable, oh clear;
The spirit's dove-flights gleam in the sun of truth.

The pool moved by God is, even troubled, clear!
First the sun of spirit will set the moon
Alight; then turning, the earth will come clear too.

JEAN RACINE (1639–1699)
France

Jean Racine, the greatest French tragic playwright, was born at La Ferté-Milon in 1639. He received a strict and thorough education under religious auspices and became the most prominent playwright of his time, receiving extensive patronage from Louis XIV. *Phaedra* was first performed and published in 1677. Immediately thereafter Racine left the commercial theater and was named official historian to the king, a post he held until his death in 1699. *Phaedra* focuses on a subject drawn from ancient Greek drama: the story of Phaedra's desperate love for her stepson Hippolytus. It is widely admired as one of Racine's greatest tragedies.

Racine's Preface to Phaedra†

> HERE is another tragedy of which I have borrowed the subject from Euripides. Although I have followed a slightly different route from that author as regards the plot, I have not failed

---

*Translated by Mary Ann Caws and Fred J. Nichols.
†Translated by John Cairncross.

to enrich my play with everything which seemed to me to be most striking in his. Even if I owed him only the idea of Phaedra's character, I should be justified in saying that I owe him what is probably the clearest and most closely-knit play I have written. I am not surprised that this character should have met with such a favourable reception in Euripides' day and that it should still be so successful in our time, since it possesses all the qualities required by Aristotle in a tragic hero, that is, the ability to arouse pity and terror. For Phaedra is neither entirely guilty nor altogether innocent. She is involved by her destiny, and by the anger of the gods, in an unlawful passion at which she is the very first to be horrified. She makes every effort to overcome it. She prefers to let herself die rather than declare it to anyone. And, when she is forced to disclose it, she speaks with such embarrassment that it is clear that her crime is a punishment of the gods rather than an urge flowing from her own will.

I have even been at pains to make her slightly less odious than in the tragedies of the ancients, where she resolves of her own accord to accuse Hippolytus. I felt that calumny was somewhat too low and foul to be put in the mouth of a princess whose sentiments were otherwise so noble and virtuous. This baseness seemed to me to be more appropriate to a nurse, who could well have more slave-like inclinations, and who nevertheless launches this false accusation only in order to save the life and honour of her mistress. Phaedra consents to it only because she is in such a state of excitement as to be out of her mind, and she appears a moment later in order to exculpate her innocent victim and declare the truth.

In Euripides and Seneca, Hippolytus is accused of having violated his stepmother: Vim corpus tulit. But here he is only accused of having intended to do so. I wished to spare Theseus a degree of agitation which could have detracted from the sympathy aroused by him among the spectators.

As regards the role of Hippolytus, I had noticed that the ancients reproached Euripides with having portrayed him as a sage free from any imperfection. As a result, the young prince's death caused much more indignation than pity. I felt obliged to leave him one weakness which would make him slightly guilty towards his father, without however depriving him in any way of the nobility with which he spares Phaedra's honour and allows himself to be mistreated without accusing her. I regard as a weakness the passion he feels in spite of himself for Aricia, who is the daughter and sister of his father's mortal enemies.

This character—Aricia—was not invented by me. Virgil says that Hippolytus married her, and had a son by her, after Aesculapius had brought him back to life. And I have also read in certain authors that Hippolytus married and took to Italy a young Athenian lady of high birth who was called Aricia and who gave her name to a small Italian town.

I cite these authorities, because I have been very scrupulous in trying to follow the classical account. I have even been faithful to the story of Theseus as recounted by Plutarch.

It was in this historian that I found that what gave rise to the belief that Theseus went down to the underworld to abduct Proserpine was a journey by this prince in Epirus towards the source of the Acheron to a king whose wife Pirithous wished to carry off and who kept Theseus prisoner after having put Pirithous to death. In this way, I have endeavoured to retain the credibility of the story without losing anything of the ornaments of the legend which constitutes a rich source of poetry. And the rumor of Theseus' death, based on this legendary journey, gives rise to Phaedra's profession of love which becomes one of the main causes of her downfall, since she would never have dared to speak had she believed that her husband was alive.

For the rest, I do not as yet dare to affirm that this play is my best tragedy. I leave it to the readers and to time to decide as to its real value. What I can affirm is that in no other play of mine is virtue given greater prominence. The slightest transgressions are severely punished. The very thought of crime is regarded with as much horror as crime itself. Weaknesses caused by love are treated as real weaknesses. The passions are portrayed merely in order to show the aberrations to which they give rise; and vice is painted throughout in colours which bring out its hideousness and hatefulness. That is really the objective which everyone working for the public should have in mind. And it is what the tragedians of early times aimed at above all else. Their theatre was a school in which virtue was taught not less well than in the schools of the philosophers. Hence it was that Aristotle *did not disdain to lend a hand to the composition of Euripides' tragedies. It would be greatly to be desired that modern writings were as sound and full of useful precepts as the works of these poets. This might perhaps provide a means of reconciling to tragedy a host of people famous for their piety and their doctrine who have recently condemned it and who would no doubt pass a more favourable judgement on it if writers were as keen to edify their spectators as to amuse them, thereby complying with the real purpose of tragedy.*

Phaedra

Characters

THESEUS, *son of Aegeus, King of Athens*

HIPPOLYTUS, *son of Theseus and Antiope, Queen of the Amazons*

THERAMENES, *Hippolytus' mentor*

ISMENE, *Aricia's confidante*

PHAEDRA, *wife of Theseus, daughter of Minos and Pasiphae*

ARICIA, *princess of the blood royal of Athens*

OENONE, *Phaedra's nurse and confidante*

PANOPE, *a woman of Phaedra's retinue*

The scene is in Troezen, a town in the Peloponnese

Act I

Scene I

HIPPOLYTUS: It is resolved, Theramenes. I go.
    I will depart from Troezen's pleasant land.
    Torn by uncertainty about the King,
    I am ashamed of standing idly by.
    For over half a year I have not heard   5
    Of my dear father Theseus' destiny
    Nor even by what far sky he is concealed.

THERAMENES: And, where, my lord, would you make search for him?
    Already, to allay your rightful fears,
    I have scoured both the seas that Corinth joins;[1]   10
    I have sought news of Theseus on the shores
    Of Acheron, the river of the dead;
    Elis I searched, then sailed past Tenaros

Translated by John Cairncross.

---

1. The isthmus of Corinth links the main part of Greece with the peninsula of the Peloponnese. The two seas are the Ionian and the Aegean. The River Acheron has its source in the mountains of Epirus in north-west Greece. Theramenes' wanderings took him from there southward to Elis, a province on the western shore of the Peloponnese, then to Tenaros on its southern tip, and finally to the Aegean Sea on the east side of Greece.

On to the sea where Icarus came down.
What makes you hope that you may find his trace   15
In some more favoured region of the world?
Who knows indeed if it is his desire
To have the secret of his absence known?
And whether, as we tremble for his life,
He is not tasting all the joys of love,   20
And soon the outraged victim of his wiles. . . .

HIPPOLYTUS: No more of this, Theramenes. The King
Has seen the errors of his amorous youth.
He is above unworthy dalliance,
And, stronger than his old inconstancy,   25
Phaedra has in his heart long reigned alone.
But, to be brief, I must make search for him
Far from this city where I dare not stay.

THERAMENES: Since when do you, my lord, fear to frequent
These peaceful haunts you cherished as a boy,   30
Which I have seen you many a time prefer
To the loud pomp of Athens and the court?
What peril, or what trouble, drives you hence?

HIPPOLYTUS: Those happy days are gone, and all is changed,
Since to these shores the mighty gods have sent   35
The child of Minos and Pasiphae.[2]

THERAMENES: I understand. The cause of your distress
Is known to me. Phaedra distresses you.
Theseus' new wife had scarcely seen you than
Your exile gave the measure of her power.   40
But now her hate that never let you be
Has vanished or is greatly on the wane.
Besides what perils threaten you from her—
A woman dying or who seeks to die?
Racked by a malady she will not name,   45
Tired of herself and of the light of day,
Phaedra has not the strength to do you ill.

HIPPOLYTUS: I do not fear her vain hostility.
If I go hence, I flee, let me confess,
Another enemy . . . Aricia,   50
Last of a line that plotted Theseus' death.

THERAMENES: What! Would you stoop to persecute her too?
Though she is sprung of Pallas' cruel race,[3]

---

2. Minos was King of Crete, and later judge in Hades. Pasiphae was the daughter of the Sun. She had two daughters by Minos—Ariadne and Phaedra (the latter being the one that Hippolytus has in mind). Aphrodite, the goddess of love, inspired Pasiphae with a monstrous passion for a bull, and from this union there was born the Minotaur, half man, half bull. Theseus brought back Phaedra from Greece after killing the monster in its labyrinth.

55

She never joined in her false brothers' schemes.
Why hate her then if she is innocent?
HIPPOLYTUS: I would not flee her if I hated her.
THERAMENES: My lord, may I explain your sudden flight?
    Are you no more the man that once you were,
    Relentless foe of all the laws of love
    And of a yoke Theseus himself has borne?
    Will Venus whom you haughtily disdained
    Vindicate Theseus after all these years
    By forcing you to worship with the throng
    Of ordinary mortals at her shrine?
    Are you in love?
HIPPOLYTUS: My friend, what have you said?
    You who have known me since I first drew breath,
    You ask me shamefully to disavow
    The feelings of a proud disdainful heart?
    The Amazon, my mother, with her milk[4]
    Suckled me on that pride you wonder at.
    And I myself, on reaching man's estate,
    Approved my nature when I knew myself.
    Serving me with unfeignéd loyalty,
    You would relate my father's history.
    You know how, as I hung upon your words,
    My heart would glow at tales of his exploits
    When you portrayed Theseus, that demi-god,
    Consoling mortals for Alcides' loss.[5]
    Monsters suppressed and brigands brought to book—
    Procrustes, Sciron, Sinis, Cercyon;
    The giants' bones in Epidaurus strewn
    And Crete red with the slaughtered Minotaur.
    But, when you told me of less glorious deeds,
    His word pledged and believed in countless lands:
    Helen in Sparta ravished from her home,
    Salamis, scene of Periboea's tears;
    Others whose very names he has forgot,
    Too trusting spirits all deceived by him;
    Wronged Ariadne crying to the winds;[6]

60
65
70
75
80
85

3. Pallas was descended from Erechtheus, the original King of Athens and son of the earth god. Aegeus, Theseus's father, had obtained the throne by adoption. Aricia's brothers plotted Theseus's downfall, but were discovered and put to death.

4. Antiope (Hippolyta).

5. Hercules.

6. Minos' daughter, Phaedra's sister, who led Theseus through the labyrinth and thus enabled him to kill the Minotaur; she eloped with Theseus, and was abandoned by him on the island of Naxos.

Phaedra abducted, though for lawful ends;   90
You know how, loath to hear this sorry tale,
I often urged you quickly to conclude,
Happy could I have kept the shameful half
Of these adventures from posterity.
And am I to be vanquished in my turn?   95
And can the gods have humbled me so far?
In base defeat the more despicable
Since countless exploits plead on his behalf,
Whereas no monsters overcome by me
Have given me the right to err like him.   100
And, even if I were fated to succumb,
Should I have chosen to love Aricia?
Should not my wayward feelings have recalled
That she is barred from me eternally?
King Theseus frowns upon her and decrees   105
That she shall not prolong her brothers' line:
He fears this guilty stock will blossom forth,
And has, so that her name shall end with her,
Condemned her to be single till she dies—
No marriage torch shall ever blaze for her.   110
Should I espouse her cause and brave his wrath?
Set an example to foolhardiness?
And, on a foolish passion launched, my youth . . .

THERAMENES: Ah! when your hour has once but struck, my lord,   115
    Heaven of our reasons takes but little heed.
Theseus opens your eyes despite yourself.
His hatred of Aricia has fanned
Your passion and has lent her added grace.
Besides, my lord, why fear a virtuous love?
If it is sweet, will you not dare to taste?   120
And will you always shyly flee from it?
Can you go wrong where Hercules has trod?
What hearts has Venus' power not subdued?
Where would you be yourself, who fight her now,
If, combating her love, Antiope   125
Had never been consumed for Theseus?
However, what avails this haughty tone?
Confess it, all is changed; for some days past
You are less often seen, aloof and proud,
Speeding your chariot along the shore,   130
Or, skilful in the seagod Neptune's art,
Bending an untamed courser to the curb.
The woods less often to your cries resound;
Your eyes grow heavier with secret fire.
There is no doubt, you are consumed with love.   135

>   You perish from a malady you hide.
>   Has fair Aricia enraptured you?
> HIPPOLYTUS: Theramenes, I go to seek the King.
> THERAMENES: And will you see Phaedra before you leave,
>   My lord?   140
> HIPPOLYTUS: I mean to. You may tell her so.
>   See her I must, since duty so commands.
>   But what new burden weighs Oenone down?

Scene 2

> OENONE: Alas, my lord what cares can equal mine?
>   The Queen is almost at her destined end.
>   In vain I watch over her night and day.
>   She's dying from a hidden malady;
>   Eternal discord reigns within her mind.   5
>   Her restless anguish tears her from her bed.
>   She longs to see the light, and yet, distraught
>   With pain, she bids me banish everyone . . .
>   But here she comes.
> HIPPOLYTUS: Enough. I'll take my leave   10
>   And will not show her my detested face.

Scene 3

> PHAEDRA: No further. Here, Oenone, let us stay.
>   I faint, I fall; my strength abandons me.
>   My eyes are dazzled by the daylight's glare,
>   And my knees, trembling, give beneath my weight.
>   Alas!   5
> OENONE: May our tears move you, mighty gods!
> PHAEDRA: How these vain jewels, these veils weigh on me!
>   What meddling hand has sought to re-arrange
>   My hair, by braiding it across my brow?
>   All things contrive to grieve and thwart me, all.
> OENONE: How all her wishes war among themselves!   10
>   Yourself, condemning your unlawful plans,
>   A moment past, bade us adorn your brow;
>   Yourself, summoning up your former strength,
>   Wished to come forth and see the light again.
>   Scarce have you seen it than you long to hide;   15
>   You hate the daylight you come forth to see.
> PHAEDRA: O shining founder of an ill-starred line,
>   You, whom my mother dared to boast her sire,[7]

---

7. The Sun was Pasiphae's father and hence
    Phaedra's grandfather.

Who blush perhaps to see me thus distraught,
Sungod, for the last time, I look on you.   20

OENONE: What? you will not give up this fell desire?
And will you, always saying no to life,
Make mournful preparation for your death?

PHAEDRA: Would I were seated in the forest's shade!
When can I follow through the swirling dust   25
The lordly chariot's flight along the course?

OENONE: What?

PHAEDRA: Madness! Where am I, what have I said?
Whither have my desires, my reason strayed?
Lost, lost, the gods have carried it away.
Oenone, blushes sweep across my face;   30
My grievous shame stands all too clear revealed,
And tears despite me fill my aching eyes.

OENONE: If you must blush, blush for your silence, for
It but inflames the fury of your ills.
Deaf to our wild entreaties, pitiless,   35
Will you allow yourself to perish thus?
What madness cuts you off in mid career?
What spell, what poison, has dried up the source?
Thrice have the shades of night darkened the skies
Since sleep last made its entry in your eyes,   40
And thrice the day has driven forth dim night
Since last your fainting lips took nourishment.
What dark temptation lures you to your doom?
What right have you to plot to end your life?
In this you wrong the gods from whom you spring,   45
You are unfaithful to your wedded lord;
Unfaithful also to your hapless sons,
Whom you would thrust beneath a heavy yoke.
Remember, that same day their mother dies,
Hope for the alien woman's son revives,   50
For that fierce enemy of you and yours,
That youth whose mother was an Amazon,
Hippolytus . . .

PHAEDRA: God!

OENONE: *That* reproach struck home.

PHAEDRA: Ah! wretched woman, what name crossed your lips?

OENONE: Your anger now bursts forth, and rightly so.   55
I love to see you shudder at the name.
Live then. Let love and duty spur you on.
Live. Do not give a Scythian's son a chance
To lord it with his harsh and odious rule
Over the pride of Greece and of the gods.   60
Do not delay! for every moment kills.

	Haste to replenish your enfeebled strength
	While yet the fires of life, though all but spent,
	Are burning and can still flame bright again.
PHAEDRA:	I have prolonged my guilty days too far.
OENONE:	What, are you harried by some keen remorse?
	What crime could ever bring you to this pass?
	Your hands were never stained with guiltless blood.
PHAEDRA:	Thanks be to Heaven, my hands have done no wrong.
	Would God my heart were innocent as they!
OENONE:	What fearful project then have you conceived
	Which strikes such terror deep into my heart?
PHAEDRA:	I have revealed enough. Spare me the rest.
	I die, and my grim secret dies with me.
OENONE:	Keep silence then, inhuman one, and die;
	But seek some other hand to close your eyes.
	Although the candle of your life burns low,
	I will go down before you to the dead.
	Thither a thousand different roads converge,
	My misery will choose the shortest one.
	When have I ever failed you, cruel one?
	Remember, you were born into my arms.
	For you I have lost country, children, all.[8]
	Is this how you reward fidelity?
PHAEDRA:	What do you hope to gain by violence?
	If I should speak, you would be thunderstruck.
OENONE:	And what, ye gods, could be more terrible
	Than seeing you expire before my eyes?
PHAEDRA:	Even when you know my crime and cruel fate,
	I yet will die, and die the guiltier.
OENONE:	By all the tears that I have shed for you,
	And by your faltering knees I hold entwined,
	Deliver me from dire uncertainty.
PHAEDRA:	You wish it. Rise.
OENONE:	Speak. I await your words.
PHAEDRA:	What shall I say to her and where begin?
OENONE:	Wound me no longer by such vain affrights!
PHAEDRA:	O hate of Venus! Anger-laden doom!
	Into what dark abyss love hurled my mother![9]
OENONE:	Ah, Queen, forget; and for all time to come
	Eternal silence seal this memory.
PHAEDRA:	O sister Ariadne, of what love
	You died deserted on a barren shore!

Line numbers: 65, 70, 75, 80, 85, 90, 95, 100

---

8. The nurse had accompanied Phaedra from her native Crete to Athens.

9. An allusion to Pasiphae's monstrous passion for the bull.

OENONE: What ails you, and what mortal agony
    Drives you to fury against all your race?
PHAEDRA: Since Venus wills it, of this unblest line   105
    I perish, I, the last and wretchedest.
OENONE: You are in love?
PHAEDRA: Love's furies rage in me.
OENONE: For whom?
PHAEDRA: Prepare to hear the crowning woe.
    I love . . . I tremble, shudder at the name;
    I love . . .   110

    [Oenone leans forward]

PHAEDRA: You know that prince whom I myself
    So long oppressed, son of the Amazon?
OENONE: Hippolytus?
PHAEDRA: *You* have pronounced his name.
OENONE: Merciful heavens! My blood chills in my veins.
    O grief! O crime! O lamentable race!
    Ill-fated journey and thrice ill-starred coast!   115
    Would we had never neared your dangerous shores!
PHAEDRA: My malady goes further back. I scarce
    Was bound by marriage to Aegeus' son;[10]
    My peace of mind, my happiness seemed sure.
    Athens revealed to me my haughty foe.   120
    As I beheld, I reddened, I turned pale.
    A tempest raged in my distracted mind.
    My eyes no longer saw. I could not speak.
    I felt my body freezing, burning; knew
    Venus was on me with her dreaded flames,   125
    The fatal torments of a race she loathes.
    By sleepless vows, I thought to ward her off.
    I built a temple to her, rich and fair.
    No hour went by but I made sacrifice,
    Seeking my reason in the victims' flanks.   130
    Weak remedies for love incurable!
    In vain my hand burned incense on the shrine.
    Even when my lips invoked the goddess' name,
    I worshipped *him*. His image followed me.
    Even on the altar's steps, my offerings   135
    Were only to the god I dared not name.
    I shunned him everywhere. O crowning woe!
    I found him mirrored in his father's face!
    Against myself at last I dared revolt.
    I spurred my feelings on to harass him.   140

---

10. Theseus.

To banish my adoréd enemy,
I feigned a spite against this stepson, kept
Urging his exile, and my ceaseless cries
Wrested him from a father's loving arms.
I breathed more freely since I knew him gone.   145
The days flowed by, untroubled, innocent.
Faithful to Theseus, hiding my distress,
I nursed the issue of our ill-starred bed.
Ah vain precautions! Cruel destiny!
Brought by my lord himself to Troezen's shores,   150
I saw once more the foe I had expelled.
My open wound at once poured blood again.
The fire no longer slumbers in the veins.
Venus in all her might is on her prey.
I have a fitting horror for my crime;   155
I hate this passion and I loathe my life.
Dying, I could have kept my name unstained,
And my dark passion from the light of day;
Your tears, your pleas have forced me to confess,
And I shall not regret what I have done,   160
If you, respecting the approach of death,
Will cease to vex me with reproaches, and
Your vain assistance will not try to fan
The last faint flicker still alight in me.

Scene 4

PANOPE: Would I could hide from you the grievous news,
My lady, but I cannot hold it back.
Death has abducted your unconquered lord
And this mischance is known to all but you.

OENONE: What, Panope?

PANOPE: The Queen in vain, alas!   5
Importunes heaven for Theseus' safe return,
For, from the vessels just arrived in port,
Hippolytus, his son, has learned his death.

PHAEDRA: God!

PANOPE: Athens is divided in its choice
Of master. Some favour the prince, your son,   10
Others, forgetful of the State's decrees,[11]
Dare to support the foreign woman's son.
Rumour even has it that a bold intrigue
Wishes to give Aricia the throne.
I deemed it right to warn you of this threat.   15

---

11. Which ruled out the succession of anyone
even partly of non-Greek blood.

Hippolytus is ready to set sail,
And in this turmoil it is to be feared
He may win fickle Athens to his cause.
OENONE: Panope, cease! You may be sure the Queen
    Will give due heed to this important news.   20

Scene 5

OENONE: Ah Queen, I had relinquished you to death
    And thought to follow you down to the tomb.
    I had no longer words to turn you back;
    But this news bids you steer another course.
    Now all is changed, and fortune smiles on you.   5
    The King is dead, and you must take his place.
    He leaves a son with whom your duty lies—
    A slave without you; if you live, a king.
    On whom in his misfortune can he lean?
    If you are dead, no hand will dry his tears;   10
    And his fond cries, borne upwards to the gods,
    Will bring his forbears' anger down on you.
    Live then, no longer tortured by reproach.
    Your love becomes like any other love.
    Theseus, in dying, has dissolved the bonds   15
    Which made your love a crime to be abhorred.
    You need no longer dread Hippolytus,
    And you may see him and be guiltless still.
    Perhaps, convinced of your hostility,
    He is prepared to captain the revolt.
    Quick, undeceive him; bend him to your will.
    King of these fertile shores, Troezen is his.
    But well he knows the laws assign your son   20
    The soaring ramparts that Minerva built,[12]
    Both of you have a common enemy.
    Join forces then against Aricia.
PHAEDRA: Then be it so. Your counsels have prevailed.
    I'll live, if I can be recalled to life,   25
    And if the love I bear my son can still
    In this grim hour revive my failing strength.

Act II

Scene 1

ARICIA: Hippolytus has asked to see me here?
    Hippolytus wishes to say farewell?
    Ismene, are you not mistaken?

---

12. Athens.

ISMENE: No.
     This is the first result of Theseus' death.
     Make ready to receive from every side   5
     Allegiances that Theseus filched from you.
     Aricia is mistress of her fate,
     And soon all Greece will bow the knee to her.
ARICIA: This was no rumour then, Ismene. Now
     My enemy, my tyrant is no more.   10
ISMENE: Indeed. The gods no longer frown on you,
     And Theseus wanders with your brother's shades.
ARICIA: By what adventure did he meet his end?
ISMENE: The tales told of his death are past belief.
     They say that in some amorous escapade   15
     The waters closed over his faithless head.
     The thousand tongues of rumour even assert
     That with Pirithous he went down to Hell,
     Beheld Cocytus[13] and the sombre shores,
     Showed himself living to the shades below,   20
     But that he could not, from the house of death,
     Recross the river whence is no return.
ARICIA: Can mortal man, before he breathes his last,
     Descend into the kingdom of the dead?
     What magic lured him to that dreaded shore?   25
ISMENE: You alone doubt it. Theseus is no more.
     Athens is stricken; Troezen knows the news,
     And now pays tribute to Hippolytus.
     Here in this palace, trembling for her son,   30
     Phaedra takes counsel with her anxious friends.
ARICIA: But will Hippolytus be kinder than
     His father was to me, loosen my chains,
     And pity my mishaps?
ISMENE: I think he will.
ARICIA: Do you not know severe Hippolytus?   35
     How can you hope that he will pity me,
     Honouring in me alone a sex he spurns?
     How constantly he has avoided us,
     Haunting those places which he knows we shun!
ISMENE: I know the tales of his unfeelingness;   40
     But I have seen him in your presence, and
     The legend of Hippolytus' reserve
     Doubled my curiosity in him.
     His aspect did not tally with his fame;
     At the first glance from you he grew confused.   45

---

13. The river of the underworld.

His eyes, seeking in vain to shun your gaze,
Brimming with languor, took their fill of you.
Although the name of lover wounds his pride,
He has a lover's eye, if not his tongue.

ARICIA: How avidly, Ismene, does my heart,   60
Drink in these sweet, perhaps unfounded words!
O you who know me, can it be believed
That the sad plaything of a ruthless fate,
A heart that always fed on bitterness,
Should ever know the frenzied pangs of love?   65
Last of the issue of Earth's royal son,[14]
I only have escaped the scourge of war.
I lost, all in their springtime's flowering,
Six brothers, pride of an illustrious line.
The sword swept all away and drenched the earth,   70
Which drank, unwillingly, Erechtheus' blood.
You know that, since their death, a cruel law
Forbids all Greeks to seek me as their wife,
Since it was feared my marriage might some day
Kindle my brothers' ashes into life.   75
But you recall with what disdain I viewed
These moves of a suspicious conqueror,
For, as a lifelong enemy of love,
I rendered thanks to Theseus' tyranny,
Which merely helped to keep me fancy free.   80
My eyes had not yet lighted on his son.
Not that my eyes alone yield to the charm
Of his much vaunted grace, his handsomeness,
Bestowed by nature, but which he disdains,
And seems not even to realize he owns.   85
I love and prize in him far nobler gifts—
His father's virtues, not his weaknesses.
I love, let me confess, that manly pride,
Which never yet has bowed beneath love's yoke.
Phaedra in vain gloried in Theseus' sighs.   90
I am more proud, and spurn the easy prize
Of homage to a thousand others paid
And of a heart accessible to all.
But to bring an unbending spirit down,
To cause an aching where no feeling was,   95
To stun a conqueror with his defeat,
In vain revolt against a yoke he loves,
That rouses my ambition, my desire.

---

14. Erechtheus.

Even Hercules was easier to disarm.
Vanquished more often than Hippolytus,   100
He yielded a less glorious victory.
But, dear Ismene, what rash hopes are these?
For his resistance will be all too strong.
You yet may hear me, humble in my grief,
Bewail the very pride I now admire.   105
Hippolytus in love? By what excess
Of fortune could I . . .

ISMENE: You yourself will hear.
Hither he comes.

Scene 2

HIPPOLYTUS: Princess, before I go
I deemed it right to let you know your fate.
My father is no more. My fears divined
The secret of his lengthy absence. Death,
Death only, ending his illustrious deeds,
Could hide him from the universe so long.   5
The gods at last deliver to the Fates
Alcides' friend, companion, and his heir.
I feel that, silencing your hate, even you
Hear in good part the honours due to him.
One hope alone tempers my mortal grief.   10
I can release you from a stern control,
Revoking laws whose harshness I deplore.
Yourself, your heart, do with them what you will;
And in this Troezen, now assigned to me
As my sage grandsire Pittheus' heritage,   15
Which with a single voice proclaimed me king,
I leave you free as I am; nay, more free.

ARICIA: Limit your boundless generosity.
By honouring me, despite adversity,
My lord, you place me, more than you believe,   20
Beneath those laws from which you set me free.

HIPPOLYTUS: Athens, uncertain whom to choose as heir,
Talks of yourself, of me, and the Queen's son.

ARICIA: Me?

HIPPOLYTUS: I would not wish to deceive myself.
My claim appears to be annulled by law   25
Because my mother was an Amazon.
But, if my only rival for the throne
Were Phaedra's son, my stepbrother, I could
Protect my rights against the law's caprice.
If I do not assert my claim, it is   30

To hand, or rather to return, to you
A sceptre given to your ancestors
By that great mortal whom the earth begot.
Adoption placed it in Aegeus' hands.
Theseus, his son, defended and enlarged   35
The bounds of Athens, which proclaimed him king
And left your brothers in oblivion.
Athens recalls you now within her walls.
Too long has she deplored this endless feud;
Too long your noble kinsmen's blood has flown,   40
Drenching the very fields from which it sprang.
If Troezen falls to me, the lands of Crete
Offer a rich domain to Phaedra's son.
But Attica is yours. And I go hence
To unify our votes on your behalf.   45

ARICIA: At all I hear, astounded and amazed,
I almost fear a dream deceives my ears.
Am I awake? Is it to be believed?
What god, my lord, inspired you with the thought?
How rightly is your glory spread abroad!   50
And how the truth surpasses your renown!
You in my favour will renounce your claim?
Surely it was enough to keep your heart
So long free from that hatred of my line,   55
That enmity . . .

HIPPOLYTUS: I hate you, Princess? No.
However my aloofness be decried,
Do you believe a monster gave me birth?
What churlish breeding, what unbending hate
Would not have melted at the sight of you?
Could I resist the soft beguiling spell . . .   60

ARICIA: What! My lord . . .

HIPPOLYTUS: No, I cannot now draw back!
Reason, I see, gives way to violence.
And, since I have begun to speak my mind,
Princess, I must go on: I must reveal
A secret that my heart can not conceal.   65
Before you stands a pitiable prince,
Signal example of rash arrogance.
I who, in proud rebellion against love,
Have long mocked other captives' sufferings,
Who, pitying the shipwrecks of the weak,   70
Had thought to watch them always from the shore,
Am now, in bondage to the common law,
Cut from my moorings by a surging swell.

A single blow has quelled my recklessness:
My haughty spirit is at last in thrall.   75
For six long months ashamed and in despair,
Pierced by the shaft implanted in my side,
I battle with myself, with you, in vain.
Present I flee you; absent, you are near.
Deep in the woods, your image follows me.   80
The light of day, the shadows of the night,
Everything conjures up the charms I flee;
Each single thing delivers up my heart.
And, sole reward for all my fruitless care,
I seek but cannot find myself again.   85
Bow, chariot, javelins, all importune me;
The lessons Neptune taught me are forgot.[15]
My idle steeds no longer know my voice,
And only to my cries the woods resound.
Perhaps the tale of so uncouth a love   90
Brings, as you listen, blushes to your face.
What words with which to offer you a heart!
How strange a conquest for so fair a maid!
But you should prize the offering the more.
Remember that I speak an unknown tongue,
And do not scorn my clumsy gallantry,   95
Which, but for you, I never would have known.

> *Scene 3*

THERAMENES: The Queen is coming, Prince. She looks for you.
HIPPOLYTUS: For me?
THERAMENES: I do not know what she intends.
    You have been sent for by her messenger.
    Before you leave, Phaedra would speak with you.
HIPPOLYTUS: What can I say? And what can she expect . . .   5
ARICIA: Consent at least, my lord, to hear her speak.
    Although she was your bitter enemy,
    You owe some shade of pity to her tears.
HIPPOLYTUS: Meanwhile you go. I leave, and am in doubt
    Whether I have offended my beloved,   10
    Or if my heart that I commit to you . . .
ARICIA: Go, Prince. Pursue your generous designs.
    Make Athens' state pay homage to me. All
    The gifts you offer to me I accept.
    But Athens' empire, glorious though it be,   15
    Is not your most endearing offering.

---

15. The seagod was also the god of horses.

Scene 4

HIPPOLYTUS: Are you all ready? But I see the Queen.
                Let everyone prepare with all despatch
                To sail. Go, give the signal; hasten back,
                And free me from a tedious interview.

Scene 5

PHAEDRA:

[To Oenone at the back of the stage.]

                He comes . . . My blood sweeps back into my heart.
                Forgotten are the words I had prepared.
OENONE: Think of your son, who hopes in you alone.
PHAEDRA: They say that you are leaving us at once.
                My lord. I come to join my tears to yours.   5
                I come to tell you of a mother's fears.
                My son is fatherless, and soon, too soon,
                He must behold my death as well. Even now,
                Numberless enemies beset his youth.
                You, only you, can see to his defence.   10
                But I am harried by remorse within.
                I fear lest you refuse to hear his cries.
                I tremble lest you visit on a son
                Your righteous anger at a mother's crimes.
HIPPOLYTUS: How could I ever be so infamous?   15
PHAEDRA: If you should hate me, I would not complain,
                For I appeared resolved to do you ill.
                Deep in my inmost heart you could not read.
                I drew upon myself your enmity,
                And where I dwelt, I would not suffer you.   20
                With unrelenting hate, I sought to be
                Divided from you by a waste of seas.
                I even ordained by an express decree
                That in my presence none should speak your name.
                But, if the punishment should fit the crime,   25
                If hate alone could bring your hate on me,
                Never did woman merit pity more
                And less, my lord, deserve your enmity.
HIPPOLYTUS: A mother jealous of her children's rights
                Rarely forgives another woman's son,   30
                I realize; and from a second bed
                Awkward suspicion all too often springs.
                Another would have taken like offence,
                And at her hands I might have suffered more.

PHAEDRA: Ah! My lord, heaven, I dare here attest,   35
     Has quite dispensed me from the common rule.
     Far other is the care that weighs on me.
HIPPOLYTUS: Lady, it is too early yet to grieve.
     Who knows, your husband may be still alive.
     Heaven may vouchsafe him to your tears again.   40
     Protected by the seagod, not in vain
     Will Theseus call on mighty Neptune's aid.
PHAEDRA: No mortal visits twice the house of death.
     Since Theseus has beheld the sombre shores,
     In vain you hope a god will send him back,   45
     And hungry Acheron holds fast his prey.
     But no, he is not dead; he lives, in you.
     Always I think I see my husband's face.
     I see him, speak to him, and my fond heart . . .
     My frenzied love bursts forth in spite of me.   50
HIPPOLYTUS: In this I see the wonder of your love.
     Dead as he is, Theseus still lives for you.
     Still does his memory inflame your heart.
PHAEDRA: Yes, Prince, I pine, I am on fire for him.
     I love King Theseus, not as once he was,   55
     The fickle worshipper at countless shrines,
     Dishonouring the couch of Hades' god;[16]
     But constant, proud, and even a little shy;
     Enchanting, young, the darling of all hearts,
     Fair as the gods; or fair as you are now.   60
     He had your eyes, your bearing, and your speech.
     His face flushed with your noble modesty.
     When towards my native Crete he cleft the waves,[17]
     Well might the hearts of Minos' daughters burn!
     What were you doing then? Why without you   65
     Did he assemble all the flower of Greece?
     Why could you not, too young, alas, have fared
     Forth with the ship that brought him to our shores?
     You would have slain the monstrous Cretan bull
     Despite the windings of his endless lair.   70
     My sister[18] would have armed you with the thread,
     To lead you through the dark entangled maze—
     No. *I* would have forestalled her. For my love
     Would instantly have fired me with the thought.
     I, only I, would have revealed to you   75

---

16. Pluto, King of the underworld.   **18.** Ariadne.
17. On the expedition to Crete against the
     Minotaur.

The subtle windings of the labyrinth.
What care I would have lavished on your head!
A thread would not have reassured my fears.
Affronting danger side by side with you,
I would myself have wished to lead the way,   80
And Phaedra, with you in the labyrinth,
Would have returned with you or met her doom.

HIPPOLYTUS: What do I hear? Have you forgotten that
    King Theseus is my father, you his wife?

PHAEDRA: What makes you think, my lord, I have forgot,   85
    Or am no longer mindful of my name?

HIPPOLYTUS: Forgive me. Blushing, I confess your words
    Were innocent, and I misunderstood.
    For very shame I cannot bear your gaze.
    I go . . .   90

PHAEDRA: Ah, cruel, you have understood
    Only too well. I have revealed enough.
    Know Phaedra then, and all her wild desires.
    I burn with love. Yet, even as I speak,
    Do not imagine I feel innocent,
    Nor think that my complacency has fed   95
    The poison of the love that clouds my mind.
    The hapless victim of heaven's vengeances,
    I loathe myself more than you ever will.
    The gods are witness, they who in my breast
    Have lit the fire fatal to all my line.   100
    Those gods whose cruel glory it has been
    To lead astray a feeble mortal's heart.
    Yourself recall to mind the past, and how
    I shunned you, cruel one, nay, drove you forth.
    I strove to seem to you inhuman, vile;   105
    The better to resist, I sought your hate.
    But what availed my needless sufferings?
    You hated me the more, I loved not less.
    Even your misfortunes lent you added charms.
    I pined, I drooped, in torments and in tears.   110
    Your eyes alone could see that it is so,
    If for a moment they could look at me.
    Nay, this confession to you, ah! the shame,
    Think you I made it of my own free will?
    I meant to beg you, trembling, not to hate   115
    My helpless children, whom I dared not fail.
    My foolish heart, alas, too full of you,
    Could talk to you of nothing but yourself.
    Take vengeance. Punish me for loving you.
    Come, prove yourself your father's worthy son,   120

And of a vicious monster rid the world.
I, Theseus' widow, dare to love his son!
This frightful monster must not now escape.
Here is my heart. Here must your blow strike home.
Impatient to atone for its offence,   125
I feel it strain to meet your mighty arm.
Strike. Or if it's unworthy of your blows,
Or such a death too mild for my deserts,
Of if you deem my blood too vile to stain
Your hand, lend me, if not your arm, your sword.   130
Give me it!

OENONE: Ah! What are you doing? God!
           Someone is coming. You must not be seen.
           Come, let's go in, quick, to avoid disgrace.

Scene 6

THERAMENES: Can that be Phaedra who was dragged away?
           Why, my lord, why this sudden, sharp dismay?
           I find you without sword, aghast and pale.

HIPPOLYTUS: Flee, flee, Theramenes. I cannot speak,
           Nor without horror look upon myself.   5
           Phaedra. . . . No, mighty gods, let us consign
           This shameful secret to oblivion.

THERAMENES: If you will leave, the sails are all unfurled.
           But Athens has already made her choice.
           Her chieftains have consulted all the tribes.
           Your brother rules; and Phaedra wins the day.[19]   10

HIPPOLYTUS: Phaedra?

THERAMENES: A herald speaking Athens' will
           Into her hands conveyed the reins of state.
           Her son is king, my lord.

HIPPOLYTUS: Oh God, who knows
           Her heart, is it her virtue you reward?   15

THERAMENES: Meanwhile, vague rumours say the King still lives,
           And even that in Epirus he was seen.
           But I, who sought him there, my lord, I know . . . .

HIPPOLYTUS: No matter. Let us study every clue.
           Have this new rumour traced back to its source.   20
           But, if it does not then prove credible,
           Let us depart and, at whatever cost,[20]
           Replace the sceptre in more worthy hands.

---

19. I.e. half-brother, son of Theseus and
Phaedra, whereas Hippolytus' mother was
Antiope (Hippolyta).

20. That is, even at the cost of a rebellion.

ACT III

Scene 1

PHAEDRA: Ah, take away those royal honours. How
    Can you importune me to show myself?
    And why seek to beguile my grieving heart?
    Rather conceal me. I have said too much.
    My frantic passion has revealed itself.   5
    I have said what should never have been heard.
    God! how he listened to me. By what shifts
    He long pretended not to understand.
    How his whole being hankered to be gone.
    And how his blushes added to my shame.   10
    Why did you ever thwart my baneful plan?
    Ah! when his sword was pointed at my breast,
    Did he turn pale for me, or did he wrench
    It from me? I had but to touch it once
    To make it horrible for him, and for   15
    The wretched sword to soil his cruel hands.

OENONE: Thus your misfortunes breed self-pity, and
    Only inflame a fire you ought to quench.
    Daughter of Minos, should you not aspire
    To seek your peace of mind in nobler cares?   20
    Resort to flight from an ungrateful youth,
    Reign, and assume the guidance of the State?

PHAEDRA: I reign? I bring a State beneath my rule,
    When reason reigns no longer over me;
    When I have lost my self-dominion; when   25
    Beneath a shameful sway I scarcely breathe;
    When I am dying?

OENONE: Flee.

PHAEDRA: I cannot go.

OENONE: You sent him into exile. Shun him now.

PHAEDRA: Too late, too late. He knows my mad desires.
    I have transgressed the bounds of modesty.   30
    I to Hippolytus have bared my shame,
    And hope, despite me, has seduced my heart,
    You yourself, rallying my failing strength
    When on my lips my soul was hovering,
    By guileful counsels brought me back to life.   35
    You gave me glimpses of a sinless love.

OENONE: Alas! guilty or no of your mishaps,
    What would I not have done to save your life?
    But, if by insults you were ever stung,
    Can you forget a haughty youth's disdain?   40
    God! with what cruel, stern, unfeeling heart

He left you well-nigh prostrate at his feet!
How odious his uncompromising pride!
Why did not Phaedra see him with my eyes?

PHAEDRA: He may discard this pride that angers you. 45
Bred in the forests, he is wild like them.
Hardened by rude upbringing, he perhaps
For the first time listens to words of love.
Perhaps his silence mirrors his surprise,
And our reproaches are too violent. 50

OENONE: An Amazon, forget not, gave him birth.

PHAEDRA: Though a barbarian, yet did she love.

OENONE: He hates all women with a deadly hate.

PHAEDRA: No rival, then, will triumph over me.
In short, the time for good advice is past. 55
Serve my wild heart, Oenone, not my head.
If he is inaccessible to love,
Let us attack him at some weaker point.
He seemed attracted by an empire's rule.
He could not hide it; Athens beckoned him. 60
Thither his vessels' prows were headed, and
The white sails fluttered, streaming in the wind.
Oenone, play on his ambition. Go,
Dazzle him with the glitter of the crown.
Let him assume the sacred diadem. 65
Myself to bind it on is all I ask,
Yielding to him the power I cannot hold.
He will instruct my son how to command;
Perhaps he will be father to the boy.
Mother and son I will commit to him. 70
In short, try every means to win him round.
Your words will find a readier ear than mine.
Urge! Weep! Paint Phaedra at death's door.
You may assume a supplicating tone.
I will endorse it, whatsoe'er you do. 75
Go. Upon your success depends my fate.

Scene 2

PHAEDRA: O you who see the depths of this my shame,
Relentless Venus, is my fall complete?
Your cruelty could go no further. Now
You triumph. All your arrows have struck home.
O cruel goddess! if you seek new fame, 5
Attack a more rebellious enemy.
Frigid Hippolytus, flouting your wrath,
Has at your altars never bowed the knee.

Your name seems to offend his haughty ear.
Goddess, avenge yourself. Our cause is one. 10
Make him love . . . but Oenone, you are back.
Did he not listen? Does he loathe me still?

Scene 3

OENONE: Your love is vain and you must stifle it,
O Queen, and summon up your former strength.
The King we thought was dead will soon be here;
Theseus is come; Theseus is on his way.
Headlong, the crowd rushes to welcome him. 5
I had gone out to seek Hippolytus
When, swelling to the heavens a thousand cries . . .

PHAEDRA: My husband lives. Oenone, say no more.
I have confessed a love that soils his name.
He is alive, and more I will not know.

OENONE: What? 10

PHAEDRA: I foretold it but you would not hear.
Your tears prevailed over my keen remorse.
I died this morning worthy to be mourned;
I took your counsel and dishonoured die.

OENONE: You mean to die? 15

PHAEDRA: Great God, what have I done?
My husband and his son are on their way.
I will behold the witness of my guilt
Observe me as I dare approach the King,
My heart heavy with sighs he heard unmoved,
My eyes wet with the tears the wretch disdained. 20
Mindful of Theseus' honour, as he is,
Will he conceal from him my fierce desires?
Will he be false to father and to king,
Restrain the horror that he feels for me?
His silence would be vain, Oenone, for 25
I know my baseness, and do not belong
To those bold wretches who with brazen front
Can revel in their crimes unblushingly.
I know my transports and recall them all.
Even now I feel these very walls, these vaults, 30
Will soon give tongue and, with accusing voice,
Await my husband to reveal the truth.
Then, death, come free me from so many woes.
Is it so terrible to cease to live?
Death holds no terrors for the wretched. No. 35
I fear only the name I leave behind,
For my poor children what a heritage.

The blood of Jove should make their spirit swell;[21]
But, whatsoever pride that blood inspires,
A mother's crime lies heavy on her sons.   40
I tremble lest reports, alas, too true,
One day upbraid them with a mother's guilt.
I tremble lest, crushed by this odious weight,
Neither will ever dare hold up his head.

OENONE: Ah! do not doubt it. Pity both of them.
Never was fear more justified than yours.   45
But why expose them to such base affronts?
And why bear witness now against yourself?
That way lies ruin. Phaedra, they will say,
Fled from the dreaded aspect of her lord.
Hippolytus is fortunate indeed.   50
By laying down your life, you prove him right.
How can I answer your accuser's charge?
I shall be all too easy to confound.
I shall behold his hideous triumph as
He tells your shame to all who care to hear.   55
Ah! sooner let the flames of heaven descend.
But tell me frankly do you love him still?
How do you view this overweening prince?

PHAEDRA: He is a fearful monster in my eyes.   60

OENONE: Then why concede him such a victory?
You fear him. Dare then to accuse him first
Of the offence he soon may charge you with.
Nothing is in his favour; all is yours—
His sword, left by good fortune in your hands,   65
Your present agitation, your past grief,
His father, turned against him by your cries,
And, last, his exile you yourself obtained.

PHAEDRA: Should I oppress and blacken innocence?

OENONE: All I need is your silence to succeed.
Like you I tremble and I feel remorse.   70
Sooner would I affront a thousand deaths,
But, since without this remedy you die,
For me your life must come before all else.
Therefore I'll speak. Despite his wrath, the King   75
Will do naught to his son but banish him.
A father when he punishes is still
A father, and his judgement will be mild.
But, even if guiltless blood must still be shed,
What does your threatened honour not demand?   80

---

21. Jove (Zeus) was father to Minos and
grandfather to Phaedra.

It is too precious to be compromised.
Its dictates, all of them, must be obeyed.
And, to safeguard your honour, everything,
Yes, even virtue, must be sacrified.
But who comes here? Theseus!   85

PHAEDRA: Hippolytus!
          In his bold gaze my ruin is writ large.
          Do as you will. My fate is in your hands.
          My whirling mind has left me powerless.

Scene 4

THESEUS: Fortune at last ceases to frown on me,
          O Queen, and in your arms again . . .

PHAEDRA: No more.
          Do not profane your transports of delight.
          No more do I deserve this tenderness.
          You have been outraged. Jealous fortune's blows   5
          During your absence have not spared your wife.
          I am unworthy to approach you, and
          Henceforth my only thought must be to hide.

Scene 5

THESEUS: Why this cold welcome to your father?

HIPPOLYTUS: Sire,
          Phaedra alone can solve this mystery.
          But, if my ardent wish can move you still,
          Allow me never to set eyes on her.
          Suffer your trembling son to disappear   5
          For ever from the place where Phaedra dwells.

THESEUS: You, my son, leave me?

HIPPOLYTUS: Yes. It was not I
          Who sought her. You, my lord, you brought her here.
          For you, on leaving, brought Aricia
          And your Queen, Phaedra, here to Troezen's shore.   10
          You even committed them into my care.
          But, since your safe return, why should I stay?
          Long have I squandered in the woods of Greece
          My manhood's skill on paltry enemies.
          Should not I, fleeing shameful idleness,   15
          Redden my javelins in more glorious blood?
          Before you had attained my present years,
          More than one tyrant, monsters more than one,
          Had felt the might of your unconquered arm;
          Even then, you were the scourge of insolence.   20
          You had cleared all the shores of both the seas.
          The traveller now fares freely through the land.

Hercules, resting on his laurels' fame,
Already for his labours looked to you.
And I, a glorious father's unknown son,   25
Lag far behind even my mother's deeds.
Let me at least show you my mettle and,
If some fell monster has escaped your sword,
Place at your feet its honourable spoils.
Or let the memory of a glorious death,   30
Engraving in eternity my life,
Prove to the universe I was your son.

THESEUS: What do I see? What horror spread around
Drives back from me, distraught, my family?
If I return, so feared, so undesired,   35
O heaven! why did you free me from my gaol?
I had one friend alone.[22] He rashly tried
To seize the consort of Epirus' King.
I served his amorous plan reluctantly;
But fate in anger blinded both of us.   40
The tyrant took me by surprise unarmed.
Pirithous I beheld, a woeful sight,
Thrown to fierce monsters by the barbarous king,
Who fed them on the blood of helpless men.
Me he confined in sombre caves profound   45
Nearby the shadowy kingdom of the dead.
The gods at last relented towards me and
Allowed me to outwit my guardian.
I purged the world of a perfidious knave,
And his own monsters battened on his flesh.   50
But when I joyfully prepare to meet
My dearest ones, all that the gods have spared,
Nay, when my soul, that is its own again,
Would feast itself upon so dear a sight,
Only with shudders am I welcomed home;   55
Everyone flees, rejecting my embrace.
Myself, filled with the horror I inspire,
Would I were prisoner in Epirus still.
Speak! Phaedra tells of outrage done to me.
Who played me false? Why am I unavenged?   60
Has Greece, so often guarded by my arm,
Afforded shelter to the criminal?
You do not answer. Is my son, my own
Dear son, in league, then, with my enemies?
Let us go in and end this grim suspense.   65

---

22. Pirithous.

Let us discover criminal and crime,
And Phaedra tell us why she is distraught.

Scene 6

HIPPOLYTUS: What meant these words that made my blood run cold?
Will Phaedra, still in her delirium,
Denounce herself, bring ruin on her head?
O God! What will the King say then? How love
Has spread its baleful poison through the house!   5
Myself, full of a passion he condemns,
As once he knew me, so he finds me still.
Gloomy forebodings terrify my soul.
But innocence has surely naught to fear.
Come, let me with some new and happier   10
Approach revive my father's tenderness,
And tell him of a love he may oppose
But which it is not in his power to change.

Act IV

Scene 1

THESEUS: What do I hear? A reckless libertine
Conceived this outrage on his father's name?
How harshly you pursue me, destiny.
I know not where I am, whither I go.
O son! O ill-rewarded tenderness!   5
Daring the scheme, detestable the thought.
To gain his lustful and nefarious ends,
The shameless villain had resort to force.
I recognized the sword he drew on her,
That sword I gave him for a nobler use.   10
Could all the ties of blood not hold him back?
Phaedra was slow in bringing him to book?
In keeping silent, Phaedra spared the knave?
OENONE: Rather did Phaedra spare a father's tears.
Ashamed of a distracted lover's suit,   15
And of the vicious passion she had caused,
Phaedra, my lord, was dying and her hand
Was on the point of cutting short her days.
I saw her raise her arm, I ran to her.
I, only I, preserved her for your love,   20
And, pitying her distress and your alarm,
Reluctantly I lent her tears a voice.
THESEUS: The criminal! He blenched despite himself.
As I drew near, I saw him start with fear.

I was astonished by his joyless mien;   25
His cold embraces froze my tenderness
But had this guilty love that eats him up
Already, even in Athens, shown itself?

OENONE: My lord, recall how oft the Queen complained.
Infamous love gave rise to all her hate.   30

THESEUS: And here in Troezen this flamed up again?

OENONE: My lord, I have related all I know.
The grieving Queen too long remains alone;
Allow me to withdraw and go to her.

Scene 2

THESEUS: Ah, it is he. Great gods! what eye would not
Be duped like mine by such nobility?
Must needs the brow of an adulterer
Be bright with virtue's sacred character?
And ought we not by fixed and certain signs   5
To see into perfidious mortals' hearts?

HIPPOLYTUS: May I inquire of you what baleful cloud
Has overcast, my lord, your regal brow?
Will you not venture to confide in me?

THESEUS: Villain! How dare you come before me now?   10
Monster, the thunderbolt too long has spared!
Last of the brigands whom I swept away!
After the frenzy of your wicked lust
Has driven you to assault your father's bed,
You dare to show your hateful face to me,   15
Here in this place full of your infamy,
And seek not out, under an unknown sky,
Countries to which your fame has never spread.
Flee, villain, flee. Brave not my hatred here
Not tempt my anger that I scarce restrain.   20
I have my portion of eternal shame
To have begot so criminal a son,
Without his death, disgrace to my renown,
Soiling the glory of my labours past.
Flee, and if you desire not to be joined   25
To all the villains fallen by my hand,
Take care that never does the shining sun
Behold you in these palaces again.
Flee then, and never more return;
And of your hideous presence purge my realm.   30
And, Neptune, in time past if my strong hand
Of infamous assassins cleared your shores,
Remember that, to recompense my deeds,

You swore to grant the first of my desires.
In the long hardships of a cruel gaol   35
I did not call on your immortal power;
With miser's care I put aside your aid,
Holding it in reserve for greater needs.
I call upon you now. Revenge my wrong.
I give this villain over to your wrath;   40
Drown in his blood his shameless foul desires.
Your favours will be measured by your rage.

HIPPOLYTUS: Phaedra accuses me of sinful love?
So infinite a horror numbs my soul.
So many unforeseen and heavy blows   45
Rain down upon me that I cannot speak.

THESEUS: Villain, you thought that Phaedra would conceal
In craven silence your vile insolence.
You should not, as you fled, have dropped the sword
That, in her hands, established your guilt.   50
Rather should you have crowned your perfidy
And at one stroke robbed her of speech and life.

HIPPOLYTUS: Rightly indignant at so black a lie,
I ought, my lord, to let the truth speak out,
But I shall not resolve this mystery   55
Out of the deep respect that seals my lips.
And, if you will not deepen your distress,
Look at my life; remember who I am.
Like virtue, crime advances by degrees,
Whoever goes beyond the bounds of law   60
Can in the end flout the most sacred rules.
No less than virtue, crime has its degrees,
And innocence has never yet been known
To swing at once to licence's extreme.
A single day cannot change virtuous men   65
To craven and incestuous murderers.
Reared by a virtuous Amazon from birth,
I never had belied my mother's blood.
Pittheus, esteemed the wisest far of men,
Instructed me after I left her hands.   70
I do not seek to paint myself too fair;
But, if one virtue is my birthright, that
Is above all, my lord, as I have shown,
Hate of the crime that they accuse me of.
That is what I am famous for in Greece,   75
I carried virtue to the sternest lengths,
My obdurate austerity is known;
The daylight is not purer than my heart.
Yet I, they say, fired by unholy love . . .

THESEUS: Yes, by that very pride you stand condemned.   80
        The reason why you were so cold is clear;
        Phaedra alone entranced your lustful eyes.
        And, by all other charms unmoved, your heart
        Disdained to glow with innocent desire.

HIPPOLYTUS: No, father, for this may not be concealed,   85
        I have not scorned to glow with virtuous love,
        And at your feet confess my real offence.
        I am in love; in love despite your ban.
        Aricia is mistress of my heart
        And Pallas' daughter has subdued your son.   90
        I worship her and, flouting your command,
        For her alone I pine, I am consumed.

THESEUS: You love her? God! The ruse is gross indeed!
        You feign to err to justify yourself.

HIPPOLYTUS: For half a year I have been deep in love.   95
        Trembling, I came to tell you so myself.
        What! Can no word of mine unseal your eyes?
        What fearful oath, to move you, must I swear?
        May heaven and earth and everything that is . . .

THESEUS: Foulness goes hand in hand with perjury.   100
        Cease! Spare me an importunate harangue,
        If your false virtue has no other stay.

HIPPOLYTUS: To you I may seem false and full of guile.
        Phaedra does justice to me in her heart.

THESEUS: Ah! how my wrath grows at your shamelessness.   105

HIPPOLYTUS: What time and what the place of banishment?

THESEUS: Were you beyond Alcides' pillars, still[23]
        Would I believe your villainy too near.

HIPPOLYTUS: Crushed by the crime that you suspect me of,
        If you desert me who will pity me?   110

THESEUS: Go seek out friends who in their viciousness
        Applaud adultery and incest. These
        Villains and ingrates, lawless, honourless,
        Will shelter evildoers such as you.

HIPPOLYTUS: You harp on incest and adultery.   115
        I will say nought; but Phaedra, as you know,
        My lord, is of a mother, of a line,
        Richer in all these horrors than my own.

THESEUS: What! are there no bounds to your frantic rage?
        For the last time, begone from out my sight.   120

---

23. The Pillars of Hercules, at the western end
    of the Mediterranean; hence any ex-
    tremely remote locality.

Go, libertine, before a father's wrath
Has you with ignominy torn from hence.

Scene 3

THESEUS: Unhappy youth! Haste to your certain doom.
By the stream dreaded even of the gods
Neptune has given and will fulfil his word.
A god of vengeance follows hard on you.
I loved you and, in spite of your offence,   5
My heart is stirred for you forebodingly.
But you have forced me to pronounce your doom.
Was ever wretched father outraged so?
O God who see my overwhelming grief,
How could I have begot so foul a child?   10

Scene 4

PHAEDRA: My Lord, I come stricken with terror, for
Your dreaded voice has reached me and I fear
Your menace may be given prompt effect.
If it is not too late, then spare your son.
Respect your flesh and blood, I beg of you,   5
And save me from the horror of his cries.
Do not lay up for me the endless grief
Of causing bloodshed by a father's hand.
THESEUS: No, Queen, my hand has not bathed in his blood,
But still the villain will not now escape.   10
Immortal hands are with his downfall charged.
This Neptune owes me. You will be avenged.
PHAEDRA: This Neptune owes you. What? Your anger calls . . .
THESEUS: How! You already fear I may be heard?
Rather unite your wishes with my own.   15
In all their heinousness depict his crimes;
Stir up my sluggish cold resentment, for
You do not know the measure of his crimes.
His fury showers affronts upon your name.
Your mouth, he says, speaks nothing but deceit;   20
He swears Aricia has won his heart,
And that he loves her.
PHAEDRA: What!
THESEUS: Those were his words.
But I am not the dupe of vain pretence.
Let us expect swift justice from the god.   25
I shall myself to Neptune's altars, there
To urge fulfilment of immortal oaths.

Scene 5

PHAEDRA: He's gone. What tidings have assailed my ears!
　　　　What smouldering fire awakens in my heart!
　　　　God! What a thunderbolt! What baleful news!
　　　　Flying with but one thought to aid his son,
　　　　I tore myself from pale Oenone's arms,　　　　　　　　　5
　　　　Yielding to the remorse that tortured me.
　　　　Who knows how far repentance would have gone?
　　　　Perhaps I might even have accused myself?
　　　　Perhaps, had not my voice died in my throat,
　　　　The frightful truth would have escaped my lips.　　　　10
　　　　Hippolytus can love but loves not me.
　　　　Aricia has won his heart, his troth.
　　　　Ah! when, inexorable to my pleas,
　　　　Hippolytus put on a front of steel,
　　　　I thought his heart for ever closed to love,　　　　　15
　　　　And against women all alike was armed.
　　　　Another none the less has conquered him.
　　　　She has found favour in his cruel eyes.
　　　　Perhaps he has a heart easy to move.
　　　　Alone of women me he cannot bear.　　　　　　　　　20
　　　　And I was hastening to his defence!

Scene 6

PHAEDRA: Oenone, do you know what I have heard?
OENONE: No, but I still am trembling, to be frank.
　　　　As you rushed forth, I blenched at your intent.
　　　　I was afraid you would destroy yourself.
PHAEDRA: Who would have thought it? There was someone else.　5
OENONE: What!
PHAEDRA: Yes. Hippolytus is deep in love.
　　　　This shy, unconquerable enemy,
　　　　Whom my respect displeased, my tears annoyed,
　　　　Whom I could never speak to unafraid,
　　　　Submissive, tamed, proclaims his own defeat.　　　　10
　　　　Aricia is mistress of his heart.
OENONE: Aricia?
PHAEDRA: Ah! unplumbed depths of woe!
　　　　For what new torments have I spared myself?
　　　　All I have suffered, jealous torments, fears,
　　　　Raging desire, the horror of remorse,　　　　　　　15
　　　　A cruel, harsh, intolerable slight,
　　　　Were a mere foretaste of my torments now.
　　　　They love each other. By what spell did they
　　　　Deceive me? How, where did they meet, since when?
　　　　You knew. Why did you let me be misled?　　　　　20

Why did you keep from me their stealthy love?
Were they seen oft exchanging looks and words?
Deep in the forests were they wont to hide?
Alas! They had the utmost liberty.
Heaven smiled upon their innocent desires.   25
They followed where love led them, conscience free.
For them the dawn rose shining and serene.
And I, rejected by all living things,
I hid myself from day, I shunned the light;
Death was the only god I dared invoke.   30
I waited for the moment of my end,
Feeding on gall and drinking deep of tears.
Too closely watched, I did not even dare
Give myself up in freedom to my grief.
Trembling, this baleful pleasure I enjoyed   35
And, cloaking with a feignéd calm my woes,
Was often driven to forego my tears.

OENONE: What good will their love do them? Never will
They meet again.

PHAEDRA: Their love will always live.
Even as I speak, ah cruel, deadly thought!   40
They flout the fury of my insane rage.
Despite this exile which will sever them
They swear a thousand oaths never to part.
No. No. Their happiness is gall to me.
Oenone, pity my wild jealousy.   45
Aricia must perish, and the King
Be stirred to wrath against her odious race.
No trifling retribution will suffice.
The sister has outdone her brothers' crime.
I will implore him in my jealous rage.   50
What am I doing? I have lost my mind!
I, jealous? and 'tis Theseus I implore!
My husband is alive and yet I pine.
For whom? Whose heart have I been coveting?
At every word my hair stands up on end.   55
Henceforth the measure of my crimes is full.
I reek with foulest incest and deceit.
My hands, that strain for murder and revenge,
Burn with desire to plunge in guiltless blood.
Wretch! and I live and can endure the gaze   60
Of the most sacred sun from which I spring.
My grandsire is the lord of all the gods;
My forebears fill the sky, the universe.
Where can I hide? In dark infernal night?
No, there my father holds the urn of doom.   65

Destiny placed it in his ruthless hands.
Minos judges in hell the trembling dead.
Ah! how his horror-stricken shade will start
To see before him his own daughter stand,
Forced to admit to such a host of sins   70
And some, perhaps, unknown even in hell!
What, father, will you say to that dread sight?
I see your hand slip from the fateful urn;
I see you searching for new punishments,
Yourself your own kin's executioner.   75
Forgive me. Venus' wrath has doomed your race.
Your daughter's frenzy shows that vengeance forth.
Alas, my sad heart never has enjoyed
The fruits of crimes whose dark shame follows me.
Dogged by misfortune to my dying breath,   80
I end upon the rack a life of pain.

OENONE: Ah, Queen! dismiss these unbecoming fears,
And of your error take a different view.
You are in love. We cannot change our fate.
By destined magic you were swept along.   85
Is that so strange or so miraculous?
Has love then triumphed only over you?
Frailty is human and but natural.
Mortal, you must a mortal's lot endure.
This thraldom was imposed long, long ago.   90
The gods themselves that in Olympus dwell,
Who smite the evildoer with their bolt,
Have sometimes felt unlawful passions' fire.

PHAEDRA: Great gods! What counsels dare you offer me?
Even to the last you seek to poison me.   95
Wretch! Thus it is that you have caused my doom.
You, when I fled from life, you called me back;
At your entreaties duty was forgot;
It was you made me see Hippolytus.
You meddling fool. Why did your impious lips,   100
Falsely accusing him, besmirch his life?
You may have killed him, if the gods have heard
A maddened father's sacrilegious wish.
I'll hear no more. Hence, loathsome monster, hence.
Go, leave me to my pitiable fate.   105
May the just heavens reward you fittingly,
And may your punishment forever fright
All who, as you have done, by base deceit
Pander to ill-starred princes' weaknesses,
Urging them on to yield to their desires,   110

And dare to smooth the path of crime for them,
Vile flatterers, the most ill-fated boon
The anger of the gods can make to kings!

OENONE: Ah God! to save her what have I not done;
But this is the reward I have deserved.   115

Act V

Scene 1

ARICIA: What, in this peril you refuse to speak?
You leave a loving father undeceived?
Cruel one, can you, by my tears unmoved,
Consent without a sigh to part from me?
Go hence and leave me to my grieving heart.   5
But, if you go, at least preserve your life.
Defend your honour from a foul reproach
And force your father to revoke your doom.
There still is time. Wherefore, from what caprice,
Will you let Phaedra's slander hold the field?   10
Tell Theseus all.

HIPPOLYTUS: Ah, what have I not said?
Should I make known the outrage to his bed
And by an all too frank confession bring
Over my father's brow a blush of shame?
This odious secret you alone have pierced.   15
My sole confidants are the gods and you.
Judge of my love, I have not hid from you
All I desired to hide even from myself.
But, since you have been sworn to secrecy,
Forget, if it be possible, my words.   20
And never may your pure unsullied lips
Recount the details of this horrid scene.
Let's trust the justice of the gods above.
Their interest lies in vindicating me.
Sooner or later Phaedra will be brought   25
To book and meet an ignominious doom.
That is the only boon I ask of you.
My anger takes all other liberties.
Reject the bondage under which you pine;
Dare to accompany me in my flight.   30
Tear yourself free from an unhallowed spot
Where virtue breathes a foul, polluted air.
Let us to cover our escape exploit
The wild confusion that my downfall spreads.

I can provide you with the means for flight.   35
The only guards controlling you are mine.
Mighty defenders will take up our cause.
Argos awaits us; Sparta summons us.
Let's bear our grievance to our new allies.
Phaedra must never profit from our fall[24]   40
And drive us both from off my father's throne,
Making her son the heir to our estates.
Now is our chance. We must lay hands on it.
What holds you back? You seem to hesitate.
Only your interest thus emboldens me.   45
When I am ardent, why are you so cold?
Are you afraid to share an exile's lot?

ARICIA: Alas! How pleasant to be banished thus!
With what delight, linking my fate with yours,
By all the world forgotten I would live!   50
But, since we are not joined by that sweet bond,
Could I in honour flee from here with you?
I know that, even by the strictest code,
I may throw off your father's tutelage.
No bond of home or parents holds me back,   55
And flight from tyrants is permissible.
You love me, though, my lord, and my good name ...

HIPPOLYTUS: No. No. Your honour is too dear to me.
I come before you with a nobler plan.
Flee from my foes. Flee as my wedded wife.   60
Alone in exile, since heaven wills it so,
We need no man's consent to pledge our faith.
Not always torches blaze for Hymen's rites.
Not far from Troezen's gates, among these tombs,
My princely forebears' ancient burial place,   65
There stands a shrine dreaded of perjurers.
There mortals never swear an oath in vain.
Who breaks his word is punished instantly,
And men forsworn, afraid of certain death,
Are held in check by this most dreaded threat.   70
There, if you trust me, we will ratify
By solemn oath our everlasting love,
Taking to witness this old temple's god.
We'll pray him to be father to us both.
I'll call to witness the most sacred gods,   75
And chaste Diana, Juno the august,

---

24. I.e. profit by obtaining the kingdom which
    normally would have gone to Hippolytus
    and Aricia.

And all the gods, witnesses of my love,
Will lend their blessing to my holy vows.
ARICIA: The King is coming. Flee, make haste. To cloak
My own departure, I will stay awhile.   80
Go now, but leave me someone I can trust
To lead my steps to the appointed place.

Scene 2

THESEUS: O God! lighten the darkness of my mind.
Show me the truth that I am searching for.
ARICIA: Make ready, dear Ismene, for our flight.

Scene 3

THESEUS: Your colour changes and you seem aghast,
Lady. What was the young prince doing here?
ARICIA: My lord, he took eternal leave of me.
THESEUS: You have subdued that proud rebellious heart,
And his first raptures were inspired by you.   5
ARICIA: My lord, I cannot well deny the truth.
Your unjust hatred is not shared by him.
He did not treat me like a criminal.
THESEUS: I know. He swore eternal love to you.
Do not rely on that inconstant heart,   10
For he to others swore the self same oaths.
ARICIA: He, Sire?
THESEUS: You ought to have restrained him. How
Could you endure to share his fickle heart?
ARICIA: And how could you allow such calumny
To tarnish the bright glory of his life?   15
Have you so little knowledge of his heart?
Can you not tell baseness from innocence?
Must from your eyes alone an odious cloud
Conceal his virtues which shine bright to all?
I cannot let him further be maligned.   20
Stop and repent of your assassin's prayer.
Fear, my lord, fear lest the unbending heavens
Hate you enough to grant you your desire.
Oft in their wrath they take our sacrifice.
Often their gifts are sent to scourge our sins.   25
THESEUS: In vain you seek to cover his offence.
Your passion blinds you to his faults. But I
Have faith in sure, trustworthy witnesses.
I have seen tears which surely were not feigned.
ARICIA: Take care, my lord. Invincible, your hands   30
Have freed the world from monsters numberless;
But all are not destroyed. You still let live

One . . . But your son forbids me to proceed.
Knowing his wishes, I respect you still.
I would not grieve him if I dared to speak.   35
Following his restraint, I shall withdraw
Rather than let the truth escape my lips.

Scene 4

THESEUS (*alone*) What does she mean, and what do these words hide,
Begun and broken off, begun again?
Is it their aim to trick me by a feint?
Are they in league to put me on the rack?
But I myself, despite my stern resolve,   5
What plaintive voice cries in my inmost heart?
A lurking flash of pity harrows me.
I'll have Oenone questioned once again;
I must have more light thrown upon the crime.
Guards, bring Oenone out to me alone.   10

Scene 5

PANOPE: I do not know what the Queen purposes,
But her distraction is a fearful sight.
Mortal despair cries from her haggard face,
And death has laid its paleness on her cheeks.
Oenone, driven out with shame, has plunged   5
Already into the unsounded sea.
We do not know what led her to this death;
The waves have closed for ever over her.
THESEUS: What?
PANOPE: This dark action did not calm the Queen.
Distraction seems to swell her wavering heart.   10
Sometimes, to soothe her secret sufferings,
She takes her children, bathes them in her tears;
Then, suddenly, renouncing mother's love,
Shuddering with horror, will have none of them.
This way and that, she wanders aimlessly;   15
Wildly she looks at us, but knows us not.
She thrice has written, then has changed her mind,
And thrice torn up the letter she began.
See her, we beg you. We implore your help.
THESEUS: Oenone's dead, and Phaedra seeks to die.   20
Call back my son, let him defend himself
And speak to me! I'll lend a willing ear.

[*Alone.*]

Do not be overhasty with your gifts,
Neptune! I wish my prayer may not be heard.   25
Perhaps I have believed false witnesses,
Lifting too soon my cruel hand to you.
Ah! if you act, how endless my despair!

  Scene 6

THESEUS: What have you done with him. Theramenes?
          I put him as a boy into your hands.
          But why the tears that trickle down your cheeks?
          What of my son?
THERAMENES: O tardy vain concern!
          O unavailing love! Your son's no more.   5
THESEUS: God!
THERAMENES: I have seen the best of mortals die,
          And the most innocent, I dare to add.
THESEUS: Dead? When I open wide my arms to him,
          The gods, impatient, hasten on his death?
          What blow, what thunderbolt snatched him away?   10
THERAMENES: Scarce were we issuing from Troezen's gates;
          He drove his chariot; round about him ranged,
          Copying his silence, were his cheerless guards.
          Pensive, he followed the Mycenae road,
          And let the reins hang loose upon his steeds.   15
          These haughty steeds, that once upon a time,
          Noble, high-spirited, obeyed his voice,
          Now dull of eye and with dejected air
          Seemed to conform to his despondent thoughts.
          A ghastly cry from out the water's depths   20
          That moment rent the quiet of the air.
          From the earth's entrails then a fearful voice
          Made answer with a groan to that dread cry.
          Deep in our hearts our blood with horror froze.
          The coursers' manes, on hearing, stood erect.   25
          And now, there rose upon the liquid plain
          A watery mountain seething furiously.
          The surge drew near, dissolved and vomited
          A raging monster from among the foam.
          His forehead huge was armed with fearsome horns   30
          And his whole body sheathed in yellow scales,
          Half bull, half dragon, wild, impetuous.
          His crupper curved in many a winding fold.
          The shore quaked with his long-drawn bellowings.
          The heavens beheld the monster, horror-struck;   35

It poisoned all the air; it rocked the earth.
The wave that brought it in recoiled aghast.
Everyone, throwing courage to the winds,
Took refuge in the temple near at hand.
Hippolytus alone, undaunted, stayed,   40
Reined in his steeds and seized his javelins,
Had at the monster and, with sure-flung dart,
Dealt him a gaping wound deep in his flank.
With rage and pain the monster, starting up,
Collapsed and, falling at the horses' feet,   45
Rolled over, opening wide his flaming jaws,
And covered them with smoke and blood and fire.
Carried away by terror, deaf, the steeds
No more responded to his curb or voice.
Their master spent his efforts all in vain.   50
They stained the bridle with their bloody foam.
In this wild tumult, it is even said,
A god appeared, goading their dusty flanks.
Over the rocks fear drove them headlong on;
The axle groaned and broke. Hippolytus   55
Saw his whole chariot shattered into bits.
He fell at last, entangled in the reins.
Forgive my grief. For me this picture spells
Eternal sorrow and perpetual tears.
I have beheld, my lord, your ill-starred son   60
Dragged by the horses that his hand had fed.
His voice that called them merely frightened them.
Onward they flew—his body one whole wound.
The plain resounded with our cries of woe.
At last they slackened their impetuous course.   65
They halted near the old ancestral tombs
Where all his royal forebears lie in state.
I and his guards hastened to him in tears.
The traces of his blood showed us the way.
The rocks were stained with it, the cruel thorns   70
Dripped with the bleeding remnants of his hair.
I saw him, called him; giving me his hand,
He opened and then straightway closed his eyes.
'Heaven takes my life, though innocent,' he cried.
'When I am dead, protect Aricia.   75
Friend, if my father ever learns the truth,
And pities the misfortunes of his son,
And would appease me in the life to come,
Tell him to show that princess clemency,

To give her back . . .'. And then he passed away,   80
And in my arms lay a disfigured corpse,
A tribute to the anger of the gods
That even his father would not recognize.

THESEUS: My son, fond hope I have myself destroyed!
    Inexorable, all too helpful gods!   85
    What keen remorse will haunt me all my life!

THERAMENES: Aricia then came upon the scene.
    She came, my lord, fleeing your royal wrath,
    Before the gods to pledge her faith to him.
    As she drew near, she saw the reeking grass.   90
    She saw, a grim sight for a lover's eyes,
    Hippolytus, disfigured, deadly pale.
    A while she tried to doubt her evil fate.
    She sees the body of Hippolytus,
    Yet still pursues the quest for her beloved.   95
    But, in the end, only too sure 'tis he,
    With one sad look, accusing heaven's spite,
    Cold, moaning, and well nigh inanimate,
    She falls, unconscious, at her sweetheart's feet.
    Ismene, bending over her, in tears,   100
    Summons her back to life, a life of pain.
    And I have come, my lord, hating the world,
    To tell you of Hippolytus' last wish
    And to discharge the bitter embassy
    Which he entrusted to me as he died.   105
    But hither comes his deadly enemy.

Scene 7

THESEUS: Well, then, you triumph and my son's no more.
    What grounds I have for fear! What cruel doubt
    Gnaws at my heart, pleading his innocence!
    But he is dead. Accept your victim. Joy
    In his undoing, justified or no,   5
    For I am willing to deceive myself.
    Since you accuse him, I accept his guilt.
    His death will make my tears flow fast enough
    Without my seeking for enlightenment
    Which could not ever bring him back to me   10
    And might perhaps but sharpen my distress.
    Let me flee, far from you and from these shores,
    The bloody vision of my mangled son.
    Stunned and pursued by this grim memory,
    Would I were in another universe!   15

Everything seems to brand my wicked wrath.
My very name increases my despair.
Less known of mortals, I could hide myself.
I hate even the favours of the gods.
And now I must bewail their murderous gifts,   20
No longer tiring them with fruitless prayers.
Whatever they have done for me, their aid
Cannot give back what they have robbed me of.

PHAEDRA: No, Theseus. No, I must at last speak out.
I must redress the wrong I did your son,   25
For he was innocent.

THESEUS: Wretch that I am!
If I condemned him, it was on your word.
Cruel one, do you hope to be forgiven . . . .

PHAEDRA: Each moment's precious. Listen. It was I,
Theseus, who on your virtuous, filial son   30
Made bold to cast a lewd, incestuous eye.
Heaven in my heart lit an ill-omened fire.
Detestable Oenone did the rest.
She feared your son, knowing my frenzy, might
Reveal a guilty passion he abhorred.   35
The wretch, exploiting my enfeebled state,
Rushed to denounce Hippolytus to you.
She has exacted justice on herself
And found beneath the waves too mild a death.
By now I would have perished by the sword,   40
But first I wished to clear my victim's name.
I wished, revealing my remorse to you,
To choose a slower road down to the dead.
I have instilled into my burning veins
A poison that Medea brought to Greece.   45
Already it has reached my heart and spread
A strange chill through my body. Even now
Only as through a cloud I see the bright
Heaven and the husband whom I still defile.
But death, robbing my eyes of light, will give   50
Back to the sun its tarnished purity.

PANOPE: Ah! she is dying.

THESEUS: Would the memory
Of her appalling misdeeds die with her!
Let us, now that my error's all too clear,
Go out and mourn over my ill-starred son.   55
Let us embrace my cherished son's remains
And expiate my mad atrocious wish,

Rendering him the honours he deserves,
And, to appease the anger of his shade,
Let his beloved, despite her brothers' crime,
Be as a daughter to me from this day.   60

San Agustin National Archeological Park. Monolith of a warrior (left) and a god of war, on mound dedicated to gods of war.

SECTION VIII
The Early Americas

The first inhabitants of the Americas—the peoples we know collectively as Indians—migrated across the Bering Strait from Asia between 25,000 and 40,000 years ago. Over the ensuing millennia, they migrated gradually over the North and South American continents, developing cultures suited to diverse geographic and climatic conditions. Our earliest evidence for the emergence of regional cultures dates from about 10,000 B.C.E.

Mexico, and Central and South America

Although advanced civilizations existed in the Americas from as early as 800 C.E., the most sophisticated Indian cultures—the Mayas (first century B.C.E.), the Aztecs (thirteenth century C.E.), and the Incas (thirteenth century C.E.) respectively—occupied central Mexico, Central America, and the high valleys of the Andes. When the Spanish conquistadors landed in the "new" world, the indigenous population may have been as large as forty-five million. We are including here selections from the cultural traditions of the three best-known societies: the Aztecs of Mexico, the Mayas of the Yucatan and Central America, and the Incas of what is now called Peru. These three groups represent, however, a tiny fraction of the 350 major tribal groups, fifteen cultural centers or advanced civilizations, and more than 160 linguis-

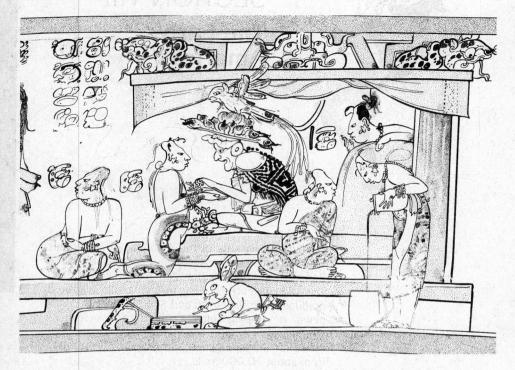

AND THEN THEY TOOK HOLD OF A HUMAN SACRIFICE: A classic Maya funerary vase painting from northern Guatemala, showing head lord of Xibalba, One Death, seated on his throne at right; (*The vase is in the Princeton University Art Museum.*)

tic groups that occupied Latin America. Building on the legacies of the societies that came before them, these civilizations were to develop advanced agricultural technology, sophisticated astronomical knowledge, stratified societies, and imperial political systems.

When speaking of the Aztecs it is usually the Mexicas, a Nahuatl-speaking warrior tribe, that is being referred to. The Mexicas, an uncultivated people, formed an alliance around 1246 C.E. with the aristocracy of the surviving Toltecs who preceded them as leaders of the Aztec state. The Mexicas built their capital city of Tenochtitlan in what is now central Mexico around 1325 and by 1376 they had made the transition from a clan (*calpulli*) society to a monarchy. In 1428, allied with the peoples of Texcoco and Tlacopan, they conquered the seat of the state in Atzcapotzalco. From then on the Mexicas reigned supreme, subjugating many other peoples who in retaliation were to later provide material and military help to Cortés, who conquered them in 1521.

Under the Mexicas, the Aztec empire became a warrior state. Although human sacrifice was practiced to an extent by other peoples in the empire, the Mexicas undertook such rituals to an unprecedented degree. Such fanaticism can be partly explained by the prominence that the deity Huitzilopochtli gained over the other deities of the Aztec pantheon. Huitzilopochtli, the Mexicas believed, required the daily sacrifice of human hearts in order for the sun to rise. This belief legitimized the casualties of their military expansion. By the mid-fifteenth century, when military expansion slowed down, the Mexicas resorted to the infamous "flower wars" or tournaments in which they battled other peoples, particularly the Tlaxcalans, in order to exchange captives, who were then sacrificed to the deities.

It is in this context that Aztec "literary" production should be understood. The "flower songs" included here are not "poetry" as we traditionally understand it. Rather they are the words forming a part of a ritual in which "ghost warriors" were called down from heaven to help in battle.

Our knowledge of the Mayan peoples can be traced back to around 2000 B.C.E., when they began to settle in the areas known today as Guatemala, Honduras, and El Salvador, and the Mexican states of Yucatan, Campeche, Tabasco, and Chiapas. Like the Mexicas, the Mayans had their roots in a civilization (the Olmecs) which flourished before them. Two of the most sophisticated achievements of the Mayas, hieroglyphic writing and the calendar, were developed as early as 500 C.E. but were not inscribed on stone until the first century B.C.E. There were two Mayan empires. The first was the Classic Period, which flourished between 317 and 889 C.E. in Petén, in what is today northern Guatemala. The richly inscribed architectural and sculptural wonders of Palenque, Tikal, and Copán date from this period. As the first empire declined because of overpopulation, environmental blight, and malnutrition, the center of Mayan civilization shifted northward to the Yucatan around 900 C.E. This second or New Empire was shaped by the Toltecs, a Nahuatl-speaking people of Mayan descent. They were militaristic and worshipped the god-king Quetzalcoatl or "Plumed Serpent," who figures prominently in the *Popol Vuh* or "Council Book" of the Maya-Quiché kingdom founded by their descendants.

The Mayas of both periods had a highly developed culture that was expressed in musical, dramatic, philosophical, and historical forms. Among the thousands of hieroglyphic works that they produced, only four survived the destruction wreaked by the conquistadors. The first, *Xahoh-Tun* [The Dance of Tun], is also known as *Rabinal Achí* in reference to the place—Rabinal—in which the transcribed Mayan oral text was found in the mid-nineteenth century. The events, which are thought to have taken place in the mid-fifteenth century C.E., revolve around the young warrior Cavek Quiché Vinak's challenge to an enemy lord, who in the end has him sacrificed. The other three—the *Popol Vuh, The Annals of the Cakchikels,* and *The Books of Chilam Balam*—all reproduce the cosmogonies of various Mayan peoples. Discovered on different dates in the seventeenth, eighteenth, and nineteenth centuries, these works are thought to have been created in the fifteenth century. Some, like the *Popol Vuh,* were written down in Mayan, just after the Spanish conquest in the sixteenth century. Like the *Popol Vuh,* which is a sacred book of counsel and prophesy, the various books of *Chilam Balam* (Chilam signifies *priest* and Balam, which denotes *jaguar,* refers to the last and greatest prophet before the conquest), were meant to be interpreted in ritual ceremonies. The *Annals of the Cakchiquels* describes in historical detail the bloody fight between the Cakchiquels and the Quichés in the middle of the fifteenth century. All of these reveal some Christian influence, a result of Indian scribes having been trained by the Spaniards. The scribes were used to aid the Spaniards in their evangelizing mission by translating Christian prayers, sermons, and catechisms into the Mayan languages.

The third civilization discussed here, the Incas, were the most sophisticated. They built their empire by skillful political organization, efficient administration of resources, and the invention and use of advanced military technology. Their religion tended toward monotheism, with the sun being their principal deity, whom they worshipped in sumptuous temples. Around 1100 C.E., the Incas began to populate the valley which was to become Cuzco, their capital city. By the time the Spaniards arrived, the Incas had extended their dominion over a territory that included today's Peru and Ecuador, and large portions of Bolivia, Chile, and Argentina. The Inca, which means "child of the sun," was a kind of emperor believed to be descended from the sun deity. He was the highest authority in the hereditary monarchy and had both military and priestly functions. Incan society was highly stratified, but its economy was predominantly collectivist. The success of the Incas was primarily due to their organizational abilities, which were perfected in a highly developed mathematical system. Like the Romans in Europe, the Incas were able to build an excellent highway system, stretching over 25,000 kilometers. They also constructed aqueducts, bridges, and large-scale buildings, such as those at Machu Picchu, and organized an efficient communication network of messenger-runners. Like the Romans, too, they imposed their language, Quechua, throughout their empire.

The Incas had an extensive and varied culture. Although they did not have writing, they did have a system of memorization based on knotted strings or *kipus* of different sizes, colors, and shapes. They had ritual dramatic forms that included dance, song, and pantomime. Their "lyric" forms were metaphysical, ritual, or epic in character. When the Spaniards conquered the Incan empire in the 1530s, it was at the height of its splendor under the rule of Atahualpa. As in the defeat of Moctezuma, the Spaniards took advantage of the rivalries among different groups, particularly that of Atahualpa's brother Huascar.

When we look back today at the legacies of the Aztecs, the Mayas, and the Incas, we find that the native texts recorded during the period of the Spanish conquests register a note of profound despondency, not only at the destruction of life and the great works of civilization, but more importantly at the loss of a guiding vision, whether epistemological or cosmological. The world as they had known it was no more. The Mayan books of *Chilam Balam*—for there are Chilam books from various Mayan sites—characterize this loss as the destruction of understanding and wisdom: "There was no longer any great teacher, any great orator, any supreme priest, when the change of rulers occurred upon [the] arrival [of the Spaniards]."* Similarly, in one of the surviving Aztec accounts of the defeat of Moctezuma, we can read: "Broken spears lie in the roads;/we have torn our hair in grief./The houses are roofless now, and their walls/are red with blood."† Worse still, there was no longer communication with the gods, as Durán's *History of the Indies* notes: "[The Aztecs] had no further answer from their oracles; then they regarded the gods as mute or dead."‡

The problems of transliteration and transcription that we encounter in dealing with Hispanic texts attest to a certain duality in Latin American cultures that continues even today—for example, in the literature of magical or marvelous realism (a noncontradictory combination of the rational and the supernatural) and in Cuban *santería* or Brazilian *candomblé*, African-based popular religions that combine Catholic saints and Yoruban *orixas* or deities in syncretic figures, each with its own style of dress, food and rhythm. Initially, this duality was related to

---

The Book of Chilam Balam of Chumayel (Norman: University of Oklahoma Press, 1967) p. 5.

†"The Story of the Conquest as Told by the Anonymous Authors of Tlatelolco," *The Broken Spears. The Aztec Account of the Conquest of Mexico*, trans. from Nahuatl into Spanish by Angel Maria Garibay K., trans. into English by Lysander Kemp, ed. Miguel León-Portilla (Boston: Beacon Press, 1962), p. 137.

‡D. Durán, *The Aztecs, The History of the Indies of New Spain* (New York: Orion, 1964) 77.

the reconciling of two entirely different visions of the world. This is most evident in the conquerors' accounts—letters to the kings, journals, chronicles, histories, etc.—of the nature of the places and peoples they encountered. For example, in the attempts made by Christopher Columbus to explain what he saw, there are constant references to his own repository of knowledge: from Christian scripture, Pliny's *Natural History*—the Latin text regarded as a scientific source book during the Middle Ages—and Marco Polo's *Travels* to chivalry romances and Renaissance epic poems. In many cases, this knowledge took precedence over what Columbus saw or heard. For example, when he heard the word "Cariba," supposedly an appellative for a neighboring tribe of warlike Indians, he assimilated it to "Caniba," which were the subjects of the Grand Khan of which Marco Polo writes.§ Likewise, certain beliefs that he had—that the lands he encountered bordered on Paradise, or that he expected to meet up with Cyclopes and mermaids—demonstrate that his episte- mological framework overrode what he actually witnessed. However, despite such assimilations he was also careful to note the exoticism of many things: "I saw many trees very unlike ours, and many of them had branches of different kinds, and all coming from one root; one branch is of one kind and one of another, and they are so unlike each other that it is the greatest wonder in the world."**

The literature of conquest, colonization, and evangelization tells us much about native societies and their destruction. The oscillation between assimilation and differentiation, as noted by Columbus in his journal, however, was to remain a problem in most accounts of such "encounters" between civilizations and, more generally, for most interpretations of the nature of Latin American culture right up to the present.

The Dominican priest Bartolomé de Las Casas, who himself came with the conquistadors as an evangelist and was granted an *encomienda* or tract of land, underwent so strong a conversion to abolitionism that he eventually came to value the Indians more than his fellow Christians. His characterization of the natives as innocents—"poor lambs" in the excerpts from *The History of the Indies* presented here—and his energetic protest against the brutality of the conquistadors were put forth in many arguments and writings, but most notably in the *Very Brief Account of the Destruction of the Indies* (1522), which was immediately translated into six European languages. This work constituted the immediate pretext for the so-called Black Legend, according to which Spain was considered to have wreaked a destruction of indigenous peoples far more brutal than the violence of conquest by other European nations. The Black Legend was elaborated as a means to legitimize the challenges by England, the Low Countries, and France to Spain's possession of the Indies by papal and other international law.

The selections included here from Felipe Guamán Poma de Ayala, a Chris- tianized Indian of noble, Incan lineage, and Garcilaso de la Vega (El Inca), a *mestizo* (part Native American and part European) of double royal lineage, offer two interesting variations on the interaction of identity, recognition, and knowledge. Both, as Indians, claim to have privileged knowledge that has enabled them to write a truer history of their native Peru. This knowledge is also used as a pretext for criticizing their respective targets—the colonial administration in Guamán Poma's case, European historiography as it relates to Peru in Garcilaso's—and for making a case for their own worth.

§*The Journal of Christopher Columbus* (London: Anthony Blond, 1968), 11/23/92, 11/26/92, 12/11/92.
***The Journal of Christopher Columbus*, 10/16/92.

Colonial literature was not, of course, institutionalized as such in its own time; it is, rather, the construct of literary scholarship dating from the nineteenth century and is currently in the process of reconstruction. It is this scholarship, intimately linked to intellectual projects to legitimize particular countries and Latin America in general by grounding cultural identity in a historical foundation, which led us to include all kinds of genres as literature, be they chronicles, ethnographies written by missionaries, the epic poetry of the elites, *autos sacramentales* or religious drama, the satirical writing of disgruntled *letrados* (administrative functionaries and others who disseminated information and knowledge) and those who were at odds with colonial rule, which was the exclusive domain of Spaniards. There was, of course, strictly literary writing, but it was the exception and it was very much under the influence of the Baroque ethos that the Catholic Church and the Spanish and Portuguese crowns propagated throughout Latin America.

The Baroque influence — showy, intricate artifices interwoven with a mood of disillusionment and the signs of Iberian decadence and the Counter-Reformation — was taken to extremes in Latin America. There the formal acquires an almost independent existence, for the source of power is always distant and the mixture of races leads to a heterogeneous society in which strategies of simulation and dissimulation are required to "pass" from one stratum to another. The complication and proliferation of forms, intensified by recourse not only to this social and linguistic heterogeneity but also to the panoply of natural elements different from the European ones, mark Latin American literature. An excess of style, which was initially a means to approximate and even better models of European culture, became a way of life and art among many writers, enduring to this day in such expressive modes as magical or marvelous realism and the neobaroque (a twentieth-century reworking, in strictly literary terms, of this stylization).

North America

At the time of the first European contacts, the area currently occupied by the lower United States was home to some 240 tribes (or nations) distributed across six broad cultural regions: Northwest Coast, Plateau, Plains, Southwest, Eastern Woodlands, and Southeast.

There is no doubt that a rich and varied literary culture—from songs, stories, and dramatic oratory to chants and charms and curing spells—existed for thousands of years before the arrival of the Europeans. But the indigenous cultures of the present-day United States were oral cultures; they did not use alphabetic writing to record their thought or "literature." For an anthology such as this—indeed, for any anthology—the problem is apparent: how to represent the literature of a period when literature was not represented in textual form? Strictly speaking, of course, there is no way to do so; we cannot *read* Indian literature from a time before the incursion of the Europeans because a written literature simply did not exist.

But because oral cultures are oriented toward continuity rather than change, it is at least possible to suggest that some later texts that we do have may serve as approximate representations of what we do not have. Any such assumptions, of course, must amount to at best an informed guess. We have decided that it is a guess worth chancing—at least in a limited way. Thus we have included a lengthy excerpt from a Navajo creation story, which, although it was first recorded in a written form in the nineteenth century, is probably not very different from versions of the story told hundreds of years earlier. (But that is something we can only guess, not know.) We have also included in this section a few examples classified as songs, charms, prophecies—genres that are entirely Western categories, that we can only speculate are consistent with the actual Native American oral versions that existed long before Columbus. The North American peoples whose works are included in this section are the Navajo, Kwakiutl, Crow, Iroquois, and Cherokee.

The Navajo migrated from southern Canada to the southwestern United States between the years 1000 and 1300 C.E., settling among the sedentary Pueblo peoples who had preceded them to the region far earlier. Although the Navajo raided their Pueblo neighbors, they also learned from them, adapting Pueblo techniques in agriculture, in the arts of pottery and weaving, and in ritual practices such as sand painting. The Navajo were also influenced by the Mexicans, from whom they later learned the silver-working techniques for which they are well-known today. In the seventeenth century, sheep—introduced to the New World by the Spanish—became important to the Navajo economy. Today, even after the disastrous "sheep reduction" program instituted by the federal government in the 1930s and 1940s, sheepherding remains important to the Navajo people. In 1864 the Navajo, caught up in the fighting between the Union and the Confederacy in the Civil War, were violently subdued in Santa Fe by Kit Carson, a colonel in the Union army and onetime "friend" of the Indian. They were then sent upon the "Long Walk" some 300 miles to imprisonment at Fort Sumner, southeast of Santa Fe. This was a traumatic event for the Navajo as the "Trail of Tears" was for the Cherokee (see below). In 1868 the Navajo were permitted to return to their homelands and to settle on a reservation that had been surveyed so that most of the best pastureland was left to the more numerous white settlers. The Navajo today are the most populous tribe in the United States.

The Kwakiutl are a Northwest Coast people. Their traditional homelands included the northern portion of Vancouver Island and the facing mainland. In common with several other peoples of the Northwest, Kwakiutl subsistence was heavily dependent upon salmon fishing, and important ritual activities were focused on the life cycle of the salmon. As Navajo silverwork and weaving are well-known throughout the world, so, too, are the woodworking skills of the Kwakiutl—their elaborately carved and painted memorial poles, house posts, and ceremonial utensils are among the best known of Indian arts.

Kwakiutl society was elaborately stratified, with each person holding an inherited position. The potlatch, a ceremonial distribution of gifts undertaken for a variety of reasons—to celebrate an important event or to affirm or establish status—is perhaps the Kwakiutl ritual activity most intensely studied by anthropologists. Dancing societies were another important institution; each society had a hierarchical repertoire of dances that told of ancestral encounters with supernatural beings in which gifts, social rankings, crests, and privileges were originally bestowed in a sort of potlatch of the gods.

The Crow are a Plains people who occupied the Yellowstone River country in what are today the states of Oregon and Montana. After obtaining horses from the Spanish (the horse had become extinct in the New World), Plains Indians developed a distinctive culture based on hunting the extensive buffalo herds that provided food, clothing, and housing. (For example, buffalo skins were used to construct the familiar conical *tipi,* or what we call the tepee, of the Plains.) They also conducted ritualized raiding activities designed to increase the supply of horses or to bring prestige to those who carried them out successfully (e.g., to warriors who killed or counted *coup* upon—touched—an enemy in battle).

The spiritual life of young Crow males, typical of Plains tribes generally, was rooted in individual mystical experience. A vision induced in an adolescent male by fasting and self-torture would reveal the supernatural guardian, usually an animal, who would confer upon him certain powers. The Lakota and the Cheyenne were traditional enemies of the Crow, and, as the whites advanced upon the Plains, the Crow made common cause with them against these enemy tribes. Thus, in 1868, when the Crow agreed to settle upon a reservation carved from some of their former territories in Montana, their history of cooperation with the whites helped them to obtain a better deal, relatively speaking, than the resisting Plains tribes. The Sun Dance of the Crow, once outlawed as a "heathenish practice," has, in somewhat modified form, had a great revival today, and serves as the center of the ritual life of many contemporary, traditional Crow people.

The Cherokee originally dwelt around the Great Lakes, but after defeat by the Delaware and Iroquois, they migrated south, and, around the year 1700, were settled around the northern Allegheny Mountains of eastern Tennessee and the western Carolinas. The southernmost group of Iroquoian speakers, the Cherokee, developed an economy based upon advanced agricultural techniques; social organization emphasized a division between red (war) villages, whose chiefs were under the rule of the supreme war chief, and white (peace) villages, whose chiefs answered to the supreme peace chief. Each village consisted of some thirty to sixty log cabins and a council house.

The response of the Cherokee to the increasing numbers of white invaders intruding upon Cherokee lands after the turn of the nineteenth century involved a complex and subtle combination of resistance and accommodation. In 1821 the mixed-blood Cherokee, George Guess, or Sequoyah, performed the extraordinary task of singlehandedly inventing a writing system—strictly speaking, a syllabary rather than an alphabet—for the Cherokee language. As result, many Cherokee persons also became literate in English.

Nonetheless, in 1830, under pressure from President Andrew Jackson, Congress passed the Indian Removal Act, which gave the president the authority to remove Indians east of the Mississippi from their traditional homelands to Indian Territory (present-day Oklahoma) west of the Mississippi. This was done in 1838, when approximately twelve thousand eastern Cherokee were forced by federal troops to set out, in the dead of winter, on the "Trail of Tears." Fully one third—four thousand people—died on that march. Today, the majority of Cherokee people live in the state of Oklahoma. Next to the Navajo, the Cherokee are the most populous tribe in the United States today.

The people called the Iroquois are not a single tribe but rather a loose confederation of five (the Mohawk, Oneida, Onondaga, Cayuga, and Seneca), and later (with the addition of the Tuscarora) six peoples speaking similar languages (the "Iroquoian" language group). The Iroquois lived in an area around the southern Great Lakes, and, in the seventeenth and eighteenth centuries, controlled a wide expanse of territory from the Great Lakes as far south and east as Albany.

The Iroquoian peoples relied on both agriculture and hunting for sustenance. The basic economic and social unit was the village, a grouping of "longhouses," each of which lodged many families. Indeed, the longhouse served as a central metaphor of society for the Iroquois. For example, the nations of the Iroquois League spoke of themselves as "people of the longhouse," meaning that the tribes together were as families in a dwelling. Society was matrilineal, with property owned by the women. The women also played a major role in the frequent and lengthy council meetings through which decisions involving the people were made. Renowned as fierce warriors, the Iroquois were able to organize effective resistance against French expansion south from Canada, and westward expansion by those English who would become Americans. The Iroquois supported the British in the Revolutionary War because, among other reasons, they were obviously in agreement with the British wish to contain the line of colonial settlement east of the Allegheny Mountains. American victory led to harsh consequences for the Iroquois. Today Iroquoian culture flourishes in a variety of complex ways, on both sides of the border between the United States and Canada.

Further Readings

Adorno, Rolona. *Guamán Poma de Ayala: Writing and Resistance in Colonial Peru*. Austin: University of Texas Press, 1986.

Allen, Paula Gunn, ed. *Studies in American Indian Literature*. New York: Modern Language Association, 1983.

Astrov, Margot, ed. *American Indian Prose and Poetry*. New York: Fawcett, 1973 [1946].

Bierhorst, John, ed. *Four Masterworks of American Indian Literature: Quetzalcoatl, The Ritual of Condolence, Cuceb, The Night Chant*. New York: Farrar, Straus & Giroux, 1974.

———. *In the Trail of the Wind: American Indian Poems and Ritual Orations*. New York: Farrar, Straus & Giroux, 1987 [1971].

———. *The Red Swan: Myths and Tales of the American Indians*. New York: Farrar, Straus & Giroux, 1976.

Burns, Allan F. *An Epoch of Miracles: Oral Literature of the Yucatec Maya*. Austin: University of Texas Press, 1983.

Jara, René and Spadaccini, Nicholas, eds. *1492–1992: Re/Discovering Colonial Writing*. Hispanic Issues No. 4. Minneapolis: The Prisma Institute, 1989.

Klor de Alva, Jorge. "Language, Politics, and Translation: Colonial Discourse and Classic Nahuatl in New Spain." In *The Art of Translation: Voices from the Field*. Ed. Rosanna Warren. Boston: Northeastern University Press, 1989.

Kroeber, Karl, ed. *Traditional American Indian Literatures: Texts and Interpretations*. Lincoln: University of Nebraska Press, 1981.

León-Portilla, Miguel. *Aztec Thought and Culture: A Study of the Ancient Nahuatl Mind*. Norman: University of Oklahoma Press, 1963.

———. *Pre-Columbian Literatures of Mexico*. Norman: University of Oklahoma Press, 1969.

MacCormak, Sabine. *Children of the Sun and Reason of State: Myths, Ceremonies, and Conflicts in Incan Peru*. 1992 Lecture Series, Working Papers No. 6, Department of Spanish and Portuguese, University of Maryland, College Park (1990).

Murray, David. *Forked Tongues: Speech, Writing and Representation in North American Indian Texts*. Bloomington: Indiana University Press, 1991.

O'Gorman, Edmundo. *The Invention of America*. Bloomington: Indiana University Press, 1961.

Ruoff, A. LaVonne Brown. *American Indian Literatures: An Introduction, Bibliographic Review, and Selected Bibliography*. New York: Modern Language Association, 1990.

Swann, Brian, and Arnold Krupat, eds. *Recovering the Word: Essays on Native American Literature*. Berkeley: University of California Press, 1987.

Wachtel, Nathan. *The Vision of the Vanquished. The Spanish Conquest of Peru Through Indian Eyes: 1530–1570*. Trans. Ben and Siân Reynolds. New York: Harper and Row, 1977.

Wiget, Andrew. *Native American Literature*. Boston: Twayne Publishers, 1985.

ANONYMOUS (MID-SIXTEENTH CENTURY)
Guatemala

The *Popol Vuh*—which can be translated as "Council Book" or "Council Paper"—of the Maya-Quiché Indians was written down in the Latin alphabet in the middle of the sixteenth century. The manuscript was found at a church in Chiche-castenango, Guatemala. At the beginning of the eighteenth century, it was translated into Spanish by a Dominican priest named Francisco Jimenez. The *Popol Vuh* is the most complete creation myth to survive the devastation wreaked by the Spanish conquistadors.

The *Popol Vuh* consists of four major sections. The first, excerpted here, contains the creation account and is analogous to the first chapter of Genesis, although contradicting it since the mud beings created by the Makers, apparent Adams, are destroyed because they have no understanding. The first part also tells of the deeds of Hunahpu and Xbalanque, twin gods who control the morning-star aspect of Venus or One Hunahpu, their father, and respectively become the sun and the moon ("little jaguar sun"). They were sent to earth to curb the pride of Zipacna, a self-aggrandizing figure who, like his father Seven Macaw, claimed to be the Maker. The second part includes other mythic accounts, such as that of the Ahup people who played ball with the lords of the Xibalba, the region of the dead, and the story, excerpted here, of Ixquic, the maiden who became pregnant from the saliva that dripped from the skull of one of the Ahub lords defeated in the ball game. The third and fourth parts tell the history of the Quichés under their first four leaders.

The *Popol Vuh* was originally a hieroglyphic "council book," which the Lords of Quiché consulted to determine the future, that is, to see as the first four humans had seen, "everything under the sky perfectly."* The most recent translator of the *Popol Vuh* into English, Dennis Tedlock, explains that the original hieroglyphic book probably contained astronomical tables that permitted diviners to set appropriate dates for ceremonies and political events. The book was not just read but performed in the interpretation and conduct of Quiché life.

Prayer Suggested by the Maya Andrés Xiloj to Help the Reading of the *Popol Vuh*

Make my guilt vanish,
Heart of Sky, Heart of Earth;
do me a favor,
give me strength, give me courage
in my heart, in my head,
since you are my mountain and my plain;
may there be no falsehood and no stain,

Translated by Dennis Tedlock, Popol Vuh: The Definitive Edition of the Mayan Book of the Dawn of Life and the Glories of Gods and Kings.

and may this reading of the Popol Vuh
come out clear as dawn,
and may the shifting of ancient times
be complete in my heart, in my head;
and make my guilt vanish,
my grandmothers, grandfathers,
and however many souls of the dead there may be,
you who speak with the Heart of Sky and Earth,
may all of you together give strength
to the reading I have undertaken.

from *Popol Vuh*

[And now for the messengers of One and Seven Death]

And now for the messengers of One and Seven Death: "You're going, you Military Keepers of the Mat, to summon One and Seven Hunahpu. You'll tell them, when you arrive:

" 'They must come,' the lords say to you. 'Would that they might come to play ball with us here. Then we could have some excitement with them. We are truly amazed at them. Therefore they should come,' say the lords, 'and they should bring their playthings, their yokes and arm guards should come, along with their rubber ball,' say the lords, you will say when you arrive," the messengers were told.

And these messengers of theirs are owls: Shooting Owl, One-legged Owl, Macaw Owl, Skull Owl, as the messengers of Xibalba are called.

There is Shooting Owl, like a point, just piercing.

And there is One-legged Owl, with just one leg; he has wings.

And there is Macaw Owl, with a red back; he has wings.

And there is also Skull Owl, with only a head alone; he has no legs, but he does have wings.

There are four messengers, Military Keepers of the Mat in rank.

And when they came out of Xibalba they arrived quickly, alighting above the ball court where One and Seven Hunahpu were playing, at the ball court called Great Abyss at Carchah. The owls, arriving in a flurry over the ball court, now repeated their words, reciting the exact words of One Death, Seven Death, Pus Master, Jaundice Master, Bone Scepter, Skull Scepter, House Corner, Blood Gatherer, Trash Master, Stab Master, Wing, Packstrap, as all the lords are named. Their words were repeated by the owls.

"Don't the lords One and Seven Death speak truly?"[1]

"Truly indeed," the owls replied. "We'll accompany you."

Translated by Dennis Tedlock.

---

1. That this line is part of the dialogue rather
   than part of the narrative is made obvious
   by the next line, which is clearly a reply.

"They're to bring along all their gaming equipment," say the lords.

"Very well, but wait for us while we notify our mother," they replied.

And when they went to their house, they spoke to their mother; their father had died:

"We're going, our dear mother, even though we've just arrived.[2] The messengers of the lord have come to get us:

" 'They should come,' he says," they say, giving us orders. "We'll leave our rubber ball behind here," they said, then they went to tie it up under the roof of the house. "Until we return—then we'll put it in play again."

They told One Monkey and One Artisan:

"As for you, just play and just sing,[3] write and carve to warm our house and to warm the heart of your grandmother." When they had been given their instructions, their grandmother Xmucane sobbed, she had to weep.

"We're going, we're not dying. Don't be sad," said One and Seven Hunahpu, then they left.

[After that One and Seven Hunahpu Left, guided down the road by the messengers]

After that One and Seven Hunahpu left, guided down the road by the messengers.

And then they descended the road to Xibalba, going down a steep cliff, and they descended until they came out where the rapids cut through, the roaring canyon narrows named Neck Canyon. They passed through there, then they passed on into the River of Churning Spikes. They passed through countless spikes but they were not stabbed.

And then they came to water again, to blood: Blood River. They crossed but did not drink. They came to a river, but a river filled with pus. Still they were not defeated, but passed through again.

And then they came to the Crossroads, but here they were defeated, at the Crossroads.

Red Road was one and Black Road another.

White road was one and Yellow Road another.

There were four roads, and Black Road spoke:

"I am the one you are taking. I am the lord's road," said the road. And they were defeated there: this was the Road of Xibalba.

And then they came to the council place of the lords of Xibalba, and they were defeated again there. The ones seated first there are just manikins, just woodcarvings dressed up by Xibalba. And they greeted the first ones:

"Morning,[4] One Death," they said to the manikin. "Morning, Seven Death," they said to the woodcarving in turn.

---

2. "Even though" is my translation of *xaet*. Antitheses are rather frequent in the speech of Hunahpu and Xbalanque.

3. The playing here (*tzuan-*) is specifically on the flute.

4. This is *calah [zalah]*, literally "clear, bright, plainly visible," used as a morning greeting in classical Quiché. Today the preferred greeting for the morning is *zakiric*, "it is getting light (or dawning)."

So they did not win out, and the lords of Xibalba shouted out with laughter over this. All the lords just shouted with laughter because they had triumphed; in their hearts they had beaten One and Seven Hunahpu. They laughed on until One and Seven Death spoke:

"It's good that you've come. Tomorrow you must put your yokes and arm guards into action," they were told.

"Sit here on our bench," they were told, but the only bench they were offered was a burning-hot rock.

So now they were burned on the bench; they really jumped around on the bench now, but they got no relief. They really got up fast, having burned their butts. At this the Xibalbans laughed again, they began to shriek with laughter, the laughter rose up like a serpent in their very cores,[5] all the lords of Xibalba laughed themselves down to their blood and bones.

"Just go in the house. Your torch and cigars will be brought to your sleeping quarters," the boys were told.

After that they came to the Dark House, a house with darkness alone inside. Meanwhile the Xibalbans shared their thoughts:

"Let's just sacrifice them tomorrow. It can only turn out to be quick; they'll die quickly because of our playing equipment, our gaming things," the Xibalbans are saying among themselves.

This ball of theirs is just a spherical knife. White Dagger is the name of the ball, the ball of Xibalba. Their ball is just ground down to make it smooth; the ball of Xibalba is just surfaced with crushed bone to make it firm.

[And One and Seven Hunahpu went inside Dark House]

And One and Seven Hunahpu went inside Dark House.

And then their torch was brought,[6] only one torch, already lit, sent by One and Seven Death, along with a cigar for each of them, also already lit, sent by the lords. When these were brought to One and Seven Hunahpu they were cowering,[7] here in the dark. When the bearer of their torch and cigars arrived, the torch was bright as it entered; their torch and both their cigars were burning. The bearer spoke:

" 'They must be sure to return them in the morning—not finished, but just as they look now. They must return them intact,' the lords say to you," they were told, and they were defeated. They finished the torch and they finished the cigars that had been brought to them.

And Xibalba is packed with tests, heaps and piles of tests.

This is the first one: the Dark House, with darkness alone inside.

---

5. *Cumatz* or "serpent" is a term for various kinds of disabling cramps.
6. The torch is *chah*, literally "pine"; in the present context it is the Quiché term for what is more widely known in Mesoamer-ica as *ocote* (a Nahua-derived term), a split-off stick of extremely resinous pine wood, still widely used for torches and kindling.
7. The verb here is *chocochoh*, which means to crouch "in a cowering manner."

Ceremonial ax - represents the
Olmec Rain God, which the Olmec
conceived of as part jaguar, part
''crying baby.''

And the second is named Rattling House, heaving with cold inside, whistling with drafts, clattering with hail. A deep chill comes inside here.

And the third is named Jaguar House, with jaguars alone inside, jostling one another, crowding together, with gnashing teeth. They're scratching around; these jaguars are shut inside the house.

Bat House is the name of the fourth test, with bats alone inside the house, squeaking, shrieking, darting through the house. The bats are shut inside; they can't get out.

And the fifth is named Razor House, with blades alone inside. The blades are moving back and forth, ripping, slashing through the house.

These are the first tests of Xibalba, but One and Seven Hunahpu never entered into them, except for the one named earlier, the specified test house.

And when One and Seven Hunahpu went back before One and Seven Death, they were asked:

"Where are my cigars? What of my torch? They were brought to you last night!"

"We finished them, your lordship."

"Very well. This very day, your day is finished, you will die, you will disappear, and we shall break you off. Here you will hide your faces: you are to be sacrificed!" said One and Seven Death.

And then they were sacrificed and buried. They were buried at the Place of Ball Game Sacrifice, as it is called. The head of One Hunahpu was cut off; only his body was buried with his younger brother.

"Put his head in the fork of the tree that stands by the road," said One and Seven Death.

And when his head was put in the fork of the tree, the tree bore fruit. It would not have had any fruit, had not the head of One Hunahpu been put in the fork of the tree.

This is the calabash tree, as we call it today, or "the head of One Hunahpu," as it is said.

And then One and Seven Death were amazed at the fruit of the tree. The fruit grows out everywhere, and it isn't clear where the head of One Hunahpu is; now it looks just the way the calabashes look. All the Xibalbans see this, when they come to look.

The state of the tree loomed large in their thoughts, because it came about at the same time the head of One Hunahpu was put in the fork. The Xibalbans said among themselves:

"No one is to pick the fruit, nor is anyone to go beneath the tree," they said. They restricted themselves; all of Xibalba held back.

It isn't clear which is the head of One Hunahpu; now it's exactly the same as the fruit of the tree. Calabash tree came to be its name, and much was said about it. A maiden heard about it, and here we shall tell of her arrival.

[And here is the account of a maiden, the daughter of a lord named Blood Gatherer]

And here is the account of a maiden, the daughter of a lord named Blood Gatherer.

And this is when a maiden heard of it, the daughter of a lord. Blood Gatherer is the name of her father, and Blood Woman is the name of the maiden.

And when he heard the account of the fruit of the tree, her father retold it. And she was amazed at the account:

"I'm not acquainted with that tree they talk about. ' "Its fruit is truly sweet!" they say,' I hear," she said.

Next, she went all alone and arrived where the tree stood. It stood at the Place of Ball Game Sacrifice:

"What? Well! What's the fruit of this tree? Shouldn't this tree bear something sweet? They shouldn't die, they shouldn't be wasted. Should I pick one?" said the maiden.

And then the bone spoke; it was here in the fork of the tree:

"Why do you want a mere bone, a round thing in the branches of a tree?" said the head of One Hunahpu when it spoke to the maiden. "You don't want it," she was told.

"I do want it," said the maiden.

"Very well. Stretch out your right hand here, so I can see it," said the bone.

"Yes," said the maiden. She stretched out her right hand, up there in front of the bone.

And then the bone spit out its saliva, which landed squarely in the hand of the maiden.

And then she looked in her hand, she inspected it right away, but the bone's saliva wasn't in her hand.

"It is just a sign I have given you, my saliva, my spittle. This, my head, has nothing on it—just the bone, nothing of meat. It's just the same with the head of a great lord: it's just the flesh that makes his face look good. And when he dies, people get frightened by his bones. After that, his son is like his saliva, his spittle, in his being, whether it be the son of a lord or the son of a craftsman, an orator. The father does not disappear, but goes on being fulfilled. Neither dimmed nor destroyed is the face of a lord, a warrior, craftsman, orator. Rather, he will leave his daughters and sons. So it is that I have done likewise through you. Now go up there on the face of the earth; you will not die. Keep the word. So be it," said the head of One and Seven Hunahpu—they were of one mind when they did it.

This was the word Hurricane, Newborn Thunderbolt, Raw Thunderbolt had given them. In the same way, by the time the maiden returned to her home, she had been given many instructions. Right away something was generated in her belly, from the saliva alone, and this was the generation of Hunahpu and Xbalanque.

And when the maiden got home and six months had passed, she was found out by her father. Blood Gatherer is the name of her father.

[And after the maiden was noticed by her father, when he saw that she was now with child, all the lords then shared their thoughts]

And after the maiden was noticed by her father, when he saw that she was now with child, all the lords then shared their thoughts—One and Seven Death, along with Blood Gatherer:

"This daughter of mine is with child, lords. It's just a bastard," Blood Gatherer said when he joined the lords.

"Very well. Get her to open her mouth.[8] If she doesn't tell, then sacrifice her. Go far away and sacrifice her."

"Very well, your lordships," he replied. After that, he questioned his daughter:

"Who is responsible for the child in your belly, my daughter?" he said.

"There is no child, my father, sir; there is no man whose face I've known,"[9] she replied.

---

8. This is *chacoto uchi [uchii]*, literally "Dig it out of her mouth," an idiom for close questioning. In terms of the somatic mapping of actual or potential speech, as conceived by Quichés, this implies that she knows perfectly well what her father wants her to say; if her word were "in her belly," on the other hand, it would mean that she

could not readily articulate a response even if she wanted to.

9. This statement is not only true in its figurative reference to Blood Woman's sexual innocence, but in its literal sense: she has never known the (fleshly) face of the man responsible for her miraculous pregnancy.

"Very well. It really is a bastard you carry! Take her away for sacrifice, you Military Keepers of the Mat. Bring back her heart in a bowl, so the lords can take it in their hands this very day," the owls were told, the four of them.

Then they left, carrying the bowl. When they left they took the maiden by the hand, bringing along the White Dagger, the instrument of sacrifice.

"It would not turn out well if you sacrificed me, messengers, because it is not a bastard that's in my belly. What's in my belly generated all by itself when I went to marvel at the head of One Hunahpu, which is there at the Place of Ball Game Sacrifice. So please stop: don't do your sacrifice, messengers," said the maiden. Then they talked:

"What are we going to use in place of her heart? We were told by her father: 'Bring back her heart. The lords will take it in their hands, they will satisfy themselves, they will make themselves familiar with its composition. Hurry, bring it back in a bowl, put her heart in the bowl.' Isn't that what we've been told? What shall we deliver in the bowl? What we want above all is that you should not die," said the messengers.

"Very well. My heart must not be theirs, nor will your homes be here.[10] Nor will you simply force people to die, but hereafter, what will be truly yours will be the true bearers of bastards. And hereafter, as for One and Seven Death, only blood,[11] only nodules of sap, will be theirs. So be it that these things are presented before them, and not that hearts are burned before them. So be it: use the fruit of a tree,"[12] said the maiden. And it was red tree sap she went out to gather in the bowl.

After it congealed, the substitute for her heart became round. When the sap of the croton tree was tapped, tree sap like blood, it became the substitute for her blood. When she rolled the blood around inside there, the sap of the croton tree, it formed a surface like blood, glistening red now, round inside the bowl. When the tree was cut open by the maiden, the so-called cochineal croton, the sap is what she called blood, and so there is talk of "nodules of blood."

"So you have been blessed with the face of the earth. It shall be yours," she told the owls.

"Very well, maiden. We'll show you the way up there. You just walk on ahead; we have yet to deliver this apparent duplicate of your heart before the lords," said the messengers.

And when they came before the lords, they were all watching closely:

"Hasn't it turned out well?" said One Death.

"It has turned out well, your lordships, and this is her heart. It's in the bowl."

---

10. In the biological sense, this means that future owls will be free to move around the surface of the earth. If I am right in suspecting that the messenger owls of Xibalba correspond to the planet Mercury, the astronomical sense of this same statement would be that Mercury appears above the horizon on more days than it remains below.

11. "Blood" is a literal translation of *quic* [qui4], which also refers to gums and resins from trees (including latex), in this case the blood-red resin of the cochineal croton or "red tree."

12. This is a figurative reference to nodules of sap from the cochineal croton.

"Very well. So I'll look," said One Death, and when he lifted it up with his fingers, its surface was soaked with gore, its surface glistened red with blood.

"Good. Stir up the fire, put it over the fire," said One Death.

After that they dried it over the fire, and the Xibalbans savored the aroma. They all ended up standing here, they leaned over it intently. They found the smoke of the blood to be truly sweet!

And while they stayed at their cooking, the owls went to show the maiden the way out. They sent her up through a hole onto the earth, and then the guides returned below.

In this way the lords of Xibalba were defeated by a maiden; all of them were blinded.

And here, where the mother of One Monkey and One Artisan lived, was where the woman named Blood Woman arrived.

[And when the Blood Woman came to the mother of One Monkey and One Artisan]

And when the Blood Woman came to the mother of One Monkey and One Artisan,[13] her children were still in her belly, but it wasn't very long before the birth of Hunahpu and Xbalanque, as they are called.

And when the woman came to the grandmother, the woman said to the grandmother:

"I've come, mother, madam. I'm your daughter-in-law and I'm your child,[14] mother, madam," she said when she came here to the grandmother.

"Where do you come from? As for my lastborn children,[15] didn't they die in Xibalba? And these two remain as their sign and their word: One Monkey and One Artisan are their names. So if you've come to see my children, get out of here!" the maiden was told by the grandmother.

"Even so, I really am your daughter-in-law. I am already his, I belong to One Hunahpu. What I carry is his. One Hunahpu and Seven Hunahpu are alive, they are not dead. They have merely made a way for the light to show itself, madam mother-in-law, as you will see when you look at the faces of what I carry," the grandmother was told.

And One Monkey and One Artisan have been keeping their grandmother

---

13. In fact the mother (in the literal sense) of One Monkey and One Artisan has already died by this time; in the present passage the term "mother" is being used in its role-designating sense rather than in its genealogical sense. One Monkey and One Artisan are living alone with Xmucane, their father's mother, at this point; she is the only person they have who could fill the role of "mother."

14. The use of "child" here is metaphorical. A Quiché daughter-in-law takes up resi-

dence with her husband's family; in offering herself not only as a daughter-in-law but as a "child," Blood Woman both seeks the kind of acceptance a daughter would have and makes an offer of loyalty.

15. Given that Xmucane is never mentioned as having had any children other than One and Seven Hunahpu, she may be using *chipa [4hipa]* or "lastborn (youngest)" endearingly, in effect calling her sons, who were adults when they left home, "my little babies."

entertained: all they do is play and sing, all they work at is writing and carving, every day, and this cheers the heart of their grandmother.

And then the grandmother said:

"I don't want you, no thanks, my daughter-in-law. It's just a bastard in your belly, you trickster! These children of mine who are named by you are dead," said the grandmother.

"Truly, what I say to you is so!"[16]

"Very well, my daughter-in-law, I hear you. So get going, get their food so they can eat. Go pick a big netful of corn, then come back—since you are already my daughter-in-law,[17] as I understand it," the maiden was told.

"Very well," she replied.

After that, she went to the garden; One Monkey and One Artisan had a garden. The maiden followed the path they had cleared and arrived there in the garden, but there was only one clump,[18] there was no other plant, no second or third. That one clump had borne its ears. So then the maiden's heart stopped:

"It looks like I'm a sinner, a debtor! Where will I get the netful of food she asked for?" she said. And then the guardians of food were called upon by her:

> "Come thou, rise up, come thou, stand up:
> Generous Woman, Harvest Woman,
> Cacao Woman, Cornmeal Woman,
> thou guardian of the food of One Monkey, One Artisan,"

said the maiden.

And then she took hold of the silk, the bunch of silk at the top of the ear. She pulled it straight out, she didn't pick the ear, and the ear reproduced itself to make food for the net. It filled the big net.

And then the maiden came back, but animals carried her net. When she got back she went to put the pack frame in the corner of the house, so it would look to the grandmother as if she had arrived with a load.

And then, when the grandmother saw the food, a big netful:

"Where did that food of yours come from? You've leveled the place! I'm going to see if you've brought back our whole garden!" said the grandmother.

And then she went off, she went to look at the garden, but the one clump was still there, and the place where the net had been put at the foot of it was still obvious.

And the grandmother came back in a hurry, and she got back home, and she said to the maiden:

"The sign is still there. You really are my daughter-in-law! I'll have to keep

---

16. I take it that this sentence belongs to Blood Woman rather than Xmucane, given that it is followed with *utz bala*, "Very well," which signals the beginning of a reply and definitely belongs to Xmucane.

17. The grandmother isn't so much accepting Blood Woman's claim to kinship here as she is saying (with sarcasm) something

like, "If you *say* you're my daughter-in-law, then *act* like one." Quiché daughters-in-law, who live with the families of their husbands, are subject to the commands of their mothers-in-law, who give them heavy household tasks to do.

18. In Mesoamerica corn is properly grown in thick clumps, not stalk by stalk in single file; clumps survive high winds better.

watching what you do. These grandchildren of mine are already showing genius," the maiden was told.

Now this is where we shall speak of the birth of Hunahpu and Xbalanque.

[And this is their birth; we shall tell of it here]

And this is their birth; we shall tell of it here.

Then it came to the day of their birth, and the maiden named Blood Woman gave birth. The grandmother was not present when they were born; they were born suddenly. Two of them were born, named Hunahpu and Xbalanque. They were born in the mountains, and then they came into the house. Since they weren't sleeping:

"Throw them out of here! They're really loudmouths!" said the grandmother.

After that, when they put them on an anthill, they slept soundly there. And when they removed from there, they put them in brambles next.

And this is what One Monkey and One Artisan wanted: that they should die on the anthill and die in the brambles. One Monkey and One Artisan wanted this because they were rowdyish and flushed with jealousy. They didn't allow their younger brothers in the house at first, as if they didn't even know them, but even so they flourished in the mountains.

And One Monkey and One Artisan were great flautists and singers, and as they grew up they went through great suffering and pain. It had cost them suffering to become great knowers. Through it all they became flautists, singers, and writers, carvers. They did everything well. They simply knew it when they were born, they simply had genius. And they were the successors of their fathers who had gone to Xibalba, their dead fathers.

Since One Monkey and One Artisan were great knowers, in their hearts they already realized everything when their younger brothers came into being, but they didn't reveal their insight because of their jealousy. The anger in their hearts came down on their own heads;[19] no great harm was done. They were decoyed[20] by Hunahpu and Xbalanque, who merely went out shooting every day. These two got no love from the grandmother, or from One Monkey and One Artisan. They weren't given their meals; the meals had been prepared and One Monkey and One Artisan had already eaten them before they got there.

But Hunahpu and Xbalanque aren't turning red with anger; rather, they just let it go, even though they know their proper place, which they see as clear as day. So they bring birds when they arrive each day, and One Monkey and One Artisan

---

19. Andrés Xiloj remarked, "We see a person; we speak behind his back and he doesn't hear what we are murmuring. Then this murmur doesn't fall upon that person, but we are the ones who pay for it." A daykeeper, taking on the task of defending a person who has been the victim of witchcraft, asks in prayer that "the one who did this work should be the one to receive it."

20. The verb here is *poizaxic [poyizaxic]*; if English "doll" were a verb, this could be translated literally as "to be dolled"—that is, to be misled by a doll. Today *poyizaxic* is most commonly employed with reference to the use of scarecrows in fields.

eat them. Nothing whatsoever is given to Hunahpu and Xbalanque, either one of them. All One Monkey and One Artisan do is play and sing.

And then Hunahpu and Xbalanque arrived again, but now they came in here without bringing their birds, so the grandmother turned red:

"What's your reason for not bringing birds?" Hunahpu and Xbalanque were asked.

"There are some, our dear grandmother, but our birds just got hung up in a tree,"[21] they said, "and there's no way to get up the tree after them, our dear grandmother, and so we'd like our elder brothers to please go with us, to please go get the birds down," they said.

"Very well. We'll go with you at dawn," the elder brothers replied.

Now they had won, and they gathered their thoughts, the two of them, about the fall of One Monkey and One Artisan:

"We'll just turn their very being around with our words. So be it, since they have caused us great suffering. They wished that we might die and disappear—we, their younger brothers. Just as they wished us to be slaves here, so we shall defeat them there. We shall simply make a sign of it," they said to one another.

And then they went there beneath a tree, the kind named yellowwood, together with the elder brothers. When they got there they started shooting. There were countless birds up in the tree, chittering, and the elder brothers were amazed when they saw the birds. And not one of these birds fell down beneath the tree:

"Those birds of ours don't fall down; just go throw them down," they told their elder brothers.

"Very well," they replied.

And then they climbed up the tree, and the tree began to grow, its trunk got thicker.

After that, they wanted to get down, but now One Monkey and One Artisan couldn't make it down from the tree. So they said, from up in the tree:

"How can we grab hold?[22] You, our younger brothers, take pity on us! Now this tree looks frightening to us, dear younger brothers," they said from up in the tree. Then Hunahpu and Xbalanque told them:

"Undo your pants, tie them around your hips, with the long end trailing like a tail behind you, and then you'll be better able to move," they were told by their younger brothers.

"All right," they said.

And then they left the ends of their loinclothes trailing, and all at once these became tails. Now they looked like mere monkeys.

After that they went along in the trees of the mountains, small and great. They went through the forests, now howling, now keeping quiet in the branches of trees.

Such was the defeat of One Monkey and One Artisan by Hunahpu and Xbalanque. They did it by means of their genius alone.

---

21. When birds are shot they sometimes close their feet around the branch where they were sitting and then hang there, dead.
22. The verb stem here is *chanic,* translated on the basis of *chanih,* "keep in the fist." The tree is too thick for One Monkey and One Artisan to use their hands in coming down.

And when they got home they said, when they came to their grandmother and mother:

"Our dear grandmother, something has happened to our elder brothers. They've become simply shameless, they're like animals now," they said.

"If you've done something to your elder brothers, you've knocked me down and stood me on my head. Please don't do anything to your elder brothers, my dear grandchildren," the grandmother said to Hunahpu and Xbalanque. And they told their grandmother:

"Don't be sad, our dear grandmother. You will see the faces of our elder brothers again. They'll come, but this will be a test for you, our dear grandmother. Will you please not laugh[23] while we test their destiny?" they said.

And then they began playing. They played "Hunahpu Monkey."

[And then they sang, they played, they drummed]

And then they sang, they played, they drummed. When they took up their flutes and drums, their grandmother sat down with them, then they played, they sounded out the tune, the song that got its name then. "Hunahpu Monkey" is the name of the tune.

And then One Monkey and One Artisan came back, dancing when they arrived.

And then, when the grandmother looked, it was their ugly faces the grandmother saw. Then she laughed, the grandmother could not hold back her laughter, so they just left right away, out of her sight again, they went up and away in the forest.

"Why are you doing that, our dear grandmother? We'll only try four times; only three times are left. We'll call them with the flute, with song. Please hold back your laughter. We'll try again," said Hunahpu and Xbalanque.

Next they played again, then they came back, dancing again, they arrived again, in the middle of the patio of the house. As before, what they did was delightful; as before, they tempted their grandmother to laugh. Their grandmother laughed at them soon enough. The monkeys looked truly ridiculous, with the skinny little things below their bellies[24] and their tails wiggling in front of their breasts.[25] When they came back the grandmother had to laugh at them, and they went back into the mountains.

---

23. Among the contemporary Jacaltec Maya there are myths in which the hero tricks his elder brother or his mother's brothers into going up a tree that grows taller and maroons them, after which they turn into monkeys. The hero's mother than tries to reverse this transformation but fails.

24. This is *chi xiriric xe quipam;* Andrés Xiloj read it as "round little thing," chuckling as he did so. This refers not to the "bellies" of the monkeys (*quipam*) but to what is "be-

low" or "at the bottom of" (*xe*) their bellies.

25. This is *chi chilita he pu chuchi quiqux,* "that wag tails and at-edge-of their-breasts." Andrés Xiloj read *chuchi* as "up against" in this context. Spider monkeys and howler monkeys both have very long prehensile tails; howlers are seldom observed, but spider monkeys are given to winding their tails around to the front of their bodies and all the way up to their chins.

"Please, why are you doing that, our dear grandmother? Even so, we'll try it a third time now," said Hunahpu and Xbalanque.

Again they played, again they came dancing, but their grandmother held back her laughter. Then they climbed up here, cutting right across the building, with thin red lips, with faces blank, puckering their lips, wiping their mouths and faces, suddenly scratching themselves. And when the grandmother saw them again, the grandmother burst out laughing again, and again they went out of sight because of the grandmother's laughter.

"Even so, our dear grandmother, we'll get their attention."

So for the fourth time they called on the flute, but they didn't come back again. The fourth time they went straight into the forest. So they told their grandmother:

"Well, we've tried, our dear grandmother. They came at first, and we've tried calling them again. So don't be sad. We're here—we, your grandchildren. Just love our mother, dear grandmother. Our elder brothers will be remembered. So be it: they have lived here and they have been named; they are to be called One Monkey and One Artisan," said Hunahpu and Xbalanque.

So they were prayed to by the flautists and singers among the ancient people, and the writers and carvers prayed to them. In ancient times they turned into animals, they became monkeys, because they just magnified themselves, they abused their younger brothers. Just as they wished them to be slaves, so they themselves were brought low. One Monkey and One Artisan were lost then, they became animals, and this is now their place forever.

Even so, they were flautists and singers; they did great things while they lived with their grandmother and mother.

ANONYMOUS (LATE SIXTEENTH CENTURY)
Tenochtitlán (Mexico City)

The flower song presented here was originally part of a bound manuscript dating from the end of the sixteenth century that contains ninety-one songs in Nahuatl, the Aztec language, transliterated into the Latin alphabet. A friar named Francisco Ximénez found the manuscript in his parish (Chichicastenango, Guatemala) sometime between 1701 and 1703, copied it, and added a Spanish translation. The manuscript remained with the Dominican order until 1830, when it was purchased by the library of the University of San Carlos in Guatemala City. Several scholars consulted it there, copied it, published Ximénez's translation or translated it into other languages. In 1861 Etienne Brasseur de Bourbourg, a Jesuit priest interested in indigenous texts, stole the manuscript and translated it into French. In 1911 the manuscript was acquired by the Newberry Library in Chicago. Exactly what term should be used to characterize the genre of these compositions is, as in the case of other pre-Hispanic Native American expressive

Sculpture of the god Xochipilli seated on a throne decorated with flowers and jewels; his body is tattooed with flowers and he has a mask over his face. He was the god of music, dancing, and love. Mexica (Aztec) culture. From Mexico City. Postclassic: 1300–1521 A.D. Museo Nacional de Antropologia. *Mexico City.*

forms, a matter of interpretation that must consider the cultural environment of the Aztecs rather than European literary forms. To call them lyric poetry, for example, would be to overlook their ritual nature, which included the accompaniment of drumming, dancing, and often a peculiar form of "flying" or "whirling" to earth from a platform placed on top of a pole. John Bierhorst, the translator of this excerpt, departs from the traditional translation of xochitl/cuicatl (flower song) as "poetry."* He believes that the two Nahuatl words are versions of each other, a kind of fixed metaphor that refers to persons, particularly "ghost warriors" whom the singer summoned back from the afterworld to earth. This return, enacted in the "flying" or "whirling" down from the platform, is also understood to be the source of music. Bierhorst cites the following examples: "From heaven, ah, come good flowers, good songs"; "As a song you're born, O Montezuma: as a flower you come to bloom on earth," and "God has formed you, has given you birth as a flower. He paints you as a song"; and "My songs are marching forth." The return of these ghost warriors permits, again according to Bierhorst, the reenactment of historical battles in such a way that the singer and his comrades emerge victorious, thus adding to the prestige of the Mexicas. This Flower Song is summarized as follows in Bierhorst's "Commentary," which is a gloss on each song: Revenant muses from the enemy city-states of Huexotzinco and Tlaxcala (that had joined Cortés against the Aztecs) summon ghost warriors from the afterworld to join the battle. An unnamed singer, most likely Aztec, declares having summoned the victim revenants. He then proceeds to call Aztec warriors to battle. In a fantasized battle the Huexotzincans and Tlaxcalans are defeated and sent to paradise as payment for the newly arrived ghosts, who now establish the Aztec kingdom or Mexico as paradise on earth.†

from *Cantares Mexicanos: Songs of the Aztecs*

Aztec Flower song

Where are you, singer? Here, let the flower drums appear. They're twirling down
    as plumes. They're littered as golden flowers.
You'd pleasure princes, lords, eagles, jaguars.
Ah, he's descended. The singer's at the drum. He's setting them free as plumes.
    He's dispersing the songs of Life Giver. Bellbird gives him the echo, singing
    along, spreading flowers. Let's have these flowers!
And how do I hear his songs? Ah! It's Life Giver who gives him the echo. Bellbird
    gives him the echo, singing along, spreading flowers. Let's have *these flowers!*
These jades are falling as a mist of plumes. Ah! They're your songs. And this is how
    Ayocuan, *yes,* Cuetzpal, utters them. It would seem indeed that this one has
    acquaintance with Life Giver.

Translated by John Bierhorst.

*John Bierhorst, trans. and introd., Cantares Mexicanos: Songs of the Aztecs *(Stanford: Stanford University Press, 1985) 3–122.*

†This account is based on Bierhorst, p. 438.

So this is how that lord, that vaunted one, comes creating them. Yes, with plumelike bracelet beads he pleasures the Only Spirit. How *else* would Life Giver acquiesce? How *else* could there be anything good on earth?

"Let me borrow for a moment, for a while, these jades and bracelets, these princes. I flower-spin these nobles. Here! As songs of mine I whirl them, ah! beside the drum.

"For a moment I have companions here in Huexotzinco, I, King Tecayehuatzin. I'm assembling jades, emeralds, princes. I flower-spin these nobles, ah!"

From heaven, ah, come good flowers, good songs. They put away our cares, they put away our pain. Ah, it's the Chichimec lord, Tecayehuatzin! Be pleasured.

Comrades are scattering down as plumelike popcorn flowers, spinning down as white morning glories, lords, princes, moving along these branches, inhaling this plumelike cornsilk flower *tree*.

A golden bellbird! A beautiful song! You're singing a beauty. And you that are warbling are there, it would seem, on the flower-*tree* branches, where flowers are swelling.

It would seem that you're a swan for Life Giver, a singer for God, you, the first of these singers to watch for the dawn.

"Though my heart desires shield flowers, Life Giver's flowers, what might happen to this heart of mine? Alas, it's for nothing that we've come to be born here on earth.

"I'm to pass away like a ruined flower. My fame will be nothing, my renown here on earth will be nothing. There may be flowers, there may be songs, but what might happen to this heart of mine? Alas, it's for nothing that we've come to be born here on earth.

"Friends, be pleasured! Let us put our arms around each other's shoulders here. We're living in a world of flowers here. No one when he's gone can enjoy the flowers, the songs, that lie outspread in this home of Life Giver.

"Earth is but a moment. Is the Place Unknown the same? Is there happiness and friendship? Is it not just here on earth that acquaintances are made?"

I've heard a song. I hear the fluting of the garland, Lord Ayocuan.

He's answered you. From within the house of flowers Aquiahuatzin has answered you. And Commander Ayapancatl.

"Life Giver, Spirit, where are you! I seek you time and again. For you I grieve, I, the singer. I give you pleasure.

"Popcorn flowers, plumelike popcorn flowers are drizzling into this house of green places, this house of paintings. I give you much pleasure."

It seems that there in Tlaxcala they're singing as jade gongs beside the drum. And there's a narcotic that's flower-narcotic. And Lord Xicotencatl, and Tizatlacatzin, and Camaxochitzin are entertained with this music, awaited with these flowers—they that are songs of the Only Spirit.

O Life Giver, it seems your home is everywhere. The Flower Mat is here! And princes, whirled as flowers there, are making prayers to you.

That multitude of flower trees is standing up beside the drum. As baby maize ears, yes, as plumes, they're spun. They're scattered. They're holy flowers.

Bellbird is singing in the plume arbor. He echoes the lords, he delights those eagle jaguars.

Flowers are sprinkling down. Let there be dancing beside the drum, O friends. Whom do we await? Our hearts are grieving.

He's the one. It's God! Hear him! He descends from heaven, singing. Angels echo him. They come fluting.

"I grieve, I, Cuauhtencoztli. Our flower drums stand wrapped in sadness. Is it true? Let it not be so. Our songs are good no more."

But let them arise! Let them appear! We live beyond, exist beyond. You're poor, my friend. Let me take you away. Arise beyond!

"I'm singing, alas." O friends, whatever you utter sings here!

"From where the Flower Court lies comes one of the nobles. Ah, it's Coyolchiuhqui. He comes singing through tears from the house of green places. Unhappy are the flowers, unhappy the songs. Everything created here is misery.

"The pain is hard. We move along in anguish. Motenchuatzin am I, and in grieving songs I plume-spin princes, lords, rulers, and Telpoloatl, Lord Tepoloatl. We're all alive in this house of green places. Unhappy the flowers, unhappy the songs. Everything created *here* is misery."

I've heard a song. I see him in Green Places, walking in Dawn's House along the flower shore, calling to turquoise swans and green-corn birds. It's the roseate swan Lord Monencauhtzin.

O friends, who are they that dwell within God's house of green-swan cacao flowers? Keep on tilling this plume garden. Let me, let me see them laughing like jade flutes, conversing like flower log drums. And might these lords and princes strike and resonate the turquoise-brilliant drums within this house of flowers?

Hear it! He's shrilling, warbling on the branches of the flower tree. He's shaking! It's the golden flower-bell, the rattle hummingbird, the swan, Lord Monencauhtzin. Like a gorgeous troupial fan he spreads his wings and soars beside the flower drum.

They've reached the top. Flowers have reached the top. The flowers are blooming in the presence of Life Giver. And He's given you the echo. Oh, heart!

You've brought down precious birds of God. Your songs, your riches, are plentiful. You're giving pleasure. Flowers are stirring.

"A singer am I, and everywhere I walk, everywhere I speak, the plume-like popcorn flowers sprinkle down on this flower court, this house of butterflies.

"From Flower Place come all the whirling flowers that make hearts spin. They themselves come scattering, come strewing flowers, whirled ones, narcotic flowers."

They're entered upon the Flower Mat. And he who wings abundantly, who warbles in this home of yours, this picture house, is Xayacamach. Cacao flowers intoxicate his heart.

There's a beautiful song. And the one who shrills, who lifts his song, is Tlapalteuccitzin. Great is his pleasure. His flowers are sifting down. And the flowers are cacao flowers.

O friends, I seek you, running through all these gardens. And here you are. Pass away in gladness, pass away producing *songs*. I've arrived, I, your comrade, your comrade.

Among these flowers am I introducing tzitzi-weed flowers, mozo-weed flowers? Is that the way it is? Am I simple? Am I poor? O friends!

Who am I that soar? I compose. I flower-sing, *I*, a butterfly of song. Let my cares be put aside. Let my heart enjoy it.

I come from Home. I've descended, I, a swan of Green Places, arriving on earth. I spread my wings beside the flower drum. My songs are lifted. They're born on earth.

It seems that I myself am cultivating songs, keeping company with those who work the soil. I, your humble comrade, am snaring my plumelike ancestors as golden garlands.

I'm on guard in the flower fields, I, your poor little friend. With gorgeous flower fronds I thatch my troopers' flower tents, rejoicing in these fields of God. Be pleasured!

Pass away rejoicing greatly, you flower jewels, for He is Lord. Will you live again? Ah, your heart knows that you live forever.

I've arrived in the branches of the flower tree, I, Flower Hummingbird, delighting in the aroma, rejoicing. Sweet, fragrant, are my words.

With flowers you are prayed to, O God, O Life Giver. We bow down, we pleasure you beside the flower drum, O Water-Palace Lord.

The drums are kept: they're kept beyond in the house of green places. Your comrades War Declarer, Arrow Snake, and Rattle Eagle are awaiting You. These lords are sighing in flowers.

"This city of Huexotzinco has been coveted: it's hated: it lies encased with spines, bristling with javelins, this Huexotzinco."

Gongs, rattles, are ringing at your home in Huexotzinco. Tecayehuatzin, Lord Quecehuatl, stands guard there, fluting, singing in his home, in Huexotzinco.

Listen! God the father is descending. Jaguar eagle drums are ringing in his home. Gong music is ringing.

It would seem to be so. Ah, these flowers are plumes—yes, a trailing cape *of plumes*. It's in a house of pictures that the realm is held *in safety*, that the Only Spirit is held *in veneration*.

Your city in the Jade Land is ascending on an arrow fire of flowers. My city of the golden pictures is your home, O Only Spirit.

Friends, hear the words of a dream: the golden milk corn sustains us in summer, the roseate-swan green corn gives us life, and it bejewels us to know that friends' hearts have been converted to the faith.

CHRISTOPHER COLUMBUS [CRISTOFORO COLOMBO]

(1451–1506)

Italy

The long-standing controversy regarding Columbus and his "discovery" of a "new" world in 1492 received renewed attention in 1992, 500 years after his historic voyage. The undeniable events are that Columbus did land, due to a navigational error, on an island in what is now the Caribbean Sea. The landing was to become a symbol of the emergence of European modernity, of unprecedented developments in knowledge, politics, economics, and society. Columbus had set out on an expedition, financed by Ferdinand and Isabella, the king and queen of Spain, to find a westward sea route for the spice trade in the Far East. Much as he tried to persuade his royal sponsors of his success, he found no spices and was to return with only a few nuggets of gold. His journal compensates for such missing riches with a treasure trove of fantastic and marvelous descriptions. Many critics have remarked that he did not actually see what he recorded, but rather recorded what he had gleaned from his extensive readings: Amazons, mermaids, men with dogs' heads and tails. It is precisely because of the awe with which Columbus and other conquistadors viewed the New World that their accounts have been considered traditionally as founding texts of Latin American literature. This is especially evident in those works that can be characterized as exponents of "marvelous realism"—that is, a world view whose rationality includes supernatural events and explanations, at least from the perspective of an archetypically modern mentality.

The excerpts presented here register Columbus's ambivalence toward the people he encounters. He expresses wonder and admiration at their appearance and dwellings, but he considers them quite gullible and incapable of defending themselves, thus making them likely candidates for servitude and enslavement. Indeed, these latter attitudes manifested themselves markedly in Columbus's efforts to wrest gold and other riches from the native peoples.

The diary of Columbus's first voyage is available only in Father Bartolomé de Las Casas's edition of extracted passages, linked together by the priest's own summaries and enunciative indicators, such as "The admiral says" or "he says." Consequently, the priest's voice sometimes seems to intervene in Columbus's own account.

from *The Journal of Christopher Columbus*

THURSDAY/FRIDAY, OCTOBER 11/12, 1492

[Columbus describes the people of the new world]

"I,"[1] he says, " in order that they might feel great amity towards us, because I knew that they were a people to be delivered and converted to our holy faith rather by love than by force, gave to some among them some red caps and some glass beads, which they hung round their necks, and many other things of little value. At this they were greatly pleased and became so entirely our friends that it was a wonder to see. Afterwards they came swimming to the ships' boats, where we were, and brought us parrots and cotton thread in balls, and spears and many other things, and we exchanged for them other things, such as small glass beads and hawks' bells, which we gave to them. In fact, they took all and gave all, such as they had, with good will, but it seemed to me that they were a people very deficient in everything. They all go naked as their mothers bore them, and the women also, although I saw only one very young girl. And all those whom I did see were youths, so that I did not see one who was over thirty years of age; they were very well built, with very handsome bodies and very good faces. Their hair is coarse almost like the hairs of a horse's tail and short; they wear their hair down over their eyebrows, except for a few strands behind, which they wear long and never cut. Some of them are painted black, and they are the colour of the people of the Canaries, neither black nor white, and some of them are painted white and some red and some in any colour that they find. Some of them paint their faces, some their whole bodies, some only the eyes, and some only the nose. They do not bear arms or know them, for I showed to them swords and they took them by the blade and cut themselves through ignorance. They have no iron. Their spears are certain reeds, without iron, and some of these have a fish tooth at the end, while others are pointed in various ways. They are all generally fairly tall, good looking and well proportioned. I saw some who bore marks of wounds on their bodies, and I made signs to them to ask how this came about, and they indicated to me that people came from other islands, which are near, and wished to capture them, and they defended themselves. And I believe and still believe that they come here from the mainland to take them for slaves. They should be good servants and of quick intelligence, since I see that they very soon say all that is said to them, and I believe that they would easily be made Christians, for it appeared to me that they had no creed. Our Lord willing, at the time of my departure I will bring back six of them to Your Highnesses, that they may learn to talk. I saw no beast of any kind in this island, except parrots."

Translated by Cecil Jane.

---

1. When the speech is inside quotation marks, Columbus is speaking. Otherwise, it is Bartolomé de Las Casas, who is linking together Columbus's words.

SATURDAY, OCTOBER 13, 1492

[Exchanges]

The men were all of a good height, very handsome people. Their hair is not curly, but loose and coarse as the hair of a horse; all have very broad foreheads and heads, more so than has any people that I have seen up to now. Their eyes are very lovely and not small. They are not at all black, but the colour of Canarians, and nothing else could be expected, since this is in one line from east to west with the island of Hierro in the Canaries. Their legs are very straight, all alike; they have no bellies but very good figures.

. . .

This island is fairly large and very flat; the trees are very green and there is much water. In the centre of it, there is a very large lake; there is no mountain, and all is so green that it is a pleasure to gaze upon it. The people also are very gentle and, since they long to possess something of ours and fear that nothing will be given to them unless they give something, when they have nothing, they take what they can and immediately throw themselves into the water and swim. But all that they do possess, they give for anything which is given to them, so that they exchange things even for pieces of broken dishes and bits of broken glass cups.

SUNDAY, OCTOBER 14, 1492

[The people of the new world greet Columbus]

And I soon saw two or three villages, and the people all came to shore, calling us and giving thanks to God. Some brought us water, others various eatables: others, when they saw that I was not inclined to land, threw themselves into the sea and came, swimming, and we understood that they asked us if we had come from heaven. One old man got into the boat, and all the rest, men and women, cried in loud voices: "Come and see the men who have come from heaven; bring them food and drink." Many came and many women, each with something, giving thanks to God, throwing themselves on the ground and raising their hands to the sky, and then shouting to us that we should land.

. . .

These people are very unskilled in arms, as Your Highnesses will see from the seven whom I caused to be taken in order to carry them off that they may learn our language and return. However, when Your Highnesses so command, they can all be carried off to Castile or held captive in the island itself, since with fifty men they would be all kept in subjection and forced to whatever may be wished.

. . .

MONDAY, OCTOBER 15, 1492

[At daybreak, I hoisted sail]

To this island I gave the name *Santa Maria de la Concepción,*" and about sunset, I anchored off the said point to learn if there were gold there, because those whom I had caused to be taken in the island of San Salvador told me that there they wore very large golden bracelets on the legs and arms. I can well believe that all that they said was a ruse in order to get away. It was nevertheless my wish not to pass any island without taking possession of it, although when one had been annexed, all might be said to have been. And I anchored and was there until to-day, Tuesday, when at dawn I went ashore in the armed boats and landed. The people, who were many, were naked and of the same type as those of the other island of San Salvador; they allowed us to go through the island and gave us what we asked of them.

This island is very green and flat and very fertile, and I have no doubt that all the year they sow and reap Indian corn, and equally other things. I saw many trees very unlike ours, and many of them had many branches of different kinds, and all coming from one root; one branch is of one kind and one of another, and they are so unlike each other that it is the greatest wonder in the world. How great is the difference between one and another! For example: one branch has leaves like those of a cane and another leaves like those of a mastic tree, and thus, on a single tree, there are five or six different kinds all so diverse from each other. They are not grafted, for it might be said that it is the result of grafting; on the contrary, they are wild and these people do not cultivate them. No creed is known to them and I believe that they would be speedily converted to Christianity, for they have a very good understanding. There are here fish, so unlike ours that it is a marvel; there are some shaped like dories, of the finest colours in the world, blue, yellow, red and of all colours, and others painted in a thousand ways, and the colours are so fine that no man would not wonder at them or be anything but delighted to see them.

FRIDAY, NOVEMBER 23, 1492

[Columbus is told of cannibals]

Beyond this cape there stretched out another land or cape, which also trended to the east, which those Indians whom he had with him called "Bohio." They said that this land was very extensive and that in it were people who had one eye in the forehead, and others whom they called "Canibals." Of these last, they showed great fear, and when they saw that this course was being taken, they were speechless, he says, because those people ate them and because they are very warlike.

TUESDAY, DECEMBER 11, 1492

[Understanding and misunderstanding]

"The Caniba are nothing else than the people of the Grand Khan, who must be very near here and possess ships, and they must come to take them captive, and as the prisoners do not return, they believe that they have been eaten. Every day we understand these Indians better and they us, although many times there has been misunderstanding."

BARTOLOMÉ DE LAS CASAS

(1474–1566)

Spain

Born in Seville, Bartolomé de Las Casas was the son of a military officer that accompanied Columbus on his first voyage to the "Indies." He was educated in the humanist tradition of the period at the University of Salamanca, graduating as a *licenciado* (equivalent to a master's degree) and eventually going on to complete his studies for the priesthood. In 1502 he accompanied the conquistador Nicolás de Ovando (1460–1518) who sailed to Santo Domingo (Hispaniola) to take over the governorship (1502–1509). After taking his vows as a Dominican priest in 1510, he moved to Cuba, where he gave a sermon critical of Spanish colonizers and in defense of the Indians. At age seventy he was named Bishop of Chiapas; he died in his nineties while on a trip to Spain.

Las Casas is a major historian, although a polemical and activist one. Since he was engaged in day-to-day administrative, legal, and Church matters—as a high Church official he was a major arbiter in the conduct of Church and State law, writing legal tracts and engaging in legal arguments—he did not have the time to write history as a scholar. Consequently, his major historical work, *The History of the Indies* took many years to complete, from 1527 to 1564. Las Casas made several trips to the Spanish court of the Emperor Charles V. There he debated with noted scholars such as Juan Ginés de Sepúlveda, a philosopher and translator of Aristotle's *Politics* into Latin, who in "The Just Causes of War Against the Indians" (1548) invoked the authority of classical antiquity, especially Aristotle and Aquinas, "on behalf of his concept of natural slavery."

Las Casas argued that the Indians were as rational as Christians and certainly more faithful to their religion, for they were willing to sacrifice life, the most precious gift to humankind, to serve their gods. "The nations who offered human sacrifices to their gods thereby showed, as deluded idolators, the high idea they had of the excellence of divinity, of the value of their gods, and how noble and high was their veneration of divinity. They consequently demonstrated that they possessed, better than other nations, natural reflection, rectitude of speech, and the judgment of reason; they employed their understanding better than the others. And in religious feeling they exceeded all the other nations, for the latter are the most religious nations in the world who, for the good of their peoples, offer their own children as sacrifices."* Las Casas was victorious against Sepúlveda, and laws protecting the Indians from enslavement were enacted. These laws, of course, were worth about as much as the paper they were printed on, as abuses against the Indians continued throughout the colonial period.

What makes Las Casas so remarkable to the modern reader is the extent to which he fought for the rights of the oppressed. Las Casas was the only defender of the Indians who tried to see things from their side. Others, like Francisco de Vitoria, theologian, jurist and professor at the University of Salamanca, although arguing against contemporary justifications of the wars waged in America against the Indians, nevertheless conceived of circumstances in which "just wars" are possible, such as when innocents seek protection against tyranny, thus leaving a loophole for those who argued that the Indians' cannibalism required action to protect the sacrificed victims. If at first he condoned the enslavement of Africans in order to save the "weaker" indigenous Native American peoples from painful toil, he eventually came to reject all forms of imposed labor. If at first he argued on behalf of Indian freedom together with a peaceful evangelization, he ultimately came to reject all forms of religious imposition.

from *The History of the Indies*

[The Horrors of the Conquest: The Conquest of Cuba]

At this time, when it was known in the island of Jamaica that Diego Velázquez had gone to settle and pacify . . . the island of Cuba, Juan de Esquivel, the deputy in Jamaica, agreed to send one Pánfilo de Narváez, a native of Valladolid . . . with thirty Spaniards, to aid Diego Velázquez—or else they bestirred themselves and asked permission to go there. All were archers, with their bows and arrows, in the use of which they were more practiced than the Indians.

This Pánfilo de Narváez was a man with an air of authority, tall of stature, and rather fair-haired, tending toward red. He was honorable and wise, but not very prudent; good company, with good habits, valiant in fighting against the Indians and would perhaps have been valiant against other peoples—but above all he had this defect, that he was very careless. . . .

With his band of bowmen he was well received by Diego Velázquez. . . . Velázquez promptly gave them shares of Indians, as if these were heads of cattle, so that the Indians would serve them, although they had brought some Jamaican Indians to do that wherever they went. Diego Velázquez made this Narváez his chief captain and always honored him in such a way that, after Velázquez, Narváez held first place in that island.

A few days later I went there, the said Diego Velázquez having sent for me because of our past friendship in this island of Hispaniola. We went together,

Translated by George Sanderlin.

Bartolomé de Las Casas Apologtica Historia Summaria, vol. 2 (Mexico City: Universidad Nacional Autónoma de México, 1967) 183.

Narváez and I, for about two years, and secured the rest of that island, to the detriment of all of it, as will be seen.

[Las Casas tells how Velázquez terrorized the natives of eastern Cuba, near Cape Maisi, executed the chieftain Hatuey, and went on to Baracoa. Narváez landed at the Gulf of Guacayanabo, on the south coast near Maisi, and, on orders from Velázquez, invaded the province of Camagüey, in central Cuba.]

The Spaniards entered the province of Camagüey, which is large and densely populated . . . and when they reached the villages, the inhabitants had prepared as well as they could cassava bread from their food; what they called *guaminiqui-najes* from their hunting; and also fish, if they had caught any.

Immediately upon arriving at a village, the cleric Casas would have all the little children band together; taking two or three Spaniards to help him, along with some sagacious Indians of this island of Hispaniola, whom he had brought with him, and a certain servant of his, he would baptize the children he found in the village. He did this throughout the island . . . and there were many for whom God provided holy baptism because He had predestined them to glory. God provided it at a fitting time, for none or almost none of those children remained alive after a few months. . . .

When the Spaniards arrived at a village and found the Indians at peace in their houses, they did not fail to injure and scandalize them. Not content with what the Indians freely gave, they took their wretched subsistence from them, and some, going further, chased after their wives and daughters, for this is and always has been the Spaniards' common custom in these Indies. Because of this and at the urging of the said father, Captain Narváez ordered that after the father had separated all the inhabitants of the village in half the houses, leaving the other half empty for the Spaniards' lodging, no one should dare go to the Indians' section. For this purpose, the father would go ahead with three or four men and reach a village early; by the time the Spaniards came, he had already gathered the Indians in one part and cleared the other.

Thus, because the Indians saw that the father did things for them, defending and comforting them, and also baptizing their children, in which affairs he seemed to have more command and authority than others, he received much respect and credit throughout the island among the Indians. Further, they honored him as they did their priests, magicians, prophets, or physicians, who were all one and the same.

Because of this . . . it became unnecessary to go ahead of the Spaniards. He had only to send an Indian with an old piece of paper on a stick, informing them through the messenger that those letters said thus and so. That is, that they should all be calm, that no one should absent himself because he would do them no harm, that they should have food prepared for the Christians and their children ready for baptism, or that they should gather in one part of the village, and anything else that it seemed good to counsel them—and that if they did not carry these things out, the father would be angry, which was the greatest threat that could be sent them.

They performed everything with a very good will, to the best of their ability.

And great was the reverence and fear which they had for the letters, for they saw that through these what was being done in other, distant regions was known. It seemed more than a miracle to them. . . .

The Spaniards thus passed through certain villages of that province on the road they were taking. And because the folk of the villages . . . were eager to see such a new people and especially to see the three or four mares being taken there, at which the whole land was frightened—news of them flew through the island—many came to look at them in a large town called Caonao, the penultimate syllable long. And the Spaniards, on the morning of the day they arrived at the town, stopped to breakfast in a riverbed that was dry but for a few small pools. This riverbed was full of whetstones, and all longed to sharpen their swords on them and did. When they had finished their breakfast, they continued on the road to Caonao.

Along the road for two or three leagues there was an arid plain, where one found oneself thirsty after any work; and there certain Indians from the villages brought them some gourds of water and some things to eat.

They arrived at the town of Caonao in the evening. Here they found many people, who had prepared a great deal of food consisting of cassava bread and fish, because they had a large river close by and also were near the sea. In a little square were 2,000 Indians, all squatting because they have this custom, all staring, frightened, at the mares. Nearby was a large *bohio,* or large house, in which were more than 500 other Indians, close-packed and fearful, who did not dare come out.

When some of the domestic Indians the Spaniards were taking with them as servants (who were more than 1,000 souls . . .) wished to enter the large house, the Cuban Indians had chickens ready and said to them: "Take these—do not enter here." For they already knew that the Indians who served the Spaniards were not apt to perform any other deeds than those of their masters.

There was a custom among the Spaniards that one person, appointed by the captain, should be in charge of distributing to each Spaniard the food and other things the Indians gave. And while the captain was thus on his mare and the others mounted on theirs, and the father himself was observing how the bread and fish were distributed, a Spaniard, in whom the devil is thought to have clothed himself, suddenly drew his sword. Then the whole hundred drew theirs and began to rip open the bellies, to cut and kill those lambs—men, women, children, and old folk, all of whom were seated, off guard and frightened, watching the mares and the Spaniards. And within two credos, not a man of all of them there remains alive.

The Spaniards enter the large house nearby, for this was happening at its door, and in the same way, with cuts and stabs, began to kill as many as they found there, so that a stream of blood was running, as if a great number of cows had perished. Some of the Indians who could make haste climbed up the poles and woodwork of the house to the top, and thus escaped.

The cleric had withdrawn shortly before this massacre to where another small square of the town was formed, near where they had lodged him. This was in a large house where all the Spaniards also had to stay, and here about forty of the Indians who had carried the Spaniards' baggage from the provinces farther back were stretched out on the ground, resting. And five Spaniards chanced to be with the cleric. When these heard the blows of the swords and knew that the Spaniards were killing the Indians—without seeing anything, because there were certain houses between—they put hands to their swords and are about to kill the forty Indians . . . to pay them their commission.

The cleric, moved to wrath, opposes and rebukes them harshly to prevent them, and having some respect for him, they stopped what they were going to do, so the forty were left alive. The five go to kill where the others were killing. And as the cleric had been detained in hindering the slaying of the forty carriers, when he went he found a heap of dead, which the Spaniards had made among the Indians, which was certainly a horrible sight.

When Narváez, the captain, saw him he said: "How does Your Honor like what these our Spaniards have done?"

Seeing so many cut to pieces before him, and very upset at such a cruel event, the cleric replied: "That I commend you and them to the devil!"

The heedless Narváez remained, still watching the slaughter as it took place, without speaking, acting, or moving any more than if he had been marble. For if he had wished, being on the horseback and with a lance in his hands, he could have prevented the Spaniards from killing even ten persons.

Then the cleric leaves him, and goes elsewhere through some groves seeking Spaniards to stop them from killing. For they were passing through the groves looking for someone to kill, sparing neither boy, child, woman, nor old person. And they did more, in that certain Spaniards went to the road to the river, which was nearby. Then all the Indians who had escaped with wounds, stabs, and cuts—all who could flee to throw themselves into the river to save themselves—met with Spaniards who finished them.

Another outrage occurred which should not be left untold, so that the deeds of our Christians in these regions may be observed. When the cleric entered the large house where I said there were about 500 souls—or whatever the number, which was great—and saw with horror the dead there and those who had escaped above by the poles or woodwork, he said to them:

"No more, no more. Do not be afraid. There will be no more, there will be no more."

With this assurance, believing that it would be thus, an Indian descended, a well-disposed young man of twenty-five or thirty years, weeping. And as the cleric did not rest but went everywhere to stop the killing, the cleric then left the house. And just as the young man came down, a Spaniard who was there drew a cutlass or half sword and gives him a cut through the loins, so that his intestines fall out. . . .

The Indian, moaning, takes his intestines in his hands and comes fleeing out of the house. He encounters the cleric . . . and the cleric tells him some things about the faith, as much as the time and anguish permitted, explaining to him that if he wished to be baptized he would go to heaven to live with God. The sad one, weeping and showing pain as if he were burning in flames, said yes, and with this the cleric baptized him. He then fell dead on the ground. . . .

Of all that has been said, I am a witness. I was present and saw it, and I omit many other particulars in order to shorten the account.

FELIPE GUAMÁN POMA DE AYALA (1526–1613)
Peru

Felipe Guamán Poma de Ayala was a Christianized Indian of noble, Incan lineage. His *New Chronicle and Good Government,* addressed to the Spanish king in order to redress certain colonialist inequities, and thus also known as *Letter to a King,* offers an interesting perspective on the interaction of identity, valuation, and knowledge. In the first place, as an Indian, he claims to have privileged knowledge that enables him to write a truer history of his native Peru than that contained in previous chronicles. This knowledge is also used as a pretext for criticizing the colonial administration and for making a case for his own worth. Guamán, semieducated in the cultural forms of the Spaniards, opted for the chronicle, a genre of medieval origin analogous to "mythistory," whose starting point is always the beginning of the world, making its way through dynasties and generations, and finally reaching the present. The underlying purpose of his *Nueva Crónica* (New Chronicle) was the denunciation of Spanish injustices and the proposal of a *Buen Gobierno* or Good Government: "[I]t is not the Spanish administrators and employers who are the rightful owners of Peru. According to the laws of both God and man, we Indians are the proprietors." Guamán also subverts the apparent conformity to colonial rule by a deft masking of Andean ideas in European expressive forms. Most important in his critique of the Spaniards is his use of pictures, which unlike European illustrations do not follow the meaning of the text but, rather, precede it and guide it. Like all syncretic expression, these pictures accommodate a double reading. On one level of interpretation narrative events are represented; on another level this narrative representation is subverted by a subliminal message. The mapping of values in Andean space follows a different hierarchy than that of European space. While the center is the position of preferred value, as in European topology, the left always, signifies greater importance than the right. By placing Indian figures on the left and Spaniards on the right, Guamán thus inverts their status and by implication the hierarchy of colonialism.

from **Letter to a King**

The First Part of this Chronicle: The Indians of Peru

AUTHOR'S FAMILY

My history begins with the exemplary life which was led by my father Huaman Mallqui and my mother Curi Ocllo Coya, daughter of Tupec Inca Yupanqui, the Peruvian ruler.

My father interested himself in the education of his adopted son Martín de Ayala, a half-caste of mixed Spanish and Indian blood. He caused this boy to enter the service of God and take the habit of a Christian friar when only 12 years old. This was a happy chance for myself. For my half-brother Martín, once he had grown into a man, gave instruction to his brothers including myself. Thus I came to be able to write my "First New Chronicle," having been taught my letters at an early age.

As one of the principal Indians of Peru, my father had duly presented himself to the envoy of the Emperor Charles V, Don Francisco Pizarro, and other Spaniards in order to kiss their hands and offer peace and friendship to the Emperor. He was received by them at the port of Tumbes before their march to Caxamarca. My father was on the side of Inca Huascar, the legitimate ruler, whom he served as Viceroy. After his reception by the Christians he returned to his province.

My father served in an important capacity during all the wars, battles and revolts against the Spanish Crown. In one of these wars he was in the service of a loyal Captain named Luis de Avalos de Ayala, the father of the half-caste Martín about whom I have written, and they both took part in the bloody battle of Huarina. The Captain was umhorsed by a lance-thrust while fighting against the partisans of Gonzalo Pizarro. He was defended and saved from certain death by my father, who knocked down and killed Martín de Olmos, one of the rebel side. The Captain, on rising from the ground, acknowledged his debt and declared that my father, even though an Indian, deserved a grant of land from the Crown. Thus my father, having gained some honour from this service, thenceforward took the name of Ayala and adopted the style of Don Martín de Ayala.[1]

Translated by Christopher Dilke.

---

1. This story, in the precise form in which it is told, appears improbable or indeed impossible. Ayala arrived in Spain a year after the battle of Huarina in 1547. In other battles he fought on the same side as Martín de Olmos, who survived to be mayor of Cuzco in 1573.

The Second Part of this Chronicle: The Conquest

The first inhabitant of the Old World to discover our country was St. Bartholomew, who arrived from Jerusalem during the reign of the Inca Sinchi Roca.

It was much later that the way across the sea was opened up. Alexander VI, a Spaniard, was Pope and Maximilian I was the Holy Roman Emperor. Queen Joan was on the throne of Spain.[2] Already it was known that another ocean existed to the west of the Indies.

Our countries were properly discovered by two men: one of Columbus' companions and Pedro de Candia. When the former died he left his papers to his friend. Candia returned to Castile and reported that he had been ashore at Santa.

The way it happened was that the Inca Huayna Capac, who was in Cuzco, was told that some men with long beards and the appearance of corpses had landed in his Empire. He immediately gave the order that one of them—who turned out to be Candia—was to be brought by his messengers as freight to Cuzco, so that he could see him with his own eyes. In this way the two of them, the Inca and the Spaniard, got to know one another.

They communicated by signs. When Candia was asked what he ate, he replied that he lived on silver and gold. The Inca thereupon gave him some silver and gold-dust and a quantity of gold plate and had him returned by the messengers to Santa, where he found his companion lying dead. Candia travelled back to Spain alone, taking with him the precious gifts which he had obtained.[3]

He spread the news of the wealth to be found in Peru and reported that our people were dressed and shod in gold and silver, wore ornaments of these metals on their heads and hands and even walked on gold and silver floors. This was true to the extent that our Indians decorated themselves for their feasts and entertainments with bracelets, diadems and brooches made of the precious metals. And Candia added that a small kind of camel was to be found in our country, meaning the llama.

The greed for gold which was awakened by Candia's story caused a number of Spaniards to enlist themselves for the Conquest of our country. They were assisted by a Peruvian Indian who had been brought back to Spain as a captive and who was given the name of Felipe or Felipillo. This Indian learnt the Castilian tongue in order to be able to act as interpreter. The Spaniards could hardly wait for their arrival in Peru, so anxious were they to lay their hands on our treasures.

. . .

In 1532, when Charles V was King of Spain and also Holy Roman Emperor, Pizarro and Almagro, acting in their capacity as his ambassadors, received an envoy from the legitimate ruler Capac Apo Inca Tupac Cucihualpa Huascar, who came with a message of peace to greet them at the port of Tumbes. This envoy was my father Huaman Mallqui, who carried credentials from the capital city of Cuzco.

. . .

---

2. Ferdinand and Isabella were the Sovereigns in 1492.

3. Candia met, not the Inca, but an Incan nobleman at Tumbes.

The second ambassador to be received by the Spaniards was Rumiñavi, the commanding general of Atahuallpa. He presented himself with great ceremony before Pizarro and Almagro and requested them to remove their troops from the country. In exchange for their departure he offered them a large amount of gold and silver. The Spaniards refused the request, saying that they wished to meet and kiss hands with the Inca in their capacity as ambassadors of their King-Emperor and that they could not leave the country until they had done so.

The presents which Atahuallpa sent to Pizarro and Almagro and the factor Illán consisted of male servants and sacred virgins. Some of the virgins were also offered to the Spaniards' horses because, seeing them eating maize, the Peruvians took them for a kind of human being. Until that time, horses were unknown to our people and it seemed advisable to treat them with respect.

. . .

To our Indian eyes, the Spaniards looked as if they were shrouded like corpses. Their faces were covered with wool, leaving only the eyes visible, and the caps which they wore resembled little red pots on top of their heads. Sometimes they also decorated their heads with plumes. Their swords appeared very long, since they had to be carried with the points turned in a backward direction. They were all dressed alike and talked together like brothers and ate at the same table. Only one of them seemed to have powers of command and he had a dark face, white teeth and flashing eyes. He often shouted at the others and they obeyed his orders.

. . .

Franciso Pizarro, speaking for himself and Almagro, explained through the Indian interpreter Felipe that he was the messenger and ambassador of a great ruler who desired friendship with the Inca and that this was the only object of his mission to Peru. Atahuallpa listened with close attention to the words spoken by Pizarro and then by the interpreter. He answered with great dignity that he had no reason to doubt the fact of the Spaniards' long journey or their mission from an important ruler. However, he had no need to make any pact of friendship with them because he too was a great ruler in his own country.

After this reply Friar Vicente joined in the conversation. He came forward holding a crucifix in his right hand and a breviary in his left and introduced himself as another envoy of the Spanish ruler, who according to his account was a friend of God, and who often worshipped before the cross and believed in the Gospel. Friar Vicente called upon the Inca to renounce all other gods as being a mockery of the truth.

Atahuallpa's reply was that he could not change his belief in the Sun, who was immortal, and in the other Inca divinities. He asked Friar Vicente what authority he had for his own belief and the friar told him it was all written in the book which he held. The Inca then said: "Give me the book so that it can speak to me." The book was handed up to him and he began to eye it carefully and listen to it page by page. At last he asked: "Why doesn't the book say anything to me?" Still sitting on his throne, he threw it on to the ground with a haughty and petulant gesture.

Friar Vicente found his voice and called out that the Indians were against the Christian faith. Thereupon Pizarro and Almagro began to shout orders to their men, telling them to attack these Indians who rejected God and the Emperor. The

Spaniards began to fire their muskets and charged upon the Indians, killing them like ants.

It was 32 years since the outbreak of civil war between the two Inca brothers Huascar and Atahuallpa. During that period of time Franciso Pizarro, Diego de Almagro the elder and the younger, Gonzalo Pizarro, Carbajal and Hernández Girón had committed treason to the Crown and instigated disorder and unrest. They had all of them been driven by the ambition of poor men to make a fortune and become great lords in our country.

GARCILASO DE LA VEGA (EL INCA) (1539–1616)
Peru

Garcilaso de la Vega was part Native American, part European, of royal lineage on both sides. His father, Captain Sebastián de la Vega Vargas, opted to marry not Garcilaso's mother, the Incan princess Ñusta Champu Ocllo, whom he met in Peru, but a Spanish noble woman of his own status, Doña Luisa de los Ríos, who eventually became his sole heir when he died in 1560. Garcilaso continued to live with his father, the *Corregidor,* serving as his amanuensis. When Don Sebastián died, he left a sum of money for Garcilaso, now twenty-one, to go to Spain and continue his education. The young Garcilaso went to seek redress in the Spanish courts, but it was to no avail. He never returned to Peru, and remained in Spain, settling with relatives in Montilla, Andalusia. His brief absences, included taking part in the War of the Alpujarras (1570), in which he received the title of captain. Garcilaso eventually joined a religious order in Cordova after his relative, the marquis of Priego, died. Garcilaso had received an annuity from the marquis but when a cousin inherited the title, he was left without means. Losing all hope of inheritance, he turned to literature, particularly the Greeks and Italians: Plutarch, Boccaccio, and Ariosto. He seemed to be modeling himself after his illustrious forebear and namesake, Garcilaso de la Vega, the poet, who had ushered the Renaissance into Spain half a century earlier. In 1590 he published a translation of Leon Hebreo's *Dialoghi di amore (Dialogues on Love),* a very influential neoplatonic treatise of the time. In Cordova he wrote *La Florida* (1605), an account of Hernando de Soto's explorations of Florida and his masterpiece, *The Royal Commentaries,* a two-volume work published between 1609 and 1617.* Unlike Guamán, Garcilaso chose to work the lofty genre of history, which, however, he mixed with autobiographical passages and the oral lore of native informants. Motivated by the desire to exalt the history of the Incas and to cast them as the first and greatest civilization of Peru, he disturbed the Spanish readers of his time and was subsequently criticized by professional historians for injecting heavy doses of myth. However, Garcilaso shrewdly justified his approach by pointing out that Greek and Roman histories also made use of legendary material. He also criticized the lapses and errors of Spanish historians like

"El Castillo," Chichén Itzá.

Francisco López de Gómara, Hernán Cortés's chaplain and biographer and author of an early and highly influential *General History of the Indies* (1552). Either for lack of direct information or ignorance of Quechua, the Incan language, Spanish historians misconstrued and mistranslated the history of the Incas.

from *Royal Commentaries of the Incas and General History of Peru*

Preface to the Reader

Though there have been learned Spaniards who have written accounts of the states of the New World, such as those of Mexico and Peru and the other kingdoms of the heathens, they have not described these realms so fully as they might have done. This I have remarked particularly in what I have seen written about Peru, concerning which, as a native of the city of Cuzco, which was formerly the Rome of that empire, I have fuller and more accurate information than that provided by

Translated by Harold V. Livermore.

*The title that Garcilaso gave his book is *Royal Commentaries*, which was published in 1609; *Of the Incas* has been added in English editions. *General History of Peru* is the title given by the Royal Council to Part Two, which appeared seven months after Garcilaso's death, as a way of disavowing connections with its implicit critiques of the Spaniards.

previous writers. It is true that these have dealt with many of the very remarkable achievements of that empire, but they have set them down so briefly that, owing to the manner in which they are told, I am scarcely able to understand even such matters as are well known to me. For this reason, impelled by my natural love for my native country, I have undertaken the task of writing these *Commentaries,* in which everything in the Peruvian empire before the arrival of the Spaniards is clearly and distinctly set down, from the rites of their vain religion to the government of their kings in time of peace and war, and all else that can be told of these Indians, from the highest affairs of the royal crown to the humblest duties of its vassals. I write only of the empire of the Incas, and do not deal with other monarchies, about which I can claim no similar knowledge. In the course of my history I shall affirm its truthfulness and shall set down no important circumstances without quoting the authority of Spanish historians who may have touched upon it in part or as a whole. For my purpose is not to gainsay them, but to furnish a commentary and gloss, and to interpret many Indian expressions which they, as strangers to that tongue, have rendered inappropriately. This will be fully seen in the course of my history, which I commend to the piety of those who may peruse it, with no other interest than to be of service to Christendom.

The Idolatry of the Indians and the Gods They Worshipped Before the Incas

For the better understanding of the idolatry, way of life, and customs of the Indians of Peru, it will be necessary for us to divide those times into two periods. First we shall say how they lived before the Incas, and then how the Inca kings governed, so as not to confuse the one thing with the other, and so that the customs and gods of one period are not attributed to the other. It must therefore be realized that in the first age of primitive heathendom there were Indians who were little better than tame beasts and others much worse than wild beasts. To begin with their gods, we may say that they were of a piece with the simplicity and stupidity of the times, as regards the multiplicity of gods and the vileness and crudity of the things the people worshipped. Each province, each tribe, each village, each quarter, each clan, each house had gods different from the rest, for they considered that other people's gods, being busy with other people's affairs, could not help them, but they must have their own. Thus they came to have so great a variety of gods, which were too numerous to count. They did not understand, as the gentile Romans did, how to create abstract gods such as Hope, Victory, Peace, and so on, for their thoughts did not rise to invisible things, and they worshipped what they saw, some in one way and others in another. They did not consider whether the things they worshipped were worthy of their worship and they had no self-respect, in the sense of refraining from worshipping things inferior to themselves. They only thought of distinguishing themselves from one another, and each from all the rest. Thus they worshipped grasses, plants, flowers, trees of all kinds, high hills, great rocks and nooks in them, deep caves, pebbles, and little pieces of stone of various colors found in rivers and streams, such as jasper. They worshipped the emerald, especially in the province now called Puerto

Viejo. They did not worship diamonds or rubies because these stones did not exist there. Instead they worshipped various animals, some for their ferocity, such as the tiger, lion, and bear: and consequently, regarding them as gods, if they chanced to meet them, they did not flee but fell down and worshipped them and let themselves be killed and eaten without escaping or making any defence at all. They also worshipped other animals for their cunning, such as the fox and monkeys. They worshipped the dog for its faithfulness and nobility, the wild cat for its quickness, and the bird they call *cuntur* for its size; and some natives worshipped eagles, because they boast of descending from them and also from the *cuntur*. Other peoples adored hawks for their quickness and ability in winning their food. They adored the owl for the beauty of its eyes and head; the bat for the keenness of its sight—it caused them much wonder that it could see at night. They also adored many other birds according to their whims. They adored great snakes for their monstrous size and fierceness (some of those in the Antis are about twenty-five or thirty feet long and as thick round as a man's thigh). They also considered other smaller snakes—where there were none so big as in the Antis—to be gods, and they adored lizards, toads, and frogs. In a word, there was no beast too vile and filthy for them to worship as a god, merely in order to differ from one another in their choice of gods, without adoring any real god or being able to expect any benefit from them. They were very simple in everything, like sheep without a shepherd. But we need not be surprised that such unlettered and untaught people should have fallen into these follies, for it is well known that the Greeks and Romans, who prided themselves so greatly on their learning, had thirty thousand gods when their empire was at its height.

The Great Variety of Other Gods They Had

There were many other Indians of various nations in this first period who chose their gods with rather more discrimination than these. They worshipped certain objects that were beneficial, such as streaming fountains and great rivers, which they argued gave them water to irrigate their crops.

Others adored the earth and called it "mother," because it gave them its fruits. Others the air they breathed, saying that men lived by it; others fire, because it warmed them and they cooked their food with it. Others worshipped a ram, because of the great flocks reared in their region; others the great chain of the Sierra Nevada, because of its height and wonderful grandeur and because many rivers used for irrigation flow from it; others maize or *sara,* as they call it, because it was their usual bread; others other cereals or legumes, according to what grew most abundantly in their provinces.

The coastal Indians, in addition to an infinity of other gods they had, even including those already mentioned, generally worshipped the sea, which they called *Mamacocha,* or "Mother Sea," implying that it was like a mother to them in sustaining them with its fish. They also worshipped the whale on account of its monstrous greatness. Besides these cults, which were common to the whole coast, various provinces and regions worshipped the fish most commonly caught there, holding that the first fish that was in the upper world (their word for heaven) was the origin of all other fish of the kind they ate and that it took care to send them plenty of its children to sustain their tribe. Thus in some provinces they worshipped the sardine, which they killed in greater quantity than any other fish, in others the skate, in others the dogfish, in others the goldfish for its beauty, in others the crab and other shellfish for lack of anything better in their waters or because they could not catch or kill anything else. In short, they worshipped and considered gods any fish that was more beneficial to them than the rest. So they had for gods not only the four elements, each separately, but also the compounds and forms of them, however vile and squalid. Other tribes, such as the Chirihuanas and the people of Cape Passau (that is, the southernmost and northernmost provinces of Peru) felt no inclination to worship anything, high or low, either from interest or fear, but lived and still live exactly like beasts, because the doctrine and teaching of the Inca kings did not reach them.

The Origin of the Inca Kings of Peru

While these peoples were living or dying in the manner we have seen, it pleased our Lord God that from their midst there should appear a morning star to give them in the dense darkness in which they dwelt some glimmerings of natural law, of civilization, and of the respect men owe to one another. The descendants of this leader should thus tame those savages and convert them into men, made capable of reason and of receiving good doctrine, so that when God, who is the sun of justice, saw fit to send forth the light of His divine rays upon those idolaters, it might find them no longer in their first savagery, but rendered more docile to receive the Catholic faith and the teaching and doctrine of our Holy Mother the Roman Church, as indeed they have received it—all of which will be seen in the course of this history. It has been observed by clear experience how much prompter and quicker to receive the Gospel were the Indians subdued, governed, and taught by the Inca kings than the other neighboring peoples unreached by the Incas' teachings, many of which are still today as savage and brutish as before, despite the fact that the Spaniards have been in Peru seventy years. And since we stand on the threshold of this great maze, we had better enter and say what lay within.

After having prepared many schemes and taken many ways to begin to give an account of the origin and establishment of the native Inca kings of Peru, it seemed to me that the best scheme and simplest and easiest way was to recount what I often heard as a child from the lips of my mother and her brothers and uncles and other elders about these beginnings. For everything said about them from other sources comes down to the same story as we shall relate, and it will be better to have it as told in the very words of the Incas than in those of foreign authors. My mother dwelt in Cuzco, her native place, and was visited there every week by the few relatives, both male and female, who escaped the cruelty and tyranny of Atahuallpa (which we shall describe in our account of his life). On these visits the ordinary subject of conversation was always the origin of the Inca kings, their greatness, the grandeur of their empire, their deeds and conquests, their government in peace and war, and the laws they ordained so greatly to the advantage of their vassals. In short, there was nothing concerning the most flourishing period of their history that they did not bring up in their conversations.

From the greatness and prosperity of the past they turned to the present, mourning their dead kings, their lost empire, and their fallen state, etc. These and similar topics were broached by the Incas and Pallas on their visits, and on recalling their departed happiness, they always ended these conversations with tears and mourning, saying: "Our rule is turned to bondage" etc. During these talks, I, as a boy, often came in and went out of the place where they were, and I loved to hear them, as boys always do like to hear stories. Days, months, and years went by, until I was sixteen or seventeen. Then it happened that one day when my family was talking in this fashion about their kings and the olden times, I remarked to the senior of them, who usually related these things: "Inca, my uncle, though you have no writings to preserve the memory of past events, what information have you of the origin and beginnings of our kings? For the Spaniards and the other peoples who live on their borders have divine and human histories from which they know when their own kings and their neighbors' kings began to reign and when one empire gave way to another. They even know how many thousand years it is since God created heaven and earth. All this and much more they know through their books. But you, who have no books, what memory have you preserved of your antiquity? Who was the first of our Incas? What was he called? What was the origin of his line? How did he begin to reign? With what men and arms did he conquer this great empire? How did our heroic deeds begin?"

The Inca was delighted to hear these questions, since it gave him great pleasure to reply to them, and turned to me (who had already often heard him tell the tale, but had never paid as much attention as then) saying:

"Nephew, I will tell you these things with pleasure: indeed it is right that you should hear them and keep them in your heart (this is their phrase for 'in the memory'). You should know that in olden times the whole of this region before you was covered with brush and heath, and people lived in those times like wild beasts, with no religion or government and no towns or houses, and without tilling or sowing the soil, or clothing or covering their flesh, for they did not know how to weave cotton or wool to make clothes. They lived in twos and threes as chance brought them together in caves and crannies in rocks and underground caverns. Like wild beasts they ate the herbs of the field and roots of trees and fruits growing wild and also human flesh. They covered their bodies with leaves and the bark of trees and animals' skins. Others went naked. In short, they lived like deer or other game, and even in their intercourse with women they behaved like beasts, for they knew nothing of having separate wives."

I must remark, in order to avoid many repetitions of the words "our father the Sun," that the phrase was used by the Incas to express respect whenever they mentioned the sun, for they boasted of descending from it, and none but Incas were allowed to utter the words: it would have been blasphemy and the speaker would have been stoned. The Inca said:

"Our father the Sun, seeing men in the state I have mentioned, took pity and was sorry for them, and sent from heaven to earth a son and a daughter of his to indoctrinate them in the knowledge of our father the Sun that they might worship him and adopt him as their god, and to give them precepts and laws by which they would live as reasonable and civilized men, and dwell in houses and settled towns, and learn to till the soil, and grow plants and crops, and breed flocks, and use the fruits of the earth like rational beings and not like beasts. With this order and mandate our father the Sun set these two children of his in Lake Titicaca, eighty leagues from here, and bade them go where they would, and wherever they stopped to eat or sleep to try to thrust into the ground a golden wand half a yard long and two fingers in thickness which he gave them as a sign and token: when this wand should sink into the ground at a single thrust, there our father the Sun wished them to stop and set up their court.

"Finally he told them: 'When you have reduced these people to our service, you shall maintain them in reason and justice, showing mercy, clemency, and mildness, and always treating them as a merciful father treats his beloved and tender children. Imitate my example in this. I do good to all the world. I give them my light and brightness that they may see and go about their business; I warm them when they are cold; and I grow their pastures and crops, and bring fruit to their trees, and multiply their flocks. I bring rain and calm weather in turn, and I take care to go round the world once a day to observe the wants that exist in the world and to fill and supply them as the sustainer and benefactor of men. I wish you as children of mine to follow this example sent down to earth to teach and benefit those men who live like beasts. And henceforward I establish and nominate you as kings and lords over all the people you may thus instruct with your reason, government, and good works.'

"When our father the Sun had thus made manifest his will to his two children he bade them farewell. They left Titicaca and travelled northwards, and wherever they stopped on the way they thrust the golden wand into the earth, but it never sank in. Thus they reached a small inn or resthouse seven or eight leagues south of this city. Today it is called Pacárec Tampu, 'inn or resthouse of the dawn.' The Inca gave it this name because he set out from it about daybreak. It is one of the towns the prince later ordered to be founded, and its inhabitants to this day boast greatly of its name because our first Inca bestowed it. From this place he and his wife, our queen, reached the valley of Cuzco which was then a wilderness."

THE NAVAJO PEOPLE
Southwestern United States

People the world over have stories of how the world began, and these stories serve—as Genesis does for the Judeo-Christian tradition—to provide a general world view for the culture in question. The Navajo creation story is not, as Genesis is not, made up of a single story, told or written by a named individual. Rather, any single *text* of the creation story is inevitably a composite made up of what various Navajo people have narrated or explained to one or another Euro-American at various times.

Although the Navajo came into contact with Europeans as early as the sixteenth century, it was not until the nineteenth century that informed and careful efforts to record their extensive ceremonial and, as we might say, "literary" expression were undertaken. Foremost among these efforts were those of Washington Matthews whose publications date from the early 1880s until the time of his death in 1905. In Matthews's *Navaho Legends* (1897) is found what author Paul Zolbrod calls "one of the earliest renditions of the Navajo account of the creation and the most comprehensive English text" available. Zolbrod's own text of the Navajo creation story, from which our selection is taken, began, as Zolbrod writes, as "an experiment in text retrieval," since his "original intention was to present an English version of the Navajo creation story as evidence of an ongoing pre-Columbian literary tradition in North America."* In the end, he may have done something like that—although as Zolbrod himself notes, his work mostly led him to "an expanded view of poetry and poetics, or an uncertain one," inasmuch as it is not and cannot be clear to what extent any "text retrieval" process, however careful and sophisticated, can actually retrieve what was never textualized.

An Athabascan people whose language is related to that of Canadian and Alaskan tribes, the Navajo arrived in the southwestern United States from a much more northerly point at a relatively recent date—between 1000 and 1300 C.E. They learned farming and weaving techniques from long-settled Pueblo people, acquired livestock from the Spanish in the seventeenth century, and developed silver-working skills from contact with Mexicans in the nineteenth century.

The creation story describes how the *Diné*—the name the Navajo use for themselves, meaning, roughly, "earth surface people"—ascended to the surface from the many worlds below the earth. Together with the Holy People, who lived in the twelfth and lowest level beneath the earth, the ancestors of the present-day Navajo, after a series of adventures, came to their homes and established their traditional ways of life. The most important figure in Navajo mythology is Changing Woman, daughter of First Man and First Woman (themselves created from two ears of corn). Her mating with the Sun and with Water produced two twins sons who were able to slay the monsters that disrupted the life of the *Diné* on this earth. As the anthropologist James F. Downs puts it, "The record of their victories is written in the landscape of the Navajo country. Prominent mountains, lava flows, and other natural features are identified with the carcasses of slain monsters."

from The Navajo Creation Story [Diné Bahane]

One

Of a time long, long ago these things are said.

It is said[1] that at *Tó bił dahisk'id* white arose in the east and was considered day. We now call that spot Place Where the Waters Crossed.

Translated by Paul Zolbrod.

*Our selections come from pages 35–51 of Paul Zolbrod's Diné Bahanè: The Navajo Creation Story (Albuquerque: University of New Mexico Press, 1984). The quotation is from p. 5.

Blue arose in the south. It too was considered day. So the *Nítch'i dine'é*, who already lived there, moved around. We would call them Air-Spirit People in the language spoken today by those who are given the name *Bilagáana*, which means White Man.

In the west yellow arose and showed that evening had come. Then in the north black arose. So the Air-Spirit People lay down and slept.

. . . .

At *Tó bił dahisk'id* where the streams came together water flowed in all directions. One stream flowed to the east. One stream flowed to the south. One stream flowed to the west. One stream flowed to the north.

Along three of those streams there were dwelling places. There were dwelling places along the stream that flowed east. There were dwelling places along the stream that flowed south. There were dwelling places along the stream that flowed west. But along the stream that flowed north there were no dwellings.

. . . .

To the east there was a place called *Dą́ą́*. In the language of *Bilagáana*, the White Man that name means food. To the south there was a place called *Nahodoolá*. It is unknown what that name means. And to the west there was a place called *Lók'aatsoh sikaad*. In the White Man's language that name means Standing Reed. Nothing is said about a place to the north.

Also to the east there was a place called *Ásaa'łáá'ii*, which means One Dish. And also to the south there was a place called *Tó hadziłtił*, which means A Big Amount of Water Coming Out in the language of *Bilagáana*. And also to the west there was a place called *Dził łichíí' bee hooghan*. That name means House of Red Mountain. To the north there are no places that have been given names.

Then there was a place called *Leeyaa hooghan* to the east. In his language the White Man would give it the name Underground House. And there was another place called *Chiiłchintah* to the south. In the language he speaks *Bilagáana* would give it the name Among Aromatic Sumac. And there was another place called *Tsé łichíí' bee hooghan* to the west. In the language of his people the White Man would give it the name House of Red Rock. We hear of no places with names to the north.

. . .

In those early times dark ants dwelled there. Red ants dwelled there. Dragonflies dwelled there. Yellow beetles dwelled there.

Hard beetles lived there. Stone-carrier beetles lived there. Black beetles lived there. Coyote-dung beetles lived there.

Bats made their homes there. Whitefaced beetles made their homes there. Locusts made their homes there. White locusts made their homes there.

Those are the twelve groups who started life there. We call them *Nítch'idine'é*. In the language of *Bilagáana* the White Man that name means Air-Spirit People. For they are people unlike the five-fingered earth-surface people who come into the world today, live on the ground for a while, die at a ripe old age, and then leave the world. They are people who travel in the air and fly swiftly like the wind and dwell nowhere else but here.

Far to the east there was an ocean. Far to the south there was an ocean. Far to the west there was an ocean. And far to the north there was an ocean.

In the ocean to the east dwelled *Tééhoołtsódii,* who was chief of the people there. In the White Man's language he can be called The One That Grabs Things In the Water. In the ocean to the south lived *Táłtł'ááh alééh.* His name means Blue Heron. In the ocean to the west *Ch'ał* made his home and was chief of those people. In the language of the White Man he would be called Frog. And in the ocean to the north dwelled *Ii'ni'jiłgaii.* In the White Man's language that name means Winter Thunder. He was chief among whoever those people were who lived there, it is said.

Two

It is also said that the Air-Spirit People fought among themselves. And this is how it happened. They committed adultery, one with another. Many of the men were to blame, but so were many of the women.

They tried to stop, but they could not help themselves.

Tééhoołtsódii The One That Grabs Things In the Water, who was chief in the east, complained, saying this:

"They must not like it here," he said.

And *Táłtł'ááh alééh* the Blue Heron, who was chief in the south, also complained:

"What they do is wrong," he complained.

Ch'ał the Frog, who was chief in the west, also complained. But he took his complaint directly to the Air-Spirit people, having this to say to them:

"You shall no longer be welcome here where I am chief," is what he said.

"That is what I think of you."

And from his home in the north where he was chief, *Ii'ni'jiłgaii* the Winter Thunder spoke to them also.

"Nor are you welcome here!" he, too, said to them.

"Go away from this land.

"Leave at once!"

But the people still could not help it: one with another they continued to commit adultery. And when they did it yet another time and then argued with each other again, *Tééhoołtsódii* The One That Grabs Things In the Water would no longer speak to them. *Táłtł'ááh alééh* the Blue Heron would no longer speak to them. Likewise *Ch'ał* the Frog would say nothing to them. And *Ii'ni'jiłgaii* the Winter Thunder refused to say anything.

Four days and four nights passed.

Then the same thing happened. Those who lived in the south repeated their sins: the men with the women and the women with the men. They committed adultery. And again they quarreled afterward.

One woman and one man sought *Tééhoołtsódii* The One That Grabs Things In the Water in the east to try to straighten things out. But they were driven away. Then they went to *Táłtł'ááh alééh* the Blue Heron in the south. But they were again driven away. And they looked for *Ch'ał* the Frog in the west. But they were driven away again. Finally they went to the north to speak with *Ii'ni'jiłgaii* the Winter Thunder. He, too, drove them away, breaking his silence to say this to them:

"None of you shall enter here," he said to them.

"I do not wish to listen to you.

"Go away, and keep on going!"

That night the people held a council at *Nahodoolá* in the south. But they could not agree on anything. On and on they quarreled, until white arose in the east and it was again day. *Tééhoołtsódii* The One That Grabs Things In the Water then spoke to them:

"Everywhere in this world you bring disorder," he said to them.

"So we do not want you here.

"Find some other place to live."

But the people did not leave right away. For four nights the women talked and squabbled, each blaming the other for what had happened. And for four nights the men squabbled and talked. They, too, blamed one another.

At the end of the fourth night as they were at last about to end their meeting, they all noticed something white in the east. They also saw it in the south. It appeared in the west, too. And in the north it also appeared.

It looked like an endless chain of white mountains. They saw it on all sides. It surrounded them, and they noticed that it was closing in on them rapidly. It was a high, insurmountable wall of water! And it was flowing in on them from all directions, so that they could escape neither to the east nor to the west; neither to the south nor to the north could they escape.

So, having nowhere else to go, they took flight. Into the air they went. Higher and higher they soared, it is said.

Three

It is also said that they circled upward until they reached the smooth, hard shell of the sky overhead. When they could go no higher they looked down and saw that water now covered everything. They had nowhere to land either above or below.

Suddenly someone with a blue head appeared and called to them:

"Here," he called to them.

"Come this way.

"Here to the east there is a hole!"

They found that hole and entered. One by one they filed through to the other side of the sky. And that is how they reached the surface of the second world.

The blue-headed creature was a member of the Swallow People. It was they who lived up there.

While the first world had been red, this world was blue. The swallows lived in blue houses, which lay scattered across a broad, blue plain. Each blue house was cone-shaped; each tapered toward the top where there was a blue entry hole.

At first the Swallow People gathered around the newcomers and watched them silently. Nobody from either group said anything to any member of the other. Finally, when darkness came and the exiled Air-Spirit People made camp for the night, the blue swallow left.

In the morning the insect people from the world below decided that someone should explore this new world. So they sent a plain locust and a white locust to the east, instructing them to look for people like themselves.

Two days came and went before the locusts returned. They said that they had traveled for a full day. And as darkness fell they reached what must have been the end of the world. For they came upon the rim of a great cliff that rose out of an abyss whose bottom could not be seen. Both coming and going, they said, they found no people, no plants, no rivers, no mountains. They found nothing but bare, blue, level ground.

Next the two messengers were sent south to explore. Again, two days came and went while they were gone. And they again reported that after traveling for a full day they reached the end of the world. And they reported again that neither in going nor in coming back could they find people or plants, mountains or rivers.

They were then sent to the west. And after that they were sent to the north. Both times they were gone for two days, and they reported each time that they reached the end of the world after traveling for a full day. They also reported that again they could find neither people nor plants and neither mountains nor rivers.

To the others they had only this to say:

"It seems that we are in the center of a vast, blue plain," was all that they could say.

"Wherever we went in this world we could find neither company nor food; neither rivers nor mountains could we find."

After the scouts had returned from their fourth trip, the Swallow People visited the camp of the newcomers. And they asked why they had sent someone to the east to explore.

This is what the insect people from the lower world replied:

"We sent them out to see what was in the land," they replied.

"We sent them out to see if there were people here like ourselves."

Then the swallows asked this:

"What did your scouts tell you?" they asked.

To which the newcomers replied this way:

"They told us that they reached the end of the world after traveling for a full day," they replied.

"They told us that wherever they went in this world they could find neither people nor plants. Neither rivers nor mountains could they find."

The swallows then asked why the insect people had sent their scouts to the south. And they were told that the locusts were sent south to see what was in the land. And when the swallows asked why scouts were sent to the west, they were told again that the locusts were to see what they could find in this blue world. Which is what they were told when they asked why scouts were sent to the north.

To all of which the Swallow People then had this to say:

"Your couriers spoke the truth," they then said.

"But their trips were not necessary.

"Had you asked us what the land contained, we would have told you.

"Had you asked us where this world ended, we would have told you.

"We could have saved you all that time and all that trouble.

"Until you arrived here, no one besides us has ever lived in this world. We are the only ones living here."

The newcomers then had this suggestion to make to the swallows:

"You are like us in many ways," they suggested.

"You understand our language.

"Like us you have legs; like us you have bodies; like us you have wings; like us you have heads.

"Why can't we become friends?"

To which the swallows replied:

"Let it be as you say," they replied.

"You are welcome here among us."

So it was that both sets of people began to treat each other as members of one tribe. They mingled one among the other and called each other by the familiar names. They called each other grandparent and grandchild, brother and sister; they called each other father and son, mother and daughter.

For twenty-three days they all lived together in harmony. But on the night of the twenty-fourth day, one of the strangers became too free with the wife of the swallow chief.

Next morning, when he found out what had happened the night before, the chief had this to say to the strangers:

"We welcomed you here among us," was what he had to say to them.

"We treated you as friends and as kin.

"And this is how you return our kindness!

"No doubt you were driven from the world below for just such disorderly acts.

"Well, you must leave this world, too; we will have you here no longer.

"Anyhow, this is a bad land. There is not enough food for all of us.

"People are dying here every day from hunger. Even if we allowed you to stay, you could not live here very long."

When they heard the swallow chief's words, the locusts took flight. And all the others followed. Having nowhere else to go, they flew skyward.

Into the air they went. Higher and higher they soared. They circled upward until they reached the smooth, hard shell of the sky overhead, it is said.

Four

It is also said that like the sky of the world below, this sky had a smooth, hard shell. And like the sky of the world below this one seemed to have no opening. When the insect people reached it they flew around and around, having nowhere to land either above or below.

But as they circled, they noticed a white face peering at them. This was the face of *Nítch'i*. In the language of *Bilagáana* the White Man he would be called Wind. And they heard him cry to them:

"Here!" he cried.

"Here to the south you will find an opening."

"Come this way."

So off they flew to the south, and soon they found a slit in the sky slanting upward in a southerly direction. One by one they flew through it to the other side. And that is how they reached the surface of the third world.

. . .

While the second world had been blue, this world was yellow. Here the exiles found no one but Yellow Grasshopper People, who lived in yellow holes in the ground along the banks of a river which flowed east through their yellow land.

At first the Yellow Grasshopper People said nothing. They gathered silently around the newcomers and stared at them. Nobody from either group spoke to anyone from the other. And when darkness finally came and the people from the world below made their camp, the grasshoppers left.

In the morning the wanderers sent out the same two locusts who had explored the second world.

First they flew to the east where they were gone for two days altogether. Then they flew to the south where they were gone for two more days. Then they flew to the west, where they were gone for another two days. And they flew to the north where for two additional days they were gone. Each time they returned with the same report.

For a full day they had journeyed, until by nightfall they arrived at the rim of a cliff that rose from some unseen place far, far below. And neither in going forth nor in coming back could they find people or plants, mountains or waters. The river along whose banks the Grasshopper People lived soon tapered off toward the east until it was a dry, narrow gully. Otherwise there was nothing to see in this world except flat, yellow countryside and the yellow grasshoppers who lived on it.

When the messengers returned from their fourth journey the two great chiefs of the Grasshopper People came to visit. And they asked the newcomers why they had someone fly to the east and to the west, to the south and to the north.

To which the insect people from the world below replied:

"We sent them to see what was in the land," they replied.

"We sent them to see if they could find people like ourselves."

Then the grasshopper chiefs asked:

"And what did they find?" they asked.

Answered the newcomers:

"They found nothing but the bare land," they answered.

"They found nothing but the cliffs that marked the edge of this world."

"They found no plants and no people. They found no mountains and no rivers.

"Even the river along whose banks your people live here in the center of this world tapers off until it is only a dry, narrow gully."

Replied the grasshopper chiefs then:

"You might have first asked us what the land contains," they replied.

"We could have saved your messengers all that trouble.

"We could have told you that there in nothing in this land but what you see right here.

"We have lived here for a long time, but we have seen nothing that you have not seen. And we have seen no other people until you came."

The insect people from the world below then spoke to the grasshopper chiefs as they had spoken to the Swallow People in the second world, saying these things to them:

"Come to think of it, you are somewhat like us," they said to them.

"Like us you have heads. Like us you have wings. Like us you have bodies. Like us you have legs.

"You even speak the way we speak.

"Perhaps we can join you here."

The grasshoppers consented, and the two groups quickly began to mingle. They embraced each other, and soon they were using the names of family and kin together. They called each other mother and daughter, father and son, brother and sister, grandparent and grandchild. It was as if they were all of the same tribe.

As before, all went well for twenty-three days. But as before, on the night of the twenty-fourth, one of the newcomers treated the chief of the grasshoppers exactly as the swallow chief had been treated in the second world.

When he discovered how he had been wronged, the grasshopper chief spoke this way to the insect people:

"No doubt you were sent away from the world below for such transgressions!" is how he spoke.

"No doubt you bring disorder wherever you go. No doubt you lack intelligence.

"Well, here too you shall drink no more of our water. Here too you shall eat no more of our food. Here too you shall breathe no more of our air.

"Get out of here!"

So the insect people took flight again. And again they circled round and round into the sky until they arrived at the smooth, hard shell of its outer crust, it is said.

Five

It is also said that they again had to circle around for quite some time, looking in vain for some way to get through the sky overhead. Finally they heard a voice bidding them fly to the west and look there. And they noticed a red head peering at them. The voice they heard and the head they saw belonged to Níłch'i łichíí. In the language of Bilagáana the White Man he would bear the name Red Wind.

Doing as they were told they found a passage which twisted around through the sky's other surface like the tendril of a vine. It had been made this way by the wind. They flew into it and wound their way to the other side. And that is how they reached the surface of the fourth world.

Four of the grasshoppers had come with them. One was white. One was blue.

One was yellow. And one was black. To this very day, in fact, we have grasshoppers of those four colors among us.

The surface of the fourth world was unlike the surface of any of the lower worlds. For it was a mixture of black and white. The sky above was alternately white, blue, yellow, and black, just as it had been in the worlds below. But here the colors were of a different duration.

In the first world each color lasted for about the same length of time each day. In the second world the blue and the black lasted just a little longer than the white and the yellow. But here in the fourth world there was white and yellow for scarcely any time, so long did the blue and black remain in the sky. As yet there was no sun and no moon; as yet there were no stars.

When they arrived on the surface of the fourth world, the exiles from the lower worlds saw no living thing. But they did observe four great snow-covered peaks along the horizon around them. One peak lay to the east. One peak lay to the south. One peak lay likewise to the west. And to the north there was one peak.

The insect people sent two scouts to the east, who returned at the end of the two days. Those two said that they had not been able to reach the eastern mountain after an entire day's flight. And although they had traveled far indeed they could see no living creature. Neither track nor trail could they see; not one sign of life were they able to detect.

Two scouts were then sent to the south. And when these two returned at the end of two full days they reported that after an entire day's flight they managed to reach a low range of mountains on this side of the great peak which lay in that direction.

They too had traveled very far. They too could see no living creature. But they did observe two different kinds of tracks the likes of which they had never seen before. They described them carefully, and from that description the tracks seemed to resemble those made these days in our own world by deer and turkey.

Two scouts were sent next to the west. And after two full days they returned, reporting that they could by no means reach the great peak which lay in that direction, no matter how fast they could fly in a single day and no matter how far. Neither in going forth nor in returning could they see any living creature. Not one sign of life were they able to see.

Finally, two scouts were sent to explore the land that lay to the north. And when they returned they had a different story to tell. For they reported that they had found a strange race unlike any other. These were people who cut their hair square in front. They were people who lived in houses in the ground. They were people who cultivated the soil so that things grew therein. They were now harvesting what they had planted, and they gave the couriers food to eat.

It was now evident to the newcomers that the fourth world was larger than any of the worlds below.

On the very next day, two members of the newly found race came to the camp of the exiles. They were called *Kiis'áanii*, they said, which in the language of

Bilagáana the White Man means People Who Live in Upright Houses. And they wished to invite the exiles to visit their village.

On the way they came to a stream which was red. The *Kiis'áanii* warned their guests not to wade through it. Otherwise the water would injure the feet of the newcomers. Instead they showed the insect people a square raft made of four logs. One log was of white pine. One log was of blue spruce. One log was of yellow pine. And one log was of black spruce. On this raft they all crossed to the opposite bank, where the people who had arrived from the third world visited the homes of the people who dwelled here in the fourth world.

The exiles were given corn and pumpkins to eat. And they were asked by their new friends to stay. For quite some time, in fact, they stayed in the village of the upright houses. There they lived well on the food that the *Kiis'áanii* gave them. Eventually they all lived together like the people of one tribe. Soon the two groups were using the names of family and kin between themselves. They called each other father and son, mother and daughter, grandparent and grandchild, brother and sister.

The land of the *Kiis'áanii* was a dry land. It had neither rain nor snow and there was little water to be found. But the people who had been dwelling there knew how to irrigate the soil to make things grow, and they taught the newcomers to do so.

Twenty-three days came and went, and twenty-three nights passed and all was well. And on the twenty-fourth night the exiles held a council meeting. They talked quietly among themselves, and they resolved to mend their ways and to do nothing unintelligent that would create disorder. This was a good world, and the wandering insect people meant to stay here, it is said.

Six

It is also said that late in the autumn of that year the newcomers heard a distant voice calling to them from far in the east.

They listened and waited, listened and waited. Until soon they heard the voice again, nearer and louder than before. They continued to listen and wait, listen and wait, until they heard the voice a third time, all the nearer and all the louder.

Continuing to listen, they heard the voice again, even louder than the last time, and so close now that it seemed directly upon them.

A moment later they found themselves standing among four mysterious beings. They had never seen such creatures anywhere before. For they were looking at those who would eventually become known as *Haashch'ééh dine'é*.

In the language of *Bilagáana* the White Man, that name means Holy People. For they are people unlike the earth-surfaced people who come into the world today, live on the ground for a while, die at a ripe old age, and then move on. These are intelligent people who can perform magic. They do not know the pain of being mortal. They are people who can travel far by following the path of the rainbow. And they can travel swiftly by following the path of the sunray. They can make the winds and the thunderbolts work for them so that the earth is theirs to control when they so wish.

The people who were then living on the surface of the fourth world were looking upon *Bits'íís łigaii,* which name means White Body. He is the one that the Navajo people who live in our own world would eventually call *Haashch'ééłti'í,* which in today's language means Talking God.

And they were looking upon *Bits'íís dootł'izh.* That name means Blue Body. He is the one that the Navajo people in our own world would eventually come to know as *Tó neinilí,* which means Water Sprinkler.

And they were looking upon *Bits'íís łitsoii,* or Yellow Body. He is the one that the Navajo people today call *Hashch'éoghan.* Nobody can be sure what that name means in today's language. Some say it means Calling God; some say that it means House God; and some say that it means Growling God.

And they were looking upon *Bits'íís łizhin.* In the White Man's language that name means Black Body. He is the one that the Navajo people living in this world would eventually come to know as *Haashch'ééshzhiní,* which means Black God. Sometimes he is also called the God of Fire.

Without speaking the Holy People made signs to those who were gathered there, as if to give them instructions. But the exiles could not understand their gestures. So they stood by helplessly and watched.

And after the gods had left, the people talked about that mysterious visit for the rest of that day and all night long, trying to determine what it meant.

. . .

As for the gods, they repeated their visit four days in a row. But on the fourth day, *Bits'íís łizhin* the Black Body remained after the other three departed. And when he was alone with the onlookers, he spoke to them in their own language. This is what he said:

"You do not seem to understand the Holy People," he said.

"So I will explain what they want you to know.

"They want more people to be created in this world. But they want intelligent people, created in their likeness, not in yours.

"You have bodies like theirs, true enough.

"But you have the teeth of beasts! You have the mouths of beasts! You have the feet of beasts! You have the claws of beasts!

"The new creatures are to have hands like ours. They are to have feet like ours. They are to have mouths like ours and teeth like ours. They must learn to think ahead, as we do.

"What is more, you are unclean!

"You smell bad.

"So you are instructed to cleanse yourselves before we return twelve days from now."

That is what *Bits'íís łizhin* the Black Body said to the insect people who had emerged from the first world to the second, from the second world to the third, and from the third world to the fourth world where they now lived.

. . .

Accordingly, on the morning of the twelfth day the people bathed carefully.

The women dried themselves with yellow corn meal. The men dried themselves with white corn meal.

Soon after they had bathed, they again heard the distant voice coming from far in the east.

They listened and waited as before, listened and waited. Until soon they heard the voice as before, nearer and louder this time. They continued to listen and wait, listen and wait, until they heard the voice a third time as before, all the nearer and all the louder.

Continuing to listen as before, they heard the voice again, even louder than the last time, and so close now that it seemed directly upon them, exactly as it had seemed before. And as before they found themselves standing among the same four *Haashch'ééh dine'é,* or Holy People as *Bilagáana* the White Man might wish to call them.

Bits'íís dootł'izh the Blue Body and *Bits'íís łizhin* the Black Body each carried a sacred buckskin. *Bits'íís łigaii* the White Body carried two ears of corn.

One ear of corn was yellow. The other ear was white. Each ear was completely covered at the end with grains, just as sacred ears of corn are covered in our own world now.

Proceeding silently, the gods laid one buckskin on the ground, careful that its head faced the west. Upon this skin they placed the two ears of corn, being just as careful that the tips of each pointed east. Over the corn they spread the other buckskin, making sure that its head faced east.

Under the white ear they put the feather of a white eagle.

And under the yellow ear they put the feather of a yellow eagle.

Then they told the onlooking people to stand at a distance.

So that the wind could enter.

Then from the east *Nítch'i łigai* the White Wind blew between the buckskins. And while the wind thus blew, each of the Holy People came and walked four times around the objects they had placed so carefully on the ground.

As they walked, the eagle feathers, whose tips protruded slightly from between the two buckskins, moved slightly.

Just slightly.

So that only those who watched carefully were able to notice.

And when the Holy People had finished walking, they lifted the topmost buckskin.

And lo! the ears of corn had disappeared.

In their place there lay a man and there lay a woman.

                                    . . .

The white ear of corn had been transformed into our most ancient male ancestor. And the yellow ear of corn had been transformed into our most ancient female ancestor.

It was the wind that had given them life: the very wind that gives us our breath as we go about our daily affairs here in the world we ourselves live in!

When this wind ceases to blow inside of us, we become speechless. Then we die.

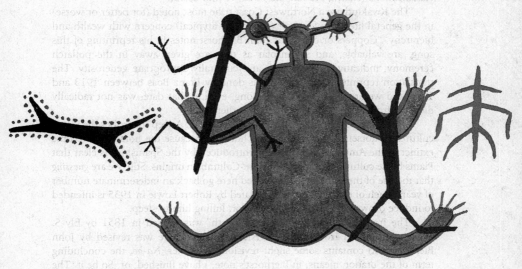

Cuyama. Curious bearlike being, showing superimposition. On a rock lying in a cave.

In the skin at the tips of our fingers we can see the trail of that life-giving wind.

Look carefully at your own fingertips.

There you will see where the wind blew when it created your most ancient ancestors out of two ears of corn, it is said.

THE KWAKIUTL PEOPLE
THE CROW PEOPLE
THE IROQUOIS PEOPLE
THE CHEROKEE PEOPLE

In contrast to *The Navajo Creation Story*, a lengthy and elaborated narrative, that tells Navajo people of their origins, the material presented next—a Kwakiutl song, a series of Crow "charms," an Iroquois oration, and a "magic formula" from the Iroquois and the Cherokee—is neither extensive nor story-like. Classifying these works by "genre," as noted earlier, is a Western practice; native people could have said *when* they were to be spoken, sung, or chanted, and *why* they would have been spoken, sung, or chanted, but they would not have offered the classifications (charm, oration, etc.) that we find useful.

The Kwakiutl are a Northwest Coast tribe most noted (for better or worse) in the general literature for their (apparently atypical) concern with wealth and hierarchy. "Coppers or coins," as John Bierhorst notes in his reprinting of this song, are valuable, and so, insofar as they are given away in the potlatch ceremony, indicative of high rank and culturally appropriate generosity. The translation reprinted by Bierhorst was done by Franz Boas between 1913 and 1914 and we are guessing that the song, even at that date, was not radically different from similar songs of a much earlier date.

"Five Charms to Make the Evening Warrior Fall Asleep" describes the Plains cultures of horsemanship and buffalo hunting. Because the horse had become extinct in the Americas, only being reintroduced by the Spanish, it is clear that Plains horse culture cannot have any pre-Columbian origins. Still, we are *guessing* that the use of the war charms discussed here go back an indeterminate number of years. Each of the five charms translated by Robert Lowie in 1935 is intended to induce drowsiness in an enemy warrior, lulling him to sleep.

The Iroquois "Oration on a Son's Death" was revised in 1851 by Ely S. Parker, himself an Iroquois; the version presented here was revised by John Bierhorst and contains some slight revisions of Parker. *Na-ho,* the concluding term of the oration means, in Bierhorst's note, I have finished; or, So be it. The Iroquois "magic formula" was translated by Arthur C. Parker in 1928.

We conclude with a charm in the form of a "medical prescription," as James Mooney called it sometime after 1888, from the Cherokee. Obviously this is not strictly "literature," for all that it has certain "poetic" properties. I have given the "free translation," for us, the "poetic" translation, but also included Mooney's interlinear "literal" translation to the original Cherokee.

THE KWAKIUTL PEOPLE

Song of a Chief's Daughter

Be ready, O chiefs' sons of the tribes! to be my husbands; for I come to make my husband a great chief through my father, for I am mistress, ha ha aya ha ha aya!

I, mistress, come to be your wife, O princes of the chiefs of the tribes! I am seated on coppers, and have many names and privileges that will be given by my father to my future husband, ha ha aya ha ha aya!

For my belt has been woven by my mother, which I use when I look after the dishes that will be given as a marriage present by my father to him who shall be my husband, when many kinds of food shall be given in the marriage feast by my father to him who shall be my husband, ha ha aya ha ha aya!

Translated by Franz Boas.

THE CROW PEOPLE

Five Charms to Make the Enemy Warrior Fall Asleep*

1

In the spring when we lie down under the young cherry-trees, with the grass green and the sun getting a bit warm, we feel like sleeping, don't we?

2

In the fall when there is a little breeze and we lie in some shelter, hearing the dry weeds rubbing against one another, we generally get drowsy, don't we?

3

In the daytime as the drizzle strikes the lodge pattering and we lie warming the soles of our feet, we fall asleep, don't we?

4

At night when we lie down, listening to the wind rustling through the bleached trees, we know not how we get to sleep but we fall asleep, don't we?

5

Having looked for a hollow among the thickest pines, we make a fresh camp there. The wind blows on us, and we, rather tired, lie down and keep listening to the rustling pines until we fall asleep.

THE IROQUOIS PEOPLE

Oration on a Son's Death†

My son, listen once more to the words of your mother. You were brought into life with her pains. You were nourished with her life. She has attempted to be faithful in raising you up. When you were young she loved you as her life. Your presence has been a source of great joy to her. Upon you she depended for support and comfort in her declining days. She had always expected to gain the end of the path of life before you. But you have outstripped her, and gone before her. Our great and wise creator has ordered it thus. By his will I am left to taste more of the miseries of this world. Your friends and relatives have gathered about your body, to look upon you for the last time. They mourn, as with one mind, your departure from among us. We, too, have but a few days more, and our journey shall be

*Translated by Robert Lowie.
†Translated by Ely S. Parker; revised by John Bierhorst.

ended. We part now, and you are conveyed from our sight. But we shall soon meet again, and shall again look upon each other. Then we shall part no more. Our maker has called you to his home. Thither will we follow. *Na-ho!*

Magic Formula*

You have no right to trouble me,
Depart, I am becoming stronger;
You are now departing from me,
You who would devour me;
I am becoming stronger, stronger.
Mighty medicine is now within me,
You cannot now subdue me—
I am becoming stronger,
I am stronger, stronger, stronger.

THE CHEROKEE PEOPLE

Charm (as a medical prescription)†

¦ι'α' ɔⁿ'	Dι·ˈniskɔ ·liˀ	Dv̀ˈnitlℚ̆ηℚ̈ˀǐˀ
this-and	their heads	whenever they are ill

αnïsGü'ya	αniˈlɔˌ'iˀ	vtsι"nαwaˀ	anɔ̈"nvGa'	α'niDɑ̈·ᵘwē
they men	they just passed by	beyond-it-stretched	they have come and said it	they (are) wizards

αniˈlɔ ¦'iˀ	vtsι"nαwaˀ	αnɔ̈ "nι.Ga'	vts "nαwaˀ	Gɔ̈ 'tℏtα ¦αⁿ
they just passed by	beyond it stretched	they have come and said it	beyond it stretched	It (has been) rubbed

vtsι"nαwaˀ	αnɔ "nι.Ga'	yǎ'		
beyond it stretched	they have come and said it	Sharp!		

¦ι"α-Nˌɔⁿ	na.ˈsGw ɔ̈ⁿ	ηι'niskɔ ·liˀ	Dv'nitlφησˀ·iˀ	¦ι'a·' nι-vsti'
this-and	also	their heads	whenever they are ill	this so far like

ɔ·ˈDali-Gù'Dli	anℚ̈·ˈskö tlʒ̆'.i	DιDzɔ·ˈt'ιstɔ .ti'		
mountain-he climbs	it used to be held in the mouth	they to be blown with it		

---

*Translated by Arthur C. Parker.
†Translated by James Mooney.

And This Is (for) When Their Heads Are Ill†

The men have just passed by, they have caused relief,
The wizards have just passed by, they have caused relief,
Relief has been rubbed, they have caused relief. Sharp!

Afterword:
A Note on Translation
by Jorge Luis Borges

No problem is more essential to literature and its small mysteries than translation. A lapse of memory spurred by vanity, the fear of divulging mental processes that we can guess to be perilously pedestrian, the attempt to maintain an incalculable reserve of mystery—all cast a veil over the alleged original. Translation, in contrast, seems destined to illustrate aesthetic debates. The model to be imitated is a visible text, and the translator is not free to follow the unfathomable labyrinths of past projects or to accept the sudden temptation of an easy solution. Bertrand Russell defined an external object as a circular system radiating many possible impressions. Given the incalculable repercussions of words, the same could be said about a text, whose translations become a partial and precious document of the changes it inevitably suffers. What are the many renderings of the *Iliad*—from Chapman's to Magnien's—if not different perspectives of a mutable fact, if not a long experimental lottery of omissions and emphases? (Changing languages is not necessary for this deliberate juggling of interpretations, which can occur within a single literature.) To assume that all recombinations of elements are necessarily inferior to their original form is to assume that draft 9 is necessarily inferior to draft H—since every text is a draft. The notion of a "definitive text" belongs to religion or perhaps merely to exhaustion.

Our superstition that translations are inferior—reinforced by the age-old Italian adage *traduttore traditore*—is the result of our naïveté: all great works that we turn to time and again seem unalterable and definitive. Hume identified our habitual idea of causality with the experience of temporal succession. Thus a good film seen a second time seems even better; we tend to take repetitions for absolutes. Our first reading of famous books is really the second, since we already know them. The cliché "rereading the classics" turns out to be an unwitting truth. But how can we know now whether the statement "In a place of La Mancha, whose name I don't care to remember, there lived not long ago a nobleman who kept a lance and shield, a greyhound, and a skinny old nag" actually proceeded from divine inspiration? I only know that any modifications would be sacrilegious and that I could not conceive of another beginning for *Don Quixote*. Cervantes, however, probably dispensed with such a frivolous superstition and may not have recognized this paragraph. I, in contrast, can only reject any divergence. Since Spanish is my native language, the *Quixote* is to me an unchanging monument, with no possible variations except those furnished by the editor, the bookbinder, and the compositor. But the *Odyssey,* thanks to my opportune ignorance of Greek, is a library of works in prose and verse, from Chapman's couplets to Andrew Lang's "authorized version" or from Berard's classic French drama and Morris's lively saga to Samuel Butler's ironic bourgeois novel. I mention mostly English names because English writers have always gravitated toward this epic of the sea, and their many versions of the *Odyssey* would be enough to illustrate the history of their literature. But the rich and even contradictory variety of this library is not attributable solely to the evolution of the English language, to the original's grand proportions, or to the deviations and diverse capacities of the translators. The main cause is the impossibility of knowing what belonged to the poet and what belonged to the language. To this fortunate impossibility we owe so many possible versions, all of them sincere, genuine, and divergent.

I do not know of a more controversial issue than the Homeric adjectives. Recurrent expressions such as "the divine Patroclus," "the nourishing earth," "the wine-dark sea," "the uncloven-hoofed horses," "the moist ways," "the dark blood," "the dear knees" stir our hearts at unexpected moments. At one point, there is mention of "rich noblemen who drink of the black waters of the Aesopos"; at another, a tragic king who, "unhappy in lovely Thebes, governed the Cadmeans by the gods' fatal decree." Alexander Pope, whose lavish translation we shall scrutinize later, believed that all these immutable epithets were liturgical in character. Rémy de Gourmont, in his long essay on style, writes that though they must have been enchanting at one time, they are no longer so. I, however, suspect that these standard epithets were what prepositions still are today: modest and obligatory sounds used to join certain words and on which no originality can be exercised. We know, for example, that the correct way to get somewhere is *on* foot and not *with* foot, just as the blind bard knew that the adjective to describe Patroclus was "divine." Neither usage is motivated by aesthetic reasons. I offer these conjectures with humble sobriety: our only certainty is that we cannot separate what belongs to the author from what belongs to the language. When we read in the seventeenth-century playwright Agustín Moreto (if we must read Agustín Moreto) the phrase "Pues en casa tan compuestas/¿Qué hacen todo el santo día?" 'What do these prim ladies do at home the whole damn day?' we know that the day's unholiness belongs to the language and not to the writer. Where Homer's accents lie, however, we can never know.

For a lyrical or elegiac poet, this uncertainty of ours regarding authorial intentions could be devastating, but not so for the conscientious narrator of vast plots. The deeds of the *Iliad* and the *Odyssey* more than survive, even though Achilles and Ulysses have disappeared, as have what Homer had in mind by choosing them and what he really thought of them. The present state of his works resembles a complex equation that delineates precise relations among unknown quantities. What a treasure trove for the translator! Browning's most famous poem, *The Ring and the Book,* consists of ten detailed accounts of a single crime, given by each of those involved. The work's variety derives entirely from the characters, not from the actions, and offers contrasts almost as intense and unfathomable as those among ten just versions of Homer.

The magnificent Newman-Arnold debate (1861–62), more significant than either of its participants, laboriously depicted the two main ways to translate. Newman defended the literal retention of all verbal singularities; Arnold argued for the literary, severe elimination of details that would distract or detain the reader and for the subordination of the ever-unpredictable Homer in each line to the essential or conventional Homer, whose forthright syntax flows and whose ideas are noble yet plain. Arnold's method provides the harmonious pleasures of uniformity; Newman's, continual little surprises.

Let us consider the various destinies of a single passage from Homer, concerning Achilles's son Neoptolemus. Ulysses relays the events to the ghost of Achilles in the city of the Cimmerians, on the night without end (*Odyssey* 11). Buckley's literal version goes like this:

> But when we had sacked the lofty city of Priam, having his share and excellent reward, he embarked unhurt on a ship, neither stricken with the sharp brass, nor wounded hand to hand, as oftentimes happens in war; for Mars confusedly raves.

Here is another literal as well as archaic rendition, by Butcher and Lang:

> But after we had sacked the steep city of Priam, he embarked unscathed with his share of the spoil, and with a noble prize; he was not smitten with the sharp spear, and got no wound in close fight: and many such chances there be in war, for Ares rageth confusedly.

Cowper, in 1791:

At length when we had sack'd the lofty town
Of Priam, laden with abundant spoils
He safe embark'd, neither by spear or shaft
Aught hurt, or in close fight by faulchion's edge
As oft in war befalls, where wounds are dealt
Promiscuous, at the will of fiery Mars.

Pope's 1725 version:

And when the Gods our arms with conquest crown'd,
When Troy's proud bulwarks smok'd upon the ground,
Greece to reward her soldier's gallant toils
Heap'd high his navy with unnumber'd spoils.
*   Thus great in glory from the din of war*
Safe he return'd, without one hostile scar:
Tho' spears in iron tempests rain'd around,
Yet innocent they play'd, and guiltless of a wound.

George Chapman, in 1614:

*   In the event,*
High Troy depopulate, he made ascent
To his fair ship, with prise and treasure store
Safe; and no touch away with him he bore

Of far-off-hurl'd lance, or of close-fought sword,
Whose wounds for favours war doth oft afford,
Which he (though sought) miss'd in war's closest wage.
In close fights Mars doth never fight, but rage.

And finally Butler's 1900 version:

> Yet when we had sacked the city of Priam he got his handsome share of the prize money and went on board (such is the fortune of war) without a wound upon him, neither from a thrown spear nor in close combat, for the rage of Mars is a matter of great chance.

The first two—the literal versions—could move us for a variety of reasons: the reverential reference to the sacking of the city; the naive statement that one gets hurt in war; the infinite disorders of combat suddenly embodied in a single, raging god. Other, lesser pleasures are also at work: in one of the texts I have reproduced, the charming pleonasm "embarked on a ship" and, in the other, the unnecessary conjunction in "*and* many such chances there be in war." The third version, Cowper's, is the most innocuous of all since it is completely literal, as far as Miltonic verse permits.

Pope's rendering is extraordinary. His luxuriant language (like Góngora's) can be distinguished by its persistent and excessive use of superlatives. For example, the hero's lone black ship becomes a fleet. Continuously subjected to this law of amplification, all the lines of Pope's text fall into two grand categories: undiluted oratory, as in "And when the Gods our arms with conquest crown'd," or visual representation, as in "When Troy's proud bulwarks smok'd upon the ground." Speeches and spectacles: this is Pope. Chapman's fiery version is also spectacular, but his mode is lyrical, not oratorical. Butler, in contrast, reveals his determination to evade all opportunities for the visual and to turn Homer's text into a sober series of news items.

Which of these many translations is faithful? the reader might ask. I repeat: none or all of them. If fidelity implies conveying Homer's inventions and the bygone people and days that the poet portrayed, none of the versions can succeed for us but all would for a tenth-century Greek. If fidelity means preserving the effects Homer intended, any one of the above might serve, except for the literal ones, whose virtue lies in their departure from current poetic practices. It is not out of the question, then, that Butler's sedate version could be the most faithful.

Appendix A: World Map

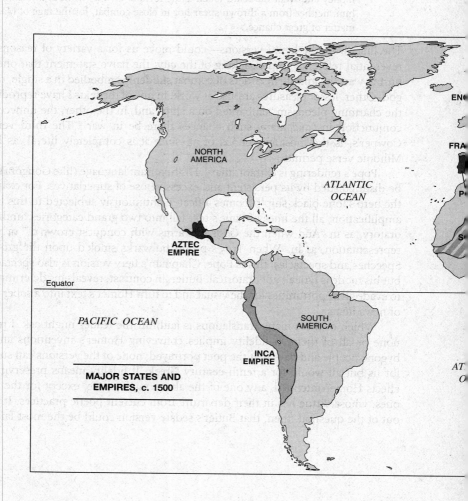

NORTH
AMERICA

ATLANTIC
OCEAN

AZTEC
EMPIRE

Equator

PACIFIC OCEAN

SOUTH
AMERICA

INCA
EMPIRE

**MAJOR STATES AND
EMPIRES, c. 1500**

EN

FRA

P

S

AT
O

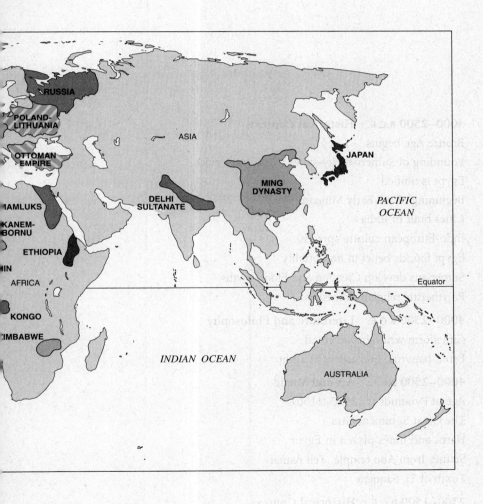

RUSSIA

POLAND-
LITHUANIA

OTTOMAN
EMPIRE

ASIA

JAPAN

MAMLUKS

DELHI
SULTANATE

MING
DYNASTY

PACIFIC
OCEAN

KANEM-
BORNU

ETHIOPIA

IN

AFRICA

Equator

KONGO

IMBABWE

INDIAN OCEAN

AUSTRALIA

Appendix B: Comparative Chronology of World Cultures

4000–2500 B.C.E.   **Historical Context**

Bronze Age begins

Founding of Sumerian city-states (Kish, Ur, Uruk)

Egypt is unified

Beginning of the Early Minoan period

Cities built in India

Indo-European culture spreads

Egypt founds belief in immortality

Sumerians develop Creation and Flood myths

Polytheistic religion flourishes

4000–2500 B.C.E.   **Literature and Philosophy**

Cuneiform writing is invented

Pepi's papyrus, *Instructions to a Son*

4000–2500 B.C.E.   **Art and Music**

Age of Pyramids (c. 2650–2150)

The Great Sphinx at Giza

Harps and flutes played in Egypt

Statues from Abu temple, Tell Asmar

Tomb of Ti, Saqqara

2500–1500 B.C.E.   **Historical Context**

Akkadian and Babylonian Empires

Elamite Dynasty of Awan (c. 2500–2180)

Old and Middle Kingdoms in Egypt

Hsia Dynasty in China

Hyskos invasions
Aryan invasions
Mycenean culture begins
Expansion of trade
Hittites use horses, wheeled carts
Hittites institute monogamy
Patriarchy of Abraham
Semites settle Palestine
Mythical King Tangun founds Old Korea (2333)
Mathematics, medical science founded

2500–1500 B.C.E. **Literature and Philosophy**
Book of the Dead, Egypt
Code of Hammurabi, Mesopotamia
Epic of Gilgamesh, Sumerian
Shih-ching, or *Book of Odes* (composed between 2205 and 600)

2500–1500 B.C.E. **Art and Music**
Minoan frescoes
Palace of Knossos constructed on Crete
Snake goddess, Crete
Stele of Hammurabi
Tomb of Tutankhamen
Ziggurat of Ur
Stonehenge, England
Chinese music employs five-tone scale
Painted pottery produced by Chinese

1500–1000 B.C.E. **Historical Context**
Iron Age begins
New Kingdom in Egypt (1575–1200)
Traditional date for sack of Troy (c. 1184)
Akhnaten introduces monotheism: Eighteenth Dynasty
Destruction of Palace of Knossos
Hebrews emphasize patriarchy
Hebrew Exodus, Moses and the Covenant
Early Assyrian Empire
Fall of Hittites
Babylon defeats the Elamites (1128–1105)

Growth of influence of the Egyptian priesthood

The flourishing of the Levantine trading states

Egypt invaded by the Sea Peoples

Beginning of Greek "Dark Age" (1100–800)

1500–1000 B.C.E.   Literature and Philosophy

Writing of early books of the Bible

Phoenicians develop alphabet

I Ching, or Book of Changes, ascribed to Wên Wang (c. 1200)

1500–1000 B.C.E.   Art and Music

Temple of Karnak built in Egypt

Reliefs from Nineveh and Nimrud

Hera from Samos

1000–600 B.C.E.   Historical Context

Sargon II founds Khorsabad

Hebrew kingdoms of David and Solomon

The age of the Hebrew Prophets

Early Greek "tyrants"

Phoenicians found Carthage (814)

Traditional date for the founding of Rome (753)

Jimmu, first Japanese monarch (legendary), begins rule (660)

Hinduism: challenges to Brahmanism by ascetic groups

First Olympic Games in honor of Zeus

Founding of the Greek polis

Beginning of the Vedic period

Fall of Assyria

Fall of Israel

Assyrian water clock invented

Zoroaster, founder of the Persian religion (630–553)

1000–600 B.C.E.   Literature and Philosophy

Homer and the Greek epics: the Iliad and the Odyssey

Hesiod, Works and Days; Theogony

Beginnings of lyric poetry in Greece: Archilochus

Earliest Chinese poem: Book of Songs

1000–600 B.C.E.   Art and Music

First Doric columns

Building of the Assyrian Palaces

Seven-string lyre in use

Chinese brush and ink painting

Gold vessels, jewelry made in Northern Europe

600–400 B.C.E. Historical Context

Rise of the Persian Empire

Solon of Athens (640–560)

Nedbuchadnezzar II of Babylon (605–562)

Babylonian Captivity of the Jews (586)

Persian conquests of Babylon and Egypt

Founding of the Roman Republic

Cyrus the Great's Rule (553–529)

Cambyses' rule (529–522)

Militarized society founded in Sparta under code of Lycurgus

Vedic period ends

Darius I's rule (522–485)

Persian Wars (499–479)

Rise of Etruscan culture

Greek expansion under Pericles (498–427)

Peloponnesian War (431–404)

Teachings of Buddha and Confucius

Zoroastrianism in Persia

Medical advances of Hippocrates

Life of Socrates

Teachings of Lao-tzu: Taoism (400–300)

600–400 B.C.E. Literature and Philosophy

Birth of Greek tragedy

Aesop's *Fables* (c. 620–560)

Lao-tzu, *Tao-te Ching* (c. 600)

Birth of Greek comedy

Herodotus, *History of the Persian Wars*

Thucydides, *History of the Peloponnesian War*

Poetry of Sappho of Lesbos

Analects, books of Confucius's sayings (fifth to fourth century)

Sophocles, *Antigone* (c. 450)

Hippocrates, *Aphorisms* (c. 415)

Euripides, *The Bacchae* (408)

600–400 B.C.E.   Art and Music

Pindar, Greek musician and poet (520–447)

Hanging Gardens of Babylon constructed

Classical Greek pottery flourishes

Theater of Dionysus in Athens (493)

Building of the Parthenon (447–432)

400–200 B.C.E.   Historical Context

Philip of Macedon

Plato (427–347) becomes student of Socrates

Alexander the Great (356–323)

Aetolian and Achaean Leagues

Fall of the Persian Empire

First Illyrian War

Italy unified under Roman conquest (272)

First Punic War (264–241)

Second Punic War (219–201)

Rise of the Mauryan Dynasty in India

End of Chavin Civilization in Latin America

Rise of Ch'in Dynasty, East Asia

400–200 B.C.E.   Literature and Philosophy

Bhagavad Gita (c. 500–200)

Plato, *Dialogues* (399–347)

Mahabharata, Indian epic, begun

Aristotle (384–322), *The Rhetoric; Constitution of Athens: The Poetics* (335–322)

Writings of Mencius (372–?), defender of Confucianism, named the Second Holy One

Xenophon, *Anabasis* (371)

Ch'ü Yüan, Chinese poet (343–277)

Greek new comedy: Menander, Philemon

Plautus, found of Roman Comedy, *Amphitryon*

Stoicism (Zeno, Epicurus)

Cynic School (Diogenes, Antisthenes)

Cyrenaic School (hedonists)

Appolonius of Rhodes, *Argonautica* (c. 295–215)

The Laws of Manu, sacred Buddhist text (c. 200)

400–200 B.C.E. Art and Music
Early Hellenistic art

Praxiteles, Greek sculptor (400–330)

Etruscan actors give first theatrical performance in Rome (365)

Corinthian columns appear (c. 350)

Aristotle's musical theory (340)

Sun Temple at Teotihuacan, Mexico (300)

Completion of Colossus of Rhodes (c. 275)

Great Wall of China built (215)

200–1 B.C.E. Historical Context
Mauryan decline; rise of Shunga Dynasty (185–30)

Revolt of the Maccabees (167)

Third Punic War (149–146)

Greece comes under control of Rome (147)

Rome conquers North Africa

Destruction of Carthage (146)

Age of Wu Ti, East Asia

Nok civilization at height in Africa

Reforms of the Gracchi

Spartacus's slave revolt (71)

Caesar's dictatorship in Rome (46–44)

Augustus begins reign (27)

Marius and Sulla

Forming of Triumvirates

Kushan Invasion, South Asia

Cleopatra VII, Egypt's last queen

200–1 B.C.E. Literature and Philosophy
Terence, Roman playwright, *Andria* (167)

Catullus, Rome poet (87–54)

Lucretius, *De rerum natura* (60)

Cicero, *De oratore* (55)

Horace, *Satires* (35–29)

Vergil, *Aeneid* (29–19)

Livy, Titus, Roman historian

200–1 B.C.E.   Art and Music

Venus of Milo, sculpture (140)

Victory (Nike) of Samothrace

Vitruvius, *De architectura* (90)

Laocoön, marble sculpture (38)

1–200 C.E.   Historical Context

Age of Augustus (30 B.C.E.–14 C.E.)

Birth of Christ

Conquest of Britain (43–51)

Roman Empire reaches its greatest extent

Nero's persecution of the Christians (64)

Sack of Jerusalem (70)

Indian envoy to Emperor Trajan of Rome (100)

Decline of Kushans, South Asia

Rise of Christianity

Bar-Kokba Rebellion of the Hebrew leader against Rome under Hadrian (132–135)

1–200 C.E.   Literature and Philosophy

Seneca, Roman dramatist and philosopher (4 B.C.E.–65 C.E.)

Ovid, *Metamorphoses* (5)

Julius Caesar, *Commentaries on the Civil War* (45)

Petronius, *Satyricon* (c. 100)

Juvenal, *Satires* (c. 100)

Tacitus, *Historiae* (117)

Apuleius, *The Golden Ass* (c. 155)

Marcus Aurelius, *Meditations* (c. 170–180)

1–200 C.E.   Art and Music

Roman Pantheon built (118–125)

Oldest Mayan monuments (c. 164)

Colosseum, Rome

Column of Trajan, Rome

200–400 C.E.   Historical Context

Neoplatonism, led by Plotinus (205–270)

Period of disorder in Roman Empire (235–284)

Reign of Constantine: Christianity becomes state religion

Diocletian's reforms (285–305)

Constantinople becomes new seat of Roman Empire (331)
Theodosius (379–395)
Monastic orders begin
Fall of Han Dynasty
Rise of Mayan culture
Christianity brought to Ethiopia
Rise of Gupta rule in South Asia

200–400 C.E.   Literature and Philosophy
Replacement of scrolls by books begins
Kalidasa, *Sakuntala,* Sanskrit drama (220)
Avesta, Zoroastrian holy text (c. 300–400)
Saint Augustine, *The Confessions* (397–401)

200–400 C.E.   Art and Music
Baths of Caracalla built (212–217)
Church of Saint Peter's built in Rome (325)
Saint Ambrose introduces the singing of hymns (386)

400–600 C.E.   Historical Context
Decline of western Roman Empire
Alaric's sack of Rome (410)
Pope Leo I (440–461)
Founding of Venice (452)
Germanic invasions
Rise of Attila the Hun
Collapse of Gupta Rule
Silk monopoly maintained by Byzantine Empire
Vandals sack Rome (455)
End of first schism; Western and Eastern Churches reconcile (484)
Mayan urban civilization flourishes in southern Mexico
Corpus juris civilis founded
Emperor Wu-ti embraces Buddhism, brings the religion to central China (517)
Age of Justinian the Great, Byzantine Emperor (527–565)
Death of the legendary King Arthur (537)
Outbreaks of plague (542–594)
Spread of Buddhism into Japan (552)

Czechs settle in Bohemia

Beginning of alchemy, search for the Philosopher's Stone

400–600 C.E.   **Literature and Philosophy**

Proclus, chief representative of later Neo-Platonism (410–485)

St. Augustine, *The City of God* (411)

Cassiodorus, Roman scholar (490–583)

Aryabhata, Hindu astronomer and mathematician, compiles his manual of astronomy (517)

Priscian, *Institutiones grammaticae* (520)

Boethius, Roman scholar, *The Consolation of Philosophy* (c. 523)

400–600 C.E.   **Art and Music**

Boethius introduces Greek system of musical notation to Western music (521)

Sophia Basilica, Constantinople, completed (537)

Golden Era of Byzantine art (c. 550)

600–800 C.E.   **Historical Context**

Muhammad's Vision (610); rise of Islam

Muslims go to Ghana and Sudan

Early Abbasids

Roots of Sunni-Shi'ite division

T'ang Dynasty in East Asia

Muslims manufacture paper

Free Byzantine peasantry established

End of barbarian invasions in Western Europe

Flowering of Korean civilization

Buddhism becomes state religion in Tibet (632)

Arabs attack North Africa (670)

Clovis III becomes king of united Franks (691)

Muslims defeated at Poitiers, ending their westward advance (732)

Water wheels drive mills throughout Europe

Saint Boniface, Benedictine monk, foe of heathen Germanic beliefs

Iconoclastic Controversy divides Byzantine Church

600–800 C.E.   **Literature and Philosophy**

Bana, Hindu poet, *Kadambari, Harsacarita* (600–650)

Printing of books in China

Lyric poetry of T'ang Dynasty promotes Chinese language

Muhammad, the Koran (c. 660)

Li Po, Chinese poet (701–762)

Tu Fu, Chinese poet (713–770)

The Book of Kells, Latin gospels in Irish (760)

600–800 C.E.   Art and Music

Classic Buddha figures produced in Bihar, northern India

Production of Chinese porcelain (620)

Pueblo period in southwestern North America

Stone churches replace wooden structures in England (700)

Gregorian liturgical music in Europe (750)

Earliest Japanese prints (779)

800–1000 C.E.   Historical Context

Empire of Charlemagne, crowned First Holy Roman Emperor by Pope Leo III (800)

Birth of feudal social structure

Commercial expansion of the Muslim world

Decline of Byzantine peasant class

Unification of England by Anglo-Saxons

Period of Viking invasions

City of Machu Picchu, Peru (800)

Decline of the Mayan Empire: Last Mayan inscriptions (879)

Rise of the Sung Dynasty

Slavic tribes migrate into territories around the Oder

Iconoclastic Debate continues in Eastern Empire

Magyars carry out raids in Germany, Italy

Fatimid Dynasty in North Africa

Hugh Capet, King of France (987–996)

Poles converted to Christianity under first ruler, Mieczyslaw I

800–1000 C.E.   Literature and Philosophy

Lady Ise, Japanese lyric poet (877–940)

The Anglo-Saxon Chronicle (c. 891–924)

The Thousand and One Nights, Arabian tales (begun 900)

Roswitha of Gandersheim, German nun, playwright (935–c. 1000)

Great Master Kyunyô, Korea, *Eleven Devotional Poems* (965–967)

Murasaki Shikibu, *The Tale of Genji* (c. 1000)

Beowulf, heroic poem in Old English (1000)

Firdawsi, Persian poet, *Shâh Nâma* (c. 1000)

Al-Mutanabbi, master poet of Abbasid period in Islam (c. tenth century)

Abū Al-Kindi, Arabian philosopher (c. ninth century)

al-Fārābi, Muslim philosopher (c. tenth century)

800–1000 C.E.   Art and Music

Poetry sung to musical accompaniment, court of Charlemagne (800)

Chandi Loro Jonggrang, Prambanam, Java constructed (c. 800)

1000–1200 C.E.   Historical Context

Rise of feudal society

Norman Conquest (1066)

Seljuk Turks defeat Byzantines (1071)

The Crusades (First Crusade, 1095)

Revival of cities

Birth of Genghis Khan, founder of Mongol Empire (1155)

Schism between Byzantine and Roman Churches

Thomas à Becket murdered at Canterbury (1170)

Guild System established

Kamakura Shogunate in East Asia

Spiritual center of Judaism moves to Spain

Climax of Mayan culture in Yucatan

First universities founded; rise of scholasticism

Decline in the social position of women

China perfects the use of gunpowder

Widespread fear of Apocalypse, Last Judgment

1000–1200 C.E.   Literature and Philosophy

Avicenna, Arabian philosopher, physician (980–1037)

Sun Tung Po, Chinese poet (1036–1101)

The Mabinogion, Welsh tales (1050)

Peter Abelard, French philosopher, theologian (1079–1142)

Song of Roland, French heroic poem (1100)

First miracle play recorded, Dunstable, England (1110)

The Rubaiyat, Omar Khayyam, Persian poet, scientist (d. 1123)

Averroes, Arabian scholar, philosopher (b. 1126)

Poema del Cid, Spanish heroic poem (c. 1140)

Chrétien de Troyes, court poet of France (1144–1190)

Wolfram von Eschenbach, German poet (1172–1220)

The Nibelungenlied (1191–1204)
The Njal Saga, Icelandic saga (c. 1300)

1000–1200 C.E.   Art and Music
Kuo Hsi, Chinese painter (1020–c. 1090)
Polyphonic singing replaces Gregorian Chant (1050)
Marcabru, Provençal troubadour (1137–1150)
Bertrand de Born, English troubadour (1140–1215)
Building of Angkor Wat (1150)
Hsia Kuei, Chinese painter (1180–1230)
Ma Yüan, Chinese painter (1190–1224)
Construction of Chartres Cathedral begun (1194)

1200–1400 C.E.   Historical Context
Early population growth, later decimated by famine, Black Death
Later Crusades
Rise of Mali Empire, Kliwa (c. 1200–1450)
Islam begins to replace Indian religions (1200)
New techniques in warfare: longbow and crossbow
Latin Empire in Constantinople (1204)
Founding of Delhi Sultanate (1206)
Madjapahit kingdom dominant in Malaysia
Opening of European embassy in China
Reign of Saint Louis (1214–1270)
Magna Carta (1215)
Period of Hōjō rule in Japan (1219–1333)
Mongol invasions of Russia (1223), China (1211–1215), Japan (1274)
Travels of Marco Polo (1254–1324)
Founding of the Sorbonne in Paris (1254)
End of the Crusades (1291)
Height of Swahili (east African) city-states (c. 1300–1500)
"Babylonian Captivity" of papacy (1309–1376)
Ashikaga Period in Japan (1336–1568)
Hundred Years' War begins (1337–1453)
Founding of Yuan Dynasty
Rise of the Aztecs
Siamese invasion of Cambodia, collapse of Khmer Empire (1350–1460)
Rise of the Ottoman Turks

Great Interregnum

Inquisition

Founding of Li Dynasty in Korea (1392)

1200–1400 C.E. Literature and Philosophy

Wang Shih-fu, *Hsi Hsiang Chi,* Chinese play (c. 1200)

Wolfram von Eschenbach, *Parzival* (1203)

Gottfried von Strassburg, *Tristan* (1210)

Roger Bacon, English philosopher, scientist (1214–1294)

Sonnet form developed in Italian poetry (1221)

Sumer is icumen in, probably earliest English round (1225)

The Romance of the Rose, Guillaume de Lorris; continued by Jean de Meun (1227)

Sa'di, *The Gulistān,* Arabian tales (c. 1240)

Kuan Han-ch'ing, "father of Chinese drama" (c. 1245–c. 1322)

Summa theologica (1273), Thomas Aquinas, theologian, philosopher (1225–1274)

Moses de Leon, *Zohar,* foundation of Jewish mysticism (1275)

Dante Alighieri, *La Vita Nuova* (1290); *The Divine Comedy* (1307)

Le Jeu D'Adam, anonymous, miracle play (c. 1300)

Hafiz, Persian poet (1300–1388)

Beginnings of *renga* poetry in Japan (c. 1300)

Tale of the Heike, anonymous, Japanese prose narrative (1310)

Liu Chi, Chinese poet (1311–1375)

Giovanni Boccaccio, *The Decameron* (1353)

The Elder Edda (late thirteenth century)

Development of Japanese Nō drama

Fang Hsiao-Ju, Chinese scholar (1357–1402)

Petrarch, *Canzonieri* (1366)

Geoffrey Chaucer, *The Canterbury Tales* (1387–1400)

1200–1400 C.E. Art and Music

Gothic period

Jesters first appear in European courts (1202)

Tannhauser, German poet, Minnesinger (1205–1270)

Great Amida Buddha, bronze sculpture, Kamakura period in Japan (1253)

Giotto, Italian painter (1266–1337)

Appearance of *jongleurs,* professional musical entertainers, France (1300)

"Bards" flourish in Ireland

Art from Around the World

Ma He-chih, Chinese, active twelfth century C.E. Colors on silk. Palace Museum, Beijing. See Section III, East Asia: Early and Middle Periods.

Attributed to Takayoshi, Japanese, Heian period, twelfth century C.E. *The Emperor Playing* Go. Illustration for *The Tale of Genji*. Colors on paper. Tokugawa Art Museum, Nagoya. See *The Tale of Genji,* Section III, East Asia: Early and Middle Periods.

Orcagna [Andrea di Cione], Italian, active c. 1343 C.E.; d. c. 1368. *The Last Judgment: Inferno.* Fresco, twisted columns and fragments. Museo dell'Opera di Santa Croce, Florence. See *The Divine Comedy,* Section IV, Medieval Europe.

Anonymous, French, thirteenth century C.E. manuscript. Illustration for *Renard the Fox* 1174–1205, the farewell scene between Renard the Fox setting off for the King's court, and his son. Bibliothèque Nationale, Paris. See *Renard the Fox,* Section IV, Medieval Europe.

قلم ـــا قرع بما ـض من شعر فـالت لـه ريـاض ا لله حسيبـ من غـرز و بجـر

و لم ينصف مع انكـار الوصـل وو جـود الـسـبيـل فعـا ل بيـا ض اهـل الوفا قليل

ثـم قالـت الـســـبـرة يا بيـا ض انـت شـا عر مغلو و اد يـب ا ر يـب ـ و نـحن نهـول مـا

روضنـا و جعلبكـا و سمعنـا بن عينـاو ا انت تقـول من تلعـا نفسـك بـار ك الله

بيعـدوو فـا لـ المخزور و تـلـسـا ند بالخمـر و الشرور في حـض الكـاس اعيـون الـيلـ و مغنجـون

10

Anonymous, thirteenth century C.E. *Bayad playing the 'ud before Riyad.*
Manuscript illustration. Vatican Library, Rome. See Section V, Early and
Classical Middle East.

Anonymous, n.d., Arabic. Frontispiece to the *Assemblies Maqāmat* of Al-Hariri. Manuscript illustration. Nationalbibliothek, Vienna. See *The Maqāmat,* Section V, Early and Classical Middle East.

Anonymous, Turcoman, 899–1495. *The Conference of the Birds*. Bodleian Library, Oxford. See *The Conference of the Birds,* Section V, Early and Classical Middle East.

Anonymous, Persian, c. 1515 C.E. *Majnum in the Wilderness*. India Office Library, London. See Section V, Early and Classical Middle East.

Painter A, Persian, c. 1525–1530 C.E., *Rustam's Fourth Course: He Cleves a Witch*. (Like the demons of the Turcoman album.) The Metropolitan Museum of Art. See *The Shāh Nāma*. See Section V, Early and Classical Middle East.

Michelangelo Buonarroti, Italian, 1510. *The Fall of Man*. Ceiling, Sistine Chapel, the Vatican. See ''To Giovanni, the one from Pistoia on Painting the Vault of the Sistine Chapel.'' See Section VII, Early Modern Europe.

Anonymous, n. d., California Indian Culture. Chumash Rock Painting, Cuyama. See Section VIII, The Early Americas.

Kumano Mandala, hanging scroll, Japan (c. 1300)

Building of Aztec capital, Tenochtitlan (c. 1325)

Mastersinger movement, Germany (1350)

Guillaume de Machaut, *Mass for Four Voices* (1364)

1400–1600 C.E.   Historical Context

Renaissance in Europe

Jan Hus (1415), Joan of Arc (1431), burned at stake

Torquemada, Grand Inquisitor (1420–1498)

Gutenberg invents the printing press (1450)

Savonarola, Italian religious reformer (1452–1498)

Hundred Years' War ends (1453)

Constantinople falls to the Ottoman Turks (1453)

Voyages of discovery to the New World

Expeditions of Cheng Ho

Wars of the Roses (1455, beginning)

Unification of Japan by Hideyoshi

Birth of Guru Nanak, founder of Sikhism (1469)

Decline of Mali

Nicolaus Copernicus's new astronomy (1473–1543)

Rise of Incas, followed by wars of the conquistadors against Aztecs and Incas

Martin Luther begins the Protestant Reformation (1517)

Haussa Confederation, led by Kebbi, dominant power east of the Niger in Africa (1517)

Reign of Suleiman the Great (1520–1566)

The sack of Rome (1527)

The Council of Trent (1545–1564)

Rise of Muscovy

Age of Akbar, Mogul Emperor of India (1556–1605)

The Battle of Lepanto (1571)

Spain unified

Recovery of the French monarchy

Tudor Dynasty in England

Empire of Kanem at height in Africa (1571–1603)

Massacre of French Protestants (1572)

Akbar's conquest of Gujarat gives him access to the sea (1572)

Revolution in warfare: cannon and muskets

Defeat of the Spanish Armada (1588)

Under Hideyoshi, Japan invades Korea, is rebuffed by Chinese (1592–1597)

Persians defeat Uzbeks (1597)

1400–1600 C.E.   Literature and Philosophy

Shih Nai-an, *Shui Hu Chuan* (c. 1400)

Yü Chiao Li, Chinese novel, anonymous (c. 1400)

Nesimi, Turkish poet (c. 1400)

François Villon, French poet (1431–?)

Pico de Mirandola, Italian humanist (1463–1494)

Thomas More, English statesman, humanist (1478–1535)

Marguerite de Navarre, French author (1492–1549)

Erh Tou Mei, or *Twice Flowering Plum Trees,* anonymous (c. 1500–1600)

Fuzûli, Turkish poet (c. 1500)

Hwang Chini, Korean woman poet (1506–1544)

Garcia Rodriguez de Montalvo, *Amadis de Gaula* (1508)

Desiderius Erasmus, Dutch humanist, *The Praise of Folly* (1509)

Everyman, anonymous, English morality play (1510)

Niccolò Machiavelli, Italian politician, playwright, *The Prince* (1513)

Ch'in P'ing Mei, Chinese novel, attributed to Wang Shih-chêng (1526–1593)

Baldassare Castiglione, *The Book of the Courtier* (1527)

François Rabelais, *Gargantua* and *Pantagruel* (1532–1564)

Tulsi Das, Hindu poet (1532–1623)

Michel de Montaigne, French essayist (1533–1592)

Miguel de Cervantes, Spanish novelist (1547–1616)

Lazarillo de Tormes, anonymous (1554)

Lope de Vega, Spanish dramatist (1562–1635)

John Donne, English metaphysical poet (1572–1631)

Li Shih-Chên, *Materia Medica* (1578)

Galileo, *De Motu,* on the behavior of falling bodies (1590)

Sir Philip Sidney, *The Defense of Poesie* (posthumous, 1595)

1400–1600 C.E.   Art and Music

Jan van Eyck, Dutch painter (c. 1390–1441)

Masaccio, Italian painter (1401–1428)

Donatello, Italian sculptor of *David* (1408), *Saint John* (1408)

Fillippo Brunelleschi, *Rules of Perspective* (1412)

Great Temple of the Dragon completed, Peking (1420)

Florence Cathedral completed (1434)

Sandro Botticelli, Italian painter (1444–1510)

Josquin des Prés, Dutch composer (1450–1521)

Hieronymus Bosch, Dutch painter (1450–1516)

Leonardo da Vinci, Italian painter, sculptor, inventor (1452–1519)

Albrecht Dürer, German artist (1471–1528)

Michelangelo, Italian sculptor, painter, architect, poet (1475–1564)

Titian, Italian painter (1477–1510)

Ch'en Shun, Chinese painter (1483–1544)

Alberti, *De re aedificatoria* (1485)

Ballet first presented at Italian courts (1490)

Benvenuto Cellini, Italian goldsmith, sculptor (1500–1571)

Jacopo Tintoretto, Italian painter (1518–1594)

Pieter Brueghel the Elder, Dutch painter (1520–1569)

Beginnings of kabuki theater in Japan

Ch'iu Ying, Chinese painter (1522–1560)

Palestrina, Italian composer (1525–1594)

Puppet theater combined with narration in Japan (1596–1614)

Cathedral of Saint Basil, Moscow, built (1554–1560)

1600–1715 C.E.   Historical Context

Decline of European aristocracy

Giordano Bruno burned at stake in Rome for heresy (1600)

Founding of Tokugawa family Shogunate in Japan (1603)

Death of Akbar (1605)

Guy Fawkes's Gunpowder Plot (1605)

Galileo discovers Jupiter's moons (1609)

Stuart dynasty

Richelieu's France

Tobacco planted in Virginia (1612)

Peak of Safavid culture, Middle East

Japan's expulsion of Westerners

Religious wars: Thirty Years' War in Germany (1618–1648)

The founding of the French Academy (1634)

English Civil War (1642–1646)

Dutch settle in western Africa

Beginning of African slave trade to North America

Glorious Revolution in England (1688): constitutional monarchy

Fall of Ming Dynasty, replaced by Manchu Dynasty (1644)

Jamestown, Quebec colonized

Ali Bey declares himself bey of Tunis (1650)

Salem witch trials (1692)

Age of Louis XIV in France

Growth of literacy

War of the Spanish Succession (1701–1713)

Chūshingura Incident, Japan (1703)

Peter the Great lays foundations of Petersburg (1703)

Hussein ibn Ali founds Husseinite dynasty in Tunis (1705)

Advances in astronomy by Kepler, Brahe

Beginning of Sikh militancy (1708)

1600–1715 C.E. Literature and Philosophy

Shakespeare's *Hamlet* (1600); *The Tempest* (1611)

Hung Lou Mêng, or *The Dream of the Red Chamber,* anonymous (c. late 1600s)

Chin Ku Ch'i Kuan, or *Marvellous Tales, Ancient and Modern,* anonymous (c. 1600s)

P'u Sung-Ling, *Liao Chai Chih I,* or *Strange Stories* (c. 1600s)

Cervantes, *Don Quixote,* Part I published (1605)

Pierre Corneille, French dramatist (1606–1684)

Francis Bacon, *Novum Organum* (1620)

Francisco Gomez de Quevedo, *Los Suenos* (1627)

Baruch Spinoza, Dutch philosopher (1632–1677)

Pedro Calderon de la Barca, *Life Is a Dream* (1636)

René Descartes, *Discourse on Method* (1637)

Bashô, poet of Japanese haiku (1644–1694)

Anne Bradstreet, *The Tenth Muse Lately Sprung Up in America* (1650)

Thomas Hobbes, *Leviathan* (1651)

Molière, *Tartuffe* (1664)

La Rochfoucauld, *The Maxims* (1665)

Racine, *Andromaque* (1667)

John Milton, *Paradise Lost* (1667–1674)

Wali, Urdu poet (1668–1744)

Blaise Pascal, *Pensées* (1670)

Chikamatsu Monzaemon, Japan's foremost kabuki playwright (flourished in 1670s)

John Bunyan, *Pilgrim's Progress* (1675)

Newtonian physics: *Principia Mathematica* (1687)

John Locke, *An Essay on Toleration* (1689)

1600–1715 C.E.   Art and Music

Baroque period

Ninsei, Japanese potter (1596–1660)

Kano Tannyu, Japanese artist (1602–1674)

Founding of Globe Theater

Claudio Monteverdi, *Orfeo,* opera (1607)

El Greco, Rubens, Van Dyck, Velasquez, Rembrandt dominate painting

Building of Taj Mahal (1628–1650)

Molière founds *Illustre Théatre* in Paris (1643)

Ogata Korin, Japanese artist (1658–1716)

Building of Versailles Palace (begun 1662)

Birth of Italian commedia dell'arte companies (1670)

Hua Yen, Chinese painter (1682–c. 1762)

1715–1750 C.E.   Historical Context

First phase of Industrial Revolution

Reign of Louis XV: "Ancien Regime" in France (1715–1774)

Peter the Great's modernization efforts in Russia

British military campaign against India

South Sea Bubble (1720)

War of the Polish Succession (1733)

English repeal of witchcraft laws (1736)

Safavid Dynasty ends

Nadir Shah reigns in Iran (1736–1747)

War of the Austrian Succession (1740–1748)

Reign of Frederick the Great (1740–1786)

China invades Tibet (1751)

Lisbon earthquake kills 30,000 people (1755)

Walpole's Ministry in England

Hapsburg-Bourbon Alliance

Voltaire joins court of Frederick the Great

1715–1750 C.E.   Literature and Philosophy

Age of Enlightenment

Founding of literary salons

Takedo Izumo, kabuki playwright (1691–1756)

Daniel Defoe, *Robinson Crusoe* (1719)

Khwāja Mir Dard, Sufi poet (1720–1784)

Mir Taqi Mir, Urdu poet (1724–1808)

Jonathan Swift, *Gulliver's Travels* (1726)

Samuel Richardson, *Pamela* (1740); *Clarissa* (1748)

David Hume, *An Enquiry Concerning Human Understanding* (1748)

Henry Fielding, *Tom Jones* (1749)

Thomas Gray, *Elegy Written in a Country Churchyard* (1750)

Denis Diderot, *Encyclopedia* (1751–1772)

Phyllis Wheatley, *Poems on Various Subjects* (1773)

Immanuel Kant, *Critique of Pure Reason* (1781)

1715–1750 C.E. Art and Music

Rococo style: Watteau, Boucher, Fragonard

Hogarth, Gainsborough, Reynolds dominate English art

Johann Sebastian Bach, German composer (1685–1750)

Suzuki Harunobu, Japanese painter (1718–1770)

Covent Garden Opera House, London, opened (1732)

Maruyama Okyo, Japanese artist (1733–1795)

Handel's *Messiah* (1742)

Kitagawa Utamaro, Japanese painter (1753–1806)

Wolfgang Amadeus Mozart, Austrian composer (1756–1791)

Appendix C:
Reading and Writing
About World Literature

According to advice offered by English novelist Virginia Woolf, you should read with a pencil in hand. Jotting down the thoughts that crowd in upon you as you read helps you to fix—for a while—some of your responses to a work. For it is the mysterious property of sensations, impressions, and thoughts that they dart about in your mind and, sometimes, disappear, Woolf compares the evanescent quality of thought to a fishing line let down in a stream:

> Thought—to call it by a prouder name than it deserved—had let its line down into the stream. It swayed, minute after minute, hither and thither among the reflections and the weeds, letting the water lift it and sink it, until—you know the little tug—the sudden conglomeration of an idea at the end of one's line. (*A Room of One's Own*)

It is important to recognize this gathering of thoughts, this tug of an idea at the end of your line, and to record your early responses to a work, both personal and cultural.

You should read knowing that you are reading with others. Not only are you having a dialogue with an author, someone who writes in a particular time and place, but you are also having a conversation with the cultures represented in *The HarperCollins World Reader,* and, eventually, with the other students in your class. Your curiosity and desire to know about other people and places should propel you into the readings even though you will sometimes feel a strangeness in encountering unfamiliar names and places. Read on. An effort of the imagination is necessary to enter other people's lives and stories, as well as to understand the different responses of other readers in your class who will have a kaleidoscope of views on culture, language, religion, class, race, ethnicity, gender, and sex. Though you read alone, silently, in a private space, you discover that you are always also reading with others as you explore different values and cultures. For example, in reading the Islamic writer Ibn Hazm's eleventh century tales of love in *The Dove's Neckring (Towq al-Hamama)*, you might be shocked to read stories of the pursuit of "slave-girls" who grow up in the houses of wealthy families. You discover through reading that slavery is a part of Arab culture in the eleventh century, but you also discover the independence in the slave-girl's position as the narrator pursues the sixteen-year-old girl and finds her "far more glamorous in her refusals and rejections" of him, as he describes an experience of unrequited love.

You might debate the value and discussion of womanly and manly beauty in this same Islamic epic. The beauty of the slave girl is described:

> She had a wonderful complexion which she always kept closely veiled. . . . For women are as aromatic herbs, which if not well tended soon lose their fragrance; they are as edifices which, if not constantly cared for quickly fall into ruin. Therefore, it has been said that manly beauty is the truer, the more solidly established, and of higher excellence since it can endure, and that without shelter, onslaughts the merest fraction of which would transform the loveliness of a woman's face beyond recognition: such enemies as the burning heat of noonday, the scorching wind of the desert, every air of heaven, and all the changing moods of the seasons. (Section V, Early and Classical Middle East)

Since the body has different meanings in different cultures, how does each culture teach its women and men to "tend" their bodies? Islamic culture may teach its women to "veil" their bodies; Chinese culture may promote "foot-binding" in a particular period to enhance the daintiness of women's feet; American culture may encourage "thinness" as an aspect of women's beauty. What Islamic culture may see as the "enemy"—"the burning heat of noonday"—may be another culture's "obsession"—suntanning of the body.

Such personal and cultural responses to other literatures grow out of your past reading experiences and your personal and social experiences, and may become the basis for a paper at a later stage of writing. You will quickly follow along from the early moments of your understanding of a text to see and see again, shape and reshape your interpretations and writing about the text as you think about it and discuss it with others. Early thoughts, feelings, and questions may very well control the later phases of writing about a work, and you should preserve these responses.

Your early observations may be recorded in three ways. First, you might want to highlight certain words or write comments in your book. Preserve your sudden sympathy for a character or your feeling of being bothered by an unfamiliar word or your feelings of difference as you read by commenting in the margins or between the lines of your text. Highlight certain words or passages that need further reflection; use question marks to note ambiguities or puzzles; draw arrows to relate different parts of a work. For example, notations on the poem, "Walking Both Sides of an Invisible Border" (stanzas five and six), by Alootook Ipellie, an Eskimo born in Canada, might look like this:

Remind me of Ruth in the Bible "amidst the alien corn."

I did not ask to be born an (Inuk)   *What?*
Nor did I ask to be forced
{ To learn an _alien_ culture
{ With an _alien_ language   *Repeats the word "alien"*
But I lucked out on fate
Which I am unable to undo.
I have resorted to fancy _dancing_
In order to survive each day
No wonder I have earned   *Images of dancing*
The dubious reputation of being
The world's premier _choreographer_
Of distinctive _dance steps_

That allow me to avoid
Potential personal paranoia   *Three "p's"*
On both sides of this invisible border

A second way of recording early responses to a work is to keep a reading notebook, what Ann Berthoff calls a "dialectical notebook." In such a notebook, the facing pages are in dialogue with one another. On the left-hand page, you write your initial impressions of a work or copy out sentences or passages that interest you. You may find a particular sentence puzzling; you may fasten on a certain character; you may be intrigued by the description of a place or you may have a strong feeling of anger. Jot down your impressions and feelings and set the notebook aside. Later, on the right-hand page, explore these impressions further, reflecting upon, questioning, and explaining remarks you made on the left-hand page. On the right-hand page, you will, in effect, be taking notes on your notes, and transforming your first impressions into new understandings. Some observations will remain relevant; some can be ignored. A "dialectical notebook" page on Alootook Ipellie's poem might look like the notes illustrated here.

Initial impressions, copied sentences and passages	Reflections, explanations, interpretations
I remember the pictures of igloos, Eskimos in parkas, fishing through a hole in the ice in my elementary school social studies book. Do Eskimos or Inuits still live in this way? Why are certain Eskimos called "Inuits." Does the word have a meaning? Another language?	Looked up Inuit in the encyclopedia but only found information on the word "Eskimo" which is of Algonquin origin and has the "pejorative meaning of eater of raw flesh." I know little about different kinds of Eskimos. The images I have are stereotypes — oversimplified views of a group of people.

A third method of recording your responses involves generating a list of questions, contradictions, ambiguities, or puzzles that come to mind as you read a work. Such questions would be reconsidered at a later stage of writing, and one or two of them might even grow into a definite subject of research for a paper. Here is a potential list of questions that you might have after reading Alootook Ipellie's poem:

Who is speaking in this poem? Is it Ipellie himself or an Inuk he created?

Why does he feel so bad about himself? Being made to feel like an "illegitimate child" or someone "sent to a torture chamber/without having committed a crime" suggests a strong sense of injustice.

Who is it that is "forcing" him to learn an alien culture? Headnote mentions French and English, but what do I know about the historical situation of Eskimos in Canada?

Why are there so many images of feet and dancing? And lines and borders?

In this first stage of reading and writing, you are actively trying to make sense of the world of Alootook Ipellie by recording the flux of your impressions, questionings, comparisons, and judgments. Writing down your impressions keeps you alert to the meanings that you are making and remaking as you read. And writing helps you to fix meaning—for a while—because once your thoughts are written down you can look at them and then look at them again. Whatever method you choose—highlighting, jotting in a book, keeping a reading notebook, or listing questions that a work provokes—you are creating, reflecting, judging, and comparing meanings from the very moment you begin to read, and you may always reconsider, change, and remake your meanings. Thoughts flutter away but writing stays.

Reading with a pencil in hand will remind you of the relationship between reading and writing. At this early stage, you move from one spot in the text to another, stressing nothing in particular, simply recording the conversation between you, the author, and the work. This, after all, is thinking. Reading, writing, and thinking are intertwined as the French literary critic Gérard Genette says: "The text is that Moebius strip in which the side of writing and the side of reading, ceaselessly turn and cross over, in which writing is constantly read, in which reading is constantly written and inscribed" (*Figures,* 70). As a reader, you enter into such interplays of reading and writing that ceaselessly turn and cross over.

But reading and writing remain in some sense unfinished until completed by others. You work from your responses and feelings outward to other stages that involve you in reading with others. Robert Scholes, an educator and literary critic, identifies three levels:

LEVEL 1: READING

LEVEL 2: INTERPRETATION

LEVEL 3: CRITICISM

These levels of reading take you beyond your inner dialogue that is largely private: the way in which you represented your thinking to yourself in your notebook or jottings or lists of questions as suggested earlier. In discussion with your classmates and your instructor, and maybe even other literary critics, certain initial ideas may be discarded; others will survive.

As meanings evolve, they are shaped and reshaped, and eventually prepared for an audience. It is thus important "how" you move back and forth from early notebook jottings about your reading to more formal discussion and writing for an audience. For example, while reading "Walking Both Sides of the Border" (in "Writing Across Boundaries," the last section featured in *The HarperCollins World Reader,* The Modern World), you may have informally jotted in your notebook:

> *Inuit in this poem being oppressed and physically tortured by somebody. Evidence in the line "having been sentenced to a Torture chamber."*

In discussion, a classmate might point out that Ipellie uses the word "like" before this clause—"like having been sentenced to a torture chamber"—forcing you to concede that Ipellie is here using a comparison (simile) to a torture chamber to convey how the Inuk feels. You realize he has not been physically tortured, and that you read the line too literally. Discussion then might lead you to revise an initial impression as you come into agreement with your classmate on the literal meaning of what you have read. Not all "readings" are equally valid. Sometimes then you must grapple with someone else to establish "what happens" in a poem or story when it is not straightforward or clear. As a reader, you fill in gaps, relate parts of a work to each other, figure out the characters: in short, you make sense of it. This is the literal level of "reading."

On the second level of interpretation, you will discuss the "meaning" of what you have read with others and with your classmates and instructor. You may have noted in the margins of your book that the image of "a border" recurs in the first few stanzas of the poem:

> The Inuk is "Walking with an invisible border" and later "Walking on both sides of an invisible border." Who is making these borders "that become so wide" that he is unable to take another step? Who is creating these difficulties and making him paranoid?

A classmate interested in dancing, may perceive something different in the poem. She might jot down all the passages that mention "feet," "steps," "dancing." The meaning of the poem may reside for her in the Inuk's coping strategies, his "fancy dancing" and refusal to be a victim of opposing cultural forces—in this case, the Inuk and the English. You, on the other hand, may be more sensitive to the Inuk's complaints, his sense of oppression and "paranoia" about his social and historical circumstances. Each of you finds different yet compatible meanings based on your personal and cultural sensitivities and experiences.

The third level of reading, "criticism," involves you in discriminating further by comparing and judging works, and sometimes, the opinions of others. You move beyond the analysis of one text—its events and meanings—to compare texts of two or more authors, cultures, or historical periods in *The HarperCollins World Reader*. You might examine who is speaking in the Ipellie poem, Ipellie himself or a lyric "I," and compare him to the *griot* who chants an epic in the West African culture. In *The Oral Epic of Askia Mohammed,* a sixteenth-century epic by the Songhay People (in Section VI, Africa: The Epic Tradition), we might compare the *griot* known in Songhay as *jésere,* and in English poetry as a "bard" or, later, a "poet." The first English version of this sixteenth-century West African epic appears in *The HarperCollins World Reader,* and was chanted again according to oral traditions in Mali in Saga, Niger, in 1980 and 1981. The tale relates how every time Kassaye, the sister of the threatened ruler, Si, delivers a baby, it is killed by Si, because it has been foretold by the "seers" that his throne will be taken from him by one of his sister's children. The tale of jealousy and power is told over and over again in Mali. Does this *griot* speak for a whole community? How does his role compare with that of the "poet," Ipellie? Does he speak for the community of Inuks in the same way as the Mali epic poet?

What is the difference in the way that you "hear" these two poems? As you experience the Mali epic, you notice that there are unusual repetitions in certain lines. For example, Si is still king, and his sister Kassaye knows that he will continue to kill any child she has; in fact, he has already killed seven of them. She waits to see whether anything will change:

> While Kassaye remained like that
> Until, until, until, until one day, much later, in the middle of the night
> A man came who was wearing beautiful clothes.

The repetition of the word "until" creates for us a sense of Kassaye's waiting: it rhythmically marks the passage of time, "until, until, until, until one day, much later." This repetition reveals the oral dimension of this epic that is chanted in the Mali culture. Reminding us of the oral origins of all poetry, we note, nevertheless, that much English and American poetry today appeals to the eye and not the ear, as it formerly did in Old English epics such as *Beowulf.*

You may have noticed that each time a point has been advanced about world literature here, the thesis is supported with quotations from the texts in *The HarperCollins World Reader.* As you write, the "evidence" you assemble in support of your positions is quotations or paraphrases from the text. Such a practice in writing a paper for the humanities is different from the practice of writing, for example, for the disciplines of psychology or chemistry. The social and physical sciences require citations of case studies or statistics or experiments as evidence in an argument. In the humanities, reading, jottings, rereadings, underlinings, writing, and rewriting provide the evidence you need to write a more formal paper at a later stage.

Reading, writing, and thinking are intertwined. You see that all of these processes are tempered by the realization that you bring your own personal and cultural experiences to any work, and impressions registered are shaped by your memories as well as your growing stock of cultural associations. Samuel Johnson once observed that "the two most engaging powers of any author are, 'to make new things familiar and familiar things new.' " Many selections in a reader marked by cultural, chronological, and geographical diversity will appear to be concerned with strange and "new things," rather than "familiar things," but as you read, you will recognize ways in which the writers have carried out both aims identified by Johnson. On one level, the customs and values of different cultures will become somewhat more familiar; at the same time, certain aspects of your own culture that you have come to take for granted may take on a different meaning and reshape your previous convictions and outlook.

Virtually all works of literature have certain elements in common, whether or not they are written in another language and at a different time. One important aspect of any text is the *point of view* from which it was written. The point of view is the author's dominant focus, from which he or she projects the story, poem, or essay. Sometimes the point of view is so clear it is taken for granted. For instance, when Alootook Ipellie writes, "I feel like an illegitimate child/Forsaken by my parents," readers presume that they are hearing the voice of the poet himself. In the Korean poem "A Ferryboat and a Traveler," by Han Yongun, which begins, "I am a ferryboat, you are a traveler," it is clear that the poet has decided to assume the *persona* of a ferryboat. Alternatively, in "Evening Faces," from the Japanese novel *The Tale of Genji*, written by Murasaki Shikibu, an aristocratic eleventh-century Japanese lady, the viewpoint is third-person. The author is sharing the thoughts of a single major character, the young Buddhist nobleman Prince Genji. The selection begins, "On his way from court to pay one of his calls at Rokujō, Genji stopped to inquire after his old nurse." Had the viewpoint suddenly shifted, and the story continued, "the old nurse was wondering if some tea would help her headache, and trying to decide if she was able to make the journey next day to visit her sister, with whom she had shared her childhood in the country," the reader might be confused; the interest in Prince Genji generated up to that point would be diluted. The viewpoint character must be consistent, supplying the emotion, conflict, and suspense of the work of literature; the reader identifies with the viewpoint and infers the message of the work through the reaction of this character.

The point of view is a necessary staple in all works of literature, though there may be variations in the way the point of view is worked out. For instance, sometimes a speaker in the first person is actually looking back at an earlier period of his or her life. This is the case, for instance, in *Narrative of the Life of Frederick Douglass, an American Slave, Written by Himself* (in The Americas sections of *The HarperCollins World Reader, The Modern World*).

At other times, a work is written in the present, with such an immediacy that the reader seems to be peering over the shoulder of the writer watching the act of composition. This is the case with Vladimir Nabokov's "An Evening of Russian Poetry" (in "Writing Across Boundaries"). The author addresses several audiences: the group of people gathered for his lecture, the person (presumably a student) helping him project slides, the student (Sylvia) who interrupts with a question, and the reader. The larger framework of the lecture embraces two smaller designs: the mechanical difficulty of projecting the slide correctly (i.e., making the visual image conform to the chosen word), and the pedagogical problem posed by Sylvia, who begs for easy packaged knowledge instead of complex linguistic theory.

> The subject chosen for tonight's discussion
> is everywhere, though often incomplete:
> when their basaltic banks become too steep,
> most rivers use a kind of rapid Russian,
> and so do children talking in their sleep.
> My little helper at the magic lantern,
> insert that slide and let the colored beam
> project my name or any such like phantom
> in Slavic characters upon the screen.
> The other way, the other way. I thank you.
>
> On mellow hills the Greek, as you remember,
> fashioned his alphabet from cranes in flight;
> his arrows crossed the sunset, then the night.
> Our simple skyline and a taste for timber,
> the influence of hives and conifers,
> reshaped the arrows and the borrowed birds.
> Yes, Sylvia?
>
> *"Why do you speak of words*
> *when all we want is knowledge nicely browned?"*
>
> Because all hangs together—shape and sound,
> heather and honey, vessel and content.

Within his larger address to the audience, he speaks to the person (presumably a student) inserting slides for him, while, at the same time he seems to be pondering the transitory nature of his own name and, possibly, his message. The slide has apparently been shown reversed or upside-down; he breaks off to ask the person to correct it. He continues his lecture, but interrupts himself to respond to a member of the audience, who has apparently raised her hand: "Yes, Sylvia?" He answers her question as to why "words" are significant, incorporating his reply within his lecture, addressing Sylvia, the audience, and the reader. "Content," or meaning, and the "vessel," or words, cannot be separated, for "all hangs together."

The point of view is only one element that might be considered a common denominator of virtually all literary works of art. Other factors you need to keep in mind are structure and diction, as well as metaphor, irony, symbolism, and other rhetorical devices. Above all, focus on the author's message; grasp the meaning of the piece of writing.

You have been writing since you began reading, making notations in your text and keeping a notebook to remind you of your initial impressions, reflections, and interpretations. At some point, however, you will need to incorporate these fragmentary notes into a public, formal essay.

You will find it helpful to tackle your essay by stages. Students who hastily scribble a paper at three A.M. rarely produce a piece of writing of which they can be proud. The steps in writing most students find useful are these: *invention, drafting,* and *revision.* If you can space out these steps, allowing periods of time away from your writing, results will be far better. The subconscious part of your mind will go on working on the material even though you are doing something else; often you return to it with renewed energy and new ideas.

Invention

"I don't know how to get started," students often say. Several rhetorical techniques may help you as you cast around for initial ideas. Read over your book jottings and your notebook, and then try one or more of these strategies.

Freewriting

Freewriting may be the easiest way to release your powers of invention and discovery. Without devising any sort of outline or plan, force yourself simply to begin writing about a text you have read and to keep writing for five minutes. Do not lift your pen or pencil; just keep writing. Let your mind wander back to the act of reading the text, and give free rein to the associations you gathered. (The reason you should keep writing and not let yourself reread what you have is so that you will not begin editing what you have; that task is reserved for a later stage.) You do not need to write complete sentences, just phrases or vague ideas. Jot down anything that made a strong impression.

As a sample text for freewriting, consider the first five paragraphs of the short story "We Blacks All Drink Coffee" by the Cuban writer Mirta Yañez (included in "Writing Across Boundaries"):

> She says that I don't even know how to wash my own clothes and yet I want to go off. What is a mother's child going to do in a place like that? Just imagine what my grandmother would say if she knew, if she were to rise from the grave and see what the apple of her eye wanted to get into. It's a good thing she is dead, because if she weren't . . . . There's a lot of talk about irresponsible mothers. But not about her.

> And so my mother goes grumbling on and on from the end of the corridor where she has gone to take refuge so that her voice will be lost, will slip in between the furniture, so the neighbours will not hear one word sounding louder than another, what would they think of this family, of this child of fifteen wanting to go off to pick coffee?

> Things were different in her time. What would a well brought up girl be doing in the middle of the bush? Who would have thought of such a thing? Going where there are so many dangers. At least that's what the books say. Right into the heart of a titanic forest, a girl from a good family. Luckily there are no wild animals in this country.

For my mother the only safe place is my room with its four walls, a roof, a floor of the most ordinary sort. And not even then is it completely worthy of her confidence.

What do I care about the neighbours? But she does. And she closes the windows so that the argument will not go beyond this castle which is the protective shell of my family life. And when the room is the way she would like it, like the cell of a cloistered nun, she rushes forward from the other side of the corridor, she claps her hands. She shouts carefully. I am what is known as a girl who was given everything she ever wanted. If I asked for a flying bird, a flying bird I would get. Now look how ungrateful I was.

Here is what freewriting might look like for the above passage:

girl 15 wants to pick coffee beans   mother won't let her   she is too nice neighbors might criticize   she is like flying bird   does she hate mother   picking beans is first job   she is too sheltered   what dangers does the mother mean grandmother would have been shocked   wants to hide girl in room   home equals castle   girl given everything

Clustering

You could take the same five paragraphs and try another strategy. Write each of your main ideas in the center of a piece of blank paper and circle it. Then "cluster" supporting ideas around it, each with relevant quotations, details, and key words. Making such a diagram will allow you to visualize the way the various pieces of your research or your argument fit together.

Your clustering might look like the diagram shown below.

Nutshelling

Nutshelling, sometimes called *looping,* is when you record your thoughts as they come for a few minutes, as you did in freewriting; this process may also be called brainstorming. Then you extract the best idea from what you have, draw a line, and start again with that phrase or sentence. You keep extracting the "kernel" or nucleus of the text and putting it in a new context. Many students find it difficult to narrow a subject and arrive at a workable thesis. This procedure can be very helpful in channeling your initial impressions and shaping them into an argument. Nutshelling might also work well for "We Blacks All Drink Coffee:"

First stage of nutshelling, *freewriting or brainstorming:*

> The girl wants to pick beans in coffee field but her mother objects because she can't even wash her own clothes and is not independent yet and has been given everything she ever wanted even a flying bird if she had wanted one; mother says her grandmother would have been shocked ancestry matters to mother but not to girl it seems like that anyway

Second stage, *first extract or loop:*

> Mother overprotective; she smothers girl who wants to be independent which is good girl wants to be a bird and go free in the fields and break out of the cage not have a bird but be a bird etc.

Third stage, *second extract or loop:*

> Symbol of the bird is good as image of independence which is what girl seems to want maybe that comparison would work

Fourth stage, *consolidation of ideas:*

Here you could go on to list points of comparison between the girl and a flying bird:

girl	bird
castle (home)	cage
sheltered	confined
frustrated	restless
pick beans	fly free

When you finally organize your thoughts, you should have a skeletal chart or list of basic points that will assist you in developing your essay.

If you use a computer and a word-processing program that offers more than one screen, you might use alternate screens or windows for the nutshelling technique. After you have assembled some promising ideas on-screen, you can block and copy (not cut) the most promising sections, move them to the other screen, and start over without the distraction of your earlier text. You could continue the process, extracting the best "kernel" from the second excerpt, clearing the first screen, and starting over for the third time. Be sure to save all your texts, though, with different file names (you could call them N1, N2, N3, etc., for Nutshelling 1, 2 and 3, for instance), so you will have access to them later if necessary.

Cubing

Cubing is a technique offering a way of swiftly considering a subject from six points of view, and is a useful preventive if you tend to be locked into a single way of looking at a subject. If you shift points of view every three to five minutes, your perspective is continually renewed. In cubing, you imagine your subject as a solid block, or cube. Then, for three to five minutes each, carry out the following steps:

Describe it

Compare it

Analyze it

Associate it

Apply it

Argue for/against it

The quick shift from one perspective to another makes cubing work. If you consider the Yáñez story as a solid block, your cubing might look like this:

Describe it: girl wants to pick beans; argues with mother.

Compare it: girl like bird, impatient in cage at home, wants to be independent

Analyze it: girl wants new ways; mother wants old ways; conflict between generations

Associate it: similar to me in high school when I wanted to be free to go out, do things; I can understand girl; who cares what neighbors and ancestors think?

Apply it: could be applied to essay on theme of innocence and experience or to essay on other cultures.

Argue for/against it: I basically agree with the girl in wanting to try new experiences and expand her thinking; the mother should realize the world has changed now; she should trust her daughter not to disgrace the family

Any of these techniques may assist you in collecting your thoughts on a particular text.

Drafting

The next step is to write your first draft. If you are writing on the Yáñez story and have carried out the preceding brainstorming techniques, it is likely that by now you might have decided on a single topic that interests you, such as the conflict between generations, the depiction of racial prejudice (undercut by the title, which implies that all Cubans have African blood, inherited from their Spanish/Moorish ancestry), the interplay of color emblems in the story (white, black, yellow, red, green), or the concept of family honor as it pertains to the treatment of daughters among the Cuban upper classes.

Now, you need to develop a thesis, as opposed to a topic. A topic is the overall subject, a rough label, but your thesis expresses your argument and is a vital part of your essay. It should set forth an explicit argument about the text to which you are responding and should be the nucleus of the introductory paragraph. This paragraph should provide a general context within which you can develop your ideas. It should not only make your thesis clear but also provide a transition to the body of the paper. It should be proportional in size to the total length of the paper.

A useful test of a thesis is whether you can convert it into a satisfactory title. The following two titles fail to suggest an argument based on the Yañez story:

> "Working in the Coffee Fields"

(This title is too vague; also the girl does not actually work in the fields.)

> "The Family's Influence on a Young Cuban Girl"

(This title is better, but it does not suggest the import of the story.)

A third title, which implies the theme of the story, is better formulated:

> "Leaving the Nest: The Empowerment of the Heroine in Yañez'
> 'We Blacks All Drink Coffee' "

A possible thesis might be the following:

> The narrator realizes that she is rapidly becoming an adult with choices of her own to make regarding her conduct, yet, at the same time, she perceives that she can never completely escape her upbringing, with its implicit familial obligations. The girl's wish to escape from her childhood is shown by the symbol of the "flying bird." If she had wanted to own a "flying bird," she would have been given one; she was very spoiled. But if she wants to *be* a "flying bird," she is constricted.

Your paper must contain examples and evidence such as the following to support your ideas:

To show she is becoming an adult:

> From the "vision" of her mother's hysterical reaction and her final remark, "do as you think best," the girl judges that she has finally been perceived as an adult, but one with responsibility to herself and her family.

To show that the symbol of a bird leaving a nest is relevant:

> The symbol of the "flying bird" works in two ways in the story: to show the girl's original imprisonment in her cage-like room in the family "castle" or home, and to show her final liberation.

You may find some of the selections in *The HarperCollins World Reader* puzzling, because they deal not only with systems of religious and philosophical thought that are foreign to you but also with habits of daily life that lie outside your immediate experience. For instance, some of the selections from Japanese literature depict subtle criteria of taste and judgment, profoundly meaningful within the social hierarchy, that may seem insignificant to you. The continual sending of poems in *The Tale of Genji* and *The Tale of the Heike* (in Section III, East Asia: Early and Middle Period) is an example. A cultivated man or woman (not just a young lover) was expected to be a close observer, sensitive to the transience of the human condition, and to express his reflections in poetry that was controlled and veiled, not spontaneous and emotional. Matters you might consider trivial, such as the color of writing paper and the quality of handwriting, were actually subjects of very serious scrutiny and were the measure of a person's fastidiousness (in itself a quality you may not consider of primary consequence). As you read, you will note many other differences—in manners, food, dress, and other matters. It may particularly surprise you to read, in "Housewife," by the Indian writer Ismat Chugtai, that the bride Lajo, a former prostitute, despises the pants, or *churidar pyjamas,* her husband Mirza insists on her wearing. She calls them the "devil's intestines" and much prefers a loose skirt, the *lehnga.* A skirt, rather than the traditional pants, symbolizes the freedom she has had before marriage and before being under the control of her husband.

You may find it difficult to tailor your writing to a given audience, assuming you need to shape it to please your instructor, your tutor, your college newspaper editor, or a prospective employer. You should realize, though, that your primary audience is actually yourself. All writing is a form of self-discovery, and it is in writing about a text that you formulate your ideas and begin to sort out your thoughts. You, in fact, collaborate with other readers to become your own teacher as you shape a written response to a text through successive drafts.

Revision

When an essay you have considered your best effort is returned by your instructor with suggestions for revisions, you may feel disheartened. Try, though, to regard the comments as supportive feedback, a good opportunity to enlarge your knowledge of writing and to refine the structure, style, and content of the essay. Feedback from other students, or "peer response," is an invaluable source of insight into your writing. Some instructors build mini-workshops into their courses, with small groups of students reading each other's papers, in order to encourage peer response. Workshops in class may not be feasible for most literature courses, but you might wish to organize informal support group sessions with classmates to try out ideas and exchange preliminary drafts. It has been said that revision is not a finite third stage of writing, but a continual, ongoing process of the "re-vision" of a text; you "re-see" it as you work. Each "re-vision" leads to further changes and improvement.

You might highlight the best sections (those with the clearest ideas), using a colored marker; underline those which are doubtful; then cross through the fuzzy or badly written parts. Begin again, with the clearest idea and the arguments and illustrations related to it. If a paper is not to be revised, make sure you understand the comments so that you can apply them to your future writing. The entire process of revision is made far easier if you can use a computer.

In a sense, reading and writing complement each other. Reading with the aim of describing your reaction to a text—that is, writing about it—heightens your sensitivity to it. Writing, or interpreting, illuminates your reading and is an important component in your assimilation of a piece of writing. Both processes make possible the understanding of a work as part of a global cultural paradigm— unified by themes common to the human condition, yet richly varied in its subtexts and individual motifs. Your acuity as both reader and writer will be sharpened, and your perceptions enlarged, as you enter into dialogue with the diverse works in *The HarperCollins World Reader*.

Comparative Table of Contents by Theme

This "alternative" table of contents is a representative grouping of poems, epics, stories, plays, and essays in *The HarperCollins World Reader* that shows how various themes are treated across different cultures, regions, and times. In no sense complete, it serves as a beginning exploration in the comparative mode intending to explore, and—in some cases—deviate from, literary expectations.

The alphabetized headings consist of a mixture of cross-cultural genres and selections grouped together around a similar theme. For example, the theme of social order in India may be juxtaposed with an ancient tale about royalty in Japan—*The Pillow Book* by Sei Shōnagon—with "The Friendly Dice Game" from the Indian epic *The Mahabharata*. From such a central focus, literary themes may be taught across cultures, genres, and times so that, for example, the family tradition described in *The Creation Story* in the Ancient Mediterranean World can be compared with *The Oral Epic of Son-Jara* in Africa and Shakespeare's romantic play, *The Tempest*.

Thematic groupings give the reader a rough idea as to what notions seem to be of particular significance in certain times and places. Thus reflections on family traditions during the ancient period can be contrasted with traditions of the early modern era.

Comparing and contrasting these cross-cultural themes will encourage student interest in the comparative mode while at the same time opening the way to further investigation of world literature.

Age and Aging

Ovid, from the *Amores,* Ancient Mediterranean World, sect. I

Li Po, "The River Merchant's Wife: A Letter," East Asia (China), sect. III

From *The Early Royal Anthologies,* Ono no Komachi, East Asia (Japan), sect. III

Sŏng Hon, [The Mountain Is Silent], East Asia (Korea), sect. III

Hŏ Nansŏrhŏn, "A Woman's Sorrow," East Asia (Korea), sect. III

William Shakespeare, *The Tempest,* Early Modern Europe, sect. VII

Violence

Marie de France, "The Wolf and the Lamb," Medieval Europe, sect. IV

Firdawsî, from *The Shâh Nâma*, Early and Classical Middle East, sect. V

Marguerite de Navarre, [Passion and Vengeance in the Naples Court], from *Heptameron*, Early Modern Europe, sect. VII

War and Battle

Anonymous, "The Babylonian Creation Epic," from *Enuma Elish*, Ancient Mediterranean World, sect. I

Homer, from the *Iliad*, Ancient Mediterranean World, sect. I

Kabti-ilani-Marduk, *The Erra Epic*, Ancient Mediterranean World, sect. I

Archilochus, Ancient Mediterranean World, sect. I

Tyrtaeus, Ancient Mediterranean World, sect. I

Thucydides, "Pericles' Funeral Oration," from *The History of the Peloponnesian War*, Ancient Mediterranean World, sect. I

Vergil, from the *Aeneid*, Ancient Mediterranean World, sect. I

Various Authors, *Love Poems from the Tamil*, South Asia, sect. II

Kampan, from *The Ramayana*, South Asia, sect. II

Anonymous, [Pick a fern, pick a fern, ferns are high], from *The Book of Songs*, East Asia (China), sect. III

Anonymous, from *Intrigues of the Warring States*, East Asia (China), sect. III

Anonymous, from *The Tale of the Heike*, East Asia (Japan), sect. III

'Ubayd-i Zākānī, [A Sequence of Satiric Anecdotes], Early and Classical Middle East, sect. V

Maninka People, from *The Oral Epic of Son-Jara*, Africa, sect. VI

François Rabelais, *Gargantua* and *Pantagruel*, Early Modern Europe, sect. VII

Michel de Montaigne, "Of Cannibals," from *Essays*, Early Modern Europe, sect. VII

Miguel de Cervantes Saavedra, *Don Quixote*, Early Modern Europe, sect. VII

Wisdom, Knowledge and Morality

Hesiod, from *Works and Days*, Ancient Mediterranean World, sect. I

Plato, [The Trial of Socrates], from *The Apology*, Ancient Mediterranean World, sect. I

Lucretius, from *On the Nature of Things*, Ancient Mediterranean World, sect. I

Ashvaghoshā, "The Four Signs," from *The Life of Buddha*, South Asia, sect. II

Basavanna, Devera Dasimayya, Mahadeviyakka, from *The Kannada*, South Asia, sect. II

Kabir, songs from *The Bijak*, South Asia, sect. II

Credits

Photo Credits

246, folio 25 verso; 6: India Office Library/The British Library; 7(T): The Metropolitan Museum of Art, Gift of Arthur A. Houghton, Jr., 1970, (1970.301.17); 7(B): Scala/Art Resource, NY; 8: From THE ROCK PAINTINGS OF THE CHUMASH: A STUDY OF A CALIFORNIA INDIAN CULTURE, written and illustrated by Campbell Grant. University of California Press, Berkeley and Los Angeles, 1965. Plate 29.

Text Credits

Index of Titles, Authors, and First Lines of Poetry

Page numbers in italics indicate the location of bibliographic headnotes.

1407